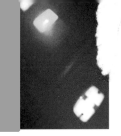

map pages

CW00531278

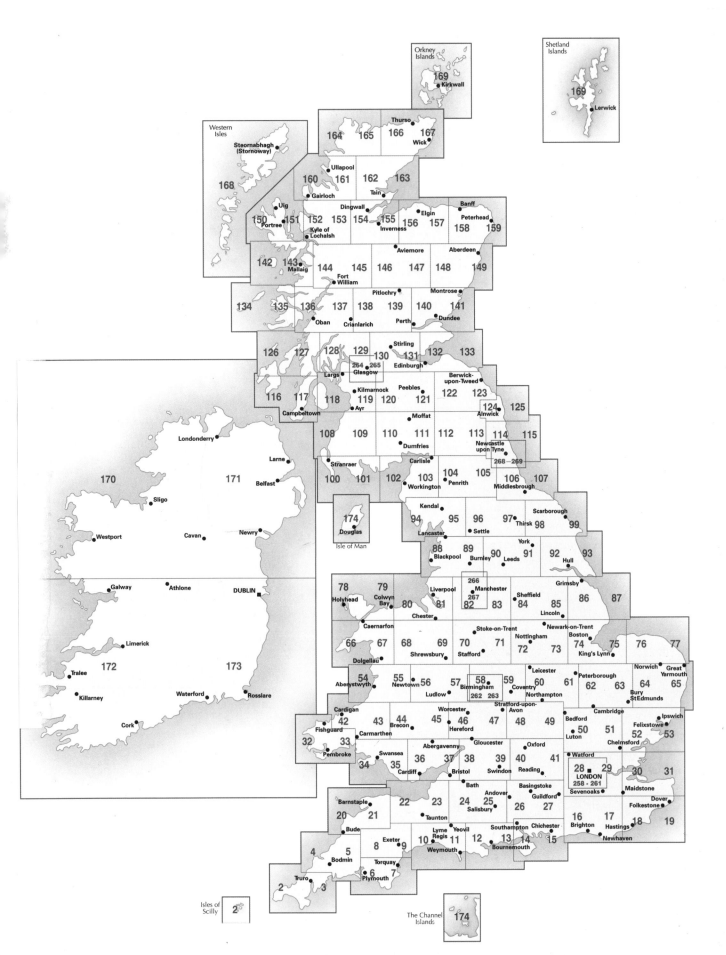

Orkney Islands
169 Kirkwall

Shetland Islands
169 Lerwick

Western Isles
Steornabhagh (Stornoway)
168
Uig
150 Portree **151** **152** **153** Kyle of Lochalsh
142 **143** Mallaig
134 **135** **136** **137** **138** Oban **139** **140** **141**
Crianlarich Perth Dundee

Thurso
164 **165** **166** Wick **167**
Ullapool
160 **161** **162** **163**
Gairloch Tain
Dingwall Elgin Banff
154 **155** **156** **157** Peterhead
Inverness **158** **159**
Aviemore Aberdeen
144 **145** **146** **147** **148** **149**
Fort William
Pitlochry Montrose

Stirling
126 **127** **128** **129** **130** **131** **132** **133**
264 **265** Edinburgh
Largs Glasgow
Kilmarnock Peebles Berwick-upon-Tweed
116 **117** **118** **119** **120** **121** **122** **123**
Campbeltown Ayr
Moffat **124** **125**
Alnwick
108 **109** **110** **111** **112** **113** **114** **115**
Dumfries Newcastle upon Tyne
268 — 269
Carlisle
Stranraer **104** **105** **106** **107**
100 **101** **102** **103** Penrith Middlesbrough
Workington
Londonderry
Larne
170 **171** Belfast
Sligo
Kendal Scarborough
94 **95** **96** **97** Thirsk **98** **99**
Lancaster Settle
174 York
Douglas **88** **89** **90** Leeds **91** **92** **93**
Isle of Man Blackpool Burnley Hull
Westport Cavan Newry
266 Grimsby
78 **79** Liverpool Manchester
Galway Athlone Holyhead **80** **81** **267** Sheffield **86** **87**
DUBLIN Colwyn Bay **82** **83** **84** **85**
Chester Lincoln
172 **173** Newark-on-Trent
Caernarfon Stoke-on-Trent Boston
Limerick **66** **67** **68** **69** **70** **71** Nottingham **74** **75** **76** **77**
Tralee Dolgellau Shrewsbury Stafford **72** **73** King's Lynn
Killarney Waterford Norwich Great Yarmouth
Rosslare Leicester
Cork **54** **55** **56** **57** **58** **59** Peterborough
Aberystwyth Newtown Birmingham Coventry **60** **61** **62** **63** **64** **65**
Ludlow **262** **263** Northampton Bury StEdmunds
Worcester Stratford-upon-Avon Cambridge Ipswich
Cardigan **42** **43** **44** **45** **46** **47** **48** **49** Bedford **50** **51** Felixstowe
Brecon Hereford Bedford Luton **52** **53**
Fishguard **32** **33** Carmarthen Gloucester Oxford Chelmsford
Pembroke Swansea **36** Abergavenny **37** **38** **39** **40** **41** Watford **30** **31**
34 **35** Cardiff Bristol Swindon Reading **28** **29**
Bath Andover Basingstoke LONDON Maidstone
Barnstaple **22** **23** **24** **25** Guildford **258 - 261** Sevenoaks Dover
20 **21** Taunton Salisbury **26** **27** **16** **17** Folkestone
Bude Lyme Yeovil Southampton Chichester Brighton **18** **19**
4 **5** **8** Exeter **10** Regis **11** **12** **13** **14** **15** Hastings
Bodmin **9** Weymouth Bournemouth Newhaven
Torquay
6 **7** Plymouth
2 **3**
Truro

Isles of Scilly **2**

The Channel Islands **174**

AA

ROAD ATLAS
OF THE
BRITISH
ISLES
2002

Scale 1:200,000
or 3.15 miles to 1 inch

contents

Distances, journey times and map pages	inside front cover
The tourist's British Isles	4–48
Traffic and travel information	IV–V
Route planner	VI–XI
Motorways	**XII–XV**
Restricted junctions	XII–XIII
M25 London orbital motorway	XIV
M60 Manchester orbital motorway	XV
Map symbols	XVI–1
Road maps	**2–174**
Scottish islands	168–169
Ireland	170–173
The Channel Islands & The Isle of Man	174
Town plans	**175–234**
Key to town plans	175
Central London	240–250
Central London street index	251–257
Ports and airports	**235–239**
Major ports	235
Major airports	236–238
Channel Tunnel	239
District maps	**258–269**
London district	258–261
Birmingham district	262–263
Glasgow district	264–265
Manchester district	266–267
Tyne & Wear district	268–269
Index to place names	**270–320**
County map (index opener)	270
Distances, journey times and map pages	inside back cover

12th edition July 2001

© Automobile Association Developments Limited 2001

Original edition printed 1990.

Ordnance Survey This product includes mapping data licensed from Ordnance Survey® with the permission of the Controller of Her Majesty's Stationery Office. © Crown copyright 2001. All rights reserved. Licence number 399221.

Northern Ireland mapping reproduced by permission of the Director and Chief Executive, Ordnance Survey of Northern Ireland, acting on behalf of the controller of Her Majesty's Stationery Office © Crown copyright 2001. Permit No. 1674.

Republic of Ireland mapping based on Ordnance Survey Ireland by permission of the Government. Permit No. MP004201 © Government of Ireland.

Published by AA Publishing (a trading name of Automobile Association Developments Limited, whose registered office is Norfolk House, Priestley Road, Basingstoke, Hampshire RG24 9NY. Registered number 1878835).

Mapping produced by the Cartographic Department of The Automobile Association. This atlas has been compiled and produced from the Automaps database utilising electronic and computer technology.

ISBN 0 7495 2974 1

A CIP catalogue record for this book is available from The British Library.

Printed in Italy by Pizzi, Milan.

The contents of this atlas are believed to be correct at the time of the latest revision. However, the publishers cannot be held responsible for loss occasioned to any person acting or refraining from action as a result of any material in this atlas, nor for any errors, omissions or changes in such material. The publishers would welcome information to correct any errors or omissions and to keep this atlas up to date. Please write to the Cartographic Editor, Publishing Division, The Automobile Association, Fanum House, Basing View, Basingstoke, Hampshire RG21 4EA.

Information on National Parks provided by the Countryside Agency for England and the Countryside Council for Wales.

Information on National Scenic Areas in Scotland provided by Scottish Natural Heritage.

Information on Forest Parks provided by the Forestry Commission.

The RSPB sites shown are a selection chosen by the Royal Society for the Protection of Birds.

National Trust properties shown are a selection of those open to the public as indicated in the handbooks of the National Trust and the National Trust for Scotland.

Automobile Association Developments Limited would like to thank the following photographers, libraries and associations for their assistance in the preparation of this book.

British Waterways Board, Waterways Museum 22a, 23b
The Mansell Collection 6a, 6b, 7a, 7c
Museum of Rural Llife 26a
Nature Photographers Ltd 32a (P R Sterry), 41a (C Palmer), 41b (W S Paton), 41c (P R Sterry)
Pictures Colour Library Ltd 25c
Rex Features Ltd 18b (N Jorgensen)
Spectrum Colour Library 10, 11a, 11c, 25d

All remaining pictures are held in the Association's own library (AA Photo Library) with contributions from the following photographers:

M Alexander, A Baker, P Baker, V & S Bates, J Beazley, M Birkitt, I Burgum, D Corrance, S L Day, E Ellington, P Enticknap, A J Hopkins, C Jones, A Lawson, S & O Mathews, E Meacher, C Molyneux, J Morrison, R Mort, J Mottershaw, R Newton, A Perkins, M Short, R Strange, T Teegan, T D Timms, M Trelawny, A Tryner, R Victor, W Voysey, R Weir, L Whitwam, P Wilson, T Woodcock, T Wyles

CHURCH & HOME:
BUILDINGS IN THE LANDSCAPE

LOCAL STONE

In the border country of Somerset and Dorset some of the finest building stone is found. The exquisite golden stone of Somerset's Ham Hill was transported across the county border to give such splendid buildings as Sherborne Abbey their mellow hue. Hamstone has been lavished on great Somerset houses too, as much as on the charming vernacular buildings of so many of the county's villages. In the immediate hinterland of Ham Hill are the Tudor and Jacobean piles of Montacute House, Tintinhull and the restored Barrington Court, the latter further enhanced by the 20th-century development of its gardens. All three are in the care of the National Trust and are open to the public.

In Cornwall the availability of durable granite has produced the solid four-square certainty of church tower and farmhouse alike, the roughness and earthy colour of the unadorned stone merging with the knuckly landscape of Dartmoor and the Atlantic coast of Cornwall. But in the non-granite country of Devon, cottages were often built of 'cob', unbaked mud that was remarkably durable. In Cornwall and Devon too, the use of less attractive slates and shales has resulted in darker, more sombre buildings that still merge satisfyingly with the landscape from which they emerged.

Granite is a rock that is often at its best when low to

*T*op: Egypt cottage at Chulmleigh is of Devon cob and thatch; right: Forde Abbey, a superb example of an ecclesiastical conversion into a home

For many people, the West Country means the picture-postcard thatched cottages of Dorset, Somerset and Devon, the cobbled streets of the famous coastal villages of Clovelly and St Ives, and the elaborate façades of seaside hotels in Torquay and Ilfracombe. But memorable images apart, it is the building materials that characterise the different parts of a region, as represented by cottages and castles, churches and cathedrals. Above all else the best buildings appear to have grown from the very landscape that they adorn.

the ground, absorbed by the landscape rather than set monumentally upon it. Yet types of Cornish granite have produced such great buildings as Lanhydrock, near Bodmin, and the magnificent Antony House on the banks of the River Lynher opposite Plymouth.

CHURCH ARCHITECTURE

An enduring motif of West-Country architecture is the local church, with its stately tower rising fortress-like from surrounding woods, or dominating the lower roof-line of numerous towns and villages. Somerset is particularly noted for its elegant church towers. Spires were few in Somerset; instead the tall, square tower, with its characteristic Somerset tracery and its elegant lace-like pinnacles and statue niches, big windows and ornamental string courses, has been the glory of the West Country for centuries. There are especially fine church buildings at Glastonbury, Wells, Taunton, Shepton Mallet, Yeovil and Huish Episcopi.

There was less church building during the 17th and 18th centuries. That period saw the rise of non-conformist chapels and meeting places, and it was not until the 19th century that a new religious self-confidence produced such fine Regency churches as Teignmouth's St James's and the Norman-influenced St Paul's at Honiton.

Large numbers of non-conformist churches were built throughout the West Country during the 19th century. They were simple preaching places, although neo-classical and

Gothic themes emerged. Throughout Cornwall, stern-faced Methodist chapels still dominate the rural landscape, their main façades seeming always to face the unsmiling north as if to deny even the sun its elevated place.

CHANGING STYLES

The Romans left few traces of their presence west of Exeter, the Anglo-Saxons likewise, but Norman influence was substantial in churches and castles, and there are numerous West-Country churches that have some element of Norman work that has survived the repeated restorations and extensions of the ensuing centuries.

It is the 15th and 16th centuries, however, that have bequeathed us fairly complete buildings. Rural buildings of the period were still vulnerable to structural erosion and decay from the impact of the heavy work that went on around them, but in Devon, good examples of larger farmhouses still exist. These include Sir Walter Raleigh's birthplace of Hayes Barton near Budleigh Salterton, constructed of cob and with a fine Devon thatch.

Good stone buildings of the period include the outstanding George Inn at Norton St Philip, between Bath and Frome. The George is pure medieval, its ground floor of stone with a fine entrance archway, the upper storeys timber-framed.

In Glastonbury High Street is another famous inn – The George and Pilgrim – this time in three storeys of ornamented stone. A few yards further along is the 15th-century Gothic building known as the Tribunal.

The great buildings of the late 16th century are well represented in the West Country by beautiful houses such as Montacute and by town buildings such as the Guildhall at Exeter. Later developments of the Stuart period produced Dorset's Forde Abbey, an example of how buildings evolve from earlier forms. Forde lies on the site of a 12th-century Cistercian Abbey and parts of the abbey are incorporated into the 17th-century house. Tintinhull, near Yeovil, is another example of incorporation, the mainly 17th-century building having absorbed parts of a 16th-century farmhouse.

The George Inn at Norton St Philip is a fine medieval building

Above: the wonderful West Front of Wells Cathedral; above right: Montacute House has the lovely golden glow of Hamstone

THE LAST 200 YEARS

By the 18th century urban architecture was becoming increasingly sophisticated, as the burgeoning merchant class expressed its aspirations. Great country houses also reflected this. Devon's Saltram House, the county's finest country mansion, is an outstanding early Georgian building with fine interiors, the whole maintained by the National Trust. But it was urban building that became the focus for fashionable architecture. The legacy of the Georgian and Regency periods, so evident in our great cities and in such places as Bath, can be seen in most West Country towns of any size. Even as far west as Truro the stylish neo-classicism of entire terraces, such as those of Lemon Street, matched the sophistication of those of Bath, and the red-brick elegance of Taunton's Hammet Street and The Crescent match the crescents and terraces of Exeter.

During the late 18th century and well into the Victorian period the 'seaside' architecture peculiar to holiday resorts produced some outstanding buildings in towns such as Sidmouth, Ilfracombe and Torquay.

Sidmouth still has some very fine Regency buildings, including the fascinating *cottage ornée*, a mock-rustic style incorporating Gothic façades topped with lavish thatch. At Ilfracombe, the use of polychromatic brickwork resulted in some outstanding Victorian Gothic buildings.

It was a stylishness soon to be overtaken by the bland and brutal convenience architecture of the 20th century, as technology and commercial enterprise ensured the triumph of function over style. Yet good modern architecture is still given breathing space, even in the featureless world of supermarkets and tower blocks. Award-winning buildings include Truro's Crown Court, designed by the same architects who were responsible for the Tate Gallery at St Ives, and in 1995 Sainsbury's superstore at Plymouth won an award for its bold design that features a white canopy made of overlapping sail-like armatures.

But it is in the surviving older buildings of Dorset, Somerset, Devon and Cornwall that the great legacy of good West-Country architecture is enshrined – the Hamstone villages, the thatched houses of quiet hamlets, and the lichened and mossy cottages of fishing villages. Above all, the marvellous churches and cathedrals and the great country houses of the West remain as priceless jewels within the landscape.

LITERARY SETTINGS: WRITERS IN THE WEST COUNTRY

The poet John Heath-Stubbs captured, grudgingly it seems, both the inspiration and the awe of the wildest parts of the west of England, when he spoke of '...a hideous and wicked country/Sloping to hateful sunsets and the end of time...' Most writers have been more happily captivated than that. For Heath-Stubbs, it seems, too much raw nature was unnerving. The poet's uneasy words were inspired by the powerful Atlantic coast of Gurnard's Head near Land's End, itself the *Belerium*, the 'Seat of Storms', of the Roman writer Tacitus, an early commentator within the literary setting.

From those Roman times until the present day, the West Country has continued to attract poets and writers. From the beautiful countryside of Dorset, Thomas Hardy created his own landscape of 'Wessex', at the gates of the West Country, yet he too was drawn further west, to the spectacular coastline of North Cornwall. Here he met his wife Emma at the exquisite little church of St Juliot, near Boscastle, and much bitter-sweet romance ensued. The pair strolled out at Beeny Cliff, just north of Boscastle, and above 'the opal and the sapphire of that wandering western sea' – lines in which Hardy captured the essence of the Cornish coast better, perhaps, than generations of writers since. But before Hardy, the north coast of Devon gave inspiration to Charles Kingsley, who grew up at the charming village of Clovelly, lived later at Bideford, and gave the breezy name of *Westward Ho!* to his most famous novel – and subsequently to a seaside village.

EVOCATIVE LANDSCAPES

The coast of North Cornwall more recently inspired John Betjeman, whose lifelong association with Padstow, further south from Hardy's Beeny Cliff, added a richer, more robust tone to the poetry of suburbia. South of Padstow, the rugged tin-mining coast of St Agnes and Perranporth inspired Winston Graham's marvellous *Poldark* saga, an epic narrative of life in 18th- and 19th-century Cornwall from the pen of a modern master.

The Atlantic coast of the west was ever inspirational, but so too were the high moors of Exmoor and the Quantocks. Amidst the wooded combes and soft rolling heaths of the Quantocks, the poet Samuel Taylor Coleridge and his friends, William and Dorothy Wordsworth, found the intensely pastoral inspiration for their great Romantic poems, even before the Lake District claimed them for its own.

Between Exmoor and the sea, Coleridge wrote his fevered, flawed masterpiece 'Kubla Khan', its opium-induced fantasies rudely interrupted by the unannounced visit of 'a person from Porlock', who was thus immortalised as perhaps the most notorious full stop in literary history.

Directly inland from Porlock, around the heathland wastes of Badgworthy Water, is 'Doone Country', the inspiration for R D Blackmore's famously romantic novel *Lorna Doone*. The legends of the robber Doones of Badgworthy, said to originate from an exiled and disaffected Scottish noble family, were part of Exmoor lore long before Blackmore's masterly embellishment, but with all its lonely, compelling beauty, the moorland wilderness cried out for just such a rattling good tale. Blackmore's novel merged romance with reality, and turned into shrines of literary pilgrimage such places as the little church at Oare where Lorna was shot and wounded by Carver Doone during her wedding to John Ridd.

Main picture: Thomas Hardy's study, in Dorchester's County Museum; above left: Samuel Taylor Coleridge; right: R D Blackmore

ROMANCE AND MYSTERY

R D Blackmore's 20th-century counterpart was undoubtedly Daphne du Maurier, whose grasp of the romantic and the picturesque gave rise to such popular novels as *Jamaica Inn* and *Frenchman's Creek*. The former borrowed some of its imagery from the forlorn heights of Cornwall's Bodmin Moor; the latter focused on the tree-shrouded creeks of the Helford River on the county's south-west coast. But du Maurier's true literary setting was the lovely landscape of the River Fowey. Here, amidst the wooded parkland of Menabilly House, were shaped the novels *My Cousin Rachel* and *Rebecca*, who woke and 'dreamt of Manderley'. It was here too that du Maurier was inspired to write a short story about predatory seabirds – subsequently filmed by Alfred Hitchcock as *The Birds* – after watching a cloud of screaming gulls foraging in the wake of a tractor as it drew its plough through the rich earth of the Cornish fields.

Similar inspiration for one of the greatest detective stories ever written, *The Hound of the Baskervilles*, was drawn from Dartmoor by Sir Arthur Conan Doyle. The novelist had stayed on the south-eastern edge of the moor, at Manaton, and had been gripped by the changing moods of its great waste, and by the Gothic atmosphere of the lonely granite tors that rise eerily like castles above the marshy low ground.

Following in the romantic spirit set by Blackmore in *Lorna Doone* and Hardy in *Tess of the D'Urbervilles*, 20th-century writer John Fowles established Lyme Regis as the setting for his powerful novel, *The French Lieutenant's Woman*, with its more complex literary romanticism. The novel is now

Jane Austen knew Lyme Regis well

immortalised on film, most dramatically by the image of the tragic heroine, the black-cloaked Sarah Woodruff, precarious in body and soul, on the storm-battered harbour wall of The Cobb at Lyme. Here also, the more formal romance of Jane Austen's *Persuasion* depicts the headstrong Louisa Musgrove falling from the Higher Cobb, intent on landing in Captain Wentworth's arms, but knocking herself unconscious instead; and so precipitating a crisis for all the characters in the novel.

CONTINUING INSPIRATION

The literary inspiration of the West Country continues today, its dramatic landscapes inspiring even those writers whose themes may not necessarily reflect a West-Country setting. Near Land's End lives the novelist John Le Carré, whose books range the cosmopolitan world of Europe and Asia, yet whose hard work of writing is often carried out against the background of the restless Atlantic. A near neighbour of Le Carré's is Derek Tangye, author of a gently sentimental series of autobiographical novels about his beloved west Cornwall. The novelist Mary Wesley lives in Totnes and writes more sophisticated novels than perhaps Daphne du Maurier would ever have dared. Wesley based her scintil-

Sir Arthur Conan Doyle wrote of the mysteries of brooding Dartmoor

lating *Camomile Lawn* on Cornwall's Roseland Peninsula.

The popular novelist Rosamund Pilcher has strong connections with the north coast of west Cornwall near St Ives, and the film version of her novel *The Shell Seekers* was filmed in the town.

Earlier literary figures connected with the St Ives area included Virginia Woolf, who based her novel *To the Lighthouse* on the nearby Godrevy lighthouse. D H Lawrence lived at Zennor, along the coast from St Ives, for a period during World War I, hounded by the authorities because of his pacifist stance and because of his wife Frieda's German nationality. Lawrence described vividly his experiences during his time in Cornwall when he wrote the nightmare sequence in his novel *Kangaroo*.

Locations in the West Country have inspired some of the most seminal works of English poetry and prose. Near Yeovil is East Coker, ancestral

Top: the Boscastle coastline has romantic associations with Thomas Hardy; above: the Doone Valley

home of T S Eliot, whose ashes are buried here, and who attached the name of this archetypal English village to the second poem of his *Four Quartets*. Coleridge was born at Ottery St Mary. John Galsworthy lived for 18 years at Manaton in east Dartmoor, where he worked on *The Forsyte Saga*. At the unlikely setting of nearby Chagford, Evelyn Waugh wrote *Brideshead Revisited*, whose characters would have felt positively uneasy amidst Dartmoor's ruggedness. Torquay was the birthplace of Agatha Christie, who also lived on the inspiring Dart Estuary and wrote several of her famous crime novels on the nearby Burgh Island off Salcombe. And in the delightful valleys of the Rivers Taw and Torridge in North Devon Henry Williamson wrote *Tarka the Otter* and *Salar the Salmon*.

THE NEW FOREST

THE LIVING AND WORKING FOREST

Occupying a large part of south-west Hampshire, the New Forest is both a major tourist attraction and an area of wildlife and landscape conservation. A wide-ranging and detailed New Forest Heritage Area Management Strategy seeks to reconcile these conflicting functions, together with a third element – commercial timber production. Negotiations are underway to make the New Forest a national park, but the process is expected to be protracted because of the number of landowners and other interested parties involved. A suggested park boundary has been drawn on a map, but so far has not met with universal approval.

If the forest becomes a fully fledged national park, it will be in the English rather than the international sense, because it encompasses not just beautiful scenery and flora and fauna, but towns and villages too, and, of course people who earn their living from the land. The forest's 1,500 deer belong to the Crown and are managed by the Commission, but the 3,000 or so New Forest ponies belong to the Commoners – local people whose 11th-century predecessors secured grazing and other rights when the savage Forest Law deprived them of the right to hunt.

The 'capital' of the forest is Lyndhurst, seat of the Commission's local administration, of the ancient but still important Court of Verderers, and the New Forest District Council. A town of a few thousand people, it is idyllically set with great forestry 'inclosures' to north and south, and open heathlands to east and west.

The name, it has been observed, is doubly misleading. The New Forest was 'new' only in 1097, when William the Conqueror declared it a royal hunting preserve, and 'forest' then meant not a large area of woodland, as we think of today, but an area of land reserved for hunting. Then, as now, trees occupied less space than the heathland and the often rather marshy fields, but today, though 130sq miles (336sq km) of New Forest are still 'preserved', it is for public enjoyment and for conservation as an ecological and landscape asset, rather than for a monarch's days out in the saddle.

Above: thatch amidst the forest at Swan Green; right: the famous and sturdy little New Forest ponies can be seen grazing any clearings between the woodland

The New Forest Museum and Visitor Centre adjoining the main car park at Lyndhurst provides both general tourist information and audio-visual and other displays on how the New Forest came into existence, its way of life and its customs and traditions.

FOREST ATTRACTIONS

As well as the obvious attractions of the landscape and wildlife, the Forest has a number of places of interest to visit. The thrill of seeing native species in the wild is always an uncertainty, but visitors can be sure of seeing some of the animals at close hand at a number of attractions: New Forest Nature Quest, at Longdown, houses Britain's largest native wildlife collection in a lovely woodland setting, with sections on back garden wildlife, riverbank species, nocturnal animals and reptiles; there is a Deer Sanctuary at Bolderwood (west of Lyndhurst), with a Reptiliary near by; the Owl Sanctuary at Crow, near Ringwood, dedicated to putting birds back into the wild, has over 100 spacious aviaries; New Forest Badger Watch at Ringwood provides a wonderful opportunity to view these delightful but elusive creatures both above and below ground. There is a hide and an observation set, and headphones provide an instructive commentary. You need to book about a month in advance to take part in an evening watch. The Longdown Dairy Farm near Ashurst is a working farm which welcomes visitors.

A reminder of the forest's days as a Norman hunting preserve exists in the Rufus Stone, which commemorates the allegedly accidental shooting of the unpopular, red-headed King William II (Rufus) while he was out hunting.

A good way to appreciate the best of the woodland is to venture along the magnificent Rhinefield and Bolderwood ornamental drives, and there are horse-drawn wagon rides as well as waymarked woodland walks, all with skilfully sited car parks.

Of the Forest's half-dozen villages, Minstead is among the most visited, with its thatched cottages and well-preserved, largely 18th-century All Saints Church, notable for its three-decker pulpit, box pews and two galleries, one above the other. Furzey Gardens at Minstead consists of 8 acres (3ha) of flowering trees and shrubs. More famous are the Exbury Gardens, which are spectacularly colourful during the rhododendron season, and Spinners at Boldre, near Lymington is another lovely garden to visit. Burley in the south-east of the Forest, set amidst bracing open heathland, is a good centre for walkers. Castle Hill, 1¼ miles (2km) north, is an Iron-Age camp and one of the best vantage points to view the Forest.

In the south-east of the Forest stands Beaulieu Abbey, founded by King John for the Cistercians, but home of the Montagu family since 1538. Its battlemented Palace House was once the abbey's gatehouse, though its present appearance owes much to an 1870s 'restoration'. Understanding of the medieval remains is greatly helped by an exhibition about monastic life. Alongside the Abbey is the 3rd Lord Montagu's pride and joy, his splendid National Motor Museum, with 250 exhibits, including cars, commercial vehicles and motorcycles. There is also 'Wheels', described as 'a futuristic ride on space-age pods through 100 years of motoring', as well as a monorail and veteran bus rides.

Buckler's Hard, 2½ miles (4km) down the Beaulieu River, is a remnant of an early 18th-century plan to build Montagu Town, a port to rival Southampton. Two rows of attractive brick cottages were as far as the project got, but the little settlement was important for 80 years as a shipyard – Nelson's *Agamemnon* was built here, using 2,000 New Forest oaks. Buckler's Hard's Maritime Museum vividly evokes that era. On the next little river to the west stands Lymington, a lively yachting and ferry port and the New Forest's main market town. Its mellow streetscape and roof-scape, mixed with masts and the steeple of St Michael's Church, are as lively as the Saturday high-street market.

Exbury Gardens are a riot of colour during the rhododendron and azalea season in early summer

A CITY ON THE FOREST FRINGE

A large, modern city, port, and regional shopping and commercial centre, Southampton nonetheless has a long history. There was a Roman town on the east bank of the Itchen at Bitterne, and on the west bank a Saxon town called Hamwic. Despite World War II bombs and post-war development, a great deal of the past remains. South of the modern shopping centre Above Bar is a surviving gateway of the medieval town, the fortified Bargate. Beyond stretches the high street, with the Red Lion, Dolphin and Star hotels reminding us that this was Southampton's 18th-century equivalent of a railway station or airport.

To right and left of Bargate run the impressive remains of the town walls with defensive towers, including the picturesquely named Catchcold Tower and Blue Anchor Postern. The Tudor House, a fine example of a rich merchant's town house of around

Lymington harbour is a delightful scene, popular with weekend sailors as well as with Isle of Wight ferry passengers

1500, is now a museum, and its finest exhibit is arguably its handsome banqueting hall. Other medieval and Tudor buildings have been converted to museum use, including the Museum of Archaeology in God's House Tower on the old Town Quay, and the Maritime Museum, housed in the early 15th-century Wool House.

More recent history is celebrated in the Hall of Aviation, which tells the story of aviation – particularly flying boats and seaplanes – in and around the Solent. The name 'Supermarine' attaches not only to the Spitfire, first built in Southampton, but also to the racing seaplanes that took part in the Schneider Trophy races here in 1929 and 1931. The modern helicopter was also created in Southampton, and several are on show.

Southampton is very green, with a series of six parks right in the heart of the city, while to the north the 368 acres (149ha) of Southampton Common drive a generous green wedge between the adjacent suburbs. The waterfront is also a pleasant public amenity, with Mayflower Park looking out over the Test estuary between Town Quay and the Western Docks, and the more recent development of Ocean Village, focusing on the 'festival market' concept.

CUSTOMS AND FESTIVALS

Traditional customs and festivals in southern England are many and varied. Some, like 'first footing' on New Year's Eve, pancakes on Shrove Tuesday, and bonfires and fireworks on Guy Fawkes Day, are nationwide, but sometimes may have peculiar local variants. Many go back to pagan times, though the early Christian church took them over. The variety of traditional festivals celebrated is, moreover, being interestingly extended and enriched as schools and communities respond to an increasingly multicultural population.

Thus primary school children in Kent or Oxfordshire are quite likely to know about Holi (when Hindus celebrate the end of winter), Id-ul-Fitr (the end of the Ramadan fast for Muslims), Vesak (when Buddhists leave gifts on the doorsteps of the poor), Shavuot (when Jews celebrate the first fruits of the harvest), or the Chinese New Year marked with fire-crackers and (as in London's Chinatown) dragon dancers. But in these two pages we look at some of the more traditional customs and festivals of the south and south-east.

THE FIRST QUARTER

One curious New Year custom is Queen's College, Oxford's Needle and Thread Gaudy (feast), when the college bursar presents each guest at table with a needle threaded with silk, and says: 'Take this and be thrifty'. Sound advice, no doubt, but all a bit of a joke, in arcane Oxford style. Needle and thread in Norman French is *aiguille* and *fil* – a pun on the college's 14th-century founder, Robert de Eglesfield.

Solemnity and fun are mixed in a different way in London in February, with the annual Clowns' Service at Holy Trinity Church, Dalston. Clowns in full costume and make-up attending this service end with a prayer thanking God 'for causing me to share with others your precious gift of laughter'. It began relatively recently, in 1946, as a tribute to the great 19th-century clown Joseph Grimaldi.

In March people at Stockbridge in Hampshire elect jurors to the Courts Leet and Baron, which traditionally resolved disputes over the local commons. These now belong to the National Trust, but the revived ceremony is fun and provides a useful forum for discussion of local matters.

RITES OF SPRING

Easter and the period preceding it are rich in quaint and colourful customs, starting with Shrove Tuesday, which is traditionally associated with pancakes. This, it seems, is because pancake-making used up perishable foodstuffs before the 40 days of Lent.

A well-known variant is the pancake race at Olney, Buckinghamshire. Contrary to general belief, dropping the pancake does not disqualify the racer, though it may spoil the appetite.

On Maundy Thursday the sovereign distributes Maundy Money – specially minted silver coins – at Westminster Abbey and varying cathedrals. In London Easter Sunday sees the Easter Parade in Battersea Park, followed on Easter Monday by the Harness Horse Parade in Regents Park. On Dunstable Down in Bedfordshire they roll oranges down the hill to waiting children.

May Day ceremonies are perhaps most spectacular in Oxford, where at 6am choristers climb the 144ft (44m) tower of Magdalen College to sing a Latin hymn to the (surprisingly large) assembled crowd. The tower's bells ring out, and a day of celebrations begins with morris dancing, punting parties and picnics.

Towards the end of May at Rye, Sussex, the inauguration of the new mayor is strangely celebrated by the new incumbent throwing hot pennies to children from the town hall. Along the coast, the Vicar of Hastings blesses the sea, presumably to enhance local fishermen's catches (these days his pulpit is a lifeboat). Also in May, the charter trustees of High Wycombe, Buckinghamshire choose a mayor, who

The country moves into the city with maypole dancers performing outside St Margaret's Church in London

is then weighed by the mayoress, out-going mayor and various others, the presiding weights-and-measures official pronouncing either 'Some more' (meaning 'You've put on weight since last year') or 'No more' (meaning 'You haven't').

SUMMER CELEBRATIONS

On a June Saturday in each leap year, Great Dunmow in Essex is the scene of the well-known Dunmow Flitch, a 900-year-old custom in which married couples seek to convince a local jury of 'six maids and six bachelors' that they have never been unfaithful nor had cross words. National celebrities dressed in wig and gown act as prosecuting and defending counsel; the prize for successful defendants is the flitch – a whole side of bacon.

On the second Wednesday in July the new Master of the Vintners' Company (a City of London livery company) processes from Vintners' Hall in Upper Thames Street to the Church of St James Garlickhithe, he and his entourage carrying nosegays against noxious fumes or infection, and preceded by their Wine Porter who sweeps a clean path with his broom. Later in the month the Vintners are concerned with Swan Upping on the Thames – the nicking of the beak of each swan to show whether it belongs to the Queen, the Vintners or the Dyers.

In August the Thames hosts the Doggett's Coat and Badge Race, when recently qualified Thames Watermen compete in a sculling race from London Bridge to Chelsea's Cadogan Pier. Thomas Doggett, an Irish actor-manager who died in 1721, inaugurated the race to show his patriotic support for George I and his new Hanoverian dynasty – the

Top: swan upping on the River Thames; above: the best-known of all English traditions – morris dancing: right: Pearly Kings and Queens are a long-established London tradition

prizes being £5, a scarlet coat, breeches and shoes, and a huge silver badge.

WINTER CUSTOMS

The first day of October sees the Lord Chancellor processing from a service in Westminster Abbey to the House of Lords where he greets his guests and gives them 'Breakfast' (a reception for lawyers and others). On the first Sunday London's

Costermongers congregate for their service in St Martin-in-the-Fields, many of them kitted out in the dressy manner of 19th-century street traders, including 'Pearly Kings and Queens', their clothes studded with pearl buttons.

Following Guy Fawkes' unsuccessful attempt to blow up King and Parliament in 1605, bonfires and fireworks in England are mostly not at the New Year but on 5 November. Nowhere is this festival so thoroughly celebrated as in Lewes, Sussex, where the memory of 17 Protestant martyrs in the reign of Queen Mary led to a (these days not serious) anti-Papist tradition. Lewes has a number of bonfire societies in different parts of the town, who dress up, go in procession, and burn effigies of currently-hated politicians and others on giant bonfires. In London, the second Saturday in November sees the City's new Lord Mayor ride in his state coach to be sworn in at the Royal Courts of Justice. The accompanying procession consists of mobile floats on various aspects of a theme chosen by the incoming Lord Mayor.

On Christmas Day the Serpentine in Hyde Park is the scene of a swimming race for the Peter Pan Cup, originally presented in 1864 by Peter Pan's creator Sir James Barrie. The swimmers, meet at 9am, and sometimes need to break ice.

DAILY EVENTS

Some customs and ceremonies take place every day of the year. At the ancient Hospital of St Cross in Winchester, the first 32 people to arrive can claim a slice of bread (presented on a wooden platter) and a drink of ale from a horn cup.

And each evening at the Tower of London the Chief Yeoman Warder and his escort are challenged by a sentry, leading to the following ex-change. 'Halt, who goes there?' 'The Keys'. 'Whose keys?' 'Queen Elizabeth's keys'. The sentry then presents arms, the Chief Warder removes his hat and proclaims, 'God preserve Queen Elizabeth', and the whole guard responds 'Amen!'

LONDON BUILDINGS, OLD AND NEW

London's architectural riches range from great set-pieces like the Palace of Westminster and Wren's two great waterside 'hospitals', or retirement homes (for old soldiers at Chelsea and old sailors at Greenwich) through to smaller, more hidden gems like the Blewcoat School in Caxton Street, Westminster, and the more out of the way City churches.

London has its grand sequences, like the Mall, with Nash's stuccoed, columned sweep of Carlton House Terrace, his great processional route from Regent's Park along Portland Place and Regent Street, and Pall Mall with its succession of Italianate 19th-century gentlemen's clubs. But the capital generally eschews grand gestures; its townscape tends to be both more reticent and more anarchic.

THE HEART OF THE CAPITAL

Perhaps the place to start is at Charing Cross in the heart of London, and the hotel which fronts the station (Decimus Burton, 1834) is worth more than a glance. Trafalgar Square has two fine classical buildings. The first, St Martin-in-the-Fields Church (Gibbs, 1726), has a magnificent temple-like portico and steeple.

The other is the National Gallery (Wilkins, 1838), with its controversial but extremely likeable 1991 Sainsbury Wing, designed by American architect Robert Venturi after criticism by Prince Charles scotched the original plan.

Whitehall is full of architectural delights, outstandingly the Banqueting House (Inigo Jones), which, in the early 17th century, was shockingly modern. There is also the Horse Guards (1760), the ceremonial gateway to the parade ground and park beyond, and Richmond Terrace. A 1960s scheme for a new government precinct would have swept away this and the famous New Scotland Yard, but by 1970 the tide of conservation was running strongly enough to stop it. William Whitfield's attractive Department of Heath building, alongside Richmond Terrace, shows how modern infill can possess strength and character, and yet still exist in sympathy with its surroundings.

More MPs' offices on the Parliament Square corner await completion of a new station

for the Jubilee Line. The architects of the 11 new stations on the line's extension have a brief to bring light and spaciousness into the underworld.

The Houses of Parliament and Westminster Abbey are, of course, the great architectural features of this square, but the Queen Elizabeth II Conference Centre (1986) demonstrates how large modern buildings can sit happily in a historic townscape.

Other notable buildings hereabouts include Westminster Cathedral (Bentley, 1903); and Channel 4's television studios and headquarters in Horseferry Road (Rogers, 1994).

THE CITY AND DOCKLANDS

The City of London has rather different planning policies from neighbouring Westminster, most of which is now a conservation area. The City has its historic jewels – Wren's St Paul's Cathedral, his 'wedding cake' St Bride's and a string of other churches, built after the Great Fire of 1666. The tranquil and beautiful Inns of Court are here, along with such monuments to commerce as the Bank of England, Royal Exchange, Custom House and the Mansion House and Guildhall. Just over the City boundary is that great riverside fortress, the Tower of London.

Because it is a money-making machine, the City has looked favourably on new developments designed to give

*T*op: *St Paul's Cathedral is an impressive sight amidst the towering modern office blocks of the city*

*A*bove: *Westminster Cathedral and St Pancras Station both reflect the flamboyance of the 19th century*

*L*eft: Canary Wharf, in the docklands area, has been transformed by this splendid development; above: Westminster's Roman Catholic cathedral houses many works of art

its money-makers the accommodation they want, resulting in many large, dull or ugly buildings, some bold and beautiful ones, and a striking new City skyline. Notable recent buildings include Rogers' 1986 Lloyds building in steel and glass, with a lofty atrium looking down on its underwriting room. Another is the stylishly upgraded Liverpool Street Station (British Rail architects) with the huge Broadgate office development (Arup Associates, Skidmore Owings Merrill). And there is the 1950s–1980s Barbican development, combining accommodation with entertainment venues and restaurants (Chamberlin Powell & Bon).

These days the Square Mile has a rival in its near neighbour to the east – London's renascent Docklands. Here is the capital's most spectacular and controversial group of buildings, Canary Wharf. Conceived as a sort of Wall Street-on-Thames, this £4 billion development extends more than half a mile (1km) across the Isle of Dogs, and includes London's tallest tower, by American architect Cesar Pelli. It has its own shopping centre and waterside restaurants, with a mixture of architectural styles that are often pastiche. Canary Wharf is best approached by the elevated Docklands Light Railway, but do get out and walk all round it!

AROUND THE CENTRE

On the north-central fringe of central London are four buildings of particular merit – the British Museum (1847, Smirke), University College's original Gower Street group (Wilkins, 1829), St Pancras Station and the new British Library. St Pancras's spectacular and recently restored High Victorian hotel front (1874, G G Scott) faces Barlow's great 1868 train shed, being adapted for trains from the planned Channel Tunnel fast rail link (completion due 2007); the Library next door, designed by Colin St John Wilson, is clad in red brick to match the station.

The 'museums area' of South Kensington also merits a good, long look. Here is the expression of Queen Victoria's and (especially) Prince Albert's belief in the nation's intellectual and cultural advancement, and stylistically the site reflects that age. Impressively self-confident buildings in brick, terracotta and stone line spacious boulevards. They include the Victoria and Albert, Natural History and Science Museums; Imperial College tower and the Royal Albert Hall. There are plans to enhance the overall area ('Albertopolis') by submerging the road in front of the Royal Albert Hall and creating a piazza connecting it with the Albert Memorial.

Everything on the South Bank is now dwarfed by the London Eye. The two most notable buildings of the cultural complex here are the Royal Festival Hall (Robert Matthew, Leslie Martin, 1951) and the Royal National Theatre (Denys Lasdun, 1975). Wide-ranging plans currently on the drawing board include refurbishment of the existing buildings, the building of another concert hall, the creation of public squares, the provision of shops and cafés in the area, the expansion of the Jubilee Gardens to stretch from County Hall to Hungerford Bridge, and improved access in the form of new footbridges, tramways and even cable cars. The conversion of the Bankside Power Station into the impressive Tate Modern art gallery has proved to be a powerful magnet.

Just downstream you see the thatched roof of the replica Globe Theatre, part of an international Shakespeare centre close to the site of the original Globe. Further on are Southwark Cathedral, London Bridge City, where lofty Hay's Galleria rises from a former dock basin, and (below Tower Bridge) Butler's Wharf, an area of 19th-century warehouses recycled into flats, restaurants and design studios – an ideal site for the Design Museum.

*T*he familiar Albert Memorial, restored to its full splendour after an extensive overhaul and cleaning-up operation

THE GREEN LUNGS OF LONDON

CENTRAL LONDON PARKS

Centuries ago these parks were mostly royal hunting forests outside the confines of a much smaller capital. Central London has now engulfed many of them, and the oldest is St James's Park, with its neat lawns, colourful flower beds and shrubberies around a lovely lake.

It is hard to imagine this as marshland, as it was until it was drained to provide Henry VIII with a bowling alley, tiltyard and deer nursery. Charles II redesigned it, and by the late 17th century it was already home to many species of wading birds, including two pelicans given to the king by the Russian ambassador. The variety and profusion of birdlife around the lake is one of its attractions; another is the splendid roofscape seen from the bridge.

St James's Park forms the first link in a great green chain, leading past Buckingham Palace into Green Park, then into the wide expanses of Hyde Park and Kensington Gardens. Lush and restful

*A*bove: *sweeping lawns beside the Serpentine in Hyde Park bring a taste of the countryside into central London; left: the ornate gates which lead into Green Park*

Cities, and the people in them, need to breathe, and one feature of London that appeals to visitors and residents alike is the number and richness of green spaces. A recent survey carried out for the Royal Parks Agency showed that in that particular year its parks attracted some 30 million visitors, which put them collectively above such national tourist attractions as St Paul's Cathedral (2.6 million) and the Tower of London (2.4 million). Other research among visitors from abroad shows that they are drawn to London by the relaxed, civilised image created by its parks – particularly the Royal Parks.

Green Park is the smallest Royal Park, while Hyde Park is the largest of those in central London – quite exhilarating amidst this densely built-up area. Deer-hunting ceased here in the 1750s, and the deer have long gone, but people still ride horses along a sandy track called Rotten Row. The name is a corruption of *Route du Roi* (the king's road), because it is

on the line of the road which led to Kensington Palace. Just north of Rotten Row is the Serpentine, which, with the Long Water, forms a long curving lake. In the park's north-east corner are Marble Arch and Speakers' Corner, where assorted soap-box orators, from anarchists to evangelists to flat-earthers, by tradition harangue passers-by.

Across the Broad Water lie Kensington Gardens, originally the gardens of Kensington Palace and now effectively a westward extension of Hyde Park, though it is more intimate and sedate. Features include the magnificently restored Albert Memorial, the Round Pond, Broad and Flower Walks, the Sunken Garden and the Orangery. Don't miss the intricately carved Elfin Oak, Frampton's statue of J M Barrie's eternally youthful hero, Peter Pan, and (near Lancaster Gate) the recently restored Italian Water Gardens with their fountains and statuary.

Regent's Park formed part of an inspired 19th-century property development scheme, a collaboration between architect John Nash and the Prince Regent. It was originally to be the grounds of a new palace, which was never built, and consists of landscaped, wooded parkland with a lake; villas lie hidden within it, and the park

is ringed by a sequence of grand stucco terraces. It is a magical combination of landscape and water, with a well-preserved architectural backdrop. Other features include the delightful Queen Mary's Rose Garden and the open-air theatre's summer season. On the northern boundary of the park are London Zoo and the Regent's Canal. The adjacent Primrose Hill, once part of the same hunting forest, retains a more rural atmosphere and where it rises to 207ft (63m) there are panoramic views over London.

FURTHER AFIELD

The outer Royal Parks include three huge open spaces near the Thames in west London, all associated with former royal palaces. Richmond Park still has ancient oak trees, a large herd of deer and lots of other wildlife. From Robin Hood Gate a pedestrian link connects with another huge belt of parkland – Wimbledon Common, with its lake and windmill, and adjoining Putney Heath. Bushy Park and Hampton Court Park lie west and north of Hampton Court Palace and are somewhat similar to Richmond's landscaped parkland, except that Hampton Court's gardens have a more urbane, cultivated character, with formal vistas, a canal lined with lime trees, statuary and the famous maze.

Greenwich Park, too, was a royal hunting park, walled in from adjoining Blackheath. Today it forms part of a unique sequence, which starts on the Thames waterside with Sir Christopher Wren's Royal Naval College. It then moves through the National Maritime Museum's grounds, along the twin colonnades flanking Inigo Jones's superb Queen's House and into the park, which contains Wren's charming hill-top Old Observatory, standing at zero degrees longitude. The sequence continues along a broad chestnut-lined avenue to the windswept, kite-flying Blackheath and terminates at the spire of All Saint's Church in Blackheath Village.

HEATHS, COMMONS AND SQUARES

London's unique inheritance of Royal Parks constitutes only the *crème de la crème* of its green open spaces, but there are many other appealing tracts of land. Hampstead Heath, Kenwood and Parliament Hill to the north are famous for their wonderful views (Guy Fawkes' compatriots intended to watch the result of their conspiracy to blow up Parliament from here). Epping Forest, a huge green wedge stretching from Wanstead out into Essex, is real countryside on London's doorstep, and on the eastern edge are Lee Valley Park and Thames Chase, the latter a new forest, planted by the Countryside Commission.

Clapham, Tooting, Streatham, Wandsworth and Barnes all have their commons, and London also has a number of big municipal parks, providing relief from urban sprawl and a refuge for wildlife. The Grand Union and Regent Canals, forming an arc of waterways with towpaths round north inner London, offer tranquil walking and are an important part of a network of ecological corridors.

There remain many parts of London which are not so fortunate in having a green open space in their vicinity, and their saving grace is the London square. These railing-enclosed gardens with mature trees are sometimes open to the public, sometimes the private reserve of the residents, but are always a green lung among busy streets. There are over 600 squares in Greater London, with a huge diversity of character. They range from such fashionable and architecturally magnificent ensembles as Belgrave and Eaton Squares to unnumbered squares, crescents, and circuses with soft green centres all over London. These – like the parks – bring delight and refreshment to Londoners and visitors alike.

*B*elow: colourful flower beds in St James's Park; below left: the Regent's Canal is a peaceful backwater in North London; bottom: Richmond Hill looks down over the Thames

*T*ower Bridge is a spectacular and dramatic sight when floodlit against the night sky of the capital

CROSSING THE THAMES

CENTRAL LONDON BRIDGES

When it comes to bridges in London, most people tend to think first of Tower Bridge, London Bridge and Westminster Bridge. Tower Bridge – until 1991 the lowest bridge on the Thames – reflects the Victorian obsession with Gothic architecture. A glass-covered walkway, 142ft (43m) above the water, links the two towers and gives panoramic views along the river. The opening mechanism was electrified in 1976, but the original hydraulic machinery is now the centrepiece of a museum, which uses state-of-the-art effects to tell the story of the bridge in a dramatic and exciting way. Recent surveys suggest that the bridge is suffering from heavy traffic; its life may be prolonged by providing a replacement tunnel a little

The River Thames was once London's greatest thoroughfare – it was by far the easiest means of travelling in and out of the capital in the days of horses and carriages, rough, muddy tracks, footpads and highwaymen. But the great river always needed to be crossed, and there have been bridges over the Thames for about 1,000 years. Today there are some 30 of them within Greater London – for road, rail and pedestrians – not to mention the tunnels or the towering Queen Elizabeth II suspension bridge downstream, which doubles up with the twin Dartford Tunnels to carry the busy M25 across the river.

downstream and restricting Tower Bridge's use to pedestrians, cyclists and perhaps buses.

The next bridge upstream is London Bridge, the oldest and most famous, which has its origins in a wooden bridge built to connect Roman *Londinium* via the Kent section of Watling Street to the Roman ports of *Dubris* (Dover) and *Rutupiae* (Richborough). It was broken or burnt down several times until, in 1176, Peter de Colechurch erected the first stone bridge, with a chapel on

it dedicated to St Thomas à Becket. Soon after, houses were built alongside its roadway, and the gruesome custom developed of displaying the impaled heads of executed rebels and traitors on the bridge.

De Colechurch's bridge was not well designed. It had many narrow arches, and their piers obstructed the river's flow and made navigation hazardous. But it saw service until the 18th century, when the houses were removed and a wider central channel was created. In

1801 Thomas Telford designed a new and revolutionary single-span iron bridge, but it was too innovative for the powers-that-be. They built instead a five-arched stone bridge, designed by engineer, John Rennie, and built by his more famous son who was knighted upon its completion in 1831. Rennie's bridge was bought and transported, stone by stone, to the USA, where it now stands incongruously in the Arizona desert.

The latest incarnation of London Bridge is a three-span construction, opened in 1972.

Next come Southwark Bridge and Blackfriars road and railway bridges before we reach Waterloo Bridge, which opened in 1942, replacing Rennie's much admired stone bridge of 1817. Hungerford (or Charing Cross) railway bridge, with a well-used pedestrian way, connects Charing Cross to the South Bank arts complex. Dating from 1864, the rail

bridge replaced Brunel's suspension bridge, but used its brick piers; the chains were recycled into his Clifton Suspension Bridge in Bristol.

Westminster Bridge, alongside the Houses of Parliament, was the second bridge to be built in what is now central London. The present structure, was completed in 1862, but it replaced an earlier bridge, which opened in 1750. That was the bridge on which Wordsworth wrote his famous sonnet ('Earth has not anything to show more fair...'), but it later suffered – like others – from the notorious scouring action of strong Thames tides.

The idea of a second crossing at Westminster provoked strong opposition from vested interests – the Thames Watermen had to be bought off with £25,000 compensation; the Archbishop, of Canterbury, owner of the horse ferry at Lambeth, collected £21,000 – considerable amounts in those days. Later, in 1862, Lambeth Bridge was completed, right where the Archbishop's ferry used to be – on its east side stands Lambeth Palace, the Archbishop's official residence; its western approach, Horseferry Road, is a lasting reminder of the ferry. The present bridge was built in 1932.

Upstream again are Vauxhall Bridge, Grosvenor railway bridge (carrying the lines out of Victoria) and Chelsea Bridge, a handsome suspension bridge. On the other side of Battersea Park is perhaps the most attractive of them all, Albert Bridge. Opened in 1873, it was designed by R M Ordish and may be described as a 'semi-suspension' bridge – the diagonal stays radiating so picturesquely from the towers to support the deck are rigid; the light suspension chains take only the weight of the stays.

Eighteen London bridges lie upstream of this, starting with Battersea (designed by Sir Joseph Bazalgette, who built

the Victoria Embankment). They include the monumental Hammersmith Bridge with its rather Empire-style towers and the suspension footbridge at Teddington Weir, ending with Hampton Court Bridge, of which only one side (Hampton Court) is in London; the other is in Surrey.

Tunnels under the river are numerous, and include several carrying Underground lines. Within London there are also three road tunnels: Rotherhithe, with bends definitely for horse-drawn rather than motor vehicles, and the two Blackwall Tunnels. Also downstream of Tower bridge are two pedestrian tunnels, the one at Woolwich providing an alternative to the free Woolwich Ferry, the other at Greenwich, connecting the Cutty Sark Gardens to Island Gardens on

*T*wo contrasting bridges across the Thames are the sturdy Lambeth Bridge, right, built in the 1930s, and the Albert Bridge, below, looking like a metal cobweb across the water

the Isle of Dogs, the present terminus of the Docklands Light Railway (DLR). Another tunnel at this point will soon extend the line of the DLR to Greenwich, Deptford and Lewisham.

Just upstream of the Woolwich ferry and foot tunnel is something which is neither a bridge nor a tunnel, but is an important link between the north and south banks of the river. The Thames Barrier, completed in 1984, is a vital part of a £480 million flood defence scheme for London.

*T*he river near Westminster Bridge is busy with tourist boats, cruising the historic artery of the city

The Barrier has four enormous curving steel gates, each 200ft (61m) long, shaped like barrels sliced longways; each weighs 3,200 tonnes. These fit into concrete sills on the river bed and only rise if winds and the North Sea surge threaten to cause flooding in the capital. Immediately downstream is the South Bank Visitors' Centre, with viewing esplanades, a café, and an exhibition.

POMP AND CIRCUMSTANCE

L ondon has many odd and colourful ceremonies. Some are public, others private; some vouchsafe passers-by a glimpse of worthy-looking persons in bizarre old-fashioned costume, processing through the public street in the course of honouring some ancient tradition. Often the origins and purpose seem obscure; these are traditions kept alive when the reasons for them have long disappeared. But these quaint and colourful ceremonies can be savoured simply because they are quaint and colourful. Parliament, the monarchy, the armed forces, the law and the City of London are the main focuses of traditional ceremony.

ROYAL TRADITIONS

Ceremonial relations between Crown and Parliament reflect the struggle of the elected House of Commons in the 17th century to assert its independence from the Stuart kings. Thus, when the Queen opens each new session of Parliament, it is not in the House of Commons – no sovereign has been admitted here since the Civil War and subsequent execution of Charles I – but in the House of Lords.

The State Opening of Parliament usually takes place in late October or early November and begins with a coach carrying the imperial state crown to Parliament, followed some 20 minutes later by the Queen in the splendid Irish state coach. From Buckingham Palace they drive down the Mall, through Horseguards Arch into Whitehall and thus to Parliament. As the Queen enters the Lords, guns in Hyde Park fire a salute; as she takes her seat on the throne, the Lord Great Chamberlain (a hereditary royal official) raises his wand to summon the Commons.

But when Black Rod, a House of Lords official, arrives at the Commons chamber,

Far left: the 'Beefeaters' of the Tower are a daily attraction; above and left: the Lord Mayor's Show, led by his fairytale golden coach, takes place once a year in November

something odd happens. The Sergeant at Arms, a Commons official, slams the door in his face. This recalls Charles I's attempt to arrest five MPs in 1642, one of the events which led to the Civil War. However, eventually Black Rod gets to delivers his message, and MPs follow the Speaker of the House of Commons to the Lords to hear the Queen's Speech. In a curious way, this is proof of Parliament's triumph, because the speech is written not by the Queen, but by government ministers, and it sets out their policies and legislative programme for the new parliamentary session.

Earlier that day another historic ceremony is performed. The Queen's bodyguard of Yeomen of the Guard, in their picturesque red and black uniforms, search the cellars beneath of the Palace of Westminster for gunpowder – recalling the attempt on 5 November 1605 to blow up King James I and Parliament.

The most colourful of the public royal ceremonies is the annual Trooping the Colour which celebrates the sovereign's official birthday, usually on the second Saturday of June. The parade's original purpose was to show the men of a particular regiment their

'colour' or flag so that they would recognise it as a rallying point in battle. In today's ceremony, the Queen, dressed in the uniform of the Foot Guards she is reviewing, goes with an escort of Household Cavalry to Horseguards and inspects the parade; there is then a march past, and finally the Queen leads her Foot Guards back to Buckingham Palace. Until 1987, the Queen rode on horseback; now she rides in a carriage.

Beating the Retreat is another display of military precision involving the marching and drilling bands of the Household Division in their colourful uniforms. It takes place on Horseguards Parade in late May or early June and involves mounted bands, trumpeters, massed marching bands and pipes and drums. The name has nothing to do with defeat in battle – it goes back to the ancient custom of signalling or 'beating' the retreat of sunlight at nightfall.

For those who miss these annual parades, the Changing of the Guard is a colourful

daily ceremony which takes place at four royal palaces in London. Most impressive is that at Buckingham Palace, with one detachment of Foot Guards, in their scarlet tunics and tall bearskin helmets, taking over from another the duty of guarding the Queen's residence. Similar ceremonies also take place at the Horse Guards in Whitehall, St James's Palace, and the Tower of London.

CIVIC DIGNITARIES

Over the years London's local authorities have often been reorganised to suit new conditions, but the oldest, the City of London Corporation, which administers only the 'Square Mile' – the tiny area containing London's financial centre – has retained its independence. The authority combines an efficient (though arguably undemo-cratic) administration with the pomp and pageantry of 800 years of proud municipal independence.

Its figurehead is the Lord Mayor, elected each year in an unbroken 800-year tradition by the liverymen of the City livery companies, or guilds. When the reigning Lord Mayor and Sheriffs arrive at the Guildhall in their traditional robes of office, the Keeper of Guildhall presents them with nosegays of garden flowers. This tradition goes back to the days when they were believed to give protection not only against the evil smells of London streets, but against the diseases that were harboured there.

The election of the Lord Mayor takes place around Michaelmas Day (29 September), followed in November by the Lord Mayor's Procession (or Lord Mayor's Show). This dates back to Magna Carta in 1215 when King John, under pressure from his barons, sought support from the City in return for giving it a new charter allowing annual elections. His proviso was that

Trooping the Colour, with the Queen's guardsmen resplendent in their ceremonial uniforms, takes place in June to mark the official birthday of the sovereign

CEREMONY IN MUSIC

A different kind of Pomp and Circumstance is found in Elgar's five marches of that name, music redolent of the imperial pride of the Edwardian era.

At least one (Number 1) features each year at the festive Last Night of the Proms (the Henry Wood Promenade Concerts) at the Royal Albert Hall. Sung lustily by the audience of Promenaders to the words of 'Land of Hope and Glory', the enthusiastic chorus typifies the way in which Londoners enjoy celebrating the past without necessarily taking too seriously the attitudes lying behind the traditions.

The imposing Royal Albert Hall

each new Lord Mayor took an oath of allegiance before the king or his justices, and so, on a Saturday each November, the new Lord Mayor of London goes in procession to the Royal Courts of Justice in the Strand to swear loyalty to the Crown.

The processional route is along Cheapside, Ludgate Hill and Fleet Street to the Strand. The Lord Mayor's gilded coach, built in 1757 and looking for all the world as if it has come straight out of a fairy tale, has actually come straight out of the Museum of London, harnessed to six magnificent Shire horses; he is attended by a personal body-guard of pikemen in armour and musketeers from England's oldest regiment, the Honourable Artillery Company. A huge retinue of mobile floats or tableaux make up the procession, and illustrate various aspects of a theme chosen by the new Lord Mayor for his year of office.

Another highlight of the City calendar is the Lord Mayor's Banquet, held on the Monday following the Show, and the most important in a series of banquets and feasts which each Lord Mayor must enjoy or endure during his year of office. The new Lord Mayor and Sheriffs give this banquet in honour of the outgoing Lord Mayor, and invite some 700 VIPs, the most important of them welcomed with fanfares by splendidly costumed trumpeters. During the evening there is a major speech by the Prime Minister.

The Ceremony of the Keys at the Tower of London has taken place at 10pm every night for centuries

OFF-CENTRE LONDON

GREENWICH AND THE SOUTH-EAST

On a nice day, you cannot beat the boat trip to Greenwich from the city, but travel to Greenwich by the Docklands Light Railway and you will alight at Island Gardens on the opposite side of the river. From here you can enjoy the finest view of the great architectural ensemble of the Royal Naval College and National Maritime Museum, before continuing on foot through a tunnel beneath the Thames. As well as the museum, there is a historic ship collection which includes the *Cutty Sark* clipper ship and *Gipsy Moth IV*, Sir Francis Chichester's round-the-world yacht. The restored Queen's House is also open, as is the Old Royal Observatory, standing at zero degrees longitude in Greenwich Park. The Millennium Dome remains a landmark on the Greenwich waterfront, but its future is uncertain and negotiations for its sale are expected to extend well into the first decade of the 21st century.

Most visitors to London look at a few famous tourist attractions, perhaps take a bus tour round the centre, and think they have seen what the city has to offer. To do this is to miss out on some real treats, because 'off-centre London' has interesting and attractive places that are well worth visiting. Here we explore some of the more notable of them – moving clockwise, we start at about the four o'clock position at one of the best known of London's outer limits.

Woolwich, to the east, has the imposing Royal Artillery Barracks and Academy on the common, and the Museum of Artillery, housed in the Rotunda, by John Nash. Also at Woolwich is the Thames Barrier Visitor Centre, while at nearby Eltham are impressive ruins of a medieval royal palace.

To the south, near Bromley, are Chislehurst Caves, a mysterious labyrinth hewn out of the chalk over a period of 8,000 years. During World War II the caves became a huge air-raid shelter which even had its own church. North-west again, Dulwich has a historic 'village' centre, the impressive 19th-century Dulwich College and the Dulwich Picture Gallery, with many old masters.

ALONG THE THAMES

Richmond combines historic buildings and splendid Thames views with a bustling commercial centre and lively arts and restaurant scene. Architectural

Syon House, left, and magnificent Hampton Court Palace, below

set-pieces include its two greens, with delightful old lanes, and Richmond Hill, with 18th-century houses and fine views.

Kew, downstream, is best known for the Royal Botanic Gardens, 300 acres (122ha) of landscaped gardens, with some spectacular buildings. Seventeenth-century Kew Palace is the most modest but charming of royal residences, and Kew Village is charming too. In nearby Brentford is the Kew Bridge Steam Museum, a Victorian pumping station with enormous beam engines and London's only steam railway.

Upstream from Richmond are a string of splendid 18th-century buildings – Marble Hill House, a magnificent Palladian villa of the 1720s set in lovely parkland; Ham House, a large 17th-century house of exceptional interest; the early 18th-century Orleans House Octagon, its adjoining wing now an art gallery. A ferryman will row you from the Ham side to Marble Hill Park.

Further upstream is Hampton Court Palace, built by Cardinal Wolsey, Henry VIII's most powerful minister, who gave the palace to his monarch. His great gatehouse in Tudor brick dominates the main approach, and beyond the huge Base Court lies the Clock Court with its 16th-century astronomical clock and Great Hall. Later monarchs all left their mark here, notably the work carried out by Wren for William and Mary, with the arcaded Fountain Court and great East Front, looking out over the formal gardens and lovely parkland.

Downriver, the riverside is studded with attractions – Horace Walpole's 'Gothick castle' at Strawberry Hill, Syon House with its Adam interiors and spacious park, Old

Ham House is a superb riverside mansion which was built in 1610

Chiswick with its 18th-century Chiswick Mall, and Fulham Palace in Bishop's Park. Chelsea, known for its King's Road boutiques and cafés, also has Wren's Chelsea Hospital (home to the famous pensioners), a maze of streets leading to the river and the 320-year-old Physic Garden, a pioneer botanical garden.

Further north are two notable historic houses – Lord Burlington's Chiswick House, an essay in Palladian style, and Osterley Park, built in the 16th century by Sir Thomas Gresham, merchant, Lord Mayor of London and founder of the Royal Exchange, and later splendidly remodelled in classical style.

AROUND NORTH LONDON

Harrow-on-the-Hill is noted for 400-year-old Harrow School. A little way to the east, at Colindale, is the Royal Air Force Museum, with 70 aircraft and other exhibits, including flight simulators, cinema shows and the incredible 'Battle of Britain Experience'.

Hampstead's Fenton House was built in the late 17th century; it accommodates a collection of musical instruments, and often resounds to the sound of harpsichords or virginals. Keats House is now a museum devoted to the famous poet, and the house

Greenwich is the centre of London's maritime heritage, with the superb Royal Naval College and museum and a collection of historic vessels down on the river

once occupied by Sigmund Freud contains his collection of antiquities and displays relating to his work, while Kenwood, in lovely wooded grounds, contains fine art collections. Highgate has the unusual and surprisingly popular attraction of its impressive cemetery, housing the remains of luminaries such as George Eliot and Karl Marx.

The Georgian and Victorian Islington area has many delights, including the fascinating London Canal Museum.

SPORTING MUSEUMS

Sports fans are spoilt for choice, with the MCC Museum at Lord's Cricket Ground in St John's Wood, the Lawn Tennis Museum at the All England Club in Wimbledon, or the popular Wembley Stadium Tour.

WATERWAYS OF CENTRAL ENGLAND

Before the proliferation of the canal system in the late 18th and 19th centuries, the movement of freight across large distances had been a practical impossibility, effectively limited to something like 12 miles (19.3km) by both the cost and the poor state of roads. The only exceptions were those areas lucky enough to be on one of the larger rivers like the Severn and, in the eastern part of the country, the Ouse.

Attempts to find a way of improving on river navigation date back at least to the days of the Romans, who constructed artificial waterways near Lincoln and Cambridge. From the 12th century onwards the idea was resurrected and small-scale navigation allowed the passage of narrow barges here and there. The first pound locks in Britain were introduced in 1566 (having already been in existence in Holland for 200 years), after which the domestication of rivers, such as the Great Ouse, became much easier and their development and use increased throughout the 17th century. These projects were not generally government financed, but were instead in the form of investment by merchants, who were driven by the expectation of eventually being able to make a profit.

THE CANAL AGE

Large-scale construction was nonetheless surprisingly slow to get off the ground considering that most of the technical problems had already been overcome in the 17th century; the first long-distance canal was built only in the 1730s, in Ulster, running between Newry and the

Upper Bann. However, it was really with the construction of the Bridgewater Canal, designed by James Brindley, that canals began to proliferate all over the country. Brindley gained his ideas through his experience as a millwright in Leek, Staffordshire – the

*W*hole families would once live and work on the narrowboats which are so popular today for holidays

Bridgewater and the Trent and Mersey were his two greatest achievements.

The success of these canals encouraged the formation of joint stock companies to build others. Whilst this certainly led to a flurry of activity, it also created problems. These companies built their canals as they saw fit and according to local conditions. The lack of co-ordination meant that some canals were open to just about any size of craft, whilst others were restricted to narrowboats only. Nonetheless, it became clear that canals were at least of great use locally and construc-tion continued until the 1830s, at which point nearly every town of any importance was within striking distance of a stretch of navigable water.

Central England and East Anglia were two of the areas where waterways were particu-larly important. The Midlands were at the heart of the Industrial Revolution, and there are still 130 miles (209.1km) of navigable canals in Birmingham and the Black Country alone. With Wolver-hampton and Cannock to the north and Stourbridge to the south, in its great days this area had 212 working locks, with 550 factory side basins, form-ing the greatest concentration of industrial canals in the country. In its heyday canal transport carried eight million tons a year, and even as late as the 1950s a million tons a year were still being transported on the waterways.

The Grand Union Canal, 300 miles (482.8km) long and as important as its name suggests, links London with Birmingham, and, had it not been for the outbreak of World War II, might have seen wide boats of 66 tons pushing along its waters.

A spur breaks away from the Grand Union near Daventry in Northamptonshire and runs for 66 miles (106.3km) to link up with the River Trent.

This in turn is linked to the Fossdyke near Lincoln and to the Wash, also served by the River Nene which is itself linked to the Grand Union via Northampton and Wellingborough.

DECLINE AND REBIRTH

Ironically, it was this very com-prehensiveness of the canal system that led to the canal's downfall. Waterways were used to transport the coal that powered the steam locomo-tives on the railways, which were new, much faster and more efficient. Canals were gradually abandoned, and in

some cases drained in order to become railbeds. With one or two major exceptions, com-mercial traffic has all but died and canals have assumed a new role as leisure amenities. And not only on the water – the old tow paths make excellent walk and cycle ways, and many tourist offices produce routes and trails to follow.

The greatest navigation in

T op: Birmingham's Gas Street Basin is part of a canal-side development; above: the traditional dress of the boatman, c 1900–1910

Norfolk is that based on the Great Ouse, one of Britain's greatest rivers. It was first made navigable from the sea upstream to Bedford in the 17th century, when the surrounding land was drained by the Dutchman, Cornelius Vermuyden, creating new waterways. But its commercial usefulness had vanished by the late 19th century, and by the turn of the 20th century much of it lay derelict. Today, after many vicissitudes, it has been reopened through the enthusiam of the Great Ouse Restoration Society.

C olourful craft on the Shropshire Union Canal near Colemere

NEW TOWNS AND OLD TOWNS

Like many countries with long histories, Britain has had to adapt over the centuries to rapidly changing circumstances. Much that was taken for granted in the past has become redundant. Towns that were once prosperous have fallen on hard times as their once-famous products have become superfluous. New towns and communities have been planned and built, and their merits, or otherwise, continue to be debated.

Historically, with the exception of resort towns like Leamington Spa, towns have tended to grow organically. There was a moment of foundation in the sense that a family or a tribe settled at a particular place, which sometimes attracted others as time passed. Industries in turn grew according to need. The 20th century in Britain has seen the development of the 'new town', not a result of such serendipity but of philosophy.

VISIONS OF UTOPIA

Although visions of Utopia have been expressed in England since the Elizabethan era, to a large extent the ideas behind 'new' towns have been based on post-Victorian philanthropic reactions to urban poverty. The functions of towns were rationalised and organised, sorted and graded and then new ones were designed and laid out. Public buildings, entertainments and shops were to be in the centre, around this would be residential areas, and then, at the perimeter, the factories. From this grew the 'garden' towns of the early 20th century.

After World War II, the New Towns Act of 1946 promoted the construction of new towns, the first generation including Corby and the second including Peterborough and Milton Keynes. Such towns were noticeably less genteel than their 'garden city' predecessors and made much more use of strictly modern materials and designs; their planners also made provision for traffic. The express aim of the towns was to remove the poor from the slums of big cities, particularly London, to provide them with a more congenial and more humane environment. At the same time, it was hoped that they would divert potentially harmful pressure away from green belt areas.

The adventurous architecture of The Point at Milton Keynes, above, contrasts sharply with Lincoln's medieval townscape, left

In many ways the new towns appear to have been a surprising success, at least economically, and indeed there is a steady lobby for the construction of more. Yet curiously, there is still a tendency to sneer at them. The principal accusation levelled is that they are 'soulless', an accusation that carries some weight when it is borne in mind that although it has been reasonably easy to attract business and employees to Milton Keynes, for example, it has proved a great deal harder to get their

bosses to buy homes for their families there.

The attraction of the leafy suburbs of old-fashioned cities or the traditional village green with pub is still very strong. In the case of Milton Keynes, founded in 1967, the business argument has been won – with a population in excess of 150,000, it has become the 13th-largest district in the country. The challenge now is to find other reasons for people to move there. Television campaigns emphasise the mix of old and new, whilst its proximity to Cambridge, Oxford and Stratford is cited as an advantage for the tourist.

IN EASY REACH

These days, perhaps, such arguments are almost superfluous. Milton Keynes, and others of the new towns, seem to be able to weather economic stagnation better than many of the older towns. One reason is location. The sites for the new towns were deliberately chosen with their relative position in mind, and Milton Keynes is rated as being the best centre for distribution in the whole country. The older towns are, of course, stuck with their location and have to choose industries that suit them, not the other way around –

although, should rail transport ever make a comeback, it could well be to the advantage of some of Britain's most historic towns.

A good general location results in a town that will attract a broad range of companies. Milton Keynes was chosen by Coca-Cola some 25 years ago and since then at least another 3,000 businesses have followed, bringing with them over 65,000 jobs.

If, however, the accent appears to be purely on financial gain, that is not an entirely accurate impression. Another advantage to 'newness' is that heritage legislation, for the time being at least, is meaningless. Experiments can be made, therefore, and not just visual ones. The National Energy Foundation, for example, resides in Milton Keynes and as a result of the lessons learned in energy conservation there in the last 30 years, other towns are following its example. Soulless some of the new towns may be, but they are certainly not artless.

Ancient and modern can be found all over Britain; shown here are splendid examples of both. Top right: a medieval building in Lincoln; middle right: the magnificent façade of Lincoln Cathedral; bottom right and below: glass palaces in Milton Keynes

RARE BREEDS AND TRADITIONAL CROPS

Despite the Industrial Revolution and the proliferation of the great towns and cities that have become closely associated with the Midlands, England remains an essentially rural country. Gone, however, are the smallholdings that are still a significant feature of France and Italy; and gone, for the most part, are the meadows filled with orchids and other wild flowers that until recently seemed to fill summer horizons. England is one of the most advanced and efficient farming economies in the world, but it seems it has become so at the expense of a human dimension that has always appeared attractive to the romantically-inclined outsider.

The truth is that such changes have actually been taking place for centuries and resistance to them is not something new. Often it was not through the publication of letters in newspapers, but by riots and violence. The most famous example of this is the early 19th century Luddite movement which is supposed to have been named after a Leicestershire worker, Ned Ludd, who destroyed his machinery in anger.

CHANGING THE LANDSCAPE

Even as far back as the 17th century, the drainage scheme in the Norfolk fens instigated by the Duke of Bedford met with fierce opposition from local farmers who had previously made use of the marshes to rear geese, which were driven in their thousands as far away as London. Before the construction of the network of drainage ditches, the landscape of Norfolk had been essentially marshy, with rivers flowing aimlessly and with fickle unpredictability across it, ideal for geese but quite hopeless for crops.

Yet, even the construction of drainage ditches proved inadequate for the successful leaching of the fields, particularly of the peaty, black soil which tended to subside. Thus a way had to be found to pump the water from field to ditch and then from ditch to main channel. The windpump made its entry to enhance the popular vision of the Fenlands.

In the case of the Fens, a farming landscape has been created deliberately and although the sails of the windpumps no longer turn, modern pumps have taken their place. A flat landscape of hedgeless fields and farmsteads surrounded by dense, tall hedges as protection against the wind, seems to have become a permanent feature.

Norfolk and Leicestershire have both made several contributions to the changing aspect of English agriculture. The Norfolk Four Course Rotation is the foundation of modern farming, based on the principle of ploughing in compost instead of manure in sequence – roots, barley, seeds and wheat – which is said to bring the best out of the soil. Leicestershire's contribution was the development of modern sheep farming.

*B*elow: not quite the prairies, but certainly the new face of farming, near Chelmsford; right: a Cotswold ewe, of the breed that brought so much wealth to the Cotswolds in medieval times; below right: rare breeds at Stratford's Shire Horse Centre

THE COTSWOLD BREED

SELECTIVE BREEDING

There are some forty breeds of sheep still in existence in Britain, far more than in any other country in the world. Wool, after all, was the key to English prosperity in the Middle Ages, most notably in the Cotswolds and East Anglia. Yet, the breeds that provided the wool are no longer used and incredibly have come close to extinction. One reason for this is cross breeding, which is not entirely a modern phenomenon. The man behind this was Robert Bakewell, a farmer born in 1725 in the hamlet of Dishley, near Loughborough.

Before inheriting the family farm, Bakewell travelled extensively in England and Europe. By the time he started farming his own land, he had learnt the science of selective breeding, but instead of selecting the best from other herds he concentrated on inbreeding. He used his ideas for cattle rearing but his greatest successes came with sheep, the result of a programme based on the Leicester breed, which were similar to the old Lincoln and Cotswold sheep that had been the foundation of the medieval wool trade. The result was that he was able to produce early maturing sheep for the butcher. His Leicesters, and his ideas, made a vital contributions to sheep farming throughout the world.

Similarly, the Lincoln Long Wool breed was found all over the Midlands until it was later crossed with the ubiquitous Merino. Other local breeds of sheep have been less successful and are rarely found today – these include the Staffordshire Ryeland and the Norfolk Horn, although this latter is the ancestor of the Suffolk which is still sometimes crossed to produce fat lamb. Most of these local breeds of sheep, however, have disappeared from commercial farms.

The same is true of cattle, though once again breeds from

A field of buttercups and sheep near North Nibley; right: the Berney Arms Windpump in Norfolk, accessible by boat or rail, was used in draining the marshland and grinding clinker for cement; below right: a traditional rural landscape near Winchcombe in Gloucestershire

Lincolnshire and Suffolk have been important in producing modern strains. Sometimes the demise of a breed may be put down to vainglory – a strange case is that of the Lincolnshire Shorthorn, which was too often bred for its show qualities at the expense of its advantages as a producer.

As for pigs, local breeds such as the Essex Saddleback have lost out to fashion, overtaken by the popularity of the leaner Scandinavian varieties.

A certain monotony is therefore evident in the breeds which graze the landscape of our farms. But the developments that have led to this state of affairs are the fruition of centuries of striving as much as to the technocratic notions of our own time.

However, even if the old meadow flowers have gone, they have been replaced by the dazzle of yellow rape and the milky blue of flax; and no doubt the world will in due course regard them as much a part of the traditional rural panorama as were once upon a time poppies and cowslips.

THE WELSH MARCHES – A FRONTIER LAND

Aglance at Sheet 137 of the Ordnance Survey's 1:50,000 Landranger series, covering Ludlow and Wenlock Edge and the western edge of Shropshire, shows a landscape shaped by conflict and war.

Here in the heart of the troubled borderland of the Welsh Marches, many examples of the defensive structures built at various times in the region's history are still visible. Ludlow's great red sandstone keep, built by Roger Montgomery, Earl of Shrewsbury, in the 11th century to repel Welsh raiders, was succeeded by many smaller castles of the 'motte and bailey' design, such as those scattered along Offa's Dyke. A classic example can be found at New Radnor.

Later, the fortified manors of Stokesay Castle, Bromfield and Richard's Castle tell of more settled times, while the manors of Wilderhope and Croft Castle show the gradual trend away from defence towards the country houses found in more peaceful areas.

EARLY TIMES

In prehistoric times, the slopes of every major hill formed their own frontier with everything below, and settlers fortified their summits with banks, ditches and palisades, within which they enjoyed the best possible coigns of vantage. One of the most striking features of the above-mentioned map is the number of these 'forts,' 'camps' and 'earthworks' – over 20 of them – marked in the Gothic typeface which the OS uses, rather imprecisely, to indicate a 'non-Roman antiquity.'

The better-known examples include Croft Ambrey, south-west of Ludlow, where hundreds of regularly placed huts have been traced; and Caer Caradoc, overlooking the Church Stretton valley, where Caractacus is alleged to have made his last stand against the Romans. But there are many other lesser-known examples. Some, like Burfa Camp, Bury Ditches and Bagbury, are now hidden under blanket forestry plantations, but many others command the same sweeping views over the countryside which first attracted their builders over 2,000 years ago.

Magnificent views for miles around can be enjoyed from high up on Croft Ambrey Iron-Age hillfort – it is said that 14 counties are visible

Radio-carbon dating has shown that most British hillforts were built between 750 and 500 BC, though many were still in use up to the Roman invasion in the first century AD. The name 'hillfort' can be misleading, although many must have had a defensive purpose. But the idea that they were all the last outposts of the native Britons who fled there in the face of the invading Romans is one which is no longer in favour with modern archaeologists. Some believe that hillforts were the spiritual or religious centres of the Iron Age, and temples have been found in some of them. But there is no doubt that many others were settlements which were perhaps used only in the summer to watch over grazing stock, or as administrative or market centres.

AFTER THE ROMANS

Winding up from south to north through the western side of the said map is the ancient earthwork known as Offa's Dyke – now followed by the 177-mile (285km) Offa's Dyke Path, which opened in 1971. Built in the last quarter of the 8th century by King Offa of Mercia to mark the western edge of his kingdom and to control Welsh incursions, Offa's Dyke is the longest continuous earthwork in Britain, and links the Severn and Dee estuaries.

There can be little doubt from its method of construction that Offa's Dyke was primarily defensive in nature, and there is some evidence that it may once have had a permanently manned stockade along its crest. It was said to have been instigated by Offa in AD 782, but the first reference to this monumental earthwork is

When Harlech Castle was built it had a sheer drop to the sea on one side. Though the sea has receded, it still has one of the most impressive situations of all Edward I's Welsh castles. The defence of its walls during the Wars of the Roses inspired the stirring song 'Men of Harlech'

not recorded until 100 years later, when Bishop Asser notes that Offa ordered the dyke to be built between Wales and Mercia 'from sea to sea'.

Following the decline of Mercia, the usually bickering Welsh princes united under Gruffydd ap Llywelyn and began serious incursions across the Dyke into England. These were eventually thwarted by Harold, who was later to become the short-lived king of England, in a vicious campaign of retaliation in 1063.

NORMAN BARONS AND WELSH PRINCES

The next chapter in the much-troubled history of the Marches begins with the Norman conquest of 1066. William set about subduing his new nation by making grants of land to favoured 'Marcher' barons, who ruled by right of conquest and claimed special rights, not subject to the usual restraint of the law. It was these autocratic barons who built the string of earth mounds and wooden forts known as 'motte and bailey' castles, such as that still visible at New Radnor. The word 'Marches' has the same origin as 'mark', meaning a boundary.

The great stone castles of the Marches, such as Ludlow, Monmouth, Chepstow, Rhuddlan and Shrewsbury, came later, as the English overlords tried to stamp their authority over an unwilling populace. A double, and sometimes triple, line of castles was erected along the border, such as Grosmont, Skenfrith and White Castles in Monmouthshire.

But the Welsh princes like Gruffydd, now known as Llywelyn the Last, were still unwilling to bow under the English yoke, and after he evaded taking the oath of loyalty to Edward I, he was soon in open conflict with the king's army, commanded by Roger de Mortimer, Earl of Shrewsbury. Mortimer was just one of the immensely powerful Marcher Lords. Others of these included Roger de Lacy of Ludlow and Robert de Say of Clun.

Llywelyn was eventually defeated by the king in 1282, and to confirm his conquest, Edward built a series of massive fortresses throughout Wales. These castles, such as Conwy, Caernarfon, Harlech and Beaumaris, were at the forefront of medieval military architecture and even today stand as impressive ruins.

Welsh opposition was not finally stamped out until the defeat in 1410 of another great hero of nationalism, Owain Glyndwr. In 1472, in an attempt to subdue the powerful Marcher Lords as much as the still warring Welsh, Edward IV set up a Lord President and Council of the Marches, who were to supervise the affairs of Wales and the border for the next two centuries. The Council usually sat at Ludlow or Shrewsbury castles.

AFTER THE TUDORS

It was not until the reign of Henry VIII that the boundary between England and Wales was finally settled. One of the most impressive remains is Roger Montgomery's red sandstone castle towering above the River Teme at Ludlow. Started in 1085 during the first wave of castle-building, during its history it has been the prison for Edward IV's sons – 'the Princes in the Tower' – and the place where Henry VIII's elder brother, Arthur, died. On a different note, it was the scene in 1634 of the first production of John Milton's masque, *Comus*, and is still the regular venue for open-air Shakespearean productions.

Monmouth, with its rare portcullised gatehouse over the River Monnow, boasts the ruins of its 11th-century castle, where Henry V was born in 1387. Chepstow's great Norman castle still dominates the town's medieval streets, and across the border at Goodrich an almost perfectly preserved 13th-century castle still frowns down over the River Wye. At Rhuddlan, near Rhyl on the coast of north Wales, Edward I is said to have made his famous move to win over the Welsh by proclaiming his infant son as the first Prince of Wales.

Chepstow Castle is the first recorded Norman stone castle; it was used as a base for advances into Wales

THE NATIONAL PARKS OF WALES

The three National Parks of Wales – Snowdonia, the Brecon Beacons and the Pembrokeshire Coast – could hardly offer greater scenic contrasts. From the jagged volcanic peaks of Snowdonia, which includes the highest ground south of Scotland, to the sweeping sandstone escarpments of the Brecon Beacons and the dramatic cliffs and bays of the Pembrokeshire Coast, the variety is breathtaking. In their tightly controlled protected areas, the parks encapsulate the very best of the unspoilt landscapes in the Principality.

A proposal for a fourth Welsh national park in the Cambrian Mountains of mid-Wales, centred on Plynlimon and the source of the Rivers Severn and Wye, was thwarted as a result of local opposition, mainly from farmers and landowners, in the mid 1970s.

There are several well-established routes to the summit, some of which have had to be extensively restored because of overuse. If the climb is too much, you can take the rack-and-pinion railway which winds up from Llanberis to the summit, where there is a café.

Slate and forestry have been the traditional industries in Snowdonia, but tourism is now as important in the slate-built villages of Llanberis, Capel Curig, Betws-y-Coed and Blaenau Ffestiniog.

SNOWDONIA

Snowdonia, at 827sq miles (2,142sq km), is the second largest national park in Britain after the Lake District, and was the first of the three to be designated (in 1951). Outdoor campaigners such as Sir Clough Williams Ellis, who built the Italianate fantasy village of Portmeirion, had long pressed for the proper protection of this unique and precious landscape.

It was medieval English sailors crossing the Irish Sea who gave Snowdon and Snowdonia its name – the wild, rocky landscape beyond Anglesey always seemed to them to be brushed with snow. To the Welsh, though, this mountainous region had always been known as *Eryri*, the 'abode of eagles', and it was the place where their leaders, from the legendary Arthur through to the historical figures of Llywelyn the Great and Owain Glyndwr, traditionally sought refuge from the invading English.

There is still an indefinable air of nostalgia and 'Welshness' in these sometimes savage hills, where Welsh speakers are still in the majority.

The physical shape of the national park is best described as a large diamond split into three by valleys which run north-east to south-west. These deep gashes neatly separate the main mountain groups of Snowdon, the Glynders and Carneddau in the north; the rugged Rhinogs and Arenig in the centre; Cadair Idris and the Arans to the south. Most visitors gravitate to the area around Snowdon, which at 3,560ft (1,085m) is a natural magnet to the peak-bagger.

THE BRECON BEACONS

The Brecon Beacons National Park, straddling the borders of Powys, Dyfed, Gwent and Mid Glamorgan, takes its name from, and is centred on the triple peaks of the Beacons themselves, which dominate the lush valley of the River Usk. These Old Red Sandstone mountains, the highest of which is Pen-y-Fan at 2,907ft (886m), stand like a petrified wave about to break over the ancient county town of Brecon, where the Romans had a fort at Y Gaer. The ascent of Pen-y-Fan is most easily achieved from the Storey Arms on the A470; those who make the climb are rewarded with spectacular views.

There is much more to the 522sq mile (1,352sq km) park, established in 1957, than the Beacons. Two other distinct mountain masses make up the area, both of which confusingly carry the name 'Black'. The Black Mountains (plural) are a range of sandstone hills running north–south from Hay-on-Wye to Abergavenny.

In the heart of Snowdonia – the view from Beddgelert towards Nantgwynant

Offa's Dyke, the 8th-century boundary embankment and ditch which separated England and Wales, runs along its crest and makes a fine walk. The Black Mountain (singular) is a wilder, less-visited area to the west of the A406 Sennybridge to Ystradgynlais road. It is centred on the sweeping crest of Carmarthen Van, at 2,631 ft (802 m) the highest point in the Black Mountain, which has the mysterious little glacial lake of Llyn y Fan Fach at its feet. Further west, near the boundary of the national park, remote Carreg Cennen Castle has one of the most spectacular situations of any castle in Wales.

There is another, altogether different landscape which dominates the south of the park. The area of Carboniferous rocks which stretches across the southern boundary has created a landscape of tumbling waterfalls, huge caves and potholes and beautiful woodlands which are a major attraction to visitors, and is easily accessible from the valleys of South Wales. A pleasant way to view the scenery is on the Brecon Mountain Railway from Pant Station, north of Merthyr Tydfil.

The Mellte and Hepste valleys, between Ystradfellte and Pont-neddfechan, are the centre of the Beacons caving country. Dan-yr-Ogof Showcaves system, north of Abercraf, has the largest chamber in any British showcave, and in Bone Cave evidence was found of human occupation 3,000 years ago. The caves are now part of a tourist complex with a number of attractions.

THE PEMBROKESHIRE COAST

This area of Dyfed is sometimes known as 'Little England beyond Wales' and the popularity of resorts like Tenby and St David's is undeniable. But the epithet has its basis in history, since a string of castles were erected by the Norman invaders, along a line from Newgale in the west to Amroth in the east, to subdue the native Welsh. The line – known by the Norse word *landsker*, meaning frontier – can still be traced in placenames. South of the line, many places have anglicised names and English is still the most common language, but north of the *landsker*, Welsh is more commonly spoken and Welsh names abound.

The Pembrokeshire Coast National Park – at 225sq miles (583sq km) one of the smallest British national parks – is the only one which is largely coastal, and it is not hard to see why. Its main glory is its superb 230-mile (370-km) coastline, followed for most of its way by the Pembrokeshire Coast Path, a wonderful rollercoaster of a walk with rugged cliffs, sandy bays and a number of ever-changing seascapes.

The 170 miles (274 km) of the Pembrokeshire Coast Path also offer a crash-course in geology, for the route shows at a glance the story of the formation of the earth from the earliest pre-Cambrian rocks around the tiny cathedral city of St David's to the Ordovician volcanic structure of the north.

The only real uplands in this mainly coastal park are the Preseli Hills in the north, a self-contained moorland block of Ordovician rocks rising to 1,759 ft (536 m) at Foel Cwm Cerwym, south of Bryberian. The Preseli Hills are famous as the source of the blue stones which were somehow transported to far-off Wiltshire for the inner circle of Stonehenge.

Wild and remote it may be, but the reality of Black Mountain is far removed from the image of its name

The main attraction of Pembrokeshire will always be its coastline, and there are few more invigorating walking experiences in Britain than to stride along these cliffs in early spring, on a carpet of wild flowers, accompanied by the cries of the seabirds.

St David's Head separates the rocky coastline to the north from the sands of the aptly named Whitesand Bay to the south

THE PEAK DISTRICT

The Peak District stands at the crossroads of Britain – linking the hard, uncompromising landscapes of the north and the lush greenness of the lowland south. As the southernmost extremity of the Pennine Chain, the Peak is the last knobbly vertebra in the backbone of England, and the first real hill country to be met by the traveller from the south and east. The change is quite sudden, as an early 18th-century traveller reflected on leaving Ashbourne to enter the Peak; 'at the summit of the hill it was a top coat colder'.

The landscape changes too, as you climb on to the limestone plateau in the south and centre, which is known as the White Peak. Gone are the neatly hedged fields of the Midlands, replaced by tumble-down drystone walls spreading up hill and down dale, seemingly with no regard for the swelling contours.

WILD FLOWERS OF THE PEAK

To the botanist, the Peak represents the best of both worlds. Here can be found southern types, like the nettle-leaved bell-flower, at their northern limit and northern types, like the cloudberry, at their southernmost extent. But to see the delicate white flowers of the cloudberry, you must travel north, leaving the limestone of the White Peak behind.

Enclosing the limestone plateau to the north, east and west is a mantle of bleak and sometimes forbidding, peat-covered moorland known, in contrast, as the Dark Peak. This is the home of hardy species such as the cloudberry which, as its name suggests, is frequently to be found in the clouds, and of the blue or mountain hare, which changes the colour of its coat to match the winter snows.

The cloudberry is equipped to survive on the high moors

THE ROCKS BENEATH

The predominant rock in the Dark Peak is millstone grit, a coarse sandstone which takes its name from the fact that it was once much in demand for mill- and grindstones. Abandoned millstone quarries can be found beneath many gritstone edges, with piles of finished but now unwanted stones. The Peak National Park, which encompasses 555 sq miles (1,437.4sq km) and was the first in Britain to be set up, in 1951, took the millstone symbol as its boundary marker and logo.

Both limestone and gritstone were laid down under tropical seas during the Carboniferous period, about 330 million years ago, and if you look carefully in a limestone wall or gatepost, you may just be able to make out the remains of the sea lilies and shells which created the rock. The grit was laid down later over the limestone under deltaic conditions not unlike those found in the Mississippi or Nile today.

EARLY SETTLERS

The Peak District, like any upland region, is the creation of its underlying geology, and the high and dry plateaux of the Peak were particularly attractive to the first settlers who made their way across the land bridge from Europe. The remoteness of the region has resulted in the survival of a surprising number of remains of these first hunter-gatherers, including perhaps the most spectacular – the stone circles of Arbor Low, near Youlgreave and the Nine Ladies on Stanton Moors. Almost every hilltop in the Peak seems to be marked by a burial mound or barrow, most dating from the

The Nine Ladies Stone Circle is evidence of the early occupation of Stanton Moor, amidst lovely countryside above the River Derwent

Bronze Age and known by the local name of 'low'. Complete landscapes of the Bronze Age, including huts, stone circles, fields and barrows, have been identified on the now uninhabited moorlands to the east.

The Iron Age saw the construction of a number of apparently defensive hillforts, such as Mam Tor, commanding the upper Hope Valley near Castleton, and Fin Cop above Monsal Dale. Whether these defensive positions were ever the last resort of native Brigantians against the invading Romans will probably never be known, but the Imperial legions' chief interest in the Peak was in its abundant supplies of lead ore.

WEALTH FROM THE LAND

The Romans were the first to exploit the mineral wealth of the Peak District, and mining and quarrying has been a major local source of employment ever since. In the 18th and 19th centuries, lead production was a major source of Peak District wealth and over 10,000 miners were at work in the limestone area. Evidence of their passing can still be seen in White Peak meadows, where over 50,000 shafts have been identified.

The wealth won from lead and from the wool of their sheep gave landowners like the Dukes of Devonshire and Rutland the confidence to build

Mock Beggars Hall, above, is a natural rock formation, while Bakewell Pudding, bottom right, was an accidental creation

their magnificent houses of Chatsworth and Haddon Hall, both near Bakewell and superb but contrasting examples of the English country house.

Haddon Hall is the older and more intimate of the two, benefitting from the fact that it was abandoned for 200 years and therefore not significantly 'improved' since the late Middle Ages. It stands on a prominent bluff overlooking the River Wyel. Just over the hill in the Derwent Valley is Chatsworth, the palatial, Palladian-style seat of the Dukes of Devonshire, largely rebuilt in the 17th century and now a treasure house of works of art. It stands in extensive parkland landscaped by Lancelot 'Capability' Brown.

A much earlier seat of power in the Peak is the romantic ruin of Peveril Castle, high above the tiny township of Castleton in the Hope Valley. Peveril Castle was built by William Peveril shortly after the Norman Conquest as the administrative centre for the Royal Forest of the Peak – a hunting preserve for medieval kings and princes.

THE MOST VISITED NATIONAL PARK

Today, Castleton is a popular centre for the millions of visitors who throng to Britain's most-visited national park, many coming to visit the four famous caverns. Treak Cliff and the Blue John Cavern and Mine are where the rare semi-precious stone, Blue John, is found. Peak Cavern is the most spectacular, while Speedwell's flooded passages are explored by boat.

Matlock and Matlock Bath have family attractions such as Gulliver's Kingdom and the Heights of Abraham, with its cable cars, caverns, maze and water gardens, and its illuminations. Matlock Bath is also home to Temple Mine and the Peak District Mining Museum.

The 'capital' of the Peak is Bakewell, famous for the pudding (never known as a 'tart' here). The friendly little town is the natural centre, and has the biggest local livestock and street market every Monday.

Most of today's 22 million annual visitors to the Peak come from the surrounding towns and cities. Half the population of England live within day-trip distance of this precious island of unspoilt scenery. To them, the Peak District is a vital lung and breathing space – right on their doorstep.

THE ABBEYS OF THE NORTH

EARLY CHRISTIANITY

St Paulinus (d. AD 644) was the first successful Christian missionary in the north, converting King Edwin, who made him Archbishop of York. Paulinus preached, baptised and encouraged the setting up of churches throughout the north, but when his patron was killed in battle, he returned to Kent and the north reverted to paganism.

The second wave of missionaries came from the Irish, rather than Roman tradition, and were spearheaded by St Columba (AD 521–97), who founded the monastery on Iona. His monks established churches throughout the north and one of them, St Aidan (d. AD 651), became the first Bishop of Lindisfarne (Holy Island), off the coast of Northumberland. The clash between the Celtic and Roman monasticism was finally resolved at the great Synod of Whitby, held at Whitby Abbey on the North Yorkshire coast, where it was decided to adopt Roman, Papal observances.

The most famous chronicler of these events was the Venerable Bede (AD 673–735), whose reputation has stood longer than the great abbey at Jarrow, where he lived and died. Bede was born into a Saxon family who sent him, at the age of seven, to be brought up as a monk at Wearmouth Abbey; he soon moved on to Jarrow where he spent the rest of his life. He learnt Latin, Greek and Hebrew and wrote treatises on theology, natural phenomena and orthography, but his most famous work was his *Ecclesiastical History of the English People*. Full of vividly told anecdotes, the work is also

From the very earliest days of Christianity, the remoteness and wildness of the northern English landscape attracted hermits and monastic communities alike, offering opportunities for retreat from the civilised world and the adoption of a life of self-sufficiency and poverty. It is ironic then that the success of these establishments resulted not only in the building of some of the finest and richest abbeys in the kingdom, but also in a transformation of their surroundings. The Cistercian brotherhood, in particular, by a combination of sheer hard work and technical expertise, turned unproductive land into fertile, well-drained fields which supported vast numbers of sheep. Though their grandiose abbeys are now reduced to ruins, the achievement of these medieval pioneers lives on in the oases of lush pasture which they created in the midst of moorland and fells.

The dedication stone of St Paul's Church in Jarrow, which contains the chapel where Bede worshipped. The church is now at the heart of the Bede's World exhibition, which tells of the former monastery here and of the life of the great chronicler

scholarly and accurate. Its extraordinary qualities were immediately recognised and it has remained the standard textbook on the early English Church for over 1,200 years.

CISTERCIAN PIONEERS

It was the Cistercians who left the greatest legacy of monastic architecture. The oldest foundation, Rievaulx, was, as its name suggests, established by French monks from Clairvaux, where the abbot, St Bernard (1091–1153), was one of the most influential of all medieval Christians. Rievaulx was founded in 1131 and by the end of the century there were said to be over 140 monks and 500 lay brothers living there. Its evocative ruins are set in a wooded valley in the Hambleton Hills of North Yorkshire. They are best seen from the vantage point of Rievaulx Terrace, which, with its Tuscan and Ionic Temples, was built specifically for that purpose in the mid-18th century.

On an even grander scale are the ruins of Fountains Abbey, founded a year after Rievaulx, but reconstructed in the second half of the century

after a disastrous fire. Built on a site once described as 'fit more for the dens of wild beasts than for the uses of man', the abbey became the wealthiest Cistercian house in England, a pre-eminence which is still evident from the sheer size of the remaining buildings and the rich beauty of their setting. Approached through the delightful water gardens of Studley Royal, the sight is breathtaking.

Between Rievaulx and Fountains are the ruins of Byland Abbey, founded in 1134, which boasts the longest Cistercian church in England. Its daughter house, Jervaulx, was, according to tradition, founded by a group of monks from Byland who lost their way on the banks of the River Yore and were guided to safety by a vision of the Virgin and Child, who declared 'Ye are late of Byland but now of Yorevale'.

The distinctive red sandstone remains of Furness Abbey in Cumbria, which was founded in 1123 but taken over by the Cistercians in 1147, testify to the fact that it came second only to Fountains in terms of wealth, owning extensive properties in northern England and the Isle of Man. In terms of size, it belittled even Fountains, having a dormitory twice as long.

The Cistercians were not the only monks to settle in this area. Two 12th-century Augustinian foundations have been preserved to some degree. One, Brinkburn Priory, despite its pretty setting by the River Coquet, always remained impoverished, but its church survived the Reformation because it served the parish; the church was completely restored in the 19th century and is regarded as the finest example of early Gothic

The remains of Rievaulx Abbey are still substantial, showing its former importance and prosperity. The nave, which dates back to 1135, is the earliest large Cistercian nave in Britain and the choir is a notable example of 13th-century work

architecture in Northumberland. Newburgh Priory in North Yorkshire lives on only because it was incorporated into the mansion built there by Henry VIII's chaplain; the house boasts possession of the tomb of that other destroyer of churches, Oliver Cromwell. The most unusual of all is Mount Grace Priory, founded in 1398, the best-preserved Carthusian charterhouse in England. Living in individual two-storey cells, each with its own garden, the Carthusians lived the life of hermits within the Priory precincts, reviving the Irish ideal which had inspired the very first monastic foundations in the area.

Fountains Abbey is the largest monastic ruin in Britain and is in a wonderful setting, surrounded by landscaped gardens. These were created in the 18th century and include water gardens, ornamental temples, follies and magnificent views

THE DISSOLUTION

Picturesque and tranquil though their ruins may be now, the great abbeys were once at the centre of religious, social and commercial life. This might have continued, had Henry VIII not divorced Katherine of Aragon so that he could marry Anne Boleyn. Because the Pope refused to approve of the arrangement, Henry VIII made himself Supreme Head of the Church in England, and the Dissolution of the Monasteries began in 1536, with around 800 monasteries suppressed. In the south of England there was little resistance, but in the north up to 40,000 men rallied to join the Pilgrimage of Grace, a peaceful protest which soon became an armed revolt, with finance, and even physical support, from the monks of Byland, Furness, Rievaulx and Whitby. With typical guile, Henry VIII persuaded the rebels to disband by promising that the monasteries would be saved, but then reneged and exacted a terrible revenge on all who had taken part. Monks were among the leaders whom he had executed, and every religious house was forcibly disbanded, its wealth seized and its lands sold.

THE NORTH YORK MOORS

The most extensive area of moorland in England or Wales, the North York Moors covers 554 sq miles (892sq km) of glorious scenery. Rolling hills are ablaze with purple heather in late summer and there are pretty green valleys, with rock-strewn streams, and acres of forest. Apart from the busy seaside resorts, there are only a scattering of small market towns. Most settlements are villages, usually centred on a bridge over a river; the cottages are built of stone with distinctive red pantiled roofs. In the more remote dales and on the moortops, there are isolated farms and shooting lodges, reminders of the great estates which still own much of the land.

EARLY DAYS

The earliest man-made features on the North York Moors date from the Bronze Age and are appropriately mysterious. The 40 bridestones at Nab Ridge, on Nab End Moor in Bilsdale, are the remains of a stone circle, 40 feet (12.2m) in diameter, which may once have formed the retaining wall of a burial chamber. Above Grosmont, at High and Low Bridestones, there are remains of stone circles and some standing stones. The most dramatic group is on Bridestones Moor, on the western edge of Dalby Forest, where the huge rocks have been weathered into fantastic and gravity-defying shapes by the wind and rain.

The Romans also left their mark. South of Goathland, stretching across Wheeldale Moor, is one of the best-preserved examples of a Roman road in Britain, built to connect the Roman fortress of Malton with Whitby on the coast. Its culverts, kerbstones

Bilsdale, near Hornby, is flanked on one side by the ridge of Easterside Hill

and foundations, 16 feet (4.9m) wide, are visible for 16 miles (25.7km) over this remote moor. The road gave access to Roman forts, dating from AD 100, and their remains can be visited at Cawthorn Camps, to the north of Pickering. A Roman signal station, built on the cliffs at Scarborough in about AD 370, is the only one of five on the coast to have been excavated.

SAINTS AND POETS

Whitby holds a significant place in the history of early Christianity. The abbey, perched on the clifftop, was founded in AD 657 by St Hilda, and seven years later it hosted the Synod of Whitby, at which it was decided to adopt Roman, rather than Celtic practice in England. Caedmon, the first English Christian poet, appropriately had his home at the abbey. The dramatic ruins

which command the coastline today are those of a much later, 13th-century foundation – on a dark night it is easy to see why Bram Stoker used it as the setting for his novel *Dracula*. St Mary's Church, close by and reached by 199 steps from the harbour below, is a rare survivor from the 18th century, with its double-decker pulpit, galleries and box pews.

THE MIDDLE AGES

Originally a Celtic settlement founded in 270 BC, Pickering continued to thrive because it lay on the crossroads of the Malton to Whitby and Helmsley to Scarborough roads. The parish church is deservedly famous for its unusually complete set of medieval wall paintings, but it is the ruins of its motte and bailey castle which dominate this busy market town. Dating from the 12th century, the castle was reput-

edly used as a hunting lodge by every king from 1100 to 1400. Parts of the old Royal Forest of Pickering are still Crown Land, and there are forest drives, nature trails and picnic sites in nearby Dalby Forest.

The Normans built an even more impressive castle at Scarborough, with a curtain wall which envelopes the headland; its massive square keep, rising 80 feet (24.4m) high, is a landmark for miles around, though

Pickering Church contains some remarkably well-preserved medieval wall paintings

One of Britain's most picturesque villages, Robin Hood's Bay clings to the steep cliffs above the sea

the rest of the castle was almost completely destroyed during the Civil War.

SEAFARERS AND SMUGGLERS

The coastal towns of the North York Moors enjoyed their heydey in the 18th century. Whitby was then the base for a hugely successful whaling fleet, which is commemorated in Pannett Park Museum (there is a massive whalebone arch on the North cliff), and for colliers plying the North Sea. The Rev William Scoresby (1789–1857), son of a local whaling captain and explorer, unusually combined a career in the church with Arctic explorations, and became a leading authority on magnetism. Captain James Cook (1728–1779), the explorer and map-maker, also learnt his trade in Whitby and the Captain Cook Museum in Grape Lane commemorates his achievements. Whitby's Heritage Centre is also in Grape Lane. Though the town still has a fishing fleet and is famous for its shellfish, its importance as a port and har-

bour has declined.

Further down the coast, at Robin Hood's Bay, a more notorious trade was carried on. This quaint town, its cobbled streets and tiny cottages crammed into the small gap between the sea and steep cliffs, was a haven for smugglers. The only access is on foot down a long, narrow and precipitous road, though there are plenty of cafés and inns in which to break the journey.

VICTORIAN SEASIDE SPAS

It was in the 19th century that the greatest changes came to the seaside towns of Scarborough and Whitby. Scarborough had claimed healing properties for its waters, taken from the stream flowing across the South Sands, for almost 200 years. They were said to cure asthma, skin diseases and melancholy as well as to cleanse the blood and stomach.

The town also lays claim to the invention of the bathing machine which enabled bathers to maintain their modesty. The craze for sea-bathing, another highly regarded cure for all manner of ills, swept the whole of the country. Anne Brontë (1820–

1849) was one of many invalids who came to Scarborough for the sea-cure. She died here in 1849 and is buried in St Mary's churchyard.

Both Scarborough and Whitby were immensely fashionable in Victorian and Edwardian times, and many elegant buildings date from that time. Whitby's jet industry also thrived. The coal-black mineral was cut, polished and turned into mourning jewellery; it became an essential fashion item when adopted by the widowed Queen Victoria.

THE MOORS TODAY

The enduring popularity of the east coast owes much to the excellent long sandy beaches, while the lure of the

Examples of Whitby jet jewellery can be seen in the Whitby Museum

wild moorland and its communities never fades. Splendid views can be enjoyed from the steam trains of the North York Moors Railway, running 18 miles (28.9km) from Pickering to Grosmont; others can be seen along the 93 miles (149.6km) of the Cleveland Way footpath, which skirts the northern and western edges of the moors and then follows the coast towards Scarborough.

One major attraction of the moors is the Ryedale Folk Museum in Hutton-le-Hole, illustrating over 2,000 years of local history with an array of fascinating bygones. This is one of Britain's most remarkable open-air museums, with a reconstructed cruck house, Elizabethan manor and cottages from three different centuries. Here too are the oldest daylight photographic studio in England and a small glassmaking furnace of 1590 from Rosedale Abbey.

SCOTLAND'S STRONGHOLDS

Alone piper on the ramparts of Edinburgh Castle during the Military Tattoo is for many an enduring image of the Scottish castle – massively set on an impregnable rock, battlemented and guarded with cannon, manned by fierce Highlanders urged to deeds of heroism by the call of the pipes. For others, Eilean Donan on the road to Skye is the Scottish

castle *par excellence*, an island-held fairytale reflected in ruffled waters of a loch and backed by dramatic mountains. Or it may be the pepperpot turrets and crow-stepped gables of towering Craigievar in the gentler country of Scotland's north-east. Such is the variety of Scottish castles, reflecting the troubled history of this determinedly independent country.

Cannons on the battlements of Edinburgh's famous castle

ROYAL FORTRESSES

The story of the Scottish castle really starts in the 13th century. Motte and bailey castles had been built to the Norman plan by the kings Alexander I and David I, who were brought up in Norman England, and these were gradually replaced by stone fortresses. Edinburgh, sitting on its volcanic rock, was an early example. Continually fought over by the Scots and English, little other than the chapel survives from its earliest days. It last saw action in 1745 when the Young Pretender failed to take it but was incarcerated there instead.

Another royal castle, Stirling, 'the key to Scotland', has an equally formidable setting, and many great battles, including Bannockburn in 1314, were fought near by. Most of

the present buildings are late medieval, and Mary, Queen of Scots was crowned here as an infant in 1543. But it was not just monarchs who built great fortresses. Wherever a suitable site was available, and circumstances demanded, the great landowners of Scotland would build on it.

CLAN CASTLES

The MacLeods at Dunvegan in the west of the Isle of Skye still

live in their ancestral castle beside a tongue of the sea. Enlarged and made more comfortable over the centuries, it tells of a lawless past. The family has additional protection from the Fairy Flag, possibly 7th century, which legend says will save the MacLeods from destruction on three occasions – it has already worked twice.

On the opposite side of the country St Andrews Castle was the stronghold for the powerful bishops, who were as involved in worldly politics as in prayer. As Scotland fought to retain (or recapture) its independence from England, the castle frequently changed hands, as its battered walls overlooking the sea testify.

One of the best of the early castles is set in wooded, rather undramatic country down on the Solway Firth, south of Dumfries. Caerlaverock is a

wonderful triangular castle still surrounded by the waters of its moat – the very latest in military thinking when it was built in around 1280. Captured by the English king Edward I, 'the Hammer of the Scots', in 1300, it was constantly dismantled and besieged in the Middle Ages, yet managed to retain its splendour, and was later enhanced by a splendid Renaissance façade.

Not far away to the west is a much sterner castle – the massive 14th-century tower and walls of Threave. It sits on an island in the River Dee, and was built by the appropriately named Archibald the Grim, bastard son of Sir James Douglas. A later Douglas surrendered the castle to James II in 1455 after the king had bombarded it with the huge gun, 'Mons Meg', now in Edinburgh Castle. The Douglases also held the now-ruined Tantallon Castle on the southeast corner of the Firth of Forth, near North Berwick.

Some of the most impressive of Scottish castles are the result of careful restoration. Duart, on the Isle of Mull overlooking Loch Linnhe, retains 13th-century fragments, and was restored by Sir Fitzroy Maclean from 1911 onwards. It is now the home of the clan chief. The smaller castle of Eilean Donan on Loch Duich was in utter ruin after bombardment from an English warship in 1719 until it was restored in 1932.

The high walls and round towers of Caerlaverock Castle, seat of the Maxwells, have stood firm since the 13th century, though the machicolations were added during the 15th century

Eilean Donan Castle poses romantically on Loch Duich, amidst wonderful mountain scenery

THE CASTLES OF MAR

Once the crowns of England and Scotland had been united by King James VI & I, a new type of castle developed – the tower house. Times of increasing political stability demanded increasing comfort, without altogether abandoning a defensive role. These new towers are characterised by a plain lower storey – sometimes square, but more often L- or Z-shaped. On the upper floors they burst into a riot of corbelled-out

Craigevar Castle is perhaps the loveliest of all the Castles of Mar

towers and gables to increase the amount of accommodation, though access is still usually by spiral stairways.

Some of the best examples are found to the west of Aberdeen, between the Don and the Dee valleys – the former province of Mar. Among the best of the castles of Mar is Craigievar, unaltered since it was completed in 1626. Significantly, it was built not for a monarch or a clan chief, but for one of the Jacobean nouveau riche, the Aberdeen merchant William Forbes. The largest of the castles of Mar were Castle Fraser, Crathes and the extended Drum Castle. Glamis Castle, childhood home of Queen Elizabeth, the Queen Mother, has one of the most prickly rooflines, stiff with cone-topped towerlets.

At Drumlanrig, built in the 1680s, the Douglas Dukes of Queensberry built themselves a huge square palace, which succeeds in combining the appearance of a medieval stronghold with that of an early 17th-century mansion. Like many of the inhabited Scottish castles, its interiors are a luxurious contrast to its outward appearance.

SCOTTISH BARONIAL

It was not long before the style established by the castles of Mar began to influence architects. Inveraray Castle, rebuilt in the mid-18th century, uses the same vocabulary of turrets and battlements, though regulated with classical order,

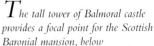

The tall tower of Balmoral castle provides a focal point for the Scottish Baronial mansion, below

which also underpins superb Culzean on the Ayrshire coast, where Robert Adam's skills blend a castellated façade with wonderful Italianate interiors.

By the middle of the 19th century the 'Scottish Baronial' style was all the rage among the landed gentry. Blair Castle was reconstructed in the favoured style, and so was Dunrobin. The most famous achievement of all is Queen Victoria's Balmoral, where Prince Albert (with professional help, it must be said) provided a huge square keep with a more comfortable country house attached, with all its main apartments tricked out in tartan – the apotheosis of the Scottish castle.

THE WILDLIFE OF SCOTLAND

From soaring crags to misty marshland, from mountain top to sea, from lowland plain to high moorland, the habitats of Scotland are about as varied as could be. Sub-tropical trees flourish less than 50 miles (80km) from the north coast in Inverewe Gardens, warmed by the Gulf Stream. On the Cairngorm plateau genuine Arctic conditions, more typical of regions 1,000 miles (1,609km) north, prevail. Between these two extremes lie the high moorland, the lush glens, the rock-bound coasts and the gentle rivers that are home to many distinctive species.

Only the luckiest visitor will see some of Scotland's most precious treasures – the golden eagle, the osprey or the red squirrel, for example. Nor are the fierce wild cats easy to spot in moorland and forest. Otters, too, are seldom seen, though they hunt beside the seashore of the west coast and among the islands as well as by inland burns. Despite their rarity, however, such species seem unlikely to go the way of others – wild reindeer died out here in the 12th century, the beaver probably in the 15th (though there are plans to reintroduce it), and the last wolf in Scotland was killed in 1743.

FORESTS OLD AND NEW

Many of the lost animals of Scotland needed the huge stretches of native pine forest which once covered much of the country. Now only one per cent of the Caledonian Forest survives, having fallen victim to man's greed for timber.

Eighteenth-century iron smelting accounted for the loss of many trees, which were felled and floated down the rivers to be burned for charcoal to fuel the furnaces. Others provided valuable timber, while deliberate clearance of forest (as well as of inhabitants) to introduce vast sheep runs accounted for many more. The bare, open, rocky landscape of much of the Highlands, although admired by visitors, is to a large extent the result of these predations.

Where there is forest today, much of it is the result of planting since the two world wars, and, although in recent years the ruler-straight edges have given way to more sensitive planting, the denseness, uniformity and blanketing effect of the trees have been much criticised. There has also been controversy over the commercial afforestation of large areas of open land, such as the unique bogland environment of the Flow Country of Sutherland and Caithness.

Where pockets of native pinewood survive – at the Black Wood of Rannoch, and Rothiemurchus Forest by the Cairngorms, for example – they are magical places, with mosses, blaeberries and junipers plentiful amid the trees, and wildflowers such as wintergreens and lady's tresses.

There are ancient oak woods, too, especially in the Argyll glens towards the Atlantic coast, where gnarled trees are hung with lichens and the forest floor is home to an amazing multitude of ferns and flowers. In places, too, are survivors of ancient birch forests – among the most accessible of them is the Birks of Aberfeldy.

Upper Loch Torridon, a beautiful sea loch on the west coast, is bordered by magnificent Highland scenery

A RECORD DOZEN

The climate of Scotland is excellent for trees of all types – which may be why 12 of Britain's 30 tallest trees are here, among them a dead heat of two Douglas firs at the Hermitage in Perthshire and Dunans in Argyll, both of which measure 212ft (64.5m). Tayside also has the tallest holly and beech – both 150ft (46m) – at Hallyburton House, as well as a Sitka spruce measuring 200ft (61m) at Strathearn. Other giants are the 206ft (63m) grand fir at Strone in Argyll and a western hemlock 167ft (51m) near by at Benmore; and – a pigmy by comparison – the 98ft (30m) silver birch at Ballogie in Grampian. Scotland holds two sequoia records – for the tallest in Britain, 174ft (53m) at Strathpeffer, and for the largest, at Clunie Gardens in Tayside, with a diameter of 11ft 4in (3.5m). And as for age, the UK's oldest known tree still survives near Aberfeldy – the Fortingall Yew. It is thought to be around 1,500 years old.

At the other extreme are the miniature willow forests that clothe some Scottish mountains, high above the normal treeline. Cold and infertile, often covered with snow which may linger into the summer, this is inhospitable terrain for vegetation. But still

plants survive, often clustered in hollows or forming dense mats of green, which may suddenly burst into colourful flower in favourable conditions. Ben Lawers in Perthshire is particularly famous for the variety of its mountain flowers, including such rarities as the vivid blue alpine gentian and the drooping saxifrage.

Animals and birds, too, need to be hardy to survive the high mountain tops. The ptarmigan is one, often seen by skiers; its mottled brown plumage turns white in winter. A summer visitor, the dotterel, is much rarer; it breeds regularly in the eastern Highlands. Snow buntings also visit from their Arctic homes in the summer, but few stay to breed. The only butterfly regularly breeding here is the mountain ringlet. Mountain hares and stoats survive on the rocky slopes; they, too, turn white in the winter.

MOORS AND SHORES

On lower moorland two game species come into their own – the red deer and the grouse. Britain's largest wild animal,

the red deer was encouraged by Victorian landowners for sport, and stalking is still important in some areas. The sight of a magnificently antlered stag in a misty valley has been a favourite image of Scotland since before Landseer painted *The Monarch of the Glen*. The managed heather moors, where regular burning helps regenerate the plants, provide the habitat for many grouse – the red is the main target for sportsmen. Larger is the black grouse; each male has its territory – called a lek – where pinewoods meet moorland. The capercaillie, hunted to extinction in Scotland by 1800, was reintroduced in 1837 and is now found deep in the woodlands of the east of the country. Where bogland predominates – in the Flow

Country, for example, and on Rannoch Moor – domes of bog moss can provide striking colours in the landscape – from the brightest greens to stabbing orange and yellow. Where the bogs are wettest, plants such as the cranberry gain a foothold, as well as the insect-eating sundew. Glittering dragonflies are often seen fluttering over the bogland.

In extreme contrast are the flower-rich sea-meadows – the machair – which lie behind many Highland beaches, and are particularly spectacular on the shores of the Outer Hebrides, where the shell sand tempers the acidity of the peat soil. Here buttercups, orchids and gentians grow in colourful profusion. The primrose banks of Barra are an especially wonderful sight.

*E*nduring symbols of the wildlife of Scotland: leaping salmon, top left, red deer, above, and the well-camouflaged ptarmigan, left

Birds, too, congregate on the islands. Remote St Kilda has its own species of wren, while Foula in Shetland has vast numbers of great skuas, and in the friable mountain-sides of Rum in the Inner Hebrides thousands of Manx sheerwaters have their burrows. On the mainland, the cliffs of Sutherland are thronged with colonies of fulmars, kittiwakes and guillemots, the mouth of the Tay is home to eider duck and the Solway estuary teems with barnacle geese.

The salmon, journeying upstream to its spawning grounds, is king of Scottish fish, but the more prosaic sea trout and trout cannot be disregarded. In mountain lochs the ferox trout – golden and spotted with black – lives alongside its red and black relative, the char. In the deepest of all – Loch Ness – may lurk the most mysterious of all Scotland's wildlife. If it does, it will add yet more to the rich diversity of the country's treasures.

Britain's Best Hotels

AA RED STAR AWARDS

Star classification is a quality scheme at five levels; the assessment rises from one star, denoting hotels with the simplest range of facilities, to five stars, denoting large, luxury hotels with a range of services and facilities that meet the best international standards. At each of the five levels, the AA recognises exceptional quality of accommodation and hospitality by awarding **AA Red Stars** for excellence. A hotel with Red Stars is judged to be the best in its star classification and this award recognises that the hotel offers outstanding levels of comfort, hospitality and customer care. Only about 3 per cent of star-rated hotels in Britain and Ireland gain this accolade. All hotels with Red Stars usually have at least one **AA Rosette** for the quality of their cuisine. The AA's hotel and restaurant inspectors award rosettes annually on a rising scale of one to five.

Red Star Hotels
ENGLAND

CENTRAL LONDON

★★★★ ⑧
ATHENAEUM HOTEL & APARTMENTS
116 Piccadilly, W1
020 7499 3464
A discreet address in the heart of Mayfair, this well-loved hotel has become a favourite with many repeat guests for its efficient service and excellent hospitality. Bedrooms are decorated to the highest standard and some have views over Green Park. The spacious and well-appointed apartments offer guests the convenience of a townhouse with all the services of a deluxe hotel. Public rooms include the contemporary Bullochs Restaurant, the Windsor lounge and the cosy, panelled cocktail bar specialising in malt whisky.

★★★★★ ⑧⑧⑧⑧⑧
THE BERKELEY
Wilton Place, Knightsbridge, SW1
020 7235 6000
Considered to be the benchmark for the very best in hotel keeping and service, the Berkeley has an excellent range of bedrooms, some with sizeable balconies, furnished with care and attention to detail. Reception rooms, including the Lutyens Writing Room, are adorned with magnificent flower arrangements, and there are superb leisure facilities. The two

restaurants offer a complete contrast in style: modern, influenced by Southeast Asia at Vong and French cuisine at La Tante Claire.

★★★★ ⑧⑧⑧
THE CAPITAL
Basil Street, Knightsbridge, SW3
020 7589 5171
Located in the heart of Knightsbridge, this small and exclusive hotel is the epitome of excellence. Individually designed bedrooms are of the highest quality, featuring handmade furniture, Egyptian cotton sheets and marble-lined bathrooms. One of the highlights of this charming hotel is dinner in the restaurant where some exquisite dishes are served.

★★★★★ ⑧⑧
CLARIDGE'S
Brook Street, W1
020 7629 8860
This renowned hotel has blended state-of-the-art modern design and technology with a traditional setting. Reception rooms and public areas are best described as opulent and immaculate, giving an overall impression that is simply majestic. In addition to the famous restaurant, refreshments are served in the lounge and reading room.

★★★★★ ⑧⑧
THE CONNAUGHT
Carlos Place, W1
020 7499 7070
The Connaught is a bastion of tradition, offering superb service in quiet comfort. Butlers and valets respond at the touch of a button. The Restaurant and the Grill Room share the same impeccable service and exhaustive menu of classical cuisine.

★★★★★ ⑧⑧⑧
THE DORCHESTER
Park Lane, W1
020 7629 8888
One of London's finest hotels, the Dorchester is sumptuously decorated in every department. Bedrooms are individually designed and beautifully furnished, and their luxurious bathrooms have huge baths which have become a Dorchester hallmark. Leading off from the foyer, the Promenade is the perfect setting for afternoon tea or drinks, and in the evenings there is live jazz in the famous bar which specialises in Italian dishes and cocktails. The Grill is a restaurant in the traditional style and there is also an acclaimed Cantonese restaurant, the Oriental.

★★★★★ ⑧⑧
FOUR SEASONS
Hamilton Place, Park Lane, W1
020 7499 0888
Set back from Park Lane, the Four Seasons Hotel offers the highest standards of attentive, friendly service. Bedrooms and their bathrooms are more spacious and better designed than most. The Lanes restaurant is contemporary in style; it has its own cocktail bar and lounge adjacent. Room and business services are available around the clock.

★★★★ ⑧⑧
GORING
Beeston Place, Grosvenor Gardens, SW1
020 7396 9000
This hotel offers traditionally furnished, well-equipped bedrooms and high levels of comfort and quality. Stylish reception rooms include the garden bar and the drawing room, both of which are popular for afternoon tea and cocktails. The restaurant menu has a classic repertoire and also a well-deserved reputation for its contemporary British cuisine.

★★★★ ⑧⑧⑧
THE HALKIN HOTEL
Halkin Street, Belgravia, SW1
020 7333 1000
Modern in design, this individual hotel offers professional service of the highest standard. Fully air-conditioned bedrooms combine comfort with practicality and include state-of-the-art communications for business visitors. The light, contemporary cuisine modifies Italian dishes to suit today's tastes.

★★★★★
LANDMARK
222 Marylebone Road, NW1
020 7631 8000
This spectacular hotel has an eight-storey central atrium where light meals and teas are served. The Cellars restaurant has a clubby atmosphere, and the main dining room serves impressive European cuisine. Bedrooms are extremely stylish, generously proportioned and air-conditioned, and the marble bathrooms feature deep tubs and separate showers. At our press date rosettes for food were not yet confirmed. Check the AA website for current information, www.theAA.com.

★★★★★ ⑧⑧⑧
THE LANESBOROUGH
Hyde Park Corner, SW1
020 7259 5599
Occupying an enviable position on Hyde Park Corner, the Lanesborough offers the highest levels of comfort in its range of bedrooms and suites. Twenty-four-hour service from a personal butler ensures that guests are well catered for, and the reception rooms, with their lavish furnishings and magnificent flower arrangements, are a delight. The popular cocktail bar has a wonderful supply of vintage cognac, whiskies and ports, and the conservatory restaurant

provides a pleasant dining atmosphere.

★★★★★ ⑧⑧⑧⑧
MANDARIN ORIENTAL HYDE PARK
66 Knightsbridge, SW1
020 7235 2000
Situated between the fashionable shopping district of Knightsbridge and the peaceful green expanse of Hyde Park, this famous hotel offers an atmosphere of luxury. Marble is used to elegant effect in the reception areas, which include a popular cocktail lounge and the principal restaurant, The Park, where dishes exemplify subtle flavours and high-quality ingredients. The standard of food, accommodation and service is excellent.

★★★★★ ⑧⑧
MILESTONE HOTEL & APARTMENTS
1 Kensington Court, W8
020 7917 1000
Much care has been lavished on this townhouse property. Themed bedrooms are individually decorated to a high standard and their wide range of facilities includes DVD players. There are superb suites and some duplexes such as the Safari, complete with colonial fan, safari print fabrics, tiger soaps and tented ceiling. Staff are very friendly and the bar and kitchen produce fresh, enjoyable cocktails and meals. In addition to a luxurious lounge, there is a snug bar with a conservatory extension.

★★★★★ ⑧⑧⑧
THE SAVOY
Strand, WC2
020 7836 4343
This splendid hotel of international repute retains its enviable position as one of the best. Bedrooms provide very high standards of comfort, with quality linens and fabrics throughout. The marble bathrooms, with their thunderstorm showers, are superb and guests will find all the luxurious extras one would expect in a hotel of this calibre. The American Bar is an excellent watering-hole for the discerning and the Grill a popular choice for dining. The River Room is renowned for the flavours and precision of its menu. Afternoon tea is a highlight and Saturday night 'Stomping at the Savoy' is a real treat.

★★★★ ⑧⑧
THE STAFFORD
16-18 St James's Place, SW1
020 7493 0111
Quietly located in exclusive St James, this charming hotel retains the friendly formality and understated luxury that have been its trademark for decades. Elegant, individual bedrooms include carriage houses. Afternoon tea is a long-standing tradition in the comfortable drawing room and the American Bar is famous for its collection of celebrity photos, caps and ties. In the restaurant, menus balance traditional grills with more creative dishes. There are several private dining rooms, including the 350-year-old wine cellars.

The Berkeley

Athenaeum Hotel & Apartments

BERKSHIRE

★ ★ ★ ★ ⑧ ⑧ ⑧
FREDRICK'S HOTEL
Shoppenhangers Road,
Maidenhead
01628 581000
Quietly located, this delightful
hotel provides individually
decorated, well-equipped
bedrooms. The enthusiastic staff
are friendly and efficient, and a
highlight of any visit is a meal
in the restaurant, which serves
memorable modern dishes.

★ ★ ★ ★ ⑧ ⑧ ⑧
THE VINEYARD AT STOCKCROSS
Stockcross, Newbury
01635 528770
Guests can enjoy first-class
service and food at this
outstanding hotel and
restaurant, which has a very
special atmosphere created by
the well-drilled, discreet and
friendly staff. The grounds,
public rooms and bedrooms are
all artistically designed, and
accurate, seasonal cooking is
complemented by an
outstanding wine list.

BUCKINGHAMSHIRE

★ ★ ★ ★ ⑧ ⑧ ⑧
HARTWELL HOUSE
Oxford Road, Aylesbury
01296 747444
This friendly hotel, set in 90
acres of grounds, has truly
magnificent reception rooms.
Bedrooms are spacious and pay
great consideration to guest
comfort. The health centre
houses the Buttery coffee shop
and the cuisine served in the
main dining room is
consistently good.

★ ★ ★ ★ ★ ⑧ ⑧ ⑧
CLIVEDEN
Taplow
01628 668561
Cliveden Hotel is approached
through a 375-acre National
Trust managed estate. Visitors
are treated as house guests and
staff recapture the country
house tradition of fine
hospitality and service.
Bedrooms are steeped in quality
and individual style. Guests can
dine in the Terrace Restaurant
with views across the parterre,
or in the discreet luxury of
Waldo's Restaurant.

CHESHIRE

★ ★ ★ ⑧ ⑧
NUNSMERE HALL COUNTRY HOUSE
Tarporley Road, Sandiway
01606 889100
This impeccably maintained

lakeside house dates back to
1900. The bedrooms are
individually styled, tastefully
appointed to a very high
standard and thoughtfully
equipped. Guests can relax in a
choice of elegant lounges, in the
library or in the oak-panelled
bar. The restaurant menu offers
a cosmopolitan range of dishes.

CORNWALL & ISLES OF SCILLY

★ ★ ⑧ ⑧ ⑧
WELL HOUSE
St Keyne, Liskeard
01579 342001
This charming small hotel offers
tastefully furnished, spacious
and very well equipped
bedrooms. There is an elegant
sitting room with log fire, and
an intimate bar. Guests can
relax over afternoon tea on the
terrace overlooking the splendid
grounds. Carefully prepared,
award-winning cuisine is served
in the comfortable dining room.

★ ★ ★ ⑧ ⑧ ⑧
ST MARTIN'S ON THE ISLE
Lower Town,
St Martin's,
Isles of Scilly
01720 422090
This island hideaway is the
perfect choice for those seeking
a peaceful break. The hotel has
its own beach, jetty and yacht,
and enjoys an unrivalled
panorama across the waves.
Bedrooms are individually
decorated and furnished, while
public rooms offer comfort and
quality in equal measure. The
impressive, accomplished
cuisine is particularly welcome
after all that fresh air!

CUMBRIA

★ ★ ★ ⑧ ⑧
FARLAM HALL
Hallbankgate,
Brampton
016977 46234
A delightful 16th-century house
in extensive landscaped
gardens, Farlam Hall has a
warm and welcoming
atmosphere. Bedrooms are
furnished to the highest
standards as guest comfort is
paramount. Public areas too are
elegantly decorated. Service is
attentive throughout.

★ ★ ★ ⑧ ⑧ ⑧ ⑧
MICHAEL'S NOOK COUNTRY HOUSE
Grasmere
015394 35496
This fine Victorian house has
been transformed into a country
house hotel of the highest
standard. Public areas are

elegant, comfortable and retain
a homely feel. Bedrooms have
interesting features: one is on
two levels and another has a
private patio. Dinner sets a
standard for others to follow.

★ ⑧ ⑧
WHITE MOSS HOUSE
Rydal Water,
Grasmere
015394 35295
This traditional Lakeland house,
once owned by Wordsworth, is
a friendly, intimate country
hotel with a loyal following.
Bedrooms are individually
decorated, and there is a two-
room suite in a cottage on the
hillside above the hotel. The set
five-course dinner uses local
ingredients. There is no bar;
pre-dinner drinks are served in
the lounge.

★ ★ ★ ⑧ ⑧ ⑧
SHARROW BAY COUNTRY HOUSE
Sharrow Bay,
Howtown
017684 86301
Standing at the water's edge
with views across the lake to
the mountains, Sharrow Bay is
often described as the first
country house hotel.
Individually furnished bedrooms
are split between the main
house and the Elizabethan
farmhouse, complete with its
own service staff, lounges and
breakfast room. There is a
choice of inviting lounges in
which to relax after the six-
course meal.

★ ⑧
HIPPING HALL
Cowan Bridge,
Kirkby Lonsdale
015242 71187
This comfortable 15th-century
house has spacious, attractively
furnished bedrooms. There are
two cottage suites with spiral
staircases from the lounge to
the bedroom. Public areas
include the original great hall
and a cosy drawing room
adjacent to the dining room.
Service is friendly and attentive.

★ ⑧
OLD CHURCH
Old Church Bay,
Watermillock
017684 86204
This comfortable, well-equipped
hotel is set in an idyllic location.
The bedrooms at the front enjoy
views of the lake and
mountains. The two lounges,
one of which is a bar in the
evening, and fireside seating in
the lobby offer a choice of quiet
places for contemplation. Board
games and reading material are
provided for guests' use and a
soft furnishings course is often
run at the hotel.

★ ★ ★ ⑧ ⑧ ⑧
GILPIN LODGE COUNTRY HOUSE HOTEL & RESTAURANT
Crook Road,
Windermere
015394 88818
Gilpin Lodge is an impeccable
Victorian residence set in
picturesque woodlands and
gardens. The sumptuous day
rooms are furnished with fine
antiques and provide
exceptional comfort. Some of

the individually styled bedrooms
have four-poster beds and
private sun terraces.
Imaginative and exciting food is
served in the three dining
rooms.

★ ★ ★ ⑧ ⑧ ⑧
HOLBECK GHYLL COUNTRY HOUSE
Holbeck Lane,
Windermere
015394 32375
In an area not short of dramatic
views, Holbeck Ghyll still
manages to stand out.
Panoramic vistas stretch across
Lake Windermere to the
magnificent Langdale Fells
beyond. The gently sloping
grounds include a tennis court,
and there is also a health spa.
Bedrooms, each individually
furnished to the same high
standard, are thoughtfully
equipped and some have
private balconies. Some rooms
are in a separate cottage.

★ ★ ⑧ ⑧
MILLER HOWE HOTEL
Rayrigg Road,
Windermere
015394 42536
For a real flavour of the Lake
District, try this popular hotel;
its stunning views of
Windermere from the
sumptuous public rooms are
unrivalled. Bedrooms are both
elegant and stylish and offer
many thoughtful extras. Dinner
remains a highlight of any visit
and the set menu offers a good
choice of creative dishes.

DERBYSHIRE

★ ★ ★ ⑧
CAVENDISH
Baslow
01246 582311
This country house hotel on the
edge of the Chatsworth estate
offers comfortable bedrooms
with many thoughtful extras.
Adorning the walls are works of
art loaned by the Duke and
Duchess of Devonshire. There is
a relaxing lounge and light
meals are served in the Garden
Room conservatory. More
formal cuisine, using fresh local
produce where possible, is
served in the restaurant.

★ ★ ⑧ ⑧ ⑧
FISCHER'S BASLOW HALL
Calver Road,
Baslow
01246 583259
This cosy country house hotel
has sumptuous bedrooms,
several with period bathroom
fittings. Public rooms centre
around the restaurant and the
slightly more casual Café-Max,

Hipping Hall

with its brasserie-style menu.
The hotel cuisine is worth
travelling for and the smart staff
are efficient and friendly.

DEVON

★ ★ ⑧ ⑧
HALMPSTONE MANOR
Bishop's Tawton,
Barnstaple
01271 830321
This historic manor house is
surrounded by lush farmland.
Bedrooms, including two with
four-poster beds, have many
useful extras and thoughtful
touches. A log fire burns in the
comfortable, spacious lounge.
Dinner, which is expertly
cooked from quality local
produce, is served in the
panelled dining room.

★ ★ ★ ⑧ ⑧ ⑧ ⑧
GIDLEIGH PARK
Chagford
01647 432367
Gidleigh Park is a now a legend
in hotel keeping. It is the
epitome of relaxed luxury, set in
pretty gardens and surrounded
by 45 acres of the Dartmoor
National Park. Bedrooms vary
in size and outlook but all
guarantee excellent levels of
comfort. Outstanding dishes,
many using local ingredients,
are offered in the restaurant
and there is an excellent wine
list.

★ ★ ★ ⑧ ⑧
LEWTRENCHARD MANOR
Lewdown
01566 783256 & 783222
This delightful Jacobean manor
house is set in an elevated
position amidst beautifully kept
gardens. Spacious, well-
equipped bedrooms enjoy far-
reaching views. The public
rooms have ornate ceilings, oak
panelling, large open fireplaces
and rich furnishings.
Imaginative and innovative
dishes are complemented by an
extensive and carefully
considered wine cellar.

DORSET

★ ★ ★ ⑧ ⑧ ⑧
SUMMER LODGE
Evershot
01935 83424
Surrounded by beautiful
countryside, this delightful hotel
enjoys a peaceful village setting.
Public rooms and the
individually decorated
bedrooms are very comfortable.
Flower arrangements, log fires
and watercolours add to the
charm. An imaginative, daily set
menu draws upon the strength
of local produce.

The Vineyard at Stockcross

Kennel Holt

★★★⊛⊛
PRIORY HOTEL
Church Green, Wareham
01929 551666
Set amidst four acres of well-tended gardens on the banks of the River Frome, this former priory is steeped in history and balances true professionalism with friendliness. A choice of comfortable lounges is available, enhanced by log fires during cooler weather. Bedrooms are luxurious and full of character, especially those in the adjacent boathouse, which are particularly spacious. At dinner, both carte and set menus are offered in the vaulted, stone cellar restaurant; lunches are served in the Garden Room during the week.

ESSEX

★★★⊛⊛
MAISON TALBOOTH
Stratford Road, Dedham
01206 322367
Overlooking the tranquil Dedham Vale, this pretty Georgian hotel offers a warm welcome. There is a comfortable drawing room where guests may take afternoon tea or snacks. Excellent breakfasts are served in the spacious bedrooms. Residents are chauffeured to the popular Le Talbooth Restaurant for dinner, just half a mile away.

GLOUCESTERSHIRE

★★★⊛⊛⊛
BUCKLAND MANOR
Buckland
01386 852626
This imposing 13th-century manor house stands in extensive grounds with beautiful gardens. Bedrooms and public areas are furnished with high-quality pieces and decorated in keeping with the style of the manor. Cuisine, based on carefully chosen raw ingredients, displays skill and the confidence to combine traditional favourites with more modern interpretations.

★★★⊛⊛⊛
THE GREENWAY
Shurdington, Cheltenham
01242 862352
The Greenway is a charming Elizabethan manor house. The dining room offers high standards of cuisine, taking full advantage of fresh local produce. The spacious, individually decorated bedrooms are divided between the main house and the smartly refurbished Georgian coach house. Rooms retain many original features and offer thoughtful extras.

★★★⊛⊛⊛
HOTEL ON THE PARK
38 Evesham Road, Cheltenham
01242 518898
Close to the centre of town, this beautiful hotel is brimming with style. The bar, restaurant and drawing room are decorated in Regency style and fine soft furnishings provide a note of opulence. Bedrooms are stunningly furnished and many little extras are offered. Cuisine is distinctive and accomplished.

★★★⊛⊛
COTSWOLD HOUSE
The Square, Chipping Campden
01386 840330
Overlooking the town square, this elegant 17th-century house offers individually decorated, comfortable bedrooms with many thoughtful extras. A choice of eating options is available.

★★⊛⊛
THE NEW INN AT COLN
Coln St-Aldwyns
01285 750651
In a peaceful setting, this delightful inn, dating back to the reign of Elizabeth I, offers genuine hospitality and enchanting bedrooms, divided between the main building and the Dovecote. Features include flagstone floors, wooden beams and inglenook fireplaces. The popular bar and restaurant serve enjoyable food prepared to a high standard.

★★★⊛⊛⊛
LOWER SLAUGHTER MANOR
Lower Slaughter
01451 820456
This charming Grade II listed manor dates mainly from the 17th century and enjoys a tranquil location at the heart of one of the Cotswolds' most famous villages. Spacious bedrooms are tastefully furnished and thoughtfully equipped. The appealing public areas include an inviting lounge and drawing room with log fires.

★★★⊛⊛
CALCOT MANOR
Calcot, Tetbury
01666 890391
Originally farmed by Cistercian monks, Calcot Manor has a 14th-century tithe barn amongst its outbuildings. Retaining much charm, this beautiful country house offers high standards of accommodation. Log fires burn in the elegant sitting rooms, and the stylish restaurant extends into a conservatory. The cooking is imaginative with a Mediterranean bias and good robust flavours. Children are made welcome with some specially designed family rooms and a superb playroom. The Gumstool bar offers informal dining in a country pub atmosphere.

★★★⊛⊛
THORNBURY CASTLE
Castle St, Thornbury
01454 281182
Located in splendid grounds, this Tudor castle's guests have included Henry VIII, Anne Boleyn and Mary Tudor, and modern-day visitors have the unrivalled opportunity to sleep in the same historic rooms. Now a fine country house hotel, its sumptuous handmade furnishings combine with modern comforts to create a truly luxurious atmosphere. The staff are professional yet approachable, and the galleried dining rooms make a memorable setting for some enjoyable meals.

★★★⊛⊛⊛
LORDS OF THE MANOR
Upper Slaughter
01451 820243
This 17th-century country manor house sits in eight acres of gardens and parkland. The spacious, deeply comfortable lounges and the luxuriously appointed restaurant overlook the front lawn and the formal rear garden. The restaurant offers cuisine that combines modern British and classical French styles in some impressive, well-judged dishes, supplemented by an excellent wine list. The bedrooms vary in size, but all are appointed to a very high standard.

HAMPSHIRE

★★★★★⊛⊛⊛
CHEWTON GLEN
Christchurch Road,
New Milton
01425 275341
Sumptuous accommodation and an abundance of thoughtful touches are provided at this internationally recognised hotel. A delightful haven of peace and tranquillity, the dedicated team ensure a memorable stay. The restaurant serves imaginative and innovative dishes, which make good use of excellent raw ingredients. The extensive wine list is a must for the wine enthusiast. Service and hospitality is of the highest standard.

★★★★⊛⊛
TYLNEY HALL
Rotherwick
01256 764881
This splendid Victorian country house, set in beautiful parkland, offers high standards of comfort in elegant surroundings. The restored water gardens, originally laid out by Gertrude Jekyll, are stunning. Public rooms, including the Wedgwood drawing room and the panelled Oak Room, are filled with fresh flowers and warmed by eleven log fires. The comfortable bedrooms are traditionally furnished.

ISLE OF WIGHT

★★★⊛⊛⊛
GEORGE HOTEL
Quay Street, Yarmouth
01983 760331
Superbly located between the quay and the castle in this picturesque yachting town, the George offers great character and quality throughout. Bedrooms have been individually decorated with great taste and style. The elegant restaurant offers excellent cooking, and the bright brasserie provides a less formal dining option.

KENT

★★⊛⊛
KENNEL HOLT
Goudhurst Road, Cranbrook
01580 712032
This Elizabethan manor house is a charming retreat with immaculately kept gardens. The relaxing public rooms are full of original features. Individually styled bedrooms, some with four-poster beds, are traditional, comfortable and furnished in keeping with the style of the property. The food is good and the wine list is a real treat.

LEICESTERSHIRE

★★★★⊛⊛
STAPLEFORD PARK
Stapleford, Melton Mowbray
01572 787522
Set in a 500-acre estate, this delightful stately home is surrounded by woods and parkland, originally laid out by Capability Brown, which now include a superb scenic championship golf course. The main reception rooms of the house are sumptuously decorated and furnished in grand country-house style. The dining room features carvings by Grinling Gibbons and makes a fine setting for the daily-changing menu. Each of the bedrooms has been designed by a sponsor, such as Turnbull & Asser and David Hicks, and those in a cottage in the grounds by companies such as IBM and Coca Cola. For the golfing widow there is a range of indoor leisure facilities and therapy rooms.

LINCOLNSHIRE

★★⊛⊛⊛
WINTERINGHAM FIELDS
Winteringham
01724 733096
This is a stylish restaurant with rooms, quietly located in the centre of the village. Bedrooms vary in size and are comfortably furnished. Public areas are very inviting but it is the inspired quality of the cooking that is the main draw, combining Swiss recipes with modern touches to provide memorable meals.

NORFOLK

★★⊛⊛⊛
MORSTON HALL
Morston, Holt, Blakeney
01263 741041
Seventeenth-century Morston Hall enjoys lovely views from its tranquil location amidst well-kept gardens. There is a choice of attractive lounges and a sunny conservatory. The elegant dining room serves enjoyable, award-winning cuisine. Bedrooms are spacious and individually decorated.

★★★⊛⊛
CONGHAM HALL COUNTRY HOUSE
Lynn Road, Grimston
01485 600250
Attractive landscaped grounds and 30 acres of parkland surround this Georgian country house. Inside, the elegant reception rooms are comfortable and beautifully furnished. Quality cuisine is served in the Orangery Restaurant through a choice of interesting menus; service is both attentive and friendly. Many of the bedrooms, mostly furnished in period style, look out over the attractive gardens.

OXFORDSHIRE

★★★★⊛⊛⊛⊛
LE MANOIR AUX QUAT' SAISONS
Great Milton
01844 278881
This delightful mellow stone 15th-century manor house lies in immaculate gardens, complete with sculptures, kitchen garden, and a traditional Japanese tea house. Period and contemporary bedrooms and suites are quite stunning and offer a superb level of comfort. The luxurious public rooms are furnished and decorated with great taste. The highlight of any stay has to be the outstanding cuisine which earns our supreme accolade of five Rosettes.

RUTLAND

★★★⊛⊛⊛
HAMBLETON HALL
Hambleton, Oakham
01572 756991
Hambleton Hall, in its landscaped grounds edging Rutland Water, is the epitome of the English country hotel. Stunning public rooms include a bar and elegant drawing room. The restaurant showcases inspired cuisine with its superb seasonal and locally sourced menu. Each of the stylish bedrooms is individually decorated.

SHROPSHIRE

★★★⊛⊛⊛
OLD VICARAGE
Worfield
01746 716497
This delightful hotel, quietly situated in the unspoilt Shropshire countryside, was an Edwardian vicarage. The bedrooms are thoughtfully furnished and well equipped. There is a lounge and a restaurant where the cuisine receives great acclaim.

SOMERSET

★★★⊛⊛
THE QUEENSBERRY
Russel Street, Bath
01225 447928
This carefully restored Bath stone townhouse is conveniently situated for the city centre.

Bedrooms are individually decorated and tastefully furnished with sofas, fresh flowers and marble bathrooms. A lounge and bar open onto a courtyard garden. The Olive Tree Restaurant offers freshly cooked cuisine with a Mediterranean influence.

★★ 🏵
ASHWICK HOUSE
Dulverton
01398 323868
This small Edwardian hotel is peacefully set in six acres on the edge of Exmoor. Public areas are extensive, the main feature being the galleried hall with its welcoming log fire. Bedrooms are spacious and comfortable and include every conceivable facility. Each evening a set menu is served using the finest local produce.

★★★ 🏵 🏵
HOMEWOOD PARK
Hinton Charterhouse
01225 723731
Set in delightful grounds, Homewood Park offers relaxed surroundings and maintains high standards of quality and comfort throughout. Bedrooms, all individually decorated, include thoughtful extras to ensure a comfortable stay. The hotel has a reputation for its excellent standard of cuisine which imaginatively interprets classical dishes. The impressive, eight-course tasting dinner should not be missed.

★★ 🏵 🏵
THE OAKS
Porlock
01643 862265
This Edwardian country house enjoys distant views of Porlock Bay and Exmoor. Bedrooms are comfortably furnished, vary in size and have many thoughtful extras. Public rooms are attractively furnished with period pieces. In winter guests can relax in front of real coal fires. During the summer, the garden is the perfect place to enjoy an aperitif before sampling the mouth-watering cuisine.

★★★ 🏵 🏵 🏵
CHARLTON HOUSE
Charlton Road,
Shepton Mallet
01749 342008
Situated in landscaped grounds just outside the town, this delightful country house dates back in parts to the 1500s. Bedrooms and public areas are decorated with high quality fabrics and furnishings; the staff are friendly and professional and the surroundings conducive to relaxation. The restaurant provides some very accomplished and distinctive cooking, with a focus on high-quality local ingredients.

★★★★ 🏵 🏵
STON EASTON PARK
Ston Easton
01761 241631
Built in 1740, this Grade I Palladian mansion is surrounded by tranquil parkland. Public areas are beautifully adorned with period features, and the bedrooms have great individuality,

reflecting the attention to detail which is a hallmark here. The enthusiastic staff make every effort to enhance the experience, and the cuisine shows both imagination and considered care.

★★★ 🏵 🏵 🏵
CASTLE HOTEL
Castle Green,
Taunton
01823 272671
This longstanding hotel, owned and run by the same family for many years, occupies an enviable position in the heart of the town. Instantly recognisable by its wisteria-covered front, the hotel has delightful bedrooms and public rooms, which offer every creature comfort. The kitchen team creates pleasing British dishes and there is a stunning brasserie.

★★ 🏵 🏵
LANGLEY HOUSE
Langley Marsh,
Wiveliscombe
01984 623318
Nestling in peaceful countryside at the foot of the Brendon Hills, parts of Langley House date back to the 16th century, although it is predominantly Georgian. There are deep armchairs and comfortable sofas in the sitting room where a log fire burns on colder evenings. Bedrooms vary in size and design, but all have thoughtful touches. Hospitality is warm and service is attentive. The award-winning cuisine should not be missed.

★ 🏵 🏵 🏵
LITTLE BARWICK HOUSE
Barwick Village,
Yeovil
01935 423902
This delightful listed Georgian dower house, situated in a quiet hamlet on the edge of Yeovil, is an ideal retreat for those seeking peaceful surroundings and good food. Guests can enjoy the informal atmosphere of a private home combined with the facilities and comforts of a modern hotel. The bedrooms are individually decorated and each has its own character and a range of thoughtful touches. The restaurant is but one of the highlights of a stay here.

★★ 🏵 🏵 🏵
OLD BEAMS RESTAURANT WITH ROOMS
Leek Road, Waterhouses
01538 308254
The dedicated proprietors are now in their 20th year at the Old Beams, a mid-18th-century property in a village setting on the edge of the Staffordshire Moorlands. The charming restaurant is characterised by its low-beamed ceilings and the conservatory extension which overlooks the lovely garden. A separate building has been converted to provide five tasteful, luxurious bedrooms. The warmth, friendliness and attentiveness of the service never falters. Only the best available fresh produce is used for the frequently changing set-price menus.

SUFFOLK

★★★★ 🏵 🏵 🏵
HINTLESHAM HALL
Hintlesham
01473 652334
Hintlesham Hall is a fine country house hotel where service is polished yet friendly. The magnificent Georgian façade belies the Tudor origins of the house. The main dining room, the Salon, is grand and elegant and serves classical cuisine. Bedrooms vary in style and design, each with individual decor and furniture. Guests may take advantage of the 18-hole golf facilities for a fee, or enjoy the smart health and leisure complex in the Orangery.

SUSSEX, EAST

★★★★ 🏵 🏵
ASHDOWN PARK
Wych Cross,
Forest Row
01342 824988
An extended country house overlooking a lake and set in unrivalled grounds, Ashdown Park has some magnificent features such as its converted-chapel conference venue. Bedrooms are spacious and decorated in a traditional style. The kitchen serves classically based dishes with light touches.

SUSSEX, WEST

★★★ 🏵 🏵
AMBERLEY CASTLE
Amberley
01798 831992
Few hotels boast the status of being a listed monument and fewer, if any, have enjoyed the honour of having a Royal Navy frigate named after it. This 11th-century luxury hotel is certainly unique, a treasure trove of history featuring a massive gate-house, portcullis and delightful gardens. Bedrooms are charming and individually decorated, some with direct access to the ramparts. The antique-dotted day rooms are cosy and stacked full of interesting books and historic bijouterie. The Queens Room restaurant offers accomplished cooking.

★★★ 🏵 🏵 🏵
GRAVETYE MANOR
East Grinstead
01342 810567
Gravetye, built in 1598, was one of the first country house hotels and remains a shining example in its class. The day rooms are comfortable and the bedrooms are decorated in traditional English style, furnished with antiques and include many thoughtful extras. The cuisine uses home-grown fruit and vegetables as well as local spring water.

★★★★ 🏵 🏵 🏵
SOUTH LODGE
Brighton Road,
Lower Beeding
01403 891711
Enjoying splendid views over the Downs, this Victorian mansion stands in 90 acres of gardens. Bedrooms are individually furnished and have lots of personal touches. Dishes such as duck confit with

Castle Hotel

Hintlesham Hall

pumpkin risotto characterise the excellent cuisine served in the elegant restaurant, where traditional Sunday lunch is also very popular.

★★★ 🏵 🏵 🏵
ALEXANDER HOUSE
East Street,
Turners Hill
01342 714914
Dating in part from the 17th century, this fine house is set in 135 acres of grounds. Reception rooms include the sunny south drawing room and the oak-panelled library. Individually decorated bedrooms include some full suites, one with a four-poster bed believed to have been made for Napoleon. The restaurant serves confident modern British cooking.

WARWICKSHIRE

★★★ 🏵 🏵 🏵
MALLORY COURT
Harbury Lane,
Bishop's Tachbrook,
Royal Leamington Spa
01926 330214
This English country house is set amidst ten acres of beautifully landscaped grounds. Most of the tastefully appointed bedrooms enjoy views over the gardens and each one is individually styled. Public areas include two elegant and comfortable lounges, a drawing room, conservatory, private dining room and an impressive panelled restaurant.

WEST MIDLANDS

★★★ 🏵 🏵
NUTHURST GRANGE COUNTRY HOUSE
Nuthurst Grange Lane,
Hockley Heath
01564 783972
This charming country house, set in an idyllic landscaped environment, provides excellent accommodation and fine cuisine. Bedrooms are thoughtfully furnished and

include a wealth of extras. The restaurant offers accomplished cooking and an imaginative selection of dishes. Staff are committed to providing a warm and relaxing atmosphere.

★★★★ 🏵 🏵
NEW HALL
Walmley Road,
Sutton Coldfield
0121 378 2442
Set in immaculately maintained grounds and gardens, this hotel is reputedly the oldest moated manor house in England. The day rooms are delightful. Divided between a purpose-built wing and the main house, the bedrooms vary in size but all are individually and decorated to a high standard. The restaurant offers imaginative dishes of a consistently high quality.

WILTSHIRE

★★★★ 🏵 🏵 🏵
MANOR HOUSE
Castle Combe
01249 782206
Set in 26 acres of grounds with a romantic Italian-style garden, this 14th-century country house offers superbly furnished rooms. Public areas include a number of cosy lounge areas with roaring fires. The bedrooms stand in a row of original stone cottages within the hotel's grounds and fully reflect the high quality of the main house.

★★★★ 🏵 🏵
LUCKNAM PARK
Colerne
01225 742777
Dating back to 1720, this magnificent Palladian mansion is set in 500 acres of glorious parkland. Style and grace are evident in both the elegant day rooms and the individually decorated bedrooms and suites. A choice of interesting menus offers a carefully balanced selection of accomplished cuisine.

Longueville Manor

★ ★ ⑥ ⑥ ⑥
HOWARD'S HOUSE
Teffont Evias,
01722 716392
This charming hotel is located in the quintessential English village of Teffont Evias. Spacious bedrooms are comfortably furnished and feature thoughtful extras such as fresh fruit, home-made biscuits and magazines. The cooking is always popular – the culmination of excellent ingredients and experienced culinary skills.

WORCESTERSHIRE

★ ★ ★ ⑥ ⑥
THE LYGON ARMS
High Street, Broadway
01386 852255
This 16th-century coaching inn is in a prime location in the heart of Broadway and features a wealth of historical charm and character. Bedrooms vary in style and layout, offering comfort, modern facilities and fine antique furniture. There is a variety of lounge areas, some with open fires.

★ ★ ★ ⑥ ⑥ ⑥
BROCKENCOTE HALL COUNTRY HOUSE
Chaddesley Corbett
01562 777876
This magnificent, personally run Victorian mansion is set in beautiful grounds. Spacious bedrooms are appointed to a high standard with many thoughtful extras, and enjoy views of the lake or surrounding parkland. There are comfortable lounges and the elegant dining room serves a high standard of cuisine.

YORKSHIRE, NORTH

★ ★ ★ ⑥ ⑥
THE DEVONSHIRE ARMS COUNTRY HOUSE
Bolton Abbey
01756 710441
With stunning views of the

The Howard

Wharfedale countryside this beautiful hotel, owned by the Duke and Duchess of Devonshire, dates back to the 17th century and has the feel of a private country house. Bedrooms are all stylishly furnished and those in the old part of the house are particularly spacious, complete with four-poster beds and fine antique pieces. Public areas include the elegant Burlington Restaurant, which offers traditional cooking, and the modern, informal Brasserie. There is a well-equipped leisure club.

★ ★ ★ ⑥ ⑥
THE GRANGE
1 Clifton, York
01904 644744
This bustling Regency townhouse is just a few minutes' walk from York's centre. The individually designed bedrooms are thoughtfully equipped. Public rooms are comfortable and tastefully furnished. There are two dining options: The Brasserie in the cellar offering an informal, relaxed atmosphere, and The Ivy with its impressive *trompe l'oeil* and fine dining menu.

★ ★ ★ ⑥ ⑥ ⑥
MIDDLETHORPE HALL
Bishopthorpe Road,
Middlethorpe, York
01904 641241
Close to the racecourse, this splendid country house nestles amid 20 acres of grounds and countryside. The elegant drawing room is impressive and enjoys delightful views of the beautiful garden. The kitchen produces an ambitious menu, served in the panelled dining room. Individually furnished bedrooms are split between the main house and a nearby courtyard. The smart spa facility includes a pool, gymnasium and several beauty treatment rooms.

CHANNEL ISLANDS

★ ★ ★ ⑥ ⑥
CHATEAU LA CHAIRE
Rozel Bay, Jersey
01534 863354
High up over Rozel Bay, Château la Chaire is positioned on the side of a wooded valley and surrounded by five acres of terraced gardens. Built as a gentleman's residence in 1843, the Château retains much of the atmosphere of a private country house, including some exquisite decorative plasterwork in the drawing room. The oak-panelled dining room, with its conservatory extension, is a fine setting for the skilful, consistent cooking. Individually styled bedrooms feature a host of comforting extras.

★ ★ ★ ★ ⑥ ⑥
LONGUEVILLE MANOR
St Saviour, Jersey
01534 725501
Dating back in part to the 13th century, Longueville Manor is set in 17 acres of well-kept grounds that include many fine specimen trees as well as a lake, swimming pool and tennis court. The various day rooms give guests an ideal excuse to enjoy a sumptuous afternoon tea or quiet hour with a book. Antique-furnished bedrooms are individually decorated with great style; ornaments, fresh flowers and fine embroidered bed linen provide the personal touch. The twin dining rooms, one with ancient, heavily carved oak panelling, are appointed to the highest standard and provide an appropriate setting for some fine cooking. Good use is made of produce from the hotel's extensive kitchen garden in sophisticated dishes.

SCOTLAND

ABERDEENSHIRE

★ ★ ⑥ ⑥
BALGONIE COUNTRY HOUSE
Braemar Place, Ballater
013397 55482
This charming Edwardian-style country house is a peaceful haven set in secluded gardens, with views of Glen Muick. A short walk from the village, the house is impeccably maintained and has a friendly atmosphere. Comfortable bedrooms come in two styles, period or more contemporary. There is a cosy bar with an adjoining lounge. Food is foremost at Balgonie, from the excellent breakfasts to the scrumptious afternoon teas and daily-changing four course dinners. Service is exemplary.

ARGYLL & BUTE

★ ★ ★ ★ ⑥ ⑥ ⑥
ISLE OF ERISKA
Eriska, Ledaig
01631 720371
This Victorian mansion house is situated on a private island approached by a small bridge. Guests are encouraged to explore the island, visiting the beaches, woodland and natural gardens. Spacious bedrooms provide good levels of comfort and boast some fine antique pieces. Public areas include a

choice of different lounges as well as the part wood-panelled dining room. Here local seafood features prominently in the carefully prepared meals.

★ ★ ★ ⑥ ⑥
AIRDS HOTEL
Port Appin
01631 730236
This relaxing hotel overlooks Loch Linnhe. Bedrooms are furnished with flair, and the lounges invite guests to relax and unwind. There is an enclosed sun porch from which to take in the stunning views. In the kitchen, top quality ingredients are prepared with a light touch.

DUMFRIES & GALLOWAY

★ ⑥ ⑥
WELL VIEW HOTEL
Ballplay Road, Moffat
01683 220184
Located on a quiet road within walking distance of town, Well View Hotel retains many of its original Victorian features. Individually furnished bedrooms are comfortable and thoughtfully equipped. Dinner is a six-course affair, using fine ingredients which are locally sourced whenever possible.

★ ★ ★ ⑥ ⑥ ⑥
KIRROUGHTREE HOUSE
Minnigaff, Newton Stewart
01671 402141
Standing in eight acres of landscaped gardens on the edge of Galloway Forest park, this 17th-century mansion offers comfort and elegance in impressive surroundings. Lounges have deep sofas and antique furniture. Spacious bedrooms are individually decorated with many personal touches. The hotel is justly proud of its high levels of hospitality. Dinner is a highlight, served in the formal dining rooms.

EAST LOTHIAN

★ ★ ★ ⑥ ⑥
GREYWALLS HOTEL
Muirfield, Gullane
01620 842144
Designed by Lutyens, and with gardens created by Gertrude Jekyll, Greywalls overlooks the famous Muirfield Golf Course and guests may find themselves sleeping in the bedrooms occupied by many of the game's past greats. Public areas include a library with a log fire and grand piano and a lovely sun lounge. At dinner a simple cooking style allows top quality ingredients to shine through. The smart bedrooms are furnished in period style and are exceptionally well equipped.

EDINBURGH, CITY OF

★ ★ ★ ★ ⑥
THE HOWARD
34 Great King Street,
Edinburgh
0131 315 2220
Comfortable and inviting bedrooms, including some half and full suites, are a feature of this townhouse, made up of three linked Georgian houses. Ornate chandeliers and lavish drapes characterise the drawing

room; the adjacent restaurant, 36, has a much more contemporary style. Service is professional and, above all, friendly and caring.

FIFE

★ ★ ★ ★ ⑥ ⑥
BALBIRNIE HOUSE
Balbirnie Park,
Markinch
01592 610066
This luxury hotel has been lovingly restored to provide well-equipped, spacious accommodation. Opulent day rooms furnished with antiques include three sitting rooms, one of which has a well-stocked bar. A stylish conservatory restaurant provides an elegant venue in which guests can enjoy the imaginative cooking.

★ ★ ⑥ ⑥ ⑥
THE PEAT INN
Peat Inn
01334 840206
Just six miles from St Andrews, this popular restaurant with rooms was originally a coaching inn. The creative cooking is of a consistently high quality, based mainly on local produce. Although a cooked breakfast is not served, superb continental trays are served in the bedrooms. The luxurious, split-level bedroom suites offer a host of thoughtful extras including smart bathrooms adorned with Italian marble.

★ ★ ★ ⑥ ⑥
RUFFLETS COUNTRY HOUSE & GARDEN RESTAURANT
Strathkinness Low Road,
St Andrews
01334 472594
The committed team at Rufflets Country House have nurtured an ethos of top class hotel-keeping and fine hospitality. The success of this approach is clear in the number of guests who return time and again. A choice of welcoming and individually furnished lounges, overlooking the award-winning gardens, is complemented by a comfortable restaurant, where imaginative Scottish cuisine is served, and a separate, popular brasserie. Thoughtfully equipped bedrooms, many with striking colour schemes, complete the picture.

GLASGOW, CITY OF

★ ★ ★ ⑥ ⑥ ⑥
ONE DEVONSHIRE GARDENS
1 Devonshire Gardens,
Glasgow
0141 339 2001
Three townhouses form this highly individual hotel. Luxurious bedrooms follow an individual and distinctive decorative theme. One house has a stylish drawing room, and there is a cocktail bar and restaurant in another, where guests can enjoy classic dishes with a modern touch.

HIGHLAND

★ ★ ★ ⑥ ⑥ ⑥
ARISAIG HOUSE
Beasdale, Arisaig
01687 450622
This splendid Scottish mansion enjoys a peaceful setting amid

extensive woodland and carefully tended gardens; there are beautiful azaleas and rhododendrons. Bedrooms include some Prime Rooms and many of the bathrooms are luxurious. There is a choice of wonderfully relaxing sitting rooms enhanced by fine furnishings, fresh floral displays and welcoming open fires. The elegant panelled dining room provides an appropriate setting for creative cooking. The finest ingredients are used and natural flavours are allowed to shine through.

★ ★ ⊛ ⊛ ⊛
THREE CHIMNEYS RESTAURANT & HOUSE OVER-BY
Colbost, Isle of Skye
01470 511258
The House Over-By provides accommodation par excellence in spacious split-level rooms, all individually designed in harmony with the environment. An outstanding Scottish cold breakfast, featuring fresh fruits, locally smoked meats and fish and other regional produce, is served in a bright room overlooking the sea loch. In the cottage-style Three Chimneys Restaurant visitors are enchanted by flavoursome cooking and unfussy treatment of prime Scottish ingredients. Put this on your 'don't miss' list for your next visit to Scotland.

★ ★ ★ ★ ⊛ ⊛ ⊛
INVERLOCHY CASTLE
Torlundy,
Fort William
01397 702177
Set amidst glorious scenery, this impressive Victorian building has 500 acres of grounds. Bedrooms are lavishly appointed and spacious, some facing Ben Nevis. Private dining rooms are available, but the main dining room, adjacent to the elegant drawing room, has stunning loch and mountain views. Top quality ingredients are carefully cooked.

★ ★ ⊛ ⊛ ⊛
THE CROSS
Tweed Mill Brae,
Ardbroilach Road,
Kingussie
01540 661166
A former tweed mill, this delightful restaurant with rooms provides high standards of comfort, excellent hospitality and refined service. Bedrooms combine contemporary fittings with traditional furnishings and there is an attractive lounge with ample reading material. Imaginative cooking at dinner and an impressive wine list are offered in the stylish, stone-walled dining room.

★ ⊛ ⊛
THE DOWER HOUSE
Highfield, Muir of Ord
01463 870090
This small and charming hotel in four acres of secluded grounds has a splendid sitting room featuring an open fire and plenty to read. The bedrooms offer quality and comfort; the house is full of thoughtful touches such as fresh flowers. Set dinners and hearty breakfasts are prepared with

much care using fresh herbs and seasonal produce.

★ ★ ⊛
KILMICHAEL COUNTRY HOUSE
Glen Cloy, Brodick,
Isle of Arran
01770 302219
Believed to be the oldest house on the island, Kilmichael Country House is a friendly haven of elegance and luxury. The house nestles in a peaceful glen amidst well-tended gardens. Bedrooms are stylishly decorated, well equipped and furnished in traditional country house style; those in the converted barns are particularly elegant. Dinner in the smart restaurant is a treat and the recipes make excellent use of fresh local produce.

★ ★ ★ ★ ★ ⊛ ⊛
THE GLENEAGLES HOTEL
Auchterarder
01764 662231
With its wealth of sporting activities, including the famous championship golf courses, falconry, angling, shooting and cycling, as well as the equestrian centre and indoor leisure club, this renowned hotel has something to suit most sporting guests. Set in beautiful countryside, it also offers a peaceful retreat for visitors who want to relax and unwind. Bedrooms offer a choice between traditional comfort and a more contemporary theme. Afternoon tea is served in the smart lounge. Among the choice of eating areas, the Strathearn restaurant is the fine dining option; service is professional and diners are entertained by a pianist.

★ ★ ★ ⊛ ⊛
KINLOCH HOUSE
Blairgowrie
01250 884237
This country house hotel stands in 25 acres of wood and parkland. The bar, with its conservatory extension and extensive range of malt whiskies, is the ideal place to relax and unwind. The elegant dining room is the appropriate setting for fine dining. Bedrooms in the main house are individually decorated, while the spacious wing rooms have a more contemporary feel and boast luxurious bathrooms.

★ ★ ★ ⊛ ⊛
KINNAIRD
Kinnaird Estate,
Dunkeld
01796 482440
Part of a 9000-acre estate in the heart of the Perthshire countryside, this Edwardian mansion provides a very warm welcome. There are several inviting sitting rooms and a snooker room warmed by open fires. Innovative cooking is served in one of the two dining rooms. Bedrooms are generously proportioned and luxurious in appointment; living flame gas fires are a unique feature.

★ ★ ⊛
LADYBURN
Maybole
01655 740585
This charming country house is ideally situated in open countryside and surrounded by an attractive natural garden. Comfortable bedrooms are complemented by a choice of sitting areas, a drawing room and a library. Dinner comprises a carefully cooked three-course set menu, which is discussed with guests beforehand. The welcome is genuinely warm and services are provided willingly.

★ ★ ★ ⊛ ⊛
LOCHGREEN HOUSE
Monktonhill Road,
Southwood, Troon
01292 313343
Lochgreen is situated in 30 acres of wooded and landscaped gardens enjoying views over the Royal Troon golf course to the Clyde. Inside, the house offers the charm and elegance of past eras with antique furnishings and wood panelling. Bedrooms are well proportioned, stylish and very comfortable. Public areas include two sumptuous sitting rooms, one of which contains the bar and malt whisky collection. The restaurant is unique in design; its high ceilings and tapestried walls lend a baronial feel to the surroundings.

★ ★ ★ ★ ★ ⊛ ⊛
TURNBERRY HOTEL, GOLF COURSES & SPA
Turnberry
01655 331000
This world-famous hotel enjoys tremendous views over to the Isle of Arran, the Mull of Kintyre and Ailsa Craig. A recent addition is the excellent Colin Montgomerie Golf Academy and the new lodge rooms. Spacious bedrooms and suites in the main hotel are equipped to high standards. The restaurant serves classical cuisine in a traditional setting and the modern brasserie is more informal in style.

★ ★ ★ ⊛ ⊛
CROMLIX HOUSE
Kinbuck, Dunblane
01786 822125
This fine Edwardian mansion lies amidst neatly tended gardens in a 3000-acre estate. Comfortable bedrooms, many with private sitting rooms, have the character of a country house. There is a choice of sitting rooms, and both the drawing room and the library are heated by log fires. Dinner, prepared using local ingredients wherever possible, is served in one of two elegant dining rooms. Breakfast is taken in the conservatory overlooking the gardens.

★ ⊛ ⊛
CREAGAN HOUSE
Strathyre
01877 384638
A cosy hotel of distinction, with a lovely friendly atmosphere, this restored 17th-century

Kilmichael Country House

The Old Rectory Country House

farmhouse lies just outside the village and is backed by forest walks within the Queen Elizabeth Park. Carefully chosen pieces furnish the attractive bedrooms which are thoughtfully equipped to include CD players; TVs are available on request. The little lounge is inviting and refreshments are served here before and after an enjoyable meal in the impressive baronial-style dining room. Cuisine is bold and imaginative, and the two different menus are both very tempting.

WALES

★ ★ ★ ⊛ ⊛
YNYSHIR HALL
Eglwysfach
01654 781209
This fine country house hotel is set in 12 acres of scenic gardens. The bedrooms vary in size and all are individually designed, furnished with antiques and equipped with a range of thoughtful extras. Both the bar and the drawing room are adorned with striking paintings of local scenes, and excellent cuisine is served in the smart dining room.

★ ★ ★ ⊛ ⊛
TAN-Y-FOEL COUNTRY HOUSE HOTEL
Capel Garmon, Betws-y-Coed
01690 710507
On a wooded hillside overlooking the Conwy Valley and the town below, Tan-y-Foel appears the archetypal country house. A 16th-century stone-built house, it leaves some traditions at the front door whilst valuing those of comfort, service and hospitality. The interior design and colour schemes are both bold and modern: the lounge is furnished

and decorated in earthy tones, the restaurant is verdant, cosy and warmed by a wood-burning stove, and the breakfast room features stunning lighting effects. Bedrooms are individually designed with brighter colour schemes. The cooking is also vibrant and modern, using organic produce where possible to great effect.

★ ★ ⊛ ⊛
THE OLD RECTORY COUNTRY HOUSE
Llanrwst Road,
Llansanffraid Glan Conwy,
Conwy
01492 580611
This charming hotel in delightful terraced gardens overlooks the Conwy Estuary and Snowdonia beyond. Inside, the intimate public rooms are complemented by classical interior design and antique pieces. Bedrooms, most of which have sea or estuary views, are tastefully furnished in keeping with the building. Two bedrooms are located in the grounds and can be used as a family suite. The cuisine is excellent, with well-selected ingredients carefully put together in appealing yet reassuring combinations on the Anglo-French menu. The warm and caring hospitality is outstanding.

★ ★ ★ ⊛ ⊛
BODYSGALLEN HALL
Llandudno
01492 584466
From its elevated position on the outskirts of Llandudno, this 17th-century country house, set in 220 acres of parkland and superb gardens, enjoys views of Conwy Castle and Snowdonia. There is much charm and character in the wood-panelled walls adorned with old masters, elegant furnishings and open fires. Spacious bedrooms include many thoughtful extras and some rooms are in converted cottages. The

Glenlo Abbey

Longueville House

restaurant offers imaginative cooking using the finest local ingredients. A high level of customer care is provided by a friendly and dedicated team.

★ ★ ⑥ ⑥ ⑥
ST TUDNO
The Promenade, Llandudno
01492 874411
Although not the place for buckets and spades, this high-quality resort hotel will receive toddlers as warmly as adults. Bedrooms, some with sea views, come in a wide choice of sizes and individual styles, so discuss exact requirements at the time of booking. Public rooms include a non-smoking lounge, a convivial bar lounge and a small indoor pool. The air-conditioned Garden Room Restaurant is the focal point for enjoyable cuisine using good local produce.

DENBIGHSHIRE

★ ★ ⑥ ⑥
TYDDYN LLAN COUNTRY HOTEL & RESTAURANT
Llandrillo
01490 440264
Set in landscaped gardens amidst fine scenery, this Georgian house has been carefully restored to provide an idyllic, comfortable country retreat. Individually styled bedrooms are tastefully furnished and the delightful lounges are warmed by roaring log fires. The elegant restaurant serves an imaginative selection

of excellent dishes, created from quality local produce.

GWYNEDD

★ ★ ⑥ ⑥ ⑥
HOTEL MAES Y NEUADD
Talsarnau
01766 780200
Dating back in parts to the 14th century, with various additions over the intervening centuries, this substantial stone-built house enjoys fine views over the mountains and across the bay to the Llyn Peninsula. Bedrooms, some in an adjacent coach house, are individually furnished and many have fine antique pieces. Public areas display a similar welcoming character, including the restaurant, where the team make good use of locally sourced ingredients.

POWYS

★ ★ ★ ⑥ ⑥
LAKE COUNTRY HOUSE
Llangammarch Wells
01591 620202
This Victorian country house hotel comes complete with a golf course, lake, wooded grounds and river. Bedrooms are individually decorated and furnished with designer fabrics and many extra comforts come as standard. Great afternoon teas are served in the lounge in front of a log fire. In addition to the elegant restaurant there is a separate bar and billiard room. The kitchen produces a good standard of cuisine.

TOWNHOUSE HOTELS are small, individual, town-centre hotels which provide a high degree of privacy. They concentrate on luxuriously furnished bedrooms and suites with high-quality room service, rather than the public rooms or formal dining rooms more often associated with hotels. Townhouse hotels are usually in areas well served by restaurants.

★ ★ ★ ★ ⑥ ⑥
LLANGOED HALL
Llyswen
01874 754525
Set amidst beautiful countryside, this imposing country house has an exterior remodelled by Clough Williams-Ellis of Portmeirion fame. Inside there is a splendid balance between comfort, grandeur and interest, with wood-burning fires, deep-cushioned sofas and a range of artwork and artefacts. Bedrooms are furnished with a pleasing mix of antiques and Laura Ashley designs and feature smart bathrooms. The accomplished, imaginative cuisine complements the opulent surroundings.

SWANSEA

★ ★ ⑥ ⑥ ⑥
FAIRYHILL
Reynoldston
01792 390139
Set in 24 acres of grounds, this impressive stone-built 18th-century mansion benefits from a tranquil location in the heart of the Gower Peninsula. Bedrooms are individually decorated and furnished with style. There is a choice of comfortable seating areas, with log fires contributing to the warm and relaxed atmosphere. The cuisine is imaginative and accomplished and features many local specialities.

IRELAND

CLARE

★ ★ ★ ⑥ ⑥
GREGANS CASTLE
Ballyvaughan
065 7077 005
Standing at the foot of Corkscrew Hill, with dramatic views over Galway Bay, this hotel is situated in an area which is rich in archaeological, geological and botanical interest. A high level of personal service and hospitality has earned the hotel special commendations in recent years and the welcoming staff fulfill their reputation. The cuisine is excellent, with the emphasis placed on good food using fresh local produce.

CORK

★ ★ ★ ★ ⑥ ⑥
HAYFIELD MANOR
Perrott Avenue,
College Road, Cork
021 315600
Hayfield Manor offers privacy and seclusion within a mile of Cork city centre. This fine hotel is part of a grand two-acre estate and gardens, and offers every modern comfort. It maintains an atmosphere of tranquility and the spacious bedrooms contain many thoughtful extras. Public rooms feature elegant architecture, carefully combined with fine furnishings and real fires to create an atmosphere of intimacy. The Manor Room restaurant serves dishes from the interesting carte. Guests have access to the exclusive health club.

★ ★ ★ ⑥ ⑥ ⑥
LONGUEVILLE HOUSE
Mallow
022 47156
Set in a wooded estate, this 18th-century Georgian mansion has many fine features. The comfortable bedrooms overlook the river valley and the courtyard maze. The two elegant sitting rooms feature fine examples of Italian plasterwork and an Adams mantelpiece graces the Presidents Restaurant. Cuisine is exciting and inventive, and makes good use of excellent fresh produce.

DUBLIN

★ ★ ★ ★ ⑥ ⑥
THE CLARENCE
6-8 Wellington Quay, Dublin
01 4070800
The Clarence is an individual and very tasteful hotel offering richly furnished bedrooms. For sheer luxury, the two-bedroom penthouse suite is outstanding. Public areas include a long gallery with luxurious sofas. The bar is smart and the restaurant serves fine cuisine.

GALWAY

★ ★ ★ ⑥ ⑥
CASHEL HOUSE
Cashel
095 31001
Award-winning gardens are the setting for this gracious country house hotel. The comfortable lounges have turf fires and antique furnishings. The restaurant offers local produce such as Connemara lamb. Bedrooms are appealing and luxury suites are available.

★ ★ ★ ★ ⑥ ⑥
GLENLO ABBEY
Bushypark, Galway
091 526666
Standing in a landscaped 134-acre estate, this restored 18th-century abbey overlooks a beautiful loch. The original building houses a boardroom, business centre, conference and banqueting facilities. The bedrooms are in a modern wing along with a library, restaurants, cocktail and cellar bars.

KERRY

★ ★ ★ ★ ⑥ ⑥ ⑥
PARK HOTEL KENMARE
Kenmare
064 41200
The Park is a luxurious country house hotel on the famous Ring of Kerry. It stands above terraced gardens which overlook the estuary of the Kenmare River, with a glorious mountain backdrop. Warm hospitality and professional service are provided. The restaurant offers very good food and fine wines.

★ ★ ★ ★ ⑥ ⑥
SHEEN FALLS LODGE
Kenmare
064 41600
This beautiful hotel beside the Sheen River is surrounded by stunning lakes and mountains. The cascading Sheen Falls are floodlit at night, creating a magical atmosphere which can

be enjoyed from the the restaurant. A luxurious lounge, library, billiards room and cocktail bar complete the public rooms and there are three grades of comfortable bedrooms.

KILDARE

★ ★ ★ ★ ★ ⑥ ⑥ ⑥
THE KILDARE HOTEL & COUNTRY CLUB
Straffan
01 6017200
This luxurious hotel is set in 330 acres of park and woodland, with a golf course designed by Arnold Palmer – the venue for the 2005 Ryder Cup. Opulent reception rooms include the Chinese Drawing Room, overlooking the gardens and the River Liffey. Richly furnished bedrooms are most comfortable and extremely well equipped. Staff are very attentive, and there are extensive leisure and conference facilities.

KILKENNY

★ ★ ★ ★ ⑥ ⑥
MOUNT JULIET
Thomastown
056 73000
Set in 1500 acres of parkland, including a Jack Nicklaus designed golf course where the Irish Opens were played in 1993 and 1994, this beautiful Palladian mansion is now a very special hotel. The elegant and spacious public rooms retain much of the original architectural features, including ornate plasterwork and fine Adam fireplaces in the cocktail bar, restaurant and drawing room.

WEXFORD

★ ★ ★ ⑥ ⑥
MARLFIELD HOUSE
Gorey
055 21124
This distinctive Regency house was once the residence of the Earl of Courtown. The current hotel retains an atmosphere of elegance and luxury throughout. Public areas include a library, drawing room and dining room leading into a conservatory which overlooks the grounds and a wildlife preserve. Bedrooms are in keeping with the style of the downstairs rooms and there are some superb suites. Druids Glen and several other golf courses are nearby.

WICKLOW

★ ★ ★ ⑥ ⑥
TINAKILLY COUNTRY HOUSE & RESTAURANT
Rathnew
0404 69274
Built in 1870, this elegant house is set in seven acres of 19th-century gardens with breathtaking views of the sea. The highest standards of accommodation and hospitality are offered and the bedrooms are tastefully decorated with period furnishings and some four-poster beds. Country house cuisine is served, including fresh fish, game and home-grown vegetables.

AA

ROAD ATLAS
OF THE
BRITISH
ISLES
2002

traffic and travel information

The Automobile Association is Britain's largest motoring organisation, providing accurate and up-to-date information for all motorists. Our information detailing traffic congestion, road conditions and public transport news is collected from more than 8,000 sources, including, among others, local authorities, roadside cameras and our own registered mobile phone service 'Jambusters'.

AA Roadwatch operates 24 hours a day, giving traffic information on all UK motorways, major trunk roads and local roads. The result is one of the most comprehensive and up-to-the-minute traffic report services available.

Instant traffic reports

09003 401 100/401 100 mobile

www.theAA.com

These numbers give you direct access to a range of traffic and travel information services, including: the latest traffic reports for your local area, or for any region of the UK; a traffic report on any motorway or A-road of your choice; and local and national five-day weather forecasts.

UK and european routes

0870 5500 600

www.theAA.com

AA routes are available for the UK, Ireland and continental Europe, to help you map out a detailed plan of the best way to get to your destination. Route planning is also available online and, if you tell us your usual routes, we can send you e-mail alerts at times pre-determined by you to let you know what traffic incidents and delays are occurring.

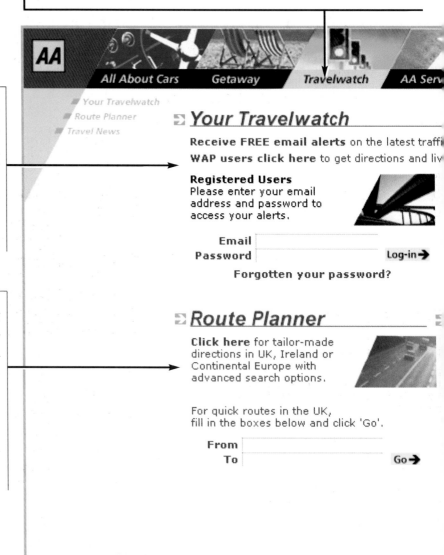

In-car information systems and radio

AA traffic and travel information can also be received by intelligent in-car navigation systems that warn of delays, provide detailed routes and even recommend a suitable hotel for a stopover. Alternatively, use your WAP-enabled mobile device to access this information on the AA's website. AA Roadwatch reports are also available over many local radio stations.

Air ambulance

0800 3899 899

For information about the work of the National Association of Air Ambulance Services, or to make a donation to NAAAS by debit or credit card, call the number above.

CALL NOW 0800 085 3007

■ Site Map   ■ Contact Us   ■ About the AA

Quick Links : Pick from List

problems on your route.
travel news on your phone.

New user
Give us the details of your trip and Travelwatch will **email you** personalised traffic reports.

New User **Register Now →**

Travel News

Click here to search for travel updates in cities, towns & motorways.

For live **traffic & weather information** on the move in Great Britain, call 09003 401 100 or **401 100** from your mobile. (Calls cost 60p per minute.)

   12. A4, Major roadworks, Uxbridge Road, E.
   13. A4, Temporary traffic lights, Saltford, E.
   14. A5, Roadworks. Delays expected, Staples Corner, N.
   15. A5, Temporary traffic lights, Dunstable, N.

Pause

✉ **Email Us: customer.services@theAA.com** ℂ
        Phone Us: 0870 600 0371
iation Limited 2001   **Web Site Terms & Conditions**

Road user information line (Highways Agency)

0845 750 040 30

For information on motorways and trunk roads, to make a complaint or comment on road conditions or roadworks, for MoT and vehicle licence enquiries.

Air ambulances are a vital part of emergency services, providing a rapid response and transfer from incident to hospital.

AA The Driving School

0800 60 70 80
www.theAA.com

The AA's Driving School is the only national driving school to use fully qualified instructors exclusively. Attractive packages are available to people pre-paying for 12 hours' tuition.

Petrolbusters

www.theAA.com

Click on the Petrolbusters symbol to locate the cheapest petrol in your area.

Call tariffs

0800 – free to caller, 0845 – charged at BT local rate, 0870 – charged at BT national rate, 09003 – 60p per minute at all times. Availability and prices for mobile calls can vary – contact your service provider for details.

Information correct at time of going to press.

V

route planner

Motorway

Primary route
dual carriageway

Primary route
single carriageway

Other A roads

0	10	20	30 miles
0	10	20	30 40 kilometres

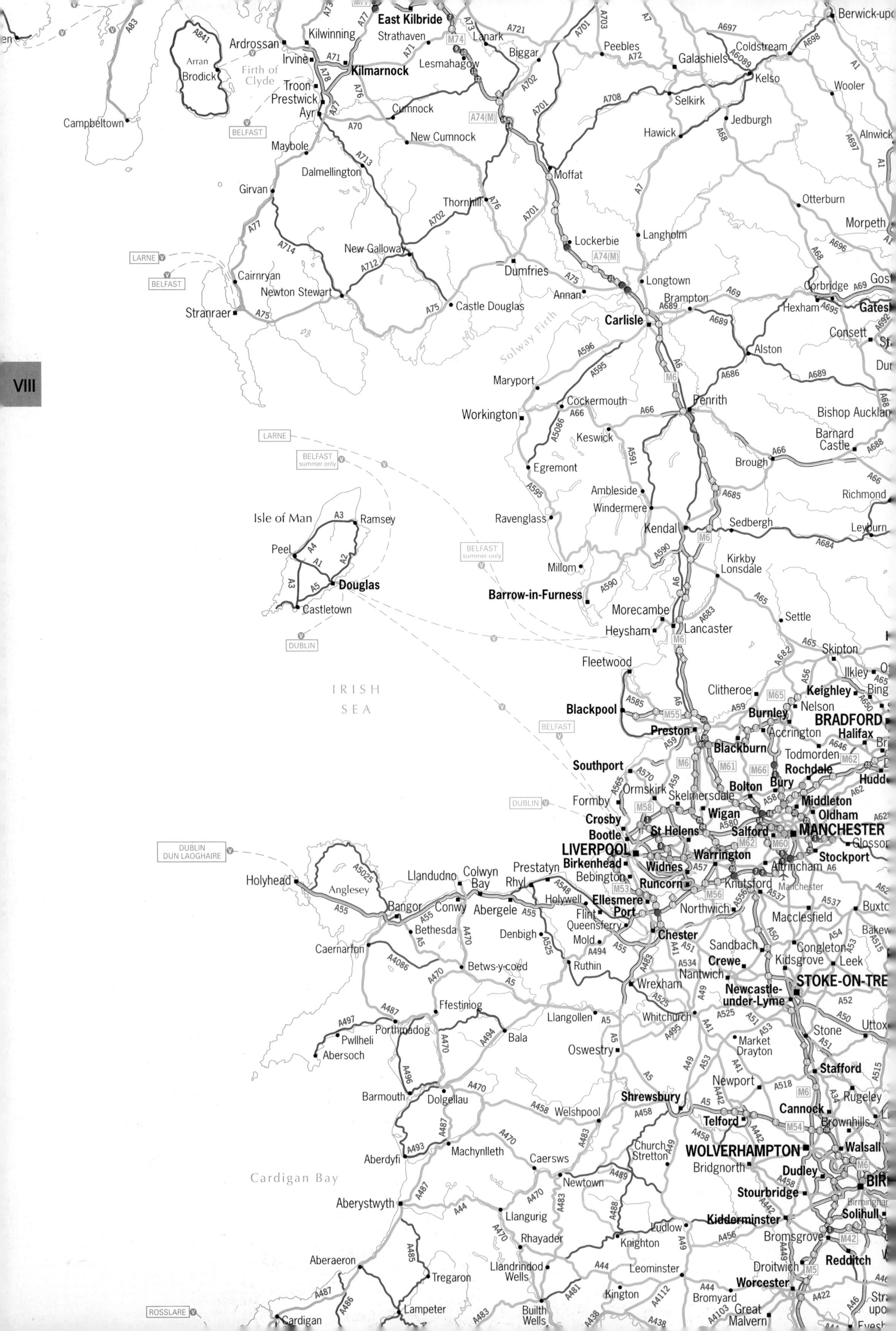

Berwick-upon
East Kilbride
Kilwinning
Ardrossan
Irvine
Strathaven
Lanark
Biggar
Peebles
Galashiels
Coldstream
Kelso
Wooler
Arran
Brodick
Firth of Clyde
Kilmarnock
Troon
Prestwick
Ayr
Lesmahagow
Hawick
Selkirk
Jedburgh
Alnwick
Campbeltown
Maybole
Cumnock
New Cumnock
Moffat
Langholm
Otterburn
Morpeth
BELFAST
Girvan
Dalmellington
Thornhill
Corbridge Gos
LARNE
BELFAST
Cairnryan
New Galloway
Lockerbie
Annan
Longtown
Brampton
Hexham
Gates
Newton Stewart
Dumfries
Carlisle
Consett St
Dun
Stranraer
Castle Douglas
Solway Firth
Maryport
Penrith
Bishop Auckland
Workington
Cockermouth
Barnard Castle
Richmond
Keswick
Brough
A66
Egremont
Ambleside
Windermere
Leyburn
Ravenglass
Kendal
Sedbergh
Isle of Man
Ramsey
Peel
Millom
Kirkby Lonsdale
Douglas
BELFAST summer only
Castletown
Barrow-in-Furness
Morecambe
Settle
DUBLIN
Heysham
Lancaster
Skipton
IRISH SEA
Fleetwood
Ilkley
Bing
Clitheroe
Keighley
Blackpool
Nelson
BRADFORD
Preston
Burnley
Halifax
Accrington
Todmorden
Br
Southport
Blackburn
Rochdale
Hudd
Formby
Ormskirk
Skelmersdale
Bolton
Bury
Crosby
Wigan
Middleton
Oldham
Bootle
St Helens
Salford
MANCHESTER
Glossop
LIVERPOOL
Warrington
Stockport
Holyhead
Anglesey
Birkenhead
Widnes
Altrincham
Bebington
Runcorn
Knutsford
Buxto
Llandudno
Colwyn Bay
Prestatyn
Ellesmere Port
Northwich
Macclesfield
Bangor
Conwy
Rhyl
Holywell
Flint
Chester
Sandbach
Congleton
Leek
Bethesda
Abergele
Queensferry
Crewe
Kidsgrove
Bakew
Caernarfon
Denbigh
Mold
Nantwich
STOKE-ON-TRE
Betws-y-coed
Ruthin
Newcastle-under-Lyme
Ffestiniog
Wrexham
Whitchurch
Stone
Uttox
Porthmadog
Bala
Llangollen
Market Drayton
Pwllheli
Oswestry
Stafford
Abersoch
Newport
Rugeley
Barmouth
Dolgellau
Welshpool
Shrewsbury
Cannock
Telford
Brownhills
Aberdyfi
Machynlleth
Caersws
Church Stretton
WOLVERHAMPTON
Walsall
Cardigan Bay
Newtown
Bridgnorth
Dudley
BIR
Aberystwyth
Stourbridge
Llangurig
Ludlow
Kidderminster
Solihull
Rhayader
Knighton
Bromsgrove
Aberaeron
Llandrindod Wells
Leominster
Worcester
Redditch
Tregaron
Lampeter
Builth Wells
Kington
Bromyard
Droitwich
Great Malvern
ROSSLARE
Cardigan

Motorway

Primary route
dual carriageway

Primary route
single carriageway

Other A roads

0   10   20   30 miles

0 10 20 30 40 kilometres

motorways – restricted junctions

Motorway junctions which have access and exit restrictions,
as shown by ⇥3⇤ on atlas pages
(Motorways and Service Areas booklet also available tel: **0870 5500 600**)

M1 LONDON–LEEDS
Junction

2
(pg 28)
Northbound No exit.
Access only from A1 *(northbound)*
Southbound No access. Exit only to A1 *(southbound)*

4
(pg 28)
Northbound No exit.
Access only from A41 *(northbound)*
Southbound No access. Exit only to A41 *(southbound)*

6A
(pg 50)
Northbound No exit. Access only from M25
Southbound No access. Exit only to M25

7
(pg 50)
Northbound No exit. Access only from M10
Southbound No access. Exit only to M10

17
(pg 60)
Northbound No exit. Access only from M45
Southbound No access. Exit only to M45

19
(pg 60)
Northbound Exit only to northbound M6
Southbound No access from A14.
Access only from M6

21A
(pg 60)
Northbound No access. Exit only to A46
Southbound No exit. Access only from A46

23A
(pg 72)
Northbound No exit. Access only to A42
Southbound No access. Exit only to A42

24A
(pg 72)
Northbound No exit. Access only from A50
Southbound No access. Exit only to A50

34
(pg 84)
Staggered junction; follow signs
Northbound No restriction
Southbound No restriction

35A
(pg 84)
Northbound No access. Exit only to A616
Southbound No exit. Access only from A616

43
(pg 90)
Northbound No access. Exit only to M621
Southbound No exit. Access only from M621

48
(pg 90)
Northbound No exit. Access only from A1(M)
Southbound No access. Exit only to A1(M)

M2 ROCHESTER–FAVERSHAM
Junction

1
(pg 29)
Westbound Exit only to A289 *(eastbound)*
Eastbound Access only from A289 *(westbound)*

M3 SUNBURY–SOUTHAMPTON
Junction

8
(pg 26)
Southwestbound No access. Exit only to A303
Northeastbound No exit. Access only from A303

10
(pg 26)
Southwestbound No exit.
Access only from Winchester & A31
Northeastbound No access. Exit only to
Winchester & A31

11
(pg 26)
Staggered junction; follow signs
Southwestbound No restriction
Northeastbound No restriction

13
(pg 14)
Southwestbound Access only to
M27 *(westbound)* & A33
Northeastbound No restriction

14
(pg 14)
Southwestbound No access.
Exit only to M27 *(eastbound)* & A33
Northeastbound No exit. Access only

M4 LONDON–SOUTH WALES
Junction

1
(pg 28)
Westbound Access only from A4 *(westbound)*
Eastbound Exit only to A4 *(eastbound)*

2
(pg 28)
Staggered junction; follow signs
Westbound No restriction
Eastbound No restriction

4A
(pg 28)
Southbound No exit to A4 *(westbound)*
Northbound No restriction

21
(pg 37)
Westbound No access. Exit only to M48
Eastbound No exit. Access only from M48

23
(pg 37)
Westbound No exit. Access only from M48
Eastbound No access. Exit only to M48

25
(pg 36)
Westbound No access. Exit only to B4596
Eastbound No exit. Access only from B4596

25A
(pg 36)
Westbound No access. Exit only to A4042
Eastbound No exit. Access only from A4042

29
(pg 36)
Westbound No access. Exit only to A48(M)
Eastbound No exit. Access only from A48(M)

38
(pg 35)
Westbound No access. Exit only to A48
Eastbound No restriction

39
(pg 35)
Westbound No exit. Access only from A48
Eastbound No access or exit

41
(pg 35)
Staggered junction; follow signs
Westbound No restriction
Eastbound No restriction

42
(pg 35)
Staggered junction; follow signs
Westbound Exit only to A483
Eastbound Access only from A483

M5 BIRMINGHAM–EXETER
Junction

10
(pg 47)
Southwestbound No access. Exit only to A4019
Northeastbound No exit. Access only from A4019

11A
(pg 38)
Southwestbound Exit only to A417 *(eastbound)*
Northeastbound Access only from A417 *(westbound)*

12
(pg 38)
Southwestbound No exit. Access only from A38
Northeastbound No access. Exit only

18A
(pg 37)
Southwestbound No exit. Access only from M49
Northeastbound Exit only to M49

M6 RUGBY–CARLISLE
Junction

4
(pg 59)
Northwestbound No access from M42 *(southbound)*.
No exit to M42 *(northbound)*
Southeastbound No access from M42 *(southbound)*.
No exit to M42

4A
(pg 59)
Northwestbound No access. Access only from
M42 *(southbound)*
Southeastbound No access. Exit only to M42

5
(pg 58)
Northwestbound No access. Exit only to A452
Southeastbound No exit. Access only from A452

10A
(pg 58)
Northbound No access. Exit only to M54
Southbound No exit. Access only from M54

20
(with M56)
(pg 82)
Staggered junction; follow signs
Northbound No restriction
Southbound No restriction

24
(pg 81)
Northbound No exit. Access only from A58
Southbound No access. Exit only to A58

25
(pg 81)
Northbound No access. Exit only
Southbound No exit. Access only

29
(pg 88)
Northbound No direct access, use adjacent
slip road to junction 29A
Southbound No direct exit, use adjacent
slip road from junction 29A

29A
(pg 88)
Northbound No direct exit, use adjacent
slip road from junction 29
Southbound No direct access, use adjacent
slip road to junction 29

30
(pg 88)
Northbound No exit. Access only from M61
Southbound No access. Exit only to M61

31A
(pg 88)
Northbound No access. Exit only
Southbound No exit. Access only

M8 EDINBURGH–GLASGOW–BISHOPTON
Junction

3A
(pg 131)
Staggered junction; follow signs
Westbound No restriction
Eastbound No restriction

8
(pg 130)
Westbound No access from M73 *(southbound)*
or from A8 *(eastbound)* & A89
Eastbound No exit to M73 *(northbound)*
or to A8 *(westbound)* & A89

9
(pg 130)
Westbound No exit. Access only
Eastbound No access. Exit only

13
(pg 130)
Westbound Access only from M80 *(southbound)*
Eastbound Exit only to M80 *(northbound)*

14
(pg 130)
Westbound No exit. Access only
Eastbound No access. Exit only

16
(pg 129)
Westbound No access. Exit only to A804
Eastbound No exit. Access only from A879

17
(pg 129)
Westbound Exit only to A82
Eastbound No restriction

18
(pg 129)
Westbound Access only from A82 *(eastbound)*
Eastbound No access. Exit only to A814

19
(pg 129)
Westbound No access from A814 *(westbound)*
Eastbound No access.
Exit only to A814 *(westbound)*

20
(pg 129)
Westbound No access. Exit only
Eastbound No exit. Access only

21
(pg 129)
Westbound No exit. Access only
Eastbound No access. Exit only to A8

22
(pg 129)
Westbound No access.
Exit only to M77 *(southbound)*
Eastbound No exit.
Access only from M77 *(northbound)*

23
(pg 129)
Westbound No access. Exit only to B768
Eastbound No exit. Access only from B768

25
(pg 129)
Westbound No access/exit from/to A8
Eastbound No access/exit from/to A8

25A
(pg 129)
Westbound No access. Exit only
Eastbound No exit. Access only

28
(pg 129)
Westbound No access. Exit only
Eastbound No exit. Access only

M9 EDINBURGH–DUNBLANE
Junction

1A
(pg 131)
Northwestbound No access. Exit only to A8000
Southeastbound No exit. Access only from A8000

2
(pg 131)
Northwestbound No exit. Access only
Southeastbound No access. Exit only

3
(pg 131)
Northwestbound No access. Exit only
Southeastbound No exit. Access only

6
(pg 131)
Northwestbound No exit. Access only from A904
Southeastbound No access. Exit only to A905

8
(pg 131)
Northwestbound No access. Exit only to
M876 *(southwestbound)*
Southeastbound No exit. Access only from
M876 *(northeastbound)*

M10 ST ALBANS–M1
Junction

with M1
(jct 7)
(pg 50)
Northwestbound Exit only to M1 *(northbound)*
Southeastbound Access only from M1 *(southbound)*

M11 LONDON–CAMBRIDGE
Junction

4
(pg 29)
Northbound Access only from A406
Southbound Exit only to A406

5
(pg 29)
Northbound No access. Exit only to A1168
Southbound No exit. Access only from A1168

9
(pg 50)
Northbound No access. Exit only to A11
Southbound No exit. Access only from A11

13
(pg 62)
Northbound No access Exit only to A1303
Southbound No exit. Access only from A1303

14
(pg 62)
Northbound Exit only to A14 *(eastbound)*
Southbound Access only from A14

M20 SWANLEY–FOLKESTONE
Junction

2
(pg 29)
Staggered junction; follow signs
Southeastbound No access. Exit only to A227
Northwestbound No exit. Access only from A227

3
(pg 29)
Southeastbound No exit. Access only from
M26 *(eastbound)*
Northwestbound No access.
Exit only to M26 *(westbound)*

5
(pg 30)
Southeastbound For access follow signs.
Exit only to A20
Northwestbound No exit. Access only from A20

6
(pg 30)
Southeastbound For exit follow signs
Northwestbound No restriction

11A
(pg 19)
Southeastbound No access. Exit only
Northwestbound No exit. Access only

M23 HOOLEY–CRAWLEY
Junction

7
(pg 28)
Southbound Access only from A23 *(southbound)*
Northbound Exit only to A23 *(northbound)*

10A
(pg 16)
Southbound No access. Exit only to B2036
Northbound No exit. Access only from B2036

M25 LONDON ORBITAL MOTORWAY
(refer also to atlas pg xiv)
Junction

1B
(pg 29)
Clockwise No access (use slip road via
jct 2).Exit only to A225 & A296
Anticlockwise No exit (use slip road via jct 2).
Access only from A225 & A296

5
(pg 29)
Clockwise No exit to M26
Anticlockwise No access from M26

9
(pg 28)
Staggered junction; follow signs
Clockwise No restriction
Anticlockwise No restriction

19
(pg 28)
Clockwise No access. Exit only to A41
Anticlockwise No exit. Access only from A41

21
(pg 50)
Clockwise Access only from M1 *(southbound)*.
Exit only to M1 *(northbound)*
Anticlockwise Access only from M1 *(southbound)*.
Exit only to M1 *(northbound)*

21A
(pg 50)
Clockwise No link from M1 to A405
Anticlockwise No link from M1 to A405

31
(pg 29)
Clockwise No exit (use slip road via jct 30)
Anticlockwise For access follow signs

M26 SEVENOAKS–WROTHAM
Junction

with M25
(jct 5)
(pg 29)
Eastbound Access only from
anticlockwise M25 *(eastbound)*
Westbound Exit only to clockwise M25 *(westbound)*

with M20
(jct 3)
(pg 29)
Eastbound Exit only to M20 *(southeastbound)*
Westbound Access only from M20 *(northwestbound)*

M27 CADNAM–PORTSMOUTH
Junction

4
(pg 14)
Staggered junction; follow signs
Eastbound Access only from M3 *(southbound)*.
Exit only to M3 *(northbound)*
Westbound Access only from M3 *(southbound)*.
Exit only to M3 *(northbound)*

10
(pg 14)
Eastbound No exit. Access only from A32
Westbound No access. Exit only to A32

12
(pg 15)
Staggered junction; follow signs
Eastbound Access only from M275 *(northbound)*
Westbound Exit only to M275 *(southbound)*

M40 LONDON–BIRMINGHAM
Junction

3
(pg 41)
Northwestbound No access. Exit only to A40
Southeastbound No exit. Access only from A40

7
(pg 41)
Northwestbound No access. Exit only to A329
Southeastbound No exit. Access only from A329

8 (pg 40)	Northwestbound	No access. Exit only to A40
	Southeastbound	No exit. Access only from A40
13 (pg 48)	Northwestbound	No access. Exit only to A452
	Southeastbound	No exit. Access only from A452
14 (pg 48)	Northwestbound	No exit. Access only from A452
	Southeastbound	No access. Exit only to A452
16 (pg 58)	Northwestbound	No exit. Access only from A3400
	Southeastbound	No access. Exit only to A3400

M42 BROMSGROVE–MEASHAM

Junction		
1 (pg 58)	Northeastbound	No exit. Access only from A38
	Southwestbound	No access. Exit only to A38
7 (pg 59)	Northeastbound	No access. Exit only to M6 *(northwestbound)*
	Southwestbound	No exit. Access only from M6 *(northwestbound)*
7A (pg 59)	Northeastbound	No access. Exit only to M6 *(southeastbound)*
	Southwestbound	No access or exit
8 (pg 59)	Northeastbound	No exit. Access only from M6 *(southeastbound)*
	Southwestbound	No access. Exit only to M6 *(northwestbound)*

M45 COVENTRY–M1

Junction		
unnumbered (Dunchurch) (pg 60)	Eastbound	No access. Exit only to A45 & B4429
	Westbound	No exit. Access only from A45 & B4429
with M1 (jct 17) (pg 60)	Eastbound	Exit only to M1 *(southbound)*
	Westbound	Access only from M1 *(northbound)*

M53 MERSEY TUNNEL–CHESTER

Junction		
1 (pg 81)	Southwestbound	No exit. Access only from A554 & A5139
	Northeastbound	No access. Exit only to A554 & A5139
11 (pg 81)	Southeastbound	Access only from M56 *(westbound)*. Exit only to M56 *(eastbound)*
	Northwestbound	Access only from M56 *(westbound)*. Exit only to M56 *(eastbound)*

M54 TELFORD

Junction		
with M6 (jct 10A) (pg 58)	Westbound	No exit. Access only from M6 *(northbound)*
	Eastbound	No access. Exit only to M6 *(southbound)*

M56 NORTH CHESHIRE

Junction		
1 (pg 82)	Westbound	No exit. Access only from M60 *(westbound)*
	Eastbound	No access. Exit only to M60 *(eastbound)* & A34 *(northbound)*
2 (pg 82)	Westbound	No access. Exit only to A560
	Eastbound	No exit. Access only from A560
3 (pg 82)	Westbound	No exit. Access only from A5103
	Eastbound	No access. Exit only to A5103 & A560
4 (pg 82)	Westbound	No access. Exit only
	Eastbound	No exit. Access only
7 (pg 82)	Staggered junction; follow signs	
	Westbound	No restriction
	Eastbound	No restriction
9 (pg 82)	Westbound	Exit to M6 *(southbound)* via A50 interchange
	Eastbound	Access from M6 *(northbound)* via A50 interchange
15 (pg 81)	Westbound	No access. Exit only to M53
	Eastbound	No exit. Access only from M53

M57 LIVERPOOL OUTER RING ROAD

Junction		
3 (pg 81)	Northwestbound	No exit. Access only from A526
	Southeastbound	No access. Exit only to A526
5 (pg 81)	Northwestbound	No exit. Access only from A580 *(westbound)*
	Southeastbound	No access. Exit only to A580

M58 LIVERPOOL–WIGAN

Junction		
1 (pg 81)	Eastbound	No exit. Access only
	Westbound	No access. Exit only

M60 MANCHESTER ORBITAL

(refer also to atlas pg xv)

Junction		
2 (pg 82)	Clockwise	No exit. Access only from A560
	Anticlockwise	No access. Exit only to A560
3 (pg 82)	Clockwise	No access from M56
	Anticlockwise	No exit. Access only from A34 *(northbound)*
4 (pg 82)	Clockwise	Access only from A34 *(northbound)*. Exit only to M56
	Anticlockwise	Access only from M56 *(eastbound)*. Exit only to A34 *(southbound)*
5 (pg 82)	Clockwise	Access/exit only from/to A5103 *(northbound)*
	Anticlockwise	Access/exit only from/to A5103 *(southbound)*
7 (pg 82)	Clockwise	No access (use adjacent slip road to junction 8). Exit only to A56
	Anticlockwise	No exit (use adjacent slip road from junction 8). Access only from A56
14 (pg 82)	Clockwise	No exit. Access to M60 from A580 *(eastbound)*. Access to M61 *(westbound)* from A580 *(westbound)*
	Anticlockwise	No access. Exit from M61 *(eastbound)* to A580 *(eastbound)*. No exit from M60
15 (pg 82)	Clockwise	Access only from M61 *(eastbound)*. Exit to M61 *(westbound)*
	Anticlockwise	No access. Exit to M61 *(westbound)* & A580 *(westbound)*
16 (pg 82)	Clockwise	No exit. Access only from A666
	Anticlockwise	No access. Exit only to A666

20 (pg 82)	Clockwise	No access. Exit only to A664
	Anticlockwise	No exit. Access only from A664
22 (pg 82)	Clockwise	No restriction
	Anticlockwise	No access. Exit only to A62
25 (pg 82)	Clockwise	No access. Exit only to A6017
	Anticlockwise	No restriction
26 (pg 82)	Clockwise	No restriction
	Anticlockwise	No access or exit
27 (pg 82)	Clockwise	No exit. Access only from A626
	Anticlockwise	No access. Exit only to A626

M61 GREATER MANCHESTER–PRESTON

Junction		
1 (pg 82)	No restriction; follow signs	
2 (pg 82)	No restriction; follow signs	
3 (pg 82)	Northwestbound	No access or exit
	Southeastbound	No access. Exit only to A660
with M6 (jct 30) (pg 82)	Northwestbound	Exit only to M6 *(northbound)*
	Southeastbound	Access only from M6 *(southbound)*

M62 LIVERPOOL–HUMBERSIDE

Junction		
23 (pg 90)	Eastbound	No access. Exit only to A640
	Westbound	No exit. Access only from A640

M65 PRESTON–COLNE

Junction		
1 (pg 88)	Northeastbound	Access and exit to M6 only
	Southwestbound	Access and exit to M6 only
9 (pg 89)	Northeastbound	No access. Exit only to A679
	Southwestbound	No exit. Access only from A679
11 (pg 89)	Northeastbound	No exit. Access only
	Southwestbound	No access. Exit only

M66 GREATER MANCHESTER

Junction		
with A56 (pg 89)	Southbound	Access only from A56 *(southbound)*
	Northbound	Exit only to A56 *(northbound)*
1 (pg 89)	Southbound	No exit. Access only from A56
	Northbound	No access. Exit only to A56

M67 HYDE BYPASS

Junction		
1 (pg 82)	Eastbound	No access. Exit only to A6017
	Westbound	No exit. Access only from A6017
2 (pg 82)	Eastbound	No exit. Access only
	Westbound	No access. Exit only to A57
3 (pg 82)	Eastbound	No restriction
	Westbound	No access. Exit only to A627

M69 COVENTRY–LEICESTER

Junction		
2 (pg 59)	Northbound	No exit. Access only from B4669
	Southbound	No access. Exit only to B4669

M73 EAST OF GLASGOW

Junction		
2 (pg 130)	Northbound	No access from or to A89. No access from M8 *(eastbound)*
	Southbound	No access from or to A89. No exit to M8 *(westbound)*
3 (pg 130)	Northbound	Exit only to A80 *(northeastbound)*
	Southbound	Access only from A80 *(southwestbound)*

M74 GLASGOW–ABINGTON

Junction		
2 (pg 120)	Southbound	No exit. Access only from A763
	Northbound	No access. Exit only to A763
3 (pg 120)	Southbound	No access. Exit only
	Northbound	Exit via junction 4. Access only
7 (pg 120)	Southbound	No access. Exit only to A72
	Northbound	No exit. Access only from A72
9 (pg 120)	Southbound	No access. Exit only to B7078
	Northbound	No access or exit
10 (pg 120)	Southbound	No exit. Access only from B7078
	Northbound	No restrictions
11 (pg 120)	Southbound	No access. Exit only to B7078
	Northbound	No exit. Access only from B7078
12 (pg 120)	Southbound	No exit. Access only from A70
	Northbound	No access. Exit only to A70

A74(M) ABINGTON–GRETNA

Junction		
14 (pg 120)	Staggered junction; follow signs	
	Southbound	No restriction
	Northbound	No restriction
18 (pg 111)	Southbound	No exit. Access only from B723
	Northbound	No access. Exit only to B723
21 (pg 111)	Southbound	No access. Exit only to B6357
	Northbound	No exit. Access only from B6357
with B7076 (pg 111)	Southbound	No exit. Access only
	Northbound	No access. Exit only
Gretna Green (pg 111)	Southbound	No access. Exit only (use B7076 through Gretna to access A75)
	Northbound	No exit. Access only
with A75 (pg 111)	Southbound	No exit. Access only from A75
	Northbound	No access. Exit only to A75
with A6071 (pg 111)	Southbound	Exit only to A74 *(southbound)*
	Northbound	Access only from A74 *(northbound)*

M77 WEST OF GLASGOW

Junction		
with M8 (pg 119)	Southbound	No access from M8 *(eastbound)*
	Northbound	No exit to M8 *(westbound)*
4 (pg 119)	Southbound	No access. Exit only
	Northbound	No exit. Access only
with A77 (pg 119)	Southbound	Exit only to A77 *(southbound)*
	Northbound	Access only from A77 *(northbound)*

M80 STEPPS BYPASS

Junction		
3 (pg 130)	Northeastbound	No access. Exit only
	Southwestbound	No exit. Access only

M80 BONNYBRIDGE–STIRLING

Junction		
5 (pg 130)	Northbound	No access. Exit only to M876 *(northeastbound)*
	Southbound	No exit. Access only from M876 *(southwestbound)*

M90 FORTH ROAD BRIDGE–PERTH

Junction		
2A (pg 131)	Northbound	No access. Exit only to A92 *(eastbound)*
	Southbound	No exit. Access only from A92 *(westbound)*
7 (pg 131)	Northbound	No exit. Access only from A91
	Southbound	No access. Exit only to A911
8 (pg 131)	Northbound	No access. Exit only to A91
	Southbound	No exit. Access only from A91
10 (pg 140)	Northbound	No access from A912. No exit to A912 *(southbound)*
	Southbound	No access from A912 *(northbound)*. No exit to A912

M180 SOUTH HUMBERSIDE

Junction		
1 (pg 84)	Eastbound	No access. Exit only to A18
	Westbound	No exit. Access only from A18

M606 BRADFORD SPUR

Junction		
2 (pg 90)	Northbound	No access. Exit only
	Southbound	No restriction

M621 LEEDS–M1

Junction		
2A (pg 90)	Eastbound	No exit. Access only
	Westbound	No access. Exit only
4 (pg 90)	Southeastbound	No access. Exit only
	Northwestbound	No restriction
5 (pg 90)	Southeastbound	No exit. Access only
	Northwestbound	No access. Exit only
6 (pg 90)	Southeastbound	No access. Exit only
	Northwestbound	No exit. Access only
with M1 (jct 43) (pg 90)	Southbound	Exit only to M1 *(southbound)*
	Northbound	Access only from M1 *(northbound)*

M876 BONNYBRIDGE–KINCARDINE BRIDGE

Junction		
with M80 (jct 5) (pg 130)	Northeastbound	Access only from M80 *(northbound)*
	Southwestbound	Exit only to M80 *(southbound)*
2 (pg 131)	Northeastbound	No access. Exit only to A9
	Southwestbound	No exit. Access only from A9
with M9 (jct 8) (pg 131)	Northeastbound	Exit only to M9 *(eastbound)*
	Southwestbound	Access only from M9 (westbound)

A1(M) SOUTH MIMMS–BALDOCK

Junction		
2 (pg 50)	Northbound	No access. Exit only to A1001
	Southbound	No exit. Access only from A1001
3 (pg 50)	Northbound	No restriction
	Southbound	No access. Exit only to A414
5 (pg 50)	Northbound	No exit. Access only
	Southbound	No access or exit

A1(M) ALCONBURY–PETERBOROUGH

Junction		
14 (pg 61)	Staggered junction; follow signs	
	Northbound	No restriction
	Southbound	No restriction
15 (pg 61)	Staggered junction; follow signs	
	Northbound	No restriction
	Southbound	No restriction

A1(M) EAST OF LEEDS

Junction		
44 (pg 90)	Northbound	Access only from M1 *(northbound)*
	Southbound	Exit only to M1 *(southbound)*

A1(M) SCOTCH CORNER–TYNESIDE

Junction		
57 (with A66(M)) (pg 106)	Northbound	No access. Exit only to A66(M) *(eastbound)*
	Southbound	No exit. Access only from A66(M) *(westbound)*
65 (with A194(M)) (pg 114)	Northbound	No access. Exit only to A194(M) & A1 *(northbound)*
	Southbound	No exit. Access only from Access only from A194(M) *(southbound)*

A3(M) HORNDEAN–HAVANT

Junction		
1 (pg 15)	Southbound	No access. Exit only to A3
	Northbound	No exit. Access only from A3
4 (pg 15)	Southbound	No exit. Access only
	Northbound	No access. Exit only

A48(M) CARDIFF SPUR

Junction		
29 (with M4) (pg 37)	Westbound	Access only from M4 *(westbound)*
	Eastbound	Exit only to M4 *(eastbound)*
29A (pg 37)	Westbound	Exit only to A48 *(westbound)*
	Eastbound	Access only from A48 *(eastbound)*

A66(M) DARLINGTON SPUR

Junction		
with A1(M) (jct 57) (pg 106)	Eastbound	Access only from A1(M) *(northbound)*
	Westbound	Exit only to A1(M) *(southbound)*

A194(M) TYNESIDE

Junction		
with A1(M) (jct 65) (pg 114)	Northbound	Access only from A1(M) *(northbound)*
	Southbound	Exit only to A1(M) *(southbound)*

XIV

M25 London orbital motorway

Refer also to atlas pages 28–29

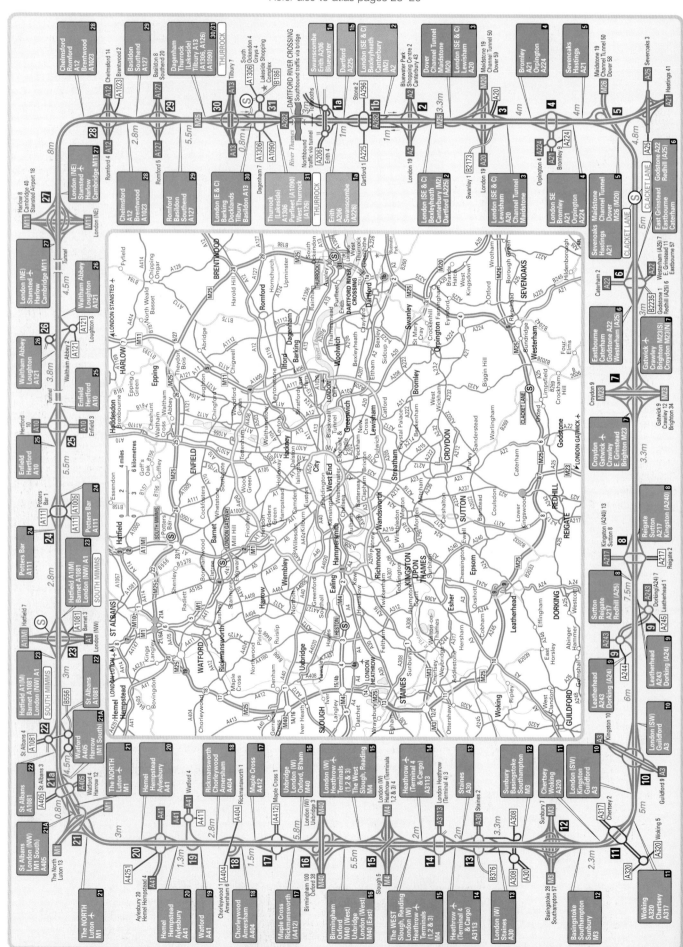

M60 Manchester orbital motorway

Refer also to atlas page 82

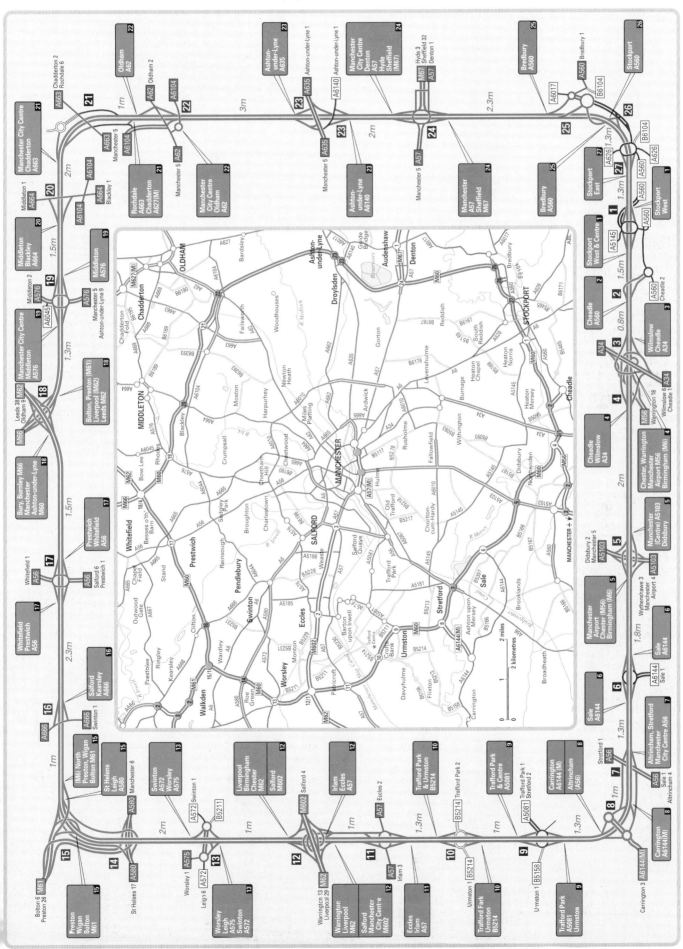

map symbols

Motoring information

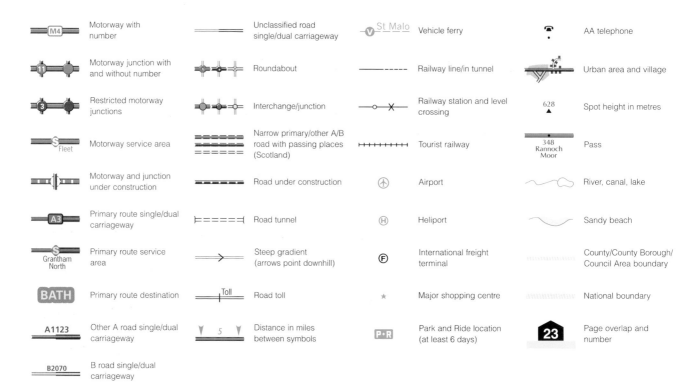

M4	Motorway with number	Unclassified road single/dual carriageway	St Malo Vehicle ferry	AA telephone
11	Motorway junction with and without number	Roundabout	Railway line/in tunnel	Urban area and village
3	Restricted motorway junctions	Interchange/junction	Railway station and level crossing	628 Spot height in metres
S Fleet	Motorway service area	Narrow primary/other A/B road with passing places (Scotland)	Tourist railway	348 Rannoch Moor Pass
	Motorway and junction under construction	Road under construction	Airport	River, canal, lake
A3	Primary route single/dual carriageway	Road tunnel	Heliport	Sandy beach
S Grantham North	Primary route service area	Steep gradient (arrows point downhill)	International freight terminal	County/County Borough/ Council Area boundary
BATH	Primary route destination	Toll Road toll	Major shopping centre	National boundary
A1123	Other A road single/dual carriageway	5 Distance in miles between symbols	P+R Park and Ride location (at least 6 days)	23 Page overlap and number
B2070	B road single/dual carriageway			

Tourist information   Places of interest are also shown on town plans. See pages 175–234

Tourist Information Centre	Agricultural showground	Prehistoric monument	Ski slope – natural
Tourist Information Centre (seasonal)	Theme park	Battle site with year 1066	Ski slope – artificial
Visitor or heritage centre	Farm or animal centre	Steam centre (railway)	NT National Trust property
Abbey, cathedral or priory	Zoological or wildlife collection	Cave	NTS National Trust for Scotland property
Ruined abbey, cathedral or priory	Bird collection	Windmill	Other place of interest
Castle	Aquarium	Monument	Boxed symbols indicate attractions within urban areas
Historic house or building	Nature reserve	Golf course	National Park (England & Wales)
Museum or art gallery	RSPB site	County cricket ground	National Scenic Area (Scotland)
Industrial interest	Forest drive	Rugby Union national stadium	Forest Park
Aqueduct or viaduct	National trail	International athletics stadium	Heritage coast
Garden	Viewpoint	Horse racing	Little Chef Restaurant (7am–10pm)
Arboretum	Picnic site	Show jumping/equestrian circuit	Travelodge
Vineyard	Hill-fort	Motor-racing circuit	Little Chef Restaurant and Travelodge
Country park	Roman antiquity	Air show venue	Granada Burger King site

XVI

Ireland (see pages 170–173) For tourist information see opposite page

M1 Motorway	N17 National primary route (Republic of Ireland)	A4 Primary route (Northern Ireland)	Road under construction
Motorway junction with and without number	N54 National secondary route (Republic of Ireland)	A21 A road (Northern Ireland)	5 Distance in miles between symbols
3 Restricted motorway junctions	R182 Regional road (Republic of Ireland)	B75 B road (Northern Ireland)	International boundary

1

Central London (see pages 240–250)

Motorway	Restricted road (access only/private)	↰ Banned turn (restricted periods only)	PO Post Office
Primary route single/dual	Footpath	↕ Ahead only	POL Police station
Other A road single/dual	Track	• Mini-roundabout	A&E 24-hour Accident & Emergency hospital
B road single/dual	Pedestrian street	Barrier	Steps
Unclassified road single/dual	Railway line/in tunnel	⇄ Railway station	✝ Church
Unclassified road wide/narrow	← One-way street	London Regional Transport (LRT) station	🛈 Tourist Information Centre
Road under construction	↱ Compulsory turn	Docklands Light Railway (DLR) station	🛈 Tourist Information Centre (seasonal)
Road tunnel wide/narrow	↰ Banned turn	P Parking	

Royal Parks (opening and closing times for traffic)
Green Park   Constitution Hill: closed Sundays, 08.00–dusk
Hyde Park   Open 05.00–midnight
Regent's Park   Open 05.00–midnight
St James's Park The Mall: closed Sundays, 08.00–dusk

Traffic regulations in the City of London include security checkpoints and restrict the number of entry and exit points.

Note: Oxford Street is closed to through-traffic (except buses & taxis) 07.00–19.00, Monday–Saturday. Restricted parts of Frith Street/Old Compton Street are closed to vehicles 12.00–01.00 daily.

District maps (see pages 258–269) For tourist information see opposite page

Motorway	Unclassified road single/dual	● Railway station	A&E 24-hour Accident & Emergency hospital
Motorway under construction	Road under construction	Inner London Regional Transport (LRT) station	H Hospital
Primary route single/dual	Restricted road	Outer London Regional Transport (LRT) station	Crem Crematorium
Other A road single/dual	Railway line/in tunnel	Railway station/LRT interchange	★ Shopping centre
B road single/dual	Tourist railway	○ Light railway/tramway station	Sports stadium

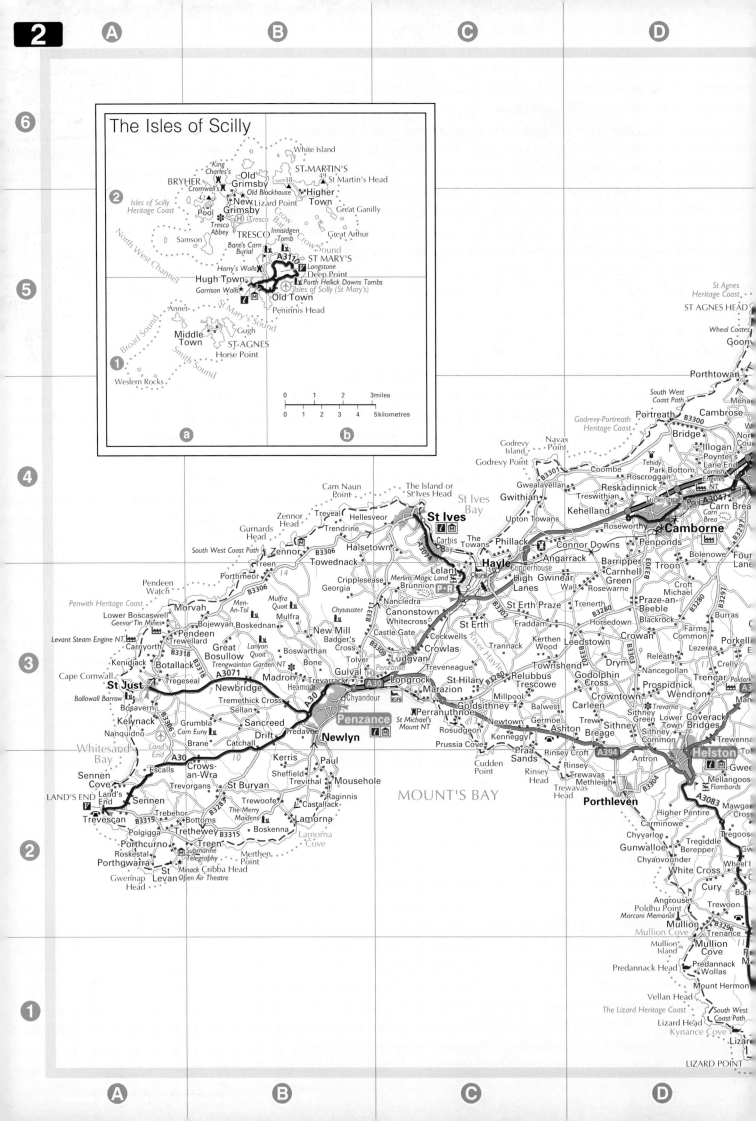

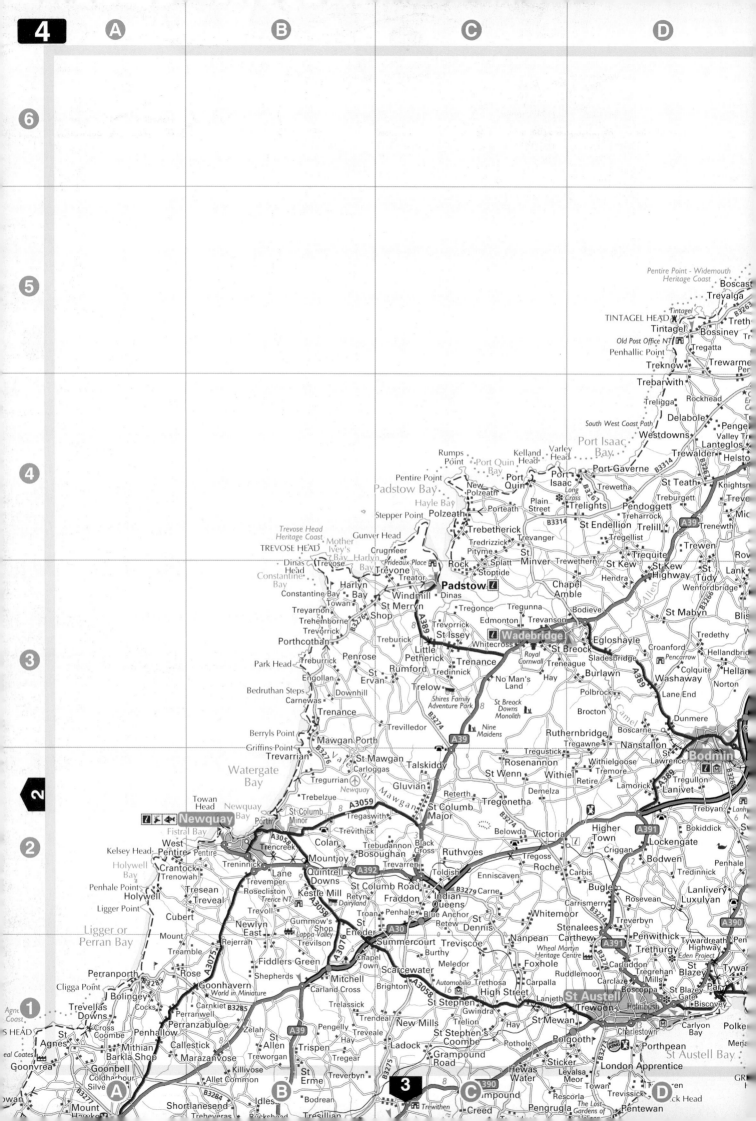

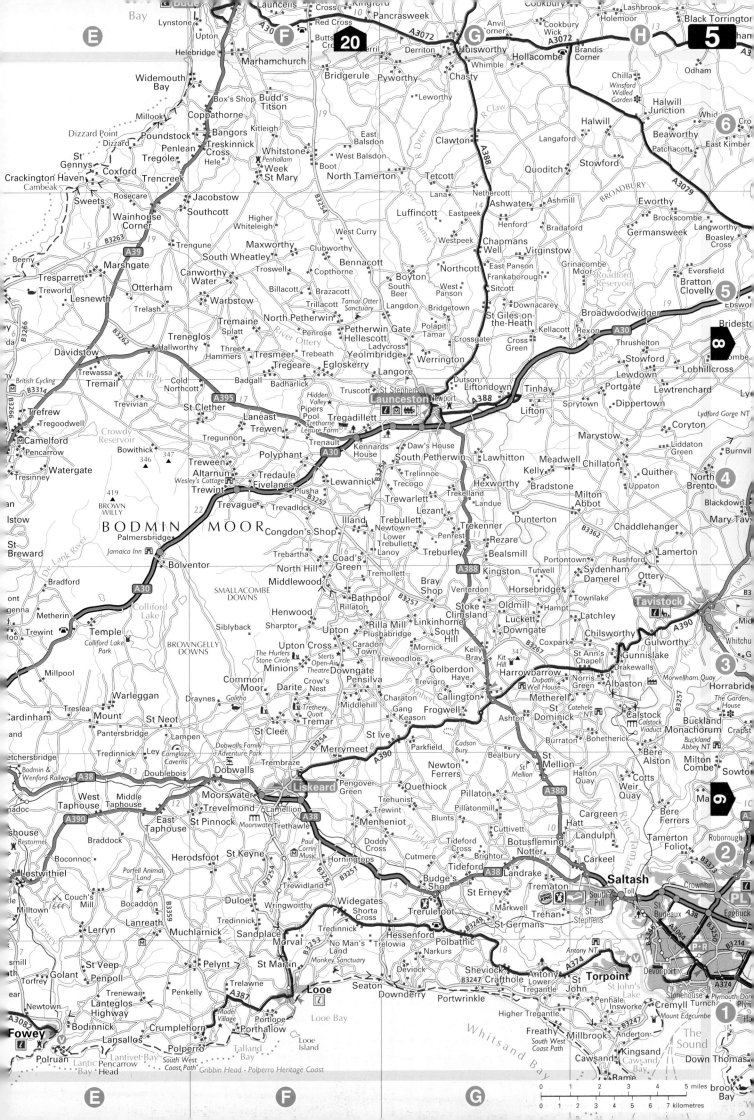

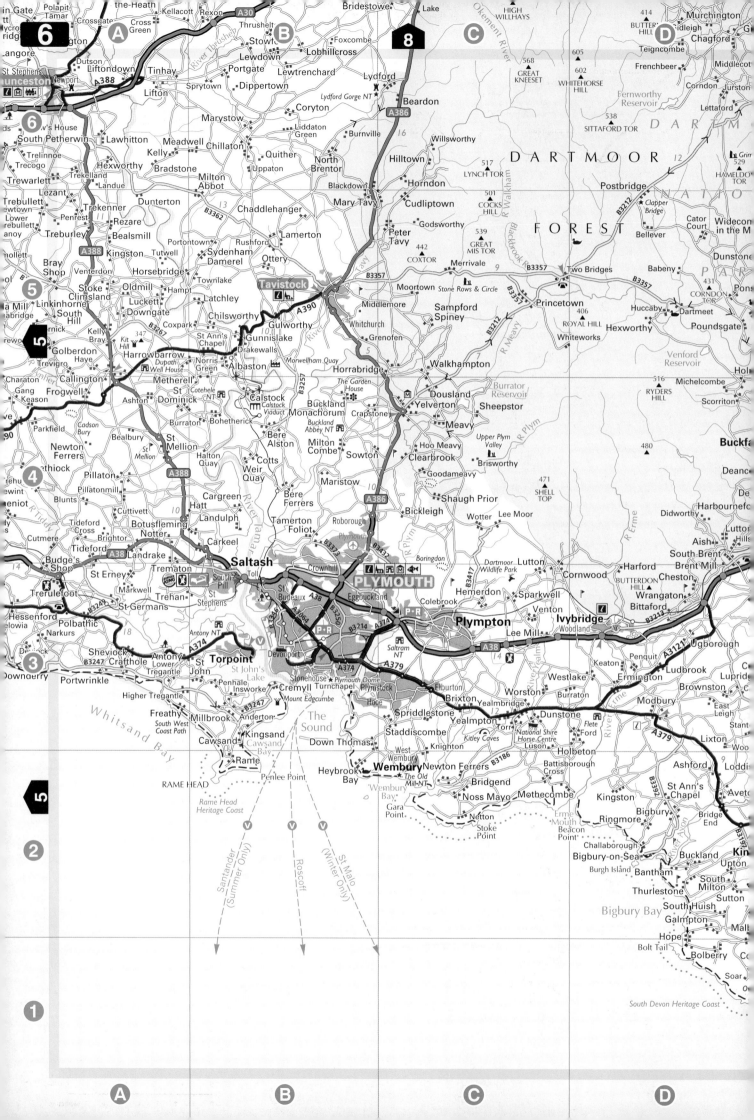

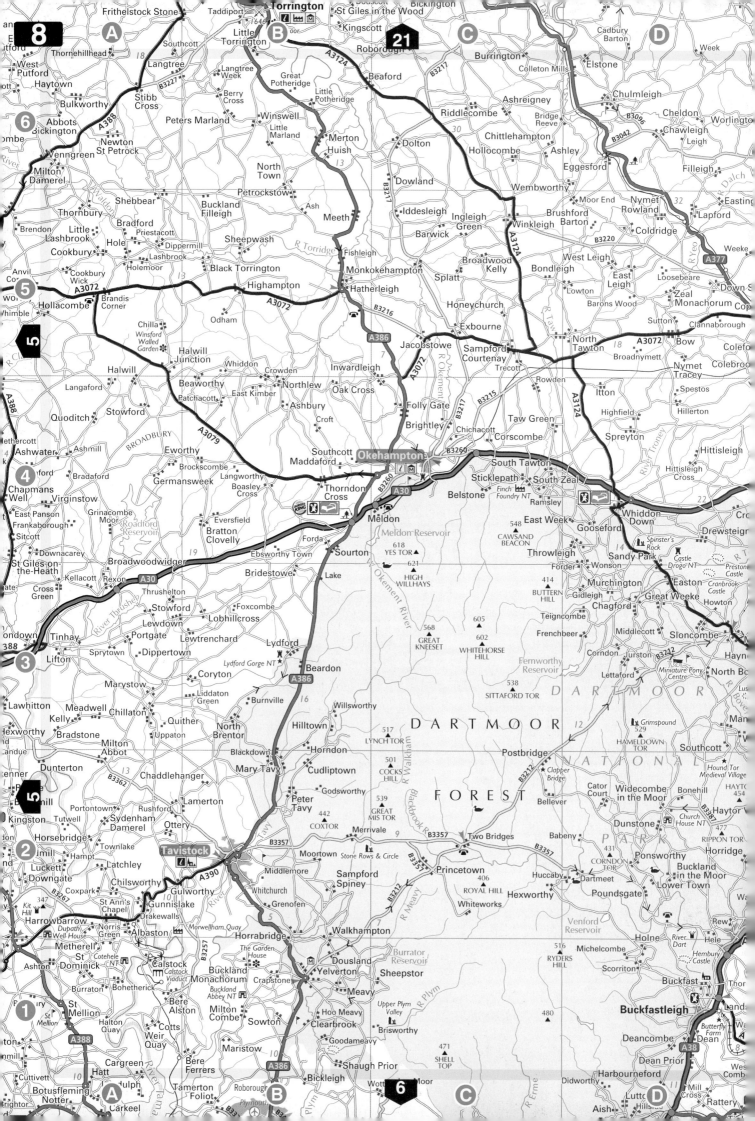

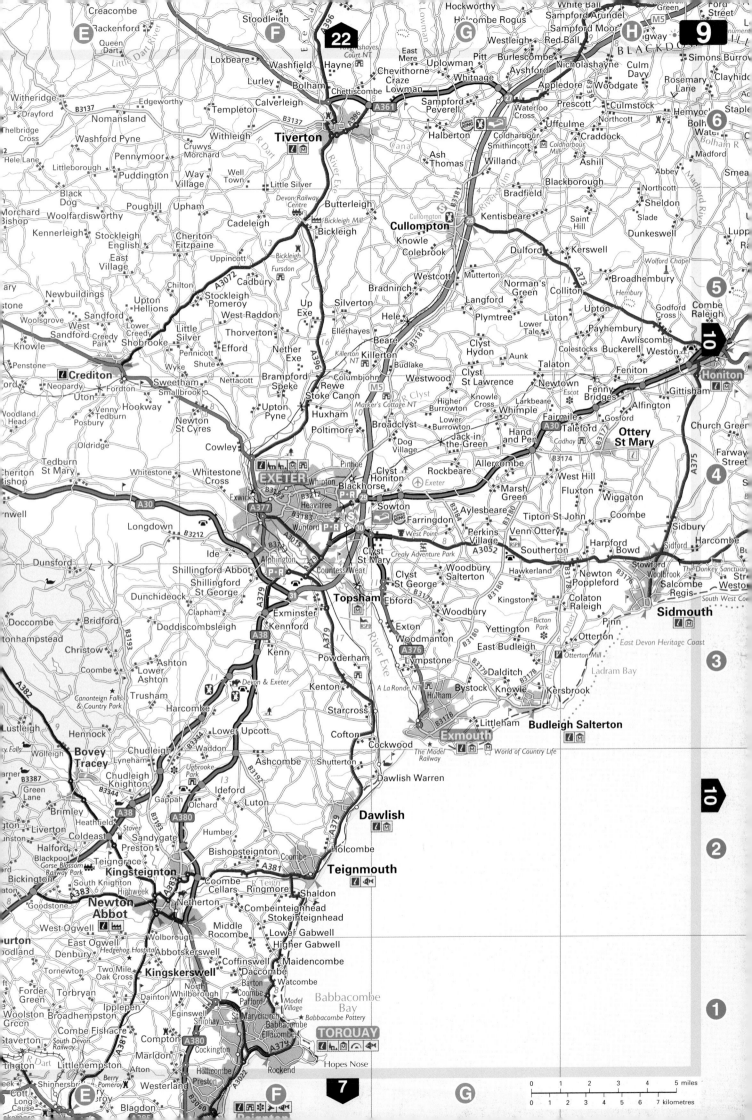

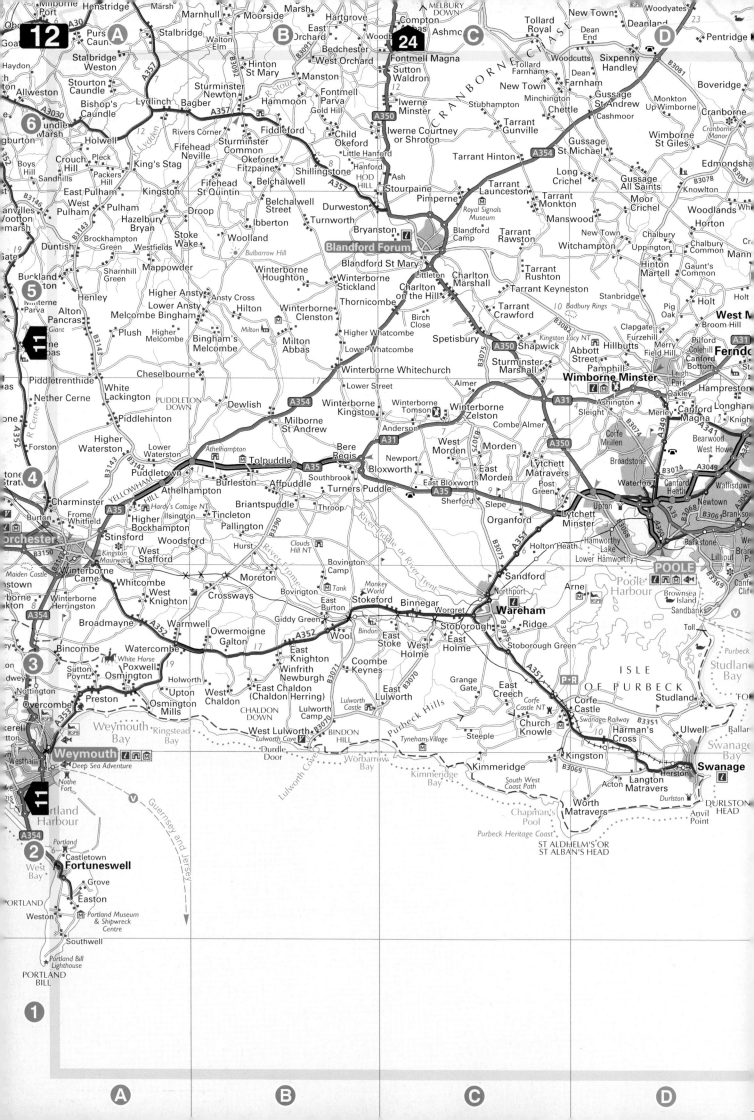

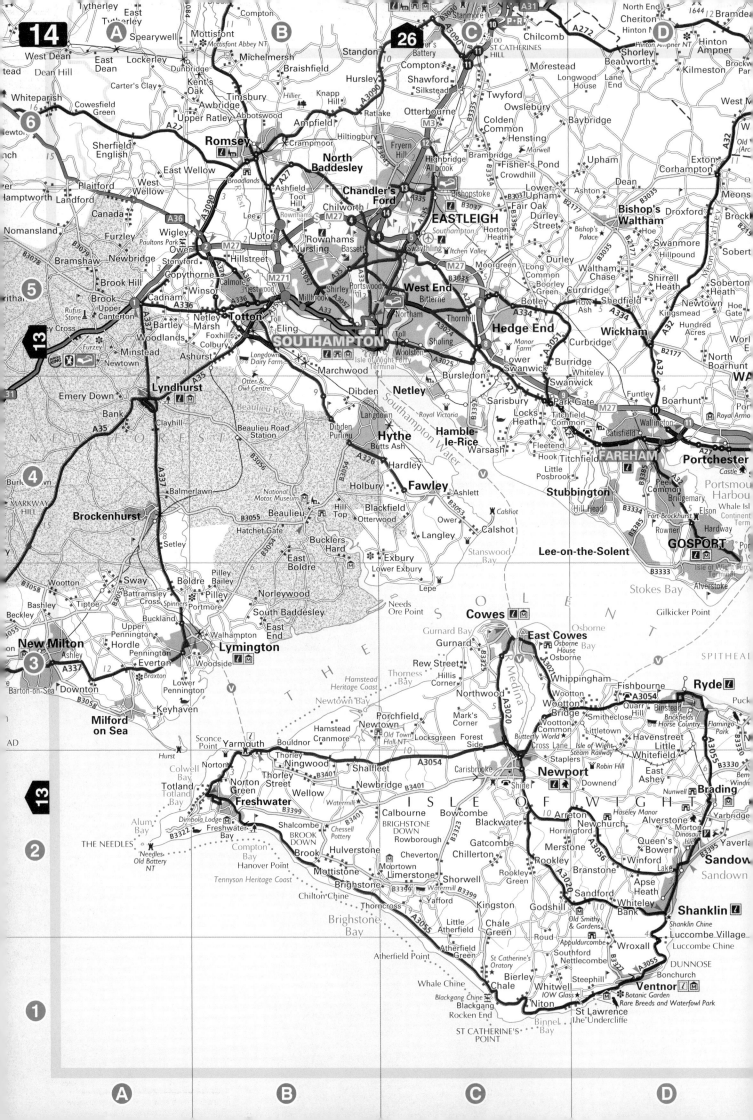

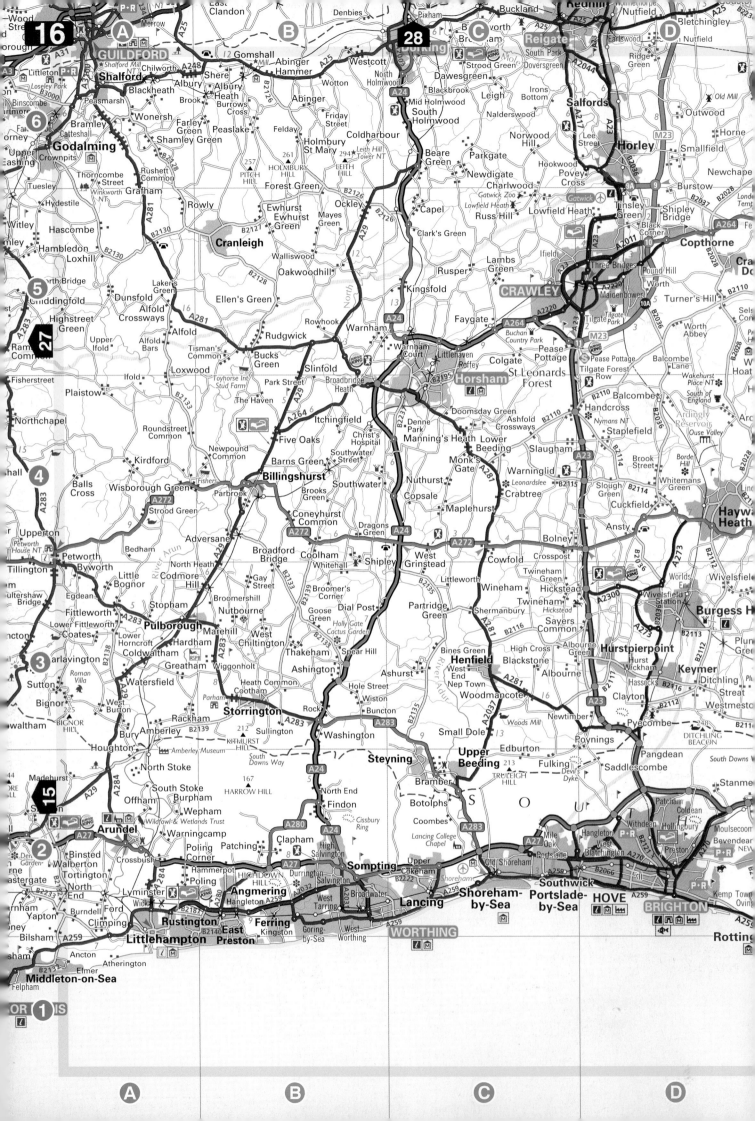

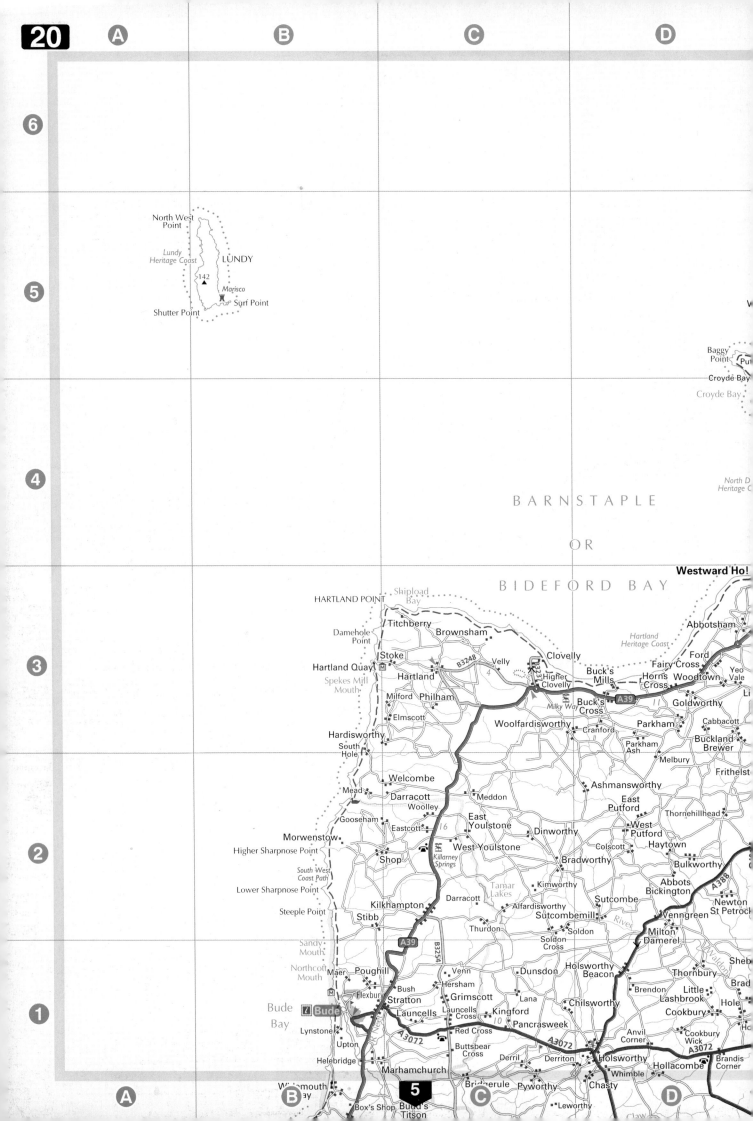

A   B   C   D

6

North West Point

Lundy Heritage Coast   **LUNDY**

▲ 142

✕ *Marisco*

5   **Surf Point**

Shutter Point

Baggy Point   Pu

Croyde Bay

Croyde Bay

4   **B A R N S T A P L E**

North D
Heritage C

O R

B I D E F O R D   B A Y   **Westward Ho!**

Shipload Bay

HARTLAND POINT   Abbotsham

Titchberry   Brownsham   *Hartland Heritage Coast*

Damehole Point   Clovelly   Ford   Fairy Cross

3   Stoke   B3248   Velly   Buck's Mills   Horns   Woodtown
Hartland Quay   Hartland   Higher Clovelly   Cross   Yeo Vale
Spekes Mill Mouth   4   Milky Way   **A39**   Li
Milford   Philham   Buck's Cross   Goldworthy

Elmscott   Woolfardisworthy   Cranford   Parkham   Cabbacott
Hardisworthy   Buckland Brewer
South Hole   Parkham Ash   Melbury   Frithelst

Welcombe   Ashmansworthy
Mead   Darracott   Meddon   East Putford   Thornehillhead
Woolley   East Youlstone   Dinworthy   West Putford   Haytown
Gooseham   Eastcott   16   Colscott   Bulkworthy
2   Morwenstow   West Youlstone   Bradworthy   Abbots Bickington
Higher Sharpnose Point   Shop   *Killarney Springs*   Newton St Petroc
Kimworthy   Sutcombe   A388
South West Coast Path   Darracott   *Tamar Lakes*   Alfardisworthy   Sutcombemill
Lower Sharpnose Point   Soldon   Milton Damerel   Sheb
Steeple Point   Kilkhampton   Thurdon   Soldon Cross   Thornbury
Stibb   Brendon   Little Lashbrook   Brad
Sandy Mouth   **A39**   B3254   Venn   Dunsdon   Holsworthy Beacon   Hole
Northcott Mouth   Poughill   Hersham   Lana   Chilsworthy   Cookbury
Maer   Grimscott   Kingford   Anvil Corner   Cookbury Wick
1   Bush   Pancrasweek   10   Brandis
ℹ Bude   Stratton   Launcells   A3072
Bude Bay   Flexbury   Launcells Cross   Red Cross   Holsworthy   Hollacombe   Corner
Lynstone   Buttsbear Cross   Derril   Derriton   Whimble
Upton   A3072   A3072
Helebridge   Marhamchurch   Bridgerule   Pyworthy   Chasty
Box's Shop   Bridgerule   Leworthy
Wi?mouth Bay   **5**   Budd's   Claw
Titson

A   B   C   D

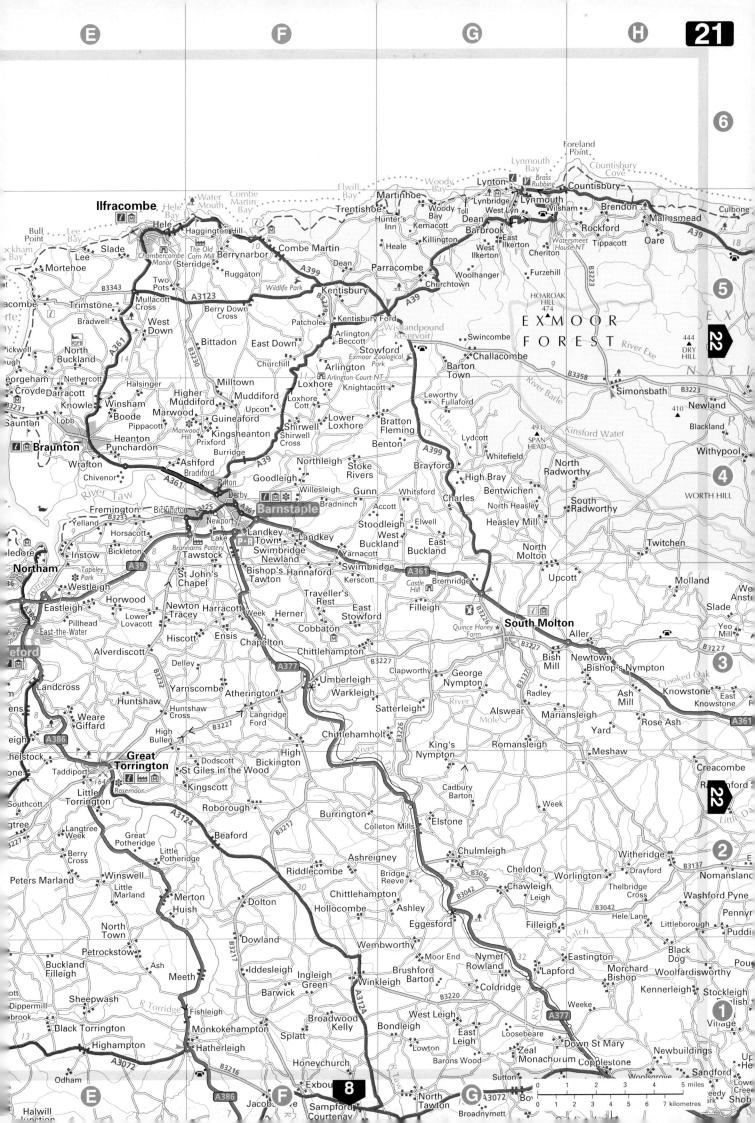

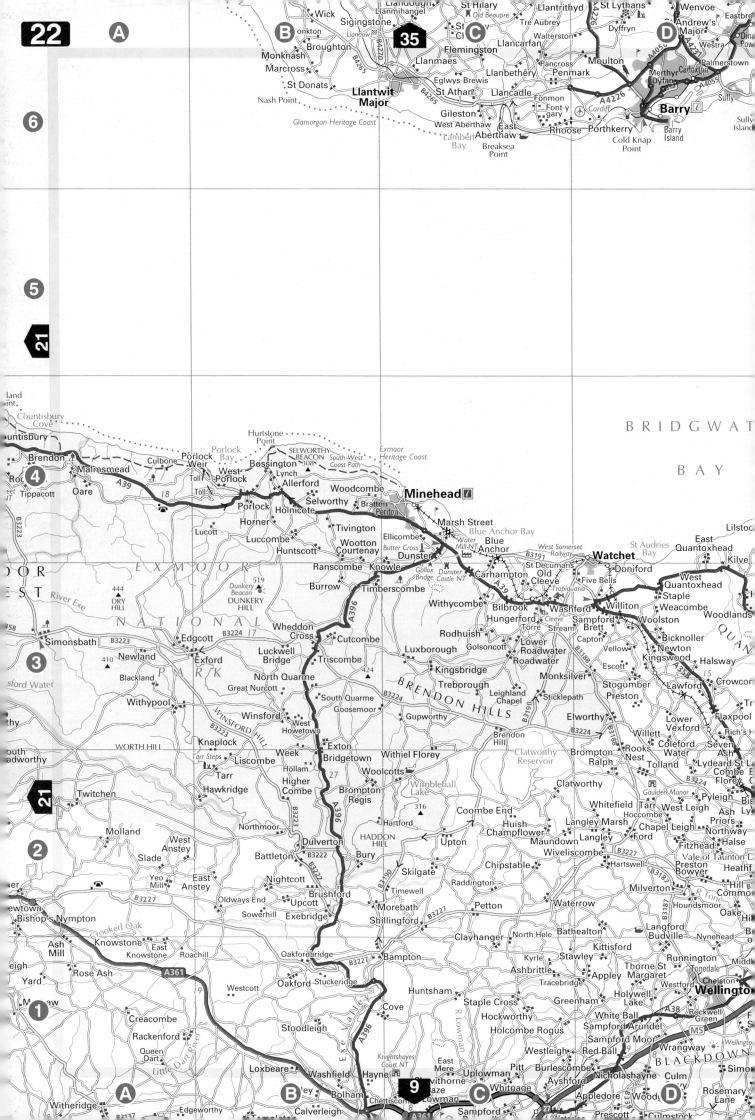

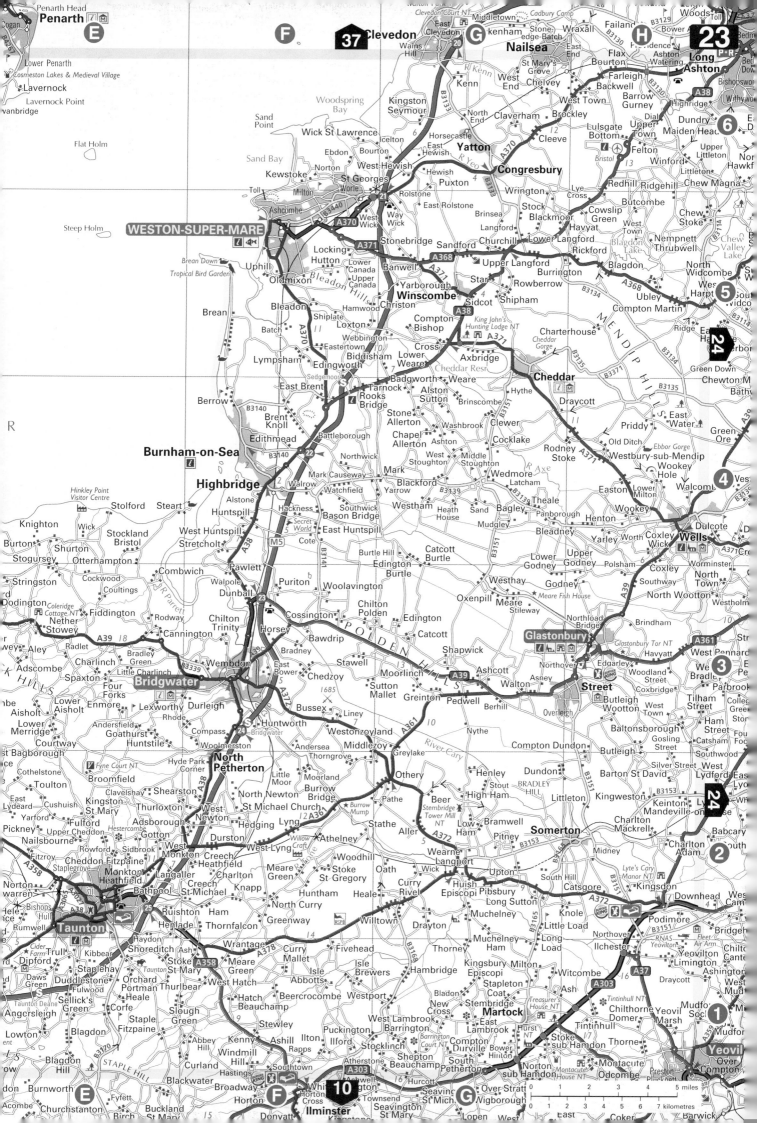

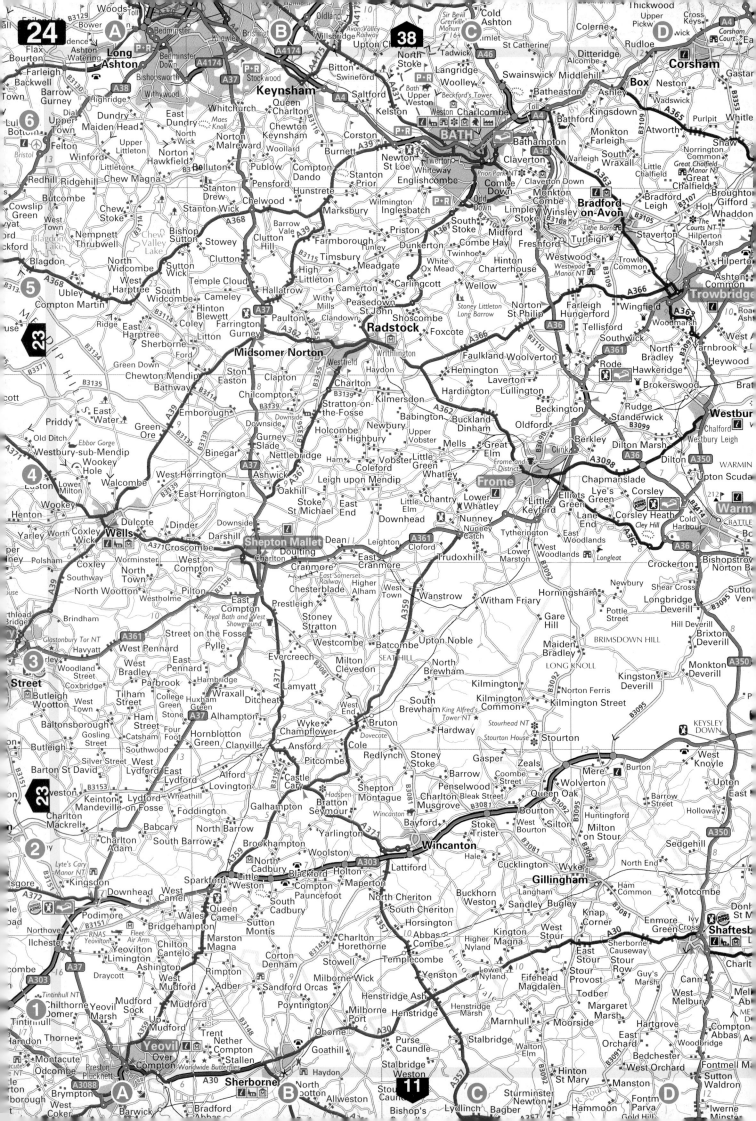

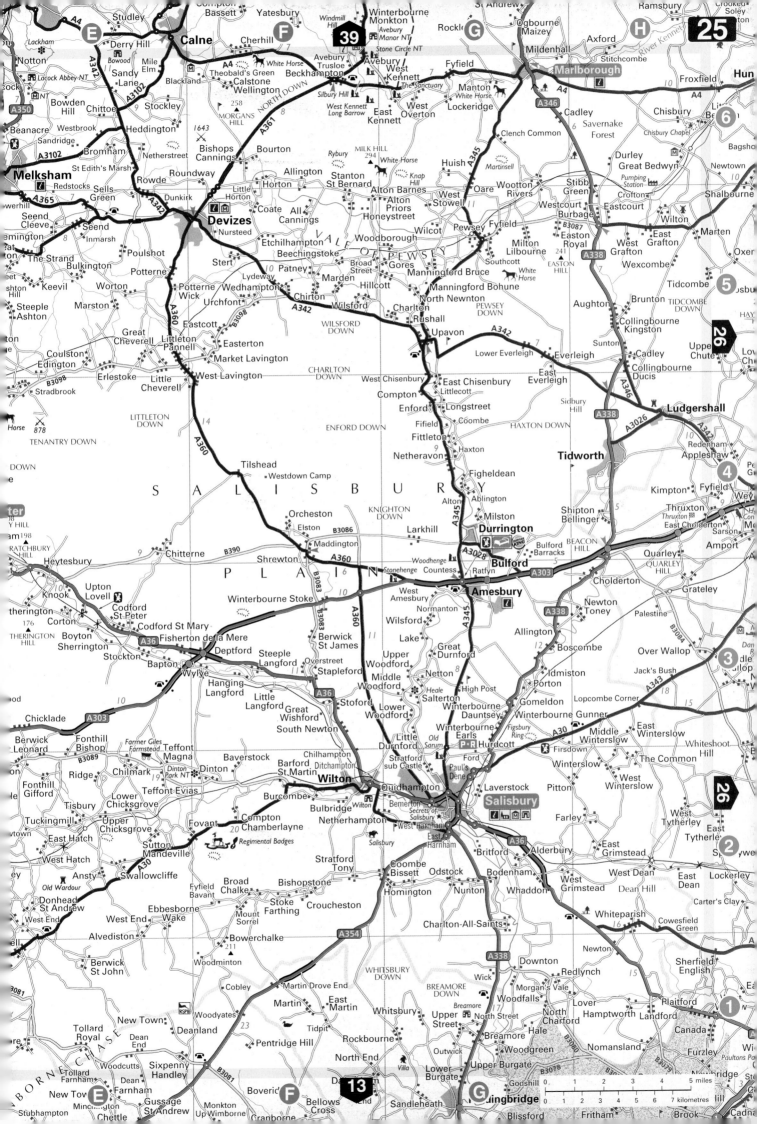

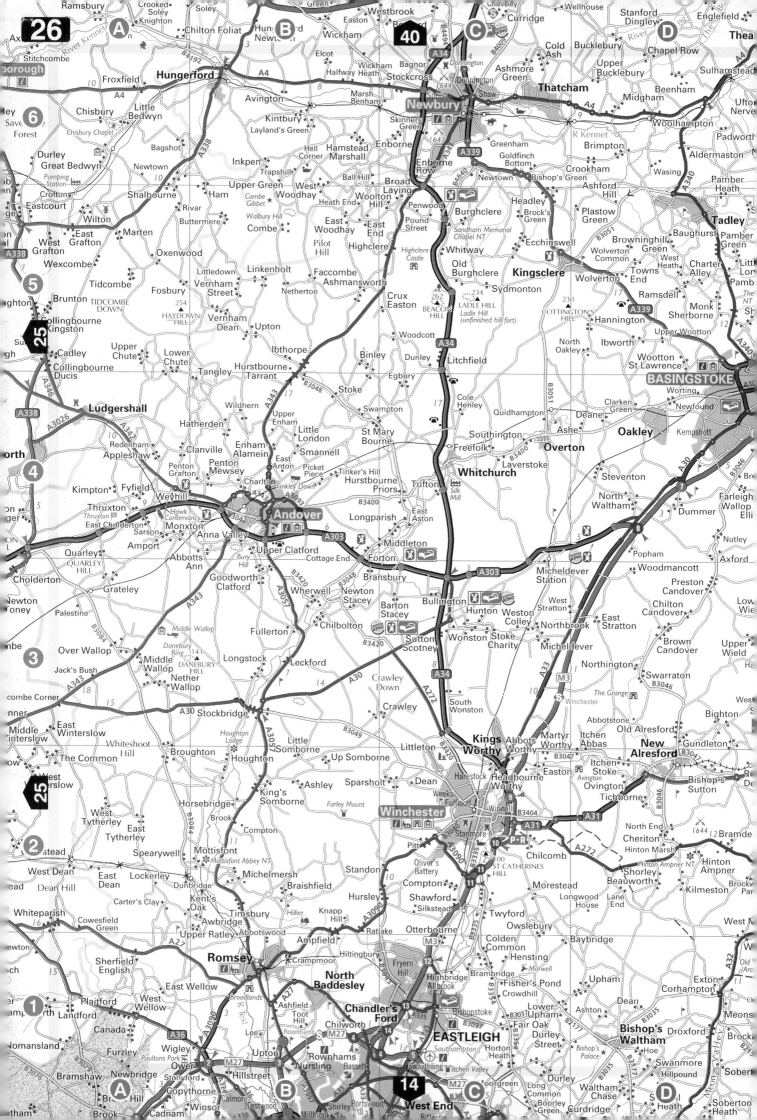

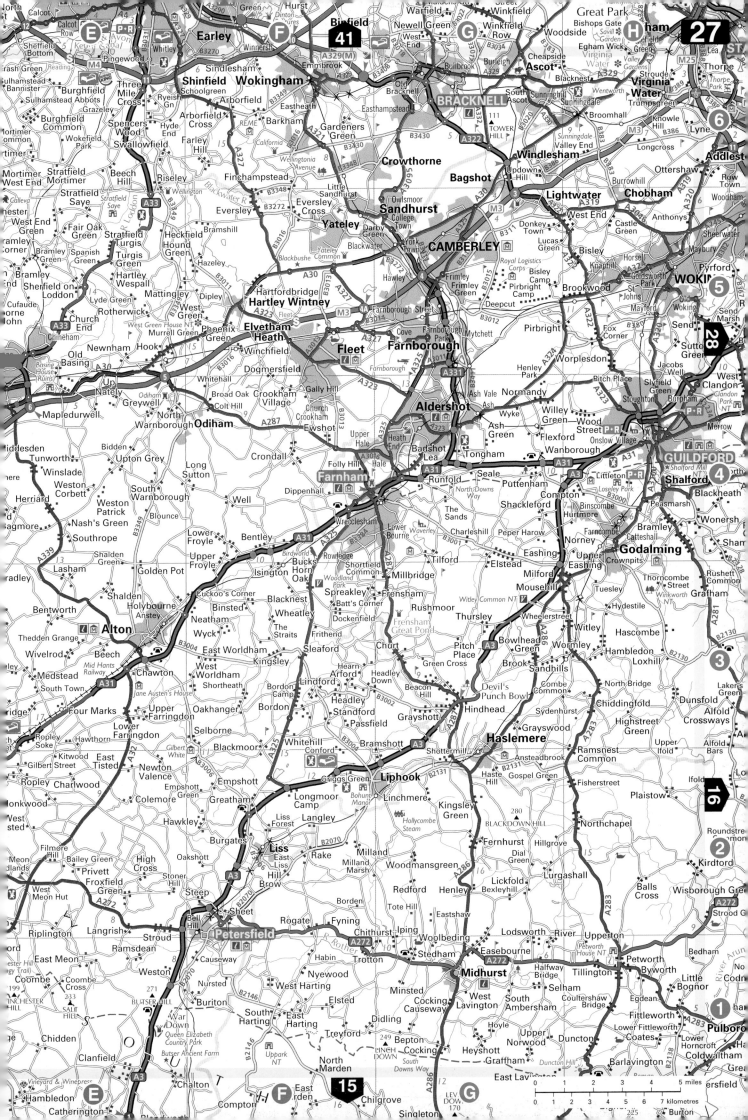

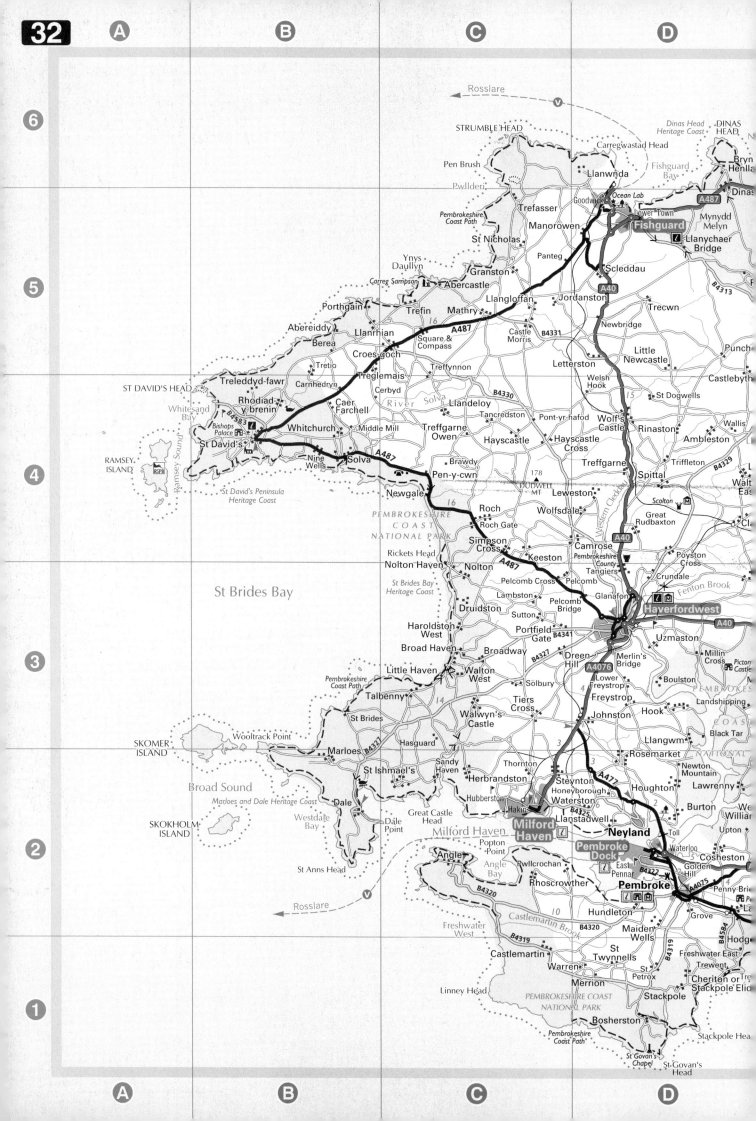

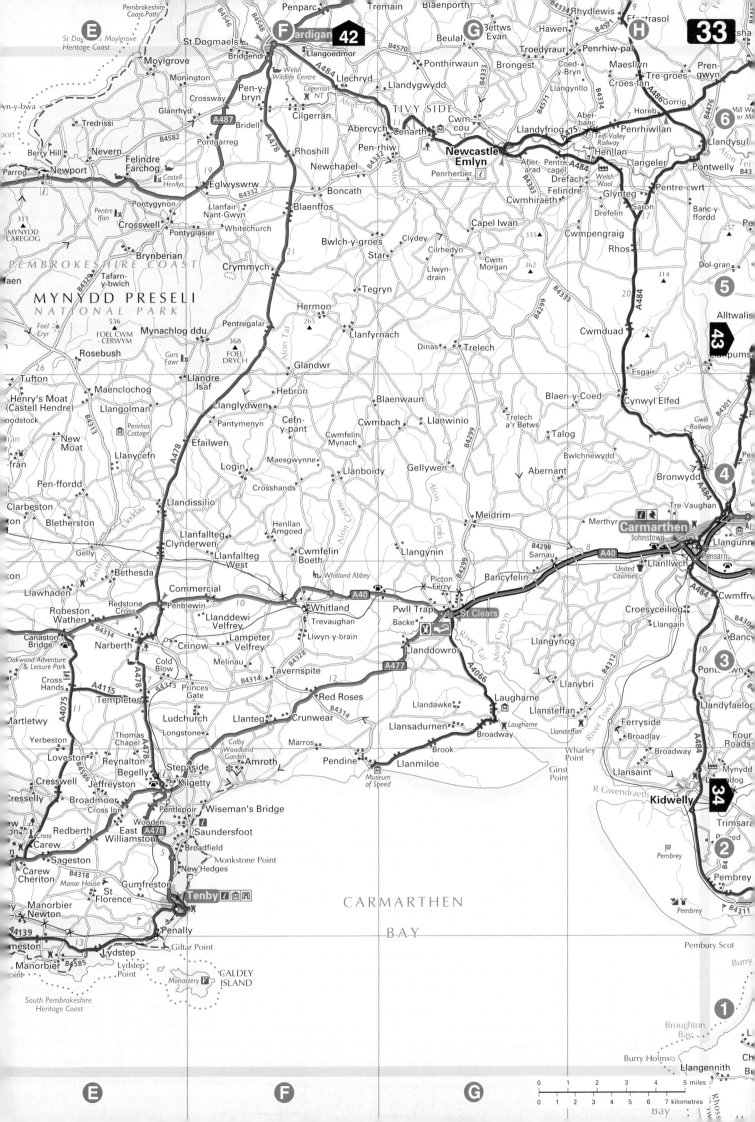

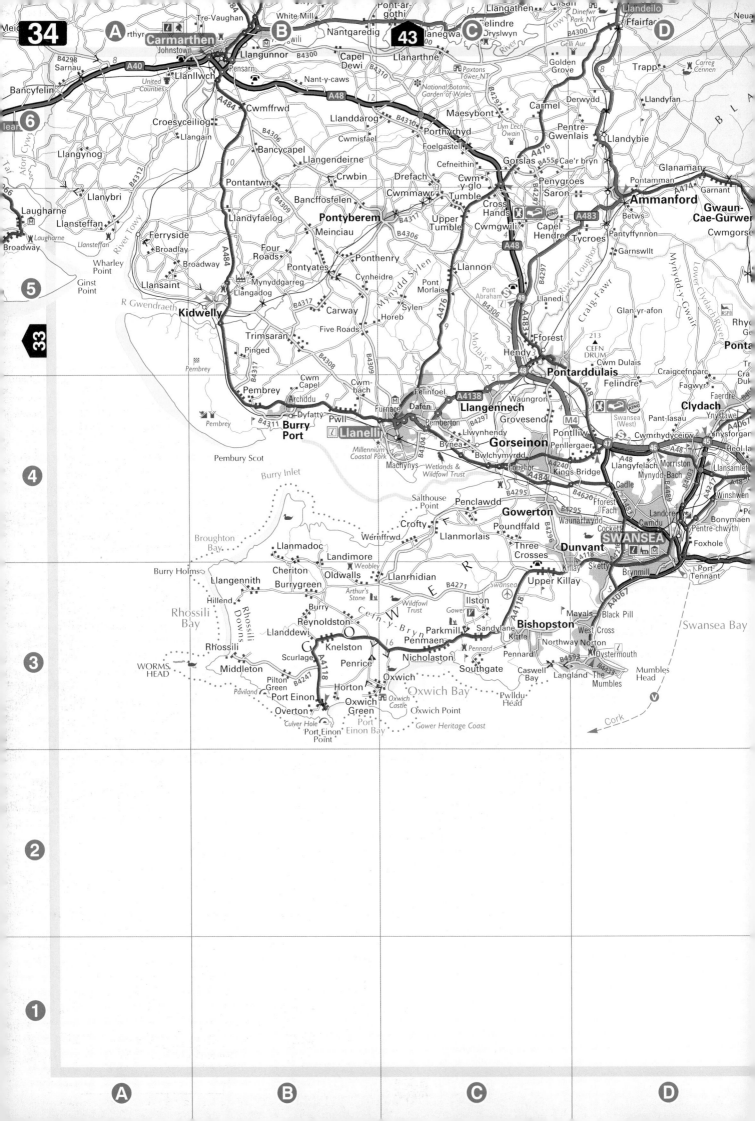

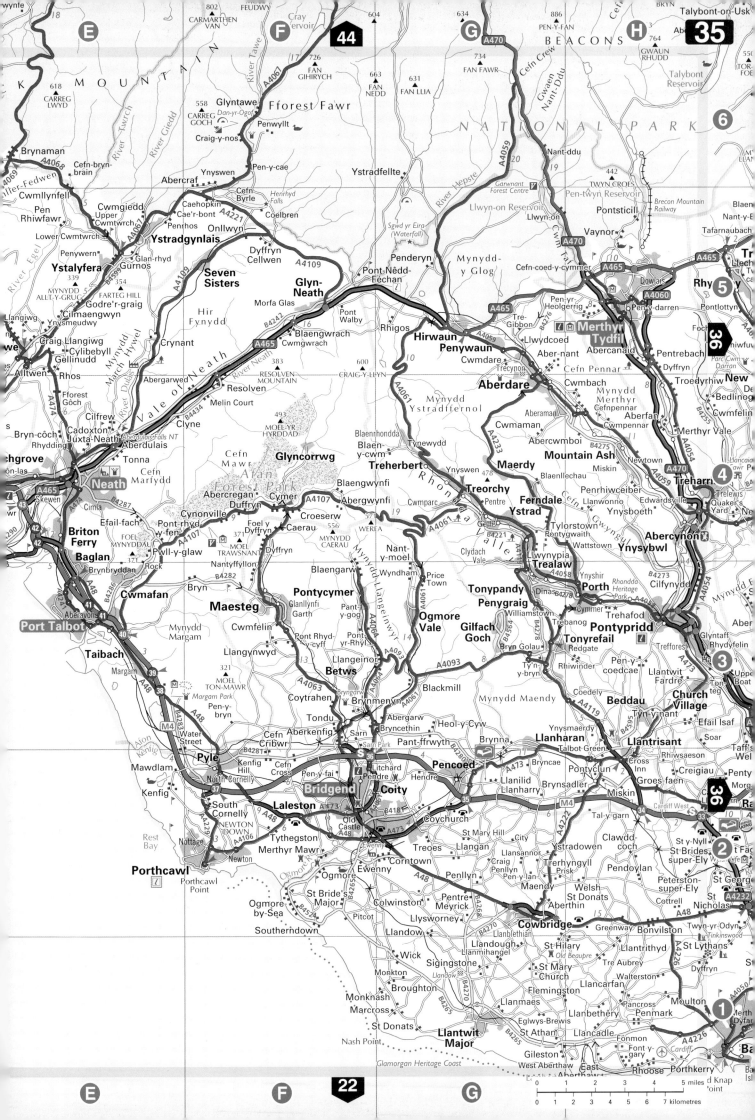

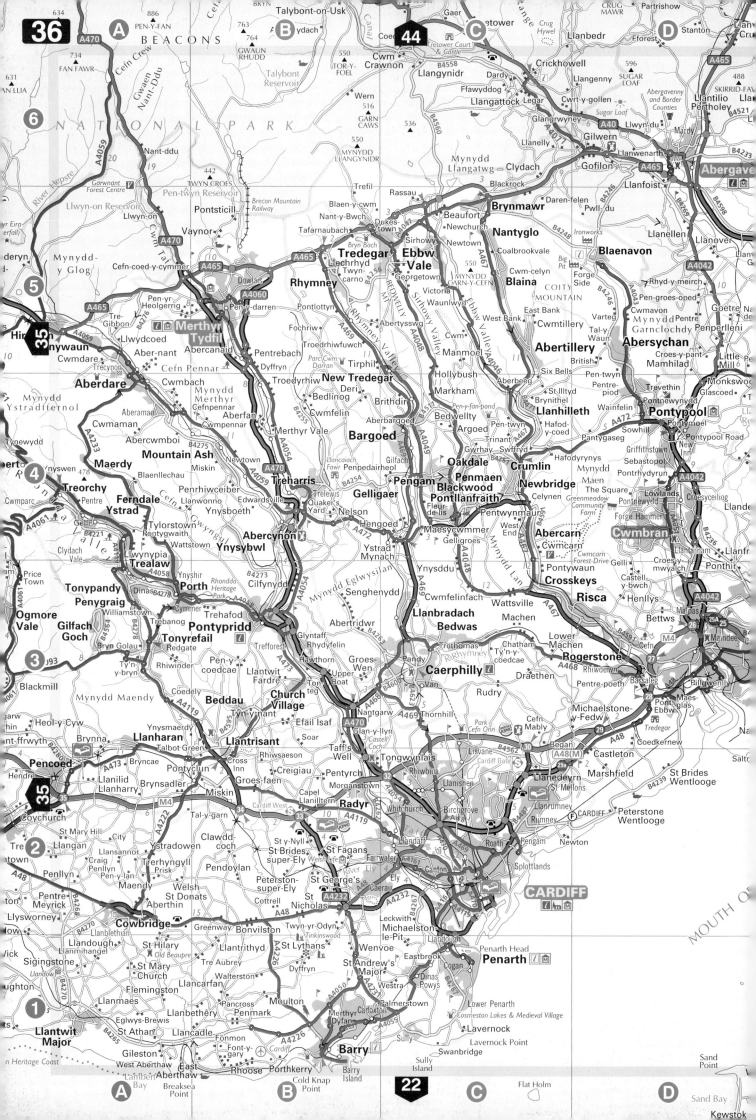

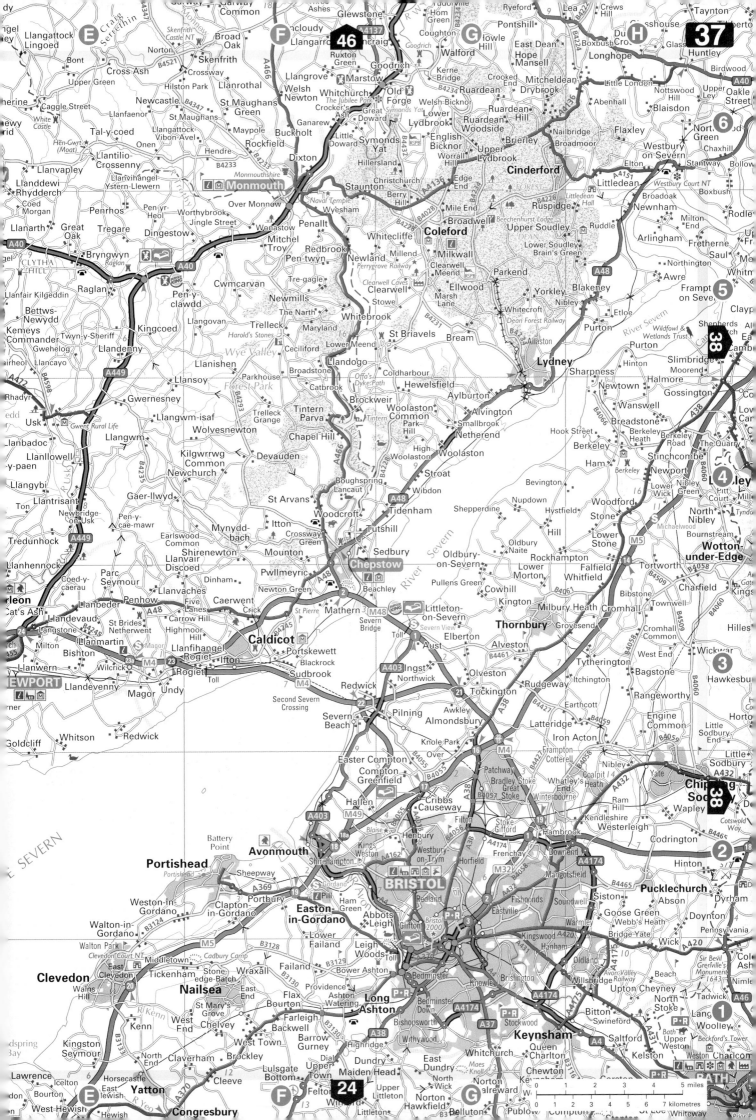

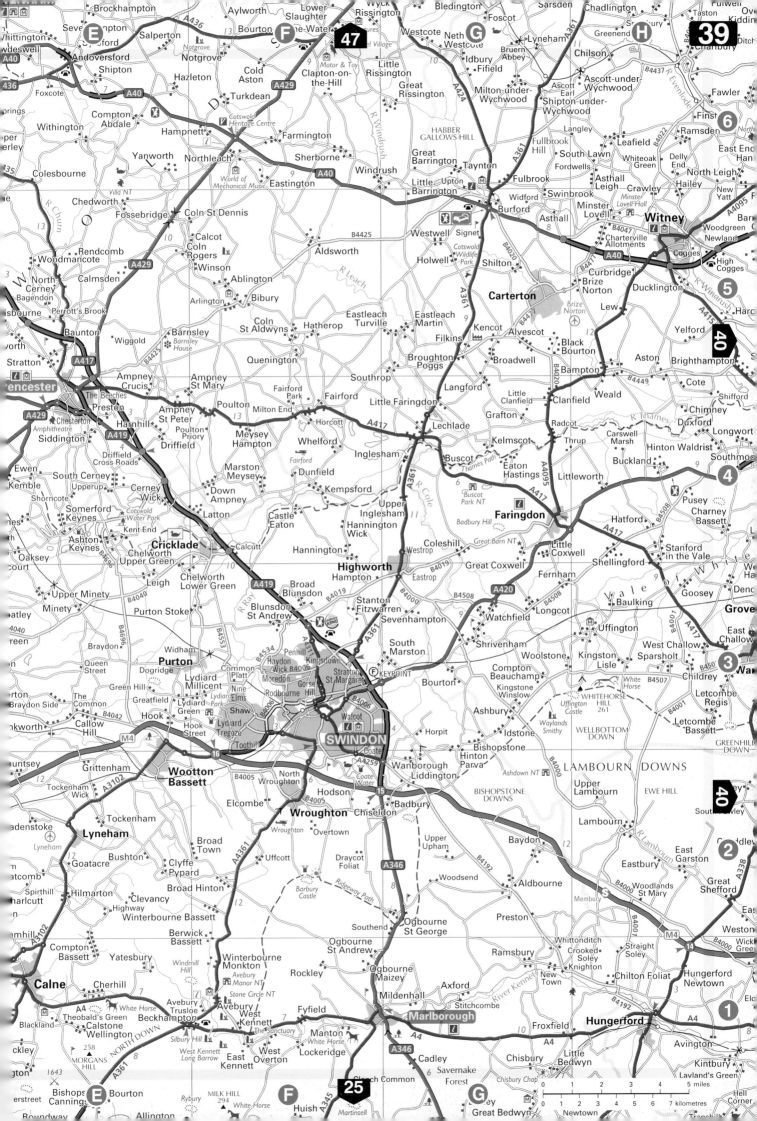

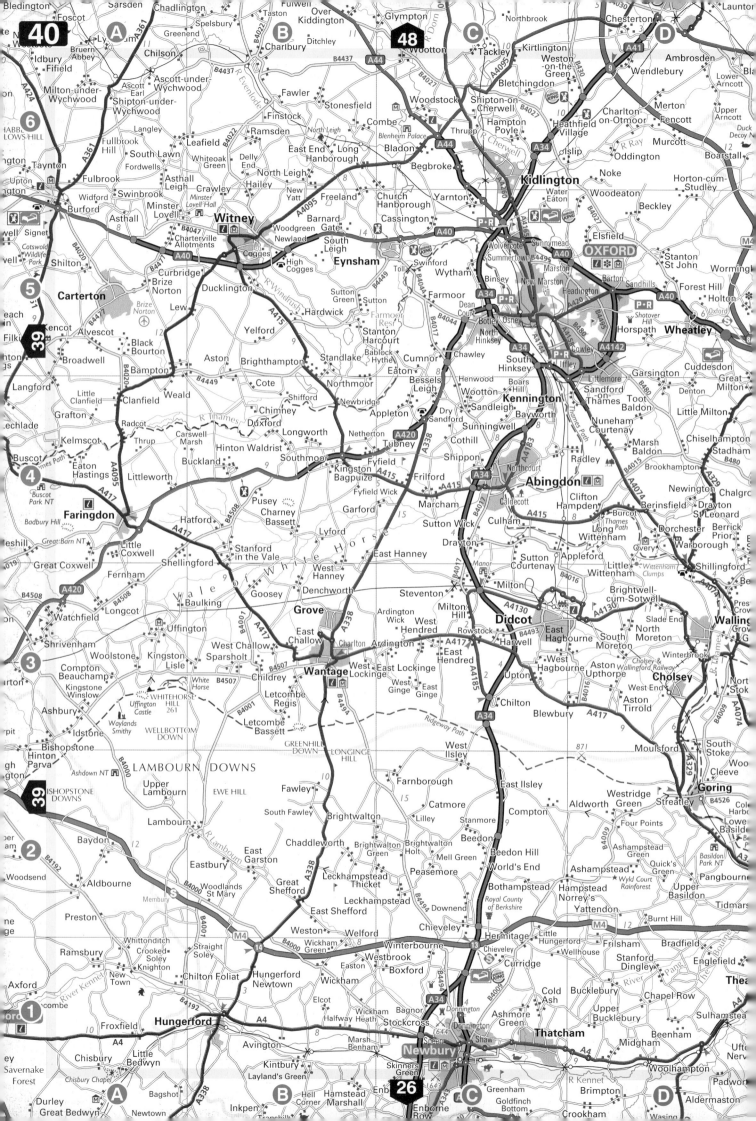

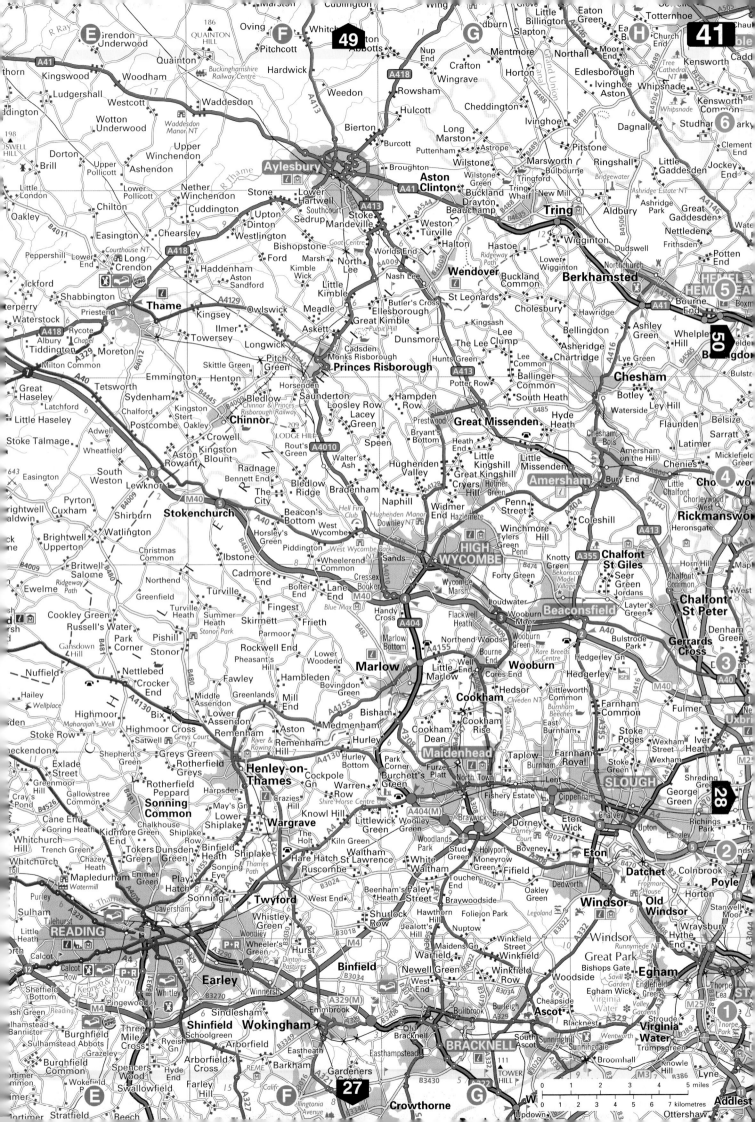

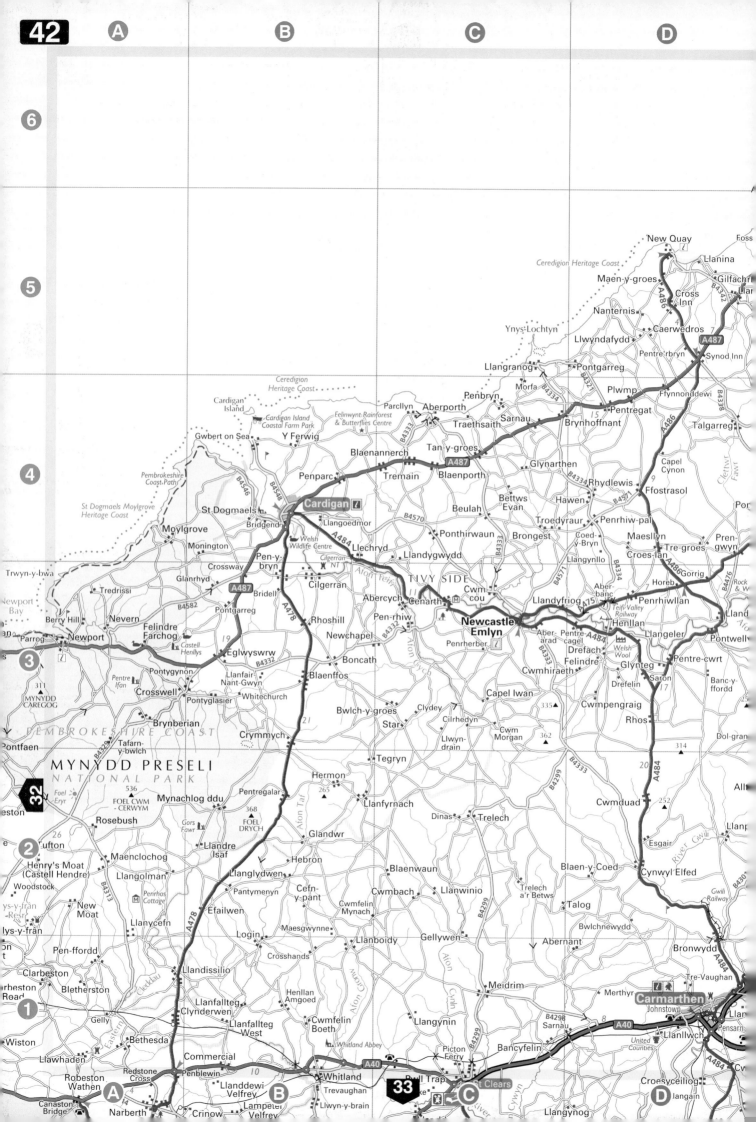

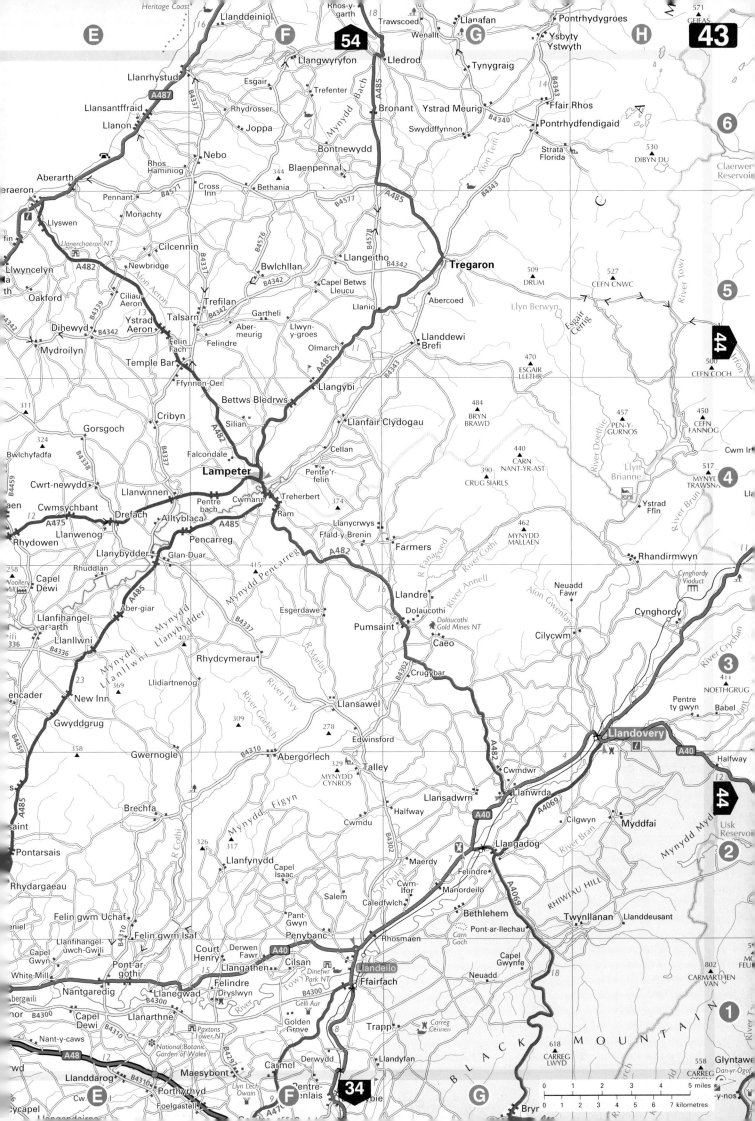

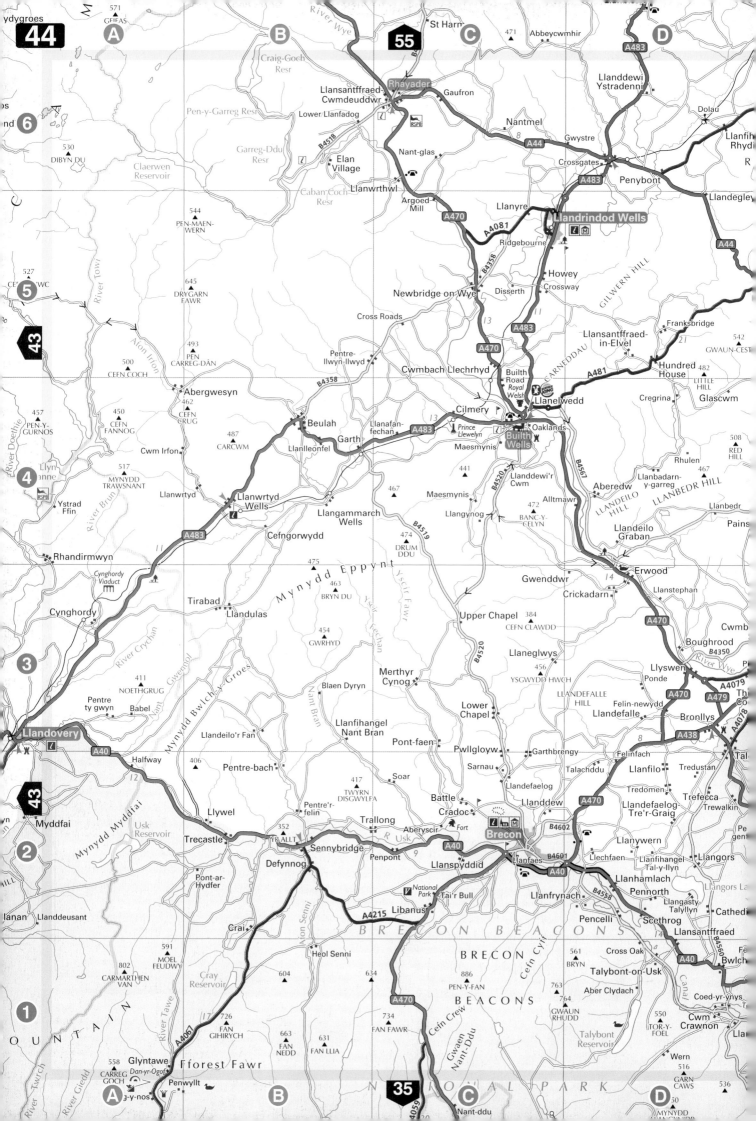

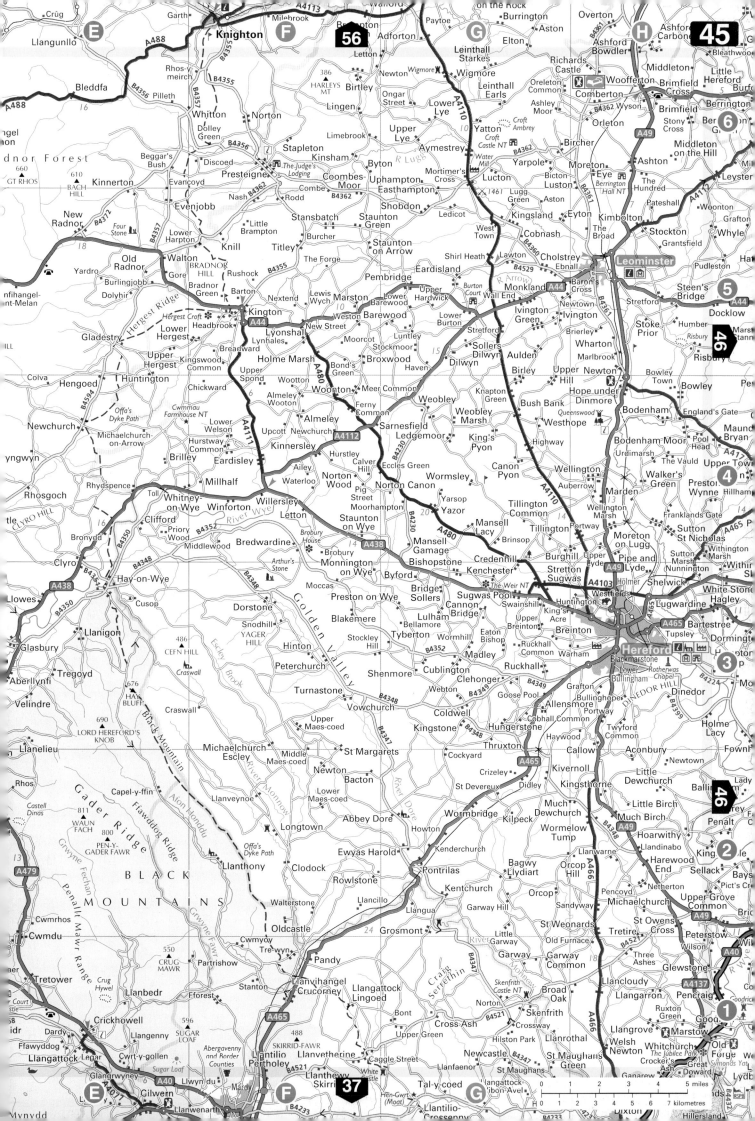

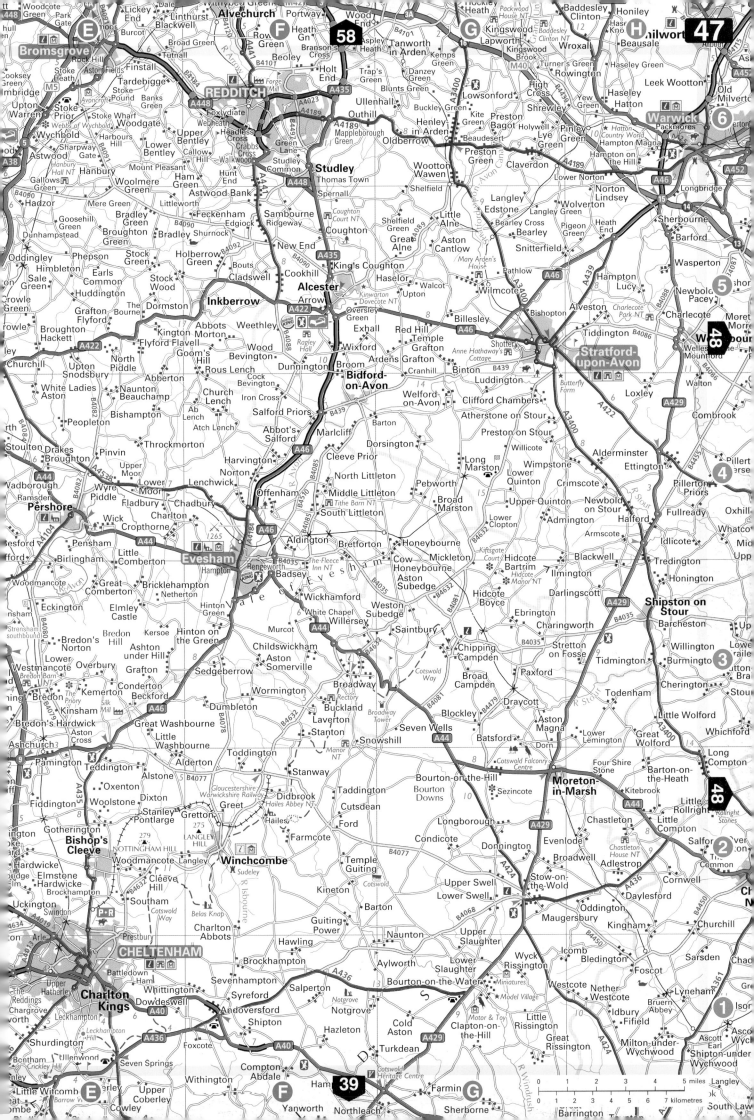

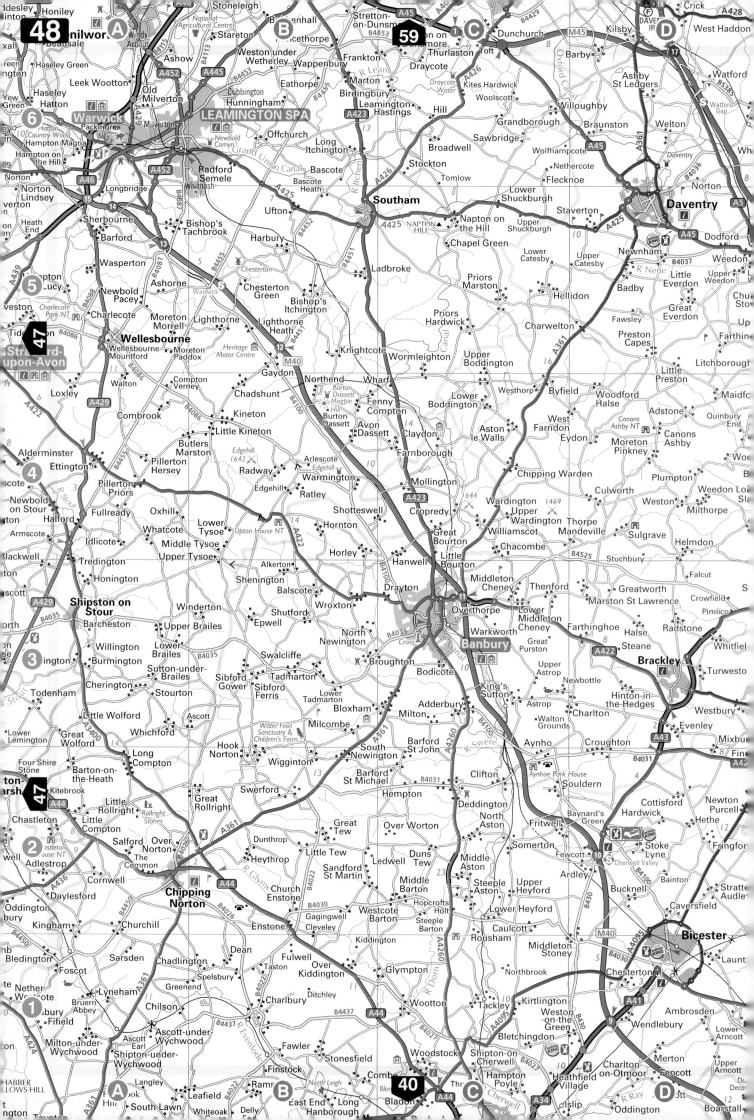

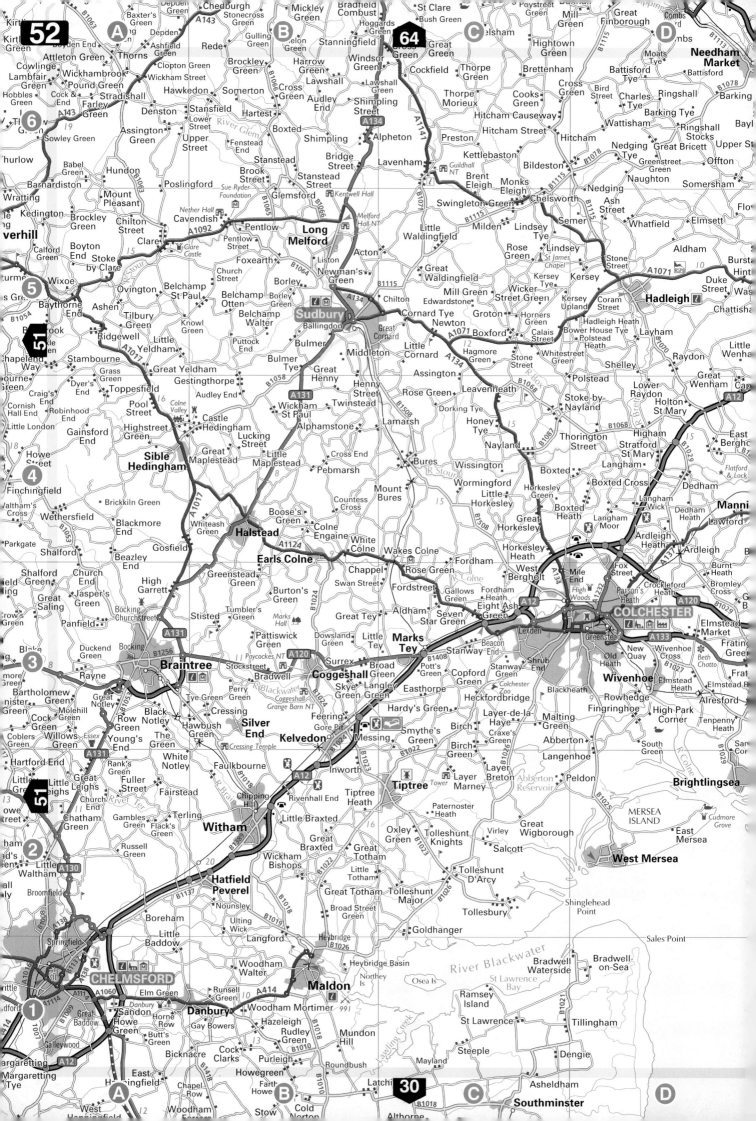

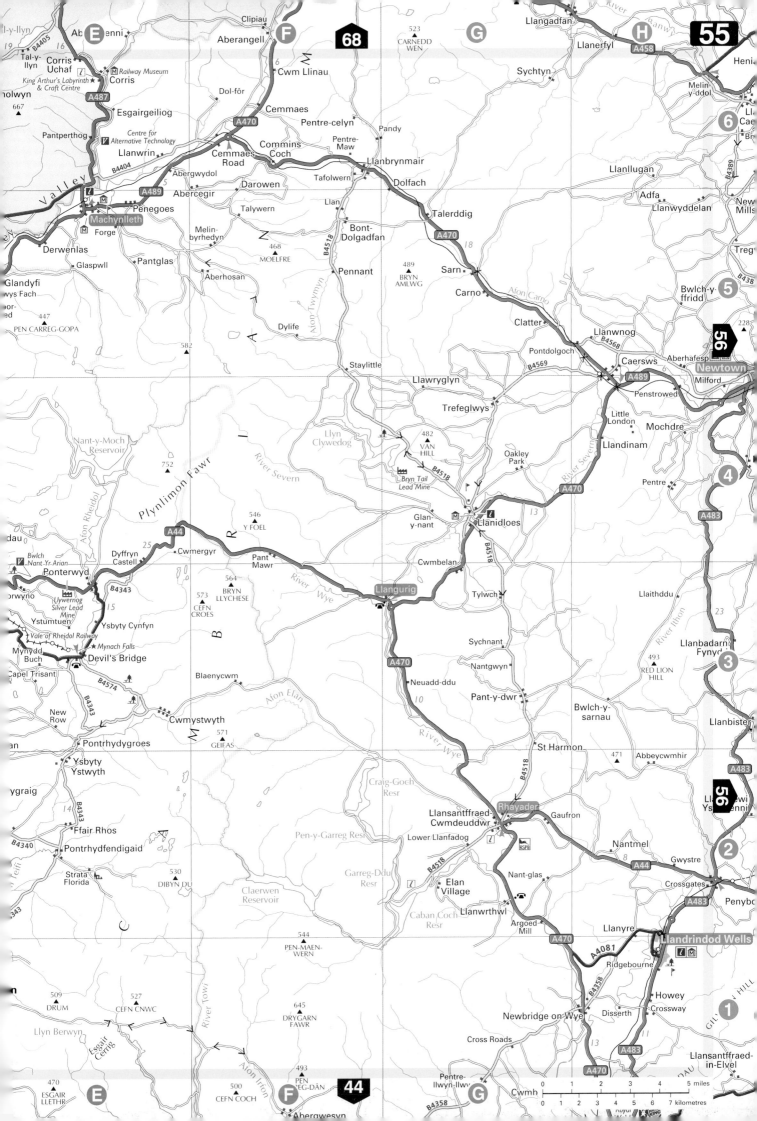

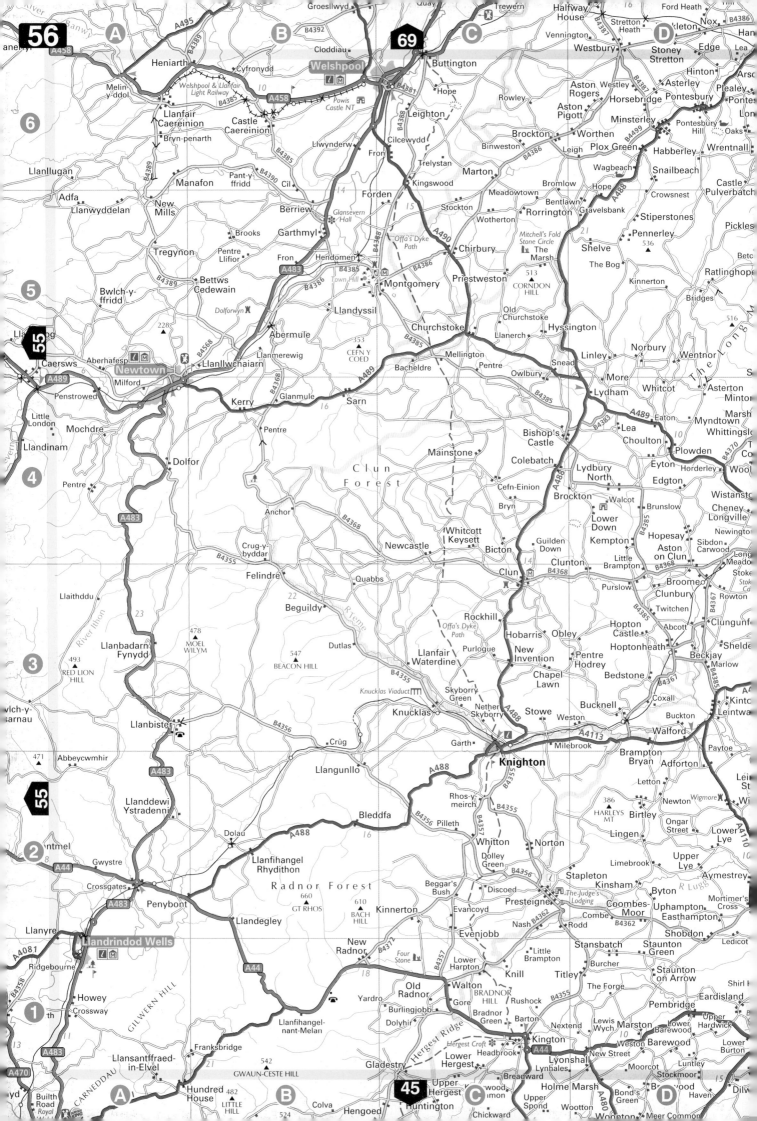

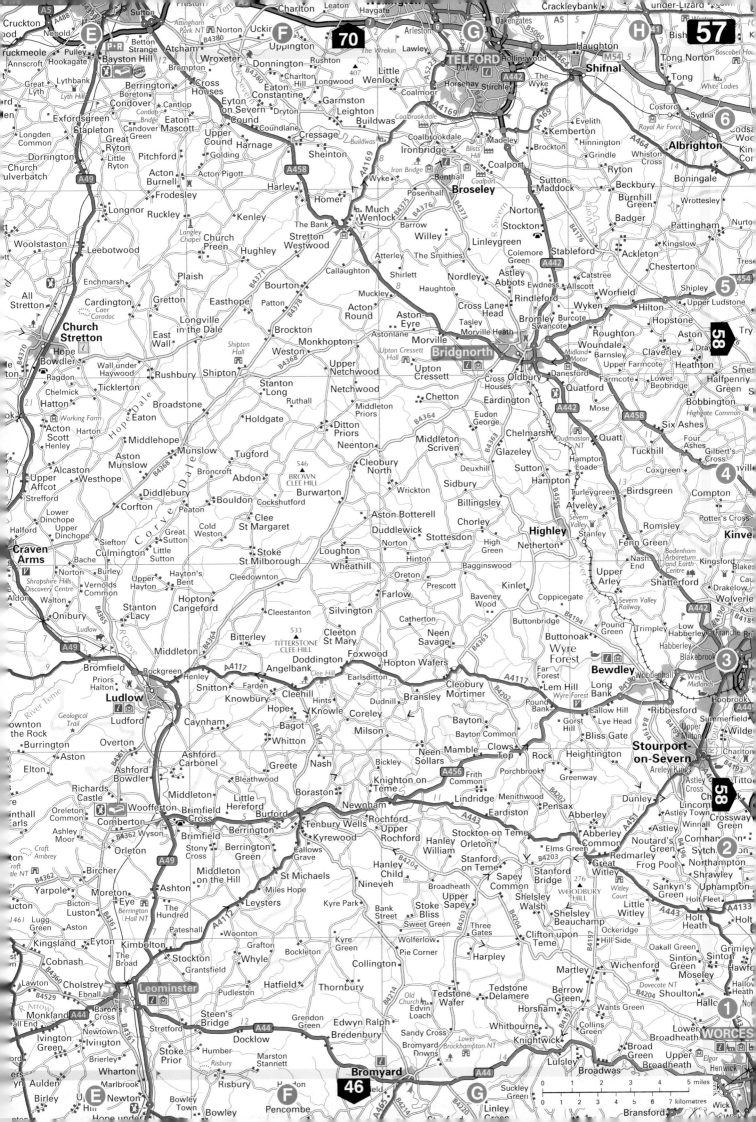

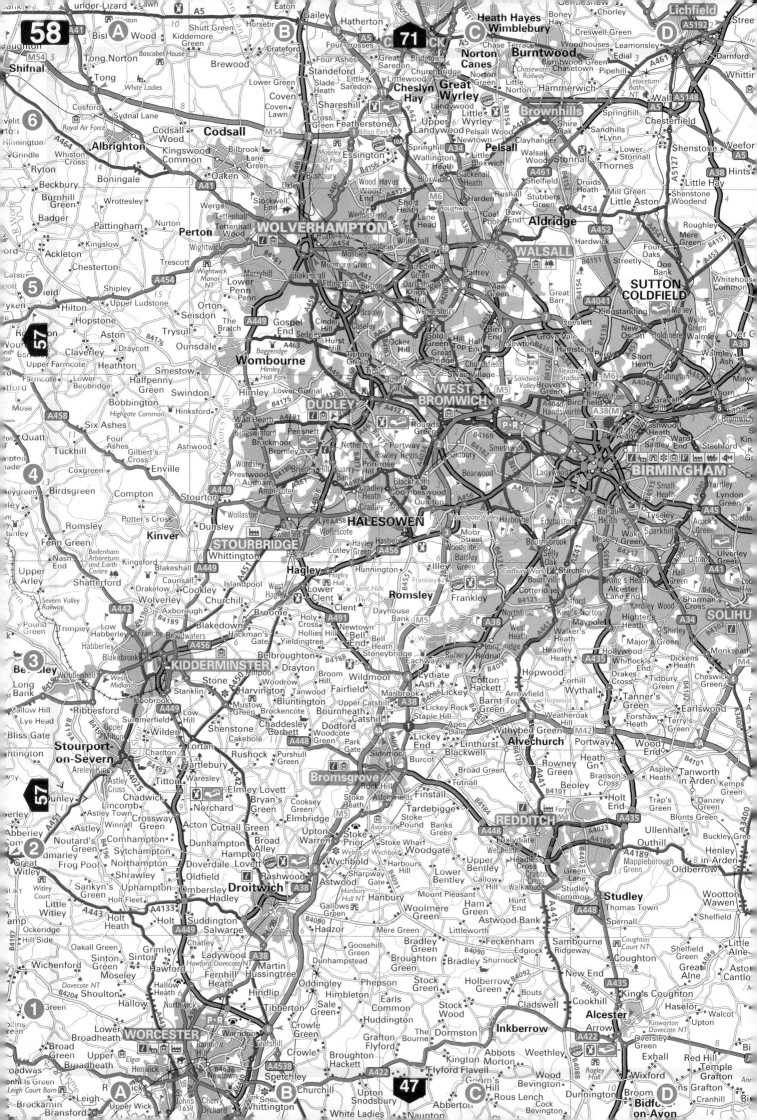

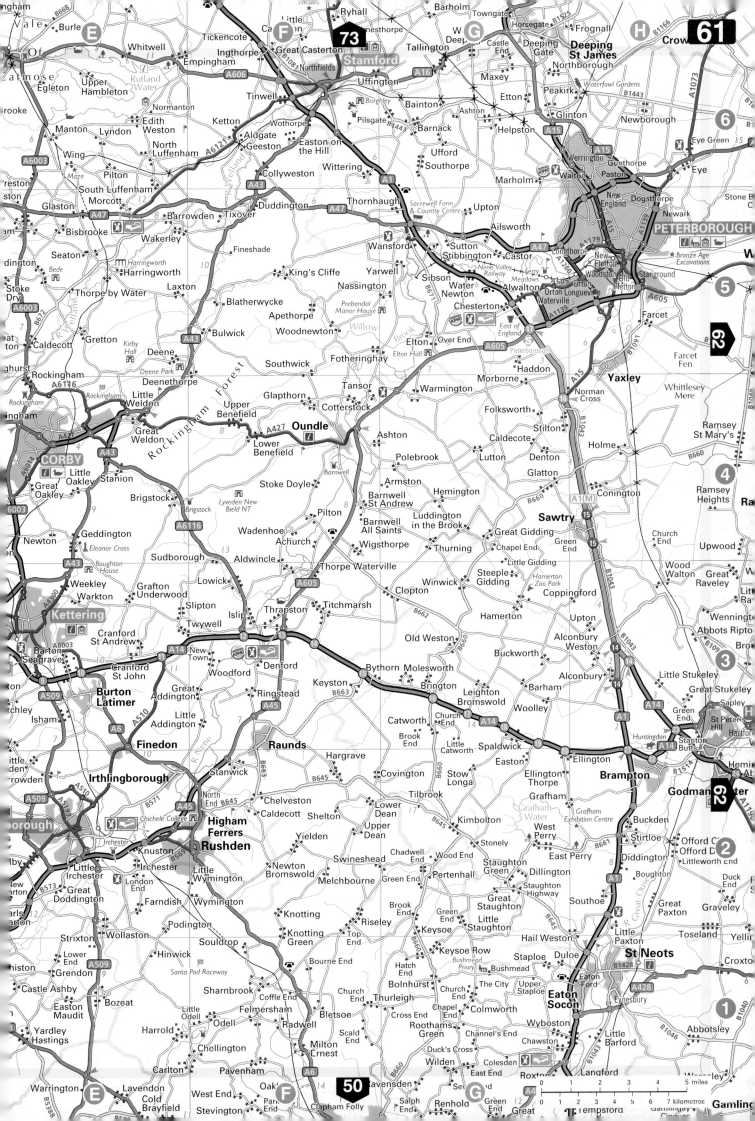

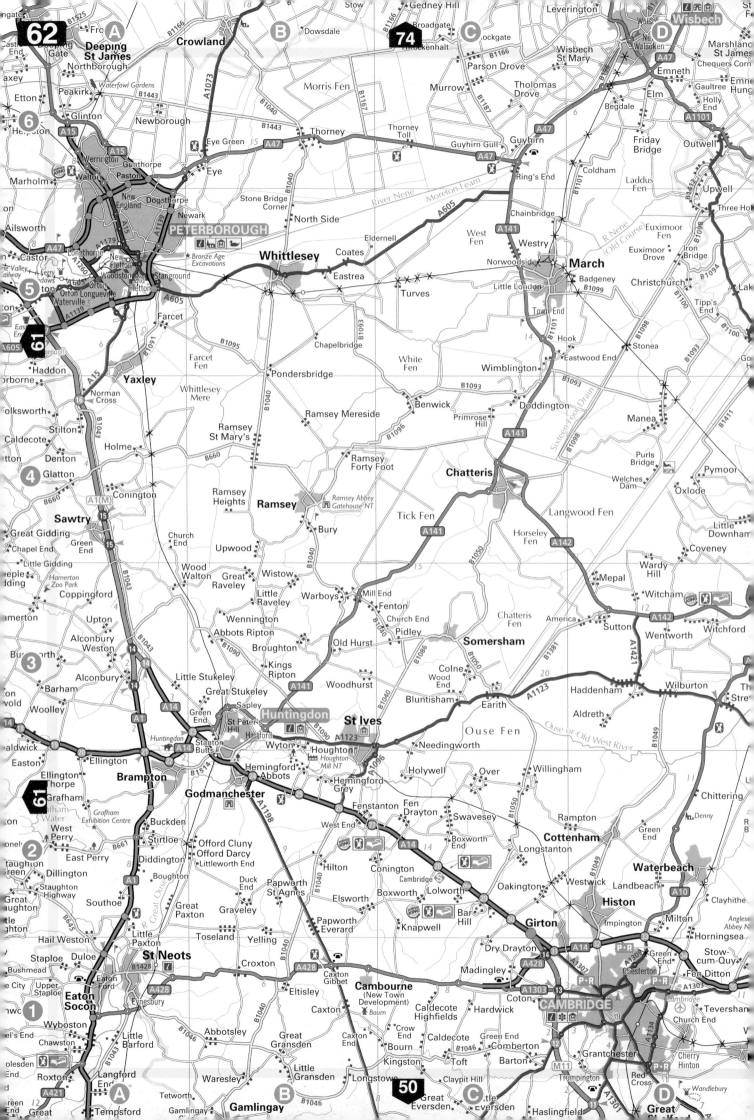

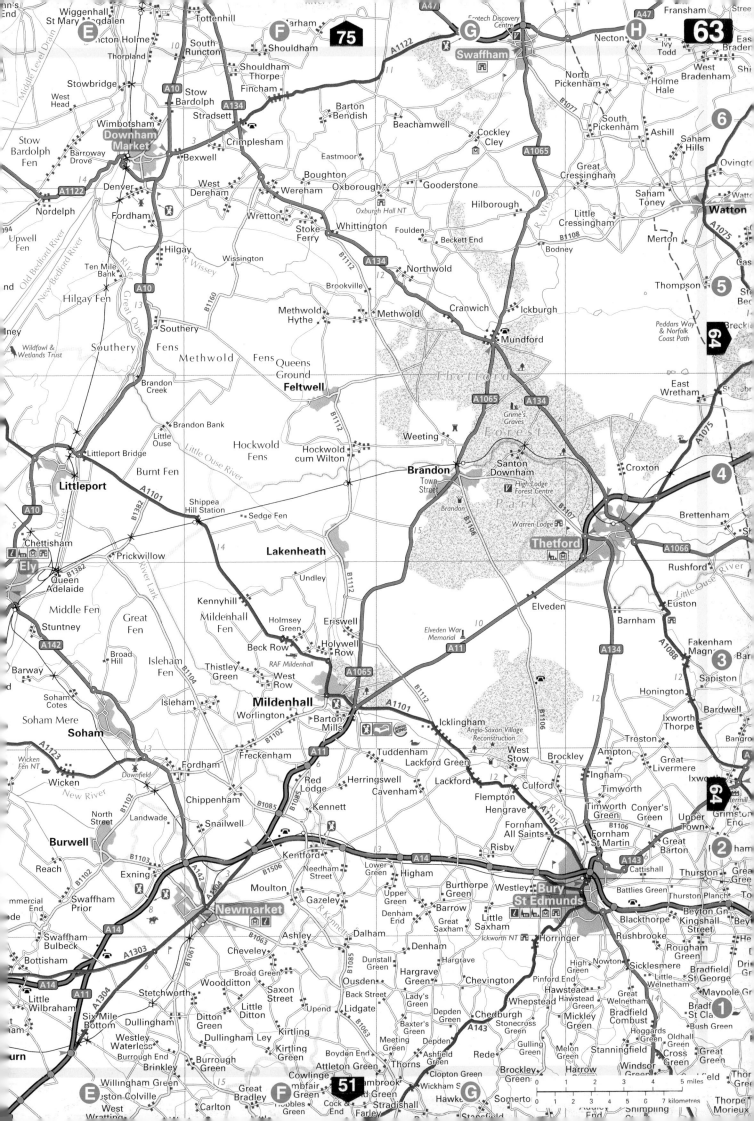

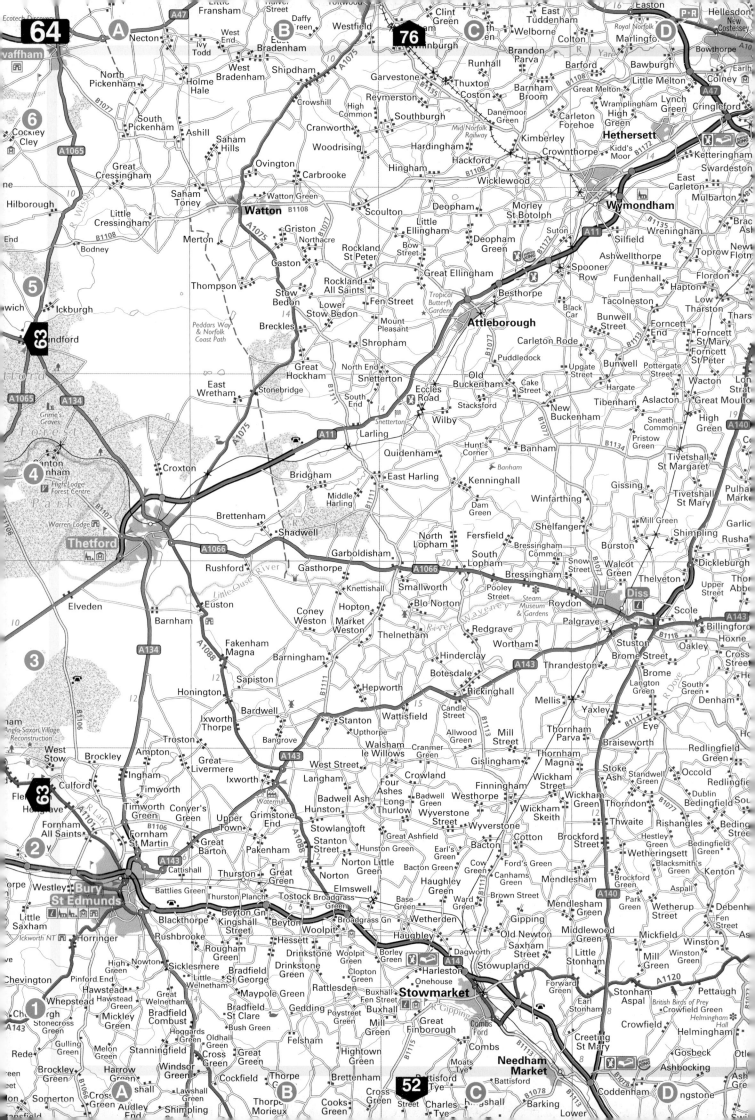

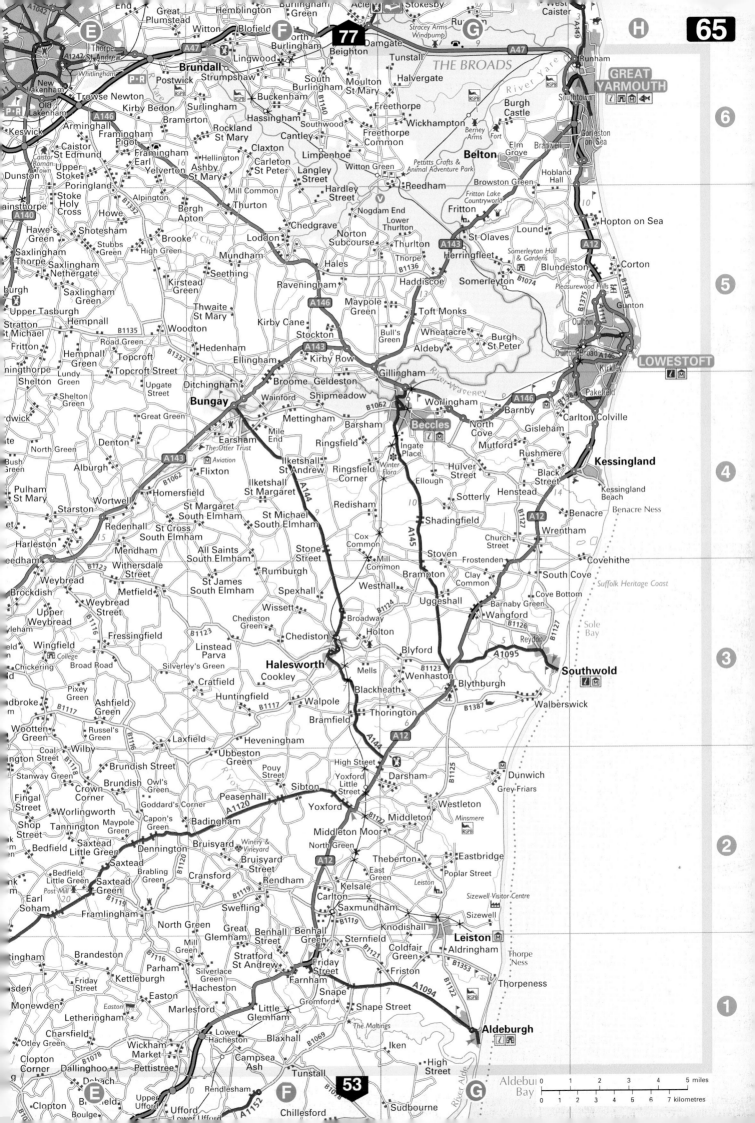

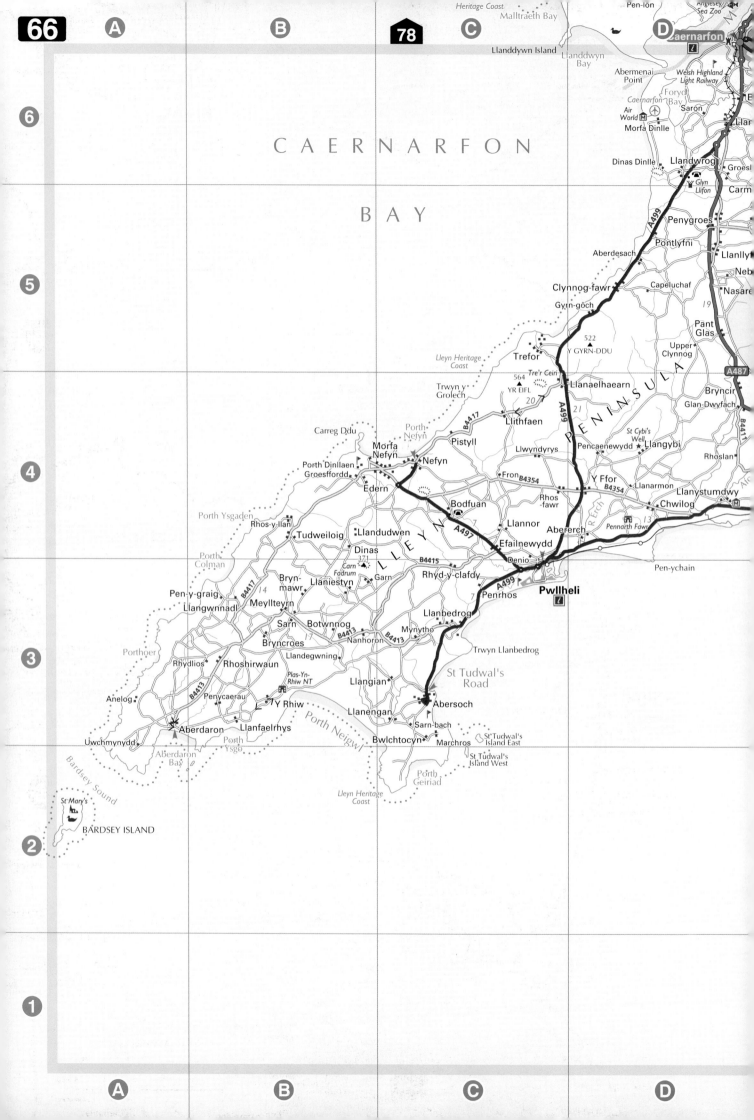

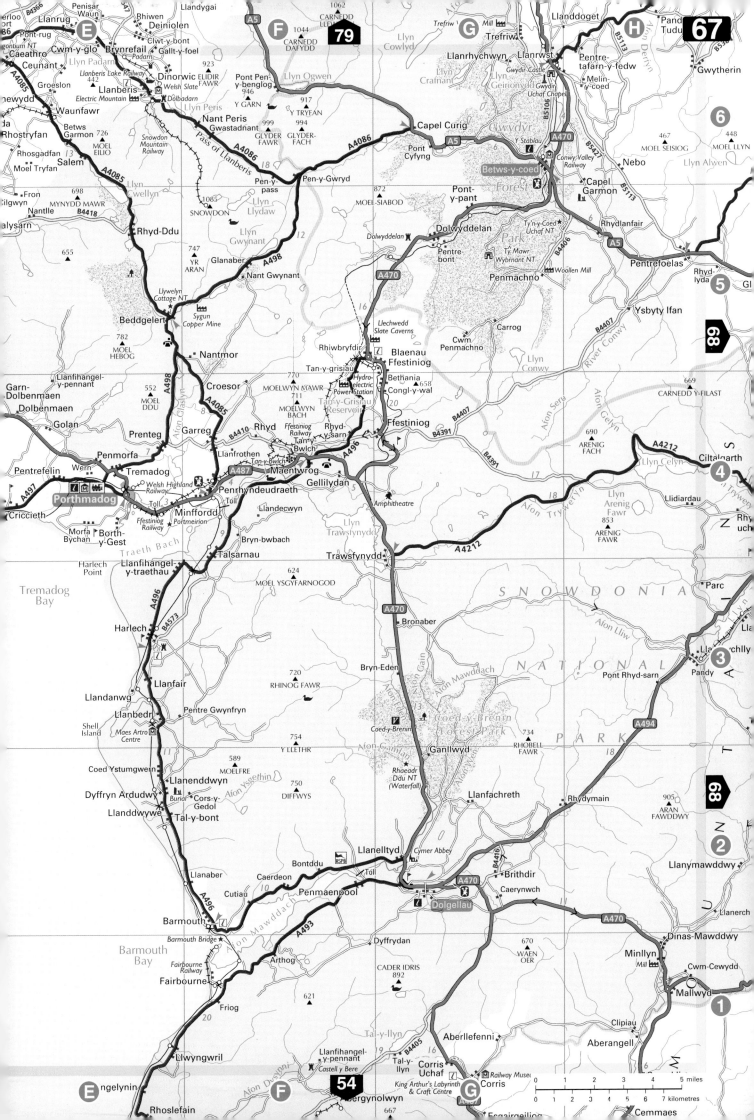

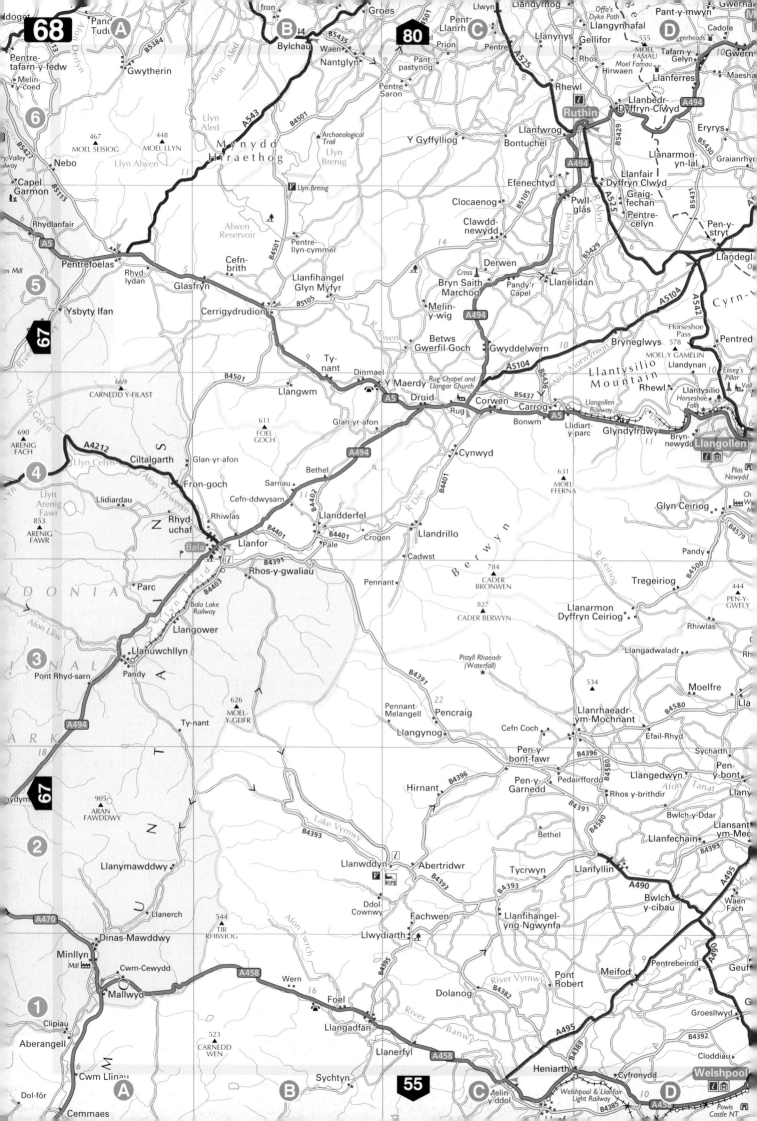

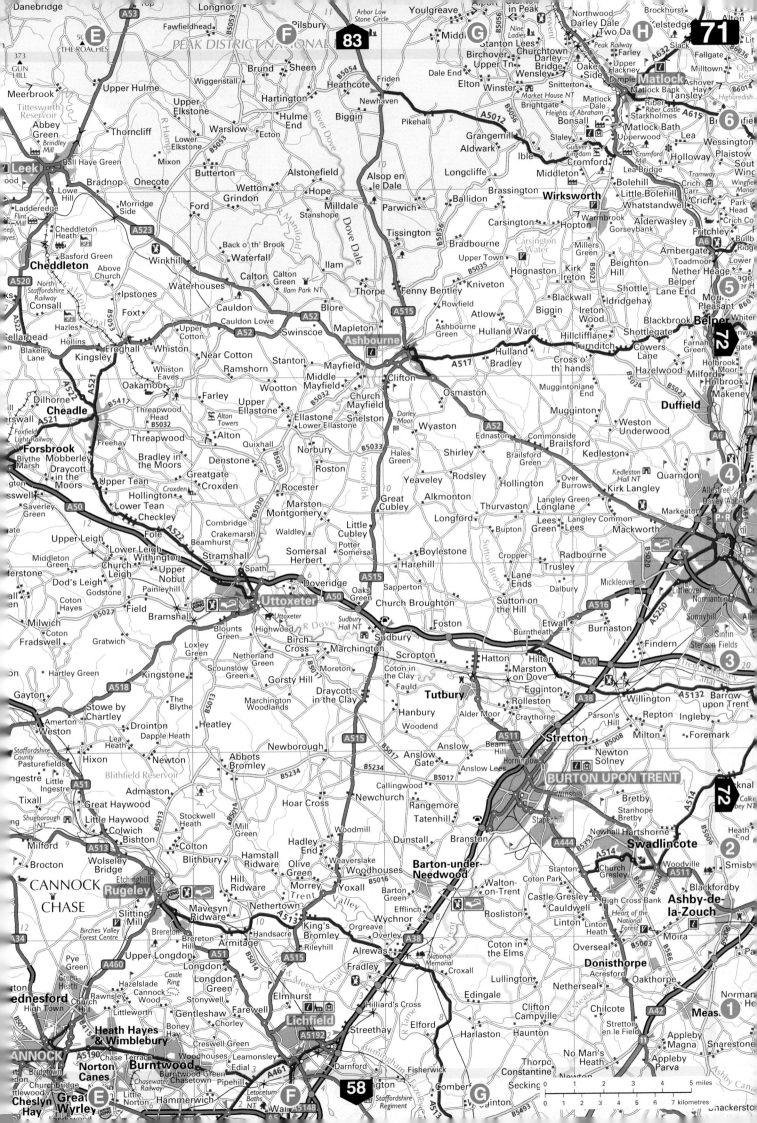

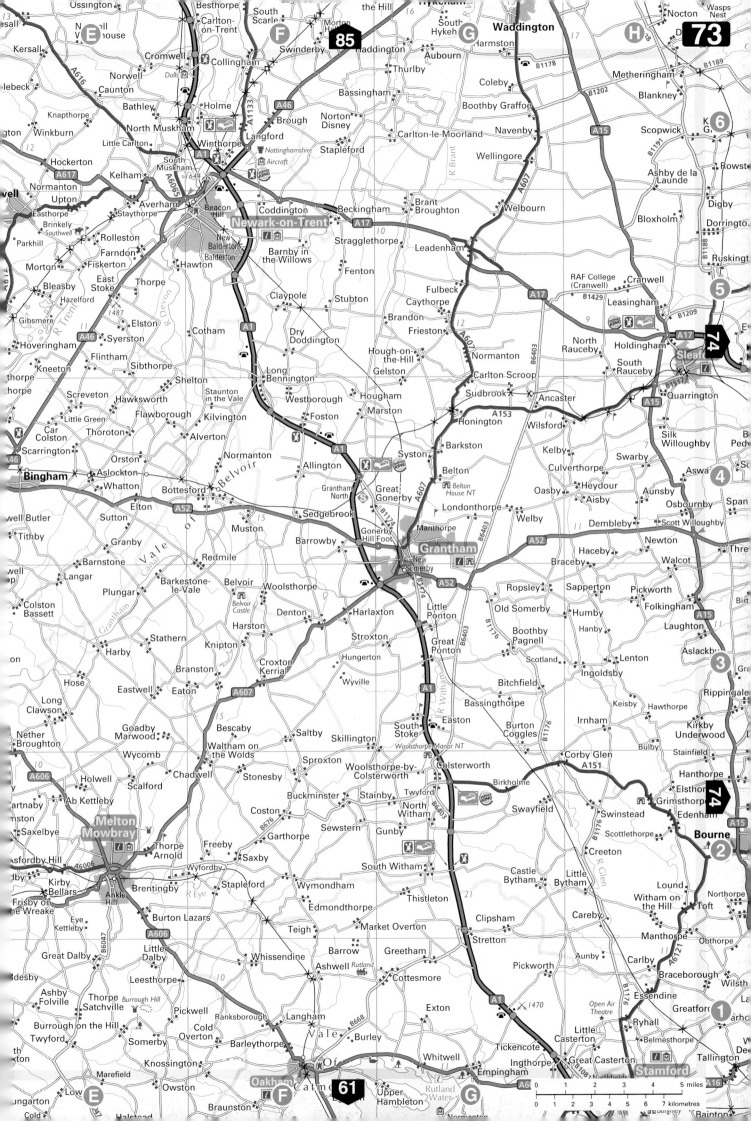

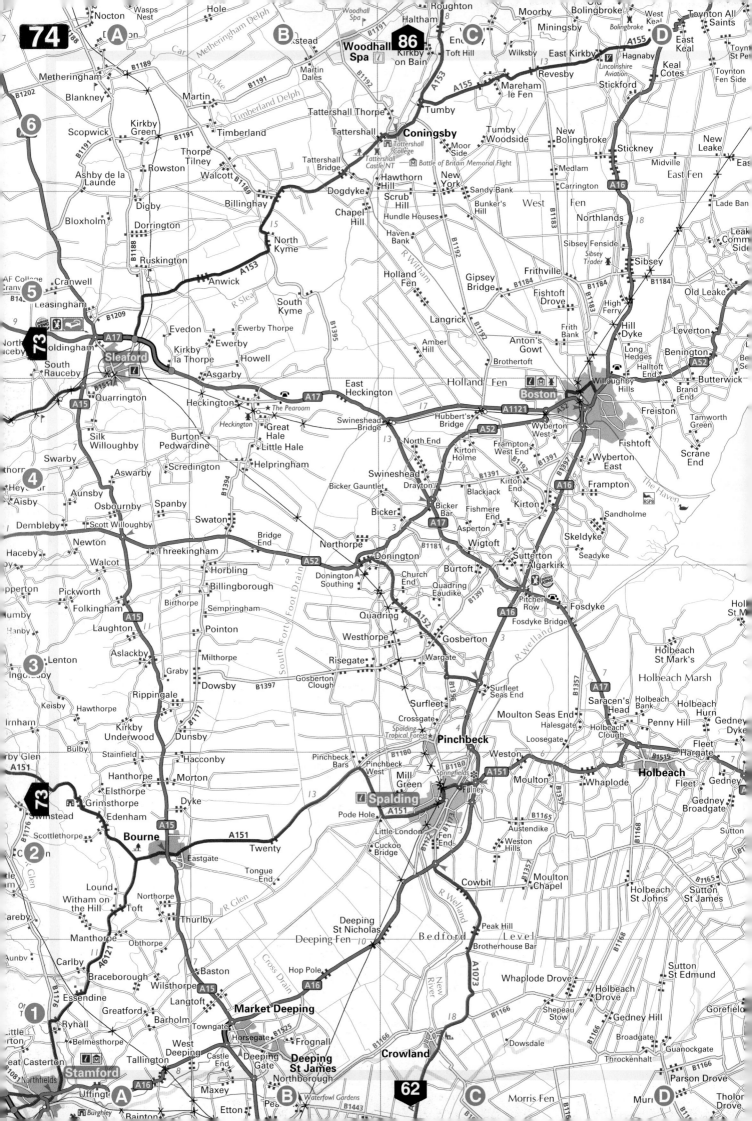

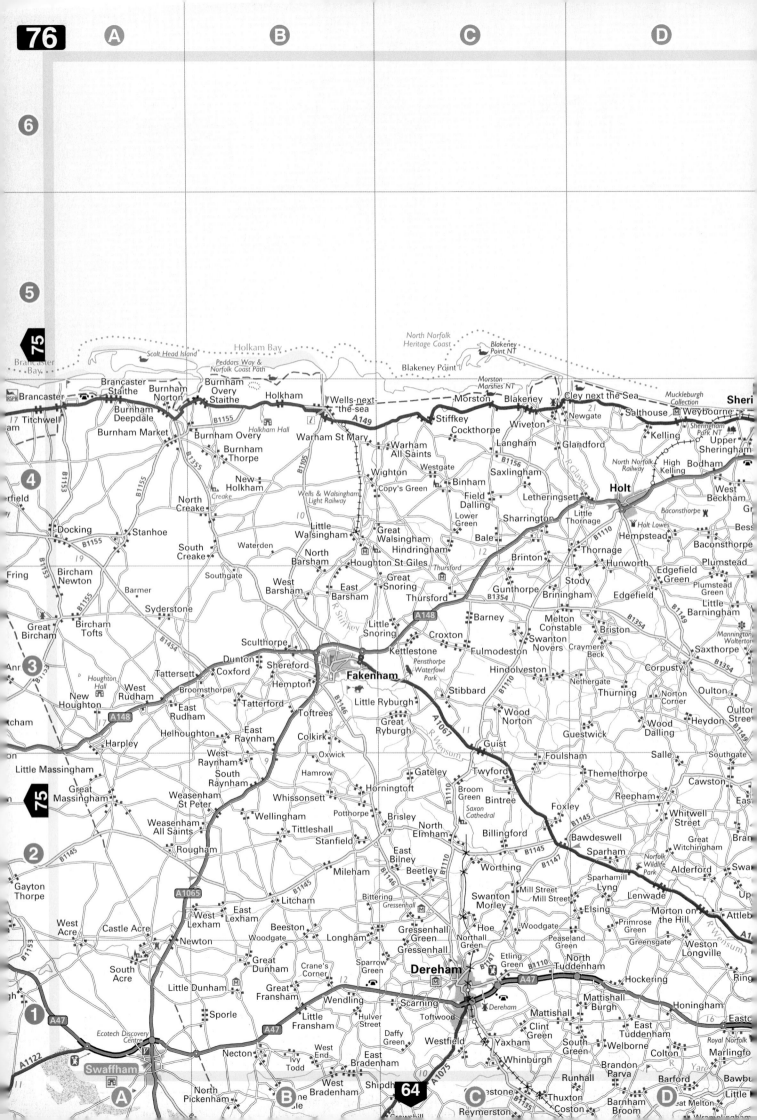

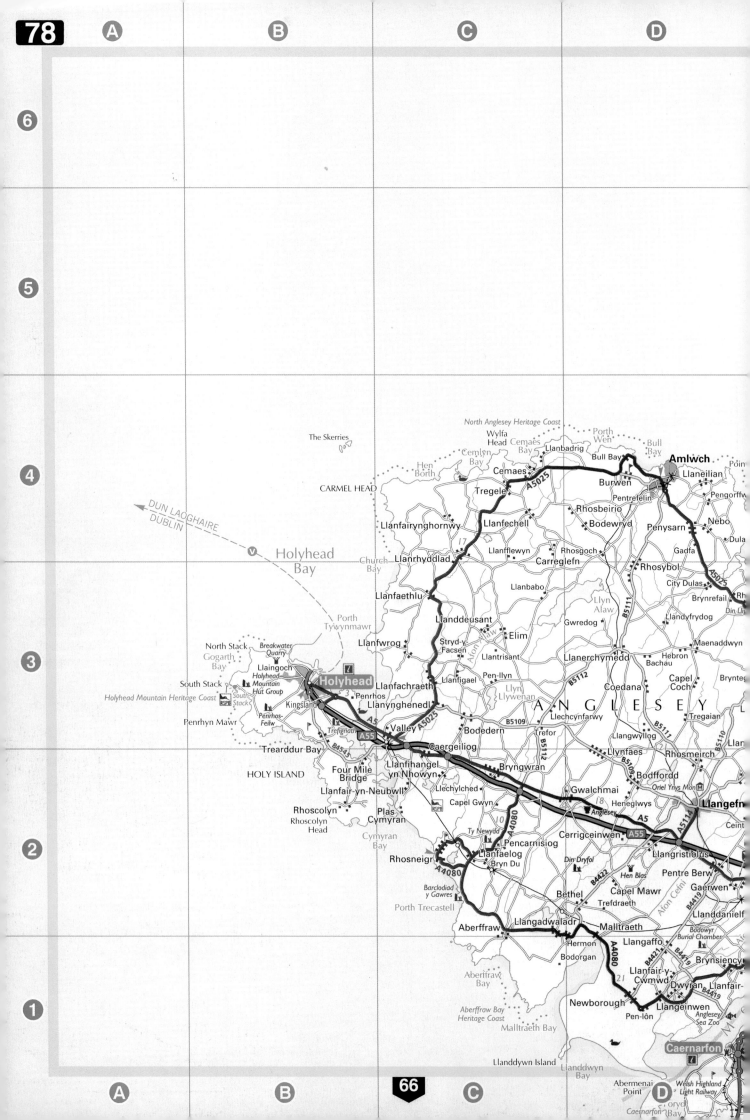

A   B   C   D

6

5

4

The Skerries

North Anglesey Heritage Coast

Wylfa Head   Cemaes Bay   Llanbadrig   Porth Wen   Bull Bay

Hen Borth   Cemlyn Bay   Cemaes   Bull Bay   **Amlwch**   Poin

CARMEL HEAD   Tregele   A5025   Burwen   Llaneilian

Pentrefelin   Pengorffw

Llanfairynghornwy   Llanfechell   Rhosbeirio   Pengorffw

Church Bay   Bodewryd   Penysarn   Nebo   Dula

Llanrhyddlad   Llanflewyn   Rhosgoch   Gadfa

DUN LAOGHAIRE DUBLIN   Carreglefn   Rhosybol   Gadfa

Holyhead Bay   Llanbabo   City Dulas   A5025

Llanfaethlu   Llyn Alaw   Brynrefail   Rh

Din Lli

Llandyfrydog

Llanddeusant   Gwredog

Stryd-y-Facsen   Elim   Maenaddwyn

Porth Tywynmawr   Afon Alaw   Llanerchymedd   Hebron   Bachau

North Stack   Breakwater Quarry   Llantrisant   Pen-llyn   Coedana   Capel Coch   Bryntec

Gogarth Bay   Llanfwrog   Llanfigael   Llyn Llywenan   Llechcynfarwy   A N G L E S E Y   L

South Stack   Llaingoch   Holyhead Mountain Hut Group   **Holyhead**   Llanfachraeth   B5112   Coedana

Holyhead Mountain Heritage Coast   RSPB   South Stack   Kingsland   Penrhos   Valley   A5025   Bodedern   Trefor   Llangwyllog   Rhosmeirch   Llar

Penrhyn Mawr   Penrhos-Feilw   Trefignath   A5   Llanynghenedl   B5109   Llynfaes   B5109   Bodffordd

Trearddur Bay   A55   Caergeiliog   Bryngwran   Oriel Ynys Mon   Llangefni

HOLY ISLAND   B4545   Four Mile Bridge   Llanfihangel yn Nhowyn   Llechylched   Gwalchmai   Anglesey   Heneglwys   A5   A5114   **Llangefn**

Llanfair-yn-Neubwll   Capel Gwyn   A4080   Cerrigceinwen   A55   Ceint

Rhoscolyn   Plas Cymyran   RSPB   Ty Newydd   Pencarnisiog   Din Dryfol   Llangristiolus   Pentre Berw

Rhoscolyn Head   Cymyran Bay   Rhosneigr   Llanfaelog   Bryn Du   Hen Blas   Capel Mawr   Gaerwen

Barclodiad y Gawres   A4080   Bethel   Trefdraeth   B4419   Llanddanielf

Porth Trecastell   Aberffraw   Llangadwaladr   Malltraeth   Bodowyr Burial Chamber

Aberffraw Bay   Hermon   A4080   Llangaffo   B4421   Brynsiencyn

Aberffraw Bay Heritage Coast   Bodorgan   Llanfair-y-Cwmwd   Dwyran   Llanfair-

Newborough   Llangeinwen   Anglesey Sea Zoo

Aberffraw Bay Heritage Coast   Pen-lôn

Malltraeth Bay   **Caernarfon**

Llanddwyn Island   Llanddwyn Bay   Abermenai Point   Welsh Highland Light Railway

3

2

1

A   B   C   D

6

5

4

-Dulas
Bay

3

Moelfre
Llanallgo
Marian-glas

GREAT ORMES HEAD

Great Orme
Heritage Coast

Little Ormes Head

Benllech

ygongl
drgoch   Red Wharf Bay
Red Wharf
Bay   Glan-
yr-afon   Penmon
Priory
Caim   Toll

Puffin Island

Black Point

Llandudno   Penrhyn Bay
Rhos-on-Sea

Conwy
Bay   Llanrhos
Penrhyn-
side

Llandrillo yn Rhos

Llanddona   Penmon   Deganwy   Pydew   Colwyn Bay

Pentraeth   Llangoed   Esgyryn
Mochdre   Old
Colwyn

Llanfaes

Gaol & Courthouse   Dwygyfylchi   Conwy   Llandudno   Llanelian-
yn-Rhos
Beaumaris   Penmaenmawr   Capelulo   Junction   Bryn-
y-Maen

Llansadwrn   Garizim   Penmaenan   Llansanffraid   Dolwen
Glan Conwy

Llandegfan   Henryd   2

Menai
Bridge   Bangor   Llanfairfechan   Nant-y-pandy   SNOWDONIA   Rowen   Bodnant NT   Trofarth   Dawn   yn-R

Anglesey
Column   Abergwyngregyn   Gorddinog   TAL-Y-FAN   610   Graig   Eglwysbach   River Elwy
Britannia   Afon Anafon   Ty'n-y-Groes   Tal-y-Cafn

Bridge   Penrhos   Llandygái   NATIONAL   Caerhun   Pentre'r   17

Plas Newydd   Tal-y-   Aber   Castell   Felin
NT   Glasinfryn   bont   MOEL   Waterfall   Llanbedr-y-Cennin

Capel-y-graig   Llanllechid   WINION   580   Tal-y-Bont   Llangernyw

Y Felinheli   Rhyd-y-   Rachub   PARK   Dolgarrog   16   Hafodunos
Pentir   groes   Gerlan   757   942   Pont Dolgarrog
Seion   Tregarth   Y DROSGL   FOEL-FRAS   Maenan

Llanddeiniolen   Sling   Bethesda   Afon Caseg   Llyn   Llanddoget   A548   Pandy
Rhiwlas   Waen-pentir   Ogwen Bank   Eigiau   Tudur
Mynydd   Trefriw Woollen Mill

Rhiwen   Llandygai   1062   Pentre-
Deiniolen   CARNEDD   Llanrhychwyn   Llanrwst   B5113

Llanrug   Clwt-y-bont   Gallt-y-foel   LLEWELYN   Trefriw   wytherin
Pont-rug   1044   923   Llyn   Gwydir   B5384
Caeathro   Cwm-y-glo   Brynrefail   CARNEDD   Cowlyd   Llyn
Ceunant   Llyn Padarn   DAFYDD   Crafnant   Llyn

E   F   67   G   Geirionydd

Dinorwic   ELIDIR   Pont Per   Llyn Ogwen
Groeslon   Welsh Slate   FAWR   y-benglog
wydd   Llanberis   Dolbadarn   946   0 1 2 3 4 5 miles
Electric Mountain   Y GARN   0 1 2 3 4 5 6 7 kilometres
Llyn Peris   917

6

5

79

LIVERPOOL
BAY

4

Hoylake

Hilbre Island

Middle Eye
Little Eye

West
Kirby

3

Point of Ayr

Prestatyn

Talacre

Gwespyr

Gronant

Ffynnongroyw

Rhyl

Llanasa

Picton

Rhewl-
fawr

Meliden

Gwaenysgor

Mostyn

Trelogan

Glan-y-don

Axton

Tre-
Mostyn

Buarth-draw

Kinmel
Bay

Abergele Roads

Kinmel Bay

Berthengam

Green

Penrhyn Bay

Towyn

Walwen

Whitford

Downing

Greenfield
Valley

Colwyn Bay

Pensarn

Trelawnyd

Basingwe

Dyserth

Llandrillo-yn-Rhos

Old
Colwyn

Llanddulas

Rhyd-
y-foel

Abergele

St George

Rhuddlan

Cwm

Walwen

Lloc

Gorsedd

Carmel

Holway

Wal

Mochdre

Pengwern

Bodelwyddan

Rhuallt

Pen-y-cefn

Pantasaph

St. Winefride's
Well

Holywell

Llandudno
Junction

79

Llanelian-
yn-Rhos

Bryn-y-Maen

Llysfaen

Bodelwyddan

St Asaph

Calcot

Milwr

Dolwen

Glascoed

Tremeirchion

Caerwys

Brynford

Dolphin

2

Craig

Trofarth

Dawn

Betws-
yn-Rhos

Groesffordd
Marli

Graig

Sodom

Afon-wen

Ysceifiog

Babell

Mynydd-
llan

Lixwm

Rhes-y-cae

Pentre
Halkyn

Ha

Pentre Isaf

Bodfari

Pen-y-felin

Nannerch

Catch

Llanfair
Talhaiarn

Llannefydd

Trefnant

Wern-y-gaer

Hendre

Rhydymwyn

River Elwy

Cefn
Berain

Green

Llangwyfan

Llyn-y-pandy

1

Hafodunos

Llangernyw

Henllan

Fron

Waen

Kilford

Brook
House

Cilcain

Gelli

Llandyrnog

Fford-las

Pant-y-mwyn

Llansannan

Denbigh

Llwyn

Gellifor

Cadole

Tan-y-fron

Rhydgaled

Groes

Pentre
Llanrhaeadr

Prion

Llanynys

Llangynhafal

Loggerheads

MOEL
FAMAU

Tafarn-y-
Gelyn

Gwer

idoget

A548

Pandy
Tudur

Bylchau

Waen

Pentre

Rhos

Moel Famau

Hirwaen

Pentre-
tafarn-y-fedw

Gwytherin

Nantglyn

Pant

Rhewl

Llanbedr-

Maes

Melin-
y-coed

Pentre
Saron

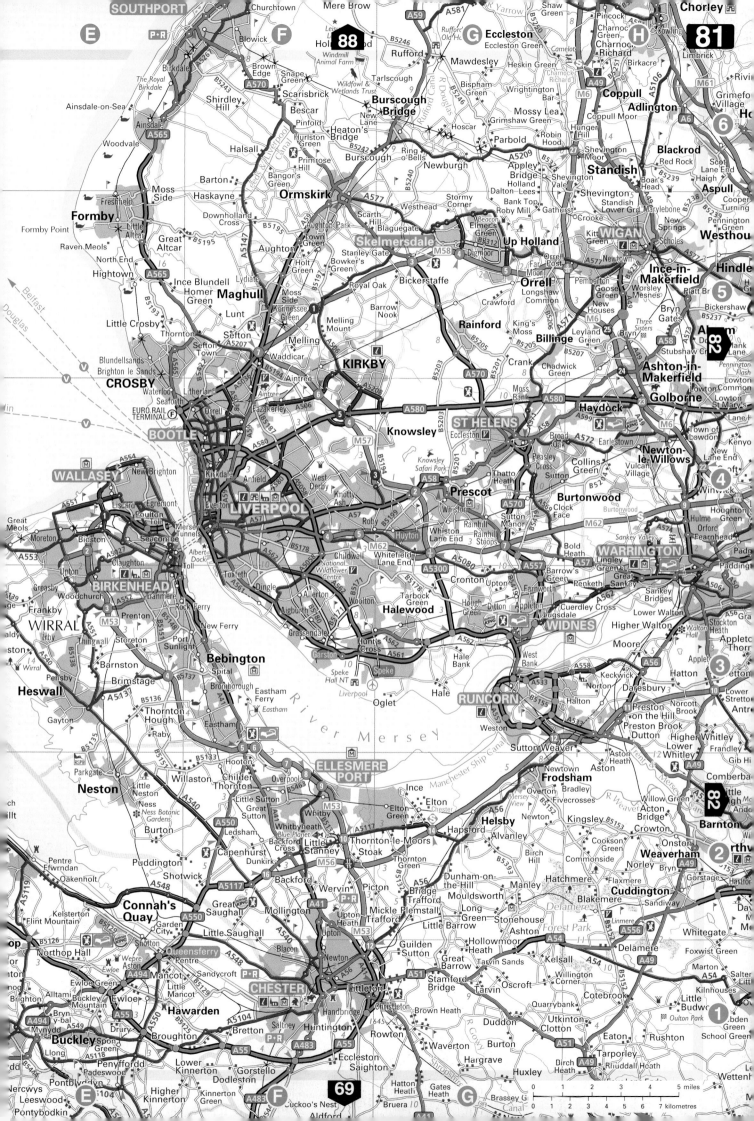

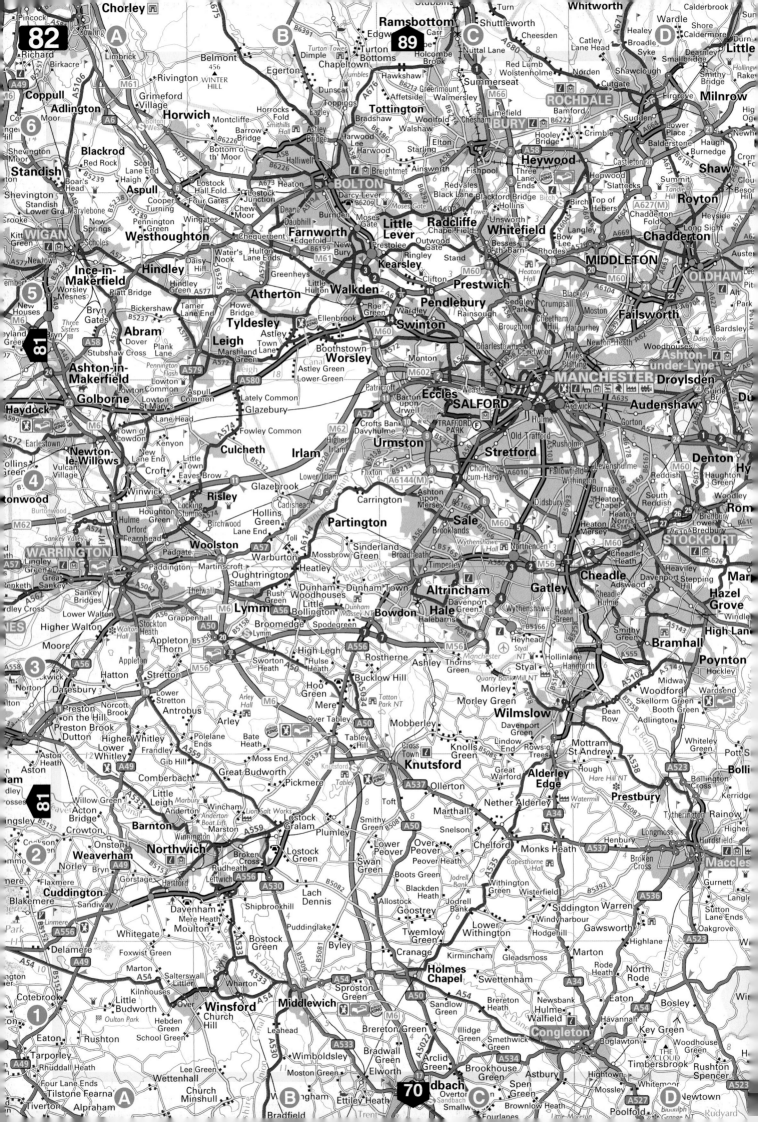

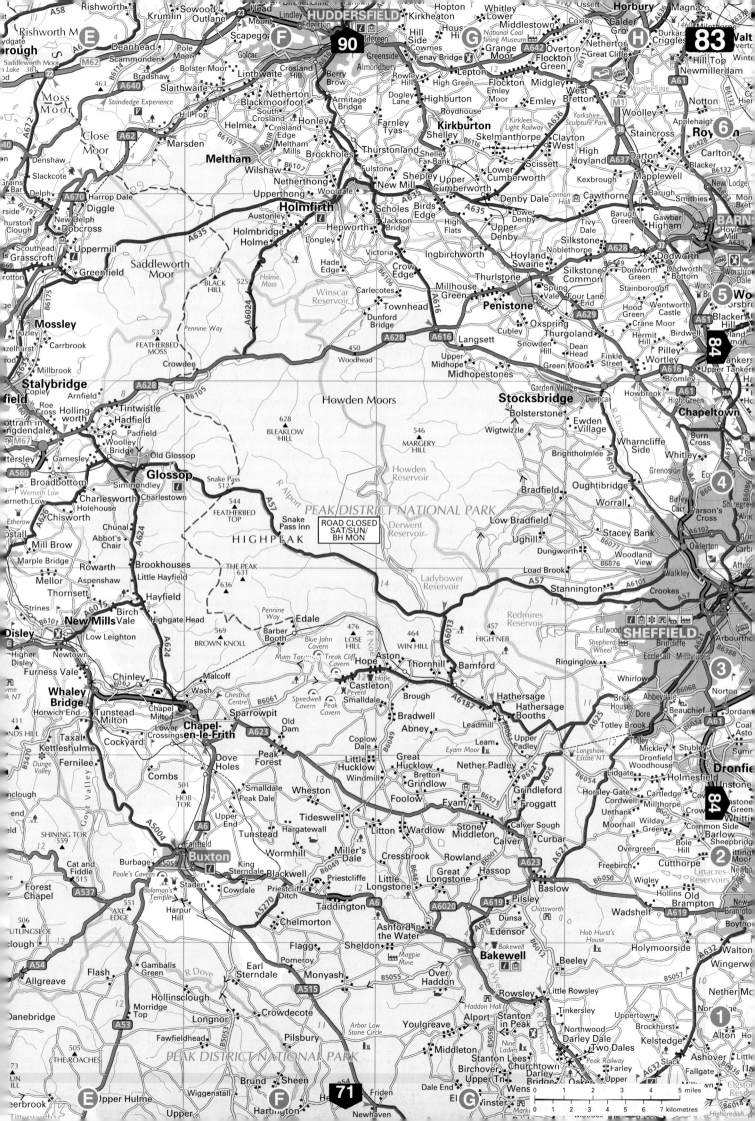

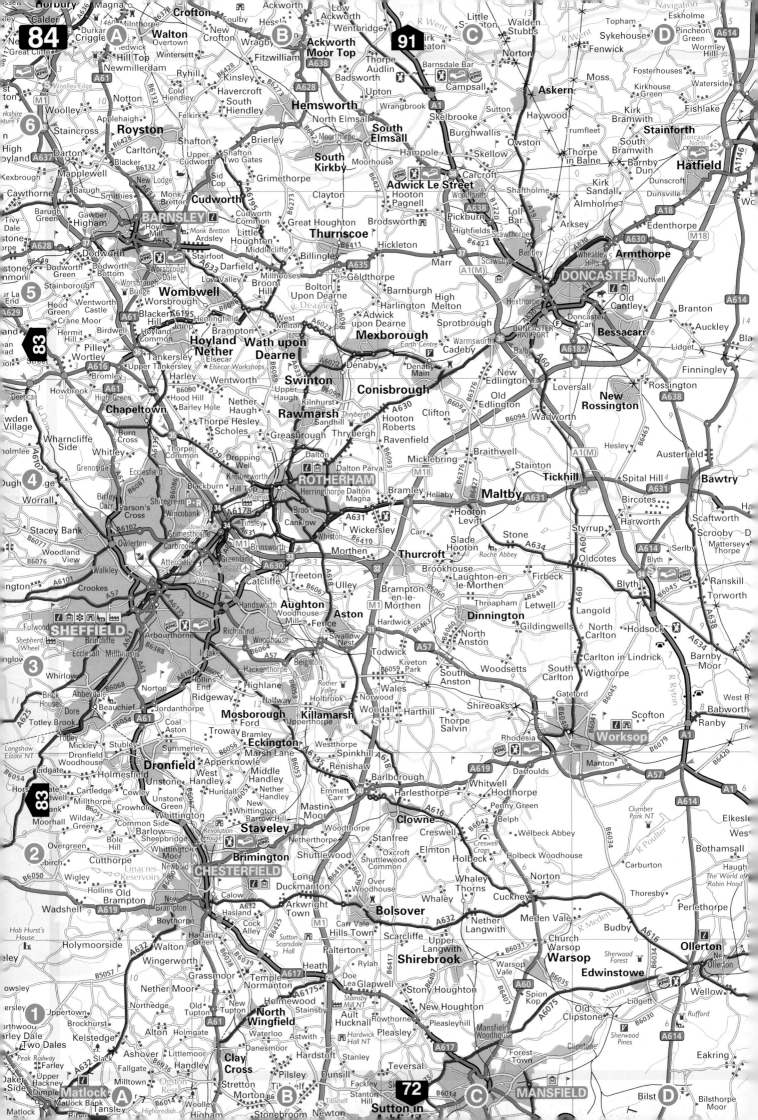

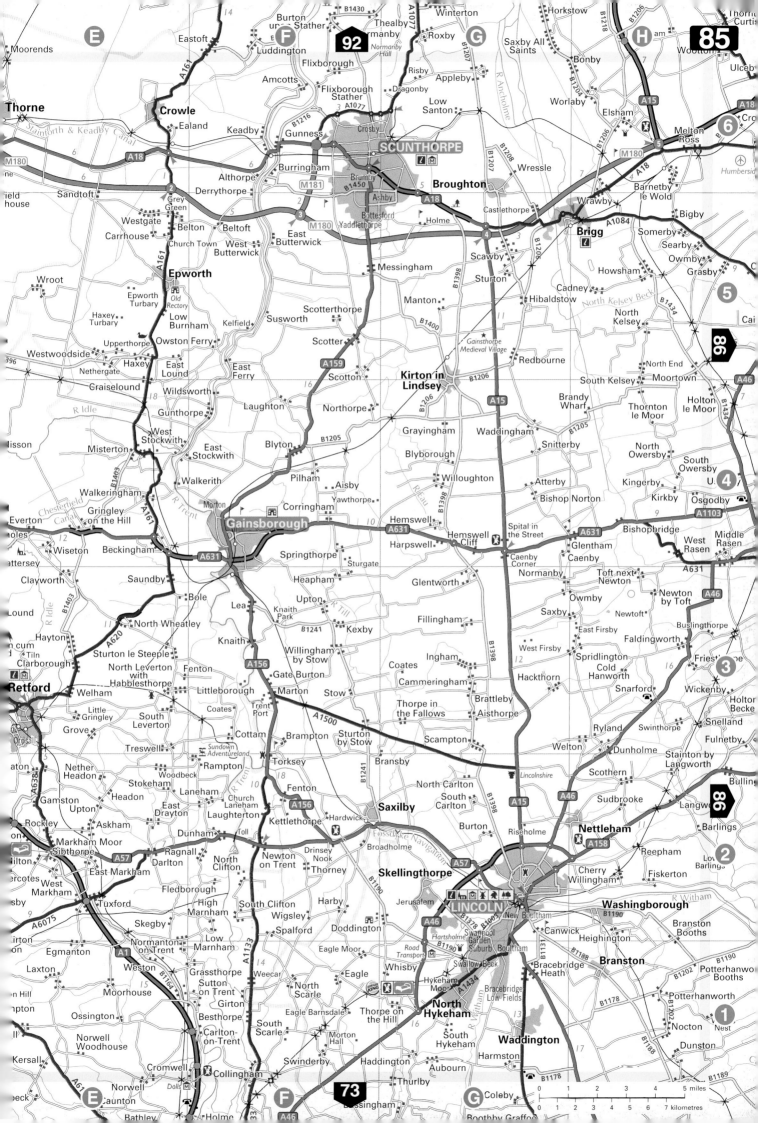

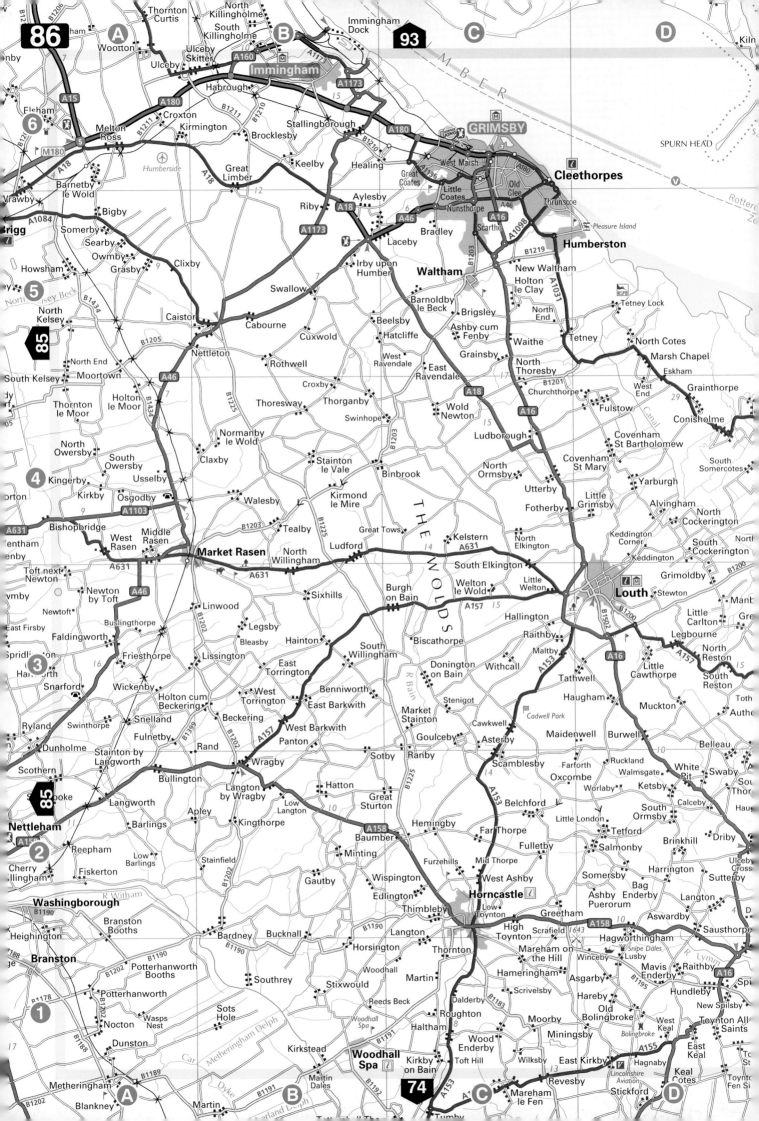

6

5

4

n Heritage Coast

n (Europoort)
rugge

North
Somercotes
A1031
Skidbrooke North End
ch
Saltfleet
brooke
Saltfleetby St Clement
Saltfleetby All Saints
Saltfleetby
St Peter
Theddlethorpe
St Helen
A1031
Theddlethorpe
All Saints
rlton
Great Eau
Mablethorpe
ayton le Marsh
A1104
Trusthorpe
Strubby
Thorpe
Sutton on Sea
Withern
Maltby
le Marsh
A52
Sandilands
B1373
A1111
Hagnaby
Beesby
Hannah
Saleby
Markby
Asserby
Thoresthorpe
Asserby
Turn
Ailby
Huttoft
Bilsby
Thurlby
Anderby Creek
Alford
B1449
Anderby
sby
B1196
Farlesthorpe
Mumby
Authorpe
Row
Chapel Point
Well
Cumberworth
Helsey
Mawthorpe
Bonthorpe
Chapel St Leonards
ceby
Hogsthorpe
Willoughby
Slackholme
End
Claxby
Sloothby
028
Skendleby
Hasthorpe
Fantasy Island
Grebby
Habertoft
Addlethorpe
Ingoldmells
y
Scremby
Welton le Marsh
A52
Ingoldmells
Point
Ashby by
Partney
Candlesby
Gunby
Orby
ton
Monksthorpe
Winthorpe
gate
Great
Steeping
Burgh le Marsh
Bratoft
A158
B1195
Irby in the Marsh
Skegness
nside
Firsby
Little
Steeping
Croft
Seacroft

3

2

1

Fendike
Corner
Thorpe St Peter
Wainfleet
Have

0 1 2 3 4 5 miles
0 1 2 3 4 5 6 7 kilometres

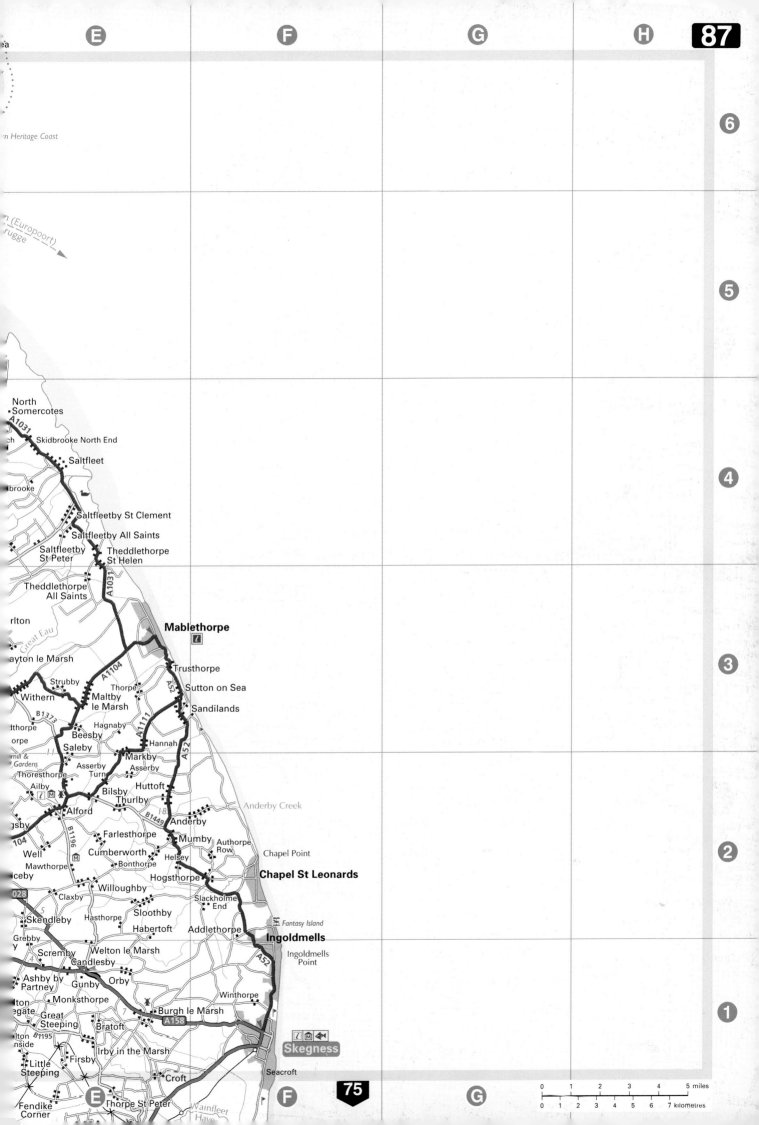

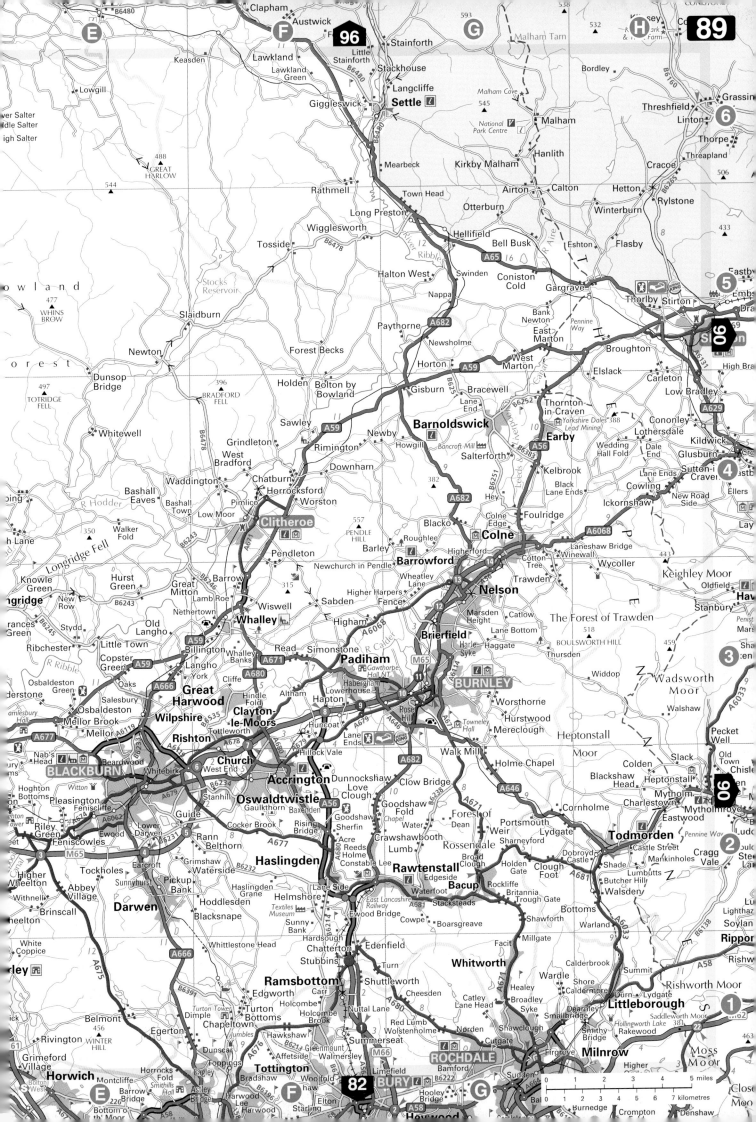

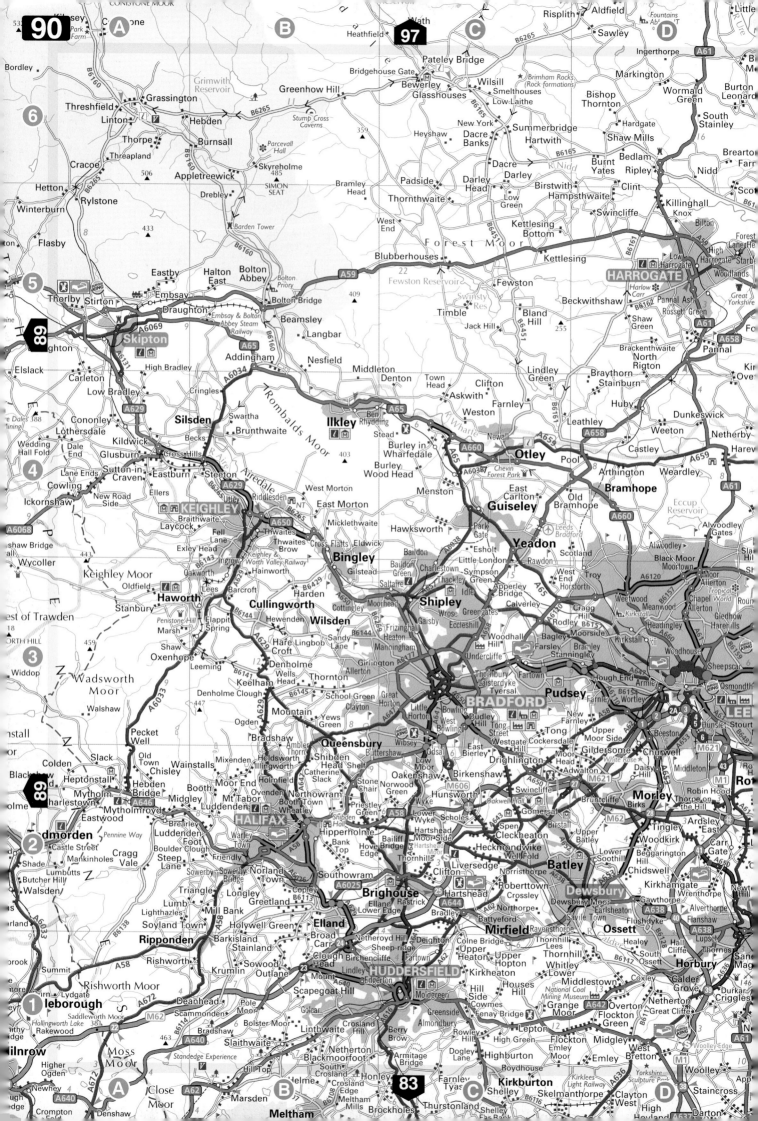

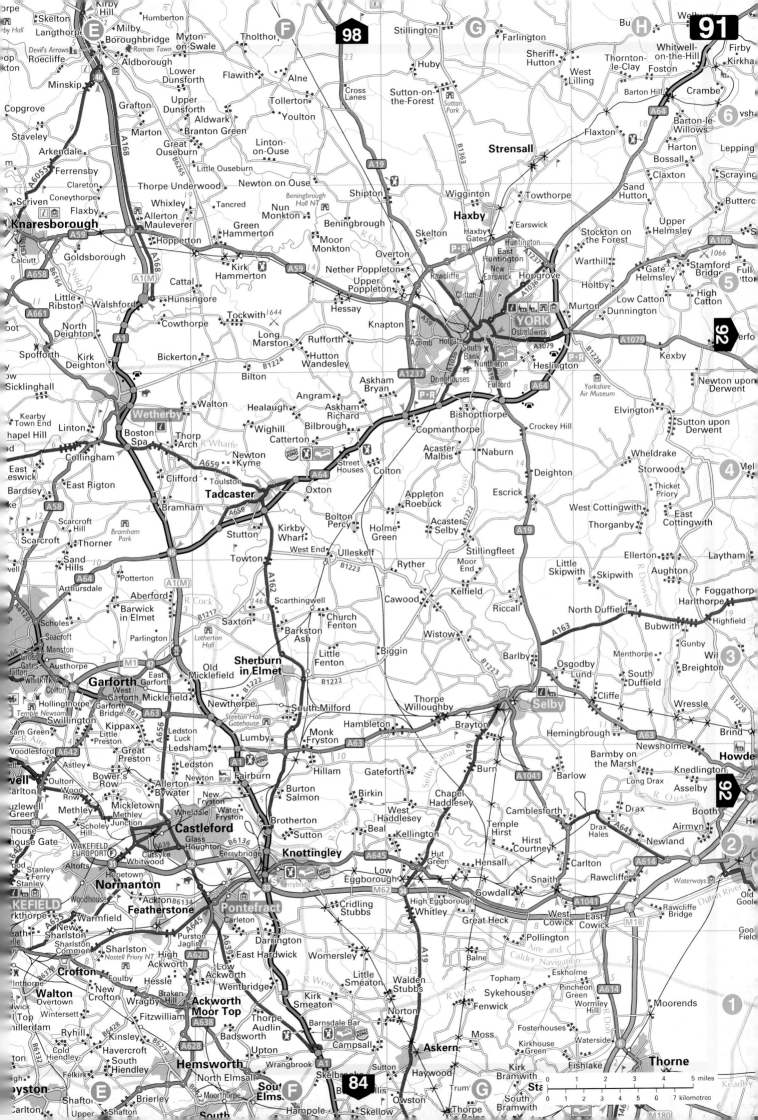

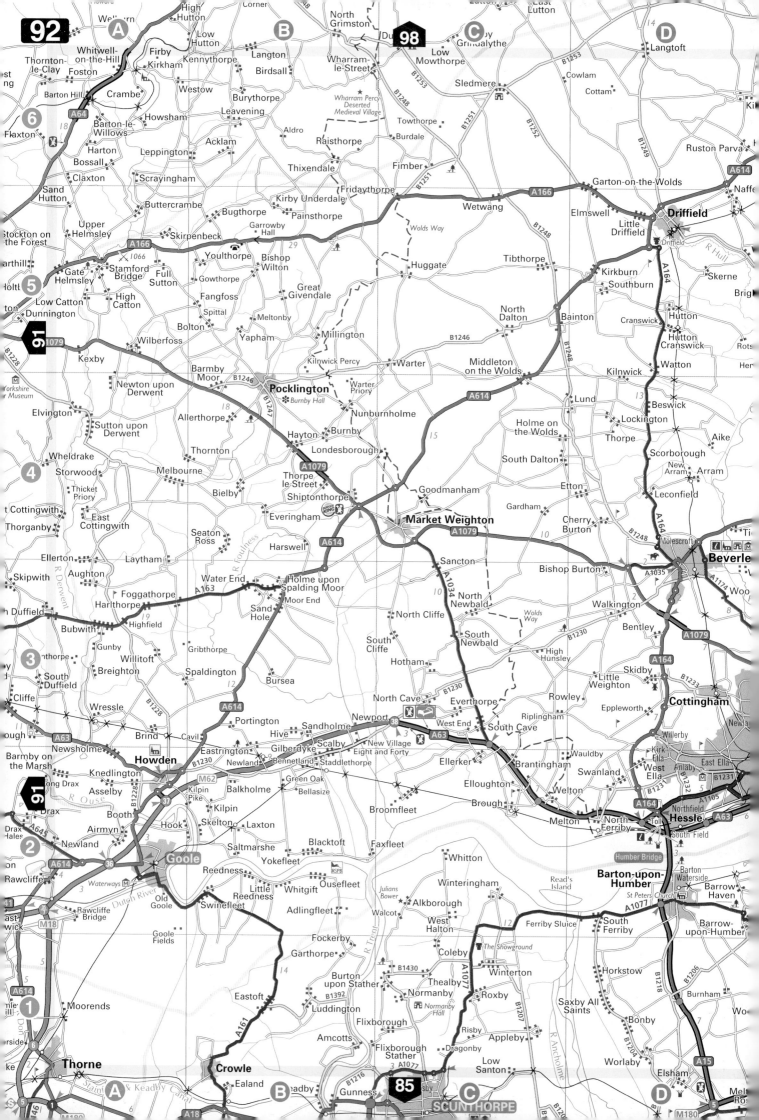

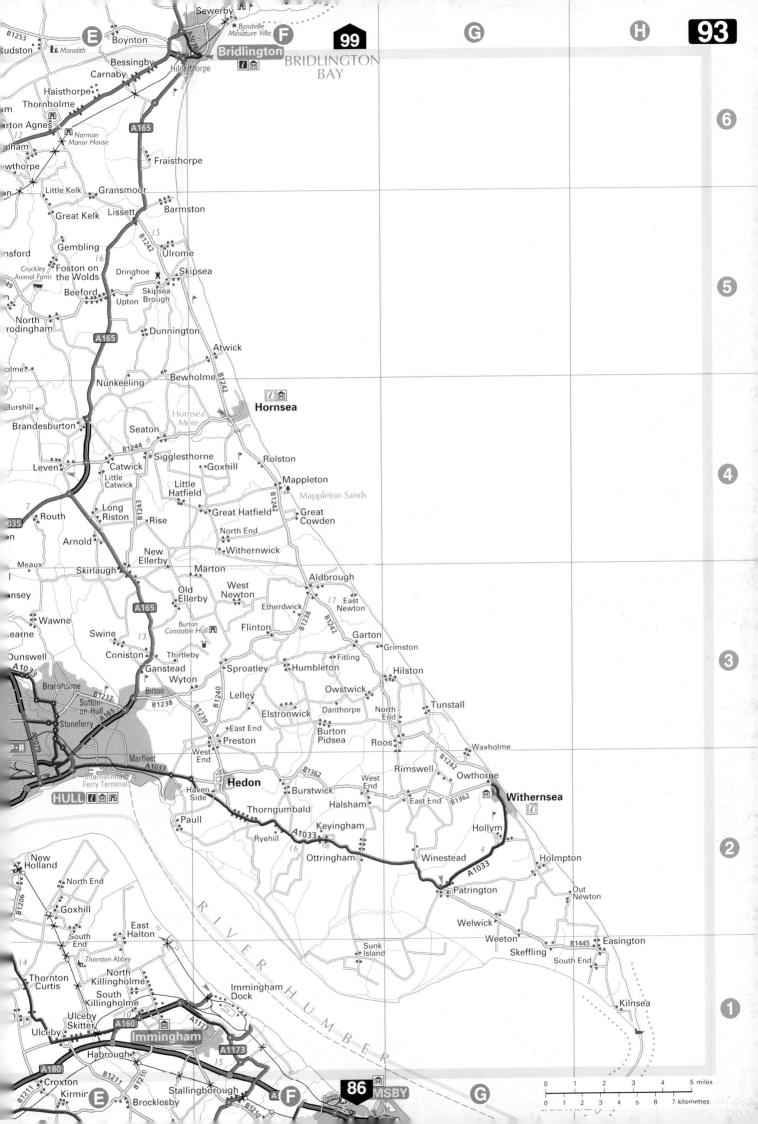

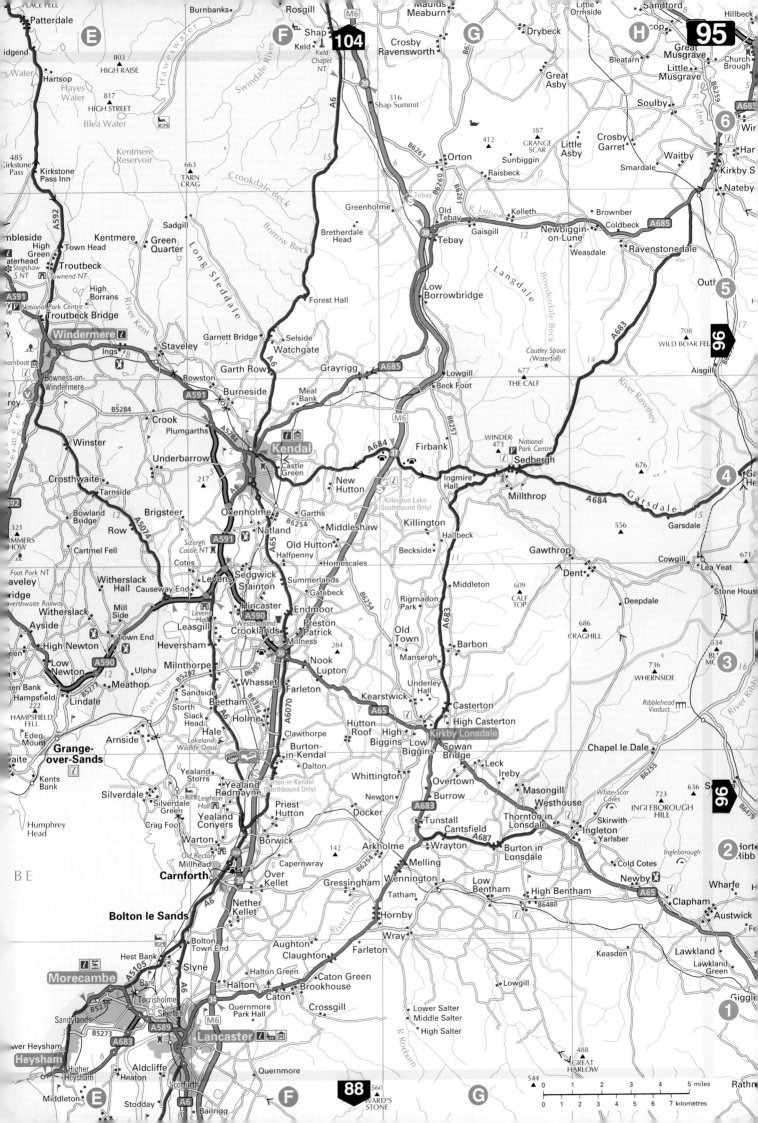

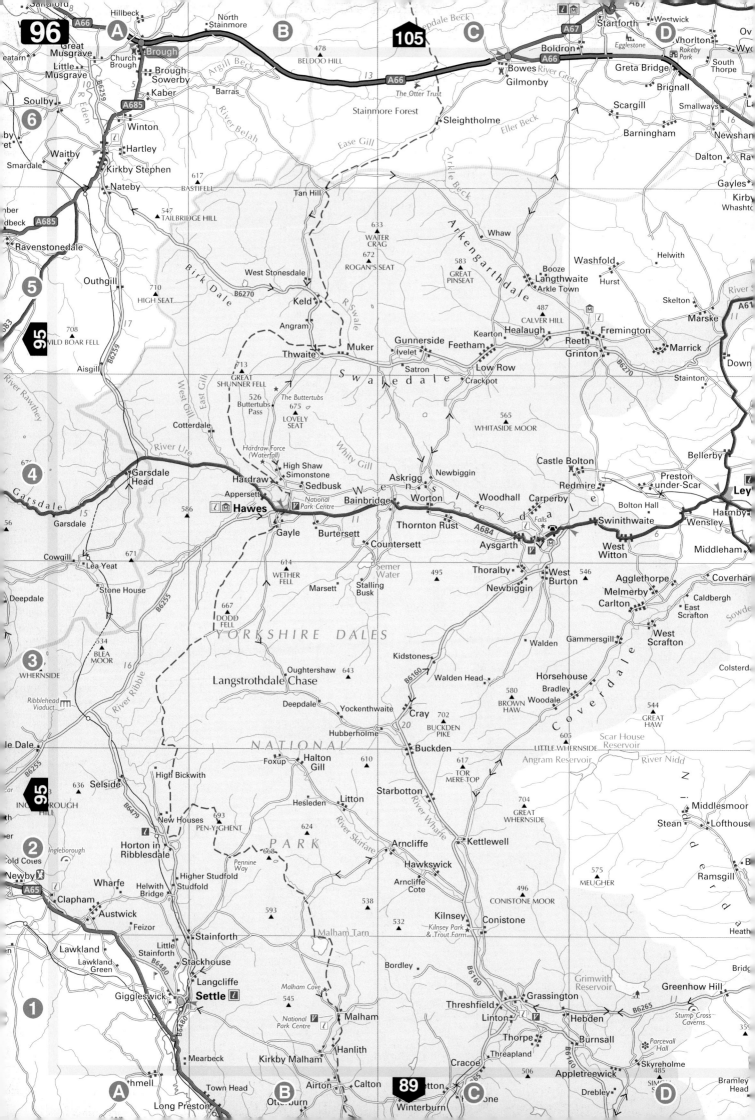

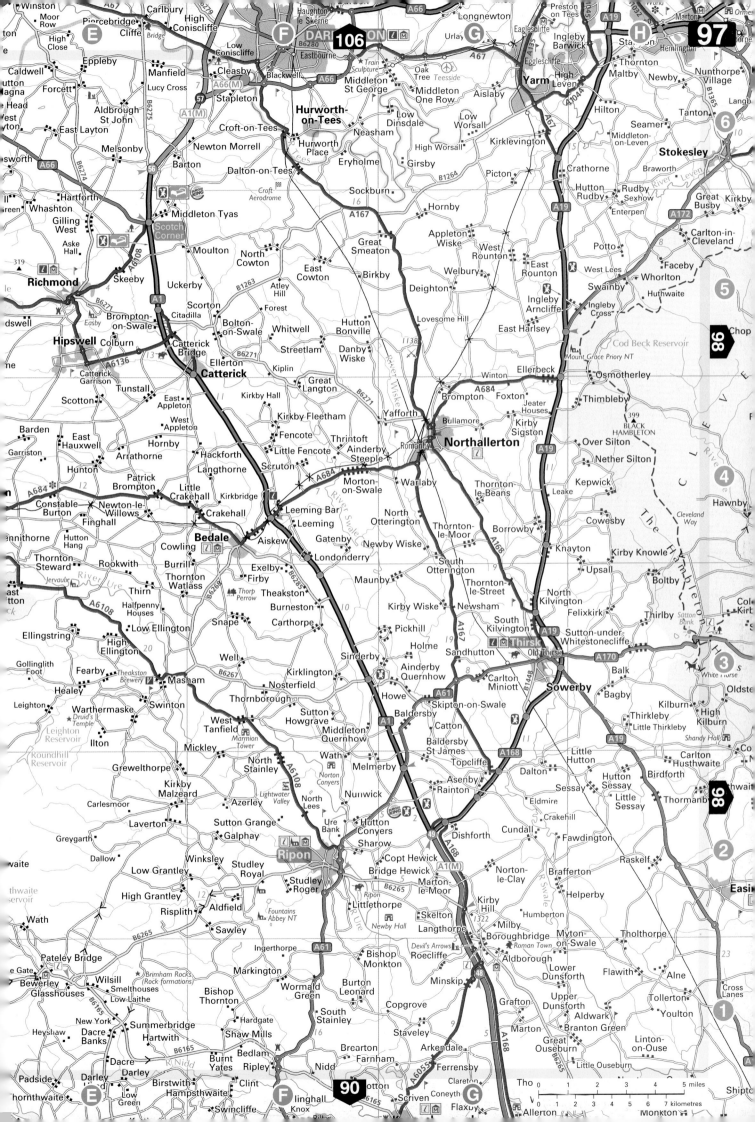

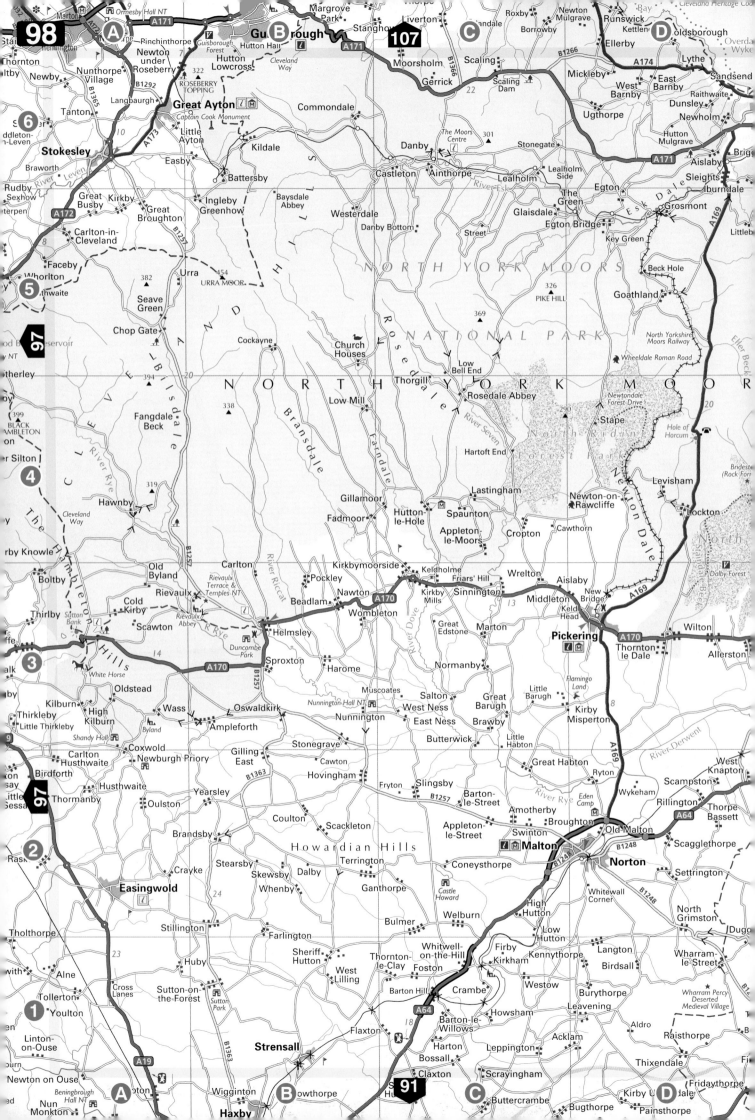

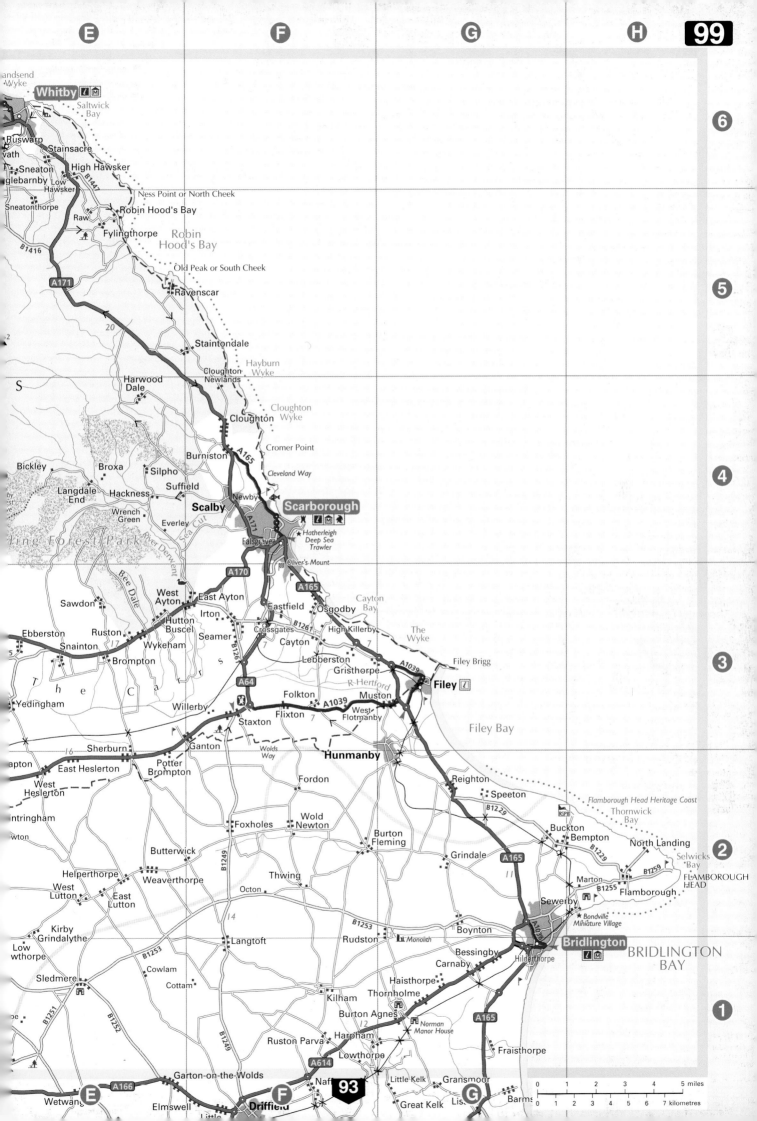

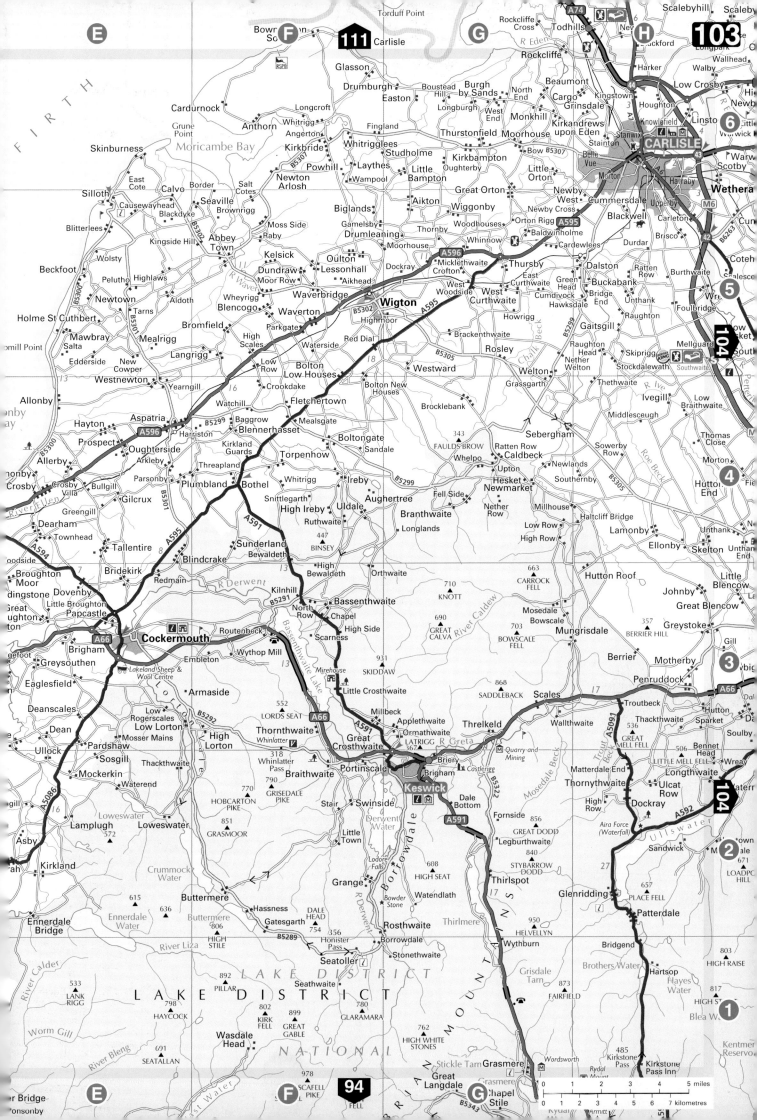

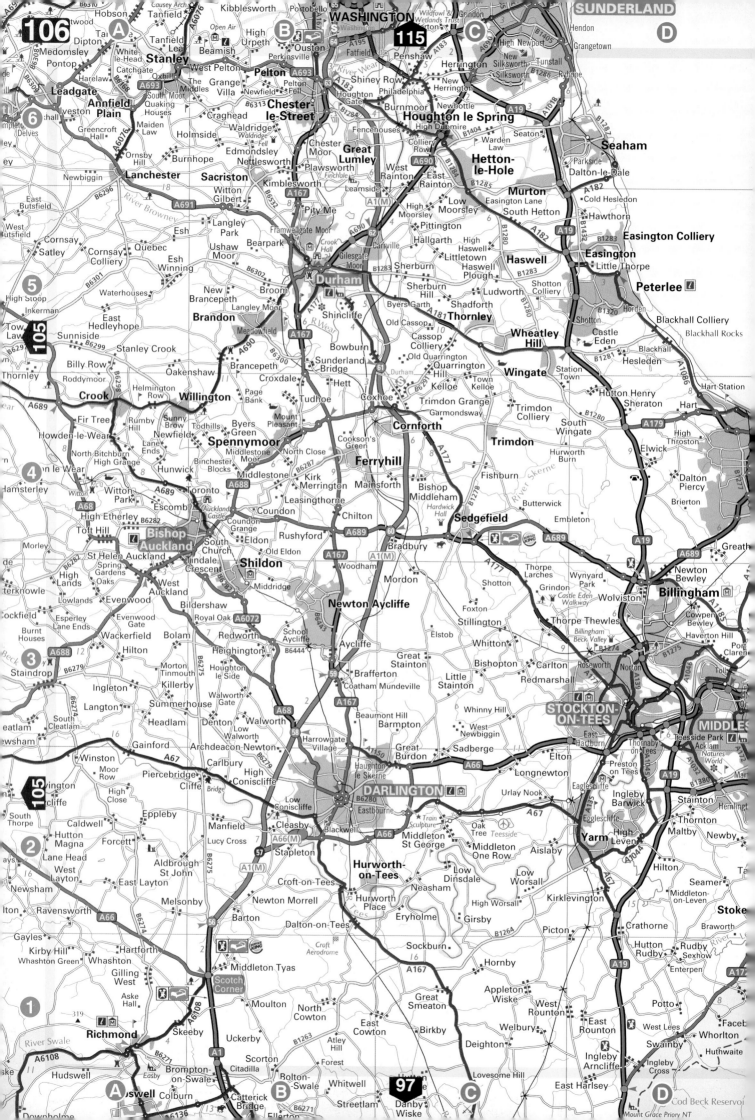

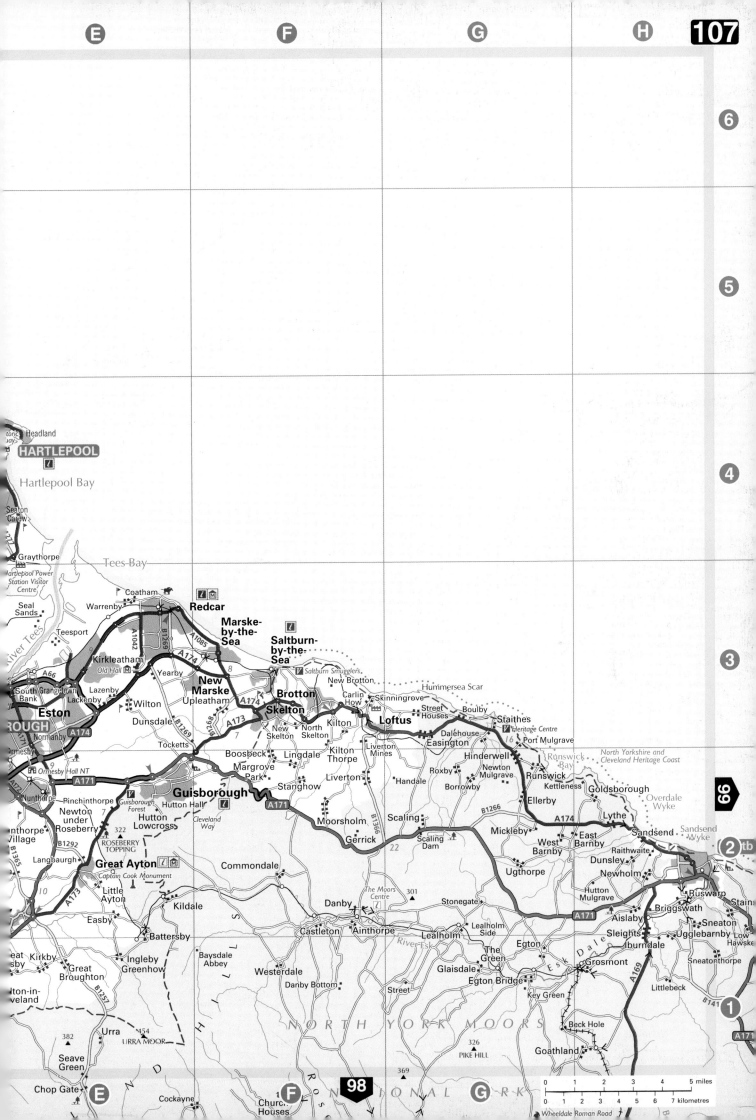

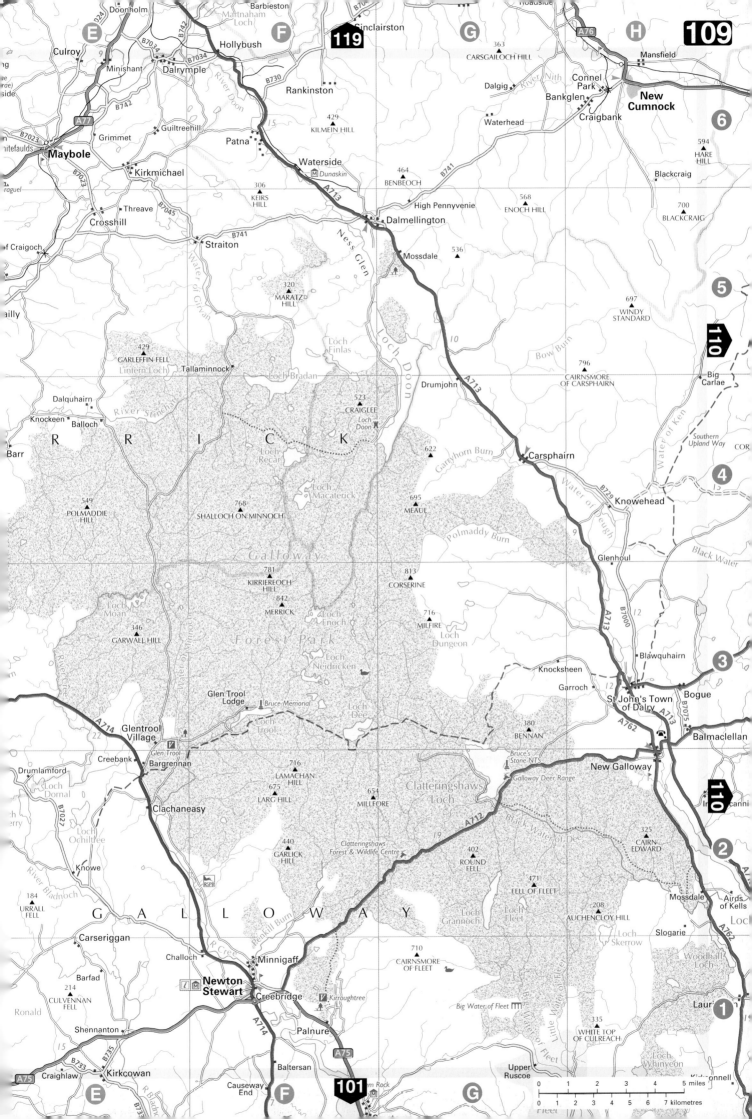

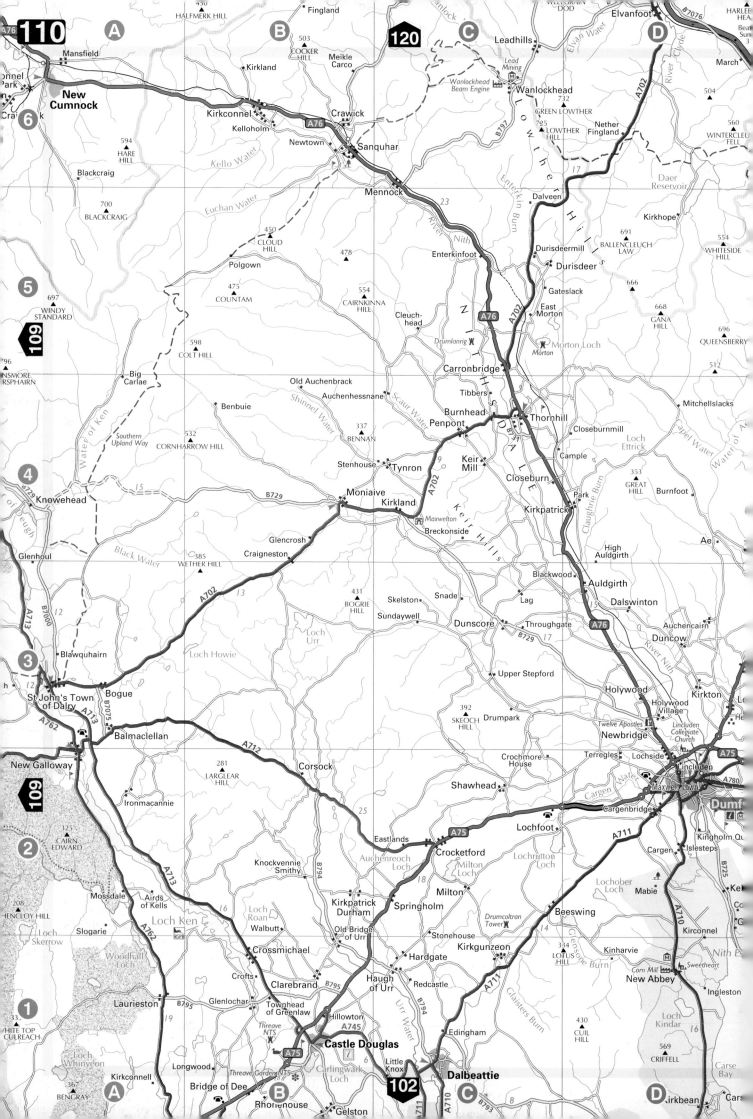

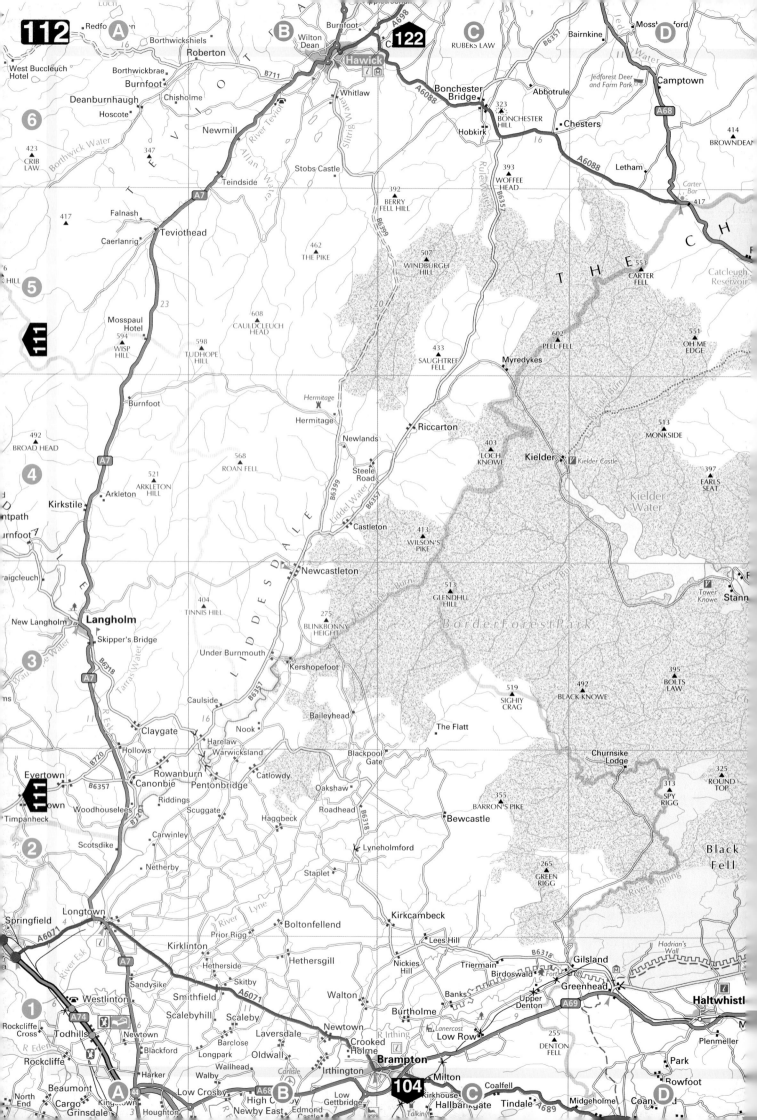

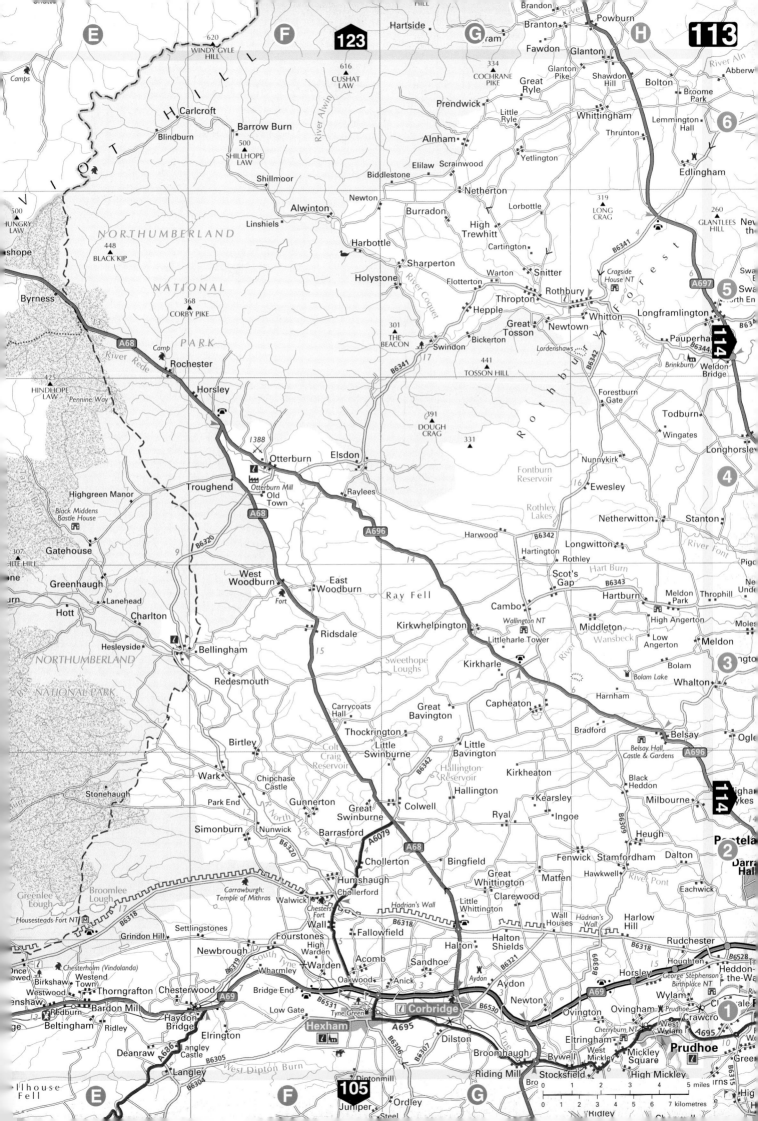

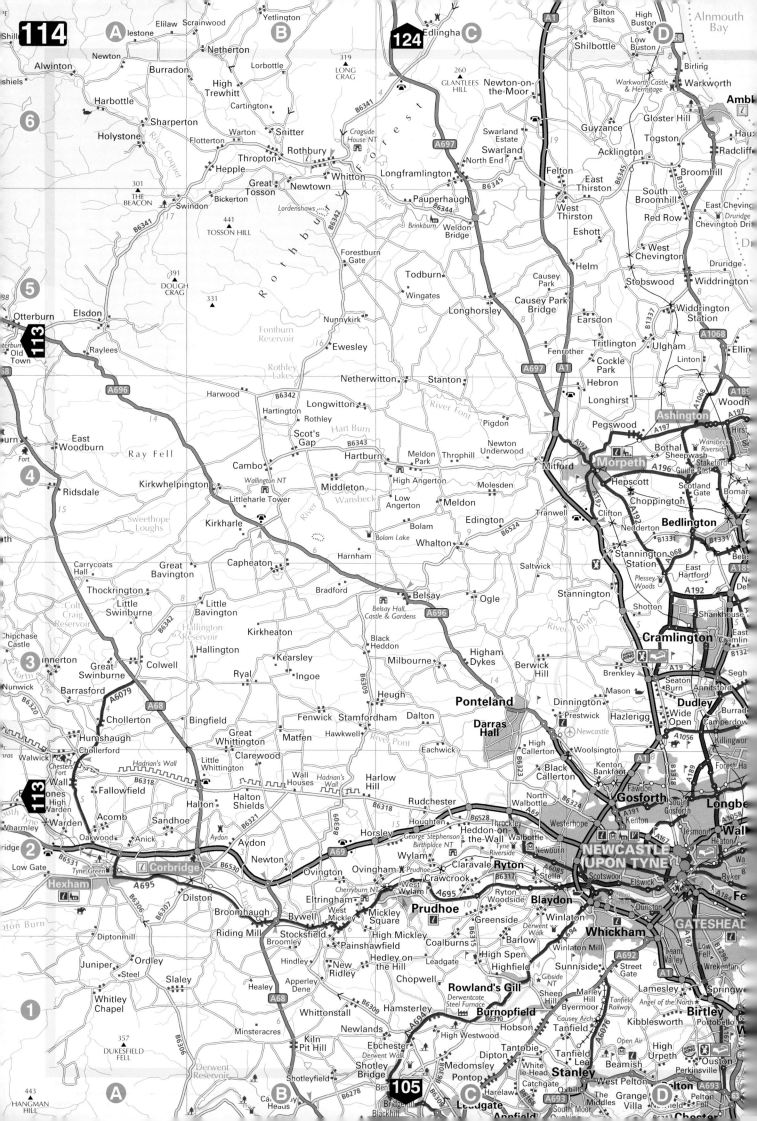

Coquet Island

th Northumberland
Heritage Coast

esswell

Lynemouth

Beacon Point

Woodhorn Demesne

Newbiggin-by-the-Sea

Seaton Colliery

Sleekburn

Cambois

North Blyth

Blyth

wsham

ew
artley

Seaton
Sluice

Seaton Hartley

**Seaton
Delaval**

Holywell

★ St Mary's Lighthouse

Earsdon

Backworth

Monkseaton

**Whitley
Bay**

Cullercoats

Shiremoor

Murton

Tynemouth

New
York

Stavanger

Haugesund

Bergen

Kristiansand

**North
Shields**

Göteborg

Rising
Sun

Willington
Quay

**SOUTH
SHIELDS**

Int. Ferry
Terminal

Toll

Tyne Tunnel

Westoe

Jarrow

Harton

Marsden
Bay

Hebburn

Monkton

Marsden

★ Souter Lighthouse NT

Cleadon

Souter Point

West
Boldon

Whitburn

ardley

Boldon
Colliery

Hamburg
(Summer Only)

Amsterdam

East
Boldon

Whitburn
Bay

Seaburn

Hylton

Southwick

Roker

Castletown

Monkwearmouth

South
Hylton

SUNDERLAND

1231

Wildfowl &
Wetlands Trust

Offerton

Grindon

Hendon

INGTON

Penshaw

High Newport

Grangetown

Penshaw

Herrington

New
Silksworth

Tunstall

ney Row

Silksworth

Rhyhope

Philadelphia

0 1 2 3 4 5 miles

0 1 2 3 4 5 6 7 kilometres

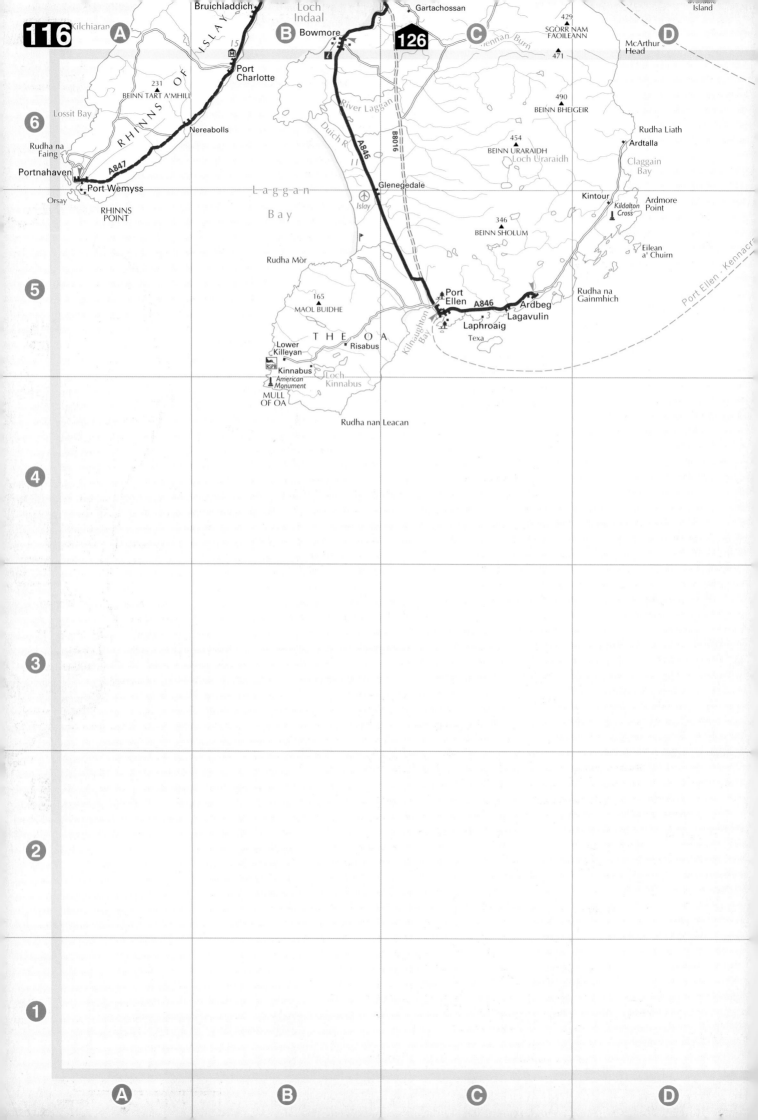

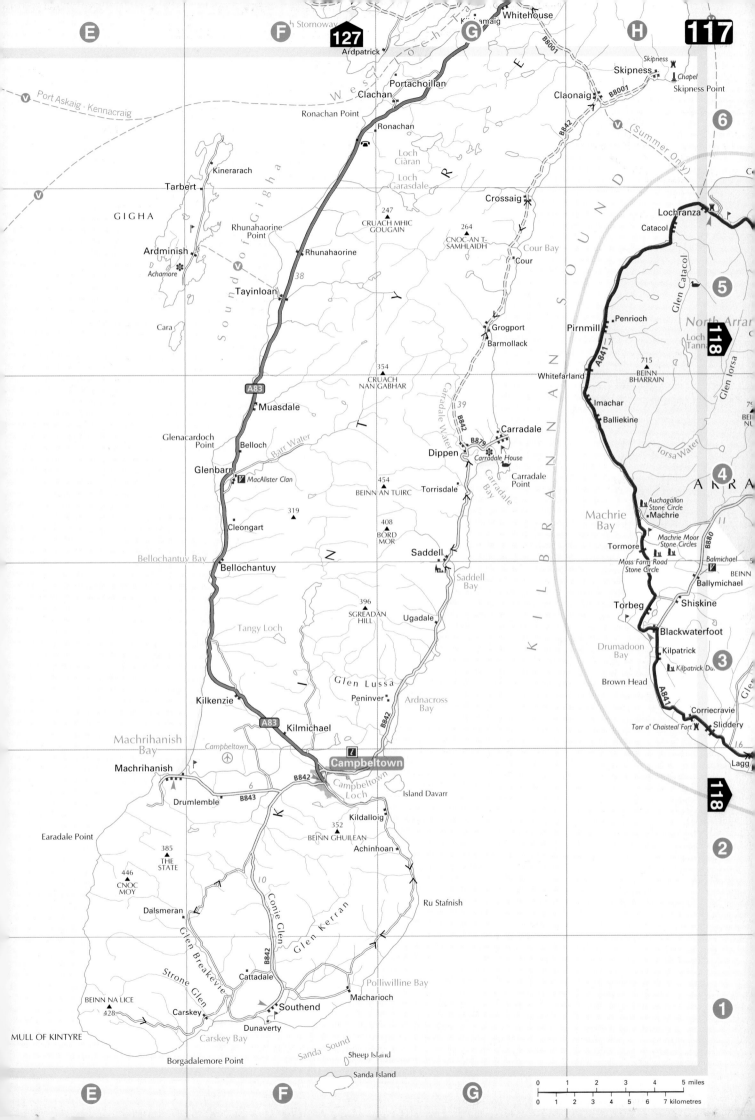

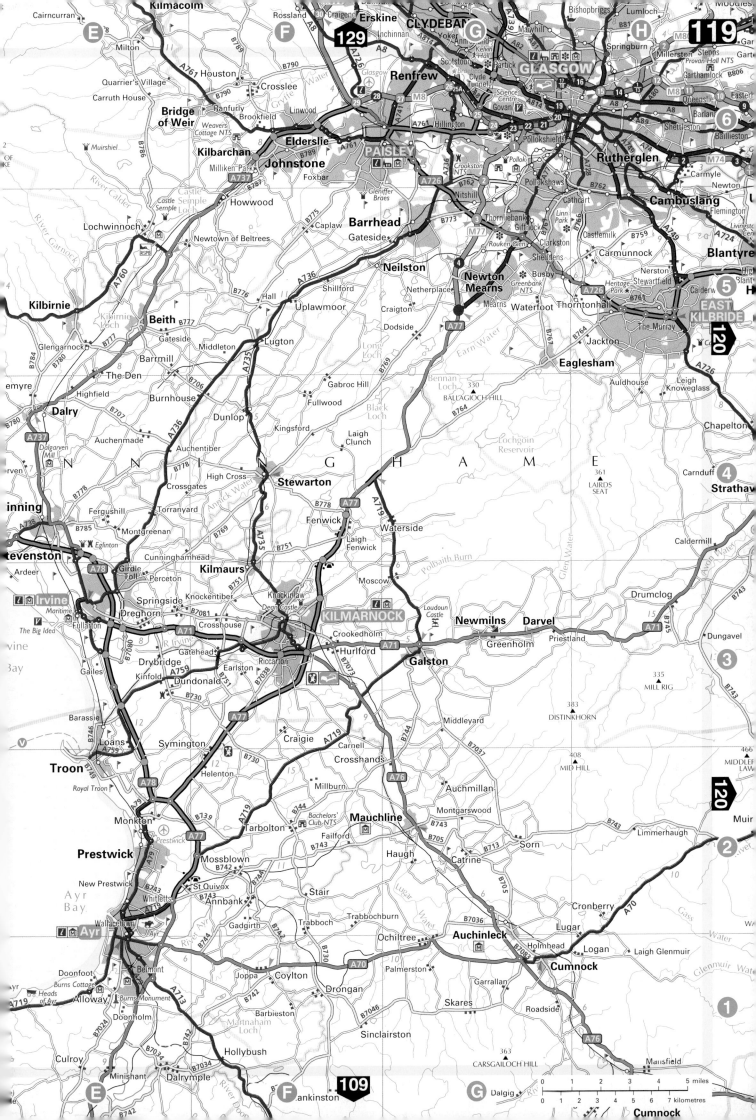

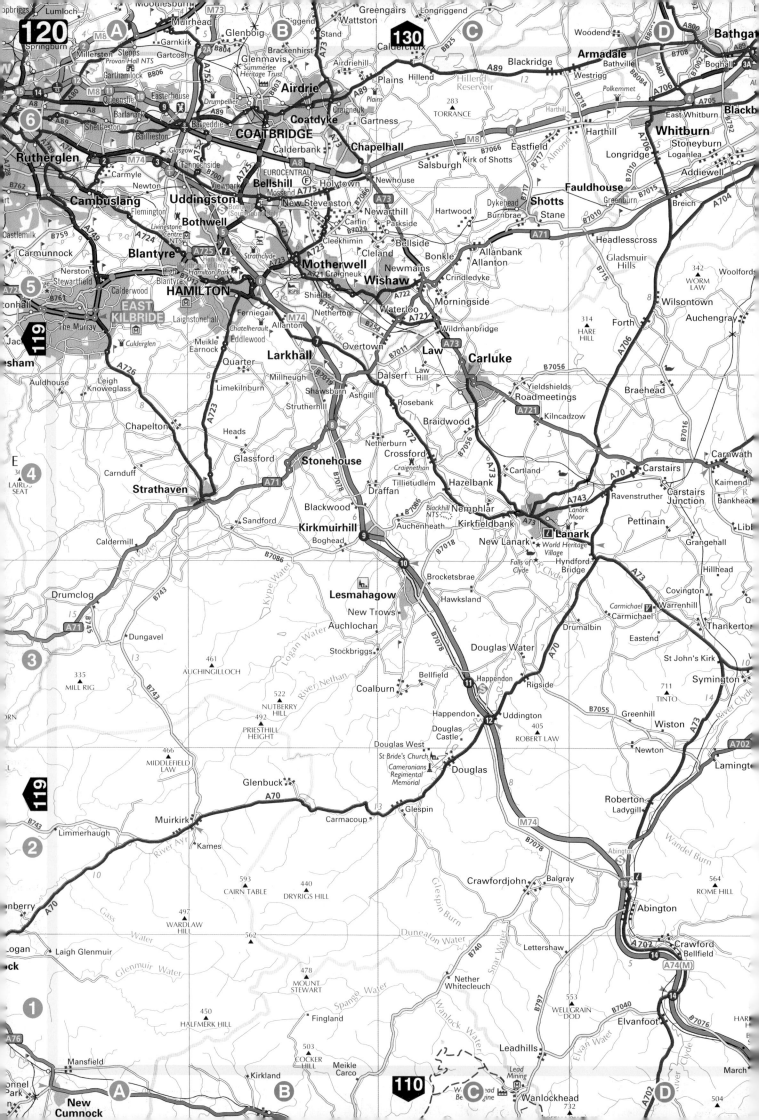

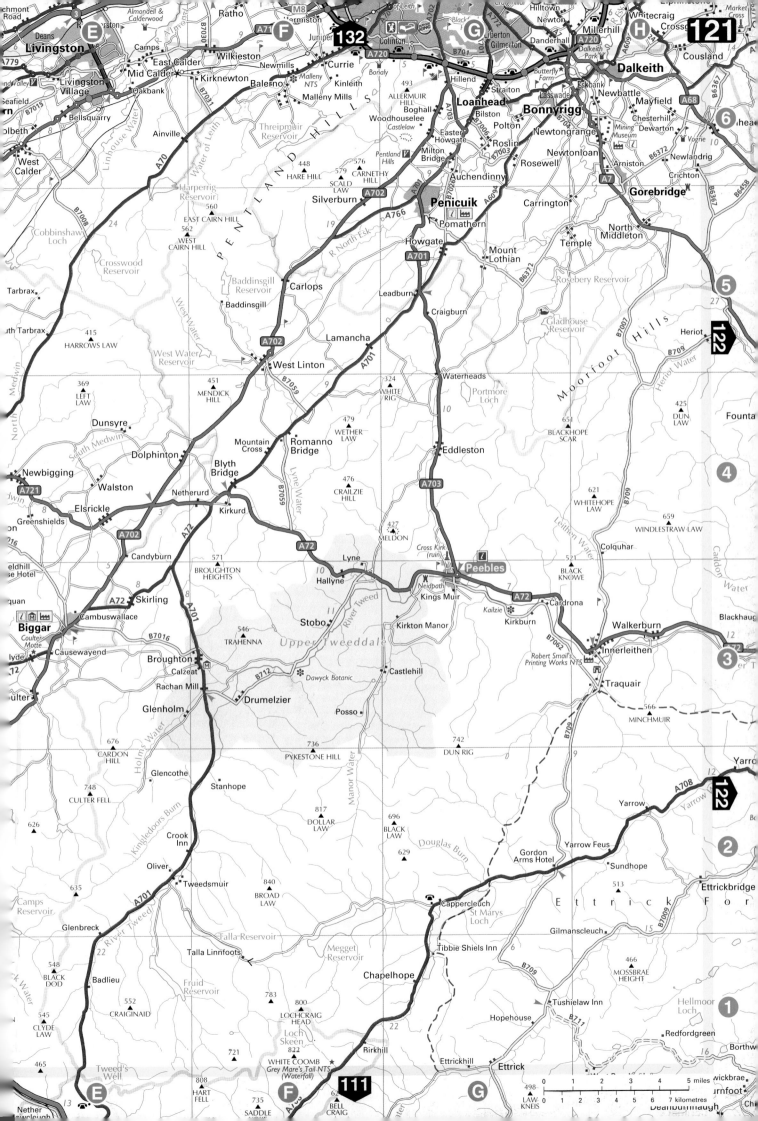

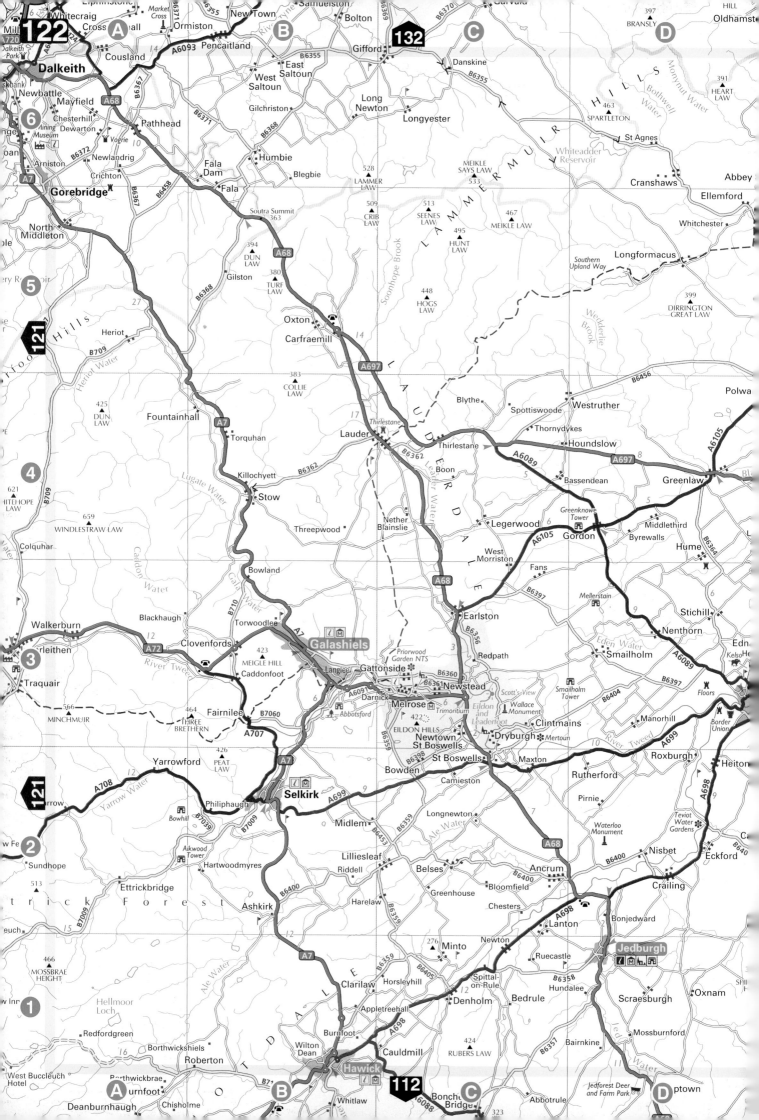

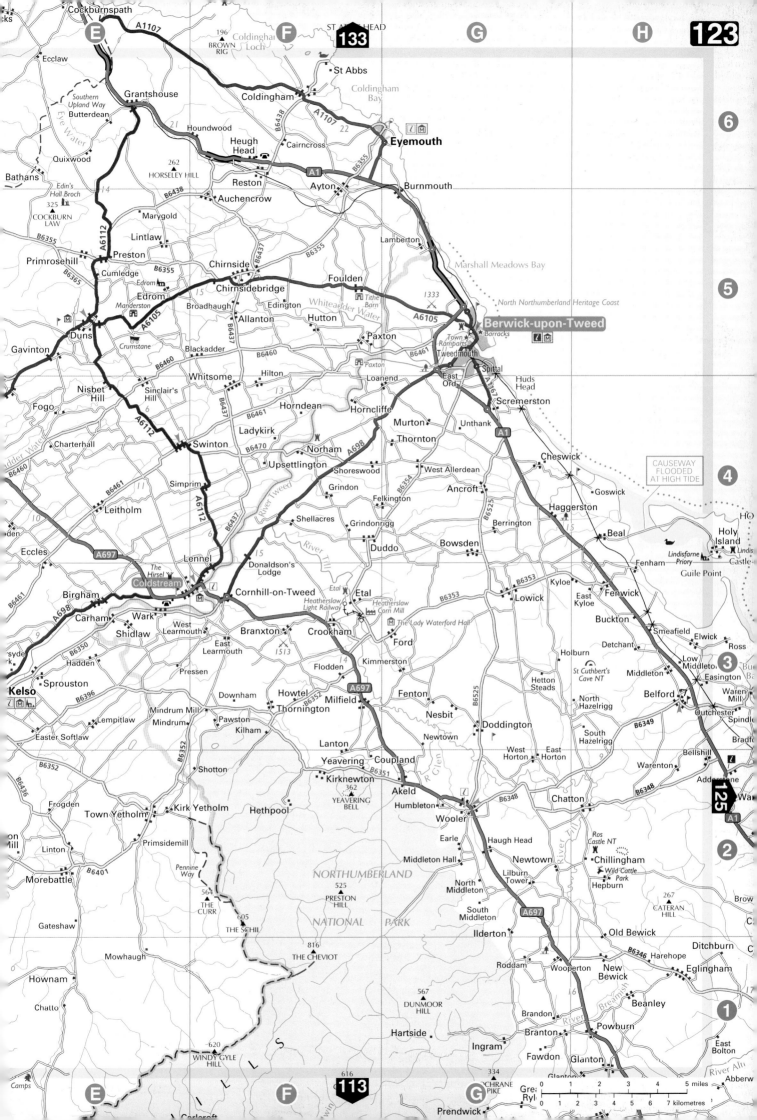

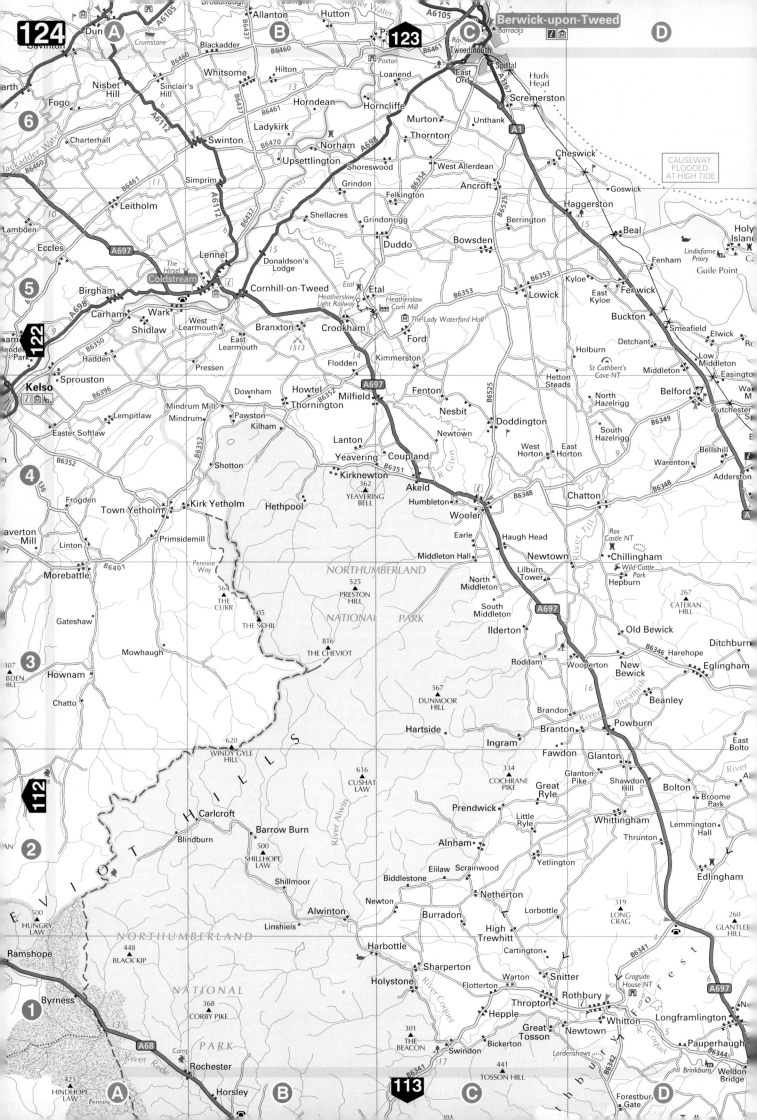

6

5

HOLY ISLAND

disfarne NT
e Point

FARNE
ISLANDS

Staple
Sound

North Northumberland
Heritage Coast

Inner
Sound

udle
Bay

Bamburgh

B1342

Budle Bamburgh

New
Glororum Shoreston

dlestone Burton

lford Elford North Sunderland

Seahouses

Lucker

Beadnell

renford Newham

Swinhoe

Beadnell
Bay

Chathill
Newstead Tughall

Ellingham

Preston

Newton-by-the-Sea

Preston
Pele Tower Brunton

Christon
Bank Embleton

wnieside Doxford

Embleton
Bay

North
Charlton Falloden

Dunstan
Steads Dunstanburgh
NT

South
Charlton

Dunstan Craster

Rock Stamford

Rennington

Howick
Hall Howick

Broxfield

Cullernose Point

Littlehoughton

Longhoughton

Denwick

Boulmer

vick

Alnwick

Seaton Point

Hawkhill Lesbury

Bilton Hipsburn

Bilton
Banks High
Buston

Alnmouth

Alnmouth
Bay

Shilbottle Low
Buston

A1068

8

Birling

wton-on-
he-Moor

Warkworth Castle
& Hermitage Warkworth

Amble

Coquet Island

Gloster Hill

arland
Estate Guyzance

Togston

Hauxley

adland
nd Acklington

Radcliffe

Felton

East
Thirston

Broomhill

West
Thirston

South
Broomhill Red Row

East Chevington

Druridge Bay

Eshott

Chevington Drift

West
Chevington

Druridge
B

Helm Druridge

4

3

2

1

0 1 2 3 4 5 miles
0 1 2 3 4 5 6 7 kilometres

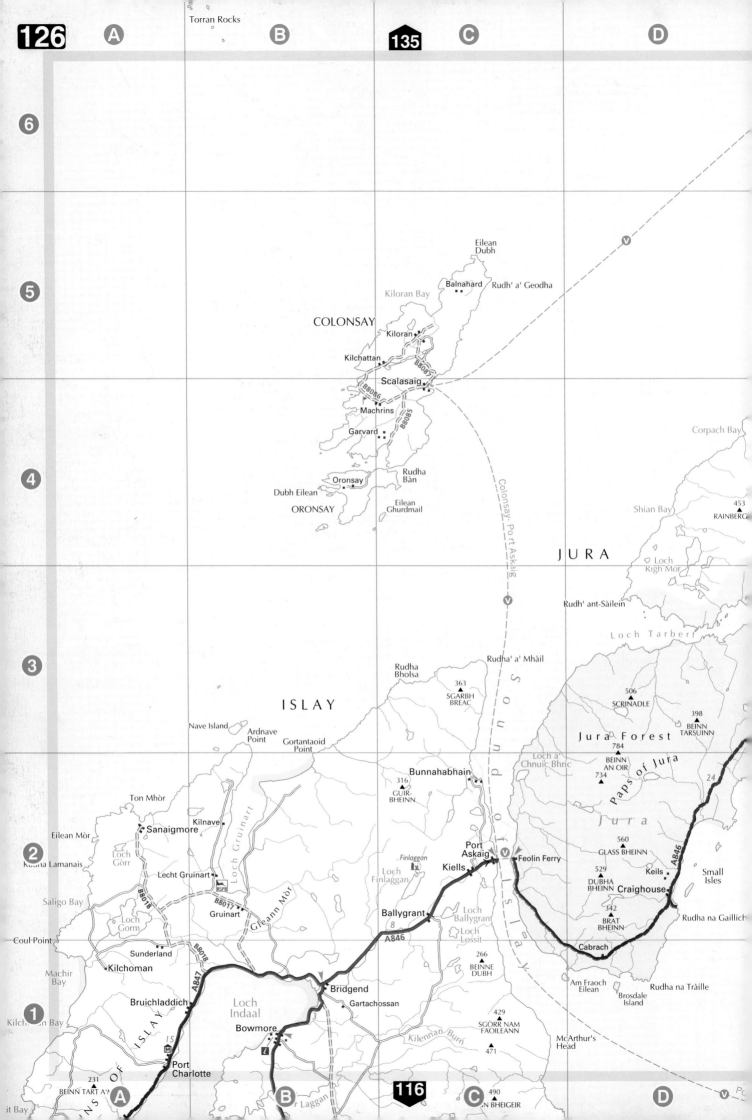

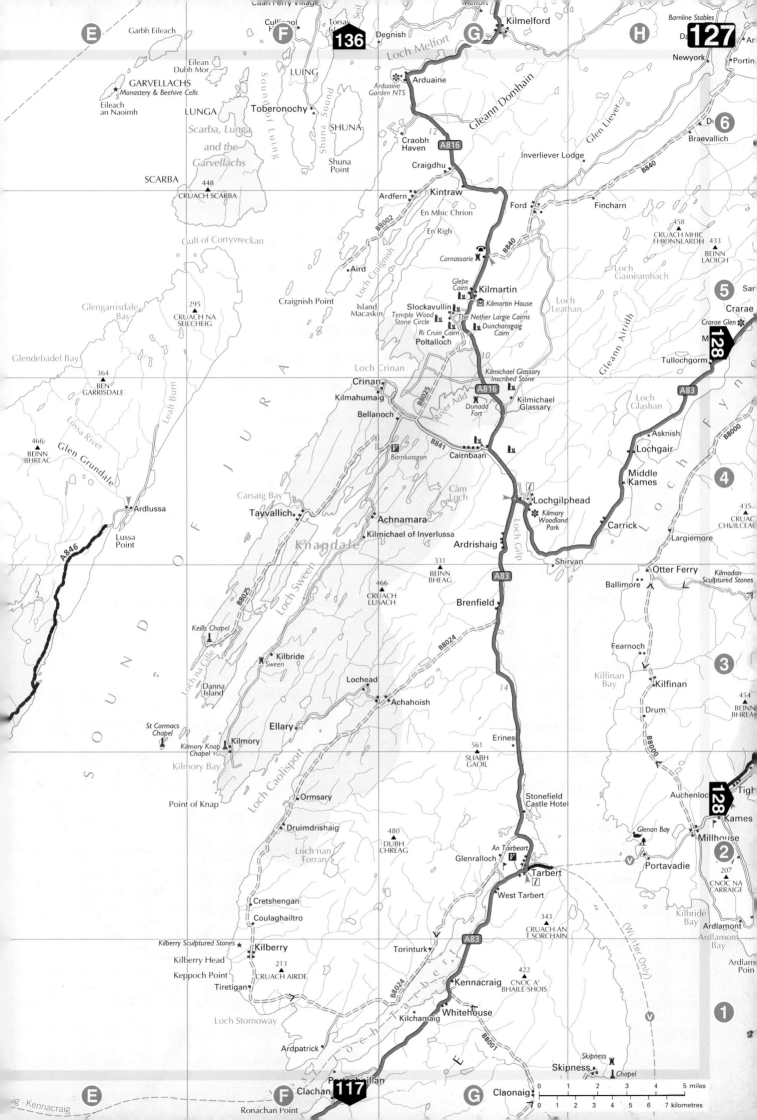

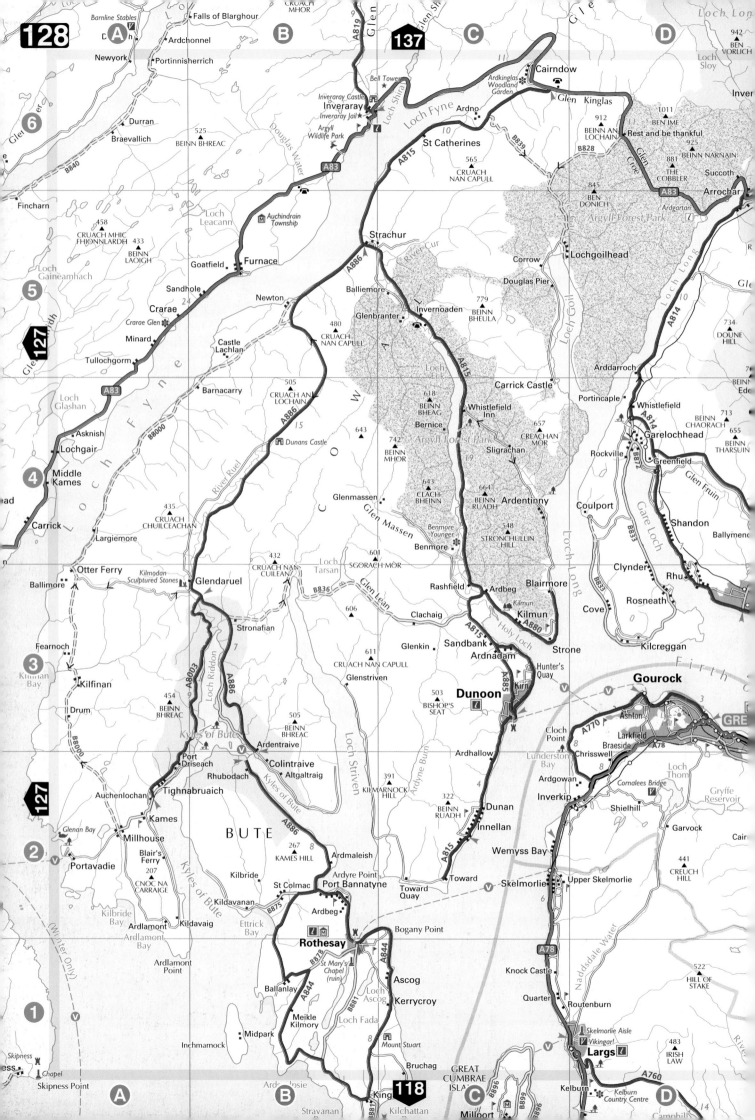

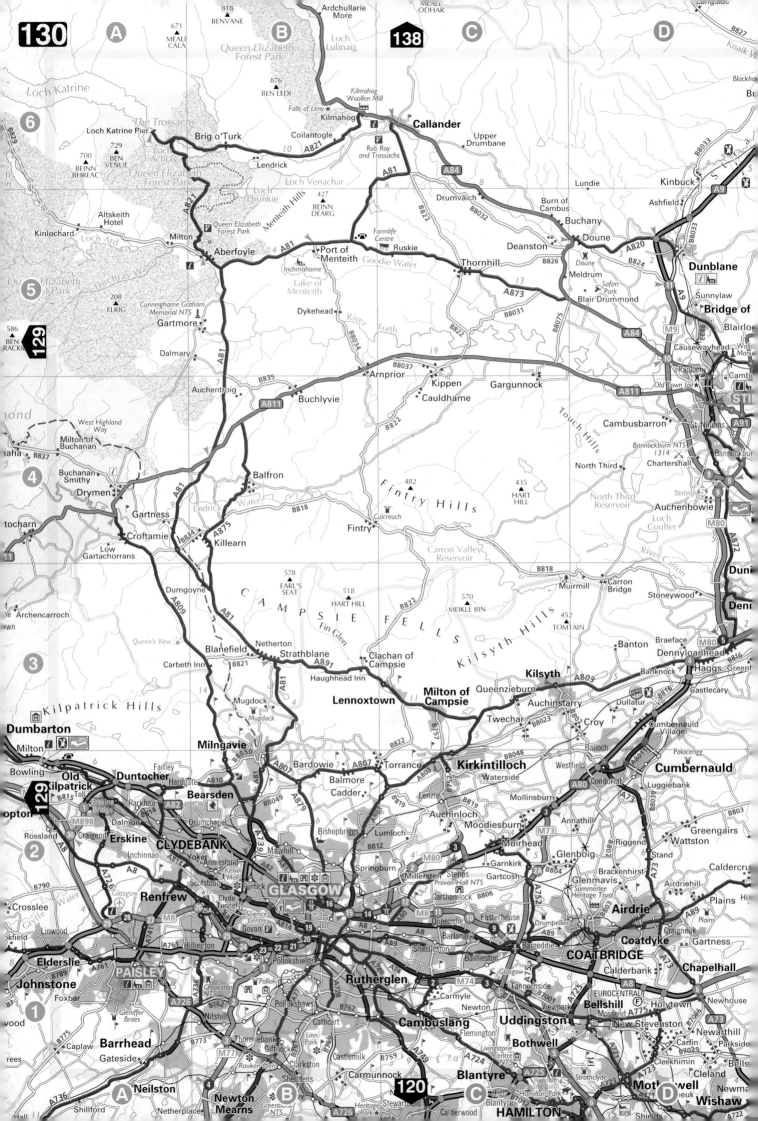

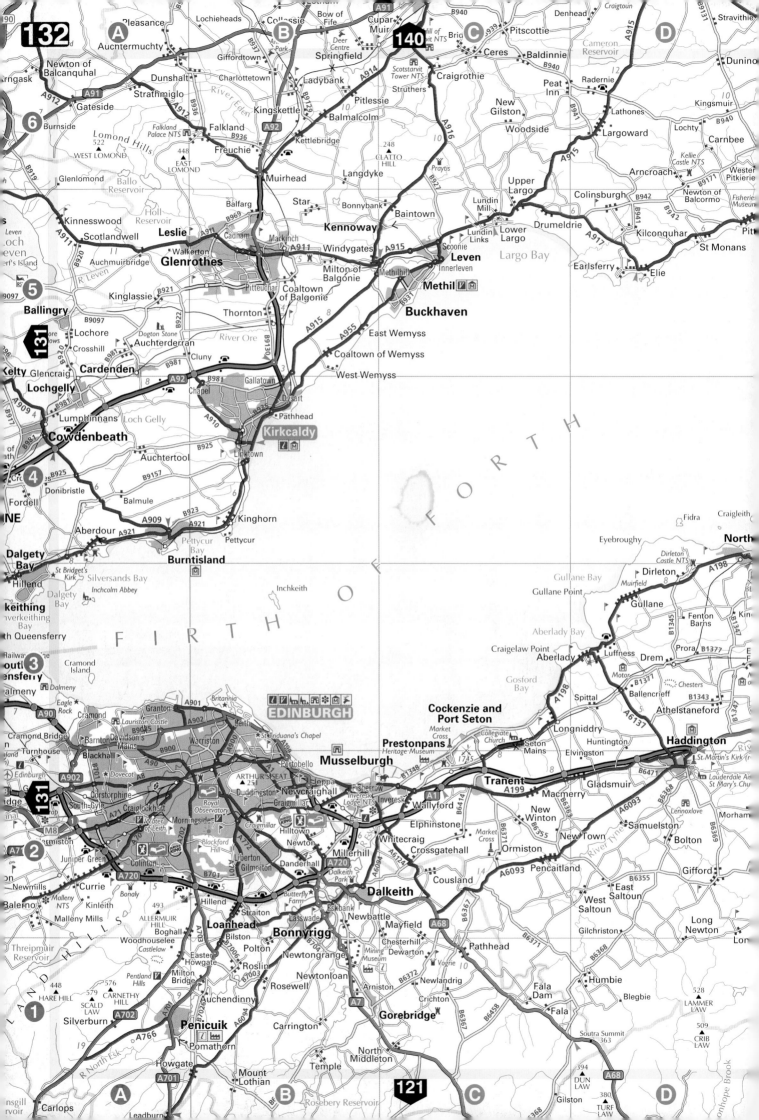

6

5

4

3

2

1

Boarhills

Kingsbarns

Balcomie Links

FIFE NESS

B940

Scotland's secret Bunker

B9171

Crail

Easter Pitkierie

A917

B9131

Kilrenny

Cellardyke

★ North Carr Lightship

Anstruther

weem

Isle of May

Bass Rock

rwick

Scottish Seabird

Tantallon

Cleghornie

8

Whitekirk

A198

St Baldred's Cradle

Tyne Mouth

Belhaven Bay

B1377

Preston Mill & Phantassie Doocot NTS

Markle

B1407

Tyninghame

John Muir

Belhaven

Dunbar

ast Linton

A1087

West Barns

Broxburn

Barns Ness

Hailes

B6370

1650

East Barns

Chapel Point

Traprain

Spott

A1

1 2

Skateraw

Torness Power Station

Pitcox

Doonhill Homestead

Thorntonloch

Traprain Law

Dry Brook

Luggate Burn

Stenton

Papple

The Brunt

Innerwick

Crowhill

Garvald

B370

319

COCKLAW HILL

Oldhamstocks

Reed Point

Cove

Pease Bay

Siccar Point

Fast Castle Head

397

BRANSLY HILL

Collegiate Church

Cockburnspath

196

BROWN RIG

Coldingham Loch

ST ABB'S HEAD

Danskine

B6355

Monynut Water

Bothwell Water

391

HEART LAW

Ecclaw

A1107

Grantshouse

Coldingham

A1107

St Abbs

Coldingham Bay

463

SPARTLETON

St Agnes

Southern Upland Way

Butterdean

Eye Water

Houndwood

B6438

A1107

22

Eyemou

MEIKLE SAYS LAW

533

Whiteadder Reservoir

Quixwood

Heugh Head

Cairncross

HUMMERMUIR HILLS

Cranshaws

Abbey St Bathans

262

HORSELEY HILL

Reston

A1

B6355

Ayton

rnm

467

MEIKLE LAW

Ellemford

Edin's Hall Broch

14

Auchencrow

Lamberton

495

HUNT LAW

Whitchester

COCKBURN LAW

Marygold

B6438

Longformacus

Southern Upland Way

rosehill

A6112

B6355

Preston

Lintlaw

B6365

399

Cumledge

G6355

Edrom

Tithe

0 1 2 3 4 5 miles

0 1 2 3 4 5 6 7 kilometres

A B C D

6

Rudha
Mòr

Cliad
Bay

B8072

Bo

Arnabost

Grishipoll
Clabhach

B8071

Loch
Cliad

Hogh Bay   Ballyhaugh   Arinagour

Totronald

CO

5

Feall
Bay

Arileod   Acha

B8070

Uig

Friesland
Bay

Eilean
Ornsay

RSPB

Calgary Point

Crossapol
Bay

Rudha
Fasachd

Loch Breachacha

Gunna

Rudha Dubh

Caoles

Tiree – Oban

V

B8069

Ruaig

Rudha Port
Bhiosd   Clachan
Mor   Balephetrish
Bay

B8068

Haugh
Bay   Loch
Bhasapoll

Ballevullin   Cornoigmore

Kenovay

Gott
Bay

4

Kilkenneth

B8068

Tiree

Moss   Heylipoll

B8065

Scarinish

Middleton

Barrapoll   B8065   Crossapoll

TIREE

Balephuil
Bay   Loch a
Phuill   B8067   Balemartine   Hynish Bay

TRESHNIS
ISLES

Rinn
Thorbhais   Mannel

Bac N

Balephuil
Bay   Hynish

Bac Bea

3

2

Soa Island

1

A B C D

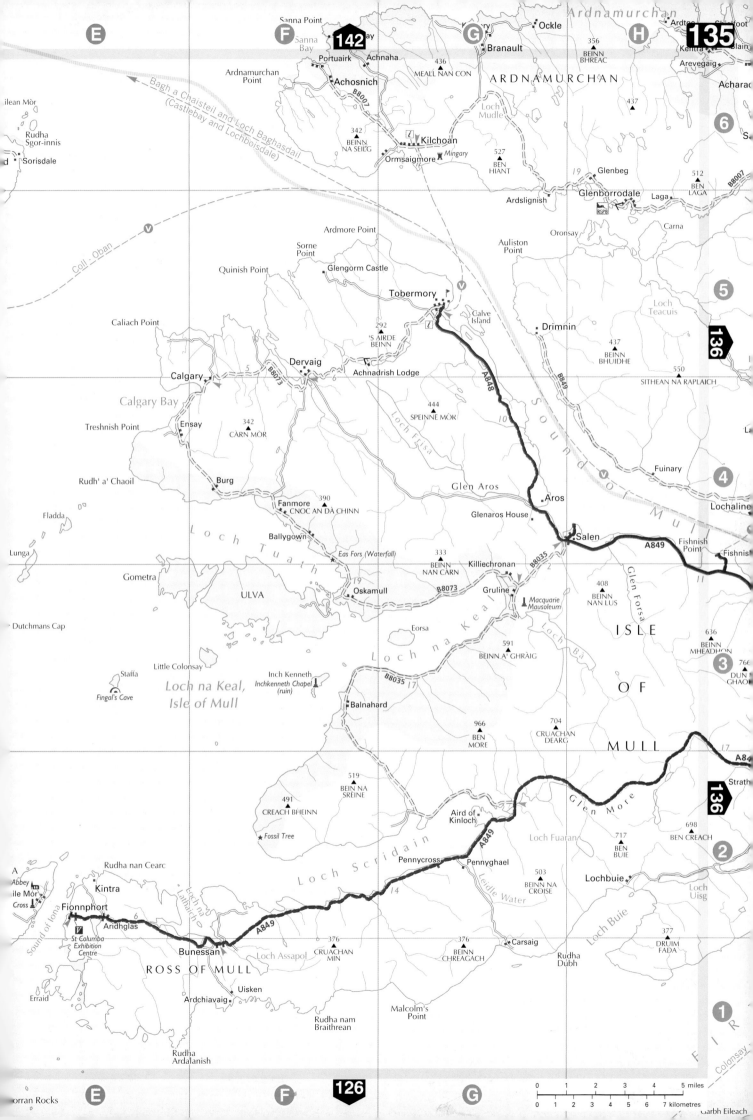

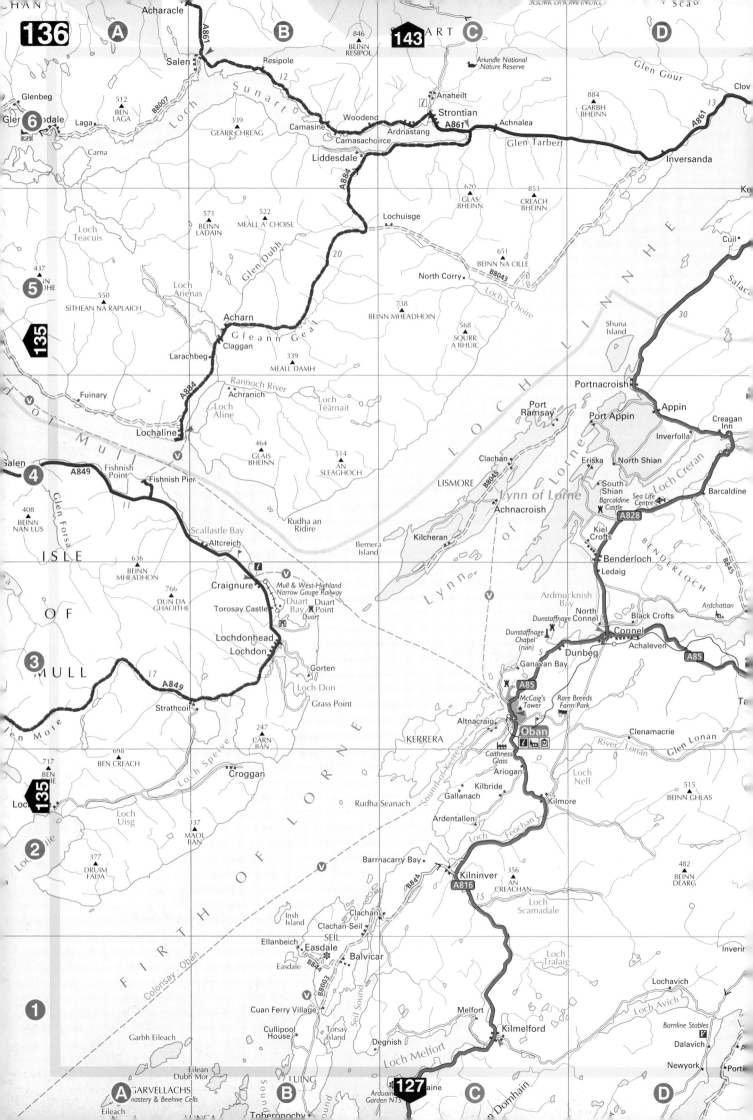

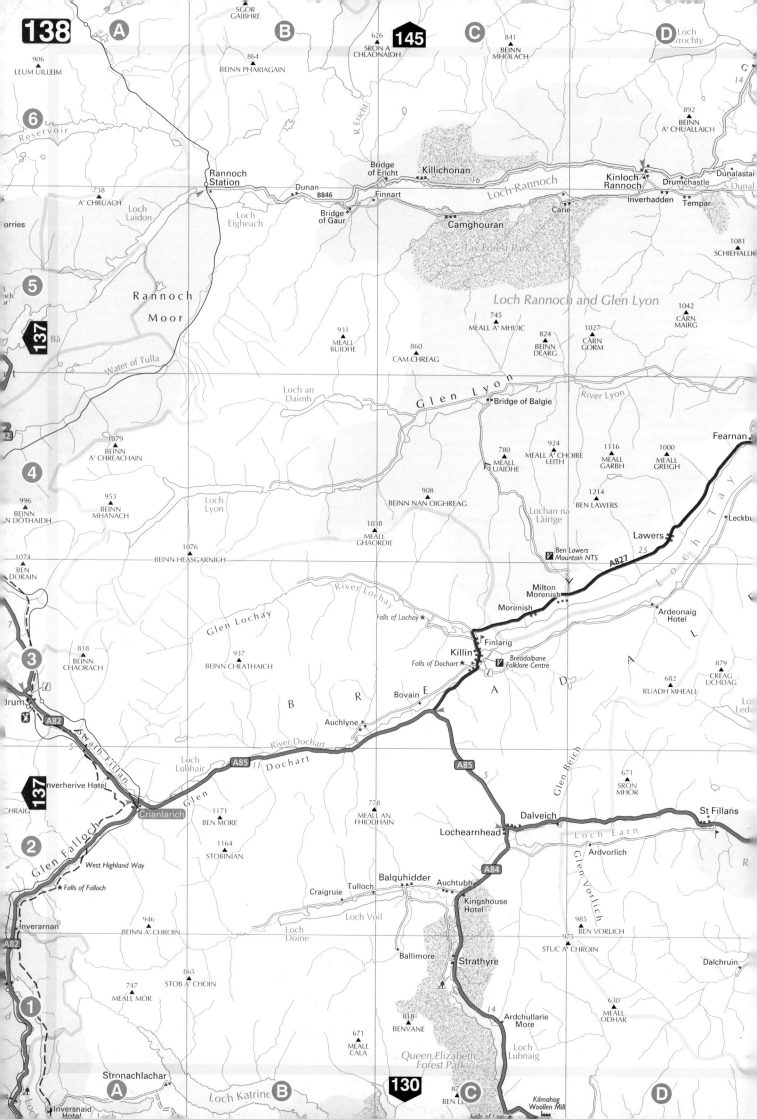

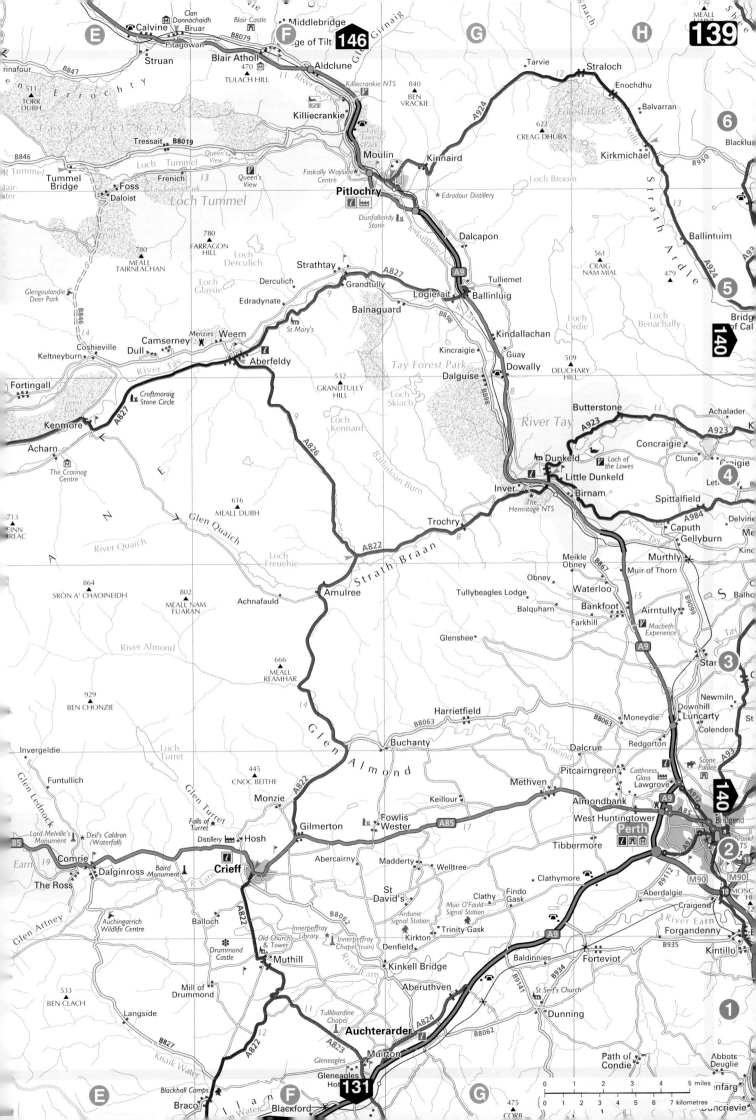

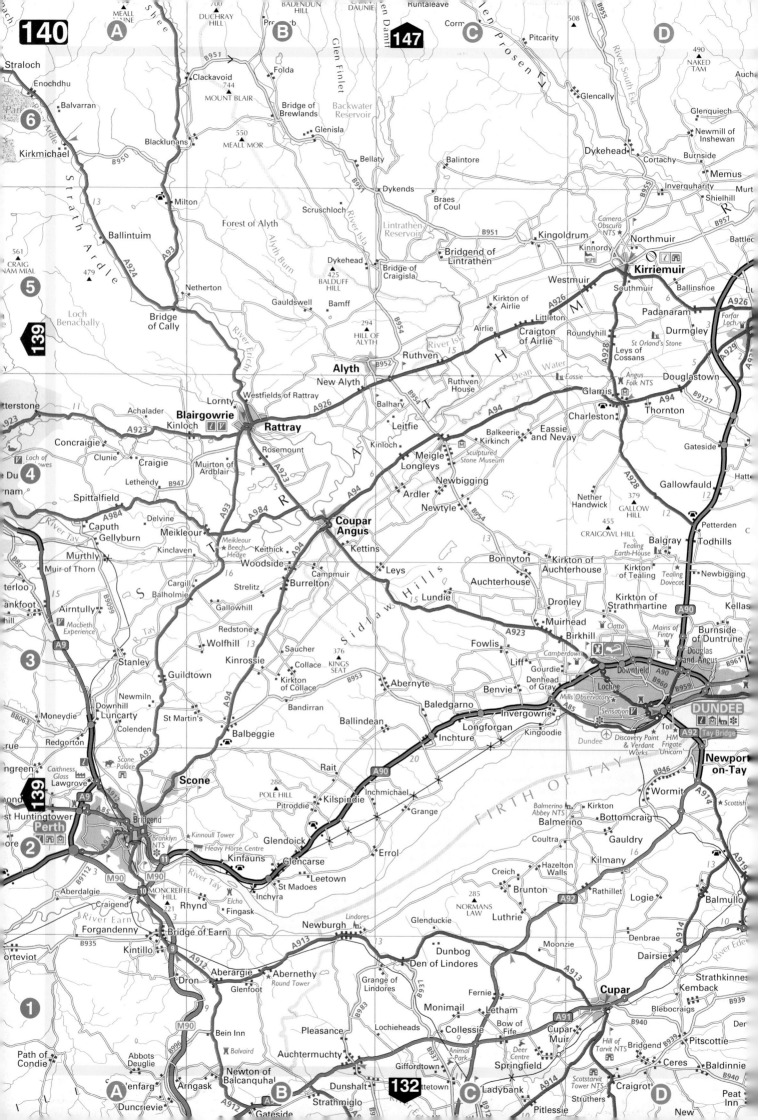

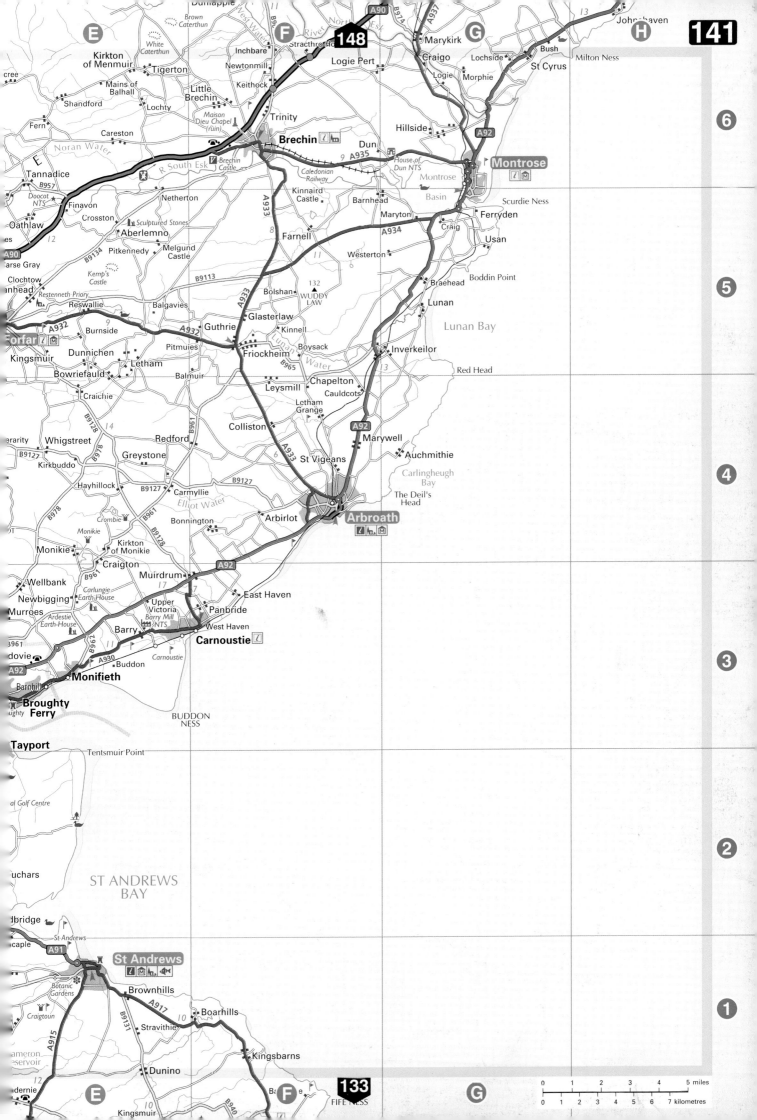

Loch Eynort

SGURR NAN GILLEAN

The Cu

434
AN CRUACHAN

SGURR
A' GHEADAIDH

Glenbrittle House

Cuillin Hills

Bualintur

1009
▲
SGURR
ALASDAIR

Loch
Coruisk

Loch Brittle

894
▲
GARS
BHEINN

225
▲
CEANN NA BEINNE

6

Rudh' an Dùnain

Soay Sound

Lo
Sc

139
▲
BEINN
BHREAC

■ Mol-chlach

SOAY

Rudh'
Aonghais

Loch Baghasdail (Lochboisdale)

5

C U I L L I N   S O U N D

CANNA

210
▲
CARN A' GHAILL

Garrisdale Point

A'Chill ■

Canna
Harbour

Rudha
Shamhnan Insir

Ⓥ

Sanday

Sound of Canna

302
▲
MULLACH
MÒR

A Bhrideanach

570
▲
ORVAL

■ ■ Kinloch

Rudha na Roinne

Loch
Scresort

4

Oigh-sgeir

RUM

810
▲
ASKIVAL

763
▲
SGURR NAN
GILLEAN

Bay of
Laig

■ ■ Clead

The Small Isles

Rudha nam
Meirleach

Sound of Rum

299
▲
AN
CRUACH

Rudha an Fhasaidh

Laig ■

3

EIGG

K

393
▲
AN SGURR

Sand

Sound of Eigg

Eilean
Chathasta

Eilean
nan Each

MUCK

2

Port Mor ■

1

Sanna Point

Sanna Bay ■

Sanna
Bay

Portuairk ■ ■

Achnaha

Ardnamurchan
Point

chosnich

B8007

Eilean Mòr

agh a Chaisteil
(Cas

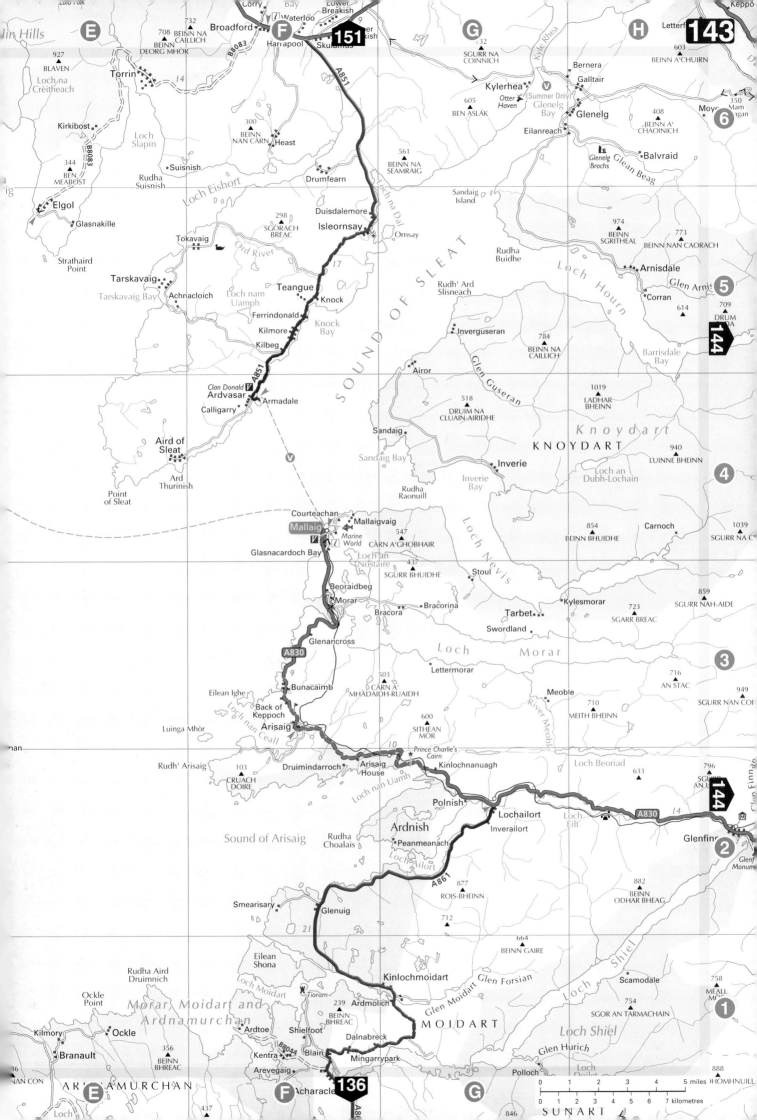

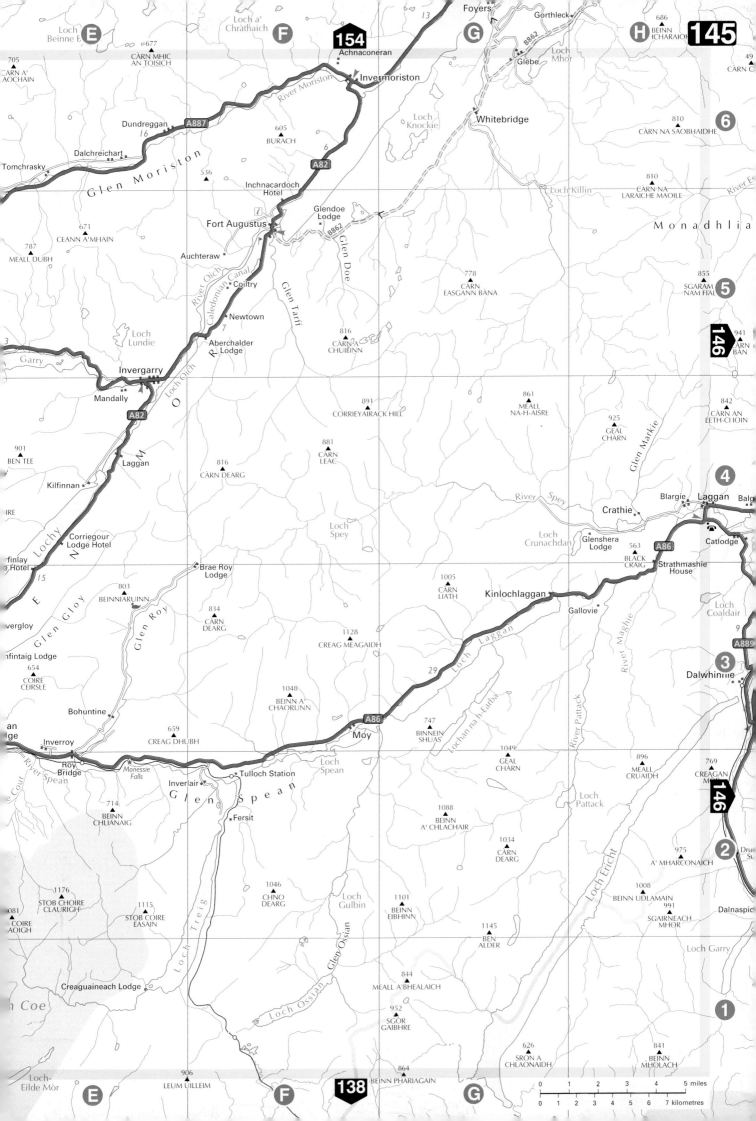

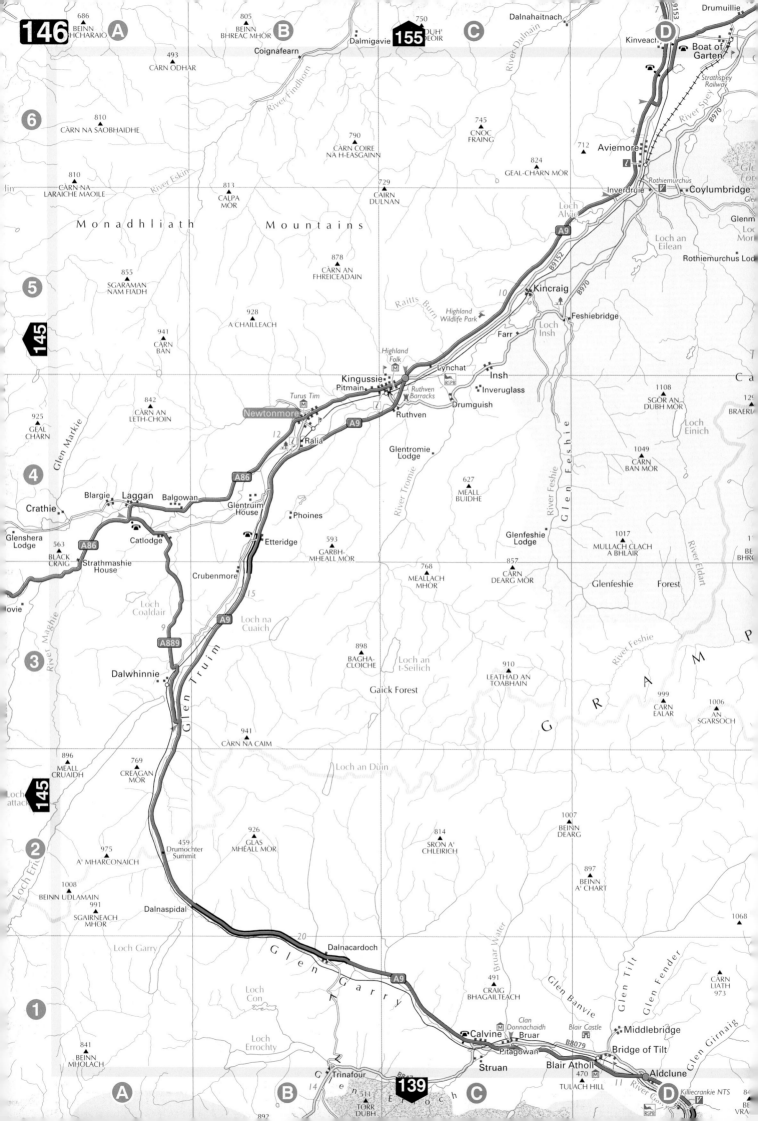

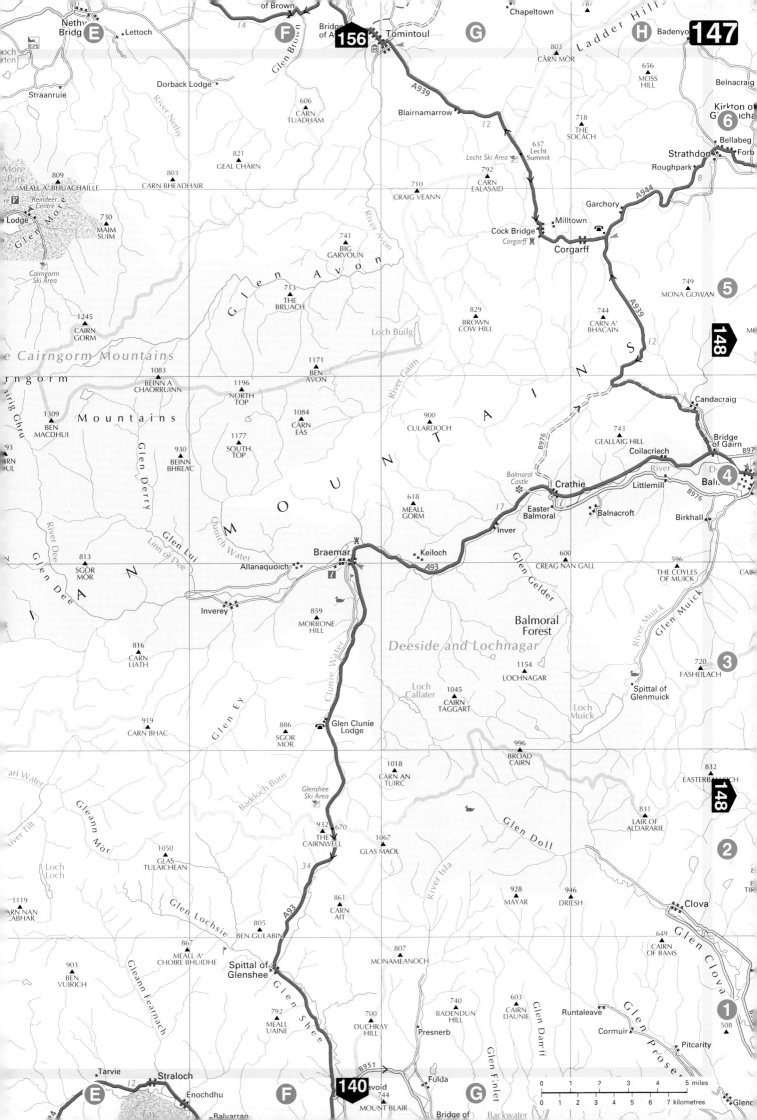

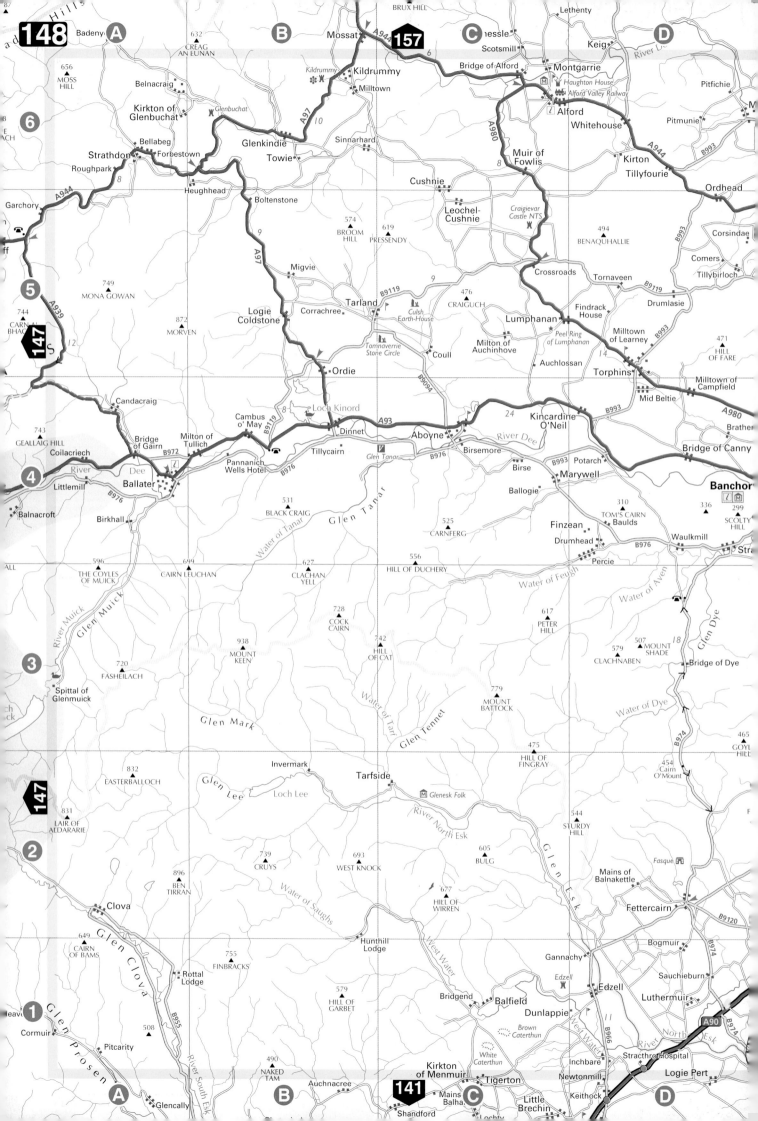

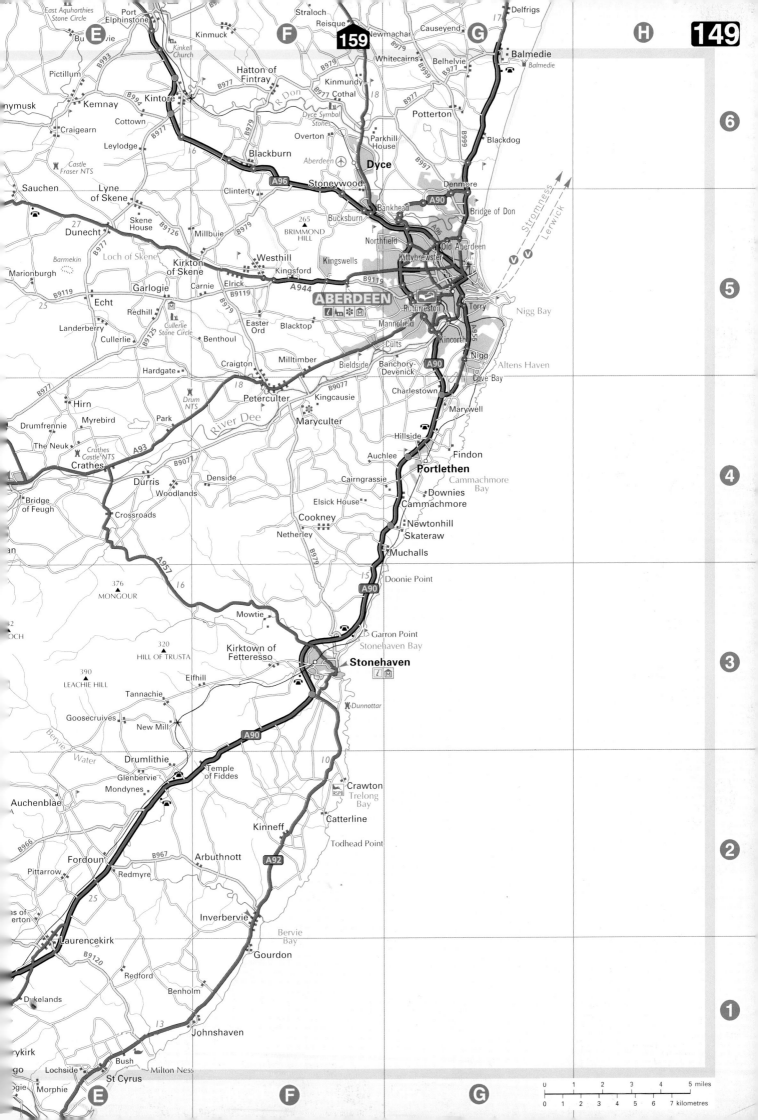

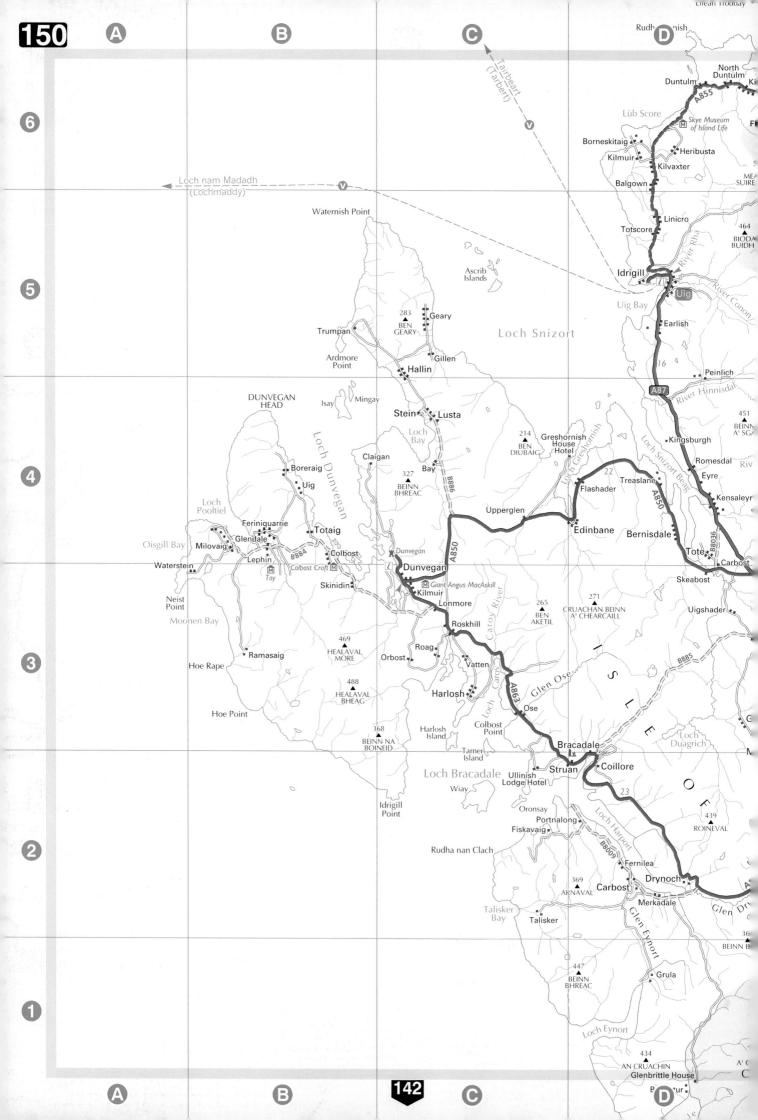

A B C D

6

Ellean Trodday

Rudh...nish

North
Duntulm
Duntulm
A855
Kilmuir...

Lùb Score

Skye Museum
of Island Life

Borneskitaig
Kilmuir
Kilvaxter
Heribusta
Balgown

Linicro

Totscore

464
BIODA
BUIDH

Tairbeart
(Tarbert)

V

Idrigill

River Rha

River Conon

Loch nam Madadh
(Lochmaddy) V

Uig

Uig Bay

Earlish

16

Waternish Point

Ascrib
Islands

Loch Snizort

Peinlich

A87

River Hinnisdal

5

283
BEN
GEARY
Geary

Trumpan

Ardmore
Point

Gillen

Hallin

Kingsburgh

451
BEINN
A' SGA

Romesdal

Eyre

Loch Snizort Beag

4

DUNVEGAN
HEAD

Isay Mingay

Stein Lusta

Loch
Bay

Greshornish
House
Hotel

214
BEN
DIUBAIG

Loch Greshornish

22

Treaslane

Flashader

Kensaleyr

A850

Boreraig

Uig

Claigan

Bay

327
BEINN
BHREAC

B886

Upperglen

Edinbane

Bernisdale

B8036

Tote

Carbost

Loch Pooltiel

Feriniquarrie

Totaig

Dunvegan

A850

Skeabost

Loch Dunvegan

Oisgill Bay

Milovaig
Glendale
Lephin

Colbost

Colbost Croft

Dunvegan
Kilmuir
Giant Angus MacAskill

271
CRUACHAN BEINN
A' CHEARCAILL

Uigshader

Waterstein

B884

Toy

Skinidin

Lonmore

265
BEN
AKETIL

Neist
Point

Moonen Bay

Roskhill

Caroy River

I
S
L
E

B885

3

469
HEALAVAL
MORE

Roag

Orbost

Vatten

Glen Ose

Loch
Duagrich

Ramasaig

Hoe Rape

488
HEALAVAL
BHEAG

Harlosh

Ose

A863

O
F

Hoe Point

368
BEINN NA
BOINEID

Harlosh
Island

Colbost
Point

Bracadale

Coillore

439
ROINEVAL

Tarner
Island

Struan

Loch Harport

Idrigill
Point

Loch Bracadale

Ullinish
Lodge Hotel

Wiay

23

2

Oronsay
Portnalong

Fiskavaig

B8009

Fernilea

Rudha nan Clach

369
ARNAVAL

Carbost

Drynoch

A

Merkadale

Glen Dr

Talisker
Bay

Talisker

Glen Eynort

447
BEINN
BHREAC

Grula

36
BEINN B

1

Loch Eynort

434
AN CRUACHIN

Glenbrittle House

A'
C

A B C D

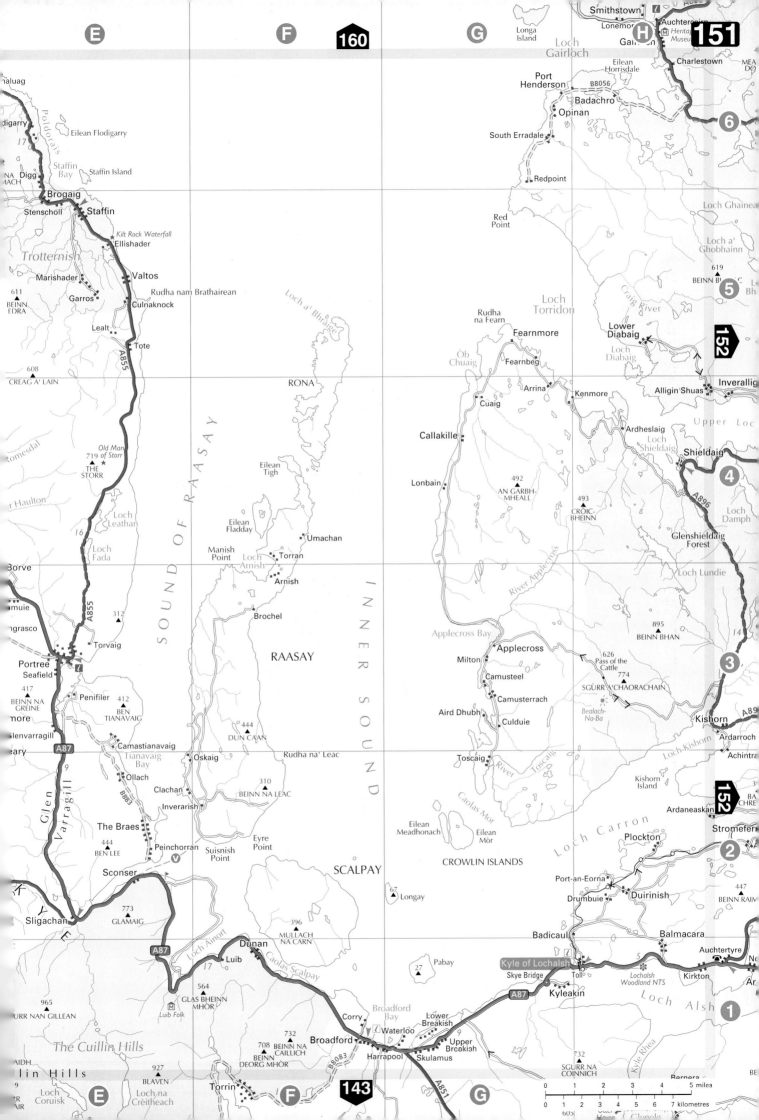

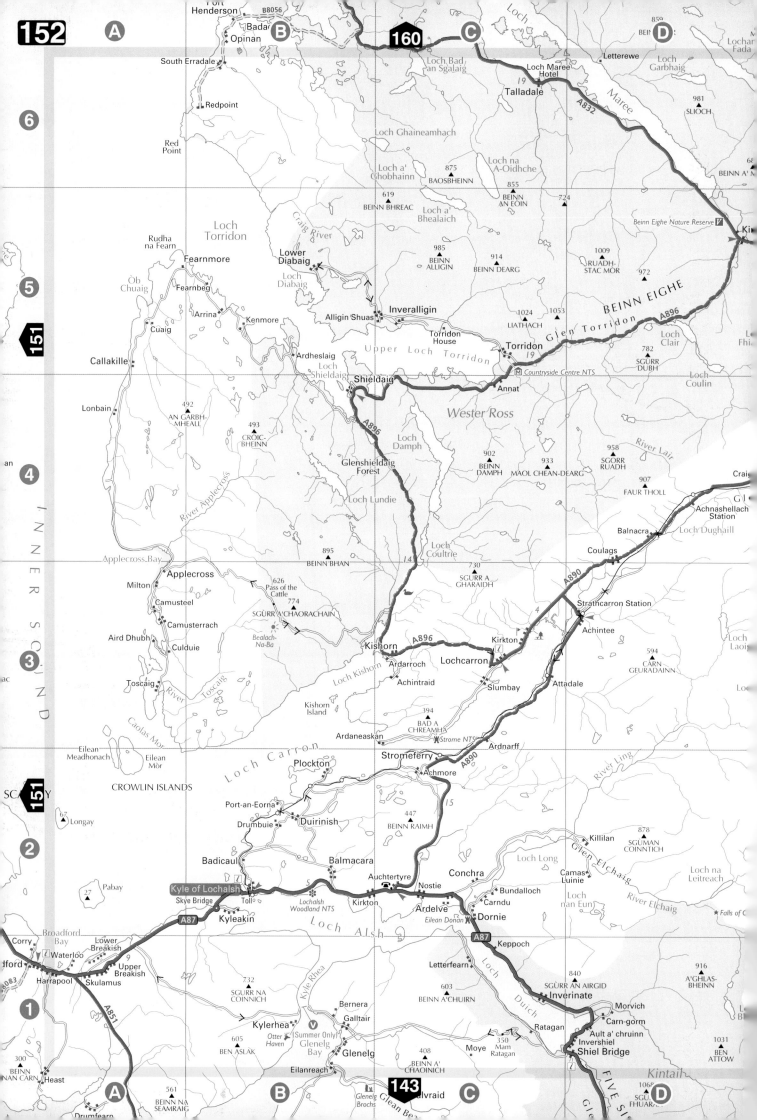

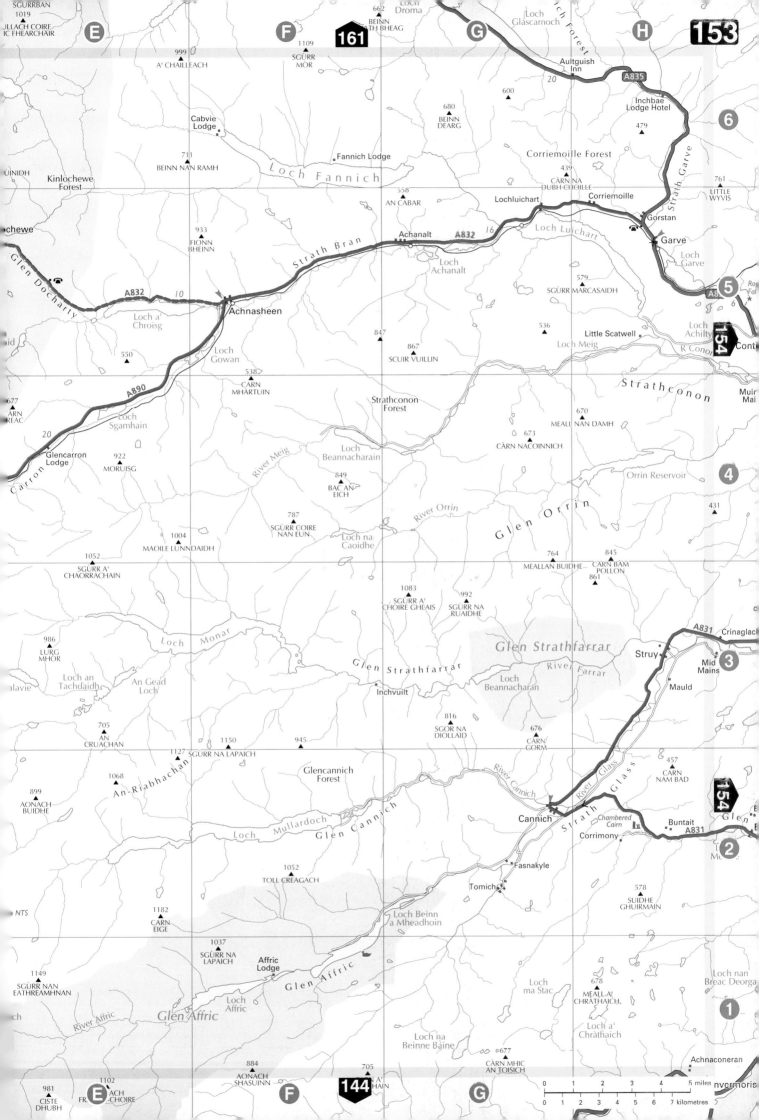

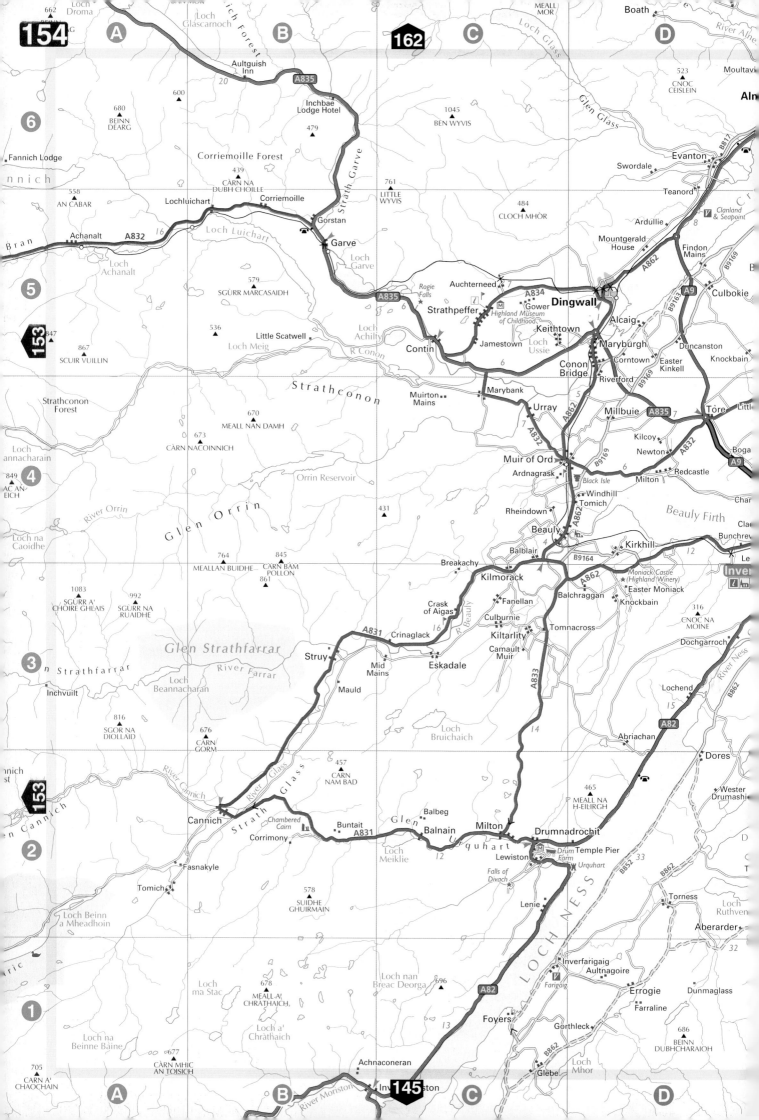

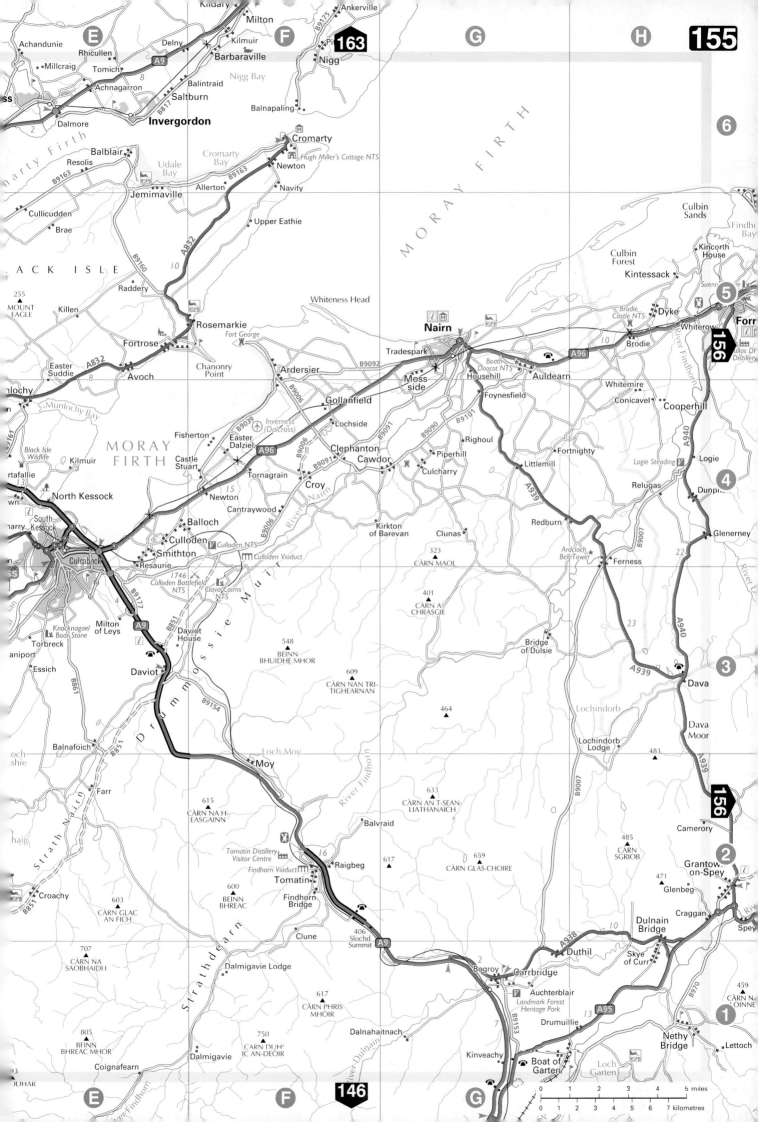

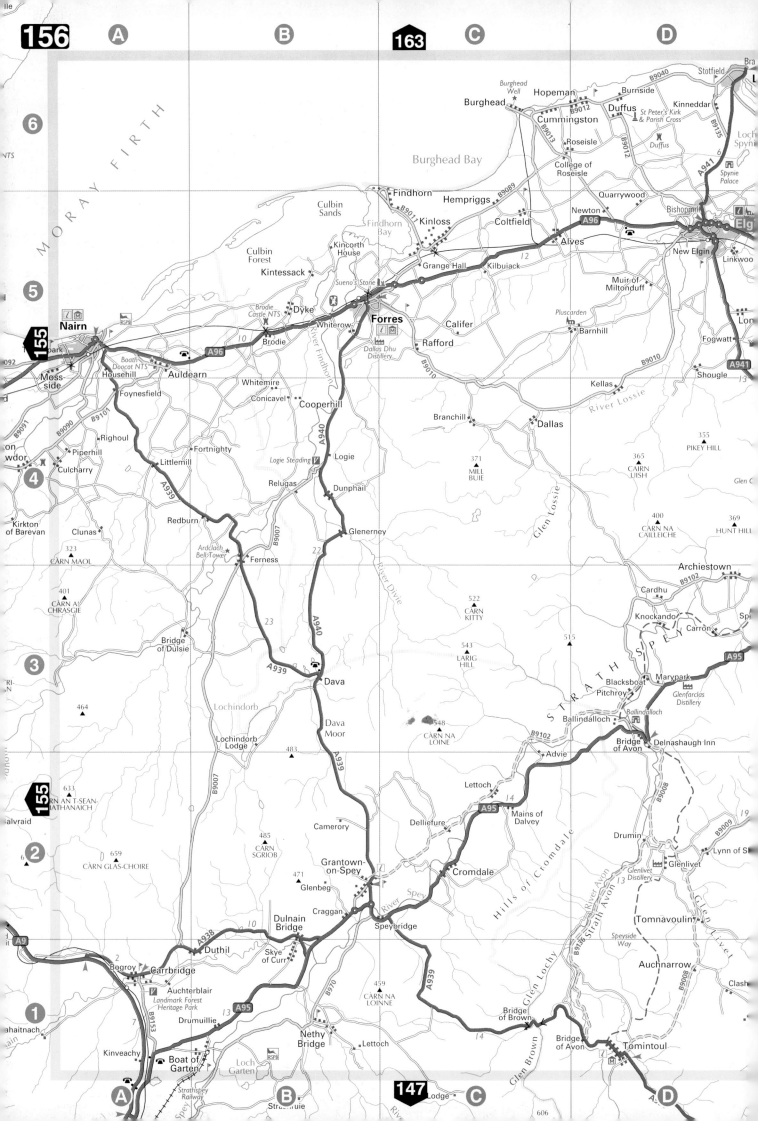

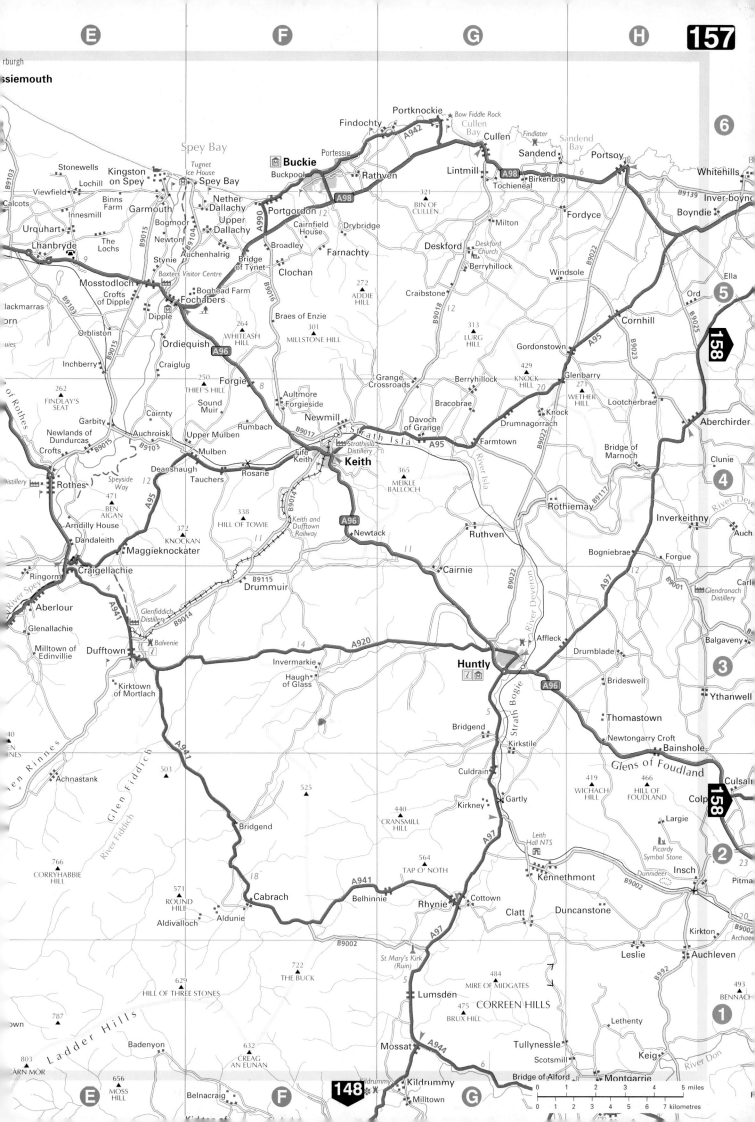

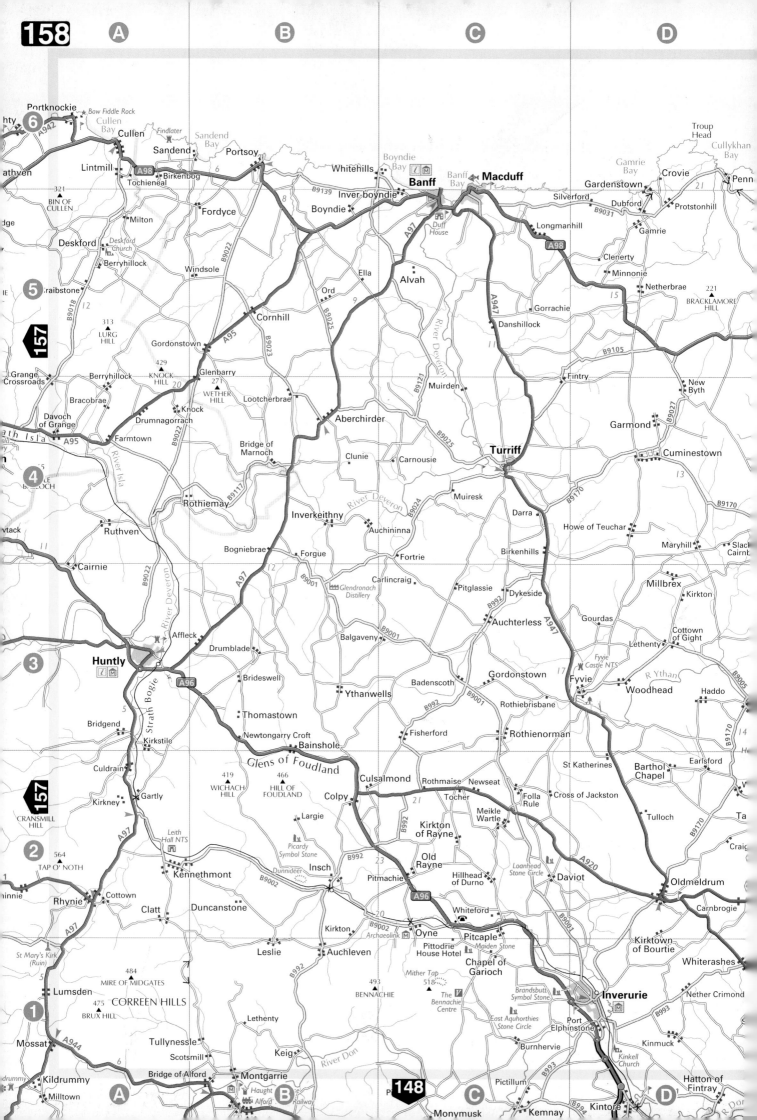

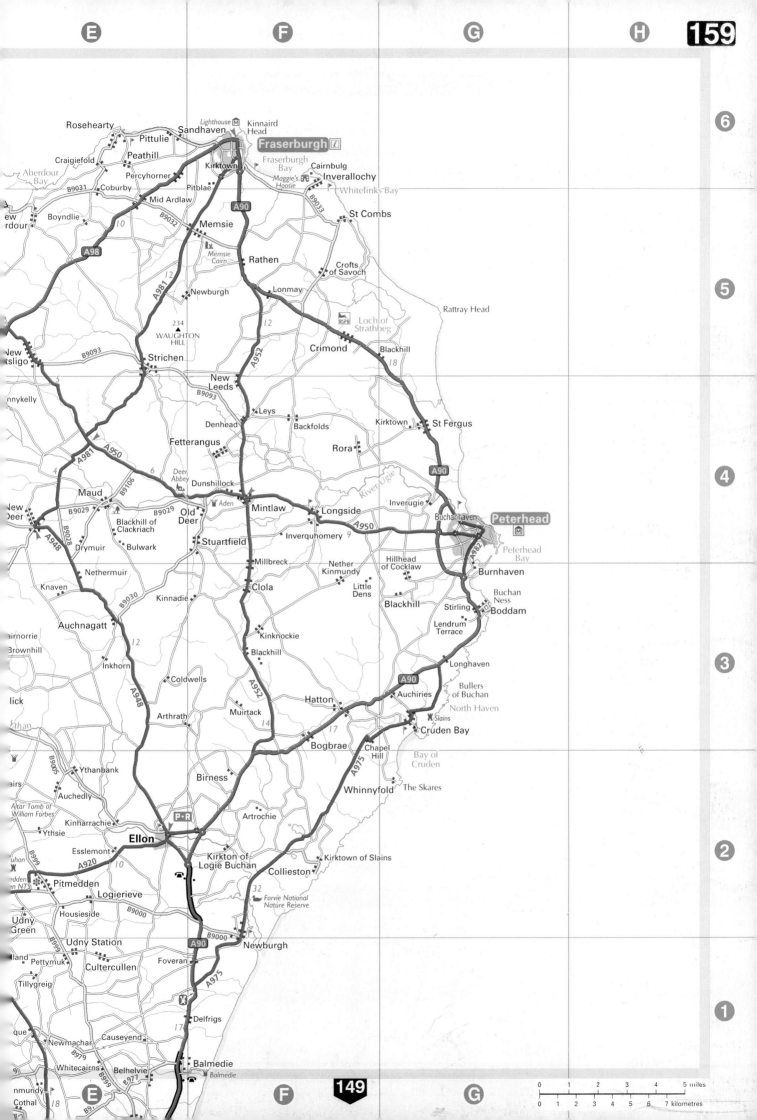

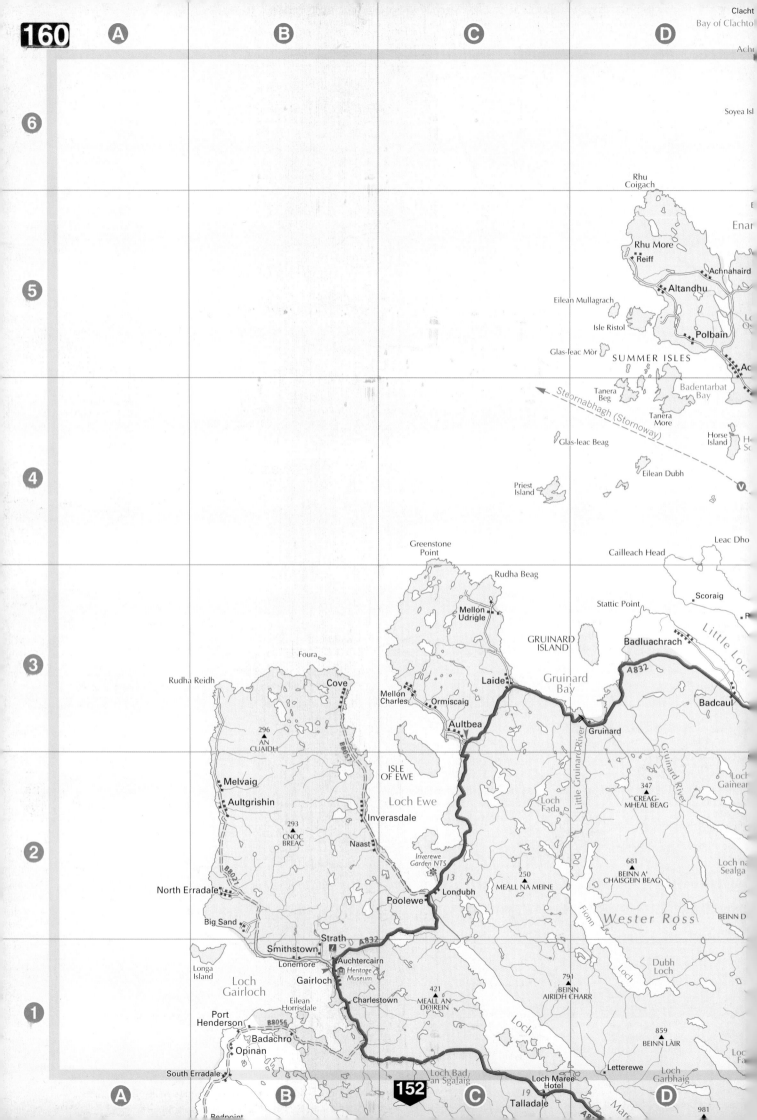

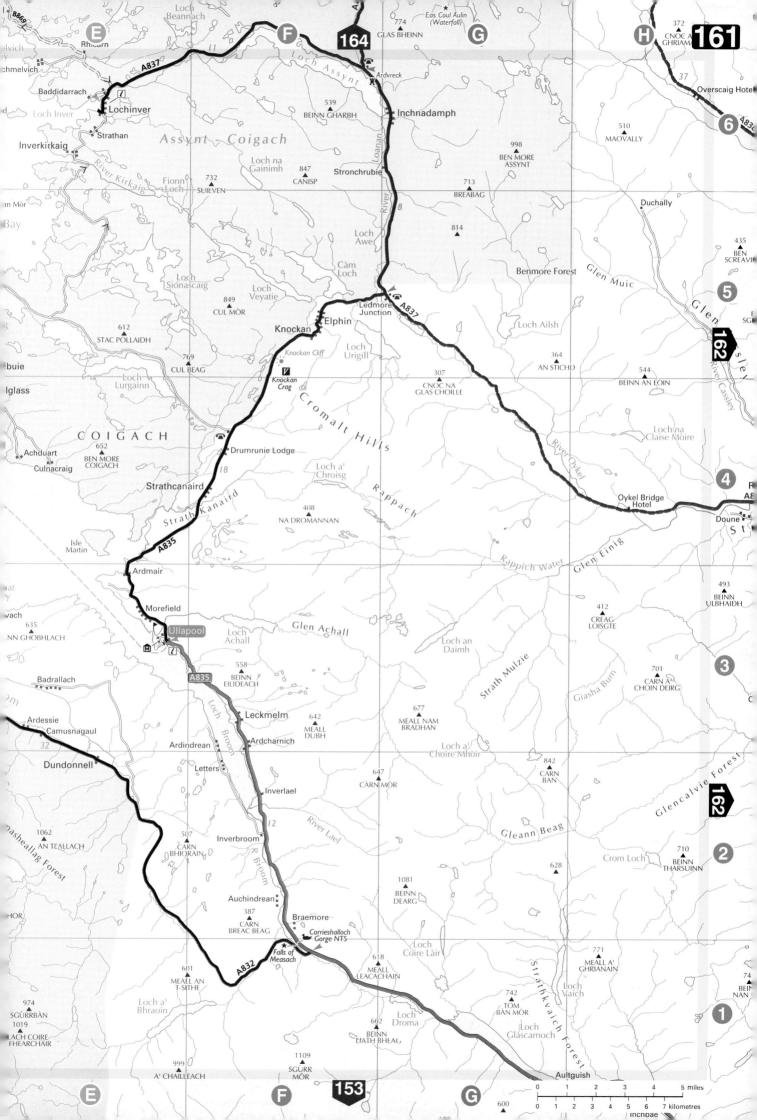

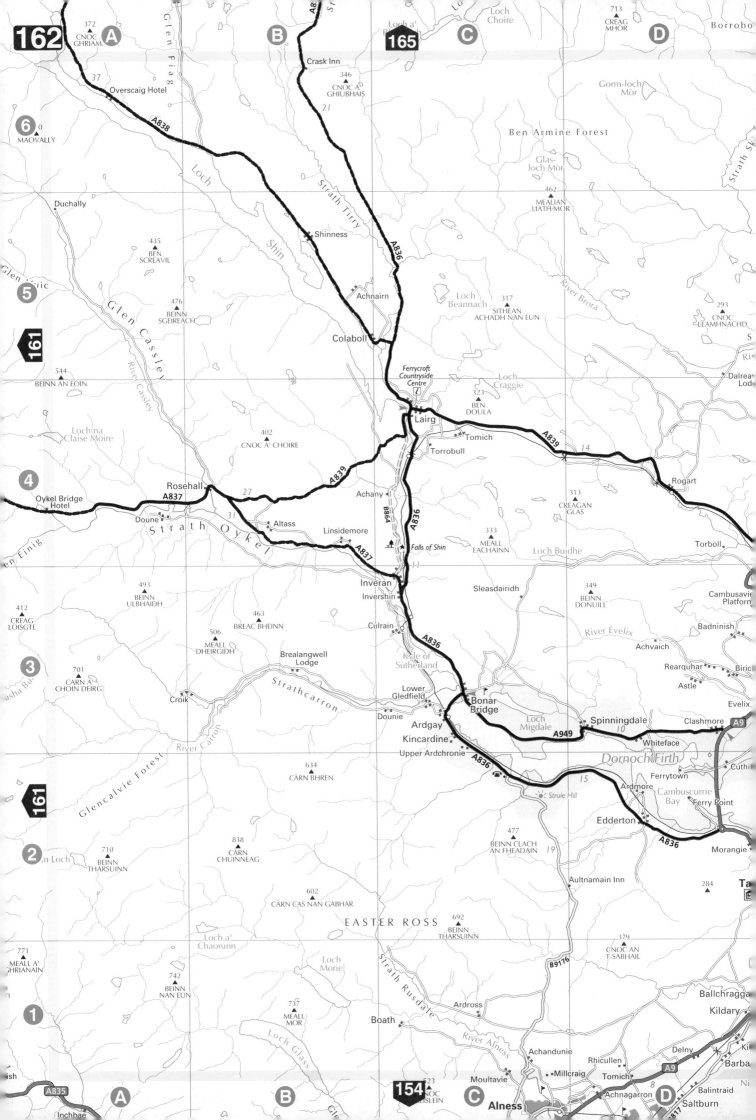

A   B   C   D

6

5

4

3

2

1

CAPE WRATH

Cléit
Dhubh

▲ 371
SGRIBHIS-
BHEINN

▲ 297
CNOC A
GHIUBHAIS

▲ 300
MAOVALLY

THE PARPH

▲ 457
FASHVEN

Loch Àir
na Bein

Sandwood
Bay

Sandwood
Loch

Rudh' an Fhir Leithe

Strath Shinary

▲ 485
CREAG
RIABACH

▲ 468
BEINN
DEARG MHÒR

▲ 464
MEALL
NA MOINE

▲ 331
GHLAS-
BHEINN

Sheigra

Balchreick   Blairmore

▲ 355
AN
SOCACH

▲ 521
FARVEALL

19

Oldshoremore

Kinlochbervie

Loch Clash

Badcall

B801

Achriesgill

Strath Dionard

Rhiconich

River

Rudha Ruadh

Loch na
Claise Càrnaich

CRA

Fanagmore

Skerricha

Loch Laxford

▲ 908
FOINAVEN

Tarbet

Foindle

North-west Sutherland

A838

HANDA
ISLAND

7

Laxford
Bridge

River Laxford

▲ 786
ARKLE

Loch na Tuac

Scourie
Bay

A894

Loch
Stack

Scourie More   Scourie

Badcall

▲ 721
BEN STACK

Strath Stack

Achfary

▲ 333
BEN
SCREAVIE

Badcall Bay

▲ 386
BEN
AUSKAIRD

A838

Loch More

Rudh' a'
Mhucard

17

Point of Stoer

OLDANY
ISLAND

Eddrachillis
Bay

Locha Chàirn Bhàin

▲ 419
BEN
STROME

Loch an
Leathaid Bhuain

Glen Dhu

Old Man
of Stoer

Culkein
Drumbeg

Kylestrome

Kylesku

Loch Glendhu

Culkein

Clashnessie
Bay

Oldany

Drumbeg

Unapool

▲ 525
BEINN AIRD
DA LOCH

Achnacarnin

B869

Nedd

Loch an
Leothaid

▲ 776
SAIL
GHORM

Loch Glencoul

Clashmore

Clashnessie

Loch
Poll

Glen

Leirg

▲ 809
QUINAG

A894

▲ 792
BEINN LEOID

Stoer

Eas Coul Aulin
(Waterfall)

Clachtoll   B869

Loch
Beannach

▲ 774
GLAS BHEINN

Bay of Clachtoll

Rhicarn

11

Achmelvich
Bay

A837

Loch Assynt

Ardvreck

Achmelvich

Baddidarrach

539

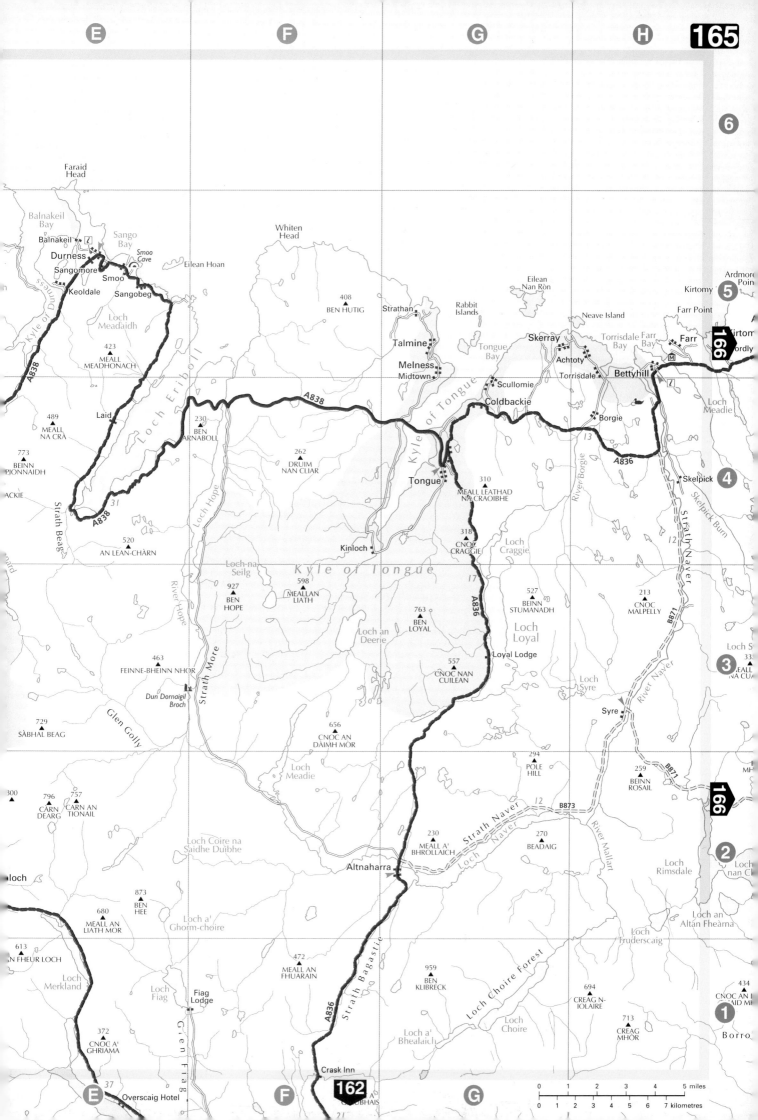

6

Faraid
Head

Balnakeil
Bay

Balnakeil   Sango
Bay

Durness   Smoo
Cave

Sangomore

Smoo

Keoldale   Sangobeg

Loch
Meadaidh

Eilean Hoan

Whiten
Head

5

408
BEN HUTIG

Strathan

Rabbit
Islands

Eilean
Nan Ròn

Kirtomy

Ardmore
Point

Farr Point

166

Kirtom
ordly

Loch Eriboll

423
MEALL
MEADHONACH

Talmine

Melness
Midtown

Tongue
Bay

Neave Island

Skerray

Achtoty

Torrisdale

Torrisdale
Bay

Farr
Bay

Farr

M

Bettyhill

Laid

489
MEALL
NA CRÀ

230
BEN
ARNABOLL

A838

Scullomie

Coldbackie

Loch Meadie

773
BEINN
PJONNAIDH

262
DRUIM
NAN CLIAR

Kyle of Tongue

Borgie

13

A836

Skelpick

4

ACKIE

Strath Beag

31

A838

520
AN LEAN-CHÀRN

Tongue

310
MEALL LEATHAD
NA CRAOIBHE

Skelpick Burn

Strath Naver

12

Loch Hope

318
CNOC
CRAGGIE

Loch
Craggie

Loch
Loyal

Kinloch

17

3

MEALL
NA CU

Loch-na-
Seilg

Kyle of Tongue

598
MEALLAN
LIATH

927
BEN
HOPE

763
BEN
LOYAL

A836

527
BEINN
STUMANADH

213
CNOC
MALPELLY

B871

Loch S

Strath More

Loch an
Deerie

Loyal Lodge

Loch
Syre

River Hope

463
FEINNE-BHEINN NHOR

557
CNOC NAN
CUILEAN

Syre

River Naver

33

Dun Dornaigil
Broch

Glen Golly

729
SÀBHAL BEAG

656
CNOC AN
DÀIMH MÒR

294
POLE
HILL

259
BEINN
ROSAIL

B871

166

2

300

796
CÀRN
DEARG

757
CARN AN
TIONAIL

Loch Coire na
Saidhe Duibhe

Loch
Meadie

Strath Naver

12

B873

MH

River Mallart

Loch
Rimsdale

Loch
nan C

loch

230
MEALL A'
BHROLLAICH

Loch Naver

270
BEADAIG

Altnaharra

Loch an
Altàn Fhearna

873
BEN
HEE

680
MEALL AN
LIATH MOR

Loch a'
Ghorm-choire

Loch Choire Forest

Loch
Truderscaig

613
N FHEUR LOCH

Loch
Merkland

Loch
Fiag

Fiag
Lodge

472
MEALL AN
FHUARAIN

Strath Bagastie

959
BEN
KLIBRECK

Loch a'
Bhealaich

Loch
Choire

694
CREAG N-
IOLAIRE

434
CNOC AN
AID M

1

713
CREAG
MHÒR

Borro

372
CNOC A'
GHRIAMA

Glen Fiag

A836

Overscaig Hotel

Crask Inn

21

| 0 | 1 | 2 | 3 | 4 | 5 miles |
| 0 | 1 | 2 | 3 | 4 | 5 | 6 | 7 kilometres |

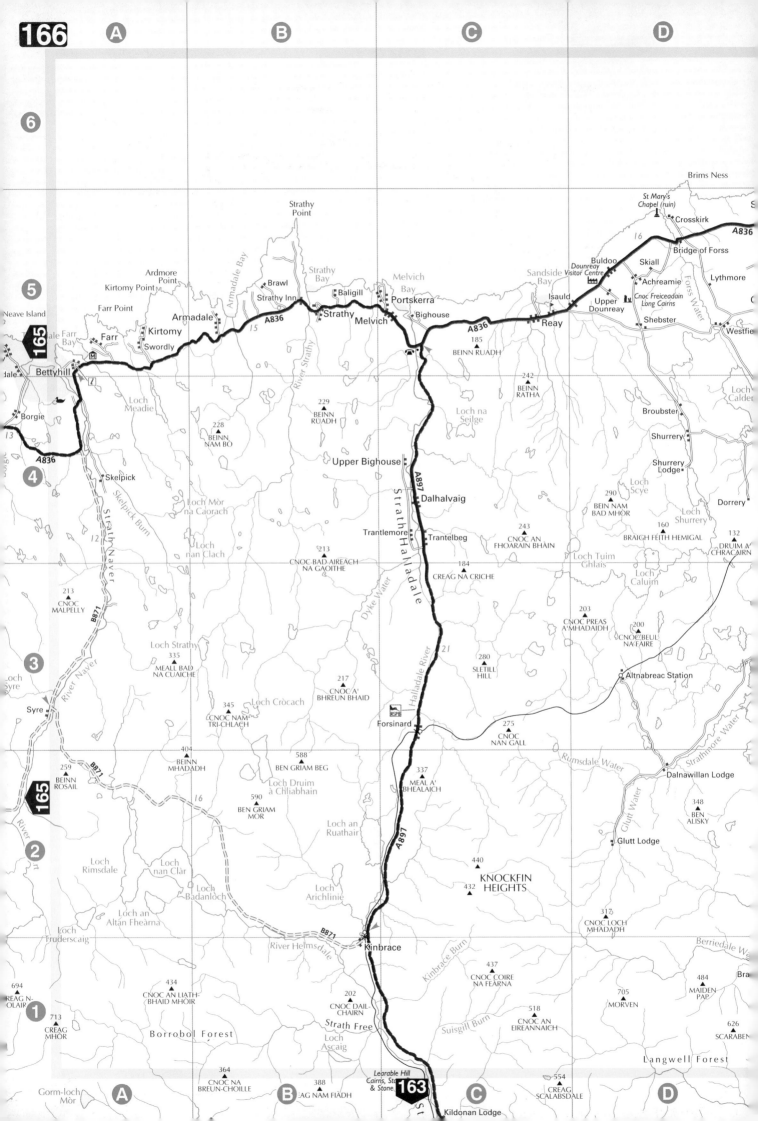

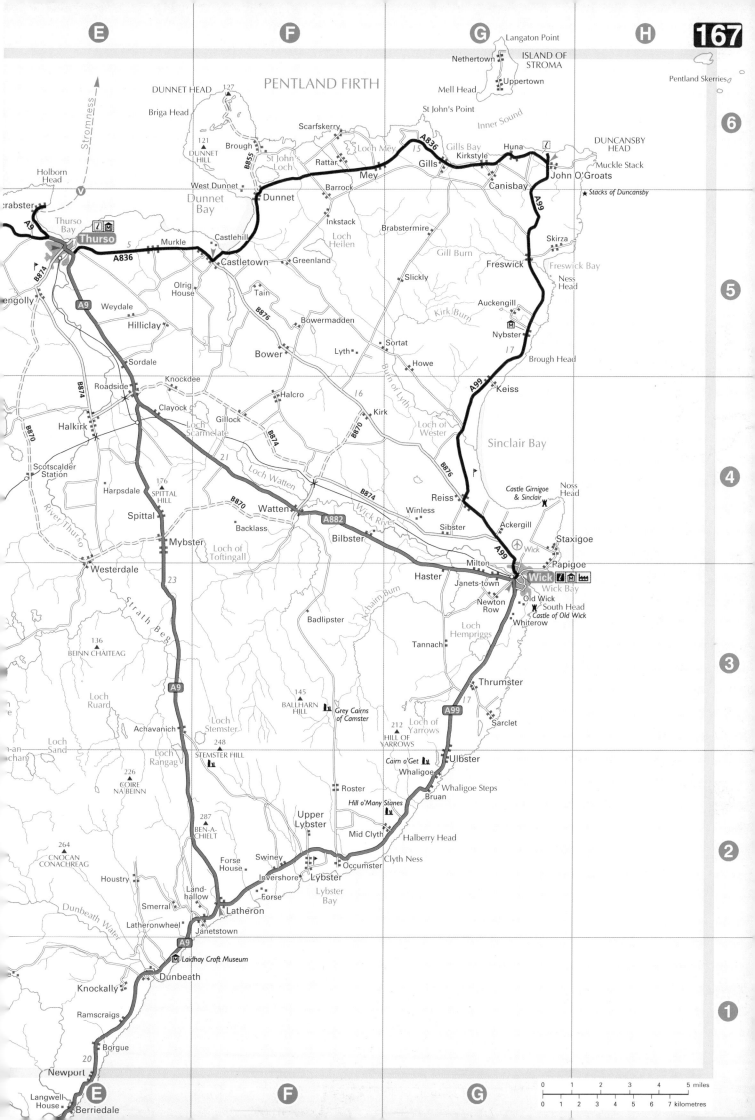

Western Isles

0 5 10 miles
0 5 10 kilometres

RUDHA RHOBHANAIS
(BUTT OF LEWIS)

Port Nis
(Port of Ness)
Lional
Sgiogarstaigh
(Skigersta)
Cros
NESS
Borgh
(Borve)
Cellar Head
Siadar
(Shader)
28
Steinacleit Cairn
& Stone Circle
DIAVAL
158
Tolastadh
(Tolsta)
Tolsta Head
Arnol
Barabhas
(Barvas)
ISLE
Bragar Blockhouse
A858
Col
A857
Carlabhagh
(Carloway)
Siabost
(Shawbost)
Loch
Breivat
OF
Broad
Bay
Port nan Giuran
(Portnaguran)
Tiumpan Head
Aird
EYE PENINSULA
Dun Carloway Broch
Breascleit
(Breasclete)
BEN-
BRAVAS
280
LEWIS
Newmarket
Garrabost
A866
Great
Bernera
West
Loch Roag
Gallan Head
Calanais
(Callanish)
Standing
Stones
Steornabhagh
(Stornoway)
A858
Sanndabhaig
(Sandwick)
Stornoway
Cnoc
(Knock)
Pabail
(Bayle)
Timsgearraidh
(Timsgarry)
Aird Uig
(Uig)
Bhaltos
(Valtos)
Colbost
231
EITSHAL
Chicken Head
Islibhig
(Islivig)
Miabhig
(Miavaig)
Acha Mor
(Achmore)
37
B8011
Liurbost
(Liurbost)
Griomaisiader
(Grimshader)
Aird Brenish
496
B8059
Lacasaigh
(Laxay)
A859
Crosbost
Breanais
(Brenish)
Mealasta
Island
TEINNASVAL
Baile Ailein
(Balallan)
Loch Erisort
Cromor
Gearraidh Bhaird
(Garyvard)
B8060
Scarp
Loch
Langavat
Airidh a bhruaich
(Aribruach)
Cearsiadar
(Kershader)
Grabhair (Gravir)
Loch Ouirn
Kebock Head
Hushinish Point
679
401
Amhuinnsuidhe
B887
TIRGA MORE
MOR MHONADH
Seaforth
Island
571
Leumrabhagh
(Lemreway)
OUTER
Aird a Mhulaidh
(Ardvourlie)
799
A859
PARK
BEINN MHOR
Loch
Shell
Taransay
West Loch
Tarbert
CLISHAM
Soay Mor
Aird Asaig (Ardhasig)
HEBRIDES
Rudha Sgeirigin
Sound of Taransay
Tairbeart
(Tarbert)
Caolas Scalpaigh
(Kyles Scalpay)
Loch Seaforth
Scalpay
Rudha Bocaig
Loch
Brollum
Sound of Shiant
Shiant
Islands
Toe Head
Na Buirgh
(Borve)
Greosabhagh
(Grosebay)
A859
24
HARRIS
333
CHAIPAVAL
Manais (Manish)
Shillay
Taobh Tuath
(Northton)
Pabbay
An T-ob
(Leverburgh)
Fionnsbhagh (Finsbay)
Berneray
Roghadal (Rodel)
St Clements Church
Renish Point
Boreray
Killegray
Sound of Pabbay
Otternish
Griminish
Point
Port nan Long
(Newton Ferry)
Vallay
196
Hermetray
Sound of Harris
Tigh a Ghearraidh
(Tigharry)
Solas
A865
231
MAIRIVAL
Weaver's Point
Loch nam Madadh - Uig
(Lochmaddy)
UIBHIST A TUATH
(NORTH UIST)
Ceann a Bhaigh
(Bayhead)
A867
Loch nam Madadh
(Lochmaddy)
Uig
Rudha Port
Scolpaig
A865
Kirkibost Island
Clachan na Luib
(Clachan-a-Luib)
Loch Euphoirt (Locheport)
Heisker or
Monach Islands
Cairinis
(Carinish)
Griomsaigh
EAVAL
347
RONA
Benbecula
Ronay
Baile a Mhanaich
(Balivanich)
B892
Gramsdal
(Gramsdale)
A865
BEINN NA FAOGHLA
(BENBECULA)
Lionacleit
Wiay
Creag Ghoraidh
(Creagorry)
B891
Hornish Point
Iochdar
Loch
Bee
Loch nam Faoileann
Our Lady of the Isles
Groigearraidh
(Grogarry)
BEN TARBERT
167
Stadhlaigearraidh (Stilligarry)
B890
Rudha Hallagro
Tobha Mor
(Howmore)
27
Loch
Druidbeg
606
HECLA
Staoinebrig
(Stoneybridge)
620
A865
BEINN MHOR
UIBHIST A DEAS
(SOUTH UIST)
Rudha Ardvule
620
Rudha Bolum
South Uist
Machair
374
Rudha Eyenort
STULAVAL
Staley
Dalabrog
(Daliburgh)
A865
Loch Baghasdail
(Lochboisdale)
A888
Loch
Boisdale
Ludag
201
Mallaig
RONEVAL
Rubha Ban
BEN SCREN
Fiaray
Scurrival
Point
Sound of Barra
ERISKAY
CANNA
Eolaigearraidh
Oitir
Mhor
BARRAIGH
(BARRA)
Bagh a Tuath
Hellisay
Borgh
(Borve)
A888
Gighay
HEAVAL
384
Tangusdale
Bruernish
Point
Bagh a Chaisteil
(Castlebay)
Kismul
Vatersay
Muldoanich
Bhatarsaigh
Sandray
Pabbay
Mingulay
Barra Head

THE MINCH
Ullapool
THE LITTLE MINCH
ISLE OF SKYE
RAASAY
SEA OF THE HEBRIDES
Mallaig
Oban
Bagh a Chaisteil / Loch Baghasdail (Castlebay) (Lochboisdale)

e f g

WESTERN ISLES

The Western Isles, na h-Eileanan Siar, stretch for 130 miles along the edge of the Atlantic, fringed on the west by mile after mile of clean, sandy beaches. The islands have a distinctive culture and Gaelic is the first language of the majority of islanders. Roadside place name signs are in Gaelic. Although one island, Lewis (north) and Harris (south) are very different. Lewis is low-lying and covered with bleak peat moors, whereas Harris is rocky and mountainous, with fertile green 'machair' land to the west.

North Uist, Benbecula and South Uist offer beaches and low-lying 'machair' to the west, and mountains and moorland to the east, while Barra has a rocky, broken east coast and fine-sand bays on the west, rising to a summit at Heaval.

Ferry Services

Lewis is linked by ferry to the mainland at Ullapool, with daily sailings (except Sunday). There are ferry services from Harris (Tairbeart) and North Uist (Loch nam Madadh) to Uig on Skye. Harris and North Uist are connected by a ferry service between An T-ob (Leverburgh) and Otternish. South Uist and Barra are served by ferry services from Oban, and a ferry service operates between South Uist and Barra. South Uist and North Uist are connected by causeways via Benbecula.

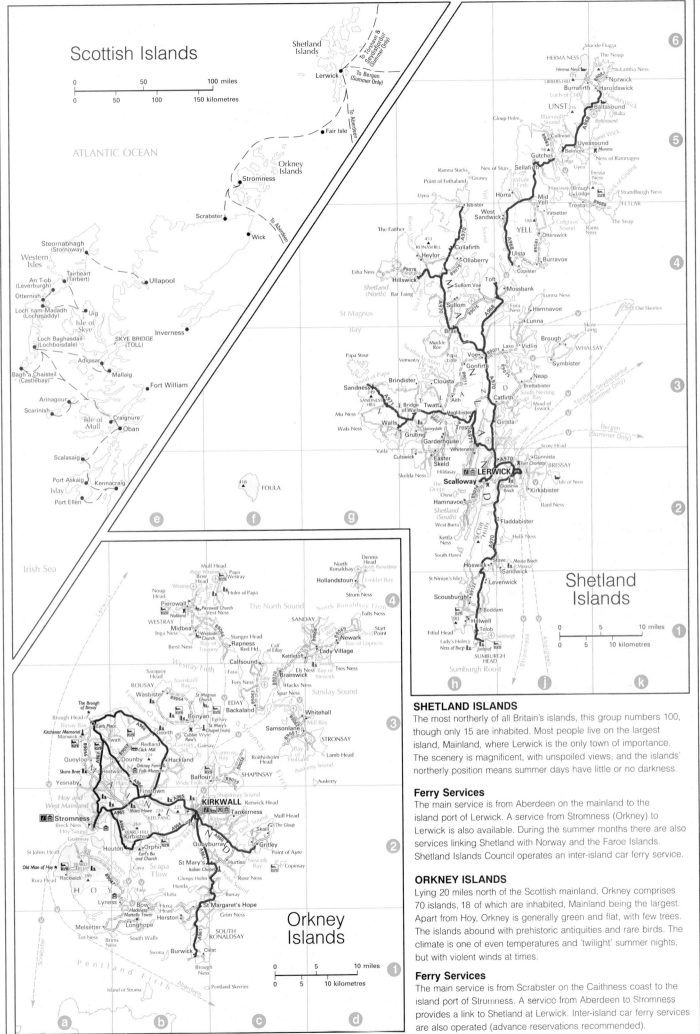

Scottish Islands

0   50   100 miles
0   50   100   150 kilometres

ATLANTIC OCEAN

Shetland Islands

Orkney Islands

SHETLAND ISLANDS

The most northerly of all Britain's islands, this group numbers 100, though only 15 are inhabited. Most people live on the largest island, Mainland, where Lerwick is the only town of importance. The scenery is magnificent, with unspoiled views, and the islands' northerly position means summer days have little or no darkness.

Ferry Services

The main service is from Aberdeen on the mainland to the island port of Lerwick. A service from Stromness (Orkney) to Lerwick is also available. During the summer months there are also services linking Shetland with Norway and the Faroe Islands. Shetland Islands Council operates an inter-island car ferry service.

ORKNEY ISLANDS

Lying 20 miles north of the Scottish mainland, Orkney comprises 70 islands, 18 of which are inhabited, Mainland being the largest. Apart from Hoy, Orkney is generally green and flat, with few trees. The islands abound with prehistoric antiquities and rare birds. The climate is one of even temperatures and 'twilight' summer nights, but with violent winds at times.

Ferry Services

The main service is from Scrabster on the Caithness coast to the island port of Stromness. A service from Aberdeen to Stromness provides a link to Shetland at Lerwick. Inter-island car ferry services are also operated (advance reservations recommended).

Ireland

Abbeydorney B3
Abbeyfeale B3
Abbeyleix D3
Adamstown D7
Adare B3
Adrigole B2
Ahascragh C4
Ahoghill E6
Allihies A2
Anascaul A2
Annalong E5
Annestown D2
Antrim E6
Ardagh B3
Ardara C6
Ardcath E4
Ardee D5
Ardfert B3
Ardfinnan C3
Ardglass E5
Ardgroom A2
Arklow E3
Arless D3
Armagh D6
Armoy E7
Arthurstown D2
Arvagh D5
Ashbourne E4
Ashford E4
Askeaton B3
Athboy D5
Athea B3
Athenry C4
Athleague C4
Athlone C4
Athy D4
Augher D6
Aughnacloy D6
Aughrim E3
Avoca E3

Bagenalstown D3
(Muine Bheag)
Bailieborough D5
Balbriggan E4
Balla B5
Ballacolla D3
Ballaghaderreen C5
Ballina B5
Ballina B3
Ballinafad C5
Ballinagh D5
Ballinakill D3
Ballinalee C5
Ballinamallard D6
Ballinamore C5
Ballinascarty B2
Ballinasloe C4
Ballindine B5
Ballineen B2
Ballingarry C3
Ballingarry B3
Ballingeary B2
(Béal Átha an Ghaorthaidh)
Ballinhassig C2
Ballinlough C5
Ballinrobe B5
Ballinspittle C2
Ballintober C5
Ballintra C6
Ballivor D4
Ballon D3
Ballybaun C4
Ballybay D5
Ballybofey C6
Ballybunion B3
Ballycanew E3
Ballycarry E6
Ballycastle B6
Ballycastle E7
Ballyclare E6
Ballyconneely A4
Ballycotton C2
Ballycumber C4
Ballydehob B1
Ballydesmond B2
Ballyduff C2
Ballyduff B3
Ballyfarnan C5
Ballygalley E6
Ballygar C4
Ballygawley D6
Ballygowan E6
Ballyhaise D5
Ballyhale D3
Ballyhaunis C5
Ballyhean B5
Ballyheige B4
Ballyjamesduff D5
Ballykeeran C4
Ballylanders C3
Ballylongford B3
Ballylooby C3
Ballylynan D3
Ballymahon C4
Ballymakeery B2
Ballymena E6
Ballymoe C5
Ballymoney D7
Ballymore C4
Ballymore Eustace D4
Ballymote C5
Ballynahinch E6
Ballynure E6
Ballyporeen C3
Ballyragget D3
Ballyroan D4
Ballyronan D6
Ballysadare C5
Ballyshannon C6
Ballyvaughan B4
Ballywalter E6
Balrothery E4
Baltimore B1
Baltinglass D3
Banagher C4
Banbridge E6
Bandon C2
Bangor E6
Bangor Erris B5
Bansha C3

Banteer B2
Bantry B2
Beaufort B2
Belcoo C6
Belfast E6
Belgooly C2
Bellaghy D6
Belleek E6
Belmullet B6
(Béal an Mhuirhead)
Belturbet D5
Benburb D6
Bennett's Bridge D3
Beragh D6
Birr C4
Blacklion C6
Blackwater E3
Blarney C2
Blessington D4
Boherbue B2
Borris D3
Borris-in-Ossory C4
Borrisokane C4
Borrisoleigh C3
Boyle C5
Bracknagh D4
Bray E4
Bridgetown D2
Brittas D4
Broadford C3
Broadford B3
Broughshane E6
Bruff C3
Bruree C3
Bunclody D3
Buncrana D7
Bundoran C6
Bunmahon D2
Bunnahowen B6
Bunnyconnellan B5
Burnfort C2
Bushmills D7
Butler's Bridge D5
Buttevant B2

Cadamstown C4
Caherconlish C3
Caherdaniel A2
Cahersiveen A2
Cahir C3
Caledon D6
Callan D3
Caltra C4
Camp A3
Cappagh White C3
Cappamore C3
Cappoquin C2
Carlanstown D5
Carlingford E5
Carlow D3
Carndonagh D7
Carnew D3
Carnlough E7
Carracastle C5
Carrick C6
(An Charraig)
Carrickfergus E6
Carrickmacross D5
Carrickmore D6
Carrick-on-Shannon C5
Carrick-on-Suir D3
Carrigaholt B3
Carrigaline C2
Carrigallen D5
Carriganimmy B2
Carrigans D7
Carrigart C7
(Carraig Airt)
Carrigtohill C2
Carrowkeel D7
Carryduff E6
Cashel C3
Castlebar B5
Castlebellingham E5
Castleblayney D5
Castlebridge D3
Castlecomer D3
Castlederg D6
Castledermot D3
Castleisland B3
Castlemaine B2
Castlemartyr C2
Castleplunket C5
Castlepollard D5
Castlerea C5
Castlerock D7
Castleshane D5
Castletown D4
Castletown
Bearhaven A2
Castletownroche C2
Castletownshend B1
Castlewellan E5
Causeway B3
Cavan D5
Celbridge D4
Charlestown C5
Charleville B3
(Rath Luirc)
Clady D6
Clane D4
Clara C4
Clarecastle B3
Claremorris B5
Clarinbridge B4
Clashmore C2
Claudy D7
Clifden A4
Cliffoney C6
Clogh D3
Clogheen C3
Clogher D6
Clohamon D3
Clonakilty B2
Clonard D4
Clonaslee D4
Clonbulloge D4
Clonbur B5
(An Fhairche)
Clondalkin E4

Clones D5
Clonmany D7
Clonmel C3
Clonmellon D5
Clonmore C3
Clonony C4
Clonoulty C3
Clonroche D3
Clontibret D5
Cloondara C5
Cloonlara C3
Clough E6
Cloughjordan C4
Cloyne C2
Coagh D6
Coalisland D6
Cobh C2
Coleraine D7
Collinstown D5
Collon D5
Collooney C5
Comber E6
Cong B5
Conna C2
Cookstown D6
Coole D5
Cooraclare B3
Cootehill D5
Cork C2
Cornamona B4
Corofin B4
Courtmacsherry B2
Courtown Harbour E3
Craigavon D6
Craughwell C4
Creeslough C7
Creggs C5
Croagh B3
Crookedwood D4
Crookhaven B1
Crookstown B2
Croom B3
Crossakeel D5
Crosshaven C2
Crossmaglen D5
Crossmolina B5
Crumlin E6
Crusheen B4
Culdaff D7
Culleybackey E6
Curracloe D3
Curraghboy C4
Curry B3
Cushendall E7

Daingean D4
Delvin D5
Derrygonnelly C6
Derrylin D5
Dervock E7
Dingle A2
(An Daingean)
Doagh E6
Donaghadee E6
Donaghmore C3
Donegal C6
Doneraile C2
Doon C4
Doonbeg B3
Douglas C2
Downpatrick E6
Dowra C5
Draperstown D6
Drimoleague B2
Dripsey B2
Drogheda E5
Dromahair C6
Dromcolliher B3
Dromod D5
Dromore D6
Dromore D6
Dromore West C6
Drum D5
Drumcliff C6
Drumconrath D5
Drumkeeran C5
Drumlish C5

Drumquin D6
Drumshanbo C5
Drumsna C5
Duagh B3
Dublin E4
Duleek E5
Dunboyne D4
Duncormick D2
Dundalk E5
Dunderrow C2
Dundrum E5
Dunfanaghy C7
Dungannon D6
Dungarvan C2
Dungarvan D3
Dungiven D7
Dungloe C7
(An Clochan Liath)
Dungourney C2
Dunkineely C6
Dun Laoghaire E4
Dunlavin D4
Dunleer E5
Dunloy E7
Dunmanway C5
Dunmore C5
Dunmore East D2
Dunmurry E6
Dunshaughlin D4
Durrow D3
Durrus B2
Dysart C4

Easky B6
Edenderry D4
Edgeworthstown D5
Eglinton D7
Elphin C5
Emyvale D6
Enfield D4
Ennis B3
Enniscorthy D3
Enniscrone B6
Enniskean B2
Enniskillen C6
Ennistymon B4
Eyrecourt C4

Farnaght C5
Farranfore B2
Feakle C4
Fenagh C5
Ferbane C4
Fermoy C2
Ferns D3
Fethard D2
Fethard C3
Finnea D5
Fintona D6
Fivemiletown D6
Fontstown D4
Foxford B5
Foynes B3
Freemount C3
Frenchpark C5
Freshford D3
Fuerty C5

Galbally C3
Galway B4
Garrison C6
Garristown E4
Garvagh D7
Geashill D4
Gilford E5
Glandore B1
Glanworth C2
Glaslough D6
Glassan C4
Glenamaddy C5
Glenarm E7
Glenavy E6
Glenbeigh A2
Glencolumbkille C6
(Gleann Cholm
Cille)
Glendalough E4
Glenealy E3
Glengarriff B2

Glenmore D3
Glenties C6
Glin B3
Glinsk B4
(Glinsce)
Golden C3
Goleen B1
Goresbridge D3
Gorey E3
Gort B4
Gortin D6
Gowran D3
Graiguenamanagh D3
Granard D5
Grange D5
Greyabbey E6
Greystones E4
Gulladuff D6

Hacketstown D3
Headford B4
Herbertstown C3
Hillsborough E6
Hilltown E5
Hospital C3
Holycross C3
Holywood E6
Howth E4

Inch A2
Inchigeelagh B2
Inishannon B2
Irvinestown D6

Johnstown C3

Kanturk B2
Keadue C5
Keady D5
Keel A5
Keenagh C5
Kells E6
Kells D5
Kenmare B2
Kesh C6
Kilbeggan D4
Kilberry D5
Kilbrittain B2
Kilcar C6
(Cill Charthaigh)
Kilcock D4
Kilcolgan B4
Kilconnell C4
Kilcoole E4
Kilcormac C4
Kilcullen D4
Kilcurry E5
Kildare D4
Kildavin D3
Kildorrery C2
Kilfenora B4
Kilgarvan B2
Kilkee B3
Kilkeel E5
Kilkelly C5
Kilkenny D3
Kilkieran B4
Kilkinlea B3
Kill D2
Killadysert B3
Killala B6
Killaloe C3
Killarney B2
Killashee C5
Killeigh D4
Killenaule C3
Killashandra D5
Killimer B3
Killimor C4
Killiney E4
Killinick D2
Killorglin B2
Killough E5
Killucan D4
Killybegs C6
Killyleagh E6
Kilmacanoge E4
Kilmacrenan C7
Kilmacthomas C2

Kilmaganny D3
Kilmaine B5
Kilmallock C3
Kilmeadan D2
Kilmeage D4
Kilmeedy B3
Kilmichael B2
Kilmore Quay D2
Kilnaleck D5
Kilrea D7
Kilrush B3
Kilsheelan C3
Kiltealy D3
Kiltegan D3
Kiltimagh B5
Kiltoom C4
Kingscourt D5
Kinlough C6
Kinnegad D4
Kinnitty C4
Kinsale C2
Kinvarra B4
Kircubbin E6
Knock B5
Knockcroghery C4
Knocklofty C3
Knocktopher D3

Lahinch B4
Laragh E4
Larne E6
Lauragh A2
Laurencetown C4
Leap B2
Leenane B5
Leighlinbridge D3
Leitrim C5
Leixlip D4
Lemybrien C2
Letterfrack B5
Letterkenny D7
Lifford D6
Limavady D7
Limerick C3
Lisbellaw D6
Lisburn E6
Liscannor B4
Liscarroll B3
Lisdoonvarna B4
Lismore C2
Lisnaskea D6
Lisryan D5
Listowel B3
Loghill B3
Londonderry D7
Longford C5
Loughbrickland E5
Loughgall D6
Loughglinn C5
Loughrea C4
Louisburgh B5
Lucan D4
Lurgan E6
Lusk E4

Macroom B2
Maghera E5
Maghera D6
Magherafelt D6
Maguiresbridge D6
Malahide E4
Malin D7
Malin More C6
Mallow C2
Manorhamilton C6
Markethill D6
Maynooth D4
Mazetown E6
Middletown D6
Midleton C2
Milford D7
Millstreet B2
Milltown B2
Milltown Malbay B3
Mitchelstown C3
Mohill C5
Monaghan D5

Monasterevin D4
Moneygall D4
Moneymore D6
Monivea C4
Mooncoin D2
Moorfields E6
Mount Bellew C4
Mount Charles C6
Mountmellick D4
Mountrath D4
Mountshannon C4
Moville D7
Moy D6
Moynalty D5
Moyvore C4
Muckross B2
Muff D7
Mullinavat D2
Mullingar D4
Mulrany B5
Myshall D3

Naas D4
Naul E4
Navan D5
Neale B5
Nenagh C3
Newbliss D5
Newbridge D4
(Droichead Nua)
Newcastle E5
Newcastle West B3
Newinn C3
Newmarket B2
Newmarket-on
Fergus B3
Newport C3
Newport B5
New Ross D3
Newry E5
Newtown D3
Newtownabbey E6
Newtownards E6
Newtownbutler D5
Newtownhamilton D5
Newtown-
mountkennedy E4
Newtownstewart D6
Newtown Forbes C5
Nobber D5

Oilgate D3
Oldcastle D5
Omagh D6
Omeath E5
Oola C3
Oranmore B4
Oughterard B4
Ovens B2

Pallas Green C3
Parknasilla A2
Partry B5
Passage East D2
Passage West C2
Patrickswell C3
Paulstown D3
Pettigo C6
Plumbridge D6
Pomeroy D6
Portadown E6
Portaferry E6
Portarlington D4
Portavogie E6
Portglenone E6
Portlaoise D4
Portmarnock E4

Portrane E4
Portroe C3
Portrush D7
Portstewart D7
Portumna C4
Poulgorm Bridge B2
Poyntzpass E6

Raharney D4
Randalstown E6
Rasharkin E7
Rathangan D4
Rathcoole D4
Rathcormack C2
Rathdowney C3
Rathdrum E3
Rathfriland E5
Rathkeale B3
Rathmelton D7
Rathmolyon D4
Rathmore B2
Rathmullan D7
Rathnew E4
Rathowen D4
Rathvilly D3
Ratoath D4
Ray E4
Ring (An Rinn) C2
Ringaskiddy C2
Rockcorry D5
Roosky C5
Rosapenna C7
Rosbercon D3
Roscommon C5
Roscrea C4
Ross Carbery B1
Rosscor C6
Rosses Point C6
Rosslare Harbour D2
Rosslea C5
Rostrevor E5
Roundstone A4
Roundwood E4
Rush E4

St Johnston D7
Saintfield E6
Sallins D4
Scarriff C4
Scartaglen B3
Scarva E6
Schull B1
Scramoge C5
Seskinore D6
Shanagarry C2
Shanagolden B3
Shannonbridge C4
Shercock D5
Shillelagh D3
Shinrone C4
Shrule B4
Silvermines C3
Sion Mills D6
Sixmilebridge B3
Skerries E4
Skibbereen B1
Slane D5
Sligo C6
Smithborough D5
Sneem A2
Spiddal B4
(An Spideal)
Stewartstown D6
Stonyford D3
Strabane D6
Stradbally D4
Stradone D5

Strandhill C6
Strangford E6
Stranorlar C6
Strokestown C5
Summerhill D4
Swanlinbar C5
Swatragh D6
Swinford B5
Swords E4

Taghmon D3
Tagoat D2
Tahilla A2
Tallaght E4
Tallow C2
Tallowbridge C2
Tandragee E6
Tang C4
Tarbert B3
Templemore C3
Templetouhy C3
Termonfeckin E5
Thomastown D3
Thurles C3
Timahoe D4
Timoleague B2
Tinahely D3
Tipperary C3
Tobercurry C5
Tobermore D6
Toomyvara C3
Toormore B1
Tralee B3
Tramore D2
Trim D4
Tuam B4
Tuamgraney C3
Tulla B3
Tullamore D4
Tullow D3
Tulsk C5
Turlough B5
Tyrellspass D4

Urlingford C3

Virginia D5

Warrenpoint E5
Waterford D2
Watergrasshill C2
Waterville A2
Westport B5
Wexford D3
Whitegate C2
Whitehead E6
Wicklow E4
Woodenbridge E3
Woodford C4

Youghal C2

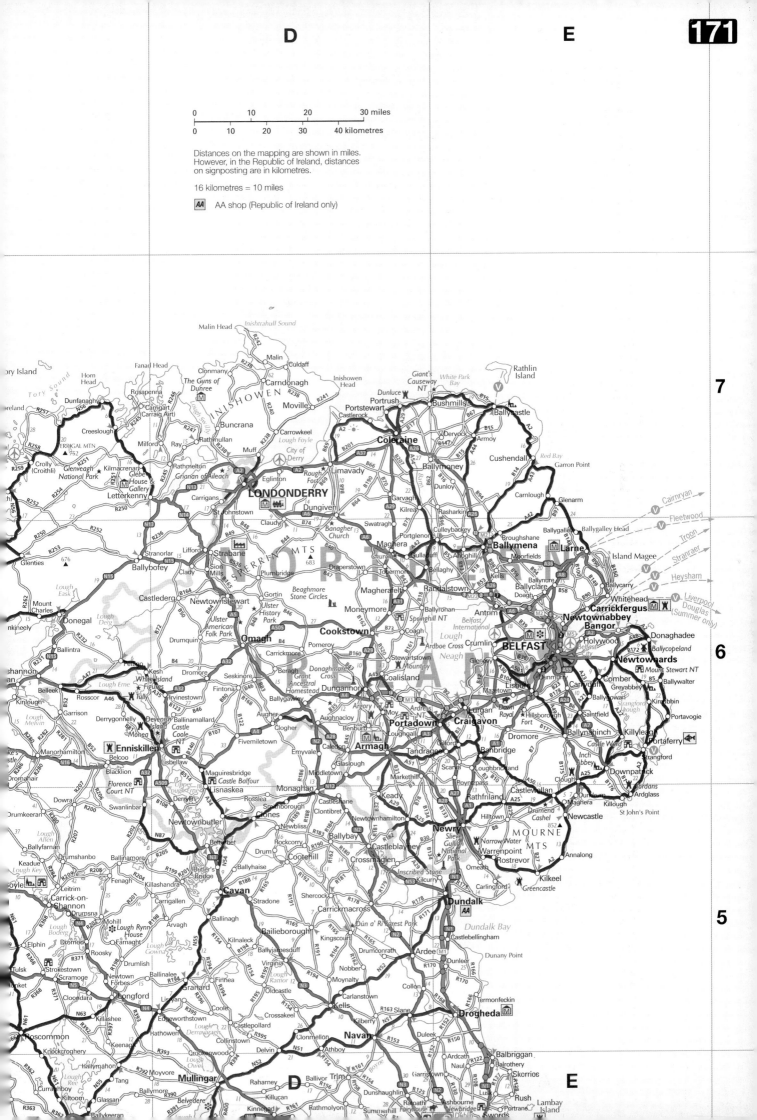

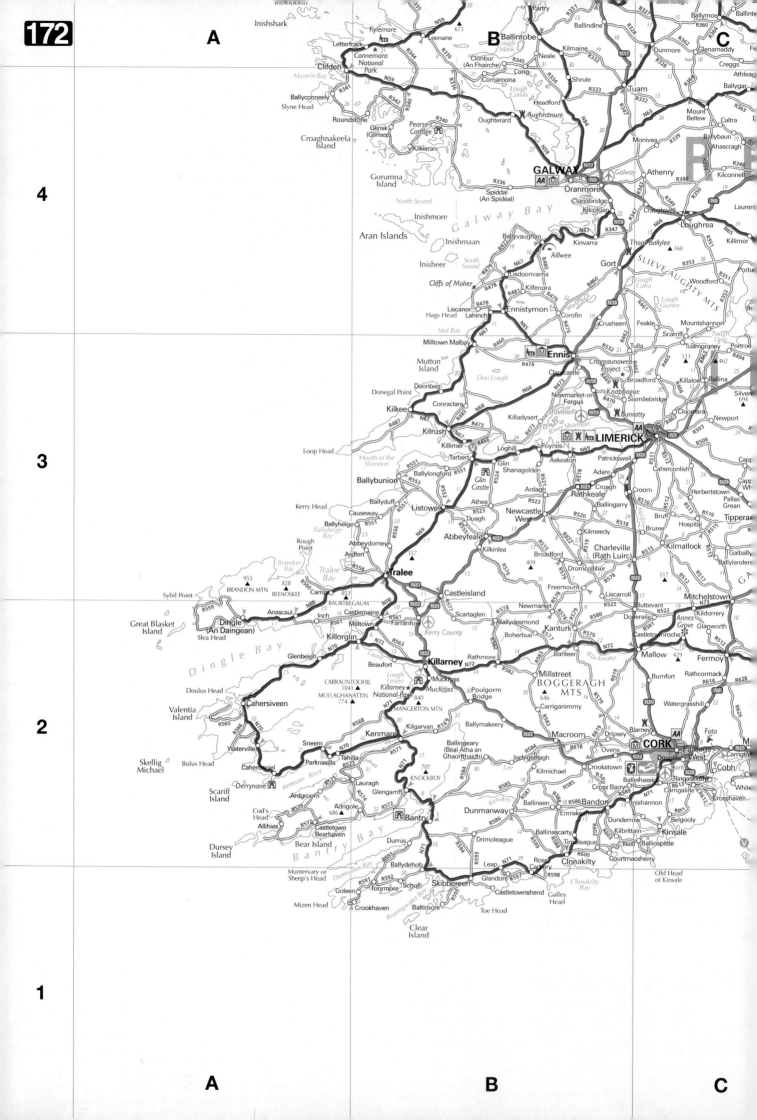

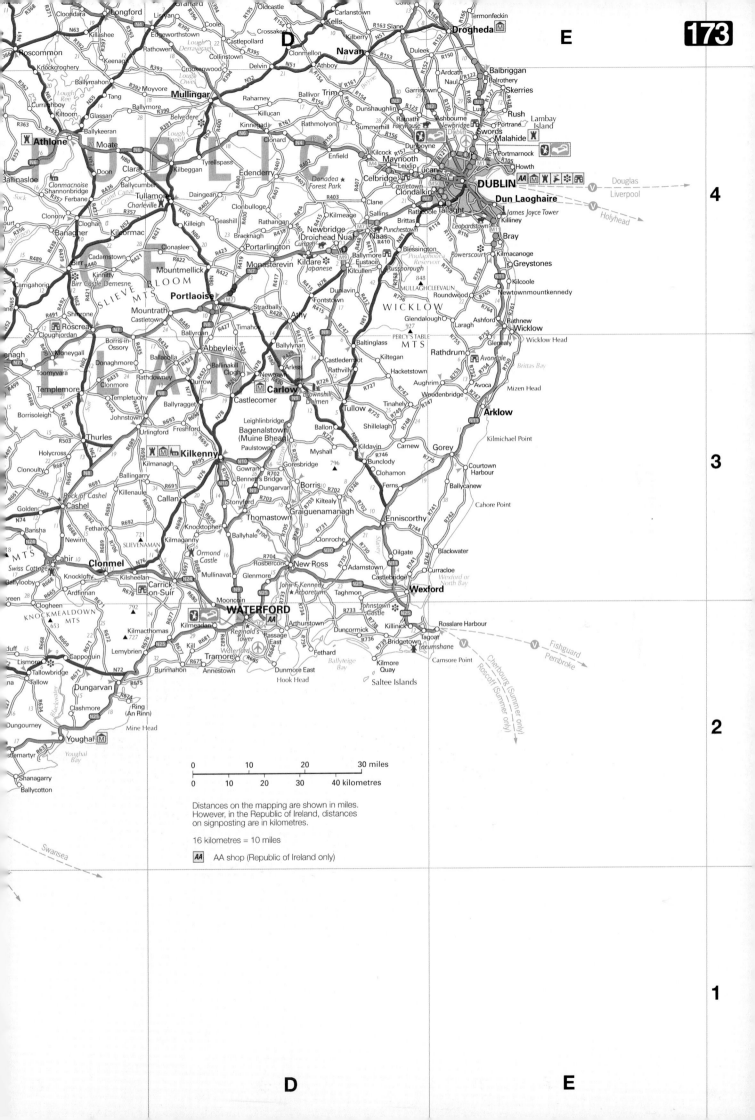

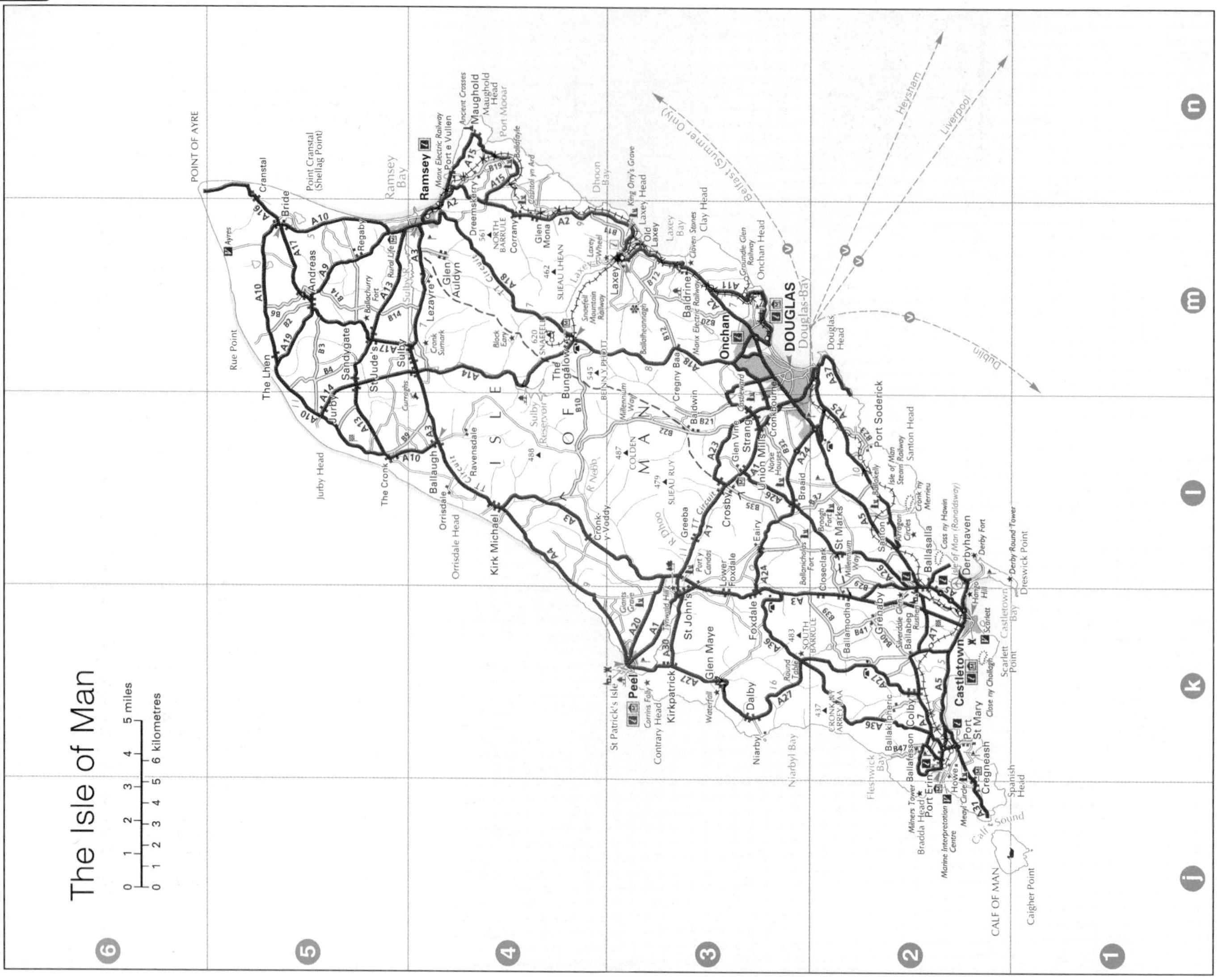

The Isle of Man

0 1 2 3 4 5 miles
0 1 2 3 4 5 6 kilometres

POINT OF AYRE

Ayres · Rue Point · The Lhen · Jurby Head · Jurby · The Cronk · Orrisdale Head · Orrisdale · Ballaugh · Kirk Michael

Cranstal · Bride · Regaby · Ballachurry · St Jude's · Sulby · Sandygate · Andreas · Lezayre · Glen Auldyn

Ramsey · Point Cranstal (Shellag Point) · Ramsey Bay · Manx Electric Railway · Port e Vullen · Ancient Crosses · Maughold · Maughold Head · Port Mooar

Dhoon Bay · Glen Mona · Ballaglass · Old Laxey · Laxey · Laxey Bay · Clay Head · North Barrule · Snaefell Mountain Railway · Snaefell · The Bungalow · Black Hut

King Orry's Grove · Onchan Head · Onchan · DOUGLAS · Douglas Bay · Douglas Head

Crosby · Union Mills · Baldrine · Groudle Glen · Port Soderick · Santon Head

St John's · Tynwald · Peel · St Patrick's Isle · Contrary Head · Kirkpatrick · Dalby · Niarbyl · Niarbyl Bay · Fleshwick Bay

Foxdale · Glen Maye · Waterfall · South Barrule · Round Table · Ballamodha · Ballasalla · Castletown · St Mary · Derbyhaven · Derby Fort · Isle of Man (Ronaldsway) · Derby Round Tower · Derbyhaven Bay · Langness Point · Dreswick Point

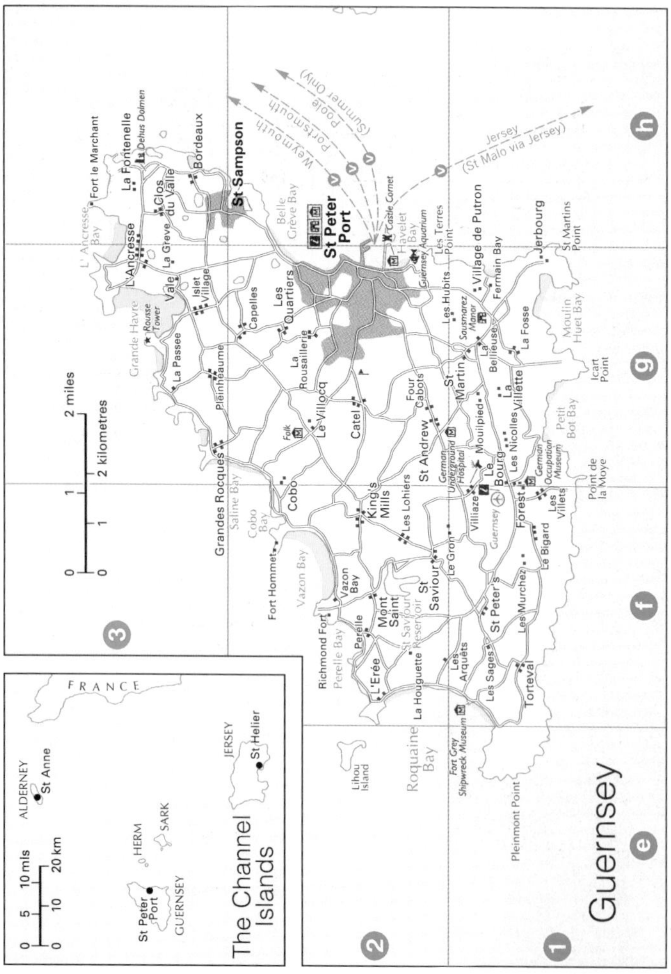

Colby · Ballabeg · Port St Mary · Port Erin · Cregneash · Howe · Bradda Head · Spanish Head · Calf of Man · Calf Sound · Chicken Rock · Kitterland

Liverpool · Belfast (Summer Only) · Heysham · Dublin

Guernsey

0 1 2 miles
0 1 2 kilometres

Fort le Marchant · La Fontenelle · Bordeaux · L'Ancresse Bay · L'Ancresse · Les Amarreurs · La Passee · Grandes Rocques · Cobo · Cobo Bay · Saline Bay · Vazon Bay · Perelle Bay · L'Erée · Lihou Island · Rocquaine Bay · Pleinmont Point · Fort Grey Shipwreck Museum · Torteval · Les Sages · Les Arquets · La Houguette · Mont Saint · St Saviour · St Peter's · Les Villets · Petit Bot Bay · Icart Point · Pointe de la Moye · Moulin Huet Bay · St Martin · Jerbourg · Jerbourg Point · St Martins Point · Village de Putron · Fermain Bay · La Fosse · St Peter Port · Belle Greve Bay · St Sampson · Vale

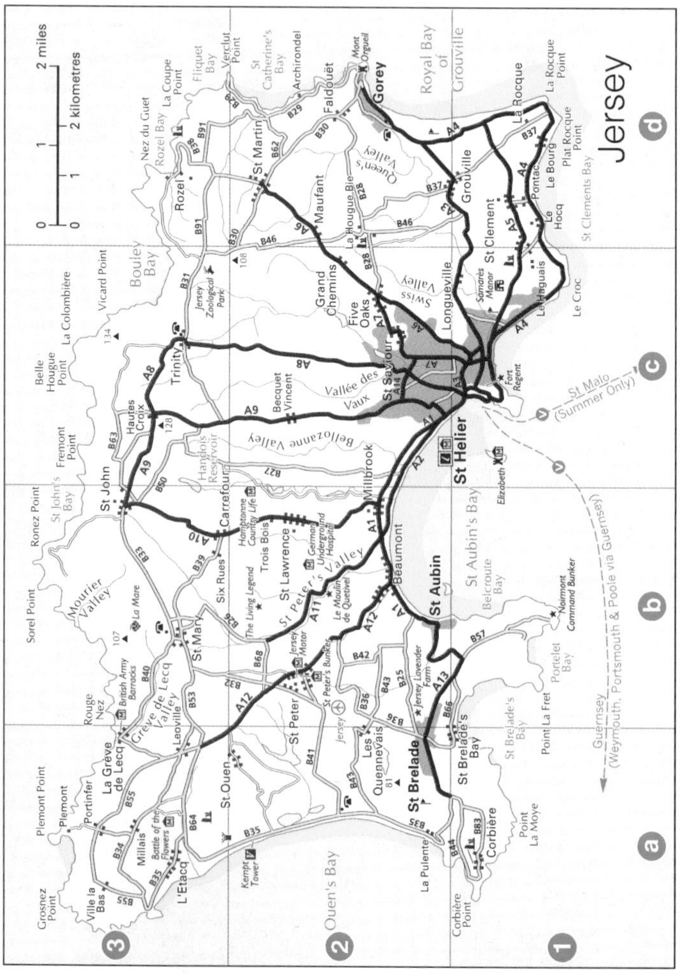

Weymouth · Poole (Summer Only) · Portsmouth · Jersey (St Malo via Jersey)

Jersey

0 1 2 miles
0 1 2 kilometres

Grosnez Point · Plemont Point · Plemont · Grève de Lecq · La Grève de Lecq · Le Val · Sorel Point · Ronez Point · St John's Bay · Bonne Nuit Bay · Bouley Bay · Rozel Bay · Rozel · Nez du Guet · Fliquet Bay · La Coupe Point · Verclut Point · St Catherine's Bay · Archirondel · Mont Orgueil · Gorey · Faldouet · St Martin · La Hougue Bie · Grouville · Royal Bay of Grouville · La Rocque · La Rocque Point · Le Bourg · Pontac · Plat Rocque Point · St Clement · Le Hocq · Samarès Manor · Le Croc · Longueville · St Saviour · St Helier · St Aubin · St Aubin's Bay · Beaumont · St Lawrence · Millbrook · Trinity · St John · Carrefour Selous · Six Rues · St Mary · St Ouen · St Brelade · St Brelade's Bay · Corbière · Corbière Point · La Pulente · La Moye · St Ouen's Bay · Le Braye

St Malo (Summer Only) · Guernsey (Weymouth, Portsmouth & Poole via Guernsey)

The Channel Islands

0 5 10 mils
0 10 20 km

FRANCE · ALDERNEY · St Anne · HERM · SARK · GUERNSEY · St Peter Port · JERSEY · St Helier

key to town plans

Aberdeen..................Page 176
Aberystwyth......................177
Basingstoke.......................177
Bath...............................178
Birmingham........................179
Blackpool..........................180
Bournemouth.......................178
Bradford..........................181
Brighton...........................181
Bristol............................182
Brixham...........................183
Cambridge.........................184
Canterbury........................183
Cardiff............................185
Carlisle...........................186
Chatham...........................186
Cheltenham........................187
Chester...........................187
Colchester........................188
Coventry..........................188
Darlington........................189
Derby.............................190
Doncaster.........................189
Dover.............................191
Dundee............................191
Durham............................192
Eastbourne........................192
Edinburgh.........................193
Exeter............................194
Glasgow...........................195
Gloucester........................194
Great Yarmouth....................196
Guildford.........................196
Harrogate.........................197
Huddersfield......................197
Hull..............................198
Inverness.........................198
Ipswich...........................199
Lancaster.........................199
Leeds.............................200
Leicester.........................201
Lincoln...........................202
Liverpool.........................203
Llandudno.........................202
LONDON..................240–250
Luton.............................204
Maidstone.........................204

Manchester.............Page 205
Margate...........................206
Middlesbrough.....................206
Milton Keynes.....................207
Newcastle-under-Lyme.....208
Newcastle upon Tyne........209
Newport...........................208
Newquay...........................210
Northampton.......................210
Norwich...........................211
Nottingham........................212
Oldham............................213
Oxford............................214
Paignton..........................213
Perth.............................215
Peterborough......................215
Plymouth..........................216
Poole.............................218
Portsmouth........................217
Preston...........................218
Ramsgate..........................219
Reading...........................219
St Andrews........................220
Salisbury.........................221
Scarborough.......................220
Sheffield.........................222
Shrewsbury........................223
Southampton.......................224
Southend-on-Sea...................223
Stirling..........................225
Stockton-on-Tees..................225
Stoke-on-Trent (Hanley).....226
Stratford-upon-Avon........226
Sunderland........................227
Swansea...........................228
Swindon...........................228
Taunton...........................229
Torquay...........................229
Tunbridge Wells...............230
Warwick...........................230
Watford...........................231
Weston-Super-Mare.......231
Winchester........................232
Windsor...........................232
Wolverhampton...............233
Worcester.........................233
York..............................234

175

Central London

Ports and airports

⛴	Ports....................................235
✈	Airports......................236–238
⏛	Channel Tunnel................239

Town plan legend

	AA-recommended routes
	Restricted roads / pedestrians only
	Other roads
COLLEGE ■	Buildings of interest
†	Churches
	Parks and open spaces
P	Car parks
C C	Toilets
←	One-way streets
	Shopmobility
P+	Park and ride
M	Metrolink stations

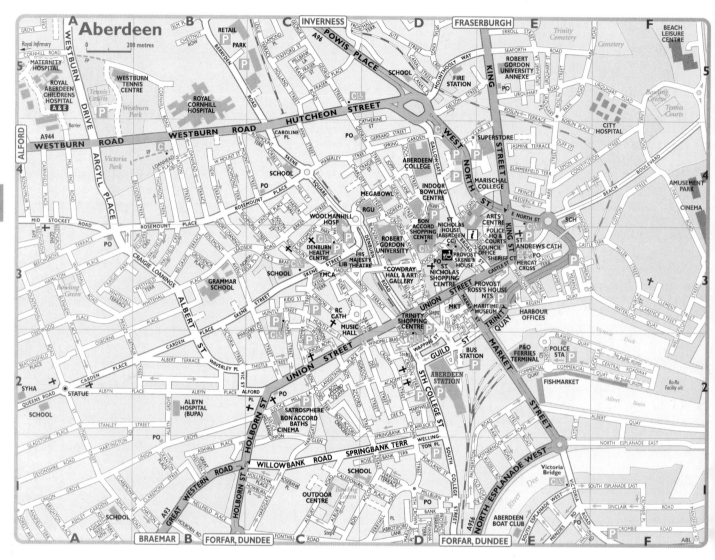

Aberdeen

Aberdeen is found on atlas page **149 G5**

Academy Street	D2	Brighton Place	A1	Deeswood Place	A2-A3	Jopps Lane	D4	Poynernook Road	E1-E2	Springbank Terrace	C1-D1
Affleck Street	D2	Broad Street	D3-E3	Denburn Road	D3-D4	Justice Mill Lane	C2	Prince Arthur Street	A3-A2-B2	Stafford Street	C5
Albert Quay	E2-F2	Cairnfield Place	A4	Devonshire Road	A1	Justice Mill Bank	C2	Princes Street	E4	Stanley Street	A2-B2
Albert Street	B2-B3	Caledonian Place	C1-D1	East North Street	E4	Jute Street	D5	Queen Street	D3-E3-E4	Stell Road	E1-E2
Albert Terrace	B2	Canal Street	D5	Erroll Street	E5	Kidd Street	C2	Queens Road	A2	Stirling Street	D2-D3
Albury Place	C1	Carden Place	A2-B2-B3	Esslemont Avenue	B4-B3-C3	King Street	E3-E4-E5	Raik Road	E1-E2	Summer Street	C2-C3
Albury Road	C1	Caroline Place	C4	Exchange Street	D3	Kintore Place	C4	Regent Quay	E3	Summerfield Terrace	E4
Albyn Grove	B1-B2	Castle Street	E3	Farmers Hall	C4	Lamond Place	C5	Regent Road	E2	Thistle Street	C2
Albyn Place	A2-B2	Castle Terrace	E3-F3	Ferryhill Road	D1	Langstane Place	C2-D2	Richmond Street	B4-C4-C3	Thomson Street	B4
Alford Place	B2-C2	Catherine Street	C5-D5	Ferryhill Terrace	D1	Leadside Road	B3-C3	Richmond Terrace	B4	Trinity Quay	E3
Ann Street	C4	Central Roadway	F2	Forbes Street	C4	Lemon Street	E4	Rose Street	C2-C3	Union Glen	C1-C2
Annfield Terrace	A1	Chapel Street	C2-C3	Fountainhall Road	A2-A3	Leslie Terrace	C5	Rosebank Place	C1	Union Grove	A1-B1-B2-C2
Argyll Place	A4	Charlotte Street	C4-D4	Fraser Place	C5	Links Road	F3-F4-F5	Rosebank Terrace	C1-D1	Union Row	C2
Ashley Gardens	A1	Chestnut Row	B5	Fraser Road	C5	Littlejohn Street	D4	Rosemount Place	A4-B4-C4	Union Street	C2-D2-D3
Ashley Road	A1-B1	Church Street	F3	Frederick Street	E4	Loanhead Terrace	B4	Rosemount Terrace	C4	Union Terrace	C3-D3
Ashvale Place	B1-B2	Claremont Place	A1-B1	Gallowgate	D4	Loch Street	D4	Rosemount Viaduct	C3	Union Wynd	C2-C3
Back Wynd	D3	Claremont Street	B1	George Street	C5-C4-D4	Maberley Street	C4-D4	Roslin Place	E4-E5	Urquhart Lane	E5
Baker Street	C3-C4	Clarence Street	F3	Gerrard Street	D4	Margaret Street	B2-C3	Roslin Street	E5	Urquhart Place	E5
Bank Street	D1	Clyde Street	E2	Gilcomston Park	C3	Marischal Street	E3	Roslin Terrace	E5	Urquhart Road	E5-F5
Beach Boulevard	E4-F4	Commerce Street	E3	Gladstone Place	A1-A2	Market Street	D3-E3-E2	Russell Road	E1	Urquhart Street	E5
Beechgrove Avenue	A3-A4	Commercial Quay	E2-F2	Gordon Street	C2-D2	Marywell Street	D2	St Andrews Street	D4	Victoria Road	E1-F1
Beechgrove Gardens	A3-A4	Constitution Street	E4-F4	Granton Place	B1	Mearns Street	E3	St Clair Street	D4-E4-E5	Victoria Street	B2-B3
Beechgrove Terrace	A3	Cornhill Road	A5	Great Western Place	B1	Menzies Road	E1	St Clement Street	F3	View Terrace	C3
Belgrave Terrace	B3	Cornhill Road	B4-B5	Great Western Road	B1	Mid Stocket Road	A3-A4	St Swithin Street	A1-A2	Wallfield Crescent	B3
Belmont Street	D3	Cotton Street	F3-F4	Grosvenor Place	B3	Mile End Road	A4	School Hill	D3	Wallfield Place	B3
Belvidere Street	A4-B4	Craigie Loanings	B3	Guild Street	D2-D3	Millburn Street	D1	Seaforth Road	E5	Wapping Street	D2-D3
Berry Street	D4	Craigie Park	A3	Hamilton Place	A3	Miller Street	F3	Short Loanings	B3-B4	Waterloo Quay	F2-F3
Berryden Road	B5-C5	Craigie Street	C4-D4	Hanover Street	E3-E4	Mount Street	B4-C4	Silver Street North	C3	Watson Street	B4
Blackfriar Street	D3-D4	Crimon Place	C3	Hardgate	C1-C2	Mounthooly Way	D5-E5	Sinclair Road	E1-F1	Waverley Place	B2
Blaikies Quay	E3-E2-F2	Crombie Place	F1	Hartington Road	A1-A2	Nellfield Place	B1	Skene Square	C4	Wellington Place	D1-D2
Blenheim Place	A2-A3	Crombie Road	F1	Hill Street	C4	Nelson Street	D5	Skene Street	B3-C3	Wellington Street	F2-F3
Bon Accord Crescent	C2	Crooked Lane	D3-D4	Holborn Street	B1-C1-C2	North Esplanade East	E1-F1	Skene Terrace	C3	West Mount Street	B4
Bon Accord Square	C2	Crown Street	D1-D2	Holland Street	C5	North Esplanade West	D1-E1	South College Street	D1-D2	West North Street	D5-D4-E4
Bon Accord Street	C1-D1-D2-C2	Crown Terrace	D2	Hollybank Place	C1	Northfield Place	B3-C3	South Crown Street	D1	Westburn Drive	A4-A5
Bon Accord Terrace	C2	Dee Place	D2	Howburn Place	C1	Old Ford Road	E1	South Esplanade East	E1-F1	Westburn Road	A4-B4-C4
Bridge Street	D2-D3	Dee Street	D2	Huntly Street	C2-C3	Osborne Place	A2-A3-B3	South Esplanade West	E1	Westfield Terrace	B3
				Hutcheon Street	C4-C5-D5	Palmerston Road	D1-E1-E2	South Mount Street	C3-C4	Whitehall Place	A3-B3
				Jack's Brae	C1-C2	Park Road	E5-F5	Spa Street	C3-C4	Whitehall Road	A3
				James Street	E3	Park Street	E4	Spital Kings Crescent	D5	Whitehall Terrace	A3-B3
				Jasmine Terrace	E4	Portland Street	D1	Spring Garden	D4	Willowbank Road	C1
				John Street	C4-D4	Powis Place	C5-D5	Springbank Street	D2	Windmill Brae	D2

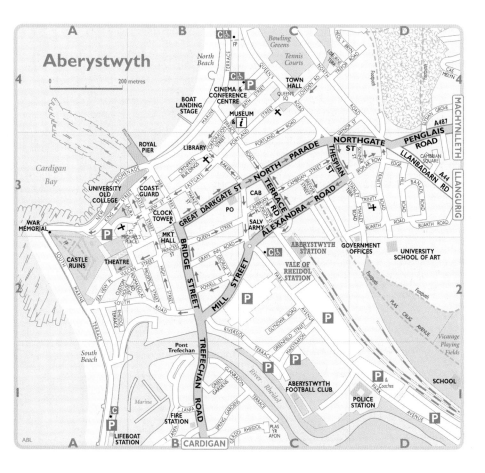

Aberystwyth

Aberystwyth is found on atlas page **54 C3**

Alexandra Road	C2-C3	Poplar Row	D3
Baker Street	B3-C3	Portland Road	C3-C4
Banadl Road	D3	Portland Street	B3-C3-C4
Bath Street	B4-C4	Powell Street	B2
Brewer Street	C3	Princess Street	B2
Bridge Street	B2-B3	Prospect Street	B2
Buarth Road	D3	Queen Street	B2-B3-C3
Cae Melyn	D4	Queen's Road	C3-C4
Cambrian Place	C3	Queen's Square	C4
Cambrian Square	D3	Rheidol Terrace	A2
Cambrian Street	C3	Riverside Terrace	B2-C2-C1
Castle Street	B3	St Michael's Place	B2-B3
Corporation Street	B3-B4	Sea View Place	A2
Crynfryn Buildings	B3	Skinner Street	D3
Custom House Street	A2-B2	South Marine Terrace	A1-A2-A3
Eastgate	B3	South Road	A2-B2
Edge Hill Road	D3	Spring Gardens	B1-C1
Elysian Grove	D4	Stanley Road	D3
George Street	B2	Stanley Terrace	C3
Gerddi Rheidol	B1-C1	Terrace Road	B4-B3-C3
Glanrafon Terrace	B1-C1	Thespian Street	C3
Glyndwr Road	C2	Trefechan Road	B1-B2
Grays Inn Road	B2-C2	Trefor Road	C4-D4
Great Darkgate Street	B3-C3	Trinity Place	D3
Green Gardens	B1	Trinity Road	D3
Greenfield Street	C1-C2	Union Street	C3
Heoly Bryn	C4-D4	Vaynor Street	C3-C4-D4
High Street	B2	Vulcan Street	A2-B2
King Street	A3-B3	Y Lanfa	B1
Laura Place	A3-B3		
Lisburne Terrace	C4		
Llanbadarn Road	D3		
Loveden Road	C4		
Maesyrafon	C1-C2		
Marine Terrace	B3-B4		
Market Street	B3		
Mill Street	B2-C2		
New Promenade	A3-B3		
New Street	B3		
North Parade	C3		
North Road	C4-D4-D3		
Northgate Street	C3-D3		
Park Avenue	C2-C1-D1		
Penglais Road	D3-D4		
Penmaesglas	B2		
Pier Street	B3		
Plas Crug Avenue	D1-D2		
Plas Yr Afon	C1		

Basingstoke

Basingstoke is found on atlas page **27 E4**

Alencon Link	A4-B4-C4	Rayleigh Road	A2-A3
Allnutt Avenue	D3	Red Lion Lane	C2
Basing View	C4-D4	Rochford Road	A3
Beaconsfield Road	B1-C1	St Mary's Court	C3-D3
Bounty Rise	A1	Sarum Hill	A2-B2
Bounty Road	A1-B1	Southend Road	A3
Bramblys Close	A2	Southern Road	B1-C1
Bramblys Drive	A2	Timberlake Road	A3-B3-B2, C3
Budds Close	A2	Victoria Street	B1-B2
Bunnian Place	C4	Vyne Road	B4
Castle Road	C1	White Hart Lane	D2
Chapel Hill	A4-B4	Winchester Road	A1-A2-B2
Chequers Road	C3-D3	Winchester Street	B2
Chester Place	A1	Winterthur Way	A4-B4
Church Hill	B4	Worting Road	A2
Church Square	B3	Wote Street	B2-C2
Church Street	B2-B3		
Churchill Way	A3-B3-B4-C4		
Churchill Way East	C4-D4		
Churchill Way West	A3		
Cliddesden Road	C1		
Clifton Terrace	B4-C4		
Council Road	B1		
Cross Street	B2		
Crossborough Gardens	D1-D2		
Crossborough Hill	D1-D2		
Eastfield Avenue	D2-D3		
Eastrop Lane	D2-D3		
Eastrop Way	D3		
Essex Road	A2-A3		
Fairfields Road	B1-C1		
Flaxfield Court	A2-A3		
Flaxfield Road	A2-B2		
Frances Road	A1		
Frescade Crescent	A1		
Goat Lane	C3-D3		
Hackwood Road	C1-C2		
Hardy Lane	A1		
Jubilee Road	B1		
London Road	C2-D2		
London Street	C2		
Lytton Road	D2		
Mortimer Lane	A3		
New Road	B2-C2-C3		
New Street	B2		
Old Market Square	B2		
Old Reading Road	C4		
Penrith Road	A1-A2		

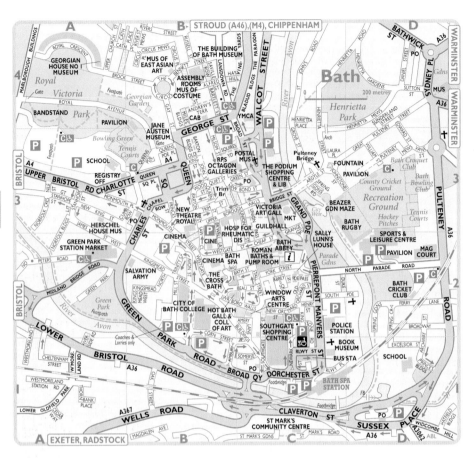

Bath

Bath is found on atlas page **24 C6**

Abbey Square	C2	Lower Oldfield Park	A1
Alfred Street	B4	Manvers Street	C1-C2
Ambury	B1	Midland Bridge Road	A2
Argyle Street	C3	Mill Street	A2
Avon Street	B2	Milsom Street	B3-B4
Barton Street	B3	Monmouth Place	A3-B3
Beau Street	B2-C2	Monmouth Street	B2-B3
Bennett Street	B4	New Bond Street	B3-C3
Bladud Buildings	B4-C4	New King Street	A3-B3
Bridewell Lane	B2-B3	New Orchard Street	C2
Bridge Street	C3	North Parade Road	C2-D2
Bristol Road	A2-A1-B1	Oak Street	B1
Broad Quay	B1-C1	Old Orchard Street	C2
Broad Street	B4-C3	Pierrepont Street	C2
Broadway	D2	Princes Street	B3
Brock Street	A4-B4	Pulteney Road	D1-D2-D3
Chapel Row	B3	Queen Square	B3
Charles Street	A2-B2-B3	Queen Square Place	B3
Charlotte Street	A3-B3	Queen Street	B3
Cheap Street	C2-C3	Quiet Street	B3
Circus Mews	B4	Railway Street	C1
Claverton Street	C1	Royal Avenue	A4-B4-B3
Corn Street	B2	Royal Crescent	A4
Dorchester Street	C1	Russell Street	B4
Edward Street	D3-D4	St John's Road	C4
Ferry Lane	D2	Saw Close	B2-B3
Gay Street	B4	South Parade	C2-D2
George Street	B3-B4	Southgate Street	C1-C2
Grand Parade	C3	Stall Street	C2
Grange Grove	C3	Sussex Place	D1
Great Pulteney Street	C3-D3-D4	Sydney Place	D4
Great Stanhope Street	A3	The Circus	B4
Green Park	A2	The Paragon	C4
Green Park Road	A2-B2-B1	The Vineyards	B4-C4
Green Street	B3-C3	Trim Street	B3
Grove Street	C3-C4	Union Passage	C2-C3
Henrietta Gardens	D4	Union Street	C2-C3
Henrietta Mews	C4-D4	Upper Borough Walls	B3-C3
Henrietta Road	C4-D4	Upper Bristol Road	A3
Henrietta Street	C3-C4	Upper Church Street	A4
Henry Street	C2	Walcot Street	C4
James Street West	A2-A3	Wells Road	A1-B1
John Street	B3	Westgate	B2
Kingsmead North	B2	Westgate Street	B2-C2
Kingsmead Street	B2	Westmoreland Road	A1
Lansdown Road	B4	William Street	D3
Little Stanhope Street	A3	Wood Street	B3
Lower Borough Walls	B2-C2	York Street	C2

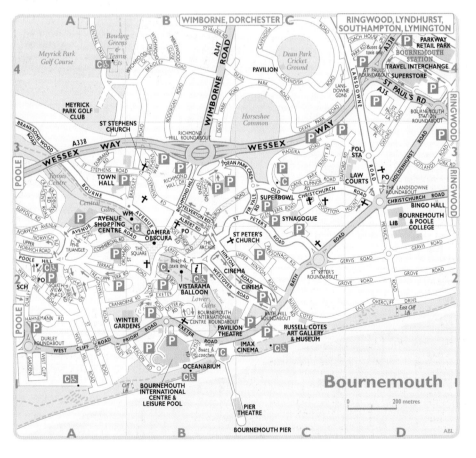

Bournemouth

Bournemouth is found on atlas page **13 E4**

Albert Road	B2-B3	Park Road	D4
Avenue Lane	A2	Parsonage Road	C2
Avenue Road	A2-A3-B2	Poole Hill	A2
Bath Road	C2-D2-D3	Post Office Road	B2
Beacon Road	B1	Priory Road	A1-B1-B2
Bodorgan Road	B3-B4	Purbeck Road	A2
Bourne Avenue	A3-B3-B2	Richmond Gardens	B3
Bradburne Road	A3	Richmond Hill	B3
Braidley Road	B3-B4	Richmond Hill Drive	B3
Branksome Wood Road	A3-A4	Russell Cotes Road	C2
Cavendish Road	C4	St Michael's Road	A1-A2
Central Drive	A3-A4	St Paul's Lane	D4
Christchurch Road	D3	St Paul's Place	D3
Coach House Place	D4	St Paul's Road	D4
Commercial Road	A2-B2	St Peter's Road	B2-B3-C3-C2
Cumnor Road	C3	St Stephens Road	A3-B3
Cotlands Road	D3	St Stephens Way	B3
Cranborne Road	A2-B2	St Valerie Road	B4
Crescent Road	A3	South Cliff Road	B1
Dean Park Crescent	B3-C3	South View Place	A2
Dean Park Road	B3-B4-C4-C3	Stafford Road	C3-D3
Durley Road	A2	Suffolk Road	A3
Durrant Road	A3	Terrace Road	A2-B2
East Overcliff Drive	C2-D2	The Square	B2
Exeter Crescent	B2	The Triangle	A2
Exeter Park Road	B2	Tregonwell Road	A1-A2
Exeter Road	B1-B2	Trinity Road	C3
Fir Vale Road	C3	Upper Hinton Road	B2-C2
Gervis Place	B2	Upper Norwich Road	A2
Gervis Road	C2-D2	Upper Terrace Road	A2-B2
Glen Fern Road	C3	Wessex Way	A3-B3-C3-D4
Grove Road	C2-D2	West Cliff Gardens	A1
Hahnemann Road	A2	West Cliff Road	A1
Hinton Road	B2-C2	West Hill Road	A1-A2
Holdenhurst Road	D3-D4	Westover Road	B2-C2
Kerley Road	A1-B1	Wimborne Road	B3-B4
Lansdowne Gardens	C4-D4	Wootton Mount	C3-D3
Lansdowne Road	C4-D4-D3	Wychwood Close	B4
Lorne Park Road	C3	Wychwood Drive	B4
Madeira Road	C3	Yelverton Road	B3
Merlewood Close	B4	York Road	D3
Meyrick Road	D2-D3		
Norwich Avenue	A2-A3		
Norwich Road	A2		
Old Christchurch			
Road	B2-B3-C3-D3		
Orchard Street	A2-B2		
Oxford Road	D3-D4		

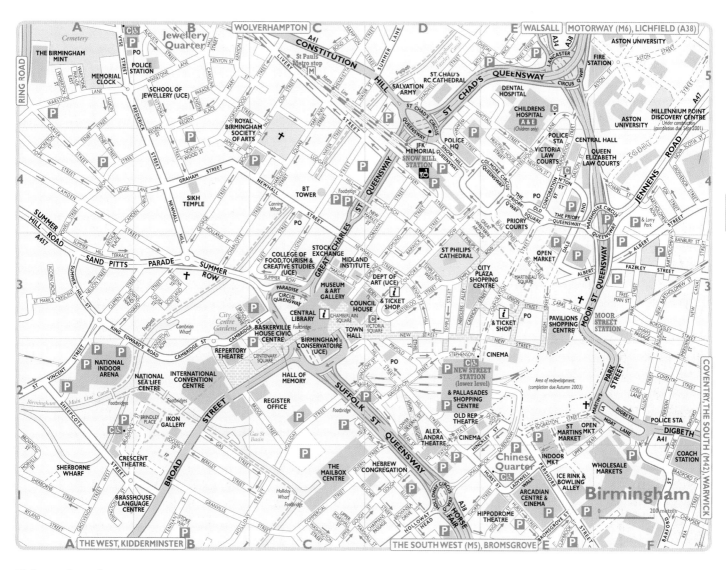

Birmingham

Birmingham is found on atlas page **58 D4**

Acorn Grove	A3	Carrs Lane	E3	Freeman Street	F3
Albert Street	E3-F3-F4	Carver Street	A4-A5	Gas Street	B2-B1-C1
Albion Street	A4-B4	Centenary Square	C2	George Street	B3-B4
Allison Street	F2-F3	Chamberlain Square	C3	Gough Street	D1
Arthur Place	A3-A4	Chapel Street	F4	Graham Street	B4
Aston Street	E5-F5	Chapmans Passage	D1	Granville Street	B1-C1
Augusta Street	B5	Charlotte Street	B3-B4-C4	Great Charles Street	
Banbury Street	F3	Cheapside	F1	Queensway	C3-C4-D4
Barford Street	F1	Church Street	D3-D4	Grosvenor Street	F4
Bartholomew Row	F4	Claybrook Street	E1	Grosvenor Street West	A1
Bartholomew Street	F3-F4	Clement Street	A3-B3	Hall Street	B5
Barwick Street	D3-D4	Coleshill Street	F4-F5	Hampton Street	C5-D5
Bath Street	D5-E5	Colmore Circus		Helena Street	B3
Beak Street	D1-D2	Queensway	D4-E4	Henrietta Street	C5-D5
Bennetts Hill	D3	Colmore Row	D3-D4	High Street	E2-E3
Berkley Street	B1-C1	Commercial Street	C1	Hill Street	C2-D2
Blucher Street	C1-D1	Constitution Hill	C5-D5	Hinckley Street	D1-E2
Bond Street	C5	Cornwall Street	C3-D3-D4	Holland Street	B3-B4
Bordesley Street	F2-F3	Corporation Street	E3-E4-E5	Holliday Street	B1-C1-C2
Bradford Street	F1	Coventry Street	F2	Holloway Circus Queensway	D1
Bridge Street	B2-C2-C1	Cox Street	C5	Holloway Head	D1
Brindley Drive	B3	Dale End	E3-E4	Horse Fair	D1
Brindley Place	B2	Dalton Street	E4	Hurst Street	E1
Broad Street	A1-B1-B2-C2	Digbeth	F2	Inge Street	E1
Bromsgrove Street	E1	Dudley Street	E2	James Street	B4
Brook Street	B4-C4	Eden Place	C3-D3	Jennens Road	F4-F5
Browning Street	A1-A2	Edgbaston Street	E2	John Bright Street	D1-D2
Brownsea Drive	D1	Edmund Street	C3-D3-D4	Kenyon Street	B5
Brunel Street	C2-D2	Edward Street	A3-B3	King Edward's Road	A3-A2-B2
Brunswick Street	A1-A2-B2	Ellis Street	D1	Kingston Row	B2-B3
Bull Street	E3-E4	Essington Street	A1	Ladywell Walk	E1
Cambridge Street	B2-B3-C3	Ethel Street	D2	Lancaster Circus Queensway	E5
Camden Drive	A4-B4	Fazeley Street	F3	Legge Lane	A4-B4
Camden Street	A4-B3	Fleet Street	C3-C4	Lionel Street	C3-C4
Cannon Street	D3-E3	Fox Street	F4	Livery Street	C5-C4-D4
Caroline Street	B5-C5	Frederick Street	A5-B5-B4	Louisa Street	B3

Loveday Street	D5-E5	Pinfold Street	D2	Summer Lane	D5
Lower Severn Street	D2	Pope Street	A4	Summer Row	B3-C3
Ludgate Hill	C4	Powell Street	A3-A4	Swallow Street	C2-D2
Margaret Street	C3	Price Street	E5	Temple Row	D3-E3
Marshall Street	C1-D1	Printing House Street	E4	Temple Row West	D3
Martin's Lane	E2-F2	Rea Street	F1	Temple Street	D3
Mary Ann Street	C5	Regent Parade	B5	Tenby Street	A4
Mary Street	B5-C5	Regent Place	B5	Tenby Street North	A4-A5
Masshouse Circus		Regent Street	B4-B5	Tennant Street	B1
Queensway	E3-E4-F4-F3	Royal Mail Street	C2-D2	The Priory Queensway	E4
Meriden Street	F2	Ryland Street	A1	Thorpe Street	D1-E1
Mill Lane	F1-F2	St Chad's Circus		Townsend Way	A3-B3
Moat Lane	F2	Queensway	D4-D5	Union Street	E3
Moor Street Queensway	E3-F3	St Chad's Queensway	D5-E5	Upper Dean Street	E1-F2
Moreton Street	A4	St Mark's Crescent	A3	Upper Gough Street	C1-D1
Morville Street	A1	St Paul's Square	C4-C5	Upper Marshall Street	C1
Navigation Street	D2	St Philips Place	D4-D3-E3	Vesey Street	E5
Needless Alley	D3	St Vincent Street	A2-A3	Victoria Square	D3
Nelson Street	A3	Sand Pitts	A3	Vittoria Street	B4-B5
New Bartholomew Street	F3	Scotland Street	B3	Vyse Street	A5
New Canal Street	F3-F4	Severn Street	C1-D1	Warstone Lane	A5-B5
New Market Street	C4-D4	Shadwell Street	D5	Warstone Parade East	A5
New Street	D3-E3-E2	Shaws Passage	F2-F3	Washington Street	C1
Newhall Hill	B3-B4	Sheepcote Street	A1-A2	Water Street	C4-C5-D5
Newhall Street	B4-C4-C3-D3	Sherborne Street	A1	Waterloo Street	D3
Newton Street	E4	Smallbrook Queensway	D1-E1-E2	Weaman Street	D4-D5
Northwood Street	B4-B5-C5	Snow Hill Queensway	D4	Well Lane	F2
Nova Scotia Street	F4	Station Street	D1-D2	Whittall Street	D5-E5-E4
Old Square	E4	Steelhouse Lane	E4-E5		
Oozel's Street	B1-B2	Stephenson Street	D2-E2		
Oxford Street	F2	Stoke Way	B1		
Parade	B3	Suffolk Street			
Paradise Circus Queensway	C3	Queensway	C2-D2-D1		
Park Street	F2-F3	Summer Hill Road	A3-A4		
Pemberton Street	A5	Summer Hill Street	A3		
Pershore Street	E1-E2	Summer Hill Terrace	A3-B3		

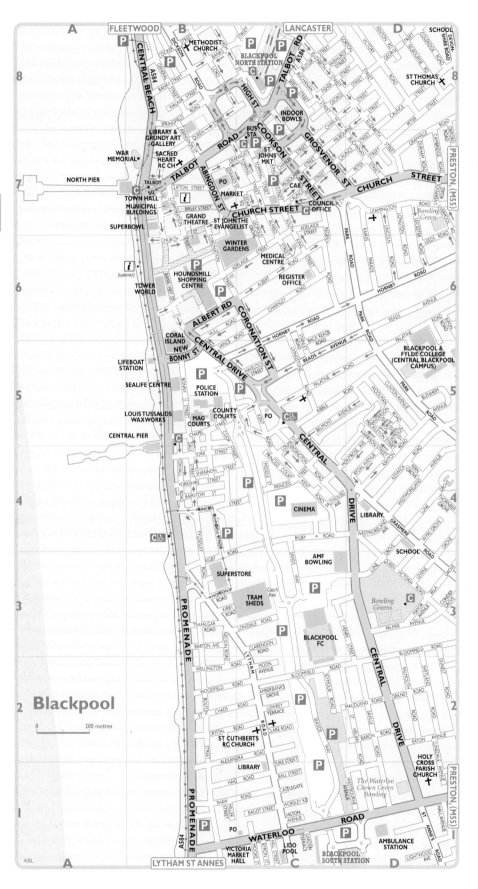

Blackpool

Blackpool is found on atlas page **88 B3**

Abingdon Street	B7-B8	Longton Road	D6-D7
Adelaide Street	B6-C6-C7	Lonsdale Road	B3-C3
Albert Road	B6-C6	Lord Street	B8
Alexandra Road	B1-B2-C2	Louise Street	C4-C5
Alfred Street	C6-C7	Lowrey Terrace	C2
Amberbanks Grove	C2	Lune Grove	D3-D4
Anderson Street	D5	Lunedale Avenue	D1-D2
Ashton Road	D4-D5	Lytham Road	B3-C3-C2-C1
Back Reads Road	C5-C6	Maudland Road	C2-D2
Bagot Street	C1	Mayor Avenue	D3
Bairstow Street	B4	Middle Street	C4
Ball Street	C1	Milbourne Street	C7-D8
Bank Hey Street	B6	Miller Street	B1
Banks Street	B8-C8	Montrose Avenue	C4-D4-D5
Baron Road	D2	Moon Avenue	C2
Barton Avenue	B3	Moore Street	C1
Bela Grove	D3	Nelson Road	B2-B3
Belmont Avenue	C5-D5	New Bonny Street	B5
Birley Street	B7	Orkney Road	D2
Blenheim Avenue	D5	Orme Street	D5
Bloomfield Road	C2-D2-D3	Oxford Road	D7-D8
Blundell Street	B3-B4	Palatine Road	C5-D5-D6
Bolton Street	B2	Palmer Avenue	D7
Bonny Street	B5	Park Road	C7-D6-D5
Buchanan Street	C8-C7-D7	Peter Street	C7-D7-D8
Butler Street	C8	Princess Court	C4
Byron Street	C1	Princess Street	B4-C4
Cambridge Road	D7	Promenade	B1-B2-B3
Castlegate	C1	Queen Street	B7-B8
Caunce Street	C7-D7-D8	Queen Victoria Road	D3
Cedar Square	C7	Raikes Parade	D6-D7
Central Beach	B8	Reads Avenue	C5-C6-D6
Central Drive	B6-C5-D3-D1	Regent Road	C6-C7
Chapel Street	B5	Ribble Road	C5-D5
Charles Street	C7-C8-D8	Rigby Street	B3-C4
Charnley Road	C6	Ripon Road	D6
Church Street	B6-B7-C7-D7	Rydal Avenue	D4
Clare Road	C2	St Anne's Road	D1
Clarendon Road	C3	St Chads Road	B2-C2
Clifton Street	B7	St Heliers Road	C2-D2-D3
Clinton Avenue	D5	Salthouse Avenue	C4
Cocker Street	B8	Sands Way	C3-C4
Coleridge Road	D8	Saville Road	D1-D2
Conder Grove	D3	Seaside Way	C1-C2
Cookson Street	C7-C8	Seed Street	C8
Coop Street	B4-B5	Selbourne Road	C7-D8
Coronation Street	B7-B6-C6-C5	Seymour Road	C2
Corporation Street	B6-B7	Shannon Street	B4
Crystal Road	B2-C2	Shaw Road	B1-C1
Dale Street	B4-B5	Shetland Road	D2-D3
Deansgate	B7-C7	South King Street	C6-C7
Devonshire Road	D8	Springfield Road	B8
Dickson Road	B8	Stanley Road	C5-C6
Duke Street	C1-C2	Talbot Road	B7-C8
Dunelt Road	D2-D3	Talbot Square	B7
Durham Road	D7	Thornber Grove	D4
East Topping Street	C7	Topping Street	C7
Eaton Avenue	D2	Trafalgar Road	B3
Edward Street	B7	Tyldesley Road	B3-B4
Elizabeth Street	C8-D8-D7	Vance Road	B5-B6-C6
Erdington Road	C4-C5	Victory Road	D8
Fairhurst Street	C8	Walker Street	B8
Falmouth Road	D2	Waterloo Road	B1-C1-D1
Fenton Road	D8	Wellington Road	B2-C2
Fern Grove	D4	Westbourne Avenue	C1-D1
Fisher Street	C8-D8	Westmoreland Avenue	D4
Foxhall Road	B4	Woodfield Road	B2-C2
Freckleton Street	D5	Woolman Road	D5
Garden Terrace	C1	Worsley Road	C1
General Street	B8	Wyre Grove	D4
George Street	C8-D8	York Street	B4
Gorton Street	C8-D8	Yorkshire Street	B4
Granville Road	D7-D8		
Grasmere Road	D3-D4		
Grosvenor Street	C7		
Haig Road	B1-C1		
Hall Avenue	D1		
Harrison Street	D4-D5		
Havelock Street	C5		
Henry Street	C3-D3		
High Street	B8-C8		
Hill Street	C1		
Hilton Avenue	C1		
Hopton Road	B3		
Hornby Road	C5-C6-D6		
Hull Road	B6		
Jameson Street	D5		
Kent Road	C4-C5		
Keswick Road	D4-D5		
King Street	C7		
Kirby Road	B3		
Leamington Road	D7		
Leeds Road	D6-D7		
Leicester Road	D6-D7		
Leopold Grove	C6-C7		
Levens Grove	D3-D4		
Lightwood Avenue	D1		
Lincoln Road	D6-D7		
Liverpool Road	D6-D7		
Livingstone Road	C5-C6		

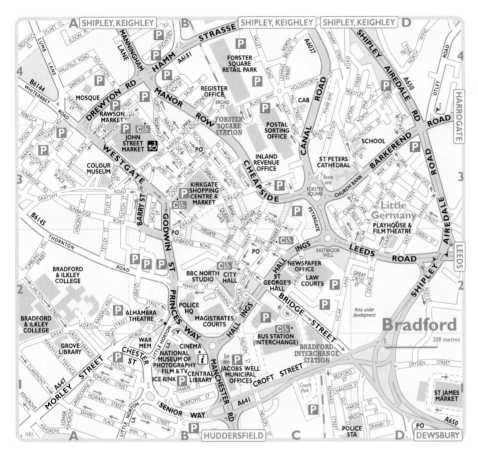

Bradford

Bradford is found on atlas page **90 C3**

Bank Street	B3-C3-C2	Manchester Road	B1
Barkerend Road	D3-D4	Manningham Lane	A4-B4
Barry Street	B3	Mannville Terrace	A1
Bolton Road	C3-C4	Manor Row	B3-B4
Bridge Street	B2-C2-C1	Market Street	B2-C2-C3
Broadway	C2-C3	Melbourne Place	A1
Burnett Street	D3	Morley Street	A1-B1-B2
Canal Road	C3-C4	Neal Street	B1
Captain Street	C3-C4-D4	Nelson Street	C1-C2
Carlton Street	A2	Norfolk Gardens	B2-C2
Channing Way	B2	North Brook Street	C4
Chapel Street	D2-D3	North Parade	B3-B4
Charles Street	C2-C3	North Street	D4
Cheapside	B3-C3	Northgate	B3-B4
Chester Street	A2-A1-B1	Otley Road	D4
Church Bank	C3-D3	Peckover Street	D3
Claremont	A1	Petergate	C3
Croft Street	C1	Piccadilly	B3
Currer Street	C3-D3	Princes Way	B1-B2
Dale Street	B3-C3	Quebec Street	B2
Darfield Street	A4	Rawson Place	C3
Darley Street	B3	Rawson Road	A3-A4-B4
Drake Street	C2	Rawson Square	B3
Drewton Road	A4-B4	St Blaise Way	B3-C3
Dryden Street	D1	St Thomas Road	A3-A4
Duke Street	B3	Salem Street	B4
East Parade	D2-D3	Sawrey Place	A1
Edmund Street	A1-B1	Sedgwick Close	A4
Edward Street	C1	Senior Way	B1
Forester Square	C3	Sharpe Street	B1
Godwin Street	B2-B3	Shipley Airedale Road	D1-D3-D4
Grammar School Street	B4	Simes Street	A3-A4-B4
Grattan Road	A3-B3	Stott Hill	C4-C3-D3
Great Horton Street	A1-A2-B2	Sunbridge Road	A3-B3-B2
Guy Street	B1	Sylhet Close	A4
Hall Ings	B1-B2-C2	Tetley Street	A2-A3
Hallfield Road	A4	Thornton Road	A3-A2-B2
Hamm Strasse	B4-C4	Tumbling Hill Street	A2
Holdsworth Street	C4	Tyrrel Street	B2-B3
Houghton Place	A4	Upper Parkgate	D3
Howard Street	A1	Upper Piccadilly	B3-B4
Ivegate	B2-B3	Valley Road	C3-C4
James Street	B3	Well Street	C2-C3
John Street	B3	Wellington Street	D3-D4
Kirkgate	B2-B3-C3	Westgate	A3-B3
Leeds Road	C2-D2	Wharf Street	C4
Little Horton Lane	A1-B1-B2	Whiteabbey Road	A4
Lumb Lane	A4	Wigan Street	A3

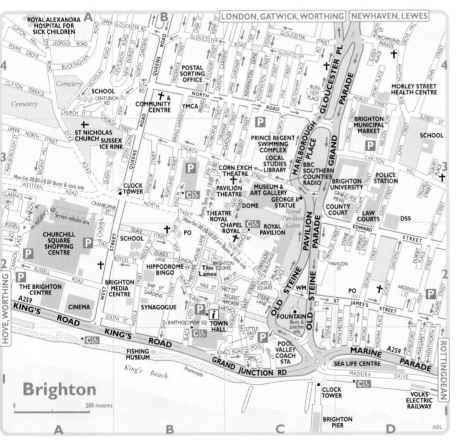

Brighton

Brighton is found on atlas page **16 D2**

Ashton Rise	D4	Marlborough Place	C3
Bartholomews	B2-C2	Meeting House Lane	B2
Black Lion Street	B1-B2	Middle Street	B2
Blenheim Place	C4	Morley Street	D4
Bond Street	B3	New Dorset Street	B4
Brighton Square	B2	New Road	C2-C3
Broad Street	D1-D2	Nile Street	B2
Buckingham Road	A4	North Gardens	B4
Camelford Street	D1-D2	North Road	B4-C4
Cannon Place	A2-A3	North Street	B3-B2-C2
Carlton Hill	D3	Old Steine	C1-C2
Castle Square	C2	Palace Place	C2
Centurion Road	A4-B4	Pavilion Buildings	C2
Charles Street	D1-D2	Pavilion Parade	C2-C3
Cheltenham Place	C4	Pool Valley	C1
Church Street	A4-B3-C3	Portland Street	B3
Circus Street	D3-D4	Powis Grove	A4
Clifton Terrace	A4	Prince Albert Street	B2
Dorset Gardens	D2	Prince's Place	C2
Duke Street	B2	Princes Street	C2-D2
Duke's Lane	B2	Queen Square	A3-B3
Dyke Road	A3-A4	Queens Gardens	B4-C4
East Street	C1-C2	Queens Road	B3-B4
Edward Street	D2	Regency Road	A2-A3
Foundry Street	B4	Regent Arcade	B2-C2
Frederick Street	B4	Regent Hill	A3
Gardner Street	C3-C4	Regent Street	C3-C4
George Street	D2	Robert Street	C4
Gloucester Place	C4-D4	Russell Road	A2
Gloucester Road	B4-C4	St James's Street	C2-D2
Gloucester Street	C4-D4	St Nicholas Road	A4-B4
Grand Junction Road	B1-C1	Ship Street	B1-B2-B3
Grand Parade	C3-D3-D4	Ship Street Gardens	B2
High Street	D2	Spring Gardens	B3-B4
Ivory Place	D4	Steine Lane	C2
John Street	D2-D3-D4	Steine Street	C1-C2
Kensington Gardens	C4	Tichborne Street	B3-B4-C4
Kensington Street	C4	Union Street	B2
Kew Street	B3-B4	Upper Gardner Street	C4
King's Road	A2-B1-C1	Upper Gloucester Road	A4-B4
Leopold Road	A4	Upper North Street	A3
Little East Street	C1	Vine Street	C4
Madeira Drive	C1-D1	Wentworth Street	D1-D2
Madeira Place	D1-D2	West Street	A2-B2-B3
Manchester Street	D1-D2	Western Road	A3
Margaret Street	D1-D2	White Street	D2-D3
Marine Parade	C1-D1	William Street	D3
Market Street	B2-C2	Windsor Street	B3

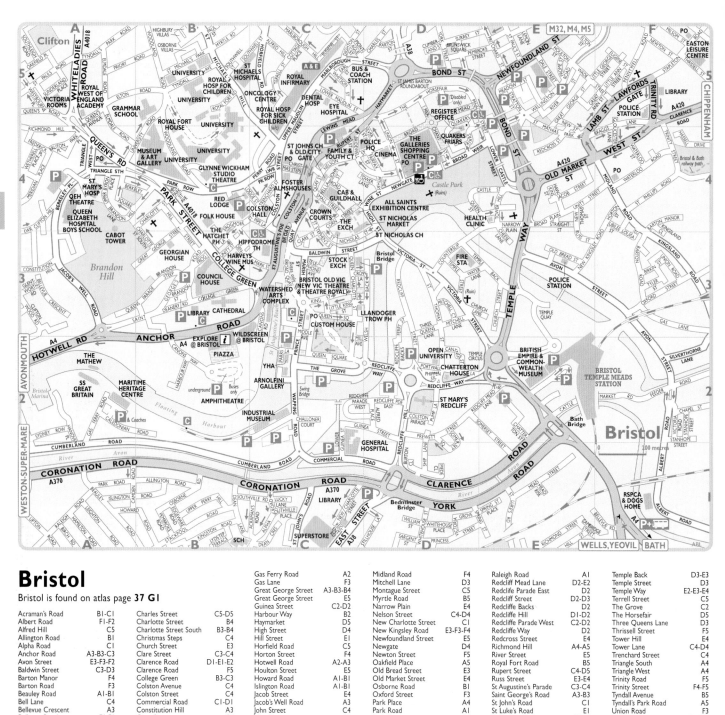

Bristol

Bristol is found on atlas page **37 G1**

Acraman's Road	B1-C1	Charles Street	C5-D5	Gas Ferry Road	A2	Midland Road	F4	Raleigh Road	A1	Temple Back	D3-E3
Albert Road	F1-F2	Charlotte Street	B4	Gas Lane	F3	Mitchell Lane	D3	Redcliff Mead Lane	D2-E2	Temple Street	D3
Alfred Hill	C5	Charlotte Street South	B3-B4	Great George Street	A3-B3-B4	Montague Street	C5	Redcliffe Parade East	D2	Temple Way	E2-E3-E4
Allington Road	B1	Christmas Steps	C4	Great George Street	E5	Myrtle Road	B5	Redcliff Street	D2-D3	Terrell Street	C5
Alpha Road	C1	Church Street	E3	Guinea Street	C2-D2	Narrow Plain	E4	Redcliffe Backs	D2	The Grove	C2
Anchor Road	A3-B3-C3	Clare Street	C3-C4	Harbour Way	B2	Nelson Street	C4-D4	Redcliffe Hill	D1-D2	The Horsefair	D5
Avon Street	E3-F3-F2	Clarence Road	D1-E1-E2	Haymarket	D5	New Charlotte Street	C1	Redcliffe Parade West	C2-D2	Three Queens Lane	D3
Baldwin Street	C3-D3	Clarence Road	E5	High Street	D4	New Kingsley Road	E3-F3-F4	Redcliffe Way	D2	Thrissell Street	F5
Barton Manor	F4	College Green	B3-C3	Hill Street	E1	Newfoundland Street	E5	Redcross Street	E4	Tower Hill	E4
Barton Road	F3	Colston Avenue	C4	Horfield Road	C5	Newgate	D4	Richmond Hill	A4-A5	Tower Lane	C4-D4
Beauley Road	A1-B1	Colston Street	C4	Horton Street	F4	Newton Street	F5	River Street	E5	Trenchard Street	C4
Bell Lane	C4	Commercial Road	C1-D1	Hotwell Road	A2-A3	Oakfield Place	A5	Royal Fort Road	B5	Triangle South	A4
Bellevue Crescent	A3	Constitution Hill	A3	Houlton Street	E5	Old Bread Street	E3	Rupert Street	C4	Triangle West	A4
Bellevue Road	E1-F1	Corn Street	C4	Howard Road	A1-B1	Old Market Street	E4	Russ Street	E3-E4	Trinity Road	F5
Berkeley Place	A4	Cottage Place	C5	Islington Road	A1-B1	Osborne Road	B1	St Augustine's Parade	C3-C4	Trinity Street	F4-F5
Berkeley Square	A4-B4	Countership	D3	Jacob Street	E4	Oxford Street	F3	Saint George's Road	A3-B3	Tyndall Avenue	B5
Birkin Street	F3	Cumberland Road	A1-B2-B1-C1	Jacob's Well Road	A3	Park Place	A4	St John's Road	C1	Tyndall's Park Road	A5
Bond Street	D5-E5-E4	Dale Street	E5	John Street	C4	Park Road	A1	St Luke's Road	E1	Union Road	F4
Braggs Lane	E4-F4-F5	Dean Lane	B1	King Street	C3	Park Row	B4	St Mathias Park	E4-E5	Union Street	D4-D5
Brandon Hill Lane	A4	Deanery Road	B3	Kingsland Road	F3	Park Street	B3-B4	St Michael's Hill	B5-C5-C4	Unity Street	B3
Brandon Steep	B3	Denmark Street	C4	Kingston Road	B1	Park Street Avenue	B4	St Michael's Park	B5	University Road	A4-B4-B5
Bridewell Street	C4	Dighton Street	C5	Lamb Street	E4-E5-F5	Pembroke Road	B1	St Nicholas Street	C4-C3-D4	Upper Byron Place	A4
Broad Mead	D4-D5	Earl Street	C5	Lawfords Gate	F5	Pembroke Street	D5-E5	St Paul's Street	E5	Upper Maudlin Street	C4-C5
Broad Plain	E4	East Street	C1-D1	Leighton Road	A1	Penn Street	D5-E5-E4	St Pauls Road	A5	Upper Perry Hill	B1
Broad Quay	C3-C4	Edgeware Road	B1	Lewins Mead	C4-C5	Pennywell Road	F5	St Phillips Road	F4	Victoria Grove	D1
Broad Street	C4	Elmdale Road	A4-A5	Little Ann Street	F5	Perry Road	C4	St Stephen's Street	C3-C4	Victoria Road	F2
Broad Weir	D4-E4	Elton Road	A5-B5	Little George Street	E5-F5	Pipe Lane	C4	St Thomas Street	D2-D3	Victoria Street	D3-E3-E2
Bruton Place	A4	Eugene Street	C5	Little King Street	C3	Prewett Street	D2	Ship Lane	D1-D2	Wade Street	E5-F5
Caledonian Road	A2-B2	Eugene Street	F5	Lodge Street	B4-C4	Prince Street	C2-C3	Silver Street	D4-D5	Wapping Road	C1-C2
Cambridge Street	E1-F1	Fairfax Street	D4	Lower Castle Street	E4	Princess Street	D1	Silverthorne Lane	F2	Waterloo Road	F4
Canons Road	C3	Feeder Road	F2	Lower Clifton Hill	A4	Priory Road	A5-B5	Small Street	C4	Waterloo Street	F4
Canons Way	B2	Ferry Street	D3	Lower Guinea Street	C1-C2	Pritchard Street	E5	Somerset Street	D2-E2-E1	Wellington Street	F5
Canynge Street	D2	Frederick Place	A4	Lower Maudlin Street	C5	Pump Lane	D2	Southville Road	B1-C1	Welsh Back	D2-D3
Castle Street	D4-E4	Frog Lane	B3	Lower Park Row	C4	Quakers Friars	D4-D5	Spring Street	D1-E1	West Street	F4-F5
Cattle Market Road	E2-F2	Frogmore Street	B3-B4-C4	Marlborough Hill	C5	Quay Street	C4	Stackpool Road	B1	Whitehouse Street	D1
Chapel Street	F2			Marlborough Street	C5-D5	Queen Charlotte Street	D3	Stapleton Road	F5	Whiteladies Road	A5
				Marsh Street	C4	Queen Square	C2-C3	Stoke's Croft	D5	Wilson Street	E5
				Mead Street	E1	Queen Street	D4-E4	Stratton Street	E5	Wine Street	D4
				Merchant Street	D4-D5	Queen's Avenue	A5	Surrey Street	D5-E5	Woodland Road	B4-B5
				Meridian Place	A4	Queen's Road	A4-A5	Sydney Row	A2	York Road	D1-E1
				Middle Avenue	C3	Queens Parade	A3-B3	Telephone Avenue	C3	York Street	D5

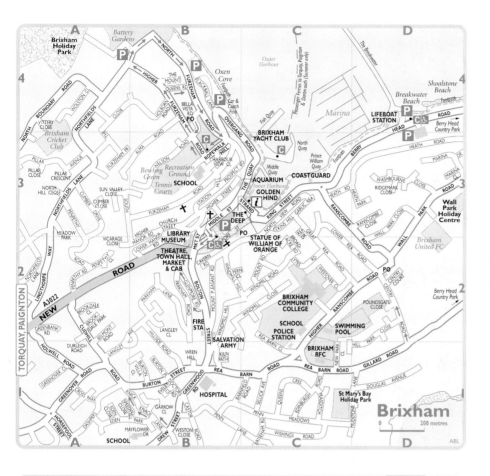

Brixham

Brixham is found on atlas page **7 G3**

Alma Road	A3-B3-B4	Lindthorpe Way	A2
Barnfield Road	B1-C1	Lower Manor Road	B2-B3
Bella Vista Road	B4	Lower Rea Road	C3-C2-D2
Berry Head Road	C3-D3-D4	Lytes Road	C2
Blackball Lane	B4	Marina Drive	D3
Bolton Street	B1-B2	Market Street	B2-B3
Briseham Road	C1	Middle Street	B3
Broadacre Road	C2	Mount Pleasant Road	B2
Burton Street	B1	Mount Road	C2
Castor Road	B1	Mudstone Lane	D1
Cavern Road	B2	Nelson Road	B3
Centry Court	B1	New Park Close	C1
Centry Road	D1-D2	New Road	A2-B2
Church Street	B3	North Boundary Road	A3-A4
Cross Park	A1	North Furzeham Road	B3-B4
Cudhill Road	A1-A2	North View Close	C3
Cumber Drive	A2-A3	Northfields Lane	A2,A3-A4
Dashpers	A1	Overgang Road	B4-C3
Doctors Road	B1	Parkham Lane	B2
Douglas Avenue	D1	Parkham Road	B2
Drew Street	B1	Peasditch	C1
Eden Park	A1-B1	Penn Lane	B1-C1
Edinburgh Road	C1	Penn Meadows	B1-C1
Elkins Hill	C3	Penpethy Road	A2-A3
Fore Street	B2-B3-C3	Pillar Avenue	A3
Furzeham Park	A3	Prospect Road	B3-C3
Garlic Rea	C3	Queens Crescent	C1
Gillard Road	D1	Queens Road	B4
Glenmore Road	B2	Ranscombe Road	C3-D3-D2
Great Rea Road	C3-C2-D2	Rea Barn Close	C1-C2
Greenbank Road	A2	Rea Barn Road	B1-C1-D1
Greenover Road	A1	Ropewalk Hill	B3
Greenwood Road	B1	Sellick Avenue	C1
Harbour View Close	B3	South Furzeham Road	A3-B3
Heath Park	D3	Station Hill	B3
Heath Road	C3-D3	Strand	B3-C3
Higher Furzeham Road	B3-B4	The Close	A3-A4
Higher Manor Road	B2-B3	The Mount	B4
Higher Ranscombe Road	C1-D2	The Quay	B3-C3
Higher Street	B3	Wall Park Close	D2-D3
Hill Park Close	D1-D2	Wall Park Road	D2-D3
Hillside Road	B1-B2	Washbourne Close	D3
Holborn Road	B4	Westover Close	C2
Holwell Road	A1-A2	Windmill Close	B2-C2
Horsepool Street	A1	Windmill Hill	B1-B2
King Street	C3	Windmill Road	C2
Knick Knack Lane	A1-B1	Wishings Road	C1
Langley Avenue	A1-A2-B2	Wolston Close	A4

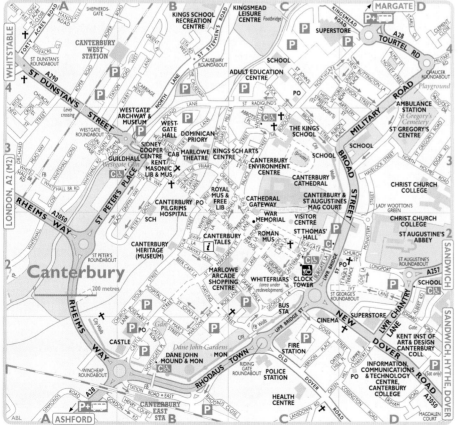

Canterbury

Canterbury is found on atlas page **31 E2**

Albion Place	C3-D3	Oaten Hill	C1-D1
Artillery Street	C4-D4-D3	Old Dover Road	C1-D1
Beer Cart Lane	B2	Orange Street	B3-C3
Best Lane	B3	Orchard Street	A3-A4
Black Griffin Way	A2-B2-B3	Palace Street	C3
Blackfriars Street	B3	Parade	C2
Broad Street	C3-D3-D2	Pound Lane	B3-B4
Burgate	C2	Rheims Way	A1-A2-A3
Butchery Lane	C2	Rhodaus Town	B1-C1
Canterbury Lane	C2	Roper Road	A4-B4
Castle Row	B2	Rose Lane	B2-C2
Castle Street	B1-B2	Roseacre Close	A4
Church Street	D2	Rosemary Lane	B1-B2
Cross Street	A3-A4	St Alphege Street	C3
Dover Street	C2-C1-D1	St Dunstan's Street	A4-A3-B3
Duck Lane	C4	St George's Street	C2
Edward Road	D1-D2	St John's Lane	B1-B2
Forty Acres Road	A4	St John's Place	C4
George's Lane	C1-C2	St Margaret's Street	B2-C2
Gordon Road	A1-B1	St Mary's Street	B1-B2
Gravel Walk	C2	St Peter's Grove	B2-B3
Guildhall Street	B2-B3-C3	St Peter's Lane	B3-B4
Havelock Street	D3	St Peter's Place	A2-A3-B3
Hawks Lane	B2	St Peter's Street	B3
High Street	B3-B2-C2	St Radigund's Street	C3-C4
Hospital Lane	B2	St Stephen's Road	B4
Iron Bar Lane	C2	Simmonds Road	A1
Ivy Lane	C2-D2	Station Road East	B1
Jewry Lane	B2	Stour Street	B2-B3
King Street	B3-C3	Sun Street	C3
Kingsmead Road	C4-D4	The Causeway	B4
Kirby's Lane	A3-B3-B4	The Borough	C3
Lansdown Road	C1	The Friars	B3
Linden Grove	A3	Tourtel Road	B3
Longport	D2	Tower Way	B3
Lower Bridge Street	C2	Union Street	D3-D4
Lower Chantry Lane	D1-D2	Upper Bridge Street	C1-C2
Marlowe Avenue	B1-B2	Upper Chantry Lane	D1
Mercery Lane	C2	Vernon Place	C1
Mill Lane	B3-C3-C4	Victoria Row	C4-D4
Monastery Street	D2-D3	Watling Street	B2-C1
New Dover Road	C2-D2-D1	Westgate Grove	A3-B3
New Ruttington Lane	D4	White Horse Lane	B2
New Street	A3-A4	Whitehall Bridge Road	A3
North Holmes Road	D3	Whitehall Close	A2-A3
North Lane	B3-B4	Whitehall Gardens	A3
Northgate	C4-D4	Whitehall Road	A3
Notley Street	D4	Worthgate Place	B1

183

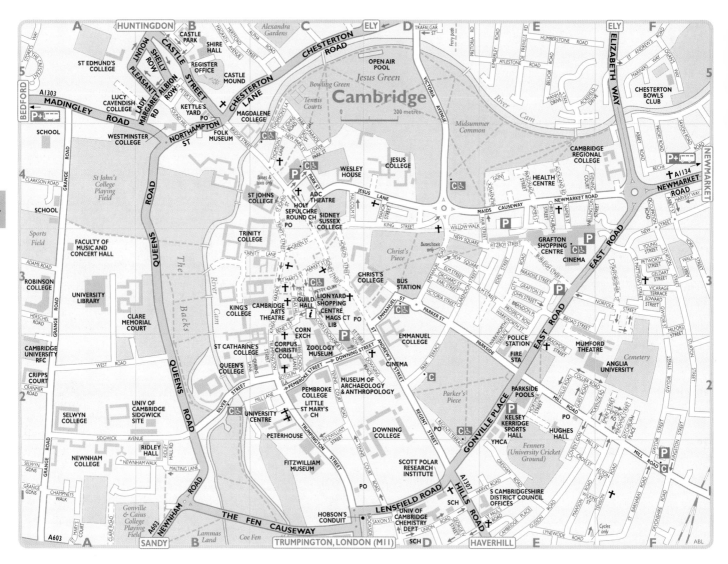

Cambridge

Cambridge is found on atlas page **62 D1**

Abbey Road	F4-F5	Devonshire Road	F1	Hobson Street	C3	Newmarket Road	E4-F4	St Matthew's Street	F3
Abbey Street	F4	Ditchburn Place	F2	Humberstone Road	E5-F5	Newnham Road	B1	St Paul's Road	E1
Abbey Walk	F3	Downing Place	C2-D2	James Street	E4	Newnham Walk	A1-B1	St Peter's Street	B5
Acrefield Drive	E5	Downing Street	C2-D2	Jesus Lane	C4-D4	Norfolk Street	E3-F3	St Tibbs Row	C2-C3
Adams Road	A3	Earl Street	D3	John Street	E3	Northampton Street	B4-B5	Saxon Road	F4-F5
Albion Row	B5	East Road	E2-E3-F3-F4	Kimberley Road	E5	Occupation Road	F4	Saxon Street	D1
Alpha Road	B5-C5	Eden Street	E3	King Street	C4-D4	Orchard Street	D3	Selwyn Gardens	A1
Auckland Road	E4	Edward Street	F3	Kings Parade	C3	Paradise Street	E3	Shelly Row	B5
Aylestone Road	E5	Elizabeth Way	F5	Kingston Street	F1-F2	Park Parade	C4-C5	Sidgwick Avenue	A2-B2
Beche Road	F4	Elm Street	D3-E3	Lady Margaret Road	B5	Park Street	C4	Sidney Street	C3
Belvoir Road	E5	Emery Road	F2	Lensfield Road	C1-D1	Park Terrace	D2-D3	Silver Street	B2-C2
Bene't Street	C3	Emery Street	F2	Logan's Way	F5	Parker Street	D3	Staffordshire Street	F3
Botolph Lane	C2	Emmanuel Road	D3-D4	Lower Park Street	C4	Parkside	D3-D2-E2	Storeys Way	A5
Bradmore Street	E2	Emmanuel Street	D3	Lynewode Road	E1	Parsonage Street	E4	Sturton Street	F2-F3
Brandon Place	E2	Evening Court	E3	Madingley Road	A5-B5-B4	Peas Hill	C3	Tenison Road	E1-F1
Bridge Street	B5-B4-C4	Fair Street	D4-E3	Magrath Avenue	B5	Pembroke Street	C2	Tennis Court Road	C2-C1-D1
Broad Street	E3	Felton Street	F1	Maids Causeway	D4-E4	Perowne Street	F2	The Crescent	A5
Brookside	D1	Fitzroy Street	E3	Malcolm Street	C4	Petty Cury	C3	The Fen Causeway	B1-C1
Brunswick Gardens	E4	Fitzwilliam Street	C2	Malting Lane	B1	Petworth Street	F3	Thomson's Lane	C4-C5
Burleigh Street	E3	Free School Lane	C2	Manhattan Drive	E5	Portugal Street	C4	Trafalgar Street	D5
Cambridge Place	E1	Geldart Street	F3	Manor Street	D4	Pound Hill	B5	Trinity Lane	B3-C3
Castle Street	B5	George IV Street	D1	Mariners Way	F5	Pretoria Road	D5	Trinity Street	C3-C4
Champneys Walk	A1	Glisson Road	E1	Market Hill	C3	Priory Road	F4-F5	Trumpington Street	C1-C2
Chesterton Lane	B5-C5	Gonville Place	D1-D2-E2	Market Street	C3	Prospect Row	E3	Union Road	D1
Chesterton Road	C5-D5	Grafton Street	E3	Mawson Road	E1	Queens Lane	B2	Vicarage Terrace	F3
Christchurch Street	E4	Grange Gardens	A1	McKenzie Road	E2-F2	Queens Road	B1-B2-B3-B4	Victoria Avenue	D4-D5
City Road	E3	Grange Road	A1-A3-A5	Milford Street	F3	Regent Street	D1-D2	Victoria Street	D3
Clare Road	A1	Green Street	C3	Mill Lane	B2-C2	Regents Terrace	D1-D2	Warkworth Street	E3
Clarendon Street	D3-E3	Gresham Road	E1	Mill Road	E2-F2-F1	Ridley Hall Road	B1	Warkworth Terrace	E2-E3
Clarkson Road	A4	Guest Road	E2	Mill Street	E2-E1-F1	St Andrew's Street	D2-D3	Wellington Street	E4
Collier Road	E2-F2	Gwydir Street	F1-F2-F3	Mortimer Street	E2	St Andrew's Road	F5	West Road	A2-B2
Corn Exchange Street	C2-C3	Harvest Way	F4	Mount Pleasant	A5-B5	St Barnabas Road	F1	Wilkins Street	E1
Covent Garden	E1-E2	Harvey Road	D1-E1	Napier Street	E4	St Johns Road	C4-C5	Willis Road	E2
Cranmer Road	A2	Herschel Road	A3	New Park Street	C4	St Johns Street	C4	Willow Walk	D4
Cross Street	E1	Hertford Street	B5-C5	New Square	D3	St Mary's Court	A1	York Street	F3-F4
De Freiville Road	E5	Hills Road	D1-E1	New Street	F3-F4	St Mary's Street	C3	Young Street	F3

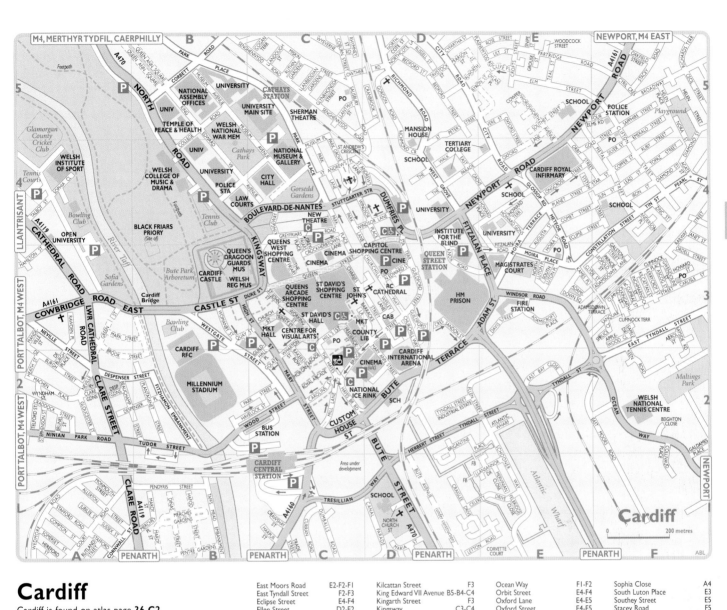

Cardiff

Cardiff is found on atlas page **36 C2**

Adam Street	D3-E3	Clive Place	E5
Adamscroft Place	E3	Clyde Street	E3-F3
Adamsdown Lane	F3	Coburn Street	C5
Adamsdown Square	E3	College Road	B4-B5
Adamsdown Terrace	F3	Comet Street	E4-F4
Allerton Street	A1	Compton Street	A1
Ascog Street	F3	Constellation Street	E3-F3-F4
Atlantic Wharf	E2	Copper Street	F4
Augusta Street	E3-E4	Corbett Road	B5
Bakers Row	C2	Cornwall Street	A1
Barracks Lane	C3-D3	Court Road	A1
Bayside Road	F2-F3	Cowbridge Road East	A3-B3
Beauchamp Street	A2-B2	Cowper Place	E5
Bedford Street	D5	Craddock Street	A2
Boulevard de Nantes	B4-C4	Cranbrook Street	D5
Bridge Street	C2-D3	Craiglee Drive	D1
Brigantine Place	D2-E2	Crockherbtown Lane	C3-C4
Broadway	F5	Crofts Street	E5
Brook Street	A3-A2-B2	Cumnock Place	F3
Bute Avenue	D1	Cumnock Terrace	F3
Bute Street	D1-D2	Cumrae Street	F3
Bute Terrace	D2-D3	Curran Road	C1
Byron Street	D5-E5	Custom House Street	C2
Canal Parade	D1	Cyril Crescent	F5
Carlisle Street	F3	Davis Street	E3
Caroline Street	C2	De Burgh Street	A2-A3
Castle Street	B3	Despenser Gardens	A2
Cathedral Road	A3-A4	Despenser Place	A2-B2
Celerity Drive	D1-E1	Despenser Street	A2-B2
Charles Street	C3-D3	Diamond Street	F4
Church Street	C3	Dinas Street	B1
Churchill Way	D2-D3	Duke Street	B3-C3
City Road	D5-E5-E4	Dumballs Road	C1
Clare Road	A2-A1-B1	Dumfries Place	D4
Clare Street	A2	East Bay Close	E2
Clifton Street	F4-F5	East Grove	D4-E4

East Moors Road	E2-F2-F1	Kilcattan Street	F3
East Tyndall Street	F2-F3	King Edward VII Avenue	B5-B4-C4
Eclipse Street	E4-F4	Kingarth Street	F3
Ellen Street	D2-E2	Kingsway	C3-C4
Elm Street	E5-F5	Knox Road	D3
Emerald Street	F4-F5	Lead Street	F4
Fitzalan Place	D4-D3-E3	Letton Road	D1-E1
Fitzalan Road	E5	Lily Street	E5
Fitzhamon Embankment	B2	Llanbeddian Gardens	C5
Four Elms Road	E5-F5	Llandough Street	C5
Frederick Street	C2-C3	Llansannor Drive	D1-E1
Galston Street	F3	Llantwit Street	C5
Glossop Road	E4	Longcross Street	E4
Gloucester Street	A2	Lower Cathedral Road	A2-A3
Glynrhondda Street	C5	Lowther Road	C5-D5
Golate	C2	Machen Place	A2
Gold Street	E4-F4-F5	Mardy Street	B1
Gordon Road	D5	Mark Street	A3-B3
Green Street	A3	Mary Ann Street	D2
Greyfriars Place	C3-C4	Merches Gardens	B1
Greyfriars Road	C3-C4	Mervinian Close	E1
Guildford Crescent	D3	Metal Street	F4
Guildford Street	D3	Meteor Road	E3-E4
Guildhall Place	C2	Mill Lane	C2
Gwendoline Street	F3	Miskin Street	C5
Hafod Street	B1	Moira Place	E3
Havelock Street	B2-C2	Moira Street	E3-E4
Hayes Bridge Road	C2	Moira Terrace	E3-E4
Heath Street	A2	Monmouth Street	A1
Helen Street	F5	Morgan Arcade	C2
Herbert Street	D1-D2	Museum Avenue	B5-C4
High Street	B3-C3	Museum Place	C4
Hill's Street	C3	Neville Place	A2
Howard Gardens	E4	Neville Street	A2-A3
Howard Place	E4	Newport Road	D4-E4-E5-F5
Howard Terrace	E4	Ninian Park Road	A2
Inchmarnock Street	F3	Nora Street	F4-F5
Iron Street	F4	North Edward Street	D3
Kames Place	E3	North Luton Place	E3
Keen Road	F2	North Road	A5-B5-B4
Kerrycroy Street	F3	Northcote Lane	D5

Ocean Way	F1-F2	Sophia Close	A4
Orbit Street	E4-F4	South Luton Place	E3
Oxford Lane	E4-E5	Southey Street	F3
Oxford Street	E4-E5	Stacey Road	F5
Park Grove	C4	Stafford Road	A1
Park Lane	C4-D3	Star Street	F4
Park Place	B5-C5-C4-C3	Station Terrace	D3-D4
Park Street	B2-C2	Stuttgarter Strasse	C4-D4
Partridge Road	E5-F5	Sun Street	F4
Pearl Street	F4	System Street	E4-F4
Pearson Street	D5	Taffs Mead Embankment	B1
Pendyris Street	B1	Talbot Street	A4
Planet Street	E4	Talworth Street	D5
Plantagenet Street	B2	Teal Street	E5
Plasnewydd Road	D5-E5	The Friary	C3
Prince Leopold Street	F3	The Hayes	C2
Quay Street	B3-C3	The Parade	D4-E4
Queen Ann Square	A5-B5	The Walk	D4
Queen Street	C3	Tin Street	F4
Rawden Place	A3	Topaz Street	F4
Richmond Crescent	D4-D5	Tresillian Way	C1-D1
Richmond Road	D4-D5	Trinity Street	C2
Royal Arcade	C2	Tudor Street	A2-B2-B1
Ruby Street	F4-F5	Tyndall Street	D2-E2
Russell Street	D5	Tyndall Street Industrial Estate	D2
Ruthin Gardens	C5	Vere Street	E5
St Andrews Crescent	C4	Wedmore Road	A1
St Andrews Lane	C4-D4	Wesley Lane	D3
St Andrews Place	C4	West Canal Wharf	C1
St John Street	C3	West Grove	D4
St Mary Street	C2-C3	Westgate Street	B3-B2-C2
St Peter's Street	D4-D5	Wharton Street	C2-C3
Salisbury Road	C5-D5-D4	Windsor Lane	C4-D4
Sandon Street	D3	Windsor Place	C4-D4
Sanquar Street	E3-F3	Windsor Road	E3
Sapele Drive	F3	Womanby Street	B3
Sapphire Street	F5	Wood Street	B2-C2
Schooner Way	E1-E2	Wordsworth Avenue	E4-E5
Senghennydd Road	B5-C5-D4	Working Street	C3
Silver Street	F4	Wyndham Street	A2
Somerset Street	A1	Zinc Street	F4

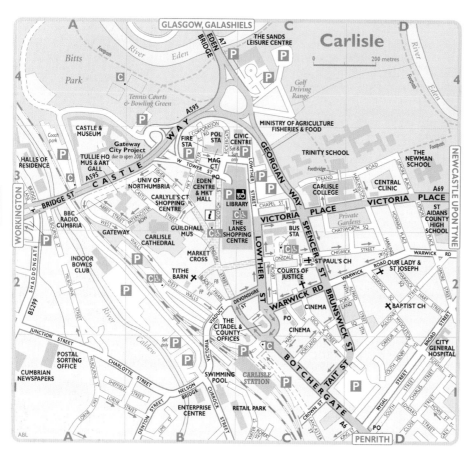

Carlisle

Carlisle is found on atlas page **103 H6**

Abbey Street	A3	Mary Street	C1-C2
Aglionby Street	D1-D2	Milbourne Street	A1-A2-A3
Alfred Street North	D2	Myddleton Street	D1-D2
Alfred Street South	D2	Nelson Bridge	B1
Blackfriars Street	B2	Orfeur Street	D1-D2
Botchergate	C1-D1	Paternoster Row	B3
Bridge Lane	A3	Peter Street	B3
Bridge Street	A3	Portland Place	C1-C2
Broad Street	D1-D2	Portland Square	C2-D2
Brunswick Street	C2-D1	Rickergate	B3
Castle Street	B2-B3	Robert Street	C1
Castle Way	A3-B3-B4	Rydal Street	D1
Cecil Street	C1-C2	Scotch Street	B2-B3
Chapel Street	C3	Shaddongate	A2
Charles Street	D1	Sheffield Street	A1-B1
Charlotte Street	A1-B1	South Henry Street	D1
Chatsworth Square	C3-D3	South Street	D1
Chiswick Street	C2-D2	Spencer Street	C2-C3
Close Street	D1	Strand Road	C3-D3
Corporation Road	B3-B4	Tait Street	C1-D1
Crosby Street	C2	Victoria Place	C3-D3
Crown Street	C1	Victoria Viaduct	B1-B2
Currock Street	B1	Warwick Road	C2-D2
Denton Street	B1	Warwick Square	D2
Devonshire Street	B2-C2	Water Street	B1-C1
Eden Bridge	B4	West Tower Street	B3
Edward Street	D1	West Walls	A3-A2-B2
English Street	B2		
Fisher Street	B3		
Fusehill Street	D1		
Georgian Way	C3-C4		
Grey Street	D1		
Harlington Place	D2		
Harlington Street	D3		
Hart Street	D2		
Howard Place	D2-D3		
Howe Street	D1		
Junction Street	A1-A2		
King Street	C1-D1		
Lancaster Street	C1		
Lime Street	B1		
Lismore Place	D2-D3		
Lismore Street	D2		
Lonsdale Street	C2		
Lorne Crescent	A1		
Lorne Street	A1-B1		
Lowther Street	C2-C3		
Market Street	B3		

Chatham

Chatham is found on atlas page **30 A3**

Afghan Road	A1-B1	New Street	B1
Albany Terrace	B2	Old Road	B2-B1-C1
Amherst Redoubt	C4	Ordnance Street	A1-B1
Armada Way	B1	Ordnance Terrace	B2
Best Street	B2-C2-C1	Otway Street	D1
Bingley Road	A2	Otway Terrace	D1
Boundary Road	A1-A2	Pagitt Street	B1
Bryant Street	C1-D1	Perry Street	A1
Carpeaux Close	D2	Port Rise	B1-C1
Charles Street	A1	Prospect Row	C1-D1
Chilham Close	B1	Queen Street	C2
Clover Street	C2	Railway Street	B2
Cressey Close	A2	Rhode Street	C2
Cromwell Terrace	C1-D1	Richard Street	C2
Cross Street	C2-D2	Rochester Street	B1
Dock Road	B4-C4	Rome Terrace	B2-C2
Eldon Street	D2	Rope Way	C3
Fort Pitt Hill	A2	Salisbury Road	D1
Fort Pitt Street	A1-B1-B2	Silver Hill	C1
Globe Lane	C3	Singapore Drive	D4
Great Lines	D4	Sir John Hawkins Way	B2-B3
Gundulph Road	A2-B2	Sir Thomas Longley Road	A4
Hamond Hill	B2	Solomons Road	C2
Hards Town	D2	The Brook	C3-C2-D2
Hartington Street	C1-D1	The Paddock	B2-C2
Hayman Street	B1	Upbury Way	D2
Herman Terrace	D1	Watts Street	B1
High Street	A2-B3-C2-D1	Westmount Avenue	B1-C1
Hills Terrace	B1	Whiffin's Lane	C3
Hillside Road	D1		
Institute Road	D1-D2		
Jenkins Dale	C1		
Khartoum Road	C4		
King Street	C2		
Kings Bastion	D4		
Lester Road	D1		
Lines Terrace	C3-C2-D2		
Lumsden Terrace	A2-B1		
Magpie Hall Road	D1		
Maidstone Road	B1-B2		
Manor Road	B2-B3		
Maxwell Road	D4		
Medway Street	B3		
Military Road	B3-C3		
Mills Terrace	D1		
Mount Road	C1		
New Road	A2, B2-C1-D1		
New Road Avenue	A2-B2		

Cheltenham

Cheltenham is found on atlas page **47 E1**

Albion Street	C3	Oxford Street	D1-D2
All Saints Road	D3-D4	Parabola Road	A1-A2
Ambrose Street	B4	Park Street	A4
Argyll Road	D1	Pittville Circus	D4
Back Albert Place	D4	Pittville Circus Road	D4
Bath Parade	C1-C2	Pittville Lawn	C4-D4
Bath Road	B1-B2-C2	Pittville Street	C3
Bath Street	C2	Portland Square	D4
Bayshill Road	A2-A3	Portland Street	C4
Bennington Street	B3-B4-C4	Prestbury Road	C4-D4
Berkeley Street	C2-D2	Priory Street	D2
Burton Street	A4	Priory Terrace	D2
Cambray Place	C2-C3	Priory Walk	D2
Carlton Street	D2	Promenade	A2-B2-B3
Clarence Road	C4	Regent Street	B2-B3
Clarence Street	B3-B4	Rodney Road	B2-C2-C3
College Road	C1-C2	Royal Crescent	B3
Devonshire Street	A4	Royal Well Place	B3
Duke Street	D2	Royal Well Road	B3
Fairview Road	C4-C3-D3	St Anne's Road	D2-D3
Fairview Street	D3-D4	St Anne's Terrace	D3
Fauconberg Road	A2	St George's Place	A3-B3-B4
Glenfall Street	D4	St George's Road	A3
Gloucester Place	C3	St George's Street	B4
Great Western Road	A4	St James Square	A3
Grosvenor Street	C2-C3	St James Street	C2
Grove Street	A4	St John's Avenue	C3-D3
Henrietta Street	B4	St Luke's Place	C1-C2
Hewlett Road	D2-D3	St Luke's Road	B1-C1
High Street	A4-B4-C3-C2	St Margaret's Road	B4-C4
Imperial Lane	B2	St Paul's Street South	B4
Imperial Square	B2	Sandford Road	B1
Jessop Avenue	A3	Sandford Street	C2
Keynsham Road	D1	Selkirk Street	D4
King Street	A4-B4	Sherbourne Place	C3-D3
Knapp Road	A4	Sherbourne Street	D3-D4
London Road	D1-D2	Southwood Lane	A1
Monson Avenue	B4-C4	Suffolk Square	A1
Montpellier Drive	B1	Sydenham Villas Road	D1-D2
Montpellier Parade	B1	Trafalgar Street	B1-B2
Montpellier Spa Road	A2-B2-B1	The Broadwalk	A2-B2-B1
Montpellier Street	A1-A2-B2	Union Street	D3-D4
Montpellier Walk	A1-A2	Victoria Place	D3
Montpellier Terrace	A1-B1	Vittoria Walk	B1-B2
New Street	A4-B4	Wellington Street	B2-C2
North Place	C3-C4	Winchcomb Street	C3-C4
Northfield Terrace	C4	Winstonian Road	D3-D4
Oriel Road	B2	York Street	D4

187

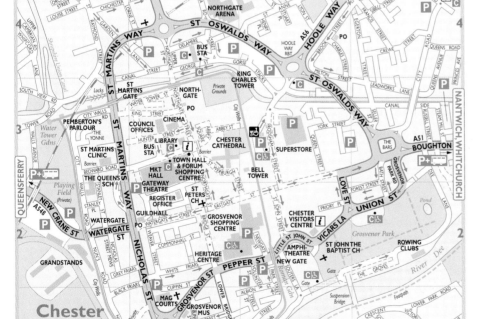

Chester

Chester is found on atlas page **81 F1**

Abbey Square	B3	New Crane Street	A2
Abbey Street	B3	Newgate Street	C2
Albion Street	B1-C1-C2	Nicholas Street	B1-B2
Bath Street	D2-D3	Nicholas Street Mews	A2
Bedward Road	A3	Northgate Street	B2-B3-B4
Black Friars	A1-B2	Nun's Road	A2-A1-B1
Bridge Street	B2	Park Street	C1-C2
Bunce Street	B1	Pepper Street	B2-C2
Canal Side	D3	Queen Street	C3
Canal Street	A3-B4	Queens Avenue	D3-D4
Castle Drive	B1-C1	Queens Drive	D1
Castle Street	B1	Queens Park Road	C1-D1
Charles Street	C4	Queens Road	D4
Chichester Street	A4-B4	Raymond Street	A4
City Road	D3-D4	Russell Street	D3
City Walls Road	A2-A3	St Anne Street	C4
Commonhall Street	B2	St John Street	C2
Crewe Street	D4	St Johns Road	D1
Cuppin Street	B1-B2	St Martins Way	B2-A3-A4-B4
Dee Lane	D2-D3	St Oswalds Way	B4-C4-C3-D3
Delamere Street	B4	St Werburgh Street	B3-C2
Duke Street	C1	Seller Street	D3
Eastgate Street	B2-C2	Sibell Street	D4
Edinburgh Way	D1	Souters Lane	C1-C2
Egerton Street	D3-D4	South Crescent Road	D1
Forest Street	C2-D2-D3	South View Road	A3
Francis Street	D4	Stanley Street	A2
Frodsham Street	C3	Station Road	D4
Garden Lane	A4-B4	Steam Mill Street	D3
George Street	B4	Steele Street	C1
Gorse Stacks	B4-C4-C3	Stuart Place	C4
Granville Street	A4	The Bars	D3
Grey Friars	A2-B2	The Groves	C2-D2
Grosvenor Park Road	D3	Tower Road	A3
Grosvenor Street	B1-B2	Trafford Street	C4
Hoole Way	C4-D4	Union Street	D2
Hunter Street	A3-B3	Upper Northgate Street	B4
King Street	A3-B3	Vicars Lane	C2
Leadworks Lane	D3	Victoria Crescent	D1
Little St John Street	C2	Victoria Road	B4
Lorne Street	A4-B4	Volunteer Street	C2
Louise Street	A4	Walls Avenue	A2-A3
Love Street	C2-C3	Water Tower Street	A3-B3
Lower Bridge Street	B2-B1-C1	Watergate Street	A2-B2
Lower Park Road	D1-D2	Weaver Street	B2
Lyon Street	C4	West Lorne Street	A4
Mason Street	B4	Whipcord Lane	A3-A4
Milton Street	C4-C3-D3	York Street	C3-D3

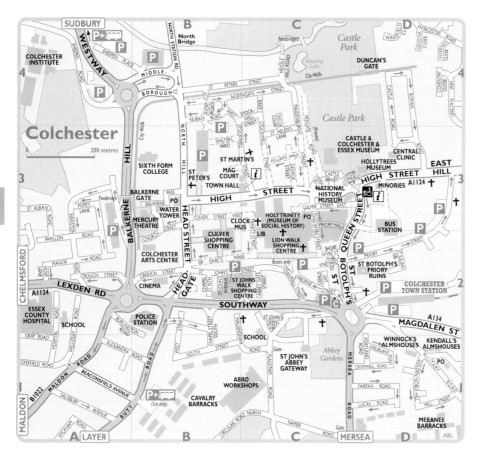

Colchester

Colchester is found on atlas page **52 D3**

Abbey Gate Street	C2	Museum Street	C3
Alexandra Road	A1-B1	Napier Road	C1
Art Street	C2	North Hill	B3-B4
Balkerne Hill	A2-A3-A4	North Station Road	B4
Balkerne Passage	B3	Northgate Street	B4-C4
Beaconsfield Avenue	A1	Nunn's Road	B4
Burlington Road	A2-B2-B1	Osborne Street	C2
Butt Road	A1-B1-B2	Papillon Road	A2
Castle Bailey	C3	Pope's Lane	A3
Castle Road	D3-D4	Portland Road	D1-D2
Chapel Street North	B2	Priory Street	C2-D2-D3
Chapel Street South	B1-B2	Priory Walk	C3
Church Street	B2-B3	Queen Street	C2-D3
Circular Road North	B1-C1	Rawston Road	A2-A3
Coventry Close	D4	Roman Road	D3-D4
Cowdray Crescent	C3-D3	Ryegate Road	C3-C4
Creffield Road	A1	St Alban's Road	A2-A3
Cromwell Road	D1	St Botolph's Street	C2
Crouch Street	A2-B2	St Helen's Lane	C3-C4
Culver Street East	C3-D3	St John's Avenue	B2
Culver Street West	B3-C3	St John's Green	C2
East Hill	D3	St John's Street	B2-C2
East Stockwell Street	C3-C4	St Julian Grove	D2
Fairfax Road	D1	St Peters Street	B4-C4
Flagstaff Road	C1	Salisbury Avenue	A1
George Street	C2	Sheepen Place	A4-B4
Golden Noble Hill	D1	Sheepen Road	A4
Gray Road	A1	Short Cut Road	B4
Head Street	B2-B3	Short Wyre Street	C2
Headgate	B2	Shrubland Road	D1
High Street	B3-C3, D3	Sir Isaac's Walk	B2-C2
Hospital Lane	A2	South Street	B1
Hospital Road	A1-A2	Southway	B2-C2
Inverness Close	D4	Stanwell Street	C2
Leicester Close	D4	Stockwell Street	B4-C4
Lexden Road	A2	Taylor Court	C3-C4
Lincoln Way	D4	Trinity Street	C2-C3
Long Wyre Street	C2-C3	Vineyard Street	C2
Lucas Road	D1	Wakefield Close	D4
Magdalen Street	D2	Walsingham Road	B2-B1-C1
Maidenburgh Street	C3-C4	Walters Yard	B3
Maldon Road	A1-A2	Wellesley Road	A1-A2
Manor Road	A1	West Stockwell Street	B4-B3-C3
Mersea Road	C1-D1	West Street	B1-B2
Middle Mill Road	C4	Westway	A4
Middleborough	A4-B4	Wickham Road	A1
Military Road	D1-D2	William's Walk	C3
Mill Street	D1	Worcester Road	D4

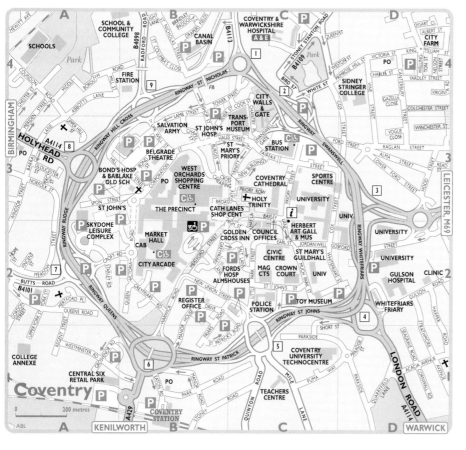

Coventry

Coventry is found on atlas page **59 F3**

Abbotts Lane	A4	Meriden Street	A3-A4
Acacia Avenue	D1	Middleborough Road	A4-B4
Alma Street	D3	Mile Lane	C1
Barras Lane	A3	Much Park Street	C2
Bayley Lane	C2-C3	New Buildings	C3
Bird Street	C4	New Union Street	B2-C2
Bishop Street	B3-B4	Norfolk Street	A3
Bond Street	B3	Park Road	B1-C1
Broadgate	B3-C3	Parkside	C1-D1
Burges	B3	Primrose Hill Street	C4-D4
Butts Road	A2	Priory Row	C3
Canterbury Street	D3-D4	Priory Street	C3
Chantry Place	C3-C4	Puma Way	C1-D1
Charles Street	D4	Quarryfield Lane	C1-D1
Colchester Street	D4	Queen Victoria Road	B2-B3
Cook Street	C4	Queens Road	A2
Corporation Street	B3	Quinton Road	C1
Coundon Road	A4	Radford Road	B4
Cox Street	C4-D3-C3-C2	Raglan Street	D3
Croft Road	A2-B2	Regent Street	A1-A2
Cross Cheaping	B3-C3	Ringway Hill Cross	A3-B3-B4
Drapers Fields	B4	Ringway Queens	A2-B1
Earl Street	C2	Ringway Rudge	A2-A3
Eaton Road	B1	Ringway St Johns	C1-C2
Fairfax Street	C3	Ringway St Nicholas	B4
Ford Street	C3-D3	Ringway St Patrick	B1-C1
Friars Road	B1-B2-C2	Ringway Swanswell	C4-C3-D3
Gosford Street	C2-D2	Ringway Whitefriars	D2-D3
Greyfriars Lane	B2	St John's Street	C2
Greyfriars Road	B2	St Nicholas Street	B4
Grosvenor Road	A1	St Patrick's Road	B1-C1-C2
Gulson Road	D2	Salt Lane	B2-C2
Hales Street	B3-C3	Silver Street	B3-B4-C4
Hay Lane	C2-C3	Spon Street	A3-B3
Hertford Street	B2	Stoney Road	B1-C1
High Street	B3-C2	Stoney Stanton Road	C4
Hill Street	A3-B3	Strathmore Avenue	D1-D2
Holyhead Road	A3	Swanswell Gate	C3
Hood Street	D3	Tower Street	B3-C3
Jordan Well	C2	Trinity Street	B3
King William Street	D4	Upper Well Street	B3
Lamb Street	B3-B4	Victoria Street	D4
Little Park Street	C2	Vine Street	D3-D4
London Road	D1	Warwick Road	B1-B2
Lower Ford Street	D3	Westminster Road	A1
Manor House Drive	B1-B2	White Street	C4
Manor Road	B1	Whitefriars Street	C2-D2
Meadow Street	A2-A3	Yardley Street	D4

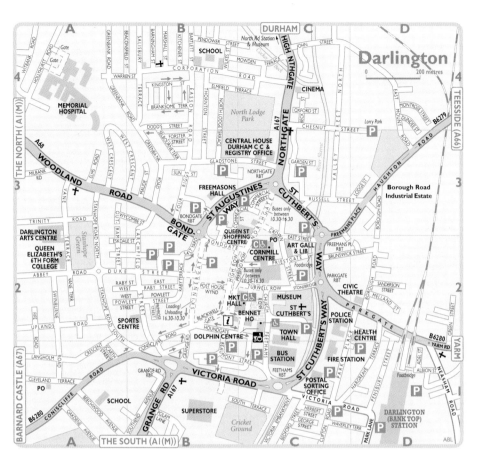

Darlington

Darlington is found on atlas page **106 B2**

Abbey Road	A2	Larchfield Street	B2-B3
Albion Street	D1	Marshall Street	B4
Barningham Street	B4	Maude Street	B3
Bartlett Street	B4	Melland Street	D2
Beaconsfield Street	A4	Mowden Terrace	B4-C4
Beaumont Street	B2-B1-C1	Neasham Road	D1
Beck Street	C4	North Lodge Terrace	B3-B4
Bedford Street	C1	Northgate	C2-C3-C4
Beechwood Avenue	A1	Oakdene Avenue	A1
Blackwell Gate	B2	Outram Street	A2-A3
Bondgate	B2-B3	Oxford Street	C4
Borough Road	D2-D3	Park Lane	D1
Branksome Terrace	B4	Park Place	C1-D2
Brunswick Street	C2-D2	Parkgate	C2-D2
Chesnut Street	C4-D4-D3	Pendower Street	B4-C4
Church Row	C2	Pensbury Street	D1
Cleveland Terrace	A1	Post House Wynd	B2
Clifton Road	C1	Powlett Street	B2
Commercial Street	B3-C3	Prebend Row	B2-C2
Coniscliffe Road	A1-B1-B2	Priestgate	C2
Corporation Road	B4-C4	Raby Terrace	B2
Crown Street	C2-C3	Russell Street	C3-D3
Dodd's Street	B4	St Augustines Way	B3-C3
Duke Street	A2-B2	St Cuthbert's Way	C1-C2-C3
Easson Road	B3-B4	Salisbury Terrace	B4
East Mount Road	D3-D4	Salt Yard	B2
East Raby Street	B2	Selbourne Terrace	B3
East Street	C2	Skinnergate	B2
Elmfield Terrace	B4-C4	South Terrace	B1-C1
Eskale Street	A2-B2	Southend Avenue	A1-B1
Feethams	C1-C2	Stanhope Road North	A2-A3
Forster Street	B3	Stanhope Road South	A2-A1-B1
Four Riggs	B3	Stonebridge	C2
Freemans Place	C2-C3-D3	Swinburne Road	A1-A2
Garden Street	C3	Thornton Street	B3-B4
Gladstone Street	B3-C3	Trinity Road	A3
Grange Road	B1	Tubwell Row	C2
Greenbank Road	A4-B4-B3	Uplands Road	A2
Hargreave Terrace	C1-D1-D2	Valley Street North	C3-C4
Haughton Road	D3-D4	Vane Terrace	A2-A3
High Northgate	C4	Victoria Embankment	C1
High Row	B2	Victoria Road	B1-C1-D1
Hollyhurst Road	A4	Waverley Terrace	C1-D1
Houndgate	B2-C2	West Crescent	A4-A3-B3
John Street	C4	Wilkes Street	B4
Kingston Street	B4	Woodland Road	A3-B3
Kitchener Street	B4	Wycombe Street	A3-B3
Langholm Crescent	A1-A2	Yarm Road	D1

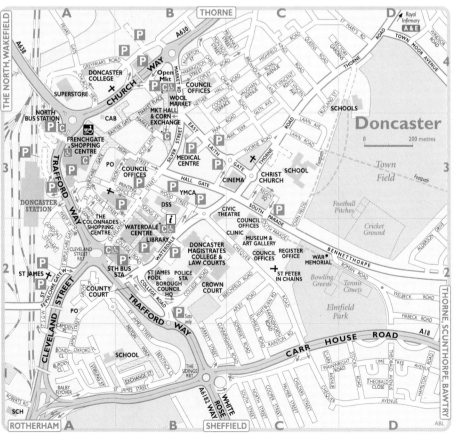

Doncaster

Doncaster is found on atlas page **84 C5**

Alderson Drive	D2	Montague Street	B4-C4
Allerton Street	B4	Nether Hall Road	B4-C4
Apley Road	C2	North Street	C1
Baxter Gate	A3-B3	Oxford Place	A1
Beechfield Road	B2-C2	Palmer Street	C1
Bennetthorpe	C2-D2	Park Road	B3-C3-C4
Bentinck Close	B1	Park Terrace	B3-C3
Bond Close	A1	Printing Office Street	B3
Broxholme Lane	C4	Priory Place	B3
Camden Place	A1	Queens Road	C4
Carr House Road	B1-C1-D1	Rainton Road	C1
Chequer Avenue	C1-D1	Ravensworth Road	C1-C2
Chequer Road	B2-C2-C1	Rectory Gardens	C4-D4
Childers Street	C1	Regent Square	C3
Christ Church Road	B4-C4-C3	Roberts Road	A1
Church View	A4	Roman Road	D2
Church Way	A4-B4	Royal Avenue	C4
Clark Avenue	C1	Rutland Street	C4
Cleveland Street	A1-A2-B2-B3	St James Street	A1-A2-B2-B1
College Road	B2	St Mary's Road	D4
Cooper Street	C1	St Sepulchre Gate	A3
Coopers Terrace	B4-C4	St Sepulchre Gate West	A1-A2
Copley Road	B4-C4	St Vincent Avenue	C4
Cunningham Road	B2-B1-C1	St Vincent Road	C4
Duke Street	A3-B3	Scot Lane	B3
East Laith Gate	B3-C3	Silver Street	B3
Elmfield Road	C1-C2	Somerset Road	C1-C2
Exchange Street	B1	South Parade	C2-C3
Firbeck Road	D2	South Street	C1
Friars Gate	A4	Spring Gardens	A3
Glyn Avenue	C4	Sterling Street	A1
Gordon Street	A2	Stewart Street	A2
Greyfriars Road	A4-B4	Stockil Road	D1
Grove Place	A2	Theobald Avenue	D1
Hall Gate	B3	Thorne Road	C3-C4-D4
Hamilton Road	D1	Town Fields	C2-C3
Harrington Street	B4	Town Moor Avenue	D4
High Street	B3	Trafford Way	A3-A2-B2-B1
Highfield Road	C4	Vaughan Avenue	C4
Jarrett Street	B1	Wainwright Road	C1-D1
Kings Road	C4	Waterdale	B2-B3
Lawn Avenue	C3	Welbeck Road	D2
Lawn Road	C3	West Street	A2-A3
Lime Tree Avenue	D1	Whitburn Road	C2
Market Place	B3-B4	White Rose Way	B1-C1
Market Road	B3-B4	Windsor Road	D4
Milbanke Street	C4	Wood Street	B3
Milton Walk	B1-B2	Young Street	B2-B3

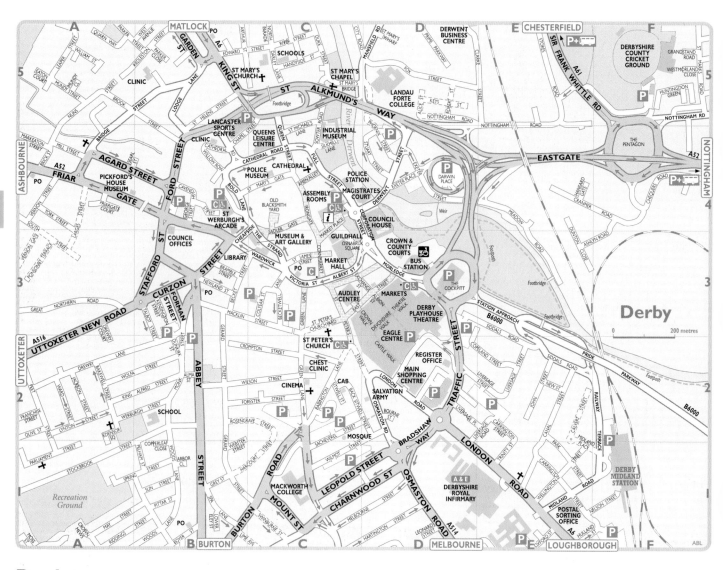

Derby

Derby is found on atlas page **72 A4**

Abbey Street	B1-B2-B3	Colyear Street	C3	Gerard Street
Agard Street	A4-B4	Copeland Street	D3-D2-E2	Grandstand Road
Albert Street	C3	Copperleaf Close	B1	Great Northern Road
Albion Street	D3	Cornmarket	C3	Green Lane
Alice Street	D5	Corporation Street	C4-D3	Grey Street
Alma Street	B2	Cranmer Road	E4-F4	Handyside Street
Amen Alley	C4	Crompton Street	B2-C2	Hansard Gate
Arbor Close	B1	Crown Mews	A1	Harcourt Street
Arthur Street	B5-C5	Crown Walk	C3-D3	Hartington Street
Ashlyn Road	E3-F3-F4	Curzon Street	B3	Hulland Street
Babington Lane	C2	Darley Lane	C5	Huntingdon Green
Back Sitwell Street	C2-D2	Derwent Street	D4	Irongate
Bakewell Street	A2	Devonshire Walk	D3	Jackson Street
Becket Street	B3-C3	Drewry Court	A2-A3	John Street
Becketwell Lane	C3	Drewry Lane	A2-B2-B3	Kedleston Street
Bold Lane	B4	Duke Street	C5	Kensington Street
Bourne Street	D2	Dunkirk Street	B2	Keys Street
Boyer Street	B1	Dunton Close	E3-E4	King Alfred Street
Bradshaw Way	D1-D2	East Street	C3-D3	King Street
Bramble Street	B3	Eastgate	E4	Larges Street
Brick Street	A4	Eaton Court	A5	Leaper Street
Bridge Street	A4-A5-B5	Edensor Square	A1-A2	Leonard Street
Brook Street	A5-B5-B4	Edward Street	B5-C5	Leopold Street
Burton Road	B1-C1-C2	Exchange Street	C3-D3	Lime Avenue
Calvert Street	E2	Exeter Place	D4	Liversage Place
Canal Street	E2	Exeter Street	D4	Liversage Road
Carrington Street	E1, E2	Ford Street	B4	Liversage Street
Castle Walk	D2	Forester Street	B2-C2	Lodge Lane
Cathedral Road	B4-C4	Forman Street	B3	London Road
Cavendish Street	B4	Fox Street	D5	Lower Eley Street
Chapel Street	B4-C5	Franchise Street	A2	Lynton Street
Charnwood Street	C1-D1	Friar Gate	A4-B4	Macklin Street
Cheapside	B3-C3	Friargate Court	A4	Mansfield Road
Chequers Road	F4	Full Street	C4	Markeaton Street
City Road	C5	Garden Street	B5	Market Place
Clarke Street	D5-E5	George Street	B4	May Street

Gerard Street	B3-B2-B1-C1	Meadow Road	E3-E4	River Street
Grandstand Road	F5	Melbourne Street	C1-D1	Robert Street
Great Northern Road	A3	Midland Place	E1-E2	Rosengrave Street
Green Lane	C2-C3	Midland Road	E1	Sacheverel Street
Grey Street	B1	Mill Street	A4	Sadler Gate
Handyside Street	C5	Monk Street	B2-B3	St Alkmund's Way
Hansard Gate	E4	Morledge	D3	St Helens Street
Harcourt Street	B1-C1	Moss Street	A1	St James Street
Hartington Street	C1-D1	Mount Street	C1	St Marks Road
Hulland Street	E1-F1	Mundy Close	A5	St Mary's Bridge
Huntingdon Green	F5	Mundy Street	A5	St Mary's Wharf
Irongate	C4	Nelson Street	E1-F1	St Marys Gate
Jackson Street	A2	New Street	E2	St Michael's Lane
John Street	B5	Newland Street	B3	St Peter's Churchyard
Kedleston Street	A5-B5	North Parade	C5	St Peter's Street
Kensington Street	B3	Nottingham Road	D5-E5, F5	Searl Street
Keys Street	D5	Nuns Street	A4-A5	Siddals Road
King Alfred Street	A2-B2	Olive Street	A2	Silkmill Lane
King Street	B5	Osmaston Road	D1-D2	Sir Frank Whittle Road
Larges Street	A3-A4	Osnabrük Square	C3	Sitwell Street
Leaper Street	A5	Oxford Street	E1	South Street
Leonard Street	D1	Park Street	E1-E2	Sowter Road
Leopold Street	C1-D1	Parker Close	B5	Spa Lane
Lime Avenue	B1-C1	Parker Street	A5-B5	Spring Street
Liversage Place	D2-E2	Parliament Street	A1	Stafford Street
Liversage Road	D2-E2	Peet Street	A1-A2	Station Approach
Liversage Street	D2-E2	Pelham Street	B1	Stockbrook Street
Lodge Lane	B4-B5	Phoenix Street	D4-D5	Stores Road
London Road	D2-D1-E1	Pittar Street	B1	Stuart Street
Lower Eley Street	B1	Ponsonby Terrace	A3	Sun Street
Lynton Street	A2	Pride Parkway	E3-E2-F2	Swinburne Street
Macklin Street	B3-C3	Prime Parkway	D5	Talbot Street
Mansfield Road	D5	Quarn Way	A5	The Strand
Markeaton Street	A4	Queen Street	C4-C5	Theatre Walk
Market Place	C3-C4	Railway Terrace	E2-F2-F1	Traffic Street
May Street	A1-B1	Riddings Street	A1-B1	Trinity Street

River Street	C5	Uttoxeter New Road	A2-A3
Robert Street	D5	Vernon Gate	A3
Rosengrave Street	B2-C2	Vernon Street	A4
Sacheverel Street	C1-C2	Victoria Street	C3
Sadler Gate	C3-C4	Ward Street	A2
St Alkmund's Way	C5-D5	Wardwick	B3-C3
St Helens Street	B5	Webster Street	B1-B2
St James Street	C3	Wellington Street	E1
St Marks Road	F5	Werburgh Street	A2-B2
St Mary's Bridge	C5	West Avenue	B5
St Mary's Wharf	D5	Westmorland Close	F5
St Marys Gate	B4-C4	William Street	A5
St Michael's Lane	C4-C5	Willow Row	B4
St Peter's Churchyard	C3	Wilmot Street	C1-D2
St Peter's Street	C3-C2-D2	Wilson Street	B2-C2
Searl Street	A4-B4	Wolfa Street	A2-B2
Siddals Road	D3-E3-E2	Woods Lane	B1-B2
Silkmill Lane	C4	York Street	A4
Sir Frank Whittle Road	E5-F5		
Sitwell Street	C2		
South Street	A3-A4		
Sowter Road	C4-C5		
Spa Lane	B1		
Spring Street	A1-B1		
Stafford Street	B3-B4		
Station Approach	D3-E3		
Stockbrook Street	A1-B1-B2		
Stores Road	E5		
Stuart Street	D4		
Sun Street	B1		
Swinburne Street	C1		
Talbot Street	B2-B3		
The Strand	C3-C4		
Theatre Walk	D3		
Traffic Street	D2-D3		
Trinity Street	E1		

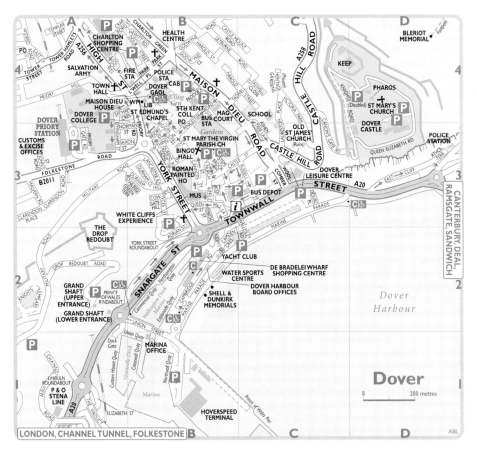

Dover

Dover is found on atlas page **19 G6**

Adrian Street	B2-B3	Mill Lane	B3
Ashen Tree Lane	C3-C4	New Bridge	B2
Athol Terrace	D3	New Street	B3
Bench Street	B3	Norman Street	A3-B3
Biggin Street	B3-B4	Park Place	B4
Bowling Green Terrace	B3	Park Street	B4
Cambridge Road	B2	Pencester Road	B3-B4
Camden Crescent	B2-C2	Princes Street	B3
Cannon Street	B3	Priory Gate Road	A3
Canon's Gate Road	C3-C4	Priory Hill	A4
Castle Hill Road	C3-C4	Priory Road	B3-B4
Castle Mount Road	B4-C4	Priory Street	B3
Castle Street	B3-C3	Queen Elizabeth Road	D3
Channel View Road	A1	Queen Street	B3
Charlton Green	B4	Queens Gardens	B3
Church Street	B3	Russell Street	C3
Clarendon Road	A3	St John's Road	A3
Cowgate Hill	B3	Saxon Street	A3-B3
Crafford Street	A4-B4	Snargate Street	B2
Dour Street	A4-B4	Stem Brook	B3
Douro Place	C3	Taswell Close	C4
Drop Redoubt Road	A2	Taswell Street	B4-C4
Durham Close	B3	Templar Street	A4
Durham Hill	B3	The Paddock	B4
East Cliff	D3	The Viaduct	A1
East Street	A4	Tower Hamlets Road	A4
Effingham Crescent	A4-B4	Tower Street	A4
Effingham Street	A3-A4	Townwall Street	B3-C3
Elizabeth Street	A1	Union Street	B1-B2
Folkestone Road	A3-B3	Victoria Park	C3-C4
Godwyne Close	B4	Wellesley Road	C2-C3
Godwyne Road	B4	Widred Road	A4
Harold Street	B4-C4	Wood Street	A4
Heritage Gardens	C4	Woolcomber Street	C3
Hewitt Road	A4	Worthington Street	B3
High Street	A4-B4	York Street	B3
King Street	B3		
Knights Road	C4-D3		
Knights Templars	A2		
Ladywell	B4		
Lancaster Road	B3		
Laureston Place	C3-C4		
Leyburne Road	B4-C4		
Maison Dieu Road	B4-C4-C3		
Malvern Road	A3		
Marine Parade	B2-C2-C3		
Market Square	B3		
Military Road	A2-A3-B3		

191

Dundee

Dundee is found on atlas page **140 D3**

Airlie Place	A1	Nicoll Street	B3
Balfour Street	A2	North Lindsay Street	B2-B3
Bank Street	B3	North Marketgait	A4-B4-C4
Barrack Road	A4	Panmure Street	B3-C3-C4
Barrack Street	B3	Park Place	A2-A1-B1
Bell Street	B3-B4-C4	Park Wynd	A2
Blackscroft	D4	Perth Road	A1
Blinshall Street	A2-A3	Prospect Place	A4-B4
Brown Street	A2-A3	Queen Street	C4-D4
Candle Lane	C3-D3	Rattray Street	B3
Castle Street	C2-C3	Reform Street	B3-C3
Commercial Street	C3	Riverside Drive	B1-C1-C2
Constable Street	D4	Roseangle	A1
Constitution Road	A4-B4-B3	St Andrews Street	C4
Cowgate	C4	St Roques Lane	D4
Crichton Street	C2	Seabraes Court	A1
Cross Lane	A2-B2	Seagate	C3-C4-D4
Dens Street	D4	Session Street	A2-A3
Dock Street	C2-C3	Small's Lane	A2
Douglas Street	A3	Small's Wynd	A1-A2
Dudhope Street	B4	South Marketgait	B2-C2-D3
Dudhope Terrace	A4	South Tay Street	A2-B2
East Dock Street	D3-D4	South Victoria Dock Road	D3
East Marketgait	C4-D4-D2	South Ward Road	B2-B3
Euclid Crescent	B3	Trades Lane	C3-D3
Euclid Street	B3	Union Street	B2-C2
Exchange Street	C2-C3	Union Terrace	A4
Foundry Lane	D4	Victoria Road	B4-C4
Gellatly Street	C3-D3	Ward Road	A3-B3
Greenmarket	B1-B2	West Bell Street	A3-B3
Guthrie Street	A3	West Marketgait	A3-A2-B2
Hawkhill	A2	West Port	A2
High Street	C2-C3	Whitehall Crescent	C2
Hilltown	B4-C4	Whitehall Street	C2
Hilltown Terrace	B4	Willison Street	B2-B3
Horsewater Wynd	A2		
Irvine's Square	B4		
Johnston Street	A3-B3		
King Street	C4-D4		
Ladywell Avenue	C4-D4		
Laurel Bank	B4		
Lochee Road	A4		
Mary Anne Lane	D3-D4		
McDonald Street	B4		
Meadowside	B3-C3-C4-B4		
Middle Street	D4		
Miln Street	A3		
Nethergate	A1-B1-B2		

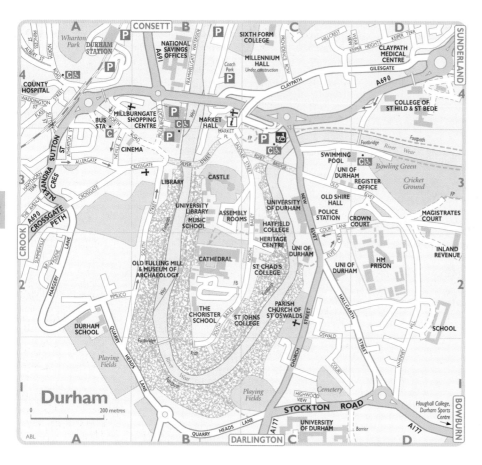

Durham

Durham is found on atlas page **106 B5**

Albert Street	A4
Alexandra Crescent	A3
Allergate	A3
Atherton Street	A3-A4
Briardene	A2
Church Street	C1-C2
Claypath	C4
Court Lane	C3-D3
Crossgate	A3-B3
Crossgate Peth	A2-A3
Elvet Bridge	C3
Elvet Crescent	C2-C3
Flass Street	A3-A4
Framwellgate	B4
Gilesgate	D4
Hallgarth Street	C2-D2-D1
Hawthorn Terrace	A3
Highwood View	C1
Hillcrest	C4
Keiper Heights	C4-D4
Keiper Terrace	D4
Margery Lane	A2-A3
Market Place	B3-B4
Millburngate	B3-B4
Neville Street	A3
New Elvet	C2-C3
North Bailey	C2-C3
North Road	A4-A3-B3
Old Elvet	C3-D3
Oswald Court	C2-C1-D1
Pimlico	A2
Princess Street	A4
Providence Row	C4
Quarry Heads Lane	A2-A1-B1-C1
Saddler Street	B3-C3
Silver Street	B3
South Bailey	B1-B2
South Street	B2-B3
Stockton Road	C1-D1
Summerville	A2-A3
Sutton Street	A3-A4
The Avenue	A3
Waddington Street	A4
Wear View	D4
Whinney Hill	D1-D2

Eastbourne

Eastbourne is found on atlas page **17 G1**

Arlington Road	A2-A3	Lascelles Terrace	B1-C1
Ashford Road	B3-B4-C4	Latimer Road	D4
Ashford Square	B4	Leaf Road	B4
Bedford Grove	A4	Lismore Road	B2-B3-C3
Belmore Road	C4-D4	Longstone Road	B3-C3-C4
Blackwater Road	A1-B1-B2	Lushington Lane	B2
Bolton Road	B2-B3	Lushington Road	B2
Bourne Street	C4-C3-D3	Marine Parade	D3
Burlington Place	B2-C2-C1	Marine Road	D3-D4
Burlington Road	C2-C3	Mark Lane	B2-B3
Camden Road	A2	Meads Road	A1-A2
Carew Road	A4-B4	Melbourne Road	C4
Carlisle Road	A1-B1-C1	New Road	C4
Cavendish Avenue	C4	North Street	C3
Cavendish Bridge	B4	Old Orchard Road	A2-A3
Cavendish Place	C3-C4	Old Wish Road	A1-B1
Ceylon Place	C3-D3-D4	Pevensey Road	C3-C4-D4
Chiswick Place	B1-B2	Queens Gardens	C3-D3
College Road	B1-B2	Royal Parade	D4
Commercial Road	B3-B4	St Anne's Road	A4-A3-B3
Compton Street	B1-C1-C2	St Aubyn's Road	D4
Connaught Road	B2	St Leonard's Road	A3-B3-B4
Cornfield Lane	B2	Saffrons Road	A2
Cornfield Road	B2-B3	Seaside	D4
Cornfield Terrace	B2	Seaside Road	C3-D3
Devonshire Place	B2-C2	South Street	A2-B2
Dursley Road	C4	Southfields Road	A3
Elms Avenue	C2-C3	Spencer Road	B2
Elms Road	C2-C3	Station Parade	A3
Enys Road	A4	Station Street	B3
Eversfield Road	A4-B4	Susans Road	B4-B3-C3
Furness Road	A2-B2	Sydney Road	C4
Gildredge Road	A3-B2	Terminus Road	B3-C3-C2
Grand Parade	C1-C2	The Avenue	A3-A4
Grange Road	A1-A2	Tideswell Road	B3-C3-C4
Granville Road	A1	Trinity Place	A3
Grassington Road	A1-A2	Trinity Trees	B2-C2
Grove Road	A2-A3	Upper Avenue	A4-B4
Hardwick Road	B1-B2	Upperton Gardens	A3-A4
Hartfield Road	A3-A4	Upperton Road	A3
Hartington Place	C2	West Street	A2-B2
Howard Square	C1	West Terrace	A2-A3
Hyde Gardens	B2-B3	Wharf Road	A3
Hyde Road	A2	Willowfield Road	C4-D4
Ivy Terrace	A3	Wilmington Gardens	B1
Junction Road	B3	Wilmington Square	B1
King Edward's Parade	B1-C1	Wish Road	B2
Langney Road	C3-C4-D4	York Road	A2

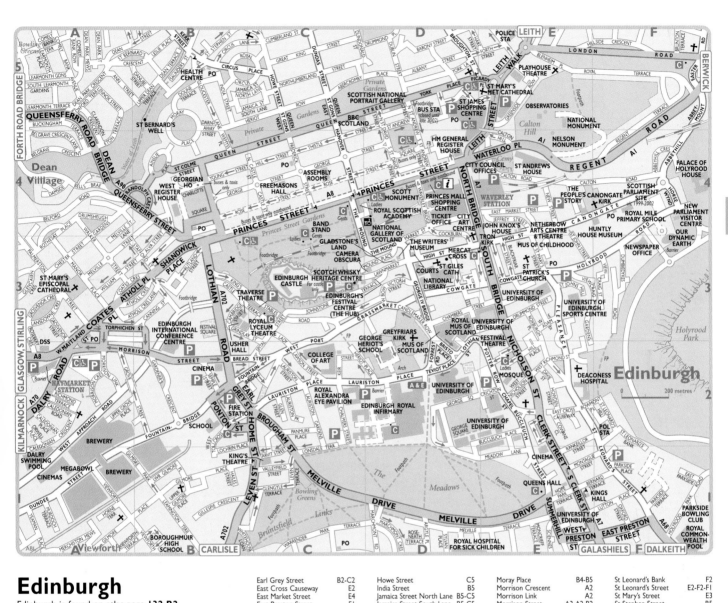

Edinburgh

Edinburgh is found on atlas page **132 B2**

Abbeyhill	F4	Castle Terrace	B3-C3	Earl Grey Street	B2-C2	Howe Street	C5	Moray Place	B4-B5	St Leonard's Bank	F2
Abbeyhill Crescent	F4	Chalmers Street	C2	East Cross Causeway	E2	India Street	B5	Morrison Crescent	A2	St Leonard's Street	E2-F2-F1
Abbeymount	F5	Chambers Street	D3-E3	East Market Street	E4	Jamaica Street North Lane	B5-C5	Morrison Link	A2	St Mary's Street	E3
Abercromby Place	C5-D5	Chapel Street	E2	East Preston Street	F1	Jamaica Street South Lane	B5-C5	Morrison Street	A3-A2-B2	St Stephen Street	B5
Ainslie Place	B4	Charlotte Square	B4	Eton Terrace	A4-A5	Jeffrey Street	E4	Mound Place	C3-D3	Semple Street	B2
Albany Street	D5	Chester Street Gardens	A3-A4	Festival Square	B3	Johnstone Terrace	C3-D3	Murdoch Terrace	A1	Shandwick Place	B3
Alva Street	B3-B4	Circus Lane	B5-C5	Forrest Road	D2-D3	Keir Street	C2	New Street	E4	South Bridge	D4
Ann Street	A5-B5	Circus Place	B5-C5	Forth Street	D5-E5	Kerr Street	B5	Nicholson Street	E2-E3	South Clerk Street	E1-F1
Argyle Place	D1	Clarendon Crescent	A4-A5	Fountainbridge	A2-B2-C2	King's Stables Road	B3-C3	North Bridge	D4-E4	South Learmonth Gardens	A5
Atholl Crescent	A3-B3	Clerk Street	E1-E2	Frederick Street	C4	Lady Lawson Street	C2-C3	North Castle Street	B4-C4	South St Andrew Street	D4
Atholl Crescent Lane	A3-B3	Coates Crescent	A3-B3	Gardener's Crescent	B2	Lansdowne Crescent	A3	North St Andrew Street	D5	South St David Street	D4
Atholl Place	A3-B3	Coates Place	A3	George IV Bridge	D3	Lauriston Gardens	C2	North St David Street	D4-D5	Spital Street	C2-C3
Barony Street	D5	Cockburn Street	D3-D4	George Square	D2	Lauriston Park	C2	Northumberland Street	C5	Stafford Street	B3
Belford Road	A4	Comely Bank Avenue	A5	George Street	B4-C4-D4	Lauriston Place	C2-D2	Oxford Street	F1	Summerhill	E1
Belgrave Crescent	A4	Cowgate	D3-E3	Gillespie Crescent	B1	Lauriston Street	C2	Palmerston Place	A3-A4	Tarvit Street	C1-C2
Belgrave Crescent Lane	A4-A5	Crichton Street	E2	Gilmore Park	A2-A1-B1	Lawnmarket	D3	Panmure Place	C2	Teviot Place	D2
Bells Brae	A4	Dalkeith Road	F1	Gilmore Place	A1-B1-C1	Leamington Terrace	B1	Parkside Terrace	F1	The Mound	C4-D3
Bernard Terrace	E1-F1	Dalry Road	A2	Gladstone Terrace	E1	Learmonth Terrace	A5	Picardy Place	D5-E5	Thistle Street	C4-C5-D5
Blackfriar Street	E3	Damside	A4	Glen Street	C2	Leith Street	D4-E5	Pleasance	E2-E3	Torphichen Street	A3-B3
Bowmont Place	E2-F2	Danube Street	A5-B5	Glengyle Terrace	C1	Leith Walk	E5	Ponton Street	B2	Upper Dean Terrace	B5
Bread Street	B2-C2	Darnaway Street	B5	Gloucester Lane	B4-B5	Lennox Street	A5	Potter Row	E2-E3	Upper Gilmore Place	B1
Bristo Place	D2-D3	Davie Street	E2	Grassmarket	C3-D3	Leslie Place	B5	Princes Street	B4-C4-D4	Upper Grove Place	A2
Brougham Street	C2	Dean Bridge	A4	Great King Street	C5	Leven Street	B1-C1	Queen Street	B4-C4-C5-D5	Valleyfield Street	C1
Broughton Street	D5	Dean Park Crescent	A5	Greenside Row	E5	Leven Terrace	C1	Queen Street Gardens East	C5	Victoria Street	D3
Buccleuch Place	D2-E2	Dean Park Mews	A5	Grindlay Street	B3-C3	Livingstone Place	E1	Queen Street Gardens West	C5	Viewcraig Gardens	E3
Buccleuch Street	E1-E2	Dean Park Street	A5	Grosvenor Crescent	A3	Lochrin Place	B2	Queensferry Road	A4-A5	Viewcraig Street	F3
Buckingham Terrace	A4-A5	Dean Street	A5-B5	Grosvenor Street	A3	London Road	E5-F5	Queensferry Street	A4-B4	Viewforth	A1-B1
Caledonian Crescent	A2	Dean Terrace	B5	Grove Street	A2-B2	Lonsdale Terrace	C1-C2	Randolph Crescent	A4-B4	Walker Street	A3-A4
Caledonian Place	A2	Doune Terrace	B5	Hanover Street	C4-C5	Lothian Road	B2-B3	Rankeillor Street	E2	Warrender Park Terrace	C1-D1
Caledonian Road	A2	Drummond Place	D5	Heriot Place	C2-D2	Lothian Street	D2-D3	Regent Road	E4-F4-F5	Waterloo Place	D4-E4
Calton Hill	E4-E5	Drummond Street	E3	Heriot Row	B5-C5	Lutton Place	E1-F1	Regent Terrace	F4-F5	Waverley Bridge	D4
Calton Road	E4-F4	Drumsheugh	A4	High Street	D3-E3-E4	Manor Place	A3-A4	Rose Street	B4-C4-D4	West Approach Road	A1-A2-B2
Cambridge Street	B3	Dublin Street	D5	Hill Place	E2-E3	Marchmont Crescent	D1	Rothesay Place	A3-A4	West Bow	D3
Candlemaker Row	D3	Dumbiedykes Road	F3	Hill Street	C4	Marchmont Road	D1	Royal Circus	B5-C5	West Maitland Street	A2-A3
Canongate	E4-F4	Dundas Street	C5	Hillside Crescent	E5-F5	Market Street	D3-D4	Royal Terrace	E5-F5	West Nicholson Street	E2
Castle Street	C4	Dundee Street	A1	Holyrood Park Road	F1	Meadow Lane	E1-E2	Rutland Street	B3	West Port	C2-C3
				Holyrood Road	E3-F3-F4	Melville Drive	C1-D1-E1	St Andrew Square	D4-D5	West Preston Street	E1
				Home Street	C1-C2	Melville Street	A3-B4	St Bernard's Crescent	A5-B5	West Richmond Street	E1
				Hope Park Terrace	E1	Melville Street Lane	A4	St Colme Street	B4	William Street	A3-B3
				Horse Wynd	F4	Melville Terrace	D1-E1	St John Street	E3-E4	York Place	D5
				Howden Street	E2	Montague Street	E1-F1	St Johns Hill	E3	Young Street	B4

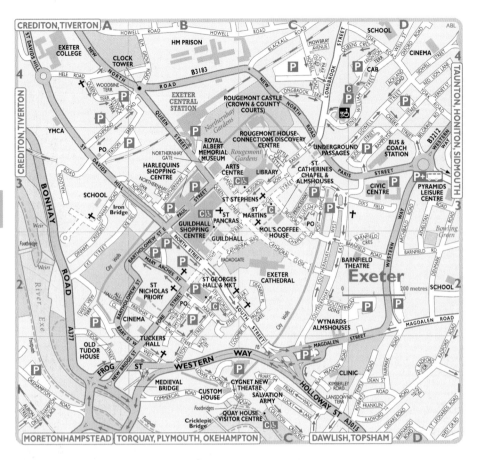

Exeter

Exeter is found on atlas page **9 F4**

Archibald Road	D2-D3	Leighton Terrace	D4
Athelstan Road	D2-D3	Little Castle Street	C3
Bailey Street	C3	Longbrook Street	C3-C4
Bampflyde Street	D3-D4	Longbrook Terrace	C4
Barnfield Road	C2-D2	Lower Coombe Street	B1
Bartholomew Street	A2-B2	Lower North Street	B3
Bartholomew Street East	B2-B3	Lucky Lane	C1
Bartholomew		Magdalen Road	D2
Street West	A2-A1-B1	Magdalen Street	C1-D1-D2
Bedford Street	C2-C3	Market Street	B2
Belgrave Road	D3-D4	Mary Arches Street	B2
Blackall Road	C4	Musgrove Row	B3-B4
Bluecoat Lane	C3	New Bridge Street	A1-B1
Bonhay Road	A1-A2-A3	New North Road	A4-B4-C4-C3
Broadgate	B2	North Street	B2-B3
Bude Street	D3	Northernhay Street	B3
Bull Meadow Road	C1	Okehampton Road	A1
Castle Street	C3	Oxford Road	D4
Cathedral Close	C2-C3	Palace Gate	C2
Cathedral Yard	B2-C2	Paris Street	C3-D3
Chapel Street	C2-C3	Paul Street	B3
Cheeke Street	D3-D4	Post Office Lane	C2-C3
Colleton Crescent	C1	Preston Street	B1-B2
Commercial Road	B1	Princesway	C1
Coombe Street	B1-B2-C2	Queen Street	B4-B3-C3
Dean Street	D1	Queens Terrace	A4
Deanery Place	C2	Radford Road	D1-D2
Denmark Road	D2-D3	Red Lion Lane	D4
Dinham Crescent	A2-A3	Richmond Road	A3-A4-B2
Dinham Road	A3	Roberts Road	D1
Dix's Field	D3	St Davids Hill	A4-A3-B3
Elm Grove Road	B4	St Leonards Road	D1
Exe Hill	A3-B3	Sidwell Street	C3-D3-D4
Exe Street	A2	Smythen Street	B2
Fairpark Road	D1-D2	South George Street	B3
Fore Street	B1-B2	South Street	B2-C2-C3
Friars Walk	C1	Southernhay East	C1-C2-C3
Frienhay Street	B2	Southernhay Gardens	C2-D2
Frog Street	A1-B1	Southernhay West	C2-C3
Gandy Street	B3-C3	Station Yard	A3-B3-B4
Haldon Road	A3	Temple Road	D1
Hele Road	A4	The Quay	B1-C1
High Street	B2-B3-C3	Tudor Street	A1-A2
Holloway Street	C1-D1	West Street	B1
Howell Road	A4-B4-C4	West View Terrace	A2
John Street	B2	Western Way	B1-C1
King Street	B1-B2	Western Way	D2-D3-D4
King William Street	C4-D4	York Road	C4-D4

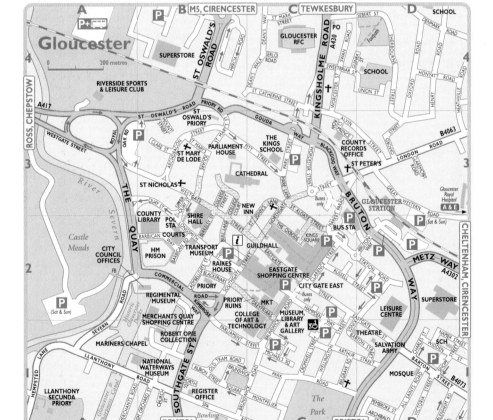

Gloucester

Gloucester is found on atlas page **46 D1**

Albion Street	B1	Market Parade	C2-C3
All Saints Road	D1	Merchants Road	A1-B1
Alvin Street	C3-D3	Mercia Road	B4
Archdeacon Street	B3	Metz Way	D2
Arthur Street	C1-D1	Montpelier	C1
Barbican Road	B2	Mount Street	B3
Barbican Way	B2	Napier Street	D1
Barton Street	D1	North Street	B1
Belgrave Road	C1	Northgate Street	C2-C3
Berkeley Street	B2-B3	Old Tram Road	B1
Blackdog Way	C3	Oxford Road	D3-D4
Blackfriars	B2	Oxford Street	D3
Blenheim Road	D1	Park Road	C1
Brunswick Road	B1-C1-C2	Park Street	C1
Brunswick Square	B1-C1	Parliament Street	B2-B1-C1
Bruton Way	C3-D2-D1	Pembroke Street	D1
Bull Lane	B2	Pitt Street	B3-C3
Clare Street	B3	Priory Road	B4
Claremont Road	D3	Quay Street	A3-B3
Clarence Row	C3	Royal Oak Road	A3
Clarence Street	C2	Russell Street	C2-D2
College Court	B3	St Aldate Street	C2-C3
College Street	B3	St Catherine Street	C4
Commercial Road	B2	St John's Lane	B2-C2-C3
Cromwell Street	C1	St Mark Street	C4
Dean's Walk	C4	St Mary's Square	B3
Dean's Way	C4	St Mary's Street	B3
Denmark Road	D1	St Michael's Square	C1
Eastgate Street	C2-D1	St Oswald's Road	B3-B4
Gouda Way	B3-B4-C3	Sebert Street	C4-D4
Great Western Road	D2-D3	Serlo Road	C4
Greyfriars	B2-C2	Severn Road	A1-A2
Guinea Street	C4-D4	Sherbourne Street	D3-D4
Hampden Way	C1-C2	Sinope Street	D1
Hare Lane	C3	Southgate Street	B1-B2-C2
Heathville Road	D3-D4	Spa Road	B1-C1
Hempsted Lane	A1	Station Road	D2
Henry Road	D3-D4	Swan Road	C4
High Orchard Street	A1-B1	Sweetbriar Street	C4-D4
Honyatt Road	D4	The Oxbode	C2
Kimbrose Way	B2	The Quay	A2-A3
Kings Barton Street	C1-D1	Union Street	C4-D4
Kings Square	C2	Upper Quay Street	B3
Kingsholme Road	C3-C4	Victoria Street	D1
Ladybellgate Street	B2	Wellington Street	C1-C2
Llanthony Road	A1-B1	Westgate Street	A3-B3-B2
London Road	D3	Widden Street	D1
Longsmith Street	B2	Worcester Street	C3,C4

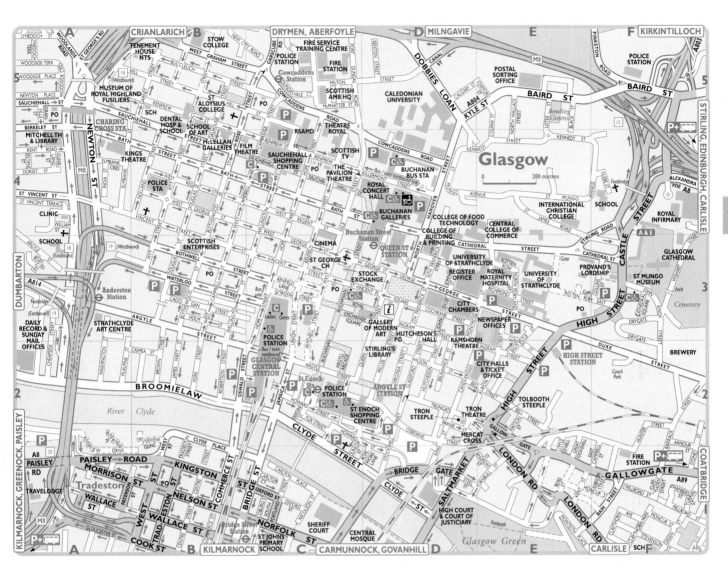

Glasgow

Glasgow is found on atlas page **130 B2**

Albion Street	D2-E2-E3	Claythorn Park	F1	Granville Street	A5	Moncur Street	E1-F1	Rotten Row East	E3-F3	West Street	B1-B2
Alexandra Parade	F4	Claythorn Street	F1	Great Dovehill	E1-E2	Monteith Place	E1	Royal Exchange Square	C3-D3	William Street	A4
Argyll Arcade	C2	Cleveland Street	A4	Green Street	F1	Montrose Street	D3-E3	St Andrews Street	D1-E1	Wilson Street	D2
Argyle Street	A3-B3-C2-D2	Clyde Place	B1-B2	High Street	E2-E3-F3	Morrison Street	A1-B1	St Georges Road	A5	Wishart Street	F3
Armour Street	F1-F2	Clyde Street	C2-C1-D1	Hill Street	A5-B5-C5	Nelson Street	B1	St James Road	E3-E4	Woodlands Road	A5
Bain Street	E1-F1	Coburg Street	C1	Holland Street	B4	Newton Place	A5	St Mungo Avenue	D4-E4-F4	Woodside Crescent	A5
Baird Street	E5-F5	Cochrane Street	D3	Holm Street	B3	Nicholson Street	C1	St Vincent Place	C3-D3	Woodside Place	A5
Barrack Street	F1-F2	College Street	E2-E3	Hope Street	C2-C3-C4-C5	Nile Street	C3-C4	St Vincent Street	A4-B4-B3-C3	Woodside Terrace	A5
Bath Street	A4-B4-C4-D4	Collins Street	F3	Howard Street	C2-D1	Norfolk Street	B1-C1	St Vincent Terrace	A4	York Street	B2-B3
Bell Street	D2-E2	Coupar Street	E4-E5	Hunter Street	F1-F2	North Frederick Street	D3	Saltmarket	D1		
Beltane Street	A4	Cowcaddens Road	C5-C4-D4	Hutcheson Street	D2	North Hanover Street	D3-D4-D5	Sauchiehall Street	A5-B4-C4-D4		
Berkeley Street	A4-A5	Crimea Street	A2-B2	India Street	A4	North Portland Street	E3	Scott Street	B4-B5		
Black Street	E4-E5	Dalhousie Street	B4-B5	Ingram Street	D3-D2-E2	North Wallace Street	E4-E5	Shuttle Street	E2-E3		
Blythswood Street	B3-B4	Dixon Street	C2	Jamaica Street	C2	Osborne Street	D1-D2	South Frederick Street	D3		
Bothwell Street	B3-C3	Dobbies Loan	D4-D5	James Watt Street	B2-B3	Oswald Street	B2	South Portland Street	C1		
Bridge Gate	D1	Douglas Street	B3-B4	John Knox Street	F2-F3	Oxford Street	C1	Stafford Street	E5		
Bridge Street	B1-C1	Drygate	F2-F3	John Street	D3	Paisley Road	A1-B1	Steel Street	D1		
Broomielaw	A2-B2	Duke Street	E3-E2-F2	Kennedy Street	D4-E4	Parnie Street	D2	Stevenson Street	F1		
Brown Street	B2-B3	Dundasvale Court	C5	Kent Road	A4	Paterson Street	A1	Stirling Road	E3-F4		
Brunswick Street	D2	Dunlop Street	C1	Kent Street	E1	Pinkston Road	F5	Stockwell Street	D1-D2		
Buccleuch Street	B5-C5	East Campbell Street	F1	Killermont Street	C4-D4	Pitt Street	B3-B4	Sydney Street	F1-F2		
Buchanan Street	C2-C3	Elmbank Crescent	A4	King Street	D1-D2	Port Dundas Road	C5	Tradeston Street	B1-B2		
Cadogan Street	B3-C3	Elmbank Street	A4-A5	Kingston Street	B1	Queen Street	C2-D2-D3	Trongate	D2		
Calgary Street	D5	Fox Street	C2	Kyle Street	D5-E5	Renfield Street	C3-C4	Turnbull Street	D1-E1		
Cambridge Street	C4-C5	Gallowgate	E2-E1-F1	Lister Street	E4-E5	Renfrew Street	A5-B5-B4-C4	Union Street	C2-C3		
Canal Street	D5	Garnet Street	B5	Little Dovehill	E1-E2	Renton Street	D5	Virginia Street	D2		
Carlton Court	C1	Garscube Road	C5	London Road	E1-F1	Richmond Street	E3	Wallace Street	A1-B1		
Carlton Place	C1	George Square	D3	Lynedoch Street	A5	Riverview Drive	A2-A1-B1	Washington Street	A2-A3		
Castle Street	F3-F4	George Street	D3-E3	Lynedoch Terrace	A5	Riverview Gardens	B2	Waterloo Street	B3-C3		
Cathedral Square	F3	Gibson Street	F1	McAlpine Street	A2-A3	Riverview Place	A2-A1	Watson Street	E2		
Cathedral Street	D3-E3-F3	Glassford Street	D2-D3	McIntyre Street	A3	Robertson Street	B2	Wellington Street	B3-C3-C4		
Centre Street	B1	Glebe Street	F4	McPhatter Street	C5	Rope work Lane	C1-D1	West Campbell Street	B3-B4-C4		
Chambers Street	F1	Gloucester Street	A1	Miller Street	D2-D3	Rose Street	B4-B5-C5	West George Street	B4-C4-D3		
Cheapside Street	A2-A3	Gordon Street	C3	Millroad Street	F1	Ross Street	E1	West Graham Street	B5-C5		
Claythorn Avenue	F1			Milton Street	C5-D5	Rotten Row	E3	West Nile Street	C3-C4-D4		
				Mitchell Street	C2-C3			West Regent Street	B4-C4		

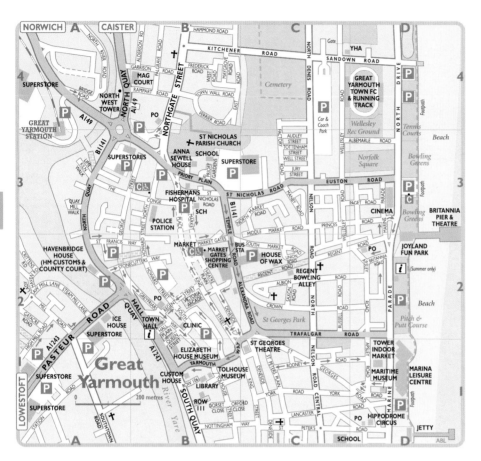

Great Yarmouth

Great Yarmouth is found on atlas page **65 H6**

Albemarle Road	C3-D3	Nottingham Way	B1-C1
Albion Road	C2-D2	Orford Close	B1-C1
Alderson Road	B4	Paget Road	C3-D3
Alexandra Road	C2	Palgrave Road	B4
Apsley Road	D1-D2	Pasteur Road	A1-A2
Audley Street	C3	Princes Road	C3-D3
Bridge Road	A4	Priory Gardens	B3
Britannia Road	D2	Priory Plain	B3
Crittens Road	A2	Quay Mill Walk	A3
Crown Road	C2-D2	Queen Street	B1-B2
Deneside	B2-C1	Rampart Road	B4
Dorset Close	B1	Regent Road	C2-D2
East Road	B4	Regent Street	B2
Euston Road	C3-D3	Rodney Road	C1-D1
Factory Road	C3-C4	Row 106	B1
Ferrier Road	B4	Russell Road	C2
Frederick Road	B4	St Francis Way	A2-B2
Garrison Road	A4-B4	St Georges Road	C1-D1
Gatacre Road	A2	St Nicholas Road	B3-C3
George Street	A2-A3-B3	St Peter's Road	C1-D1
Greyfriars Way	A2-B2-B1	St Peters Plain	C1
Hall Plain	B2	Sandown Road	C4-D4
Hall Quay	B2	Saw Mill Lane	A2
Hammond Road	B4	Saxon Road	C2
High Mill Road	A1-A2	South Market Road	B2-C2
Howard Street North	B2-B3	South Quay	B1
Howard Street South	B2	Southtown Road	A1
Jury Street	C3	Station Road	A1
King Street	B2-C1	Steam Mill Lane	A2
Kitchener Road	B4-C4	Stonecutters Way	A2-B2
Lady Haven Road	A2	Temple Road	B3-B2
Lancaster Road	C1-D1	The Conge	A3-B3
Lime Kiln Walk	A3	Theatre Plain	B2
Manby Road	C3	Tolhouse Street	B1
Marine Parade	D1-D2-D3	Tottenham Street	C3
Market Gates	B2	Town Wall Road	B4
Market Place	B2-B3	Trafalgar Road	C2-D2
Maygrove Road	B4	Union Road	B4
Middle Market Road	C2-C3	Victoria Arcade	B2
Mill Road	A2	Well Street	C3
Nelson Road Central	C1	Wellesley Road	C2-C3-C4
Nelson Road North	C2-C3	West Road	B4
North Denes Road	C4	Yarmouth Way	B1-C1-C2
North Drive	D3-D4	York Road	C1-D1
North Market Road	B3-C3		
North Quay	A2-A3-A4		
North River Road	A4		
Northgate Street	B3-B4		

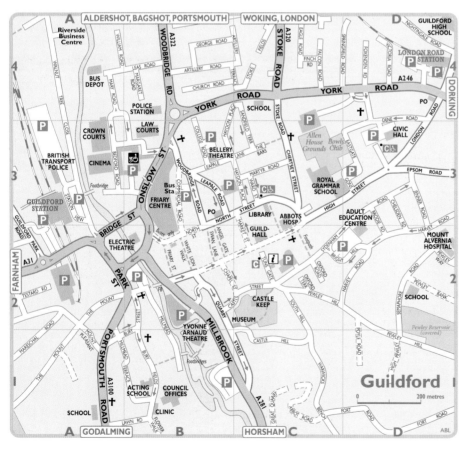

Guildford

Guildford is found on atlas page **27 H4**

Abbot Road	C1	Millmead Terrace	A1-B1
Angel Gate	B2	Mount Pleasant	A1-A2
Artillery Road	B4	Nightingale Road	D4
Artillery Terrace	B4-C4	North Street	B2-B3-C3
Bedford Road	A3	Onslow Street	B3
Bridge Street	A2-A3-B3	Oxford Road	C2
Bright Hill	C2-D2	Oxford Terrace	C2
Brodie Road	D2-D3	Park Street	A2-B2
Bury Fields	B1	Pewley Bank	D2
Bury Street	A1-B1-B2	Pewley Hill	C2-D2-D1
Castle Hill	C1-C2	Pewley Way	D2
Castle Street	B2-C2	Portsmouth Road	A1-A2-B2
Chapel Street	B2-C2	Poyle Road	D1-D2
Chelsden Road	D2-D3	Quarry Street	B2-B1-C1
Chertsey Street	C3	Sandfield Terrace	C3-C4
Church Road	B4	Semaphore Road	D1-D2
College Road	B3-B4	South Hill	C1-C2
Commercial Road	B2-B3	Springfield Road	C4-D4
Dene Road	D3-D4	Station View	A3
Eagle Road	C4	Stoke Fields	C4
Eastgate Gardens	D3	Stoke Road	C3-C4
Epsom Road	D3	Swan Lane	B2
Falcon Road	C4	Sydenham Road	C2-D2-D3
Finch Road	C4	Testard Road	A2
Flower Walk	B1	The Bars	A2
Fort Road	C1-D1	The Mount	A1-A2
Foxenden Road	D4	Tuns Gate	C2
Friary Street	B2	Victoria Road	D4
George Road	B4	Walnut Tree Close	A3-A4
Great Quarry	C1	Ward Street	C3
Guildford Park Road	A2-A3	Warwicks Bench	C1
Harvey Road	C2-D2-D3	White Lion Walk	B2
Haydon Place	C3-B3-B4-C4	William Road	A4
High Pewley	D1	Woodbridge Road	B3-B4
High Street	C3-D3	York Road	B4-C4-D4
Jenner Road	D2-D3		
Lawn Road	A1-B1		
Leapale Lane	B3-C3		
Leapale Road	B3		
Leas Road	B4		
London Road	D3-D4		
Mareschal Road	A1-A2		
Margaret Road	B4		
Market Street	C2-C3		
Martyr Road	C2		
Mary Road	A4		
Millbrook	B2-B1-C1		
Millmead	B1-B2		

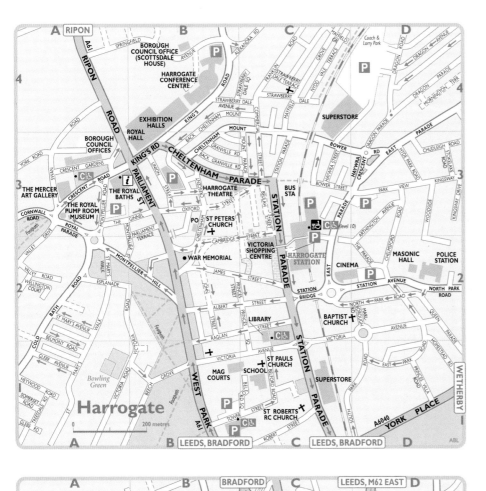

Harrogate

Harrogate is found on atlas page **90 D5**

Albert Street	B2-C2	Mornington Terrace	D4
Alexandra Road	B4-C4	Mount Parade	C3
Arthington Avenue	D2-D3	North Park Road	C2-D2
Back Cheltenham Mount	B3-B4-C4	Nydd Vale Terrace	C4
Back Granville Road	B3	Oxford Street	B3-C3
Beech Grove	A1-B1	Park View	D3
Belford Road	C1	Parliament Street	B3
Belford Square	C1	Parliament Terrace	B3
Belmont Road	A1-A2	Princes Square	B2-C2
Beulah Street	C3	Princes Street	B2-C2
Bower Road	C3-D3	Princes Villa Road	D1
Bower Street	C3	Queen Parade	D1-D2
Cambridge Street	B2-C3	Raglan Street	B1-B2-C2
Chelmsford Road	D2-D3	Ripon Road	A3-A4
Cheltenham Crescent	B2-B3	Robert Street	C1
Cheltenham Mount	B3-B4-C4	Royal Parade	A3
Cheltenham Parade	B3-C3	St Mary's Avenue	A2
Chudleigh Road	D3	St Mary's Walk	A1-A2
Cold Bath Road	A1-A2	Somerset Road	A1
Commercial Street	C3-C4	South Park Road	C1-D1
Cornwall Road	A3	Springfield Avenue	A4-B4
Crescent Gardens	A3	Station Avenue	C2-D2
Crescent Road	A3	Station Bridge	C2
Dragon Avenue	D4	Station Parade	C1-C2-C3
Dragon Parade	D3-D4	Stonelake Road	D3
Dragon Road	D4	Strawberry Dale	C4
East Parade	C2-C3-D3-D4	Strawberry Dale Avenue	B4-C4
East Park Road	D1-D2	Strawberry Dale Square	B4-C4
Esplanade	A2	Strawberry Dale Terrace	C4
Franklin Road	C4	Swan Road	A3-A4
Glebe Avenue	A1	The Ginnel	A3-B3
Glebe Road	A1	The Parade	D2
Granville Road	B3	Tower Street	B1-C1
Haywra Crescent	D3	Treesdale Road	A1
Haywra Street	C3	Union Street	B3
Heywood Road	A1	Valley Drive	A2-A3
Homestead Road	D1-D2	Valley Road	A2
Hyde Park Road	D3	Victoria Avenue	B1-C1-C2-D2
James Street	B2-C2	Victoria Road	A1-B1-B2-A2
John Street	B2	Wellington Court	A2
King's Road	B3-B4	West Park	B1
Kingsway	D3	Woodside	D2-D3
Kingsway Drive	D3	York Place	D1
Marlborough Road	D2	York Road	A3
Mayfield Grove	C4		
Montpellier Hill	A2-B2		
Montpellier Road	A3		
Montpellier Street	A2-A3		

Huddersfield

Huddersfield is found on atlas page **90 C1**

Albion Street	B1-B2	New North Road	A4-A3-B3
Alfred Street	C1	New Street	B1-B2-C2
Back Spring Street	A2	Northumberland Street	C3
Bath Street	B4	Old Leeds Road	D3-D4
Beast Market	C3	Old Gate	C2-C3
Belmont Street	A4-B4	Old South Street	A2
Bow Street	A1-A2	Outcote Bank	A1-B1
Brook Street	B3-C3	Page Street	C1
Byram Street	C3	Park Avenue	A2-A3
Cambridge Road	B4	Peel Street	C1-C2
Castlegate	B1-B2-B3-B4	Pine Street	C3-D3
Cecil Street	A2	Portland Street	A3
Chapel Street	B1-C1	Princess Street	B1-C1
Claremont Street	B4	Prospect Street	A1-B1
Cloth Hall Street	B2-C2	Quay Street	D3
Colne Street	D1	Queen Street	C2
Corporation Street	B1-C1-C2	Queensgate	C1-C2-D2
Cross Church Street	C2	Railway Street	B3
Crossgrove Street	A1	Ramsden Street	C2
Day Street	D1	Rook Street	B4
Dundas Street	B2	St Andrews Road	D2-D3-D4
Elmwood Avenue	A4-B4	St John's Road	B4
Fenton Square	A1	St Peter's Street	C3
Firth Street	D1	Southgate	C3-C2-D2
Fitzwilliam Street	A3-B3-B4	Springrove Street	A1
Fox Street	B2	Spring Street	A2
Garforth Street	D1	Springwood Avenue	A2
Gasworks Street	D4	Springwood Street	A2
George Street	B2	Station Street	B3
Great Northern Street	C4	Trinity Street	A3-A2-B2
Greenhead Road	A2	Westgate	B2-C2
Half Moon Street	B2	Upper George Street	A2
Henry Street	B2	Upperhead Row	B2
High Street	B2	Venn Street	C2-C3
Highfields Road	A4	Victoria Lane	C2
Imperial Arcade	B2	Wakefield Road	D1-D2
John William Street	B3-C3	Water Street	A1-A2
King Street	C2	Watergate	D3
Kings Mill Lane	D1	Waverley Road	A3
Kirkgate	C2-C3	William Street	C4
Lord Street	C2-C3	Wood Street	C3
Lower Fitzwilliam Street	C4-D4	Zetland Street	C2
Lynton Avenue	A2		
Manchester Road	A1-B1		
Market Place	C2		
Market Street	B2		
Merton Street	A1-A2-B2		
New North Parade	B3		

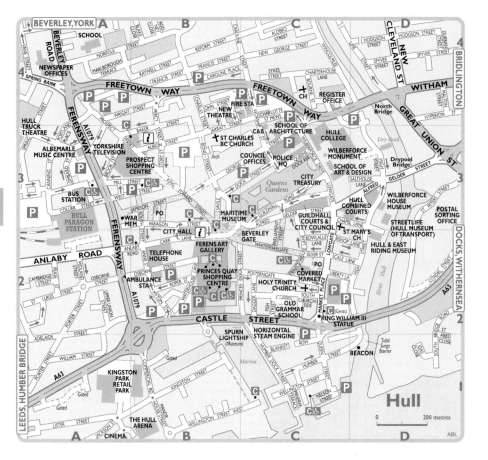

Hull

Hull is found on atlas page **93 E2**

Adelaide Street	A1-A2	Market Place	C2
Albion Street	B3	Marlborough Terrace	A4
Alfred Gelder Street	C3-D3	Midland Street	A2
Anlaby Road	A2-B2	Mill Street	A3-B3
Anne Street	B2	Myton Street	B2
Baker Street	A3-B3-B4	New Cleveland Street	D4
Beverley Road	A4	New George Street	C4
Bishop Lane	C2-D2	Norfolk Street	A4-B4
Blanket Row	C1	Osborne Street	A2-B2
Bond Street	B3	Paragon Street	B3
Bourne Street	C4	Parliament Street	C2-C3
Bowlalley Lane	C2	Pease Street	A2
Brook Street	A3	Percy Street	B3-B4
Canning Street	A3	Porter Street	A1-A2
Caroline Place	B4	Posterngate	C2
Caroline Street	B4-C4	Princes Dock Street	B2-C2
Carr Lane	B2	Prospect Street	A4-A3-B3
Castle Street	B2-C2	Queen Street	C1
Chapel Lane	C3-D3	Queens Dock Avenue	C3
Charles Street	B3-B4	Raywell Street	B4
Charlotte Street Mews	C4	Reform Street	B4
Charterhouse Lane	C4	Roper Street	B2
Collier Street	A3	St Lukes Street	A2
Commercial Road	B1	St Peters Street	D3
Dagger Lane	C2	Savile Street	B3
Dock Street	B3-C3	Scale Lane	C2-D2
Ferensway	A2-A3-A4	Silver Street	C2
Fish Street	C2	South Bridge Road	D1-D2
Freetown Way	A4-B4-C4	South Churchside	C2
George Street	B3-C3	South Street	B2-B3
Great Union Street	D3-D4	Spring Bank	A4
Guildhall Road	C3	Spring Street	A3-A4
High Street	D3	Spyvee Street	D4
Hodgson Street	D4	Story Street	B3
Humber Dock Street	C1-C2	Sykes Street	C4
Humber Street	C1-D1	Trinity House Lane	C2-C3
Hyperion Street	D4	Upper Union Street	A2
Jameson Street	A3-B3	Waterhouse Lane	B2
Jarratt Street	B3-C4	Wellington Street	C1
John Street	B4	Wellington Street West	B1-C1
King Edward Street	B3	West Street	A3-B3
Kingston Street	B1	Whitefriargate	C2
Liberty Lane	C2	Wilberforce Drive	C3
Lime Street	C4-D4	William Street	A1
Lister Street	A1	Wincolmlee	C4-D4
Lombard Street	A3	Witham	D4
Lowgate	C2-C3	Worship Street	C3-C4
Manor House Street	B1	Wright Street	A4-B4

Inverness

Inverness is found on atlas page **155 E4**

Abertarff Road	D3	Glendoe Terrace	A4
Academy Street	B3-C3	Glenurquhart Road	A1-B1-B2
Anderson Street	B4	Grant Street	A4-B4
Annfield Road	D1	Greig Street	B2-B3
Ardconnel Street	C2	Harbour Road	B4-C4-D4
Ardconnel Terrace	C2	Harrowden Road	A2-A3
Ardross Street	B2	Haugh Road	B1-C1-C3
Argyll Street	C2	High Street	C2-C3
Argyll Terrace	C2	Hill Street	C2
Attadale Road	A2-A3	Huntley Street	B2-B3
Auldcastle Road	D3	India Street	A4-B4
Ballifeary Lane	A1-B1	Kenneth Street	A3-B3-B2
Ballifeary Road	B1	King Street	B2-B3
Bank Street	B2-B3	Kingsmills Road	C2-D2-D1
Beaufort Road	D3	Laurel Avenue	A1-A2
Benula Road	A4	Leys Drive	D1-D2
Bishop's Road	B1-B2	Lochalsh Road	A2-A3-A4
Bridge Street	B2-C2	Lovat Road	D2-D3
Broadstone Park	D2	Lower Kessock Street	A4
Bruce Avenue	A1	Macewen Drive	D2
Bruce Gardens	A1-A2-B2	Maxwell Drive	A1
Burnett Road	C4	Mayfield Road	C1
Caledonian Road	A2	Midmills Road	C2-D2
Cameron Road	A3-A4	Millburn Road	C3-D3
Carse Road	A3-A4	Muirfield Road	C1-D1
Castle Road	B2-C2	Muirtown Street	A3-B3
Castle Street	C2	Ness Bank	B1-B2-C2
Cawdor Road	D2-D3	Ness Walk	B1-B2
Celt Street	B3	Old Edinburgh Road	C2-C1-D1
Chapel Street	B3	Old Mill Road	D1
Charles Street	C2	Planefield Road	B2
Church Street	B3	Rangemore Road	A2
Columba Road	A1-A2	Seafield Road	D4
Crown Avenue	C3	Shore Street	B4
Crown Circus	C3-D3	Southside Place	C2-D2-D2
Crown Drive	D2-D3	Southside Road	C1-C2
Crown Road	C3	Stephens Brae	C2
Crown Street	C2	Strother's Lane	C3
Culduthel Road	C1-C2	Telford Gardens	A3
Dalneigh Road	A1	Telford Road	A3-A4
Damfield Road	D1	Telford Road	A3
Darnaway Road	D1-D2	Tomnahurich Street	B2
Dochfour Drive	A1-A2	Union Road	C2-D2
Douglas Row	B3	Union Street	C3
Dunain Road	A3	Victoria Drive	D3
Fairfield Road	A3-A2-B2	Walker Road	B4-C4
Friars Street	B3	Wells Street	A3-B3
Gilbert Street	B3-B4	Young Street	B2

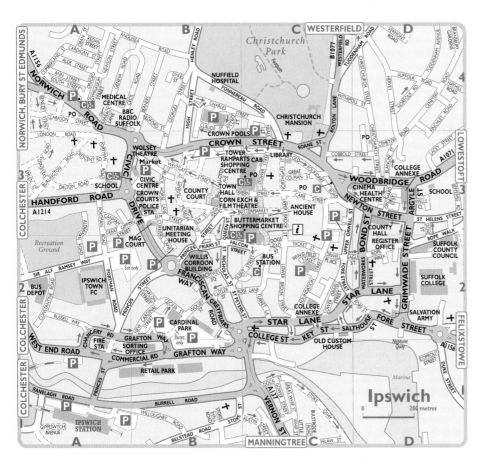

Ipswich

Ipswich is found on atlas page **53 E5**

Street	Grid	Street	Grid
Alderman Road	A2-A3	High Street	B3-B4
Anglesea Road	A4-B4	Key Street	C1-C2
Ann Street	A4	London Road	A3
Argyle Street	D3	Lower Brook Street	C2
Belstead Road	B1	Museum Street	B3
Berners Street	B4	New Cardinal Street	B2
Black Horse Lane	B3	Newton Street	C3-D3
Bolton Lane	C3-C4	Northgate Street	C3
Bond Street	D2-D3	Norwich Road	A3-A4
Burlington Road	A3	Old Foundary Road	C3
Burrell Road	B1	Orford Street	A4
Buttermarket	B3-C3	Orwell Place	C2
Cardigan Street	A4	Portman Road	A2-A3
Carr Street	C3	Princes Street	A1-A2-B2-B3
Cecil Road	A4-B4	Queen Street	B2-B3
Cecilia Street	B2	Ranelagh Road	A1
Cemetery Road	D3-D4	Rope Walk	D2-D3
Chancery Road	A1-A2	Rose Lane	B2-C2
Charles Street	B4-C4	Russell Way	A2
Christchurch Street	D3-D4	St Georges Street	B3-B4
Civic Drive	A3-B3-B2	St Helens Street	D3
Clarkson Street	A4	St Nicholas Street	B2
Claude Street	B4	St Peters Street	B2-C2
Cobbold Street	C3-D3	Salthouse Street	C2-D2
College Street	C1-C2	Silent Street	B2-C2
Commercial Road	A1-B1	Sir Alf Ramsey Way	A2
Constantine Road	A2	Soane Street	C3
Crown Street	B3-C3	Star Lane	C2-D2
Cumberland Street	A4	Stevenson Road	A3
Cutler Street	B2	Stoke Quay	C1
Dalton Road	A3	Stoke Street	B1
Dock Street	C1	Suffolk Road	D4
Dogs Head Street	C2	Tacket Street	C2
Duke Street	D1	Tavern Street	B3-C3
Elm Street	B3	Tower Street	C3
Falcon Street	B2-C2	Tuddenham Avenue	D4
Fonnereau Road	B4-C4-C3	Tuddenham Road	C4-D4
Fore Street	C2-D2	Turret Lane	C2
Foundation Street	C2	Upper Brook Street	C2-C3
Franciscan Way	B2	Upper Orwell Street	C2-C3
Friars Street	B2	Vernon Street	C1
Geneva Road	A4-B4	Waterworks Street	D2
Grafton Way	A2-B2-B1	West End Road	A1-A2
Greyfriars Road	B2	Westerfield Road	C4
Grimwade Street	D2-D3	Westgate Street	B3
Handford Road	A3	Willoughby Road	B1
Henley Road	B4	Wolsey Street	B2
Hervey Street	D3-D4	Woodbridge Road	C3-D3

199

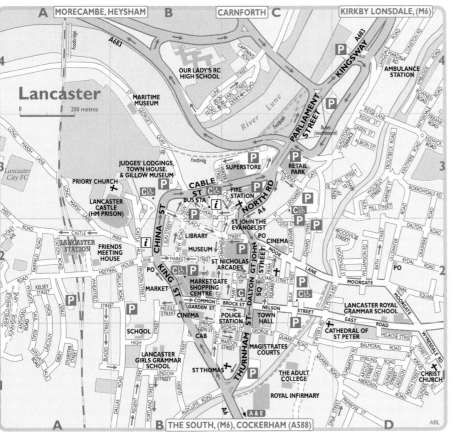

Lancaster

Lancaster is found on atlas page **88 C6**

Street	Grid	Street	Grid
Aberdeen Road	D1	Long Marsh Lane	A2-A3
Albert Road	B4-C4	Lord Street	B3-B4
Aldcliffe Road	B1	Lune Street	B4-C4
Ambleside Road	D4	Market Street	B2
Balmoral Road	D1	Marton Street	B1-C1
Bath Street	D2	Mary Street	C2
Blades Street	A1-A2	Meeting House Lane	A2-B2
Borrowdale Road	D3	Melrose Street	D1
Brewery Lane	C2	Middle Street	B2
Brock Street	C2	Moor Lane	B2
Bulk Street	C2	Moorgate	D1-D2
Cable Street	B3	Nelson Street	C2
Captain's Row	C4	New Road	B2-B3
Castle Hill	B2	North Road	C3
Castle Park	A2-B2	Park Square	D2
Chapel Street	C3	Parliament Street	C3-C4
Cheapside	B2-C2	Patterdale Road	D3-D4
China Street	B2-B3	Penny Street	B1-B2
Church Street	B3-B2-C2	Perth Street	D1
Common Garden Street	B2	Phoenix Street	C3
Dale Street	C1-D1	Portland Street	B1
Dallas Road	B1-B2	Quarry Road	C1-D1
Dalton Square	C2	Queen Street	B1
Damside Street	B3-B2-C2	Regent Street	B1
De Vitre Street	C3-D3	Ridge Lane	D3-D4
Derby Road	C4	Rydal Road	D2
Dumbarton Road	D1	St George's Quay	B3-B4
Dunkeld Street	D1	St Leonard's Gate	C2-C3
Earl Street	C4	St Peter's Road	C1-C2-D2
East Road	D1-D2	Sibsey Street	A1-A2
Edward Street	C2	Spring Garden Street	B1
Elgin Street	D1	Station Road	A2
Fairfield Road	A2	Stirling Road	D1
Friar Street	C2	Sulyard Street	C2
Gage Street	C2	Sun Street	B2
George Street	C1	Sunnyside Lane	A1-A2
Gladstone Terrace	D3	Thurnham Street	C1-C2
Grasmere Road	D2-D3	Troutbeck Road	D3
Great John Street	C2	Ullswater Road	D2-D3
Gregson Road	D1	Water Street	B3
High Street	B1-B2	West Road	A2-A3
Kentmere Road	D3	Westbourne Place	A2
King Street	B2	Westbourne Road	A2
Kingsway	C4-D4	Wheatfield Street	A2-B2
Kirkes Road	D1	Williamson Road	D2
Langdale Road	D4	Wingate Saul Road	A1-A2
Lincoln Road	A1-A2	Wolseley Street	D3
Lodge Street	C2	Wyresdale Road	D1

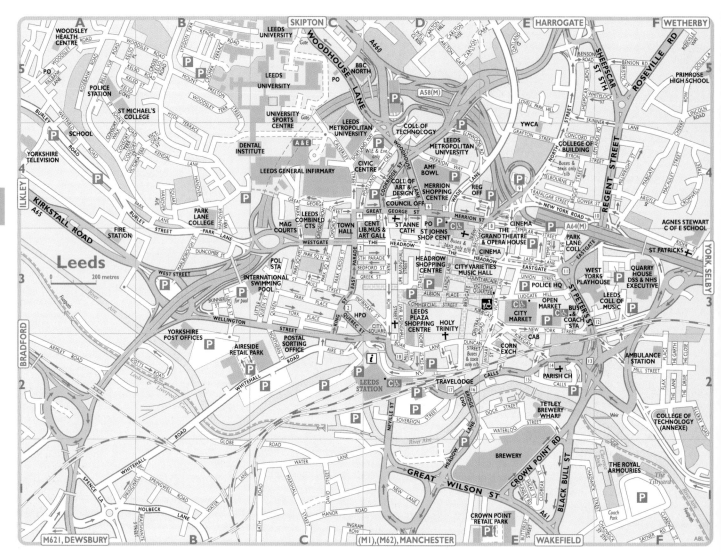

Leeds

Leeds is found on atlas page **90 D3**

Aire Street	C2
Albion Place	D3
Albion Street	D2-D3
Argyle Street	F4
Armley Road	A2
Bath Road	C1
Bedford Street	C3-D3
Belle Vue Road	A5
Benson Road	E5-F5
Black Bull Street	E1
Boar Lane	D2
Braithwaite Street	B1
Bridge End	D2
Bridge Street	E3-E4
Briggate	D2-D3
Bristol Street	F5
Burley Road	A4-A5
Burley Street	A4-B4-B3
Butterley Street	E1
Byron Street	E4-F4
Calls	D2-E2
Calverley Street	C4
Carlton Carr	D5-E5
Carlton Gate	D5
Carlton Hill	D5
Carlton Rise	D5
Central Road	D2-E2-E3
Chadwick Street	E1-F1
Chadwick Street South	F1
Cherry Row	F4-F5
Clarence Street	F1
Commercial Street	D3
Concord Street	E4
Consort Street	A4-B4
Consort Terrace	A4
Consort Walk	A4
Cookridge Street	D4
County Arcade	D3-E3
Cromer Terrace	B5
Cromwell Street	F4
Cross Kelso Road	B5
Crown Point Road	E1-E2
Cudbear Street	E1
David Street	C1
Dock Street	D2-E2
Dolly Lane	F5
Duncan Street	D2-E2
Duncombe Street	B3
East Parade	C3
Eastgate	E3-F3
Ellerby Road	F2
Elmwood Road	D4-E4
Flax Place	F2
Globe Road	B2-B1-C1
Gotts Road	A2-B2
Gower Street	E4-F4
Grafton Street	E4
Great George Street	C4-D4
Great Wilson Street	D1-E1
Greek Street	C3-D3
Hanover Avenue	B4
Hanover Square	B4
Hanover Way	B3-B4
Holbeck Lane	A1-B1
Hunslet Road	E1
Hyde Terrace	B4-B5
Infirmary Street	C3-D3
Ingram Row	C1
Kelso Gardens	A5-B5
Kelso Place	A5
Kelso Road	A5-B5
Kelso Street	A5-B5
Kendal Lane	B4
Kendal Road	B5-C5
King Street	C3
Kirkgate	D3-E3-E2
Kirkstall Road	A3-A4
Lady Lane	E3
Lands Lane	D3
Leylands Road	E4-F4
Lincoln Road	F5
Lisbon Street	B3
Little Queen Street	C3
Lovell Park Hill	E5
Lower Basinghall Street	D2-D3
Ludgate Hill	E3
Lyddon Terrace	B5
Mabgate	F4
Macauley Street	F4
Manor Road	C1-D1
Marlborough Street	B3
Marshall Street	C1
Meadow Lane	D1-D2
Melbourne Street	E4
Merrion Street	D4-E4
Merrion Way	D4
Mill Hill	D2
Mill Street	F2
Millwright Street	F4
Mount Preston Street	B4-B5
Neville Street	D1-D2
New Briggate	D3-E3-E4
New Lane	D1
New Station Street	D2
New York Road	E4
New York Street	E3
North Street	E4-E5
Northern Street	C2-C3
Oatland Court	E5
Oxford Place	C3-C4
Oxford Row	C3-C4
Park Cross Street	C3
Park Lane	A4-B4-B3
Park Place	C3
Park Row	D2-D3-D4
Park Square East	C3
Park Square North	C3
Park Square West	C3
Park Street	C3-C4
Portland Crescent	C4-D4
Portland Way	C4-D4
Quebec Street	C3-D2
Queen Street	C3
Regent Street	F4-F5
Rider Street	F3
Rillbank Lane	A5
Rosebank Road	A5
Roseville Road	F5
Roseville Way	F5
St John's Road	A5-A4-B4
St Pauls Street	C3
St Peter's Street	E3
Sayner Road	F1
Sheaf Street	E1
Sheepscar Grove	E5
Sheepscar Street South	E5-F5
Skinner Lane	E5-F4
Skinner Street	B3
South Parade	C3-D3
Sovereign Street	D2
Spence Lane	A1
Springwell Road	B1
Springwell Street	A1-B1
Templar Place	E3
Templar Street	E3-E4
The Close	F2
The Drive	F2
The Garth	F2
The Headrow	C3-D3-E3
The Lane	F2
Trafalgar Street	E4
Union Street	E3
Upper Basinghall Street	D3
Vicar Lane	E3
Victoria Quarter	D3-E3
Victoria Street	B4
Victoria Terrace	A4-B4
Wade Lane	D4-E4
Water Lane	B1-C1-D1
Waterloo Street	E2
Well Close Rise	D5
Wellington Street	B3-C3-C2
West Street	B3
Westfield Road	A4-A5
Westgate	C3
Wharf Street	E2
Whitehall Road	A1-B1-B2-C2
Whitelock Street	E5-F5
Woodhouse Lane	C5-D5-D4
Woodsley Road	A5-B5
Woodsley Terrace	B5
York Place	C3

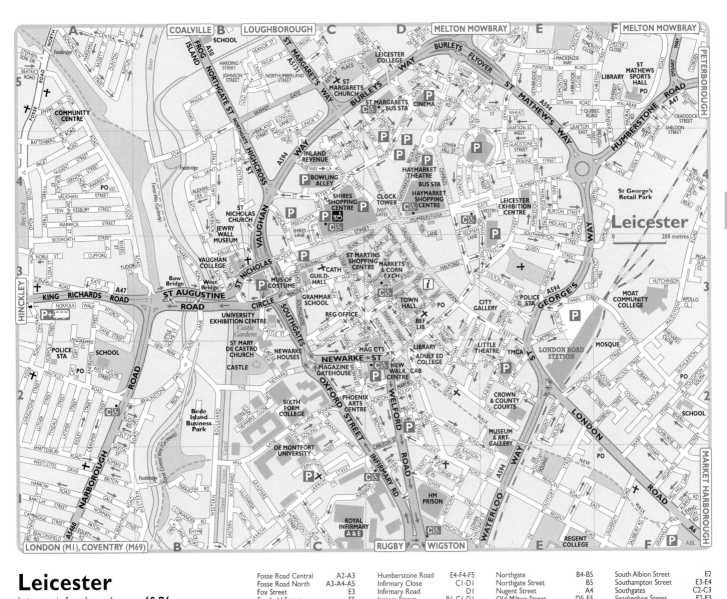

Leicester

Leicester is found on atlas page **60 B6**

Abbey Street	D5	Castle View	C2	Fosse Road Central	A2-A3	Humberstone Road	E4-F4-F5	Northgate	B4-B5	South Albion Street	E2
Albion Street	D2-D3	Causeway Lane	C4	Fosse Road North	A3-A4-A5	Infirmary Close	C1-D1	Northgate Street	B5	Southampton Street	E3-E4
All Saints Road	B4	Chancery Street	C2-D3	Fox Street	E3	Infirmary Road	D1	Nugent Street	A4	Southgates	C2-C3
Andrewes Street	A2-A3	Charles Street	D4-D3-E3	Freehold Street	F5	Jarrom Street	B1-C1-D1	Old Milton Street	D5-E5	Sparkenhoe Street	F2-F3
Applegate	C3	Chatham Street	D2-D3	Freeschool Lane	C4	Jarvis Street	B4	Orchard Street	D5	Stamford Street	D2-D3
Barclay Street	A1	Cheapside	D3-D4	Friar Lane	C3-D3	Kamloops Crescent	E5	Ottawa Road	E5	Sussex Street	F4
Bath Lane	B3-B4	Christow Street	F5	Friday Street	C5	Kent Street	F4	Oxford Street	C2	Swain Street	E3-F3
Battenberg Road	A4-A5	Church Gate	C5-C4-D4	Frog Island	B5	King Richards Road	A3-B3	Paget Road	A4	Swan Street	B4-B5
Bay Street	C5	Clarence Street	D4	Gallowtree Gate	D3-D4	King Street	D1-D2	Peacock Lane	C3	Tarragon Road	B1
Bedford Street North	E5	Clyde Street	E4	Garden Street	D5	Lancaster Road	D1-E1	Pelham Street	D1	Tewkesbury Street	A4
Bedford Street South	D4-D5	College Street	F2	Gateway Street	C1	Latimer Street	A1-A2	Pingle Street	B5	The Gateway	C1-C2
Belgrave Gate	D4-D5	Colton Street	E3	Gaul Street	A1-B1	Lee Street	D4-E4	Pocklingtons Walk	D2-D3	The Newarke	B2-C2
Bell Lane	F4	Conduit Street	E2-F2	Gladstone Street	E4	Lincoln Street	F2	Prebend Street	F2	Tichborne Street	F1-F2
Belvoir Street	D2-D3	Coriander Road	B1	Glebe Street	E2-F2	Livingstone Street	A2	Princess Road East	E1-F1	Tower Street	D1-E1
Bishop Street	D3	Cranmer Street	A1-A2	Glenfield Road	A3	London Road	E2-F2-F1	Princess Road West	D2-E1	Tudor Road	A5-A4-B3
Blackfriars Street	B4	Craven Street	C5	Gotham Street	F1-F2	Loseby Lane	C3	Queen Street	E3	Turner Street	D1
Bonchurch Street	A5	Cumberland Street	C4-C5	Grafton Place	C5-D5	Lower Brown Street	D2	Regent Road	D2-D1-E1-F1	Tyndale Street	A2
Bosworth Street	A3-A4	Dane Street	A3	Grafton Street East	E4-E5-F4	Lower Hill Street	D4	Regent Street	E2	Tyrrell Street	A4
Bowling Green Street	D3	De Montfort Street	E1-E2	Grafton Street West	E4-E5	Luther Street	A2	Repton Street	A5-B5	Ullswater Street	B1-C1
Braunstone Gate	A2-B2	Deacon Street	C1-C2	Graham Street	F4-F5	Maidstone Road	F2-F3-F4	Richard III Road	B3	University Road	F1
Briton Street	A1	Dover Street	D2-E2-E3	Granby Street	D3-E3-E2	Malabar Road	F5	Ridley Street	A1-A2	Upper Brown Street	C2
Brunswick Street	F4-F5	Dryden Street	D5-E5	Grange Lane	C1-C2	Manitoba Road	E5-F5	Rutland Street	D3-E3-E4	Vaughan Street	A4
Burgess Street	C4-C5	Duke Street	D2	Grasmere Street	B1-C1	Mansfield Street	D4-D5	St Augustine Road	B3	Vaughan Way	C3-C4-C5
Burleys Flyover	D5-E5	Dunkirk Street	E2	Gravel Street	C4-C5-D5	Marble Street	C2-C3	St George's Way	E2-E3-E4	Vernon Street	A4
Burleys Way	C5-D5	Duns Lane	B2-B3	Great Central Street	B4-C4	Market Place	D3	St Georges Street	E3	Warwick Street	A4
Burton Street	E4	Dunton Street	A5	Greyfriars	C3	Market Place South	D3	St Margaret's Way	C5	Waterloo Way	E1-E2
Butt Close Lane	C4	Dysart Way	F5	Guildhall Lane	C3	Market Street	D2-D3	St Margarets Street	C5	Welford Road	D1-D2
Byron Street	D4-D5	East Bond Street	C4-D4	Guthlaxton Street	F2	Marlborough Street	D2	St Martins	C3	Welles Street	B3-C3
Calais Hill	E2	East Gates	D3	Halford Street	D3-E3	Melbourne Street	F4	St Mathew's Way	E4-E5	Wellington Street	D2-E2
Cambridge Street	A1	East Street	E2	Harrow Road	A1	Mill Lane	B1-C1-C2	St Nicholas Circle	B3-C3	West Street	D1-E1
Campbell Street	E2-E3	Eastern Boulevard	B1	Havelock Street	C1	Millstone Lane	C2-C3	St Nicholas Place	C3	Westcotes Drive	A1
Cank Street	D3	Edmonton Road	E5	Haymarket	D4	Morledge Street	E4	St Peter's Lane	C4-D4	Western Boulevard	B1-B2
Canning Place	C5	Empire Road	A5	High Street	C3-C4-D4	Narborough Road	A1-A2-B2-B3	Samuel Street	F3-F4	Western Road	B1-A1-B2
Canning Street	C5-D5	Erskine Street	E4	Highcross Street	C3-C4	Nelson Street	E1-E2	Sanvey Gate	B5-C5	Wharf Street North	E5
Carlton Street	D1-D2	Every Street	D3	Highfield Street	F1-F2	New Park Street	B2-B3	Saxby Street	F1-F2	Wharf Street South	E4-E5
Carlton Street	D1-D2	Fitzroy Street	A3	Hill Street	D4	New Street	C3	Severn Street	F2	Wilberforce Road	A1
Castle Street	C3			Hinckley Road	A2	Newarke Close	B2-C2	Seymour Street	F2	William Street	F4
				Hobart Street	F2	Newarke Street	C2-D2	Shaftesbury Road	A1-A2	Wimbledon Street	E3
				Horsefair Street	D3	Newtown Street	D1	Short Street	D4	Yeoman Street	D4-E4-E3
				Hotel Street	C3-D3	Norfolk Street	A2-A3	Silver Street	C3-D3-D4	York Road	C2-D2
				Humberstone Gate	D4-E4	Norman Street	A1-B1	Soar Lane	B4-B5	York Street	D2-D3

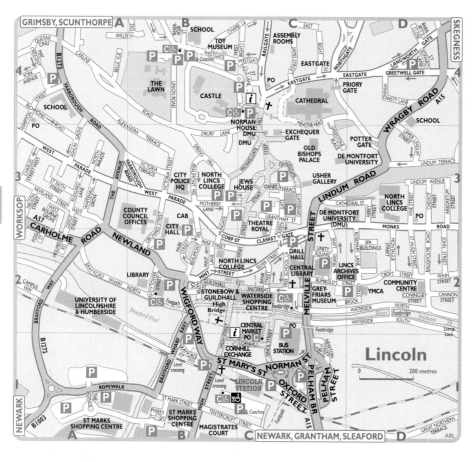

Lincoln

Lincoln is found on atlas page **85 G2**

Abbey Street	D3	Monks Road	D3
Alexandra Terrace	A4-A3-B3	Montague Street	D2
Arboretum Street	D3	Motherby Lane	B3
Ashlin Grove	A3-A4	Newland	A2-B2
Baggholme Road	D2	Newland Street West	A3
Bailgate	C4	Newton Street	C1
Bank Street	C2	Norman Street	C1
Beaumont Fee	B2-B3	North Parade	A3
Brayford Way	A1-A2	Northgate	C4-D4
Brayford Wharf East	B1-B2	Orchard Street	B2-B3
Brayford Wharf North	A2-B2	Oxford Street	C1
Brook Street	C2-D2	Park Street	B2
Carholme Road	A2-A3	Pelham Bridge	C1
Carline Road	A4-B4-B3	Pelham Street	C1
Cathedral Street	C3-D3	Queens Crescent	A4
Charles Street West	A3	Reservoir Street	B4
Cheviot Street	D3	Richmond Road	A3-A4
Clasket Gate	C2	Ropewalk	A1-B1
Coningsby Street	D2	Rosemary Lane	D2
Cornhill	C1	Rudgard Lane	A3
Corporation Street	B2-C2	Rumbold's Street	C2-D2
Croft Street	D2	St Hugh Street	D2
Danesgate	C3	St Mark Street	B1
Depot Street	A2-A3	St Mary's Street	B1-C1
Drury Lane	B3-C3	St Paul's Lane	C4
East Bight	C4	Saltergate	B2-C2
Eastgate	C4-D4	Silver Street	C2
Flaxengate	C2-C3	Sincil Street	C1-C2
Free School Lane	C2	Spring Hill	B3
Friars Lane	C2	Steep Hill	C3-C4
Grantham Street	C3	Strait	C3
Greetwell Gate	D4	Tentercroft Street	B1-C1
Guildhall Street	B2	The Avenue	A3
Hampton Street	A3-A4	Union Road	B4
High Street	B1-B2-C2-C3	Upper Lindum Street	D3
Hungate	B2-B3	Victoria Street	B3
James Street	C4	Victoria Terrace	B3
John Street	D2	Vine Street	D3
Langworth Gate	D4	Waterside North	C2-D2
Lindum Avenue	D3	Waterside South	C2-D2
Lindum Road	C3-D3	West Parade	A3-B3
Lindum Terrace	D3	Westgate	B4-C4
May Crescent	A4	Whitehall Grove	A3
Melville Street	C2-C3	Wigford Way	B1-B2
Michaelgate	B3-C3	Winn Street	D2
Minster Yard	C3-C4	Winnowsty Lane	D4
Mint Lane	B2	Wragby Road	D3-D4
Mint Street	B2	Yarborough Road	A4-A3-B3

Llandudno

Llandudno is found on atlas page **79 G3**

Abbey Road	A3-A4	Jacksons Court	C1
Adelphi Street	C2-C3	James Street	A3
Albert Street	B2	Jubilee Street	B2
Argyll Road	B2-C2	King's Avenue	A1
Arvon Avenue	A3-A4	King's Place	A1
Augusta Street	B2	King's Road	A1
Back Madoc Street	B3	Llewelyn Avenue	A4
Bodafon Street	B3-C3	Lloyd Street	A2-A3-B3
Bodhyfryd Road	A4	Llwynon Gardens	A4
Brookes Street	A3-B3-B2	Madoc Street	A3-B3
Builder Street	B1-B2	Maelgwyn Road	A3
Builder Street West	A1-B1	Maesdu Road	C1
Cae Bach	B1	Market Street	A3
Cae Clyd	D1	Masonic Street	A4
Cae Mawr	A1	Mostyn Broadway	C2-D2
Caroline Road	A3-B3-B2	Mostyn Crescent	C3
Chapel Street	A3	Mostyn Street	A4-B3-C3
Charlotte Road	C1-C2-D2	Nevill Crescent	C3
Charlton Street	B2	New Street	A3
Church Walks	A4-B4	Norman Road	B1-B2
Claremont Road	A2	North Parade	B4
Clarence Crescent	D1-D2	Old Road	A4
Clarence Drive	D1	Oxford Road	B2-C2
Clement Avenue	A3-A4	Penrhyn Crescent	D2-D3
Clifton Road	A3	Plas Road	A4
Clonmell Street	B3	St Andrews Avenue	A1-A2
Conway Road	C2-C1-D1	St David's Place	A2
Council Street West	B1	St David's Road	A2
Court Street	A4	St George's Crescent	B3
Cwm Road	B1-B2	St George's Place	B3
Deganwy Avenue	A3	St Mary's Road	A3-A2-B2
Dyffryn Road	A1	St Seiriol's Road	A2
Ffordd Dewi	C1	Somerset Street	B3
Ffordd Gwynedd	B1	South Parade	A4-B4
Ffordd Las	C1	Taliesin Street	A3
Ffordd Morfa	C1	Thorpe Street	B2
Ffordd Penrhyn	B1-C1	Trinity Avenue	A1-A2-B2
Ffordd Tudno	C1	Trinity Square	B2-B3
Garage Street	B2-C2	Tudno Street	A4
Garden Street	A3	Tudor Crescent	C2
George Street	A4-A3-B3	Tudor Road	C2-D2
Glan Y Mor Parade	B3-B4	Ty Gwyn Road	A4
Gloddaeth Crescent	B3-C3	Ty Isa Road	B3-B4
Gloddaeth Street	A3-A4	Ty'n Y Ffrith Road	D2
Hill Terrace	A4-B4	Vardre Lane	A4
Howard Place	B1	Vaughan Street	B2-C2-C3
Howard Road	B1-B2	Wern Y W Ylan	B1
Hywel Place	B1	York Road	A3

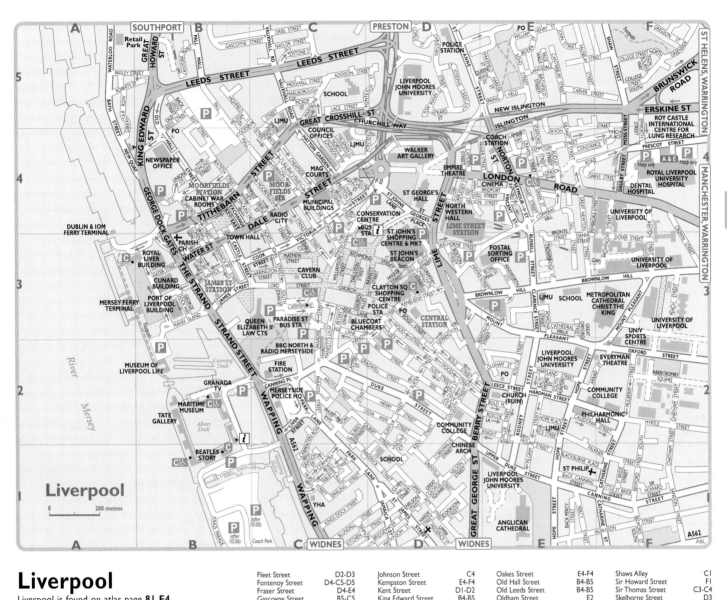

Liverpool

Liverpool is found on atlas page **81 F4**

Abercromby Square	F2	Church Alley	C3	Fleet Street	D2-D3	Johnson Street	C4	Oakes Street	E4-F4	Shaws Alley	C1
Addison Street	C5-D5	Church Street	C3-D3	Fontenoy Street	D4-C5-D5	Kempston Street	E4-F4	Old Hall Street	B4-B5	Sir Howard Street	F1
Ainsworth Street	E3	Churchill Way	C5-C4-D4	Fraser Street	D4-E4	Kent Street	D1-D2	Old Leeds Street	B4-B5	Sir Thomas Street	C3-C4
Argyle Street	C2	Clarence Street	E3	Gascoyne Street	B5-C5	King Edward Street	B4-B5	Oldham Street	E2	Skelhorne Street	D3
Arrad Street	E2-F2	Cockspur Street	B4-C5	George Dock Gates	B3-B4	Kings Dock Street	C1	Oxford Street	F2	Slater Street	D2
Ashton Street	F3-F4	College Lane	C3	George Dock Way	B3	Kings Parade	B1	Paisley Street	A5-B5	Smithfield Street	C4-C5
Audley Street	E4	College Street North	F5	Gerard Street	D5	Kitchen Street	C1-D1	Pall Mall	B5-B4-C4	Soho Street	E5
Basnett Street	C3-D3	College Street South	F5	Gibraltar Row	A4-A5	Knight Street	E2	Paradise Street	C2-C3	South John Street	C3
Bath Street	A4-A5	Colquitt Street	D2	Gilbert Street	C2-D2-D1	Lace Street	C5	Park Lane	C2-C1-D1	Sparling Street	C1
Bedford Street South	F1-F2	Constance Street	E4-F4	Gildart Street	E4-E5	Langsdale Street	E5-F5	Parker Street	D3	Springfield	E5
Benson Street	D2-E3	Cook Street	B3-C3	Gill Street	E3-E4	Leece Street	E2	Peach Street	F3	Stafford Street	E4-E5
Berry Street	D2-E2	Cookson Street	D1	Gladstone Street	C5	Leeds Street	B5-C5-D5	Pembroke Street	E3-E4-F4	Stanley Street	C3-C4
Bixteth Street	B4	Copperas Hill	E4	Gradwell Street	C2-D2	Lime Street	D3-D4	Peters Lane	C3	Strand Street	B3-B2-C2
Blackburne Place	E1-F1	Cornhill	C1	Great Charlotte Street	D3	Little St Bride Street	F1	Pilgrim Street	E1-E2	Suffolk Street	D2
Blundell Street	C1-D1	Cornwallis Street	D1-D2	Great Crosshill Street	C5-D5	Liver Street	C2	Pomona Street	E3	Surrey Street	C2
Bold Street	D2-D3	Covent Garden	B3-B4	Great George Street	D1	London Road	D4-E4-F4	Prescot Street	F4	Tabley Street	C1
Bolton Street	D3	Craven Street	E4	Great Howard Street	B5	Lord Nelson Street	D4-E4	Preston Street	C4	Tarleton Street	D3
Bridport Street	D4-E4	Crosshill Street	C4	Great Newton Street	E3-E4	Lord Street	C3	Prussia Street	B5	Tempest Hey	B4-C4
Bronte Street	E3	Crown Street	F3-F4	Greek Street	E4	Lydia Ann Street	C2-D2	Pudsey Street	D4	Temple Court	C3
Brownlow Hill	D3-E3-F3	Cunliffe Street	C4	Greenside	F5	Manchester Street	C4-D4	Raneleigh Street	D3	Temple Street	C3-C4
Brownlow Street	F3-F4	Dale Street	B3-B4-C4	Gregson Street	F5	Manesty's Lane	C2-C3	Rice Street	E2	The Strand	B3
Brunswick Road	F5	Dansie Street	E4	Grenville Street	D1	Mann Island	C2	Richmond Street	C3-D3	Tichbourne Way	F5
Brunswick Street	B3	Daulby Street	F4	Hackins Hey	B4-C4	Marlborough Street	C5	Roberts Street	A5-B5	Titheborn Street	B4-C4
Caledonia Street	E2-F2	Devon Street	E5-E4-F4	Hanover Street	C2-D3	Marybone	C5	Rodney Street	E1-E2	Tom Mann Close	D5
Camden Street	D4	Dover Street	F3	Hardman Street	E2	Maryland Street	E2	Roscoe Street	E1-E2	Trowbridge Street	E3
Campbell Street	C2	Drury Lane	B3	Harker Street	E5	Mathew Street	C3	Royal Mail Street	E3	Trueman Street	C4
Canning Place	C2	Duke Street	C2-D2	Harrington Street	C3	Midghall Street	C5	Rumford Street	B3-B4	Upper Duke Street	D1-E1
Canning Street	E1-F1	East Street	B4-B5	Hart Street	E4	Moorfields	C4	Russell Street	E3-E4	Upper Frederick Street	C2-C1-D1
Canterbury Street	E5	Eberle Street	C4	Hatton Garden	C4	Moss Street	F4-F5	St Anne Street	D5-E5	Upper Pitt Street	D1
Carpenters Row	C1-C2	Edmund Street	B4	Hawke Street	D3-E3	Mount Pleasant	D3-E3-F2-F3	St Bride Street	F1	Vauxhall Road	C5
Carver Street	E5-F5	Elliot Street	D3	Henry Street	C2-D2	Mount Street	E1	St Georges Place	D4	Vernon Street	C5
Castle Street	B3-C3	Epworth Street	F4-F5	Highfield Street	B5-C4	Mulberry Street	F2	St James Street	D1	Victoria Street	C3-C4-D4
Catharine Street	F1-F2	Erskine Street	F5	Hope Place	E2	Myrtle Street	F2	St Johns Lane	D4	Vincent Court	D1-D2
Chatham Street	F1-F2	Exchange Street East	B4	Hope Street	E1-E2	Naylor Street	C5	St Josephs Crescent	D5	Wakefield Street	E5
Cheapside	C4	Falkner Street	E2-E1-F1	Hotham Street	D4	Nelson Street	D1	St Vincent Street	E4	Wapping	C1-C2
Christian Street	D5	Fenwick Street	B3	Hurst Street	C1	New Islington	E5	Salisbury Street	E5	Water Street	B3
				Huskisson Street	E1-F1	New Quay	A4-B4	Sandon Street	F1	Waterloo Road	A5
				Islington	E4-E5	Newington	D2-D3	School Lane	C3-D3	Whitechapel	C3-C4
				Jamaica Street	D1	North John Street	C3-C4	Seel Street	D2	Williamson Street	C3
				James Street	B3	North Street	C4	Seymour Street	E4	Wood Street	D2-D3
				John Street	E5	Norton Street	E4	Shaw Street	F5	York Street	C2

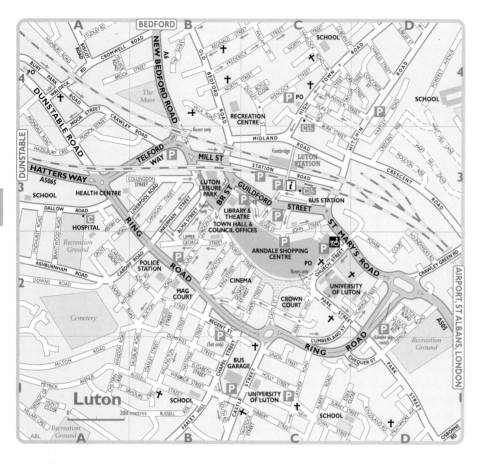

204

Luton

Luton is found on atlas page **50 B3**

Adelaide Street	B2	Hazelbury Crescent	A3
Albert Road	C1	Hibbert Street	C1
Alma Street	B2-B3	High Town Road	C3-C4-D4
Ashburnham Road	A2	Hitchin Road	C3-D3-D4
Avondale Road	A3-A4	Holly Street	C1
Back Street	C4	Inkerman Street	B2-B3
Biscot Road	A4	John Street	C3
Brantwood Road	A2-A3	Jubilee Street	D4
Bridge Street	B3	King Street	B2
Brook Street	A4-B4	Latimer Road	C1
Brunswick Street	C4-D4	Liverpool Road	B3
Burr Street	C3-C4	Manor Road	D1-D2
Bury Park Road	A4	Meyrick Avenue	A1
Buxton Road	B2	Midland Road	B3-C3
Cardiff Grove	A2	Mill Street	B2
Cardigan Street	B3	Milton Road	A1
Castle Street	B1-C1-C2	Moor Street	A4
Chapel Street	B1-B2-C2	Napier Road	A2-B2
Charles Street	D4	New Bedford Road	B4
Chequer Street	C1-D1	New Town Street	C1-D1
Church Street	C2	Old Bedford Road	B3-B4
Cobden Street	C4	Park Street	C2-D2-D1
Concorde Street	D4	Park Street West	C2
Crawley Green Road	D2	Power Court	D2
Crawley Road	A4-B3	Regent Street	B2
Crescent Rise	D3-D4	Reginald Street	B4-C4
Crescent Road	D2-D3	Ring Road	A3-B2-C1-D2
Cromwell Road	A4-B4	Rothesay Road	A2-B2
Cumberland Street	C1-C2	Russell Rise	B1
Dallow Road	A3	Russell Street	A1-B1
Downs Road	A2	St Mary's Road	C3-C2-D2
Dudley Street	C3-C4	Salisbury Road	B1-B2
Duke Street	C4	Silver Street	C2-C3
Dumfries Street	B1-B2	Stanley Street	B1-B2
Duns Place	B2	Station Road	B3-C3
Dunstable Road	A3-A4	Surrey Street	C1-D1
Farley Hill	B1	Telford Way	A3-B3
Frederick Street	B4-C4	Tenzing Grove	A1
George Street	B2-C2	Union Street	C1
George Street West	B2-C2	Upper George Street	B2
Gordon Street	B2-B3	Vicarage Street	D2
Grove Road	A2-A3	Waldeck Road	A4
Guildford Street	B3-C3	Wellington Street	B1-B2
Hart Hill Drive	D3	Wenlock Street	C4
Hartley Road	D3-D4	William Street	C4
Hastings Street	B1-B2	Windsor Street	B1
Hatters Way	A3	Winsdon Road	A1-A2
Havelock Road	C4	York Street	C4-D4

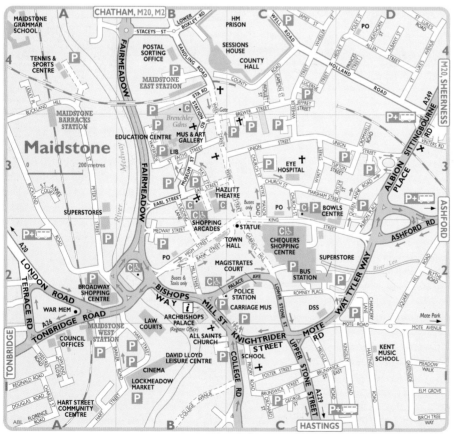

Maidstone

Maidstone is found on atlas page **30 A2**

Albion Place	D2-D3	Market Street	B3
Allen Street	D4	Marsham Street	C3-D3
Ashford Road	D2-D3	Meadow Walk	D1
Astley Street	C3-D3	Medway Street	B2
Bank Street	B2-C2	Melville Road	C1-D1
Barker Road	A1-B1	Mill Street	B2-C1
Birch Tree Way	D1	Mote Avenue	D1
Bishops Way	B2	Mote Road	C1-C2-D2-D1
Blythe Road	D2	Museum Street	B3
Brewer Street	B3-C3-C4	Orchard Street	C1
Brunswick Street	C1	Palace Avenue	B2-C2
Brunswick Street East	C1-D1	Princes Street	D4
Buckland Hill	A3-A4	Priory Road	C1
Buckland Road	A2-A3	Pudding Lane	B2-B3
Camden Street	C4	Queen Anne Road	D2-D3
Chancery Lane	D2	Reginald Road	A1
Charles Street	A1	Romney Place	C2
Church Street	C3	Rowland Close	A1
College Avenue	B1-C1	St Annes Court	A3
College Road	C1	St Faiths Street	B3
County Road	B4-C4	St Luke's Avenue	D4
Cromwell Road	D3	St Luke's Road	D4
Douglas Road	A1	St Peter's Street	A2-A3
Earl Street	B3	Sandling Road	B4
Elm Grove	D1	Sittingbourne Road	D3-D4
Fairmeadow	B2-B3-B4	Square Hill Road	D2
Florence Road	A1	Staceys Street	B4
Foley Street	D4	Station Road	B3-B4
Foster Street	C1	Terrace Road	A1-A2
Gabriel's Hill	C2	Tonbridge Road	A1-A2-B2
George Street	C1	Tufton Street	C3-D3
Greenside	D1	Union Street	C3-D3
Hart Street	A1-B1-B2	Upper Stone Street	C1
Hastings Road	D1	Vinters Road	D3
Heathorn Street	D4	Wat Tyler Way	D2
Hedley Street	C4	Waterside	B3
High Street	B2-C2-C3	Week Street	B4-B3-C3
Holland Road	C4-D4	Well Road	C4
James Street	C4	Westree Road	A1
Jeffrey Street	C4	Wheeler Street	C3-C4-D4
King Street	C3-C2-D2	Wollett Street	C3
Kingsley Road	D1	Wyatt Street	C3
Knightrider Street	C1	Wyke Manor Road	C3
Lesley Place	A4		
London Road	A2		
Lower Boxley Road	B4		
Lower Stone Street	C1-C2		
Lucerne Street	C4		

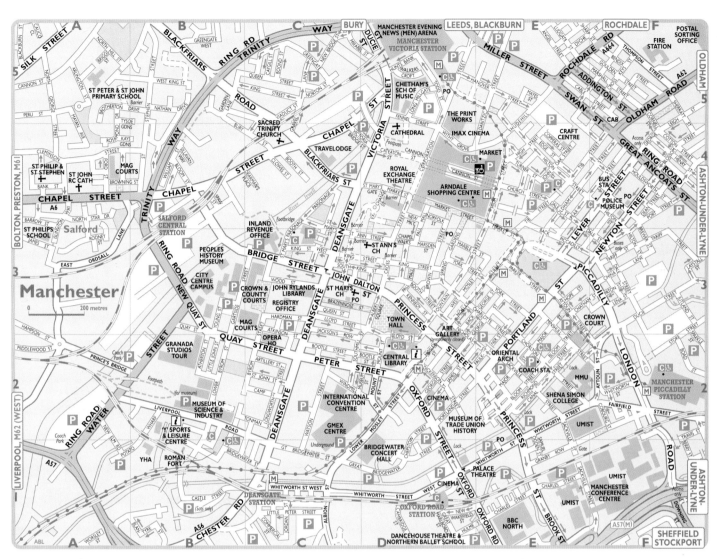

Manchester

Manchester is found on atlas page **82 C4**

Addington Street	E5-F5	Bury Street	B5-B4-C4	Dearman's Place	C4	Jordan Street	C1	Nicholas Street	D3-D2-E2	Shudehill	E4-E5
Albert Square	D3	Byrom Street	B2-C2-C3	Dickenson Street	D2	Jutland Street	F3	Norfolk Street	D4	Silk Street	A5
Albion Street	C1	Cable Street	E5-F5	Downing Street	F1	Kays Gardens	A4-B4	North George Street	A4-A5	Sillavan Way	B4
Angel Street	E5	Calico Close	A5	Ducie Street	F3	Kennedy Street	D3	North Hill Street	A5	South King Street	C3-D3
Arlington Street	A5	Cambridge Street	D1	Dyche Street	E5-F5	King Street	B5-C5	North Star Drive	A4	Southmill Street	C2-D3
Artillery Street	C2	Camp Street	C2	East Ordsall Lane	A3-A4	King Street	C3-D3	Norton Street	C5	Sparkle Street	F2-F3
Atherton Street	B2	Canal Street	E2	Edge Street	E4	King Street West	C3	Oak Street	E4	Spaw Street	B4
Atkinson Street	C2-C3	Cannon Street	A5	Exchange Street	D4	Laystall Street	F3	Oldham Road	F4-F5	Spear Street	E3-E4-F4
Aytoun Street	E3-E2-F2	Cannon Street	D4-E4	Fairfield Street	F2	Lena Street	F3	Oldham Street	E4-F4	Spring Gardens	D3-D4
Back George Street	D3-E3	Castle Street	B1	Faulkner Street	D2-E2-E3	Lever Street	E3-E4-F4	Oxford Road	E1	Store Street	F2-F3
Back Piccadilly	E4-E3-F3	Cateaton Street	D4	Fennel Street	D4-D5	Little John Street	B2	Oxford Street	D1-D2	Swan Street	E5-F5-F4
Bank Street	A4	Caygill Street	C5	Ford Street	A4	Little Peter Street	C1	Pall Mall	D3-D4	Tariff Street	F4
Barrow Street	A4	Chapel Street	A4-B4-C4-D5	Fountain Street	D3-E3-E4	Liverpool Road	A2-B2-C1	Parker Street	E3	Thompson Street	F5
Bendix Street	F5	Chapel Walks	D3	Garden Lane	B5	Lloyd Street	C3-D3-D2	Parsonage	C4	Tib Street	E4-F4
Berry Street	F1	Charles Street	E1	Gartside Street	B3-C3	London Road	F1-F2	Paton Street	F3	Todd Street	D5
Blackburn Street	A5	Charlotte Street	D3-E3-E2	George Leigh Street	F4-F5	Long Millgate	D5	Peru Street	A5	Tonman Street	B2-C2
Blackfriars Road	B5-C5	Chatham Street	E3-F3	George Street	D2-D3-E3	Longworth Street	C2	Peter Street	C2-D2	Travis Street	F2
Blackfriars Street	C4	Chepstow Street	D1-D2	Goulden Street	F5	Lower Byrom Street	B2	Piccadilly	E3-F3	Trinity Way	B3-B4-B5-C5
Blantyre Street	A1-B1	Chester Road	B1-C1	Granby Row	E1	Lower Mosley Street	C1-D2	Port Street	E4	Turner Street	E4
Bloom Street	B4	China Lane	F3	Gravel Lane	C4-C5	Ludgate Street	E5	Portland Street	D2-E2-E3	Tysoe Gardens	A5-B5
Bloom Street	E2-E3	Chorlton Street	E2-E3	Great Ancoats Street	F4	Major Street	E2-E3	Potato Wharf	A1-B1-B2	Viaduct Street	C5
Blossom Street	F4	Church Street	E4	Great Bridgewater Street	C1-D1	Marble Street	D3-E3	Prince's Bridge	A2-B2	Victoria Bridge Street	C4-D4
Boad Street	F2	Cleminson Street	A4-B4	Great Ducie Street	D5	Market Street	D4-E4-E3	Princess Street	D3-D2-E2-E1	Victoria Street	C4-D4-D5
Boond Street	C5	Clowes Street	C4	Great Marlborough Street	D1	Marsden Street	D3	Quay Street	B3-B2-C2	Walkers Croft	D5
Booth Street	C4	Cobourg Street	F2	Greengate	C5	Marshall Street	E5-F5	Queen Street	B5-C5	Water Street	A1-A2-B2-B3
Booth Street	D3	Commercial Street	C1	Greengate West	B5	Mayan Avenue	A4-A5	Queen Street	C3	Watson Street	C1-C2
Bootle Street	C2-D2	Copperas Street	E4	Hampson Street	A2-A3	Mayes Street	E5	Richmond Street	E2	West King Street	B5
Brazennose Street	C3-D3	Cornell Street	F4-F5	Hanover Street	D5-E5	Middlewood Street	A2	Rochdale Road	E5-F5	West Mosley Street	D3-E3
Brewer Street	F3-F4	Corporation Street	D4-D5-E5	Hardman Street	C3	Miller Street	E5	Rodney Street	A3	Whitworth Street	D1-E1-E2-F2
Bridge Street	B3-C3	Cotton Street	F4	Henry Street	F4	Minshull Street	E3-E2-F2	Rosamond Drive	A4-A5	Whitworth Street West	C1-D1
Bridgewater Street	B1-C1	Cross Keys Street	F4	High Street	E4	Mirabel Street	C5-D5	Sackville Street	E2-E1-F1	William Street	B4
Briggs Street	A5	Cross Street	D3-D4	Hilton Street	E4-F4-F3	Mosley Street	D2-D3-E3	St Ann Street	C3-D3	Windmill Street	C2-D2
Brook Street	E1	Dale Street	E4-F3	Hope Street	E3	Mount Street	D2	St James Street	D2	Withy Grove	D4
Brotherton Drive	A5-B5	Dantzic Street	D4-E4-E5	Houldsworth Street	F4	Museum Street	C2-D2	St John Street	C2	Wood Street	C3
Brown Street	D3-D4	Dean Street	F4	Hulme Street	D1-E1	Nathan Drive	B5	St Mary's Gate	D4	York Street	D3-E3
Browning Street	A4-B4	Deansgate	C2-C3-C4	Hunts Bank	D5	New Bridge Street	C5	St Mary's Parsonage	C3-C4	Young Street	B3
				Islington Way	A3-A4	New Elm Road	A1-A2	St Mary's Street	C3-C4		
				Jackson's Row	C2-C3	New Market	D4	St Stephen Street	B4-B5		
				James Street	A3	New Quay Street	B3	Samuel Ogden Street	E1-E2		
				John Dalton Street	C3-D3	New Wakefield Street	D1	Sharp Street	E5-F5		
				John Street	E4	Newton Street	E3-F3-F4	Sherratt Street	F4-F5		

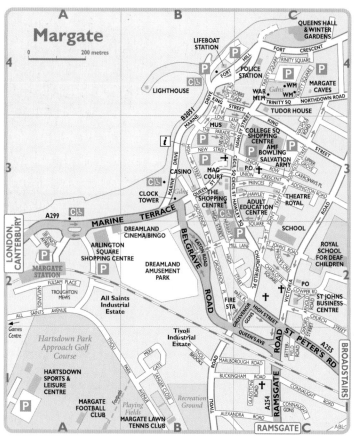

Margate

Margate is found on atlas page **31 G3**

Addington Road	C3	St John's Road	C2
Addington Street	C3	St John's Street	C2-C3
Alexandra Road	B1-C1	St Peter's Road	C1
All Saints Avenue	A2	Sanger Close	B1
Arnold Road	C2	Setterfield Road	C1
Belgrave Road	B2-B3	The Parade	B3
Buckingham Road	B1-C1	Tivoli Brooks	B1
Buenos Ayres	A2	Tivoli Park Avenue	A2-A1-B1
Carroways Place	C3	Tivoli Road	B1
Cecil Square	B3-C3	Trinity Square	C4
Cecil Street	B3-C3	Troughton Mews	A2
Charlotte Square	C2	Union Crescent	C3
Church Street	C1-C2	Union Row	C3
Churchfield Place	C2	Upper Grove	C3
Cobbs Place	B4-C4	Victoria Road	C2-C3
Connaught Gardens	C1	Walpole Road	C3
Connaught Road	C1		
Cowper Road	C2		
Eaton Road	B2		
Fort Crescent	C4		
Fort Hill	B4-C4		
Fort Road	B4		
Fulsam Place	A2		
Gladstone Road	C1		
Grosvenor Gardens	C2		
Grosvenor Place	B2-B3		
Hawley Square	C2-C3		
Hawley Street	C3		
Herbert Place	B2		
High Street	B3-B2-C2		
King Street	B4-C4-C3		
Love Lane	B3-C3		
Marine Drive	B3-B4		
Marine Terrace	A2-B3		
Marlborough Road	B1-C1		
Mere Gate	B1		
Mill Lane	B2-C2		
Naylands	A2		
New Cross Street	B3		
New Street	B3		
Northdown Road	C4		
Oxford Street	C1-C2		
Park Place	C2		
Prince's Crescent	C2		
Princes Street	C3		
Queen Street	B3		
Queens Avenue	C1		
Ramsgate Road	C1		

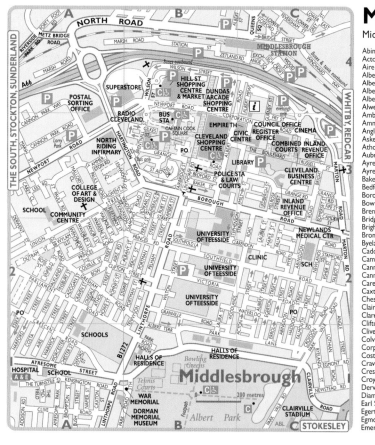

Middlesbrough

Middlesbrough is found on atlas page **106 D3**

Abingdon Road	C1-C2-C3	Emily Street	C3	Outram Street	A2
Acton Street	C1-C2	Enfield Street	A2	Oxford Street	A1
Aire Street	A1-A2	Errol Street	C1-C2	Palm Street	C2
Albert Mews	C4	Esher Street	C2	Park Lane	B1-C1
Albert Road	B3-B4-C4	Eshwood Square	A3-B3	Park Road North	B1
Albert Street	B4-C4	Essex Street	A1-A2	Park Road South	A1-B1
Albert Terrace	B1	Exchange Square	C4	Park Vale Road	C1-C2
Alwent Road	A3-B3	Fairbridge Street	B3	Parliament Road	A2-A1-B1
Amber Street	B3	Falkland Street	A2	Pelham Street	B2
Ammerston Road	A3	Falmouth Street	C1-C2	Percy Street	B2-B3
Angle Street	C1-C2	Fife Street	C3	Portman Street	B2
Aske Road	A2	Finsbury Street	A2	Princes Road	A2-B2
Athol Street	A2	Fleetham Street	A2-A3	Queens Square	C4
Aubrey Street	C1-C2	Fry Street	C3	Romney Street	A2
Ayresome Park Road	A1	Garnet Street	B2-B3	Roscoe Street	C2
Ayresome Street	A1	Glebe Road	A2	Ruby Street	B3
Baker Street	B3	Grange Road	B3-C3	Russell Street	C3
Bedford Street	B3	Granville Road	B1-B2	St Aidens Drive	B3
Borough Road	B3-C3-C2	Gresham Road	A2-B2	St Pauls Road	A2-A3
Bow Street	A2	Gurney Street	C3-C4	Somerset Street	C2-C3
Brentnall Street	B3	Haddon Street	C1-C2	Southfield Road	B2-C2
Bridge Street	C4	Harford Street	A1-A2	Southfold Lane	B2
Bright Street	C3	Hartington Road	A3-B3	Stamford Street	C2
Brompton Street	A1	Howe Street	A2	Station Street	B4
Byelands Street	C1	Jedburgh Street	C3	Stephenson Street	B2-B3
Cadogan Street	A2	Kensington Road	A1	Stowe Street	A2-B2
Camden Street	C2-C3	Kingston Street	A3-B2	Talbot Street	C2
Cannon Park Road	A3	Laura Street	B1-B2	Tennyson Street	B1-B2
Cannon Park Way	A3-A4	Laurel Street	C2	The Boulevard	C3
Carey Close	A3	Lees Road	A3	The Midfield	A1
Caxton Street	A1	Linthorpe Road	A1-B1-B2-B3	The Turnstile	A1
Chester Street	A1	Lonsdale Street	A2	Union Street	A2-A3-B3
Clairville Road	C1	Lothian Road	C1	Victoria Road	B2-C2
Clarendon Road	B2-C2	Lower Feversham Street	C4	Walpole Street	A2-A3
Clifton Street	A2-B2	Lower Gosford Street	C4	Warren Street	A2-A3
Clive Road	A1	Manor Street	A2	Warwick Street	A1-A2
Colville Street	A2	Maple Street	C2	Waterloo Road	B2-C2-C1
Corporation Road	B4-B3-C3	Marsh Road	A4, A4-B4	Waverley Street	B4
Costa Street	A1-A2	Marsh Street	A3	Wentworth Street	A1
Craven Street	A2	Marton Road	C2-C3	Wilson Street	B4
Crescent Road	A1-A2	Melrose Street	C3	Wilton Street	B2
Croydon Road	C1-C2	Metz Bridge Road	A4	Windsor Street	B3
Derwent Street	A2-A3	Myrtle Street	C2	Windward Way	C4
Diamond Road	B2-B3	Napier Street	A1	Wood Street	C4
Earl Street	B3	Newlands Road	C2	Woodlands Road	B1-B2-C2-C3
Egerton Street	C1-C2	Newport Road	A3-B4	Worcester Street	A1-A2
Egmont Road	C1	Newstead Road	C1	Wylam Street	A2
Emerald Street	B3	North Road	A4-B4	Zetland Road	B4-C4

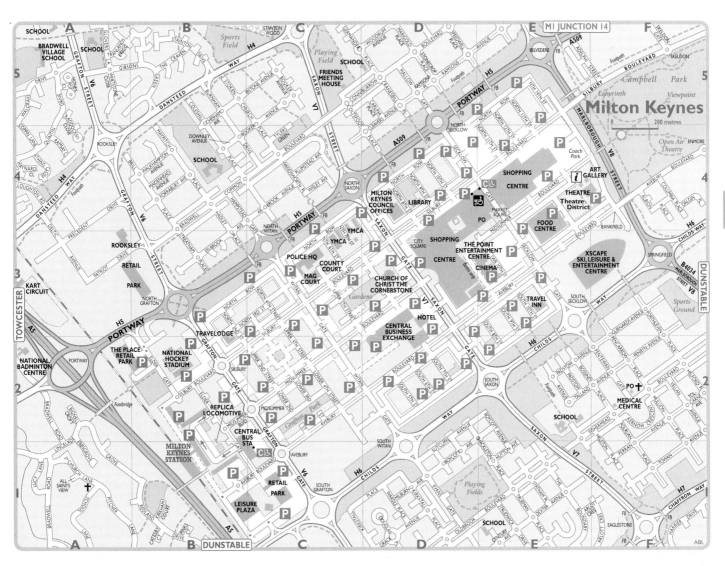

Milton Keynes

Milton Keynes is found on atlas page **49 G3**

Adelphi Street	E5-F5	Downley Avenue	B4	Maynard Close	A4	Ramsons Place	D5	Walkhampton Avenue	B4
Albion Place	F4	Ebbsgrove	A1-A2	Maypitch Place	B4	Redland Drive	B1	Wandsworth Place	C4
All Saints View	A1	Eelbrook Avenue	B3-B4	Midsummer		Saxon Gate	D4-D3-D2-E2	Wardle Place	D1
Arbrook Avenue	C4	Elder Gate	B2-B1-C1	Boulevard	B2-C2-D3-E4	Saxon Street	C5-C4, E2-E1-F1	Whetstone Close	A5
Arlott Crescent	E1-F1	Evans Gate	D1	Milburn Avenue	D1	School Lane	A1	Wisley Avenue	C4
Athins Close	A4	Fishermead Boulevard	E2-F2	Mullion Place	F1-F2	Secklow Gate	D4-E4-E3	Witan Gate	C3-C2-D2
Avebury Boulevard	B1-C2-E3-F4	Forrabury Avenue	B4	North 2nd Street	B2-B3	Shackleton Place	D2-E1	Woodruff Avenue	D5
Bignell Croft	A2	Germander Place	C5-D5	North 3rd Street	B3-C3	Silbury Boulevard	B2-C3-D4-F5		
Booker Avenue	B4-C4-C5	Gibsons Green	A5-B5	North 4th Street	C3	Skeldon Gate	F5		
Bossiney Place	E2-F2	Glovers Lane	A5	North 6th Street	C3	South 5th Street	D2		
Boycott Avenue	D1-E1-E2	Grace Avenue	D1	North 7th Street	C3-C4	South 6th Street	D2		
Bradwell Common		Grafton Gate	B3-B2-C2-C1	North 8th Street	D4	South 7th Street	D2		
Boulevard	B3-B4-C4-C5	Grafton Street	A5-A4-B4-B3	North 9th Street	D4	South 8th Street	E2-E3		
Bradwell Road	A1, A2	Gurnards Avenue	F3	North 10th Street	D4	South 9th Street	E3		
Brill Place	A4-B4	Hadley Place	B3-B4	North 11th Street	E4	South 10th Street	E3		
Burnham Drive	B5-B4-C4	Hampstead Gate	B4-C4-C3	North 12th Street	E4-E5	Speedwell Place	D5		
Caruna Place	D5	Harrier Drive	F1	North 13th Street	E4-E5	Stainton Drive	B5		
Catesby Court	B1	Helford Place	F2	North 14th Street	E5	Statham Place	E1		
Century Avenue	E1	Helston Place	F1-F2	North Row	B3-C3-D4-E5	Stokenchurch Place	B5-C5-C4		
Chaffron Way	F1	Honey Pot Close	A5	Oldbrook Boulevard	D1-E1	Stonecrop Place	D5		
Chesham Avenue	B5	Hutton Avenue	E1-E2	Padstow Avenue	E2	Streatham Place	B3		
Childs Way	C1-D2-E3-F5	Ibstone Avenue	B5-C5	Patriot Drive	A3-B3	Strudwick Drive	E1		
Church Lane	A1	Kernow Crescent	F2	Pencarrow Place	F2	Sutcliffe Avenue	D1-D2-E2		
Cleavers Avenue	D4-D5	Kirkham Court	B1	Penryn Avenue	F2	Talland Avenue	E2-F2		
Coleshill Place	B4-B5	Kirkstall Place	C1-D1	Pentewan Gate	F2	The Boundary	E1		
Coltsfoot Place	C5-D4	Lincelade Grove	A2-A1-B1	Perran Avenue	F1-F2	The Craven	B5		
Columbia Place	F4	Loughton Road	A4	Pinks Court	B1	Tolcarne Avenue	F2		
Conniburrow Boulevard	C5-D5	Lower 2nd Street	C2	Pitcher Lane	A1-B1	Towan Avenue	F1-F2		
Coppin Lane	A4	Lower 3rd Street	C2	Plumstead Avenue	C4	Tranlands Brigg	A5		
Craddocks Close	A4-A5	Lower 4th Street	C2	Polruan Place	F1-F2	Trueman Place	E1		
Cranesbill Place	D5	Lower 10th Street	E3	Porthleven Place	F2-F3	Tylers Green	C4-C5		
Dalgin Place	F4	Lucy Lane	A1	Portway	A2-B3-C4-E5	Upper 2nd Street	C2		
Dansteed Way	A3-A4-B5-C5	Maidenhead Avenue	B4	Precedent Drive	A3-A4	Upper 4th Street	C2-C3		
Deltic Avenue	A3-A4	Mallow Gate	D5	Quintin Drive	A4-A5	Upper 5th Street	C3		
Dexter Avenue	E1	Marigold Place	D5	Ramsay Close	A4	Vellan Avenue	F2		
Douglas Place	D1	Marlborough Street	E5-F4-F3	Ramsons Avenue	D5-E5	Walgrave Drive	A5		

208

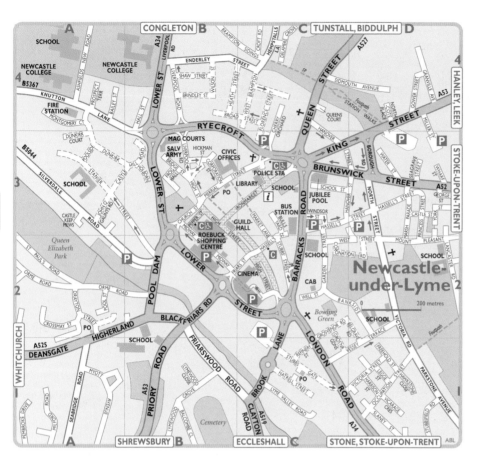

Newcastle-under-Lyme

Newcastle-under-Lyme is found on atlas page **70 C5**

Ashfields New Road	A4	Legge Street	D1
Bankside	C2-D2	Liverpool Road	B3-B4
Barracks Road	C2-C3	London Road	C2-C1-D1
Belgrave Road	D2	Lower Street	B4-B3-B2-C2
Blackfriars Road	B2	Lyme Valley Road	C1
Borough Road	D3	Lymewood Grove	B1
Brampton Sidings	B4-C4	Market Lane	C2-C3
Bridge Street	B3	Marsh Parade	D3
Brindley Street	B4	Merrial Street	B3-C3
Broad Street	B4-C4	Midway	B2-B3
Brook Lane	C1-C2	Miller Street	D3-D4
Brunswick Street	C3-D3	Montgomery Court	A4
Bulls Yard	C3	Mount Pleasant	D2
Castle Hill Road	A3-B3	Myott Avenue	A1
Castle Street	D3	North Street	D3
Cherry Orchard	C3-C4	Northcote Place	D4
Church Street	B3	Occupation Street	D1
Clayton Road	C1	Orme Road	A2-B2
Coronation Road	C2-D2	Parkstone Avenue	D1
Corporation Street	B3	Pepper Street	B3
Crossmay Street	A2	Pool Dam	B2
Deansgate	A1	Poolside	A3
Drayton Street	A2	Princess Street	D3
Dunkirk	A3	Priory Road	B1-B2
Enderley Street	B4-C4	Queen Street	C3-C4-D4
Florence Street	C3-C4	Refinery Street	C1
Freehold Street	D1	Ryecroft	B3-B4-C3
Friars Street	B2-C2	St Paul's Road	A2-A3
Friarswood Road	B2-B1-C1	School Street	C3
Frog Hall	B3	Seabridge Road	A1
Garden Street	C2-C3	Seagrave Street	D3
Gower Street	D4	Shaw Street	A1
Granville Avenue	D4	Sidmouth Avenue	C4-D4
Grosvenor Gardens	C1-C2	Silverdale Road	A3-A2-B2
Grosvenor Road	C2	Slaney Street	D1
Hall Street	B4	Stanier Street	A3-B3-B2
Hanover Street	C4-C3-D3	Station Walks	C4-D4
Harrison Street	D1	Stubbs Gate	C1
Hassell's Street	C2-C3-D3	Stubbs' Street	C1
Hatrell Street	C1	Vessey Terrace	C1-D1-D2
Heath Street	B4-C4	Victoria Road	D1-D2
Hempstalls Lane	C4	Victoria Street	C1-D1
High Street	C2-B3	Water Street	D3
Higherland	A1-A2-B2	Well Street	C2
Ironmarket	B3-C3	West Brampton	C4
John O'Gaunts Road	A3	West Street	C2-D2
King Street	C3-D3-C4	Wilson Street	B4
Knutton Lane	A4-B4	Windsor Street	C3

Newport

Newport is found on atlas page **36 D3**

Albert Terrace	B2	Keynsham Avenue	C1
Allt Yr Yn Avenue	A4	King Street	C1
Allt Yr Yn Road	A4	Kingsway	C1-C2-C3
Bailey Street	B2	Llanthewy Road	A2
Baneswell Road	B2-B3	Llanvair Road	D4
Bedford Road	D3	Locke Street	B4
Blewitt Street	B2	Lower Dock Street	C1-D1
Bond Street	C4-D4	Lucas Street	B4
Bridge Street	A3-B3	Mellon Street	C1
Bryngwyn Road	A2	Mill Street	B3-B4
Brynhyfryd Avenue	A1	North Street	B2
Brynhyfryd Road	A1-A2	Oakfield Road	A2-A3
Caerau Crescent	A1-A2	Park Square	C1
Caerau Road	A1-A2	Queen Street	C1
Caerleon Road	D2	Queen's Hill	B4
Cardiff Road	C1	Queen's Hill Crescent	A4-B4
Caroline Street	C1-C2-D2	Queensway	B3-C3
Cedar Road	D3	Riverside	D4
Charles Street	B2-C2	Rodney Parade	C3-D3
Chepstow Road	D3-D4	Rodney Road	C3-D3
Clarence Place	C3-D4	Rose Street	B4
Clifton Place	B1-B2	Rudry Street	D4
Clifton Road	B1	Rugby Road	D3
Clyffard Crescent	A2	Ruperra Street	C1-D1
Clytha Park Road	A3	St Edward Street	A2-B2
Colne Street	D3	St Julian Street	B1-B2
Coltsfoot Close	A4	St Marks Crescent	A4-B4
Comfrey Close	A4	St Mary Street	B2
Commercial Street	C1-C2-C3	St Vincent Road	C3-D3
Corelii Street	D4	School Lane	B2-C2
Corporation Road	D3	St Woolos Road	B1-B2
Cross Lane	C2	Serpentine Road	A3-B3
Devon Place	A3-B3	Skinner Street	C3
Dewsland Park Road	B1	Sorrel Drive	A4
East Street	B2	Spencer Road	A2
East Usk Road	D4	Stanley Road	B3
Factory Road	B4	Stow Hill	A1-B1-B2
Fields Park Road	A3	Stow Park Avenue	A1
Fields Road	A3-A4-B4-B3	Tregare Street	D4
Friars Road	A2	Tunnel Terrace	A2
George Street	C1-D1	Usk Way	C2-D2
Godfrey Road	A3	Vicarage Hill	B1
Gold Tops	A3-B3	Victoria Place	B1-B2
Grafton Road	C3-D3	Victoria Road	B1-C1
Graham Street	A2-B2	West Street	B2
Granville Street	D1	Westfield Road	A3
Hill Street	C1-C2	Windsor Terrace	A2
Jones Street	B2	York Place	A2-A1-B1

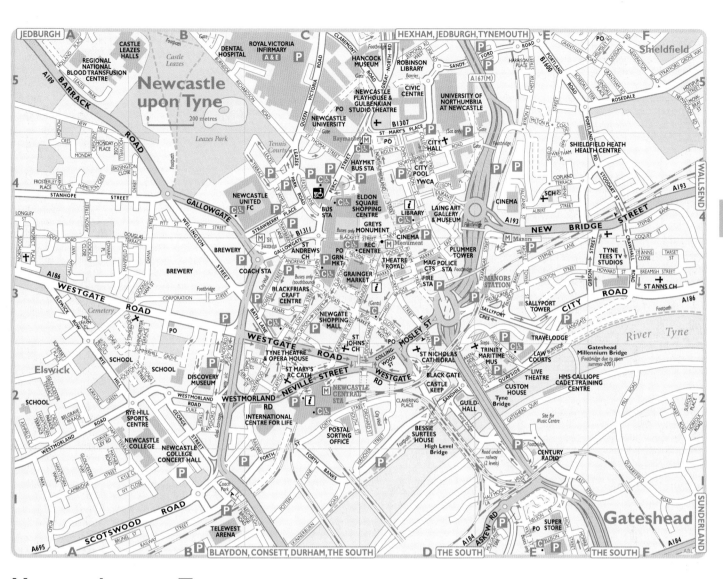

Newcastle upon Tyne

Newcastle upon Tyne is found on atlas page **114 D2**

Akenside Hill	D2-E2	Crawhall Road	F3-F4	Half Moon Lane	E1	Market Street	D3	Queen Victoria Road	C4-C5	Tower Street	E3
Albert Street	E4	Cross Parade	A2	Hamilton Crescent	A4	Market Street East	D3-D4	Railway Street	A1-B1-C1-C2	Trafalgar Street	E3-E4
Argyle Street	E3	Darnell Place	A4	Hanover Street	C1-D1-D2	Mather Road	A1-A2	Redheugh Bridge Road	B1-C1	Vallum Way	A3
Ashfield Close	A2	Dean Street	D2-D3	Harrison Place	E5	Mill Farm Close	A3	Richardson Road	B5-C5-C4	Victoria Street	B2
Askew Road	D1-E1	Derby Court	B4	Hawthorn Terrace	A2	Mill Road	F2	Ridley Place	D4	Waterloo Street	C2
Avison Street	A4	Diana Street	B3-B4	Hawthorn Walk	A1	Milton Place	E5	Rosedale	F5	Waverley Road	A2
Barrack Road	A5-B4	Dinsdale Place	A4-B3	Helmsley Road	E5-F5	Monday Crescent	A4-A5	Rosedale Terrace	E5-F5	Wellington Street	B3-B4
Bassington Close	A4-B4	Dinsdale Road	F5	Henry Square	A4	Monday Place	A4	Rye Hill	A2-B2	West Street	E1
Bath Lane	C3	Dorset Road	F2	High Bridge	D3	Mosley Street	D3	St Andrews Street	C3	Westgate Road	A3-B3-C3-D2
Belgrave Parade	A2	Douglas Terrace	A4-B3	High Street	E1	Mowbray Street	F5	St Anns Close	F3	Westmorland Road	A1-A2-B2-C2
Bigg Market	C3-D3	Drybeck Court	A2-A3	Holland Place	A5	Mulgrave Terrace	E1	St James Street	C4	Winchester Terrace	B2-B3
Blackett Street	C4-D4	Duke Street	B2	Hills Street	E1	Nelson Street	C3-D3	St Mary's Place	D5	Wretham Place	E4
Blandford Square	B2-B3	Durant Road	D4	Holywell Close	A4	Nelson Street (Gateshead)	E1	St Thomas Street	C4-C5	York Street	A2-A3
Blandford Street	B2	East Street	E1-F1	Hood Street	D3	New Bridge Street	E4-F4	Sallyport Crescent	E3		
Breamish Street	F3	Edward Place	A3	Hopper Street	E1	New Bridge Street	D4	Sandgate	E3		
Broad Chare	E2-E3	Ellison Place	D4	Hotspur Street	F5	New Mills	A5-A4	Sandhill	D2		
Brunel Street	A1-B1	Ellison Street	E1	Houston Street	A2-B2	Newgate	C3	Sandyford Road	D5-E5		
Buckingham Street	B3	Elswick Row	A3	Howard Street	F3	Newington Road	F5	Scotswood Road	A1-B1		
Burnside	B5	Falcaner Street	E4	Ivy Close	A1-B1	Norfolk Road	F2	Shield Street	E4-E5		
Buryside	E2	Fenckle Street	C3	Jesmond Road West	D5	Northcote Street	A3-A4	Skinnerburn Road	C1		
Buxton Street	E3	Forth Banks	C1-C2	John Dobson Street	D4	Northumberland Road	D4-E4	Somerset Place	A2		
Byron Street	E5	Forth Street	C1-C2-D2	King Street	E2	Northumberland Street	D4	South Street	C2-D2		
Cambridge Street	A1	Friars Street	C3	Kirkdale Green	A2	Nun Street	C3	Stanhope Street	A4-B4		
Chester Street	E5	Frosterley Place	A4	Kyle Close	A1-B1	Orchard Street	D2	Stepney Bank	F3-F4		
City Road	E3-F3	Gallowgate	B4-C3-C4	Leazes Lane	C4	Pandon Bank	E3	Stepney Lane	E3-E4		
Claremont Road	C5-D5	Gateshead Quay	E2	Leazes Park	A5	Park Road	A1	Stoddart Street	F4		
Clavering Place	D2	George Street	B1-B2	Leazes Park Road	C4	Peel Lane	C2	Stowell Street	C3		
Clayton Street	C2-C3	Gibson Street	F3-F4	Leazes Terrace	C4	Percy Street	C4	Stratford Grove West	F5		
Cloth Market	D3	Gloucester Terrace	A2	Liddle Road	A3-A4	Pilgrim Street	D3	Strawberry Lane	C3-C4		
College Street	D4-D5	Gloucester Way	A1	Link Road	D5	Pitt Street	B4	Strawberry Place	C4		
Collingwood Street	D2	Grainger Street	C3-D3	Lombard Street	D2-E2	Portland Road	E5-F5-F4	Suffolk Place	F2		
Cookson Close	A3	Grainger Street West	C2-C3	Longley Street	A4	Pottery Lane	C1	Summerhill Grove	B2		
Copland Terrace	E4	Grantham Road	E5-F5	Low Friar Street	C3	Prospect Place	A3-A4	Summerhill Street	A3-B3		
Coppice Way	E4-E5	Great North Road	D5	Melbourne Street	E3	Pudding Chare	D2-D3	Sunderland Street	B2-C2		
Coquet Street	F4	Grey Street	D3	Mansfield Street	A3	Quarryfield Road	F1-F2	Tarset Street	F3		
Corporation Street	B3	Groat Market	D3	Maple Terrace	A2-B1	Quayside	E2	Temple Street	B2-C2		

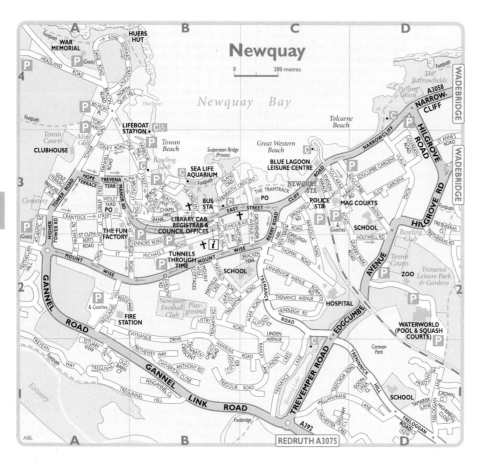

Newquay

Newquay is found on atlas page 4 B2

Agar Road	C2	Marcus Hill	B2-B3
Albany Road	C3-D3	Mayfield Road	B2
Alma Place	A3-B3	Meadowside	D1
Anthony Road	B1	Mellanvrane Lane	C1-D1
Atlantic Road	A2-A3	Mitchell Avenue	B3-B2-C2
Bank Street	B3	Mount Wise	A2-B2-C2
Beach Road	B3	Narrowcliff	D3-D4
Beachfield Avenue	B3	North Quay Hill	A4-B4
Beacon Road	A4	Pargolla Road	C2-C3
Berry Road	C2-C3	Pennannel Close	B1
Bracken Terrace	C2	Quarry Park Road	D2
Broad Street	B3	Rawley Lane	C1
Chapel Hill	B3	Robartes Road	C2
Chichester Crescent	C1-D1	St Cuthberts Road	A2
Chynance Drive	A2-B2-B1	St George's Road	A3-B3-B2
Chyverton Close	B1	St John's Road	A2-A3
Cliff Road	C3	St Michael's Road	A2-B2-B3
Colvreath Road	D3	St Piran's Road	A2-A3
Crantock Street	A3	St Thomas Road	C3
Dane Road	A4	Seymour Avenue	B3-C3
East Street	B3-C3	Springfield Road	C3
Edgcumbe Avenue	C2-D2-D3	Station Parade	C3
Edgcumbe Gardens	D3	Sydney Road	A3
Eliot Gardens	D3	The Crescent	B3
Ennors Road	B2	Tolcarne Road	C3-D3
Fernhill Road	A3	Tor Road	C3
Fore Street	A4-A3-B3	Tower Road	A3-A4
Gannel Link Road	A1-B1-B2	Trebarwith Crescent	B3-C3
Gannel Road	A2	Tredour Road	B1-C1
Gover Lane	B3	Treforda Road	C1-D1
Grosvenor Avenue	C2-C3	Tregunnel Hill	A2-A1-B1
Harbour Hill	B3	Trelawney Road	B2-C2
Hawkins Road	B1-C1	Treloggan Lane	D1
Headland Road	A4	Treloggan Road	D1
Headleigh Road	C2	Trembath Crescent	B1
Higher Tower Road	A2-A3	Trenance Avenue	C2
Hilgrove Road	D3-D4	Trenance Lane	C1-C2
Holywell Road	D2	Trenance Road	C2
Hope Terrace	A3	Trenarth Road	C2
Island Crescent	B3	Treninnick Hill	C1-D1
Jubilee Street	A3	Tretherras Road	D2-D3
King Edward Crescent	A4	Trethewey Way	B1-B2
King Street	B3	Trevean Way	A1-A2
Lanhenvor Avenue	C2	Trevemper Road	C1
Linden Avenue	C1-C2	Trevena Terrace	A3
Linden Crescent	C1	Ulalia Road	D3
Listry Road	B2-C2	Vivian Close	D2
Manor Road	A3	Wesley Yard	A3

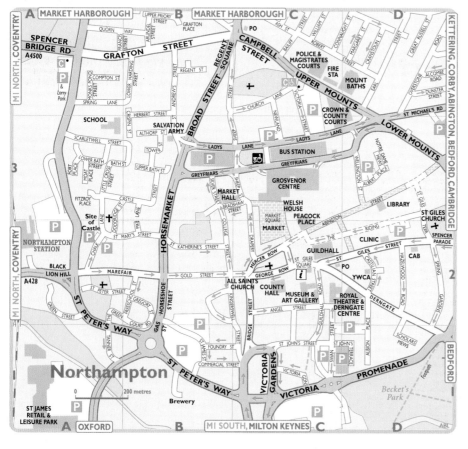

Northampton

Northampton is found on atlas page 49 F5

Abington Street	C2-C3-D3	Lower Bath Street	A3
Albert Place	D3	Lower Harding Street	B4
Albion Place	D1-D2	Lower Mounts	D3
Alcombe Road	D4	Marefair	A2-B2
Althorp Street	B3	Margaret Street	D4
Angel Street	C2	Mercer Row	C2
Arundel Street	B4	Moat Place	A3
Ash Street	C4	Monks Pond Street	A4
Bailiff Street	C4	Newland	C3-C4
Bath Street	A3-B3	Overstone Road	D4
Black Lion Hill	A2	Pike Lane	B2-B3
Bradshaw Street	B3-C3	Quorn Way	A4-B4
Bridge Street	C1-C2	Regent Square	B4
Broad Street	B3-B4	Regent Street	B4
Campbell Street	C4	Robert Street	C4-D4
Castilian Street	D2	St Andrews Street	B3-B4
Castle Street	A2-A3	St Giles Square	C2
Chalk Lane	A2-A3	St Giles Street	C2-D2
Church Lane	C4	St Giles Terrace	D2-D3
College Street	B2-B3	St James Street	B1
Commercial Street	B1-C1	St John's Street	C1
Compton Street	A4	St John's Terrace	C1-D1
Connaught Street	C4-D4	St Katherine's Street	B2
Court Road	B1-B2	St Mary's Street	A2-B2
Cranstoun Street	D4	St Michael's Road	D3-D4
Crispin Street	B3-B4	St Peter Street	A2-B2
Derngate	C2-D2-D1	St Peter's Way	A2-A1-B1-C1
Doddridge Street	A2-A3-B2	Scarletwell Street	A3-B3
Dunster Street	D4	Sheep Street	B4-B3-C3
Earl Street	D4	Silver Street	B3
Foundry Street	B1-C1	Spencer Bridge Road	A4
Francis Street	A4	Spencer Parade	D2
Freeschool Street	B2	Spring Gardens	A4
Gas Street	B1-B2	Spring Lane	A4
George Row	C2	Swan Street	C1-C2
Gold Street	B2	Tanner Street	A1
Grafton Street	A4-B4	The Drapery	C2-C3
Green Street	A2	The Green	A2
Gregory Street	B2	The Riding	C2-D2-D3
Greyfriars	B3-C3	Tower Street	B3
Guildhall Road	C1-C2	Upper Bath Street	B3
Hazelwood Road	D2	Upper Mounts	C4-D4
Herbert Street	B3-B4	Upper Priory Street	B4
Horsemarket	B2-B3	Victoria Gardens	C1
Horseshoe Street	B2	Victoria Promenade	C1-D1
Kingerswell Street	B2-C1	Victoria Street	C3-C4
Lady's Lane	B3-C3-D3	Wellington Street	D3
Little Cross Street	A3	William Street	C4

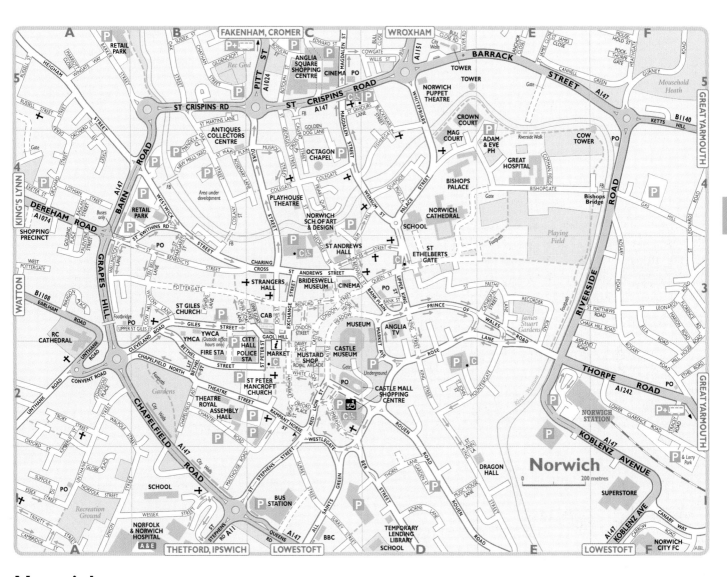

211

Norwich

Norwich is found on atlas page **77 E1**

All Saints Green	C1	Cow Hill	B3	Johnson Place	A2	Raglan Street	A4	Thorpe Road	E2-F2
Anchor Close	E5	Cowgate	C5-D5	Ketts Hill	F5	Rampant Horse Street	C2	Timberhill	C2
Aspland Road	E3-F2	Cross Lane	C4	Kimberley Street	A1-A2	Recorder Road	E3	Trinity Street	A1
Bank Plain	D3	Davey Place	C2	King Street	D3-D2-D1-E1	Red Lion Street	C2	Trory Street	A2
Bank Street	D3	Derby Street	A4-A5	Koblenz Avenue	E2-F2-F1	Redwell Street	C3-D3	Union Street	A1-B1
Barker Street	A5-B5	Dove Street	C3	Little Bethel Street	B2	Riverside	E1-E2	Unthank Road	A2-A3
Barn Road	A4-B4-B5	Duke Street	C3-C4-C5	London Street	C3-D3	Riverside Road	E3-F3-F4-F5	Unthank Street	A1-A2
Barrack Street	D5-E5-F5	Earlham Road	A3	Lothian Street	A4	Rosary Road	F2-F3-F4	Upper Goat Lane	B3-C3
Bedford Street	C3	Edward Street	C5	Lower Clarence Road	F1-F2	Rose Lane	D2-D3-E3	Upper King Street	D3
Ber Street	D2-D1	Ella Road	F2-F3	Lower Goat Lane	C3	Rosemark Lane	B4-C4	Upper St Giles Street	A3-B3
Bethel Street	B3-B2-C2	Elm Hill	C3-D4	Magdalen Street	C4-C5	Rouen Road	D2-D1-E1	Valentine Street	A3-A4
Bishopgate	E4-F4	Ely Street	A4-A5	Malthouse Road	B1-C1	Royal Arcade	C2	Walpole Street	A2-B2
Blackfriars Street	D5	Essex Street	A1	Mandela Close	B4	Russell Street	A5	Wellington Lane	A3
Botolph Street	C5	Ethel Road	F2	Marion Road	F3	St Andrews Street	C3	Wensum Street	C4-D4
Brigg Street	C2	Exchange Street	C3	Market Avenue	D2-D3	St Ann Lane	D1-D2	Wessex Street	A1-B1
Bull Close	D5	Exeter Street	A4	Marriott Close	A5	St Benedicts Street	B3	West Pottergate	A3
Calvert Street	C4-C5	Fishergate	D4-D5	Mountergate	D2-E2	St Faiths Lane	D3-E3	Westlegate	C1-C2
Canary Way	F1	Fishers Lane	B3	Music House Lane	D1-E1	St Georges Street	C3-C4-C5	Westwick Street	B3-B4
Cambridge Street	A1	Florence Road	F3	Muspole Street	C4	St James Close	E5	White Lion Street	C2
Cannell Green	E5-F5	Friars Quay	C4	New Mills Yard	B4	St John Street	D2	Whitefriars	D4-D5
Carrow Road	F1	Gas Hill	F4	Norfolk Street	A1	St Leonards Road	F3-F4	Willis Street	D5
Castle Meadow	C2-C3-D3	Gaol Hill	C3	Oak Street	B4-B5	St Margarets Street	B3-B4	Willow Lane	B3
Castle Street	C2-C3	Garden Street	D1	Opie Street	C3	St Martins Lane	B5	Wingate Way	A5
Cathedral Street	E3	Gildencroft	B5	Orchard Street	A4-A5	St Marys Plain	B4-C4		
Chalk Hill Road	E3-F3	Giles Street	B3-C3	Orford Place	C2	St Matthews Road	E3-F3		
Chantry Road	B2-C2-C1	Globe Place	A1	Oxford Street	A1-A2	St Peter Street	C2-C3		
Chapelfield East	B2	Golden Dog Lane	C4-C5	Palace-Street	D4	St Saviours Lane	C5-D5		
Chapelfield North	B2	Golding Place	A3-A4	Paragon Place	A3	St Stephens Street	B1-C1-C2		
Chapelfield Road	A2-B2-B1	Grapes Hill	A3	Pigg Lane	D4	St Swithins Road	B3-B4		
Charing Cross	C3	Gurney Road	F5	Pitt Street	C5	Stracey Road	F2		
Chatham Street	B5	Haymarket	C2	Pockthorpe Gate	F5	Suffolk Square	A1		
Cleveland Road	A2-B2-B3	Heathgate	F5	Pottergate	A3-B3-C3	Surrey Street	C1-D1		
Colegate	C4	Heigham Street	A5-A4-B4	Prince of Wales Road	D3-E3	Ten Bell Lane	B3		
Convent Road	A2	Hill House Road	F2-F3	Princes Street	C3-D3	Theatre Street	B2-C2		
Coslany Street	B4	Horns Lane	D1	Quayside	D4	Thorn Lane	D1		
Cotman Fields	E4			Queen Street	D3				

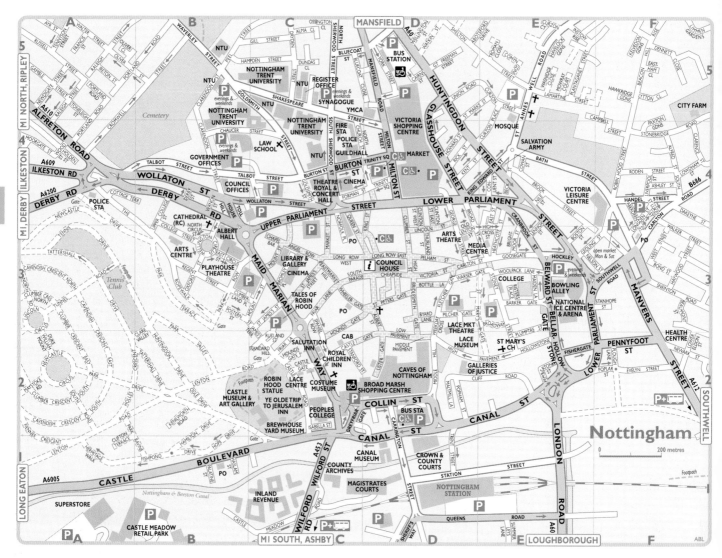

Nottingham

Nottingham is found on atlas page **72 C4**

Aberdeen Street	F3-F4	Castle Road	C2	Fiennes Crescent	A1-A2	Lamartine Street
Albert Street	D3	Cavendish Crescent East	A2-A3	Fishergate	E2	Lennox Street
Alfred Street South	F4	Cavendish Crescent North	A3	Fishpond Drive	A1-B1	Lenton Road
Alfreton Road	A4-A5	Cavendish Crescent South	A2	Fletcher Gate	D3	Lincoln Circus

Aberdeen Street	F3-F4
Albert Street	D3
Alfred Street South	F4
Alfreton Road	A4-A5
Alma Close	C5
Angel Row	C3
Barker Gate	E3
Bath Street	E4-F4
Beacon Hill Rise	F5
Beastmarket Hill	C3
Beaumont Street	F3
Beck Street	E4
Bellargate	E2-E3
Belward Street	E3
Bluecoat Close	C5-D5
Bluecoat Street	C5
Bond Street	F3
Boston Street	E3
Bottle Lane	D3
Bridlesmith Gate	D3
Brightmoor Street	E3-E4
Broad Street	D4-D3-E3
Broadway	E3
Bromley Place	C3
Brook Street	E4-E3-F3
Burton Street	C4
Byard Lane	D3
Cairns Street	D5
Campbell Street	E5-F5-F4
Canal Street	C2-D2-E2
Carlton Road	F3-F4
Carlton Street	D3-E3
Carrington Street	D1-D2
Castle Boulevard	A1-B1-C1-C2
Castle Gate	C2-D2
Castle Meadow Road	B1-C1

Castle Road	C2
Cavendish Crescent East	A2-A3
Cavendish Crescent North	A3
Cavendish Crescent South	A2
Chapel Bar	C3
Chaucer Street	B4-C4
Cheapside	D3
Clare Valley	B2-B3
Clarence Street	F4
Clarendon Street	B4-B5
Cliff Road	D2-E2
Clifton Terrace	A1
Clinton Street East	D4
Clinton Street West	D4
Clumber Crescent East	A2-A3
Clumber Crescent North	A3
Clumber Crescent South	A2
Clumber Street	D3-D4
College Street	B3-B4
Collin Street	D2
Comyn Gardens	E5
Conuent Street	E4
Cowan Street	E4
Cranbrook Street	E3-E4
Cromwell Street	A4-A5-B5
Cumberland Place	B3-C3
Curzon Place	D4-E4-E5
Curzon Street	E4
Dakeyne Street	F4
Dennett Close	F5
Derby Road	A4-B4
Dryden Street	C5
Duke William Mount	A2
East Circus Street	B3
East Street	E4
Evelyn Street	F2

Fiennes Crescent	A1-A2
Fishergate	E2
Fishpond Drive	A1-B1
Fletcher Gate	D3
Forman Street	C4-D4
Friar Lane	C2-C3
Gamble Street	A5
Gedling Street	E3-F3
George Street	D3-D4
Gill Street	C3
Glasshouse Street	D4-D5
Goldsmith Street	B5-C5-C4
Goosegate	E3
Great Freeman Street	D5
Greyfriar Gate	C2
Hamilton Drive	B1-B2
Hampden Street	B5-C5
Handel Street	F4
Haslam Street	B1
Haywood Street	F3
Heathcote Street	E3-E4
Hermitage Walk	A1
High Cross Street	E3-E4
High Pavement	D2-E2
High Street	D3
Hockley	E3
Holles Crescent	A2-B2
Hollowstone	E2
Hope Drive	B1-B2
Hounds Gate	C2-C3
Howard Street	D4
Huntingdon Drive	B2-B3
Huntingdon Street	D5-D4-E4
Ilkeston Road	A4
Instow Rise	E5
Ireton Street	A5
Isabella Street	C2
Kenilworth Road	B2
Kent Street	D4-E4
King Edward Street	D4-E4
King Street	D3-D4

Lamartine Street	E5-F5
Lennox Street	E3-E4
Lenton Road	A1-A2-B2-C2
Lincoln Circus	A3
Lincoln Street	D3-D4
Lister Gate	D2
Liverpool Street	F4
London Road	E1-E2
Long Row East	D3
Long Row West	C3
Longden Street	F3-F4
Low Pavement	D2
Lowdham Street	F4
Lower Parliament Street	D4-E4-E3-E2
Lytton Close	F5
Maid Marian Way	B3-C3-C2
Maiden Lane	E3
Mansfield Road	C5-D5
Manvers Street	F2-F3
Market Street	C3-C4
Middle Hill	D2
Middle Pavement	D2
Milton Street	D4
Moorgate Street	A4
Mount Street	C3
Mowray Court	E5
Nelson Street	E3-F3
Newark Street	F2
Newcastle Circus	A2
Newcastle Drive	A3-A4-B3
Newdigate Street	A5
Nile Street	E4
Norfolk Place	C3-C4
North Church Street	C4-D4
North Circus Street	B3-B4
North Road	A3
North Sherwood Street	C5
Ogle Drive	B2
Old Lenton Street	D3
Oliver Close	A5

Oliver Street	A5-B5
Oxford Street	B3
Palatine Street	B1
Park Drive	A2-B2
Park Ravine	A2-B1
Park Row	B3-C3
Park Terrace	B3
Park Valley	B2-B3
Peel Street	B5-C5
Pelham Street	D3
Pemberton Street	E2
Pennyfoot Street	F2
Pilcher Gate	D3
Plantaganet Street	E5
Plough Lane	F2
Plumptre Street	E2-E3
Popham Street	D2
Poplar Street	F2
Portland Road	A4-A5-B5
Postern Street	B3
Queen Street	C4-C3-D3
Queens Road	D1-E1
Raleigh Street	A5
Regent Street	B3
Rick Street	D4
Risters Place	E3
Robin Hood Street	F4
Roden Street	F4
Russell Street	A5
Rutland Street	C2-C3
St Annes Well Road	E4-E5
St James's Street	C3
St James's Terrace	B3-C3-C2
St Lukes Street	F4
St Marks Street	D5-E5
St Mary's Gate	D3-E3-E2
St Peters Gate	D3
Shakespeare Street	B5-C5-D4
Shelton Street	D5-E5
Sneinton Road	F3
South Parade	C3-D3

South Sherwood Street	C4-C5
Southwell Road	F3
Spaniel Row	C2-C3
Standard Hill	C2
Stanford Street	C2-D2
Station Street	D1-E1
Stonebridge Road	F4-F5
Stoneleigh Street	A5
Stoney Street	E2-E3
Talbot Street	A4-B4-C4
Tattershall Drive	A3-A2-B2
Tennis Drive	A3
Tennyson Street	A5
The Ropewalk	A4-B4-B3
Thurland Street	D3
Toll House Hill	B4
Trent Street	D1-D2
Trinity Square	D3
Troman Close	E5
Tunnel Road	A3
Union Road	D5
Upper College Street	B3-B4
Upper Parliament Street	C3-C4-D4
Victoria Street	D3
Walker Street	F3-F4
Walter Street	A5
Warser Gate	D3-E3
Wasnidge Close	E5
Watkin Street	D5
Waverley Street	B5
Weekday Cross	D3
Wellington Circus	B3
West Street	F3
Wheeler Gate	C3
Wilford Road	C1
Wilford Street	C1
Wollaton Street	A4-B4-C4
Wood Street	A4
Woolpack Lane	E3
York Street	D5

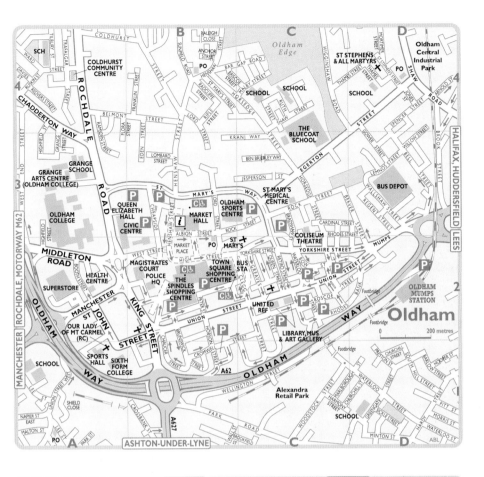

Oldham

Oldham is found on atlas page **82 D5**

Street	Grid	Street	Grid
Albion Street	B3	Market Place	B2
Bar Gap Road	B4-C4	Marlborough Street	C1-D1
Barlow Street	D1	Middleton Road	A2
Beever Street	C3-D3-D2	Morris Street	D1
Bell Street	D3	Mortimer Street	D4
Belmont Street	A4-B4	Mumps	D2-D3
Ben Brierley Way	C3	Oldham Way	B1-C1-C2-D2
Booth Street	A2	Park Road	B1-C1
Bow Street	C2-D2	Peter Street	B2
Bradshaw Street	C2-C3	Preston Street	D1
Brook Street	D3-D4	Queen Street	C2
Brunswick Street	B1-B2	Radcliffe Street	B4
Cardinal Street	C3-D3	Ramsden Street	A3-A4
Chadderton Way	A3-A4	Redvers Street	A4
Chaucer Street	B1-B2	Regent Street	D3
Cheapside	B2-B3	Retiro Street	C2
Churchill Street	C1-D1, D1	Rhodes Bank	C2-D2
Clegg Street	B2-C2-C1	Rhodes Street	C3-D3
Coldhurst Street	A4-B4	Rifle Street	B4
Cromwell Street	B1-C2	Rochdale Road	A2-A3-A4
Crossbank Street	B1	Rock Street	B3-C3
Eden Street	B3-B4	Roscoe Street	C2-D2
Egerton Street	C3-D4	Ruskin Street	A4
Franklin Street	B4	Ruth Street	C4
Gower Street	D3-D4	Shaw Road	D4
Grange Street	A3	St Mary's Street	B4
Greaves Street	C1-C2	St Mary's Way	A3-B3-C3-C2
Greengate Street	D1	St Stephen's Street	D4
Hardy Street	D1	Shaw Street	C4
Harmony Street	C1-D1	Sickle Street	D1
Henshaw Street	B2-B3-B4	South Hill Street	D1
Higginshaw Road	C4	Spencer Street	D4
High Street	B2	Sunfield Road	B4
Highfield Street	A2-A3, A3-A4	Thames Street	C4-D4
Hobson Street	B1-B2	Tilbury Street	A4
Hooper Street	D1	Trafalgar Street	A4
Horsedge Street	B4-C4-C3	Union Street	B2-C2-D2
Jesperson Street	B3-C3	Union Street West	A1
John Street	A2-A1-B1-B2	Wall Street	B1
Jones Street	D4	Wallshaw Street	D3
King Street	B1-B2	Ward Street	A4
Kranj Way	B3-C3	Waterloo Street	C2-C1-D1
Lee Street	A1	Wellington Street	B1-C1
Lemnos Street	D3	West End Street	A2-A3-A4
Lombard Street	B3	West Street	A2-B2
Lord Street	B2-B3, B3-B4	Willow Street	D3-D4
Malby Street	C4	Woodstock Street	C1
Manchester Street	A1-A2	Yorkshire Street	C2-D2

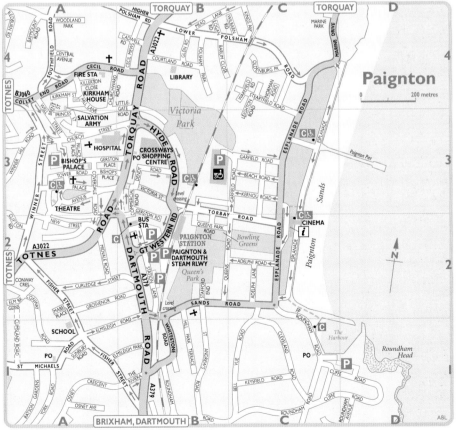

Paignton

Paignton is found on atlas page **7 F4**

Street	Grid	Street	Grid
Adelphi Lane	C2	Leighton Road	C3-C4
Adelphi Road	C2	Littlegate Road	A4-B4
Barum Close	B4	Logan Road	B4
Batson Gardens	A1	Lower Polsham Road	B4-C4
Baymount Road	A4	Mabel Place	A2
Beach Road	C3	Marine Drive	C4
Bell Vue Road	C1	Marine Park	C4
Bishops Place	A3-B3	Mead Lane	B4-C4
Brent Street	A3-A4	Midvale Road	A2
Cadwell Road	B4	Mill Lane	A3-A4
Cecil Mews	B4	New Street	A2
Cecil Road	A4-B4	Norman Road	C4
Central Avenue	A4	Oldenburg Park	C4
Church Street	A3-B3	Osney Avenue	A1
Churchward Road	A4	Osney Crescent	A1
Cleveland Road	C1	Palace Avenue	A3
Cliffe Road	C1-D1	Palace Place	A3
Clifton Road	A2-A3	Polsham Park	B4
Climsland Road	A1-A2	Princes Street	A3
Colley End Road	A4	Queens Park Road	B2
Commercial Road	B3	Queens Road	B2-C2
Conway Crescent	A2	Redburn Road	A4
Conway Road	A1-A2	Roundham Road	B1-C1-C2
Courtland Road	B4	St Andrews Road	B1-B2
Coverdale Road	A3	St Michaels Road	A1
Curledge Road	A2-B2	Sands Road	B2-C2
Dartmouth Road	B1-B2	Southfield Road	A4
Dendy Road	B3	Stafford End	B2
Elm Bank Gardens	A2	Station Lane	B2
Elmsleigh Park	A1-B1	Steartfield Road	C3-C4
Elmsleigh Road	A1-B1-B2	Sunbury Road	A1
Esplanade	C2-C3-C4	The Riviera	B1
Esplanade Road	C2-C3-C4	Torbay Road	B3-B2-C2
Fisher Street	A2-A1-B1	Torquay Road	B3-B4
Garfield Road	C3	Totnes Road	A2-A3
Gerston Place	A3-B3	Tower Road	A3
Gerston Road	B2-B3	Victoria Street	B3
Glen Road	B4	Warefield Road	C4
Great Western Road	B2-B3	Well Street	A3-A4
Grosvenor Road	A2-B2	Whitestone Road	B1
Higher Polsham Road	A4-B4	Wilbarn Road	C4
Hill Park Terrace	B1-B2	Winner Hill Road	A3
Hyde Road	B3	Winner Street	A2-A3-A4
Kernou Road	C3	Woodland Park	A4
Keysfield Road	C1	York Road	A1
Killerton Close	A4		
Kings Avenue	C4		
Kirkham Street	A4		

213

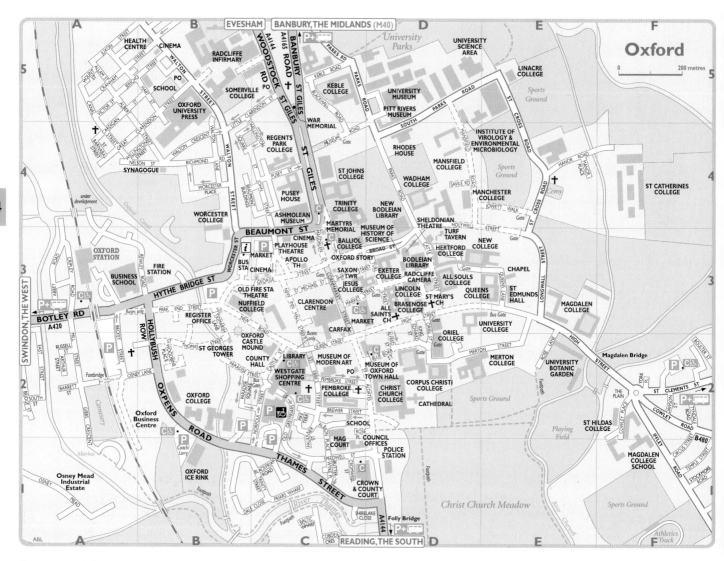

Oxford

Oxford is found on atlas page **40 C5**

Abbey Road	A3	Faulkner Street	C1-C2	Paradise Square	B2	Tyndale Road	F2
Albert Street	A5-B4	Friars Wharf	C1	Paradise Street	B2-C2	Victor Street	A5
Albion Place	C1-C2	George Street	B3-C3	Park End Street	A3-B3	Walton Crescent	B4
Alfred Street	D2-D3	Gibbs Crescent	A1-A2	Parks Road	C5-D5-D4	Walton Lane	B4-B5
Allam Street	A5	Great Clarendon Street	A4-B4-B5	Pembroke Street	C2	Walton Street	B4-B5
Arthur Street	A2	Hart Street	B5	Pike Terrace	C2	Wellington Square	B4-C4
Baltic Wharf	C1	High Street	C2-D3-E2-F2	Pusey Street	C4	Wellington Street	A4-B4
Banbury Road	C5	Hollybush Row	B2-B3	Queen Street	C2	Woodbine Place	B2
Barrett Street	A2	Holywell Street	D4-E4-E3	Queens Lane	E3	Woodstock Road	C5
Beaumont Buildings	B4-C4	Hythe Bridge Street	B3	Rewley Road	A3-B3	Worcester Place	B4
Beaumont Street	B3-C3-C4	Iffley Road	F1-F2	Richmond Road	B4	Worcester Street	B3
Becket Street	A2-A3	Jericho Street	A5-B5	Rose Lane	E2-E3	York Place	F2
Blackfriars Road	C1	Jowett Walk	D4-E4	Rose Place	C2		
Blackhall Road	C4-C5	Juxon Street	A5	Russell Street	A2		
Blue Boar Street	D2	Keble Road	C5	St Aldates	C2-D2-D1		
Botley Road	A3	King Edward Street	D2-D3	St Barnabas Street	A4		
Boulter Street	F2	Little Clarendon Street	B4-B5-C5	St Clements Street	F2		
Brewer Street	C2	Longwall Street	E3	St Cross Road	E3-E4-E5		
Bridge Street	A2	Magdalen Street	C3	St Ebbe's Street	C2		
Broad Street	C3-D3	Manor Place	E4	St Giles	C4-C5		
Butterwyke Place	C1	Manor Road	E4-F4	St John Street	C3-C4		
Canal Street	A4-A5	Mansfield, Road	D4-D5	St Michael Street	C3		
Cardigan Street	A4-A5-B5	Market Street	C3-D3	St Thomas Street	B2		
Castle Street	C2	Merton Street	D2-E2-E3	Savile Road	D4		
Cattle Street	D3	Mill Street	A2-A3	Ship Street	C3-D3		
Circus Street	F1-F2	Mount Street	A5	Shirelake Close	C1		
Cobden Crescent	C1	Museum Road	C4	South Parks Road	D4-D5-E5		
Cornmarket Street	C3	Nelson Street	A4-B4	South Street	A2		
Cowley Place	F2	New Inn Hall Street	C2-C3	Speedwell Street	C1-D1		
Cowley Road	F2	New Road	B3-C3-C2	Stockmore Road	F1		
Cranham Street	A5-B5	Norfolk Street	C1-C2	Temple Street	F1-F2		
Cripley Road	A3	Old Greyfriars Street	C1-C2	Thames Street	B1-C1-D1		
Cromwell Street	C1	Oriel Street	D2-D3	The Plain	F2		
Dale Close	B1-C1	Osney Lane	A2-B2	Tidmarsh Lane	B2-B3		
Dawson Street	F2	Osney Mead	A1	Trinity Street	C1		
East Street	A2-A3	Oxpens Road	B1-B2	Turl Street	D3		

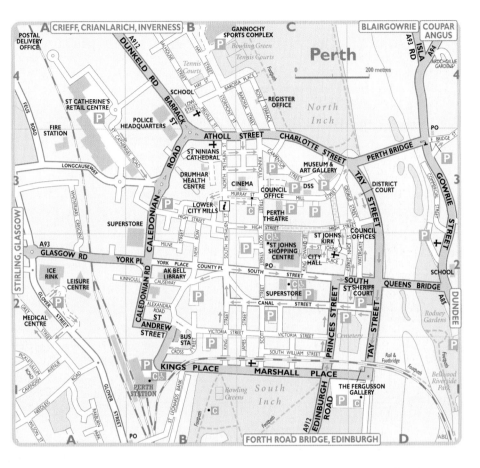

Perth

Perth is found on atlas page **140 A2**

Alexandra Road	B2	Rose Terrace	C4
Ardchoillie Gardens	D4	St Andrew Street	B2
Atholl Street	B3-C3	St Catherines Road	A4-A3-B3
Balhousie Street	B4	St John Street	C2-D3
Barossa Place	C4	St Johns Place	C2
Barossa Street	B4-C4	St Leonards Bank	BI
Barrack Street	B4	Scott Street	CI-C2-C3
Caledonian Road	B2-B3	South Methuen Street	B2-B3
Canal Street	B2-C2	South Street	B2-C2-D2
Carpentor Street	C3	South William Street	CI
Cavendish Avenue	AI	Stormont Street	B3-B4
Charlotte Street	C3	Tay Street	DI-D2-D3
Commercial Street	D3	Victoria Street	B2-C2
County Place	B2	Watergate	D2-D3
Cross Street	BI-B2	Whitefriars Crescent	A2-A3
Dunkeld Road	A4-B4	Wilson Street	AI
East Bridge Street	D3	York Place	A2-B2
Edinburgh Road	CI		
Feus Road	A3-A4		
George Street	C3-D3		
Glasgow Road	A2		
Glover Street	AI-A2		
Gowrie Street	D2-D3		
Grey Street	AI-A2		
Hay Street	B4		
High Street	B3-C3-D3		
Isla Road	D4		
James Street	CI-C2		
King Edward Street	C2		
King Street	BI-B2		
Kings Place	BI		
Kinnoull Causeway	A2-B2		
Kinnoull Street	C3		
Longcauseway	A3-B3		
Low Street	B4		
Marshall Place	CI-DI		
Melville Street	B3-B4		
Mill Street	C3		
Milne Street	B2-B3		
Murray Street	B3-C3		
Needless Road	AI		
New Row	B2-B3		
North Methuen Street	B3		
Perth Bridge	D3		
Pickletullum Road	AI		
Princes Street	CI-C2		
Queens Bridge	D2		
Raeburn Park	AI		

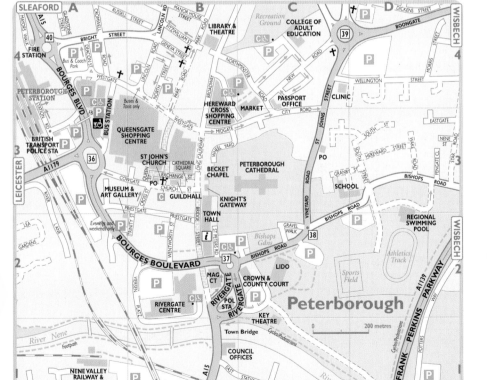

Peterborough

Peterborough is found on atlas page **62 A5**

Bishops Road	C2-C3-D3	South Street	D3
Boongate	D4	Star Road	D3
Bourges Boulevard	A4-A2-B2	Station Road	A3-A4
Bridge Street	B2-B3	Trinity Street	B2-B3
Bright Street	A4-B4	Versen Platz	BI-B2
Broadway	B3-B4	Vineyard Road	C2-C3
Cathedral Square	B3	Wake Road	D3
Church Street	B3	Wellington Street	C4-D4
City Road	C3-C4	Wentworth Street	B2
Cowgate	A3-B3	Westgate	A4-B4-B3
Cromwell Road	A4	Wheel Yard	B3
Cross Street	B3		
Deacon Street	A4		
Dickens Street	D4		
East Station Road	BI-CI		
Eastgate	D3		
Exchange Street	B3		
Fengate Close	D3		
Fitzwilliam Street	B4		
Frank Perkins Parkway	DI-D2		
Geneva Street	B4		
George Street	AI		
Gladstone Street	A4		
Granby Street	C3-D3		
Gravel Walk	C2		
Hereward Street	D3		
Jubilee Street	AI		
Lea Gardens	A2		
Lincoln Road	B4		
Long Causeway	B3		
Manor House Street	B4		
Mayors Walk	A4		
Midgate	B3-C3		
Morris Street	D4		
Nene Street	D3		
New Road	C4		
North Street	B4		
Northminster Road	B4-C4-C3		
Oundle Road	AI-BI		
Park Road	B3-B4		
Potters Way	DI-D2		
Priestgate	A3-B3-B3		
Queen Street	B3		
River Lane	A2-A3		
Rivergate	BI-B2-C2		
Russell Street	A4-B4		
St Johns Street	C3-C4		
St Peters Road	B2		

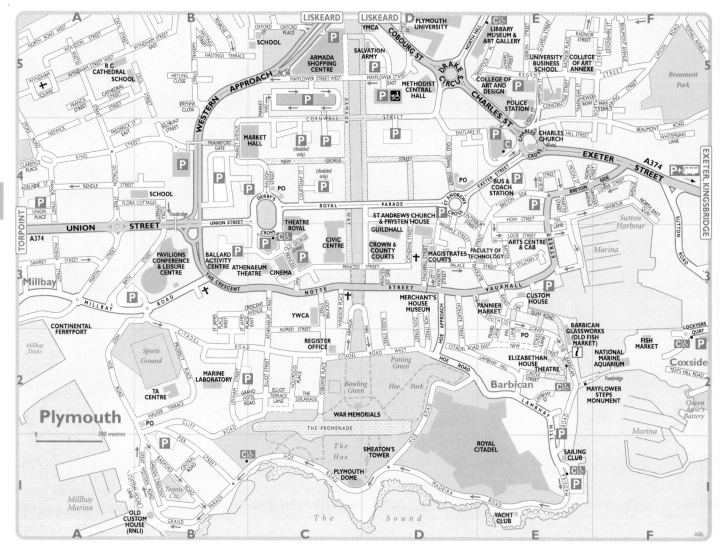

Plymouth

Plymouth is found on atlas page **6 B3**

Adelaide Street	A4	Eastlake Street	D4-E4	Kinterbury Street	D4-D3-E3	Phoenix Street	A3	Union Place	A4
Alfred Street	C2	Elliot Street	C2	Lambhay Hill	D2-E2-E1	Pier Street	B1-B2	Union Street	A3-C3
Anstis Street	A4-A5	Elliot Terrace Lane	C2	Lambhay Street	E2	Pin Lane	E2	Vauxhall Street	E3
Armada Way	C2-C3-D3-D2	Exeter Street	D4-E4-F4	Leigham Street	B2	Princess Street	C3-D3	Walker Terrace	B2
Armada Way	C3-C4-C5	Fineswell Street	D3	Lipson Road	F5	Princess Street Ope	D3	West Hoe Road	A2-A3-B3
Athenaeum Street	C2-C3	Flora Cottages	A4-B4	Lockyer Street	C3	Princess Way	C3	Western Approach	B4-B5-C5
Basket Ope	E3	Flora Street	B4	Lockyers Quay	F2	Prospect Place	B2	Whimple Street	D3
Bath Street	A3-B3	Francis Street	A5	Looe Street	E3	Prynne Close	B5	Whitefriars Lane	F4
Batter Street	E3	Frankfort Gate	B4	Lower Street	E2	Quay Road	E3	Windsor Place	C3
Beaumont Avenue	F5	Frederick Street East	A4-B4	Madeira Road	D1-E1-E2	Radford Road	B1	Wolsdon Street	A5
Beaumont Road	F4-F5	Friars Lane	E2-E3	Manor Street	A3-A4	Radnor Place	E5	Wyndham Square	A5
Belmont Street	B4	Garden Crescent	B1	Market Avenue	B4	Radnor Street	E5-F5	Wyndham Street East	A5-B5
Bilbury Street	E4	Gasking Street	F5	Market Way	C4-C5	Raleigh Street	C4	Wyndham Street West	A5
Breton Side	E4-F4	Gibbon Street	E5	Martin Street	A3	Regent Street	E5-F5	Zion Street	D2-D3
Buckwell Street	D3-E3	Gilwell Street	E5	Martin Street	E4	Rendle Street	A4-B4		
Castle Street	E2	Grand Hotel Road	B2-C2	Mayflower Street East	D5	Royal Parade	C4-D4		
Cathedral Street	A5	Grand Parade	B1	Mayflower Street West	C5	St Andrew Street	D3		
Catherine Street	D3	Great Western Road	B1	Millbay Road	A3-B3	St Andrews Cross	D4		
Cecil Street	A5-B5-B4	Green Street	E4-E5	Moon Street	E4	St James Place East	B2-B3		
Central Road	B1	Hampton Street	E5	Neswick Street	A4-A5-B5	St James Place West	B2-B3		
Chapel Street	E5	Harbour Avenue	F4	New George Street	C4-D4	Sawrey Street	A3		
Charles Cross	E4	Harwell Street	B5	New Street	E2	Southside Street	D3-E3-E2		
Charles Street	D5-E5-E4	Hastings Street	B5	North East Quay	F3-F4	Stillman Street	E3		
Citadel Road	B3-B2-C2-D2	Hastings Terrace	B5-C5	North Hill	D5-E5	Stoke Road	A4-A5		
Citadel Road East	D2-E2	Hawkers Avenue	E4-F4	North Road West	A5	Stokes Lane	E2		
Clarence Place	A4	Hetling Close	B5	North Street	E4-F4-F5	Sussex Street	D2-D3		
Cliff Road	B1-B2-C2	Hewers Row	E5	Notte Street	C3-D3	Sutton Road	F3-F4		
Cobourg Street	D5	Hill Street	E4	Octagon Street	A4	Tavistock Place	D5-E5		
Constantine Street	E5	Hoe Approach	D2-D3	Old George Street	C3	Teats Hill Road	F2		
Cornwall Street	B4-C4-D4-D5	Hoe Road	B1-C1-D1-D2	Old Town Street	D4	The Barbican	E2		
Courtenay Street	C4	Hoe Street	D2-D3	Oxford Place	C2	The Crescent	B3-C3		
Crescent Avenue	B3-C3	Hoegate Street	D2-D3	Oxford Street	B5-C5	The Esplanade	C2		
Custom House Lane	A1-B1	Holyrood Place	C2	Palace Street	D3-E3	The Promenade	C2-D2		
Derry's Cross	C3-C4	How Street	E3-E4	Park Terrace	F5	Tin Lane	E3-E4		
Devonshire Street	F5	James Street	D5	Penrose Street	B5	Tothill Avenue	F5		
Drake Circus	D5	King Street	A4-B4			Trafalgar Street	E5		

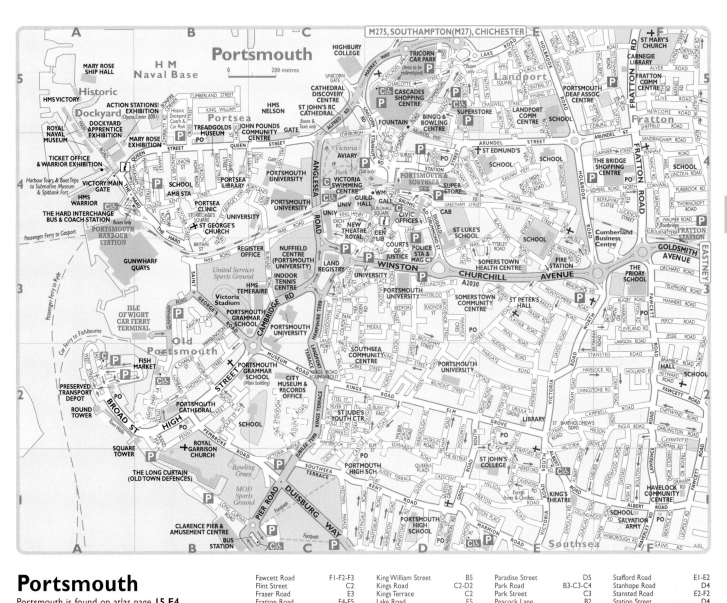

Portsmouth

Portsmouth is found on atlas page **15 E4**

Admiralty Road	B4-B5	Canal Walk	E4	Fawcett Road	F1-F2-F3	King William Street	B5	Paradise Street	D5	Stafford Road	E1-E2
Albany Road	E1-E2	Carlisle Road	E3-E4	Flint Street	C2	Kings Road	C2-D2	Park Road	B3-C3-C4	Stanhope Road	D4
Albert Grove	E1-E2	Cascades Approach	D5	Fraser Road	E3	Kings Terrace	C2	Park Street	C3	Stansted Road	E2-F2
Albert Road	E2-E1-F1	Castle Road	C1-C2-D2	Fratton Road	F4-F5	Lake Road	E5	Peacock Lane	B2	Station Street	D4
Alec Rose Lane	D3-D4	Cavendish Road	E1	Garnier Street	F4	Landport Street	C3	Pelham Road	D1-D2	Stone Street	C2
Alexandra Road	E5	Charles Street	E5	Gold Street	C2	Landport Terrace	C2	Pembroke Road	B2-B1-C1	Surrey Street	D4
Alfred Road	C5	Charlotte Street	D5	Goldsmith Avenue	F3	Lansdowne Street	C3	Penhale Road	F4	Sussex Terrace	D1
Alver Road	F5	Chelsea Road	E1-F1-F2	Goodwood Road	F1-F2	Lawrence Road	F1-F2	Penny Street	B2	Telephone Road	F3
Anglesea Road	C4	Chetwynd Road	F2	Great Southsea Street	C2-D2	Lawson Road	F2-F3	Percy Road	F3	Temple Street	D5
April Square	E5	Church Road	E5-F5	Green Road	D2	Lincoln Road	F4	Pier Road	C1	The Hard	A4-B4-B3
Ariel Road	F4	Claremont Road	F4	Greetham Street	D4-E4	Little Southsea Street	C2	Playfair Road	E3	The Retreat	D1
Armory Lane	B3	Cleveland Road	F3	Grosvenor Street	D3	Livingstone Road	E2-F2	Purbrook Road	F4	The Thicket	E2
Arundel Street	D4-E4-F4	Clifton Street	F5	Grove Road North	E2	Lombard Street	B2	Queen Street	A4-B4-C4	Unicorn Road	C5-D5
Arundel Way	D4-D5	Clive Road	F5	Grove Road South	D1-D2	Long Curtain Road	B1	Queens Crescent	D1	Union Place	E5
Ashburton Road	D1	Coburg Street	E5-F5	Guildhall Square	D4	Lords Street	E5	Queens Grove	D1	Upper Arundel Street	D4-E4
Astley Street	C3	Collingwood Road	E1-F1	Guildhall Walk	C3-D4	Lorne Road	F2	Queens Place	D1	Victoria Avenue	C1-C2
Aylward Street	B4	Commercial Road	D4-D5	Gunwharf Road	B3	Lucknow Street	F4	Raglan Street	E4	Victoria Grove	E2-F2
Baileys Road	E3	Cornwall Road	F4	Hambrook Street	C2	Main Road	A4-A5	Railway View	E4	Victoria Road North	E2-E3-F3
Belmont Street	D2	Cottage Grove	D2-E2	Hampshire Terrace	C3	Manners Road	F3	Rugby Road	F3	Victoria Road South	E1-E2
Bishop Street	B4	Cottage View	E4	Hanover Street	B4	Margate Road	D2-E2	St Andrews Road	E2-E3	Victory Road	B4
Blackfriars Road	E3-E4	Crasswell Street	B5	Harold Road	F1	Market Way	C5-D5	St Davids Road	E2-E3	Vivash Road	F4
Bonfire Corner	B5	Cross Street	B4-B5	Havant Street	B5	Marmion Road	D1-E1	St Edward's Road	D1-D2	Walmer Road	F4
Boulton Road	F1-F2	Cumberland Street	B5	Havelock Road	E2-F2	Melbourne Place	C3-D3	St Faith's Road	E5	Waltham Street	C3
Bramble Road	F2	Curzon Howe Road	B4	Hawke Street	B4	Merton Road	D1-E1	Saint George's Road	B3	Warblington Street	B2-B3
Bridgeside Close	E4	Darlington Road	F2	Hereford Road	E1	Middle Street	D3	St George's Way	B4	Warwick Crescent	D3
Bridport Street	D4-E4	Dugald Drummond Street	D3-D4	High Street	B2	Milford Road	E4	St James's Road	D2-D3	Waterloo Street	D3
Britannia Road	F2-F3	Duisburg Way	C1	Highbury Street	B2	Montgomerie Road	E3	St James's Street	B4-C4	Waverley Road	F1
Britannia Road North	F3	Duncan Road	E1-F1	Holbrook Road	E5-E4-F3	Museum Road	C2	St Nicholas Street	B2	Wellington Street	D3
Broad Street	A2-B2	Durham Street	D4	Hudson Road	E2-E3	Nancy Road	F4	St Paul's Road	C3	West Street	A2
Brougham Street	D2-D3	Earlsdon Street	D3	Hyde Park Road	D3-E3-E4	Napier Road	F1	St Paul's Street	C2	Western Parade	C1
Buck Street	D4-D5	East Street	A2	Inglis Road	F2	Nelson Road	D1-E1	St Peter's Grove	E2	White Hart Lane	B2
Buriton Street	E5	Edinburgh Road	C4-D4	Isambard Brunel Road	D4	Newcome Road	F5	St Thomas's Street	B2-B3	Wickham Street	A4-B4
Burnaby Road	C3	Eldon Street	D2-D3	Jacobs Street	D5	Nightingale Road	C1	Sandringham Road	F4	Willis Street	D4
Butcher Street	B3-B4	Elm Grove	D2-E2	Jessie Road	F3	Norfolk Street	D2	Selbourne Terrace	F4	Wilson Grove	E2-F2
Cambridge Road	C3	Elphinstone Road	D1	Jubilee Terrace	C1-C2	Norman Road	F2	Shaftesbury Road	D1	Wiltshire Street	C3
Campbell Road	E2-F2	Exmouth Road	E1	Kent Road	C1-D1	North Street	B4-B5	Sheffield Road	F5	Winston Churchill Avenue	C3-E3
				Kent Street	B4	Oxford Road	F1-F2	Silver Street	C2	Wisborough Road	F1
				King Albert Street	F5	Orchard Road	F3	Slindon Street	D4	Woodpath	D1-D2
				King Charles Street	B2	Oyster Street	B2	Somers Road	D2-D3-E3-E4	Woodville Drive	C2
				King Henry I Street	C4-D4	Pains Road	E2-E3	Somers Road North	E4-F4	Yarborough Road	D2
				King Street	D2	Palmerston Road	D1	Southsea Terrace	C1	Yorke Street	C2-D2

217

218

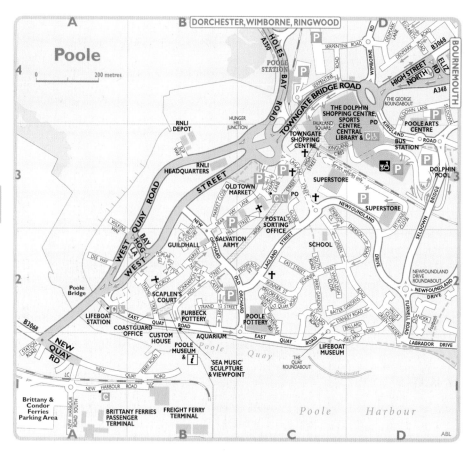

Poole

Poole is found on atlas page **12 D4**

Baiter Gardens	C2-D2	Prosperous Street	C2
Ballard Close	C2-D2	St Aubyns Court	B2-B3
Ballard Road	C2-C1-D1-D2	Seldown	D4
Bay Hog Lane	B2	Seldown Bridge	D2-D3
Blandford Road	A1-A2	Seldown Lane	D3-D4
Castle Street	B2	Serpentine Road	C4-D4
Chapel Lane	C3	Skinner Street	C2
Church Street	B2	Slip Way	B3
Cinnamon Lane	B2	South Road	C2
Dear Hay Lane	B3-C3	Stanley Road	C2-D2
Dee Way	A2	Station Road	A1
Denmark Lane	D4	Sterte Road	C4
Denmark Road	D4	Strand Street	B2
Drake Road	C2	Taylors Buildings	C2
East Quay Road	A2-B2-C1-C2	Thames Street	B2
East Street	C2	Towngate Bridge Road	C3-C4-D4
Elizabeth Road	D4	Vallis Close	D2
Emerson Close	C3	West Street	A2-B2-B3-C3
Emerson Road	C3-D3-D2	West Quay Road	A2-B3
Falkland Square	C3-C4	Whatleigh Close	C2
Ferry Road	B1	Wilkins Way	A2-A3
Fishermans Road	C2	Wimborne Road	D4
Furnell Road	D2		
Globe Lane	C3		
Green Gardens	D1-D2		
Green Road	C3-C2-D2		
High Street	B2-C2-C3		
High Street North	C3		
Hill Street	B2-B3-C3		
Holes Bay Road	C4		
Kingland Crescent	C3-D3		
Kingland Road	D3-D4		
Labrador Drive	D1		
Lagland Street	C2-C3		
Lander Close	D2		
Levet's Lane	B2		
Market Close	B3		
Market Street	B2		
New Harbour Road	A1-B1		
New Harbour Road South	A1		
New Orchard	B2-B3		
New Quay Road	A1-B1		
New Street	B2		
Newfoundland Drive	C3-D3-D2		
Old Orchard	B2-C2		
Perry Gardens	C2		
Pitwines Close	D2-D3		
Poplar Close	B2		

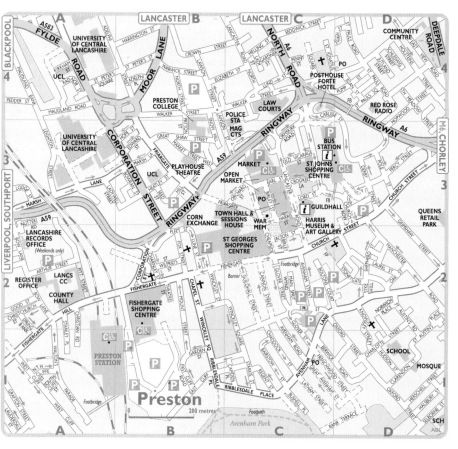

Preston

Preston is found on atlas page **88 D3**

Adelphi Street	A4-B4	Jutland Street	D4
Arthur Street	A2	Knowsley Street	D1-D2
Avenham Lane	C1-C2	Ladywell Street	A3-B3
Avenham Road	C1-C2	Lancaster Road	C2-C3
Avenham Street	C2	Lancaster Road North	B4-C4
Bairstow Street	C1	Laurel Street	D2
Berwick Road	C1-D1	Lawson Street	B4-B3-C3
Bow Lane	A2	Leighton Street	A3-A4
Bowran Street	B3	Lord Street	C3
Cannon Street	C2	Lund Street	C4
Carlisle Street	C4-D4-D3	Lune Street	B2
Chaddock Street	C1-C2	Manchester Road	D2-D3
Chapel Street	B2	Market Street West	B3
Charlotte Street	D1-D2	Maudland Bank	A4
Cheapside	C2	Melling Street	C4
Christchurch Street	A2	Moor Lane	B4
Church Row	D3	Mount Street	B1-B2
Church Street	C2-D2-D3	North Road	C4
Clarendon Street	D1	North Street	B4
Corporation Street	A3-B3-B2	Oak Street	D2
Crooked Lane	C3	Old Vicarage Street	C3
Crown Street	B4-C4	Orchard Street	C3
Derby Street	D3	Ormskirk Road	C3
Earl Street	C3	Oxford Street	C2-D2-D1
East Cliff	B1	Percy Street	C3
East Cliff Road	B1	Pitt Street	A2-A3
East View Road	D4	Pole Street	D3
Egan Street	D4	Pump Street	C4-D4
Elizabeth Street	B4-C4	Ribblesdale Place	B1-C1
Fishergate	B2-C2	Ringway	B3-C4-D4-D3
Fishergate Hill	A1-A2	St Austin's Place	D1-D2
Fleet Street	B2	St Austin's Road	D1-D2
Fox Street	B2	St Ignatius Square	C4
Frenchwood Street	C1-D1	St Pauls Road	D4
Friargate	B3-C3	St Pauls Square	D4
Fylde Road	A4	St Peter's Square	A4-B4
Great Avenham Street	C1-D1	St Peter's Street	B4
Great Shaw Street	B3	Seed Street	B3
Grimshaw Street	D2-D3	Shepherd Street	D2
Guildhall Street	C2	South Meadow Street	D3-D4
Harrington Street	A4-B4	Starkie Street	C1
Harris Street	C3	Syke Street	C2
Heatley Street	B3	Walker Street	B4-C4
Herschell Street	D1	Walton's Parade	A1-A2
Hill Street	B3	Warwick Street	B4
Holsteins Street	D4	West Cliff	A1
Hopwood Street	D3-D4	Winckley Square	B1-B2-C2-C1
Jacson Street	C2	Winckley Street	B2

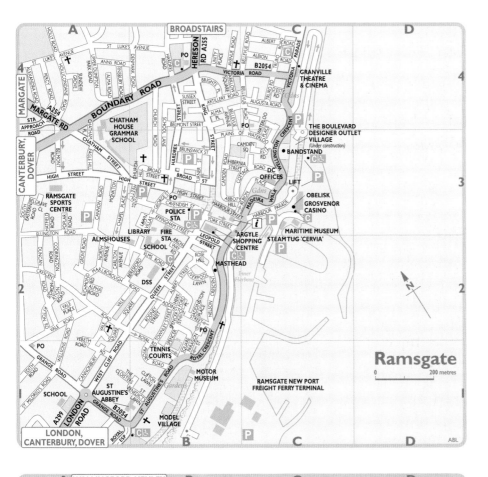

Ramsgate

Ramsgate is found on atlas page **31 G2**

Abbots Hill	B3	Hardres Road	B4
Addington Street	B2	Hardres Street	B3-B4
Albert Road	C4	Hereson Road	B4
Albert Street	B2	Hibernia Street	B3-C3
Albion Place	B3-C3	High Street	A3-B3
Albion Road	C4	Hollicondane Road	A4
Alma Road	A4	King Street	B3-B4
Anns Road	A4-B4	Lawn Villas	B3
Arklow Square	B4	Leopold Street	B2-B3
Artillery Road	B4-C4	Liverpool Lawn	B2
Augusta Road	C4	London Road	A1
Avenue Road	B4	Madeira Walk	C3
Belgrave Close	A3	Margate Road	A4
Bellevue Avenue	B4	Marlborough Road	A2-B2
Bellevue Road	C4	Meeting Street	B3
Belmont Road	A3	Monkton	A3
Belmont Street	B4	Nelson Crescent	B2
Beresford Road	B2	North Avenue	A2
Boundary Road	A4-B4	Paragon Street	B1-B2
Brights Place	B4	Percy Road	A4
Broad Street	B3	Plains of Waterloo	B3-C3
Brunswick Street	B3	Priory Road	B1
Camden Road	B3	Queen Street	B2
Cannon Road	A3	Richmond Road	A2
Cannonbury Road	A1	Rose Hill	B2
Carlton Avenue	A2	Royal Crescent	B1-B2
Cavendish Street	B3	Royal Esplanade	A1-B1
Chapel Place	B3	Royal Road	B1-B2
Chatham Place	A3-A4	Ryton Road	A2
Chatham Street	A3-B3	St Augustine's Road	B1
Church Road	B3-B4	St Benedict's Lawn	B1
Codrington Road	A2	St Luke's Avenue	A4-B4
Coronation Road	A2	School Lane	B3-B4
Cottage Road	B3-C3	Spencer Square	B1-B2
Crescent Road	A2	Station Approach Road	A4
Denmark Road	B4	Sussex Street	B4
Duncan Road	A2	Townley Street	B2
Eagle Hill	A3	Truro Road	C4
Effingham Street	B3	Turner Street	B3
Elizabeth Road	C3	Upper Dumpton Park Road	A4
Ellington Road	A3	Vale Road	A2
Elms Road	B2	Vale Square	A2-B2
Finsbury Road	A4	Victoria Parade	C4
George Street	B3	Victoria Road	B4-C4
Grange Road	A1	Wellington Crescent	C3-C4
Grove Road	A2-A3	West Cliff Road	A1-A2
Harbour Parade	C3	Willsons Road	A1-A2
Harbour Street	B3-C3	York Street	B3

219

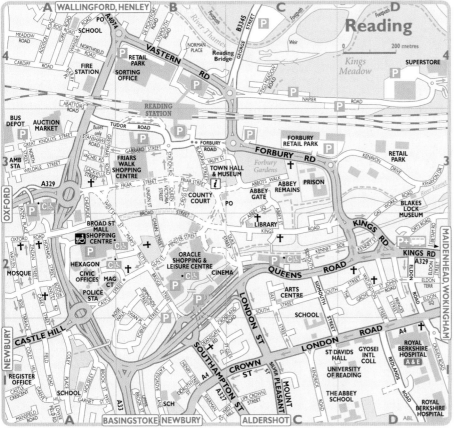

Reading

Reading is found on atlas page **41 E2**

Abattoirs Road	A4	Katesgrove Lane	B1
Abbey Square	C2-C3	Kenavon Drive	D3
Abbey Street	C2-C3	Kendrick Road	C1
Abbots Walk	C3	Kennet Side	C2-D2
Addison Road	A4	Kennet Street	D2
Anstey Road	A2	Kings Meadow Road	C4
Barry Place	A4	Kings Road	C2-D2
Betam Road	D2	London Road	C1-D1-D2
Blagrave Street	B3	London Street	C1-C2
Bridge Street	B2	Meadow Road	A4
Broad Street	B2-B3	Minster Street	B2
Brook Street West	A1-B1	Mount Pleasant	C1
Cardiff Road	A4	Napier Road	C4-D4
Carey Street	A1-A2	Northfield Road	A4
Castle Street	A2-B2	Orts Road	D2
Castle Hill	A1	Oxford Road	A2
Chain Street	B2	Pell Street	B1
Chatham Street	A3	Queen Victoria Street	B3
Cheapside	A2-A3	Queens Road	C2-D2
Coley Hill	A1	Redlands Road	D1
Coley Park Road	A1	Rose Walk	B2
Coley Place	A1	Ross Road	A4
Craven Road	D1	St Giles Close	B1-C1
Cross Street	B3	St Johns Road	D2
Crossland Road	B1-C2	St Mary's Butts	B2
Crown Street	C1	Sherman Road	B1
Deansgate Road	B1	Sidmouth Street	C2-C1
Duke Street	C2	Silver Street	C1
East Street	C1-C2	Simmonds Street	B2
Eaton Place	A2-A3	South Street	C2-D2
Eldon Road	D2	Southampton Street	B1-C1
Eldon Terrace	D2	Stanshawe Road	A3
Field Road	A1	Station Road	B3
Fobney Street	B1-B2	Swan Place	B1-B2
Forbury Road	B3-C3	Swansea Road	A4
Friar Street	A3-B3	The Grove	D2
Garnet Hill	A1	Tudor Road	A3-B3
Garnet Street	A1	Union Street	B3
Garrard Street	B3	Upper Brook Street	B1
Gas Works Road	D2-D3	Valpy Street	B3-C3
George Street	C4	Vastern Road	B4
Great Knollys Street	A3	Watlington Street	D1-D2
Greyfriars Road	A3	Waylen Street	A2
Gun Street	B2	Weldale Street	A3
Henry Street	B1	West Street	A3-B2
Hill Street	B1	Wolseley Street	A1
Howard Street	A2	York Road	A4
Jesse Terrace	A1-A2	Zinzan Street	A2

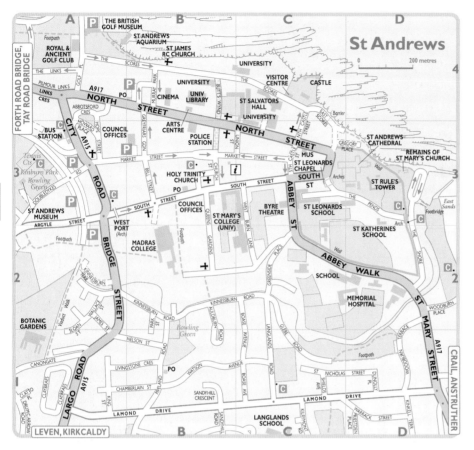

220

St Andrews

St Andrews is found on atlas page 141 E1

Abbey Street	C2-C3	St Nicholas Street	C1-D1
Abbey Walk	C2-D2	Sandyhill Crescent	B1
Abbotsford Crescent	A4	Sandyhill Road	B1
Argyle Street	A2-A3	Shields Avenue	C1
Auldburn Road	B1-B2	Sloan Street	A1-A2
Bell Street	B3	South Castle Street	C3
Boase Avenue	C1-C2	South Street	A3-B3-C3
Bridge Street	A1-A2-A3	The Links	A4
Butts Wynd	B4	The Pends	C3-D3
Canongate	A1	The Scores	A4-B4-C4
Chamberlain Street	A1-B1	The Shore	D2-D3
Church Street	B3	Union Street	B3-C3
City Road	A3-A4	Wallace Street	A2
Clatto Place	A1	Warrack Street	C1-D1
Claybraes	A1	Watson Avenue	B1-C1
Doubledykes Road	A3	West Burn Lane	C2-C3
Drumcarrow Road	A1	Woodburn Place	D2
Dunolly Place	D1	Woodburn Terrace	D1-D2
East Scores	C3-C4		
Glebe Road	C1-C2		
Golf Place	A4		
Greenside Place	C2		
Gregory Place	C3-D3		
Greyfriars Garden	B3-B4		
Hope Street	A3-A4		
Howard Place	A3-A4		
James Street	A1-A2		
Kilrymont Road	C1		
King Street	A1		
Kinkell Terrace	D1		
Kinnessburn Road	A2-B2-C2		
Kinnessburn Terrace	A2		
Lamond Drive	A1-B1-C1-D1		
Langlands Road	C1-C2		
Largo Road	A1		
Links Crescent	A4		
Livingstone Crescent	A1-B1		
Market Street	A3-B3-C3		
Murray Park	B4		
Nelson Street	A1-B1		
North Castle Street	C3-C4		
North Street	A4-B4-B3-C3		
Park Street	B1-B2		
Pilmour Links	A4		
Pipeland Road	B1-B2		
Priestden Place	D1		
Queens Gardens	B2-B3		
St Mary Street	D1-D2		

Scarborough

Scarborough is found on atlas page 99 F4

Aberdeen Walk	A2-B2	Peasholm Crescent	A3-A4
Albermarle Crescent	A1-A2	Peasholm Drive	A4
Albert Road	B3-B4	Princess Street	C3
Alma Square	A1-A2	Prospect Road	A2
Auborough Street	B3	Quay Street	D2
Bar Street	B2	Queen Street	B2-B3
Barwick Street	A1-A2	Queens Parade	A4-B4-B3
Bedford Street	B2	Queens Terrace	B3
Bellevue Parade	A1	Ramshill Road	B1
Bellevue Street	A1	Rutland Terrace	B3-C3
Brook Street	A2	St Mary's Street	C3
Cambridge Street	A2	St Marys Walk	C3
Castle Road	A2-B2-B3-C3	St Nicholas Street	B1-B2
Castlegate	C3-D3	St Sepulchre Street	C2-C3
Church Lane	C3	St Thomas Street	B2-B3
Clark Street	B3	Sandringham Street	A3-B3
Cliff Bridge Terrace	B1	Sandside	C2-D2
Columbus Ravine	A3-A4	Sherwood Street	A1
Cooks Row	C3	Somerset Terrace	A1-B1
Cross Street	B3-B2-C2	Springfield	C2-C3
Dean Road	A2-A3	Sussex Street	B2
Durham Street	A3-B3	Tennyson Avenue	A3-A4
Eastborough	C2	The Crescent	B1
Elders Street	B2	Tindall Street	A1
Falconer's Road	A1	Tollergate	B3-C3
Falsgrave Road	B1-C1-C2	Trafalgar Road	A3-A4
Foreshore Road	B1-C1-C2	Trafalgar Square	A3-B3
Friargate	C2-C3	Trafalgar Street West	A2-A3
Friars Way	B3	Union Street	A2-B2
Graham Close	C3	Valley Bridge Road	A1-B1
Hanover Road	A1	Valley Road	A1
Hope Street	B3	Vernon Road	B1-B2
Hoxton Road	A2	Victoria Park	A4
James Street	A3-B3	Victoria Park Avenue	A4
King Street	B2	Victoria Road	A1-A2
Langdale Road	A3	Victoria Street	A2
Longwestgate	B3-C3	Vine Street	A2
Marlborough Street	B3	Westborough	B1-B2
Melrose Street	A2	Woodall Avenue	A4
Moorland Road	A3-A4	Wrea Lane	A3
Nelson Street	A2	York Place	B1
New Queen Street	B3		
Newborough	B2-C2		
North Marine Road	A4-B4-B3		
North Street	B2-B3		
North Way	A2		
Oxford Street	A3-B2		
Paradise	C3		

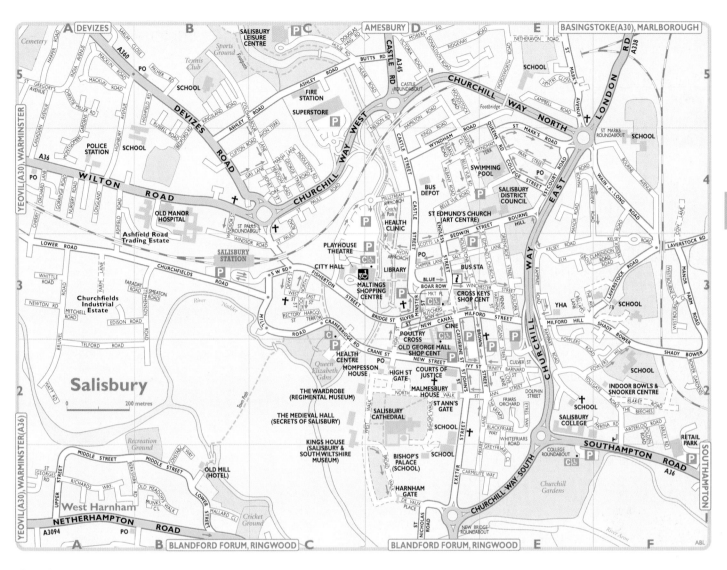

Salisbury

Salisbury is found on atlas page **25 G2**

Albany Road	D4	Churchill Way South	D1-E1	Gorringe Road	A4
Ashfield Road	A3-A4	Churchill Way West	C4-C5-D5	Greencroft Street	E3-E4
Ashley Road	B4-B5-C5	Clarendon Road	E3-F3	Greyfriars Close	E1
Avon Approach	D3	Clifton Road	B4-C4	Guilder Street	E3
Avon Terrace	C4-C5	Coldharbour Lane	B5-C4	Hamilton Road	D4-D5
Barnard Street	E2	College Street	E4	Harcourt Terrace	C3
Bedford Road	B4	Constable Way	B1	Harper Road	A5
Bedwin Street	D3-D4-E4	Cow Lane	F3-F4	High Street	D2-D3
Bellamy Lane	E3	Crane Street	D2	Highbury Avenue	A4-A5
Belle Vue Road	D4	Cranebridge Road	C2-C3	Highfield Road	B5
Berkshire Road	A1-B1	Culver Street	E2	Hulse Road	C5-D5
Bishops Walk	D1-D2	De Vaux Place	D1	India Avenue	A5
Blackfriars Way	E2	Devizes Road	A5-B5-B4-C4	Ivy Street	D2
Blakey Road	F2	Dews Street	C3	Kelsey Road	E3-F3
Blue Boar Row	D3	Dolphin Street	E2	Kings Road	D4-D5
Bourne Avenue	F4	Donaldson Road	D5-E5	Kingsland Road	B5
Bourne Hill	E4	Douglas Haig Road	C5-D5	Laverstock Road	F3
Bower Gardens	F2	East Street	C3	London Road	E4-F5
Bridge Street	D3	Edison Road	A3-B3	Longland	A4
Broad Walk	D1	Elm Grove Road	E3-F3	Love Lane	E2
Brown Street	D3-E2	Endless Street	D3-D4	Lower Road	A3
Brunel Road	A2-A3	Estcourt Road	E4	Lower Street	B1
Butchers Row	D3	Exeter Street	D1-D2	Macklin Road	A5
Butts Road	C5-D5	Eyres Way	E2	Mallard Close	B1
Campbell Road	E5	Fairview Road	E4-E3-F3	Manor Farm Road	F3
Canadian Avenue	A4-A5	Faraday Road	A3-B3	Manor Road	E3-E4
Carmelite Way	D1-E1	Farley Road	F1-F2	Marina Road	F2
Castle Road	D5	Farm Lane	A3	Marsh Lane	C4
Castle Street	D3-D4-D5	Fisherton Street	C3	Meadow Road	C4
Catherine Street	D2-D3	Fowlers Hill	E2-F2	Middle Street	A1-B1
Cherry Orchard Lane	A3-A4	Fowlers Road	E3-E2-F2	Middleton Road	C4
Chipper Lane	D3	Friars Orchard	E2	Milford Lane	E3
Christie Miller Road	A5	Friary Lane	D1-E1-E2	Milford Street	D3-E3
Churchfields Road	B3-C3	Gas Lane	B4-C4	Mill Road	C3
Churchill Way East	E2-E3-E4	George Street	C4	Millstream Approach	D4
Churchill Way North	D5-E5-E4	Gigant Street	E2-E3	Minster Street	D3

Mitchell Road	A3	Shady Bower	F2-F3
Moberly Road	D5	Sidney Street	C4
Montgomery Gardens	A4-A5	Silver Street	D3
Munks Close	B1	Smeaton Road	B3
Nelson Road	D4-D5	South Street	C3
Netheravon Road	E5	South West Road	C3
Netherhampton Road	A1-B1	Southampton Road	E2-E1-F1
New Canal	D3	Stephenson Road	B2-B3
New Street	D2	Swaynes Close	D4
Newton Road	A3	Telford Road	A2-B2
North Street	C3	The Avenue	E3
North Walk	D2	The Beeches	F2
Nursery Road	A4	The Friary	E2
Old Meadows Walk	B1	Tollgate Road	E2-F2-F1
Palmer Road	B5	Trinity Street	E2
Park Street	E4	Upper Street	A1
Pennyfarthing Street	E3	Ventry Close	E5
Polden Road	F1-F2	Victoria Road	D5
Queens Road	E4	Wain a Long Road	F3-F4
Rampart Road	E2-E3	Waterloo Road	F2
Rectory Road	C3	Watt Road	A2
Richards Way	A1	Wessex Road	F3-F4
Ridgeway Road	D5-E5	West Street	C3
Rollerstone Street	D3	West Walk	D1-D2
Russell Road	B4-B5	Westbourne Close	F3
St Ann Street	D2-E2	Whitefriars Road	E1-E2
St Edmund's Church Street	E3	Whittle Road	A3
St Georges Road	A1	Wilton Road	A4-B4-C4
St Gregory's Avenue	A5	Winchester Street	D3-E3
St John's Street	D2	Windsor Road	B3-C3
St Mark's Avenue	E4	Windsor Road	B3-B4
St Mary's Road	E4	Woodstock Road	D5
St Nicholas Road	D1	Wordsworth Road	E5
St Pauls Road	C3-C4	Wyndham Road	D4-E5
Salt Lane	D3-E3	Wyndham Terrace	D4-E4
Scotts Lane	D3	York Road	C4

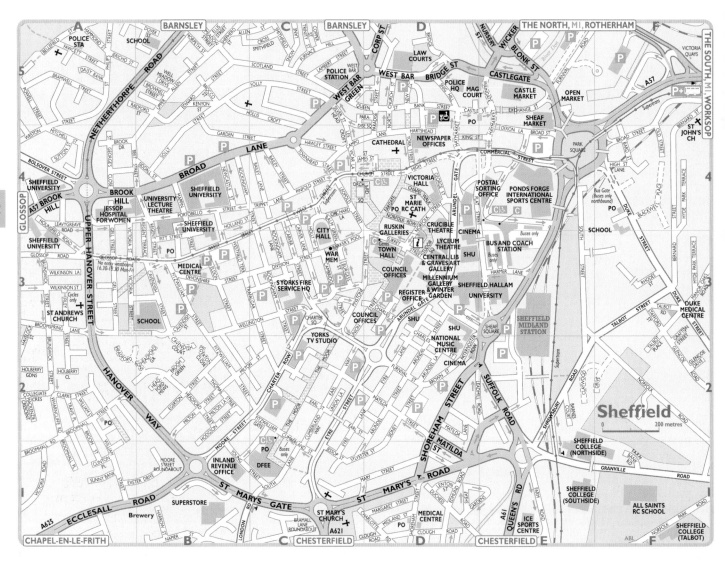

Sheffield

Sheffield is found on atlas page **84 A3**

Allen Street	B5-C5	Carver Lane	C3-C4	Egerton Street	B2	Holberry Close	A2	Nursery Street	D5-E5	Suffolk Road	E2
Arundel Gate	D2-D3-D4	Carver Street	C3-C4	Eldon Street	B3	Holberry Gardens	A2	Old Street	F4	Sunny Bank	A1
Arundel Lane	D2	Castle Street	D5-E5	Ellis Street	B5	Holland Street	B4	Orchard Lane	C4	Surrey Street	D3
Arundel Street	C1-D1-D2-D3	Castlegate	E5	Exchange Street	E5	Hollis Croft	B5-C5	Orchard Square	C4-D4	Sutton Street	A4
Bailey Lane	C4	Cavendish Court	B2	Exeter Drive	A1-B1	Holly Street	C3-C4	Paradise Square	C5-D5	Sylvester Street	C1-D1
Bailey Street	C4	Cavendish Street	B3	Eyre Lane	C1-C2-D2-D3	Hounsfield Road	A3-A4	Paradise Street	D4-D5	Talbot Place	F2-F3
Balm Green	C3-C4	Chapel Walk	D4	Eyre Street	C1-C2-D2	Hyde Park Terrace	F3, F3-F4	Park Square	E4-F4	Talbot Road	F3
Bank Street	D5	Charles Street	D2-D3	Fargate	D4	Jericho Street	A5-B5	Paternoster Row	D2	Talbot Street	F3
Bard Street	F4	Charlotte Road	C1-D1	Farm Bank Road	F1	Jessop Street	C1	Pinfold Street	C4	The Moor	C2
Barker's Pool	C3	Charter Row	C2-C3	Farm Road	E1	Kenyon Street	B5	Pinstone Street	C3-D3	Thomas Street	B2
Barnes Court	E2	Charter Square	C3	Fawcett Street	A5	King Street	D4-E4	Pitt Street	B3	Townhead Street	C4
Beet Street	A4-B4	Church Street	C4-D4	Filey Street	A2-A3	Lambert Street	C5	Portobello Street	A4-B4	Trafalgar Street	B3-C3-C2
Bellefield Street	A5	Clarke Street	A2	Fitzwilliam Gate	C2	Leadmill Road	D2-E2	Powell Street	A5	Travis Place	A2
Bernard Street	F3-F4-F5	Claywood Drive	E2-F2	Fitzwilliam Street	B3-B2-C2	Leavygreave Road	A4	Queen Street	C5-D5	Trinity Street	C5
Blackwell Place	F4	Clinton Place	A1	Flat Street	D4-E3	Lee Croft	C4	Queen's Road	E1	Trippet Lane	C4
Blonk Street	E5	Clough Road	C1-D1	Furnace Hill	C5	Lenton Street	D1	Radford Street	A5-B5	Tudor Square	D3-D4
Bolsover Street	A4	Collegiate Crescent	A2	Furnival Road	E5-F5	Leopold Street	C4	Regent Street	B3-B4	Union Lane	C2
Bramwell Street	A5	Commercial Street	E4	Furnival Street	D2	London Road	B1-C1	Regent Terrace	B3-B4	Union Street	C3-D3
Bridge Street	D5	Copper Street	C5	Garden Street	B5-B4-C4	Mackenzie Crescent	A2	Rhodes Street	F3	Upper Allen Street	B4-B5
Broad Lane	B4-C4	Corporation Street	D5	Gell Street	A3-A4	Manor Oaks Road	F3	Rockingham Lane	C3-C4	Upper Hanover Street	A3-A4
Broad Street	E4, F4-F5	Cross Smithfield	B5-C5	George Street	D4	Mappin Street	B3-B4	Rockingham Street	B4-C4-C3-C2	Vicar Lane	C4
Brocco Street	B5	Cumberland Street	C1-C2	Glencoe Drive	F2	Margaret Street	D2	St George's Close	A4	Victoria Road	A1
Brook Drive	A4	Cumberland Way	C1-C2	Glencoe Road	F2	Mary Street	C1-D1	St James Street	C4-D4	Victoria Street	A3-A4
Brook Hill	A4	Daisy Bank	A5	Glossop Road	A3-B3	Matilda Lane	D2	St Marys Gate	B1-C1	Waingate	E5
Broom Green	B2	Devonshire Street	B3	Grafton Street	F2-F3	Matilda Street	C2-D2-D1	St Mary's Road	C1-D1	Well Meadow Drive	B5
Broom Street	A1-A2	Division Street	C3	Granville Road	E1-F1	Meadow Street	B5	St Philip's Road	A5	Wellington Street	B3-C4
Broomhall Place	A1	Dixon Lane	E4	Hammond Street	A5	Midland Street	D1	Scotland Street	B5-C5	West Bar	D5
Broomhall Road	A1-A2	Dover Street	A5-B5	Hanover Way	A2-B2-B1	Milton Lane	B2	Sheaf Gardens	D1-E1	West Bar Green	C5
Broomhall Street	A2	Duchess Road	D1-E1	Harmer Lane	E3	Milton Street	B2-C2	Shepherd Street	B5	West Street	B3-C4
Broomspring Lane	A3	Duke Street	F2-F3-F4	Harrow Street	B1	Mitchell Street	A4	Shoreham Street	D1-D2	Westfield Terrace	B3
Brown Street	D2	Earl Street	C2-D2	Hartshead	D4	Moore Street	B1-B2-C2	Shrewsbury Road	E2	Weston Street	A4-A5
Brownell Street	B5	Earl Way	C2	Havelock Street	A2-A3	Morpeth Street	B5	Siddall Street	B4	Wharncliffe Road	A2
Brunswick Street	A2-A3	Ecclesall Road	A1-B1	Hawley Street	C4	Napier Street	A1	Sidney Street	D2	Wilkinson Lane	A3
Burgess Street	C3	Edmund Road	D1	Haymarket	D4-D5, E4-E5	Netherthorpe Road	A4-A5-B5	Silver Street Head	C5	Wilkinson Street	A3
Cambridge Street	C3	Edward Street	B5	Headford Gardens	A2-B2	New Street	D5	Smithfield	C5	William Street	A1-A2
Campo Lane	C4-D4	Egerton Close	B2	Headford Grove	B2	Newcastle Street	B4	Snig Hill	D5	York Street	D4
				Headford Mews	B2	Norfolk Park Road	F1	Snow Lane	C5	Young Street	B1-C1
				Headford Street	B2	Norfolk Road	F2	Solly Street	B4-B5-C5		
				High Street	D4	Norfolk Row	D4	South Lane	C1		
				High Street Lane	F4	Norfolk Street	D3-D4	South Street	E3-E4		
				Hodgson Street	B1-B2	North Church Street	D4-D5	Stafford Street	F3		

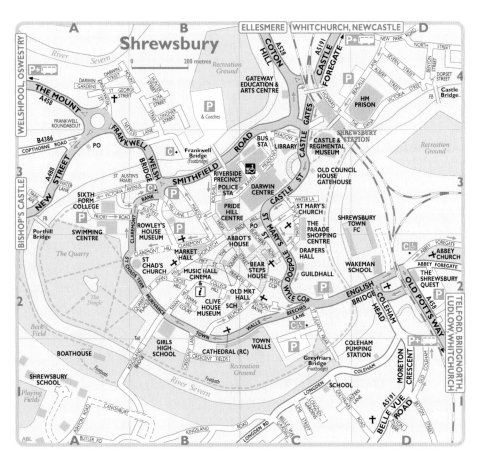

Shrewsbury

Shrewsbury is found on atlas page **69 G1**

Abbey Foregate	D2	Mardol	B3
Albert Street	D4	Market Street	B2
Alma Street	B4	Meadow Place	C3
Alton Terrace	D1	Moreton Crescent	D1
Ashton Road	A1	Mount Street	A4-B4
Beacalls Lane	C4-D4	Murivance	B2
Beeches Lane	C2	Nettles Lane	A4-B3-B4
Belle Vue Gardens	C1	New Park Road	D4
Belle Vue Road	D1	New Street	A3
Belmont	B2-C2	North Street	D4
Belmont Bank	C2	Old Coleham	D1
Benyon Street	D4	Old Potts Way	D1-D2
Betton Street	D1	Park Avenue	A3
Butchers Row	C2-C3	Pride Hill	B3-C3
Butler Road	A1	Princess Street	B2-C2
Canonbury	A1-B1	Priory Road	A3-B3
Castle Foregate	C4	Quarry Place	B2
Castle Gates	C3-C4	Raven Meadows	B3-C3
Castle Street	C3	Roushill	B3
Claremont Bank	B2-B3	St Austin's Friars	A3
Claremont Hill	B2	St Austin's Street	B3
Claremont Street	B2	St Chads Terrace	B2
Coleham Head	D2	St George Street	A4-B4
College Hill	B2	St John's Hill	B2
Copthorne Road	A3	St Julian's Friar	C1-C2
Coton Hill	C4	St Mary's Place	C2-C3
Crescent Fields	B1	St Mary's Street	C2-C3
Crescent Lane	B1-B2	Salters Lane	C1-D1
Cross Hill	B2	Severn Street	D4
Darwin Gardens	A4	Shoplatch	B2
Darwin Street	A4	Smithfield Road	B3-C3-C4
Dogpole	C2	Swan Hill	B2
Dorset Street	D4	Swan Hill Court	B2
Drinkwater Street	A4	The Dana	C4-D4
English Bridge	C2-D2	The Mount	A4
Frankwell	A4-A3-B3	The Square	B2
Greyfriars Road	C1-D1	Town Walls	B2-B1-C2
High Street	B3-B2-C2	Victoria Avenue	A3-B3
Hill Lane	B3	Victoria Street	D4
Howard Street	C4	Water Lane	A3
Hunter Street	B4	Water Lane	C3
Kingsland Bridge	A1-B1-B2	Welsh Bridge	B3
Kingsland Road	B1-C1	Wyle Cop	C2
Lime Street	C1		
Longden Coleham	C1-D1		
Longden Gardens	C1		
Longden Road	B1-C1		
Longner Street	B4		

223

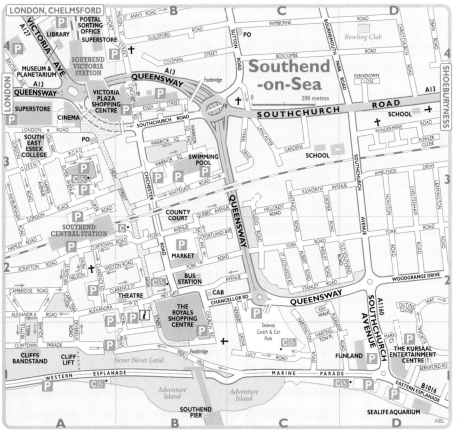

Southend-on-Sea

Southend-on-Sea is found on atlas page **30 B5**

Albert Road	C2	London Road	A3
Alexandra Road	A2	Lucy Road	C1
Alexandra Street	A2-B2	Luker Road	A3
Ambleside Drive	D3	Marine Parade	C1-D1
Ash Walk	C2	Marks Court	D1
Ashburnham Road	A2-A3	Milton Street	B4
Baltic Avenue	B2	Napier Avenue	A3
Baxter Avenue	A4	Nelson Mews	A2
Beresford Road	D1	Nelson Street	A2
Boscombe Road	C4-D4	Oban Road	D4
Bournemouth Park Road	C4-D4	Old Southend Road	D2
Cambridge Road	A2	Outing Close	D2
Capel Terrace	A2	Pier Hill	B1-C1
Chancellor Road	B2-C2	Pleasant Road	C2-C1-D1
Cheltenham Road	D2-D3	Portland Avenue	B2-C2
Chichester Road	B2-B3-B4	Prittlewell Square	A1-A2
Christchurch Road	D4	Quebec Avenue	B3-C3
Church Road	B1-B2	Queen's Road	A3
Clarence Road	A2	Queensway	A4-B4-C2-D2
Clarence Street	A2-B2	Royal Mews	B1
Clifftown Parade	A1	St Ann's Road	B4
Clifftown Road	A2-B2	St Leonards Road	C2
Coleman Street	B4-C4	Scratton Road	A2
College Way	A3	Short Street	A4-B4
Cromer Road	C2-C3	Southchurch Avenue	D1-D2-D3
Devereux Road	A1-A2	Southchurch Road	B3-C3-C4-D4
Elmer Avenue	A3	Stanley Road	C2-D2
Eastern Esplanade	D1	Sutton Road	C4
Essex Street	B4	Toledo Road	C2-C3
Ferndown Close	D4	Tylers Avenue	B2
Fowler Close	D3	Tyrrel Drive	C3
Gordon Place	A2-A3	Victoria Avenue	A4
Gordon Road	A3	Warrior Square East	B3
Great Eastern Avenue	A4	Warrior Square	B3
Guildford Road	B4	Wesley Road	C2
Hamlet Road	A2	Western Esplanade	A1-B1
Hartington Place	C1	Weston Road	A2-B2
Hartington Road	C1-C2	Whitegate Road	B3
Hastings Road	C2-C3	Wimborne Road	C4-D4
Herbert Grove	C1-C2	Windermere Road	D3
Heygate Avenue	B2-C2	Woodgrange Drive	D2
High Street	A3-B3-B2-B1	York Road	B2-C2-D2
Hillcrest Road	C3		
Honiton Road	D2-D3		
Kilworth Avenue	C3-D3		
Kursaal Way	D1-D2		
Lancaster Gardens	C3		
Leamington Road	D2-D3		

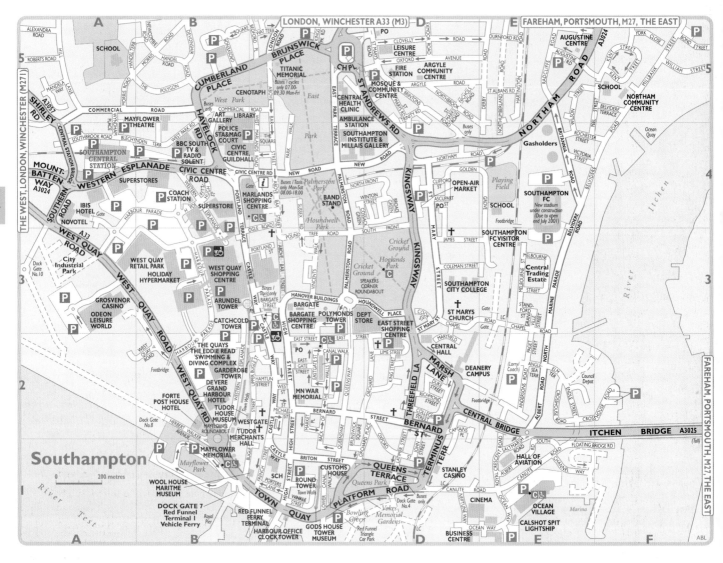

Southampton

Southampton is found on atlas page **14 B5**

Above Bar Street	C3-C4-C5	Coleman Street	D3-E3	John Street	D1-D2	Platform Road	C1-D1	West Park Road	B4-B5
Albert Road North	E2	College Street	D2	Kent Street	F5	Porters Lane	C1	West Quay Road	A4-A3-B3-B2
Albert Road South	E1-E2	Commercial Road	A5-B5-C5	King Street	D2	Portland Street	C3	West Street	C2
Alexandra Road	A5	Cook Street	D3	Kings Park Road	C5	Portland Terrace	B3-B4	Western Esplanade	A4-B4, B2-B3
Andersons Road	E2	Cossack Green	C4-D4	Kingsway	D3-D4	Pound Tree Road	C3	William Street	F5
Anglesea Terrace	E2	Crosshouse Road	E2-F2	Latimer Street	D1-D2	Queens Terrace	D1	Wilson Street	E4-E5
Argyle Road	D5-E5	Cumberland Place	B5-C5	Lime Street	D2	Queensway	C1-C2	Winkle Street	C1
Ascupart Street	D4	Derby Road	E4-E5	London Road	C5	Radcliffe Road	E5	Winton Street	C4-D4
Augustine Road	E5	Devonshire Road	B5	Lower Canal Walk	C1	Richmond Street	D2	Wyndham Place	A4-A5
Back of the Walls	C1-C2	Duke Street	D2	Mandela Way	A5	Rochester Street	E4-F4	York Close	F5
Bargate Street	C3	Durnford Road	E5	Marine Parade	E3	Roberts Road	A5	
Bedford Place	C5	East Park Terrace	C4-C5	Market Place	C2	Royal Crescent Road	E1-E2	
Belvidere Road	E3-E4-F4-F5	East Street	C2-D2-D3	Marsh Lane	D2	St Albans Road	E5	
Belvidere Terrace	F5	Eastgate Street	C2	Maryfield	D2	St Andrews Road	C5-D5-D4	
Bernard Street	C2-D2	Elm Terrace	E2	Melbourne Street	E3	St Marks Road	D5	
Blechynden Terrace	A4-B4	Endle Street	E2	Millbank Street	F5	St Mary Street	D3-D4	
Bond Street	F5	Exmoor Road	D5	Morris Road	A5-B5	St Marys Road	D5	
Brintons Road	D4-D5	Fitzhugh Street	B4	Mountbatten Way	A4	St Michaels Street	C2	
Britannia Road	E4-E5	Floating Bridge Road	E1-F1	Neptune Way	D1	Saltmarsh Road	E1-E2	
Briton Street	C1	French Street	C1	New Road	C4-D4	Shirley Road	A4-A5	
Broad Green	D4	Golden Grove	D4-E4-E3	Newcombe Road	B5	South Front	C3-D3-D4	
Brunswick Place	C5	Granville Street	E3	Nichols Road	D5	Southbrook Road	A4	
Brunswick Square	C1-C2	Grosvenor Square	B5	North Front	C4-D4	Southern Road	A4	
Bugle Street	B1-C2	Hamtun Street	C2	Northam Road	D4-E4-E5-F5	Standford Street	E3	
Canal Walk	C2	Handel Road	B5	Northbrook Road	D5	Sussex Road	C4	
Canute Road	D1-E1	Handel Terrace	A5-B5	Northumberland Road	E4-E5	Terminus Terrace	D1-D2	
Captains Place	D2	Hanover Buildings	C3	Ocean Way	D1-E1	The Polygon	B5	
Castle Way	B3-C3-C2-C1	Harbour Parade	A4-B4-B3-B2	Ogle Road	B3-C4	The Square	C4	
Central Bridge	D2-E2	Hartington Road	E5	Orchard Lane	C2-D2	Threefield Lane	D2	
Central Station Bridge	A4	Havelock Road	B4-B5	Orchard Place	C1-D1-D2	Town Quay	B1-C1	
Channel Way	E1	Herbert Walker Avenue	B2	Oxford Avenue	D5-E5	Trinity Road	D5	
Chapel Road	D3-E3	High Street	C1-C2-C3	Oxford Street	D1-D2	Upper Bugle Street	C2	
Charlotte Place	C5	Hill Lane	A5	Paget Street	E2-E3	Victoria Street	E4	
Civic Centre Road	B4-C4	Houndwell Place	C3-D3	Palmerston Road	C3-C4	Vincents Walk	C3	
Clifford Street	D4	Itchen Bridge	E2-F2	Park Walk	C4-C5	Waterloo Terrace	C5	
Clovelly Road	D5-E5	James Street	D3-E3	Peel Street	E4-F5	West Marlands Road	C4-C5	

Stirling

Stirling is found on atlas page **130 D4**

Abbey Road	D3	Rosebery Terrace	C3-D3
Abbotsford Place	D4	Royal Gardens	A2
Abercromby Place	B1	St John Street	B2
Albert Place	A2-B2	St Mary's Wynd	B2-B3
Alexandra Place	D4	Seaforth Place	C2-C3
Allan Park	B1-C1	Shiphaugh Place	D4
Argyll Avenue	D3-D4	Spittal Street	B2-C2
Back O' Hill Road	A4-B4	Springbank Road	D1
Baker Street	B2-C2	Sutherland Avenue	D4
Ballengeich Road	A4-A3-B3	Union Street	B4-C4
Barn Road	B3	Upper Bridge Street	B3-B4
Barnton Street	C2-C3	Upper Craigs	C1
Bayne Street	B4	Victoria Place	A2-B2
Bow Street	B2	Victoria Road	B2
Broad Street	B2-B3	Victoria Square	A1-B1
Bruce Street	B4-C4	Wallace Street	C3-C4
Burghmuir Road	C4-C2-D1	Waverley Crescent	D4
Clarendon Place	B1-B2	Well Green	C1
Cowane Street	B4-B3-C3	Windsor Place	B1
Dean Crescent	C4-D4		
Douglas Street	B3-C4		
Duff Crescent	A4		
Dumbarton Road	B1-C1		
Edward Avenue	D4		
Edward Road	C4		
Esplanade	A3-B3		
Forest Road	D3-D4		
Forth Crescent	C3-D3		
Forth Street	C3-C4		
Friars Street	C2		
Glebe Avenue	B1		
Glendevon Road	A4		
Harvey Wynd	B3-B4		
Irvine Place	B3-C2		
James Street	C3-C4		
King Street	C2		
Lower Bridge Street	B4		
Lower Castle Hill	B3		
Maxwell Place	C2-C3		
Millar Place	D3-D4		
Morris Terrace	B2		
Murray Place	C2		
Park Avenue	B1-C1		
Port Street	C1		
Princes Street	B3-B2-C2		
Queen Street	B3-C3		
Queenshaugh Drive	D4		
Queen's Road	A1-A2		

225

Stockton-on-Tees

Stockton-on-Tees is found on atlas page **106 D3**

Allison Street	B4	Outram Street	A1
Alma Street	B4	Oxbridge Lane	A1
Bath Lane	B4-C4	Palmerston Street	A3
Bedford Street	A4	Park Road	A1
Bishop Street	B3-C3	Parkfield Road	B1
Bishopton Lane	A4-B4	Parkfield Way	B1
Bishopton Road	A4	Parliament Street	A1-B1
Boathouse Lane	C1	Petch Street	A3
Bowesfield Lane	A1-B1	Phoenix Sidings	A4
Bridge Road	B1-B2	Portrack Lane	C4-D4
Bright Street	B3	Prince Regent Street	B2-B3
Brunswick Street	B2	Princess Avenue	B4-C4
Buchanan Street	A1-A2	Princeton Drive	D1
Chalk Close	B1	Radcliffe Crescent	D1-D2
Chapel Street	B3	Riverside	B1-C1-C2-C3
Church Road	B3-C3-C4-D4	Russell Street	B3
Claremont Court	D1	Ryan Avenue	C4
Clarence Row	C4	St Bernard Road	A2
Columbia Drive	C2-C3	St Johns Close	A4-B4
Commercial Street	C3	Shaftesbury Street	A1
Corporation Street	A3-A4	Silver Street	B3
Council of Europe Boulevard	C2-C3	Skinner Street	B2
Cromwell Avenue	B4-C4	Smith Street	B3-B4
Derby Street	A3	Stamp Street	A3-A4
Dixon Street	A3	Stanford Close	D1
Dovecot Street	A2-B2-B3	Station Street	D1
Durham Road	A4	Sydney Street	A3-B3
Durham Street	A4	Tarring Street	A2-A3
Edward Street	A1	The Square	B3-C3
Egglestone Terrace	A2	Thistle Green	B3-C3
Ewbank Drive	A2	Tower Street	B2-C2
Finkle Street	B2	Union Street East	C4
Frederick Street	B4	University Boulevard	C2-D2
Fudan Way	D2	Vasser Way	C2
Garbutt Street	B4-C4	Vicarage Avenue	A4
Hartington Road	A2-B2	Vicarage Street	A4
Harvard Avenue	D1-D2	Wade Avenue	C4
High Street	B2-B3-B4	Webster Street	A2
Hume Street	B4	Wellington Street	A3-B3
Hutchison Street	A3	West Row	B2-B3
Lawrence Street	A1	Westbourne Street	A1
Limeoak Way	D4	Westpoint Road	C2-D2
Mandale Road	D1	William Street	B2
Maritime Road	C4	Woodland Street	A1
Massey Road	D2-D3	Worthing Street	A2
Melbourne Street	A3	Yale Crescent	C1-D1-D2
Mill Street West	A3-B3	Yarm Lane	A1-B2
Norton Road	B4	Yarm Road	A1

226

Stoke-on-Trent (Hanley)

Stoke-on-Trent (Hanley) is found on atlas page **70 D5**

Albion Street	B2	Lower Bethesda Street	B1-C1
Bagnall Street	B2	Lower Foundry Street	B3
Balfour Street	D2	Lower Mayer Street	D4
Baskerville Street	D3-D4	Lowther Street	A4
Berkeley Street	C1	Margill Close	A1
Bethesda Street	B1-B2	Market Lane	B3-C3
Birch Terrace	C2	Market Square	C3
Botteslow Street	C2-D1	Marsh Street North	B2-B3
Brewery Street	B4	Marsh Street South	C3
Broad Street	B2	Mayer Street	C4-D4
Broom Street	C4-D4	Meigh Street	C3
Brunswick Street	B2-B3	Morley Street	A2-B2
Bryan Street	B3-B4	Mynors Street	D3-D4
Bucknall New Road	C3-D3-D2	New Hall Street	B3
Bucknall Old Road	D3	Old Hall Street	C2-C3
Cannon Street	A1-B1	Old Town Road	C4
Century Street	A4-B3	Pall Mall	B2
Charles Street	C2	Parliament Row	B2
Cheapside	B2	Percy Street	B3-C3-C2
Clough Street	A2-B2	Piccadilly	B2-B3
Clyde Street	A1	Picton Street	D1-D2
Commercial Road	D1-D2	Portland Street	A4
Denbigh Street	A4	Potteries Way	B1-C2-C4-B4
Derby Street	C1-C2	Quadrant Road	B3-B4-C4
Dresden Street	D2	Regent Road	B1-C1
Eastwood Road	C1-D1	Robson Street	A1
Eaton Street	D3-D4	St Ann Street	D3
Etruria Road	A3	St John Street	D3-D4
Festing Street	C4-D4	Sampson Street	A4-B4
Foundry Street	B3	Slippery Lane	A1-A2
Fountain Square	B3-C3	Snow Hill	A1
Garth Street	C3	Stafford Street	B3-B2-C2
Gilman Street	C2-D2	Statham Street	A1-A2
Gitana Street	B2-B3	Sun Street	A1
Glass Street	C3	Talbot Street	C1
Goodson Street	C3	Tontine Street	C2-C3
Grafton Street	C3-C4	Town Road	C3-C4
Hanover Street	B4	Trinity Street	B3
Hillchurch Street	C3	Union Street	B4-C4
Hillcrest Street	C3-D3	Upper Hillchurch Street	C3-C4-D4
Hope Street	B3-B4	Upper Huntbach Street	C3-D3
Hordley Street	C2-D2	Vale Place	B4
Huntbach Street	C3	Warner Street	B1-B2
Jervis Street	D4	Waterloo Street	D2
John Bright Street	D4	Wellington Road	D2
John Street	B2-C2	Wells Street	C2-D2
Lamb Street	B3-C3	Yates Street	A1
Lichfield Street	C1-C2	York Street	B3-B4

Stratford-upon-Avon

Stratford-upon-Avon is found on atlas page **47 G5**

Albany Road	A3-A2-B2	New Street	B1
Alcester Road	A3-B3	Old Town	B2-B1-C1
Arden Street	B3-B4	Orchard Way	A1-A2
Avenue Road	C4	Payton Street	C3
Bancroft Place	D3	Percy Street	C4
Birmingham Road	B4	Rother Street	B2-B3
Bordon Place	A1	Rowley Crescent	D4
Brewery Street	B4	Ryland Street	B1
Bridge Foot	D3	St Andrew's Crescent	A2
Bridge Street	C3-D3	St Gregory's Road	C4-D4
Broad Street	B2	St Martin's Close	A2
Broad Walk	B1-B2	Sanctus Drive	B1
Brookvale Road	A1-A2	Sanctus Road	A1-B1
Bull Street	B1-B2	Sanctus Street	B1
Cedar Close	D4	Sandfield Road	A1
Chapel Lane	C2	Scholars Lane	B2-C2
Chapel Street	C2	Seven Meadows Road	A1-B1
Cherry Orchard	A1	Shakespeare Street	B4-C4
Cherry Street	B1	Sheep Street	C2
Chestnut Walk	B2	Shipston Road	D1-D2
Church Street	B2-C2	Shottery Road	A2
Clopton Bridge	D2-D3	Southern Lane	C1-C2
Clopton Court	B4	Station Road	A3
Clopton Road	B4	Swans Nest Lane	D2
College Lane	B1	The Willows	A2-A3
College Street	B1	The Willows North	A3
Ely Street	B2-C2	Tiddington Road	D2
Evesham Place	B2	Trinity Street	B1
Evesham Road	A1	Tyler Street	C3
Great Williams Street	C3-C4	Union Street	C3
Greenhill Street	B3	Warwick Court	C4
Grove Road	B2-B3	Warwick Crescent	D4
Guild Street	B3-C3	Warwick Road	D4
Henley Street	B3-C3	Waterside	C2-C3
High Street	C2-C3	Welcombe Road	D4
Holtom Street	B1	Wellesbourne Grove	A3-B3
John Street	C3	West Street	B1-B2
Kendall Avenue	B4-C4	Western Road	A4-B4
Lock Close	C3-C4	Windsor Street	B3
Maidenhead Road	C4	Wood Street	B3-C3
Mansell Street	B4		
Mayfield Avenue	C4		
Mayfield Court	C4		
Meer Street	B3-C3		
Mill Lane	C1		
Mulberry Street	C4		
Narrow Lane	B1		
New Broad Street	B1		

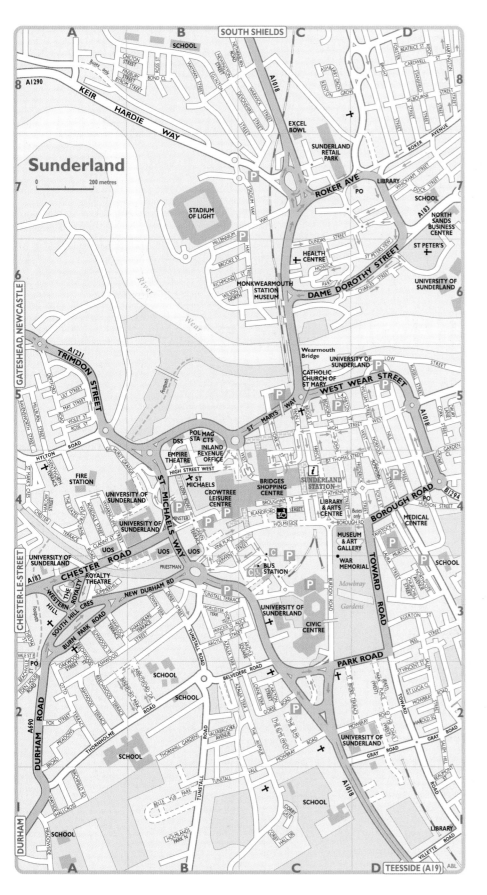

Sunderland

Sunderland is found on atlas page **115 F1**

Abbotsford Grove	B2	Park Place East	D2
Alice Street	B3-C3	Park Place West	D2
Argyle Square	C3	Park Road	C2-C3-D3
Ashberry Grove	C8	Peel Street	D3
Ashwood Street	A2-A3-B3	Princess Street	B3
Ashwood Terrace	A2	Ravensworth Street	A5
Athenaeum Street	C4-D4	Richmond Street	B6-C6
Azalea Terrace North	B2-B3	Ripon Street	D8
Azalea Terrace South	B2-C2	Roker Avenue	C7-D7-D8
Beachville Street	A2	Rose Street	A5
Beatrice Street	D8	Rosedale Street	A4
Beaumont Street	D1-D2	Ross Street	B8
Bedford Street	C5	Russell Street	D5
Beechwood Street	A2-A3	St Bedes Terrace	C2-D2
Beechwood Terrace	A2	St Lucia Close	D2
Belle Vue Park	B1	St Mark's Crescent	A4
Belvedere Road	B2-C2-C3	St Marys Way	C5
Beresford Park	A2-B2	St Michaels Way	B3-B4
Birchfield Road	A1	St Peters View	D6-D7
Blandford Street	C4	St Thomas Street	C4-C5
Bond Close	B8	St Vincent Street	D2-D3
Borough Road	C4-D4	Salem Hill	D1-D2
Bridge Street	C5	Salem Street	D2-D3
Bright Street	D7-D8	Selbourne Street	D8
Broad Meadows	A1-A2	Shakespeare Terrace	A3-B3
Brooke Street	B6-C6	Shallcross	A1
Brougham Street	C4	South Hill Crescent	A3
Burdon Road	C3-C4	Spring Garden Close	D4-D5
Burn Park Road	A3	Stadium Way	C7
Byrom Street	A8-B8	Stansfield Street	D8
Cardwell Street	D8	Summerhill	A3
Carlton Street	C2	Tavistock Place	D4
Charles Street	C6-D6	The Avenue	C2
Chester Road	A3-B4	The Elms	C2
Chester Terrace	A4	The Elms West	C2
Chilton Street	A8-B8	The Leazes	A4
Churchill Street	D3	The Oaks West	D2
Clanny Street	A4	The Royalty	A3
Corby Gate	C1	Thelma Street	A3
Corby Hall Drive	C1	Thornhill Gardens	B2
Cork Street	D5	Thornholme Road	A1-A2-B2
Dame Dorothy Street	C6-D6	Toward Road	D1-D2-D3-D4
Deptford Road	A5	Trimdon Street	A5-A6
Derby Street	B3	Tunstall Road	B1-B2-B3
Derwent Street	B3-B4-C4	Tunstall Terrace	B3-C3
Devonshire Street	B8-C8-C7	Tunstall Vale	B1-C1-C2
Dock Street	D7	Valerbrooke Road	B2
Drury Lane	D5	Villette Road	D1
Dundas Street	C6-C7-D7	Vine Place	B3-B4-C4
Durham Road	A1-A2-A3	Violet Street	A5
Eden House Road	A2	Warwick Street	C8
Edwin Terrace	B3	Wayman Street	B8
Egerton Street	D3	Wayside	A1
Eglinton Street	B8-C8-C7	Wentworth Terrace	A4
Elmwood Street	A3	West Street	C4-C5
Fawcett Street	C4-C5	West Sunniside	D4-D5
Finsbury Street	A8-B8	West Wear Street	C5-D5
Forster Street	D7-D8	Westbourne Road	A3-A4
Fox Street	A2	Western Hill	A3
Foyle Street	D4	Wharncliffe Street	A4
Frederick Street	D4	Whickham Street	D7
Gilhurst Grange	A5-A4-B4	William Street	D5
Gorse Road	C2	Wilson Street North	B6-C6
Gray Road	D2	Worcester Street	B3
Green Terrace	B4	Worcester Terrace	B3
Harlow Street	A4	Yale Street	A3
Harold Square	D2	York Street	C4-C5
Hartington Street	D8		
Havelock Terrace	A3		
Hay Street	C6-C7		
High Street West	B4, C5-D5		
Holmlands Park North	B1		
Holmside	C4		
Howick Park	C6		
Hudson Street	D4		
Hylton Road	A4-A5		
John Street	C4-C5		
Keir Hardie Way	A8-B8-B7		
Kenton Grove	C8		
Lambton Street	C5		
Laura Street	D3-D4		
Lily Street	A5		
Lorne Terrace	C2		
Low Row	B4		
Low Street	C5-D5		
May Street	A5		
Meadowside	A1		
Millburn Street	A5		
Millennium Way	B6-B7-C7		
Mowbray Road	C2-D2		
Murton Street	D3-D4		
Netherburn Road	B8-C8		
New Durham Road	A3-B3		
Newington Street	B8		
Nile Street	D4-D5		
Norfolk Street	D4-D5		
Northcote Avenue	D3		
Oakwood Street	A2-A3		
Otto Terrace	A2		
Pann Lane	C4-C5		

227

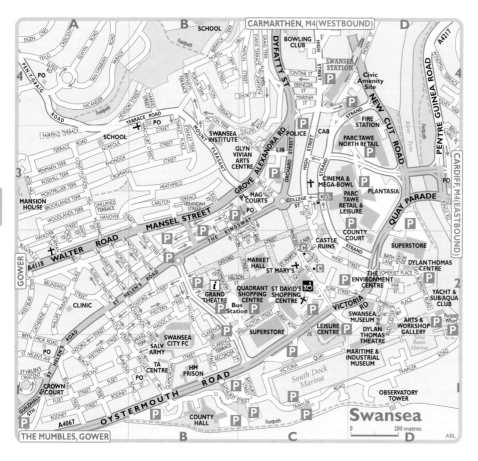

Swansea

Swansea is found on atlas page **34 D3**

Albert Row	C2	Nicander Parade	A4-B4
Alexandra Road	C3	Nicholl Street	A2-B2
Argyle Street	A2-A1-B1	Norfolk Street	A3-B3
Bath Lane	D2	North Hill	B4-C4
Bathurst Street	B1-C1	Orchard Street	C3
Beach Street	A1	Oxford Street	A1-B2-C2-C3
Belle Vue Way	C3	Oystermouth Road	A1-B1-C1
Bond Street	A1	Page Street	B2
Brooklands Terrace	A3	Pen y Graig Road	A3-A4
Brunswick Street	A2	Penmaen Terrace	A3
Bryn-y-Mor Road	A1	Pentre Guinea Road	D3-D4
Brynsyfi Terrace	B4	Phillips Parade	A1-A2
Burrows Road	A1-B1	Picton Terrace	B3-B4
Cambrian Place	D2	Pier Street	D2
Carlton Terrace	B3	Plymouth Street	B2
Castle Street	C3	Portland Street	C2-C3
Catherine Street	A1-A2	Portia Terrace	B4
Clifton Hill	C3	Princess Way	C2-C3
College Street	C3	Quay Parade	D3
Constitution Hill	A3	Rhondda Street	A3-B3
Cromwell Street	A3-B3	Richardson Street	A2-B2-B1
Duke Street	A2	Rodney Street	A1-B1
Dyfatty Street	C4	Rosehill Terrace	A3
East Burrows Road	D2	Russell Street	A2
Evans Terrace	C4	St Helen's Avenue	A1
Fairfield Terrace	A3	St Helen's Road	A1-A2-B1
Firm Street	B4	St Mary's Square	C2
Fleet Street	A1-B1	Somerset Place	D2
Fullers Row	B3-C3-C4	Stanley Place	B3-B4
George Street	A2-B2	Strand	D4-C3-C2-D2
Glamorgan Street	B1	Tan y Marian Road	A4
Graig Terrace	C4	Teilo Crescent	A4
Grove Place	C3	Terrace Road	A3-B4
Hanover Street	A2-A3-B3	The Kingsway	B2-C3
Harcourt Street	B3-B4	Tontine Street	C4
Heathfield	B3	Trawler Road	C1-D1
Henrietta Street	A2-B2	Union Street	B2-C2
Hewson Street	A4-B4	Victoria Quay	C1
High Street	C3-C4	Victoria Road	C2-D2
Hill Street	B4	Vincent Street	A1-B1
Islwyn Road	A4	Walter Road	A2-B2
Madoc Street	B2	Watkin Street	C4
Mansel Street	B2-B3	Wellington Street	B2-C2
Milton Terrace	B4	Western Street	A1-A2-B2
Montpellier Terrace	A3	William Street	B1-B2
Mount Pleasant	B4-B3	Wind Street	C2-D2
Nelson Street	B2-C2	Woodlands Terrace	A3
New Cut Road	D3-D4	York Street	C2-D2

Swindon

Swindon is found on atlas page **39 F3**

Albion Street	A1	Groundwell Road	C1-C2-D2
Alfred Street	C3	Havelock Street	B1-B2
Aylesbury Street	B3	Hawksworth Way	A3-A4
Bathampton Street	A2	Haydon Street	B3-C3
Bathurst Road	C3-D3	Henry Street	B2-B3
Beales Close	B3	Hunt Street	C1-D1
Beatrice Street	B4-C4	Islington Street	C2
Beckhampton Street	C2-D2	James Watt Close	A3
Belgrave Street	C1	King Street	B2
Bridge Street	B2-B3	Leicester Street	C2
Bristol Street	A2	Lincoln Street	C2
Broad Street	C3-D3	London Street	A2
Cambria Bridge Road	A1	Manchester Road	B3-C3-C4
Cambria Place	A1	Maxwell Street	A1-A2
Canal Walk	B2	Milton Road	A2-B2
Carfax Street	C3	Morley Street	B1-B2
Chester Street	A2	Morse Street	B1
Church Place	A2	Newcastle Street	D2-D3
Colbourne Street	D4	Newcombe Drive	A3
College Street	B2-C2	Newhall Street	B1
Commercial Road	B1-C1	North Star Avenue	A4-B4-B3
Corporation Street	C3	Ocotal Way	D4
County Road	C4-D4-D3	Oxford Street	A2
Crombey Street	B1-C1	Plymouth Street	C2-D2
Cross Street	C1	Ponting Street	C3-C4
Curtis Street	A1-B1	Princes Street	C2
Deacon Street	B1-B2	Queen Street	B2
Dixon Street	B1-C1	Reading Street	A2-B2
Dowling Street	B1	Regent Street	B2-C2
Drove Road	D1-D2-D3	Rosebery Street	C4-C3-D3
Dryden Street	A1-B1	Salisbury Street	C4-C3-D3
Durham Street	C1	Shrivenham Road	D3
Eastcott Hill	C1	Southampton Street	D2
Edgeware Road	B2-C2	Stafford Street	B1-C1
Edmund Street	C1	Stanier Street	B1
Elmina Road	C4	Station Road	B3-C4
Emlyn Square	A2	Tennyson Street	A1-B2
Euclid Street	C2-D2	The Parade	B2
Exeter Street	A2	Theobald Street	A1-A2
Faringdon Road	A1-A2-B2	Upham Road	D1
Farnsby Street	A2-B2	Victoria Road	C1
Fleet Street	B2-B3	Villett Street	B2
Fleming Way	B3-C3-D3	Wellington Street	B3
Gladstone Street	C3-C4	Whitehead Street	A1-B1
Gloucester Street	B3	Whitehouse Road	B4
Gooch Street	C3-C4	Whitney Street	B1-C1
Graham Street	C4-C3-D3	William Street	A1
Great Western Way	A4-B4-C4	York Road	D1-D2-D3

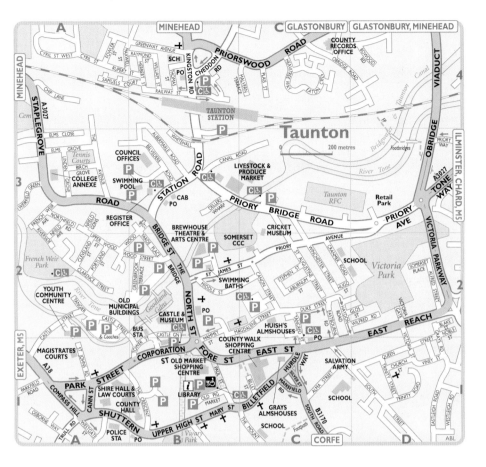

Taunton

Taunton is found on atlas page **23 E2**

Albermarle Road	B3-B4	Middle Street	B2-C2
Alfred Street	D2	North Street	B2
Alma Street	C1	Northfield Road	A3
Belvedere Road	B3	Obridge Road	C4-D4
Billetfield	C1	Obridge Viaduct	D3-D4
Birch Grove	A3	Old Pig Market	B1
Bridge Street	B2-B3	Park Street	A1
Canal Road	B3-C3	Paul Street	B1
Cann Street	A1	Plais Street	C4
Canon Street	C2	Portland Street	A2
Castle Green	B2	Priorswood Road	B4-C4
Castle Street	A1-A2-B2-B1	Priory Avenue	C2-D2-D3
Cheddon Road	B4	Priory Bridge Road	B3-C3-D3
Church Street	D1	Queen Street	D1-D2
Clarence Street	A2	Railway Street	B4
Cleveland Street	A2-A3	Raymond Street	B4
Compass Hill	A1	Rupert Street	A4-B4
Corporation Street	B1	St Augustine Street	C2
Cranmer Road	C2	St James Street	B2-C2
Cyril Street	A4	St Johns Road	A1
Cyril Street West	A4	Shuttern	A1-B1
Dellers Wharf	B3	Silver Street	C1
Duke Street	C2	South Road	C1
East Reach	C1-D1-D2	South Street	C1-D1
East Street	C1	Staplegrove Road	A4-A3-B3
Eastbourne Road	C1-C2	Station Road	B3
Eastleigh Road	D1	Stephen Street	C2
Eaton Crescent	C4	Tancred Street	C1-C2
Elms Grove	A3	Tangier	A2
Fore Street	B1	The Avenue	A3-A4
Fowler Street	A4	The Bridge	B2
French Weir Avenue	A3	The Crescent	A1-B1
Grays Road	D1-D2	Thomas Street	B4
Greenbrook Terrace	B2	Tone Way	D3
Greenway Avenue	B4	Tower Street	B1-B2
Hammet Street	B1-B2	Trinity Road	D1
Haydon Road	C2	Trinity Street	D1
Heavitree Way	C4	Trull Road	A1
Herbert Street	B4	Upper High Street	B1
Hurdle Way	C1	Upper Wood Street	A2-A3
Kingston Road	B4	Victoria Gate	D2
Laburnum Street	C2	Victoria Parkway	D2-D3
Linden Grove	A3	Victoria Street	D1-D2
Magdalene Street	B2-C2	Viney Street	D1
Malvern Street	C4	William Street	B4
Mansfield Road	C1	Winchester Street	C2
Mary Street	B1	Wood Street	B3-B2-A2
Maxwell Street	A4-B4	Yarde Place	B2-B3

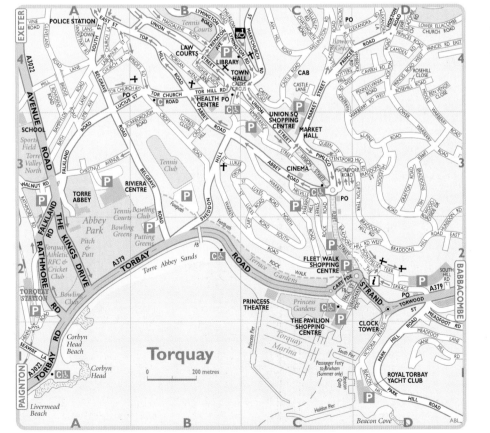

Torquay

Torquay is found on atlas page **7 F4**

Abbey Road	B4-B3-C3	Melville Street	C2-C3
Alexandra Road	C4-D4	Middle Warberry Road	D3-D4
Alpine Road	C3-D3	Mill Lane	A4
Ash Hill Road	C4	Montpelier Terrace	D2
Avenue Road	A3-A4	Morgan Avenue	B4
Bampfylde Road	A3-A4	Palk Street	C2-D2
Bath Lane	A3-A4	Park Hill Road	D1-D2
Beacon Hill	D1	Pennsylvania Road	D4
Belgrave Road	A4-A3-B3-B2	Pimlico	C3
Braddons Hill Road	D2	Potters Hill	C4-D4
Braddons Hill Road East	D2	Princes Road	C4-D4
Braddons Hill Road West	C2-D2	Princes Road West	D4
Braddons Street	D3	Queen Street	C3
Bridge Road	A3-A4	Rathmore Road	A2-A3
Camden Road	D4	Rock Road	C2-C3
Cary Parade	C2	Rosehill Road	D4
Cary Road	C2-C3	St Efride's Road	A4-B4
Castle Circus	B4-C4	St Lukes Road	B3-C4
Castle Lane	C4	St Lukes Road North	B3-C3-C2
Castle Road	C4	St Lukes Road South	B3-C3-C2
Cavern Road	D4	St Marychurch Road	C4
Chatsworth Road	C4	Scarborough Road	A3-B3
Chestnut Avenue	A3	Seaway Lane	A1
Church Lane	A4	Sheddon Hill	B2-B3
Church Street	A4	South Hill Road	D2
Cleveland Road	A4	South Street	A4
Clifton Terrace	D3	Stentiford Hill Road	C3-D3
Croft Hill	B3	Strand	D2
Croft Road	B3-B4	Temperance Street	C3-C4
East Street	A4	The Kings Drive	A2-A3
Ellacombe Road	C4	The Terrace	D2
Falkland Road	A2-A3-A4	Thurlow Road	B4
Fleet Street	C3-C2-D2	Tor Church Road	A4-B4
Grafton Road	D3	Tor Hill Road	B4
Hennapyn Road	A1-A2	Torbay Road	A1-A2-B2-C2
Higher Union Lane	B4	Torwood Street	D2
Hillesdon Road	D3	Trematon Avenue	B4
Hoxton Road	D4	Union Street	B4-C4-C3
Laburnum Street	A4	Upper Braddons Hill Road	D2-D3
Lower Ellacombe Church Road	D4	Vansittart Road	A4
Lower Warberry Road	D3-D4	Vaughan Parade	C2-D2
Lucius Street	A4-B4	Victoria Parade	D1-D2
Lymington Road	B4-C4	Victoria Road	C4-D4
Madrepore Road	C3-D3	Walnut Road	A3
Magdalene Road	B4	Warberry Road West	C4-C3-D3
Market Street	C3-C4	Warren Hill	C3
Meadfoot Lane	D1	Warren Road	B3-B2-C2-C3
Meadfoot Road	D1-D2	Wellington Road	C4

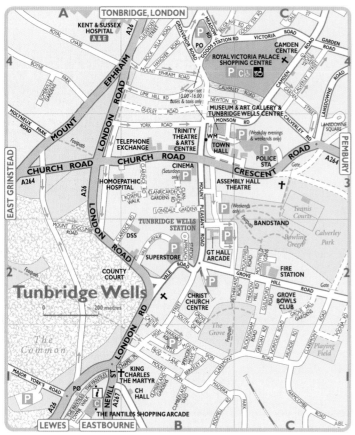

Tunbridge Wells

Tunbridge Wells is found on atlas page **17 G5**

Arundel Road	C1	Mount Ephraim	A3-A4-B4
Belgrave Road	B4-C4	Mount Ephraim Road	B4
Berkeley Road	B1	Mount Pleasant Road	B2-B3
Boyne Park	A4	Mount Sion	B1
Buckingham Road	C1-C2	Mountfield Gardens	C2
Calverley Road	B4-C4-C3	Mountfield Road	C2
Calverley Street	C4	Nevill Street	A1
Camden Road	C4	Newton Road	B4-C4
Castle Street	B1-B2	Norfolk Road	C1-C2
Chapel Place	A1-B1	Poona Road	C1-C2
Church Road	A3-B3	Rock Villa Road	B4
Clanricarde Gardens	B3	Rodmell Road	B1
Clanricarde Road	B3	Rosehill Walk	B3
Claremont Road	B1-C1-C2	Royal Chase	A4
Clarence Road	A2-B2-B3, B3	Somerville Gardens	A4
Crescent Road	B3-C3	South Grove	B1-B2
Culverden Street	B4	Spencer Mews	B1
Cumberland Gardens	B1	Station Approach	B2
Cumberland Yard	B1	Sutherland Road	B2-C2
Dale Street	C4	The Pantiles	A1
Dudley Road	A4-B4	The Pantiles Lower Walk	A1
Farmcombe Road	C1	Vale Avenue	B2
Frog Lane	B1	Vale Road	B2
Garden Road	C4	Victoria Road	C4
Garden Street	C3-C4	Warwick Road	B1
Goods Station Road	B4-C4	York Road	A3-B3
Grecian Road	C1		
Grosvenor Road	B4		
Grove Avenue	B2		
Grove Hill Gardens	C2		
Grove Hill Road	B2-C2		
Grover Street	C4		
Guildford Road	C2		
Hanover Road	B4		
High Street	B1-B2		
Lansdowne Road	C3-C4		
Lansdowne Square	C3-C4		
Lime Hill Road	B4		
Little Mount Sion	B1		
London Road	A1-B2-A3-B4		
Lonsdale Gardens	B3		
Madeira Park	B1-C1		
Major York's Road	A1		
Meadow Hill Road	C2		
Meadow Road	B4		
Molyneux Park Road	A3-A4		
Monson Road	B3-C3		
Mount Edgcumbe Road	A2		

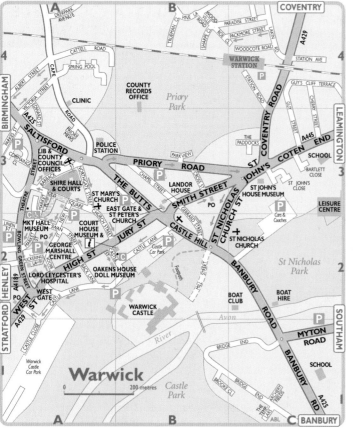

Warwick

Warwick is found on atlas page **59 F2**

Albert Street	A4	St Nicholas Church Street	B2-C3
Archery Fields	C1	Saltisford	A3
Back Lane	A2	Sharpe Close	B4
Banbury Road	B2-C2-C1	Smith Street	B3-C3
Barrack Street	A3	Spring Pool	A4
Bartlett Close	C3	Station Avenue	C4
Bowling Green Street	A2	Station Road	C4
Bridge End	B1-C1	Swan Street	A2
Brook Street	A2	The Butts	A3-B3
Brooke Close	B1-C1	The Paddocks	C3
Cape Road	A3-A4	The Templars	C1
Castle Close	A1-A2	Theatre Street	A2-A3
Castle Hill	B2	Trueman Close	B4
Castle Lane	A2-B2	Victoria Street	A4
Castle Street	A2-B2	Vine Lane	B4
Cattell Road	A4	West Street	A1-A2
Chapel Street	B3	Woodcote Road	C4
Cherry Street	C3-C4	Woodville Road	B4
Church Street	A2-A3		
Commainge Close	A3		
Coten End	C3		
Coventry Road	C3-C4		
Cross Street	B3		
Deerpark Avenue	A4		
Edward Street	A3-A4		
Gerrard Street	B2-B3		
Guy Street	C3-C4		
Guy's Cliff Terrace	C4		
High Street	A2		
Jury Street	B2-B3		
Lakin Road	C4		
Linen Street	A2		
Market Place	A3		
Market Street	A2		
Myton Road	C1		
New Street	A2-A3		
Northgate Street	A3		
Old Square	A3		
Packmore Street	B4-C4		
Paradise Street	B4-C4		
Parkes Street	A3		
Parkview	B3		
Priory Mews	A3		
Priory Road	A3-B3-C3		
Puckerings Lane	A2		
Roe Close	B4-C4		
St John's	C3		
St John's Close	C3		

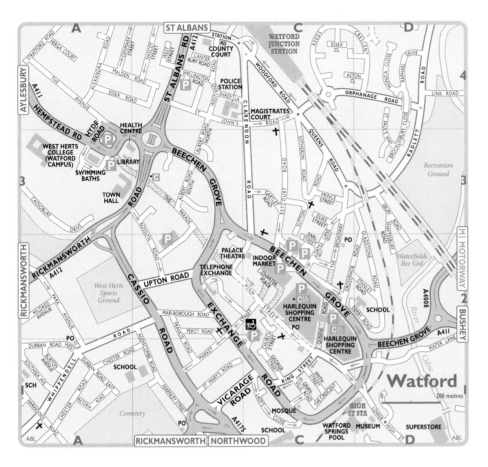

Watford

Watford is found on atlas page **28 B6**

Addiscombe Road	B1-B2	Nascot Street	B4
Albert Road North	B3-B4	Orphanage Road	C4-D4
Albert Road South	B3	Park Avenue	A1-A2
Alexandra Road	A4	Percy Road	B2
Aston Close	C4-D4	Pretoria Road	A1
Beechen Grove	B3-C2-D2-D1	Prince Street	C3
Brocklesbury Close	D3-D4	Queens Road	C1-C2, C3-C4
Burton Avenue	A1	Radlett Road	D3-D4
Canterbury Road	B4	Raphael Drive	D4
Cassio Road	A2-B2-B1	Reeds Crescent	C4-D4
Cassiobury Drive	A3	Rickmansworth Road	A2-A3-B3
Charter Place	C2	Rosslyn Road	B2-B3
Chester Road	A1-B1	St Albans Road	B4
Church Street	C1-C2	St John's Road	B4-C4
Clarendon Road	C3-C4	St Mary's Road	B1
Denmark Street	A4-B4	St Paul's Way	D3-D4
Derby Road	C2-D2	Shady Lane	B4
Duke Street	C3	Shaftesbury Road	D2-D3
Durban Road East	A1	Smith Street	C1
Durban Road West	A1	Sotheron Road	C3-C4
Earl Street	C2	Southsea Avenue	A1
Ebury Road	D2-D3	Stanley Road	C2-D2
Essex Close	C4	Station Road	B4
Essex Road	A4-B4	Stratford Road	A4
Estcourt Road	C2-C3-C4	Sutton Road	C3
Exchange Road	B2-B1-C1	The Avenue	A4
Fearnley Street	B1	The Broadway	C2-C3
Francis Road	B1-B2	The Crescent	C1
Gartlet Road	C3	The Parade	B3
George Street	C1	Upton Road	B2
Gladstone Road	D2-D3	Vicarage Road	B1-C1
Granville Road	C1	Water Lane	D1-D2
Grosvenor Road	C2-D2	Wellington Road	B4
Harwoods Road	A1	West Street	B4
Hempstead Road	A3-A4	Westland Road	B4
Herga Court	A4	Whippendell Road	A1-A2-B2
High Street	B2-C1-C2	Woodford Road	C4
Hyde Road	A3-A4		
King Street	C1		
Lady's Close	C1		
Link Road	D4		
Loates Lane	C2-C3		
Lower High Street	D1		
Malden Road	A4-B4		
Market Street	B1-B2-C2		
Marlborough Road	B2		
Mildred Avenue	A2		
Monica Close	D4		

231

Weston-Super-Mare

Weston-Super-Mare is found on atlas page **23 F5**

Albert Avenue	D1-D2	Waterloo Street	C4-D4
Albert Road	C1-D1	West Street	C4
Alexandra Parade	C3-D3	Whitecross Road	D1
Alfred Street	D3-D4	Wilton Gardens	C2
Alma Street	D3	Worthy Lane	D4
Beach Road	C1-C2	Worthy Place	C4-D4
Beaconsfield Road	D2	York Street	C3
Boulevard	D4		
Burlington Street	D3		
Carlton Street	C2		
Clevedon Road	C1		
Connaught Place	C4-D4		
Ellenborough Crescent	D1		
Ellenborough Park North	C1-D1		
Ellenborough Park Road	D1-D2		
Ellenborough Park South	C1-D1		
Gloucester Street	C3		
Graham Road	D2		
Grove Road	C4		
High Street	C3-C4		
Hopkins Street	D3-D4		
Knightstone Road	B4-C4		
Locking Road	D3		
Longton Grove Road	D4		
Lower Bristol Road	C4-D4		
Marine Parade	B1-C1-C2-C3		
Market Lane	C4		
Meadow Street	C3-D3		
Neva Road	C2-D2		
North Street	C3-D4		
Orchard Street	D3-D4		
Oxford Street	C3-D2		
Palmer Row	D4		
Palmer Street	D3-D4		
Prospect Place	D4		
Regent Street	C3-D3		
Ridgeway Avenue	D1-D2		
Royal Parade	C3-C4		
St James Street	C3		
South Parade	C4		
South Terrace	C4		
Southside	D4		
Station Road	D2		
Sunnyside Road North	D1		
Victoria Quadrant	D4		
Victoria Square	C3		
Wadham Street	C4		
Walliscote Road	C1-C2-D2-D3		

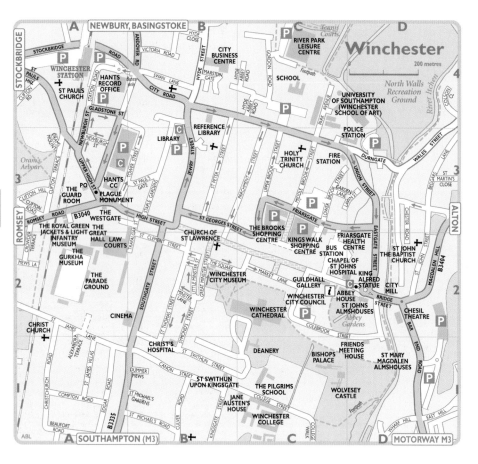

232

Winchester

Winchester is found on atlas page **26 C2**

Alexandra Terrace	A1-A2	Park Avenue	C3-C4
Andover Road	B4	Romsey Road	A3
Bar End Road	D1-D2	St Clement Street	B2
Beaufort Road	A1	St Georges Street	B3-C3
Beggars Lane	D3	St James Lane	A1-A2
Bridge Street	D2	St James Villas	A1
Canon Street	B1	St John Street	D2-D3
Chester Road	D2-D3	St Martin's Close	D3
Christchurch Road	A1-A2	St Michael's Gardens	B1
City Road	B4	St Michael's Road	A1-B1
Clifton Hill	A3	St Paul's Gate	B3
Clifton Road	A3-A4	St Pauls Hill	A4
Clifton Terrace	A3	St Peter Street	B3-B4
Colebrook Street	C2-D2-D1	St Swithun Street	B1
College Street	C1	St Thomas Street	B1-B2
College Walk	C1	Southgate Street	B1-B2-B3
Colson Close	D4	Staple Gardens	B3
Compton Road	A1	Station Road	A4
Crowder Terrace	A2-A3	Stockbridge Road	A4-B4
Culver Road	B1	Swan Lane	B4
Dummer Mews	B1	Symond's Street	B1-B2
Durngate	D3	The Square	B2-C2
East Hill	D1	Tower Street	A4-B4-B3-A3
Eastgate Street	D2-D3	Trafalgar Street	B2-B3
Edgar Road	A1	Union Street	D3
Friarsgate	C3	Upper Brook Street	C3
Garden Lane	C3	Upper High Street	A3
Gladstone Street	A4	Victoria Road	B4
Gordon Road	C4	Wales Street	D3-D4
Great Minster Street	B2	Wharf Hill	D1
High Street	A3-B3		
Hyde Abbey Road	B4-C4		
Hyde Close	B4		
Hyde Street	B4		
Jewry Street	B3-B4		
Kingsgate Street	B1		
Lawn Street	C3-D3		
Little Minster Street	B2		
Lower Brook Street	C3		
Magdalen Hill	D2-D3		
Market Lane	C2		
Marston Gate	B4		
Mews Lane	A2		
Middle Brook Street	C3		
Minster Lane	B2		
Newburgh Street	A3-A4		
Orams Mount	A3		
Parchment Street	B3-C3-C4		

Windsor

Windsor is found on atlas page **41 H2**

Adelaide Square	C2-D2	High Street, Eton	C4
Albany Road	C3	High Street, Windsor	C3-D3
Albert Street	A3-B3	Imperial Road	A1-A2-A3
Alexandra Road	C2-C3	Kings Road	C1-D1-D2
Alma Road	B2-B3-B4	Lammas Court	C2
Arthur Road	B3-B4	Madeira Walk	C3-D3
Bachelors Acre	C3	Maidenhead Road	A4-B4
Bailey Close	A2	Meadow Lane	C4
Balmoral Gardens	C1	Mill Lane	A4
Barry Avenue	B4-C4	Nightingale Walk	C1
Beaumont Road	C2	Orchard Avenue	A3
Bexley Street	B3	Osborne Road	B2-C2-C1
Bolton Avenue	C1-C2	Oxford Road	B3
Bolton Crescent	C1	Park Street	D3
Bolton Road	B1-C1	Parsonage Lane	A3-A4
Bridgeman Drive	A2	Peascod Street	C3
Brook Street	D2	Peel Close	A1
Bulkeley Avenue	B1-B2	Princes Avenue	A1-B1
Carey Close	B1	Queens Road	B2-C2
Castle Hill	C3-D3	River Street	C4
Cavalry Crescent	B1	Riverside Walk	D4
Charles Street	C3-C4	Russell Street	C3
Claremont Road	B3-C3	St Leonards Avenue	C2
Clarence Crescent	B3-C3	St Leonards Road	B1-C2-C3
Clarence Road	A3-B3-C3	St Marks Place	B2-C2
Clewer Avenue	A2	St Marks Road	B2-C2
Clewer Court Road	A4	Sheet Street	D2-D3
Clewer New Town	A2-A3	Springfield Road	A2-B2
Clewer Park	A4	Stowell Road	B4
College Crescent	B2	Temple Road	C2
Dagmar Road	C2	Thames Street	C3-C4
Datchet Road	C4-D4	The Arches	C4
Devereux Road	C2	Trinity Road	C3
Dorset Road	B3	Upcroft	A1-B1
Duke Street	B4	Vantissart Road	B3
Dyson Close	B1	Victor Road	B1-C1
Elm Road	B2	Victoria Street	C3-D3
Farm Yard	C4-D4	Ward Royal	B3-C3
Fountain Gardens	C1	Westmead	A1-A2
Frances Road	C1-C2-D2	William Street	C3
Gloucester Place	C2-D2	Wood Close	C1
Goslar Way	A3-B3-B2	York Avenue	B2
Goswell Road	C3	York Road	A2-B2
Green Lane	A3-A2-B2		
Grove Road	C2-D2		
Helena Road	C2		
Helston Lane	A3		
Hermitage Lane	A1		

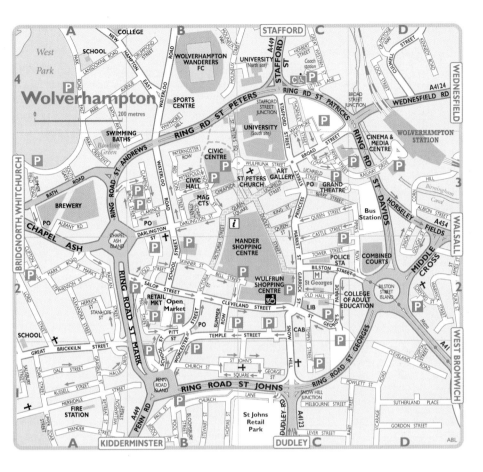

Wolverhampton

Wolverhampton is found on atlas page **58 B5**

Alexandra Street	A1-A2	Penn Road	B1
Bath Avenue	A4-A3-B3	Piper's Row	D2-D3
Bath Road	A3	Pitt Street	B2
Bell Street	B2-C2	Princess Street	C3
Berry Street	C3-D3	Queen Square	B3-C3
Bilston Street	C2-D2	Queen Street	C3-D3
Birch Street	B3	Raby Street	C1-D1
Broad Street	C3-D4	Raglan Street	A2
Castle Street	C2-C3-D3	Railway Drive	D3
Chapel Ash	A2-A3	Red Lion Street	B3
Cheapside	B3-C3	Retreat Street	A1
Church Lane	B1-C1	Ring Road St Andrews	A3-B3
Church Street	B1	Ring Road St Davids	D2-D3
Clarence Road	B3	Ring Road St Georges	C1-D1-D2
Clarence Street	B3	Ring Road St Johns	B1-C1
Cleveland Road	D1	Ring Road St Mark	A2-B2-B1
Cleveland Street	B2-C2	Ring Road St Patricks	C4-D4
Corn Hill	D3	Ring Road St Peters	B3-B4-C4
Corporation Street	B3	Russell Street	A1
Culwell Street	D4	St George's Parade	C2
Dale Street	A1	St John's Square	B1-C1
Darlington Street	B3	St Mark's Road	A2
Dudley Road	C1	St Mark's Street	A2
Dudley Street	C2-C3	St Peter's Square	B4-B3-C3
Fold Street	B2	Salop Street	B2
Fryer Street	C3-D3	School Street	B1-B2, B2-B3
Garrick Street	C2	Skinner Street	B2
Graiseley Street	A1	Snow Hill	C1-C2
Great Brickkiln Street	A1	Stafford Street	C3-C4
Great Western Street	C4	Stephenson Street	A2
Hallet Drive	A1	Stewart Street	B1
Horseley Fields	D3	Summer Row	B2
King Street	C3	Sutherland Place	D1
Lichfield Street	C3-D3	Tempest Street	C1-C2
Littles Lane	C4	Temple Street	B2-C2
Long Street	C3	Thomas Street	B1
Lord Street	A1-A2	Thornley Street	C3-C4
Market Street	C2-C3	Tower Street	C2-D2
Merridale Street	A1-B1	Vicarage Road	D1
Middle Cross	D2	Victoria Street	B2-B3
Mitrefold	B3	Warwick Street	D2
Molineux Street	B4-C4	Waterloo Road	B3-B4
New Hampton East	A4-B4	Wednesfield Road	D4
North Street	B3	Whitmore Hill	B4
Old Hall Street	C2	Whitmore Street	C3-C4
Park Avenue	A4-B4	Worcester Street	B1-B2
Park Road East	A4	Wulfruna Street	C3
Peel Street	B2	Zoar Street	A1

233

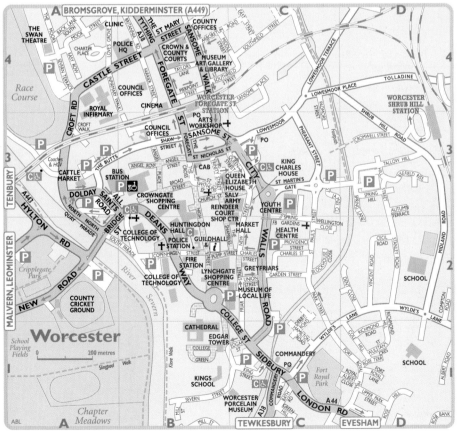

Worcester

Worcester is found on atlas page **46 D5**

All Saints Road	A3	New Road	A2
Angel Place	B3	New Street	C2-C3
Angel Row	B3	North Parade	A2
Angel Street	B3	North Quay	A2-A3
Arboretum Road	B4-C4	Park Street	C1-C2
Bath Road	C1	Pheasant Street	C3
Bridge Street	A2	Pierpoint Street	B4
Britannia Road	B4	Providence Street	C2
Broad Street	B3	Pump Street	B2-C2
Byefield Rise	D3	Queen Street	B3-C3
Castle Street	A4-B4	Richmond Hill	D1-D2
Cecil Road	D2	Richmond Road	D1
Charles Street	C2	Rose Terrace	D1
Charter Place	A4	St James Close	C3
Church Street	B3	St Martin's Gate	C3
City Walls Road	C1-C2-C3	St Mary Street	B4
Cole Hill	D1	St Nicholas Street	B3-C3
College Green	B1	St Paul's Street	C2-C3
College Street	B2-C2-C1	St Swithuns Street	B3
Commandery Road	C1	St Wulstan's Crescent	D1
Copenhagen Street	B2	Sansome Place	C4
Croft Road	A3-A4	Sansome Street	B3-C3
Cromwell Street	D3	Sansome Walk	B3-B4
Deans Way	B2-B3	Severn Street	B1-C1
Dent Close	D2	Severn Terrace	A4
Dolday	A3	Shaw Street	B3
Easy Row	A4	Shrub Hill Road	C4-D4-D3
Farrier Street	B3-B4	Sidbury	C1
Foregate Street	B3-B4	South Parade	A2-B2
Fort Royal Hill	C1-D1	Southfield Street	C4
Friar Street	C1-C2	Spring Gardens	C2-C3
Garden Street	C2	Spring Hill	D3
Green Hill	C1	Spring Lane	D2-D3
Hamilton Road	C1	Stanley Road	D2
High Street	B2-B3	Tallow Hill	D3
Hill Street	D3	Taylors Lane	B4
Hylton Road	A2-A3	The Butts	A3-B3
Infirmary Walk	A4-B4	The Cross	B3
King Street	C1	The Foregate	B3
Little Southfield Street	B4-C4	The Shambles	B3-C3
London Road	C1-D1	The Tything	B4
Love's Grove	A4	Tolladine	D4
Lowesmoor	C3	Trinity Street	B3
Lowesmoor Place	C4-D4	Union Street	C2
Lowesmoor Terrace	C4-D4	Upper Park Street	D1
Middle Street	B4-C4	Vincent Road	D2
Midland Road	D2-D3	Wellington Close	C2
Moor Street	A4	Wylde's Lane	C1-D2

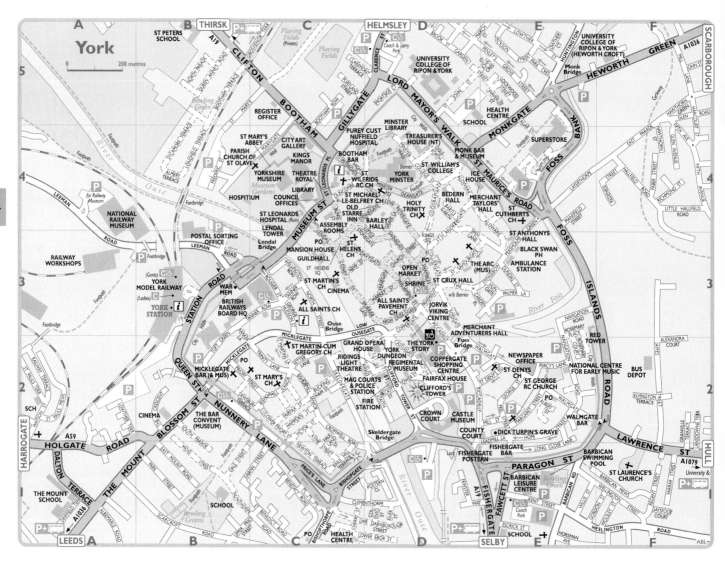

York

York is found on atlas page **91 G5**

Agar Street	E4-E5	Cromwell Road	C1-C2	Goodramgate	D3-D4	Long Close Lane	E1-E2	Park Street	B1	St Saviourgate	D3-E3
Albemarle Road	A1	Dale Street	B1	Gordon Street	E1-F1	Longfield Terrace	B4	Parliament Street	D3	Scarcroft Road	A1-B1
Albert Street	E2	Dalton Terrace	A1	Granville Terrace	F1-F2	Lord Mayor's Walk	D4-D5	Pavement	D3	Shambles	D3
Aldwark	D4-E4-E3	Davygate	C3-D3	Grape Lane	D4	Low Ousegate	C2-D3	Peasholme Green	E3-E4	Skeldergate	C2
Alexandra Court	F2	Daysfoot Court	F1	Grosvenor Terrace	B5-C5	Low Petergate	D3-D4	Peckitt Street	D2	South Parade	B1-B2
Almery Terrace	B4	Deangate	D4	Hallfield Road	F4	Lower Darnborough Street	C1-D1	Peel Street	E2	Spen Lane	D3
Baile Hill Terrace	C1	Dewsbury Terrace	B2-C2	Hampden Street	C2	Lower Ebor Street	C1-D1	Penley's Grove Street	D5-E5	Spurrier Gate	C3-D3
Barbican Mews	F1	Driffield Terrace	A1	Harcourt Street	F4-F5	Lower Priory Street	C2	Percy's Lane	E2	Station Road	B2-B3
Barbican Road	E1	Duncombe Place	C4	Hawthorn Green	F5	Lowther Court	E5	Piccadilly	D1-D2-D3	Stonegate	C3-C4-D4
Barker Lane	B2-B3	Dundas Street	E3	Hawthorn Street	F5	Lowther Street	E5	Portland Street	C5	Swann Street	B1-C1
Bartle Garth	D4	East Mount Road	B1	Heslington Road	E1-F1	Lowther Terrace	A2	Postern Close	D1	Swinegate	D3
Bishopgate Street	C1-D1	East Parade	F4	Heworth Green	E5-F5	Mansfield Street	E4	Price's Lane	C1	Sycamore Terrace	B4-B5
Bishopmill Junior	C2	Elvington Terrace	F2	High Ousegate	D3	March Street	D5-E5	Priory Street	B2-C2	Tanner Row	B3-C3
Bishopmill Senior	C2	Escrick Street	E1	High Petergate	C4	Margaret Street	E2	Queen Anne's Road	B5	The Crescent	B2
Bishopthorpe Road	C1	Faber Street	F4	Holgate Road	A1-B2	Market Street	D3	Queen Street	B2	The Mount	A1-B1
Blake Street	C3-C4	Fairfax Street	C2	Hope Street	E2	Marygate	B4-C4-C5	Railway Terrace	A2	The Stonebow	D3-E3
Blossom Street	B1-B2	Falkland Street	C1-C2	Horsman Avenue	E1	Micklegate	B2-C2	Redeness Street	F4	Toft Green	B2
Bootham	C4-C5	Farrar Street	F1	Hungate	E3	Mill Lane	F5	Regent Street	F1	Tower Street	D2
Bootham Row	C4-C5	Fawcett Street	E1	Huntington Road	E5	Mill Street	E2	Richmond Street	F4	Trinity Lane	C2
Bootham Terrace	B5	Feasegate	D3	Jackson Street	E5	Minster Yard	D4	River Street	D1	Upper Price Street	B1
Brook Street	D5	Fetter Lane	C2	James Street	F1-F2-F3	Moatside Court	D5	Rosemary Court	E2	Victor Street	C2
Buckingham Street	C2	Fewster Way	D1-E1	John Street	F5	Monkgate	D4-E4-E5	Rosemary Place	E2-E3	Walmgate	D2-E2-F2
Castlegate	D2	Fifth Avenue	F4	Kent Street	E1	Moss Street	B1	Rougier Street	C3	Watson Street	A2
Cherry Street	C1	Fishergate	D1-E1	Kings Square	D3	Museum Street	C3-C4	St Andrewgate	D3-D4	Waverley Street	E5
Church Street	D3	Foss Bank	E4-E5	Kings Staith	C2-D2	Navigation Road	E2-E3	St Benedict Road	C1	Wellington Row	C3
Claremont Terrace	C5-D5	Foss Islands Road	E4-E3-F3-F2	Kyme Street	C1-C2	New Street	C3	St Denys Road	E2	Wellington Street	E1-F1
Clarence Street	D5	Fossgate	D3	Lansdowne Terrace	F1-F2	Newton Terrace	C1	St Helen's Square	C3	Willis Street	E1
Clementhorpe	C1-D1	Frederic Street	B4	Lawrence Street	F1-F2	North Parade	B5	St John Crescent	E5	Wolsley Street	F1
Clifford Street	D2	Garden Place	D3-E3	Layerthorpe	E4-F4	North Street	C2-C3	St John Street	D5		
Clifton	B5-C5	Garden Street	D5-E5	Leadhill Lane	E1-E2	Nunnery Lane	B2-C2-C1	St Leonards Place	C4		
Colenso Street	D1	George Hudson Street	C2-C3	Leeman Road	A4-A3-B3	Nunthorpe Road	B1-C1	St Martins Lane	C2		
College Street	D4	George Street	E2	Lendal	C3-C4	Ogle Forth	D4	St Mary's	B4-B5-C5		
Colliergate	D3	Gillygate	C4-C5-D5	Little Hallfield Road	F4	Palmer Lane	E3	St Maurice's Road	D5-E5		
Coney Street	C3-D3	Glen Avenue	F4	Little Stonegate	C4-D3	Paragon Street	E1	St Pauls Mews	A2		
Coppergate	D2-D3	Glen Road	F5	Lockwood Street	E5	Park Crescent	E5	St Pauls Terrace	A2		

ports and airports

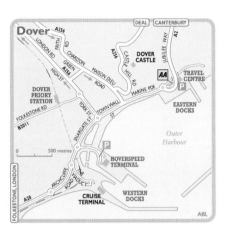

Pay-on-return parking is available at the Dover Eastern Docks and pay-and-display at the Hoverspeed Terminal.
For further information tel: 01304 241427
A long-stay parking facility with a collection and delivery service is also available.
For details tel: 01304 201227

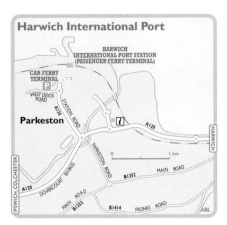

Open air parking is available at the terminal.
For charge details tel: 01255 242000
Further parking is available 5 miles from Harwich International Port with a collection and delivery service.
For charge details tel: 01255 870217

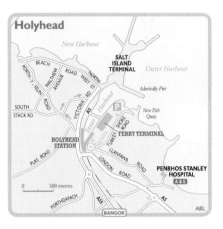

Open-air 'park and ride' car park is available close to the Ferry Terminal.
For charge details tel: 01407 762304 or 606732

Free open-air parking is available at King George Dock (left at owners' risk).
Tel: 01482 795141
Undercover parking is also available.
For charge details tel: 01482 781021

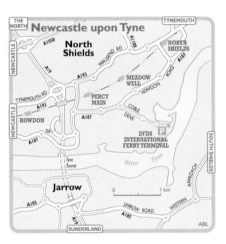

Open-air secure parking is available at the DFDS International Ferry Terminal, Royal Quays.
For charge details tel: 0191 296 0202

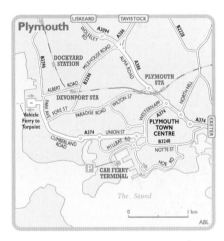

Free open-air parking is available outside the terminal building.
Tel: 0990 360360

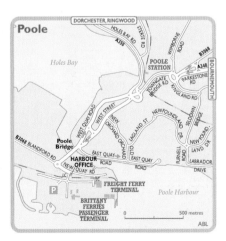

Open-air parking for 600 vehicles is available adjacent to the Ferry Terminal.
For charge details tel: 01202 440220

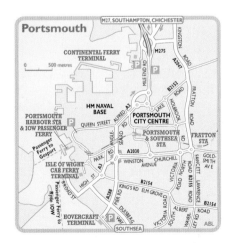

Secure parking facilities are available at the Continental Ferry Terminal and long-stay parking off Mile End Rd.
For charge details tel: 023 9275 1261
Pay-and-display parking is available opposite the Hovercraft Terminal.
Multi-storey parking is available close to the Isle of Wight Passenger Ferry Terminal.
For charge details tel: 023 9282 3153

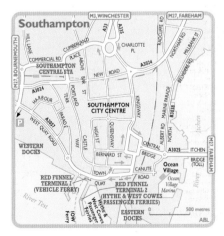

Covered or fenced compound parking for 2,000 vehicles is available within the Western Docks with a collection and delivery service.
For charge details tel: 023 8022 8001
Fax: 023 8063 5699

major airports

London Heathrow Airport – 16 miles west of London

Telephone: 0870 0000 123 or visit www.baa.co.uk
Parking: short-stay, long-stay and business parking is available.
For charge details tel: 0800 844844
Public Transport: coach, bus, rail and London Underground.
There are several 4-star and 3-star hotels within easy reach of the airport.
Car hire facilities are available.

London Gatwick Airport – 35 miles south of London

Telephone: 01293 535353 or visit www.baa.co.uk
Parking: short and long-stay parking is available at both the North and South terminals.
For charge details tel: 0800 844844
Public Transport: coach, bus and rail.
There are several 4-star and 3-star hotels within easy reach of the airport.
Car hire facilities are available.

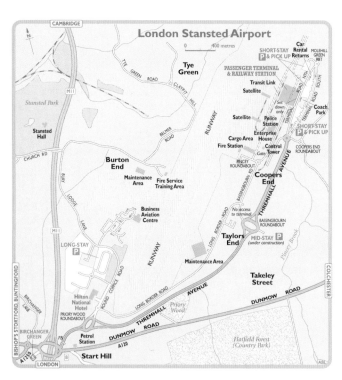

London Stansted Airport – 36 miles north east of London

Telephone: 0870 000 0303 or visit www.baa.co.uk
Parking: short and long-stay open-air parking is available.
For charge details tel: 01279 681192
Public Transport: coach, bus and direct rail link to London on the Stansted Express.
There is one 3-star hotel within easy reach of the airport.
Car hire facilities are available.

London Luton Airport – 33 miles north of London

Telephone: 01582 405100 or visit www.london-luton.com
Parking: short and long-stay open-air parking is available.
For charge details tel: 01582 395249
Public Transport: coach, bus and rail.
There are several 3-star hotels within easy reach of the airport.
Car hire facilities are available.

major airports

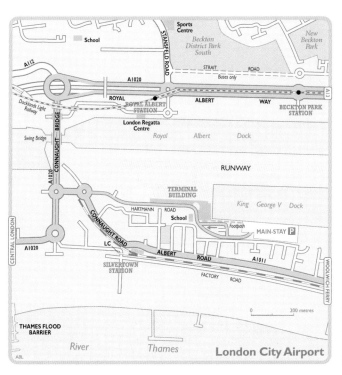

London City Airport – 7 miles east of London

Telephone: 020 7646 0088 or visit www.londoncityairport.com
Parking: open-air parking is available.
For charge details tel: 020 7646 0088
Public Transport: shuttle-bus service into London (Liverpool Street). Easy access to the rail network, Docklands Light Railway and the London Underground.
There are 5-star, 4-star and 3-star hotels within easy reach of the airport.
Car hire facilities are available.

Birmingham International Airport – 8 miles east of Birmingham

Telephone: 0121 767 5511 (Main Terminal), 0121 767 7502 (Eurohub Terminal) or visit www.bhx.co.uk
Parking: short and long-stay parking is available. For charge details tel: 0121 767 7861
Public Transport: shuttle-bus service to Birmingham International railway station and the NEC.
There is one 3-star hotel adjacent to the airport and several 4 and 3-star hotels within easy reach of the airport. Car hire facilities are available.

East Midlands Airport – 15 miles south west of Nottingham, next to the M1 at junctions 23A and 24

Telephone: 01332 852852 or visit www.eastmidlandsairport.com
Parking: short and long-stay parking is available.
For charge details tel: 01332 852852 ext 3263
Public Transport: bus and coach services to major towns and cities in the East Midlands.
There are several 3-star hotels within easy reach of the airport.
Car hire facilities are available.

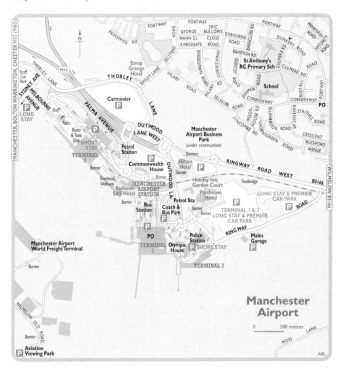

Manchester Airport – 10 miles south of Manchester

Telephone: 0161 489 3000 or visit www.manchesterairport.co.uk
Parking: short and long-stay parking is available. For charge details tel: 0161 489 3723
Public Transport: bus, coach and rail. Manchester airport railway station connects with the rail network.
There are several 4-star and 3-star hotels within easy reach of the airport.
Car hire facilities are available.

major airports

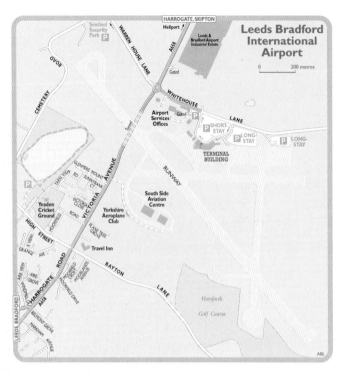

Leeds Bradford International Airport – 7 miles north east of Bradford and 9 miles north west of Leeds

Telephone: 0113 250 9696 or visit www.lbia.co.uk
Parking: short and long-stay parking is available.
For charge details tel: 0113 250 9696 ext 2214
Public Transport: regular bus and coach services operate from Bradford and Leeds.
There is one 4-star and several 3-star hotels within easy reach of the airport.
Car hire facilities are available.

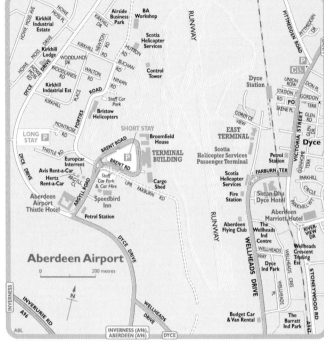

Aberdeen Airport – 7 miles north west of Aberdeen

Telephone: 01224 722331 or visit www.baa.co.uk
Parking: open-air parking is available.
For charge details tel: 01224 722331 ext 5142
Public Transport: regular bus service to central Aberdeen.
There are several 4-star and 3-star hotels within easy reach of the airport.
Car hire facilities are available.

Edinburgh Airport – 7 miles west of Edinburgh

Telephone: 0131 333 1000 or visit www.baa.co.uk
Parking: open-air parking is available.
For charge details tel: 0131 344 3197
Public Transport: regular bus services to central Edinburgh.
There are two 4-star hotels and several 3-star hotels within easy reach of the airport.
Car hire facilities are available.

Glasgow Airport – 8 miles west of Glasgow

Telephone: 0141 887 1111 or visit www.baa.co.uk
Parking: short and long-stay parking is available, mostly open-air.
For charge details tel: 0141 889 2751
Public Transport: regular coach services operate direct to central Glasgow and Edinburgh.
There are several 3-star hotels within easy reach of the airport.
Car hire facilities are available.

the Channel Tunnel

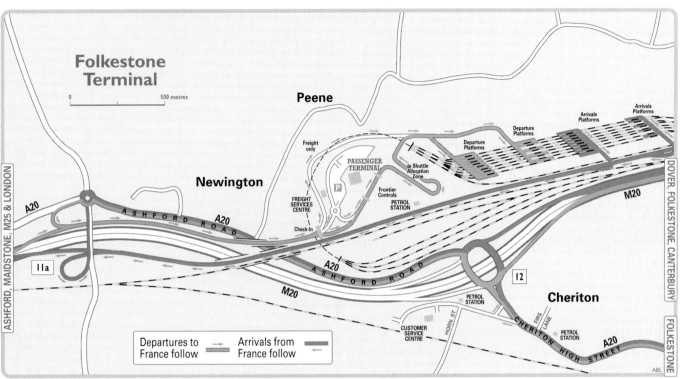

Services to Europe

The Eurotunnel shuttle service for cars, cars towing caravans and trailers, motorcycles, coaches and HGV vehicles runs between terminals at Folkestone and Calais/Coquelles.
It takes just over one hour to travel from the M20 motorway in Kent, via the Channel Tunnel, to the A16 autoroute in France. The service runs 24 hours a day, every day of the year.
Call the Eurotunnel Call Centre (tel: 08705 353535) or visit www.eurotunnel.com for the latest ticket and travel information.

There are up to four departures per hour at peak times, with the journey in the tunnel from platform to platform taking just 35 minutes (45 minutes at night). Travellers pass through British and French frontier controls on departure, saving time on the other side of the Channel. Each terminal has bureaux de change, restaurants and a variety of shops. In Calais/Coquelles, the Cité de l'Europe contains numerous shops, restaurants and a hypermarket.

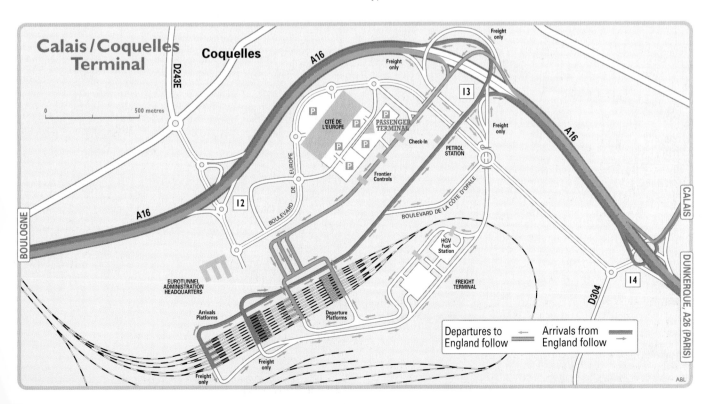

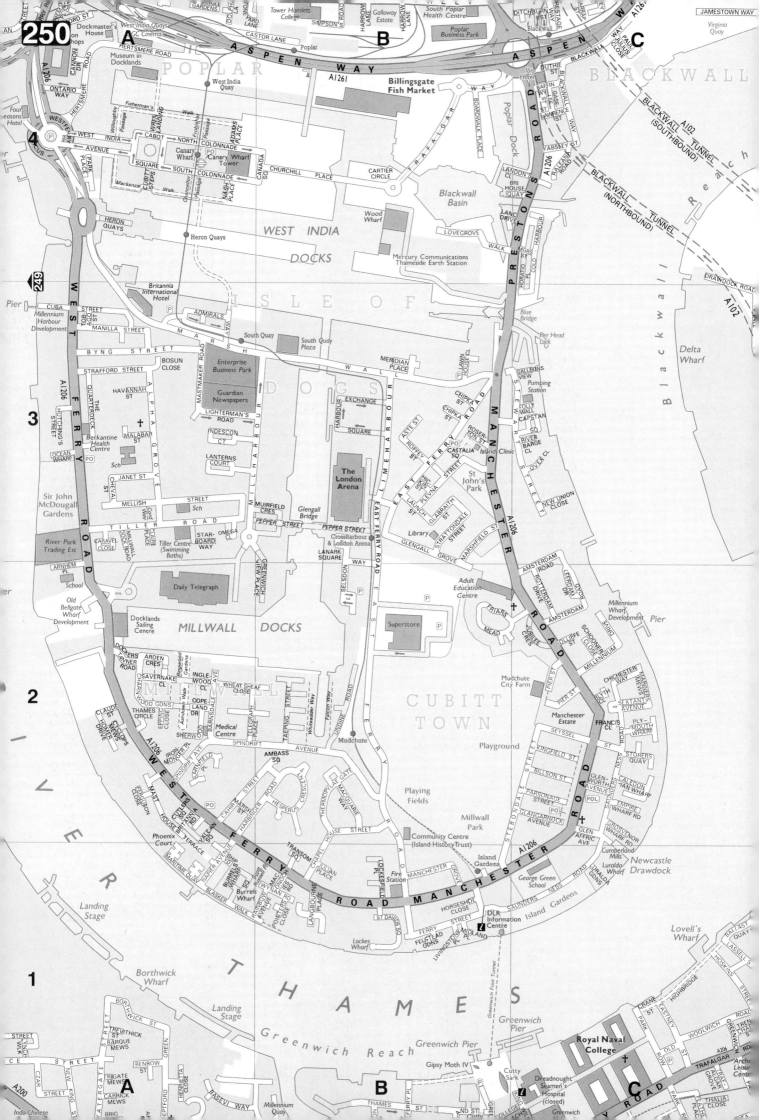

Central London street index

In the index the street names are listed in alphabetical order and written in full, but may be abbreviated on the map. Postal codes are listed where information is available. Each entry is followed by its map page number in bold type, and an arbitrary letter and grid reference number. For example, for Exhibition Road SW7 **244** C3, turn to page 244. The letter 'C' refers to the grid square located at the bottom of the page; the figure '3' refers to the grid square located at the left-hand side of the page. Exhibition Road is found within the intersecting square. SW7 is the postcode. A proportion of street names and their references are also followed by the name of another street in italics. These entries do not appear on the map due to insufficient space but can be located adjacent to the name of the road in italics.

A

Abbey Orchard Street SW1 **246** B3
Abbey Street SE1 **248** A1
Abbots Gardens W8 **244** A3
  St Mary's Place
Abbots Lane SE1 **248** A2
Abbots Walk W8 **244** A3
  St Mary's Place
Abbotshade Road SE16 **249** E2
Abchurch Lane EC4 **243** F1
Abercorn Close NW8 **240** B4
Abercorn Place NW8 **240** B4
Aberdeen Place NW8 **240** C3
Aberdour Street SE1 **247** F2
Abingdon Road W8 **244** A3
Abingdon Street SW1 **246** B3
Abingdon Villas W8 **244** A3
Achilles Way W1 **245** E4
Ackroyd Drive E3 **249** F4
Acorn Walk SE16 **249** F2
Acton Street WC1 **242** C4
Adam And Eve Mews W8 **244** A3
Adam and Eve Court W1 **241** E1
  Oxford Street
Adam Street WC2 **242** B1
Adam's Row W1 **241** E1
Adams Place E14 **250** A4
Addington Street SE1 **246** C3
Addle Hill EC4 **243** E1
Addle Street EC2 **243** E2
Adelaide Street WC2 **242** B1
  William IV Street
Adelina Grove E1 **248** D4
Adeline Place WC1 **242** B2
Adelphi Terrace WC2 **242** B1
  Adams Street
Adler Street E1 **248** B4
Admiral Place SE16 **249** E2
Admiral Way W9 **240** A3
Admirals Way E14 **250** A3
Adpar Street W2 **240** C3
Adrian Mews SW10 **244** A1
Agar Street WC2 **242** B1
Agatha Close E1 **248** C2
Agdon Street EC1 **243** D3
Agnes Street E14 **249** F4
Ainstey Street SE16 **249** D1
  Brunel Road
Air Street W1 **242** A1
Alaska Street SE1 **246** C4
Albany Mews SE5 **247** E1
Albany Road SE5 **247** E1
Albany Street NW1 **241** F4
Albatross Way SE16 **249** D1
Albemarle Street W1 **241** F1
Albemarle Way EC1 **242** C3
  Clerkenwell Road
Albert Court SW7 **244** C3
Albert Embankment SE1 **246** B1
Albert Gardens E1 **249** D3
Albert Hall Mansions SW7 **244** C3
Albert Mews W8 **244** B3
Albert Place W8 **244** B3
Alberta Street SE17 **247** D1
Albion Close E1 **241** D1
Albion Mews W2 **241** D1
Albion Place EC1 **243** D3
Albion Street SE16 **249** D1
Albion Street W2 **241** D1
Albion Way EC1 **243** E2
Albion Yard E1 **248** C4
Aldbugh Mews W1 **241** E2
  Marylebone Lane
Aldenham Street NW1 **242** A4
Aldermanbury EC2 **243** E2
Aldermanbury Square EC2 **243** E2
  Aldermanbury
Alderney Street SW1 **245** F2
Aldersgate Street EC1 **243** E3
Aldford Street W1 **241** E1
Aldgate EC3 **248** A3
Aldgate High Street EC3 **248** A3
Aldsworth Close W9 **240** A3
Aldwych WC2 **242** C1
Alexander Place SW7 **244** C2
Alexander Square SW3 **244** C2
Alexander Street W2 **240** A2
Alford Place N1 **243** E4
Alfred Mews W1 **242** A3
Alfred Place W1 **242** A3
Alfred Road W2 **240** A2
Alice Street SE1 **247** F3
Alie Street E1 **248** B3
All Hallows Lane EC4 **243** F1
All Soul's Place W1 **241** F2
  Langham Street
Allen Street W8 **244** A3
Allington Street SW1 **245** F3
Allsop Place NW1 **241** D3
Alma Square NW8 **240** B4
Alpha Grove E14 **250** A3
Alpha Place SW3 **245** D1
Alsace Road SE17 **247** F1
Alscot Road SE1 **248** B1
Alvey Street SE17 **247** F2
Ambassador Square E14 **250** B2
Ambergate Street SE17 **247** D1
Amberley Road W9 **240** A3
Amelia Street SE17 **247** E2
Amen Corner EC4 **243** D2
Amen Court EC4 **243** D2
America Square EC3 **248** A3
America Street SE1 **247** E4

Amoy Place E14 **249** F3
Ampton Place WC1 **242** C4
Ampton Street WC1 **242** C4
Amsterdam Road E14 **250** C2
Amwell Street EC1 **242** C4
Anderson Street SW3 **245** D2
Andrew Borde Street WC2 **242** B2
  Charing Cross Road
Angel Court EC2 **243** F2
Angel Court SW1 **246** A4
  King Street
Angel Mews E1 **248** C3
Angel Passage EC4 **243** F1
Angel Place SE1 **247** E4
Angel Street EC2 **243** E2
Ann Moss Way SE16 **249** D1
Ansdell Street W8 **244** A3
Antill Terrace E1 **249** D4
Apothecary Street EC4 **243** D2
  New Bridge Street
Apple Tree Yard SW1 **242** A1
Appold Street EC2 **243** F3
Aquinas Street SE1 **247** D4
Arbour Square E1 **249** D4
Archangel Street SE16 **249** E1
Archer Street W1 **242** A1
Arden Crescent E14 **250** A2
Argent Street SE1 **247** E4
  Loman Street
Argyle Square WC1 **242** B4
Argyle Street WC1 **242** B4
Argyle Walk WC1 **242** B4
Argyll Road W8 **244** A3
Argyll Street W1 **241** F2
Arlington Street SW1 **245** F4
Arlington Way EC1 **243** D4
Arne Street WC2 **242** B2
Arneway Street SW1 **246** A2
Arnhem Place E14 **250** A2
Arnside Street SE17 **247** E1
Arthur Street EC4 **243** F1
Artichoke Hill E1 **248** C3
Artillery Lane E1 **248** A4
Artillery Passage E1 **248** A4
  Artillery Lane
Artillery Row SW1 **246** A3
Artizan Street E1 **248** A4
  Harrow Place
Arundel Street WC2 **242** C1
Ashbridge Street NW8 **240** C3
Ashburn Gardens SW7 **244** B2
Ashburn Mews SW7 **244** B2
Ashburn Place SW7 **244** B2
Ashby Street EC1 **243** D4
Ashdown Walk E14 **250** A2
Asher Drive E1 **248** B3
Ashfield Street E1 **248** C4
Ashfield Yard E1 **249** D4
  Ashfield Street
Ashland Place W1 **241** E3
Ashley Place SW1 **245** F3
Ashmill Street NW1 **240** C3
Ashworth Road W9 **240** A4
Aske Street N1 **243** F4
Asolando Drive SE17 **247** E2
  King & Queen Street
Aspen Way E14 **250** B4
Assam Street E1 **248** B4
Assembly Passage E1 **249** D4
Aste Street E14 **250** B3
Aston Street E14 **249** E4
Astwood Mews SW7 **244** B2
Atherstone Mews SW7 **244** B2
Atterbury Street SW1 **246** B2
Attneave Street WC1 **242** C4
Aubrey Place NW8 **240** B4
Auckland Street SE11 **246** C1
Augustus Street NW1 **241** F4
Aulton Place SE11 **247** D1
Austin Friars EC2 **243** F2
Austin Friars Square EC2 **243** F2
  Austin Friars
Austral Street SE11 **247** D2
Ave Maria Lane EC4 **243** E2
Aveline Street SE11 **246** C1
Avenue Row W1 **241** F1
Avis Square E1 **249** E4
Avon Place SE1 **247** E3
Avonmouth Street SE1 **247** E3
Aybrook Street W1 **241** E2
Aylesbury Road SE17 **247** F1
Aylesbury Street EC1 **243** D3
Aylesford Street SW1 **246** A1
Aylward Street E1 **249** D4
Ayres Street SE1 **247** E4

B

Babmaes Street SW1 **246** A4
  Jermyn Street
Bacchus Walk N1 **243** F4
Bache's Street N1 **243** F4
Back Church Lane E1 **248** B4
Back Hill EC1 **243** D3
Bacon Grove SE1 **248** A1
Baffin Way E14 **250** C4
Bainbridge Street WC1 **242** B2
Baker Street W1 & NW1 **241** D3
Baker's Mews W1 **241** E2
Baker's Row EC1 **243** D3
Baker's Yard EC1 **243** D3
  Baker's Row

Bakers Hall Court EC3 **248** A3
  Harp Lane
Balcombe Street NW1 **241** D3
Balderton Street W1 **241** E1
Baldwin Street EC1 **243** F4
Baldwin's Gardens EC1 **242** C3
Bale Road E1 **249** F4
Balfe Street N1 **242** B4
Balfour Mews W1 **241** E1
Balfour Place W1 **241** E1
Balfour Street SE17 **247** F2
Ballast Quay SE10 **250** C1
Balniel Gate SW1 **246** A1
Baltic Street East EC1 **243** E3
Baltic Street West EC1 **243** E3
Balvaird Place SW1 **246** B2
Bancroft Road E1 **246** C1
Bank End SE1 **247** E4
Bankside SE1 **247** E4
Bankside Jetty SE1 **243** E1
Banner Street EC1 **243** E3
Banyard Road SE16 **248** C1
Barbon Close WC1 **242** C3
Barge House Street SE1 **243** D1
Bark Place W2 **240** A1
Barkston Gardens SW5 **244** A2
Barleycorn Way E14 **249** F3
Barlow Place W1 **241** F1
Barlow Street SE17 **247** F2
Barnaby Place SW7 **244** C2
Barnardo Street E1 **249** D3
Barnby Street NW1 **242** A4
Barnes Street E14 **249** E4
Barnfield Place E14 **250** A2
Barnham Street SE1 **248** A2
Barnsdale Avenue E14 **250** A2
Barnwood Close W9 **240** A3
Baron Street N1 **242** C4
Baron's Place SE1 **247** D3
Barque Mews SE8 **250** A1
Barrett Street W1 **241** E2
Barrie Street W2 **240** B1
Barrow Hill Road NW8 **240** C4
  St Johns Wood High Street
Barter Street WC1 **242** B2
Barth Lane EC2 **243** F2
Bartholomew Close EC1 **243** E2
Bartholomew Square EC1 **243** E3
Bartholomew Street SE1 **247** F2
Barton Street SW1 **246** B3
Basevi Way SE8 **250** A1
Basil Street SW3 **245** D3
Basin Approach E14 **249** E3
Basinghall Avenue EC2 **243** E2
Basinghall Street EC2 **243** E2
Basswick Street EC1 **243** E3
Bate Street E14 **249** F3
Bateman Street W1 **242** A2
Bateman's Buildings W1 **242** A2
Bath Court EC1 **242** C3
  Warner Street
Bath Place N1 **243** F4
Bath Street EC1 **243** E4
Bath Terrace SE1 **247** E3
Bathurst Mews W2 **240** C1
Bathurst Street W2 **240** C1
Battle Bridge Lane SE1 **247** F4
Batty Street E1 **248** B4
Bayley Street WC1 **242** A2
Baylis Road SE1 **246** C3
Bayswater Road W2 **240** A1
Baythorne Street E3 **249** F4
Beaconsfield Road SE17 **247** F1
Beak Street W1 **242** A1
Bear Alley EC4 **243** D2
  Farringdon Street
Bear Gardens SE1 **243** E1
Bear Lane SE1 **247** D4
Bear Street WC2 **242** B1
  Cranbourn Street
Beatrice Place W8 **244** A2
Beauchamp Place SW3 **245** D3
Beauchamp Street EC1 **243** D3
  Brooke Street
Beaufort Gardens SW3 **245** D3
Beaufort Street SW3 **244** B1
Beaumont Mews W1 **241** E2
Beaumont Place W1 **242** A3
Beaumont Street W1 **241** E3
Beccles Street E14 **249** F3
Beckway Street SE17 **247** F2
Bedale Street SE1 **247** E3
  Borough High Street
Bedford Avenue WC1 **242** B2
Bedford Court WC2 **242** B1
Bedford Gardens W8 **244** A4
Bedford Place WC1 **242** B3
Bedford Row WC1 **242** C3
Bedford Square WC1 **242** B2
Bedford Street WC2 **242** B1
Bedford Way WC1 **242** B3
Bedfordbury WC2 **242** B1
Bedser Close SE11 **246** C1
Beech Street EC2 **243** E3
Beeston Place SW1 **245** F3
Bekesbourne Street E14 **249** E3
Belgrave Mews North SW1 **245** E3
Belgrave Mews South SW1 **245** E3
Belgrave Mews West SW1 **245** E3
Belgrave Place SW1 **245** E3
Belgrave Road SW1 **245** F2
Belgrave Square SW1 **245** E3
Belgrave Street E1 **249** E3
Bell Lane E1 **248** A4
Bell Street NW1 **240** C3
Bell Yard WC2 **242** C2
Bellamy Close E14 **250** A3
  Manilla Street
Belvedere Buildings SE1 **247** E3

Belvedere Road SE1 **246** C4
Ben Jonson Road E1 **249** E4
Ben Smith Way SE16 **248** C1
Benbow Street SE8 **250** A1
Bendall Mews W1 **241** D3
Bennet's Hill EC4 **243** E1
  Castle Baynard Street
Benson Quay E1 **249** D3
Bentinck Mews W1 **241** E2
  Marylebone Lane
Bentinck Street W1 **241** E2
Bere Street E1 **249** E3
Bergen Square SE16 **249** E1
Bering Square E14 **250** A1
  Maritime Quay
Berkeley Gardens W8 **244** A4
Berkeley Mews W1 **241** D2
Berkeley Square W1 **241** F1
Berkeley Street W1 **241** F1
Bermondsey Square SE1 **243** E2
  Long Lane
Bermondsey Street SE1 **248** A2
Bermondsey Wall East SE16 **248** B1
Bermondsey Wall West SE16 **248** B2
Bernard Street WC1 **242** B3
Berners Mews W1 **242** A2
Berners Street W1 **242** A2
Berry Street EC1 **243** E3
Berryfield Road SE17 **247** E1
Berwick Street W1 **242** A2
Bessborough Gardens SW1 **246** B2
Bessborough Place SW1 **246** A1
Bessborough Street SW1 **246** A1
Betterton Street WC2 **242** B2
Betts Street E1 **248** C3
Bevenden Street N1 **243** F4
Beverston Mews W1 **241** D2
Bevin Close SE16 **249** E2
Bevin Way WC1 **242** C4
Bevington Street SE16 **248** B1
Bevis Marks EC3 **248** A4
Bewley Street E1 **248** C3
Bickenhall Street W1 **241** D3
Bidborough Street WC1 **242** B4
Biddulph Road W9 **240** A4
Bigland Street E1 **248** C3
Billiter Square EC3 **248** A3
  Fenchurch Avenue
Billiter Street EC3 **248** A3
Billson Street E14 **250** C2
Bina Gardens SW5 **244** B2
Bingham Place W1 **241** E3
Binney Street W1 **241** E1
Birchfield Street E14 **249** E3
Birchin Lane EC3 **243** F1
Bird Street W1 **241** E2
Birdcage Walk SW1 **246** A3
Birkenhead Street WC1 **242** B4
Bishop's Court EC4 **243** D2
  Old Bailey
Bishop's Court WC2 **242** C2
  Chancery Lane
Bishop's Terrace SE11 **247** D2
Bishops Bridge Road W2 **240** B2
Bishopsgate EC2 **243** F2
Bishopsgate Arcade EC2 **248** A4
Bishopsgate Churchyard EC2 **243** F2
Bittern Street SE1 **247** E3
Black Prince Road SE1 & SE11 **246** C2
Black Swan Yard SE1 **248** A2
Blackall Street EC2 **243** F3
Blackburne's Mews W1 **241** E1
Blackfriars Bridge EC4 & SE1 **243** D1
Blackfriars Lane EC4 **243** D1
Blackfriars Passage EC4 **243** D1
Blackfriars Road SE1 **247** D4
Blacklands Terrace SW3 **245** D2
Blackwall Tunnel E14 & SE10 **250** C4
Blackwood Street SE17 **247** F1
Blandford Square NW1 **241** D3
Blandford Street W1 **241** E2
Blasker Walk E14 **250** A1
Bleeding Heart Yard EC1 **243** D2
  Greville Street
Blenheim Street W1 **241** F1
  New Bond Street
Bletchley Street N1 **243** E4
Blithfield Street W8 **244** A3
Blomfield Road W9 **240** A3
Blomfield Street EC2 **243** F2
Blomfield Villas W2 **240** A2
Bloomburg Street SW1 **245** F2
  Vauxhall Bridge Road
Bloomfield Place W1 **241** F1
  Bourdon Street
Bloomfield Terrace SW1 **245** E2
Bloomsbury Court WC1 **242** B2
  High Holborn
Bloomsbury Place WC1 **242** B3
  Southampton Row
Bloomsbury Square WC1 **242** B2
Bloomsbury Street WC1 **242** B2
Bloomsbury Way WC1 **242** B2
Blount Street E14 **249** E4
Blue Anchor Yard E1 **248** B3
Blue Ball Yard SW1 **246** A4
  St James's Street
Blyth Close E14 **250** C2
Boardwall Place E14 **250** B4
Bohn Road E1 **249** F4
Bolsover Street W1 **241** F3
Bolt Court EC4 **243** D2
Bolton Gardens SW5 **244** A2
Bolton Gardens Mews SW10 **244** B1
Bolton Street W1 **245** F4
Boltons Place SW10 **244** B2
Bond Way SW8 **246** B1
Bonding Yard Walk SE16 **249** E1
Bonhill Street EC2 **243** F3

Bonnington Square SW8 **246** C1
Booker Close E14 **249** F4
Boot Street N1 **243** F4
Booth's Place W1 **241** F2
  Wells Street
Boreas Walk N1 **243** E4
  Nelson Place
Borough High Street SE1 **247** E3
Borough Road SE1 **247** E3
Borrett Close SE17 **247** E1
Borthwick Street SE8 **250** A1
Boscobel Place SW1 **245** E2
Boscobel Street NW8 **240** C3
Boss Street SE1 **248** A2
Boston Place NW1 **241** D3
Bosun Close E14 **250** A3
Boswell Court WC1 **242** B3
  Boswell Street
Boswell Street WC1 **242** B3
Botolph Lane EC3 **243** F1
Bott's Mews W2 **240** A2
Boulcott Street E1 **249** E3
Boundary Lane SE17 **247** E1
Boundary Road SE1 **247** D4
Bourdon Street W1 **241** F1
Bourlet Close W1 **241** F2
Bourne Street SW1 **245** E2
Bourne Terrace W2 **240** A2
Bouverie Street EC4 **243** D1
Bow Lane EC4 **243** E1
Bow Street WC2 **242** B2
Bowden Street SE11 **247** D1
Bower Street E1 **249** D3
Bowling Green Lane EC1 **243** D3
Bowling Green Place SE1 **247** F4
  Newcomen Street
Bowling Green Street SE11 **246** C1
Bowling Green Walk N1 **243** F4
Boyd Street E1 **248** B3
Boyfield Street SE1 **247** D3
Boyle Street W1 **241** F1
  Savile Row
Boyson Road SE17 **247** E1
Brackley Street EC1 **243** E3
Brad Street SE1 **247** D4
Braden Street W9 **240** A3
Bradenham Close SE17 **247** F1
Braganza Street SE17 **247** D1
Braham Street E1 **248** B3
Bramerton Street SW3 **244** C1
Bramham Gardens SW5 **244** A2
Branch Road E14 **249** E3
Brandon Street SE17 **247** E2
Brangton Road SE11 **246** C1
Brass Tally Alley SE16 **249** E1
Bray Crescent SE16 **249** D2
Bray Place SW3 **245** D2
Bread Street EC4 **243** E1
Bream's Buildings EC **242** C2
Brechin Place SW7 **244** B2
Breezer's Hill E1 **248** C3
Bremner Road SW7 **244** B3
Brendon Street W1 **241** D2
Brenton Street E14 **249** E4
Bressenden Place SW1 **245** F3
Brettell Street SE17 **247** F1
Brewer Street W1 **242** A1
Brewers' Green SW1 **246** A3
  Caxton Street
Brewhouse Lane E1 **248** C2
Brewhouse Walk SE16 **249** E2
Brick Court EC4 **242** C2
  Middle Temple Lane
Brick Street W1 **245** E4
Bride Lane EC4 **243** D2
Bridewain Street SE1 **248** B1
Bridewell Place EC4 **243** D1
Bridford Mews W1 **241** F3
Bridge House Quay E14 **250** C4
Bridge Place SW1 **245** F2
Bridge Street SW1 **246** B3
Bridge Yard SE1 **247** F4
Bridgeport Place E1 **248** B2
  Kennet Street
Bridgewater Square EC2 **243** E3
  Beech Street
Bridgewater Street EC2 **243** E3
  Beech Street
Bridgeway Street NW1 **242** A2
Bridle Lane W1 **242** A1
Bridstow Place W2 **240** A2
Brightlingsea Place E14 **249** F3
Brill Place NW1 **242** A4
Briset Street EC1 **243** D3
Bristol Gardens W9 **240** A3
Bristol Mews W9 **240** A3
Britannia Road E14 **250** A2
Britannia Street WC1 **242** C4
Britannia Walk N1 **243** F4
Britten Street SW3 **244** C1
Britton Street EC1 **243** D3
Broad Court WC2 **242** B2
Broad Sanctuary SW1 **246** B3
Broad Walk W2 **245** E4
Broadbent Street W1 **241** F1
Broadley Street NW8 **240** C4
Broadley Terrace NW1 **241** D3
Broadstone Place W1 **241** E2
Broadwall SE1 **247** D4
Broadway SW1 **246** A3
Broadwick Street W1 **242** A1
Brockham Street SE1 **247** E3
Brodlove Lane E1 **249** D3
Bromley Place W1 **241** F2
Brompton Place SW3 **245** D3
Brompton Road SW3 **245** D3
Brompton Square SW3 **244** C3
Bronti Close SE17 **247** E1
Brook Drive SE11 **247** D2

Brook Gate W1 ... 241 E1
Brook Mews North W2 ... 240 B1
Brook Street W1 ... 241 E1
Brook Street W2 ... 240 C1
Brook's Mews W1 ... 241 F1
Brooke Street EC1 ... 243 D2
Brooke's Court EC1 ... 242 C2
Brooke's Market EC1 ... 243 D2
  Brooke Street
Brown Hart Gardens W1 ... 241 E1
Brown Street W1 ... 241 D2
Browning Close W9 ... 240 B3
Browning Street SE17 ... 247 E2
Brownlow Mews WC1 ... 242 C3
Brownlow Street WC1 ... 242 C2
Brune Street E1 ... 248 A4
Brunel Road SE16 ... 249 D1
Brunswick Gardens W8 ... 244 A3
Brunswick Mews W1 ... 241 D2
Brunswick Place N1 ... 243 F4
Brunswick Quay SE16 ... 249 E1
Brunswick Square WC1 ... 242 B3
Brunton Place E14 ... 249 E3
Brushfield Street E1 ... 248 A4
Bruton Lane W1 ... 241 F1
Bruton Place W1 ... 241 F1
Bruton Street W1 ... 241 F1
Bryan Road SE16 ... 249 F2
Bryanston Mews East W1 ... 241 D2
Bryanston Mews West W1 ... 241 D2
Bryanston Place W1 ... 241 D2
Bryanston Square W1 ... 241 D2
Bryanston Street W1 ... 241 D2
Buck Hill Walk W2 ... 240 C1
Buck Street WC2 ... 242 B1
Buckingham Gate SW1 ... 245 F3
Buckingham Palace Road SW1 ... 245 F2
Buckingham Place SW1 ... 245 F3
Buckland Street N1 ... 243 F4
Buckle Street E1 ... 248 B4
Bucklersbury EC4 ... 243 E2
Bucknall Street WC2 ... 242 B2
Buckters Rents SE16 ... 249 E2
Budge's Walk W2 ... 240 B4
Bulleid Way SW1 ... 245 F2
Bulstrode Place W1 ... 241 E2
  Marylebone Lane
Bulstrode Street W1 ... 241 E2
Bunhill Row EC1 ... 243 F3
Bunhouse Place SW1 ... 245 E2
Burbage Close SE1 ... 247 F3
Burdett Street SE1 ... 247 D3
Burge Street SE1 ... 247 F3
Burgess Street E14 ... 249 F4
Burgon Street EC4 ... 243 D2
  Carter Lane
Burleigh Place WC2 ... 242 B1
Burlington Arcade W1 ... 241 F1
Burlington Gardens W1 ... 241 F1
Burne Street NW1 ... 240 C3
Burnsall Street SW3 ... 245 D1
Burnside Close SE16 ... 249 E2
Burr Close E1 ... 248 B2
Burrell Street SE1 ... 247 D4
Burrells Wharf Square E14 ... 250 A1
Burrows Mews SE1 ... 247 D4
Bursar Street SE1 ... 248 A2
  Tooley Street
Burslem Street E1 ... 248 C3
Burton Grove SE17 ... 247 F1
Burton Street WC1 ... 242 B4
Burwell Close E1 ... 248 C3
Burwood Place W2 ... 241 D2
Bury Close SE16 ... 249 E2
Bury Court EC3 ... 248 A4
Bury Place WC1 ... 242 B2
Bury Street EC3 ... 248 A3
Bury Street SW1 ... 246 A4
Bury Walk SW3 ... 244 C2
Bush Lane EC4 ... 243 E2
Bushell Street E1 ... 248 B2
  Wapping High Street
Butcher Row E1 ... 249 E3
Bute Street SW7 ... 244 C1
Butler Place SW1 ... 245 F3
  Buckingham Gate
Butterfield Close SE16 ... 248 C1
Buttesland Street N1 ... 243 F4
Byelands Close SE16 ... 249 E2
Byfield Close SE16 ... 249 F2
Byng Place WC1 ... 242 A3
Byng Street E14 ... 250 A3
Byward Street EC3 ... 248 A3
Bywater Place SE16 ... 249 E2
Bywater Street SW3 ... 245 D2

C

Cabbell Street NW1 ... 240 C2
Cable Street E1 ... 248 C2
Cabot Square E14 ... 250 A4
Cadiz Street SE17 ... 247 F1
Cadogan Gardens SW3 ... 245 D2
Cadogan Gate SW1 ... 245 D2
Cadogan Lane SW1 ... 245 E3
Cadogan Place SW1 ... 245 D2
Cadogan Square SW1 ... 245 D2
Cadogan Street SW3 ... 245 D2
Cahill Street EC1 ... 243 E3
  Dufferin Street
Cahir Street E14 ... 250 A2
Cale Street SW3 ... 244 C2
Caleb Street SE1 ... 247 E4
  Marshalsea Road
Caledonia Street N1 ... 242 B4
Caledonian Road N1 & N7 ... 242 B4
Caledonian Wharf E14 ... 250 C2
Callingham Close E14 ... 249 F4
Callow Street SW3 ... 244 B1
Calthorpe Street WC1 ... 242 C3
Camberwell Road SE5 ... 247 E1
Cambridge Circus WC2 ... 242 B1
Cambridge Gate NW1 ... 241 F3
Cambridge Gate Mews NW1 ... 241 F4
  Albany Street
Cambridge Place W8 ... 244 B3
Cambridge Road NW6 ... 240 A4
Cambridge Square W2 ... 240 C2
Cambridge Street SW1 ... 245 F2
Cambridge Terrace Mews NW1 ... 241 F4
  Chester Gate
Camdenhurst Street E14 ... 249 E4
Camera Place SW10 ... 244 B1
Cameron Place E1 ... 248 C4
Camomile Street EC3 ... 248 A4
Campden Grove W8 ... 244 A4
Campden Hill Road W8 ... 244 A4
Camperdown Street E1 ... 248 B3
Canada Square E14 ... 250 B4
Canada Street SE16 ... 249 E1
Canal Street SE5 ... 247 F1
Candover Street W1 ... 241 F2
  Foley Street
Canning Passage W8 ... 244 B3
Canning Place W8 ... 244 B3
Cannon Beck Road SE16 ... 249 D2
Cannon Drive E14 ... 249 F3
Cannon Row W1 ... 246 B3
Cannon Street EC4 ... 243 E2
Cannon Street Road E1 ... 248 C3
Canterbury Place SE17 ... 247 E2
Canvey Street SE1 ... 247 E4
Cape Yard E1 ... 248 B3
Capland Street NW8 ... 240 C3
Capper Street WC1 ... 242 A3
Capstan Square E14 ... 250 C3
Capstan Way SE16 ... 249 E2
Caravel Close E14 ... 250 A3
Carbis Road E14 ... 249 F4
Carburton Street W1 ... 241 F3
Cardale Street E14 ... 250 B3
  Plevina Street
Cardigan Street SE11 ... 246 C1
Cardington Street NW1 ... 242 A4
Carey Lane EC2 ... 243 E2
Carey Street WC2 ... 242 C2
Carlisle Avenue EC3 ... 248 A3
Carlisle Lane SE1 ... 246 C3
Carlisle Place SW1 ... 245 F2
Carlisle Street W1 ... 242 A2
Carlos Place W1 ... 241 E1
Carlton Gardens SW1 ... 246 A4
Carlton House Terrace SW1 ... 246 A4
Carlton Vale NW6 ... 240 A4
Carlyle Square SW3 ... 244 C1
Carmelite Street EC4 ... 243 D1
Carnaby Street W1 ... 242 A1
Caroline Place Mews W2 ... 240 A1
Caroline Place W2 ... 240 A1
Caroline Terrace SW1 ... 245 E2
Carpenter Street W1 ... 241 E1
Carr Street E14 ... 249 E4
Carrick Mews SE8 ... 250 A1
Carrington Street W1 ... 245 E4
  Shepherd Street
Carter Lane EC4 ... 243 D2
Carter Place SE17 ... 247 E1
Carter Street SE17 ... 247 E1
Carteret Street SW1 ... 246 A3
Carthusian Street EC1 ... 243 E3
Cartier Circle E14 ... 250 B4
Carting Lane WC2 ... 242 C1
Cartwright Gardens WC1 ... 242 B4
Cartwright Street E1 ... 248 B3
Casson Street E1 ... 248 B4
Castalia Square E14 ... 250 B3
Castellain Road W9 ... 240 A3
Castle Baynard Street EC4 ... 243 E1
Castle Lane SW1 ... 246 A3
Castle Yard SE1 ... 247 D4
Castlebrook Close SE11 ... 247 D2
  Brook Drive
Castlereagh Street W1 ... 241 D2
Castor Lane E14 ... 250 A4
Catesby Street SE17 ... 247 F2
Cathay Street SE16 ... 248 C1
Cathcart Road SW10 ... 244 B1
Cathedral Piazza SW1 ... 245 F3
Cathedral Street SE1 ... 247 F4
  Winchester Walk
Catherine Place SW1 ... 245 F3
Catherine Street WC2 ... 242 C1
Catherine Wheel Alley E1 ... 248 A4
Catherine Wheel Yard SW1 ... 246 A4
  Little St James's Street
Cato Street W1 ... 241 D2
Catton Street WC1 ... 242 C2
Causton Street SW1 ... 246 B2
Cavaye Place SW10 ... 244 B1
Cavell Street E1 ... 248 C4
Cavendish Avenue NW8 ... 240 C4
Cavendish Close NW8 ... 240 C4
Cavendish Mews North W1 ... 241 F3
  Hallam Street
Cavendish Mews South W1 ... 241 F2
  Hallam Street
Cavendish Place W1 ... 241 F2
Cavendish Square W1 ... 241 F2
Caversham Street SW3 ... 245 D1
Caxton Street SW1 ... 246 A3
Cayton Place EC1 ... 243 F4
  Cayton Street
Cayton Street EC1 ... 243 E4
Cecil Court WC2 ... 242 B1
  St Martin's Lane
Centaur Street SE1 ... 246 C3
Central Street EC1 ... 243 E4
Chadwell Street EC1 ... 243 D4
Chadwick Street SW1 ... 246 B3
Chagford Street NW1 ... 241 D3
Chalton Street NW1 ... 242 A4
Chamber Street E1 ... 248 B3
Chambers Street SE16 ... 248 B1
Chancel Street SE1 ... 247 D4
Chancellor Passage E14 ... 250 A4
  South Colonnade
Chancellor Passage E14 ... 250 A4
Chancery Lane WC2 ... 242 C2
Chandler Street E1 ... 248 C2
Chandos Place WC2 ... 242 B1
Chandos Street W1 ... 241 F2
Chantry Square W8 ... 244 A3
Chapel Court SE1 ... 247 F4
Chapel House Street E14 ... 250 B1
Chapel Place W1 ... 241 F2
Chapel Side W2 ... 240 A1
Chapel Street NW1 ... 240 C2
Chapel Street SW1 ... 245 E3
Chapman Street E1 ... 248 C3
Chapter Road SE17 ... 247 E1
Chapter Street SW1 ... 246 B2
Chapter Terrace SE17 ... 247 D1
Chargrove Close SE16 ... 249 E2
Charing Cross Road WC2 ... 242 B2
Charles II Street SW1 ... 246 A4
Charles Square N1 ... 243 F4
Charles Street W1 ... 245 F4
Charleston Street SE17 ... 247 E2
Charlie Chaplin Walk SE1 ... 246 C4
  Waterloo Road
Charlotte Place W1 ... 242 A2
  Goodge Street
Charlotte Place SW1 ... 245 F2
  Wilton Road
Charlotte Road EC2 ... 243 F4
Charlotte Street W1 ... 242 A2
Charlwood Street SW1 ... 246 A1
Charnwood Gardens E14 ... 250 A2
Chart Street N1 ... 243 F4
Charterhouse Square EC1 ... 243 E3
Charterhouse Street EC1 ... 243 D2
Chaseley Street E14 ... 249 E4
Chatham Street SE17 ... 247 F2
Cheapside EC4 ... 243 E2
Chelsea Bridge SW1 & SW8 ... 245 E1
Chelsea Bridge Road SW1 ... 245 E1
Chelsea Embankment SW3 ... 245 D1
Chelsea Manor Gardens SW3 ... 245 D1
Chelsea Manor Street SW3 ... 245 D1
Chelsea Park Gardens SW3 ... 244 C1
Chelsea Square SW3 ... 244 C1
Cheltenham Terrace SW3 ... 245 D2
Chenies Mews WC1 ... 242 A3
Chenies Street WC1 ... 242 A3
Cheniston Gardens W8 ... 244 A3
Chepstow Place W2 ... 240 A1
Chepstow Road W2 ... 240 A2
Chequer Street EC1 ... 243 E3
Cherbury Street N1 ... 243 F4
Cherry Garden Street SE16 ... 248 C1
Cherry Tree Terrace SE1 ... 248 A2
Chesham Place SW1 ... 245 E3
Chesham Street SW1 ... 245 E3
Chester Close North NW1 ... 241 F4
Chester Close South NW1 ... 241 F4
Chester Court NW1 ... 241 F4
  Albany Street
Chester Gate NW1 ... 241 F4
Chester Mews SW1 ... 245 E3
Chester Place NW1 ... 241 F4
Chester Row SW1 ... 245 E2
Chester Square SW1 ... 245 E2
Chester Street SW1 ... 245 E3
Chester Terrace NW1 ... 241 F4
Chester Way SE11 ... 247 D2
Chesterfield Gardens W1 ... 245 E4
Chesterfield Hill W1 ... 241 E1
Chesterfield Street W1 ... 245 E4
Cheval Place SW7 ... 245 D3
Cheval Street E14 ... 250 A3
Cheyne Gardens SW3 ... 244 D1
Cheyne Walk SW3 & SW10 ... 244 C1
Chicheley Street SE1 ... 246 C4
Chichester Parade E14 ... 250 C2
Chichester Rents WC2 ... 242 C2
  Chancery Lane
Chichester Road W2 ... 240 A3
Chichester Street SW1 ... 246 A1
Chicksand Street E1 ... 248 B4
Chigwell Hill E1 ... 248 C3
  The Highway
Child's Place SW5 ... 244 A2
Child's Street SW5 ... 244 A2
Childs Mews SW5 ... 244 A2
Chiltern Street W1 ... 241 E3
Chilworth Mews W2 ... 240 B2
Chilworth Street W2 ... 240 B2
Chipka Street E14 ... 250 B3
Chiswell Street EC1 ... 243 E3
Chitty Street W1 ... 242 A3
Christchurch Street SW3 ... 245 D1
Christian Court SE16 ... 249 F2
Christian Street E1 ... 248 C3
Christopher Close SE16 ... 249 E2
Christopher Street EC2 ... 243 F3
Chudleigh Street E1 ... 249 E4
Chumleigh Street SE5 ... 247 F1
Church Place SW1 ... 245 F4
  Piccadilly
Church Street NW8 ... 240 C3
Church Yard Row SE11 ... 247 D2
Churchill Gardens Road SW1 ... 245 F1
Churchill Place E14 ... 250 B4
Churchway NW1 ... 242 A4
Churton Street SW1 ... 246 A2
Cinnamon Street E1 ... 248 C2
Circus Mews W1 ... 241 D3
  Enford Street
Circus Road EC2 ... 243 F2
  Finsbury Circus
Circus Road NW8 ... 240 C4
Cirencester Street W2 ... 240 A3
Citadel Place SE11 ... 246 C2
City Garden Row N1 ... 243 E4
City Road EC1 ... 243 F3
Clabon Mews SW1 ... 245 D2
Clack Street SE16 ... 249 D1
Claire Place E14 ... 250 A3
Clanricarde Gardens W2 ... 240 A1
Clare Market WC2 ... 242 C2
Claremont Close N1 ... 243 D4
Claremont Square N1 ... 243 D4
Clarence Gardens NW1 ... 241 F4
Clarence Mews SE16 ... 249 E1
Clarendon Close W2 ... 240 C1
Clarendon Gardens W9 ... 240 B3
Clarendon Place W2 ... 240 C1
Clarendon Road W11 ... 245 F1
Clarendon Street SW1 ... 245 F1
Clarendon Terrace W9 ... 240 B3
Clareville Grove SW7 ... 244 B2
Clareville Street SW7 ... 244 B2
Clarges Mews W1 ... 245 F4
Clarges Street W1 ... 245 F4
Clark Street E1 ... 248 C4
Clark's Orchard SE16 ... 248 C1
Claude Street E14 ... 250 A2
Clave Street E1 ... 248 C2
Claverton Street SW1 ... 246 A1
Clay Street W1 ... 241 D2
Clayton Street SE11 ... 246 C1
Clearbrook Way E1 ... 249 D4
Clearwell Drive W9 ... 240 A3
Cleaver Square SE11 ... 247 D1
Cleaver Street SE11 ... 247 D1
Clegg Street E1 ... 248 C2
Clemence Street E14 ... 249 F4
Clement's Inn WC2 ... 242 C2
Clement's Road SE16 ... 248 C1
Clements Lane EC4 ... 243 F1
Clenston Mews W1 ... 241 D2
Clere Street EC2 ... 243 F3
Clerkenwell Close EC1 ... 243 D3
Clerkenwell Green EC1 ... 243 D3
Clerkenwell Road EC1 ... 242 C3
Cleveland Gardens W2 ... 240 B2
Cleveland Mews W1 ... 241 F3
Cleveland Place SW1 ... 246 A4
  King Street
Cleveland Row SW1 ... 246 A4
Cleveland Square W2 ... 240 B2
Cleveland Street W1 ... 241 F3
Cleveland Terrace W2 ... 240 B2
Clifford Street W1 ... 241 F1
Clifton Gardens W9 ... 240 B3
Clifton Place W2 ... 240 C1
Clifton Road W9 ... 240 B3
Clifton Street EC2 ... 243 F3
Clifton Villas W9 ... 240 B3
Clink Street SE1 ... 247 F4
Clipper Close SE16 ... 249 D2
  Kinburn Street
Clipstone Mews W1 ... 241 F3
Clipstone Street W1 ... 241 F3
Cliveden Place SW1 ... 245 E2
Cloak Lane EC4 ... 243 E1
Cloth Fair EC1 ... 243 E3
Cloth Street EC1 ... 243 E3
Clunbury Street N1 ... 243 F4
  Cherbury Street
Cluny Place SE1 ... 247 F3
Coach & Horses Yard W1 ... 241 F1
  Old Burlington Street
Coach House Mews SE1 ... 247 F3
Cobb Street E1 ... 248 A4
Cobourg Street NW1 ... 242 A4
Cock Lane EC1 ... 243 D2
Cockpit Yard WC1 ... 242 C3
Cockspur Street SW1 ... 246 B4
Codling Close E1 ... 248 C1
Coin Street SE1 ... 247 D4
Coke Street E1 ... 248 B4
Colbeck Mews SW7 ... 244 B2
Colchester Street E1 ... 248 B4
  Drum Street
Coldbath Square EC1 ... 242 C3
Coldharbour E14 ... 250 C4
Cole Street SE1 ... 247 E3
Colebrooke Row N1 ... 243 D1
Coleherne Mews SW10 ... 244 A1
Coleherne Road SW10 ... 244 A1
Coleman Street EC2 ... 243 E2
Coley Street WC1 ... 242 C3
College Hill EC4 ... 243 E1
College Street EC4 ... 243 E1
  College Street
Collett Road SE16 ... 248 C1
Collier Street N1 ... 242 C4
Collingham Gardens SW5 ... 244 A2
Collingham Place SW4 ... 244 A2
Collingham Road SW5 ... 244 A2
Collinson Street SE1 ... 247 E3
Colnbrook Street SE1 ... 247 D3
Colombo Street SE1 ... 247 D4
Colonnade WC1 ... 242 B3
Colworth Grove SE17 ... 247 E2
Commercial Road E1 & E14 ... 248 B4
Commercial Street E1 ... 248 A4
Compton Passage EC1 ... 243 D3
Compton Place WC1 ... 242 B3
Compton Street EC1 ... 243 D3
Comus Place SE17 ... 247 F2
Concert Hall Approach SE1 ... 246 C4
Conder Street E14 ... 249 E4
  Salmon Lane
Conduit Mews W2 ... 240 C2
Conduit Place W2 ... 240 C2
Conduit Street W1 ... 241 F1
Congreve Street SE17 ... 247 F2
Connaught Place W2 ... 241 D1
Connaught Square W2 ... 241 D2
Connaught Street W2 ... 240 C2
Cons Street SE1 ... 247 D4
Constitution Hill SW1 ... 245 E3
Content Street SE17 ... 247 E2
Conway Street W1 ... 241 F3
Cook's Road E15 ... 247 D1
Cookham Crescent SE16 ... 249 D2
Coombs Street N1 ... 243 E4
Cooper Close SE1 ... 247 D3
Cooper's Row EC3 ... 248 A3
Cope Place W8 ... 244 A3
Copeland Drive E14 ... 250 A2
Copenhagen Place E14 ... 249 F3
Copley Close SE17 ... 247 E1
Copperfield Street SE1 ... 247 E4
Copthall Avenue EC2 ... 243 F2
Coptic Street WC1 ... 242 B2
Coral Street SE1 ... 247 D3
Coram Street WC1 ... 242 B3
Cord Way E14 ... 250 A3
Cork Square E1 ... 248 C2
Cork Street W1 ... 241 F1
Corlett Street NW1 ... 240 C3
  Bell Street
Corner House Street WC2 ... 246 B4
  Northumberland Street
Cornhill EC3 ... 243 F2
Cornwall Gardens SW7 ... 244 B3
Cornwall Gardens Walk SW7 ... 244 A2
Cornwall Mews South SW7 ... 244 A2
Cornwall Mews West SW7 ... 244 A3
Cornwall Road SE1 ... 246 C4
Cornwall Square SE11 ... 247 D1
Cornwall Street E1 ... 248 C3
Cornwall Terrace NW1 ... 241 D3
Cornwood Drive E1 ... 249 D4
Coronet Street N1 ... 243 F4
Corporation Row EC1 ... 243 D3
Corsham Street N1 ... 243 F4
Cosmo Place WC1 ... 242 B3
Cosser Street SE1 ... 246 C3
Cosway Street NW1 ... 241 D3
Cotham Street SE17 ... 247 E2
Cottage Place SW3 ... 244 C3
Cottesloe Mews SE1 ... 247 D3
Cottesmore Gardens W8 ... 244 B3
Cottingham Close SE11 ... 247 D2
Cottington Street SE11 ... 247 D2
Cottons Lane SE1 ... 247 F4
Counter Street SE1 ... 247 F4
County Street SE1 ... 247 E2
Court Street E1 ... 248 C4
Courtenay Square SE11 ... 246 C1
Courtenay Street SE11 ... 246 C1
Courtfield Gardens SW5 ... 244 A2
Courtfield Road SW7 ... 244 B2
Cousin Lane EC4 ... 243 F1
Coventry Street W1 ... 242 A1
Coverley Close E1 ... 248 B4
Cowcross Street EC1 ... 243 D3
Cowley Street SW1 ... 246 B3
Cowper Street EC2 ... 243 F3
Coxon Place SE1 ... 248 A1
Crace Street NW1 ... 242 A4
Crail Row SE17 ... 247 F2
Cramer Street W1 ... 241 E2
Crampton Street SE17 ... 247 E2
Cranbourn Street WC2 ... 242 B1
Crane Street SE10 ... 250 C1
Cranford Street E1 ... 249 E3
Cranley Gardens SW7 ... 244 B2
Cranley Mews SW7 ... 244 B2
Cranley Place SW7 ... 244 C2
Cranmer Court SW3 ... 245 D2
Cranwood Street EC1 ... 243 F4
Craven Hill W2 ... 240 B1
Craven Hill Gardens W2 ... 240 B1
Craven Hill Mews W2 ... 240 B1
Craven Road W2 ... 240 B1
Craven Street WC2 ... 242 B1
Craven Terrace W2 ... 240 B1
Crawford Passage EC1 ... 243 D3
Crawford Place W1 ... 241 D2
Crawford Street W1 ... 241 D2
Creasy Street SE1 ... 247 F3
  Swan Mead
Creechurch Lane EC3 ... 248 A3
Creechurch Place EC3 ... 248 A3
Creed Lane EC4 ... 243 E2
Crescent EC3 ... 248 A3
Crescent Place SW3 ... 245 D2
Crescent Row EC1 ... 243 E3
Cresswell Place SW10 ... 244 B1
Cressy Place E1 ... 249 D4
Crestfield Street WC1 ... 242 B4
Cricketers' Court SE11 ... 247 D1
  Kennington Park Road
Crimscott Street SE1 ... 248 A1
Cripplegate Street EC1 ... 243 E3
  Viscount Street
Crispin Street E1 ... 248 A4
Crofts Street E1 ... 248 B3
Cromer Street WC1 ... 242 B4
Crompton Street W2 ... 240 B3
Cromwell Mews SW7 ... 244 C2
Cromwell Place SW7 ... 244 C2
Cromwell Road SW7 & SW5 ... 244 A2
Crondall Street N1 ... 243 F4
Crosby Row SE1 ... 247 F3
Crosby Square EC3 ... 243 F2
  Great St Helen's
Cross Keys Close W1 ... 241 E2
  Marylebone Lane
Cross Lane EC3 ... 248 A3
  St Dunstan's Hill
Crosslet Street SE17 ... 247 F2
Crosswall EC3 ... 248 A3
Crowder Street E1 ... 248 C3
Crown Court WC2 ... 242 B2
Crown Office Row EC4 ... 243 D1
Crown Passage SW1 ... 246 A4
Crown Place EC2 ... 243 F3
Crucifix Lane SE1 ... 248 A2
Cruikshank Street WC1 ... 242 C4
Crutched Friars EC3 ... 248 A3
Cuba Street E14 ... 250 A3
Cubitt Steps E14 ... 250 A4
Cubitt Street WC1 ... 242 C4
Cubitts Yard WC2 ... 242 B1
  James Street
Culford Gardens SW3 ... 245 D2
Culling Road SE16 ... 249 D1
Cullum Street EC3 ... 248 A3
Culross Street W1 ... 241 E1
Culworth Street NW8 ... 240 C4
Cumberland Gardens WC1 ... 242 C4
  Great Percy Street
Cumberland Gate W1 & W2 ... 241 D1
Cumberland Market NW1 ... 241 F4
Cumberland Street SW1 ... 245 F1
Cumberland Terrace NW1 ... 241 F4
Cumberland Terrace Mews NW1 ... 241 F4
  Albany Street
Cumming Street N1 ... 242 C4
Cundy Street SW1 ... 245 E2
Cunningham Place NW8 ... 240 C3
Cureton Street SW1 ... 246 B2
Curlew Street SE1 ... 248 B2
Cursitor Street EC4 ... 242 C2
Curzon Gate W1 ... 245 E4
Curzon Place W1 ... 245 E4
Curzon Street W1 ... 245 E4
Cuthbert Street W2 ... 240 C3
Cutler Street E1 ... 248 A4
Cutlers Square E14 ... 250 A2
Cyclops Mews E14 ... 250 A2
Cynthia Street N1 ... 242 C4
Cypress Place W1 ... 242 A3
Cyrus Street EC1 ... 243 D3
Czar Street SE8 ... 250 A1

D

D'Arblay Street W1 ... 242 A2
D'Oyley Street SW1 ... 245 E2
Da Gama Place E14 ... 250 A1
  Maritime Quay
Dacre Street SW1 ... 246 A3
Dalgleish Street E14 ... 249 E4
Dallington Square EC1 ... 243 D3
Dallington Street EC1 ... 243 D3
Damien Street E1 ... 248 C4
Dane Street WC1 ... 242 C2
Dante Road SE11 ... 247 D2
Daplyn Street E1 ... 248 B4
Dark House Walk EC3 ... 243 F1
Dartford Street SE17 ... 247 E1
Dartmouth Street SW1 ... 246 A3
Darwin Street SE17 ... 247 F2
Date Street SE17 ... 247 E1
Davenant Street E1 ... 248 B4
Daventry Street NW1 ... 240 C3
Davidge Street SE1 ... 247 D3
Davies Mews W1 ... 241 E1
Davies Street W1 ... 241 E1
Dawes Street SE17 ... 247 F2
Dawson Place W2 ... 240 A1
De Laune Street SE17 ... 247 D1
De Vere Gardens W8 ... 244 B3
De Walden Street W1 ... 241 E2
  Westmorland Street
Deacon Way SE17 ... 247 E2
Deal Porters Way SE16 ... 249 D1
Deal Street E1 ... 248 B4
Dean Bradley Street SW1 ... 246 B2
Dean Close SE16 ... 249 E2
Dean Farrar Street SW1 ... 246 A3
Dean Ryle Street SW1 ... 246 B2
Dean Stanley Street SW1 ... 246 B2
  Millbank
Dean Street W1 ... 242 A2
Dean Trench Street SW1 ... 246 B3
Dean's Buildings SE17 ... 247 F2
Dean's Court EC4 ... 243 E2
  Carter Lane
Dean's Mews W1 ... 241 F2
Deancross Street E1 ... 248 C3
Deanery Street W1 ... 245 E4
Decima Street SE1 ... 247 F3
Deck Close SE16 ... 249 E2
Defoe Close SE16 ... 249 F1
Delamere Terrace W2 ... 240 A3
Delaware Road W9 ... 240 A3
Dellow Street E1 ... 248 C3
Delverton Road SE17 ... 247 E1
Denbigh Street SW1 ... 245 F2
Denman Street W1 ... 242 A1
Denmark Place WC2 ... 242 B2
  Charing Cross Road
Denmark Street WC2 ... 242 B2
Denning Close NW8 ... 240 B4
Denny Crescent SE11 ... 247 D2
Denny Street SE11 ... 247 D2
Denyer Street SW3 ... 245 D2
Deptford Green SE8 ... 250 A1
Derby Gate SW1 ... 246 B3
Dering Street W1 ... 241 F2
Deverell Street SE1 ... 247 F3
Devereux Court WC2 ... 242 C1
  Strand
Devonport Street E1 ... 249 D3
Devonshire Close W1 ... 241 F3
Devonshire Mews South W1 ... 241 E3
Devonshire Mews West W1 ... 241 E3
Devonshire Place W1 ... 241 E3
Devonshire Place Mews W1 ... 241 E3
  St Mary's Place
Devonshire Row EC2 ... 248 A4
Devonshire Square EC2 ... 248 A4
Devonshire Street W1 ... 241 E3
Devonshire Terrace W2 ... 240 B1
Diadem Court W1 ... 242 A2
  Dean Street
Dickens Square SE1 ... 247 E3
Dilke Street SW3 ... 245 D1
Dingle Gardens E14 ... 250 A4
Dingley Place EC1 ... 243 E4
Dingley Road EC1 ... 243 E4
Disney Place SE1 ... 247 E3

Disney Street SE1 ...... 247 E4
Redcross Way
Distaff Lane EC4 ...... 243 E1
Distin Street SE11 ...... 246 C2
Dixon's Alley SE1 ...... 248 C1
West Lane
Dock Hill Avenue SE16 ...... 249 E2
Dock Street E1 ...... 248 B3
Dockers Tanner Road E14 ...... 250 A2
Dockhead SE1 ...... 248 B1
Dockley Road SE16 ...... 248 B1
Dod Street E14 ...... 249 F4
Doddington Grove SE17 ...... 247 D1
Doddington Place SE17 ...... 247 D1
Dodson Street SE1 ...... 247 D3
Dolben Street SE1 ...... 247 D4
Dolland Street SE11 ...... 246 C1
Dolphin Close SE16 ...... 249 D2
Dombey Street WC1 ...... 242 C3
Domingo Street EC1 ...... 243 E3
Old Street
Dominion Street EC2 ...... 243 F2
Donegal Street N1 ...... 242 C4
Dongola Road E1 ...... 249 F4
Donne Place SW3 ...... 245 D2
Doon Street SE1 ...... 246 C4
Dora Street E14 ...... 249 F4
Doric Way NW1 ...... 242 A4
Dorrington Street EC1 ...... 243 D3
Brooke Street
Dorset Close NW1 ...... 241 D3
Dorset Mews SW1 ...... 245 E3
Dorset Rise EC4 ...... 243 D1
Dorset Square NW1 ...... 241 D3
Dorset Street W1 ...... 241 D2
Doughty Mews WC1 ...... 242 C3
Doughty Street WC1 ...... 242 C3
Douglas Place SW1 ...... 246 A2
Douglas Street
Douglas Street SW1 ...... 246 A2
Douro Place W8 ...... 244 B3
Dove Mews SW5 ...... 244 B2
Dove Walk SW1 ...... 245 E2
Dovehouse Street SW3 ...... 244 C1
Dover Street W1 ...... 241 F1
Dowgate Hill EC4 ...... 243 F1
Down Street W1 ...... 245 E4
Downfield Close W9 ...... 240 A3
Downing Street SW1 ...... 246 B4
Downton Road SE16 ...... 249 E2
Doyce Street SE1 ...... 247 E4
Draco Street SE17 ...... 247 D1
Drake Street WC1 ...... 242 C2
Drawdock Road SE10 ...... 250 C4
Draycott Avenue SW3 ...... 245 D2
Draycott Place SW3 ...... 245 D2
Draycott Terrace SW3 ...... 245 D2
Drayson Mews W8 ...... 244 A3
Drayton Gardens SW10 ...... 244 B1
Druid Street SE1 ...... 248 A2
Drum Street E1 ...... 248 B4
Drummond Crescent NW1 ...... 242 A4
Drummond Gate SW1 ...... 246 A1
Drummond Road SE16 ...... 248 C1
Drummond Street NW1 ...... 241 F3
Drury Lane WC2 ...... 242 B2
Dryden Court SE11 ...... 247 D2
Duchess Mews W1 ...... 241 F2
Duchess Street W1 ...... 241 F2
Duchy Street SE1 ...... 247 D4
Duck Lane W1 ...... 242 A2
Dudley Street W2 ...... 240 B2
Dudmaston Mews SW3 ...... 244 C2
Dufferin Street EC1 ...... 243 E3
Dufour's Place W1 ...... 242 A4
Dugard Way SE11 ...... 247 D2
Renfrew Road
Duke of Wellington Place SW1 ...... 245 E3
Duke of York Street SW1 ...... 242 A1
Duke Street W1 ...... 241 E2
Duke Street Hill SE1 ...... 247 F4
Duke's Lane W8 ...... 244 A4
Duke's Place EC3 ...... 248 A4
Duke's Road WC1 ...... 242 B4
Duke's Yard W1 ...... 241 E2
Duke Street
Duncannon Street WC2 ...... 242 B1
Dundee Street E1 ...... 248 C2
Dundee Wharf E14 ...... 249 F3
Dunelm Street E1 ...... 249 D4
Dunlop Place SE16 ...... 248 B1
Dunraven Street W1 ...... 241 E1
Dunstable Mews W1 ...... 241 E3
Dunster Court EC3 ...... 248 A3
Dunsterville Way SE1 ...... 247 F3
Duplex Ride SW1 ...... 245 E3
Dupont Street E14 ...... 249 E4
Durham House Street WC2 ...... 242 B1
Durham Row E1 ...... 249 E4
Durham Street SE11 ...... 246 C1
Durham Terrace W2 ...... 240 A2
Durward Street E1 ...... 248 C4
Durweston Street W1 ...... 241 D2
Crawford Street
Duthie Street E14 ...... 250 C4
Dyott Street WC1 ...... 242 B2
Dysart Street EC2 ...... 243 F3

E

Eagle Court EC1 ...... 243 D3
Eagle Place SW1 ...... 246 A4
Piccadilly
Eagle Street WC2 ...... 242 C2
Eardley Crescent SW5 ...... 244 A1
Earl Street EC2 ...... 243 F3
Earl's Court Gardens SW5 ...... 244 A2
Earl's Court Square SW5 ...... 244 A1
Earlham Street WC2 ...... 242 B2
Earls Court Road W8 ...... 244 A2
Earlstoke Street EC1 ...... 243 D4
Spencer Street
Earnshaw Street WC2 ...... 242 B2
Easley's Mews W1 ...... 241 E2
Wigmore Street
East Arbour Street E1 ...... 249 D4
East Ferry Road E14 ...... 250 B2
East Harding Street EC4 ...... 243 D2
East India Dock Wall Road E14 ...... 243 D2
East Lane SE16 ...... 248 B1
East Mount Street E1 ...... 248 C4
East Road N1 ...... 243 F4
East Smithfield E1 ...... 248 B3
East Street SE17 ...... 247 E1
East Tenter Street E1 ...... 248 B3
Eastbourne Mews W2 ...... 240 C2
Eastbourne Terrace W2 ...... 240 B2
Eastcastle Street W1 ...... 242 A2
Eastcheap EC3 ...... 243 F1
Eastney Street SE10 ...... 250 C1
Easton Street WC1 ...... 242 C3
Eaton Gate SW1 ...... 245 E2
Eaton Mews North SW1 ...... 245 E2

Eaton Mews South SW1 ...... 245 E2
Eaton Place SW1 ...... 245 E2
Eaton Square SW1 ...... 245 E2
Eaton Terrace SW1 ...... 245 E2
Ebbisham Drive SW8 ...... 246 C1
Ebenezer Street N1 ...... 243 F4
Ebury Bridge SW1 ...... 245 E2
Ebury Bridge Road SW1 ...... 245 E1
Ebury Mews SW1 ...... 245 E2
Ebury Mews East SW1 ...... 245 E2
Ebury Square SW1 ...... 245 E2
Ebury Street SW1 ...... 245 E2
Eccleston Bridge SW1 ...... 245 F2
Eccleston Mews SW1 ...... 245 E3
Eccleston Place SW1 ...... 245 E2
Eccleston Square SW1 ...... 245 F2
Eccleston Square Mews SW1 ...... 245 F2
Eccleston Street SW1 ...... 245 E2
Edbrooke Road W9 ...... 240 A3
Edge Street W8 ...... 244 A4
Edgware Road W2 ...... 240 C3
Edward Mews NW1 ...... 241 F4
Edward Mews W1 ...... 241 E2
Edward Square SE16 ...... 249 F3
Egerton Crescent SW3 ...... 244 C2
Egerton Gardens SW3 ...... 244 C2
Egerton Terrace SW3 ...... 245 D2
Elba Place SE17 ...... 247 E2
Eldon Road W8 ...... 244 B3
Eldon Street EC2 ...... 243 F2
Eleanor Close SE16 ...... 249 D2
Elephant and Castle SE1 ...... 247 E2
Elephant Lane SE16 ...... 248 C2
Elephant Road SE17 ...... 247 E2
Elf Row E1 ...... 249 D3
Elgar Street SE16 ...... 249 F1
Elgin Avenue W9 ...... 240 A3
Elgin Mews North W9 ...... 240 A4
Elgin Mews South W9 ...... 240 B4
Elia Street N1 ...... 243 D4
Elim Street SE1 ...... 247 F3
Eliot Mews NW8 ...... 240 B4
Elizabeth Bridge SW1 ...... 245 F2
Elizabeth Close W9 ...... 240 B3
Elizabeth Square SE16 ...... 249 E3
Elizabeth Street SW1 ...... 245 E2
Ellen Street E1 ...... 248 B3
Elliott Road SW9 ...... 247 D2
Ellis Street SW1 ...... 245 E2
Elm Park Gardens SW10 ...... 244 C1
Elm Park Lane SW3 ...... 244 B1
Elm Park Road SW3 ...... 244 B1
Elm Place SW7 ...... 244 C1
Elm Street WC1 ...... 242 C3
Elm Tree Close NW8 ...... 240 C4
Elm Tree Road NW8 ...... 240 C4
Elmfield Way W9 ...... 240 A3
Elmos Road SE16 ...... 249 E1
Elms Mews W2 ...... 240 C1
Elnathan Mews W9 ...... 240 A4
Elsa Street E1 ...... 249 E4
Elsted Street SE17 ...... 247 F2
Elvaston Mews SW7 ...... 244 B3
Elvaston Place SW7 ...... 244 B3
Elverton Street SW1 ...... 246 A2
Ely Place EC1 ...... 243 D2
Elystan Place SW3 ...... 245 D2
Elystan Street SW3 ...... 244 C2
Embankment Gardens SW3 ...... 245 D1
Embankment Place WC2 ...... 246 B4
Emerald Street WC1 ...... 242 C3
Emerson Street SE1 ...... 247 E4
Emery Hill Street SW1 ...... 246 A2
Emery Street SE1 ...... 247 D3
Emmett Street E14 ...... 249 F3
Emperor's Gate SW7 ...... 244 B2
Empire Wharf Road E14 ...... 250 C2
Empress Place SW6 ...... 244 A1
Empress Street SE17 ...... 247 E1
Endell Street WC2 ...... 242 B2
Endsleigh Gardens WC1 ...... 242 A3
Endsleigh Place WC1 ...... 242 A3
Endsleigh Street WC1 ...... 242 A3
Enford Street W1 ...... 241 D3
English Grounds SE1 ...... 248 A2
Enid Street SE1 ...... 248 B1
Ennismore Garden Mews SW7 ...... 244 C3
Ennismore Gardens SW7 ...... 244 C3
Ennismore Mews SW7 ...... 244 C3
Ennismore Street SW7 ...... 244 C3
Ensign Street E1 ...... 248 B3
Ensor Mews SW7 ...... 244 B1
Epping Close E14 ...... 250 A2
Epworth Street EC2 ...... 243 F3
Erasmus Street SW1 ...... 246 B2
Errol Street EC1 ...... 243 E3
Essendine Road W9 ...... 240 A4
Essex Street WC2 ...... 242 C1
Esterbrooke Street SW1 ...... 246 A2
Ethel Street SE17 ...... 247 E2
Europa Place EC1 ...... 243 E4
Euston Road NW1 ...... 241 F3
Euston Square NW1 ...... 242 A4
Euston Street NW1 ...... 242 A4
Evelyn Gardens SW7 ...... 244 B1
Evelyn Walk N1 ...... 243 F4
Evelyn Yard W1 ...... 242 A2
Gresse Street
Eversholt Street NW1 ...... 242 A4
Ewer Street SE1 ...... 247 E4
Exchange Place EC2 ...... 248 A4
Exchange Square EC2 ...... 248 A4
Exeter Street WC2 ...... 242 B1
Exhibition Road SW7 ...... 244 C3
Exmouth Market EC1 ...... 243 D3
Exmouth Street E1 ...... 249 D4
Exon Street SE17 ...... 247 F2
Exton Street SE1 ...... 246 C4
Eyre Street Hill EC1 ...... 243 D3

F

Factory Place E14 ...... 250 B1
Ferry Street
Fair Street SE1 ...... 248 A2
Fairclough Street E1 ...... 248 B3
Falcon Close SE1 ...... 247 E4
Falcon Point SE1 ...... 250 B2
Falconberg Mews W1 ...... 242 A2
Sutton Row
Falmouth Road SE1 ...... 247 E3
Fann Street EC1 ...... 243 E3
Fanshaw Street N1 ...... 243 F4
Fareham Street W1 ...... 242 A2
Dean Street
Farm Street W1 ...... 241 E1
Farmer Street W8 ...... 244 A4
Farncombe Street SE16 ...... 248 C1
Farnell Mews SW5 ...... 244 A1
Farnham Place SE1 ...... 247 E4
Farnham Royal SE11 ...... 246 C1
Farrance Street E14 ...... 249 F3

Farrier Walk SW10 ...... 244 B1
Farringdon Lane EC1 ...... 243 D3
Farringdon Road EC1 ...... 242 C3
Farringdon Street EC4 ...... 243 D2
Farrins Rents SE16 ...... 249 E2
Farrow Place SE16 ...... 249 E1
Farthing Alley SE1 ...... 248 B1
Wolseley Street
Farthing Fields E1 ...... 248 C2
Raine Street
Fashion Street E1 ...... 248 B4
Faunce Street SE17 ...... 247 D1
Fawcett Street SW10 ...... 244 A1
Feather's Place SE10 ...... 250 C1
Featherstone Street EC1 ...... 243 F3
Felstead Gardens E14 ...... 250 B1
Fen Court EC3 ...... 248 A3
Fenchurch Avenue EC3 ...... 248 A3
Fenchurch Buildings EC3 ...... 243 F1
Fenchurch Street
Fenchurch Place EC3 ...... 243 F1
Fenchurch Street
Fenchurch Street EC3 ...... 243 F1
Fendall Street SE1 ...... 248 A1
Fenning Street SE1 ...... 247 F4
St Thomas Street
Fennings Circus W1 ...... 242 A2
Ferguson Close E14 ...... 250 A2
Fernsbury Street WC1 ...... 242 C4
Ferry Street E14 ...... 250 B1
Fetter Lane EC4 ...... 243 D2
Field Street WC1 ...... 242 C4
Fieldgate Street E1 ...... 248 B4
Fielding Street SE17 ...... 247 E1
Finborough Road SW10 ...... 244 A1
Finch Lane EC3 ...... 243 F2
Finland Street SE16 ...... 249 E1
Finsbury Avenue EC2 ...... 243 F2
Finsbury Circus EC2 ...... 243 F2
Finsbury Market EC2 ...... 243 F3
Finsbury Pavement EC2 ...... 243 F3
Finsbury Square EC2 ...... 243 F3
Finsbury Street EC2 ...... 243 F3
First Street SW3 ...... 245 D2
Firtree Close SE16 ...... 249 E2
Fish Street Hill EC3 ...... 243 F1
Fish Wharf EC3 ...... 243 F1
Fisher Street WC1 ...... 242 C2
Fisherman's Walk E14 ...... 250 A4
Fishermans Drive SE16 ...... 249 E2
Fisherton Street NW8 ...... 240 C3
Fishmongers' Hall Wharf EC4 ...... 243 F1
Fitzalan Street SE11 ...... 246 C2
Fitzhardinge Street W1 ...... 241 E2
Fitzmaurice Place W1 ...... 241 F1
Fitzroy Square W1 ...... 241 F3
Fitzroy Street W1 ...... 241 F3
Flamborough Street E14 ...... 249 E3
Flank Street E1 ...... 248 B3
Flaxman Terrace WC1 ...... 242 B4
Fleet Square WC1 ...... 242 C4
Fleet Street EC4 ...... 243 D2
Fleming Road SE17 ...... 247 D1
Fletcher Street E1 ...... 248 B3
Flint Street SE17 ...... 247 F2
Flitcroft Street WC2 ...... 242 B2
Flood Street SW3 ...... 245 D1
Flood Walk SW3 ...... 245 D1
Floral Street WC2 ...... 242 B1
Flower and Dean Walk E1 ...... 248 B4
Thrawl Street
Foley Street W1 ...... 241 F2
Folly Wall E14 ...... 250 C3
Forbes Street E1 ...... 248 B3
Ford Square E1 ...... 248 C4
Fordham Street E1 ...... 248 C4
Fore Street EC2 ...... 243 E2
Fore Street Avenue EC2 ...... 243 E2
Formosa Street W9 ...... 240 A3
Forset Street W1 ...... 241 D2
Forsyth Gardens SE17 ...... 247 D1
Fort Street E1 ...... 248 A4
Artillery Lane
Fortune Street EC1 ...... 243 E3
Foscote Mews W9 ...... 240 A3
Foster Lane EC2 ...... 243 E2
Foubert's Place W1 ...... 241 F1
Foulis Terrace SW7 ...... 244 C1
Foundry Close SE16 ...... 249 E2
Fountain Green Square SE16 ...... 248 C1
Fournier Street E1 ...... 248 B4
Fowey Close E1 ...... 248 C2
Fox and Knot Street EC1 ...... 243 E2
Charterhouse Square
Frampton Street NW8 ...... 240 C3
Francis Close E14 ...... 250 C2
Francis Street SW1 ...... 246 A2
Franklin's Row SW3 ...... 245 D1
Frazier Street SE1 ...... 246 C3
Frean Street SE16 ...... 248 B1
Frederick Close W2 ...... 241 D1
Frederick Road SE17 ...... 247 D1
Frederick Square SE16 ...... 249 E3
Frederick Street WC1 ...... 242 C4
Fredericks Row EC1 ...... 243 D4
Fremantle Street SE17 ...... 247 F2
French Ordinary Court EC3 ...... 248 A3
Hart Street
Friar Street EC4 ...... 243 E2
Carter Lane
Friars Mead E14 ...... 250 B2
Friday Street EC4 ...... 243 E1
Friend Street EC1 ...... 243 D4
Frigate Mews SE8 ...... 250 A1
Frith Street W1 ...... 242 A2
Frobisher Passage E14 ...... 250 A4
North Colonnade
Frobisher Passage E14 ...... 250 A4
Frostic Walk E1 ...... 248 B4
Frying Pan Alley E1 ...... 248 A4
Fulbourne Street E1 ...... 248 C4
Fulford Street SE16 ...... 248 C1
Fulham Road SW3, SW6 & SW10 ...... 244 C1
Fulwood Place WC1 ...... 242 C2
Furnival Street EC4 ...... 243 D2
Fynes Street SW1 ...... 246 A2

G

Gabriels Wharf SE1 ...... 247 D4
Gainsford Street SE1 ...... 248 A2
Galbraith Street E14 ...... 250 B3
Galen Place WC1 ...... 242 B2
Galleon Close SE16 ...... 249 D2
Kinburn Street
Galleons View E14 ...... 250 C3
Galway Street EC1 ...... 243 E4
Gambia Street SE1 ...... 247 D4
Ganton Street W1 ...... 241 F1
Garbutt Place W1 ...... 241 E2
Gard Street EC1 ...... 243 E4

Garden Mews W2 ...... 240 A1
Garden Road NW8 ...... 240 B4
Garden Row SE1 ...... 247 D3
Garden Street E1 ...... 249 E4
Gardeners Lane EC4 ...... 243 E1
High Timber Street
Garford Street E14 ...... 249 F3
Garlick Hill EC4 ...... 243 E1
Garnault Mews EC1 ...... 243 D4
Garnet Street E1 ...... 248 C3
Garrett Street EC1 ...... 243 E3
Garrick Street WC2 ...... 242 B1
Garter Way SE16 ...... 249 D1
Garway Road W2 ...... 240 A2
Gaselee Street E14 ...... 250 C4
Gasholder Place SE11 ...... 246 C1
Gaspar Close SW5 ...... 244 B2
Gaspar Mews SW5 ...... 244 B2
Gate Street WC2 ...... 242 C2
Gateway SE17 ...... 247 E1
Gatliff Road SW1 ...... 245 E1
Gaunt Street SE1 ...... 247 E3
Gavel Street SE17 ...... 247 F2
Gayfere Street SW1 ...... 246 B3
Gaywood Street SE1 ...... 247 E3
Gaza Street SE17 ...... 247 D1
Gedling Place SE1 ...... 248 B1
Gee Street EC1 ...... 243 E3
Gees Court W1 ...... 241 E2
George Mathers Road SE11 ...... 247 D2
George Mews NW1 ...... 242 A4
George Row SE16 ...... 248 B1
George Street W1 ...... 241 D2
George Yard EC3 ...... 243 F1
George Yard W1 ...... 241 E1
Gerald Road SW1 ...... 245 E2
Geraldine Street SE11 ...... 247 D3
Gerrard Place W1 ...... 242 B1
Gerrard Street
Gerrard Street W1 ...... 242 A1
Gerridge Street SE1 ...... 247 D3
Gibson Road SE11 ...... 246 C2
Gilbert Place WC1 ...... 242 B2
Gilbert Street W1 ...... 241 E2
Gildea Street W1 ...... 241 F2
Gill Street E14 ...... 249 F3
Gillingham Street SW1 ...... 245 F2
Gillison Walk SE16 ...... 248 C1
Gilpin Close W2 ...... 240 B2
Porteus Road
Gilston Road SW10 ...... 244 B1
Giltspur Street EC1 ...... 243 D2
Gladstone Street SE1 ...... 247 D3
Glamis Place E1 ...... 249 D3
Glamis Road E1 ...... 249 D3
Glangarnock Avenue E14 ...... 250 C2
Glasgow Terrace SW1 ...... 245 F1
Glasshill Street SE1 ...... 247 E3
Glasshouse Fields E1 ...... 249 D3
Glasshouse Street W1 ...... 242 A1
Glasshouse Walk SE11 ...... 246 B1
Glastonbury Place E1 ...... 249 D3
Glebe Place SW3 ...... 244 C1
Gledhow Gardens SW5 ...... 244 B2
Glenaffric Avenue E14 ...... 250 C2
Glendower Place SW7 ...... 244 C2
Glengall Grove E14 ...... 250 B3
Glentworth Street NW1 ...... 241 D3
Globe Pond Road SE16 ...... 249 E2
Globe Street SE1 ...... 247 E3
Gloucester Arcade SW7 ...... 244 B2
Gloucester Court EC3 ...... 248 A3
Gloucester Gate Mews NW1 ...... 241 F4
Albany Street
Gloucester Mews W2 ...... 240 B2
Gloucester Mews West W2 ...... 240 B2
Gloucester Park SW7 ...... 244 B2
Gloucester Place NW1 & W1 ...... 241 D3
Gloucester Place Mews W1 ...... 241 D2
Gloucester Road SW7 ...... 244 B3
Gloucester Square W2 ...... 240 C2
Gloucester Street SW1 ...... 245 F1
Gloucester Terrace W2 ...... 240 B2
Gloucester Walk W8 ...... 244 A4
Gloucester Way EC1 ...... 243 D4
Glyn Street SE11 ...... 246 C1
Goat Street SE1 ...... 248 A2
Lafone Street
Godfrey Street SW3 ...... 245 D2
Goding Street SE11 ...... 246 B1
Godliman Street EC4 ...... 243 E1
Golden Lane EC1 ...... 243 E3
Golden Square W1 ...... 242 A1
Golding Street E1 ...... 248 C3
Gomm Road SE16 ...... 249 D1
Goodge Place W1 ...... 242 A2
Goodge Street W1 ...... 242 A2
Goodhart Place E14 ...... 249 E3
Goodman's Stile E1 ...... 248 B4
Goodman's Yard E1 ...... 248 B3
Goodwin Close SE16 ...... 248 B1
Gophir Lane EC4 ...... 243 F1
Bush Lane
Gordon Place W8 ...... 244 A4
Gordon Square WC1 ...... 242 A3
Gordon Street WC1 ...... 242 A3
Gore Street SW7 ...... 244 B3
Goring Street E1 ...... 248 A4
Bevis Marks
Gosfield Street W1 ...... 241 F2
Goslett Yard WC2 ...... 242 B2
Goswell Road EC1 ...... 243 D4
Gough Square EC4 ...... 243 D2
Gough Street WC1 ...... 242 C3
Goulston Street E1 ...... 248 B4
Gower Mews WC1 ...... 242 A2
Gower Place WC1 ...... 242 A3
Gower Street WC1 ...... 242 A3
Gowers Walk E1 ...... 248 B3
Grace's Alley E1 ...... 248 B3
Gracechurch Street EC3 ...... 243 F1
Graces Mews NW8 ...... 240 B4
Grafton Mews W1 ...... 241 F3
Grafton Place NW1 ...... 242 A4
Grafton Street W1 ...... 241 F1
Grafton Way W1 ...... 241 F3
Graham Street N1 ...... 243 E4
Graham Terrace SW1 ...... 245 E2
Granby Terrace NW1 ...... 241 F4
Grand Avenue EC1 ...... 243 D2
Grand Junction Wharf N1 ...... 243 E4
Grange Court WC2 ...... 242 C2
Grange Road SE1 ...... 248 A1
Grange Walk SE1 ...... 248 A1
Grange Yard SE1 ...... 248 A1
Grant's Quay Wharf EC3 ...... 243 F1
Grantully Road W9 ...... 240 A4
Granville Place W1 ...... 241 E2
Granville Road NW6 ...... 240 A4
Granville Square WC1 ...... 242 C4
Granville Street WC1 ...... 242 C4
Granville Square
Grape Street WC2 ...... 242 B2
Gravel Lane E1 ...... 248 A4
Gray Street SE1 ...... 247 D3
Gray's Inn Place WC1 ...... 242 C2
Gray's Inn Road WC1 ...... 242 B4

Great Castle Street W1 ...... 241 F2
Great Central Street NW1 ...... 241 D3
Great Chapel Street W1 ...... 242 A2
Great College Street SW1 ...... 241 D1
Seymour Street
Great Cumberland Place W1 ...... 241 D2
Great Dover Street SE1 ...... 247 E3
Great Eastern Street EC2 ...... 243 F3
Great George Street SW1 ...... 246 B3
Great Guildford Street SE1 ...... 247 E4
Great James Street WC1 ...... 242 C3
Great Marlborough Street W1 ...... 241 F2
Great Maze Pond SE1 ...... 247 F4
Great New Street EC4 ...... 243 D2
Great Newport Street WC2 ...... 242 B1
Charing Cross Road
Great Ormond Street WC1 ...... 242 C3
Great Percy Street WC1 ...... 242 C4
Great Peter Street SW1 ...... 246 B3
Great Portland Street W1 ...... 241 F3
Great Pulteney Street W1 ...... 242 A1
Great Queen Street WC2 ...... 242 B2
Great Russell Street WC1 ...... 242 B2
Great Scotland Yard SW1 ...... 246 B4
Great Smith Street SW1 ...... 246 B3
Great St Helen's EC3 ...... 243 F2
Great St Thomas Apostle EC4 ...... 243 E1
Queen Street
Great Suffolk Street SE1 ...... 247 E3
Great Sutton Street EC1 ...... 243 D3
Great Swan Alley EC2 ...... 243 F2
Great Tower Street EC3 ...... 248 A3
Great Trinity Lane EC4 ...... 243 E1
Garlick Hill
Great Turnstile WC1 ...... 242 B2
High Holborn
Great Winchester Street EC2 ...... 243 F2
Great Windmill Street W1 ...... 242 A1
Greatorex Street E1 ...... 248 B4
Greek Street W1 ...... 242 B2
Green Bank E1 ...... 248 C2
Green Dragon Court SE1 ...... 247 F4
Green Dragon Yard E1 ...... 248 B4
Green Street W1 ...... 241 E1
Green Walk SE1 ...... 247 F3
Green Yard WC1 ...... 242 C3
Greenacre Square SE16 ...... 249 E2
Greenberry Street NW8 ...... 240 C4
Greencoat Place SW1 ...... 246 A2
Greencoat Row SW1 ...... 246 A2
Greenfield Road E1 ...... 248 B4
Greenham Close SE1 ...... 247 D3
Greenwell Street W1 ...... 241 F3
Greenwich Park Street SE10 ...... 250 C1
Greenwich View Place E14 ...... 250 C3
Greet Street SE1 ...... 247 D4
Gregory Place W8 ...... 244 A4
Greig Terrace SE17 ...... 247 E1
Grenade Street E14 ...... 249 F3
Grendon Street NW8 ...... 240 C3
Grenville Place SW7 ...... 244 B2
Grenville Street WC1 ...... 242 B3
Gresham Street EC2 ...... 243 E2
Gresse Street W1 ...... 242 A2
Greville Street EC1 ...... 243 D2
Greycoat Place SW1 ...... 246 A3
Greycoat Street SW1 ...... 246 A3
Greystoke Place EC4 ...... 243 D2
Fetter Lane
Grigg's Place SE1 ...... 248 A1
Groom Place SW1 ...... 245 E3
Grosvenor Crescent SW1 ...... 245 E3
Grosvenor Crescent Mews SW1 ...... 245 E3
Grosvenor Gardens SW1 ...... 245 F3
Grosvenor Gate W1 ...... 241 E1
Park Lane
Grosvenor Hill W1 ...... 241 F1
Grosvenor Place SW1 ...... 245 E3
Grosvenor Road SW1 ...... 245 E1
Grosvenor Square W1 ...... 241 E1
Grosvenor Street W1 ...... 241 E1
Grosvenor Wharf Road E14 ...... 250 C2
Grove End Road NW8 ...... 240 B4
Grove Gardens NW8 ...... 241 D4
Grove Hall Court NW8 ...... 240 B4
Guildhall Buildings EC2 ...... 243 E2
Basinghall Street
Guildhall Yard EC2 ...... 243 E2
Guildhouse Street SW1 ...... 245 F2
Guilford Place WC1 ...... 242 B3
Guilford Street
Guilford Street WC1 ...... 242 B3
Guinness Street SE1 ...... 247 F2
Gulliver Street SE16 ...... 249 F1
Gulston Walk SW3 ...... 245 D2
Gun Street E1 ...... 248 A4
Gunthorpe Street E1 ...... 248 B4
Gunwhale Close SE16 ...... 249 D2
Guthrie Street SW3 ...... 244 C2
Gutter Lane EC2 ...... 243 E2
Guy Street SE1 ...... 247 F3
Gwynne Place WC1 ...... 242 C4

H

Haberdasher Street N1 ...... 243 F4
Hainton Close E1 ...... 248 C3
Halcrow Street E1 ...... 248 C4
Half Moon Court EC1 ...... 243 E2
Bartholomew Close
Half Moon Street W1 ...... 241 F1
Halkin Place SW1 ...... 245 E3
Halkin Street SW1 ...... 245 E3
Hall Gate NW8 ...... 240 B4
Hall Place W2 ...... 240 C3
Hall Road NW8 ...... 240 B4
Hall Street EC1 ...... 243 E4
Hallam Mews W1 ...... 241 F3
Hallam Street W1 ...... 241 F3
Halley Place E14 ...... 249 E4
Halley Street E14 ...... 249 E4
Halsey Mews SW3 ...... 245 D2
Halsey Street SW3 ...... 245 D2
Hamilton Close NW8 ...... 240 B4
Hamilton Gardens NW8 ...... 240 B4
Hamilton Place W1 ...... 245 E4
Hamilton Square SE1 ...... 247 F3
Hamilton Terrace NW8 ...... 240 B4
Hammett Street EC3 ...... 248 A3
America Square
Hampstead Road NW1 ...... 241 F4
Hampton Street SE1 & SE17 ...... 247 E2
Hanbury Street E1 ...... 248 B4
Handel Street WC1 ...... 242 B3
Hankey Place SE1 ...... 247 F3
Hannibal Road E1 ...... 249 D4
Hanover Place WC2 ...... 242 B1
Long Acre
Hanover Square W1 ...... 241 F2
Hanover Steps W2 ...... 241 D2
Hanover Street W1 ...... 241 F2
Hanover Terrace NW1 ...... 241 D4
Hanover Terrace Mews NW1 ...... 241 D4

Hans Crescent SW1 .... 245 D3
Hans Place SW1 .... 245 D3
Hans Road SW3 .... 245 D3
Hans Street SW1 .... 245 D3
Hanson Street W1 .... 241 F2
Hanway Place W1 .... 242 A2
Hanway Street W1 .... 242 A2
Harbert Road W2 .... 240 C2
Harbinger Road E14 .... 250 A4
Harbour Exchange Square E14 .. 250 B3
Harcourt Street W1 .... 241 D2
Harcourt Terrace SW10 .... 244 B1
Harding Close SE17 .... 247 E1
Hardinge Lane E1 .... 249 D3
    Hardinge Street
Hardinge Street E1 .... 249 D3
Hardwick Street EC1 .... 243 D4
Hardwicke Mews WC1 .... 242 C4
    Lloyd Baker Street
Hardwidge Street SE1 .... 247 F4
Harewood Avenue NW1 .... 241 D1
Harewood Place W1 .... 241 F2
Harley Gardens SW10 .... 244 B1
Harley Place W1 .... 241 E2
Harley Street W1 .... 241 E3
Harleyford Road SE11 .... 246 C1
Harmsworth Mews SE11 .... 247 D2
    West Square
Harmsworth Street SE17 .... 247 D1
Harp Alley EC4 .... 243 D2
    Farringdon Street
Harp Lane EC3 .... 248 A3
Harper Road SE1 .... 247 E3
Harpur Street WC1 .... 242 C3
Harriet Street SW1 .... 245 D3
Harriet Walk SW1 .... 245 D3
Harrington Gardens SW7 .... 244 B2
Harrington Road SW7 .... 244 C2
Harrison Street WC1 .... 242 B4
Harrow Place E1 .... 248 A4
Harrow Road W2, W9, W10 &
    NW10 .... 240 B2
Harrow Road Bridge W2 .... 240 B2
Harrowby Street W1 .... 241 D2
Hart Street EC3 .... 248 A3
Harwich Lane EC2 .... 248 A4
Harwood Row NW1 .... 241 D3
Hasker Street SW3 .... 245 D2
Hastings Street WC1 .... 242 B4
Hatfields SE1 .... 247 D4
Hatherley Grove W2 .... 240 A2
Hatherley Street SW1 .... 246 A2
Hatteraick Street SE16 .... 249 D2
Hatton Garden EC1 .... 243 D3
Hatton Place EC1 .... 243 D3
Hatton Place EC1 .... 243 D3
Hatton Street NW8 .... 240 C3
Hatton Wall EC1 .... 243 D3
Haunch of Venison Yard W1 .... 240 C1
    Brook Street
Havannah Street E14 .... 250 A3
Havering Street E1 .... 249 D3
Haverstock Street N1 .... 243 E4
Hawkesmoor Mews E1 .... 248 C3
Hay Hill W1 .... 241 F1
Hay's Lane SE1 .... 247 F4
Hay's Mews W1 .... 241 F1
Hayes Place NW1 .... 241 D3
Hayles Street SE11 .... 247 D2
Haymarket SW1 .... 242 A1
Hayne Street EC1 .... 243 E3
Hayward's Place EC1 .... 243 D3
Headfort Place SW1 .... 245 E3
Heathcote Street WC1 .... 242 C3
Heckford Street E1 .... 249 E3
Heddon Street W1 .... 241 F1
Hedger Street SE11 .... 247 D2
Heiron Street SE17 .... 247 E1
Helena Square SE16 .... 249 E3
Hellings Street E1 .... 248 B4
Helmet Row EC1 .... 243 E3
Helsinki Square SE16 .... 249 E3
Hemp Walk SE17 .... 247 F2
Henderson Drive NW8 .... 240 C3
Heneage Lane EC3 .... 248 A4
Heneage Place EC3 .... 248 A4
Heneage Street E1 .... 248 B4
Henniker Mews SW3 .... 244 B1
Henrietta Close SE8 .... 250 A1
Henrietta Place W1 .... 241 E2
Henrietta Street WC2 .... 242 B1
Henriques Street E1 .... 248 B4
Henshaw Street SE17 .... 247 F2
Herald's Place SE11 .... 247 D2
Herbal Hill EC1 .... 243 D3
Herbrand Street WC1 .... 242 B3
Hercules Road SE1 .... 246 C3
Hereford Road W2 .... 240 A2
Hereford Square SW7 .... 244 B2
Hermes Street N1 .... 242 C4
Hermit Street EC1 .... 243 D4
Hermitage Street W2 .... 240 C2
Hermitage Wall E1 .... 248 B4
Heron Place SE16 .... 249 D2
Heron Quays E14 .... 250 A4
Herrick Street SW1 .... 246 B2
Hertford Street W1 .... 245 E4
Hertsmere Road E14 .... 250 A4
Hesper Mews SW5 .... 244 A2
Hesperus Crescent E14 .... 250 B2
Hessel Street E1 .... 248 C3
Heygate Street SE17 .... 247 E2
Hickin Street E14 .... 250 B3
Hide Place SW1 .... 246 A2
High Holborn WC1 .... 242 B2
High Timber Street EC4 .... 243 E1
Highbridge SE10 .... 250 C1
Hildyard Road SW6 .... 244 A1
Hill Road W9 .... 240 B4
Hill Street W1 .... 241 F2
Hillery Close SE17 .... 247 F2
Hilliard's Court E1 .... 248 C2
Hillingdon Street SE5 & SE17 .. 247 E1
    Pelier Street
Hind Court EC4 .... 243 D2
Hinde Street W1 .... 241 E2
Hindmarsh Close E1 .... 248 B3
Hobart Place SW1 .... 245 F3
Hogarth Court EC3 .... 243 F1
    Fenchurch Street
Hogarth Place SW5 .... 244 A2
Hogarth Road SW5 .... 244 A2
Holbein Mews SW1 .... 245 E2
Holbein Place SW1 .... 245 E2
Holborn EC1 .... 243 D2
Holborn Circus EC1 .... 243 D2
Holborn Viaduct EC1 .... 243 D2
Holford Place WC1 .... 242 C4
Holford Street WC1 .... 242 C4
Holland Street SE1 .... 247 D4
Holland Street W8 .... 244 A3
Hollen Street W1 .... 242 A2
    Wardour Street
Holles Street W1 .... 241 F2
Holley Mews SW10 .... 244 B1
    Drayton Gardens
Hollywood Mews SW10 .... 244 B1
Hollywood Road SW10 .... 244 B1

Holyoak Road SE11 .... 247 D2
Holyoake Court SE16 .... 249 F2
Holyrood Street SE1 .... 248 A2
Holywell Row EC2 .... 243 F3
Homer Drive E14 .... 250 A3
Homer Row W1 .... 241 D2
Homer Street W1 .... 241 D2
Honduras Street EC1 .... 243 E3
    Old Street
Hooper Street E1 .... 248 B3
Hop Gardens WC2 .... 242 B1
    St Martin's Lane
Hope Wharf SE16 .... 249 D2
Hopetown Street E1 .... 248 B4
Hopkins Street W1 .... 242 A1
Hopton Street SE1 .... 247 D4
Hopwood Road SE17 .... 247 F1
Horatio Place E14 .... 250 C4
Horley Crescent SE16 .... 249 D2
    Marlow Way
Hornton Place W8 .... 244 A3
Hornton Street W8 .... 244 A3
Horse Guards Avenue SW1 ...... 246 B4
Horse Guards Road SW1 .... 246 B4
Horse Ride SW1 .... 245 F3
Horseferry Road E14 .... 249 E3
Horseferry Road SW1 .... 246 A3
Horseydown Lane SE1 .... 248 A2
Horseshoe Close E14 .... 250 B2
Hosier Lane EC1 .... 243 D2
Hoskins Street SE10 .... 250 C1
Hothfield Place SE16 .... 249 D1
Hotspur Street SE11 .... 246 C2
Houghton Street WC2 .... 242 C1
    Aldwych
Houndsditch EC3 .... 248 A4
Howard Place SW1 .... 242 A4
    Carlisle Place
Howell Walk SE1 .... 247 E2
Howick Place SW1 .... 246 A3
Howland Street W1 .... 242 A3
Howland Street W1 .... 241 F3
Howley Place W2 .... 240 B3
Hoxton Market N1 .... 243 F4
Hoxton Square N1 .... 243 F4
Huddart Street E3 .... 249 F4
Hudson's Place SW1 .... 245 F2
Huggin Hill EC4 .... 243 E1
Hugh Street SW1 .... 245 F2
Hull Close SE16 .... 249 E2
Hull Street EC1 .... 243 E4
Hunt's Court WC2 .... 242 B1
Hunter Close SE1 .... 247 F3
    Pricress Street
Hunter Street WC1 .... 242 B3
Huntley Street WC1 .... 242 A3
Huntsman Street SE17 .... 247 F2
Huntsworth Mews NW1 .... 241 D3
Hutching's Street E14 .... 250 A3
Hutton Street EC4 .... 243 D1
Hyde Park Corner W1 .... 245 E4
Hyde Park Crescent W2 .... 240 C2
Hyde Park Gardens W2 .... 240 C1
Hyde Park Gardens Mews W2 .. 240 C1
Hyde Park Gate SW7 .... 244 B3
Hyde Park Square W2 .... 240 C2
Hyde Park Street W2 .... 240 C2

I

Idol Lane EC3 .... 248 A3
Ifield Road SW10 .... 244 A1
Ilchester Gardens W2 .... 240 A1
Iliffe Street SE17 .... 247 E2
Indescon Court E14 .... 250 A3
India Place WC2 .... 242 C1
    Montreal Place
India Street EC3 .... 248 A3
Ingestre Place W1 .... 242 A1
Inglebert Street EC1 .... 243 D4
Inglewood Close E14 .... 250 A2
Ingram Close SE11 .... 246 C2
Inigo Place WC2 .... 242 B1
    Bedford Street
Inner Temple Lane EC4 .... 243 D2
Inverness Gardens W8 .... 244 A4
Inverness Mews W2 .... 240 B1
Inverness Place W2 .... 240 B1
Inverness Terrace W2 .... 240 B1
Invicta Plaza SE1 .... 247 D4
Inville Road SE17 .... 247 F1
Ireland Yard EC4 .... 243 D1
    St Andrew's Hill
Ironmonger Lane EC2 .... 243 E2
Ironmonger Place EC1 .... 250 A2
Ironmonger Row EC1 .... 243 E4
Ironside Close SE16 .... 249 D2
Irving Street WC2 .... 242 B1
Isambard Place SE16 .... 249 D2
Island Row E14 .... 249 F3
Iverna Court W8 .... 244 A3
Iverna Gardens W8 .... 244 A3
Ives Street SW3 .... 245 D2
Ivor Place NW1 .... 241 D3
Ixworth Place SW3 .... 244 C2

J

Jacob Street SE1 .... 248 B2
Jamaica Road SE1 & SE16 ...... 248 B1
Jamaica Street E1 .... 249 D4
James Street W1 .... 241 E2
James Street WC2 .... 242 B1
    Long Acre
Jameson Street W8 .... 244 A4
Janet Street E14 .... 250 A3
Jardine Road E1 .... 249 E3
Jay Mews SW7 .... 244 B3
Jermyn Street SW1 .... 246 A4
Jerome Crescent NW8 .... 240 C3
Jewry Street EC3 .... 248 A3
Joan Street SE1 .... 247 D4
Jockey's Fields WC1 .... 242 C2
John Adams Street WC2 .... 242 B1
John Aird Court W2 .... 240 B3
John Carpenter Street EC4 ..... 243 D1
John Felton Road SE16 .... 248 B1
John Fisher Street E1 .... 248 B3
    John Islip Street
John Maurice Close SE17 .... 247 F2
John Princes Street W1 .... 241 F2
John Roll Way SE16 .... 248 C1
John Street WC1 .... 242 C3
John's Mews WC1 .... 242 C3

K

Katherine Close SE16 .... 249 D2
Kean Street WC2 .... 242 C2
Keel Close SE16 .... 249 E2
Keeley Street WC2 .... 242 C2
Keeton's Road SE16 .... 248 C1
Kelso Place W8 .... 244 A3
Kemble Street WC2 .... 242 C2
Kempsford Gardens SW5 .... 244 A1
Kempsford Road SE11 .... 247 D2
Kempton Court E1 .... 248 C4
    Durward Street
Kendal Street W2 .... 241 C2
Kendall Place W1 .... 241 D2
Kendrick Mews SW7 .... 244 C2
Kendrick Place SW7 .... 244 C2
    Reece Mews
Kennet Street E1 .... 248 B2
Kennet Wharf Lane EC4 .... 243 E1
Kenning Street SE16 .... 249 D2
Kennings Way SE11 .... 247 D1
Kennington Green SE11 .... 247 D1
Kennington Grove SE11 .... 246 C1
Kennington Lane SE11 .... 246 C1
Kennington Oval SE11 .... 246 C1
Kennington Park Gardens SE11 .. 247 D1
Kennington Park Place SE11 .... 247 D1
Kennington Park Road SE11 .... 247 D1
Kennington Road SE1 & SE11 .. 246 C3
Kenrick Place W1 .... 241 E2
Kensington Church Street W8 .. 244 A4
Kensington Church Walk W8 .... 244 A3
Kensington Court W8 .... 244 A3
Kensington Court Place W8 ..... 244 A3
Kensington Gardens Square W2 .. 240 A2
Kensington Gate W8 .... 244 B3
Kensington Gore SW7 .... 244 B3
Kensington High Street W8 &
    W14 .... 244 A3
Kensington Mall W8 .... 244 A4
Kensington Palace Gardens W8 .. 244 A4
Kensington Road W8 & SW7 .... 244 B3
Kensington Square W8 .... 244 A3
Kent Passage NW1 .... 241 D4
Kent Terrace NW1 .... 241 D4
Kenton Street WC1 .... 242 B3
Kenway Road SW5 .... 244 A2
Keppel Row SE1 .... 247 E4
Keppel Street WC1 .... 242 B3
Keyse Road SE1 .... 248 A1
Keystone Crescent N1 .... 242 B4
Keyworth Street SE1 .... 247 D3
Kilburn Park Road NW6 .... 240 A4
Kildare Gardens W2 .... 240 A2
Kildare Terrace W2 .... 240 A2
Kimbolton Row SW3 .... 244 C2
    Mossop Street
Kinburn Street SE16 .... 249 D2
Kinder Street E1 .... 248 C3
King and Queen Street SE17 ... 247 E2
King Charles Street SW1 .... 246 B3
King David Lane E1 .... 249 D3
King Edward III Mews SE16 .... 248 C1
    Paradise Street
King Edward Street EC1 .... 243 E2
King Edward Walk SE1 .... 247 D3
King James Street SE1 .... 247 E3
King Square EC1 .... 243 E4
King Street EC2 .... 243 E2
King Street SW1 .... 246 A4
King Street WC2 .... 242 B1
King William Street EC4 .... 243 F1
King's Bench Walk EC4 .... 243 D1
King's Cross Road WC1 .... 242 C4
King's Mews WC1 .... 242 C3
King's Road SW3, SW6 & SW10 .. 245 D1
King's Scholars' Passage SW1 .. 245 F2
King's Stairs Close SE16 .... 248 C2
Kingford Street E14 .... 250 C2
Kinghorn Street EC1 .... 243 E3
Kinglake Street SE17 .... 247 F2
Kingly Court W1 .... 242 A1
Kingly Street W1 .... 241 F1
Kings Arms Yard EC2 .... 243 F2
Kings Bench Street SE1 .... 247 D3
Kingscote Street EC4 .... 243 D1
Kingsway WC2 .... 242 C2
Kinnerton Street SW1 .... 245 E3
Kipling Street SE1 .... 247 F4
Kirby Grove SE1 .... 247 F3
Kirby Street EC1 .... 243 D3
Knaresborough Place SW5 ...... 244 A2
Knight's Walk SE11 .... 247 D2
Knighten Street E1 .... 248 C2
Knightrider Street EC4 .... 243 E1
    Godliman Street
Knightsbridge SW1 & SW7 ..... 245 D3
Knightsbridge Green SW1 .... 245 D3
    Brompton Road
Knox Street W1 .... 241 D3
Kramer Mews SW5 .... 244 A1
Kynance Mews SW7 .... 244 B3

L

Lackington Street EC2 .... 243 F3
Lafone Street SE1 .... 248 A2
Lagado Mews SE16 .... 249 E2
Lamb Street E1 .... 248 A4
Lamb Walk SE1 .... 247 F3
Lamb's Conduit Street WC1 .... 242 C3
Lamb's Passage EC1 .... 243 F3
Lambeth Bridge SW1 & SE11 .. 246 B2
Lambeth High Street SE1 .... 246 C2
Lambeth Hill EC4 .... 243 E1
Lambeth Palace Road SE1 ...... 246 C2
Lambeth Road SE1 .... 246 C2
Lambeth Walk SE11 .... 246 C2
Lamlash Street SE11 .... 247 D2
Lamb Place SE1 .... 247 D2
Llewellyn Street SE16 .... 248 B1
Lloyd Baker Street WC1 .... 242 C4
Lloyd Square WC1 .... 242 C4
Lloyd Street WC1 .... 242 C4
Lloyd's Avenue EC3 .... 248 A3
Lanark Road W9 .... 240 A4
Lanark Square E14 .... 250 B3

L (right column)

Lancaster Drive E14 .... 250 B4
Lancaster Gate W2 .... 240 B1
Lancaster Mews W2 .... 240 B1
Lancaster Place WC2 .... 245 D3
Lancaster Street SE1 .... 247 D3
Lancaster Terrace W2 .... 240 C1
Lancaster Walk W2 .... 240 B1
Lancelot Place SW7 .... 245 D3
Lancing Street NW1 .... 242 A4
Landon Place SW1 .... 245 D3
Landon's Close E14 .... 250 B4
Langbourne Place E14 .... 250 B1
Langdale Close SE17 .... 247 E1
Langham Place W1 .... 241 F2
Langham Street W1 .... 241 F2
Langley Lane SW8 .... 246 B1
Langley Street WC2 .... 242 B1
Langton Close WC1 .... 242 C3
Lansdowne Row W1 .... 241 F1
Lansdowne Terrace WC1 .... 242 B3
Lant Street SE1 .... 247 E3
Lanterns Court E14 .... 250 A3
Larcom Street SE17 .... 247 E2
Lassell Street SE10 .... 250 C1
Lauderdale Road W9 .... 240 A4
Launcelot Street SE1 .... 246 C3
    Lower Marsh
Launceston Place W8 .... 244 B3
Lancelot Place SW7 .... 245 D3
Laurence Pountney Lane EC4 .. 244 C1
Lavender Close SW3 .... 249 E2
Lavender Road SE16 .... 244 A2
Laverton Place SW5 .... 247 E4
Lavington Street SE1 .... 247 F3
Law Street SE1 .... 247 F3
Lawn House Close E14 .... 250 B3
Lawn Lane SW8 .... 246 B1
Lawrence Lane EC2 .... 243 E2
    Trump Street
Lawrence Street SW3 .... 244 C1
Laxton Place NW1 .... 241 F3
Laystall Street EC1 .... 242 C3
Layton's Buildings SE1 .... 247 E4
    Borough High Street
Leadenhall Place EC3 .... 243 F1
Leadenhall Street EC3 .... 243 F2
Leake Street SE1 .... 246 C3
Leather Lane EC1 .... 243 D3
Leathermarket Court SE1 .... 247 F3
    Leathermarket Street
Leathermarket Street SE1 .... 247 F3
Lecky Street SW7 .... 244 C1
Leerdam Drive E14 .... 250 C2
Lees Place W1 .... 241 E1
Leicester Court WC2 .... 242 B1
    Cranbourn Street
Leicester Place WC2 .... 242 B1
    Lisle Street
Leicester Square WC2 .... 242 B1
Leicester Street WC2 .... 242 B1
Leigh Hunt Street SE1 .... 247 E3
Leigh Street WC1 .... 242 B4
Leinster Gardens W2 .... 240 B1
Leinster Mews W2 .... 240 B1
Leinster Place W2 .... 240 B1
Leinster Square W2 .... 240 A1
Leinster Terrace W2 .... 240 B1
Leman Street E1 .... 248 B3
Lennox Gardens SW1 .... 245 D2
Lennox Gardens Mews SW1 .... 245 D2
Leonard Street EC2 .... 243 F3
Leopold Street E3 .... 249 F4
Leroy Street SE1 .... 247 F2
Lever Street EC1 .... 243 E4
Leverett Street SW3 .... 245 D2
    Culford Gardens
Lewisham Street SW1 .... 246 B3
Lexham Gardens W8 .... 244 A2
Lexham Mews W8 .... 244 A2
Lexham Walk W8 .... 244 A2
Lexington Street W1 .... 242 A1
Leyden Street E1 .... 248 A4
Leydon Close SE16 .... 249 E2
Library Place E1 .... 248 C3
Library Street SE1 .... 247 D3
Lighterman Mews E1 .... 249 E4
Lightermans Road E14 .... 250 A3
Lilestone Street NW8 .... 240 C3
Lilley Close E1 .... 248 B2
Lillie Road SW6 .... 244 A1
Lillie Yard SW6 .... 244 A1
Lime Close E1 .... 248 B2
Lime Street EC3 .... 243 F1
Lime Street Passage EC3 .... 243 F1
    Lime Street
Limeburner Lane EC4 .... 243 D2
Limeharbour E14 .... 250 B3
Limehouse Causeway E14 .... 249 F3
Limehouse Link Tunnel E14 .... 249 E3
Limerston Street SW10 .... 244 B1
Lincoln Street SW3 .... 245 D2
Lincoln's Inn Fields WC2 .... 242 C2
Linden Gardens W2 .... 240 A1
Linden Mews W2 .... 240 A1
Lindley Street E1 .... 248 C4
Lindsay Square SW1 .... 246 B2
Lindsey Street EC1 .... 243 E3
Linhope Street NW1 .... 241 D3
Links Yard E1 .... 248 B4
Linsey Street SE16 .... 248 B1
Lipton Road E1 .... 249 D3
Lisle Street W1 .... 242 A1
Lisson Grove NW1 & NW8 ...... 240 C3
Lisson Street NW1 .... 240 C3
Litchfield Street WC2 .... 242 B1
Little Argyll Street W1 .... 246 A2
    Regent Street
Little Britain EC1 .... 243 E2
Little Chester Street SW1 .... 245 E3
Little College Street SW1 .... 246 B3
Little Dorrit Close SE1 .... 247 E4
Little Edward Street NW1 .... 241 F4
Little George Street SW1 .... 246 B3
    Great George Street
Little London Court SE1 .... 248 B1
    Mill Street
Little Marlborough Street W1 .. 241 F1
    Kingly Street
Little New Street EC4 .... 243 D2
    New Street Square
Little Newport Street WC2 ...... 242 B1
Little Portland Street W1 .... 241 F2
Little Russell Street WC1 .... 242 B2
Little Sanctuary SW1 .... 246 B3
    Broad Sanctuary
Little Smith Street SW1 .... 246 B3
Little Somerset Street E1 .... 248 A4
Little St James's Street SW1 ... 246 A4
Little Titchfield Street W1 .... 241 F2
Little Trinity Lane EC4 .... 243 E1
Liverpool Grove SE17 .... 247 E1
Liverpool Street EC2 .... 243 F2
Livingstone Place E14 .... 250 B1
Livonia Street W1 .... 242 A2
Lizard Street EC1 .... 243 E4
Llewellyn Street SE16 .... 248 B1
Lloyd Baker Street WC1 .... 242 C4
Lloyd Square WC1 .... 242 C4
Lloyd Street WC1 .... 242 C4
Lloyd's Avenue EC3 .... 248 A3

Lloyd's Row EC1 .... 243 D4
Lockesfield Place E14 .... 250 B1
Locksley Street E14 .... 249 F4
Lockwood Square SE16 .... 248 C1
Lodge Road NW8 .... 240 C4
Loftie Street SE16 .... 248 B1
Lolesworth Close E1 .... 248 B4
Lollard Street SE11 .... 246 C2
Loman Street SE1 .... 247 E4
London Bridge SW1 .... 245 D3
London Place SW1 .... 245 D3
Landon's Close E14 .... 250 B4
Langbourne Place E14 .... 250 B1
Lombard Court EC4 .... 243 F1
Lombard Lane EC4 .... 243 A2
    Temple Lane
London Bridge EC4 & SE1 .... 243 F1
London Bridge SE1 .... 247 F4
London Bridge Street SE1 .... 247 F4
London Street EC3 .... 248 A3
London Street W2 .... 240 C2
London Wall EC2 .... 243 E2
Long Acre WC2 .... 242 B1
Long Lane EC1 .... 243 E2
Long Lane SE1 .... 247 F3
Long Walk SE1 .... 248 A1
Long Yard WC1 .... 242 C3
Longford Street NW1 .... 241 F3
Longmoore Street SW1 .... 245 F2
Longville Road SE11 .... 247 D2
Lord Hill's Bridge W2 .... 240 A2
Lord Hill's Road W2 .... 240 A3
Lord North Street SW1 .... 246 B3
Lordship Place SW3 .... 244 C1
    Lawrence Street
Lorenzo Street WC1 .... 242 C4
Lorrimore Road SE17 .... 247 E1
Lorrimore Square SE17 .... 247 E1
Lothbury EC2 .... 243 F2
Loughborough Street SE11 ..... 246 C1
Lovat Lane EC3 .... 243 F1
Love Lane EC2 .... 243 E2
Lovegrove Walk E14 .... 250 B4
Lovell Place SE16 .... 249 E1
Lovers' Walk W1 .... 245 E4
Lowell Street E14 .... 249 E4
Lower Belgrave Street SW1 ..... 245 E3
Lower Grosvenor Place SW1 ... 245 F3
Lower James Street W1 .... 242 A1
Lower John Street W1 .... 242 A1
Lower Marsh SE1 .... 246 C3
Lower Road SE8 & SE16 .... 249 D1
Lower Robert Street WC2 .... 242 B1
    Savoy Place
Lower Sloane Street SW1 .... 245 E2
Lower Thames Street EC3 .... 243 F1
Lowndes Place SW1 .... 245 E3
Lowndes Square SW1 .... 245 E3
Lowndes Street SW1 .... 245 E3
Lowood Street E1 .... 248 C3
    Bewley Street
Loxham Street WC1 .... 242 B3
    Cromer Street
Lucan Place SW3 .... 244 C2
Lucerne Mews W8 .... 244 A4
Lucey Road SE16 .... 248 B1
Ludgate Broadway EC4 .... 243 D2
    Pilgrim Street
Ludgate Circus EC4 .... 243 D2
Ludgate Square EC4 .... 243 D2
Luke Street EC2 .... 243 F3
Lumley Street W1 .... 241 E1
    Brown Hart Garden
Lupus Street SW1 .... 245 F1
Luralda Gardens E14 .... 250 C1
Luton Street NW8 .... 240 C3
Luxborough Street W1 .... 241 E3
Lyall Street SW1 .... 245 E3
Lygon Place SW1 .... 245 F3
Lynch Walk SE8 .... 250 A1
Lyons Place NW8 .... 240 C3
Lytham Street SE17 .... 247 F1

M

Mabledon Place WC1 .... 242 B4
Macclesfield Road EC1 .... 243 E4
Mackenzie Walk E14 .... 250 A4
Macklin Street WC2 .... 242 B2
Mackworth Street NW1 .... 241 F4
Macleod Street SE17 .... 247 E1
Maconochies Road E14 .... 250 B1
Macquarie Way E14 .... 250 B2
Maddock Way SE17 .... 247 D1
Maddox Street W1 .... 241 F1
Magdalen Street SE1 .... 248 A2
Magee Street SE11 .... 247 D1
Magellan Place E14 .... 250 A1
    Maritime Quay
Maguire Street SE1 .... 248 B2
Mahogany Close SE16 .... 249 E2
Maida Avenue W2 .... 240 B3
Maida Vale W9 .... 240 B4
Maiden Lane SE1 .... 247 E4
Maiden Lane WC2 .... 242 B1
Makins Street SW3 .... 245 D2
Malabar Street E14 .... 250 A3
Malet Street WC1 .... 242 A3
Mallord Street SW3 .... 244 C1
Mallory Street NW8 .... 240 C3
Mallow Street EC1 .... 243 F3
Malta Street EC1 .... 243 D3
Maltby Street SE1 .... 248 A1
Maltravers Street WC2 .... 242 C1
Managers Street E14 .... 250 B2
Manchester Grove E14 .... 250 B3
Manchester Road E14 .... 250 B3
Manchester Square W1 .... 241 E2
Manciple Street SE1 .... 247 F3
Mandarin Street E14 .... 249 F3
Mandeville Place W1 .... 241 E2
Manette Street W1 .... 242 B2
Manilla Street E14 .... 250 A3
Manningford Close EC1 .... 243 D4
Manningtree Street E1 .... 248 B4
    Commercial Road
Manor Place SE17 .... 247 E1
Manresa Road SW3 .... 244 C1
Mansell Street E1 .... 248 B3
Mansfield Mews W1 .... 241 F2
    Mansfield Street
Mansfield Street W1 .... 241 F2
Mansion House Place EC4 .... 243 A1
    St Swithun's Lane
Manson Mews SW7 .... 244 B2
Manson Place SW7 .... 244 B2
Maple Leaf Square SE16 .... 249 E2
Maple Street W1 .... 241 F3
Maples Place E1 .... 248 C4
Marble Arch W1 .... 241 D1
Marchmont Street WC1 .... 242 B3
Margaret Court W1 .... 241 F2
    Margaret Street
Margaret Street W1 .... 241 F2

Margaretta Terrace SW3 .... **244** C1
Margery Street WC1 .... **242** C4
Marigold Street SE16 .... **248** C1
Mariners Mews E14 .... **250** C2
Maritime Quay E14 .... **250** A1
Marjorie Mews E1 .... **249** D4
Mark Lane EC3 .... **248** A1
Market Street W1 .... **241** E1
Oxford Street
Market Mews W1 .... **245** E4
Market Place W1 .... **241** F2
Market Yard Mews SE1 .... **248** A1
Markham Place SW3 .... **245** D2
Elystan Place
Markham Square SW3 .... **245** D2
Markham Street SW3 .... **245** D2
Marlborough Close SE17 .... **247** E2
Marlborough Road SW1 .... **246** A4
Marlborough Street SW3 .... **244** C2
Marloes Road W8 .... **244** A4
Marlow Way SE16 .... **249** D2
Marne Street W10 .... **248** B1
Maroon Street E14 .... **249** E4
Marsh Street E14 .... **250** A2
Marsh Wall E14 .... **250** A3
Marshall Street W1 .... **242** A1
Marshall's Place SE16 .... **248** B1
Marshalsea Road SE1 .... **247** E4
Marsham Street SW1 .... **246** B3
Marshfield Street E14 .... **250** B3
Marsland Close SE17 .... **247** E1
Martha Street E1 .... **248** C3
Martin Lane EC4 .... **243** F1
Martin's Street W1 .... **242** B1
Marlett Court WC2 .... **242** B2
Marylands Road W9 .... **240** A3
Marylebone High Street W1 ... **241** E2
Marylebone Lane W1 .... **241** E2
Marylebone Mews W1 .... **241** E2
Marylebone Road NW1 .... **241** D3
Marylebone Street W1 .... **241** E2
Marylee Way SE11 .... **246** C2
Mason Street SE17 .... **247** F2
Mason's Arms Mews W1 .... **241** F1
Maddox Street
Mason's Place EC1 .... **243** E4
Mason's Yard SW1 .... **241** E2
Duke Street
Massinger Street SE17 .... **247** F2
Mast House Terrace E14 .... **250** A2
Master's Street E1 .... **249** E4
Mastmaker Road E14 .... **250** A2
Matlock Street E14 .... **249** E4
Matthew Parker Street SW1 ... **246** B3
Maunsel Street SW1 .... **246** A2
May's Court WC2 .... **242** B1
St Martin's Lane
Mayfair Place W1 .... **245** F4
Mayflower Street SE16 .... **249** D1
Maynards Quay E1 .... **248** C3
McAuley Close SE1 .... **246** C3
McCleod's Mews SW7 .... **244** B2
Mead Row SE1 .... **247** D3
Meadcroft Road SE11 .... **247** D1
Meadow Row SE1 .... **247** E2
Meard Street W1 .... **242** A2
Mecklenburgh Place WC1 ...... **242** C3
Mecklenburgh Square WC1 .... **242** C3
Mecklenburgh Street WC1 ..... **242** C3
Mecklenburgh Square
Medway Street SW1 .... **246** A2
Melbury Terrace NW1 .... **241** D3
Melcombe Place NW1 .... **241** D3
Melcombe Street NW1 .... **241** D3
Melina Place NW8 .... **240** B4
Melior Street SE1 .... **247** F4
Snowsfields
Mellish Street E14 .... **250** A3
Melon Place W8 .... **244** A4
Kensington Church Street
Melton Street NW1 .... **242** A4
Memel Court EC1 .... **243** E3
Baltic Street
Mepham Street SE1 .... **246** C4
Mercator Place E14 .... **250** A1
Napier Avenue
Mercer Street WC2 .... **242** B1
Meredith Street EC1 .... **243** D4
Meridian Place E14 .... **250** B4
Merlin Street WC1 .... **243** D4
Mermaid Court SE1 .... **247** E4
Mermaid Court SE16 .... **250** B2
Mermaid Row SE1 .... **247** F3
Merrick Square SE1 .... **247** E3
Merrington Road SW6 .... **244** A1
Merrow Street SE17 .... **247** E1
Methley Street SE11 .... **247** D1
Mews Street E1 .... **248** B2
Meymott Street SE1 .... **247** D4
Micawber Street N1 .... **243** E4
Middle Street EC1 .... **243** E2
Middle Temple Lane EC4 .... **242** C2
Middle Yard SE1 .... **247** F4
Middlesex Street E1 .... **248** A4
Middleton Drive SE16 .... **249** E2
Midford Place W1 .... **242** A3
Tottenham Court Road
Midhope Street WC1 .... **242** B4
Midland Place E14 .... **250** B2
Midland Road NW1 .... **242** B4
Midship Close SE16 .... **249** E2
Milborne Grove SW10 .... **244** B1
Milcote Street SE1 .... **247** D3
Mile End Road E1 .... **248** C4
Miles Street SW8 .... **246** B1
Milford Lane WC2 .... **242** C1
Milk Street EC2 .... **243** E2
Milk Yard E1 .... **249** D3
Mill Place E14 .... **249** E3
Mill Street SE1 .... **248** B1
Mill Street W1 .... **241** F1
Millbank SW1 .... **246** B2
Millennium Drive E14 .... **250** C2
Millennium Square SE1 .... **248** B2
Millharbour E14 .... **250** A3
Milligan Street E14 .... **249** F3
Millman Street WC1 .... **242** C3
Millstream Road SE1 .... **248** A1
Millwall Dock Road E14 .... **250** A3
Milner Street SW3 .... **245** D2
Milton Court EC2 .... **243** F3
Milton Street EC2 .... **243** F3
Milverton Street SE11 .... **247** D1
Milward Street E1 .... **248** C4
Mincing Lane EC3 .... **248** A1
Minera Mews SW1 .... **245** E2
Minories EC3 .... **248** A3
Mint Street SE1 .... **247** E4
Miranda Close E1 .... **248** C4
Mitali Passage E1 .... **248** B4
Mitchell Street EC1 .... **243** E3
Mitre Road SE1 .... **247** D4
Mitre Square EC3 .... **248** A3
Mitre Street
Mitre Street EC3 .... **248** A3
Molyneux Street W1 .... **241** D2
Monck Street SW1 .... **246** B3
Moncorvo Close SW7 .... **244** C3
Monkton Street SE11 .... **247** D2

Monkwell Square EC2 .... **243** E2
Monmouth Road W2 .... **240** A2
Monmouth Street WC2 .... **242** B1
Montagu Mansions W1 .... **241** D3
Montagu Mews North W1 ...... **241** D2
Montagu Mews South W1 ...... **241** D2
Montagu Mews West W1 .... **241** D2
Montagu Place W1 .... **241** D2
Montagu Row W1 .... **241** D2
Montagu Square W1 .... **241** D2
Montagu Street W1 .... **241** D2
Montague Close SE1 .... **247** F4
Montague Place WC1 .... **242** B3
Montague Street EC1 .... **243** E2
Montague Street WC1 .... **242** B3
Montford Place SE11 .... **246** C1
Montpelier Mews SW7 .... **245** D3
Montpelier Place SW7 .... **245** D3
Montpelier Place W1 .... **249** D3
Montpelier Square SW7 .... **245** D3
Montpelier Street SW7 .... **245** D3
Montpelier Walk SW7 .... **245** D3
Montreal Place WC2 .... **242** C1
Montrose Court SW7 .... **244** C3
Montrose Place SW1 .... **245** E3
Monument Street EC3 .... **243** F1
Monza Street E1 .... **249** D3
Moodkee Street SE16 .... **249** D1
Moor Lane EC2 .... **243** F2
Moor Place EC2 .... **243** F2
Moorfields
Moore Street SW3 .... **242** A1
Old Compton Street
Moorfields EC2 .... **243** F2
Moorgate EC2 .... **243** F2
Mora Street EC1 .... **243** E4
Morecambe Close E1 .... **249** D4
Morecambe Street SE17 .... **247** E2
Moreland Street EC1 .... **243** E4
Moreton Place SW1 .... **246** A2
Moreton Street SW1 .... **246** A2
Moreton Terrace SW1 .... **246** A1
Morley Street SE1 .... **247** D3
Morocco Street SE1 .... **247** F3
Morpeth Terrace SW1 .... **245** F3
Morris Street E1 .... **248** C3
Morshead Road W9 .... **240** A4
Mortimer Market WC1 .... **242** A3
Capper Street
Mortimer Street W1 .... **241** F2
Morton Mews SW5 .... **244** A2
Earl's Court Gardens
Morwell Street WC1 .... **242** A2
Moscow Place W2 .... **240** A1
Moscow Road W2 .... **240** A1
Moss Close E1 .... **248** B4
Mossop Street SW3 .... **245** D2
Motcomb Street SW1 .... **245** E3
Mount Pleasant WC1 .... **242** C3
Mount Row W1 .... **241** E1
Mount Street W1 .... **241** E1
Mount Terrace E1 .... **248** C4
Moxon Street W1 .... **241** E2
Mozart Terrace SW1 .... **245** E2
Muirfield Crescent E14 .... **250** B3
Mulberry Street E1 .... **248** B4
Mulberry Walk SW3 .... **244** C1
Mulready Street NW8 .... **240** C3
Mulvaney Way SE1 .... **247** F3
Mumford Court EC2 .... **243** E2
Milk Street
Mundy Street N1 .... **243** F4
Munster Square NW1 .... **241** F4
Munton Road SE17 .... **247** E2
Murphy Street SE1 .... **246** C3
Murray Grove N1 .... **243** E4
Musbury Street E1 .... **249** D4
Muscovy Street EC3 .... **248** A3
Museum Street WC1 .... **242** B2
Myddelton Passage EC1 .... **243** D4
Myddelton Square EC1 .... **243** D4
Myddelton Street EC1 .... **243** D4
Mylne Street EC1 .... **243** D4
Myrdle Street E1 .... **248** C4
Myrtle Walk N1 .... **243** F4

N

Naoroji Street WC1 .... **242** C4
Napier Avenue E14 .... **250** A1
Narrow Street E14 .... **249** E3
Nash Place E14 .... **250** A4
Nash Street NW1 .... **241** F4
Nassau Street W1 .... **241** F2
Nathaniel Close E1 .... **248** B4
Thrawl Street
National Terrace SE16 .... **248** C1
Bermondsey Wall East
Neal Street WC2 .... **242** B2
Neathouse Place SW1 .... **245** F2
Wilton Road
Nebraska Street SE1 .... **247** E3
Neckinger SE1 .... **248** B1
Neckinger Street SE1 .... **248** B1
Nelson Court SE16 .... **249** D2
Nelson Passage EC1 .... **243** E4
Mora Street
Nelson Place N1 .... **243** E4
Nelson Square SE1 .... **247** E4
Nelson Street E1 .... **248** C4
Nelson Terrace N1 .... **243** E4
Nelson Walk SE16 .... **249** E2
Neptune Street SE16 .... **249** D1
Nesham Street E1 .... **248** B3
Netherton Grove SW10 .... **244** B1
Netley Street NW1 .... **241** F4
Nevern Place SW5 .... **244** A2
Nevern Square SW5 .... **244** A2
Neville Court EC4 .... **243** D2
Neville Street SW7 .... **244** C1
Neville Terrace SW7 .... **244** C1
New Bond Street W1 .... **241** F1
New Bridge Street EC4 .... **243** D2
New Broad Street EC2 .... **243** F2
New Burlington Mews W1 ...... **248** A3
Hart Street
New Burlington Place W1 ...... **241** F1
New Burlington Street W1 ..... **241** F1
New Cavendish Street W1 ..... **241** E2
New Change EC4 .... **243** E2
New Compton Street WC2 .... **242** B2
New Crane Place E1 .... **249** D2
New Fetter Lane EC4 .... **243** D2
New Globe Walk SE1 .... **247** E4
New Goulston Street E1 .... **248** A4
New Kent Road SE1 .... **247** E2
New King Street SE8 .... **250** A1
New North Place EC2 .... **243** F3
New North Road N1 .... **243** F4
New North Street WC1 .... **242** C3
New Oxford Street WC1 .... **242** B2
New Quebec Street W1 .... **241** D2
New Ride SW7 .... **244** C3

O

New Road E1 .... **248** C4
New Row WC2 .... **242** B1
New Spring Gardens Walk SE11 .... **246** B1
Goding Street
New Square WC2 .... **242** C2
New Street EC2 .... **248** A4
New Street Square EC4 .... **243** D2
New Turnstile WC1 .... **242** B2
High Holborn
New Union Close E14 .... **250** C3
New Union Street EC2 .... **243** F2
Newark Street E1 .... **248** C4
Newburgh Street W1 .... **242** F1
Foubert's Place
Newburn Street SE11 .... **246** C1
Newbury Street EC1 .... **243** E2
Newcastle Place W2 .... **240** C2
Newcomen Street SE1 .... **247** F4
Newell Street E14 .... **249** F3
Newgate Street EC1 .... **243** D2
Newington Butts SE1 & SE11 .... **247** D2
Newington Causeway SE1 ...... **247** E3
Newlands Quay E1 .... **249** D3
Newman Street W1 .... **242** A2
Newman's Row WC2 .... **242** C2
Lincoln's Inn Fields
Newnham Terrace SE1 .... **246** C3
Newnhams Row SE1 .... **248** A1
Newport Place WC2 .... **242** B1
Newport Street SE11 .... **246** C2
Newton Road W2 .... **240** A2
Newton Street WC2 .... **242** B2
Nicholas Lane EC4 .... **243** F1
Nicholson Street SE1 .... **247** D4
Nightingale Place SW10 .... **244** B1
Nile Street N1 .... **243** E4
Nine Elms Lane SW8 .... **246** A1
Noble Street EC2 .... **243** E2
Noel Street W1 .... **242** A2
Norbiton Road E14 .... **249** F4
Norfolk Crescent W2 .... **240** C2
Norfolk Place W2 .... **240** C2
Norfolk Square W2 .... **240** C2
Norman Street EC1 .... **243** E4
Norris Street SW1 .... **242** A1
North Audley Street W1 .... **241** E1
North Bank NW8 .... **240** C4
North Colonnade E14 .... **250** A4
North Crescent WC1 .... **242** A3
North Flockton Street SE16 ... **248** B1
Chambers Street
North Gower Street NW1 ...... **242** A4
North Mews WC1 .... **242** C3
North Ride W2 .... **240** C1
North Row W1 .... **241** E1
North Tenter Street E1 .... **248** B3
North Terrace SW3 .... **244** C2
North Wharf Road W2 .... **240** B2
Northampton Square EC1 ...... **243** D4
Northburgh Street EC1 .... **243** D3
Northchurch SE17 .... **247** F2
Northdown Street N1 .... **242** C4
Northington Street WC1 .... **242** C3
Northport Street N1 .... **243** F4
Northumberland Alley EC3 .... **248** A3
Northumberland Avenue WC2 .... **246** B4
Northumberland Street WC2 .. **246** B4
Northwick Close NW8 .... **240** C3
Northwick Terrace NW8 .... **240** B3
Northy Street E14 .... **249** E3
Norton Folgate E1 .... **248** A4
Norway Gate SE16 .... **249** E1
Norway Place E14 .... **249** F3
Norwich Street EC4 .... **243** D2
Notting Hill Gate W11 .... **240** A1
Nottingham Place W1 .... **241** E3
Nottingham Street W1 .... **241** E3
Nugent Terrace NW8 .... **240** B4

O'Leary Square E1 .... **249** D4
O'Meara Street SE1 .... **247** E4
Oak Lane E14 .... **249** F3
Oak Tree Road NW8 .... **240** C4
Oakden Street SE11 .... **247** D2
Oakfield Street SW10 .... **244** B1
Oakington Road W9 .... **240** A3
Oakley Crescent EC1 .... **243** E4
Oakley Gardens SW3 .... **245** D1
Oakley Square NW1 .... **242** A4
Oakley Street SW3 .... **244** C1
Oat Lane EC2 .... **243** E2
Observatory Gardens W8 ...... **244** A4
Observatory Mews E14 .... **250** C2
Storers Quay
Occupation Road SE17 .... **247** E1
Ocean Street E1 .... **249** E4
Ocean Wharf E14 .... **250** A3
Octagon Arcade EC2 .... **243** F2
Octagon Court SE16 .... **249** D2
Odessa Street SE16 .... **249** F1
Ogle Street W1 .... **241** F2
Old Bailey EC4 .... **243** D2
Old Bond Street W1 .... **241** F1
Old Broad Street EC2 .... **243** F2
Old Brompton Road SW5 &
SW7 .... **244** A1
Old Burlington Street W1 ...... **241** F1
Old Castle Street E1 .... **248** B4
Old Cavendish Street W1 ...... **241** F2
Old Church Road E1 .... **249** D4
Old Church Street SW3 .... **244** C1
Old Compton Street W1 .... **242** A1
Old Court Place W8 .... **244** A3
Old Fleet Lane EC4 .... **243** D2
Old Gloucester Street WC1 ... **242** B3
Old Jamaica Road SE16 .... **248** B1
Old Jewry EC2 .... **243** F2
Old Marylebone Road NW1 ... **241** D2
Old Mitre Court EC4 .... **243** D2
Fleet Street
Old Montagu Street E1 .... **248** B4
Old North Street WC1 .... **242** C3
Theobalds Road
Old Palace Yard SW1 .... **246** B3
Old Paradise Street SE11 ...... **246** C2
Old Park Lane W1 .... **245** E4
Old Pye Street SW1 .... **246** A3
Old Quebec Street W1 .... **241** D2
Old Queen Street SW1 .... **246** A3
Old School Square E14 .... **249** F4
Old Square WC2 .... **242** C2
Old Street EC1 .... **243** E3
Old Theatre Court SE1 .... **246** E4
Park Street
Old Woolwich Road SE10 ...... **250** C1
Oldbury Place W1 .... **241** E3
Olivers Yard EC1 .... **243** F3
Olliffe Street E14 .... **250** C3
Olney Road SE7 .... **247** E1
Olympia Mews W2 .... **240** B1

Omega Close E14 .... **250** A3
Onega Gate SE16 .... **249** E1
Ongar Road SW6 .... **244** A1
Onslow Gardens SW7 .... **244** B2
Onslow Mews SW7 .... **244** C2
Onslow Square SW7 .... **244** C2
Onslow Street EC1 .... **243** D3
Saffron Street
Ontario Street SE1 .... **247** E3
Ontario Way E14 .... **250** A4
Opal Street SE11 .... **247** D2
Orange Place SE16 .... **249** D1
Orange Street WC2 .... **242** B1
Orb Street SE17 .... **247** F2
Orchard Street W1 .... **241** E2
Orchardson Street NW8 .... **240** C3
Orde Hall Street WC1 .... **242** C3
Orient Street SE11 .... **247** D2
Orme Court W2 .... **240** A1
Orme Lane W2 .... **240** A1
Orme Square W2 .... **240** A1
Ormond Gate SW3 .... **245** D1
Ormonde Place SW1 .... **245** E2
Orsett Street SE11 .... **246** C2
Orsett Terrace W2 .... **240** B2
Osbert Street SW1 .... **246** A2
Osborne Street E1 .... **248** B4
Oslo Square SE16 .... **249** E1
Osnaburgh Street NW1 .... **241** F3
Osnaburgh Terrace NW1 .... **241** F4
Albany Street
Ossington Buildings W1 .... **241** E2
Moxon Street
Ossington Street W2 .... **240** A1
Ossulston Street NW1 .... **242** A4
Osten Mews SW7 .... **244** B2
Oswin Street SE11 .... **247** D2
Othello Close SE1 .... **247** D2
Otto Street SE17 .... **247** D1
Oval Way SE11 .... **246** C1
Ovex Close E14 .... **250** C3
Ovington Gardens SW3 .... **245** D3
Ovington Square SW3 .... **245** D3
Ovington Street SW3 .... **245** D2
Owen Street EC1 .... **243** D4
Oxendon Street SW1 .... **242** A1
Coventry Street
Oxford Circus W1 .... **241** F2
Regent Street
Oxford Square W2 .... **240** C2
Oxford Street W1 .... **241** E1
Oyster Row E1 .... **249** D3
Oystergate Walk EC4 .... **243** F1

P

Paddington Green W2 .... **240** C3
Paddington Street W1 .... **241** D3
Page Street SW1 .... **246** B2
Pageant Crescent SE16 .... **249** F2
Pageant Steps SE16 .... **249** E2
Pageantmaster Court EC4 ..... **243** D2
Ludgate Hill
Paget Street EC1 .... **243** D4
Pakenham Street WC1 .... **242** C4
Palace Avenue W8 .... **244** A4
Palace Court W2 .... **240** A1
Palace Gardens Mews W8 ..... **244** A4
Palace Gardens Terrace W8 ... **244** A4
Palace Gate W8 .... **244** B3
Palace Street SW1 .... **245** F3
Pall Mall SW1 .... **246** A4
Pall Mall East SW1 .... **242** B1
Pall Mall Place SW1 .... **246** A4
Palmer Street SW1 .... **246** A3
Pancras Lane EC4 .... **243** E2
Panton Street SW1 .... **242** A1
Paradise Street SE16 .... **248** C1
Paradise Walk SW3 .... **245** D1
Paragon Mews SE1 .... **247** F2
Searles Road
Pardoner Street SE1 .... **247** F3
Parfetts Street E1 .... **248** C4
Paris Garden SE1 .... **247** D4
Park Approach SE16 .... **248** C1
Park Crescent Mews East W1 .. **241** E3
Park Crescent Mews West W1 .. **241** E3
Park Lane E1 .... **241** E1
Park Place SW1 .... **245** F4
Park Place E14 .... **250** A4
Park Place Villas W2 .... **240** B3
Park Road NW1 & NW8 .... **241** D4
Park Row SE10 .... **250** C1
Park Square East NW1 .... **241** F3
Park Square Mews W1 .... **241** E3
Park Square West NW1 .... **241** E3
Park Street SE1 .... **247** E4
Park Street W1 .... **241** E1
Park Walk SW10 .... **244** B1
Park West Place W2 .... **241** D2
Parker Street WC2 .... **242** B2
Parkers Row SE1 .... **248** B1
Parliament Square SW1 .... **246** B3
Parliament Street SW1 .... **246** B4
Parnham Street E14 .... **249** E4
Parsonage Street E14 .... **250** C2
Pasley Close SE17 .... **247** E1
Passmore Street SW1 .... **245** E2
Pastor Street SE11 .... **247** D2
Pater Street W8 .... **244** A3
Paternoster Row EC4 .... **243** E2
Paternoster Square EC4 .... **243** E2
Paton Street EC1 .... **243** E3
Paul Julius Close E14 .... **250** C3
Paul's Walk EC4 .... **243** E2
Paultons Square SW3 .... **244** C1
Paveley Street NW8 .... **240** C4
Pavilion Road SW1 .... **245** D2
Pavilion Street SW1 .... **245** D2
Peabody Avenue SW1 .... **245** F1
Peacock Street SE17 .... **247** E2
Pear Tree Court EC1 .... **243** D3
Pear Tree Street EC1 .... **243** E3
Pearl Street E1 .... **248** C2
Pearman Street SE1 .... **247** D3
Peartree Lane E1 .... **249** D3
Peerless Street EC1 .... **243** E4
Pelham Crescent SW7 .... **244** C2
Pelham Place SW7 .... **244** C2
Pelham Street SW7 .... **244** C2
Pelier Street SE17 .... **247** E1
Pelling Street E14 .... **249** F4
Pemberton Row EC4 .... **243** D2
Pembridge Gardens W2 .... **240** A1
Pembridge Place W2 .... **240** A1
Pembridge Road W11 .... **240** A1
Pembridge Square W2 .... **240** A1

Pembroke Mews W8 .... **244** A2
Earls Court Road
Penang Street E1 .... **248** C2
Penfold Place NW1 .... **240** C3
Penfold Street NW1 & NW8 ... **240** C3
Peninns Mews W1 .... **244** A2
Pennington Street E1 .... **248** C3
Penrose Grove SE17 .... **247** E1
Penrose Street SE17 .... **247** E1
Penryn Street NW1 .... **244** A2
Penton Place SE17 .... **247** D2
Penton Rise WC1 .... **242** C4
Pentonville Road N1 .... **242** C4
Pepper Street E14 .... **250** B3
Pepys Street EC3 .... **248** A3
Percival Street EC1 .... **243** D3
Percy Circus WC1 .... **242** C4
Percy Street W1 .... **242** A2
Perkin's Rents SW1 .... **246** A3
Perkins Square SE1 .... **247** E4
Perry's Place W1 .... **242** A2
Perryn Road SE16 .... **248** C1
Peter Street W1 .... **242** A1
Petersham Lane SW7 .... **244** B3
Petersham Mews SW7 .... **244** B3
Petersham Place SW7 .... **244** B3
Peto Place NW1 .... **241** F3
Petticoat Lane E1 .... **248** B4
Petticoat Square E1 .... **248** A4
Petty France SW1 .... **246** A3
Petyward SW3 .... **245** D2
Phelp Street SE17 .... **247** F1
Phene Street SW3 .... **245** D1
Philchurch Place E1 .... **248** B3
Phillimore Walk W8 .... **244** A3
Philpot Lane EC3 .... **243** F1
Philpot Street E1 .... **248** C4
Phipp Street EC2 .... **243** F3
Phoenix Place WC1 .... **242** C3
Phoenix Road NW1 .... **242** A4
Phoenix Street WC2 .... **242** B2
Charing Cross Road
Piccadilly W1 .... **245** F4
Piccadilly Arcade SW1 .... **246** A4
Piccadilly
Piccadilly Circus W1 .... **242** A1
Piccadilly Place W1 .... **242** A1
Vine Street
Pickard Street EC1 .... **243** E4
Pickford Wharf N1 .... **243** E4
Pickwick Street SE1 .... **247** E3
Picton Place W1 .... **241** E2
Pier Street E14 .... **250** C2
Piggot Street E14 .... **249** F3
Pilgrim Street EC4 .... **243** D2
Pilgrimage Street SE1 .... **247** F3
Pimlico Road SW1 .... **245** E2
Pinchin Street E1 .... **248** B3
Pindar Street EC2 .... **243** F3
Pindock Mews W9 .... **240** A3
Pine Street EC1 .... **243** D3
Pitfield Street N1 .... **243** F4
Pitsea Place E1 .... **249** E3
Pitsea Street E1 .... **249** E3
Pitt Street W8 .... **244** A3
Pitt's Head Mews W1 .... **245** E4
Pixley Street E14 .... **249** F4
Platina Street EC2 .... **243** F3
Playhouse Yard EC4 .... **243** D1
Plevina Street E14 .... **250** B3
Pleydell Street EC4 .... **243** D1
Bouverie Street
Plough Place EC4 .... **243** D2
Fetter Lane
Plover Way SE16 .... **249** E1
Plumber's Row E1 .... **248** B4
Plumtree Court EC4 .... **243** D2
Plymouth Wharf E14 .... **250** C2
Plympton Street NW8 .... **240** C3
Pocock Street SE1 .... **247** D3
Pointers Close E14 .... **250** B1
Poland Street W1 .... **242** A2
Pollen Street W1 .... **241** F1
Pollitt Drive NW8 .... **240** C3
Polygon Road NW1 .... **242** A4
Pomwell Way E1 .... **248** B4
Pond Place SW3 .... **244** C2
Ponler Street E1 .... **248** C3
Ponsonby Place SW1 .... **246** B2
Ponsonby Terrace SW1 .... **246** B2
Pont Street SW1 .... **245** D3
Pont Street Mews SW1 .... **245** D3
Poolmans Street SE16 .... **249** D2
Poonah Street E1 .... **249** D3
Pope Street SE1 .... **248** A1
Poplar Place W2 .... **240** A1
Poppins Court EC4 .... **243** D2
Fleet Street
Porchester Gardens W2 .... **240** A1
Porchester Place W2 .... **240** C2
Porchester Road W2 .... **240** A2
Porchester Square W2 .... **240** A2
Porchester Terrace W2 .... **240** B1
Porlock Street SE1 .... **247** F3
Porter Street SE1 .... **247** E3
Porter Street W1 .... **241** E3
Porteus Road W2 .... **240** B2
Portland Mews W1 .... **242** A2
D'Arblay Street
Portland Place W1 .... **241** F2
Portland Square E1 .... **248** C2
Portland Street SE17 .... **247** F1
Portman Close W1 .... **241** E2
Portman Mews South W1 ...... **241** E2
Portman Square W1 .... **241** E2
Portman Street W1 .... **241** E2
Portpool Lane EC1 .... **242** C3
Portsea Place W2 .... **241** D2
Portsmouth Street WC2 .... **242** C2
Portugal Street
Portsoken Street EC3 .... **248** B3
Portugal Street WC2 .... **242** C2
Potier Street SE1 .... **247** F3
Pottery Street SE16 .... **248** C1
Poultry EC2 .... **243** E2
Praed Street W2 .... **240** C2
Pratt Walk SE11 .... **246** C2
Premier Place E14 .... **250** A4
Prescot Street E1 .... **248** B3
President Street EC1 .... **243** E4
Central Street
Presidents Drive E1 .... **248** C2
Prestage Way E14 .... **250** C4
Prestons Road E14 .... **250** C4
Prestwood Street N1 .... **243** E4
Wenlock Road
Price's Street SE1 .... **247** D4
Prideaux Place WC1 .... **242** C4
Primrose Hill EC4 .... **243** D1
Hutton Street
Primrose Street EC2 .... **248** A4
Prince Albert Road NW1 & NW8 .. **241** D4
Prince Consort Road SW7 ..... **244** C3
Prince of Wales Terrace W8 .. **244** B1
Kensington Road
Prince's Gardens SW7 .... **244** C3

255

Prince's Gate SW7 .... 244 C3
Prince's Gate Mews SW7 .... 244 C3
Prince's Mews W2 .... 240 A1
Prince's Square W2 .... 240 A1
Princelet Street E1 .... 248 B4
Princes Arcade SW1 .... 246 A4
  Piccadilly
Princes Circus WC2 .... 242 B2
Princes Court SE1 .... 248 C3
Princes Riverside Road SE16 ... 249 D2
Princes Street W1 .... 241 F2
Princess Street SE1 .... 247 D3
Princeton Street WC1 .... 242 C2
Printer Street EC4 .... 243 D2
Prioress Street SE1 .... 247 F3
Priory Walk SW10 .... 244 B1
Procter Street WC1 .... 242 C2
Prospect Place E1 .... 249 D2
Prospect Street SE16 .... 248 C1
Providence Court W1 .... 241 E1
Providence Square SE1 .... 248 B2
Provost Street N1 .... 243 F4
Prusom Street E1 .... 248 C2
Pudding Lane EC3 .... 243 F1
Puddle Dock EC4 .... 242 D1
Puma Court E1 .... 248 B4
Purbrook Street SE1 .... 248 A1

Q

Quarley Way SE15 .... 241 D2
  New Quebec Street
Quebec Way SE16 .... 249 E1
Queen Anne Mews W1 .... 241 F2
  Chandos Street
Queen Anne Street W1 .... 241 E2
Queen Anne's Gate SW1 .... 246 A3
Queen Elizabeth Street SE1 ..... 248 A2
Queen Square WC1 .... 242 B3
Queen Street EC4 .... 243 E1
Queen Street W1 .... 241 F1
Queen Street Place EC4 .... 243 E1
Queen Victoria Street EC4 .... 243 D1
Queen's Gardens SW1 .... 245 F3
Queen's Gardens W2 .... 240 B1
Queen's Gate SW7 .... 244 B3
Queen's Gate Gardens SW7 ..... 244 B3
Queen's Gate Mews SW7 .... 244 B3
Queen's Gate Place SW7 .... 244 B3
Queen's Gate Place Mews SW7 . 244 B2
Queen's Gate Terrace SW7 .... 244 B3
Queen's Mews W2 .... 240 A1
Queen's Row SE17 .... 247 E1
Queen's Walk SW1 .... 245 F4
Queenhithe EC4 .... 243 E1
Queensberry Mews West SW7 .. 244 B2
Queensberry Place SW7 .... 241 F4
  Harrington Street
Queensborough Terrace W2 ..... 240 B1
Queensway W2 .... 240 A2
Quick Street N1 .... 243 D4

R

Rabbit Row W8 .... 244 A4
Raby Street E14 .... 249 E4
Radcliffe Road SE1 .... 248 A1
Radcot Street SE11 .... 247 D1
Radley Court SE16 .... 249 E2
Radley Mews W8 .... 244 A2
Radnor Mews W2 .... 240 C2
Radnor Place W2 .... 240 C2
Radnor Street EC1 .... 243 D3
Radnor Walk SW3 .... 245 D1
Railway Approach SE1 .... 247 F4
Railway Avenue SE16 .... 249 D2
Rainbow Avenue E14 .... 250 B1
Raine Street E1 .... 248 C2
Rainsford Street W2 .... 240 C2
Raleana Road E14 .... 250 C4
Ralston Street SW3 .... 245 D1
Ramillies Place W1 .... 241 F2
Ramillies Street W1 .... 242 A2
Rampart Street E1 .... 248 C4
Rampayne Street SW1 .... 246 A2
Ramsey Mews SW3 .... 244 C1
Randall Road SE1 .... 246 C2
Randall Row SE11 .... 246 C2
Randolph Avenue W9 .... 240 A4
Randolph Crescent W9 .... 240 B3
Randolph Mews W9 .... 240 B3
Randolph Road W9 .... 240 B3
Ranelagh Bridge W2 .... 240 B2
Ranelagh Grove SW1 .... 245 E2
Ranelagh Road SW1 .... 246 A1
Ranston Street NW1 .... 240 C3
Raphael Street SW7 .... 245 D3
Ratcliff Grove EC1 .... 243 E4
Ratcliffe Cross Street E1 .... 249 E3
Ratcliffe Lane E14 .... 249 E3
Rathbone Place W1 .... 242 A2
Raven Row E1 .... 248 C4
Ravensdon Street SE11 .... 247 D1
Ravent Road SE11 .... 246 C2
Ravey Street EC2 .... 243 F3
Rawlings Street SW3 .... 245 D2
Rawstorne Place EC1 .... 243 D4
  Rawstorne Street
Rawstorne Street EC1 .... 243 D4
Ray Street EC1 .... 243 D3
Reardon Path E1 .... 248 C2
Reardon Street E1 .... 248 C2
Rebecca Terrace SE16 .... 249 D1
Rectory Square E1 .... 249 E4
Red Lion Row SE17 .... 247 E1
Red Lion Square WC1 .... 242 C2
Red Lion Street WC1 .... 242 C2
Redan Place W2 .... 240 A2
Redburn Street SW3 .... 245 D1
Redcastle Close E1 .... 249 D3
Redcliffe Gardens SW10 & SW5 . 244 A1
Redcliffe Mews SW10 .... 244 B1
Redcliffe Place SW10 .... 244 B1
Redcliffe Road SW10 .... 244 B1
Redcliffe Square SW10 .... 244 A1
Redcliffe Street SW10 .... 244 A1
Redcross Way SE1 .... 247 E4
Rede Place W2 .... 240 A1
Redesdale Street SW3 .... 245 D1
Redfield Lane SW5 .... 244 A2
Redhill Street NW1 .... 241 F4
Redman's Road E1 .... 249 D4
Redmead Lane E1 .... 248 B2
  Wapping High Street
Redriff Road SE16 .... 249 E1
Redwood Close SE16 .... 249 E2

Reece Mews SW7 .... 244 C1
Reedworth Street SE11 .... 247 D2
Reeves Mews W1 .... 241 E1
Regal Close E1 .... 248 C4
Regan Way N1 .... 243 F4
Regency Street SW1 .... 246 A2
Regent Square WC1 .... 242 B4
Regent Street W1 & SW1 .... 241 F2
Regnart Buildings NW1 .... 242 A4
  Euston Street
Relton Mews SW7 .... 245 D3
Remington Street N1 .... 243 E4
Remnant Street WC2 .... 242 C2
  Kingsway
Renforth Street SE16 .... 249 D1
Renfrew Road SE11 .... 247 D2
Rennie Street SE1 .... 243 E1
Rephidim Street SE1 .... 247 F3
Repton Street E14 .... 249 F4
Reston Place SW7 .... 244 B3
Reveley Close SE16 .... 249 E1
Rex Place W1 .... 241 E1
Rhodeswell Road E14 .... 249 F4
Rich Lane SW5 .... 244 A1
Rich Street E14 .... 249 F3
Richard's Place SW3 .... 245 D2
Richbell Place WC1 .... 242 C3
  Emerald Street
Richmond Buildings W1 .... 242 A2
  Dean Street
Richmond Mews W1 .... 242 A2
Richmond Terrace SW1 .... 246 A4
Rickett Street SW6 .... 244 A1
Ridgmount Gardens WC1 .... 242 A3
Ridgmount Street WC1 .... 242 A3
Riding House Street W1 .... 241 F2
Riley Road SE1 .... 248 A1
Ringwood Gardens E14 .... 250 A2
Risborough Street SE1 .... 247 E4
Risdon Street SE16 .... 249 D1
River Barge Close E14 .... 250 C3
River Street EC1 .... 243 D4
Riverside Walk SE1 .... 246 C4
Rivington Street EC2 .... 243 F3
Robert Adam Street W1 .... 241 E2
Robert Close W9 .... 240 B3
Robert Dashwood Way SE17 .... 247 E2
Robert Street NW1 .... 241 F4
Robert Street WC2 .... 242 B1
Roberts Close SE16 .... 249 E1
Roberts Place EC1 .... 243 D3
  Bowling Green Lane
Robinson Street SW3 .... 245 D1
  Flood Street
Rochester Row SW1 .... 246 A2
Rochester Street SW1 .... 246 A2
Rockingham Street SE1 .... 247 E3
Rocliffe Street N1 .... 243 E4
Roding Mews E1 .... 248 B2
Rodmarton Street W1 .... 241 D2
Rodney Place SE17 .... 247 E2
Rodney Road SE17 .... 247 E2
Roffey Street E14 .... 250 B2
Roger Street WC1 .... 242 C3
Roland Gardens SW7 .... 244 B1
Roland Way SE17 .... 247 F1
Roland Way SW7 .... 244 B1
Rolls Buildings EC4 .... 243 D2
Rolls Passage EC4 .... 242 C2
Romford Street E1 .... 248 C4
Romilly Street W1 .... 242 A1
Romney Mews W1 .... 241 E3
  Chiltern Street
Romney Street SW1 .... 246 B2
Ronald Street E1 .... 249 D3
Rood Lane EC3 .... 243 F1
Rope Street SE16 .... 249 E1
Ropemaker Road SE16 .... 249 E1
Ropemaker Street EC2 .... 243 F3
Ropemaker's Fields E14 .... 249 F3
Roper Lane SE1 .... 248 A1
Rosary Gardens SW7 .... 244 B2
Roscoe Street EC1 .... 243 E3
Rose & Crown Yard SW1 .... 246 A4
  King Street
Rose Alley SE1 .... 247 E4
Rose Street WC2 .... 242 B1
Rosebery Avenue EC1 .... 245 D3
Rosemoor Street SW3 .... 245 D2
Roserton Street E14 .... 250 B3
Rosman Place EC1 .... 243 D4
  Rosoman Street
Rosoman Street EC1 .... 243 D4
Rossmore Road NW1 .... 241 D3
Rotary Street SE1 .... 247 D3
Rotherhithe Street SE16 .... 249 D2
Rotherhithe Tunnel Approach
  E14 .... 249 E3
Rotherhithe Tunnel Approach
  SE16 .... 249 F1
Rothsay Street SE1 .... 247 F3
Rotten Row SW7 & SW1 .... 244 C4
Rotterdam Drive E14 .... 250 C2
Rouel Road SE16 .... 248 B1
Roupell Street SE1 .... 247 D4
Rowington Close W2 .... 240 A3
Roxby Place SW6 .... 244 A1
Roy Square E14 .... 249 F3
Royal Avenue SW3 .... 245 D1
Royal Exchange Buildings EC3 . 243 F2
  Cornhill
Royal Hospital Road SW3 .... 245 D1
Royal Mint Place E1 .... 248 B3
Royal Mint Street E1 .... 248 B3
Royal Opera Arcade SW1 .... 246 A4
Royal Road SE17 .... 247 D1
Royal Street SE1 .... 246 C3
Royalty Mews W1 .... 242 A2
Royalty Mews W1 .... 242 A2
Rudolf Place SW8 .... 246 B1
Rudolph Road NW6 .... 240 A4
Rufus Street N1 .... 243 F4
Rugby Street WC1 .... 242 C3
Rugg Street E14 .... 249 F3
Rum Close E1 .... 248 C3
Rupack Street SE16 .... 249 D1
Rupert Street W1 .... 242 A1
Rushworth Street SE1 .... 247 D3
Russell Court SW1 .... 246 A4
  Cleveland Row
Russell Place SE16 .... 249 E1
Russell Square WC1 .... 242 B3
Russia Dock Road SE16 .... 249 E2
Russia Row EC2 .... 243 E2
Russia Walk SE16 .... 249 E1
Rutherford Street SW1 .... 246 A2
Rutland Gardens SW7 .... 245 D3
Rutland Gate SW7 .... 244 C3
Rutland Gate Mews SW7 .... 244 C3
  Rutland Gate
Rutland Mews East SW7 .... 244 C3
  Ennismore Street
Rutland Mews South SW7 .... 244 C3
  Ennismore Street
Rutland Place EC1 .... 243 E3
Rutland Street SW7 .... 245 D3
Rysbrack Street SW3 .... 245 D3

S

Sackville Street W1 .... 242 A1
Saddle Yard W1 .... 245 E4
Saffron Hill EC1 .... 243 D3
Saffron Street EC1 .... 243 D3
Sage Street E1 .... 248 C3
Sage Way WC1 .... 242 C4
Sail Street SE11 .... 246 C2
St Agnes Place SE11 .... 247 D1
St Alban's Grove W8 .... 244 A3
St Alban's Street SW1 .... 242 A1
St Albans Mews W2 .... 240 C3
St Andrew's Hill EC4 .... 243 D1
St Ann's Lane SW1 .... 246 A3
St Ann's Row E14 .... 249 F3
St Ann's Street SW1 .... 246 B3
St Anne Street E14 .... 249 F3
St Anne's Court W1 .... 242 A2
St Anselm's Place W1 .... 241 E1
St Anthony's Close E1 .... 248 B2
St Barnabas Street SW1 .... 245 E2
St Botolph Street EC3 .... 248 A4
St Bride Street EC4 .... 243 D2
St Catherines Mews SW3 .... 245 D2
  Milner Street
St Chad's Place WC1 .... 242 B4
St Chad's Street WC1 .... 242 B4
St Christopher's Place W1 .... 241 E2
St Clare Street EC3 .... 248 A3
St Clement's Lane WC2 .... 242 C2
St Clements Court EC4 .... 243 F1
St Cross Street EC1 .... 243 D3
St David's Square E14 .... 250 B1
St Dunstan's Court EC4 .... 243 D2
  Fleet Street
St Dunstan's Lane EC3 .... 243 F1
  St Mary at Hill
St Dunstans Alley EC3 .... 243 F1
  St Dunstans Hill
St Dunstans Hill EC3 .... 248 A3
St Ermins Hill SW1 .... 246 A3
St George Street W1 .... 241 F1
St George's Circus SE1 .... 247 D3
St George's Court EC4 .... 243 D2
St George's Drive SW1 .... 245 F2
St George's Mews SE1 .... 247 D3
St George's Road SE1 .... 247 D3
St George's Square SW1 .... 246 A1
St George's Square E14 .... 249 E3
St George's Square Mews SW1 . 246 A1
St Georges Fields W2 .... 241 D1
St Giles High Street WC2 .... 242 B2
St Helen's Place EC3 .... 243 F2
St Helena Street WC1 .... 242 C4
St James's Court SW1 .... 246 A3
St James's Market SW1 .... 242 A1
  Haymarket
St James's Place SW1 .... 245 F4
St James's Road SE1 & SE16 ... 248 B1
St James's Row EC1 .... 243 D3
  St James's Walk
St James's Square SW1 .... 246 A4
St James's Street SW1 .... 246 A4
St James's Walk EC1 .... 243 D3
St John Street EC1 .... 243 D3
St John's Lane EC1 .... 243 D3
St John's Place EC1 .... 243 D3
St John's Square EC1 .... 243 D3
St John's Villas W8 .... 244 A3
  St Mary's Place
St John's Wood High Street NW8 . 240 C4
St John's Wood Road NW8 .... 240 C4
St Katherine's Row EC3 .... 243 F1
  Fenchurch Street
St Katherine's Way E1 .... 248 B1
St Lawrence Street E14 .... 250 C4
St Leonard's Terrace SW3 .... 245 D1
St Loo Avenue SW3 .... 245 D1
St Luke's Close EC1 .... 243 E3
St Luke's Street SW3 .... 244 C1
St Margaret's Lane W8 .... 244 A3
St Margaret's Street SW1 .... 246 B3
St Mark Street E1 .... 248 B3
St Martin's Court WC2 .... 242 B1
  St Martin's Lane
St Martin's Lane WC2 .... 242 B1
St Martin's Place WC2 .... 242 B1
St Martin's Street WC2 .... 242 B1
St Martin's-le-Grand EC1 .... 243 E2
St Mary Axe EC3 .... 248 A4
St Mary at Hill EC3 .... 243 F1
St Mary's Gardens SE11 .... 247 D2
St Mary's Gate W8 .... 244 A3
St Mary's Mansions W2 .... 240 B3
St Mary's Place W8 .... 244 A3
St Mary's Terrace W2 .... 240 B3
St Mary's Walk SE11 .... 247 D2
St Marychurch Street SE16 ..... 249 D1
St Matthew Street SW1 .... 246 A3
St Michael's Street W2 .... 240 C2
St Olav's Square SE16 .... 249 D1
  Lower Road
St Oswald's Place SE11 .... 246 C1
St Paul's Avenue SE16 .... 249 E2
St Paul's Churchyard EC4 .... 243 E2
St Paul's Terrace SE17 .... 247 E1
St Paul's Way E3 .... 249 F4
St Peter's Place W9 .... 240 A3
St Petersburgh Mews W2 .... 240 A1
St Petersburgh Place W2 .... 240 A1
St Stephen's Crescent W2 .... 240 A2
St Stephen's Gardens W2 .... 240 A2
St Stephen's Mews W2 .... 240 A2
St Swithin's Lane EC4 .... 243 F1
St Thomas Street SE1 .... 247 F4
St Vincent Street W1 .... 241 E2
Salamanca Place SE1 .... 246 C2
Salamanca Street SE1 & SE11 . 246 C2
Salem Road W2 .... 240 A1
Salisbury Close SE17 .... 247 F2
Salisbury Court EC4 .... 243 D2
Salisbury Place W1 .... 241 D3
Salisbury Street NW8 .... 240 C3
  Salisbury Court
Salmon Lane E14 .... 249 E4
Salter Road SE16 .... 249 E1
Salter Street E14 .... 249 F3
Sampson Street E1 .... 248 C2
Sancroft Street SE11 .... 246 C2
Sanctuary Street SE1 .... 247 E4
  Marshalsea Road
Sandell Street SE1 .... 247 D4
Sandland Street WC1 .... 242 C2
Sandpiper Close SE16 .... 249 F2
Sandwich Street WC1 .... 242 B4
Sandys Row E1 .... 248 A4
Sans Walk EC1 .... 243 D3
Saracens Head Yard EC3 .... 248 A3
Sardinia Street WC2 .... 242 C2

Saunders Court E14 .... 249 F3
  Limehouse Causeway
Saunders Ness Road E14 .... 250 C2
Savage Gardens EC3 .... 248 A3
  Pepys Street
Savernake Close E14 .... 250 A2
Savile Row W1 .... 241 F1
Savoy Buildings WC2 .... 242 C1
Savoy Hill WC2 .... 242 C1
  Savoy Way
Savoy Place WC2 .... 242 B1
Savoy Row WC2 .... 242 C1
Savoy Steps WC2 .... 242 C1
  Savoy Way
Savoy Street WC2 .... 242 C1
Savoy Way WC2 .... 242 C1
Sawyer Street SE1 .... 247 E4
Scala Street W1 .... 242 A3
Scandrett Street E1 .... 248 C2
Scarborough Street E1 .... 248 B3
Scarsdale Place W8 .... 244 A3
Scarsdale Villas W8 .... 244 A2
School House Lane E1 .... 249 D3
Schooner Close SE16 .... 249 D2
Schooner Close E14 .... 250 C2
Scoresby Street SE1 .... 247 D4
Scotswood Street EC1 .... 245 D3
  Sans Walk
Scott Ellis Gardens NW8 .... 240 B4
Scott Lidgett Crescent SE16 .... 248 B1
Scott Russell Place E14 .... 250 B1
Scovell Road SE1 .... 247 E3
Scrutton Street EC2 .... 243 F3
Seagrave Road SW6 .... 244 A1
Searles Road SE1 .... 247 F2
Sebastian Street EC1 .... 243 D4
Secker Street SE1 .... 246 C4
Sedan Way SE17 .... 247 F2
Sedding Street SW1 .... 245 E2
  Sloane Square
Seddon Street WC1 .... 242 C4
Sedley Place W1 .... 241 F2
  Woodstock Street
Seething Lane EC3 .... 248 A3
Sekforde Street EC1 .... 243 D3
Sellon Mews SE11 .... 246 C2
Selsdon Way E14 .... 250 B2
Selsey Street E14 .... 249 F4
Selwood Place SW7 .... 244 C1
Selwood Terrace SW7 .... 244 C2
Semley Place SW1 .... 245 E2
Senior Street W2 .... 240 A3
Senrab Street E1 .... 249 D4
Serle Street WC2 .... 242 C2
Serpentine Road W2 .... 244 C4
Seth Street SE16 .... 249 D1
Settles Street E1 .... 248 C4
Seven Dials WC2 .... 242 B2
Seville Street SW1 .... 245 D3
  Knightsbridge
Sevington Street W9 .... 240 A3
Seward Street EC1 .... 243 E3
Sextant Avenue E14 .... 250 C2
Seymour Mews W1 .... 241 E2
Seymour Place W1 .... 241 D2
Seymour Street W1 .... 241 D1
Seymour Walk SW10 .... 244 B1
Seyssel Street E14 .... 250 C2
Shad Thames SE1 .... 248 A2
Shadwell Pier Head E1 .... 249 D3
Shadwell Place E1 .... 248 C3
Shaftesbury Avenue W1 & WC2 . 242 A1
Shaftesbury Mews W8 .... 244 A2
Shafto Mews SW1 .... 245 D3
Shand Street SE1 .... 248 A2
Sharsted Street SE17 .... 247 D1
Shawfield Street SW3 .... 245 D1
Sheffield Terrace W8 .... 244 A4
Shelmerdine Close E3 .... 249 F4
Shelton Street WC2 .... 242 B2
Shepherd Market W1 .... 245 F4
Shepherd Street W1 .... 245 F4
Shepherd's Place W1 .... 241 E1
Shepherdess Place N1 .... 243 E4
  Shepherdess Walk
Shepherdess Walk N1 .... 243 E4
Sheraton Street W1 .... 242 A2
  Wardour Street
Sherlock Mews W1 .... 241 E3
Sherwood Gardens E14 .... 250 A2
Sherwood Street W1 .... 242 A1
Shillibeer Place W1 .... 241 D2
Ship Yard E14 .... 250 A1
Shipwright Road SE16 .... 249 E1
Shirland Road W9 .... 240 A3
Shoe Lane EC4 .... 243 D2
Short Street SE1 .... 247 D4
Short's Gardens WC2 .... 242 B2
Shorter Street E1 .... 248 B3
Shoulder of Mutton Alley E14 .. 249 F2
Shouldham Street W1 .... 241 D2
Shroton Street NW1 .... 240 C3
Sicilian Avenue WC1 .... 242 B2
  Vernon Place
Siddons Lane NW1 .... 241 D3
Sidford Place SE1 .... 246 C2
Sidmouth Street WC1 .... 242 C4
Sidney Square E1 .... 249 D4
Sidney Street E1 .... 248 C4
Silex Street SE1 .... 247 D3
Silk Street EC2 .... 243 E3
Silver Walk SE16 .... 249 F2
Silvester Street SE1 .... 247 E3
Simpson's Road E14 .... 250 B4
Singer Street EC2 .... 243 F3
Sise Lane EC4 .... 243 E2
  Pancras Lane
Skinner Street EC1 .... 243 D3
Skinners Lane EC4 .... 243 F4
  Queen Street
Sleaford Street SW8 .... 242 B4
Slingsby Place WC2 .... 242 B1
Slippers Place SE16 .... 248 C1
Sloane Avenue SW3 .... 245 D2
Sloane Court East SW3 .... 245 E1
Sloane Court West SW3 .... 245 E1
Sloane Gardens SW1 .... 245 E2
Sloane Street SW1 .... 245 D3
Sloane Terrace SW1 .... 245 E2
Sly Street E1 .... 248 C3
  Cannon Street Road
Smart's Place WC2 .... 242 B2
Smeaton Street E1 .... 248 C2
Smith Close SE16 .... 249 D2
Smith Square SW1 .... 246 B3
Smith Street SW3 .... 245 D1
Smith Terrace SW3 .... 245 D1
Smithfield Street EC1 .... 243 D2
Smithy Street E1 .... 249 D4
Snow Hill EC1 .... 243 D2
Snowfields SE1 .... 247 F4
Soho Square W1 .... 242 A2
Soho Street W1 .... 242 A2
Somerford Way SE16 .... 249 E1
Somers Crescent W2 .... 240 C1

Somers Mews W2 .... 240 C2
Sondes Street SE17 .... 247 F1
Sophia Square E16 .... 249 F1
Souldern Street W14 .... 241 E2
South Audley Street W1 .... 241 E1
South Bolton Gardens SW5 ..... 244 B1
South Carriage Drive SW1 &
  SW7 .... 244 C3
South Collonade E14 .... 250 A4
South Crescent W1 .... 242 A2
  Store Street
South Eaton Place SW1 .... 245 E2
South End W8 .... 244 A3
South End Row W8 .... 244 A3
South Lambeth Place SW8 .... 246 B1
South Molton Lane W1 .... 241 E1
South Molton Street W1 .... 241 E2
South Parade SW3 .... 244 C1
South Place EC2 .... 243 F3
South Street W1 .... 241 E1
South Tenter Street E1 .... 248 B3
South Terrace SW7 .... 244 C2
South Wharf Road W2 .... 240 C2
Southall Place SE1 .... 247 F3
  Long Lane
Southampton Buildings WC2 .... 242 C2
Southampton Place WC1 .... 242 B2
Southampton Row WC1 .... 242 B3
Southampton Street WC2 .... 242 B1
Southsea Street SE16 .... 249 F1
Southwark Bridge EC4 & SE1 ... 243 E1
Southwark Bridge Road SE1 .... 247 E3
Southwark Park Road SE16 ..... 248 C1
Southwark Street SE1 .... 247 D4
Southwell Gardens SW7 .... 244 B2
Southwick Street W2 .... 240 C2
  Hyde Park Crescent
Sovereign Close E1 .... 248 C3
Spa Road SE16 .... 248 B1
Spanish Place W1 .... 241 E2
Spear Mews SW5 .... 244 A2
Spelman Street E1 .... 248 B4
Spence Close SE16 .... 249 F1
Spencer Street EC1 .... 243 D4
Spenser Street SW1 .... 246 A3
Spert Street E14 .... 249 E3
Spindrift Avenue E14 .... 250 B2
Spital Square E1 .... 248 A4
Spital Street E1 .... 248 B4
Sprimont Place SW3 .... 245 D2
Spring Gardens SW1 .... 246 B4
Spring Mews W1 .... 241 D3
Spring Street W2 .... 240 C2
Spur Road SW1 .... 246 A3
Spur Road SE1 .... 246 C3
  Lower Marsh
Spurgeon Street SE1 .... 247 F3
Squire Gardens NW8 .... 240 C4
Stable Yard Road SW1 .... 246 A4
Stables Way SE11 .... 246 C1
Stacey Street WC2 .... 242 B2
Staff Street EC1 .... 243 F4
  Vince Street
Stafford Place SW1 .... 245 F3
Stag Place SW1 .... 245 F3
Stainer Street SE1 .... 247 F4
Staining Lane EC2 .... 243 E2
Stalbridge Street NW1 .... 240 C3
Stalham Street SE16 .... 248 C1
Stamford Street SE1 .... 246 C4
Stanford Road W8 .... 244 A3
Stanford Street SW1 .... 246 A2
Stanhope Gardens SW7 .... 244 B2
Stanhope Gate W1 .... 245 E4
  Hertford Street
Stanhope Mews East SW7 .... 244 B2
Stanhope Mews South SW7 ..... 244 B2
Stanhope Mews West SW7 ...... 244 B2
Stanhope Place W2 .... 241 D1
Stanhope Row W1 .... 245 F4
Stanhope Street NW1 .... 241 F4
Stanhope Terrace W2 .... 240 C1
Stannary Place SE11 .... 247 D1
Stannary Street SE11 .... 247 D1
Stanworth Street SE1 .... 248 B1
Staple Inn Buildings WC1 .... 242 C2
Staple Street SE1 .... 247 F3
Staples Close SE16 .... 249 E2
Star Place E1 .... 248 B3
Star Street W2 .... 240 C2
Star Yard WC2 .... 242 C2
Starboard Way E14 .... 250 A3
Starcross Street NW1 .... 241 A3
Station Acces Road EC2 .... 243 F3
Stave Yard Road SE16 .... 249 E2
Stead Street SE17 .... 247 E2
Stebondale Street E14 .... 250 C2
Stedham Place WC1 .... 242 B2
  New Oxford Street
Steedman Street SE17 .... 247 E2
Steel's Lane E1 .... 249 D4
Steelyard Passage EC4 .... 243 E1
Steers Way SE16 .... 249 E1
Stephen Mews W1 .... 242 A2
  Gresse Street
Stephen Street W1 .... 242 A2
Stephen's Row EC4 .... 243 F1
  Walbrook
Stephenson Way NW1 .... 242 A3
Stepney Causeway E1 .... 249 D4
Stepney Green E1 .... 249 D4
Stepney High Street E1 .... 249 E4
Stepney Way E1 .... 249 D4
Sterling Street SW7 .... 245 D3
  Montpelier Place
Sterry Street SE1 .... 247 F3
Stevedore Street E1 .... 248 C2
Stevens Street SE1 .... 248 A1
Steward Street E1 .... 248 A4
Stewart Street E14 .... 250 C3
Stewart's Grove SW3 .... 244 C2
Stillington Street SW1 .... 246 A2
Stockholm Way E1 .... 248 B2
  Vaughan Way
Stocks Place E14 .... 249 F3
Stone Buildings WC2 .... 242 C2
  Chancery Lane
Stone Hall Gardens W8 .... 244 A3
Stone Hall Place W8 .... 244 A3
  Stone Hall Gardens
Stone Stairs E1 .... 249 E3
Stonecutter Street EC4 .... 243 D2
Stones End Street SE1 .... 247 E3
Stoney Lane E1 .... 248 A4
Stoney Street SE1 .... 247 F4
Stopford Road SE17 .... 247 E1
Store Street WC1 .... 242 A2
Storers Quay E14 .... 250 C2
Storey's Gate SW1 .... 246 B3
Stork's Road SE16 .... 248 C1
Stoughton Close SE11 .... 246 C2
Stourcliffe Street W1 .... 241 D2
Strafford Street E14 .... 250 A3
Strand WC2 .... 242 B1
Stratford Avenue W8 .... 244 A3
Stratford Place W1 .... 241 E2
Stratford Road W8 .... 244 A3
Strathearn Place W2 .... 240 C1
  Hyde Park Crescent
Strathmore Gardens W8 .... 244 A4
  Palace Gardens Terrace

256

Stratton Street W1 — 245 F4
Strattondale Street E14 — 250 B3
Streatham Street WC1 — 242 B2
  Dyott Street
Strutton Ground SW1 — 246 A3
Strype Street E1 — 248 A4
Stukeley Street WC2 — 242 B2
Sturge Street SE1 — 247 E3
Sturgeon Road SE17 — 247 E1
Sturt Street E1 — 243 E4
Stutfield Street E1 — 248 B3
Sudeley Street N1 — 243 D4
Sudrey Street SE1 — 247 E3
Suffolk Lane EC4 — 243 F1
Suffolk Place SW1 — 242 B1
  Suffolk Street
Suffolk Street SW1 — 242 B1
Sugar Quay Walk EC3 — 248 A3
Sullivan Road SE1 — 247 D2
Summercourt Road E1 — 249 D4
Summers Street EC1 — 243 D3
  Back Hill
Sumner Place SW7 — 244 C2
Sumner Place Mews SW7 — 244 C2
Sumner Street SE1 — 247 E4
Sun Street EC2 — 243 F3
Sun Street Passage EC2 — 243 F2
Sun Walk E1 — 248 B3
Sunderland Terrace W2 — 240 A2
Sunningdale Gardens W8 — 244 A2
  Stratford Road
Surrenale Place W9 — 240 A3
Surrey Quays Road SE16 — 249 D1
Surrey Row SE1 — 247 D4
Surrey Square SE17 — 247 F2
Surrey Street WC2 — 242 C1
Surrey Water Road SE16 — 249 E2
Sussex Gardens W2 — 240 C1
Sussex Place NW1 — 241 D4
Sussex Place W2 — 240 C2
Sussex Square W2 — 240 C1
Sussex Street SW1 — 245 F1
Sutherland Avenue W9 — 240 A3
Sutherland Row SW1 — 245 F1
  Sutherland Street
Sutherland Square SE17 — 247 E1
Sutherland Street SW1 — 245 F1
Sutherland Walk SE17 — 247 E1
Sutton Row W1 — 242 B2
Swallow Street W1 — 242 A1
Swan Lane EC4 — 243 F1
Swan Mead SE1 — 247 F3
Swan Road SE16 — 249 D2
Swan Street SE1 — 247 E3
Swan Walk SW3 — 245 D1
Sweden Gate SE16 — 249 E1
Swedenborg Gardens E1 — 248 C3
Sweeney Crescent SE1 — 248 B4
Swinton Street WC1 — 242 C4
Swiss Court WC2 — 242 B1
  Leicester Square
Sycamore Street EC1 — 243 E3
  Old Street
Sydney Close SW3 — 244 C2
Sydney Mews SW3 — 244 C2
Sydney Street SW3 — 244 C2
Symons Street SW3 — 245 D2

T

Tabard Street SE1 — 247 F3
Tabernacle Street EC2 — 243 F3
Tachbrook Street SW1 — 246 A2
Taeping Street E14 — 250 B2
Tailworth Street E1 — 248 B4
  Chicksand Street
Talbot Square W2 — 240 C2
Talbot Yard SE1 — 247 F4
Tallis Street EC4 — 243 D1
Tamareire Street SE16 — 249 D2
Tamworth Street SW6 — 243 A1
Tankerton Street WC1 — 242 B4
  Cromer Street
Tanner Street SE1 — 248 A1
Taplow Street N1 — 243 E4
Tarbert Walk E1 — 249 D3
Tarling Street E1 — 248 C3
Tarver Road SE17 — 247 E1
Tatum Street SE17 — 247 F2
Taunton Mews NW1 — 241 D3
  Balcombe Street
Taunton Place NW1 — 241 D3
Tavistock Place WC1 — 242 B3
Tavistock Square WC1 — 242 B3
Tavistock Street WC2 — 242 B1
Taviton Street WC1 — 242 A3
Tavy Close SE11 — 247 D2
Teak Close SE16 — 249 E2
Tedworth Square SW3 — 245 D1
Telegraph Place E14 — 250 B2
Telegraph Street EC2 — 243 F2
Temple Avenue EC4 — 243 D1
Temple Lane EC4 — 243 A2
Temple Place WC2 — 242 C1
Templeton Place SW5 — 243 D1
Tench Street E1 — 248 C2
Tenison Court W1 — 241 F2
  Regent Street
Tenison Way SE1 — 246 C4
Tennis Street SE1 — 247 F3
Tenter Ground E1 — 248 A4
  White's Row
Tenterden Street W1 — 241 F2
Terminus Place SW1 — 245 F3
Thackeray Street W8 — 244 A3
Thalia Close SE10 — 250 C1
Thame Road SE16 — 249 E2
Thames Circle E14 — 250 A2
Thames Link E14 — 249 D2
Thames Street SE10 — 250 B1
Thanet Street WC1 — 242 B4
Thavies Inn EC4 — 243 D2
Thayer Street W1 — 241 E2
The Boltons SW10 — 244 B1
The Broad Walk NW1 — 241 E4
The Broad Walk W8 — 244 B4
The Cut SE1 — 247 D4
The Dial Walk W8 — 244 B4
The Economist Plaza SW1 — 246 A4
  Bury Street
The Flower Walk SW7 — 244 B3
The Grange SE1 — 248 A1
The Highway E1 & E14 — 248 C3
The Limes W2 — 240 A1
The Little Boltons SW10 & SW5 — 244 B1
The Mall SW1 — 246 A4
The Mitre E14 — 249 F3
The Piazza WC2 — 242 B1
The Quarterdeck E14 — 250 A3
The Vale SW3 — 244 C1
Theed Street SE1 — 247 D4
Theobald Street SE1 — 247 F2
  New Kent Road

Theobold's Road WC1 — 242 C3
Thermopylae Gate E14 — 250 B2
Theseus Walk N1 — 243 E4
  Rocliffe Street
Thirleby Road SW1 — 246 A3
Thistle Grove SW10 — 244 B1
Thomas Doyle Street SE1 — 247 D3
Thomas More Street E1 — 248 B2
Thomas Place W8 — 244 A3
  St Mary's Place
Thomas Road E14 — 249 F4
Thoresby Street N1 — 243 E4
Thorney Street SW1 — 246 B2
Thorngate Road W9 — 240 A3
Thornton Place W1 — 241 D3
Thrale Street SE1 — 247 E4
Thrawl Street E1 — 248 B4
Threadneedle Street EC2 — 243 F2
Three Colt Street E14 — 249 F3
Three Cranes Walk EC4 — 243 E1
Three Kings Yard W1 — 241 E1
Three Oak Lane SE1 — 248 A2
Throgmorton Avenue EC2 — 243 F2
Throgmorton Street EC2 — 243 F2
Thrush Street SE17 — 247 E1
Thurland Road SE16 — 248 B1
Thurloe Close SW7 — 244 C2
Thurloe Place SW7 — 244 C2
Thurloe Place Mews SW7 — 244 C2
Thurloe Square SW7 — 244 C2
Thurloe Street SW7 — 244 C2
Thurlow Street SE17 — 247 F2
Tiller Road E14 — 250 A3
Tillman Street E1 — 248 C3
Tilney Street W1 — 245 E3
Timber Street EC1 — 243 E3
Timberland Road E1 — 248 C3
Timberpond Road SE16 — 249 D2
Tinsley Road E1 — 249 D4
Tinworth Street SE11 — 246 B2
Titchborne Row W2 — 240 C2
Tite Street SW3 — 245 D1
Tiverton Street SE1 — 247 E3
Tivoli Court SE16 — 249 F2
Tobago Street E14 — 250 A3
Tokenhouse Yard EC2 — 243 F2
Tolmers Square NW1 — 242 A3
Tonbridge Street WC1 — 242 B4
Took's Court EC4 — 242 C2
Tooley Street SE1 — 248 A2
Topham Street EC1 — 243 D3
Tor Gardens W8 — 244 A4
Torquay Street W2 — 240 A2
Torrens Street EC1 — 243 D4
Torres Square E14 — 250 A1
  Maritime Quay
Torrington Place E1 — 248 C1
Torrington Place WC1 — 242 A3
Tothill Street SW1 — 246 A3
Tottenham Court Road W1 — 242 A3
Tottenham Street W1 — 242 A3
Toulmin Street SE1 — 247 E3
Toussaint Street SE8 — 248 B1
Tower Bridge E1 & SE1 — 248 A2
Tower Bridge Approach E1 — 248 B2
Tower Bridge Road SE1 — 248 A1
Tower Court WC2 — 242 B1
  Monmouth Street
Tower Hill EC3 — 248 A3
Tower Hill Terrace EC3 — 248 A3
  Gloucester Close
Tower Street WC2 — 242 B1
Townley Street SE17 — 247 E2
Townsend Street SE17 — 247 F2
Toynbee Street E1 — 248 B4
Tracey Street SE11 — 246 C2
Trafalgar Gardens E1 — 249 E4
Trafalgar Gardens W8 — 244 A3
  South End Row
Trafalgar Grove SE10 — 250 C1
Trafalgar Road SE10 — 250 C1
Trafalgar Square WC2 — 242 B1
Trafalgar Street SE17 — 247 F1
Trafalgar Way E14 — 250 B4
Transom Square E14 — 250 B1
Tranton Road SE16 — 248 C1
Trebeck Street W1 — 245 E4
  Curzon Street
Trebovir Road SW5 — 244 A2
Tregunter Road SW10 — 244 B1
Trenchard Street SE10 — 250 C1
Tresham Crescent NW8 — 240 C4
Treveris Street SE1 — 247 D4
  Bear Lane
Trevithick Street SE8 — 250 A1
Trevor Place SW7 — 245 D3
Trevor Square SW7 — 245 D3
Trevor Street SW7 — 245 D3
Trinidad Street E14 — 249 F3
Trinity Church Square SE1 — 247 E3
Trinity Place EC3 — 248 A3
  Trinity Square
Trinity Square EC3 — 248 A3
Trinity Street SE1 — 247 E3
Trio Place SE1 — 247 E3
Triton Square NW1 — 241 F3
Troon Street E1 — 249 E4
Trumans Street SE16 — 248 C1
Trump Street EC2 — 243 E2
Tryon Street SW3 — 245 D2
Tudor Street EC4 — 243 D1
Tufton Street SW1 — 246 B3
Tunley Street E14 — 249 F4
Tunnel Avenue SE10 — 250 C2
Tunnel Road SE16 — 249 D2
Turk's Row SW3 — 245 E1
Turner Street E1 — 248 C4
Turnmill Street EC1 — 243 D3
Turpentine Lane SW1 — 245 F1
Turquand Street SE17 — 247 E2
Twine Court E1 — 248 C3
Twyford Place WC2 — 242 C2
  Kingsway
Tyers Gate SE1 — 247 F3
Tyers Street SE11 — 246 C1
Tyers Terrace SE11 — 246 C1
Tyne Street E1 — 248 B4
Tysoe Street EC1 — 243 D4

U

Udall Street SW1 — 246 A2
Ufford Street SE1 — 247 D3
Ulster Place NW1 — 241 E3
Umberston Street E1 — 248 C4
Undershaft EC3 — 243 F2
Underwood Row N1 — 243 E4
  Shepherdess Walk
Underwood Street N1 — 243 E4
Undine Street E14 — 250 B1
Union Street SE1 — 247 E4
University Street WC1 — 242 A3
Upbrook Mews W2 — 240 B2

Upper Belgrave Street SW1 — 245 E3
Upper Berkeley Street W1 — 241 D2
Upper Brook Street W1 — 241 E1
Upper Cheyne Row SW3 — 244 C1
Upper Grosvenor Street W1 — 241 E1
Upper Ground SE1 — 243 D1
Upper Harley Street NW1 — 241 E3
Upper James Street W1 — 242 A1
Upper John Street W1 — 242 A1
Upper Marsh SE1 — 246 C3
Upper Montagu Street W1 — 241 D3
Upper St Martin's Lane WC2 — 242 B1
Upper Tachbrook Street SW1 — 246 A2
Upper Thames Street EC4 — 243 E1
Upper Wimpole Street W1 — 241 E3
Upper Woburn Place WC1 — 242 B3

V

Valcan Square E14 — 250 A2
Vale Close W9 — 240 B4
Valentine Place SE1 — 247 D3
Valentine Row SE1 — 247 D3
Vandon Passage SW1 — 246 A3
Vandon Street SW1 — 246 A3
Vandy Street EC2 — 243 F3
Vane Street SW1 — 246 A2
Vantage Mews E14 — 250 C4
  Managers Street
Varden Street E1 — 248 C4
Varndell Street NW1 — 241 F4
Vauban Street SE16 — 248 B1
Vaughan Street SE16 — 249 F1
Vaughan Way E1 — 248 B2
Vauxhall Bridge SW1 & SE1 — 246 B2
Vauxhall Bridge Road SW1 — 245 F2
Vauxhall Grove SW8 — 246 B1
Vauxhall Street SE11 — 246 C1
Vauxhall Walk SE11 — 246 C2
Venables Street NW8 — 240 C3
Vere Street W1 — 241 E2
Vernon Place WC1 — 242 B2
Vernon Rise WC1 — 242 C4
Vernon Square WC1 — 242 C4
  Penton Rise
Vernon Street W14 — 242 C4
Verulam Street WC1 — 242 C3
Vestry Street N1 — 243 F4
Vicarage Court W8 — 244 A4
Vicarage Gardens W8 — 244 A4
Vicarage Gate W8 — 244 A4
Victoria Avenue EC2 — 248 A4
Victoria Embankment SW1,WC2 & EC4 — 242 C1
Victoria Grove W8 — 244 B3
Victoria Road W8 — 244 B3
Victoria Street SW1 — 245 F3
Victory Place SE17 — 247 F2
Victory Place E14 — 249 E3
Victory Way SE16 — 249 E1
Vigo Street W1 — 242 A1
Villa Street SE17 — 247 F1
Villiers Street WC2 — 242 B1
Vince Street EC1 — 243 F4
Vincent Close SE16 — 249 E2
Vincent Square SW1 — 246 A2
Vincent Street SW1 — 246 A2
Vine Court E1 — 248 C4
Vine Lane SE1 — 248 A2
Vine Street EC3 — 248 A3
Vine Street W1 — 242 A1
Vine Street Bridge EC1 — 243 D3
  Farringdon Lane
Vinegar Street E1 — 248 C2
Vinegar Yard SE1 — 247 F4
  St Thomas Street
Vineyard Walk EC1 — 243 D3
  Pine Street
Vintner's Place EC4 — 243 E1
Violet Hill NW8 — 240 B4
Virgil Place W1 — 241 D2
  Seymour Place
Virgil Street SE1 — 246 C3
Virginia Street E1 — 248 B3
Viscount Street EC1 — 243 E3

W

Wadding Street SE17 — 247 E2
Waithman Street EC4 — 243 D2
  Pilgrim Street
Wakefield Mews WC1 — 242 B4
  Wakefield Street
Wakefield Street WC1 — 242 B4
Wakeling Street E14 — 249 E3
Wakley Street EC1 — 243 D4
Walbrook EC4 — 243 F1
Walburgh Street E1 — 248 C3
Walcorde Avenue SE17 — 247 E2
Walcot Square SE11 — 247 D2
Walden Street E1 — 248 C4
Waley Street E1 — 249 E4
Wallgrave Road SW5 — 244 A2
Wallwood Street E14 — 249 F4
Walmer Street W1 — 241 D3
  Seymour Place
Walnut Tree Walk SE11 — 246 C2
Walpole Street SW3 — 245 D2
Walton Place SW3 — 245 D3
Walton Street SW3 — 245 D3
Walton's Mews W1 — 241 D2
Walworth Place SE17 — 247 E1
Walworth Road SE1 & SE17 — 247 E2
Wansey Street SE17 — 247 E2
Wapping Dock Street E1 — 248 C2
Wapping High Street E1 — 248 B2
Wapping Lane E1 — 248 C3
Wapping Walk E1 — 248 C3
Wapping Wall E1 — 249 D2
Wardour Street W1 — 242 A2
Warner Street EC1 — 242 C3
Warren Street W1 — 241 F3
Warrington Crescent W9 — 240 B3
Warrington Gardens W9 — 240 B3
Warwick Avenue W9 — 240 A3
Warwick Court WC1 — 242 C2
Warwick Crescent W2 — 240 B3
Warwick House Street SW1 — 246 B4
Warwick Lane EC4 — 243 E2
Warwick Passage EC4 — 243 D2
  Warwick Square
Warwick Place W9 — 240 B3
Warwick Row SW1 — 245 F3
Warwick Square SW1 — 245 F2
Warwick Square EC4 — 243 D2
Warwick Street W1 — 242 A1

Warwick Way SW1 — 245 F2
Water Lane EC3 — 248 A3
Watergate SE1 — 243 D2
  New Bridge Street
Watergate Street SE8 — 250 A1
Watergate Walk WC2 — 242 B1
  Villiers Street
Wateridge Close E14 — 250 A2
  West Ferry Road
Waterloo Bridge WC2 & SE1 — 242 C1
Waterloo Place SW1 — 246 A4
Waterloo Road SE1 — 246 C4
Waterman Way E1 — 248 C2
Waterman's Walk EC4 — 243 F1
Waterside SE16 — 248 B1
Watling Street EC4 — 243 E2
Watney Market E1 — 248 C4
Watney Street E1 — 248 C3
Watson's Street SE8 — 248 C2
Watts Way SW7 — 244 C3
Waveney Close E1 — 248 B2
Waverton Street W1 — 245 E4
Weavers Lane SE1 — 248 A2
Webb Street SE1 — 247 F3
Webber Row SE1 — 247 D3
Webber Street SE1 — 247 D3
Webster Road SE16 — 248 C1
Weighouse Street W1 — 241 E1
Welbeck Street W1 — 241 E2
Welbeck Way W1 — 241 E2
Well Court EC4 — 243 E1
  Queen Street
Welland Mews E1 — 248 C1
Wellclose Square E1 — 248 B3
Wellclose Street E1 — 248 B3
  The Highway
Weller Street SE1 — 247 E3
Wellesley Street E1 — 249 D4
Wellesley Terrace N1 — 243 E4
Wellington Place NW8 — 240 C4
Wellington Road NW8 — 240 C4
Wellington Square SW3 — 245 D1
Wellington Street WC2 — 242 C1
Wells Mews W1 — 242 A2
Wells Square WC1 — 242 C4
Wells Street W1 — 241 F2
Wells Way SE5 — 247 F2 ?
Wendover SE17 — 247 F1
Wenlock Road N1 — 243 E4
Wenlock Street N1 — 243 E4
Wentworth Market E1 — 248 B4
  Wentworth Street
Wentworth Street E1 — 248 B4
Werrington Street NW1 — 242 A4
Wesley Close SE17 — 247 D2
Wesley Street W1 — 241 E2
  Weymouth Street
West Arbour Street E1 — 249 D4
West Central Street WC1 — 242 B2
West Eaton Place SW1 — 245 E2
West Ferry Road E14 — 250 A3
West Gardens E1 — 248 C3
West Halkin Street SW1 — 245 E3
West India Dock Road E14 — 249 F3
West Lane SE16 — 248 C1
West Mews SW1 — 245 F2
  Warwick Way
West Poultry Avenue EC1 — 243 D2
  West Smithfield
West Road SW4 — 245 D1
West Smithfield EC1 — 243 D2
West Square SE11 — 247 D2
West Street WC2 — 242 B1
West Tenter Street E1 — 248 B3
Westbourne Crescent W2 — 240 B1
Westbourne Gardens W2 — 240 A2
Westbourne Grove W2 & W11 — 240 A2
Westbourne Grove Terrace W2 — 240 A2
Westbourne Park Road W2 & W11 — 240 A1
Westbourne Park Villas W2 — 240 A1
Westbourne Street W2 — 240 A1
Westbourne Terrace W2 — 240 B2
Westbourne Terrace Mews W2 — 240 B2
Westbourne Terrace Road W2 — 240 B2
Westcott Road SE17 — 247 D1
Western Place SE16 — 249 D2
Westferry Circus E14 — 250 A4
Westgate Terrace SW10 — 244 A1
Westland Place N1 — 243 F4
Westminster Bridge SW1 & SE1 — 246 B3
Westminster Bridge Road SE1 — 246 C3
Westmoreland Place SW1 — 245 F1
Westmoreland Road SE17 — 247 E1
Westmoreland Street W1 — 241 E2
Westmoreland Terrace SW1 — 245 F1
Weston Rise WC1 — 242 C4
Weston Street SE1 — 247 F3
Westport Street E1 — 249 E4
Westway W12 — 240 A2
Wetherby Gardens SW5 — 244 B2
Wetherby Mews SW5 — 244 B2
  Earls Court Road
Wetherby Place SW7 — 244 B2
Weymouth Mews W1 — 241 E2
Weymouth Street W1 — 241 E2
Wharf Road N1 — 243 E4
Wharfedale Street SW10 — 244 A1
Wharton Street WC1 — 242 C4
Wheat Sheaf Close E14 — 250 A3
Wheatley Street W1 — 241 E2
  Marylebone Street
Whetstone Park WC2 — 242 C2
Whidborne Street WC1 — 242 B4
Whiskin Street EC1 — 243 D4
Whitcomb Street WC2 — 242 A1
White Church Lane E1 — 248 B4
White Hart Street SE11 — 247 D2
White Horse Lane E1 — 249 E4
White Horse Mews SE1 — 247 D3
White Horse Road E1 — 249 E3
White Horse Street W1 — 245 F4
White Kennet Street E1 — 248 A4
White Lion Hill EC4 — 243 E1
White's Grounds SE1 — 248 A1
White's Row E1 — 248 A4
Whiteadder Way E14 — 250 B2
Whitechapel High Street E1 — 248 B4
Whitechapel Road E1 — 248 B4
Whitecross Place EC2 — 243 F3
Whitecross Street EC1 — 243 E3
Whitefriars Street EC4 — 243 D2
Whitehall SW1 — 246 B4
Whitehall Court SW1 — 246 B4
Whitehall Place SW1 — 246 B4
Whitehaven Street NW8 — 240 C3
Whitehead's Grove SW3 — 245 D2
Whitfield Place W1 — 242 A3
  Whitfield Street
Whitfield Street W1 — 242 A3
Whitgift Street SE11 — 246 C2
Whittaker Street SW1 — 245 E2
Whittington Avenue EC3 — 243 F2
  Leadenhall Street
Whittlesey Street SE1 — 247 D4
Wickham Street SE11 — 246 C1
Wicklow Street WC1 — 242 C4
Widegate Street E1 — 248 A4
  Middlesex Street

Widley Road W9 — 240 A4
Wigmore Place W1 — 241 E2
Wigmore Street W1 — 241 E2
Wilbraham Place SW1 — 245 E2
Wilcox Place SW1 — 246 A3
Wild Court WC2 — 242 C2
Wild Street WC2 — 242 B2
Wild's Rents SE1 — 247 F3
Wilfred Street SW1 — 245 F3
Wilkes Street E1 — 248 B4
William IV Street WC2 — 242 B1
William Road NW1 — 241 F4
William Square SE16 — 249 E3
William Street SW1 — 245 D3
Willoughby Passage E14 — 250 A4
Willoughby Street WC1 — 242 B2
  Streatham Street
Willow Place SW1 — 246 A2
Willow Street EC2 — 243 F3
Wilmington Square WC1 — 243 D4
Wilmington Street WC1 — 243 D4
Wilson Grove SE16 — 248 C1
Wilson Street EC2 — 243 F2
Wilson's Place E14 — 249 F3
Wilton Crescent SW1 — 245 E3
Wilton Mews SW1 — 245 E3
Wilton Place SW1 — 245 E3
Wilton Road SW1 — 245 F2
Wilton Row SW1 — 245 E3
Wilton Street SW1 — 245 E3
Wilton Terrace SW1 — 245 E3
Wimpole Mews W1 — 241 E2
Wimpole Street W1 — 241 E2
Winchester Close SE17 — 247 D2
Winchester Square SE1 — 247 F4
  Winchester Walk
Winchester Street SW1 — 245 F2
Winchester Walk SE1 — 247 F4
Wincott Street SE11 — 247 D1
Windmill Row SE11 — 247 D1
Windmill Street W1 — 242 A2
Windmill Walk SE1 — 247 D4
Windrose Close SE16 — 249 D2
Windsor Terrace N1 — 243 E4
Wine Close E1 — 248 C2
Wine Office Court EC4 — 243 D2
Winnett Street W1 — 242 A1
  Rupert Street
Winsland Mews W2 — 240 C2
Winsland Street W2 — 240 C2
Winsley Street W1 — 242 A2
Winterton Place SW10 — 244 B1
Woburn Place WC1 — 242 B3
Woburn Square WC1 — 242 B3
Woburn Walk WC1 — 242 B3
  Upper Woburn Place
Wolfe Crescent SE16 — 249 D1
Wolseley Street SE1 — 248 B1
Wood Street EC2 — 243 E2
Wood's Mews W1 — 241 E1
Wood's Place SE1 — 248 A1
Woodbridge Street EC1 — 243 D3
Woodchester Square W2 — 240 A3
Woodfall Street SW3 — 245 D1
Woodland Crescent SE16 — 249 D1
Woodstock Mews W1 — 241 E2
  Westmoreland Street
Woodstock Street W1 — 241 F2
Woolaston Close SE1 — 247 E2
Wooler Street SE17 — 247 F1
Wooster Place SE1 — 247 F2
Wootton Street SE1 — 247 D4
Worgan Street SE11 — 246 C2
Wormwood Street EC2 — 243 F2
Worship Street EC2 — 243 F3
Wren Landing E14 — 250 A4
Wren Street WC1 — 242 C3
Wright's Lane W8 — 244 A3
Wyatt Close SE16 — 249 F1
Wybert Street NW1 — 241 F3
  Laxton Place
Wyclif Street EC1 — 243 D4
Wymering Road W9 — 240 A4
Wynan Road E14 — 250 B1
Wyndham Mews W1 — 241 D2
Wyndham Place W1 — 241 D2
Wyndham Street W1 — 241 D2
Wyndham Yard W1 — 241 D2
Wynnstay Gardens W8 — 244 A3
Wynyard Terrace SE11 — 246 C1
Wynyatt Street EC1 — 243 D4
Wythburn Place W1 — 241 D2

Y

Yabsley Street E14 — 250 C4
Yardley Street WC1 — 242 C4
Yarmouth Place W1 — 245 E4
Yeoman's Row SW3 — 245 D3
York Buildings WC2 — 242 B1
York Gate NW1 — 241 E3
York House Place W8 — 244 A4
York Road SE1 — 246 C3
York Square E14 — 249 E3
York Street W1 — 241 D3
York Terrace East NW1 — 241 E3
York Terrace West NW1 — 241 E3
Yorkshire Road E14 — 249 E3
Young Street W8 — 244 A3

Z

Zoar Street SE1 — 247 E4

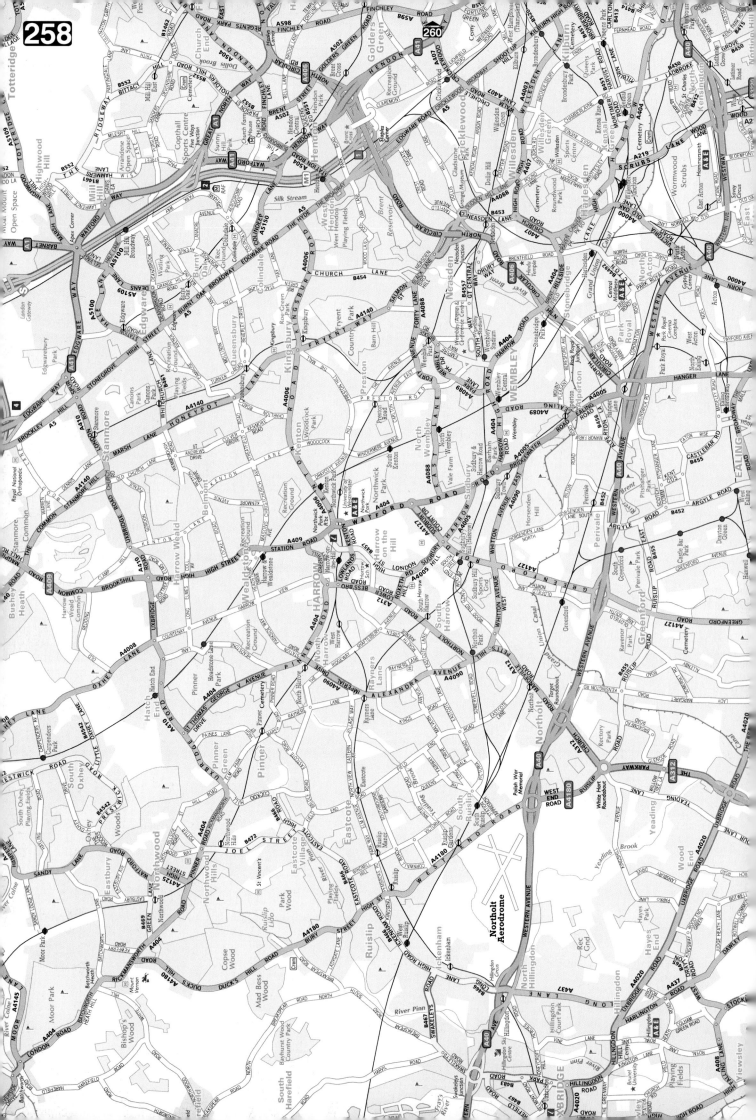

London district

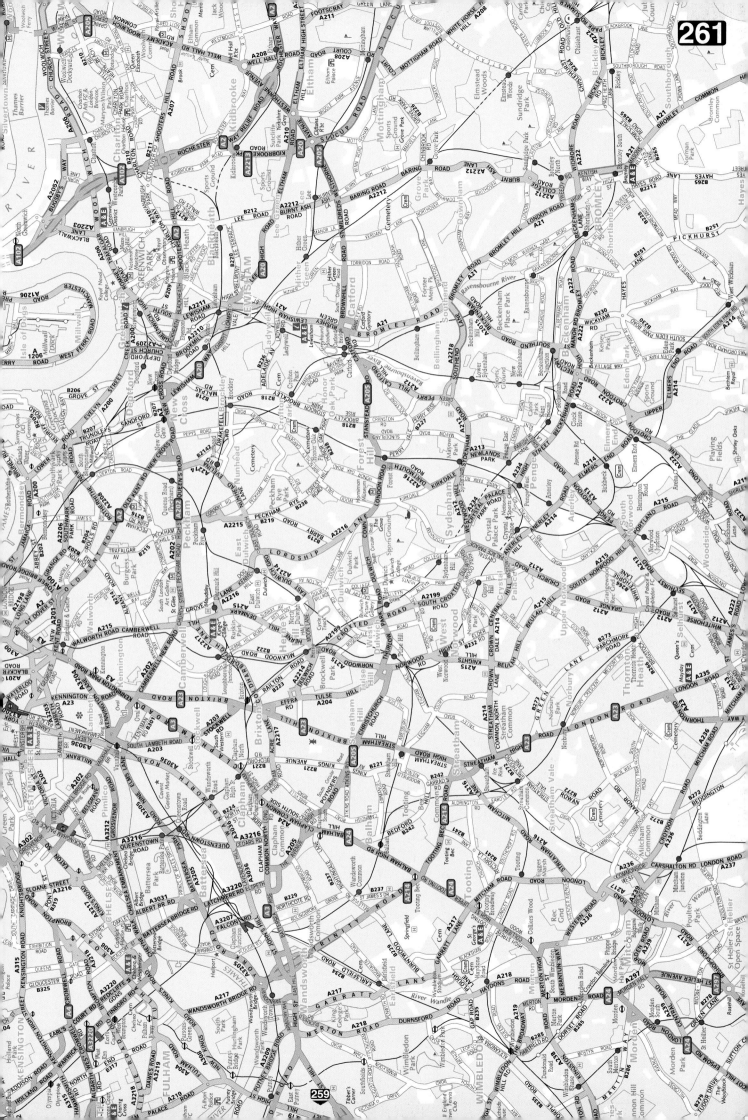

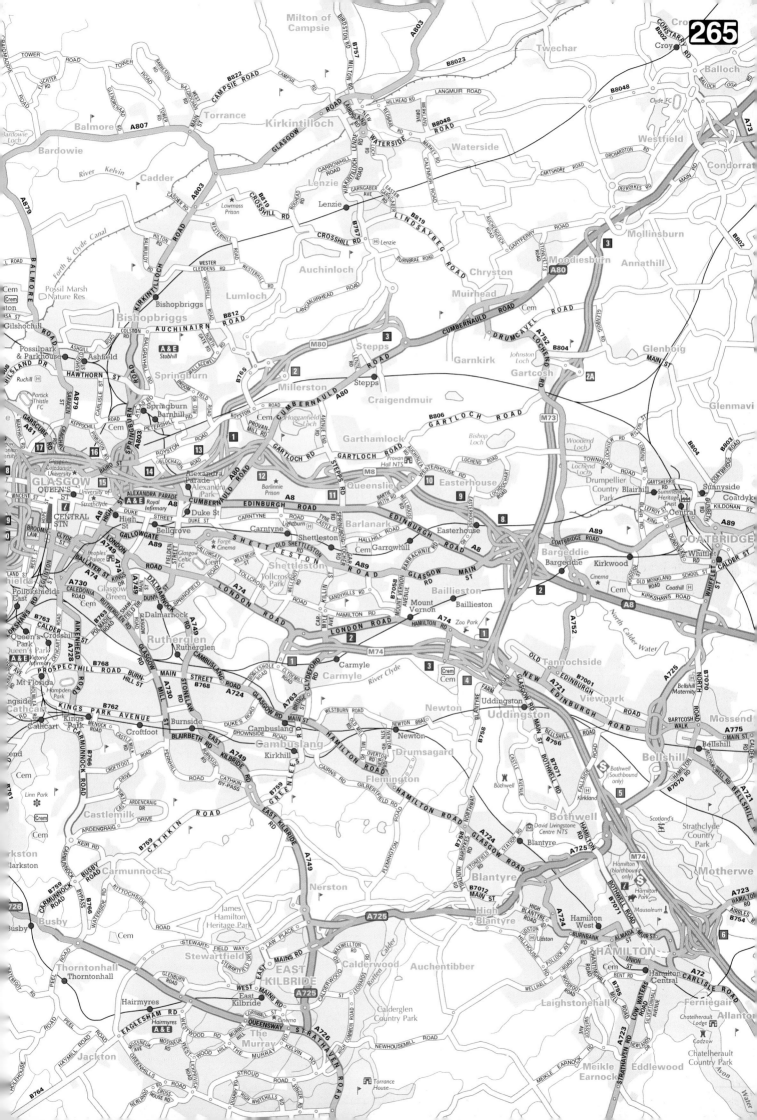

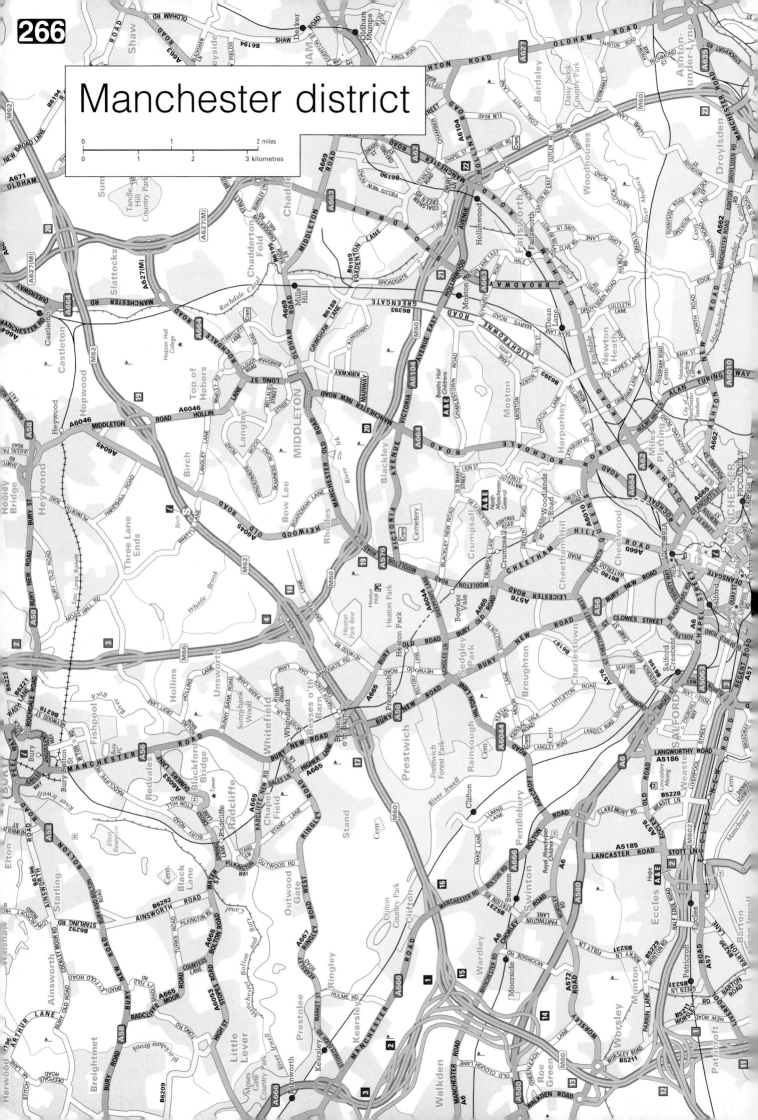

Tyne & Wear district

index to place names

Place names are listed alphabetically. Each place name is followed by its County, County Borough or Council Area name, the page number and the reference to the square in which the name is found.

100 places of interest are indexed in red.

Airports are indexed in blue.

Scotland

Aber C	Aberdeen City
Abers	Aberdeenshire
Angus	Angus
Ag & B	Argyll & Bute
Border	Borders (Scottish)
C Edin	City of Edinburgh
C Glas	City of Glasgow
Clacks	Clackmannanshire
D & G	Dumfries & Galloway
Dund C	Dundee City
E Ayrs	East Ayrshire
E Duns	East Dunbartonshire
E Loth	East Lothian
E Rens	East Renfrewshire
Falk	Falkirk
Fife	Fife
Highld	Highland
Inver	Inverclyde
Mdloth	Midlothian
Moray	Moray
N Ayrs	North Ayrshire
N Lans	North Lanarkshire
Ork	Orkney Islands
P & K	Perth & Kinross
Rens	Renfrewshire
Shet	Shetland Islands
S Ayrs	South Ayrshire
S Lans	South Lanarkshire
Stirlg	Stirling
W Isls	Western Isles
W Duns	West Dunbartonshire
W Loth	West Lothian

Wales

Blae G	Blaenau Gwent
Brdgnd	Bridgend
Caerph	Caerphilly
Cardif	Cardiff
Carmth	Carmarthenshire
Cerdgn	Ceredigion
Conwy	Conwy
Denbgs	Denbighshire
Flints	Flintshire
Gwynd	Gwynedd
IOA	Isle of Anglesey
Myr Td	Merthyr Tydfil
Mons	Monmouthshire
Neath	Neath Port Talbot
Newpt	Newport
Pembks	Pembrokeshire
Powys	Powys
Rhondd	Rhondda Cynon Taff
Swans	Swansea
Torfn	Torfaen
V Glam	Vale of Glamorgan
Wrexhm	Wrexham

The Channel Islands & Isle of Man

Guern	Guernsey
Jersey	Jersey
IOM	Isle of Man

England

Beds	Bedfordshire
Berks	Berkshire
Bristl	Bristol
Bucks	Buckinghamshire
Cambs	Cambridgeshire
Ches	Cheshire
Cnwll	Cornwall
Cumb	Cumbria
Derbys	Derbyshire
Devon	Devon
Dorset	Dorset
Dur	Durham
E R Yk	East Riding of Yorkshire
E Susx	East Sussex
Essex	Essex
Gloucs	Gloucestershire
Gt Lon	Greater London
Gt Man	Greater Manchester
Hants	Hampshire
Herefs	Herefordshire
Herts	Hertfordshire
IOW	Isle of Wight
IOS	Isles of Scilly
Kent	Kent
Lancs	Lancashire
Leics	Leicestershire
Lincs	Lincolnshire
Mersyd	Merseyside
Norfk	Norfolk
N York	North Yorkshire
Nhants	Northamptonshire
Nthumb	Northumberland
Notts	Nottinghamshire
Oxon	Oxfordshire
Rutlnd	Rutland
Shrops	Shropshire
Somset	Somerset
S York	South Yorkshire
Staffs	Staffordshire
Suffk	Suffolk
Surrey	Surrey
T & W	Tyne & Wear
Warwks	Warwickshire
W Mids	West Midlands
W Susx	West Sussex
W York	West Yorkshire
Wilts	Wiltshire
Worcs	Worcestershire

A

A'Chill *Highld* ... 142 B5
Ab Kettleby *Leics* ... 73 E2
Ab Lench *Worcs* ... 47 F4
Abbas Combe *Somset* ... 24 C1
Abberley *Worcs* ... 57 H2
Abberley Common *Worcs* ... 57 H2
Abberton *Essex* ... 52 D3
Abberton *Worcs* ... 47 E5
Abberwick *Nthumb* ... 124 D2
Abbess Roding *Essex* ... 51 F2
Abbey *Devon* ... 10 B6
Abbey Dore *Herefs* ... 45 G2
Abbey Green *Staffs* ... 71 E6
Abbey Hill *Somset* ... 23 F1
Abbey St Bathans *Border* ... 123 E6
Abbey Town *Cumb* ... 103 F5
Abbey Village *Lancs* ... 89 E2
Abbey Wood *Gt Lon* ... 29 F4
Abbeycwmhir *Powys* ... 55 H2
Abbeydale *S York* ... 83 H3
Abbeystead *Lancs* ... 88 D5
Abbot's Chair *Derbys* ... 83 E4
Abbot's Salford *Warwks* ... 47 F4
Abbotrule *Border* ... 112 C6
Abbots Bickington *Devon* ... 20 D2
Abbots Bromley *Staffs* ... 71 F2
Abbots Deuglie *P & K* ... 131 G6
Abbots Langley *Herts* ... 50 B1
Abbots Leigh *Somset* ... 37 F2
Abbots Morton *Worcs* ... 47 F5
Abbots Ripton *Cambs* ... 62 B3
Abbots Worthy *Hants* ... 26 C2
Abbotsbury *Dorset* ... 11 F3
Abbotsham *Devon* ... 20 D3
Abbotskerswell *Devon* ... 7 F4
Abbotsleigh *Devon* ... 7 E2
Abbotsley *Cambs* ... 62 B1
Abbotstone *Hants* ... 26 D3
Abbotswood *Hants* ... 26 B1
Abbott Street *Dorset* ... 12 D5
Abbotts Ann *Hants* ... 26 B4
Abcott *Shrops* ... 56 D3
Abdon *Shrops* ... 57 F4
Abenhall *Gloucs* ... 38 A6
Aber Clydach *Powys* ... 44 D1
Aber-arad *Carmth* ... 42 C3
Aber-banc *Cerdgn* ... 42 D3
Aber-giar *Carmth* ... 43 E3
Aber-Magwr *Cerdgn* ... 54 D3
Aber-meurig *Cerdgn* ... 43 F5
Aber-nant *Rhondd* ... 35 G5
Aberaeron *Cerdgn* ... 43 E5
Aberaman *Rhondd* ... 35 G4
Aberangell *Gwynd* ... 67 H1
Aberarder *Highld* ... 154 D2
Aberargie *P & K* ... 140 B1
Aberarth *Cerdgn* ... 54 B2
Aberavon *Neath* ... 35 E3
Aberbargoed *Caerph* ... 36 C4
Aberbeeg *Blae G* ... 36 C4
Abercairny *P & K* ... 139 F2
Abercanaid *Myr Td* ... 36 B5
Abercarn *Caerph* ... 36 C4
Abercastle *Pembks* ... 32 C5
Abercegir *Powys* ... 55 F6
Aberchalder Lodge *Highld* ... 145 F5
Aberchirder *Abers* ... 158 B4
Abercoed *Cerdgn* ... 46 B5
Abercraf *Powys* ... 35 F6
Abercregan *Neath* ... 35 F4
Abercwmboi *Rhondd* ... 36 A4
Abercych *Pembks* ... 42 C3
Abercynon *Rhondd* ... 36 B4
Aberdalgie *P & K* ... 139 H2
Aberdare *Rhondd* ... 35 G4
Aberdaron *Gwynd* ... 66 A3
Aberdeen *Aber C* ... 149 G5
Aberdeen Airport *Aber C* ... 149 F6
Aberdesach *Gwynd* ... 66 D5
Aberdour *Fife* ... 131 H4
Aberdulais *Neath* ... 35 E4
Aberdyfi *Gwynd* ... 54 D5
Aberedw *Powys* ... 44 D4
Abereiddy *Pembks* ... 32 B5
Abererch *Gwynd* ... 66 D4
Aberfan *Myr Td* ... 36 B4
Aberfeldy *P & K* ... 139 F5
Aberffraw *IOA* ... 78 C2
Aberffrwd *Cerdgn* ... 54 D3
Aberford *W York* ... 91 E3
Aberfoyle *Stirlg* ... 129 G5
Abergarw *Brdgnd* ... 35 G3
Abergarwed *Neath* ... 35 F4
Abergavenny *Mons* ... 36 D6
Abergele *Conwy* ... 80 B2
Abergorlech *Carmth* ... 43 F2
Abergwesyn *Powys* ... 44 A4
Abergwili *Carmth* ... 43 E1
Abergwydol *Powys* ... 55 E6
Abergwynfi *Neath* ... 35 F4
Abergwyngregyn *Gwynd* ... 79 F2
Abergynolwyn *Gwynd* ... 54 D6
Aberhafesp *Powys* ... 56 A5
Aberhosan *Powys* ... 55 F5
Aberkenfig *Brdgnd* ... 35 F3
Aberlady *E Loth* ... 132 D3
Aberlemno *Angus* ... 141 E5
Aberllefenni *Powys* ... 67 G1
Aberllynfi *Powys* ... 45 E3
Aberlour *Moray* ... 157 E3
Abermorddu *Flints* ... 69 E6
Abermule *Powys* ... 56 B5
Abernant *Carmth* ... 33 G4
Abernethy *P & K* ... 140 B1
Abernyte *P & K* ... 140 C3
Aberporth *Cerdgn* ... 42 C4
Abersoch *Gwynd* ... 66 C3
Abersychan *Torfn* ... 36 D5
Aberthin *V Glam* ... 35 G2
Abertillery *Blac G* ... 36 C5
Abertridwr *Caerph* ... 36 B3
Abertridwr *Powys* ... 68 C2
Abertysswg *Caerph* ... 36 B5

Aberuthven *P & K* ... 139 G1
Aberyscir *Powys* ... 44 C2
Aberystwyth *Cerdgn* ... 54 C3
Abingdon *Oxon* ... 40 C4
Abinger *Surrey* ... 16 B6
Abinger Hammer *Surrey* ... 16 B6
Abington *Nhants* ... 49 F5
Abington *S Lans* ... 120 D2
Abington Pigotts *Cambs* ... 50 D5
Ablington *Gloucs* ... 39 F5
Ablington *Wilts* ... 25 G4
Abney *Derbys* ... 83 G3
Above Church *Staffs* ... 71 E5
Aboyne *Abers* ... 148 C4
Abram *Gt Man* ... 82 A5
Abriachan *Highld* ... 154 D3
Abridge *Essex* ... 29 E6
Abson *Gloucs* ... 38 B2
Abthorpe *Nhants* ... 49 E4
Aby *Lincs* ... 86 D2
Acaster Malbis *N York* ... 91 G4
Acaster Selby *N York* ... 91 G4
Accott *Devon* ... 21 F4
Accrington *Lancs* ... 89 F2
Acha *Ag & B* ... 134 D5
Acha Mor *W Isls* ... 168 e8
Achachork *Highld* ... 152 D5
Achahoish *Ag & B* ... 127 F3
Achalader *P & K* ... 140 A4
Achaleven *Ag & B* ... 136 D3
Achanalt *Highld* ... 153 G5
Achandunie *Highld* ... 162 C1
Achany *Highld* ... 162 C4
Acharacle *Highld* ... 143 F1
Acharn *Highld* ... 136 B5
Acharn *P & K* ... 139 E4
Achavanich *Highld* ... 167 E3
Achduart *Highld* ... 161 E4
Achfary *Highld* ... 164 D2
Achiltibuie *Highld* ... 160 D5
Achinhoan *Ag & B* ... 117 G2
Achintee *Highld* ... 152 D3
Achintraid *Highld* ... 152 C3
Achmelvich *Highld* ... 161 E6
Achmore *Highld* ... 152 C2
Achmore *W Isls* ... 168 e8
Achnacarnin *Highld* ... 164 B2
Achnacarry *Highld* ... 144 D3
Achnacloich *Highld* ... 143 E5
Achnaconeran *Highld* ... 154 B1
Achnacroish *Ag & B* ... 136 C4
Achnadrish Lodge *Ag & B* ... 135 F5
Achnafauld *P & K* ... 139 F3
Achnagarron *Highld* ... 155 E6
Achnaha *Highld* ... 135 F6
Achnahaird *Highld* ... 160 D5
Achnairn *Highld* ... 162 B5
Achnalea *Highld* ... 136 C6
Achnamara *Ag & B* ... 127 F4
Achnasheen *Highld* ... 153 F5
Achnashellach Station *Highld* ... 152 D4
Achnastank *Moray* ... 157 E2
Achosnich *Highld* ... 135 F6
Achranich *Highld* ... 136 B4
Achreamie *Highld* ... 166 D5
Achriabhach *Highld* ... 144 D1
Achriesgill *Highld* ... 164 D4
Achtoty *Highld* ... 165 H5
Achurch *Nhants* ... 61 H4
Achvaich *Highld* ... 162 D3
Ackergill *Highld* ... 167 G4
Acklam *N York* ... 98 D3
Acklam *N York* ... 106 D3
Ackleton *Shrops* ... 57 H5
Acklington *Nthumb* ... 114 D6
Ackton *W York* ... 91 E2
Ackworth Moor Top *W York* ... 91 E1
Acle *Norfk* ... 77 G1
Acock's Green *W Mids* ... 58 D4
Acol *Kent* ... 31 G3
Acomb *N York* ... 91 G5
Acomb *Nthumb* ... 113 F1
Aconbury *Herefs* ... 45 H2
Acre *Lancs* ... 89 F2
Acrefair *Wrexhm* ... 69 E4
Acresford *Derbys* ... 71 H1
Acton *Ches* ... 70 A5
Acton *Dorset* ... 12 D2
Acton *Gt Lon* ... 28 C4
Acton *Staffs* ... 70 C4
Acton *Suffk* ... 52 C5
Acton *Worcs* ... 58 A2
Acton Beauchamp *Herefs* ... 46 B4
Acton Bridge *Ches* ... 82 A2
Acton Burnell *Shrops* ... 57 E6
Acton Green *Herefs* ... 46 C4
Acton Park *Wrexhm* ... 69 F5
Acton Pigott *Shrops* ... 57 F6
Acton Round *Shrops* ... 57 F5
Acton Scott *Shrops* ... 57 E4
Acton Trussell *Staffs* ... 70 D2
Acton Turville *Gloucs* ... 38 C2
Adbaston *Staffs* ... 70 C3
Adber *Dorset* ... 24 B1
Adbolton *Notts* ... 72 D4
Adderbury *Oxon* ... 48 C3
Adderley *Shrops* ... 70 B4
Adderstone *Nthumb* ... 124 D4
Addiewell *W Loth* ... 120 D6
Addingham *W York* ... 90 B5
Addington *Bucks* ... 49 F2
Addington *Gt Lon* ... 29 E2
Addington *Kent* ... 29 G2
Addington *Kent* ... 29 G2
Addlestone *Surrey* ... 28 A2
Addlestonemoor *Surrey* ... 28 A3
Adeney *Shrops* ... 70 B2
Adeyfield *Herts* ... 50 B1
Adfa *Powys* ... 55 H5
Adforton *Herefs* ... 56 D2
Adisham *Kent* ... 31 F1
Adlestrop *Gloucs* ... 47 H2
Adlingfleet *E RYk* ... 92 B2
Adlington *Ches* ... 82 D3
Adlington *Lancs* ... 82 A6
Admaston *Shrops* ... 70 A1
Admaston *Staffs* ... 71 E2

Admington *Warwks* ... 47 G4
Adsborough *Somset* ... 23 F2
Adscombe *Somset* ... 23 E3
Adstock *Bucks* ... 49 E2
Adstone *Nhants* ... 48 D4
Adswood *Gt Man* ... 82 D3
Adversane *W Susx* ... 16 B4
Advie *Highld* ... 156 C2
Adwalton *W York* ... 90 C2
Adwell *Oxon* ... 41 E4
Adwick Le Street *S York* ... 84 C6
Adwick upon Dearne *S York* ... 84 B5
Ae *D & G* ... 110 D4
Ae Bridgend *D & G* ... 111 E3
Affleck *Abers* ... 158 B3
Affpuddle *Dorset* ... 12 B4
Affric Lodge *Highld* ... 153 F1
Afon-wen *Flints* ... 80 D2
Afton *Devon* ... 7 F4
Agglethorpe *N York* ... 96 D3
Aigburth *Mersyd* ... 81 F3
Aike *E RYk* ... 92 D4
Aiketgate *Cumb* ... 104 B5
Aikhead *Cumb* ... 103 F5
Aikton *Cumb* ... 103 G5
Ailby *Lincs* ... 87 E2
Ailey *Herefs* ... 45 F4
Ailsworth *Cambs* ... 61 G5
Ainderby Quernhow *N York* ... 97 G3
Ainderby Steeple *N York* ... 97 F4
Aingers Green *Essex* ... 53 E3
Ainsdale *Mersyd* ... 81 E6
Ainsdale-on-Sea *Mersyd* ... 81 E6
Ainstable *Cumb* ... 104 B5
Ainsworth *Gt Man* ... 82 C6
Ainthorpe *N York* ... 107 F2
Aintree *Mersyd* ... 81 F4
Ainville *W Loth* ... 131 G1
Aird *Ag & B* ... 127 F5
Aird *D & G* ... 100 B6
Aird *W Isls* ... 168 f8
Aird a Mhulaidh *W Isls* ... 168 d7
Aird Asaig *W Isls* ... 168 d6
Aird Dhubh *Highld* ... 151 G3
Aird of Kinloch *Ag & B* ... 135 G2
Aird of Sleat *Highld* ... 143 E4
Aird Uig *W Isls* ... 168 d8
Airdeny *Ag & B* ... 137 E3
Airdrie *N Lans* ... 130 D2
Airdriehill *N Lans* ... 130 D2
Airds Bay *Ag & B* ... 137 E3
Airds of Kells *D & G* ... 110 A2
Airidh a bhruaich *W Isls* ... 168 e7
Airieland *D & G* ... 102 B6
Airlie *Angus* ... 140 D5
Airmyn *E RYk* ... 92 A2
Airntully *P & K* ... 140 A3
Airor *Highld* ... 143 G5
Airth *Falk* ... 131 E4
Airton *N York* ... 89 G5
Aisby *Lincs* ... 85 F4
Aisby *Lincs* ... 73 H4
Aisgill *Cumb* ... 96 A5
Aish *Devon* ... 6 D4
Aish *Devon* ... 7 F3
Aisholt *Somset* ... 23 E3
Aiskew *N York* ... 97 F4
Aislaby *Dur* ... 106 C2
Aislaby *N York* ... 107 H2
Aislaby *N York* ... 98 C3
Aisthorpe *Lincs* ... 85 G3
Aith *Shet* ... 169 h3
Akeld *Nthumb* ... 123 G2
Akeley *Bucks* ... 49 E3
Akenham *Suffk* ... 53 E6
Albaston *Devon* ... 5 H3
Alberbury *Shrops* ... 69 F1
Albourne *W Susx* ... 16 C3
Albourne Green *W Susx* ... 16 D3
Albrighton *Shrops* ... 69 G2
Albrighton *Shrops* ... 58 A6
Alburgh *Norfk* ... 65 E4
Albury *Herts* ... 51 E3
Albury *Oxon* ... 41 E5
Albury *Surrey* ... 16 A6
Albury End *Herts* ... 51 E3
Albury Heath *Surrey* ... 16 B6
Alby Hill *Norfk* ... 77 E3
Alcaig *Highld* ... 154 D5
Alcaston *Shrops* ... 57 E4
Alcester *Warwks* ... 47 F5
Alcester Lane End *W Mids* ... 58 D3
Alciston *E Susx* ... 17 F2
Alcombe *Wilts* ... 38 C1
Alconbury *Cambs* ... 61 H3
Alconbury Weston *Cambs* ... 61 H3
Aldborough *N York* ... 97 G1
Aldborough *Norfk* ... 77 E3
Aldbourne *Wilts* ... 39 G2
Aldbrough *E RYk* ... 93 F3
Aldbrough St John *N York* ... 106 A2
Aldbury *Herts* ... 41 H5
Aldcliffe *Lancs* ... 88 C6
Aldclune *P & K* ... 139 F6
Aldeburgh *Suffk* ... 65 G1
Aldeby *Norfk* ... 65 G5
Aldenham *Herts* ... 28 B6
Alderbury *Wilts* ... 25 G2
Aldercar *Derbys* ... 72 B5
Alderford *Norfk* ... 76 D2
Alderholt *Dorset* ... 13 E6
Alderley *Gloucs* ... 38 B3
Alderley Edge *Ches* ... 82 C2
Aldermans Green *W Mids* ... 59 F4
Aldermaston *Berks* ... 26 D6
Alderminster *Warwks* ... 47 H4
Aldershot *Hants* ... 27 G4
Alderton *Gloucs* ... 47 E2
Alderton *Nhants* ... 49 F4
Alderton *Shrops* ... 69 G2
Alderton *Suffk* ... 53 G5
Alderton *Wilts* ... 38 C2
Alderwasley *Derbys* ... 71 H5
Aldfield *N York* ... 97 F2
Aldford *Ches* ... 69 F6
Aldgate *Rutlnd* ... 61 F6

Aldham *Essex* ... 52 C3
Aldham *Suffk* ... 52 D5
Aldingbourne *W Susx* ... 15 G4
Aldingham *Cumb* ... 94 D2
Aldington *Kent* ... 18 D5
Aldington *Worcs* ... 47 F4
Aldington Corner *Kent* ... 18 D5
Aldivalloch *Moray* ... 157 F2
Aldochlay *Ag & B* ... 129 E4
Aldon *Shrops* ... 57 E3
Aldoth *Cumb* ... 103 E5
Aldreth *Cambs* ... 62 D3
Aldridge *W Mids* ... 58 C5
Aldringham *Suffk* ... 65 G1
Aldro *N York* ... 92 B6
Aldsworth *Gloucs* ... 39 F5
Aldsworth *W Susx* ... 15 F4
Aldunie *Moray* ... 157 F2
Aldwark *Derbys* ... 71 G6
Aldwark *N York* ... 97 H1
Aldwick *W Susx* ... 15 G3
Aldwincle *Nhants* ... 61 F3
Aldworth *Berks* ... 40 D2
Alexandria *W Duns* ... 129 E3
Aley *Somset* ... 23 E3
Alfardisworthy *Devon* ... 20 C2
Alfington *Devon* ... 10 B4
Alfold *Surrey* ... 16 A5
Alfold Bars *W Susx* ... 16 A5
Alfold Crossways *Surrey* ... 16 A5
Alford *Abers* ... 148 C6
Alford *Lincs* ... 87 E2
Alford *Somset* ... 24 B2
Alfreton *Derbys* ... 72 B6
Alfrick *Worcs* ... 46 C4
Alfrick Pound *Worcs* ... 46 C4
Alfriston *E Susx* ... 17 F2
Algarkirk *Lincs* ... 74 C3
Alhampton *Somset* ... 24 B3
Alkborough *Lincs* ... 92 C2
Alkerton *Gloucs* ... 38 B5
Alkerton *Oxon* ... 48 B3
Alkham *Kent* ... 19 F6
Alkington *Shrops* ... 69 G4
Alkmonton *Derbys* ... 71 G4
All Cannings *Wilts* ... 25 F5
All Saints South Elmham *Suffk* ... 65 F4
All Stretton *Shrops* ... 57 E5
Allaleigh *Devon* ... 7 E3
Allanaquoich *Abers* ... 147 F3
Allanbank *N Lans* ... 120 C5
Allanton *Border* ... 123 F5
Allanton *N Lans* ... 120 C5
Allanton *S Lans* ... 120 B5
Allaston *Gloucs* ... 37 G5
Allbrook *Hants* ... 14 C6
Allen End *Warwks* ... 59 E5
Allen's Green *Herts* ... 51 E2
Allendale *Nthumb* ... 105 E6
Allenheads *Nthumb* ... 105 E5
Allensford *Dur* ... 105 G5
Allensmore *Herefs* ... 45 G3
Allenton *Derbys* ... 72 A3
Aller *Devon* ... 21 H3
Aller *Somset* ... 23 G2
Allerby *Cumb* ... 103 E4
Allercombe *Devon* ... 9 G4
Allerford *Somset* ... 22 B4
Allerston *N York* ... 98 D3
Allerthorpe *E RYk* ... 92 B4
Allerton *Highld* ... 155 F6
Allerton *Mersyd* ... 81 F3
Allerton *W York* ... 90 B3
Allerton Bywater *W York* ... 91 E2
Allerton Mauleverer *N York* ... 91 G5
Allesley *W Mids* ... 59 F3
Allestree *Derbys* ... 72 A4
Allet Common *Cnwll* ... 3 E5
Allexton *Leics* ... 60 D5
Allgreave *Ches* ... 83 E1
Allhallows *Kent* ... 30 B4
Allhallows-on-Sea *Kent* ... 30 B4
Alligin Shuas *Highld* ... 152 C5
Allimore Green *Staffs* ... 70 C2
Allington *Dorset* ... 11 E4
Allington *Kent* ... 30 A2
Allington *Lincs* ... 73 F4
Allington *Wilts* ... 38 D2
Allington *Wilts* ... 25 F6
Allington *Wilts* ... 25 G3
Allithwaite *Cumb* ... 95 E2
Alloa *Clacks* ... 131 E4
Allonby *Cumb* ... 103 E4
Allostock *Ches* ... 82 B2
Alloway *S Ayrs* ... 119 E1
Allowenshay *Somset* ... 10 D6
Allscott *Shrops* ... 70 A1
Allscott *Shrops* ... 57 G5
Alltami *Flints* ... 81 E1
Alltchaorunn *Highld* ... 137 F5
Alltmawr *Powys* ... 44 D4
Alltwalis *Carmth* ... 43 E2
Alltwen *Neath* ... 35 E5
Alltyblaca *Cerdgn* ... 43 E4
Allweston *Dorset* ... 11 G6
Allwood Green *Suffk* ... 64 C3
Almeley *Herefs* ... 45 F4
Almeley Wooton *Herefs* ... 45 F4
Almer *Dorset* ... 12 C4
Almholme *S York* ... 84 D5
Almington *Staffs* ... 70 B3
Almondbank *P & K* ... 139 H2
Almondbury *W York* ... 90 C1
Almondsbury *Gloucs* ... 37 G3
Alne *N York* ... 97 H1
Alnesbourn Priory *Suffk* ... 53 E5
Alness *Highld* ... 155 E6
Alnham *Nthumb* ... 124 C2
Alnmouth *Nthumb* ... 125 E2
Alnwick *Nthumb* ... 125 E2
Alperton *Gt Lon* ... 28 C4
Alphamstone *Essex* ... 52 B4
Alpheton *Suffk* ... 52 B6
Alphington *Devon* ... 9 F4
Alpington *Norfk* ... 65 E5
Alport *Derbys* ... 83 G1
Alpraham *Ches* ... 69 H5

Aldham *Essex* ... 52 D3
Alrewas *Staffs* ... 71 G1
Alsager *Ches* ... 70 C6
Alsagers Bank *Staffs* ... 70 C5
Alsop en le Dale *Derbys* ... 71 F5
Alston *Cumb* ... 104 D5
Alston *Devon* ... 10 C5
Alston Sutton *Somset* ... 23 G4
Alstone *Gloucs* ... 47 E2
Alstone *Somset* ... 23 F4
Alstone Green *Staffs* ... 70 D2
Alstonefield *Staffs* ... 71 F6
Alswear *Devon* ... 21 G3
Alt *Gt Man* ... 82 D5
Altandhu *Highld* ... 160 D5
Altarnun *Cnwll* ... 5 F4
Altass *Highld* ... 162 B4
Altcreich *Ag & B* ... 136 B4
Altgaltraig *Ag & B* ... 128 B2
Altham *Lancs* ... 89 F3
Althorne *Essex* ... 30 C6
Althorpe *Lincs* ... 85 F6
Altnabreac Station *Highld* ... 166 D3
Altnacraig *Ag & B* ... 136 C3
Altnaharra *Highld* ... 165 G2
Altofts *W York* ... 91 E2
Alton *Derbys* ... 84 A1
Alton *Hants* ... 27 E3
Alton *Staffs* ... 71 F4
Alton *Wilts* ... 25 G4
Alton Barnes *Wilts* ... 25 F5
Alton Pancras *Dorset* ... 11 G5
Alton Priors *Wilts* ... 25 G5
Alton Towers *Staffs* ... 71 F4
Altrincham *Gt Man* ... 82 C3
Altskeith Hotel *Stirlg* ... 129 F5
Alva *Clacks* ... 131 E5
Alvah *Abers* ... 158 C5
Alvanley *Ches* ... 81 G2
Alvaston *Derbys* ... 72 B3
Alvechurch *Worcs* ... 58 C3
Alvecote *Warwks* ... 59 E6
Alvediston *Wilts* ... 25 E2
Alveley *Shrops* ... 57 H4
Alverdiscott *Devon* ... 21 E3
Alverstoke *Hants* ... 14 D3
Alverstone *IOW* ... 14 D2
Alverthorpe *W York* ... 90 D2
Alverton *Notts* ... 73 E4
Alves *Moray* ... 156 C5
Alvescot *Oxon* ... 39 G5
Alveston *Gloucs* ... 37 G3
Alveston *Warwks* ... 47 H5
Alvingham *Lincs* ... 86 D4
Alvington *Gloucs* ... 37 G4
Alwalton *Cambs* ... 61 G5
Alwinton *Nthumb* ... 113 F5
Alwoodley *W York* ... 90 D4
Alwoodley Gates *W York* ... 90 D4
Alyth *P & K* ... 140 B5
Amber Hill *Lincs* ... 74 C5
Amber Row *Derbys* ... 72 B6
Ambergate *Derbys* ... 72 A5
Amberley *Gloucs* ... 38 C4
Amberley *W Susx* ... 16 A3
Ambirstone *E Susx* ... 17 G2
Amble *Nthumb* ... 125 F1
Amblecote *W Mids* ... 58 B4
Ambler Thorn *W York* ... 90 B2
Ambleside *Cumb* ... 94 D5
Ambleston *Pembks* ... 32 D4
Ambrosden *Oxon* ... 48 D1
Amcotts *Lincs* ... 85 F6
America *Cambs* ... 62 D3
Amersham *Bucks* ... 41 H4
Amersham on the Hill *Bucks* ... 41 H4
Amerton *Staffs* ... 71 E3
Amesbury *Wilts* ... 25 G3
Amhuinnsuidhe *W Isls* ... 168 c7
Amington *Staffs* ... 59 E6
Amisfield Town *D & G* ... 110 D3
Amlwch *IOA* ... 78 D4
Ammanford *Carmth* ... 34 D5
Amotherby *N York* ... 98 C2
Ampfield *Hants* ... 26 B2
Ampleforth *N York* ... 98 B3
Ampney Crucis *Gloucs* ... 39 E4
Ampney St Mary *Gloucs* ... 39 E4
Ampney St Peter *Gloucs* ... 39 E4
Amport *Hants* ... 26 A4
Ampthill *Beds* ... 50 A4
Ampton *Suffk* ... 63 H2
Amroth *Pembks* ... 33 F2
Amulree *P & K* ... 139 F3
Amwell *Herts* ... 50 C2
An T-ob *W Isls* ... 168 c6
Anaheilt *Highld* ... 136 C6
Ancaster *Lincs* ... 73 G4
Anchor *Shrops* ... 56 B4
Ancroft *Nthumb* ... 123 G4
Ancrum *Border* ... 122 C2
Ancton *W Susx* ... 15 H4
Anderby *Lincs* ... 87 F2
Andersea *Somset* ... 23 F3
Andersfield *Somset* ... 23 E3
Anderson *Dorset* ... 12 C4
Anderton *Ches* ... 82 B2
Anderton *Cnwll* ... 6 B3
Andover *Hants* ... 26 B4
Andoversford *Gloucs* ... 47 F1
Andreas *IOM* ... 174 m5
Anelog *Gwynd* ... 66 A3
Anerley *Gt Lon* ... 28 D3
Anfield *Mersyd* ... 81 F4
Angarrack *Cnwll* ... 2 C4
Angarrick *Cnwll* ... 3 E3
Angelbank *Shrops* ... 57 F3
Angersleigh *Somset* ... 23 E1
Angerton *Cumb* ... 103 F6
Angle *Pembks* ... 32 C2
Angmering *W Susx* ... 16 B2
Angram *N York* ... 96 B5
Angram *N York* ... 91 F4
Angrouse *Cnwll* ... 2 D1
Anick *Nthumb* ... 113 G1
Ankerville *Highld* ... 163 E1
Ankle Hill *Leics* ... 73 E2
Anlaby *E RYk* ... 92 D2

Anmer Norfk 75 H3
Anmore Hants 15 E5
Anna Valley Hants 26 B4
Annan D & G 111 F1
Annaside Cumb 94 B3
Annat Highld 152 C4
Annathill N Lans 130 D2
Annbank S Ayrs 119 F2
Anne Hathaway's Cottage
   Warwks 47 G5
Annesley Notts 72 C5
Annesley Woodhouse Notts 72 C5
Annfield Plain Dur 106 A6
Anniesland C Glas 129 G2
Annitsford T & W 114 D3
Annscroft Shrops 57 E6
Ansdell Lancs 88 B2
Ansford Somset 24 B2
Ansley Warwks 59 F4
Anslow Staffs 71 G2
Anslow Gate Staffs 71 G2
Anslow Lees Staffs 71 G2
Ansteadbrook Surrey 27 G2
Anstey Hants 27 E3
Anstey Herts 51 E4
Anstey Leics 60 B6
Anstruther Fife 133 E5
Ansty W Susx 16 D4
Ansty Warwks 59 G4
Ansty Wilts 25 E2
Ansty Cross Dorset 12 B5
Anthill Common Hants 15 E5
Anthonys Surrey 28 A2
Anthorn Cumb 103 F6
Antingham Norfk 77 E3
Anton's Gowt Lincs 74 C5
Antony Cnwll 5 G1
Antrobus Ches 82 A3
Antron Cnwll 2 D2
Anvil Corner Devon 20 D1
Anvil Green Kent 31 E1
Anwick Lincs 74 B5
Anwoth D & G 101 G6
Aperfield Gt Lon 29 E2
Apes Dale Worcs 58 C3
Apethorpe Nhants 61 F5
Apeton Staffs 70 C2
Apley Lincs 86 A2
Apperknowle Derbys 84 B2
Apperley Gloucs 46 D2
Apperley Bridge W York 90 C3
Apperley Dene Nthumb 114 B1
Appersett N York 96 B4
Appin Ag & B 136 D4
Appleby Lincs 92 C1
Appleby Magna Leics 71 H1
Appleby Parva Leics 71 H1
Appleby Street Herts 50 D1
Appleby-in-Westmorland Cumb .. 104 D2
Applecross Highld 151 G4
Appledore Devon 21 E4
Appledore Devon 10 A6
Appledore Kent 18 C4
Appledore Heath Kent 18 C4
Appleford Oxon 40 C4
Applegarth Town D & G 111 E3
Applehaigh S York 84 A6
Appleshaw Hants 26 A4
Applethwaite Cumb 103 G3
Appleton Ches 81 G3
Appleton Ches 82 A3
Appleton Oxon 40 C4
Appleton Roebuck N York 91 G4
Appleton Thorn Ches 82 A3
Appleton Wiske N York 97 G5
Appleton-le-Moors N York 98 C4
Appleton-le-Street N York 98 C2
Appletreehall Border 122 B1
Appletreewick N York 90 B6
Appley Somset 22 D1
Appley Bridge Lancs 81 G6
Apse Heath IOW 14 D2
Apsley End Beds 50 B4
Apuldram W Susx 15 G4
Arabella Highld 163 E1
Arbirlot Angus 141 F4
Arboll Highld 163 F2
Arborfield Berks 27 F6
Arborfield Cross Berks 27 F6
Arbourthorne S York 84 A3
Arbroath Angus 141 F4
Arbuthnott Abers 149 F2
Arcadia Kent 18 B5
Archddu Carmth 34 B4
Archdeacon Newton Dur 106 B2
Archencarroch W Duns 129 F3
Archiestown Moray 156 D3
Archirondel Jersey 174 d2
Arclid Green Ches 70 C6
Ardanaiseig Hotel Ag & B 137 E2
Ardaneaskan Highld 152 C3
Ardarroch Highld 152 C3
Ardbeg Ag & B 116 C5
Ardbeg Ag & B 128 B2
Ardbeg Ag & B 128 C3
Ardcharnich Highld 161 G2
Ardchiavaig Ag & B 135 F1
Ardchonnel Ag & B 136 D1
Ardchullarie More Stirlg 138 C1
Arddarroch Ag & B 128 D5
Arddleen Powys 69 E2
Ardechive Highld 144 D3
Ardeer N Ayrs 119 E3
Ardeley Herts 50 D3
Ardelve Highld 152 C2
Arden Ag & B 129 E3
Ardens Grafton Warwks 47 G5
Ardentallen Ag & B 136 C2
Ardentinny Ag & B 128 C4
Ardentraive Ag & B 128 B2
Ardeonaig Hotel Stirlg 138 C4
Ardersier Highld 155 F5
Ardessie Highld 161 E3
Ardfern Ag & B 127 G6
Ardgay Highld 162 C3
Ardgour Highld 137 E6
Ardgowan Inver 128 C2
Ardhallow Ag & B 128 C2

Ardhasig W Isls 168 d6
Ardheslaig Highld 152 B5
Ardindrean Highld 161 F3
Ardingly W Susx 16 D4
Ardington Oxon 40 C3
Ardington Wick Oxon 40 C3
Ardlamont Ag & B 128 A2
Ardleigh Essex 52 B4
Ardleigh Heath Essex 52 B4
Ardler P & K 140 C4
Ardley Oxon 48 D2
Ardley End Essex 51 F3
Ardlui Ag & B 137 H1
Ardlussa Ag & B 127 E4
Ardmaddy Ag & B 137 E3
Ardmair Highld 161 E3
Ardmaleish Ag & B 128 B2
Ardminish Ag & B 117 F5
Ardmolich Highld 143 G1
Ardmore Ag & B 129 E3
Ardmore Highld 162 D2
Ardnadam Ag & B 128 C3
Ardnagrask Highld 154 C4
Ardnarff Highld 152 C3
Ardnastang Highld 136 C6
Ardno Ag & B 128 C6
Ardochy Lodge Hotel Highld ... 144 D5
Ardpatrick Ag & B 127 F1
Ardrishaig Ag & B 127 G4
Ardross Highld 162 C1
Ardrossan N Ayrs 118 D3
Ardsley S York 84 B5
Ardsley East W York 90 D2
Ardslignish Highld 135 G5
Ardtalla Ag & B 116 D6
Ardtoe Highld 143 F1
Arduaine Ag & B 127 G6
Ardullie Highld 154 D5
Ardvasar Highld 143 F4
Ardvorlich P & K 138 D2
Ardvourlie W Isls 168 d7
Ardwell D & G 100 B5
Ardwick Gt Man 82 D4
Areley Kings Worcs 58 A2
Arevegaig Highld 143 F1
Arford Hants 27 F3
Argoed Caerph 36 C4
Argoed Shrops 69 E2
Argoed Mill Powys 55 G2
Argos Hill E Susx 17 F4
Aridhglas Ag & B 135 E2
Arileod Ag & B 134 D5
Arinacrinachd Highld 152 A5
Arinagour Ag & B 134 D5
Ariogan Ag & B 136 C2
Arisaig Highld 143 F3
Arisaig House Highld 143 F3
Arkendale N York 91 E6
Arkesden Essex 51 F4
Arkholme Lancs 95 F2
Arkle Town N York 96 C5
Arkleby Cumb 103 E4
Arkleton D & G 112 A4
Arkley Gt Lon 28 C6
Arksey S York 84 C5
Arkwright Town Derbys 84 B2
Arle Gloucs 47 E2
Arleston Shrops 70 B1
Arley Ches 82 B3
Arley Warwks 59 F4
Arlingham Gloucs 38 B5
Arlington Devon 21 F5
Arlington E Susx 17 F2
Arlington Gloucs 39 F5
Arlington Beccott Devon 21 F5
Armadale Highld 166 B5
Armadale Highld 143 F4
Armadale W Loth 131 F2
Armaside Cumb 103 E3
Armathwaite Cumb 104 B5
Arminghall Norfk 65 E6
Armitage Staffs 71 E2
Armitage Bridge W York 83 F6
Armley W York 90 D3
Armscote Warwks 47 H4
Armshead Staffs 70 C6
Armston Nhants 61 G4
Armthorpe S York 84 D5
Arnabost Ag & B 134 D5
Arncliffe N York 96 C2
Arncliffe Cote N York 96 C2
Arncroach Fife 132 D6
Arndilly House Moray 157 E4
Arne Dorset 12 D3
Arnesby Leics 60 B5
Arnfield Derbys 83 E4
Arngask P & K 131 H6
Arnisdale Highld 143 H5
Arnish Highld 151 F3
Arniston Mdloth 121 H6
Arnol W Isls 168 e9
Arnold E R Yk 93 E4
Arnold Notts 72 D5
Arnprior Stirlg 130 D5
Arnside Cumb 95 E3
Aros Ag & B 135 G4
Arowry Wrexhm 69 G4
Arrad Foot Cumb 94 D3
Arram E R Yk 92 D3
Arrathorne N York 97 E4
Arreton IOW 14 D2
Arrina Highld 152 B5
Arrington Cambs 50 D6
Arrochar Ag & B 128 D5
Arrow Warwks 47 F5
Arrowfield Top Worcs 58 C3
Arscott Shrops 57 E6
Artafallie Highld 154 D4
Arthington W York 90 D4
Arthingworth Nhants 60 D3
Arthog Gwynd 67 F1
Arthrath Abers 159 F3
Arthursdale W York 91 E3
Artrochie Abers 159 F2

Arundel W Susx 16 A2
Asby Cumb 103 E2
Ascog Ag & B 118 C6
Ascot Berks 41 G1
Ascott Warwks 48 B3
Ascott Earl Oxon 48 A1
Ascott-under-Wychwood Oxon 48 A1
Asenby N York 97 G2
Asfordby Leics 73 E2
Asfordby Hill Leics 73 E2
Asgarby Lincs 74 B5
Asgarby Lincs 86 D1
Ash Devon 8 B5
Ash Devon 7 F3
Ash Dorset 12 C6
Ash Kent 29 G2
Ash Kent 31 F2
Ash Somset 23 F1
Ash Somset 23 G1
Ash Surrey 27 G4
Ash Green Surrey 27 G4
Ash Green Warwks 59 F4
Ash Magna Shrops 69 H4
Ash Mill Devon 21 H3
Ash Parva Shrops 69 H4
Ash Priors Somset 22 D2
Ash Street Suffk 52 D5
Ash Thomas Devon 9 G6
Ash Vale Surrey 27 G4
Ashampstead Berks 40 D2
Ashampstead Green Berks 40 D2
Ashbocking Suffk 53 E6
Ashbocking Green Suffk 53 E6
Ashbourne Derbys 71 G5
Ashbrittle Somset 22 C1
Ashburnham Place E Susx 17 H3
Ashburton Devon 7 E5
Ashbury Devon 8 B4
Ashbury Oxon 39 G3
Ashby Lincs 85 G6
Ashby by Partney Lincs 87 E1
Ashby cum Fenby Lincs 86 C5
Ashby de la Launde Lincs 73 H6
Ashby Folville Leics 73 E1
Ashby Magna Leics 60 B4
Ashby Parva Leics 60 A4
Ashby Puerorum Lincs 86 D2
Ashby St Ledgers Nhants 60 B2
Ashby St Mary Norfk 65 F6
Ashby-de-la-Zouch Leics 72 A2
Ashchurch Gloucs 47 E2
Ashcombe Devon 9 F2
Ashcombe Somset 23 F5
Ashcott Somset 23 G3
Ashdon Essex 51 G5
Ashe Hants 26 D4
Asheldham Essex 30 C6
Ashen Essex 52 A5
Ashendon Bucks 41 E6
Asheridge Bucks 41 G5
Ashfield Hants 14 B5
Ashfield Herefs 46 B1
Ashfield Stirlg 130 D5
Ashfield Suffk 65 E2
Ashfield Green Suffk 63 G1
Ashfield Green Suffk 65 E3
Ashfields Shrops 70 B3
Ashfold Crossways W Susx 16 C4
Ashford Devon 21 E4
Ashford Devon 6 D2
Ashford Kent 18 D6
Ashford Surrey 28 B3
Ashford Bowdler Shrops 57 E2
Ashford Carbonel Shrops 57 E2
Ashford Hill Hants 26 D5
Ashford in the Water Derbys ... 83 G2
Ashgill S Lans 120 B4
Ashill Devon 10 A6
Ashill Norfk 64 A6
Ashill Somset 23 F1
Ashingdon Essex 30 B5
Ashington Dorset 12 D4
Ashington Nthumb 114 D4
Ashington Somset 24 A1
Ashington W Susx 16 B3
Ashkirk Border 122 B2
Ashlett Hants 14 C4
Ashleworth Gloucs 46 D2
Ashleworth Quay Gloucs 46 D2
Ashley Cambs 63 F1
Ashley Ches 82 C3
Ashley Devon 21 G2
Ashley Dorset 13 E5
Ashley Gloucs 38 D4
Ashley Hants 26 B2
Ashley Hants 13 F4
Ashley Kent 31 G1
Ashley Nhants 60 D4
Ashley Staffs 70 C4
Ashley Wilts 38 C1
Ashley Green Bucks 41 H5
Ashley Heath Dorset 13 E5
Ashley Moor Herefs 57 E2
Ashmansworth Hants 26 B5
Ashmansworthy Devon 20 D2
Ashmead Green Gloucs 38 B4
Ashmill Devon 5 G5
Ashmore Dorset 25 E1
Ashmore Green Berks 40 C1
Ashorne Warwks 48 A5
Ashover Derbys 84 A1
Ashover Hay Derbys 72 A6
Ashow Warwks 59 F2
Ashperton Herefs 46 B3
Ashprington Devon 7 E3
Ashreigney Devon 21 F2
Ashridge Park Herts 41 H5
Ashtead Surrey 28 C2
Ashton Cambs 61 G6
Ashton Ches 81 G2
Ashton Cnwll 2 D3
Ashton Cnwll 5 G3
Ashton Devon 9 E3
Ashton Hants 14 D5
Ashton Herefs 57 E2
Ashton Inver 128 D3
Ashton Nhants 49 F4

Ashton Nhants 61 F4
Ashton Somset 23 G4
Ashton Common Wilts 24 D5
Ashton Hill Wilts 24 D5
Ashton Keynes Wilts 39 E4
Ashton under Hill Worcs 47 E3
Ashton upon Mersey Gt Man 82 C4
Ashton Watering Somset 37 F1
Ashton-in-Makerfield Gt Man ... 81 H5
Ashton-under-Lyne Gt Man 82 D5
Ashurst Hants 13 G6
Ashurst Kent 17 F5
Ashurst W Susx 16 C3
Ashurstwood W Susx 17 E5
Ashwater Devon 5 G5
Ashwell Herts 50 D5
Ashwell Rutlnd 73 F1
Ashwell Somset 10 B6
Ashwell End Herts 50 C5
Ashwellthorpe Norfk 64 D5
Ashwick Somset 24 B4
Ashwicken Norfk 75 G2
Ashwood Staffs 58 B4
Askam in Furness Cumb 94 C3
Aske Hall N York 97 E5
Askern S York 84 C6
Askerswell Dorset 11 F4
Askett Bucks 41 F5
Askham Cumb 104 B2
Askham Notts 85 E2
Askham Bryan N York 91 G4
Askham Richard N York 91 F4
Asknish Ag & B 127 H4
Askrigg N York 96 C4
Askwith N York 90 C4
Aslackby Lincs 74 A3
Aslacton Norfk 64 D4
Aslockton Notts 73 E4
Asney Somset 23 G3
Aspall Suffk 64 D2
Aspatria Cumb 103 E4
Aspenden Herts 50 D3
Aspenshaw Derbys 83 E3
Asperton Lincs 74 C4
Aspley Staffs 70 C3
Aspley Guise Beds 49 G3
Aspley Heath Beds 49 G3
Aspley Heath Warwks 58 D2
Aspull Gt Man 82 A5
Aspull Common Gt Man 82 A4
Asselby E R Yk 92 A2
Asserby Lincs 87 E2
Asserby Turn Lincs 87 E2
Assington Suffk 52 C4
Assington Green Suffk 52 A6
Astbury Ches 70 C6
Astcote Nhants 49 E4
Asterley Shrops 56 D6
Asterton Shrops 56 D4
Asthall Oxon 39 G5
Asthall Leigh Oxon 39 H6
Astle Highld 162 D3
Astley Gt Man 82 B5
Astley Shrops 69 G2
Astley W York 91 E2
Astley Warwks 59 F4
Astley Worcs 57 H2
Astley Abbots Shrops 57 G5
Astley Bridge Gt Man 82 B6
Astley Cross Worcs 58 A2
Astley Green Gt Man 82 B5
Astley Town Worcs 57 H2
Aston Berks 41 F3
Aston Ches 81 H2
Aston Ches 70 A5
Aston Derbys 83 G3
Aston Flints 81 E1
Aston Herefs 57 E2
Aston Herefs 57 E2
Aston Herts 50 D3
Aston Oxon 40 B5
Aston S York 84 B3
Aston Shrops 69 G3
Aston Shrops 70 A1
Aston Staffs 58 A5
Aston Staffs 70 C4
Aston Staffs 70 D2
Aston Staffs 70 D3
Aston W Mids 58 D4
Aston Abbotts Bucks 49 G1
Aston Botterell Shrops 57 F4
Aston Cantlow Warwks 47 G5
Aston Clinton Bucks 41 G5
Aston Crews Herefs 46 B1
Aston Cross Gloucs 47 E3
Aston End Herts 50 D3
Aston Fields Worcs 58 C2
Aston Flamville Leics 59 G5
Aston Ingham Herefs 46 B1
Aston juxta Mondrum Ches 70 B6
Aston le Walls Nhants 48 C4
Aston Magna Gloucs 47 G3
Aston Munslow Shrops 57 E4
Aston on Clun Shrops 56 D3
Aston Pigott Shrops 56 D6
Aston Rogers Shrops 56 D6
Aston Rowant Oxon 41 E4
Aston Sandford Bucks 41 F5
Aston Somerville Worcs 47 F3
Aston Subedge Gloucs 47 G3
Aston Tirrold Oxon 40 D3
Aston Upthorpe Oxon 40 D3
Aston-Eyre Shrops 57 G5
Aston-upon-Trent Derbys 72 B3
Astonlane Shrops 57 G5
Astrop Nhants 48 C3
Astrope Herts 41 G6
Astwick Beds 50 C5
Astwith Derbys 84 B1
Astwood Bucks 49 H4
Astwood Worcs 58 B2
Astwood Bank Worcs 47 F5
Aswarby Lincs 74 A4
Aswardby Lincs 86 D2
Atch Lench Worcs 47 F5
Atcham Shrops 69 H1

Athelhampton Dorset 12 B4
Athelington Suffk 65 E2
Athelney Somset 23 F2
Athelstaneford E Loth 132 D3
Atherfield Green IOW 14 C1
Atherington Devon 21 F3
Atherington W Susx 16 A1
Atherstone Somset 23 G1
Atherstone Warwks 59 F5
Atherstone on Stour Warwks 47 G4
Atherton Gt Man 82 B5
Atley Hill N York 97 F5
Atlow Derbys 71 G5
Attadale Highld 152 C3
Attenborough Notts 72 C3
Atterby Lincs 85 G4
Attercliffe S York 84 B3
Atterley Shrops 57 F5
Atterton Leics 59 G5
Attleborough Norfk 64 C5
Attleborough Warwks 59 G4
Attlebridge Norfk 76 D3
Attleton Green Suffk 52 A6
Atwick E R Yk 93 F5
Atworth Wilts 24 D6
Auberrow Herefs 45 H4
Aubourn Lincs 85 G1
Auchedly Abers 159 E2
Auchenblae Abers 149 E5
Auchenbowie Stirlg 130 D4
Auchencairn D & G 102 A5
Auchencairn D & G 110 D3
Auchencairn N Ayrs 118 G2
Auchencrow Border 123 F5
Auchendinny Mdloth 121 G6
Auchengray S Lans 120 D5
Auchenhalrig Moray 157 F5
Auchenheath S Lans 120 C4
Auchenhessnane D & G 110 C4
Auchenlochan Ag & B 128 A2
Auchenmade N Ayrs 119 E4
Auchenmalg D & G 100 D5
Auchentiber N Ayrs 119 E4
Auchindrean Highld 161 F2
Auchininna Abers 158 B4
Auchinleck E Ayrs 119 G2
Auchinloch N Lans 130 C2
Auchinstarry N Lans 130 C3
Auchintore Highld 144 C2
Auchiries Abers 159 G3
Auchlee Abers 149 F4
Auchleven Abers 158 B1
Auchlochan S Lans 120 C4
Auchlossan Abers 148 C5
Auchlunies Abers 149 F4
Auchlyne Stirlg 138 B3
Auchmillan E Ayrs 119 G2
Auchmithie Angus 141 G4
Auchmuirbridge Fife 132 A5
Auchnacree Angus 141 E6
Auchnagatt Abers 159 E3
Auchnarrow Moray 156 D1
Auchnotteroch D & G 100 A4
Auchroisk Moray 157 E4
Auchterarder P & K 139 G1
Auchteraw Highld 145 E3
Auchterblair Highld 155 G1
Auchtercairn Highld 160 B3
Auchterderran Fife 132 A5
Auchterhouse Angus 140 C3
Auchterless Abers 158 C3
Auchtermuchty Fife 140 B1
Auchterneed Highld 154 C3
Auchtertool Fife 132 A4
Auchtertyre Highld 152 C2
Auchtubh Stirlg 138 C2
Auckengill Highld 167 G5
Auckley S York 84 D5
Audenshaw Gt Man 82 D4
Audlem Ches 70 B4
Audley Staffs 70 C5
Audley End Essex 51 F4
Audley End Essex 51 F4
Audley End Suffk 52 B6
Audmore Staffs 70 C2
Audnam W Mids 58 B4
Aughertree Cumb 103 F4
Aughton E R Yk 91 H3
Aughton Lancs 81 F5
Aughton Lancs 95 F2
Aughton S York 84 B3
Aughton Wilts 25 H5
Aughton Park Lancs 81 F5
Auldearn Highld 155 G5
Aulden Herefs 45 G5
Auldgirth D & G 110 D3
Auldhouse S Lans 119 H4
Ault a' chruinn Highld 152 D1
Ault Hucknall Derbys 84 B1
Aultbea Highld 160 C2
Aultgrishin Highld 160 B2
Aultguish Inn Highld 154 B6
Aultmore Moray 157 F4
Aultnagoire Highld 154 D1
Aultnamain Inn Highld 162 D2
Aunby Lincs 73 H1
Aunk Devon 9 G5
Aunsby Lincs 73 H4
Aust Gloucs 37 G3
Austendike Lincs 74 C2
Austerfield S York 84 D4
Austerlands Gt Man 83 E5
Austhorpe W York 91 E3
Austonley W York 83 F5
Austrey Warwks 59 F6
Austwick N York 96 A4
Authorpe Lincs 86 D3
Authorpe Row Lincs 87 F2
Avebury Wilts 39 F1
Avebury Trusloe Wilts 39 F1
Aveley Essex 29 F4
Avening Gloucs 38 D4
Averham Notts 73 E5
Aveton Gifford Devon 6 D2
Aviemore Highld 146 D6
Avington Berks 26 B5
Avoch Highld 155 E5

Avon

Bath

Avon Dorset 13 E4
Avon Dassett Warwks 48 B4
Avonbridge Falk 131 E2
Avonmouth Bristl 37 F2
Avonwick Devon 6 D3
Awbridge Hants 26 B2
Awkley Gloucs 37 G3
Awliscombe Devon 10 B5
Awre Gloucs 38 B5
Awsworth Notts 72 C4
Axborough Worcs 58 B3
Axbridge Somset 23 G5
Axford Hants 26 D4
Axford Wilts 39 G1
Axminster Devon 10 C4
Axmouth Devon 10 C4
Axton Flints 80 C3
Aycliffe Dur 106 B3
Aydon Nthumb 113 G1
Aylburton Gloucs 37 G4
Ayle Cumb 104 D5
Aylesbeare Devon 9 G4
Aylesbury Bucks 41 F6
Aylesby Lincs 86 B5
Aylesford Kent 29 H2
Aylesham Kent 31 F1
Aylestone Leics 60 B5
Aylestone Park Leics 60 B5
Aylmerton Norfk 77 E4
Aylsham Norfk 77 E3
Aylton Gloucs 46 B3
Aylworth Gloucs 47 F1
Aymestrey Herefs 56 D2
Aynho Nhants 48 C2
Ayot Green Herts 50 C2
Ayot St Lawrence Herts 50 C2
Ayot St Peter Herts 50 C2
Ayr S Ayrs 119 E2
Aysgarth N York 96 C4
Ayshford Devon 9 G6
Ayside Cumb 95 E3
Ayston Rutlnd 61 E5
Aythorpe Roding Essex 51 G2
Ayton Border 123 F5
Azerley N York 97 F2

B

Babbacombe Devon 7 G4
Babbington Notts 72 C4
Babbinswood Shrops 69 F3
Babbs Green Herts 51 E2
Babcary Somset 24 A2
Babel Carmth 44 A3
Babel Green Suffk 51 H6
Babell Flints 80 D2
Babeny Devon 8 D2
Babington Somset 24 C4
Bablock Hythe Oxon 40 C5
Babraham Cambs 51 F6
Babworth Notts 84 D3
Bachau IOA 78 D3
Bache Shrops 57 E4
Bacheldre Powys 56 C5
Bachelor's Bump E Susx 18 B3
Back o' th' Brook Staffs 71 F5
Back of Keppoch Highld 143 F3
Back Street Suffk 63 G1
Backaland Ork 169 c3
Backbarrow Cumb 94 D3
Backe Carmth 33 G3
Backfolds Abers 159 F4
Backford Ches 81 F2
Backford Cross Ches 81 F2
Backies Highld 163 E4
Backlass Highld 167 F4
Backwell Somset 37 F1
Backworth T & W 115 E3
Bacon's End W Mids 59 E4
Baconsthorpe Norfk 76 D4
Bacton Herefs 45 F2
Bacton Norfk 77 F3
Bacton Suffk 64 C2
Bacton Green Suffk 64 C2
Bacup Lancs 89 G2
Badachro Highld 160 B1
Badbury Wilts 39 G2
Badby Nhants 48 D5
Badcall Highld 164 C3
Badcall Highld 164 C4
Badcaul Highld 160 D3
Baddeley Edge Staffs 70 D5
Baddeley Green Staffs 70 D5
Baddesley Clinton Warwks 59 E3
Baddesley Ensor Warwks 59 F5
Baddidarrach Highld 161 E6
Baddinsgill Border 121 F5
Badenscoth Abers 158 C3
Badenyon Abers 157 E1
Badgall Cnwll 5 F5
Badgeney Cambs 62 D5
Badger Shrops 57 H5
Badger's Cross Cnwll 2 B3
Badgers Mount Kent 29 F2
Badgeworth Gloucs 47 E1
Badgworth Somset 23 G4
Badharlick Cnwll 5 F5
Badicaul Highld 152 B2
Badingham Suffk 65 E2
Badlesmere Kent 30 D1
Badlieu Border 121 E1
Badlipster Highld 167 F3
Badluachrach Highld 160 D3
Badninish Highld 162 D3
Badrallach Highld 161 E3
Badsey Worcs 47 F3
Badshot Lea Surrey 27 G4
Badsworth W York 91 F1
Badwell Ash Suffk 64 B2
Badwell Green Suffk 64 C2
Bag Enderby Lincs 86 D2
Bagber Dorset 12 A6
Bagby N York 97 H3
Bagendon Gloucs 39 E5
Bagginswood Shrops 57 G3
Baggrow Cumb 103 F4
Bagh a Chaisteil W Isls 168 a1
Bagh a Tuath W Isls 168 b2
Bagham Kent 30 D1
Bagillt Flints 80 D2
Baginton Warwks 59 F3
Baglan Neath 35 E3
Bagley Shrops 69 F3
Bagley Somset 23 G4
Bagley W York 90 C3
Bagmore Hants 27 E4
Bagnall Staffs 70 D5
Bagnor Berks 40 C1
Bagot Shrops 57 F3
Bagshot Surrey 27 G6
Bagshot Wilts 26 A6
Bagstone Gloucs 38 B3
Bagthorpe Notts 72 B5
Bagworth Leics 59 G6
Bagwy Llydiart Herefs 45 G2
Baildon W York 90 C4
Baildon Green W York 90 C3
Baile a Mhanaich W Isls 168 b4
Baile Ailein W Isls 168 e7
Baile Mor Ag & B 135 E2
Bailey Green Hants 27 E2
Baileyhead Cumb 112 B3
Bailiff Bridge W York 90 C2
Baillieston C Glas 130 C1
Bailrigg Lancs 88 C5
Bainbridge N York 96 C4
Bainshole Abers 158 B3
Bainton Cambs 61 G6
Bainton E R Yk 92 C5
Bainton Oxon 48 D2
Baintown Fife 132 C5
Bairnkine Border 122 D1
Baker Street Essex 29 G4
Baker's End Herts 51 E2
Bakewell Derbys 83 G1
Bala Gwynd 68 B4
Balallan W Isls 168 e7
Balbeg Highld 154 C2
Balbeggie P & K 140 B3
Balblair Highld 154 C4
Balblair Highld 155 E6
Balby S York 84 C5
Balcary D & G 102 B5
Balchraggan Highld 154 D3
Balchreick Highld 164 C4
Balcombe W Susx 16 D4
Balcombe Lane W Susx 16 D5
Balcomie Links Fife 133 E6
Baldersby N York 97 G3
Baldersby St James N York 97 G2
Balderstone Gt Man 82 D6
Balderstone Lancs 89 E3
Balderton Notts 73 F5
Baldhu Cnwll 3 E4
Baldinnie Fife 132 C6
Baldinnies P & K 139 G1
Baldock Herts 50 C4
Baldovie Dund C 140 D3
Baldrine IOM 174 m3
Baldslow E Susx 18 B3
Baldwin IOM 174 l3
Baldwin's Gate Staffs 70 C4
Baldwin's Hill Surrey 17 E5
Baldwinholme Cumb 103 G5
Bale Norfk 76 C4
Baledgarno P & K 140 C3
Balemartine Ag & B 134 B3
Balerno C Edin 131 H2
Balfarg Fife 132 B5
Balfield Angus 148 C1
Balfour Ork 169 c3
Balfron Stirlg 129 G4
Balgaveny Abers 158 C3
Balgavies Angus 141 E5
Balgonar Fife 131 F4
Balgowan D & G 100 C4
Balgowan Highld 146 A4
Balgown Highld 150 D6
Balgracie D & G 100 A6
Balgray Angus 140 D4
Balgray S Lans 120 C2
Balham Gt Lon 28 D3
Balhary P & K 140 C4
Balholmie P & K 140 B3
Baligill Highld 166 B5
Balintore Angus 140 C6
Balintore Highld 163 E1
Balintraid Highld 155 E6
Balivanich W Isls 168 b4
Balk N York 97 H3
Balkeerie Angus 140 C4
Balkholme E R Yk 92 B2
Ball Green Staffs 70 D5
Ball Haye Green Staffs 71 E6
Ball Hill Hants 26 B6
Ball's Green Gloucs 38 C4
Ballabeg IOM 174 k2
Ballachulish Highld 137 E6
Ballafesson IOM 174 k2
Ballakilpheric IOM 174 k2
Ballamodha IOM 174 k2
Ballanlay Ag & B 118 B6
Ballantrae S Ayrs 108 C3
Ballards Gore Essex 30 C5
Ballards Green Warwks 59 F4
Ballasalla IOM 174 l2
Ballater Abers 148 A4
Ballaugh IOM 174 l4
Ballchraggan Highld 162 D1
Ballencrieff E Loth 132 D3
Ballevullin Ag & B 134 B4
Ballidon Derbys 71 G5
Balliekine N Ayrs 117 H4
Balliemore Ag & B 128 C5
Balligmorrie S Ayrs 108 D4
Ballimore Ag & B 127 H3
Ballimore Stirlg 138 C1
Ballindalloch Moray 156 D3
Ballindean P & K 140 C3
Ballingdon Essex 52 B5
Ballinger Common Bucks 41 G5
Ballingham Herefs 46 A2
Ballingry Fife 131 H5
Ballinluig P & K 139 G5
Ballinshoe Angus 140 D5
Ballintuim P & K 140 A5
Balloch Highld 155 E4
Balloch N Lans 130 D2
Balloch P & K 139 F2
Balloch S Ayrs 109 E4
Balloch W Duns 129 E3
Ballogie Abers 148 C4
Balls Cross W Susx 27 H2
Balls Green E Susx 17 F5
Ballygown Ag & B 135 F4
Ballygrant Ag & B 126 C2
Ballyhaugh Ag & B 134 D5
Ballymenoch Ag & B 128 D4
Ballymichael N Ayrs 118 A2
Balmacara Highld 152 B2
Balmaclellan D & G 110 A3
Balmae D & G 102 A5
Balmaha Stirlg 129 F4
Balmalcolm Fife 132 B6
Balmangan D & G 101 H5
Balmedie Abers 159 E1
Balmer Heath Shrops 69 G3
Balmerino Fife 140 D2
Balmerlawn Hants 13 G5
Balmoral Castle Grounds Abers 147 G4
Balmore E Duns 130 B2
Balmuchy Highld 163 E1
Balmuir Angus 141 F5
Balmule Fife 132 A4
Balmullo Fife 140 D2
Balnacoil Lodge Highld 163 E5
Balnacra Highld 152 D4
Balnacroft Abers 147 H4
Balnafoich Highld 155 E3
Balnaguard P & K 139 G5
Balnahard Ag & B 135 F3
Balnahard Ag & B 126 C5
Balnain Highld 154 C2
Balnakeil Highld 165 E5
Balnapaling Highld 155 F6
Balne N York 91 G1
Balquharn P & K 139 G3
Balquhidder Stirlg 138 C2
Balsall Common W Mids 59 E3
Balsall Heath W Mids 58 D4
Balsall Street W Mids 59 E3
Balscote Oxon 48 B3
Balsham Cambs 51 G6
Baltasound Shet 169 k5
Baltasound Airport Shet 169 k5
Balterley Staffs 70 C5
Balterley Green Staffs 70 C5
Balterley Heath Staffs 70 B5
Baltersan D & G 109 F1
Baltonsborough Somset 24 A3
Balvarran P & K 139 H6
Balvicar Ag & B 136 B1
Balvraid Highld 143 H6
Balvraid Highld 155 F2
Balwest Cnwll 2 C3
Bamber Bridge Lancs 88 D2
Bamber's Green Essex 51 G3
Bamburgh Nthumb 125 E4
Bamburgh Castle Nthumb 125 E5
Bamff P & K 140 B5
Bamford Derbys 83 G3
Bamford Gt Man 82 D6
Bampton Cumb 104 B2
Bampton Devon 22 B1
Bampton Oxon 40 A5
Bampton Grange Cumb 104 B2
Banavie Highld 144 C2
Banbury Oxon 48 C3
Banc-y-ffordd Carmth 42 D3
Bancffosfelen Carmth 34 B5
Banchory Abers 149 E4
Banchory-Devenick Abers 149 G5
Bancycapel Carmth 34 B6
Bancyfelin Carmth 33 G3
Bandirran P & K 140 B3
Bandrake Head Cumb 94 D4
Banff Abers 158 C5
Bangor Gwynd 79 E2
Bangor's Green Lancs 81 F6
Bangor-is-y-coed Wrexhm 69 F5
Bangors Cnwll 5 F6
Bangrove Suffk 64 B3
Banham Norfk 64 C4
Bank Hants 13 G5
Bank Ground Cumb 94 D5
Bank Newton N York 89 G5
Bank Street Worcs 57 F2
Bank Top Lancs 81 G5
Bank Top W York 90 B2
Bankend D & G 111 E2
Bankfoot P & K 139 H3
Bankglen E Ayrs 109 H6
Bankhead Aber C 149 G5
Bankhead S Lans 120 D4
Banknock Falk 130 D3
Banks Cumb 112 C1
Banks Lancs 88 B2
Banks Green Worcs 58 C2
Bankshill D & G 111 F3
Banningham Norfk 77 E3
Bannister Green Essex 51 H3
Bannockburn Stirlg 130 D4
Banstead Surrey 28 C2
Bantham Devon 6 D2
Banton N Lans 130 D3
Banwell Somset 23 G5
Bapchild Kent 30 C2
Bapton Wilts 25 E3
Bar Hill Cambs 62 C2
Barabhas W Isls 168 e9
Barassie S Ayrs 119 E3
Barbaraville Highld 162 D1
Barber Booth Derbys 83 F3
Barber Green Cumb 95 E3
Barbieston S Ayrs 119 F1
Barbon Cumb 95 G3
Barbridge Ches 70 A6
Barbrook Devon 21 G5
Barby Nhants 60 B2
Barcaldine Ag & B 136 D4
Barcheston Warwks 47 H3
Barclose Cumb 112 B1
Barcombe E Susx 17 E3
Barcombe Cross E Susx 17 E3
Barcroft W York 90 B3
Barden N York 97 E4
Barden Park Kent 17 G6
Bardfield End Green Essex 51 G4
Bardfield Saling Essex 51 H3
Bardney Lincs 86 B2
Bardon Leics 72 B1
Bardon Mill Nthumb 113 E1
Bardowie E Duns 130 B2
Bardown E Susx 17 G4
Bardrainney Inver 129 E2
Bardsea Cumb 94 D2
Bardsey W York 91 E4
Bardsley Gt Man 82 D5
Bardwell Suffk 64 B3
Bare Lancs 95 E1
Bareppa Cnwll 3 E3
Barewood Herefs 45 G5
Barfad D & G 109 E1
Barford Norfk 64 D6
Barford Warwks 48 A5
Barford St John Oxon 48 C2
Barford St Martin Wilts 25 F2
Barford St Michael Oxon 48 C2
Barfrestone Kent 31 F1
Bargate Derbys 72 A5
Bargeddie N Lans 130 C1
Bargoed Caerph 36 C4
Bargrennan D & G 109 E2
Barham Cambs 61 G3
Barham Kent 31 F1
Barham Suffk 53 E6
Barholm Lincs 74 A1
Barkby Leics 72 D1
Barkby Thorpe Leics 72 D1
Barkers Green Shrops 69 G3
Barkestone-le-Vale Leics 73 E3
Barkham Berks 27 F6
Barking Gt Lon 29 E4
Barking Suffk 52 D6
Barking Tye Suffk 52 D6
Barkingside Gt Lon 29 E5
Barkisland W York 90 B1
Barkla Shop Cnwll 3 E5
Barkston Lincs 73 G4
Barkston Ash N York 91 F3
Barkway Herts 51 E4
Barlanark C Glas 130 C1
Barlaston Staffs 70 D4
Barlavington W Susx 15 H5
Barlborough Derbys 84 B2
Barlby N York 91 G3
Barlestone Leics 59 G6
Barley Herts 51 E5
Barley Lancs 89 G4
Barley Hole S York 84 A4
Barleycroft End Herts 51 E3
Barleythorpe Rutlnd 73 F1
Barling Essex 30 C5
Barlings Lincs 86 A2
Barlochan D & G 102 B6
Barlow Derbys 84 A2
Barlow N York 91 G2
Barlow T & W 114 C2
Barmby Moor E R Yk 92 B4
Barmby on the Marsh E R Yk 91 H2
Barmer Norfk 76 A3
Barming Heath Kent 29 H1
Barmollack Ag & B 117 G5
Barmouth Gwynd 67 F2
Barmpton Dur 106 C3
Barmston E R Yk 93 E5
Barnaby Green Suffk 65 G3
Barnacarry Ag & B 128 B4
Barnack Cambs 61 G6
Barnacle Warwks 59 G4
Barnard Castle Dur 105 G2
Barnard Gate Oxon 40 B5
Barnardiston Suffk 51 H6
Barnbarroch D & G 102 B6
Barnburgh S York 84 C5
Barnby Suffk 65 G4
Barnby Dun S York 84 D6
Barnby in the Willows Notts 73 F5
Barnby Moor Notts 84 D3
Barncorkrie D & G 100 B4
Barnehurst Gt Lon 29 F4
Barnes Gt Lon 28 C4
Barnes Street Kent 17 G6
Barnet Gt Lon 28 C6
Barnet Gate Gt Lon 28 C6
Barnetby le Wold Lincs 86 A6
Barney Norfk 76 C3
Barnham Suffk 64 A3
Barnham W Susx 15 H4
Barnham Broom Norfk 64 C6
Barnhead Angus 141 G5
Barnhill Ches 69 G5
Barnhill Dund C 141 E3
Barnhill Moray 156 D5
Barnhills D & G 108 B2
Barningham Dur 96 D6
Barningham Suffk 64 B3
Barnoldby le Beck Lincs 86 C5
Barnoldswick Lancs 89 G4
Barns Green W Susx 16 B4
Barnsdale Bar N York 91 F1
Barnsley Gloucs 39 E5
Barnsley S York 84 A5
Barnsley Shrops 57 H5
Barnsole Kent 31 F2
Barnstaple Devon 21 F4
Barnston Essex 51 G3
Barnston Mersyd 81 E3
Barnstone Notts 73 E4
Barnt Green Worcs 58 C3
Barnton C Edin 131 H3
Barnton Ches 82 A2
Barnwell All Saints Nhants 61 F4
Barnwell St Andrew Nhants 61 F4
Barnwood Gloucs 46 D1
Baron's Cross Herefs 45 G5
Barons Wood Devon 8 D5
Baronwood Cumb 104 B4
Barr S Ayrs 109 E4
Barrachan D & G 101 E5
Barrapoll Ag & B 134 A4
Barra Airport W Isls 168 b2
Barras Cumb 105 E1
Barrasford Nthumb 113 F2
Barrets Green Ches 69 H6
Barrhead E Rens 119 G5
Barrhill S Ayrs 108 D3
Barrington Cambs 51 E6
Barrington Somset 23 G1
Barripper Cnwll 2 D4
Barrmill N Ayrs 119 E5
Barrnacarry Bay Ag & B 136 C2
Barrock Highld 167 F5
Barrow Gloucs 46 D2
Barrow Lancs 89 F3
Barrow Rutlnd 73 F1
Barrow Shrops 57 G5
Barrow Somset 24 C2
Barrow Suffk 63 G2
Barrow Bridge Gt Man 82 B6
Barrow Burn Nthumb 113 F6
Barrow Gurney Somset 37 F1
Barrow Haven Lincs 92 D2
Barrow Hill Derbys 84 B2
Barrow Island Cumb 94 C2
Barrow Nook Lancs 81 G5
Barrow Street Wilts 24 D2
Barrow upon Soar Leics 72 C2
Barrow upon Trent Derbys 72 A3
Barrow Vale Somset 24 B5
Barrow's Green Ches 81 G3
Barrow's Green Ches 70 B6
Barrow-in-Furness Cumb 94 C2
Barrow-upon-Humber Lincs 92 D2
Barroway Drove Norfk 63 E6
Barrowby Lincs 73 F4
Barrowden Rutlnd 61 E5
Barrowford Lancs 89 G3
Barry Angus 141 E3
Barry V Glam 36 B1
Barry Island V Glam 22 D6
Barsby Leics 73 E1
Barsham Suffk 65 F4
Barston W Mids 59 E3
Bartestree Herefs 46 A3
Barthol Chapel Abers 158 D2
Bartholomew Green Essex 51 H3
Barthomley Ches 70 C5
Bartley Hants 13 G6
Bartley Green W Mids 58 C4
Bartlow Cambs 51 G5
Barton Cambs 62 C1
Barton Ches 69 G5
Barton Cumb 104 B3
Barton Devon 7 F4
Barton Gloucs 47 F2
Barton Herefs 45 F5
Barton Lancs 81 F6
Barton Lancs 88 D3
Barton N York 106 B2
Barton Oxon 40 D5
Barton Warwks 47 F4
Barton Bendish Norfk 63 F6
Barton End Gloucs 38 C4
Barton Green Staffs 71 G2
Barton Hartshorn Bucks 49 E2
Barton Hill N York 98 C1
Barton in Fabis Notts 72 C3
Barton in the Beans Leics 59 G6
Barton Mills Suffk 63 F3
Barton Seagrave Nhants 61 E3
Barton St David Somset 24 A2
Barton Stacey Hants 26 C3
Barton Town Devon 21 G5
Barton Turf Norfk 77 F2
Barton upon Irwell Gt Man 82 C4
Barton Waterside Lincs 92 D2
Barton-le-Clay Beds 50 B4
Barton-le-Street N York 98 C2
Barton-le-Willows N York 92 A6
Barton-on-Sea Hants 13 F4
Barton-on-the-Heath Warwks 47 H2
Barton-under-Needwood Staffs 71 G2
Barton-upon-Humber Lincs 92 D2
Barugh S York 83 H5
Barugh Green S York 83 H5
Barvas W Isls 168 e9
Barway Cambs 63 E3
Barwell Leics 59 G5
Barwick Devon 8 C5
Barwick Herts 51 E3
Barwick Somset 11 F6
Barwick in Elmet W York 91 E3
Baschurch Shrops 69 F2
Bascote Warwks 59 G2
Bascote Heath Warwks 59 G2
Base Green Suffk 64 C2
Basford Green Staffs 71 E5
Bashall Eaves Lancs 89 E4
Bashall Town Lancs 89 E4
Bashley Hants 13 F4
Basildon Essex 29 H5
Basingstoke Hants 27 E4
Baslow Derbys 83 G2
Bason Bridge Somset 23 F4
Bassaleg Newpt 36 D3
Bassendean Border 122 C4
Bassenthwaite Cumb 103 F3
Bassett Hants 14 B5
Bassingbourn Cambs 50 D5
Bassingfield Notts 72 D4
Bassingham Lincs 73 G6
Bassingthorpe Lincs 73 G3
Bassus Green Herts 50 D3
Basted Kent 29 G2
Baston Lincs 74 B1
Bastwick Norfk 77 G2
Batch Somset 23 F5
Batchworth Herts 28 B5
Batchworth Heath Herts 28 B5
Batcombe Dorset 11 F5
Batcombe Somset 24 B3
Bate Heath Ches 82 B3
Batford Herts 50 B2
Bath Somset 24 C6

273

Bath Side *Essex* ... 53 F4
Bathampton *Somset* ... 24 C6
Bathealton *Somset* ... 22 D2
Batheaston *Somset* ... 24 C6
Bathford *Somset* ... 24 C6
Bathgate *W Loth* ... 131 F2
Bathley *Notts* ... 73 E6
Bathpool *Cnwll* ... 5 F3
Bathpool *Somset* ... 23 E2
Bathville *W Loth* ... 131 F2
Bathway *Somset* ... 24 B4
Batley *W York* ... 90 C2
Batsford *Gloucs* ... 47 G3
Batson *Devon* ... 7 E1
Battersby *N York* ... 107 E2
Battersea *Gt Lon* ... 28 D4
Battisborough Cross *Devon* ... 6 C2
Battisford *Suffk* ... 52 D6
Battisford Tye *Suffk* ... 52 D6
Battle *E Susx* ... 18 A3
Battle *Powys* ... 44 C2
Battle of Britain Memorial
  Flight *Lincs* ... 74 C6
Battleborough *Somset* ... 23 F4
Battledown *Gloucs* ... 47 E1
Battledykes *Angus* ... 140 D5
Battlefield *Shrops* ... 69 G2
Battlesbridge *Essex* ... 30 A5
Battlesden *Beds* ... 49 H2
Battleton *Somset* ... 22 B2
Battlies Green *Suffk* ... 64 B2
Battramsley Cross *Hants* ... 13 G4
Battyeford *W York* ... 90 C2
Baughton *Worcs* ... 46 D3
Baughurst *Hants* ... 26 D5
Baulds *Abers* ... 148 D4
Baulking *Oxon* ... 40 A3
Baumber *Lincs* ... 86 C2
Baunton *Gloucs* ... 39 E5
Baveney Wood *Shrops* ... 57 G3
Baverstock *Wilts* ... 25 F2
Bawburgh *Norfk* ... 64 D6
Bawdeswell *Norfk* ... 76 C2
Bawdrip *Somset* ... 23 F3
Bawdsey *Suffk* ... 53 G5
Bawsey *Norfk* ... 75 G2
Bawtry *S York* ... 84 D4
Baxenden *Lancs* ... 89 F2
Baxter's Green *Suffk* ... 63 G1
Baxterley *Warwks* ... 59 F5
Bay *Highld* ... 150 C4
Bay Horse *Lancs* ... 88 C5
Baybridge *Hants* ... 26 C1
Baybridge *Nthumb* ... 105 F5
Baycliff *Cumb* ... 94 D2
Baydon *Wilts* ... 39 G2
Bayford *Herts* ... 50 D1
Bayford *Somset* ... 24 C2
Bayhead *W Isls* ... 168 b5
Bayley's Hill *Kent* ... 29 F1
Baylham *Suffk* ... 53 E6
Baynard's Green *Oxon* ... 48 D2
Baysdale Abbey *N York* ... 98 B5
Baysham *Herefs* ... 46 A2
Bayston Hill *Shrops* ... 69 G1
Baythorne End *Essex* ... 51 H5
Bayton *Worcs* ... 57 G3
Bayton Common *Worcs* ... 57 G3
Bayworth *Oxon* ... 40 C4
Beach *Gloucs* ... 38 B1
Beachampton *Bucks* ... 49 F3
Beachamwell *Norfk* ... 63 G6
Beachborough *Kent* ... 19 E5
Beachley *Gloucs* ... 37 F3
Beacon *Devon* ... 10 B5
Beacon End *Essex* ... 52 C3
Beacon Hill *E Susx* ... 17 F4
Beacon Hill *Kent* ... 18 B5
Beacon Hill *Notts* ... 73 F5
Beacon Hill *Surrey* ... 27 G3
Beacon's Bottom *Bucks* ... 41 F4
Beaconsfield *Bucks* ... 41 H3
Beadlam *N York* ... 98 B3
Beadlow *Beds* ... 50 B5
Beadnell *Nthumb* ... 125 E4
Beaford *Devon* ... 21 F2
Beal *N York* ... 91 F2
Beal *Nthumb* ... 123 H4
Bealbury *Cnwll* ... 5 G3
Bealsmill *Cnwll* ... 5 G4
Beam Hill *Staffs* ... 71 G3
Beamhurst *Staffs* ... 71 E4
Beaminster *Dorset* ... 11 E5
Beamish *Dur* ... 106 B6
Beamsley *N York* ... 90 B5
Bean *Kent* ... 29 G3
Beanacre *Wilts* ... 25 E6
Beanley *Nthumb* ... 124 D3
Beardon *Devon* ... 8 B3
Beardwood *Lancs* ... 89 E2
Beare *Devon* ... 9 G5
Beare Green *Surrey* ... 16 C6
Bearley *Warwks* ... 47 G5
Bearley Cross *Warwks* ... 47 G5
Bearpark *Dur* ... 106 B5
Bearsden *W Duns* ... 129 G2
Bearsted *Kent* ... 30 B2
Bearstone *Shrops* ... 70 B4
Bearwood *Dorset* ... 12 D4
Bearwood *W Mids* ... 58 C4
Beattock *D & G* ... 111 E5
Beauchamp Roding *Essex* ... 51 G2
Beauchief *S York* ... 84 A3
Beaudesert *Warwks* ... 58 D2
Beaufort *Blae G* ... 36 C5
Beaulieu *Hants* ... 14 B4
Beaulieu House *Hants* ... 14 B4
Beaulieu Road Station *Hants* ... 13 G5
Beauly *Highld* ... 154 C4
Beaumaris *IOA* ... 79 F2
Beaumont *Cumb* ... 103 G6
Beaumont *Essex* ... 53 E3
Beaumont *Jersey* ... 174 b2
Beaumont Hill *Dur* ... 106 B3
Beaumont *Essex* ... 53 E3
Beausale *Warwks* ... 59 E2
Beauworth *Hants* ... 26 D2

Beaver *Kent* ... 18 D5
Beaver Green *Kent* ... 18 D5
Beaworthy *Devon* ... 8 B4
Beazley End *Essex* ... 52 A4
Bebington *Mersyd* ... 81 F3
Bebside *Nthumb* ... 114 D4
Beccles *Suffk* ... 65 G4
Becconsall *Lancs* ... 88 C2
Beck Foot *Cumb* ... 95 G4
Beck Hole *N York* ... 98 D5
Beck Row *Suffk* ... 63 F3
Beck Side *Cumb* ... 94 C3
Beck Side *Cumb* ... 94 D3
Beckbury *Shrops* ... 57 H5
Beckenham *Gt Lon* ... 29 E3
Beckering *Lincs* ... 86 B3
Beckermet *Cumb* ... 94 A5
Beckett End *Norfk* ... 63 G5
Beckfoot *Cumb* ... 103 E5
Beckfoot *Cumb* ... 94 B5
Beckfoot *Cumb* ... 94 C4
Beckford *Worcs* ... 47 E3
Beckhampton *Wilts* ... 39 F1
Beckingham *Lincs* ... 73 F5
Beckingham *Notts* ... 85 E4
Beckington *Somset* ... 24 D4
Beckjay *Shrops* ... 56 D3
Beckley *E Susx* ... 18 B4
Beckley *Hants* ... 13 F4
Beckley *Oxon* ... 40 D5
Becks *W York* ... 90 B4
Beckside *Cumb* ... 95 G4
Beckton *Gt Lon* ... 29 E4
Beckwithshaw *N York* ... 90 D5
Becontree *Gt Lon* ... 29 F5
Becquet Vincent *Jersey* ... 174 c2
Bedale *N York* ... 97 F4
Bedburn *Dur* ... 105 H3
Bedchester *Dorset* ... 24 D1
Beddau *Rhondd* ... 36 B3
Beddgelert *Gwynd* ... 67 E5
Beddingham *E Susx* ... 17 E2
Beddington *Gt Lon* ... 28 D3
Beddington Corner *Gt Lon* ... 28 D3
Bedfield *Suffk* ... 65 E2
Bedfield Little Green *Suffk* ... 65 E2
Bedford *Beds* ... 50 A6
Bedgebury Cross *Kent* ... 17 H5
Bedham *W Susx* ... 16 A4
Bedhampton *Hants* ... 15 E4
Bedingfield *Suffk* ... 64 D2
Bedingfield Green *Suffk* ... 64 D2
Bedingfield Street *Suffk* ... 64 D2
Bedlam *N York* ... 90 D6
Bedlam Lane *Kent* ... 18 B6
Bedlington *Nthumb* ... 114 D4
Bedlinog *Myr Td* ... 36 B4
Bedminster *Bristl* ... 37 G1
Bedminster Down *Bristl* ... 37 G1
Bedmond *Herts* ... 50 B1
Bednall *Staffs* ... 70 D2
Bedrule *Border* ... 122 C1
Bedstone *Shrops* ... 56 D3
Bedwas *Caerph* ... 36 C3
Bedwellty *Caerph* ... 36 C4
Bedworth *Warwks* ... 59 F4
Bedworth Woodlands *Warwks* ... 59 F4
Beeby *Leics* ... 60 C6
Beech *Hants* ... 27 E3
Beech *Staffs* ... 70 C4
Beech Hill *Berks* ... 27 E6
Beechingstoke *Wilts* ... 25 F5
Beedon *Berks* ... 40 C2
Beedon Hill *Berks* ... 40 C2
Beeford *E R Yk* ... 93 E5
Beeley *Derbys* ... 83 G1
Beelsby *Lincs* ... 86 B5
Beenham *Berks* ... 40 D1
Beenham's Heath *Berks* ... 41 F2
Beeny *Cnwll* ... 5 E5
Beer *Devon* ... 10 C3
Beer *Somset* ... 23 G2
Beer Hackett *Dorset* ... 11 F6
Beercrocombe *Somset* ... 23 F1
Beesands *Devon* ... 7 E2
Beesby *Lincs* ... 87 E3
Beeson *Devon* ... 7 E2
Beeston *Beds* ... 50 C6
Beeston *Ches* ... 69 H6
Beeston *Norfk* ... 76 B2
Beeston *Notts* ... 72 C4
Beeston *N York* ... 90 D3
Beeston Regis *Norfk* ... 77 E4
Beeswing *D & G* ... 110 C2
Beetham *Cumb* ... 95 F3
Beetham *Somset* ... 10 C6
Beetley *Norfk* ... 76 C2
Began *Cardif* ... 36 C3
Begbroke *Oxon* ... 40 C4
Begdale *Cambs* ... 62 D6
Begelly *Pembks* ... 33 E2
Beggar's Bush *Powys* ... 56 C2
Beggarington Hill *W York* ... 90 D2
Beguildy *Powys* ... 56 B3
Beighton *Norfk* ... 65 F6
Beighton *S York* ... 84 B3
Beighton Hill *Derbys* ... 71 H5
Bein Inn *P & K* ... 140 B1
Beith *N Ayrs* ... 119 E5
Bekesbourne *Kent* ... 31 E2
Bekesbourne Hill *Kent* ... 31 E2
Belaugh *Norfk* ... 77 F2
Belbroughton *Worcs* ... 58 B3
Belchalwell *Dorset* ... 12 B6
Belchalwell Street *Dorset* ... 12 B6
Belchamp Otten *Essex* ... 52 B5
Belchamp St Paul *Essex* ... 52 B5
Belchamp Walter *Essex* ... 52 B5
Belchford *Lincs* ... 86 C2
Belgrave *Leics* ... 60 B6
Belhaven *E Loth* ... 133 E1
Belhelvie *Abers* ... 149 G6
Belhinnie *Abers* ... 157 G2
Bell Bar *Herts* ... 50 C1
Bell Busk *N York* ... 89 G5
Bell End *Worcs* ... 58 B3
Bell Heath *Worcs* ... 58 B3

Bell Hill *Hants* ... 27 F2
Bell o' th' Hill *Ches* ... 69 G5
Bellabeg *Abers* ... 148 A6
Bellamore *Herefs* ... 45 G3
Bellanoch *Ag & B* ... 127 G4
Bellasize *E R Yk* ... 92 B2
Bellaty *Angus* ... 140 B6
Belle Vue *Cumb* ... 103 H6
Belle Vue *W York* ... 91 E1
Belleau *Lincs* ... 86 D2
Bellerby *N York* ... 96 D4
Bellever *Devon* ... 8 C2
Bellfield *S Lans* ... 120 C3
Bellfield *S Lans* ... 120 D1
Bellingdon *Bucks* ... 41 H5
Bellingham *Nthumb* ... 113 G3
Belloch *Ag & B* ... 117 F4
Bellochantuy *Ag & B* ... 117 F4
Bellows Cross *Dorset* ... 13 E6
Bells Cross *Suffk* ... 53 E6
Bells Yew Green *E Susx* ... 17 G5
Bellshill *N Lans* ... 120 B5
Bellshill *Nthumb* ... 124 D4
Bellside *N Lans* ... 120 C5
Bellsquarry *W Loth* ... 131 G2
Belluton *Somset* ... 24 B6
Belmesthorpe *Rutlnd* ... 73 H1
Belmont *Gt Lon* ... 28 C2
Belmont *Lancs* ... 89 E1
Belmont *S Ayrs* ... 119 E1
Belmont *Shet* ... 169 j5
Belnacraig *Abers* ... 148 A6
Belowda *Cnwll* ... 4 C2
Belper *Derbys* ... 72 A5
Belper Lane End *Derbys* ... 72 A5
Belph *Derbys* ... 84 C2
Belsay *Nthumb* ... 114 C3
Belses *Border* ... 122 C2
Belsford *Devon* ... 7 E3
Belsize *Herts* ... 28 A6
Belstead *Suffk* ... 53 E5
Belston *Devon* ... 8 C4
Belstone *Devon* ... 8 C4
Belthorn *Lancs* ... 89 F2
Beltinge *Kent* ... 31 E3
Beltingham *Nthumb* ... 113 E1
Beltoft *Lincs* ... 85 F5
Belton *Leics* ... 72 B2
Belton *Lincs* ... 85 E5
Belton *Lincs* ... 73 G4
Belton *Norfk* ... 65 G6
Belton *Rutlnd* ... 60 D5
Beltring *Kent* ... 17 G6
Belvedere *Gt Lon* ... 29 F4
Belvoir *Leics* ... 73 F3
Belvoir Castle *Leics* ... 73 F3
Bembridge *IOW* ... 15 E2
Bemersley Green *Staffs* ... 70 D5
Bemerton *Wilts* ... 25 G2
Bempton *E R Yk* ... 99 G2
Ben Rhydding *W York* ... 90 C4
Benacre *Suffk* ... 65 G4
Benbuie *D & G* ... 110 B4
Benderloch *Ag & B* ... 136 D4
Benenden *Kent* ... 18 B5
Benfieldside *Dur* ... 105 G5
Bengates *Norfk* ... 77 F3
Bengeworth *Worcs* ... 47 F3
Benhall Green *Suffk* ... 65 F1
Benhall Street *Suffk* ... 65 F1
Benholm *Abers* ... 149 F1
Beningbrough *N York* ... 91 F5
Benington *Herts* ... 50 D3
Benington *Lincs* ... 74 D5
Benington Sea End *Lincs* ... 74 D5
Benllech *IOA* ... 79 E3
Benmore *Ag & B* ... 128 C4
Bennacott *Cnwll* ... 5 F5
Bennan *N Ayrs* ... 118 B1
Bennet Head *Cumb* ... 104 A2
Bennetland *E R Yk* ... 92 B3
Bennett End *Bucks* ... 41 F4
Benniworth *Lincs* ... 86 B3
Benover *Kent* ... 29 H1
Benson *Oxon* ... 40 D3
Bentfield Green *Essex* ... 51 F3
Benthall *Shrops* ... 57 G6
Bentham *Gloucs* ... 38 D6
Benthoul *Aber C* ... 149 F5
Bentlawn *Shrops* ... 56 D5
Bentley *Hants* ... 27 F4
Bentley *S York* ... 84 C5
Bentley *Suffk* ... 53 E4
Bentley *Warwks* ... 59 F5
Bentley Heath *Herts* ... 28 C6
Bentley Heath *W Mids* ... 59 E3
Benton *Devon* ... 21 G4
Bentpath *D & G* ... 111 G4
Bentwichen *Devon* ... 21 G4
Bentworth *Hants* ... 27 E3
Benvie *Angus* ... 140 C3
Benville *Dorset* ... 11 F5
Benwick *Cambs* ... 62 C4
Beoley *Worcs* ... 58 D2
Beoraidbeg *Highld* ... 143 F3
Bepton *W Susx* ... 15 G5
Berden *Essex* ... 51 E4
Bere Alston *Devon* ... 6 B4
Bere Ferrers *Devon* ... 6 B4
Bere Regis *Dorset* ... 12 B4
Berea *Pembks* ... 32 B5
Berepper *Cnwll* ... 2 D2
Bergh Apton *Norfk* ... 65 E5
Berhill *Somset* ... 23 G3
Berinsfield *Oxon* ... 40 D4
Berkeley *Gloucs* ... 38 B4
Berkeley Heath *Gloucs* ... 38 B4
Berkeley Road *Gloucs* ... 38 B4
Berkhamsted *Herts* ... 41 H5
Berkley *Somset* ... 24 D4
Berkswell *W Mids* ... 59 E3
Bermondsey *Gt Lon* ... 28 D4
Bernera *Highld* ... 143 G6
Bernice *Ag & B* ... 128 C4
Bernisdale *Highld* ... 150 D4
Berrick Prior *Oxon* ... 40 D4
Berrick Salome *Oxon* ... 40 D4

Berriedale *Highld* ... 163 H6
Berrier *Cumb* ... 103 H3
Berriew *Powys* ... 56 B5
Berrington *Nthumb* ... 123 G4
Berrington *Shrops* ... 57 E6
Berrington *Worcs* ... 57 F2
Berrington Green *Worcs* ... 57 F2
Berrow *Somset* ... 23 F4
Berrow *Worcs* ... 46 C3
Berrow Green *Worcs* ... 46 C5
Berry Brow *W York* ... 83 F6
Berry Cross *Devon* ... 21 E2
Berry Down Cross *Devon* ... 21 F5
Berry Hill *Gloucs* ... 37 G5
Berry Hill *Pembks* ... 33 E6
Berry Pomeroy *Devon* ... 7 F4
Berry's Green *Gt Lon* ... 29 E2
Berryhillock *Moray* ... 157 G5
Berryhillock *Moray* ... 157 G5
Berrynarbor *Devon* ... 21 F5
Bersham *Wrexhm* ... 69 E5
Berthengam *Flints* ... 80 C3
Berwick *E Susx* ... 17 F2
Berwick Bassett *Wilts* ... 39 F2
Berwick Hill *Nthumb* ... 114 C3
Berwick St James *Wilts* ... 25 F3
Berwick St John *Wilts* ... 25 E1
Berwick St Leonard *Wilts* ... 25 E2
Berwick-upon-Tweed *Nthumb* ... 123 G5
Bescaby *Leics* ... 73 F3
Bescar *Cumb* ... 81 F6
Besford *Shrops* ... 69 H2
Besford *Worcs* ... 47 E4
Besom Hill *Gt Man* ... 83 E5
Bessacarr *S York* ... 84 D5
Bessels Leigh *Oxon* ... 40 C4
Besses o' th' Barn *Gt Man* ... 82 C5
Bessingby *E R Yk* ... 99 G1
Bessingham *Norfk* ... 77 E4
Bestbeech Hill *E Susx* ... 17 G4
Besthorpe *Norfk* ... 64 C5
Besthorpe *Notts* ... 85 F1
Beswick *E R Yk* ... 92 D4
Betchcott *Shrops* ... 57 E5
Betchworth *Surrey* ... 28 C1
Beth Chatto Garden *Essex* ... 52 D3
Bethania *Cerdgn* ... 54 C2
Bethania *Gwynd* ... 67 G4
Bethel *Gwynd* ... 79 E1
Bethel *Gwynd* ... 68 B4
Bethel *IOA* ... 78 D2
Bethel *Powys* ... 68 C2
Bethersden *Kent* ... 18 C5
Bethesda *Gwynd* ... 79 F1
Bethesda *Pembks* ... 33 E3
Bethlehem *Carmth* ... 43 G2
Bethnal Green *Gt Lon* ... 28 D4
Betley *Staffs* ... 70 C5
Betsham *Kent* ... 29 G3
Betteshanger *Kent* ... 31 G1
Bettiscombe *Dorset* ... 10 D5
Bettisfield *Wrexhm* ... 69 G3
Betton *Shrops* ... 70 B4
Betton Strange *Shrops* ... 69 G1
Bettws *Newpt* ... 36 D3
Bettws Bledrws *Cerdgn* ... 43 F4
Bettws Cedewain *Powys* ... 56 B5
Bettws Evan *Cerdgn* ... 42 C4
Bettws-Newydd *Mons* ... 37 E5
Betws *Brdgnd* ... 35 F3
Betws *Carmth* ... 34 D5
Betws Garmon *Gwynd* ... 67 E6
Betws Gwerfil Goch *Denbgs* ... 68 C5
Betws-y-coed *Conwy* ... 67 G6
Betws-yn-Rhos *Conwy* ... 80 A2
Beulah *Cerdgn* ... 42 C4
Beulah *Powys* ... 44 B4
Bevendean *E Susx* ... 16 D2
Bevercotes *Notts* ... 85 E2
Beverley *E R Yk* ... 92 D3
Beverstone *Gloucs* ... 38 C4
Bevington *Gloucs* ... 37 H4
Bewaldeth *Cumb* ... 103 F4
Bewcastle *Cumb* ... 112 C2
Bewdley *Worcs* ... 57 H3
Bewerley *N York* ... 97 E1
Bewholme *E R Yk* ... 93 E5
Bewlbridge *Kent* ... 17 H5
Bexhill *E Susx* ... 18 A2
Bexley *Gt Lon* ... 29 F3
Bexleyheath *Gt Lon* ... 29 F4
Bexleyhill *W Susx* ... 27 G2
Bexon *Kent* ... 30 C3
Bexwell *Norfk* ... 63 E6
Beyton *Suffk* ... 64 B2
Beyton Green *Suffk* ... 64 B2
Bhaltos *W Isls* ... 168 d8
Bhatarsaigh *W Isls* ... 168 a1
Bibstone *Gloucs* ... 38 B3
Bibury *Gloucs* ... 39 F5
Bicester *Oxon* ... 48 D1
Bickenhill *W Mids* ... 59 E4
Bicker *Lincs* ... 74 C4
Bicker Bar *Lincs* ... 74 C4
Bicker Gauntlet *Lincs* ... 74 C4
Bickershaw *Gt Man* ... 82 A5
Bickerstaffe *Lancs* ... 81 G5
Bickerton *Devon* ... 7 E1
Bickerton *N York* ... 91 F5
Bickerton *Nthumb* ... 113 G5
Bickford *Staffs* ... 70 D1
Bickington *Devon* ... 21 E4
Bickington *Devon* ... 7 E5
Bickleigh *Devon* ... 9 F5
Bickleigh *Devon* ... 6 C4
Bickleton *Devon* ... 21 E4
Bickley *Ches* ... 69 G5
Bickley *Gt Lon* ... 29 E3
Bickley *N York* ... 99 F4
Bickley *Worcs* ... 57 F2
Bickley Moss *Ches* ... 69 H5
Bicknacre *Essex* ... 52 B1
Bicknoller *Somset* ... 22 D3
Bicknor *Kent* ... 30 B2
Bickton *Hants* ... 13 E6
Bicton *Herefs* ... 57 E2

Bicton *Shrops* ... 69 G...
Bicton *Shrops* ... 56 C...
Bidborough *Kent* ... 17 F...
Bidden *Hants* ... 27 E...
Biddenden *Kent* ... 18 B...
Biddenden Green *Kent* ... 18 C...
Biddenham *Beds* ... 50 A...
Biddestone *Wilts* ... 38 C...
Biddisham *Somset* ... 23 G...
Biddlesden *Bucks* ... 49 E...
Biddlestone *Nthumb* ... 124 C...
Biddulph *Staffs* ... 70 D...
Biddulph Moor *Staffs* ... 70 D...
Bideford *Devon* ... 21 E...
Bidford-on-Avon *Warwks* ... 47 F...
Bidston *Mersyd* ... 81 E...
Bielby *E R Yk* ... 92 B...
Bieldside *Aber C* ... 149 F...
Bierley *IOW* ... 14 C...
Bierton *Bucks* ... 41 F...
Big Balcraig *D & G* ... 101 E...
Big Carlae *D & G* ... 110 A...
Big Pit Blaenavon *Torfn* ... 36 D...
Big Sand *Highld* ... 160 B...
Bigbury *Devon* ... 6 D...
Bigbury-on-Sea *Devon* ... 6 D...
Bigby *Lincs* ... 86 A...
Biggar *Cumb* ... 94 C...
Biggar *S Lans* ... 121 E...
Biggin *Derbys* ... 71 G...
Biggin *Derbys* ... 71 F...
Biggin *N York* ... 91 F...
Biggin Hill *Gt Lon* ... 29 E...
Biggin Hill Airport *Gt Lon* ... 29 E...
Biggleswade *Beds* ... 50 C...
Bigholms *D & G* ... 111 G...
Bighouse *Highld* ... 166 C...
Bighton *Hants* ... 26 D...
Bigland Hall *Cumb* ... 94 D...
Biglands *Cumb* ... 103 F...
Bignor *W Susx* ... 15 H...
Bigrigg *Cumb* ... 102 D...
Bilborough *Notts* ... 72 C...
Bilbrook *Somset* ... 22 C...
Bilbrook *Staffs* ... 58 B...
Bilbrough *N York* ... 91 F...
Bilbster *Highld* ... 167 F...
Bildershaw *Dur* ... 106 A...
Bildeston *Suffk* ... 52 D...
Billacott *Cnwll* ... 5 F...
Billericay *Essex* ... 29 G...
Billesdon *Leics* ... 60 C...
Billesley *Warwks* ... 47 G...
Billingborough *Lincs* ... 74 B...
Billinge *Mersyd* ... 81 G...
Billingford *Norfk* ... 76 C...
Billingford *Norfk* ... 64 D...
Billingham *Dur* ... 106 D...
Billinghay *Lincs* ... 74 B...
Billingley *S York* ... 84 B...
Billingshurst *W Susx* ... 16 B...
Billingsley *Shrops* ... 57 G...
Billington *Beds* ... 49 G...
Billington *Lancs* ... 89 F...
Billington *Staffs* ... 70 D...
Billockby *Norfk* ... 77 G...
Billy Row *Dur* ... 106 A...
Bilsborrow *Lancs* ... 88 D...
Bilsby *Lincs* ... 87 E...
Bilsham *W Susx* ... 15 H...
Bilsington *Kent* ... 18 D...
Bilsthorpe *Notts* ... 72 D...
Bilsthorpe Moor *Notts* ... 72 D...
Bilston *Mdloth* ... 132 B...
Bilston *W Mids* ... 58 B...
Bilstone *Leics* ... 59 F...
Bilting *Kent* ... 30 D...
Bilton *E R Yk* ... 93 E...
Bilton *N York* ... 91 F...
Bilton *N York* ... 90 D...
Bilton *Nthumb* ... 125 E...
Bilton *Warwks* ... 59 H...
Bilton Banks *Nthumb* ... 125 E...
Binbrook *Lincs* ... 86 B...
Binchester Blocks *Dur* ... 106 B...
Bincombe *Dorset* ... 11 G...
Binegar *Somset* ... 24 B...
Bines Green *W Susx* ... 16 C...
Binfield *Berks* ... 41 F...
Binfield Heath *Oxon* ... 41 F...
Bingfield *Nthumb* ... 113 G...
Bingham *Notts* ... 73 E...
Bingham's Melcombe *Dorset* ... 12 B...
Bingley *W York* ... 90 B...
Bings *Shrops* ... 69 H...
Binham *Norfk* ... 76 C...
Binley *Hants* ... 26 B...
Binley *W Mids* ... 59 G...
Binnegar *Dorset* ... 12 C...
Binniehill *Falk* ... 131 E...
Binns Farm *Moray* ... 157 G...
Binscombe *Surrey* ... 27 H...
Binsey *Oxon* ... 40 C...
Binstead *IOW* ... 14 D...
Binsted *Hants* ... 27 F...
Binsted *W Susx* ... 15 H...
Binton *Warwks* ... 47 G...
Bintree *Norfk* ... 76 C...
Binweston *Shrops* ... 56 C...
Birch *Essex* ... 52 C...
Birch *Gt Man* ... 82 C...
Birch Close *Dorset* ... 12 C...
Birch Cross *Staffs* ... 71 F...
Birch Green *Essex* ... 52 C...
Birch Green *Herts* ... 50 D...
Birch Heath *Ches* ... 69 H...
Birch Hill *Ches* ... 81 G...
Birch Vale *Derbys* ... 83 E...
Birch Wood *Somset* ... 10 C...
Bircham Newton *Norfk* ... 75 H...
Bircham Tofts *Norfk* ... 75 H...
Birchanger *Essex* ... 51 F...
Birchencliffe *W York* ... 90 B...
Bircher *Herefs* ... 57 E...
Birchfield *W Mids* ... 58 D...
Birchgrove *Cardif* ... 36 C...
Birchgrove *E Susx* ... 17 E...

Birchgrove *Swans* 35 E4
Birchington *Kent* 31 F3
Birchley Heath *Warwks* 59 F5
Birchmoor *Warwks* 59 E5
Birchmoor Green *Beds* 49 H3
Birchover *Derbys* 83 G1
Birchwood *Ches* 82 B4
Birchyfield *Herefs* 46 B5
Bircotes *Notts* 84 D4
Bird End *W Mids* 58 C5
Bird Street *Suffk* 52 D6
Birdbrook *Essex* 51 H5
Birdforth *N York* 97 H2
Birdham *W Susx* 15 F4
Birdingbury *Warwks* 59 G2
Birdlip *Gloucs* 38 D6
Birdoswald *Cumb* 112 C1
Birds Edge *W York* 83 G5
Birds Green *Essex* 51 G2
Birdsall *N York* 98 D1
Birdsgreen *Shrops* 57 H4
Birdsmoorgate *Dorset* 10 D5
Birdwell *S York* 84 A5
Birdwood *Gloucs* 46 C1
Birgham *Border* 123 E3
Birichin *Highld* 162 D3
Birkacre *Lancs* 88 D1
Birkby *N York* 97 F5
Birkdale *Mersyd* 88 B1
Birkenbog *Abers* 157 G6
Birkenhead *Mersyd* 81 E3
Birkenhills *Abers* 158 C4
Birkenshaw *W York* 90 C2
Birkhall *Abers* 148 A4
Birkhill *Angus* 140 C3
Birkhill *D & G* 121 F1
Birkholme *Lincs* 73 G2
Birkin *N York* 91 F2
Birks *W York* 90 D2
Birkshaw *Nthumb* 113 E1
Birley *Herefs* 45 G4
Birley Carr *S York* 84 A4
Birling *Kent* 29 H2
Birling *Nthumb* 125 F2
Birling Gap *E Susx* 17 F1
Birlingham *Worcs* 47 E3
Birmingham *W Mids* 58 D4
Birmingham Airport *W Mids* 59 E4
Birnam *P & K* 139 G4
Birness *Abers* 159 F2
Birse *Abers* 148 C4
Birsemore *Abers* 148 C4
Birstall *Leics* 72 D1
Birstall *W York* 90 C2
Birstwith *N York* 90 D6
Birthorpe *Lincs* 74 A3
Birtley *Herefs* 56 D6
Birtley *Nthumb* 113 F3
Birtley *T & W* 114 D1
Birts Street *Worcs* 46 C3
Bisbrooke *Rutlnd* 61 E5
Biscathorpe *Lincs* 86 C3
Biscovey *Cnwll* 3 H5
Bish Mill *Devon* 21 G3
Bisham *Berks* 41 G3
Bishampton *Worcs* 47 E4
Bishop Auckland *Dur* 106 B4
Bishop Burton *E R Yk* 92 D3
Bishop Middleham *Dur* 106 C4
Bishop Monkton *N York* 97 F1
Bishop Norton *Lincs* 85 G4
Bishop Sutton *Somset* 24 A5
Bishop Thornton *N York* 97 F1
Bishop Wilton *E R Yk* 92 B5
Bishop's Castle *Shrops* 56 C4
Bishop's Caundle *Dorset* 11 G6
Bishop's Cleeve *Gloucs* 47 E2
Bishop's Frome *Herefs* 46 B4
Bishop's Green *Essex* 51 G2
Bishop's Green *Hants* 26 C6
Bishop's Itchington *Warwks* 48 B5
Bishop's Norton *Gloucs* 46 D2
Bishop's Nympton *Devon* 21 H3
Bishop's Offley *Staffs* 70 C3
Bishop's Stortford *Herts* 51 F3
Bishop's Sutton *Hants* 26 D2
Bishop's Tachbrook *Warwks* 48 A5
Bishop's Tawton *Devon* 21 F4
Bishop's Waltham *Hants* 14 D5
Bishop's Wood *Staffs* 70 C1
Bishopbridge *Lincs* 85 H4
Bishopbriggs *E Duns* 130 B2
Bishopmill *Moray* 156 D5
Bishops Cannings *Wilts* 25 F6
Bishops Gate *Surrey* 41 H1
Bishops Hull *Somset* 23 E2
Bishops Lydeard *Somset* 23 E2
Bishopsbourne *Kent* 31 E1
Bishopsteignton *Devon* 7 F5
Bishopstoke *Hants* 14 C6
Bishopston *Swans* 34 C3
Bishopstone *Bucks* 41 F5
Bishopstone *E Susx* 17 F1
Bishopstone *Herefs* 45 G3
Bishopstone *Kent* 31 F3
Bishopstone *Wilts* 25 F2
Bishopstone *Wilts* 39 G3
Bishopstrow *Wilts* 24 D4
Bishopswood *Somset* 10 C6
Bishopsworth *Bristl* 37 G1
Bishopthorpe *N York* 91 G4
Bishopton *Dur* 106 C3
Bishopton *Rens* 129 F2
Bishopton *Warwks* 47 G5
Bishton *Newpt* 37 E3
Bishton *Staffs* 71 E2
Bisley *Gloucs* 38 D5
Bisley *Surrey* 27 H5
Bisley Camp *Surrey* 27 G5
Bispham *Lancs* 88 B4
Bispham Green *Lancs* 81 G6
Bissoe *Cnwll* 3 E4
Bisterne *Hants* 13 E5
Bitchet Green *Kent* 29 F1
Bitchfield *Lincs* 73 G3
Bittadon *Devon* 21 F5
Bittaford *Devon* 6 D3
Bittering *Norfk* 76 B2

Bitterley *Shrops* 57 F3
Bitterne *Hants* 14 C5
Bitteswell *Leics* 60 A4
Bitton *Gloucs* 38 B1
Bix *Oxon* 41 E3
Blaby *Leics* 60 B5
Black Bourton *Oxon* 39 G5
Black Callerton *T & W* 114 C2
Black Car *Norfk* 64 C5
Black Corner *W Susx* 16 B5
Black Corries *Highld* 137 G5
Black Crofts *Ag & B* 136 D3
Black Cross *Cnwll* 4 C2
Black Dog *Devon* 9 E6
Black Heddon *Nthumb* 114 B3
Black Lane *Gt Man* 82 C5
Black Lane Ends *Lancs* 89 H4
Black Moor *W York* 90 D4
Black Notley *Essex* 52 A3
Black Pill *Swans* 34 D3
Black Street *Suffk* 65 G4
Black Tar *Pembks* 32 D3
Black Torrington *Devon* 8 B5
Blackadder *Border* 123 F5
Blackawton *Devon* 7 E3
Blackbank *Warwks* 59 F4
Blackbeck *Cumb* 94 A6
Blackborough *Devon* 10 A5
Blackborough End *Norfk* 75 G1
Blackboys *E Susx* 17 F3
Blackbrook *Derbys* 72 A5
Blackbrook *Staffs* 70 C4
Blackbrook *Surrey* 16 C6
Blackburn *Abers* 149 F6
Blackburn *Bl w D* 89 E2
Blackburn *S York* 84 B4
Blackburn *W Loth* 131 F2
Blackcraig *E Ayrs* 109 H6
Blackdog *Abers* 149 G6
Blackdown *Devon* 8 B2
Blackdown *Dorset* 10 D5
Blackdyke *Cumb* 103 E5
Blacker *S York* 84 A6
Blacker Hill *S York* 84 A5
Blackfen *Gt Lon* 29 E3
Blackfield *Hants* 14 C4
Blackford *Cumb* 112 A1
Blackford *P & K* 131 E6
Blackford *Somset* 23 G4
Blackford *Somset* 24 B2
Blackford Bridge *Gt Man* 82 C5
Blackfordby *Leics* 72 A2
Blackgang *IOW* 14 C1
Blackhall *C Edin* 131 H3
Blackhall *Dur* 106 D5
Blackhall Colliery *Dur* 106 D5
Blackhaugh *Border* 122 A3
Blackheath *Essex* 52 D3
Blackheath *Gt Lon* 29 E4
Blackheath *Suffk* 65 G3
Blackheath *W Mids* 58 C4
Blackhill *Abers* 159 F3
Blackhill *Abers* 159 G5
Blackhill *Abers* 159 G3
Blackhill *Dur* 105 G5
Blackhill of Clackriach *Abers* 159 E4
Blackhorse *Devon* 9 G4
Blackhorse Hill *E Susx* 18 A3
Blackjack *Lincs* 74 C4
Blackland *Somset* 22 A3
Blackland *Wilts* 39 E1
Blacklaw *D & G* 111 E6
Blackley *Gt Man* 82 D5
Blacklunans *P & K* 140 B6
Blackmarstone *Herefs* 45 H3
Blackmill *Brdgnd* 35 G3
Blackmoor *Hants* 27 F3
Blackmoor *Somset* 23 G5
Blackmoorfoot *W York* 83 F6
Blackmore *Essex* 51 G1
Blackmore End *Essex* 52 A4
Blackmore End *Herts* 50 C2
Blackness *Falk* 131 G3
Blacknest *Berks* 41 H1
Blacknest *Hants* 27 F3
Blacko *Lancs* 89 G4
Blackpool *Devon* 7 F2
Blackpool *Devon* 7 E5
Blackpool *Lancs* 88 B3
Blackpool Airport *Lancs* 88 B3
Blackpool Gate *Cumb* 112 C2
Blackridge *W Loth* 131 E2
Blackrock *Cnwll* 2 D3
Blackrock *Mons* 36 C5
Blackrock *Mons* 37 F3
Blackrod *Gt Man* 82 A6
Blacksboat *Moray* 156 D3
Blackshaw *D & G* 111 E1
Blackshaw Head *W York* 89 H2
Blacksmith's Green *Suffk* 64 D2
Blacksnape *Lancs* 89 E2
Blackstone *W Susx* 16 C3
Blackthorn *Oxon* 48 D1
Blackthorpe *Suffk* 64 B2
Blacktoft *E R Yk* 92 B2
Blacktop *Aber C* 149 F5
Blackwall *Derbys* 71 G5
Blackwater *Cnwll* 3 E4
Blackwater *Hants* 27 G2
Blackwater *IOW* 14 C2
Blackwater *Somset* 10 C6
Blackwaterfoot *N Ayrs* 117 H3
Blackwell *Cumb* 103 H5
Blackwell *Derbys* 83 F2
Blackwell *Derbys* 72 B6
Blackwell *Warwks* 47 H5
Blackwell *Worcs* 58 C3
Blackwellsend Green *Gloucs* 46 C2
Blackwood *Caerph* 36 C4
Blackwood *D & G* 110 D3
Blackwood *S Lans* 120 B4
Blackwood Hill *Staffs* 70 D6
Blacon *Ches* 81 F1
Bladbean *Kent* 19 E6

Bladnoch *D & G* 101 E6
Bladon *Oxon* 40 C6
Bladon *Somset* 23 G1
Blaen Dyryn *Powys* 44 B3
Blaen-y-Coed *Carmth* 33 H4
Blaen-y-cwm *Blae G* 36 B5
Blaen-y-cwm *Rhondd* 35 G4
Blaenannerch *Cerdgn* 42 C4
Blaenau Ffestiniog *Gwynd* 67 G5
Blaenavon *Torfn* 36 D5
Blaenffos *Pembks* 42 B3
Blaengarw *Brdgnd* 35 F3
Blaengeuffordd *Cerdgn* 54 D3
Blaengwrach *Neath* 35 F5
Blaengwynfi *Neath* 35 F4
Blaenllechau *Rhondd* 35 G4
Blaenpennal *Cerdgn* 54 D2
Blaenplwyf *Cerdgn* 54 C3
Blaenporth *Cerdgn* 42 C4
Blaenrhondda *Rhondd* 35 G4
Blaenwaun *Carmth* 33 H4
Blaenycwm *Cerdgn* 55 F3
Blagdon *Devon* 7 F4
Blagdon *Somset* 23 E1
Blagdon *Somset* 23 H5
Blagdon Hill *Somset* 23 E1
Blagill *Cumb* 104 D5
Blaguegate *Lancs* 81 G5
Blaich *Highld* 144 C2
Blain *Highld* 143 F1
Blaina *Blae G* 36 C5
Blair Atholl *P & K* 146 D1
Blair Drummond *Stirlg* 130 D5
Blair's Ferry *Ag & B* 128 A2
Blairgowrie *P & K* 140 B4
Blairingone *P & K* 131 F5
Blairlogie *Stirlg* 131 E5
Blairmore *Ag & B* 128 C3
Blairmore *Highld* 164 C5
Blairnamarrow *Moray* 147 G6
Blaisdon *Gloucs* 38 B6
Blake End *Essex* 51 H3
Blakebrook *Worcs* 58 A3
Blakedown *Worcs* 58 B3
Blakeley Lane *Staffs* 71 E5
Blakemere *Ches* 81 H2
Blakemere *Herefs* 45 F3
Blakemore *Devon* 7 E4
Blakeney *Gloucs* 38 B5
Blakeney *Norfk* 76 C4
Blakenhall *Ches* 70 B5
Blakenhall *W Mids* 58 B5
Blakeshall *Worcs* 58 A3
Blakesley *Nhants* 48 D4
Blanchland *Nthumb* 105 F5
Bland Hill *N York* 90 C5
Blandford Camp *Dorset* 12 C5
Blandford Forum *Dorset* 12 C5
Blandford St Mary *Dorset* 12 C5
Blanefield *Stirlg* 129 G3
Blankney *Lincs* 74 A6
Blantyre *S Lans* 120 A5
Blar a' Chaorainn *Highld* 144 C1
Blargie *Highld* 146 A4
Blarmachfoldach *Highld* 144 C1
Blashford *Hants* 13 E5
Blaston *Leics* 60 D5
Blatherwycke *Nhants* 61 F5
Blawith *Cumb* 94 D4
Blawquhairn *D & G* 109 H3
Blaxhall *Suffk* 65 F1
Blaxton *S York* 84 D5
Blaydon *T & W* 114 C2
Bleadney *Somset* 23 H4
Bleadon *Somset* 23 F5
Bleak Street *Somset* 24 C2
Blean *Kent* 31 E2
Bleasby *Lincs* 86 B3
Bleasby *Notts* 73 E5
Bleasdale *Lancs* 88 D4
Bleatarn *Cumb* 104 D1
Bleathwood *Herefs* 57 F2
Blebocraigs *Fife* 140 D1
Bleddfa *Powys* 56 B2
Bledington *Gloucs* 47 H1
Bledlow *Bucks* 41 F4
Bledlow Ridge *Bucks* 41 F4
Bleet *Wilts* 24 D5
Blegbie *E Loth* 122 B6
Blencarn *Cumb* 104 C3
Blencogo *Cumb* 103 F5
Blendworth *Hants* 15 E5
Blennerhasset *Cumb* 103 F4
Bletchingdon *Oxon* 40 C6
Bletchingley *Surrey* 28 D1
Bletchley *Bucks* 49 G2
Bletchley *Shrops* 70 A3
Bletherston *Pembks* 33 E4
Bletsoe *Beds* 61 F1
Blewbury *Oxon* 40 D3
Blickling *Norfk* 77 E3
Blidworth *Notts* 72 D6
Blidworth Bottoms *Notts* 72 D5
Blindburn *Nthumb* 113 E6
Blindcrake *Cumb* 103 E4
Blindley Heath *Surrey* 16 D6
Blisland *Cnwll* 5 E3
Bliss Gate *Worcs* 57 H3
Blissford *Hants* 13 F6
Blisworth *Nhants* 49 E4
Blithbury *Staffs* 71 F2
Blitterlees *Cumb* 103 E5
Blo Norton *Norfk* 64 C3
Blockley *Gloucs* 47 G3
Blofield *Norfk* 77 F1
Blore *Staffs* 70 B3
Blore *Staffs* 71 F5
Blounce *Hants* 27 E4
Blount's Green *Staffs* 71 F3
Blowick *Mersyd* 88 B1
Bloxham *Oxon* 48 C3
Bloxholm *Lincs* 74 A5
Bloxwich *W Mids* 58 C6
Bloxworth *Dorset* 12 C4
Blubberhouses *N York* 90 C5
Blue Anchor *Cnwll* 4 C2
Blue Anchor *Somset* 22 C4

Blue Bell Hill *Kent* 30 A2
Blue John Cavern *Derbys* 83 F3
Blundellsands *Mersyd* 81 E5
Blundeston *Suffk* 65 H5
Blunham *Beds* 50 B6
Blunsdon St Andrew *Wilts* 39 F3
Bluntington *Worcs* 58 B3
Bluntisham *Cambs* 62 C3
Blunts *Cnwll* 5 G2
Blunts Green *Warwks* 58 D2
Blurton *Staffs* 70 D4
Blyborough *Lincs* 85 G4
Blyford *Suffk* 65 G3
Blymhill *Staffs* 70 C1
Blymhill Lawn *Staffs* 70 C1
Blyth *Notts* 84 D3
Blyth *Nthumb* 115 E4
Blyth Bridge *Border* 121 F4
Blythburgh *Suffk* 65 G3
Blythe *Border* 122 C4
Blythe *Staffs* 70 D4
Blythe End *Warwks* 59 E4
Blythe Marsh *Staffs* 71 E4
Blyton *Lincs* 85 F4
Bo'ness *Falk* 131 F3
Boar's Head *Gt Man* 81 H6
Boarhills *Fife* 141 F1
Boarhunt *Hants* 14 D4
Boarley *Kent* 30 A2
Boars Hill *Oxon* 40 C4
Boarsgreave *Lancs* 89 G2
Boarshead *E Susx* 17 F5
Boarstall *Bucks* 40 D6
Boasley Cross *Devon* 8 B4
Boat of Garten *Highld* 156 B1
Boath *Highld* 162 C1
Bobbing *Kent* 30 B2
Bobbington *Staffs* 58 A4
Bobbingworth *Essex* 51 F1
Bocaddon *Cnwll* 5 E2
Bochym *Cnwll* 2 D2
Bocking *Essex* 52 A3
Bocking Churchstreet *Essex* 52 A3
Bockleton *Worcs* 46 B5
Boconnoc *Cnwll* 5 E2
Boddam *Abers* 159 G3
Boddam *Shet* 169 h1
Boddington *Gloucs* 46 D2
Bodedern *IOA* 78 C3
Bodelwyddan *Denbgs* 80 B2
Bodenham *Herefs* 45 H4
Bodenham *Wilts* 25 G2
Bodenham Moor *Herefs* 46 A4
Bodewryd *IOA* 78 D4
Bodfari *Denbgs* 80 C2
Bodffordd *IOA* 78 D2
Bodfuan *Gwynd* 66 C4
Bodham *Norfk* 76 D4
Bodiam *E Susx* 18 A4
Bodiam Castle *E Susx* 18 B4
Bodicote *Oxon* 48 C3
Bodieve *Cnwll* 4 D3
Bodinnick *Cnwll* 5 E1
Bodle Street Green *E Susx* 17 G3
Bodmin *Cnwll* 4 D2
Bodmin Moor *Cnwll* 4 D3
Bodney *Norfk* 63 G5
Bodorgan *IOA* 78 C1
Bodrean *Cnwll* 3 F5
Bodsham Green *Kent* 19 E6
Bodwen *Cnwll* 4 D2
Bodymoor Heath *Warwks* 59 E5
Bogallan *Highld* 155 E4
Bogbrae *Abers* 159 F3
Boghall *Mdloth* 132 A2
Boghall *W Loth* 131 F2
Boghead *S Lans* 120 B4
Boghead Farm *Moray* 157 F5
Bogmoor *Moray* 157 F5
Bogmuir *Abers* 148 D1
Bogniebrae *Abers* 158 B4
Bognor Regis *W Susx* 15 G3
Bogroy *Highld* 155 G1
Bogue *D & G* 110 A3
Bohetherick *Devon* 5 H3
Bohortha *Cnwll* 3 F3
Bohuntine *Highld* 145 E3
Bojewyan *Cnwll* 2 B3
Bokiddick *Cnwll* 4 D2
Bolam *Dur* 106 A3
Bolam *Nthumb* 114 C4
Bolberry *Devon* 6 D1
Bold Heath *Mersyd* 81 G4
Boldmere *W Mids* 58 D5
Boldon Colliery *T & W* 115 E2
Boldre *Hants* 13 G4
Boldron *Dur* 105 G1
Bole *Notts* 85 E3
Bole Hill *Derbys* 84 A2
Bolehill *Derbys* 71 H6
Bolenowe *Cnwll* 2 D4
Bolham *Devon* 9 F6
Bolham Water *Devon* 10 B6
Bolingey *Cnwll* 3 E5
Bollington *Ches* 82 D2
Bollington Cross *Ches* 82 D2
Bollow *Gloucs* 38 B6
Bolney *W Susx* 16 C4
Bolnhurst *Beds* 61 F2
Bolshan *Angus* 141 F5
Bolsover *Derbys* 84 B2
Bolsterstone *S York* 83 H4
Boltby *N York* 97 H3
Bolter End *Bucks* 41 F3
Bolton *Cumb* 104 C2
Bolton *E Loth* 132 D2
Bolton *E R Yk* 92 B5
Bolton *Gt Man* 82 B6
Bolton Abbey *N York* 90 B5
Bolton Bridge *N York* 90 B5
Bolton by Bowland *Lancs* 89 F4
Bolton Hall *N York* 96 D4
Bolton le Sands *Lancs* 95 E2
Bolton Low Houses *Cumb* 103 F4
Bolton New Houses *Cumb* 103 F4

Bolton Percy *N York* 91 F4
Bolton Town End *Lancs* 95 E1
Bolton Upon Dearne *S York* 84 B5
Bolton-on-Swale *N York* 97 F5
Boltonfellend *Cumb* 112 B2
Boltongate *Cumb* 103 F4
Bolventor *Cnwll* 5 E4
Bomarsund *Nthumb* 114 D4
Bomere Heath *Shrops* 69 G2
Bonar Bridge *Highld* 162 C3
Bonawe *Ag & B* 137 E3
Bonby *Lincs* 92 D1
Boncath *Pembks* 42 B3
Bonchester Bridge *Border* 112 C6
Bonchurch *IOW* 14 D1
Bondleigh *Devon* 8 C5
Bonds *Lancs* 88 C4
Bone *Cnwll* 2 B3
Bonehill *Devon* 8 D2
Bonehill *Staffs* 59 E6
Boney Hay *Staffs* 71 E1
Bonhill *W Duns* 129 E3
Boningale *Shrops* 58 A6
Bonjedward *Border* 122 D2
Bonkle *N Lans* 120 C5
Bonnington *Angus* 141 F4
Bonnington *Kent* 18 D5
Bonnybank *Fife* 132 C5
Bonnybridge *Falk* 130 D3
Bonnykelly *Abers* 158 D4
Bonnyrigg *Mdloth* 132 B2
Bonnyton *Angus* 140 C4
Bonsall *Derbys* 71 H6
Bonshaw Tower *D & G* 111 G2
Bont *Mons* 45 G1
Bont-Dolgadfan *Powys* 55 F5
Bontddu *Gwynd* 67 F2
Bontnewydd *Cerdgn* 54 D2
Bontnewydd *Gwynd* 66 D6
Bontuchel *Denbgs* 68 C6
Bonvilston *V Glam* 36 B2
Bonwm *Denbgs* 68 C4
Bonymaen *Swans* 34 D4
Boode *Devon* 21 E4
Boohay *Devon* 7 F3
Booker *Bucks* 41 F3
Booley *Shrops* 69 H3
Boon *Border* 122 C4
Boon Hill *Staffs* 70 C5
Boorley Green *Hants* 14 C5
Boosbeck *N York* 107 F2
Boose's Green *Essex* 52 B4
Boot *Cnwll* 5 F6
Boot *Cumb* 94 C5
Boot Street *Suffk* 53 F6
Booth *E R Yk* 92 A2
Booth *W York* 90 B2
Booth Town *W York* 90 B2
Boothby Graffoe *Lincs* 73 G6
Boothby Pagnell *Lincs* 73 G3
Boothstown *Gt Man* 82 B5
Boothville *Nhants* 60 D2
Bootle *Cumb* 94 B4
Bootle *Mersyd* 81 F4
Boots Green *Ches* 82 C2
Booze *N York* 96 C5
Boraston *Shrops* 57 F2
Bordeaux *Guern* 174 h3
Borden *Kent* 30 B2
Borden *W Susx* 27 F2
Border *Cumb* 103 F5
Bordley *N York* 96 C1
Bordon *Hants* 27 F3
Bordon Camp *Hants* 27 F3
Boreham *Essex* 52 A2
Boreham *Wilts* 24 D4
Boreham Street *E Susx* 17 G2
Borehamwood *Herts* 28 C6
Boreland *D & G* 111 F4
Boreraig *Highld* 150 B4
Boreston *Devon* 7 E3
Boreton *Ches* 57 E6
Borgh *W Isls* 168 e9
Borgh *W Isls* 168 a2
Borgie *Highld* 165 H4
Borgue *D & G* 101 G5
Borgue *Highld* 167 E1
Borley *Essex* 52 B5
Borley Green *Essex* 52 B5
Borley Green *Suffk* 64 B1
Borneskitaig *Highld* 150 D6
Borness *D & G* 101 G5
Borough Green *Kent* 29 G2
Boroughbridge *N York* 97 G1
Borras Head *Wrexhm* 69 F5
Borrowash *Derbys* 72 B3
Borrowby *N York* 107 G2
Borrowby *N York* 97 G4
Borrowdale *Cumb* 103 F1
Borrowstoun *Falk* 131 F3
Borstal *Kent* 29 H3
Borth *Cerdgn* 54 C4
Borth-y-Gest *Gwynd* 67 E4
Borthwickbrae *Border* 112 A6
Borthwickshiels *Border* 122 B1
Borve *Highld* 151 E3
Borve *W Isls* 168 e9
Borve *W Isls* 168 a2
Borve *W Isls* 168 c6
Borwick *Lancs* 95 F2
Borwick Lodge *Cumb* 94 C3
Borwick Rails *Cumb* 94 C3
Bosavern *Cnwll* 2 A3
Bosbury *Herefs* 46 C4
Boscarne *Cnwll* 4 D3
Boscastle *Cnwll* 5 E5
Boscombe *Dorset* 13 E4
Boscombe *Wilts* 25 G3
Boscoppa *Cnwll* 3 H5
Bosham *W Susx* 15 F4
Bosham Hoe *W Susx* 15 F4
Bosherston *Pembks* 32 D1
Boskednan *Cnwll* 2 B3
Boskenna *Cnwll* 2 B2
Bosley *Ches* 82 D1

Place	County	Page	Grid
Bosoughan	Cnwll	4	B2
Bossall	N York	92	A6
Bossiney	Cnwll	4	D5
Bossingham	Kent	31	E1
Bossington	Somset	22	B4
Bostock Green	Ches	82	B2
Boston	Lincs	74	D4
Boston Spa	W York	91	E4
Boswarthan	Cnwll	2	B3
Boswinger	Cnwll	3	G4
Botallack	Cnwll	2	A3
Botanic Gardens	C Glas	141	E1
Botany Bay	Gt Lon	28	D6
Botcheston	Leics	59	H6
Botesdale	Suffk	64	C3
Bothal	Nthumb	114	D4
Bothampstead	Berks	40	C2
Bothamsall	Notts	84	D2
Bothel	Cumb	103	F4
Bothenhampton	Dorset	11	E4
Bothwell	S Lans	120	B5
Botley	Bucks	41	H4
Botley	Hants	14	C5
Botley	Oxon	40	C5
Botolph Claydon	Bucks	49	E2
Botolph's Bridge	Kent	19	E5
Botolphs	W Susx	16	C2
Bottesford	Leics	73	F4
Bottesford	Lincs	85	F5
Bottisham	Cambs	63	E1
Bottom o' th' Moor	Gt Man	82	B6
Bottom of Hutton	Lancs	88	C2
Bottomcraig	Fife	140	D2
Bottoms	Cnwll	2	A2
Bottoms	W York	89	H2
Botts Green	Warwks	59	E5
Botusfleming	Cnwll	5	H2
Botwnnog	Gwynd	66	B3
Bough Beech	Kent	17	F6
Boughrood	Powys	44	D3
Boughspring	Gloucs	37	G4
Boughton	Cambs	62	A2
Boughton	Nhants	60	D2
Boughton	Norfk	63	F6
Boughton	Notts	84	D1
Boughton Aluph	Kent	18	D6
Boughton End	Beds	49	H3
Boughton Green	Kent	30	A1
Boughton Malherbe	Kent	30	B1
Boughton Monchelsea	Kent	30	A1
Boughton Street	Kent	30	D2
Boulby	N York	107	G3
Boulder Clough	W York	90	B2
Bouldnor	IOW	14	B2
Bouldon	Shrops	57	F4
Boulge	Suffk	53	F6
Boulmer	Nthumb	125	F2
Boulston	Pembks	32	D3
Boultham	Lincs	85	G2
Bourn	Cambs	62	C1
Bourne	Lincs	74	A2
Bourne End	Beds	49	H4
Bourne End	Beds	61	F1
Bourne End	Bucks	41	G3
Bourne End	Herts	50	A1
Bournebridge	Essex	29	F5
Bournebrook	W Mids	58	C4
Bournemouth	Dorset	13	E4
Bournemouth Airport	Dorset	13	E4
Bournes Green	Essex	30	C5
Bournes Green	Gloucs	38	D5
Bournheath	Worcs	58	B3
Bournstream	Gloucs	38	B4
Bournville	W Mids	58	C3
Bourton	Dorset	24	C2
Bourton	Oxon	39	G3
Bourton	Shrops	57	F5
Bourton	Somset	23	G6
Bourton	Wilts	25	F6
Bourton on Dunsmore	Warwks	59	G2
Bourton-on-the-Hill	Gloucs	47	G2
Bourton-on-the-Water	Gloucs	47	G1
Bousd	Ag & B	134	D6
Boustead Hill	Cumb	103	G6
Bouth	Cumb	94	D3
Bouthwaite	N York	96	D2
Bouts	Worcs	47	F5
Bovain	Stirlg	138	C3
Boveney	Berks	41	G2
Boveridge	Dorset	12	D6
Bovey Tracey	Devon	9	E2
Bovingdon	Herts	50	A1
Bovingdon Green	Bucks	41	F3
Bovinger	Essex	51	F1
Bovington	Dorset	12	B3
Bovington Camp	Dorset	12	B3
Bovington Tank Museum	Dorset	12	B3
Bow	Cumb	103	G6
Bow	Devon	8	D5
Bow	Devon	7	E3
Bow	Gt Lon	29	E4
Bow	Ork	169	b2
Bow Brickhill	Bucks	49	G3
Bow Lee	Gt Man	82	C5
Bow of Fife	Fife	140	C1
Bow Street	Cerdgn	54	D4
Bow Street	Norfk	64	C5
Bowbank	Dur	105	F2
Bowbridge	Gloucs	38	C5
Bowburn	Dur	106	B5
Bowcombe	IOW	14	C2
Bowd	Devon	10	B4
Bowden	Border	122	C2
Bowden	Devon	7	F2
Bowden Hill	Wilts	25	E6
Bowdon	Gt Man	82	C3
Bower	Highld	167	F5
Bower Ashton	Bristl	37	G1
Bower Hinton	Somset	23	G1
Bower House Tye	Suffk	52	C5
Bower's Row	W York	91	E2
Bowerchalke	Wilts	25	F1
Bowerhill	Wilts	25	E5
Bowermadden	Highld	167	F5
Bowers	Staffs	70	C4
Bowers Gifford	Essex	30	A5
Bowershall	Fife	131	G4
Bowes	Dur	105	G1
Bowgreave	Lancs	88	C4
Bowhouse	D & G	111	E1
Bowithick	Cnwll	5	E4
Bowker's Green	Lancs	81	F5
Bowland	Border	122	B3
Bowland Bridge	Cumb	95	E4
Bowley	Herefs	46	A4
Bowley Town	Herefs	46	A4
Bowlhead Green	Surrey	27	G3
Bowling	W Duns	129	F2
Bowling	W York	90	C3
Bowling Bank	Wrexhm	69	F5
Bowling Green	Worcs	46	D4
Bowmanstead	Cumb	94	D4
Bowmore	Ag & B	126	B1
Bowness-on-Solway	Cumb	111	G1
Bowness-on-Windermere	Cumb	95	E5
Bowriefauld	Angus	141	E5
Bowscale	Cumb	103	G3
Bowsden	Nthumb	123	G4
Bowston	Cumb	95	F4
Bowthorpe	Norfk	77	E1
Box	Gloucs	38	C4
Box	Wilts	38	C1
Box End	Beds	50	A6
Box Hill	Surrey	28	C1
Box's Shop	Cnwll	5	F6
Boxbush	Gloucs	46	B1
Boxbush	Gloucs	38	B6
Boxford	Berks	40	C1
Boxford	Suffk	52	C5
Boxgrove	W Susx	15	G4
Boxley	Kent	30	A2
Boxmoor	Herts	50	A1
Boxted	Essex	52	D4
Boxted	Suffk	52	B6
Boxted Cross	Essex	52	D4
Boxted Heath	Essex	52	D4
Boxwell	Gloucs	38	C3
Boxworth	Cambs	62	C2
Boxworth End	Cambs	62	C2
Boyden End	Suffk	63	F1
Boyden Gate	Kent	31	F3
Boylestone	Derbys	71	G4
Boyndie	Abers	158	B5
Boyndlie	Abers	159	E5
Boynton	E R Yk	99	G2
Boys Hill	Dorset	11	G6
Boysack	Angus	141	F5
Boythorpe	Derbys	84	B2
Boyton	Cnwll	5	G5
Boyton	Suffk	53	G5
Boyton	Wilts	25	E3
Boyton Cross	Essex	51	G2
Boyton End	Suffk	51	H5
Bozeat	Nhants	49	G5
Braaid	IOM	174	I3
Brabling Green	Suffk	65	E2
Brabourne	Kent	19	E6
Brabourne Lees	Kent	18	D5
Brabstermire	Highld	167	G5
Bracadale	Highld	150	D2
Braceborough	Lincs	74	A1
Bracebridge Heath	Lincs	85	G1
Bracebridge Low Fields	Lincs	85	G1
Braceby	Lincs	73	H3
Bracewell	Lancs	89	G4
Brackenfield	Derbys	72	A6
Brackenhirst	N Lans	130	D2
Brackenthwaite	Cumb	103	G5
Brackenthwaite	N York	90	D5
Bracklesham	W Susx	15	F3
Brackletter	Highld	144	D3
Brackley	Nhants	48	D3
Brackley Hatch	Nhants	49	E3
Bracknell	Berks	41	G1
Braco	P & K	131	E6
Bracobrae	Moray	157	G4
Bracon Ash	Norfk	64	D5
Bracora	Highld	143	G3
Bracorina	Highld	143	G3
Bradaford	Devon	5	G5
Bradbourne	Derbys	71	G5
Bradbury	Dur	106	C4
Bradden	Nhants	49	E4
Braddock	Cnwll	5	E2
Bradeley	Staffs	70	D5
Bradenham	Bucks	41	F4
Bradenstoke	Wilts	39	E2
Bradfield	Berks	40	D1
Bradfield	Devon	9	G6
Bradfield	Essex	53	E4
Bradfield	Norfk	77	F3
Bradfield	S York	83	G4
Bradfield Combust	Suffk	64	A1
Bradfield Green	Ches	70	B6
Bradfield Heath	Essex	53	E4
Bradfield St Clare	Suffk	64	B1
Bradfield St George	Suffk	64	B1
Bradford	Cnwll	5	E3
Bradford	Devon	20	D1
Bradford	Nthumb	125	E4
Bradford	Nthumb	114	B3
Bradford	W York	90	C3
Bradford Abbas	Dorset	11	F6
Bradford Leigh	Wilts	24	D5
Bradford Peverell	Dorset	11	G4
Bradford-on-Avon	Wilts	24	D5
Bradford-on-Tone	Somset	23	E1
Bradiford	Devon	21	F4
Brading	IOW	14	D2
Bradley	Ches	81	G2
Bradley	Derbys	71	G5
Bradley	Hants	27	E3
Bradley	Lincs	86	C5
Bradley	N York	96	D3
Bradley	Staffs	70	D2
Bradley	W Mids	58	B5
Bradley	W York	90	C2
Bradley	Worcs	47	E5
Bradley	Wrexhm	69	E5
Bradley Green	Ches	69	G5
Bradley Green	Somset	23	E3
Bradley Green	Warwks	59	F5
Bradley Green	Worcs	47	E5
Bradley in the Moors	Staffs	71	E4
Bradley Stoke	Gloucs	37	G3
Bradmore	Notts	72	C3
Bradney	Somset	23	F3
Bradninch	Devon	21	F4
Bradninch	Devon	9	G5
Bradnop	Staffs	71	E6
Bradnor Green	Herefs	45	F5
Bradpole	Dorset	11	E4
Bradshaw	Gt Man	82	B6
Bradshaw	W York	90	B1
Bradshaw	W York	90	B3
Bradstone	Devon	5	G4
Bradwall Green	Ches	82	C1
Bradwell	Bucks	49	F3
Bradwell	Derbys	83	G3
Bradwell	Devon	21	E5
Bradwell	Essex	52	B3
Bradwell	Norfk	65	G6
Bradwell Waterside	Essex	52	D1
Bradwell-on-Sea	Essex	52	D1
Bradworthy	Devon	20	C2
Brae	Highld	155	E5
Brae	Shet	169	h3
Brae Roy Lodge	Highld	145	F4
Braeface	Falk	130	D3
Braehead	Angus	141	G5
Braehead	D & G	101	E5
Braehead	S Lans	120	D4
Braemar	Abers	147	F4
Braemore	Highld	167	E1
Braemore	Highld	161	F2
Braes of Coul	Angus	140	C5
Braes of Enzie	Moray	157	F5
Braeswick	Ork	169	c3
Braevallich	Ag & B	128	A6
Brafferton	Dur	106	B3
Brafferton	N York	97	G2
Brafield-on-the-Green	Nhants	49	F5
Bragar	W Isls	168	e9
Bragbury End	Herts	50	D3
Braidwood	S Lans	120	C4
Brailsford	Derbys	71	G4
Brailsford Green	Derbys	71	G4
Brain's Green	Gloucs	38	A5
Braintree	Essex	52	A3
Braiseworth	Suffk	64	D2
Braishfield	Hants	26	B2
Braithwaite	Cumb	103	F2
Braithwaite	W York	90	B4
Braithwell	S York	84	C4
Braken Hill	W York	91	E1
Bramber	W Susx	16	C2
Brambridge	Hants	26	C1
Bramcote	Notts	72	C4
Bramcote	Warwks	59	G4
Bramdean	Hants	26	D2
Bramerton	Norfk	65	E6
Bramfield	Herts	50	D2
Bramfield	Suffk	65	F3
Bramford	Suffk	53	E5
Bramhall	Gt Man	82	D3
Bramham	W York	91	E4
Bramhope	W York	90	D4
Bramley	Derbys	84	B3
Bramley	Hants	27	E5
Bramley	S York	84	C4
Bramley	Surrey	16	A6
Bramley	Norfk	90	D3
Bramley Corner	Hants	27	E5
Bramley Green	Hants	27	E5
Bramley Head	N York	90	B5
Bramling	Kent	31	F2
Brampford Speke	Devon	9	F4
Brampton	Cambs	62	A2
Brampton	Cumb	104	B6
Brampton	Cumb	104	C2
Brampton	Lincs	85	F3
Brampton	Norfk	77	E2
Brampton	S York	84	B5
Brampton	Suffk	65	G3
Brampton Abbotts	Herefs	46	B2
Brampton Ash	Nhants	60	D4
Brampton Bryan	Herefs	56	D3
Brampton-en-le-Morthen	S York	84	C3
Bramshall	Staffs	71	E3
Bramshaw	Hants	13	F6
Bramshill	Hants	27	F5
Bramshott	Hants	27	G2
Bramwell	Somset	23	G2
Bran End	Essex	51	G3
Branault	Highld	143	E1
Brancaster	Norfk	75	H4
Brancaster Staithe	Norfk	76	A4
Brancepeth	Dur	106	B5
Branchill	Moray	156	C4
Brand End	Lincs	74	D4
Brand Green	Gloucs	46	C2
Branderburgh	Moray	156	D6
Brandesburton	E R Yk	93	E4
Brandeston	Suffk	65	E1
Brandis Corner	Devon	20	D1
Brandiston	Norfk	76	D2
Brandon	Dur	106	B5
Brandon	Lincs	73	G5
Brandon	Nthumb	124	D3
Brandon	Suffk	63	G4
Brandon	Warwks	59	G3
Brandon Bank	Norfk	63	E4
Brandon Creek	Norfk	63	E5
Brandon Parva	Norfk	64	C6
Brandsby	N York	98	B2
Brandy Wharf	Lincs	85	H4
Brane	Cnwll	2	B3
Branksome	Dorset	12	D4
Branksome Park	Dorset	12	D4
Bransbury	Hants	26	B3
Bransby	Lincs	85	F3
Branscombe	Devon	10	B3
Bransford	Worcs	46	D4
Bransgore	Hants	13	F4
Bransholme	E R Yk	93	E3
Branson's Cross	Worcs	58	D2
Branston	Leics	73	F3
Branston	Lincs	85	H1
Branston	Staffs	71	G2
Branston Booths	Lincs	86	A2
Branstone	IOW	14	D2
Brant Broughton	Lincs	73	G5
Brantham	Suffk	53	E4
Branthwaite	Cumb	103	E3
Branthwaite	Cumb	103	G4
Brantingham	E R Yk	92	C2
Branton	Nthumb	124	D3
Branton	S York	84	D5
Branton Green	N York	91	E6
Branxton	Nthumb	123	F3
Brassey Green	Ches	69	G6
Brassington	Derbys	71	G5
Brasted	Kent	29	F1
Brasted Chart	Kent	29	E1
Brathens	Abers	148	D3
Bratoft	Lincs	87	E1
Brattleby	Lincs	85	G3
Bratton	Shrops	70	A1
Bratton	Somset	22	B4
Bratton	Wilts	25	E4
Bratton Clovelly	Devon	8	B4
Bratton Fleming	Devon	21	G4
Bratton Seymour	Somset	24	B2
Braughing	Herts	51	E3
Braughing Friars	Herts	51	E3
Braunston	Nhants	60	B2
Braunston	Rutlnd	60	D6
Braunstone	Leics	60	B6
Braunton	Devon	21	E4
Brawby	N York	98	C3
Brawdy	Pembks	32	C4
Brawl	Highld	166	B5
Braworth	N York	106	D2
Braybrooke	Nhants	60	D4
Braydon	Wilts	39	E3
Braydon Brook	Wilts	39	E3
Braydon Side	Wilts	39	E3
Brayford	Devon	21	G4
Braystones	Cumb	94	A5
Braythorn	N York	90	D4
Brayton	N York	91	G3
Braywick	Berks	41	G2
Bray Shop	Cnwll	5	G3
Bray's Hill	E Susx	17	G3
Breach	Kent	30	B3
Breach	Kent	19	E6
Breachwood Green	Herts	50	B3
Breaden Heath	Shrops	69	G4
Breadsall	Derbys	72	A4
Breadstone	Gloucs	38	B4
Breadward	Herefs	45	F5
Breage	Cnwll	2	D3
Breakachy	Highld	154	C3
Brealangwell Lodge	Highld	162	B3
Bream	Gloucs	37	G5
Breamore	Hants	25	G1
Brean	Somset	23	F5
Breanais	W Isls	168	c8
Brearley	W York	90	A2
Brearton	N York	90	D6
Breascleit	W Isls	168	d8
Breasclete	W Isls	168	d8
Breaston	Derbys	72	B3
Brechfa	Carmth	43	E2
Brechin	Angus	141	F6
Breckles	Norfk	64	B5
Brecon	Powys	44	C2
Breconside	D & G	110	C4
Bredbury	Gt Man	82	D4
Brede	E Susx	18	B3
Bredenbury	Herefs	46	B5
Bredfield	Suffk	53	F6
Bredgar	Kent	30	B2
Bredhurst	Kent	30	B2
Bredon	Worcs	47	E3
Bredon's Hardwick	Worcs	47	E3
Bredon's Norton	Worcs	47	E3
Bredwardine	Herefs	45	F4
Breedon on the Hill	Leics	72	B2
Breich	W Loth	120	D5
Breightmet	Gt Man	82	B6
Breighton	E R Yk	92	A3
Breinton	Herefs	45	G3
Bremhill	Wilts	38	D1
Bremridge	Devon	21	G3
Brenchley	Kent	17	H6
Brendon	Devon	20	D1
Brendon	Devon	21	H5
Brendon Hill	Somset	22	C3
Brenfield	Ag & B	127	G3
Brenish	W Isls	168	c8
Brent Eleigh	Suffk	52	C5
Brent Knoll	Somset	23	F4
Brent Mill	Devon	6	D3
Brent Pelham	Herts	51	E4
Brentford	Gt Lon	28	C4
Brentingby	Leics	73	E2
Brentwood	Essex	29	G5
Brenzett	Kent	18	D4
Brenzett Green	Kent	18	D4
Brereton	Staffs	71	E2
Brereton Green	Ches	82	C1
Brereton Heath	Ches	82	C1
Brereton Hill	Staffs	71	E1
Bressingham	Norfk	64	C3
Bressingham Common	Norfk	64	C4
Bretby	Derbys	71	H2
Bretford	Warwks	59	G3
Bretforton	Worcs	47	F4
Bretherdale Head	Cumb	95	F5
Bretherton	Lancs	88	C2
Brettabister	Shet	169	j3
Brettenham	Norfk	64	B4
Brettenham	Suffk	52	C6
Bretton	Derbys	83	G2
Bretton	Flints	81	F1
Brewer Street	Surrey	28	D1
Brewers End	Essex	51	F3
Brewood	Staffs	70	D1
Briantspuddle	Dorset	12	B4
Brick End	Essex	51	F3
Brick Houses	S York	83	H3
Brickendon	Herts	50	D1
Bricket Wood	Herts	50	B1
Brickkiln Green	Essex	52	A4
Bricklehampton	Worcs	47	E3
Bride	IOM	174	m5
Bridekirk	Cumb	103	E3
Bridell	Pembks	42	B3
Bridestowe	Devon	8	B3
Brideswell	Abers	158	B3
Bridford	Devon	9	E3
Bridge	Cnwll	2	D4
Bridge	Kent	31	E1
Bridge End	Beds	50	A6
Bridge End	Cumb	103	H5
Bridge End	Cumb	94	C3
Bridge End	Devon	6	D2
Bridge End	Dur	105	G4
Bridge End	Essex	51	G4
Bridge End	Lincs	74	B4
Bridge End	Surrey	28	B2
Bridge Green	Essex	51	E4
Bridge Hewick	N York	97	F2
Bridge of Alford	Abers	148	C6
Bridge of Allan	Stirlg	130	D5
Bridge of Avon	Moray	156	D3
Bridge of Avon	Moray	156	D1
Bridge of Balgie	P & K	138	C2
Bridge of Brewlands	Angus	140	B6
Bridge of Brown	Highld	156	C1
Bridge of Cally	P & K	140	A5
Bridge of Canny	Abers	148	D4
Bridge of Craigisla	Angus	140	C5
Bridge of Dee	D & G	102	A6
Bridge of Don	Aber C	149	G6
Bridge of Dulsie	Highld	155	G3
Bridge of Dye	Abers	148	D2
Bridge of Earn	P & K	140	A2
Bridge of Ericht	P & K	138	C6
Bridge of Feugh	Abers	149	E4
Bridge of Forss	Highld	166	D5
Bridge of Gairn	Abers	148	A4
Bridge of Gaur	P & K	138	B5
Bridge of Marnoch	Abers	158	B4
Bridge of Orchy	Ag & B	137	G4
Bridge of Tilt	P & K	146	D3
Bridge of Tynet	Moray	157	F5
Bridge of Walls	Shet	169	h3
Bridge of Weir	Rens	129	E2
Bridge Reeve	Devon	21	G2
Bridge Sollers	Herefs	45	G3
Bridge Street	Suffk	52	B6
Bridge Trafford	Ches	81	G2
Bridge Yate	Gloucs	38	B1
Bridgefoot	Cumb	103	E3
Bridgehampton	Somset	24	A2
Bridgehill	Dur	105	H5
Bridgehouse Gate	N York	97	E1
Bridgemary	Hants	14	D3
Bridgemere	Ches	70	B5
Bridgend	Abers	157	G3
Bridgend	Ag & B	126	B1
Bridgend	Angus	148	C5
Bridgend	Brdgnd	42	B4
Bridgend	Cerdgn	42	B4
Bridgend	Cumb	103	H1
Bridgend	D & G	111	E6
Bridgend	Devon	6	C2
Bridgend	Fife	140	D1
Bridgend	Moray	157	G4
Bridgend	P & K	140	A2
Bridgend	W Loth	131	G3
Bridgend of Lintrathen	Angus	140	C5
Bridgerule	Devon	5	H1
Bridges	Shrops	56	D5
Bridgetown	Devon	5	G5
Bridgetown	Somset	22	B3
Bridgham	Norfk	64	B4
Bridgnorth	Shrops	57	G5
Bridgtown	Staffs	58	C6
Bridgwater	Somset	23	F3
Bridlington	E R Yk	99	G1
Bridport	Dorset	11	E4
Bridstow	Herefs	46	A2
Brierfield	Lancs	89	G3
Brierley	Gloucs	37	G6
Brierley	Herefs	45	H5
Brierley	W York	84	B6
Brierley Hill	W Mids	58	B4
Brierton	Dur	106	D4
Briery	Cumb	103	G2
Brig o'Turk	Stirlg	129	G6
Brigg	Lincs	85	G5
Briggate	Norfk	77	F3
Briggswath	N York	107	H2
Brigham	Cumb	103	E3
Brigham	Cumb	103	G2
Brigham	E R Yk	93	E5
Brighouse	W York	90	C2
Brighstone	IOW	14	C2
Brightgate	Derbys	71	G6
Brighthampton	Oxon	40	B5
Brightholmlee	Derbys	83	H4
Brightley	Devon	8	C4
Brightling	E Susx	17	H3
Brightlingsea	Essex	52	D2
Brighton	Cnwll	3	F5
Brighton	E Susx	16	D2
Brighton le Sands	Mersyd	81	E4
Brightons	Falk	131	E3
Brightor	Cnwll	5	G2
Brightwalton	Berks	40	C2
Brightwalton Green	Berks	40	C2
Brightwalton Holt	Berks	40	C2
Brightwell	Suffk	53	F5
Brightwell Baldwin	Oxon	41	E4
Brightwell Upperton	Oxon	41	E4
Brightwell-cum-Sotwell	Oxon	40	D3
Brignall	Dur	105	G4
Brigsley	Lincs	86	C6
Brigsteer	Cumb	95	E4
Brigstock	Nhants	61	E4
Brill	Bucks	41	E6
Brill	Cnwll	3	E5
Brilley	Herefs	45	E4
Brimfield	Herefs	57	E2
Brimfield Cross	Herefs	57	E2
Brimington	Derbys	84	B2
Brimley	Devon	9	E2
Brimpsfield	Gloucs	38	D5
Brimpton	Berks	26	D6
Brimscombe	Gloucs	38	C4

Entry	Page	Grid
Brimstage Mersyd	81	E3
Brincliffe S York	84	A3
Brind E R Yk	92	A3
Brindham Somset	23	H5
Brindister Shet	169	h3
Brindle Lancs	88	D2
Brineton Staffs	70	C1
Bringhurst Leics	60	D5
Brington Cambs	61	G3
Briningham Norfk	76	C3
Brinkely Notts	73	E5
Brinkhill Lincs	86	D2
Brinkley Cambs	51	G6
Brinklow Warwks	59	G3
Brinkworth Wilts	39	E3
Brinscall Lancs	89	E2
Brinscombe Somset	23	G4
Brinsea Somset	23	G5
Brinsley Notts	72	B5
Brinsop Herefs	45	G4
Brinsworth S York	84	B4
Brinton Norfk	76	C4
Brinyan Ork	169	b3
Brisco Cumb	104	A5
Brisley Norfk	76	C2
Brislington Bristl	37	G1
Brissenden Green Kent	18	C5
Bristol Bristl	37	G1
Bristol Airport Somset	23	H6
Bristol Zoo Bristl	37	G2
Briston Norfk	76	D3
Brisworthy Devon	6	C4
Britannia Lancs	89	G2
Britford Wilts	25	G2
Brithdir Caerph	36	C4
Brithdir Gwynd	67	G2
British Torfn	36	D5
British Legion Village Kent	29	H2
Briton Ferry Neath	35	E4
Britwell Salome Oxon	41	E3
Brixham Devon	7	G3
Brixton Devon	6	C3
Brixton Gt Lon	28	D4
Brixton Deverill Wilts	24	D3
Brixworth Nhants	60	D2
Brize Norton Oxon	39	H5
Brize Norton Airport Oxon	39	H5
Broad Alley Worcs	58	B2
Broad Blunsdon Wilts	39	F3
Broad Campden Gloucs	47	G3
Broad Carr W York	90	B1
Broad Chalke Wilts	25	F2
Broad Clough Lancs	89	G2
Broad Ford Kent	17	H5
Broad Green Essex	52	B3
Broad Green Worcs	46	C5
Broad Green Worcs	58	C2
Broad Haven Pembks	32	C3
Broad Hill Cambs	63	E3
Broad Hinton Wilts	39	F2
Broad Laying Hants	26	C5
Broad Marston Worcs	47	G4
Broad Meadow Staffs	70	C5
Broad Oak Cumb	94	B4
Broad Oak E Susx	18	B3
Broad Oak E Susx	17	G4
Broad Oak Hants	27	F4
Broad Oak Herefs	45	H1
Broad Oak Kent	31	E2
Broad Oak Mersyd	81	G4
Broad Road Suffk	65	E3
Broad Street E Susx	18	B3
Broad Street Essex	51	F2
Broad Street Kent	30	A3
Broad Street Kent	30	B2
Broad Street Wilts	25	F5
Broad Street Green Essex	52	B2
Broad Town Wilts	39	F2
Broad's Green Essex	51	H2
Broadbottom Gt Man	83	E4
Broadbridge W Susx	15	F4
Broadbridge Heath W Susx	16	B4
Broadclyst Devon	9	G4
Broadfield Inver	129	E2
Broadfield Pembks	33	E2
Broadford Highld	151	F1
Broadford Bridge W Susx	16	B3
Broadgairhill Border	111	F6
Broadgate Lincs	74	D1
Broadgrass Green Suffk	64	B2
Broadhaugh Border	123	F5
Broadheath Gt Man	82	C4
Broadheath Worcs	57	G2
Broadhembury Devon	10	A5
Broadhempston Devon	7	E4
Broadholme Notts	85	F2
Broadland Row E Susx	18	B3
Broadlay Carmth	34	A5
Broadley Essex	51	E1
Broadley Gt Man	89	G1
Broadley Moray	157	F5
Broadley Common Essex	51	E1
Broadmayne Dorset	11	G3
Broadmere Hants	26	D4
Broadmoor Gloucs	37	G6
Broadmoor Pembks	33	E2
Broadnymett Devon	8	D5
Broadoak Dorset	11	E4
Broadoak Gloucs	38	B5
Broadoak Wrexhm	69	F6
Broadstairs Kent	31	G3
Broadstone Dorset	12	D4
Broadstone Mons	37	F5
Broadstone Shrops	57	F4
Broadwas Worcs	46	C5
Broadwater Herts	50	C3
Broadwater W Susx	16	B2
Broadwaters Worcs	58	A3
Broadway Carmth	33	G3
Broadway Carmth	34	A5
Broadway Pembks	32	C3
Broadway Somset	10	D6
Broadway Suffk	65	F3
Broadway Worcs	47	F3
Broadwell Gloucs	37	G5
Broadwell Gloucs	47	G2
Broadwell Oxon	39	G5
Broadwell Warwks	59	G2

Broadwey Dorset	11	G3
Broadwindsor Dorset	11	E5
Broadwoodkelly Devon	8	C5
Broadwoodwidger Devon	5	H5
Brobury Herefs	45	F4
Brochel Highld	151	F3
Brock Lancs	88	D4
Brock's Green Hants	26	C5
Brockamin Worcs	46	C5
Brockbridge Hants	14	D5
Brockdish Norfk	65	E3
Brockencote Worcs	58	B3
Brockenhurst Hants	13	G5
Brocketsbrae S Lans	120	C3
Brockford Green Suffk	64	D2
Brockford Street Suffk	64	D2
Brockhall Nhants	60	B2
Brockham Surrey	28	C1
Brockhampton Gloucs	47	E2
Brockhampton Gloucs	47	F1
Brockhampton Hants	15	E4
Brockhampton Herefs	46	B2
Brockhampton Green Dorset	11	G5
Brockholes W York	83	F6
Brockhurst Derbys	84	A1
Brockhurst Warwks	59	G4
Brocklebank Cumb	103	G4
Brocklesby Lincs	86	B6
Brockley Somset	23	G6
Brockley Suffk	63	G2
Brockley Green Suffk	51	H5
Brockley Green Suffk	52	B6
Brockleymoor Cumb	104	B4
Brockmoor W Mids	58	B4
Brockscombe Devon	8	B4
Brockton Shrops	56	C6
Brockton Shrops	57	G6
Brockton Shrops	56	D4
Brockton Shrops	57	F5
Brockton Staffs	70	C3
Brockweir Gloucs	37	F4
Brockwood Park Hants	26	D2
Brockworth Gloucs	38	D6
Brocton Cnwll	4	D3
Brocton Staffs	71	E2
Brodick N Ayrs	118	B3
Brodie Moray	156	B5
Brodsworth S York	84	C5
Brogaig Highld	151	G3
Brogborough Beds	49	H3
Broken Cross Ches	82	B2
Broken Cross Ches	82	D2
Brokenborough Wilts	38	D3
Brokerswood Wilts	24	D4
Bromborough Mersyd	81	F3
Brome Suffk	64	D3
Brome Street Suffk	64	D3
Bromeswell Suffk	53	F6
Bromfield Cumb	103	F5
Bromfield Shrops	57	E3
Bromham Beds	50	A6
Bromham Wilts	25	E6
Bromley Gt Lon	29	E3
Bromley S York	83	H5
Bromley S York	57	G5
Bromley W Mids	58	B4
Bromley Common Gt Lon	29	E3
Bromley Cross Essex	52	D3
Bromlow Shrops	56	C6
Brompton Kent	30	A3
Brompton N York	97	G4
Brompton N York	99	E3
Brompton Shrops	57	F6
Brompton Ralph Somset	22	D2
Brompton Regis Somset	22	B2
Brompton-on-Swale N York	97	E5
Bromsash Herefs	46	B2
Bromsberrow Gloucs	46	C3
Bromsberrow Heath Gloucs	46	C3
Bromsgrove Worcs	58	C2
Bromstead Heath Staffs	70	C2
Bromyard Herefs	46	B5
Bromyard Downs Herefs	46	B5
Bronaber Gwynd	67	G3
Bronant Cerdgn	54	D2
Broncroft Shrops	57	F4
Brongest Cerdgn	42	C4
Bronington Wrexhm	69	G4
Bronllys Powys	44	D3
Bronwydd Carmth	42	D1
Bronydd Powys	45	E4
Bronygarth Shrops	69	E4
Brook Carmth	33	G3
Brook Hants	13	F6
Brook Hants	26	B2
Brook IOW	14	B2
Brook Kent	18	D6
Brook Surrey	27	G3
Brook Surrey	16	B6
Brook End Beds	61	G2
Brook End Beds	50	C5
Brook End Bucks	49	G4
Brook End Cambs	61	G3
Brook Hill Hants	13	F6
Brook House Denbgs	80	C1
Brook Street Essex	29	G3
Brook Street Kent	18	C5
Brook Street Suffk	52	B6
Brook Street W Susx	16	D1
Brooke Norfk	65	G5
Brooke Rutlnd	60	D6
Brookfield Rens	129	F1
Brookhampton Oxon	40	D2
Brookhampton Somset	24	B2
Brookhouse Lancs	95	F1
Brookhouse S York	84	C4
Brookhouse Green Ches	70	C6
Brookhouses Derbys	83	E4
Brookland Kent	18	C4
Brooklands Gt Man	82	C4
Brookmans Park Herts	50	C1
Brooks Powys	56	B5
Brooks End Kent	31	F3
Brooks Green W Susx	16	B4
Brooksby Leics	72	D2
Brookthorpe Gloucs	38	C5
Brookville Norfk	63	F5
Brookwood Surrey	27	H5

Broom Beds	50	C5
Broom Dur	106	B5
Broom S York	84	B4
Broom Warwks	47	F5
Broom Green Norfk	76	C2
Broom Hill Dorset	12	D5
Broom Hill Notts	72	C5
Broom Hill S York	84	B5
Broom Hill Worcs	58	B3
Broom Street Kent	30	D2
Broom's Green Gloucs	46	C2
Broome Norfk	65	F4
Broome Shrops	56	D3
Broome Worcs	58	B3
Broome Park Nthumb	124	D5
Broomedge Ches	82	B5
Broomer's Corner W Susx	16	B3
Broomershill W Susx	16	B3
Broomfield Essex	51	H2
Broomfield Kent	30	B1
Broomfield Kent	31	E3
Broomfield Somset	23	E2
Broomfields Shrops	69	F2
Broomfleet E R Yk	92	C2
Broomhall Surrey	27	H6
Broomhaugh Nthumb	114	B2
Broomhill Nthumb	114	D6
Broomhill Green Ches	70	A5
Broomley Nthumb	114	B1
Broomsthorpe Norfk	76	B3
Brora Highld	163	F4
Broseley Shrops	57	G6
Brotherhouse Bar Lincs	74	C1
Brotherlee Dur	105	F4
Brothertoft Lincs	74	C5
Brotherton N York	91	F2
Brotton N York	107	F3
Broubster Highld	166	D4
Brough Cumb	105	E1
Brough Derbys	83	G3
Brough E R Yk	92	C2
Brough Highld	167	F6
Brough Notts	73	F6
Brough Shet	169	j3
Brough Lodge Shet	169	j5
Brough Sowerby Cumb	105	E1
Broughall Shrops	69	H4
Broughton Border	121	F3
Broughton Bucks	41	G6
Broughton Bucks	49	G3
Broughton Cambs	62	B3
Broughton Flints	81	F1
Broughton Gt Man	82	C5
Broughton Hants	26	A2
Broughton Lancs	88	D3
Broughton Lincs	85	G6
Broughton N York	89	H5
Broughton N York	98	D3
Broughton Nhants	60	D3
Broughton Oxon	48	B3
Broughton Staffs	70	C3
Broughton V Glam	35	G1
Broughton Astley Leics	60	A5
Broughton Beck Cumb	94	D3
Broughton Gifford Wilts	24	D6
Broughton Green Worcs	47	E5
Broughton Hackett Worcs	47	E5
Broughton Mains D & G	101	F5
Broughton Mills Cumb	94	C4
Broughton Moor Cumb	103	E3
Broughton Poggs Oxon	39	G5
Broughton Tower Cumb	94	C4
Broughty Ferry Dund C	141	E3
Brow End Cumb	94	C2
Brow-of-the-Hill Norfk	75	G2
Brown Candover Hants	26	D3
Brown Edge Lancs	88	B1
Brown Edge Staffs	70	D5
Brown Heath Ches	81	G1
Brown Lees Staffs	70	C4
Brown Street Suffk	64	C2
Brown's Green W Mids	58	C4
Brownber Cumb	95	H5
Brownheath Shrops	69	G3
Brownhill Abers	158	D3
Brownhills Fife	141	E1
Brownhills W Mids	58	C6
Brownieside Nthumb	125	E3
Browninghill Green Hants	26	D5
Brownlow Heath Ches	70	C6
Brownrigg Cumb	102	D3
Brownrigg Cumb	103	F5
Browns Hill Gloucs	38	D4
Brownsham Devon	20	C3
Brownsover Warwks	60	A3
Brownston Devon	6	D3
Browston Green Norfk	65	G5
Broxa N York	99	E4
Broxbourne Herts	51	E1
Broxburn E Loth	133	F3
Broxburn W Loth	131	G2
Broxfield Nthumb	125	E3
Broxted Essex	51	G3
Broxton Ches	69	G5
Broxwood Herefs	45	F5
Broyle Side E Susx	17	E3
Bruan Highld	167	G2
Bruar P & K	146	C1
Brucefield Highld	163	F3
Bruchag Ag & B	118	C5
Bruera Ches	69	G6
Bruern Abbey Oxon	47	H1
Bruichladdich Ag & B	126	B1
Bruisyard Suffk	65	F2
Bruisyard Street Suffk	65	F2
Brumby Lincs	85	F6
Brund Staffs	71	F6
Brundall Norfk	65	G5
Brundish Suffk	65	E2
Brundish Street Suffk	65	E2
Brunnion Cnwll	2	C3
Brunslow Shrops	56	D4
Bruntcliffe W York	90	D4
Brunthwaite W York	90	B4
Bruntingthorpe Leics	60	B4
Brunton Fife	140	C2
Brunton Nthumb	125	E3

Brunton Wilts	25	H5
Brushford Somset	22	B2
Brushford Barton Devon	8	D5
Bruton Somset	24	B3
Bryan's Green Worcs	58	B2
Bryanston Dorset	12	C5
Bryant's Bottom Bucks	41	G4
Brydekirk D & G	111	F2
Brympton Somset	11	E6
Bryn Ches	82	A2
Bryn Gt Man	81	H5
Bryn Neath	35	F3
Bryn Powys	56	C4
Bryn Du IOA	78	C2
Bryn Gates Lancs	82	A5
Bryn Golau Rhondd	35	G3
Bryn Saith Marchog Denbgs	68	C5
Bryn-bwbach Gwynd	67	F4
Bryn-coch Neath	35	E4
Bryn-Eden Gwynd	67	G3
Bryn-Henllan Pembks	32	D6
Bryn-mawr Gwynd	66	B3
Bryn-newydd Denbgs	68	D4
Bryn-penarth Powys	56	A6
Bryn-y-bal Flints	81	E1
Bryn-y-Maen Conwy	79	H2
Bryn-yr-Eos Wrexhm	69	E4
Brynaman Carmth	35	E6
Brynberian Pembks	42	A3
Brynbryddan Neath	35	E5
Bryncae Rhondd	35	G2
Bryncethin Brdgnd	35	G3
Bryncir Gwynd	66	D4
Bryncroes Gwynd	66	B3
Bryncrug Gwynd	54	D6
Bryneglwys Denbgs	68	D5
Brynfields Wrexhm	69	E4
Brynford Flints	80	D2
Bryngwran IOA	78	C2
Bryngwyn Mons	37	E5
Bryngwyn Powys	45	E4
Brynhoffnant Cerdgn	42	C4
Brynmawr Blae G	36	C3
Brynmenyn Brdgnd	35	F3
Brynmill Swans	34	D3
Brynna Rhondd	35	G2
Brynrefail Gwynd	79	E1
Brynrefail IOA	78	D3
Brynsadler Rhondd	36	A2
Brynsiencyn IOA	78	D1
Brynteg IOA	78	D3
Bualintur Highld	142	D6
Buarth-draw Flints	80	D3
Bubbenhall Warwks	59	F3
Bubwith E R Yk	92	A3
Buccleuch Border	121	F3
Buchanan Smithy Stirlg	129	F4
Buchanhaven Abers	159	G4
Buchanty P & K	139	G2
Buchany Stirlg	130	C5
Buchlyvie Stirlg	130	B4
Buck's Cross Devon	20	D3
Buck's Mills Devon	20	D3
Buckabank Cumb	103	H5
Buckden Cambs	62	A2
Buckden N York	96	C3
Buckenham Norfk	65	F6
Buckerell Devon	10	B5
Buckfast Devon	7	E4
Buckfastleigh Devon	7	E4
Buckhaven Fife	132	C5
Buckholt Mons	37	F6
Buckhorn Weston Dorset	24	C2
Buckhurst Hill Essex	29	E5
Buckie Moray	157	F6
Buckingham Bucks	49	E3
Buckland Bucks	41	G5
Buckland Devon	6	D2
Buckland Gloucs	47	F3
Buckland Hants	13	G4
Buckland Herts	50	D4
Buckland Kent	19	F6
Buckland Oxon	40	B4
Buckland Surrey	28	C1
Buckland Brewer Devon	20	D3
Buckland Common Bucks	41	G5
Buckland Dinham Somset	24	C4
Buckland Filleigh Devon	8	B5
Buckland in the Moor Devon	7	E5
Buckland Monachorum Devon	6	B4
Buckland Newton Dorset	11	G5
Buckland Ripers Dorset	11	G3
Buckland St Mary Somset	10	C6
Buckland-Tout-Saints Devon	7	E2
Bucklebury Berks	40	D1
Bucklers Hard Hants	14	B4
Bucklesham Suffk	53	F5
Buckley Green Warwks	58	D2
Buckley Mountain Flints	81	E1
Bucklow Hill Ches	82	B3
Buckminster Leics	73	F2
Bucknall Lincs	86	B2
Bucknall Staffs	70	D5
Bucknell Oxon	48	D2
Bucknell Shrops	56	D3
Buckpool Moray	157	F6
Bucks Green W Susx	16	B5
Bucks Hill Herts	28	B6
Bucks Horn Oak Hants	27	F3
Bucksburn Aber	149	G5
Buckshead Cnwll	3	F4
Buckton E R Yk	99	G2
Buckton Herefs	56	D3
Buckton Nthumb	123	H3
Buckworth Cambs	61	G3
Budby Notts	84	D2
Budd's Titson Cnwll	5	F6
Buddileigh Staffs	70	C5
Buddon Angus	141	E3
Bude Cnwll	20	B1
Budge's Shop Cnwll	5	G2
Budlake Devon	9	G5
Budle Nthumb	125	E4
Budleigh Salterton Devon	9	G3
Budlett's Common E Susx	17	F4

Budock Water Cnwll	3	E3
Buerton Ches	70	B4
Bugbrooke Nhants	49	E5
Bugford Devon	7	F3
Buglawton Ches	82	D1
Bugle Cnwll	4	C2
Bugley Dorset	24	C2
Bugthorpe E R Yk	92	B5
Buildwas Shrops	57	F6
Builth Road Powys	44	C4
Builth Wells Powys	44	C4
Bulbourne Herts	41	G6
Bulbridge Wilts	25	F2
Bulby Lincs	73	H3
Buldoo Highld	166	D5
Bulford Wilts	25	G4
Bulford Barracks Wilts	25	G4
Bulkeley Ches	69	G5
Bulkington Warwks	59	G4
Bulkington Wilts	25	E5
Bulkworthy Devon	20	D2
Bull Bay IOA	78	D4
Bull's Green Herts	50	D2
Bull's Green Norfk	65	G5
Bullamore N York	97	G4
Bullbridge Derbys	72	A5
Bullbrook Berks	41	G1
Bullen's Green Herts	50	C1
Bulley Gloucs	46	C1
Bullgill Cumb	103	E4
Bullinghope Herefs	45	H3
Bullington Hants	26	C3
Bullington Lincs	86	A2
Bullington End Bucks	49	F4
Bullockstone Kent	31	E3
Bulmer Essex	52	B5
Bulmer N York	98	C2
Bulmer Tye Essex	52	B5
Bulphan Essex	29	G5
Bulstone Devon	10	B4
Bulstrode Herts	50	A1
Bulstrode Park Bucks	41	H3
Bulverhythe E Susx	18	A2
Bulwark Abers	159	E4
Bulwell Notts	72	C4
Bulwick Nhants	61	F5
Bumble's Green Essex	51	E1
Bunacaimb Highld	143	F3
Bunarkaig Highld	144	D3
Bunbury Ches	69	H6
Bunbury Heath Ches	69	H6
Bunchrew Highld	154	D4
Buncton W Susx	16	B3
Bundalloch Highld	152	C2
Bunessan Ag & B	135	F1
Bungay Suffk	65	F4
Bunker's Hill Lincs	74	C5
Bunnahabhain Ag & B	126	C2
Bunny Notts	72	C3
Buntait Highld	154	B2
Buntingford Herts	50	D4
Bunwell Norfk	64	D5
Bunwell Street Norfk	64	D5
Bupton Derbys	71	G4
Burbage Derbys	83	E2
Burbage Leics	59	G5
Burbage Wilts	25	H5
Burcher Herefs	45	F5
Burchett's Green Berks	41	F2
Burchett's Green E Susx	17	G4
Burcombe Wilts	25	F2
Burcot Oxon	40	D4
Burcot Worcs	58	C2
Burcote Shrops	57	H5
Burcott Bucks	41	G6
Burcott Bucks	49	G1
Burcott Somset	23	H3
Burdale N York	92	C6
Bures Essex	52	C4
Burford Oxon	39	G5
Burford Shrops	57	F2
Burg Ag & B	135	F4
Burgates Hants	27	F2
Burge End Herts	50	B4
Burgess Hill W Susx	16	D3
Burgh Suffk	53	F6
Burgh by Sands Cumb	103	G6
Burgh Castle Norfk	65	G6
Burgh Heath Surrey	28	C2
Burgh le Marsh Lincs	87	E1
Burgh next Aylsham Norfk	77	E2
Burgh on Bain Lincs	86	C3
Burgh St Margaret Norfk	77	G1
Burgh St Peter Norfk	65	G5
Burghclere Hants	26	C5
Burghead Moray	156	C6
Burghfield Berks	41	E1
Burghfield Common Berks	27	E6
Burghill Herefs	45	H4
Burghwallis S York	84	C6
Burham Kent	29	H2
Buriton Hants	15	F6
Burland Ches	70	A5
Burlawn Cnwll	4	D3
Burleigh Gloucs	38	C4
Burlescombe Devon	22	D1
Burleston Dorset	12	B4
Burlestone Devon	7	F2
Burley Hants	13	F5
Burley Rutlnd	73	F1
Burley Shrops	57	E3
Burley Gate Herefs	46	B4
Burley in Wharfedale W York	90	C4
Burley Lawn Hants	13	F5
Burley Street Hants	13	F5
Burley Wood Head W York	90	C4
Burleydam Ches	70	A4
Burlingham Green Norfk	77	G1
Burlingjobb Powys	45	E5
Burlington Shrops	69	G3
Burlton Shrops	69	G3
Burmarsh Kent	19	E5
Burmington Warwks	47	H3
Burn N York	91	G2
Burn Cross S York	84	A4
Burn Naze Lancs	88	B4
Burn of Cambus Stirlg	130	C5

277

Burnage Gt Man 82 D4
Burnaston Derbys 71 H3
Burnbanks Cumb 104 B2
Burnbrae N Lans 120 C5
Burnby E R Yk 92 B4
Burndell W Susx 15 H4
Burnden Gt Man 82 B5
Burnedge Gt Man 82 D6
Burneside Cumb 95 F4
Burneston N York 97 F3
Burnett Somset 24 B6
Burnfoot Border 112 A6
Burnfoot Border 122 B1
Burnfoot D & G 110 D4
Burnfoot D & G 111 H4
Burnfoot D & G 112 A4
Burnfoot P & K 131 F5
Burnham Bucks 41 G2
Burnham Lincs 92 D1
Burnham Deepdale Norfk 76 A4
Burnham Green Herts 50 D2
Burnham Market Norfk 76 A4
Burnham Norton Norfk 76 A4
Burnham Overy Norfk 76 B4
Burnham Overy Staithe Norfk 76 B4
Burnham Thorpe Norfk 76 B4
Burnham-on-Crouch Essex 30 C6
Burnham-on-Sea Somset 23 F4
Burnhaven Abers 159 G3
Burnhead D & G 110 C4
Burnhervie Abers 158 C1
Burnhill Green Staffs 57 H5
Burnhope Dur 106 A6
Burnhouse N Ayrs 119 F4
Burniston N York 99 F4
Burnley Lancs 89 G3
Burnmoor Dur 106 B6
Burnmouth Border 123 H4
Burnopfield Dur 114 C1
Burnrigg Cumb 104 B6
Burnsall N York 90 B6
Burnside Angus 141 E5
Burnside Angus 140 D6
Burnside Fife 131 H6
Burnside Moray 156 D6
Burnside W Loth 131 G3
Burnside of Duntrune Angus 140 D3
Burnt Heath Essex 52 D3
Burnt Hill Berks 40 D2
Burnt Houses Dur 105 H2
Burnt Oak E Susx 17 F4
Burnt Yates N York 90 D6
Burntcommon Surrey 28 A1
Burntheath Derbys 71 G3
Burnthouse Cnwll 3 E3
Burntisland Fife 132 A4
Burntwood Staffs 71 E1
Burntwood Green Staffs 71 F1
Burnville Devon 8 B3
Burnworthy Somset 10 B6
Burpham Surrey 28 A1
Burpham W Susx 16 A2
Burradon Nthumb 113 G5
Burradon T & W 114 D3
Burrafirth Shet 169 j5
Burras Cnwll 2 D3
Burraton Cnwll 5 H3
Burraton Devon 6 D3
Burravoe Shet 169 j4
Burrells Cumb 104 C2
Burrelton P & K 140 B3
Burridge Devon 21 F4
Burridge Devon 10 D5
Burridge Hants 14 C5
Burrill N York 97 F4
Burringham Lincs 85 F6
Burrington Devon 21 F2
Burrington Herefs 57 E3
Burrington Somset 23 G5
Burrough End Cambs 63 E1
Burrough Green Cambs 63 F1
Burrough on the Hill Leics 73 E1
Burrow Lancs 95 G2
Burrow Somset 22 B3
Burrow Bridge Somset 23 F2
Burrowhill Surrey 27 H6
Burrows Cross Surrey 16 B6
Burry Swans 34 B3
Burry Port Carmth 34 B4
Burrygreen Swans 34 B3
Burscough Lancs 81 G6
Burscough Bridge Lancs 81 G6
Bursea E R Yk 92 B3
Burshill E R Yk 93 E4
Bursledon Hants 14 C4
Burslem Staffs 70 D5
Burstall Suffk 53 E5
Burstock Dorset 11 E5
Burston Norfk 64 D4
Burston Staffs 70 D3
Burstow Surrey 16 D5
Burstwick E R Yk 93 F2
Burtersett N York 96 B4
Burtholme Cumb 112 C1
Burthorpe Green Suffk 63 G2
Burthwaite Cumb 103 H5
Burthy Cnwll 3 G5
Burtle Somset 23 G4
Burtoft Lincs 74 C3
Burton Ches 81 E2
Burton Ches 81 G1
Burton Dorset 11 G4
Burton Dorset 13 E4
Burton Lincs 85 G2
Burton Nthumb 125 E4
Burton Pembks 32 D2
Burton Somset 23 E4
Burton Somset 11 F6
Burton Wilts 38 C2
Burton Wilts 24 D2
Burton Agnes E R Yk 93 E6
Burton Bradstock Dorset 11 E3
Burton Coggles Lincs 73 G3
Burton Constable Hall E R Yk 93 F3
Burton Dassett Warwks 48 B4
Burton End Essex 51 F3
Burton End Suffk 51 G5
Burton Fleming E R Yk 99 F2

Burton Green Warwks 59 F3
Burton Green Wrexhm 69 F6
Burton Hastings Warwks 59 G4
Burton in Lonsdale N York 95 G2
Burton Joyce Notts 72 D4
Burton Latimer Nhants 61 E3
Burton Lazars Leics 73 E2
Burton Leonard N York 97 F1
Burton on the Wolds Leics 72 D2
Burton Overy Leics 60 C5
Burton Pedwardine Lincs 74 B4
Burton Pidsea E R Yk 93 F3
Burton Salmon N York 91 F2
Burton upon Stather Lincs 92 C1
Burton upon Trent Staffs 71 G2
Burton's Green Essex 52 B3
Burton-in-Kendal Cumb 95 F2
Burtonwood Ches 81 H4
Burwardsley Ches 69 G6
Burwarton Shrops 57 F4
Burwash E Susx 17 G4
Burwash Common E Susx 17 G4
Burwash Weald E Susx 17 G4
Burwell Cambs 63 E2
Burwell Lincs 86 D3
Burwen IOA 78 D4
Burwick Ork 169 b1
Bury Cambs 62 B4
Bury Gt Man 82 C6
Bury Somset 22 B2
Bury W Susx 16 A3
Bury End Beds 50 B4
Bury End Bucks 41 H4
Bury Green Herts 51 E3
Bury St Edmunds Suffk 63 H2
Burythorpe N York 98 D1
Busby E Rens 119 G5
Buscot Wilts 39 G4
Bush Abers 149 E1
Bush Cnwll 20 C1
Bush Bank Herefs 45 G4
Bush Green Norfk 65 E4
Bush Green Suffk 64 B1
Bush Hill Park Gt Lon 28 D6
Bushbury W Mids 58 B6
Bushby Leics 60 C6
Bushey Herts 28 B6
Bushey Heath Herts 28 B5
Bushley Worcs 46 D3
Bushley Green Worcs 46 D3
Bushmead Beds 61 G1
Bushton Wilts 39 E2
Busk Cumb 104 C4
Buslingthorpe Lincs 86 A3
Bussage Gloucs 38 D5
Bussex Somset 23 F3
Butcher Hill W York 89 H2
Butcher's Cross E Susx 17 F4
Butcombe Somset 23 H5
Butleigh Somset 23 H3
Butleigh Wootton Somset 23 H3
Butler's Cross Bucks 41 G5
Butler's Hill Notts 72 C5
Butlers Marston Warwks 48 A4
Butley Suffk 53 G6
Butley High Corner Suffk 53 G6
Butt Green Ches 70 B5
Butt Lane Staffs 70 C5
Butt's Green Essex 52 A1
Buttercrambe N York 92 A5
Butterdean Border 133 G1
Butterknowle Dur 105 H3
Butterleigh Devon 9 G5
Buttermere Cumb 103 F2
Buttermere Wilts 26 B5
Butters Green Staffs 70 C5
Buttershaw W York 90 C2
Butterstone P & K 139 H4
Butterton Staffs 70 C4
Butterton Staffs 71 F6
Butterwick Dur 106 C4
Butterwick Lincs 74 D4
Butterwick N York 98 C3
Butterwick N York 99 F2
Buttington Powys 69 E1
Buttonbridge Shrops 57 G3
Buttonoak Shrops 57 H3
Butts Ash Hants 14 B4
Buttsbear Cross Cnwll 20 C1
Buxhall Suffk 64 C1
Buxhall Fen Street Suffk 64 C1
Buxted E Susx 17 F4
Buxton Derbys 83 E2
Buxton Norfk 77 E2
Buxton Heath Norfk 77 E2
Bwlch Powys 44 D1
Bwlch-y-cibau Powys 68 D2
Bwlch-y-Ddar Powys 68 D2
Bwlch-y-ffridd Powys 56 A5
Bwlch-y-groes Pembks 42 C3
Bwlch-y-sarnau Powys 55 H3
Bwlchgwyn Wrexhm 69 E5
Bwlchllan Cerdgn 43 F5
Bwlchnewydd Carmth 33 H4
Bwlchtocyn Gwynd 66 C3
Bwlchyfadfa Cerdgn 43 E4
Bwlchymyrdd Swans 34 C4
Byermoor T & W 114 C1
Byers Garth Dur 106 C5
Byers Green Dur 106 B4
Byfield Nhants 48 C4
Byfleet Surrey 28 B2
Byford Herefs 45 G3
Bygrave Herts 50 D4
Byker T & W 114 D2
Bylchau Conwy 80 B1
Byley Ches 82 B2
Bynea Carmth 34 C4
Byrewalls Border 122 D4
Byrness Nthumb 113 E5
Bystock Devon 9 G3
Bythorn Cambs 61 F3
Byton Herefs 56 D2
Bywell Nthumb 114 B2
Byworth W Susx 15 H6

C

Cabbacott Devon 20 D5
Cabourne Lincs 86 B5
Cabrach Ag & B 126 D1
Cabrach Moray 157 F2
Cabus Lancs 88 C4
Cabvie Lodge Highld 153 F6
Cackle Street E Susx 17 E4
Cackle Street E Susx 17 H3
Cackle Street E Susx 18 B3
Cadbury Devon 9 F5
Cadbury Barton Devon 21 G2
Cadder E Duns 130 B2
Caddington Beds 50 B3
Caddonfoot Border 122 B3
Cade Street E Susx 17 G3
Cadeby Leics 59 G6
Cadeby S York 84 C5
Cadeleigh Devon 9 F5
Cadgwith Cnwll 3 E1
Cadham Fife 132 B5
Cadishead Gt Man 82 B4
Cadle Swans 34 D4
Cadley Lancs 88 D3
Cadley Wilts 25 G6
Cadley Wilts 25 H5
Cadmore End Bucks 41 F3
Cadnam Hants 13 G6
Cadney Lincs 85 H5
Cadole Flints 80 D1
Cadoxton V Glam 36 B1

Cadoxton Juxta-Neath
   Neath 35 E4
Cadsden Bucks 41 F5
Cadwst Denbgs 68 C4
Cae'r bryn Carmth 34 C6
Cae'r-bont Powys 35 E5
Caeathro Gwynd 67 E6
Caehopkin Powys 35 F5
Caenby Lincs 85 G4
Caenby Corner Lincs 85 G4
Caeo Carmth 43 G3
Caer Farchell Pembks 32 A3
Caerau Brdgnd 35 F4
Caerau Cardif 36 B2
Caerdeon Gwynd 67 F2
Caergeiliog IOA 78 C2
Caergwrle Flints 69 E6
Caerhun Conwy 79 G2
Caerlanrig Border 112 A5
Caerleon Newpt 36 D3
Caernarfon Gwynd 78 D1
Caernarfon Airport Gwynd 66 D6
Caernarfon Castle Gwynd 78 D1
Caerphilly Caerph 36 C3
Caersws Powys 55 H5
Caerwedros Cerdgn 42 D5
Caerwent Mons 37 F3
Caerwys Flints 80 D2
Caerynwch Gwynd 67 G2
Caggle Street Mons 37 E6
Caim IOA 79 F3
Cairinis W Isls 168 b4
Cairnbaan Ag & B 127 G4
Cairnbulg Abers 159 F6
Cairncross Border 133 H1
Cairncurran Inver 129 E2
Cairndow Ag & B 128 C6
Cairneyhill Fife 131 G4
Cairnfield House Moray 157 F5
Cairngarroch D & G 100 B5
Cairngrassie Abers 149 G4
Cairnie Abers 157 G3
Cairnorrie Abers 159 E3
Cairnryan D & G 108 B2
Cairnty Moray 157 E4
Caister-on-Sea Norfk 77 H1
Caistor Lincs 86 B5
Caistor St Edmund Norfk 65 E6
Cake Street Norfk 64 C4
Cakebole Worcs 58 B3
Calais Street Suffk 52 C5
Calanais W Isls 168 d8
Calbourne IOW 14 B2
Calceby Lincs 86 D2
Calcot Berks 41 E1
Calcot Flints 80 D2
Calcot Gloucs 39 F5
Calcot Row Berks 41 E1
Calcots Moray 157 E5
Calcott Kent 31 E2
Calcott Shrops 69 G1
Calcutt N York 91 E5
Calcutt Wilts 39 F4
Caldbeck Cumb 103 G4
Caldbergh N York 96 D3
Caldecote Cambs 61 G4
Caldecote Cambs 62 C1
Caldecote Herts 50 D5
Caldecote Nhants 49 E4
Caldecote Highfields Cambs 62 C1
Caldecott Nhants 61 F2
Caldecott Oxon 40 C4
Caldecott Rutlnd 61 E5
Caldicot Mons 37 F3
Caldmore W Mids 58 C5
Caldwell N York 106 A2
Caldy Mersyd 81 D3
Caledfwlch Carmth 43 G2
Calendra Cnwll 3 G4
Calenick Cnwll 3 F4
Calford Green Suffk 51 H5
Calfsound Ork 169 c4
Calgary Ag & B 135 F4
Califer Moray 156 C5

California Falk 131 E3
California Norfk 77 H1
California Cross Devon 6 D3
Calke Derbys 72 A2
Callakille Highld 151 G4
Callander Stirlg 130 C6
Callanish W Isls 168 d8
Callaughton Shrops 57 F5
Callestick Cnwll 3 E5
Calligarry Highld 143 F4
Callington Cnwll 5 G3
Callow Herefs 45 H3
Callow End Worcs 46 D4
Callow Hill Wilts 39 E3
Callow Hill Worcs 57 H3
Callow Hill Worcs 58 C2
Callows Grave Worcs 57 F2
Calmore Hants 13 G6
Calmsden Gloucs 39 E5
Calne Wilts 39 E1
Calow Derbys 84 B2
Calshot Hants 14 C4
Calstock Cnwll 6 B4
Calstone Wellington Wilts 39 E1
Calthorpe Norfk 77 E3
Calthorpe Street Norfk 77 G2
Calthwaite Cumb 104 A4
Calton N York 89 G5
Calton Staffs 71 F5
Calton Green Staffs 71 F5
Calveley Ches 70 A6
Calver Derbys 83 G2
Calver Hill Herefs 45 F4
Calver Sough Derbys 83 G2
Calverhall Shrops 70 A4
Calverleigh Devon 9 F6
Calverley W York 90 C3
Calvert Bucks 49 E2
Calverton Bucks 49 F3
Calverton Notts 72 D5
Calvine P & K 146 C1
Calvo Cumb 103 E5
Calzeat Border 121 F3
Cam Gloucs 38 B4
Camas Luinie Highld 152 D2
Camasachoirce Highld 136 B6
Camasine Highld 136 B6
Camastianavaig Highld 151 E3
Camault Muir Highld 154 C3
Camber E Susx 18 C3
Camberley Surrey 27 G5
Camberwell Gt Lon 28 D4
Camblesforth N York 91 G2
Cambo Nthumb 114 B4
Cambois Nthumb 115 E4
Camborne Cnwll 2 D4
Cambourne Cambs 62 B1
Cambridge Cambs 62 D1
Cambridge Gloucs 38 B5
Cambridge Airport Cambs 62 D1
Cambrose Cnwll 2 D4
Cambus Clacks 131 E4
Cambus o' May Abers 148 B4
Cambusavie Platform Highld 162 D3
Cambusbarron Stirlg 130 D4
Cambuskenneth Stirlg 130 D4
Cambuslang S Lans 120 A5
Cambuswallace S Lans 121 E3
Camden Town Gt Lon 28 D4
Cameley Somset 24 B5
Camelford Cnwll 5 E4
Camelon Falk 131 E3
Camer's Green Worcs 46 C3
Camerory Highld 156 B2
Camerton Cumb 102 D3
Camerton Somset 24 B5
Camghouran P & K 138 C5
Camieston Border 122 C2
Cammachmore Abers 149 G4
Cammeringham Lincs 85 G3
Camore Highld 163 E3
Campbeltown Ag & B 117 F2
Campbeltown Airport Ag & B 117 F2
Camperdown T & W 114 D3
Campmuir Angus 140 B3
Campsall S York 84 C6
Campsea Ash Suffk 65 F1
Campton Beds 50 B4
Camptown Border 112 D6
Camrose Pembks 32 D4
Camserney P & K 139 E5
Camusnagaul Highld 161 E3
Camusnagaul Highld 144 C2
Camusteel Highld 151 E3
Camusterrach Highld 151 G3
Canada Hants 26 A1
Canal Foot Cumb 94 D3
Canaston Bridge Pembks 33 E3
Candacraig Abers 148 A4
Candle Street Suffk 64 C3
Candlesby Lincs 87 E1
Candover Green Shrops 57 E6
Candyburn Border 121 E4
Cane End Oxon 41 E2
Canewdon Essex 30 C5
Canford Bottom Dorset 12 D5
Canford Cliffs Dorset 12 D3
Canford Heath Dorset 12 D4
Canford Magna Dorset 12 D4
Canhams Green Suffk 64 C2
Canisbay Highld 167 G6
Canklow S York 84 B4
Canley W Mids 59 F3
Cann Dorset 24 D1
Cann Common Somset 23 E4
Cannich Highld 154 B2
Canning Town Gt Lon 29 E4
Cannington Somset 23 E4
Cannock Staffs 71 E1
Cannock Wood Staffs 71 E1
Canon Bridge Herefs 45 G3
Canon Frome Herefs 46 B3
Canon Pyon Herefs 45 G4
Canonbie D & G 112 A2
Canons Ashby Nhants 48 D4

Canonstown Cnwll 2 C3
Canterbury Kent 31 E2
Canterbury Cathedral Kent 31 E2
Cantley Norfk 65 F6
Cantlop Shrops 57 E6
Canton Cardif 36 C2
Cantraywood Highld 155 F4
Cantsfield Lancs 95 G2
Canvey Island Essex 30 B4
Canwick Lincs 85 G2
Canworthy Water Cnwll 5 F5
Caol Highld 144 C2
Caolas Scalpaigh W Isls 168 d6
Caoles Ag & B 134 C4
Caonich Highld 144 C4
Capel Kent 17 G6
Capel Surrey 16 C5
Capel Bangor Cerdgn 54 D3
Capel Betws Lleucu Cerdgn 43 F5
Capel Coch IOA 78 D3
Capel Curig Conwy 67 G6
Capel Cynon Cerdgn 42 D4
Capel Dewi Carmth 43 E1
Capel Dewi Cerdgn 43 E3
Capel Garmon Conwy 67 H6
Capel Green Suffk 53 G6
Capel Gwyn Carmth 43 E1
Capel Gwyn IOA 78 C2
Capel Gwynfe Carmth 43 G1
Capel Hendre Carmth 34 C5
Capel Isaac Carmth 43 F2
Capel Iwan Carmth 42 C3
Capel le Ferne Kent 19 F5
Capel Llanilltern Cardif 36 B2
Capel Mawr IOA 78 C2
Capel Seion Cerdgn 54 D3
Capel St Andrew Suffk 53 G5
Capel St Mary Suffk 52 D4
Capel Trisant Cerdgn 55 E3
Capel-Dewi Cerdgn 54 D4
Capel-y-ffin Powys 45 E2
Capel-y-graig Gwynd 79 E2
Capelles Guern 174 g2
Capeluchaf Gwynd 66 D5
Capelulo Conwy 79 G2
Capenhurst Ches 81 F2
Capernwray Lancs 95 F2
Capheaton Nthumb 114 B3
Caplaw E Rens 119 F5
Capon's Green Suffk 65 E2
Cappercleuch Border 121 G2
Capstone Kent 30 A2
Capton Devon 7 F3
Capton Somset 22 D3
Caputh P & K 139 H4
Car Colston Notts 73 E4
Caradon Town Cnwll 5 F3
Carbeth Inn Stirlg 129 G3
Carbis Cnwll 4 D2
Carbis Bay Cnwll 2 C4
Carbost Highld 150 D2
Carbost Highld 150 D3
Carbrook S York 84 B4
Carbrooke Norfk 64 B6
Carburton Notts 84 D2
Carclaze Cnwll 3 H5
Carclew Cnwll 3 E4
Carcroft S York 84 C6
Cardenden Fife 132 A5
Cardeston Shrops 69 F1
Cardewlees Cumb 103 G5
Cardhu Moray 156 D3
Cardiff Cardif 36 C2
Cardiff Airport V Glam 22 D6
Cardigan Cerdgn 42 B4
Cardinal's Green Cambs 51 G5
Cardington Beds 50 B5
Cardington Shrops 57 E5
Cardinham Cnwll 5 E3
Cardrain D & G 100 C3
Cardrona Border 121 G3
Cardross Ag & B 129 E3
Cardryne D & G 100 C3
Cardurnock Cumb 103 F6
Careby Lincs 73 H2
Careston Angus 141 E6
Carew Pembks 33 E2
Carew Cheriton Pembks 33 E2
Carew Newton Pembks 33 E2
Carey Herefs 46 A2
Carfin N Lans 120 B5
Carfraemill Border 122 B5
Cargate Green Norfk 77 G1
Cargen D & G 110 D2
Cargenbridge D & G 110 D2
Cargill P & K 140 B3
Cargo Cumb 103 H6
Cargreen Cnwll 6 B4
Cargurrel Cnwll 3 F3
Carham Nthumb 123 E3
Carhampton Somset 22 C3
Carharrack Cnwll 3 E4
Carie P & K 138 C5
Carinish W Isls 168 b4
Carisbrooke IOW 14 C2
Cark Cumb 94 D2
Carkeel Cnwll 5 H2
Carlabhagh W Isls 168 d8
Carland Cross Cnwll 3 F5
Carlbury Dur 106 B2
Carlby Lincs 73 H1
Carlcroft Nthumb 113 E6
Carlecotes S York 83 G5
Carleen Cnwll 2 D3
Carlesmoor N York 97 E3
Carleton Cumb 104 A5
Carleton Cumb 104 B3
Carleton Cumb 94 A6
Carleton Lancs 88 B3
Carleton N York 89 H4
Carleton N York 91 F2
Carleton Forehoe Norfk 64 C6
Carleton Rode Norfk 64 D5
Carleton St Peter Norfk 65 F6
Carlidnack Cnwll 3 E3
Carlin How N York 107 F3
Carlincraig Abers 158 C3
Carlingcott Somset 24 C5

Carlisle Cumb 103 H6
Carlisle Airport Cumb 104 B6
Carloggas Cnwll 4 B2
Carlops Border 121 F5
Carloway W Isls 168 d8
Carlton Beds 49 H5
Carlton Cambs 51 G6
Carlton Dur 106 C3
Carlton Leics 59 G6
Carlton N York 96 D3
Carlton N York 98 B3
Carlton N York 91 G2
Carlton Notts 72 D4
Carlton S York 84 A6
Carlton Suffk 65 F2
Carlton W York 90 D2
Carlton Colville Suffk 65 G4
Carlton Curlieu Leics 60 C5
Carlton Green Cambs 51 G6
Carlton Husthwaite N York 97 H2
Carlton in Lindrick Notts 84 B3
Carlton Miniott N York 97 G3
Carlton Scroop Lincs 73 G4
Carlton-in-Cleveland N York 97 H5
Carlton-le-Moorland Lincs 73 G6
Carlton-on-Trent Notts 85 F1
Carluddon Cnwll 3 H5
Carluke S Lans 120 C4
Carlyon Bay Cnwll 3 H5
Carmacoup S Lans 120 B2
Carmarthen Carmth 42 D1
Carmel Carmth 34 C6
Carmel Flints 80 D2
Carmel Gwynd 67 E5
Carmichael S Lans 120 D3
Carminowe Cnwll 2 D2
Carmunnock C Glas 119 H5
Carmyle C Glas 120 A6
Carmyllie Angus 141 E4
Carn Brea Cnwll 2 D4
Carn-gorm Highld 152 D1
Carnaby E R Yk 99 G1
Carnbee Fife 132 D6
Carnbo P & K 131 G5
Carnbrogie Abers 158 D2
Carndu Highld 152 C2
Carnduff S Lans 120 A4
Carne Cnwll 3 E2
Carne Cnwll 3 G4
Carne Cnwll 4 C2
Carnell E Ayrs 119 F3
Carnewas Cnwll 4 B3
Carnforth Lancs 95 F2
Carnhedryn Pembks 32 B4
Carnhell Green Cnwll 2 D3
Carnie Abers 149 F5
Carnkie Cnwll 3 E3
Carnkiet Cnwll 3 E5
Carno Powys 55 G5
Carnoch Highld 144 A4
Carnock Fife 131 G4
Carnon Downs Cnwll 3 E4
Carnousie Abers 158 C4
Carnoustie Angus 141 E3
Carnwath S Lans 120 D4
Carnyorth Cnwll 2 A3
Carol Green W Mids 59 E3
Carpalla Cnwll 3 G5
Carperby N York 96 C4
Carr Gt Man 89 F1
Carr S York 84 C4
Carr Gate W York 90 D2
Carr Shield Nthumb 105 E5
Carr Vale Derbys 84 B2
Carradale Ag & B 117 G4
Carrbridge Highld 155 G1
Carrbrook Gt Man 83 E5
Carrefour Jersey 174 b3
Carreglefn IOA 78 C4
Carrhouse Lincs 85 E5
Carrick Ag & B 127 H4
Carrick Castle Ag & B 128 C4
Carriden Falk 131 F3
Carrington Gt Man 82 B4
Carrington Lincs 74 C6
Carrington Mdloth 121 H5
Carrismerry Cnwll 4 D2
Carrog Conwy 67 G5
Carrog Denbgs 68 C4
Carron Falk 131 E3
Carron Moray 156 D3
Carron Bridge Stirlg 130 D3
Carronbridge D & G 110 C6
Carronshore Falk 131 E3
Carrow Hill Mons 37 E3
Carruth House Inver 129 E2
Carrutherstown D & G 111 E2
Carrville Dur 106 B5
Carrycoats Hall Nthumb 113 F3
Carsaig Ag & B 135 G1
Carse Gray Angus 140 D5
Carseriggan D & G 109 E1
Carsethorn D & G 102 D6
Carshalton Gt Lon 28 D2
Carsington Derbys 71 G5
Carskey Ag & B 117 F1
Carsluith D & G 101 F6
Carsphairn D & G 109 G4
Carstairs S Lans 120 D4
Carstairs Junction S Lans 120 D4
Carswell Marsh Oxon 40 B4
Carter's Clay Hants 26 A2
Carterton Oxon 39 G5
Carterway Heads Dur 105 G5
Carthew Cnwll 3 G5
Carthorpe N York 97 F3
Cartington Nthumb 124 C1
Cartland S Lans 120 C4
Cartledge Derbys 83 H2
Cartmel Cumb 95 E4
Cartmel Fell Cumb 95 E4
Carway Carmth 34 B5
Carwinley Cumb 112 A2
Cashe's Green Gloucs 38 C5
Cashmoor Dorset 12 D6
Cassington Oxon 40 C5
Cassop Colliery Dur 106 C5

Castallack Cnwll 2 B2
Castell Conwy 79 G2
Castell-y-bwch Torfn 36 D3
Casterton Lancs 95 G3
Castle Cnwll 5 E2
Castle Acre Norfk 76 A1
Castle Ashby Nhants 49 G5
Castle Bolton N York 96 D4
Castle Bromwich W Mids 58 D4
Castle Bytham Lincs 73 G2
Castle Caereinion Powys 56 B6
Castle Camps Cambs 51 G5
Castle Carrock Cumb 104 B6
Castle Cary Somset 24 B2
Castle Combe Wilts 38 C2
Castle Donington Leics 72 B3
Castle Douglas D & G 110 B1
Castle Eaton Wilts 39 F4
Castle Eden Dur 106 D5
Castle End Cambs 61 G6
Castle Frome Herefs 46 B4
Castle Gate Cnwll 2 B3
Castle Green Cumb 95 F4
Castle Green Surrey 27 H5
Castle Gresley Derbys 71 H2
Castle Hedingham Essex 52 B4
Castle Hill Kent 17 H6
Castle Hill Suffk 53 E5
Castle Kennedy D & G 100 B6
Castle Lachlan Ag & B 128 B5
Castle Morris Pembks 32 C5
Castle O'er D & G 111 G4
Castle Pulverbatch Shrops 56 D6
Castle Rising Norfk 75 G2
Castle Street W York 89 H2
Castle Stuart Highld 155 F4
Castlebay W Isls 168 a1
Castlebythe Pembks 32 D5
Castlecary Falk 130 D3
Castleford W York 91 E2
Castlehill Border 121 G3
Castlehill Highld 167 F5
Castlehill W Duns 129 E3
Castleside Dur 105 G5
Castlethorpe Bucks 49 F4
Castlethorpe Lincs 85 G5
Castleton Border 112 B4
Castleton Derbys 83 F3
Castleton Gt Man 82 D6
Castleton N York 107 F2
Castleton Newpt 36 D3
Castletown Dorset 11 G2
Castletown Highld 167 F5
Castletown IOM 174 k2
Castletown T & W 115 E1
Castley N York 90 D4
Caston Norfk 64 B5
Castor Cambs 61 G5
Caswell Bay Swans 34 C3
Cat and Fiddle Ches 83 E2
Cat's Ash Newpt 37 E3
Catacol N Ayrs 118 A4
Catbrook Mons 37 F4
Catch Flints 80 D2
Catchall Cnwll 2 B3
Catchem's Corner W Mids 59 E3
Catchgate Dur 106 A6
Catcliffe S York 84 B3
Catcomb Wilts 39 E2
Catcott Somset 23 G3
Catcott Burtle Somset 23 G3
Catel Guern 174 g2
Caterham Surrey 28 D1
Catfield Norfk 77 G2
Catfield Common Norfk 77 G2
Catfirth Shet 169 j3
Catford Gt Lon 29 E3
Catforth Lancs 88 C3
Cathcart C Glas 119 H5
Cathedine Powys 44 D2
Catherine Slack W York 90 B2
Catherine-de-Barnes W Mids 59 E3
Catherington Hants 15 E5
Catherston Leweston Dorset 10 D4
Catherton Shrops 57 G3
Catisfield Hants 14 D4
Catley Herefs 46 B4
Catley Lane Head Gt Man 89 G1
Catlodge Highld 146 A4
Catlow Lancs 89 G3
Catlowdy Cumb 112 B2
Catmere End Essex 51 F5
Catmore Berks 40 C2
Caton Devon 7 E5
Caton Lancs 95 F1
Caton Green Lancs 95 F1
Cator Court Devon 8 D2
Catrine E Ayrs 119 G2
Catsfield E Susx 17 H3
Catsfield Stream E Susx 17 H3
Catsgore Somset 23 H2
Catsham Somset 24 A3
Catshill Worcs 58 C3
Catstree Shrops 57 H5
Cattadale Ag & B 117 F1
Cattal N York 91 F5
Cattawade Suffk 53 E4
Catterall Lancs 88 C4
Catterick N York 97 F5
Catterick Bridge N York 97 E5
Catterick Garrison N York 97 E5
Catterlen Cumb 104 B3
Catterline Abers 149 F2
Catterton N York 91 F4
Catteshall Surrey 27 H4
Catthorpe Leics 60 B3
Cattishall Suffk 64 A2
Cattistock Dorset 11 F4
Catton Cumb 105 E6
Catton N York 97 G3
Catton Norfk 77 E1
Catwick E R Yk 93 E4
Catworth Cambs 61 G3

Caudle Green Gloucs 38 D5
Caulcott Beds 50 A5
Caulcott Oxon 48 C2
Cauldcots Angus 141 F4
Cauldhame Stirlg 130 C4
Cauldmill Border 122 C1
Cauldon Staffs 71 F5
Cauldon Lowe Staffs 71 F5
Caulkerbush D & G 102 C6
Caulside D & G 112 B3
Caundle Marsh Dorset 11 G6
Caunsall Worcs 58 B3
Caunton Notts 73 E6
Causeway Hants 27 F1
Causeway End D & G 101 E6
Causeway End Essex 51 H3
Causewayend S Lans 121 E3
Causewayhead Cumb 103 E5
Causewayhead Stirlg 130 D5
Causey Park Nthumb 114 C5
Causey Park Bridge Nthumb 114 D5
Causeyend Abers 159 E1
Cavendish Suffk 52 B5
Cavenham Suffk 63 G2
Caversfield Oxon 48 D2
Caversham Berks 41 E2
Caverswall Staffs 70 D4
Caverton Mill Border 123 E2
Cavil E R Yk 92 B3
Cawdor Highld 155 G4
Cawkwell Lincs 86 C3
Cawood N York 91 G3
Cawsand Cnwll 6 B3
Cawston Norfk 76 D2
Cawston Warwks 59 H3
Cawthorn N York 98 C4
Cawthorne S York 83 H5
Cawton N York 98 B2
Caxton Cambs 62 B1
Caxton End Cambs 62 B1
Caxton Gibbet Cambs 62 B1
Caynham Shrops 57 F3
Caythorpe Lincs 73 G5
Caythorpe Notts 72 D5
Cayton N York 99 F3
Ceann a Bhaigh W Isls 168 b5
Ceannacroc Lodge Highld 144 D6
Cearsiadar W Isls 168 e7
Ceciliford Mons 37 F5
Cefn Newpt 36 D3
Cefn Berain Conwy 80 B2
Cefn Byrle Powys 35 F5
Cefn Canel Powys 69 E3
Cefn Coch Powys 68 C3
Cefn Cribwr Brdgnd 35 F2
Cefn Cross Brdgnd 35 F2
Cefn Mably Caerph 36 C3
Cefn-brith Conwy 68 B5
Cefn-bryn-brain Carmth 35 E6
Cefn-coed-y-cymmer Myr Td 36 A5
Cefn-ddwysarn Gwynd 68 B4
Cefn-Einion Shrops 56 C4
Cefn-mawr Wrexhm 69 E4
Cefn-y-bedd Wrexhm 69 E6
Cefn-y-pant Carmth 33 F4
Cefneithin Carmth 34 C6
Cefngorwydd Powys 44 B4
Cefnpennar Rhondd 36 B4
Ceint IOA 78 D2
Cellan Cerdgn 43 F4
Cellardyke Fife 133 E5
Cellarhead Staffs 70 D5
Celleron Cumb 104 B3
Celynen Caerph 36 C4
Cemaes IOA 78 C4
Cemmaes Powys 55 F6
Cemmaes Road Powys 55 F6
Cenarth Cerdgn 42 C3
Cerbyd Pembks 32 B4
Ceres Fife 140 D1
Cerne Abbas Dorset 11 G5
Cerney Wick Gloucs 39 E4
Cerrigceinwen IOA 78 D2
Cerrigydrudion Conwy 68 B5
Cess Norfk 77 G2
Ceunant Gwynd 67 E6
Chaceley Gloucs 46 D2
Chacewater Cnwll 3 E4
Chackmore Bucks 49 E3
Chacombe Nhants 48 C4
Chadbury Worcs 47 F4
Chadderton Gt Man 82 D5
Chadderton Fold Gt Man 82 D5
Chaddesden Derbys 72 B4
Chaddesley Corbett Worcs 58 B3
Chaddlehanger Devon 8 B2
Chaddleworth Berks 40 B2
Chadlington Oxon 48 B1
Chadshunt Warwks 48 B4
Chadwell Leics 73 E2
Chadwell Shrops 70 C1
Chadwell End Beds 61 G2
Chadwell Heath Gt Lon 29 F5
Chadwell St Mary Essex 29 G4
Chadwick Worcs 58 A2
Chadwick End W Mids 59 E3
Chadwick Green Mersyd 81 G5
Chaffcombe Somset 10 D6
Chafford Hundred Essex 29 G4
Chagford Devon 8 D3
Chailey E Susx 17 E3
Chainhurst Kent 17 H6
Chalbury Dorset 12 D5
Chalbury Common Dorset 12 D5
Chaldon Surrey 28 D2
Chale IOW 14 C1
Chale Green IOW 14 C1
Chalfont Common Bucks 28 A5
Chalfont St Giles Bucks 41 H4
Chalfont St Peter Bucks 28 A5
Chalford Gloucs 38 D5
Chalford Oxon 41 E4
Chalford Wilts 24 D4
Chalgrave Beds 50 A3
Chalgrove Oxon 41 E4

Chalk Kent 29 G3
Chalk End Essex 51 G2
Chalkhouse Green Berks 41 E2
Chalkway Somset 10 D5
Chalkwell Kent 30 C2
Challaborough Devon 6 D2
Challacombe Devon 21 G5
Challoch D & G 109 F1
Challock Kent 30 D1
Chalmington Dorset 11 F5
Chalton Beds 50 A3
Chalton Beds 50 B6
Chalton Hants 15 E5
Chalvey Berks 41 H2
Chalvington E Susx 17 F2
Chambers Green Kent 18 C6
Chandler's Cross Herts 28 B6
Chandler's Ford Hants 14 C6
Chandlers Cross Worcs 46 C3
Channel's End Beds 61 G1
Chantry Somset 24 C4
Chantry Suffk 53 E5
Chapel Cumb 103 F3
Chapel Fife 132 B4
Chapel Allerton Somset 23 G4
Chapel Allerton W York 90 D3
Chapel Amble Cnwll 4 D3
Chapel Brampton Nhants 60 C2
Chapel Chorlton Staffs 70 C4
Chapel Cross E Susx 17 G3
Chapel End Beds 50 B5
Chapel End Beds 61 G1
Chapel End Cambs 61 G4
Chapel End Warwks 59 F5
Chapel Field Gt Man 82 C5
Chapel Green Warwks 59 F4
Chapel Green Warwks 48 C5
Chapel Haddlesey N York 91 G2
Chapel Hill Abers 159 F3
Chapel Hill Lincs 74 B5
Chapel Hill Mons 37 F4
Chapel Hill N York 90 D4
Chapel Lawn Shrops 56 C3
Chapel le Dale N York 95 H2
Chapel Leigh Somset 22 D2
Chapel Milton Derbys 83 E3
Chapel of Garioch Abers 158 C1
Chapel Rossan D & G 100 B5
Chapel Row Berks 40 D1
Chapel Row E Susx 17 G3
Chapel Row Essex 30 B6
Chapel St Leonards Lincs 87 F2
Chapel Stile Cumb 94 D5
Chapel Town Cnwll 3 F5
Chapel-en-le-Frith Derbys 83 E3
Chapelbridge Cambs 62 B5
Chapelend Way Essex 51 H5
Chapelgate Lincs 74 D2
Chapelhall N Lans 120 B6
Chapelhope Border 121 G1
Chapelknowe D & G 111 G2
Chapels Cumb 94 C3
Chapelton Angus 141 F4
Chapelton Devon 21 F3
Chapelton S Lans 120 A4
Chapeltown Lancs 89 F1
Chapeltown Moray 156 D1
Chapeltown S York 84 A4
Chapmans Well Devon 5 G5
Chapmanslade Wilts 24 D4
Chapmore End Herts 50 D2
Chappel Essex 52 C3
Charaton Cnwll 5 F3
Chard Somset 10 D5
Chard Junction Somset 10 D5
Chardleigh Green Somset 10 C6
Chardstock Devon 10 C5
Charfield Gloucs 38 B3
Chargrove Gloucs 47 E1
Charing Kent 30 C1
Charing Heath Kent 30 C1
Charing Hill Kent 30 C1
Charingworth Gloucs 47 G3
Charlbury Oxon 48 B1
Charlcombe Somset 24 C6
Charlcutt Wilts 39 E2
Charlecote Warwks 47 H5
Charles Devon 21 G4
Charles Tye Suffk 52 D6
Charleshill Surrey 27 G4
Charleston Angus 140 D4
Charlestown Aber C 149 G4
Charlestown Cnwll 3 H5
Charlestown Derbys 83 E4
Charlestown Dorset 11 G2
Charlestown Fife 131 G3
Charlestown Gt Man 82 C5
Charlestown Highld 160 B1
Charlestown Highld 155 H4
Charlestown W York 90 A2
Charlestown W York 90 C3
Charlesworth Derbys 83 E4
Charlinch Somset 23 E3
Charlottetown Fife 132 B6
Charlton Gt Lon 29 E4
Charlton Hants 26 B4
Charlton Nhants 48 D3
Charlton Nthumb 113 G3
Charlton Oxon 40 B3
Charlton Oxon 70 A1
Charlton Somset 23 F2
Charlton Somset 24 B4
Charlton Somset 24 B4
Charlton Surrey 28 B3
Charlton W Susx 15 G5
Charlton Wilts 25 E1
Charlton Wilts 38 D3
Charlton Wilts 25 G3
Charlton Worcs 58 A2
Charlton Worcs 47 F4
Charlton Abbots Gloucs 47 F2
Charlton Adam Somset 24 A2
Charlton Hill Shrops 57 F6
Charlton Horethorne Somset 24 B1
Charlton Kings Gloucs 47 E1
Charlton Mackrell Somset 23 H2
Charlton Marshall Dorset 12 C5

Charlton Musgrove Somset 24 C2
Charlton on the Hill Dorset 12 C5
Charlton-all-Saints Wilts 25 G2
Charlton-on-Otmoor Oxon 40 D6
Charlwood Hants 27 E2
Charlwood Surrey 16 C5
Charminster Dorset 11 G4
Charmouth Dorset 10 D4
Charndon Bucks 49 E2
Charney Bassett Oxon 40 B4
Charnock Green Lancs 88 D1
Charnock Richard Lancs 88 D1
Charsfield Suffk 65 E1
Chart Corner Kent 30 B1
Chart Hill Kent 30 B1
Chart Sutton Kent 30 B1
Charter Alley Hants 26 D5
Charterhall Border 123 E4
Charterhouse Somset 23 H5
Charterville Allotments Oxon 40 A5
Chartham Kent 31 E1
Chartham Hatch Kent 31 E1
Chartridge Bucks 41 G5
Chartway Street Kent 30 B1
Charwelton Nhants 48 D5
Chase Terrace Staffs 71 E1
Chasetown Staffs 58 C6
Chastleton Oxon 47 H2
Chasty Devon 5 G6
Chatburn Lancs 89 F4
Chatcull Staffs 70 C3
Chatham Caerph 36 C3
Chatham Kent 30 A3
Chatham Green Essex 51 H2
Chathill Nthumb 125 E4
Chatley Worcs 46 D5
Chatsworth House Derbys 83 G2
Chattenden Kent 30 A3
Chatter End Essex 51 F3
Chatteris Cambs 62 C4
Chatterton Lancs 89 F1
Chattisham Suffk 52 D5
Chatto Border 123 E1
Chatton Nthumb 124 D4
Chaul End Beds 50 B3
Chawleigh Devon 21 G2
Chawley Oxon 40 C5
Chawston Beds 61 G1
Chawton Hants 27 E3
Chaxhill Gloucs 38 B6
Chazey Heath Oxon 41 E2
Cheadle Gt Man 82 D3
Cheadle Staffs 71 E4
Cheadle Heath Gt Man 82 D4
Cheadle Hulme Gt Man 82 D3
Cheam Gt Lon 28 C2
Cheapside Berks 41 G1
Chearsley Bucks 41 E5
Chebsey Staffs 70 D3
Checkendon Oxon 41 E3
Checkley Ches 70 B5
Checkley Staffs 71 E4
Checkley Green Ches 70 B5
Chedburgh Suffk 63 G1
Cheddar Somset 23 G5
Cheddington Bucks 41 G6
Cheddleton Staffs 71 E5
Cheddleton Heath Staffs 71 E5
Cheddon Fitzpaine Somset 23 E2
Chedglow Wilts 38 D4
Chedgrave Norfk 65 F5
Chedington Dorset 11 E5
Chediston Suffk 65 F3
Chediston Green Suffk 65 F3
Chedworth Gloucs 39 E5
Chedzoy Somset 23 F3
Cheesden Gt Man 89 G1
Cheeseman's Green Kent 18 D5
Cheetham Hill Gt Man 82 C5
Cheetwood Gt Man 82 C5
Cheldon Devon 21 G2
Chelford Ches 82 C2
Chellaston Derbys 72 B3
Chellington Beds 49 H5
Chelmarsh Shrops 57 G4
Chelmick Shrops 57 E4
Chelmondiston Suffk 53 F4
Chelmorton Derbys 83 F2
Chelmsford Essex 51 H1
Chelmsley Wood W Mids 59 E4
Chelsea Gt Lon 28 D4
Chelsfield Gt Lon 29 E2
Chelsham Surrey 29 E2
Chelston Somset 22 D1
Chelsworth Suffk 52 C5
Cheltenham Gloucs 47 E1
Chelveston Nhants 61 F2
Chelvey Somset 37 H1
Chelwood Somset 24 B5
Chelwood Common E Susx 17 E4
Chelwood Gate E Susx 17 E4
Chelworth Wilts 38 D4
Chelworth Lower Green Wilts 39 E4
Chelworth Upper Green Wilts 39 E4
Cheney Longville Shrops 56 D4
Chenies Bucks 28 A6
Chepstow Mons 37 F4
Chequerbent Gt Man 82 B5
Chequers Corner Norfk 75 E1
Cherhill Wilts 39 E1
Cherington Gloucs 38 D4
Cherington Warwks 48 A3
Cheriton Devon 21 G5
Cheriton Hants 26 D2
Cheriton Kent 19 F5
Cheriton Swans 34 B4
Cheriton Bishop Devon 9 E4
Cheriton Fitzpaine Devon 9 E5
Cheriton or Stackpole Elidor Pembks 32 D1
Cherrington Shrops 70 B2
Cherry Burton E R Yk 92 D4
Cherry Hinton Cambs 62 D1
Cherry Orchard Worcs 46 D4
Cherry Willingham Lincs 85 H2
Chertsey Surrey 28 A3
Cheselbourne Dorset 12 B5

279

Chesham *Bucks* **41** H4
Chesham *Gt Man* **82** C6
Chesham Bois *Bucks* **41** H4
Cheshunt *Herts* **50** D1
Chesley *Kent* **30** B2
Cheslyn Hay *Staffs* **58** C6
Chessetts Wood *Warwks* **59** E3
Chessington *Surrey* **28** C2
Chessington World of
  Adventure *Gt Lon* **28** C2
Chester *Ches* **81** F1
Chester Cathedral *Ches* **81** F1
Chester Moor *Dur* **106** B6
Chester Zoo *Ches* **81** F1
Chester-le-Street *Dur* **106** B6
Chesterblade *Somset* **24** B3
Chesterfield *Derbys* **84** D2
Chesterfield *Staffs* **58** D6
Chesterhill *Mdloth* **132** C2
Chesters *Border* **122** C2
Chesters *Border* **112** C6
Chesterton *Cambs* **61** G5
Chesterton *Cambs* **62** D1
Chesterton *Gloucs* **39** E4
Chesterton *Oxon* **48** D1
Chesterton *Shrops* **57** H5
Chesterton *Staffs* **70** C5
Chesterton Green *Warwks* **48** B5
Chesterwood *Nthumb* **113** E1
Chestfield *Kent* **31** E3
Chestnut Street *Kent* **30** B2
Cheston *Devon* **6** D3
Cheswardine *Shrops* **70** B3
Cheswell *Shrops* **70** B2
Cheswick *Nthumb* **123** G4
Cheswick Green *W Mids* **58** D3
Chetnole *Dorset* **11** F5
Chettiscombe *Devon* **9** F6
Chettisham *Cambs* **63** E4
Chettle *Dorset* **12** C6
Chetton *Shrops* **57** G4
Chetwode *Bucks* **49** E2
Chetwynd *Shrops* **70** B2
Chetwynd Aston *Shrops* **70** C2
Cheveley *Cambs* **63** F1
Chevening *Kent* **29** F2
Cheverton *IOW* **14** C2
Chevington *Suffk* **63** G1
Chevington Drift *Nthumb* **114** D5
Chevithorne *Devon* **9** G6
Chew Magna *Somset* **24** A6
Chew Moor *Gt Man* **82** B5
Chew Stoke *Somset* **24** A5
Chewton Keynsham *Somset* **24** B6
Chewton Mendip *Somset* **24** B5
Chichacott *Devon* **8** C4
Chicheley *Bucks* **49** G4
Chichester *W Susx* **15** G4
Chickerell *Dorset* **11** G3
Chickering *Suffk* **65** E3
Chicklade *Wilts* **25** E3
Chickward *Herefs* **45** F4
Chidden *Hants* **15** E5
Chiddingfold *Surrey* **27** H3
Chiddingly *E Susx* **17** F3
Chiddingstone *Kent* **17** F6
Chiddingstone Causeway *Kent* **17** F6
Chideock *Dorset* **11** E4
Chidham *W Susx* **15** F4
Chidswell *W York* **90** D2
Chieveley *Berks* **40** C2
Chignall Smealy *Essex* **51** G2
Chignall St James *Essex* **51** G2
Chigwell *Essex* **29** E5
Chigwell Row *Essex* **29** E5
Chilbolton *Hants* **26** B3
Chilcomb *Hants* **26** C2
Chilcombe *Dorset* **11** F4
Chilcompton *Somset* **24** B4
Chilcote *Leics* **71** H1
Child Okeford *Dorset* **12** B6
Child's Ercall *Shrops* **70** B2
Childer Thornton *Ches* **81** F2
Childrey *Oxon* **40** B3
Childswickham *Worcs* **47** F3
Childwall *Mersyd* **81** F4
Childwick Bury *Herts* **50** B2
Childwick Green *Herts* **50** B2
Chilfrome *Dorset* **11** F4
Chilgrove *W Susx* **15** F5
Chilham *Kent* **30** D1
Chilhampton *Wilts* **25** F2
Chilla *Devon* **8** A5
Chillaton *Devon* **8** A3
Chillenden *Kent* **31** F1
Chillerton *IOW* **14** C2
Chillesford *Suffk* **53** G6
Chillingham *Nthumb* **124** D4
Chillington *Devon* **7** E2
Chillington *Somset* **10** D6
Chilmark *Wilts* **25** E2
Chilmington Green *Kent* **18** C5
Chilson *Oxon* **48** A1
Chilsworthy *Cnwll* **5** H3
Chilsworthy *Devon* **20** C1
Chiltern Green *Beds* **50** B3
Chilthorne Domer *Somset* **23** H1
Chilton *Bucks* **41** E5
Chilton *Devon* **9** E5
Chilton *Dur* **106** B4
Chilton *Kent* **19** F6
Chilton *Oxon* **40** C3
Chilton *Suffk* **52** C5
Chilton Candover *Hants* **26** D3
Chilton Cantelo *Somset* **24** A1
Chilton Foliat *Wilts* **40** A1
Chilton Polden *Somset* **23** F3
Chilton Street *Suffk* **52** A5
Chilton Trinity *Somset* **23** F3
Chilwell *Notts* **72** C4
Chilworth *Hants* **14** B5
Chilworth *Surrey* **16** A6
Chimney *Oxon* **40** B4
Chineham *Hants* **27** E5
Chingford *Gt Lon* **29** E5
Chinley *Derbys* **83** E3
Chinnor *Oxon* **41** F4
Chipchase Castle *Nthumb* **113** F2

Chipnall *Shrops* **70** B3
Chippenham *Cambs* **63** F2
Chippenham *Wilts* **38** D2
Chipperfield *Herts* **28** A6
Chipping *Herts* **50** D4
Chipping *Lancs* **89** E4
Chipping Campden *Gloucs* **47** G3
Chipping Hill *Essex* **52** B2
Chipping Norton *Oxon* **48** A2
Chipping Ongar *Essex* **51** F1
Chipping Sodbury *Gloucs* **38** B2
Chipping Warden *Nhants* **48** C4
Chipstable *Somset* **22** C2
Chipstead *Kent* **29** F2
Chipstead *Surrey* **28** D2
Chirbury *Shrops* **56** C5
Chirk *Wrexhm* **69** E4
Chirnside *Border* **123** F5
Chirnsidebridge *Border* **123** F5
Chirton *Wilts* **25** F5
Chisbury *Wilts* **26** A6
Chiselborough *Somset* **11** E6
Chiseldon *Wilts* **39** F2
Chiselhampton *Oxon* **40** D4
Chisholme *Border* **112** A6
Chislehurst *Gt Lon* **29** E3
Chislet *Kent* **31** F2
Chisley *W York* **90** A2
Chiswell Green *Herts* **50** B1
Chiswick *Gt Lon* **28** C4
Chiswick End *Cambs* **51** E5
Chisworth *Derbys* **83** E4
Chitcombe *E Susx* **18** B3
Chithurst *W Susx* **27** G1
Chittering *Cambs* **62** D2
Chitterne *Wilts* **25** E4
Chittlehamholt *Devon* **21** G3
Chittlehampton *Devon* **21** G3
Chittlehampton *Devon* **21** G2
Chittoe *Wilts* **25** E5
Chivelstone *Devon* **7** E1
Chivenor *Devon* **21** E4
Chlenry *D & G* **100** C6
Chobham *Surrey* **27** H5
Cholderton *Wilts* **25** H3
Cholesbury *Bucks* **41** G5
Chollerford *Nthumb* **113** F2
Chollerton *Nthumb* **113** F2
Cholmondeston *Ches* **70** A6
Cholsey *Oxon* **40** D3
Cholstrey *Herefs* **45** G5
Chop Gate *N York* **98** A5
Choppington *Nthumb* **114** D4
Chopwell *T & W* **114** C1
Chorley *Ches* **69** H5
Chorley *Lancs* **88** D1
Chorley *Shrops* **57** G4
Chorley *Staffs* **71** F1
Chorleywood *Herts* **28** A6
Chorleywood West *Herts* **28** A6
Chorlton *Ches* **70** B5
Chorlton Lane *Ches* **69** G5
Chorlton-cum-Hardy *Gt Man* **82** C4
Choulton *Shrops* **56** D4
Chowley *Ches* **69** G6
Chrishall *Essex* **51** E5
Christchurch *Border* **128** D2
Christ's Hospital *W Susx* **16** B4
Christchurch *Cambs* **62** D5
Christchurch *Dorset* **13** E4
Christchurch *Gloucs* **37** G6
Christchurch *Mons* **37** E3
Christian Malford *Wilts* **38** D2
Christleton *Ches* **81** G1
Christmas Common *Oxon* **41** E4
Christon *Somset* **23** G5
Christon Bank *Nthumb* **125** E4
Christow *Devon* **9** E3
Chuck Hatch *E Susx* **17** F5
Chudleigh *Devon* **9** E2
Chudleigh Knighton *Devon* **9** E2
Chulmleigh *Devon* **21** G2
Chunal *Derbys* **83** E4
Church *Lancs* **89** F2
Church Aston *Shrops* **70** B2
Church Brampton *Nhants* **60** C2
Church Brough *Cumb* **105** E1
Church Broughton *Derbys* **71** G3
Church Cove *Cnwll* **3** E1
Church Crookham *Hants* **27** F4
Church Eaton *Staffs* **70** C2
Church End *Beds* **49** H2
Church End *Beds* **49** H1
Church End *Beds* **50** A4
Church End *Beds* **61** F1
Church End *Beds* **50** C4
Church End *Cambs* **61** G3
Church End *Cambs* **62** A4
Church End *Cambs* **62** C3
Church End *Cambs* **62** D1
Church End *Essex* **51** G3
Church End *Essex* **51** H3
Church End *Essex* **52** A2
Church End *Gt Lon* **28** C5
Church End *Hants* **27** E5
Church End *Herts* **50** B2
Church End *Herts* **50** D4
Church End *Herts* **51** E3
Church End *Lincs* **74** C3
Church End *Lincs* **86** D4
Church End *Warwks* **59** E4
Church End *Warwks* **59** F5
Church Enstone *Oxon* **48** B2
Church Fenton *N York* **91** F3
Church Green *Devon* **10** B4
Church Gresley *Derbys* **71** H2
Church Hanborough *Oxon* **40** C6
Church Hill *Ches* **82** B1
Church Hill *Staffs* **71** E1
Church Houses *N York* **98** B5
Church Knowle *Dorset* **12** C3
Church Laneham *Notts* **85** F2
Church Langton *Leics* **60** C5
Church Lawford *Warwks* **59** G3
Church Lawton *Staffs* **70** C6
Church Leigh *Staffs* **71** E4
Church Lench *Worcs* **47** F4

Church Mayfield *Staffs* **71** F4
Church Minshull *Ches* **70** B6
Church Norton *W Susx* **15** G3
Church Preen *Shrops* **57** F5
Church Pulverbatch *Shrops* **57** E6
Church Stowe *Nhants* **49** G5
Church Street *Essex* **52** B5
Church Street *Kent* **29** H3
Church Street *Suffk* **65** G4
Church Stretton *Shrops* **57** F5
Church Town *Lincs* **85** E5
Church Village *Rhondd* **36** B3
Church Warsop *Notts* **84** C1
Church Wilne *Derbys* **72** B3
Churcham *Gloucs* **46** C1
Churchbridge *Staffs* **58** C6
Churchdown *Gloucs* **46** D1
Churchend *Essex* **52** C5
Churchfield *W Mids* **58** C5
Churchgate *Herts* **50** D1
Churchgate Street *Essex* **51** F2
Churchill *Devon* **21** F5
Churchill *Devon* **10** C5
Churchill *Oxon* **48** A2
Churchill *Somset* **23** G5
Churchill *Worcs* **58** B3
Churchill *Worcs* **47** E5
Churchinford *Somset* **10** C6
Churchover *Warwks* **60** A3
Churchstanton *Somset* **10** B6
Churchstoke *Powys* **56** C5
Churchstow *Devon* **6** D2
Churchthorpe *Lincs* **86** D4
Churchtown *Derbys* **83** G1
Churchtown *Devon* **21** G5
Churchtown *Lancs* **88** B4
Churchtown *Lancs* **88** C4
Churchtown *Mersyd* **88** B1
Churnsike Lodge *Nthumb* **112** D2
Churston Ferrers *Devon* **7** F3
Churt *Surrey* **27** G3
Churton *Ches* **69** F6
Churwell *W York* **90** D2
Chwilog *Gwynd* **66** D4
Chyandour *Cnwll* **2** B3
Chyanvounder *Cnwll* **2** D2
Chyeowling *Cnwll* **3** E4
Chysauster *Cnwll* **2** B3
Chyvarloe *Cnwll* **2** D2
Cil *Powys* **56** B6
Cilcain *Flints* **80** D1
Cilcennin *Cerdgn* **43** E5
Cilcewydd *Powys* **56** C6
Cilfrew *Neath* **35** E4
Cilfynydd *Rhondd* **36** B3
Cilgerran *Pembks* **42** B3
Cilgwyn *Carmth* **43** G2
Cilgwyn *Gwynd* **67** E5
Ciliau-Aeron *Cerdgn* **43** E5
Cilmaengwyn *Neath* **35** E5
Cilmery *Powys* **44** C4
Cilrhedyn *Pembks* **42** C3
Cilsan *Carmth* **43** F1
Ciltalgarth *Gwynd* **68** A4
Cilycwm *Carmth* **43** H3
Cimla *Neath* **35** E4
Cinder Hill *W Mids* **58** B5
Cinderford *Gloucs* **37** H6
Cippenham *Berks* **41** H2
Cirencester *Gloucs* **39** E4
Citadilla *N York* **97** E5
City *Gt Lon* **28** D4
City *V Glam* **35** G2
City Airport *Gt Lon* **29** E4
City Dulas *IOA* **78** D3
Clabhach *Ag & B* **134** D5
Clachaig *Ag & B* **128** C4
Clachan *Ag & B* **136** C2
Clachan *Ag & B* **136** C4
Clachan *Ag & B* **117** G6
Clachan *Ag & B* **151** E2
Clachan Mor *Ag & B* **134** B4
Clachan na Luib *W Isls* **168** b5
Clachan of Campsie *E Duns* **130** B3
Clachan-a-Luib *W Isls* **168** b5
Clachan-Seil *Ag & B* **136** B2
Clachaneasy *D & G* **109** E2
Clachanharry *Highld* **155** E4
Clachtoll *Highld* **164** B1
Clackavoid *P & K* **140** B6
Clackmannan *Clacks* **131** E4
Clackmarras *Moray* **156** D5
Clacton-on-Sea *Essex* **53** E2
Cladich *Ag & B* **137** E2
Cladswell *Worcs* **47** F5
Claggan *Highld* **136** B5
Claigan *Highld* **150** B4
Clandown *Somset* **24** B5
Clanfield *Hants* **15** E5
Clanfield *Oxon* **39** G4
Clannaborough *Devon* **8** D5
Clanville *Hants* **26** A4
Clanville *Somset* **24** B2
Claonaig *Ag & B* **117** H6
Clap Hill *Kent* **18** D5
Clapgate *Dorset* **12** D5
Clapgate *Herts* **51** E3
Clapham *Beds* **50** A6
Clapham *Devon* **9** F3
Clapham *Gt Lon* **28** D4
Clapham *N York* **95** H2
Clapham *W Susx* **16** B2
Clapham Folly *Beds* **50** A6
Clappersgate *Cumb* **94** D5
Clapton *Somset* **10** D6
Clapton *Somset* **24** B5
Clapton-in-Gordano *Somset* **37** F2
Clapton-on-the-Hill *Gloucs* **39** F6
Clapworthy *Devon* **21** G3
Clarach *Cerdgn* **54** D4
Clarbeston *Pembks* **33** E4
Clarbeston Road *Pembks* **32** D4
Clarborough *Notts* **85** E3
Clare *Suffk* **52** A5
Clarebrand *D & G* **110** B1
Clarencefield *D & G* **111** E2
Clareton *N York* **91** E5

Clarewood *Nthumb* **114** B2
Clarilaw *Border* **122** B1
Clark's Green *Surrey* **16** C5
Clarken Green *Hants* **26** D4
Clarkston *E Rens* **119** G5
Clashmore *Highld* **164** A1
Clashmore *Highld* **162** D3
Clashnessie *Highld* **164** B1
Clashnoir *Moray* **156** D1
Clathy *P & K* **139** G2
Clathymore *P & K* **139** G2
Clatt *Abers* **157** G2
Clatter *Powys* **55** G5
Clatterford End *Essex* **51** G2
Clatworthy *Somset* **22** C2
Claughton *Lancs* **88** D3
Claughton *Lancs* **95** F1
Claughton *Mersyd* **81** E3
Claverdon *Warwks* **59** E2
Claverham *Somset* **23** G6
Clavering *Essex* **51** F4
Claverley *Shrops* **57** H5
Claverton *Somset* **24** C6
Claverton Down *Somset* **24** C6
Clawdd-coch *V Glam* **36** B2
Clawdd-newydd *Denbgs* **68** C5
Clawthorpe *Cumb* **95** F3
Clawton *Devon* **5** G6
Claxby *Lincs* **86** B4
Claxby *Lincs* **87** E2
Claxton *N York* **91** H6
Claxton *Norfk* **65** F6
Clay Common *Suffk* **65** G3
Clay Coton *Nhants* **60** B3
Clay Cross *Derbys* **84** B1
Clay End *Herts* **50** D3
Claybrooke Magna *Leics* **59** H4
Claydon *Oxon* **48** C4
Claydon *Suffk* **53** E6
Claygate *D & G* **112** A3
Claygate *Kent* **17** H6
Claygate *Surrey* **28** C2
Claygate Cross *Kent* **29** G2
Clayhall *Gt Lon* **29** E5
Clayhanger *Devon* **22** C1
Clayhanger *W Mids* **58** C6
Clayhidon *Devon* **10** B6
Clayhill *E Susx* **18** B4
Clayhill *Hants* **13** G5
Clayhithe *Cambs* **62** D2
Clayock *Highld* **167** E4
Claypit Hill *Cambs* **50** D6
Claypits *Gloucs* **38** B5
Claypole *Lincs* **73** F5
Claythorpe *Lincs* **86** D3
Clayton *S York* **84** B5
Clayton *W Susx* **16** D3
Clayton *W York* **90** B3
Clayton Green *Lancs* **88** D2
Clayton West *W York* **83** G6
Clayton-le-Moors *Lancs* **89** F3
Clayton-le-Woods *Lancs* **88** D2
Clayworth *Notts* **85** E3
Cleadale *Highld* **142** D3
Cleadon *T & W* **115** E2
Clearbrook *Devon* **6** C4
Clearwell *Gloucs* **37** G5
Clearwell Meend *Gloucs* **37** G5
Cleasby *N York* **106** B2
Cleat *Ork* **169** b1
Cleatlam *Dur* **105** H2
Cleator *Cumb* **102** D1
Cleator Moor *Cumb* **102** D2
Cleckheaton *W York* **90** C2
Clee St Margaret *Shrops* **57** F3
Cleedownton *Shrops* **57** F3
Cleehill *Shrops* **57** F3
Cleekhimin *N Lans* **120** B5
Cleestanton *Shrops* **57** F3
Cleethorpes *Lincs* **86** C6
Cleeton St Mary *Shrops* **57** F3
Cleeve *Oxon* **40** D2
Cleeve *Somset* **23** G6
Cleeve Hill *Gloucs* **47** E2
Cleeve Prior *Worcs* **47** F4
Cleghornie *E Loth* **133** E3
Clehonger *Herefs* **45** G3
Cleish *P & K* **131** G5
Cleland *N Lans* **120** C5
Clement Street *Kent* **29** F3
Clement's End *Beds* **50** A2
Clenamacrie *Ag & B* **136** D3
Clench Common *Wilts* **25** G6
Clenchwarton *Norfk* **75** F2
Clenerty *Abers* **158** D5
Clent *Worcs* **58** B3
Cleobury Mortimer *Shrops* **57** G3
Cleobury North *Shrops* **57** F4
Clephanton *Highld* **155** H4
Clerkhill *D & G* **111** G5
Cleuch-head *D & G* **110** C5
Clevancy *Wilts* **39** E2
Clevedon *Somset* **37** E1
Cleveley *Oxon* **48** B2
Cleveleys *Lancs* **88** B4
Clevelode *Worcs* **46** D4
Cleverton *Wilts* **38** D3
Clewer *Somset* **23** G4
Cley next the Sea *Norfk* **76** C4
Cliburn *Cumb* **104** C3
Cliddesden *Hants* **26** D4
Cliff Warwks* **59** E5
Cliff End *E Susx* **18** B3
Cliffe *Dur* **106** B2
Cliffe *Kent* **30** A4
Cliffe *Lancs* **89** F3
Cliffe *N York* **91** H3
Cliffe Woods *Kent* **30** A3
Clifford *Herefs* **45** E4
Clifford *W York* **91** E1
Clifford Chambers *Warwks* **47** G4
Clifford's Mesne *Gloucs* **46** C1
Cliffsend *Kent* **31** G2
Clifton *Beds* **50** C5
Clifton *Bristl* **37** G2
Clifton *Cumb* **104** B3

Clifton *Derbys* **71** G4
Clifton *Gt Man* **82** C5
Clifton *Lancs* **88** C3
Clifton *N York* **90** C4
Clifton *N York* **91** G5
Clifton *Notts* **72** C3
Clifton *Nthumb* **114** D4
Clifton *Oxon* **48** C2
Clifton *S York* **84** C4
Clifton *W York* **90** C2
Clifton *Worcs* **46** D4
Clifton Campville *Staffs* **71** G1
Clifton Dykes *Cumb* **104** B3
Clifton Hampden *Oxon* **40** D4
Clifton Reynes *Bucks* **49** G4
Clifton upon Dunsmore *Warwks* **60** A3
Clifton upon Teme *Worcs* **46** C5
Cliftonville *Kent* **31** G3
Climping *W Susx* **16** A2
Clink *Somset* **24** C4
Clint *N York* **90** D6
Clint Green *Norfk* **76** C1
Clinterty *Aber C* **149** F5
Clintmains *Border* **122** C3
Clipiau *Gwynd* **67** H1
Clippesby *Norfk* **77** G1
Clipsham *Rutlnd* **73** G2
Clipston *Nhants* **60** C3
Clipston *Notts* **72** D3
Clipstone *Beds* **49** H2
Clipstone *Notts* **84** D1
Clitheroe *Lancs* **89** F4
Clive *Shrops* **69** G2
Clixby *Lincs* **86** A5
Cloatley *Wilts* **38** D3
Clocaenog *Denbgs* **68** C5
Clochan *Moray* **157** F5
Clochtow *Angus* **141** F3
Clock Face *Mersyd* **81** G4
Cloddiau *Powys* **68** D1
Clodock *Herefs* **45** F2
Cloford *Somset* **24** C4
Clola *Abers* **159** F3
Clophill *Beds* **50** B4
Clopton *Nhants* **61** G3
Clopton *Suffk* **53** F6
Clopton Corner *Suffk* **53** F6
Clopton Green *Suffk* **52** A6
Clopton Green *Suffk* **64** B1
Clos du Valle *Guern* **174** h3
Closeburn *D & G* **110** C4
Closeburnmill *D & G* **110** D4
Closeclark *IOM* **174** k2
Closworth *Somset* **11** F6
Clothall *Herts* **50** D4
Clotton *Ches* **81** G1
Cloudesley Bush *Warwks* **59** G4
Clough *Gt Man* **82** D6
Clough Foot *W York* **89** G2
Clough Head *N York* **90** B1
Cloughton *N York* **99** F4
Cloughton Newlands *N York* **99** F4
Clousta *Shet* **169** q3
Clova *Angus* **148** A2
Clovelly *Devon* **20** C3
Clovenfords *Border* **122** B3
Clovulin *Highld* **137** G6
Clow Bridge *Lancs* **89** G2
Clowne *Derbys* **84** C2
Clows Top *Worcs* **57** G3
Cloy *Wrexhm* **69** F4
Cluanie Inn *Highld* **144** C6
Cluanie Lodge *Highld* **144** C5
Clubworthy *Cnwll* **5** F5
Clugston *D & G* **101** E6
Clun *Shrops* **56** C3
Clunas *Highld* **155** G6
Clunbury *Shrops* **56** D3
Clunderwen *Carmth* **33** E4
Clune *Highld* **147** H1
Clunes *Highld* **144** D3
Clungunford *Shrops* **56** D3
Clunie *Abers* **158** B4
Clunie *P & K* **140** A4
Clunton *Shrops* **56** D3
Cluny *Fife* **132** A5
Clutton *Ches* **69** G5
Clutton *Somset* **24** B5
Clutton Hill *Somset* **24** B5
Clwt-y-bont *Gwynd* **79** E1
Clydach *Mons* **36** C6
Clydach *Swans* **34** D4
Clydach Vale *Rhondd* **35** G3
Clydebank *W Duns* **129** F2
Clydey *Pembks* **42** C3
Clyffe Pypard *Wilts* **39** E2
Clynder *Ag & B* **128** C3
Clynderwen *Carmth* **33** E4
Clyne *Neath* **35** E4
Clynnog-fawr *Gwynd* **66** D5
Clyro *Powys* **45** E4
Clyst Honiton *Devon* **9** G4
Clyst Hydon *Devon* **9** G5
Clyst St George *Devon* **9** G3
Clyst St Lawrence *Devon* **9** G5
Clyst St Mary *Devon* **9** G4
Cnoc *W Isls* **168** f8
Cnwch Coch *Cerdgn* **54** D3
Coad's Green *Cnwll* **5** F4
Coal Aston *Derbys* **84** A3
Coal Pool *W Mids* **58** C5
Coal Street *Suffk* **65** E2
Coalbrookdale *Shrops* **57** G6
Coalbrookvale *Blae G* **36** C5
Coalburn *S Lans* **120** C3
Coalburns *T & W* **114** C1
Coalcleugh *Nthumb* **105** E5
Coaley *Gloucs* **38** B4
Coalfell *Cumb* **104** C6
Coalhill *Essex* **30** A6
Coalmoor *Shrops* **57** G6
Coalpit Heath *Gloucs* **38** B2
Coalpit Hill *Staffs* **70** C5
Coalport *Shrops* **57** G6
Coalsnaughton *Clacks* **131** E4
Coaltown of Balgonie *Fife* **132** B5
Coaltown of Wemyss *Fife* **132** B5
Coalville *Leics* **72** B1
Coanwood *Nthumb* **104** D6

Coat Somset ... 23 G1
Coatbridge N Lans ... 130 D2
Coatdyke N Lans ... 130 D2
Coate Wilts ... 25 F5
Coate Wilts ... 39 F2
Coates Cambs ... 62 B5
Coates Gloucs ... 38 D4
Coates Lincs ... 85 F3
Coates Lincs ... 85 G3
Coates W Susx ... 15 H5
Coatham N York ... 107 E3
Coatham Mundeville Dur ... 106 B3
Cobbaton Devon ... 21 F3
Coberley Gloucs ... 38 D6
Cobhall Common Herefs ... 45 G3
Cobham Kent ... 29 G3
Cobham Surrey ... 28 B2
Coblers Green Essex ... 51 H3
Cobley Dorset ... 25 F1
Cobnash Herefs ... 45 G5
Cobo Guern ... 174 g2
Cobridge Staffs ... 70 D5
Coburby Abers ... 159 E5
Cock & End Suffk ... 51 H6
Cock Alley Derbys ... 84 B2
Cock Bank Wrexhm ... 69 F5
Cock Bevington Warwks ... 47 F4
Cock Bridge Abers ... 147 G5
Cock Clarks Essex ... 52 B1
Cock Green Essex ... 51 H3
Cock Marling E Susx ... 18 B3
Cock Street Kent ... 30 A1
Cockayne N York ... 98 B5
Cockayne Hatley Beds ... 50 D6
Cockburnspath Border ... 133 G2
Cocker Bar Lancs ... 88 D2
Cocker Brook Lancs ... 89 F2
Cockerham Lancs ... 88 C5
Cockermouth Cumb ... 103 E3
Cockernhoe Green Herts ... 50 B3
Cockersdale W York ... 90 C3
Cockett Swans ... 34 D4
Cockfield Dur ... 105 H2
Cockfield Suffk ... 52 C6
Cockfosters Gt Lon ... 28 D6
Cocking W Susx ... 15 G6
Cocking Causeway W Susx ... 15 G6
Cockington Devon ... 7 F4
Cocklake Somset ... 23 G4
Cockle Park Nthumb ... 114 D5
Cockley Beck Cumb ... 94 C5
Cockley Cley Norfk ... 63 G6
Cockpole Green Berks ... 41 F2
Cocks Cnwll ... 3 E5
Cockshutford Shrops ... 57 F4
Cockshutt Shrops ... 69 G3
Cockthorpe Norfk ... 76 C4
Cockwells Cnwll ... 2 C3
Cockwood Devon ... 9 G3
Cockwood Somset ... 23 E3
Cockyard Derbys ... 83 E3
Cockyard Herefs ... 45 G3
Coddenham Suffk ... 53 E6
Coddington Ches ... 69 G6
Coddington Herefs ... 46 C3
Coddington Notts ... 73 F5
Codford St Mary Wilts ... 25 E3
Codford St Peter Wilts ... 25 E3
Codicote Herts ... 50 C2
Codmore Hill W Susx ... 16 B3
Codnor Derbys ... 72 B5
Codrington Gloucs ... 38 B2
Codsall Staffs ... 58 B6
Codsall Wood Staffs ... 58 A6
Coed Morgan Mons ... 37 E5
Coed Talon Flints ... 69 E6
Coed Ystumgwern Gwynd ... 67 E2
Coed-y-Bryn Cerdgn ... 42 D4
Coed-y-caerau Newpt ... 37 E3
Coed-y-paen Mons ... 36 D4
Coed-yr-ynys Powys ... 44 D1
Coedana IOA ... 78 D3
Coedely Rhondd ... 35 H3
Coedkernew Newpt ... 36 D3
Coedpoeth Wrexhm ... 69 E5
Coedway Powys ... 69 F1
Coelbren Powys ... 35 F5
Coffinswell Devon ... 7 F4
Cofton Devon ... 9 F3
Cofton Hackett Worcs ... 58 C3
Cogan V Glam ... 36 C1
Cogenhoe Nhants ... 49 F5
Cogges Oxon ... 40 B5
Coggeshall Essex ... 52 B3
Coggin's Mill E Susx ... 17 G4
Coignafearn Highld ... 146 B6
Coilacriech Abers ... 147 H4
Coilantogle Stirlg ... 130 B6
Coillore Highld ... 150 D2
Coiltry Highld ... 145 F5
Coity Brdgnd ... 35 G2
Col W Isls ... 168 f8
Colaboll Highld ... 162 C5
Colan Cnwll ... 4 B2
Colaton Raleigh Devon ... 10 A3
Colbost Highld ... 150 A4
Colburn N York ... 97 E5
Colbury Hants ... 13 G6
Colby Cumb ... 104 C2
Colby IOM ... 174 k2
Colby Norfk ... 77 E3
Colchester Essex ... 52 D3
Cold Ash Berks ... 40 C1
Cold Ashby Nhants ... 60 C3
Cold Ashton Gloucs ... 38 B1
Cold Aston Gloucs ... 47 G1
Cold Blow Pembks ... 33 E3
Cold Brayfield Bucks ... 49 G4
Cold Cotes N York ... 95 H2
Cold Green Herefs ... 46 B3
Cold Hanworth Lincs ... 85 H3
Cold Harbour Herts ... 50 B2
Cold Harbour Oxon ... 41 E2
Cold Harbour Wilts ... 24 D4
Cold Hatton Shrops ... 70 A2
Cold Hatton Heath Shrops ... 70 A2

Cold Hesledon Dur ... 106 D5
Cold Hiendley W York ... 84 A6
Cold Higham Nhants ... 49 E4
Cold Kirby N York ... 98 A3
Cold Newton Leics ... 60 C6
Cold Northcott Cnwll ... 5 F4
Cold Norton Essex ... 30 B6
Cold Overton Leics ... 73 F1
Cold Weston Shrops ... 57 F4
Coldbackie Highld ... 165 G4
Coldbeck Cumb ... 95 H5
Coldean E Susx ... 16 D2
Coldeast Devon ... 9 E2
Colden W York ... 89 H2
Colden Common Hants ... 26 C1
Coldfair Green Suffk ... 65 G1
Coldham Cambs ... 62 D6
Coldharbour Cnwll ... 3 E5
Coldharbour Devon ... 9 G6
Coldharbour Gloucs ... 37 G5
Coldharbour Surrey ... 16 B6
Coldingham Border ... 133 H2
Coldmeece Staffs ... 70 C3
Coldred Kent ... 19 F6
Coldridge Devon ... 8 D5
Coldstream Border ... 123 F3
Coldwaltham W Susx ... 16 A3
Coldwell Herefs ... 45 G3
Coldwells Abers ... 159 E3
Cole End Warwks ... 59 E4
Cole Green Herts ... 50 D2
Cole Green Herts ... 51 E4
Cole Henley Hants ... 26 C4
Cole's Cross Devon ... 7 E2
Colebatch Shrops ... 56 C4
Colebrook Devon ... 9 G5
Colebrook Devon ... 6 C3
Colebrooke Devon ... 9 E5
Coleby Lincs ... 92 C1
Coleby Lincs ... 73 G6
Coleford Devon ... 9 E5
Coleford Gloucs ... 37 G5
Coleford Somset ... 24 B4
Coleford Water Somset ... 22 D3
Colegate End Norfk ... 64 D4
Colehill Dorset ... 12 D5
Coleman Green Herts ... 50 C2
Coleman's Hatch E Susx ... 17 E5
Colemere Shrops ... 69 F3
Colemore Hants ... 27 E2
Colemore Green Shrops ... 57 G5
Colenden P & K ... 140 A3
Coleorton Leics ... 72 B2
Colerne Wilts ... 38 C1
Coles Cross Dorset ... 10 D5
Coles Green Suffk ... 53 E5
Colesbourne Gloucs ... 39 E6
Colesden Beds ... 61 G1
Coleshill Bucks ... 41 H4
Coleshill Oxon ... 39 G4
Coleshill Warwks ... 59 E4
Colestocks Devon ... 10 A5
Coley Somset ... 24 A5
Colgate W Susx ... 16 C5
Colinsburgh Fife ... 132 D5
Colinton C Edin ... 132 A2
Colintraive Ag & B ... 128 B2
Colkirk Norfk ... 76 B3
Collace P & K ... 140 B3
Collafirth Shet ... 169 h4
Collaton Devon ... 7 E1
Collaton Devon ... 7 E3
Collaton St Mary Devon ... 7 F4
College Green Somset ... 24 A3
College of Roseisle Moray ... 156 C6
Collessie Fife ... 140 C1
Colleton Mills Devon ... 21 G2
Collier Row Gt Lon ... 29 F5
Collier Street Kent ... 17 H6
Collier's End Herts ... 51 E3
Collier's Green Kent ... 18 B4
Colliers Green Kent ... 18 A5
Colliery Row T & W ... 106 C6
Colliston Abers ... 159 F2
Collin D & G ... 111 E2
Collingbourne Ducis Wilts ... 25 H5
Collingbourne Kingston Wilts ... 25 H5
Collingham Notts ... 85 F1
Collingham W York ... 91 E4
Collington Herefs ... 46 B5
Collingtree Nhants ... 49 F5
Collins Green Ches ... 81 H4
Collins Green Worcs ... 46 C5
Colliston Angus ... 141 F4
Colliton Devon ... 10 A5
Collyweston Nhants ... 61 F6
Colmonell S Ayrs ... 108 C3
Colmworth Beds ... 61 G1
Coln Rogers Gloucs ... 39 E5
Coln St Aldwyns Gloucs ... 39 F5
Coln St Dennis Gloucs ... 39 E5
Colnbrook Berks ... 28 A4
Colne Cambs ... 62 C3
Colne Lancs ... 89 G4
Colne Bridge W York ... 90 C2
Colne Edge Lancs ... 89 G4
Colne Engaine Essex ... 52 B4
Colney Norfk ... 64 D6
Colney Heath Herts ... 50 C1
Colney Street Herts ... 50 B1
Colpy Abers ... 158 B2
Colquhar Border ... 121 H4
Colquite Cnwll ... 4 D3
Colscott Devon ... 20 D2
Colsterdale N York ... 97 E3
Colsterworth Lincs ... 73 G2
Colston Bassett Notts ... 73 E3
Colt Hill Hants ... 27 F4
Colt's Hill Kent ... 17 G6
Colton Cumb ... 94 D3
Colton N York ... 91 F4
Colton Norfk ... 76 D1
Colton Staffs ... 71 E2
Colton W York ... 91 E4

Columbjohn Devon ... 9 F5
Colva Powys ... 45 E4
Colvend D & G ... 102 C6
Colwall Herefs ... 46 C3
Colwell Nthumb ... 113 G2
Colwich Staffs ... 71 E2
Colwick Notts ... 72 D4
Colwinston V Glam ... 35 G2
Colworth W Susx ... 15 G4
Colwyn Bay Conwy ... 79 H3
Colyford Devon ... 10 C4
Colyton Devon ... 10 C4
Combe Berks ... 26 B5
Combe Devon ... 7 E1
Combe Devon ... 7 F2
Combe Herefs ... 56 D2
Combe Oxon ... 40 B6
Combe Almer Dorset ... 12 C4
Combe Common Surrey ... 27 H3
Combe Down Somset ... 24 C5
Combe Fishacre Devon ... 7 F4
Combe Florey Somset ... 22 D2
Combe Hay Somset ... 24 C5
Combe Martin Devon ... 21 F5
Combe Raleigh Devon ... 10 B5
Combe St Nicholas Somset ... 10 C6
Combeinteignhead Devon ... 7 F5
Comberbach Ches ... 82 A2
Comberford Staffs ... 59 E6
Comberton Cambs ... 62 C1
Comberton Herefs ... 57 E2
Combpyne Devon ... 10 C4
Combridge Staffs ... 71 F4
Combrook Warwks ... 48 A4
Combs Derbys ... 83 E2
Combs Suffk ... 64 C1
Combs Ford Suffk ... 64 C1
Combwich Somset ... 23 E3
Comers Abers ... 148 D5
Comhampton Worcs ... 58 A2
Commercial Pembks ... 33 F3
Commercial End Cambs ... 63 E2
Commins Coch Powys ... 55 F6
Common Edge Lancs ... 88 B3
Common End Cumb ... 102 D2
Common Moor Cnwll ... 5 F3
Common Platt Wilts ... 39 F3
Common Side Derbys ... 84 A2
Commondale N York ... 107 F2
Commonside Ches ... 81 H2
Commonside Derbys ... 71 G4
Commonwood Shrops ... 69 G3
Commonwood Wrexhm ... 69 F5
Compass Somset ... 23 F3
Compstall Gt Man ... 83 E4
Compstonend D & G ... 101 H5
Compton Berks ... 40 C2
Compton Devon ... 7 F4
Compton Hants ... 26 B2
Compton Hants ... 26 C2
Compton Staffs ... 58 A4
Compton Surrey ... 27 H4
Compton W Susx ... 15 F5
Compton Wilts ... 25 G4
Compton Abbas Dorset ... 24 D1
Compton Abdale Gloucs ... 39 E6
Compton Bassett Wilts ... 39 E1
Compton Beauchamp Oxon ... 39 G3
Compton Bishop Somset ... 23 G5
Compton Chamberlayne Wilts ... 25 F2
Compton Dando Somset ... 24 B6
Compton Dundon Somset ... 23 H2
Compton Durville Somset ... 23 G1
Compton Greenfield Gloucs ... 37 G2
Compton Martin Somset ... 24 A5
Compton Pauncefoot Somset ... 24 B2
Compton Valence Dorset ... 11 F4
Compton Verney Warwks ... 48 A4
Comrie Fife ... 131 H4
Comrie P & K ... 139 E2
Conaglen House Highld ... 144 C1
Conchra Highld ... 152 C2
Concraigie P & K ... 140 A4
Conder Green Lancs ... 88 C5
Conderton Worcs ... 47 E3
Condicote Gloucs ... 47 G2
Condorrat N Lans ... 130 D2
Condover Shrops ... 57 E6
Coney Hill Gloucs ... 38 C6
Coney Weston Suffk ... 64 B3
Coneyhurst Common W Susx ... 16 B4
Coneysthorpe N York ... 98 C2
Coneythorpe N York ... 91 E5
Conford Hants ... 27 F3
Congdon's Shop Cnwll ... 5 F4
Congerstone Leics ... 59 F6
Congham Norfk ... 75 G2
Congl-y-wal Gwynd ... 67 G4
Congleton Ches ... 82 D1
Congresbury Somset ... 23 G6
Congreve Staffs ... 70 D1
Conheath D & G ... 110 D2
Conicavel Moray ... 156 B4
Coningsby Lincs ... 74 C6
Conington Cambs ... 61 H4
Conington Cambs ... 62 B2
Conisbrough S York ... 84 C5
Conisholme Lincs ... 86 D4
Coniston Cumb ... 94 D5
Coniston E R Yk ... 93 E3
Coniston Cold N York ... 89 G5
Conistone N York ... 96 C2
Connah's Quay Flints ... 81 E2
Connel Ag & B ... 136 D3
Connel Park E Ayrs ... 109 H6
Connor Downs Cnwll ... 2 C4
Conon Bridge Highld ... 154 D5
Cononley N York ... 90 A4
Consall Staffs ... 71 E5
Consett Dur ... 105 H5
Constable Burton N York ... 97 E4
Constable Lee Lancs ... 89 F2
Constantine Cnwll ... 3 E3
Constantine Bay Cnwll ... 4 B3
Contin Highld ... 154 C5
Conwy Conwy ... 79 G2
Conyer Kent ... 30 C2

Conyer's Green Suffk ... 64 A2
Cooden E Susx ... 17 H2
Cook's Green Essex ... 53 E3
Cookbury Devon ... 20 D1
Cookbury Wick Devon ... 20 D1
Cookham Berks ... 41 G3
Cookham Dean Berks ... 41 G3
Cookham Rise Berks ... 41 G3
Cookhill Warwks ... 47 F5
Cookley Suffk ... 65 F3
Cookley Worcs ... 58 A3
Cookley Green Oxon ... 41 E3
Cookney Abers ... 149 F6
Cooks Green Suffk ... 52 C6
Cooksbridge E Susx ... 17 E3
Cooksey Green Worcs ... 58 B2
Cookshill Staffs ... 70 D4
Cooksland Cnwll ... 4 D3
Cooksmill Green Essex ... 51 G1
Cookson Green Ches ... 81 H2
Cookson's Green Dur ... 106 B4
Coolham W Susx ... 16 B4
Cooling Kent ... 30 A4
Cooling Street Kent ... 30 A3
Coombe Cnwll ... 2 D5
Coombe Cnwll ... 3 F4
Coombe Devon ... 9 E3
Coombe Devon ... 7 G5
Coombe Devon ... 10 A4
Coombe Gloucs ... 38 B4
Coombe Hants ... 15 E6
Coombe Wilts ... 25 G4
Coombe Bissett Wilts ... 25 F2
Coombe Cellars Devon ... 7 F5
Coombe Cross Hants ... 15 E6
Coombe End Somset ... 22 C2
Coombe Hill Gloucs ... 46 D2
Coombe Keynes Dorset ... 12 B3
Coombe Pafford Devon ... 7 F4
Coombe Street Somset ... 24 C2
Coombes W Susx ... 16 C2
Coombes-Moor Herefs ... 56 D2
Coombeswood W Mids ... 58 C4
Cooper Street Kent ... 31 G2
Cooper Turning Gt Man ... 82 A5
Cooper's Corner Kent ... 29 F1
Cooperhill Moray ... 156 B4
Coopers Green E Susx ... 17 F4
Coopers Green Herts ... 50 C2
Coopersale Common Essex ... 51 F1
Coopersale Street Essex ... 51 F1
Cootham W Susx ... 16 B3
Cop Street Kent ... 31 F2
Copdock Suffk ... 53 E5
Copford Green Essex ... 52 C3
Copgrove N York ... 97 G1
Copister Shet ... 169 j4
Cople Beds ... 50 B6
Copley Dur ... 105 G3
Copley Gt Man ... 83 E4
Copley W York ... 90 B2
Coplow Dale Derbys ... 83 F3
Copmanthorpe N York ... 91 G4
Compere End Staffs ... 70 C3
Copp Lancs ... 88 C3
Coppathorne Cnwll ... 5 F6
Coppenhall Staffs ... 70 D2
Coppenhall Moss Ches ... 70 B6
Copperhouse Cnwll ... 2 C3
Coppicegate Shrops ... 57 G3
Coppingford Cambs ... 61 H3
Coppins Corner Kent ... 18 C6
Copplestone Devon ... 9 E5
Coppull Lancs ... 81 H6
Coppull Moor Lancs ... 81 H6
Copsale W Susx ... 16 C4
Copster Green Lancs ... 89 E3
Copston Magna Warwks ... 59 G4
Copt Heath W Mids ... 59 E3
Copt Hewick N York ... 97 G2
Copt Oak Leics ... 72 C1
Copthall Green Essex ... 29 E6
Copthorne Cnwll ... 5 F5
Copthorne W Susx ... 16 D5
Copythorne Hants ... 13 G6
Coram Street Suffk ... 52 D5
Corbets Tey Gt Lon ... 29 F5
Corbiere Jersey ... 174 a1
Corbridge Nthumb ... 113 G1
Corby Nhants ... 61 E4
Corby Glen Lincs ... 73 G2
Corby Hill Cumb ... 104 B6
Cordon N Ayrs ... 118 B2
Cordwell Derbys ... 83 H2
Coreley Shrops ... 57 F3
Cores End Bucks ... 41 G3
Corfe Somset ... 23 E1
Corfe Castle Dorset ... 12 C3
Corfe Mullen Dorset ... 12 D4
Corfton Shrops ... 57 E4
Corgarff Abers ... 147 H5
Corhampton Hants ... 14 D6
Corks Pond Kent ... 17 G5
Corley Warwks ... 59 F4
Corley Ash Warwks ... 59 F4
Corley Moor Warwks ... 59 F4
Cormuir Angus ... 147 H1
Cornard Tye Suffk ... 52 C5
Corndon Devon ... 8 D3
Corner Row Lancs ... 88 C3
Corney Cumb ... 94 B4
Cornforth Dur ... 106 C4
Cornhill Abers ... 158 B5
Cornhill-on-Tweed Nthumb ... 123 F3
Cornholme W York ... 89 G2
Cornish Hall End Essex ... 51 H4
Cornoigmore Ag & B ... 134 B4
Cornriggs Dur ... 105 E4
Cornsay Dur ... 105 H4
Cornsay Colliery Dur ... 106 A5
Corntown Highld ... 154 D5
Corntown V Glam ... 35 G2
Cornwell Oxon ... 48 A2
Cornwood Devon ... 6 C3
Cornworthy Devon ... 7 F3
Corpach Highld ... 144 C2
Corpusty Norfk ... 76 D3

Corrachree Abers ... 148 B5
Corran Cnwll ... 3 G4
Corran Highld ... 143 H5
Corran Highld ... 137 E6
Corrany IOM ... 174 m4
Corrie D & G ... 111 F3
Corrie N Ayrs ... 118 B4
Corriecravie N Ayrs ... 118 A2
Corriegills N Ayrs ... 118 B3
Corriegour Lodge Hotel Highld ... 145 E4
Corriemoille Highld ... 154 B5
Corrimony Highld ... 154 B2
Corringham Essex ... 29 H4
Corringham Lincs ... 85 F4
Corris Gwynd ... 55 E6
Corris Uchaf Gwynd ... 67 G1
Corrow Ag & B ... 128 C5
Corry Highld ... 151 F1
Cors-y-Gedol Gwynd ... 67 F2
Corscombe Devon ... 8 C4
Corscombe Dorset ... 11 E5
Corse Gloucs ... 46 C2
Corse Lawn Gloucs ... 46 D2
Corsham Wilts ... 38 C1
Corsindae Abers ... 148 D5
Corsley Wilts ... 24 D4
Corsley Heath Wilts ... 24 D4
Corsock D & G ... 110 B2
Corston Somset ... 24 C6
Corston Wilts ... 38 D3
Corstorphine C Edin ... 132 A2
Cortachy Angus ... 140 D6
Corton Suffk ... 65 H5
Corton Wilts ... 25 E3
Corton Denham Somset ... 24 B1
Coruanan Lodge Highld ... 144 C1
Corwen Denbgs ... 68 C4
Coryates Dorset ... 11 G3
Coryton Devon ... 8 B3
Coryton Essex ... 30 A4
Cosby Leics ... 60 B5
Coseley W Mids ... 58 B5
Cosford Shrops ... 58 A6
Cosgrove Nhants ... 49 F3
Cosham Hants ... 15 E4
Cosheston Pembks ... 32 D2
Coshieville P & K ... 139 E5
Cossall Notts ... 72 C4
Cossall Marsh Notts ... 72 B4
Cossington Leics ... 72 D1
Cossington Somset ... 23 F3
Costessey Norfk ... 77 E1
Costock Notts ... 72 C3
Coston Leics ... 73 F2
Coston Norfk ... 64 C6
Cote Oxon ... 40 B4
Cote Somset ... 23 F4
Cotebrook Ches ... 81 H1
Cotehill Cumb ... 104 A5
Cotes Cumb ... 95 F3
Cotes Leics ... 72 C2
Cotes Staffs ... 70 C3
Cotes Heath Staffs ... 70 C3
Cotesbach Leics ... 60 A4
Cotgrave Notts ... 72 D4
Cothal Abers ... 149 F6
Cotham Notts ... 73 F5
Cothelstone Somset ... 23 E2
Cotherstone Dur ... 105 G2
Cothill Oxon ... 40 C4
Cotleigh Devon ... 10 B5
Cotmanhay Derbys ... 72 B4
Coton Cambs ... 62 C1
Coton Nhants ... 60 C2
Coton Shrops ... 69 G3
Coton Staffs ... 70 C2
Coton Staffs ... 71 E3
Coton Staffs ... 59 E6
Coton Clanford Staffs ... 70 D2
Coton Hayes Staffs ... 71 E3
Coton Hill Shrops ... 69 G1
Coton in the Clay Staffs ... 71 G3
Coton in the Elms Derbys ... 71 G1
Coton Park Derbys ... 71 G2
Cott Devon ... 7 E4
Cottage End Hants ... 26 B4
Cottam E R Yk ... 99 F1
Cottam Lancs ... 88 C3
Cottam Notts ... 85 F3
Cottenham Cambs ... 62 D2
Cotterdale N York ... 96 B4
Cottered Herts ... 50 D4
Cotteridge W Mids ... 58 C3
Cotterstock Nhants ... 61 F4
Cottesbrooke Nhants ... 60 C3
Cottesmore Rutlnd ... 73 G1
Cottingham E R Yk ... 92 D3
Cottingham Nhants ... 60 D4
Cottingley W York ... 90 B3
Cottisford Oxon ... 48 D2
Cotton Suffk ... 64 C2
Cotton End Beds ... 50 B5
Cotton Tree Lancs ... 89 G4
Cottown Abers ... 157 G2
Cottown Abers ... 149 E6
Cottown of Gight Abers ... 158 D3
Cottrell V Glam ... 36 B2
Cotts Devon ... 6 B4
Cotwall Shrops ... 70 A2
Cotwalton Staffs ... 70 D3
Couch's Mill Cnwll ... 5 E2
Coughton Herefs ... 46 B1
Coughton Warwks ... 47 F5
Coulaghailtro Ag & B ... 127 G2
Coulags Highld ... 152 D4
Coulderton Cumb ... 102 D1
Coull Abers ... 148 C5
Coulport Ag & B ... 128 D4
Coulsdon Gt Lon ... 28 D2
Coulston Wilts ... 25 E5
Coulter S Lans ... 121 F3
Coultershaw Bridge W Susx ... 15 H6
Coultings Somset ... 23 E3
Coulton N York ... 98 B2
Coultra Fife ... 140 C2
Cound Shrops ... 57 F6
Coundlane Shrops ... 57 F6
Coundon Dur ... 106 B4

Coundon Grange *Dur* 106 B4
Countersett *N York* 96 B4
Countess *Wilts* 25 G3
Countess Cross *Essex* 52 B4
Countess Wear *Devon* 9 F3
Countesthorpe *Leics* 60 B5
Countisbury *Devon* 21 G6
Coup Green *Lancs* 88 D2
Coupar Angus *P & K* 140 B4
Coupland *Cumb* 104 D2
Coupland *Nthumb* 123 F2
Cour *Ag & B* 117 G5
Courance *D & G* 111 E4
Court Henry *Carmth* 43 F1
Court-at-Street *Kent* 18 D5
Courteachan *Highld* 143 F4
Courteenhall *Nhants* 49 F4
Courtsend *Essex* 30 D5
Courtway *Somset* 23 E3
Cousland *Mdloth* 132 C2
Cousley Wood *E Susx* 17 G5
Cove *Ag & B* 128 D3
Cove *Border* 133 G2
Cove *Devon* 22 B1
Cove *Hants* 27 G5
Cove *Highld* 160 B3
Cove Bay *Aber C* 149 G4
Cove Bottom *Suffk* 65 G3
Covehithe *Suffk* 65 H4
Coven *Staffs* 58 B6
Coven Lawn *Staffs* 58 B6
Coveney *Cambs* 62 D4
Covenham St Bartholomew *Lincs* 86 D4
Covenham St Mary *Lincs* 86 D4
Coventry *W Mids* 59 F3
Coventry Airport *Warwks* 59 F3
Coverack *Cnwll* 3 E2
Coverack Bridges *Cnwll* 2 D3
Coverham *N York* 96 D3
Covington *Cambs* 61 F2
Covington *S Lans* 120 D3
Cow Green *Suffk* 64 C2
Cow Honeybourne *Worcs* 47 G3
Cowan Bridge *Lancs* 95 G2
Cowbeech *E Susx* 17 G3
Cowbit *Lincs* 74 C2
Cowbridge *V Glam* 35 G2
Cowdale *Derbys* 83 F2
Cowden *Kent* 17 E5
Cowden Pound *Kent* 17 E6
Cowden Station *Kent* 17 F6
Cowdenbeath *Fife* 131 H4
Cowers Lane *Derbys* 71 H5
Cowes *IOW* 14 C3
Cowesby *N York* 97 H4
Cowesfield Green *Wilts* 25 H2
Cowfold *W Susx* 16 C4
Cowgill *Cumb* 96 A3
Cowhill *Gloucs* 37 G3
Cowie *Stirlg* 131 E4
Cowlam *E R Yk* 99 E1
Cowley *Derbys* 84 A2
Cowley *Devon* 9 F4
Cowley *Gloucs* 38 D6
Cowley *Gt Lon* 28 B4
Cowley *Oxon* 40 D5
Cowley *Oxon* 49 E2
Cowling *Lancs* 88 D1
Cowling *N York* 89 H4
Cowling *N York* 97 F4
Cowlinge *Suffk* 51 H6
Cowmes *W York* 90 C1
Cowpe *Lancs* 89 G2
Cowpen *Nthumb* 115 E4
Cowpen Bewley *Dur* 106 D3
Cowplain *Hants* 15 E5
Cowshill *Dur* 105 E4
Cowslip Green *Somset* 23 H5
Cowthorpe *N York* 91 E5
Cox Common *Suffk* 65 F4
Coxall *Shrops* 56 D3
Coxbank *Ches* 70 B4
Coxbench *Derbys* 72 A4
Coxbridge *Somset* 24 A3
Coxford *Cnwll* 5 E6
Coxford *Norfk* 76 B3
Coxgreen *Staffs* 58 A4
Coxheath *Kent* 30 A1
Coxhoe *Dur* 106 C4
Coxley *Somset* 23 H4
Coxley *W York* 90 D1
Coxley Wick *Somset* 23 H4
Coxpark *Cnwll* 5 H3
Coxtie Green *Essex* 29 F6
Coxwold *N York* 98 A3
Coychurch *Brdgnd* 35 G2
Coylton *S Ayrs* 119 F1
Coylumbridge *Highld* 146 D5
Coytrahen *Brdgnd* 35 F3
Crab Orchard *Dorset* 13 E5
Crabbs Cross *Worcs* 58 C2
Crabtree *W Susx* 16 C4
Crabtree Green *Wrexhm* 69 F4
Crackenthorpe *Cumb* 104 C2
Crackington Haven *Cnwll* 5 E6
Crackley *Staffs* 70 C5
Crackley *Warwks* 59 F3
Crackleybank *Shrops* 70 C1
Crackpot *N York* 96 C4
Cracoe *N York* 90 A6
Craddock *Devon* 10 A6
Cradle End *Herts* 51 E3
Cradley *Herefs* 46 C4
Cradley *W Mids* 58 B4
Cradley Heath *W Mids* 58 B4
Cradoc *Powys* 44 C2
Crafthole *Cnwll* 5 G1
Crafton *Bucks* 49 G1
Crag Foot *Lancs* 95 E2
Cragg Hill *W York* 90 D3
Cragg Vale *W York* 90 A2
Craggan *Highld* 156 B2
Craghead *Dur* 106 B6
Crai *Powys* 44 B2
Craibstone *Moray* 157 G3
Craichie *Angus* 141 E4
Craig *Angus* 141 G5
Craig *Highld* 153 E4

Craig Llangiwg *Neath* 35 E5
Craig Penllyn *V Glam* 35 G2
Craig's End *Essex* 51 H4
Craig-y-Duke *Neath* 35 E4
Craig-y-nos *Powys* 35 F6
Craigbank *E Ayrs* 109 H6
Craigburn *Border* 121 G3
Craigcefnparc *Swans* 34 D4
Craigcleuch *D & G* 111 H3
Craigdam *Abers* 158 D2
Craigdhu *Ag & B* 127 G6
Craigearn *Abers* 149 E6
Craigellachie *Moray* 157 E4
Craigend *P & K* 140 A2
Craigend *Rens* 129 F2
Craigendoran *Ag & B* 129 E3
Craighlaw *D & G* 100 D6
Craighouse *Ag & B* 126 D2
Craigie *P & K* 140 A4
Craigie *S Ayrs* 119 F3
Craigiefold *Abers* 159 E6
Craiglockhart *C Edin* 132 A2
Craiglug *Moray* 157 E5
Craigmillar *C Edin* 132 B2
Craignant *Shrops* 69 E3
Craigneston *D & G* 110 B4
Craigneuk *N Lans* 130 D2
Craigneuk *N Lans* 120 B5
Craignure *Ag & B* 136 B3
Craigo *Angus* 141 G6
Craigrothie *Fife* 132 C6
Craigruie *Stirlg* 138 B2
Craigton *Aber C* 149 F5
Craigton *Angus* 141 E4
Craigton *E Rens* 119 G5
Craigton of Airlie *Angus* 140 C5
Crail *Fife* 133 E6
Crailing *Border* 122 D2
Craiselound *Lincs* 85 E4
Crakehall *N York* 97 F4
Crakehill *N York* 97 G2
Crakemarsh *Staffs* 71 F4
Crambe *N York* 98 C1
Cramlington *Nthumb* 114 D3
Cramond *C Edin* 132 A3
Cramond Bridge *C Edin* 131 H3
Crampmoor *Hants* 26 B1
Cranage *Ches* 82 C1
Cranberry *Staffs* 70 C4
Cranborne *Dorset* 12 D6
Cranbrook *Kent* 18 A5
Cranbrook Common *Kent* 18 B5
Crane Moor *S York* 83 H5
Crane's Corner *Norfk* 76 B1
Cranfield *Beds* 49 H3
Cranford *Devon* 20 D3
Cranford *Gt Lon* 28 B4
Cranford St Andrew *Nhants* 61 E3
Cranford St John *Nhants* 61 E3
Cranham *Gloucs* 38 D6
Cranham *Gt Lon* 29 G5
Cranhill *Warwks* 47 G4
Crank *Mersyd* 81 G3
Cranleigh *Surrey* 16 B5
Cranmer Green *Suffk* 64 C2
Cranmore *IOW* 14 B3
Cranmore *Somset* 24 B4
Cranoe *Leics* 60 D5
Cransford *Suffk* 65 F2
Cranshaws *Border* 122 D6
Cranstal *IOM* 174 n5
Cranswick *E R Yk* 92 D3
Crantock *Cnwll* 4 B2
Cranwell *Lincs* 73 H5
Cranwich *Norfk* 63 G5
Cranworth *Norfk* 64 B6
Craobh Haven *Ag & B* 127 G6
Crapstone *Devon* 6 B4
Crarae *Ag & B* 128 A5
Crask Inn *Highld* 162 B6
Crask of Aigas *Highld* 154 C3
Craster *Nthumb* 125 F3
Craswall *Herefs* 45 F3
Crateford *Staffs* 70 D1
Cratfield *Suffk* 65 F3
Crathes *Abers* 149 E4
Crathes Castle *Abers* 149 E4
Crathie *Abers* 147 G4
Crathie *Highld* 145 H4
Crathorne *N York* 106 D2
Craven Arms *Shrops* 57 E4
Crawcrook *T & W* 114 C2
Crawford *Lancs* 81 G5
Crawford *S Lans* 120 D1
Crawfordjohn *S Lans* 120 C2
Crawick *D & G* 110 B6
Crawley *Hants* 26 C3
Crawley *Oxon* 40 B5
Crawley *W Susx* 16 D5
Crawley Down *W Susx* 16 D5
Crawleyside *Dur* 105 F4
Crawshawbooth *Lancs* 89 F2
Crawton *Abers* 149 F2
Craxe's Green *Essex* 52 C3
Cray *N York* 96 C3
Cray's Pond *Oxon* 41 E2
Crayford *Gt Lon* 29 F3
Crayke *N York* 98 A2
Craymere Beck *Norfk* 76 D3
Crays Hill *Essex* 29 H5
Craythorne *Staffs* 71 G4
Craze Lowman *Devon* 9 G6
Crazies Hill *Oxon* 41 F2
Creacombe *Devon* 22 A1
Creag Ghoraidh *W Isls* 168 b4
Creagan Inn *Ag & B* 136 b4
Creagorry *W Isls* 168 b4
Creaguaineach Lodge *Highld* 145 E1
Creamore Bank *Shrops* 69 G3
Creaton *Nhants* 60 C2
Creca *D & G* 111 G3
Credenhill *Herefs* 45 G3
Crediton *Devon* 9 E5
Creebank *D & G* 109 E2
Creebridge *D & G* 109 F1
Creech Heathfield *Somset* 23 F2
Creech St Michael *Somset* 23 F2

Creed *Cnwll* 3 G4
Creedy Park *Devon* 9 E5
Creekmouth *Gt Lon* 29 E4
Creeting St Mary *Suffk* 64 C1
Creeton *Lincs* 73 H2
Creetown *D & G* 101 F6
Cregneash *IOM* 174 j2
Cregny Baa *IOM* 174 m3
Cregrina *Powys* 44 D1
Creich *Fife* 140 C2
Creigiau *Cardif* 36 B2
Crelly *Cnwll* 2 D3
Cremyll *Cnwll* 6 B3
Cressage *Shrops* 57 F6
Cressbrook *Derbys* 83 G2
Cresselly *Pembks* 33 E2
Cressex *Bucks* 41 F3
Cressing *Essex* 52 B3
Cresswell *Nthumb* 115 E5
Cresswell *Pembks* 33 E2
Cresswell *Staffs* 71 E4
Creswell *Derbys* 84 C2
Creswell Green *Staffs* 71 F1
Cretingham *Suffk* 65 E1
Cretshengan *Ag & B* 127 F2
Crew Green *Powys* 69 E2
Crewe *Ches* 69 F5
Crewe *Ches* 70 B6
Crewe Green *Ches* 70 B6
Crewkerne *Somset* 11 E6
Crews Hill *Herefs* 46 B1
Crews Hill Station *Herts* 28 D6
Crewton *Derbys* 72 B3
Crianlarich *Stirlg* 138 A2
Cribbs Causeway *Gloucs* 37 G2
Cribyn *Cerdgn* 43 E4
Criccieth *Gwynd* 67 E4
Crich *Derbys* 72 A5
Crich Carr *Derbys* 72 A5
Crich Common *Derbys* 72 A5
Crichton *Mdloth* 122 A6
Crick *Mons* 37 F3
Crick *Nhants* 60 B3
Crickadarn *Powys* 44 D3
Cricket St Thomas *Somset* 10 D5
Crickheath *Shrops* 69 E2
Crickhowell *Powys* 45 E1
Cricklade *Wilts* 39 F4
Cricklewood *Gt Lon* 28 C5
Cridling Stubbs *N York* 91 F2
Crieff *P & K* 139 F2
Criggan *Cnwll* 4 D2
Criggion *Powys* 69 E1
Crigglestone *W York* 90 D1
Crimble *Gt Man* 82 D6
Crimond *Abers* 159 F5
Crimplesham *Norfk* 63 F6
Crimscote *Warwks* 47 H4
Crinaglack *Highld* 154 C3
Crinan *Ag & B* 127 G4
Crindledyke *N Lans* 120 C5
Cringleford *Norfk* 64 D6
Cringles *N York* 90 B4
Crinow *Pembks* 33 E3
Cripp's Corner *E Susx* 18 A3
Cripplesease *Cnwll* 2 C3
Cripplestyle *Dorset* 13 E6
Crizeley *Herefs* 45 G2
Croachy *Highld* 155 E2
Croanford *Cnwll* 4 D3
Crochmore House *D & G* 110 C2
Crock Street *Somset* 10 D6
Crockenhill *Kent* 29 F3
Crocker End *Oxon* 41 E3
Crocker's Ash *Herefs* 37 F6
Crockerhill *W Susx* 15 G4
Crockernwell *Devon* 8 D4
Crockerton *Wilts* 24 D3
Crocketford *D & G* 110 C2
Crockey Hill *N York* 91 G4
Crockham Hill *Kent* 29 E1
Crockhurst Street *Kent* 17 G6
Crockleford Heath *Essex* 52 D3
Croes-goch *Pembks* 32 C5
Croes-lan *Cerdgn* 42 D4
Croes-y-mwyalch *Torfn* 36 D3
Croes-y-pant *Mons* 36 D5
Croeserw *Neath* 35 F4
Croesor *Gwynd* 67 F4
Croesyceiliog *Carmth* 34 B6
Croesyceiliog *Torfn* 36 D4
Croft *Ches* 82 A4
Croft *Devon* 8 B4
Croft *Leics* 60 A5
Croft *Lincs* 75 E6
Croft Michael *Cnwll* 2 D3
Croft-on-Tees *Dur* 106 B2
Croftamie *Stirlg* 129 F4
Crofton *Cumb* 103 G5
Crofton *N York* 91 E1
Crofton *Wilts* 25 H5
Crofts *D & G* 110 B1
Crofts *Moray* 157 E4
Crofts Bank *Gt Man* 82 C4
Crofts of Dipple *Moray* 157 E5
Crofts of Savoch *Abers* 159 F5
Crofty *Swans* 34 C4
Crogen *Gwynd* 68 B4
Croggan *Ag & B* 136 B2
Croglin *Cumb* 104 B5
Croik *Highld* 162 A3
Cromarty *Highld* 155 F6
Crombie *Fife* 131 G4
Cromdale *Highld* 156 C2
Cromer *Herts* 50 D3
Cromer *Norfk* 77 E4
Cromford *Derbys* 71 H6
Cromhall *Gloucs* 38 B3
Cromhall Common *Gloucs* 38 B3
Cromor *W Isls* 168 e7
Crompton Fold *Gt Man* 82 D6
Cromwell *Notts* 73 F6
Cronberry *E Ayrs* 119 H2
Crondall *Hants* 27 F4
Cronk-y-Voddy *IOM* 174 l4
Cronkbourne *IOM* 174 l3
Cronton *Mersyd* 81 G3
Crook *Cumb* 95 E4

Crook *Dur* 106 A4
Crook Inn *Border* 121 E2
Crook of Devon *P & K* 131 G5
Crookdake *Cumb* 103 F4
Crooke *Gt Man* 81 H5
Crooked End *Gloucs* 37 G6
Crooked Holme *Cumb* 112 B1
Crooked Soley *Wilts* 40 A1
Crookedholm *E Ayrs* 119 F3
Crookes *S York* 84 A3
Crookhall *Dur* 105 H5
Crookham *Berks* 26 D6
Crookham *Nthumb* 123 F3
Crookham Village *Hants* 27 F4
Crooklands *Cumb* 95 F3
Cropper *Derbys* 71 G3
Cropredy *Oxon* 48 C4
Cropston *Leics* 72 C1
Cropthorne *Worcs* 47 F2
Cropton *N York* 98 C4
Cropwell Bishop *Notts* 72 D4
Cropwell Butler *Notts* 72 D4
Cros *W Isls* 168 f9
Crosbie *N Ayrs* 118 C4
Crosbost *W Isls* 168 e7
Crosby *Cumb* 103 E4
Crosby *IOM* 174 l3
Crosby *Lincs* 85 F6
Crosby *Mersyd* 81 E4
Crosby Garret *Cumb* 95 H6
Crosby Ravensworth *Cumb* 104 C2
Crosby Villa *Cumb* 103 E4
Croscombe *Somset* 24 B4
Crosemere *Shrops* 69 G3
Crosland Edge *W York* 83 F6
Crosland Hill *W York* 90 B1
Cross *Somset* 23 G5
Cross Ash *Mons* 45 G1
Cross Coombe *Cnwll* 3 E5
Cross End *Beds* 61 G1
Cross End *Essex* 52 B4
Cross Flatts *W York* 90 B4
Cross Gates *W York* 91 E3
Cross Green *Devon* 5 G5
Cross Green *Staffs* 58 B6
Cross Green *Suffk* 52 B6
Cross Green *Suffk* 64 B1
Cross Green *Suffk* 52 C6
Cross Hands *Carmth* 34 C5
Cross Hands *Pembks* 33 E3
Cross Hill *Derbys* 72 B5
Cross Hills *N York* 90 A4
Cross Houses *Shrops* 57 F6
Cross Houses *Shrops* 57 G5
Cross in Hand *E Susx* 17 F3
Cross Inn *Cerdgn* 42 D5
Cross Inn *Cerdgn* 54 C2
Cross Inn *Pembks* 33 E2
Cross Inn *Rhondd* 36 B2
Cross Keys *Ag & B* 129 E4
Cross Keys *Wilts* 38 C1
Cross Lane *IOW* 14 C3
Cross Lane Head *Shrops* 57 G5
Cross Lanes *Cnwll* 2 D2
Cross Lanes *Cnwll* 3 E4
Cross Lanes *N York* 98 A1
Cross Lanes *Wrexhm* 69 F5
Cross o' th' hands *Derbys* 71 H5
Cross Oak *Powys* 44 D1
Cross of Jackston *Abers* 158 C2
Cross Roads *Powys* 44 C5
Cross Street *Suffk* 64 D3
Cross Town *Ches* 82 C2
Cross-at-Hand *Kent* 18 A6
Crossaig *Ag & B* 117 G5
Crossapoll *Ag & B* 134 B4
Crossbush *W Susx* 16 A4
Crosscanonby *Cumb* 103 E4
Crossdale Street *Norfk* 77 E4
Crossens *Mersyd* 88 B2
Crossford *Fife* 131 G4
Crossford *S Lans* 120 C4
Crossgate *Cnwll* 5 G5
Crossgate *Lincs* 74 C3
Crossgate *Staffs* 70 D4
Crossgatehall *E Loth* 132 C2
Crossgates *E Ayrs* 119 E4
Crossgates *Fife* 131 H4
Crossgates *N York* 99 F3
Crossgates *Powys* 56 A2
Crossgill *Lancs* 88 D6
Crosshands *Carmth* 33 F4
Crosshands *E Ayrs* 119 G2
Crosshill *Fife* 131 H5
Crosshill *S Ayrs* 109 E5
Crosshouse *E Ayrs* 119 E3
Crosskeys *Caerph* 36 C3
Crosskirk *Highld* 166 B5
Crosslands *Cumb* 94 D4
Crosslanes *Shrops* 69 E2
Crosslee *Rens* 129 E2
Crossley *S York* 90 C2
Crossmichael *D & G* 110 B1
Crosspost *W Susx* 16 C4
Crossroads *Abers* 148 C5
Crossroads *Abers* 149 E4
Crosston *Angus* 141 E5
Crossway *Mons* 45 G1
Crossway *Pembks* 42 B3
Crossway *Powys* 44 C5
Crossway Green *Mons* 37 F4
Crossway Green *Worcs* 58 A2
Crossways *Dorset* 12 B3
Crosswell *Pembks* 42 B3
Crosthwaite *Cumb* 95 E4
Croston *Lancs* 88 C1
Crostwick *Norfk* 77 F5
Crostwight *Norfk* 77 F3
Crouch *Kent* 30 D2
Crouch *Kent* 29 G2
Crouch End *Gt Lon* 28 D5
Crouch Fold *Gt Man* 82 D6
Crouch Hill *Dorset* 11 G5
Croughton *Nhants* 48 D2
Crovie *Abers* 158 D6
Crow *Hants* 13 E5
Crow Edge *S York* 83 G5

Crow End *Cambs* 62 C1
Crow Green *Essex* 29 G6
Crow Hill *Herefs* 46 B2
Crow's Green *Essex* 51 H3
Crow's Nest *Cnwll* 5 F3
Crowan *Cnwll* 2 D3
Crowborough *E Susx* 17 F4
Crowborough Town *E Susx* 17 F5
Crowcombe *Somset* 22 D3
Crowdecote *Derbys* 83 F1
Crowden *Derbys* 83 F5
Crowden *Devon* 8 B4
Crowdhill *Hants* 14 C6
Crowdleham *Kent* 29 F2
Crowell *Oxon* 41 F3
Crowfield *Nhants* 48 D3
Crowfield *Suffk* 64 D1
Crowfield Green *Suffk* 64 D1
Crowgate Street *Norfk* 77 F2
Crowhill *E Loth* 133 F2
Crowhole *Derbys* 84 A2
Crowhurst *E Susx* 18 A3
Crowhurst *Surrey* 17 E6
Crowhurst Lane End *Surrey* 17 E6
Crowland *Lincs* 74 C1
Crowland *Suffk* 64 C2
Crowlas *Cnwll* 2 C3
Crowle *Lincs* 85 E6
Crowle *Worcs* 47 E5
Crowle Green *Worcs* 47 E5
Crowmarsh Gifford *Oxon* 40 D3
Crown Corner *Suffk* 65 E2
Crownhill *Devon* 6 B3
Crownpits *Surrey* 27 H4
Crownthorpe *Norfk* 64 C6
Crowntown *Cnwll* 2 D3
Crows-an-Wra *Cnwll* 2 B2
Crowshill *Norfk* 64 B6
Crowsnest *Shrops* 56 D5
Crowthorne *Berks* 27 G6
Crowton *Ches* 81 H2
Croxall *Staffs* 71 G1
Croxby *Lincs* 86 B4
Croxdale *Dur* 106 B4
Croxden *Staffs* 71 F4
Croxley Green *Herts* 28 B5
Croxton *Cambs* 62 B1
Croxton *Lincs* 86 A6
Croxton *Norfk* 76 C3
Croxton *Norfk* 64 A4
Croxton *Staffs* 70 C3
Croxton Green *Ches* 69 H5
Croxton Kerrial *Leics* 73 F3
Croxtonbank *Staffs* 70 C3
Croy *Highld* 155 F4
Croy *N Lans* 130 D3
Croyde *Devon* 21 E4
Croyde Bay *Devon* 20 D5
Croydon *Cambs* 50 D6
Croydon *Gt Lon* 28 D3
Crubenmore *Highld* 146 B3
Cruckmeole *Shrops* 69 F1
Cruckton *Shrops* 69 F1
Cruden Bay *Abers* 159 G3
Crudgington *Shrops* 70 A2
Crudwell *Wilts* 38 D4
Crug *Powys* 56 B3
Crug-y-byddar *Powys* 56 B4
Crugmeer *Cnwll* 4 C4
Crugybar *Carmth* 43 G3
Crumlin *Caerph* 36 C4
Crumplehorn *Cnwll* 5 F1
Crumpsall *Gt Man* 82 C5
Crundale *Kent* 30 D1
Crundale *Pembks* 32 D3
Crunwear *Pembks* 33 F3
Cruwys Morchard *Devon* 9 F6
Crux Easton *Hants* 26 C5
Cruxton *Dorset* 11 F4
Crwbin *Carmth* 34 B6
Cryers Hill *Bucks* 41 G4
Crymmych *Pembks* 42 B3
Crynant *Neath* 35 E5
Crystal Palace *Gt Lon* 28 D3
Cuaig *Highld* 151 G4
Cuan Ferry Village *Ag & B* 136 B1
Cubbington *Warwks* 59 F2
Cubert *Cnwll* 4 B2
Cubley *S York* 83 G5
Cublington *Bucks* 49 G1
Cublington *Herefs* 45 G3
Cuckfield *W Susx* 16 D4
Cucklington *Somset* 24 C2
Cuckney *Notts* 84 C2
Cuckold's Green *Kent* 30 B4
Cuckoo Bridge *Lincs* 74 B2
Cuckoo's Corner *Hants* 27 F3
Cuckoo's Nest *Ches* 69 F6
Cuddesdon *Oxon* 40 D5
Cuddington *Bucks* 41 F5
Cuddington *Ches* 82 A2
Cuddington Heath *Ches* 69 G5
Cuddy Hill *Lancs* 88 C3
Cudham *Gt Lon* 29 E2
Cudliptown *Devon* 8 B2
Cudnell *Dorset* 12 D4
Cudworth *S York* 84 B6
Cudworth *Somset* 10 D6
Cudworth Common *S York* 84 B6
Cuerden Green *Lancs* 88 D2
Cuerdley Cross *Ches* 81 H3
Cufaude *Hants* 27 E5
Cuffley *Herts* 50 D1
Cuil *Highld* 136 D5
Culbokie *Highld* 154 D5
Culbone *Somset* 22 A4
Culburnie *Highld* 154 C3
Culcabock *Highld* 155 E3
Culcharry *Highld* 155 G4
Culcheth *Ches* 82 B4
Culdrain *Abers* 157 G2
Culduie *Highld* 151 G3
Culford *Suffk* 63 G2
Culgaith *Cumb* 104 C3
Culham *Oxon* 40 C4
Culkein *Highld* 164 A2
Culkein Drumbeg *Highld* 164 B2
Culkerton *Gloucs* 38 D4

Cullen Moray ... 157 G6
Cullercoats T & W ... 115 E3
Cullerlie Abers ... 149 E5
Cullicudden Highld ... 155 E5
Cullingworth W York ... 90 B3
Cullipool House Ag & B ... 136 B1
Cullivoe Shet ... 169 j5
Culloden Highld ... 155 E4
Cullompton Devon ... 9 G5
Culm Davy Devon ... 10 B6
Culmington Shrops ... 57 E4
Culmstock Devon ... 10 A6
Culnacraig Highld ... 161 E4
Culnaightrie D & G ... 102 B5
Culnaknock Highld ... 151 E5
Culpho Suffk ... 53 F6
Culrain Highld ... 162 C3
Culross Fife ... 131 F4
Culroy S Ayrs ... 109 E6
Culsalmond Abers ... 158 B2
Culscadden D & G ... 101 F5
Culshabbin D & G ... 100 D5
Culswick Shet ... 169 h2
Cultercullen Abers ... 159 E1
Cults Aber C ... 149 F5
Culverstone Green Kent ... 29 G2
Culverthorpe Lincs ... 73 H4
Culworth Nhants ... 48 D4
Culzean Castle S Ayrs ... 108 D6
Cumbernauld N Lans ... 130 D2
Cumbernauld Village N Lans ... 130 D3
Cumberworth Lincs ... 87 E2
Cumdivock Cumb ... 103 G5
Cuminestown Abers ... 158 D4
Cumledge Border ... 123 E5
Cummersdale Cumb ... 103 H5
Cummertrees D & G ... 111 F1
Cummingstown Moray ... 156 C6
Cumnock E Ayrs ... 119 G1
Cumnor Oxon ... 40 C5
Cumrew Cumb ... 104 B5
Cumrue D & G ... 111 E3
Cumwhinton Cumb ... 104 A5
Cumwhitton Cumb ... 104 B5
Cundall N York ... 97 G2
Cunninghamhead N Ayrs ... 119 E4
Cupar Fife ... 140 D1
Cupar Muir Fife ... 140 D1
Curbar Derbys ... 83 G2
Curbridge Hants ... 14 C5
Curbridge Oxon ... 40 B5
Curdridge Hants ... 14 C5
Curdworth Warwks ... 59 E5
Curland Somset ... 23 F1
Curridge Berks ... 40 C1
Currie C Edin ... 131 H2
Curry Mallet Somset ... 23 F1
Curry Rivel Somset ... 23 G2
Curteis Corner Kent ... 18 B5
Curtisden Green Kent ... 18 A5
Curtisknowle Devon ... 7 E3
Cury Cnwll ... 2 D2
Cushnie Abers ... 148 C6
Cushuish Somset ... 23 E2
Cusop Herefs ... 45 E3
Cutcloy D & G ... 101 F4
Cutcombe Somset ... 22 B3
Cutgate Gt Man ... 82 D6
Cuthill Highld ... 162 D2
Cutiau Gwynd ... 67 F2
Cutler's Green Essex ... 51 G4
Cutmadoc Cnwll ... 5 E2
Cutmere Cnwll ... 5 G2
Cutnall Green Worcs ... 58 B2
Cutsdean Gloucs ... 47 F2
Cutsyke W York ... 91 E2
Cutthorpe Derbys ... 84 A2
Cuttivett Cnwll ... 5 G2
Cuxham Oxon ... 41 E4
Cuxton Kent ... 29 H3
Cuxwold Lincs ... 86 B5
Cwm Blae G ... 36 C5
Cwm Denbgs ... 80 C2
Cwm Capel Carmth ... 34 B4
Cwm Crawnon Powys ... 44 D1
Cwm Dulais Swans ... 34 D5
Cwm Irfon Powys ... 44 A4
Cwm Llinau Powys ... 55 F6
Cwm Morgan Carmth ... 42 C3
Cwm Penmachno Conwy ... 67 G5
Cwm-bach Carmth ... 34 B4
Cwm-celyn Blae G ... 36 C5
Cwm-Cewydd Gwynd ... 68 A1
Cwm-cou Cerdgn ... 42 C3
Cwm-Ifor Carmth ... 43 G2
Cwm-y-glo Carmth ... 34 C6
Cwm-y-glo Gwynd ... 79 E1
Cwmafan Neath ... 35 E3
Cwmaman Rhondd ... 35 G4
Cwmann Carmth ... 43 F4
Cwmavon Torfn ... 36 D5
Cwmbach Carmth ... 33 G4
Cwmbach Powys ... 44 D3
Cwmbach Rhondd ... 35 H4
Cwmbach Llechrhyd Powys ... 44 C5
Cwmbelan Powys ... 55 G3
Cwmbran Torfn ... 36 D4
Cwmbrwyno Cerdgn ... 55 E3
Cwmcarn Caerph ... 36 C4
Cwmcarvan Mons ... 37 F5
Cwmdare Rhondd ... 35 G5
Cwmdu Carmth ... 43 F2
Cwmdu Powys ... 45 E2
Cwmdu Swans ... 34 D4
Cwmduad Carmth ... 42 D2
Cwmdwr Carmth ... 43 G2
Cwmergyr Cerdgn ... 55 E4
Cwmfelin Brdgnd ... 35 F3
Cwmfelin Myr Td ... 36 B4
Cwmfelin Boeth Carmth ... 33 F4
Cwmfelin Mynach Carmth ... 33 H4
Cwmfelinfach Caerph ... 36 C3
Cwmffrwd Carmth ... 34 B6
Cwmgiedd Powys ... 35 E5
Cwmgors Carmth ... 34 D5
Cwmgwili Carmth ... 34 C5
Cwmgwrach Neath ... 35 F5
Cwmhiraeth Carmth ... 42 D3

Cwmisfael Carmth ... 34 B6
Cwmllynfell Neath ... 35 E6
Cwmmawr Carmth ... 34 C5
Cwmparc Rhondd ... 35 G4
Cwmpengraig Carmth ... 42 D3
Cwmpennar Rhondd ... 36 B4
Cwmrhos Powys ... 45 E2
Cwmrhydyceirw Swans ... 34 D4
Cwmsychbant Cerdgn ... 43 E4
Cwmtillery Blae G ... 36 C5
Cwmwoy Mons ... 45 F1
Cwmystwyth Cerdgn ... 55 E3
Cwrt Gwynd ... 54 D5
Cwrt-newydd Cerdgn ... 43 E4
Cwrt-y-gollen Powys ... 36 C6
Cyfronydd Powys ... 56 B6
Cylibebyll Neath ... 35 E5
Cymer Neath ... 35 F4
Cymmer Rhondd ... 36 A3
Cynghordy Carmth ... 44 A3
Cynheidre Carmth ... 34 B5
Cynonville Neath ... 35 F4
Cynwyd Denbgs ... 68 C4
Cynwyl Elfed Carmth ... 42 D2

D

Daccombe Devon ... 7 F4
Dacre Cumb ... 104 A3
Dacre N York ... 90 C6
Dacre Banks N York ... 90 C6
Daddry Shield Dur ... 105 F4
Dadford Bucks ... 49 E3
Dadlington Leics ... 59 G5
Dafen Carmth ... 34 C4
Daffy Green Norfk ... 76 C1
Dagenham Gt Lon ... 29 F4
Daglingworth Gloucs ... 39 E5
Dagnall Bucks ... 41 H6
Dagworth Suffk ... 64 C1
Dailly S Ayrs ... 108 D5
Dainton Devon ... 7 F4
Dairsie Fife ... 140 D1
Daisy Hill Gt Man ... 82 B5
Daisy Hill W York ... 90 D2
Dalabrog W Isls ... 168 b3
Dalavich Ag & B ... 136 D1
Dalbeattie D & G ... 110 C1
Dalbury Derbys ... 71 G3
Dalby IOM ... 174 k3
Dalby Lincs ... 86 D2
Dalby N York ... 98 B2
Dalcapon P & K ... 139 G5
Dalchalm Highld ... 163 F4
Dalchreichart Highld ... 145 E6
Dalchruin P & K ... 138 D1
Dalcrue P & K ... 139 H2
Dalderby Lincs ... 86 C1
Daldulich Devon ... 9 G3
Dale Cumb ... 104 B4
Dale Derbys ... 72 B4
Dale Pembks ... 32 B2
Dale Bottom Cumb ... 103 G2
Dale End Derbys ... 71 G6
Dale End N York ... 89 H4
Dale Hill E Susx ... 17 H4
Dalehouse N York ... 107 G3
Dalgarven N Ayrs ... 119 E4
Dalgety Bay Fife ... 131 H3
Dalginross P & K ... 139 E2
Dalguise P & K ... 139 G4
Dalhalvaig Highld ... 166 C4
Dalham Suffk ... 63 F1
Daliburgh W Isls ... 168 b3
Dalkeith Mdloth ... 132 B2
Dallas Moray ... 156 C4
Dallinghoo Suffk ... 53 F6
Dallington E Susx ... 17 G3
Dallington Nhants ... 49 E5
Dalmally Ag & B ... 137 F2
Dalmary Stirlg ... 129 G5
Dalmellington E Ayrs ... 109 F5
Dalmeny C Edin ... 131 H3
Dalmigavie Highld ... 155 F1
Dalmigavie Lodge Highld ... 155 F1
Dalmore Highld ... 155 E6
Dalmuir W Duns ... 129 F2
Dalnabreck Highld ... 143 F1
Dalnacardoch P & K ... 146 B1
Dalnahaitnach Highld ... 155 G1
Dalnaspidal P & K ... 146 A2
Dalnawillan Lodge Highld ... 166 D2
Dalqueich P & K ... 131 G6
Dalquhairn S Ayrs ... 109 E4
Dalreavoch Lodge Highld ... 162 D5
Dalry N Ayrs ... 119 E4
Dalrymple E Ayrs ... 109 E1
Dalserf S Lans ... 120 C4
Dalsmeran Ag & B ... 117 G2
Dalston Cumb ... 103 H5
Dalston Gt Lon ... 28 D4
Dalswinton D & G ... 110 D3
Dalton Cumb ... 95 F2
Dalton D & G ... 111 F2
Dalton Lancs ... 81 G5
Dalton N York ... 96 D6
Dalton N York ... 97 G2
Dalton N York ... 114 C3
Dalton S York ... 84 B4
Dalton Magna S York ... 84 B4
Dalton Parva S York ... 84 B4
Dalton Piercy Dur ... 106 D4
Dalton-in-Furness Cumb ... 94 C2
Dalton-le-Dale Dur ... 106 C6
Dalton-on-Tees N York ... 106 B2
Dalveen D & G ... 110 C5
Dalveich Stirlg ... 138 C2
Dalwhinnie Highld ... 146 A3
Dalwood Devon ... 10 C5
Dam Green Norfk ... 64 C4

Damask Green Herts ... 50 C4
Damerham Hants ... 13 E6
Damgate Norfk ... 77 G1
Danaway Kent ... 30 B2
Danbury Essex ... 52 A1
Danby N York ... 107 F2
Danby Bottom N York ... 98 C5
Danby Wiske N York ... 97 F5
Dandaleith Moray ... 157 E4
Danderhall Mdloth ... 132 B2
Dane End Herts ... 50 D3
Dane Hills Leics ... 60 B6
Dane Street Kent ... 30 D1
Danebridge Ches ... 83 E1
Danegate E Susx ... 17 F5
Danehill E Susx ... 17 E4
Danemoor Green Norfk ... 64 C6
Danesford Shrops ... 57 G4
Danesmoor Derbys ... 84 B1
Daniel's Water Kent ... 18 C5
Danshillock Abers ... 158 C5
Danskine E Loth ... 133 E2
Danthorpe E R Yk ... 93 F3
Danzey Green Warwks ... 58 D2
Dapple Heath Staffs ... 71 E3
Darby Green Hants ... 27 F5
Darcy Lever Gt Man ... 82 B5
Dardy Powys ... 45 E1
Daren-felen Mons ... 36 C5
Darenth Kent ... 29 F3
Daresbury Ches ... 81 H3
Darfield S York ... 84 B5
Darfoulds Notts ... 84 C2
Dargate Kent ... 30 D2
Darite Cnwll ... 5 F3
Darland Kent ... 30 A3
Darland Wrexhm ... 69 F6
Darlaston Staffs ... 70 D4
Darlaston W Mids ... 58 C5
Darlaston Green W Mids ... 58 C5
Darley N York ... 90 C6
Darley Abbey Derbys ... 72 A4
Darley Bridge Derbys ... 71 G6
Darley Dale Derbys ... 83 G1
Darley Green Warwks ... 59 E3
Darley Head N York ... 90 C5
Darleyhall Herts ... 50 B3
Darlingscott Warwks ... 47 H3
Darlington Dur ... 106 B2
Darliston Shrops ... 69 H3
Darlton Notts ... 85 E2
Darnford Staffs ... 71 F1
Darnick Border ... 122 C3
Darowen Powys ... 55 F6
Darra Abers ... 158 C4
Darracott Cnwll ... 20 C2
Darracott Devon ... 20 C2
Darracott Devon ... 21 E4
Darras Hall Nthumb ... 114 C2
Darrington N York ... 91 F2
Darsham Suffk ... 65 G2
Darshill Somset ... 24 B4
Dartford Kent ... 29 F3
Dartington Devon ... 7 E4
Dartmeet Devon ... 6 D5
Dartmouth Devon ... 7 F3
Darton S York ... 83 H6
Darvel E Ayrs ... 119 G3
Darwell Hole E Susx ... 17 H3
Darwen Lancs ... 89 E2
Datchet Berks ... 41 H2
Datchworth Herts ... 50 D3
Datchworth Green Herts ... 50 D2
Daubhill Gt Man ... 82 B5
Dauntsey Wilts ... 39 E2
Dava Highld ... 156 B3
Davenham Ches ... 82 B2
Davenport Gt Man ... 82 D3
Davenport Green Ches ... 82 C3
Davenport Green Gt Man ... 82 C3
Daventry Nhants ... 48 D5
David Street Kent ... 29 G2
Davidson's Mains C Edin ... 132 A3
Davidstow Cnwll ... 5 E5
Davington D & G ... 111 G5
Davington Hill Kent ... 30 D2
Daviot Abers ... 158 C2
Daviot Highld ... 155 E3
Daviot House Highld ... 155 E3
Davis's Town E Susx ... 17 F3
Davoch of Grange Moray ... 157 G4
Davyhulme Gt Man ... 82 C4
Daw End W Mids ... 58 C5
Daw's House Cnwll ... 5 G4
Dawesgreen Surrey ... 16 C6
Dawley Shrops ... 57 G6
Dawlish Devon ... 9 F2
Dawlish Warren Devon ... 9 G2
Dawn Conwy ... 80 A2
Daws Green Somset ... 23 E1
Daws Heath Essex ... 30 B5
Dawsmere Lincs ... 75 E3
Day Green Ches ... 70 C6
Daybrook Notts ... 72 C4
Dayhills Staffs ... 70 D3
Dayhouse Bank Worcs ... 58 C3
Daylesford Gloucs ... 47 H2
Ddol Flints ... 80 D2
Ddol-Cownwy Powys ... 68 B2
Deal Kent ... 31 G1
Dean Cumb ... 103 E3
Dean Devon ... 21 F5
Dean Devon ... 21 G5
Dean Devon ... 7 E4
Dean Dorset ... 12 D6
Dean Hants ... 26 C2
Dean Hants ... 14 D6
Dean Lancs ... 89 G2
Dean Oxon ... 48 B1
Dean Somset ... 24 B4
Dean Bottom Kent ... 29 G3
Dean Court Oxon ... 40 C5
Dean End Dorset ... 25 E1
Dean Head S York ... 83 G5
Dean Prior Devon ... 7 E4
Dean Row Ches ... 82 D3
Dean Street Kent ... 30 A1
Deanburnhaugh Border ... 112 A6

Deancombe Devon ... 7 E4
Deane Gt Man ... 82 B5
Deane Hants ... 26 D4
Deanhead W York ... 90 B1
Deanland Dorset ... 25 E1
Deanlane End W Susx ... 15 F5
Deanraw Nthumb ... 113 E1
Deans W Loth ... 131 F2
Deanscales Cumb ... 103 E3
Deanshanger Nhants ... 49 F3
Deanshaugh Moray ... 157 F5
Deanston Stirlg ... 130 C5
Dearham Cumb ... 103 E4
Dearnley Gt Man ... 89 H1
Debach Suffk ... 53 F6
Debden Essex ... 51 F4
Debden Essex ... 29 E6
Debden Green Essex ... 51 G4
Debenham Suffk ... 64 D2
Deblin's Green Worcs ... 46 D4
Dechmont W Loth ... 131 G2
Dechmont Road W Loth ... 131 F2
Deddington Oxon ... 48 C2
Dedham Essex ... 52 D4
Dedham Heath Essex ... 52 D4
Dedworth Berks ... 41 G2
Deene Nhants ... 61 E5
Deenethorpe Nhants ... 61 F5
Deepcar S York ... 83 H4
Deepcut Surrey ... 27 G5
Deepdale Cumb ... 95 H3
Deepdale N York ... 96 B3
Deeping Gate Lincs ... 74 B1
Deeping St James Lincs ... 74 B1
Deeping St Nicholas Lincs ... 74 C2
Deerhurst Gloucs ... 46 D2
Deerhurst Walton Gloucs ... 46 D2
Deerton Street Kent ... 30 C2
Defford Worcs ... 47 E3
Defynnog Powys ... 44 B2
Deganwy Conwy ... 79 G3
Degnish Ag & B ... 136 B1
Deighton N York ... 97 G5
Deighton N York ... 91 G4
Deighton W York ... 90 C1
Deiniolen Gwynd ... 79 E1
Delabole Cnwll ... 4 D4
Delamere Ches ... 81 H1
Delfrigs Abers ... 159 F1
Dell Quay W Susx ... 15 F4
Delley Devon ... 21 F3
Delliefure Highld ... 156 C2
Delly End Oxon ... 40 B6
Delmonden Green Kent ... 18 A4
Delnabo Moray ... 156 C2
Delnashaugh Inn Moray ... 156 D3
Delny Highld ... 162 D1
Delph Gt Man ... 83 E5
Delves Dur ... 105 H5
Delvine P & K ... 140 A4
Dembleby Lincs ... 73 H4
Demelza Cnwll ... 4 C2
Den of Lindores Fife ... 140 C1
Denaby S York ... 84 C5
Denaby Main S York ... 84 C5
Denbies Surrey ... 28 B1
Denbigh Denbgs ... 80 C1
Denbrae Fife ... 140 D2
Denbury Devon ... 7 F4
Denby Derbys ... 72 B5
Denby Bottles Derbys ... 72 B5
Denby Dale W York ... 83 G5
Denchworth Oxon ... 40 B3
Dendron Cumb ... 94 C2
Denel End Beds ... 50 A4
Denfield P & K ... 139 G1
Denford Nhants ... 61 F3
Dengie Essex ... 52 C1
Denham Bucks ... 28 A5
Denham Suffk ... 63 G1
Denham Suffk ... 64 D3
Denham End Suffk ... 63 G2
Denham Green Bucks ... 28 A5
Denham Green Suffk ... 64 D3
Denhead Abers ... 159 F4
Denhead Fife ... 141 E1
Denhead of Gray Dund C ... 140 D3
Denholm Border ... 122 C1
Denholme W York ... 90 B3
Denholme Clough W York ... 90 B3
Denio Gwynd ... 66 C4
Denmead Hants ... 15 E5
Denmore Aber C ... 149 G6
Denne Park W Susx ... 16 C4
Dennington Suffk ... 65 E2
Denny Falk ... 130 D3
Dennyloanhead Falk ... 130 D3
Denshaw Gt Man ... 83 E6
Denside Abers ... 149 F4
Densole Kent ... 19 F6
Denston Suffk ... 52 A6
Denstone Staffs ... 71 F4
Denstroude Kent ... 31 E2
Dent Cumb ... 95 H3
Denton Cambs ... 61 G4
Denton Dur ... 106 B3
Denton E Susx ... 17 E2
Denton Gt Man ... 82 D4
Denton Kent ... 29 G3
Denton Kent ... 19 F6
Denton Lincs ... 73 F3
Denton N York ... 90 C4
Denton Nhants ... 49 F5
Denton Norfk ... 65 E4
Denton Oxon ... 40 D4
Denver Norfk ... 63 E5
Denwick Nthumb ... 125 E2
Deopham Norfk ... 64 C5
Deopham Green Norfk ... 64 C5
Depden Suffk ... 63 G1
Depden Green Suffk ... 63 G1
Deptford Gt Lon ... 29 E4
Deptford Wilts ... 25 F3
Derby Derbys ... 72 A4
Derby Devon ... 21 F4
Derbyhaven IOM ... 174 I2
Derculich P & K ... 139 F5
Dereham Norfk ... 76 C1
Deri Caerph ... 36 B4

Derril Devon ... 20 C1
Derringstone Kent ... 31 F1
Derrington Staffs ... 70 D2
Derriton Devon ... 20 D1
Derry Hill Wilts ... 38 D1
Derrythorpe Lincs ... 85 F5
Dersingham Norfk ... 75 G3
Dervaig Ag & B ... 135 F5
Derwen Denbgs ... 68 C5
Derwen Fawr Carmth ... 43 F1
Derwenlas Powys ... 55 E5
Derwydd Carmth ... 34 D6
Desborough Nhants ... 60 D4
Desford Leics ... 59 H6
Deskford Moray ... 157 G5
Detchant Nthumb ... 123 H3
Detling Kent ... 30 B2
Deuxhill Shrops ... 57 G4
Devauden Mons ... 37 F4
Devil's Bridge Cerdgn ... 55 E3
Deviock Cnwll ... 5 G1
Devitts Green Warwks ... 59 F4
Devizes Wilts ... 25 F5
Devonport Devon ... 6 B3
Devonside Clacks ... 131 E5
Devoran Cnwll ... 3 E4
Dewarton Mdloth ... 132 C1
Dewlish Dorset ... 12 B4
Dewsbury W York ... 90 D2
Dewsbury Moor W York ... 90 C2
Deytheur Powys ... 69 E2
Dial Somset ... 23 H6
Dial Green W Susx ... 27 G2
Dial Post W Susx ... 16 B3
Dibberford Dorset ... 11 E5
Dibden Hants ... 14 B4
Dibden Purlieu Hants ... 14 B4
Dickens Heath W Mids ... 58 D3
Dickleburgh Norfk ... 64 D4
Didbrook Gloucs ... 47 F2
Didcot Oxon ... 40 C3
Didcot Railway Centre Oxon ... 40 C3
Diddington Cambs ... 61 H2
Diddlebury Shrops ... 57 E4
Didley Herefs ... 45 G2
Didling W Susx ... 15 F5
Didmarton Gloucs ... 38 C3
Didsbury Gt Man ... 82 C4
Didworthy Devon ... 6 D4
Digby Lincs ... 74 A5
Digg Highld ... 151 E6
Diggle Gt Man ... 83 E5
Digmoor Lancs ... 81 G5
Digswell Herts ... 50 C2
Digswell Water Herts ... 50 C2
Dihewyd Cerdgn ... 43 E5
Dilham Norfk ... 77 F2
Dilhorne Staffs ... 71 E4
Dillington Cambs ... 61 G2
Dilston Nthumb ... 113 G1
Dilton Wilts ... 24 D4
Dilton Marsh Wilts ... 24 D4
Dilwyn Herefs ... 45 G5
Dimple Derbys ... 71 H6
Dimple Gt Man ... 89 E1
Dinas Carmth ... 33 G5
Dinas Cnwll ... 4 C3
Dinas Gwynd ... 66 B4
Dinas Pembks ... 32 D6
Dinas Rhondd ... 35 G3
Dinas Dinlle Gwynd ... 66 D6
Dinas Powys V Glam ... 36 C1
Dinas-Mawddwy Gwynd ... 68 A1
Dinder Somset ... 24 A4
Dinedor Herefs ... 45 H3
Dingestow Mons ... 37 F5
Dingle Mersyd ... 81 F3
Dingleden Kent ... 18 B4
Dingley Nhants ... 60 D4
Dingwall Highld ... 154 D5
Dinham Mons ... 37 F3
Dinmael Conwy ... 68 B4
Dinnet Abers ... 148 B4
Dinnington S York ... 84 C3
Dinnington Somset ... 10 D6
Dinnington T & W ... 114 C3
Dinorwic Gwynd ... 67 E6
Dinton Bucks ... 41 F5
Dinton Wilts ... 25 F2
Dinwoodie D & G ... 111 F4
Dinworthy Devon ... 20 C2
Dipford Somset ... 23 E1
Dipley Hants ... 27 F5
Dippen Ag & B ... 117 G4
Dippen N Ayrs ... 118 B2
Dippenhall Surrey ... 27 F4
Dippermill Devon ... 8 A5
Dippertown Devon ... 5 H4
Dipple Moray ... 157 E5
Dipple S Ayrs ... 108 D5
Diptford Devon ... 7 E3
Dipton Dur ... 114 C1
Diptonmill Nthumb ... 105 F6
Dirleton E Loth ... 132 D3
Dirt Pot Nthumb ... 105 E5
Discoed Powys ... 56 C2
Diseworth Leics ... 72 B2
Disforth N York ... 97 G2
Disley Ches ... 83 E3
Diss Norfk ... 64 D3
Disserth Powys ... 44 C5
Distington Cumb ... 102 D2
Ditcham Wilts ... 25 F2
Ditchburn Nthumb ... 124 D3
Ditcheat Somset ... 24 B3
Ditchingham Norfk ... 65 F4
Ditchley Oxon ... 48 B1
Ditchling E Susx ... 16 D3
Ditherington Shrops ... 69 G1
Ditteridge Wilts ... 38 C1
Dittisham Devon ... 7 F3
Ditton Ches ... 81 G3
Ditton Kent ... 29 H2
Ditton Green Cambs ... 63 F1
Ditton Priors Shrops ... 57 F4
Dixton Gloucs ... 47 E2
Dixton Mons ... 37 F6
Dizzard Cnwll ... 5 E6

Dobcross Gt Man ... 83 E5
Dobroyd Castle W York ... 89 H2
Dobwalls Cnwll ... 5 F2
Doccombe Devon ... 9 E3
Dochgarroch Highld ... 154 D3
Dockenfield Surrey ... 27 F3
Docker Lancs ... 95 F2
Docking Norfk ... 75 H4
Docklow Herefs ... 46 A5
Dockray Cumb ... 103 G5
Dockray Cumb ... 103 H2
Dod's Leigh Staffs ... 71 E3
Dodbrooke Devon ... 7 E2
Dodd's Green Ches ... 70 A4
Doddinghurst Essex ... 29 G6
Doddington Cambs ... 62 C4
Doddington Kent ... 30 C2
Doddington Lincs ... 85 G2
Doddington Nthumb ... 123 G3
Doddington Shrops ... 57 F3
Doddiscombsleigh Devon ... 9 E3
Doddshill Norfk ... 75 G3
Doddy Cross Cnwll ... 5 G2
Dodford Nhants ... 48 D5
Dodford Worcs ... 58 B3
Dodington Gloucs ... 38 B2
Dodington Somset ... 23 E3
Dodleston Ches ... 69 F6
Dodscott Devon ... 21 F2
Dodside E Rens ... 119 G5
Dodworth S York ... 83 H5
Dodworth Bottom S York ... 84 A5
Dodworth Green S York ... 83 H5
Doe Bank W Mids ... 58 D5
Doe Lea Derbys ... 84 B1
Dog Village Devon ... 9 G4
Dogdyke Lincs ... 74 B6
Dogley Lane W York ... 83 G6
Dogmersfield Hants ... 27 F4
Dogridge Wilts ... 39 E3
Dogsthorpe Cambs ... 62 A5
Dol-for Powys ... 55 F6
Dol-gran Carmth ... 42 D3
Dolanog Powys ... 68 C1
Dolau Powys ... 56 B2
Dolaucothi Carmth ... 43 G3
Dolbenmaen Gwynd ... 67 E4
Doley Shrops ... 70 B3
Dolfach Powys ... 55 G6
Dolfor Powys ... 56 A4
Dolgarrog Conwy ... 79 G1
Dolgellau Gwynd ... 67 G2
Dolgoch Gwynd ... 54 D6
Doll Highld ... 163 F4
Dollar Clacks ... 131 F5
Dollarfield Clacks ... 131 F5
Dolley Green Powys ... 56 C2
Dollwen Cerdgn ... 54 D3
Dolphin Flints ... 80 D2
Dolphinholme Lancs ... 88 D5
Dolphinton S Lans ... 121 E4
Dolton Devon ... 21 F2
Dolwen Conwy ... 80 A2
Dolwyddelan Conwy ... 67 G5
Dolybont Cerdgn ... 54 D4
Dolyhir Powys ... 45 E5
Domgay Powys ... 69 E2
Donaldson's Lodge Nthumb ... 123 F4
Doncaster S York ... 84 C5
Doncaster Carr S York ... 84 D5
Donhead St Andrew Wilts ... 25 E2
Donhead St Mary Wilts ... 25 E2
Donibristle Fife ... 131 H4
Doniford Somset ... 22 D3
Donington Lincs ... 74 B4
Donington on Bain Lincs ... 86 C3
Donington Southing Lincs ... 74 B3
Donisthorpe Leics ... 71 H1
Donkey Street Kent ... 19 E5
Donkey Town Surrey ... 27 G5
Donnington Berks ... 40 C1
Donnington Gloucs ... 47 G2
Donnington Herefs ... 46 C3
Donnington Shrops ... 57 F6
Donnington Shrops ... 70 B1
Donnington W Susx ... 15 G4
Donnington Wood Shrops ... 70 B1
Donyatt Somset ... 10 D6
Doomsday Green W Susx ... 16 C4
Doonfoot S Ayrs ... 119 E1
Doonholm S Ayrs ... 119 E1
Dorback Lodge Highld ... 147 F6
Dorchester Dorset ... 11 G4
Dorchester Oxon ... 40 D4
Dordon Warwks ... 59 E5
Dore S York ... 83 H3
Dores Highld ... 154 D2
Dorking Surrey ... 28 C1
Dorking Tye Suffk ... 52 C4
Dormans Land Surrey ... 17 E6
Dormans Park Surrey ... 17 E5
Dormington Herefs ... 46 A3
Dormston Worcs ... 47 E5
Dorn Gloucs ... 47 G3
Dorney Bucks ... 41 G2
Dornie Highld ... 152 C2
Dornoch Highld ... 163 E3
Dornock D & G ... 111 G1
Dorrery Highld ... 166 D4
Dorridge W Mids ... 59 E3
Dorrington Lincs ... 74 A5
Dorrington Shrops ... 57 E6
Dorrington Shrops ... 70 B4
Dorsington Warwks ... 47 G4
Dorstone Herefs ... 45 F3
Dorton Bucks ... 41 E6
Dosthill Staffs ... 59 E5
Dottery Dorset ... 11 E4
Doublebois Cnwll ... 5 E2
Doughton Gloucs ... 38 C3
Douglas IOM ... 174 m3
Douglas S Lans ... 120 C2
Douglas and Angus Dund C ... 140 D3
Douglas Castle S Lans ... 120 C3
Douglas Pier Ag & B ... 128 C5
Douglas Water S Lans ... 120 C3
Douglas West S Lans ... 120 C2
Douglastown Angus ... 140 D4

Doulting Somset ... 24 B4
Dounby Ork ... 169 b3
Doune Highld ... 162 A4
Doune Stirlg ... 130 D5
Dounepark S Ayrs ... 108 D4
Dounie Highld ... 162 C3
Dousland Devon ... 6 C4
Dovaston Shrops ... 69 F2
Dove Green Notts ... 72 B5
Dove Holes Derbys ... 83 F2
Dovenby Cumb ... 103 E3
Dover Gt Man ... 82 A5
Dover Kent ... 19 G6
Dover Castle Kent ... 19 G6
Dovercourt Essex ... 53 F4
Doverdale Worcs ... 58 B2
Doveridge Derbys ... 71 F3
Doversgreen Surrey ... 16 C6
Dowally P & K ... 139 G5
Dowbridge Lancs ... 88 C3
Dowdeswell Gloucs ... 47 E1
Dowlais Myr Td ... 36 B5
Dowland Devon ... 21 F2
Dowlish Ford Somset ... 10 D6
Dowlish Wake Somset ... 10 D6
Down Ampney Gloucs ... 39 F4
Down Hatherley Gloucs ... 46 D1
Down St Mary Devon ... 8 D5
Down Thomas Devon ... 6 B3
Downacarey Devon ... 5 G5
Downderry Cnwll ... 5 G1
Downe Gt Lon ... 29 E2
Downend Berks ... 40 C2
Downend Gloucs ... 37 G2
Downend Gloucs ... 38 C4
Downend IOW ... 14 D2
Downfield Dund C ... 140 D3
Downgate Cnwll ... 5 F3
Downgate Cnwll ... 5 G3
Downham Essex ... 29 H6
Downham Gt Lon ... 29 E3
Downham Lancs ... 89 F4
Downham Nthumb ... 123 F3
Downham Market Norfk ... 63 E6
Downhead Somset ... 24 A2
Downhead Somset ... 24 B4
Downhill Cnwll ... 4 B3
Downhill P & K ... 140 A3
Downholland Cross Lancs ... 81 F5
Downholme N York ... 96 D5
Downies Abers ... 149 G4
Downing Flints ... 80 D2
Downley Bucks ... 41 G4
Downside Somset ... 24 B4
Downside Somset ... 24 B4
Downside Surrey ... 28 B2
Downton Hants ... 13 F4
Downton Wilts ... 25 G1
Downton on the Rock Herefs ... 56 D3
Dowsby Lincs ... 74 B3
Dowsdale Lincs ... 74 C1
Dowsland Green Essex ... 52 B3
Doxey Staffs ... 70 D2
Doxford Nthumb ... 125 E3
Doynton Gloucs ... 38 B2
Draethen Caerph ... 36 C3
Draffan S Lans ... 120 B4
Dragonby Lincs ... 85 G6
Dragons Green W Susx ... 16 B4
Drakeholes Notts ... 85 E4
Drakelow Worcs ... 58 A3
Drakemyre N Ayrs ... 119 E4
Drakes Broughton Worcs ... 47 E4
Drakes Cross Worcs ... 58 D3
Drakewalls Cnwll ... 5 H3
Draughton N York ... 90 B5
Draughton Nhants ... 60 D3
Drax N York ... 91 H2
Drax Hales N York ... 91 H2
Draycot Foliat Wilts ... 39 F2
Draycote Warwks ... 59 G2
Draycott Derbys ... 72 B3
Draycott Gloucs ... 47 G3
Draycott Shrops ... 58 A5
Draycott Somset ... 23 G4
Draycott Somset ... 24 A1
Draycott Worcs ... 46 D4
Draycott in the Clay Staffs ... 71 F3
Draycott in the Moors Staffs ... 71 E4
Drayford Devon ... 21 H2
Draynes Cnwll ... 5 F3
Drayton Hants ... 15 E4
Drayton Leics ... 60 D5
Drayton Lincs ... 74 C4
Drayton Norfk ... 77 E1
Drayton Oxon ... 48 C3
Drayton Oxon ... 40 C4
Drayton Somset ... 23 G2
Drayton Worcs ... 58 B3
Drayton Bassett Staffs ... 59 E5
Drayton Beauchamp Bucks ... 41 G5
Drayton Manor Park Staffs ... 59 E5
Drayton Parslow Bucks ... 49 F2
Drayton St Leonard Oxon ... 40 D4
Drebley N York ... 90 B5
Dreemskerry IOM ... 174 n4
Dreen Hill Pembks ... 32 C3
Drefach Carmth ... 42 D3
Drefach Carmth ... 34 C6
Drefach Cerdgn ... 43 E4
Drefelin Carmth ... 42 D3
Dreghorn N Ayrs ... 119 E3
Drellingore Kent ... 19 F5
Drem E Loth ... 132 D3
Dresden Staffs ... 70 D4
Drewsteignton Devon ... 8 D4
Driby Lincs ... 86 D2
Driffield E R Yk ... 92 D5
Driffield Gloucs ... 39 E4
Driffield Cross Roads Gloucs ... 39 E4
Drift Cnwll ... 2 B3
Drigg Cumb ... 94 B5
Drighlington W York ... 90 C2
Drimnin Highld ... 135 G5
Drimpton Dorset ... 11 E5
Drimsallie Highld ... 144 B2
Dringhoe E R Yk ... 93 E5
Dringhouses N York ... 91 G4

Drinkstone Suffk ... 64 B1
Drinkstone Green Suffk ... 64 B1
Drinsey Nook Notts ... 85 F2
Drive End Dorset ... 11 F5
Driver's End Herts ... 50 C3
Drointon Staffs ... 71 E3
Droitwich Worcs ... 58 B2
Dron P & K ... 140 A1
Dronfield Derbys ... 84 A2
Dronfield Woodhouse Derbys ... 84 A2
Drongan E Ayrs ... 119 F1
Dronley Angus ... 140 C3
Droop Dorset ... 12 A5
Dropping Well S York ... 84 B4
Droxford Hants ... 14 D5
Droylsden Gt Man ... 82 D4
Druid Denbgs ... 68 C4
Druids Heath W Mids ... 58 D6
Druidston Pembks ... 32 C3
Druimachoish Highld ... 137 F4
Druimarbin Highld ... 144 C1
Druimdrishaig Ag & B ... 127 F2
Druimindarroch Highld ... 143 F2
Drum Ag & B ... 127 H3
Drum P & K ... 131 G5
Drumalbin S Lans ... 120 D3
Drumbeg Highld ... 164 B2
Drumblade Abers ... 158 B3
Drumbreddon D & G ... 100 B4
Drumbuie Highld ... 152 B2
Drumburgh Cumb ... 103 G6
Drumburn D & G ... 102 C6
Drumchapel C Glas ... 129 G2
Drumchastle P & K ... 138 D6
Drumclog S Lans ... 120 A3
Drumeldrie Fife ... 132 C5
Drumelzier Border ... 121 F3
Drumfearn Highld ... 143 F6
Drumfrennie Abers ... 149 G4
Drumguish Highld ... 146 C4
Drumhead Abers ... 148 D4
Drumin Moray ... 156 D2
Drumjohn D & G ... 109 G4
Drumlamford S Ayrs ... 109 G2
Drumlasie Abers ... 148 D5
Drumleaning Cumb ... 103 G5
Drumlemble Ag & B ... 117 F2
Drumlithie Abers ... 149 E2
Drummoddie D & G ... 101 E5
Drummore D & G ... 100 C4
Drummuir Moray ... 157 F3
Drumnadrochit Highld ... 154 C2
Drumnagorrach Moray ... 157 H3
Drumpark D & G ... 110 C3
Drumrunie Lodge Highld ... 161 F4
Drumshang S Ayrs ... 108 D6
Drumuie Highld ... 151 E3
Drumuillie Highld ... 156 B1
Drumvaich Stirlg ... 130 C5
Drunzie P & K ... 131 H6
Druridge Nthumb ... 114 D5
Drury Flints ... 81 E1
Dry Doddington Lincs ... 73 F5
Dry Drayton Cambs ... 62 C1
Dry Sandford Oxon ... 40 C4
Dry Street Essex ... 29 H5
Drybeck Cumb ... 104 C2
Drybridge Moray ... 157 F5
Drybridge N Ayrs ... 119 E3
Drybrook Gloucs ... 37 G6
Dryburgh Border ... 122 C3
Drym Cnwll ... 2 D3
Drymen Stirlg ... 129 F4
Drymuir Abers ... 159 E4
Drynoch Highld ... 150 D2
Dryslwyn Carmth ... 43 F1
Dryton Shrops ... 57 F6
Dubford Abers ... 158 D5
Dublin Suffk ... 64 D2
Duchally Highld ... 161 H5
Duck End Beds ... 50 B5
Duck End Cambs ... 62 B2
Duck End Essex ... 51 G3
Duck End Essex ... 51 H4
Duck's Cross Beds ... 61 G1
Duckend Green Essex ... 51 H3
Duckington Ches ... 69 G5
Ducklington Oxon ... 40 B5
Duddenhoe End Essex ... 51 E4
Duddingston C Edin ... 132 B2
Duddington Nhants ... 61 F5
Duddlestone Somset ... 23 E1
Duddleswell E Susx ... 17 E4
Duddlewick Shrops ... 57 G4
Duddo Nthumb ... 123 F4
Duddon Ches ... 81 G1
Duddon Bridge Cumb ... 94 C4
Dudleston Shrops ... 69 F4
Dudleston Heath Shrops ... 69 F4
Dudley T & W ... 114 D3
Dudley W Mids ... 58 B4
Dudley Hill W York ... 90 C3
Dudley Port W Mids ... 58 C4
Dudnill Shrops ... 57 G3
Dudsbury Dorset ... 13 E4
Dudswell Herts ... 41 H5
Duffield Derbys ... 72 A4
Duffryn Neath ... 35 F4
Duffus Moray ... 157 E3
Dufton Cumb ... 104 D3
Duggleby N York ... 98 D1
Duirinish Highld ... 152 B2
Duisdalemore Highld ... 143 F5
Duisky Highld ... 144 B2
Duke Street Suffk ... 52 D5
Dukestown Blae G ... 36 C5
Dukinfield Gt Man ... 82 D4
Dulas IOA ... 78 D4
Dulcote Somset ... 24 A4
Dulford Devon ... 10 A5
Dull P & K ... 139 E5
Dullatur N Lans ... 130 D3
Dullingham Cambs ... 63 E1
Dullingham Ley Cambs ... 63 F1
Dulnain Bridge Highld ... 156 B1
Duloe Beds ... 61 G1
Duloe Cnwll ... 5 F2

Dulverton Somset ... 22 B2
Dulwich Gt Lon ... 28 D3
Dumbarton W Duns ... 129 E3
Dumbleton Gloucs ... 47 F3
Dumfries D & G ... 110 D2
Dumgoyne Stirlg ... 129 G3
Dummer Hants ... 26 D4
Dumpton Kent ... 31 G3
Dun Angus ... 141 G6
Dunalastair P & K ... 138 D6
Dunan Ag & B ... 128 C2
Dunan Highld ... 151 F1
Dunan P & K ... 138 B5
Dunaverty Ag & B ... 117 F1
Dunball Somset ... 23 F3
Dunbar E Loth ... 133 F3
Dunbeath Highld ... 167 E1
Dunbeg Ag & B ... 136 C3
Dunblane Stirlg ... 130 D5
Dunbog Fife ... 140 C1
Dunbridge Hants ... 26 A2
Duncanston Highld ... 154 D5
Duncanstone Abers ... 158 B2
Dunchideock Devon ... 9 F3
Dunchurch Warwks ... 59 H2
Duncote Nhants ... 49 E4
Duncow D & G ... 110 D3
Duncrievie P & K ... 131 G6
Duncton W Susx ... 15 H5
Dundee Dund C ... 140 D3
Dundee Airport Dund C ... 140 D3
Dundon Somset ... 23 G2
Dundonald S Ayrs ... 119 E3
Dundonnell Highld ... 161 E2
Dundraw Cumb ... 103 F5
Dundreggan Highld ... 145 E6
Dundrennan D & G ... 102 B5
Dundry Somset ... 24 A6
Dunecht Abers ... 149 E5
Dunfermline Fife ... 131 G4
Dunfield Gloucs ... 39 F4
Dunford Bridge S York ... 83 F5
Dungate Kent ... 30 C2
Dungavel S Lans ... 120 A3
Dunge Wilts ... 24 D5
Dungworth S York ... 83 H4
Dunham Notts ... 85 F2
Dunham Town Gt Man ... 82 B3
Dunham Woodhouses Gt Man ... 82 B3
Dunham-on-the-Hill Ches ... 81 G2
Dunhampstead Worcs ... 47 E5
Dunhampton Worcs ... 58 A2
Dunholme Lincs ... 85 H3
Dunino Fife ... 132 D4
Dunipace Falk ... 130 D3
Dunkerton Somset ... 24 C5
Dunkeswell Devon ... 10 B5
Dunkeswick N York ... 90 D4
Dunkirk Ches ... 81 F2
Dunkirk Gloucs ... 38 C3
Dunkirk Kent ... 30 D2
Dunkirk Staffs ... 70 C5
Dunkirk Wilts ... 25 E5
Dunlappie Angus ... 148 D1
Dunley Hants ... 26 C5
Dunley Worcs ... 57 H2
Dunlop E Ayrs ... 119 F4
Dunmaglass Highld ... 154 D1
Dunmere Cnwll ... 4 D3
Dunmore Falk ... 131 E4
Dunn Street Kent ... 30 D2
Dunnet Highld ... 167 F5
Dunnichen Angus ... 141 E5
Dunning P & K ... 139 G1
Dunnington E R Yk ... 93 E5
Dunnington N York ... 91 H5
Dunnington Warwks ... 47 F5
Dunnockshaw Lancs ... 89 G2
Dunoon Ag & B ... 128 C3
Dunphail Moray ... 156 B4
Dunragit D & G ... 100 C6
Dunrostan Ag & B ... 128 C2
Duns Border ... 123 E5
Duns Tew Oxon ... 48 C2
Dunsa Derbys ... 83 G2
Dunsby Lincs ... 74 A3
Dunscar Gt Man ... 82 B6
Dunscore D & G ... 110 C3
Dunscroft S York ... 84 D6
Dunsdale N York ... 107 E3
Dunsden Green Oxon ... 41 E2
Dunsdon Devon ... 20 C1
Dunsfold Surrey ... 16 A5
Dunsford Devon ... 9 E3
Dunshalt Fife ... 132 B6
Dunshillock Abers ... 159 F4
Dunsill Notts ... 72 B6
Dunsley N York ... 107 H2
Dunsley Staffs ... 58 B4
Dunsmore Bucks ... 41 G5
Dunsop Bridge Lancs ... 89 E5
Dunstable Beds ... 50 A3
Dunstall Staffs ... 71 G2
Dunstall Common Worcs ... 46 D3
Dunstall Green Suffk ... 63 G1
Dunstan Nthumb ... 125 F3
Dunstan Steads Nthumb ... 125 F3
Dunster Somset ... 22 C4
Dunston Lincs ... 86 A1
Dunston Norfk ... 65 E6
Dunston Staffs ... 70 D2
Dunston T & W ... 114 D2
Dunston Heath Staffs ... 70 D2
Dunstone Devon ... 6 C3
Dunstone Devon ... 8 D2
Dunsville S York ... 84 D5
Dunswell E R Yk ... 93 E3
Dunsyre S Lans ... 121 E4
Dunterton Devon ... 5 G4
Dunthrop Oxon ... 48 B2
Duntisbourne Abbots Gloucs ... 38 D5
Duntisbourne Rouse Gloucs ... 39 E5
Duntish Dorset ... 11 G5
Duntocher W Duns ... 129 F2
Dunton Beds ... 49 E2
Dunton Bucks ... 49 F2
Dunton Norfk ... 76 B3

Dunton Bassett Leics ... 60 B4
Dunton Green Kent ... 29 F2
Dunton Wayletts Essex ... 29 G5
Duntulm Highld ... 150 D6
Dunure S Ayrs ... 118 D1
Dunvant Swans ... 34 C4
Dunvegan Highld ... 150 C3
Dunwich Suffk ... 65 G2
Dunwood Staffs ... 70 D6
Durdar Cumb ... 103 H5
Durgan Cnwll ... 3 E2
Durham Dur ... 106 B5
Durham Cathedral Dur ... 106 B5
Durisdeer D & G ... 110 C5
Durisdeermill D & G ... 110 C5
Durkar W York ... 90 D1
Durleigh Somset ... 23 F3
Durley Hants ... 14 C5
Durley Wilts ... 25 H6
Durley Street Hants ... 14 C5
Durlock Kent ... 31 F2
Durlock Kent ... 31 G2
Durlow Common Gloucs ... 46 B3
Durmgley Angus ... 140 D5
Durn Gt Man ... 89 H1
Durness Highld ... 165 G1
Duror Highld ... 137 E5
Durran Ag & B ... 128 A6
Durrington W Susx ... 16 B2
Durrington Wilts ... 25 G4
Durris Abers ... 149 E4
Dursley Gloucs ... 38 B4
Dursley Cross Gloucs ... 46 C1
Durston Somset ... 23 F2
Durweston Dorset ... 12 B5
Duston Nhants ... 49 E5
Duthil Highld ... 155 G1
Dutlas Powys ... 56 B3
Duton Hill Essex ... 51 G3
Dutson Cnwll ... 5 G4
Dutton Ches ... 81 H3
Duxford Cambs ... 51 F5
Duxford Oxon ... 40 B4
Duxford Aircraft Museum Cambs ... 51 E5
Dwygyfylchi Conwy ... 79 G3
Dwyran IOA ... 78 D1
Dyce Aber C ... 149 F6
Dyer's End Essex ... 51 H4
Dyfatty Carmth ... 34 A4
Dyffrydan Gwynd ... 67 F1
Dyffryn Brdgnd ... 35 F4
Dyffryn Myr Td ... 36 B5
Dyffryn V Glam ... 36 C4
Dyffryn Ardudwy Gwynd ... 67 E2
Dyffryn Castell Cerdgn ... 55 E4
Dyffryn Cellwen Neath ... 35 F5
Dyke Lincs ... 74 A2
Dyke Moray ... 156 B5
Dykehead Angus ... 140 D6
Dykehead Angus ... 140 D6
Dykehead N Lans ... 120 C5
Dykehead Stirlg ... 130 B5
Dykelands Abers ... 149 E1
Dykends Angus ... 140 C5
Dykeside Abers ... 158 C3
Dylife Powys ... 55 F5
Dymchurch Kent ... 19 E4
Dymock Gloucs ... 46 C2
Dyrham Gloucs ... 38 B2
Dysart Fife ... 132 B4
Dyserth Denbgs ... 80 C3

E

Eachway Worcs ... 58 C3
Eachwick Nthumb ... 114 C3
Eagland Hill Lancs ... 88 C4
Eagle Lincs ... 85 F1
Eagle Barnsdale Lincs ... 85 F1
Eagle Moor Lincs ... 85 F1
Eaglescliffe Dur ... 106 D2
Eaglesfield Cumb ... 103 E3
Eaglesfield D & G ... 111 G2
Eaglesham E Rens ... 119 G5
Eagley Gt Man ... 82 B6
Eairy IOM ... 174 I3
Eakley Lanes Bucks ... 49 F4
Eakring Notts ... 84 D1
Ealand Lincs ... 85 E6
Ealing Gt Lon ... 28 C4
Eals Nthumb ... 104 C4
Eamont Bridge Cumb ... 104 B3
Earby Lancs ... 89 G4
Earcroft Lancs ... 89 E2
Eardington Shrops ... 57 G4
Eardisland Herefs ... 45 G4
Eardisley Herefs ... 45 F4
Eardiston Shrops ... 69 F2
Eardiston Worcs ... 57 G2
Earith Cambs ... 62 C3
Earl Shilton Leics ... 59 G5
Earl Soham Suffk ... 65 E2
Earl Sterndale Derbys ... 83 F1
Earl Stonham Suffk ... 64 D1
Earl's Croome Worcs ... 46 D3
Earl's Down E Susx ... 17 G3
Earl's Green Suffk ... 64 C2
Earle Nthumb ... 124 C4
Earl's Croome Worcs ... 46 D3
Earlestown Mersyd ... 81 H4
Earley Berks ... 41 F1
Earlham Norfk ... 64 D6
Earlish Highld ... 150 D5
Earls Barton Nhants ... 61 E2
Earls Colne Essex ... 52 B4
Earls Common Worcs ... 47 E5
Earlsditton Shrops ... 57 F3
Earlsdon W Mids ... 59 F3
Earlsferry Fife ... 132 D5
Earlsfield Gt Lon ... 28 C3
Earlsford Abers ... 158 D3
Earlsheaton W York ... 90 D2
Earlston Border ... 122 C3
Earlston E Ayrs ... 119 F3

Earlswood Surrey ... 28 D1
Earlswood Warwks ... 58 D3
Earlswood Common Mons ... 37 F4
Earnley W Susx ... 15 F3
Earnshaw Bridge Lancs ... 88 D2
Earsdon Nthumb ... 114 D5
Earsdon T & W ... 115 E3
Earsham Norfk ... 65 F4
Earswick N York ... 91 G5
Eartham W Susx ... 15 G4
Earthcott Gloucs ... 37 G3
Easby N York ... 107 E2
Easdale Ag & B ... 136 B1
Easebourne W Susx ... 27 G1
Easenhall Warwks ... 59 G3
Eashing Surrey ... 27 H4
Easington Bucks ... 41 E5
Easington Dur ... 106 D5
Easington E R Yk ... 93 H1
Easington N York ... 107 G3
Easington Nthumb ... 124 D4
Easington Oxon ... 41 E4
Easington Colliery Dur ... 106 D5
Easington Lane T & W ... 106 C5
Easingwold N York ... 98 A2
Easole Street Kent ... 31 F1
Eassie and Nevay Angus ... 140 C4
East Aberthaw V Glam ... 22 C6
East Allington Devon ... 7 E2
East Anstey Devon ... 22 B2
East Anton Hants ... 26 B4
East Appleton N York ... 97 F4
East Ashey IOW ... 14 D2
East Ashling W Susx ... 15 F4
East Aston Hants ... 26 C4
East Ayton N York ... 99 F3
East Balsdon Cnwll ... 5 F6
East Bank Blae G ... 36 C5
East Barkwith Lincs ... 86 B3
East Barming Kent ... 29 H1
East Barnby N York ... 107 H2
East Barnet Gt Lon ... 28 D6
East Barns E Loth ... 133 F3
East Barsham Norfk ... 76 B3
East Beckham Norfk ... 77 E4
East Bedfont Gt Lon ... 28 B3
East Bergholt Suffk ... 52 D4
East Bierley W York ... 90 C2
East Bilney Norfk ... 76 C2
East Blatchington E Susx ... 17 F1
East Bloxworth Dorset ... 12 C4
East Boldon T & W ... 115 E2
East Boldre Hants ... 14 B4
East Bolton Nthumb ... 124 D3
East Bower Somset ... 23 F3
East Bradenham Norfk ... 64 B6
East Brent Somset ... 23 F4
East Bridgford Notts ... 73 E4
East Briscoe Dur ... 105 F2
East Buckland Devon ... 21 G4
East Budleigh Devon ... 9 G3
East Burnham Bucks ... 41 H3
East Burton Dorset ... 12 B3
East Butsfield Dur ... 105 H5
East Butterwick Lincs ... 85 F5
East Calder W Loth ... 131 G2
East Carleton Norfk ... 64 D6
East Carlton Nhants ... 60 D4
East Carlton W York ... 90 C4
East Chaldon (Chaldon Herring)
   Dorset ... 12 B3
East Challow Oxon ... 40 B3
East Charleton Devon ... 7 E2
East Chelborough Dorset ... 11 F5
East Chevington Nthumb ... 114 D5
East Chiltington E Susx ... 17 E3
East Chinnock Somset ... 11 E6
East Chisenbury Wilts ... 25 G4
East Cholderton Hants ... 26 A4
East Clandon Surrey ... 28 B1
East Claydon Bucks ... 49 F2
East Clevedon Somset ... 37 E1
East Coker Somset ... 11 F6
East Combe Somset ... 22 D2
East Compton Somset ... 24 B3
East Cornworthy Devon ... 7 F3
East Cote Cumb ... 103 E6
East Cottingwith E R Yk ... 91 H4
East Cowes IOW ... 14 C3
East Cowick E R Yk ... 91 H2
East Cowton N York ... 97 F5
East Cramlington Nthumb ... 114 D3
East Cranmore Somset ... 24 B4
East Creech Dorset ... 12 C3
East Curthwaite Cumb ... 103 G5
East Dean E Susx ... 17 F1
East Dean Gloucs ... 46 B1
East Dean Hants ... 26 A2
East Dean W Susx ... 15 G5
East Down Devon ... 21 F5
East Drayton Notts ... 85 E2
East Dulwich Gt Lon ... 28 D4
East Dundry Somset ... 24 A6
East Ella E R Yk ... 92 D2
East End Beds ... 49 H3
East End Beds ... 50 B6
East End Bucks ... 49 G4
East End E R Yk ... 93 F3
East End E R Yk ... 93 G2
East End Essex ... 51 E2
East End Hants ... 26 B5
East End Hants ... 14 B3
East End Herts ... 51 E3
East End Kent ... 18 B5
East End Kent ... 30 C3
East End Oxon ... 40 B6
East End Somset ... 37 F1
East End Somset ... 24 B4
East End Suffk ... 53 E4
East Everleigh Wilts ... 25 G5
East Farleigh Kent ... 30 A1
East Farndon Nhants ... 60 C4
East Ferry Lincs ... 85 F5
East Firsby Lincs ... 85 H3
East Fortune E Loth ... 132 D3
East Garforth W York ... 91 G3
East Garston Berks ... 40 B2
East Ginge Oxon ... 40 C3

East Goscote Leics ... 72 D1
East Grafton Wilts ... 25 H5
East Green Suffk ... 65 F2
East Grimstead Wilts ... 25 H2
East Grinstead W Susx ... 17 E5
East Guldeford E Susx ... 18 C3
East Haddon Nhants ... 60 C2
East Hagbourne Oxon ... 40 C3
East Halton Lincs ... 93 E2
East Ham Gt Lon ... 29 E4
East Hanney Oxon ... 40 B4
East Hanningfield Essex ... 30 A6
East Hardwick W York ... 91 F1
East Harling Norfk ... 64 B4
East Harlsey N York ... 97 G5
East Harnham Wilts ... 25 G2
East Harptree Somset ... 24 A5
East Hartburn Dur ... 106 D3
East Hartford Nthumb ... 114 D3
East Harting W Susx ... 15 F5
East Hatch Wilts ... 25 E2
East Hatley Cambs ... 50 D6
East Hauxwell N York ... 97 E4
East Haven Angus ... 141 F3
East Heckington Lincs ... 74 B4
East Hedleyhope Dur ... 106 A5
East Helmsdale Highld ... 163 G5
East Hendred Oxon ... 40 C3
East Heslerton N York ... 99 E2
East Hewish Somset ... 23 G6
East Hoathly E Susx ... 17 F3
East Holme Dorset ... 12 C3
East Horrington Somset ... 24 A4
East Horsley Surrey ... 28 B1
East Horton Nthumb ... 123 G2
East Howe Dorset ... 13 E4
East Huntington N York ... 91 G5
East Huntspill Somset ... 23 F4
East Hyde Beds ... 50 B2
East Ilkerton Devon ... 21 G5
East Ilsley Berks ... 40 C2
East Keal Lincs ... 86 D1
East Kennett Wilts ... 25 G6
East Keswick W York ... 91 E4
East Kilbride S Lans ... 119 H5
East Kimber Devon ... 8 B4
East Kirkby Lincs ... 86 D1
East Knighton Dorset ... 12 B3
East Knowstone Devon ... 22 A1
East Knoyle Wilts ... 24 D2
East Kyloe Nthumb ... 123 H3
East Lambrook Somset ... 23 G1
East Langdon Kent ... 19 G6
East Langton Leics ... 60 C5
East Laroch Highld ... 137 E6
East Lavant W Susx ... 15 G4
East Lavington W Susx ... 15 G5
East Layton N York ... 106 A2
East Leake Notts ... 72 C3
East Learmouth Nthumb ... 123 F3
East Leigh Devon ... 8 D5
East Leigh Devon ... 6 D3
East Leigh Devon ... 7 E3
East Lexham Norfk ... 76 B2
East Linton E Loth ... 133 E3
East Liss Hants ... 27 F2
East Lockinge Oxon ... 40 B3
East Lound Lincs ... 85 E5
East Lulworth Dorset ... 12 C3
East Lutton N York ... 99 E2
East Lydeard Somset ... 23 E2
East Lydford Somset ... 24 A2
East Malling Kent ... 29 H2
East Malling Heath Kent ... 29 H1
East Marden W Susx ... 15 F5
East Markham Notts ... 85 E2
East Martin Hants ... 25 F1
East Marton N York ... 89 G5
East Meon Hants ... 27 E1
East Mere Devon ... 9 G6
East Mersea Essex ... 52 D2
East Midlands Airport Leics ... 72 B3
East Molesey Surrey ... 28 B3
East Morden Dorset ... 12 C4
East Morton D & G ... 110 C5
East Morton W York ... 90 B4
East Ness N York ... 98 C3
East Newton E R Yk ... 93 F3
East Norton Leics ... 60 D5
East Ogwell Devon ... 7 F5
East Orchard Dorset ... 24 D1
East Ord Nthumb ... 123 G5
East Panson Devon ... 5 G5
East Parley Dorset ... 13 E4
East Peckham Kent ... 29 G1
East Pennar Pembks ... 32 D2
East Pennard Somset ... 24 B3
East Perry Cambs ... 61 G2
East Portlemouth Devon ... 7 E1
East Prawle Devon ... 7 E1
East Preston W Susx ... 16 B2
East Pulham Dorset ... 11 G6
East Putford Devon ... 20 D2
East Quantoxhead Somset ... 22 D4
East Rainham Nhants ... 30 B3
East Rainton T & W ... 106 C6
East Ravendale Lincs ... 86 C5
East Raynham Norfk ... 76 B3
East Rigton W York ... 91 E4
East Rolstone Somset ... 23 G5
East Rounton N York ... 97 G5
East Rudham Norfk ... 76 A3
East Runton Norfk ... 77 E4
East Ruston Norfk ... 77 F3
East Saltoun E Loth ... 132 D2
East Scrafton N York ... 96 D3
East Sheen Gt Lon ... 28 C3
East Shefford Berks ... 40 B2
East Sleekburn Nthumb ... 114 D4
East Somerton Norfk ... 77 H2
East Stockwith Lincs ... 85 E4
East Stoke Dorset ... 12 C3
East Stoke Notts ... 73 E5
East Stour Dorset ... 24 D1
East Stourmouth Kent ... 31 F2
East Stowford Devon ... 21 F3
East Stratton Hants ... 26 D3
East Studdal Kent ... 31 G1

East Sutton Kent ... 30 B1
East Taphouse Cnwll ... 5 E2
East Thirston Nthumb ... 114 D5
East Tilbury Essex ... 29 H4
East Tisted Hants ... 27 E2
East Torrington Lincs ... 86 B3
East Tuddenham Norfk ... 76 D1
East Tytherley Hants ... 26 A2
East Tytherton Wilts ... 38 D2
East Village Devon ... 9 E5
East Wall Shrops ... 57 E5
East Walton Norfk ... 75 H2
East Water Somset ... 24 A4
East Week Devon ... 8 D4
East Wellow Hants ... 26 A1
East Wemyss Fife ... 132 B5
East Whitburn W Loth ... 131 F2
East Wickham Gt Lon ... 29 E4
East Williamston Pembks ... 33 E2
East Winch Norfk ... 75 G2
East Winterslow Wilts ... 25 H3
East Wittering W Susx ... 15 F3
East Witton N York ... 97 E3
East Woodburn Nthumb ... 113 F3
East Woodhay Hants ... 26 B5
East Woodlands Somset ... 24 C4
East Worldham Hants ... 27 F3
East Wretham Norfk ... 64 B4
East Youlstone Devon ... 20 C2
East-the-Water Devon ... 21 E3
Eastbourne Dur ... 106 B2
Eastbourne E Susx ... 17 G1
Eastbridge Suffk ... 65 G2
Eastbrook V Glam ... 36 C1
Eastburn W York ... 90 A4
Eastbury Berks ... 40 B2
Eastbury Herts ... 28 B5
Eastby N York ... 90 A5
Eastchurch Kent ... 30 C3
Eastcombe Gloucs ... 38 D5
Eastcote Gt Lon ... 28 B5
Eastcote Nhants ... 49 E5
Eastcote W Mids ... 59 E3
Eastcott Cnwll ... 20 C2
Eastcott Wilts ... 25 F5
Eastcourt Wilts ... 38 D3
Eastcourt Wilts ... 25 H5
Eastdown Devon ... 7 F2
Eastend Essex ... 30 C5
Eastend S Lans ... 120 D3
Easter Balmoral Abers ... 147 G4
Easter Compton Gloucs ... 37 G2
Easter Dalziel Highld ... 155 F4
Easter Howgate Mdloth ... 132 A1
Easter Kinkell Highld ... 154 D5
Easter Moniack Highld ... 154 D3
Easter Ord Abers ... 149 F5
Easter Pitkierie Fife ... 133 E6
Easter Skeld Shet ... 169 h2
Easter Softlaw Border ... 123 E3
Easter Suddie Highld ... 155 E5
Eastergate W Susx ... 15 G4
Easterhouse C Glas ... 130 C2
Eastern Green W Mids ... 59 F3
Easterton Wilts ... 25 F5
Eastertown Somset ... 23 F5
Eastfield N Lans ... 131 E1
Eastfield N York ... 99 F3
Eastgate Dur ... 105 F4
Eastgate Lincs ... 74 A2
Eastgate Norfk ... 76 D2
Eastham Mersyd ... 81 F3
Eastham Ferry Mersyd ... 81 F3
Easthampstead Berks ... 27 G6
Easthampton Herefs ... 56 D2
Eastheath Berks ... 27 F6
Easthope Shrops ... 57 F5
Easthorpe Essex ... 52 C3
Easthorpe Notts ... 73 E5
Eastington Devon ... 8 D5
Eastington Gloucs ... 39 F6
Eastington Gloucs ... 38 C5
Eastlands D & G ... 110 C2
Eastleach Martin Gloucs ... 39 G5
Eastleach Turville Gloucs ... 39 G5
Eastleigh Devon ... 21 E3
Eastleigh Hants ... 14 C5
Eastling Kent ... 30 C2
Eastmoor Norfk ... 63 F6
Eastney Hants ... 15 E3
Eastnor Herefs ... 46 C3
Eastoft Lincs ... 92 B1
Easton Cambs ... 61 G2
Easton Cumb ... 103 G6
Easton Devon ... 8 D3
Easton Dorset ... 11 G2
Easton Hants ... 26 C2
Easton Lincs ... 73 G3
Easton Norfk ... 76 D1
Easton Somset ... 23 H4
Easton Suffk ... 65 E1
Easton Wilts ... 38 D1
Easton Grey Wilts ... 38 D3
Easton Maudit Nhants ... 49 G5
Easton on the Hill Nhants ... 61 F6
Easton Royal Wilts ... 25 G5
Easton-in-Gordano Somset ... 37 F2
Eastpeek Devon ... 5 G5
Eastrea Cambs ... 62 B5
Eastriggs D & G ... 111 G1
Eastrington E R Yk ... 92 B3
Eastrop Wilts ... 39 G3
Eastry Kent ... 31 G1
Eastshaw W Susx ... 27 G2
Eastville Bristl ... 37 G2
Eastville Lincs ... 74 D6
Eastwell Leics ... 73 E3
Eastwick Herts ... 51 E2
Eastwood Essex ... 30 B5
Eastwood Notts ... 72 B5
Eastwood W York ... 89 H2
Eastwood End Cambs ... 62 C5
Eathorpe Warwks ... 59 G2
Eaton Ches ... 81 H1
Eaton Ches ... 82 D1
Eaton Leics ... 73 F3
Eaton Norfk ... 64 D6

Eaton Notts ... 85 E2
Eaton Oxon ... 40 C5
Eaton Shrops ... 56 D4
Eaton Shrops ... 57 E4
Eaton Bishop Herefs ... 45 G3
Eaton Bray Beds ... 49 H1
Eaton Constantine Shrops ... 57 F6
Eaton Ford Beds ... 61 H1
Eaton Green Beds ... 49 H1
Eaton Hastings Oxon ... 39 G4
Eaton Mascott Shrops ... 57 F6
Eaton Socon Cambs ... 61 H1
Eaton upon Tern Shrops ... 70 B2
Eaves Brow Ches ... 82 A4
Eaves Green W Mids ... 59 E4
Ebberston N York ... 99 E3
Ebbesborne Wake Wilts ... 25 E2
Ebbw Vale Blae G ... 36 C5
Ebchester Dur ... 105 H6
Ebdon Somset ... 23 F6
Ebford Devon ... 9 G3
Ebley Gloucs ... 38 C5
Ebnal Ches ... 69 G5
Ebnall Herefs ... 45 G5
Ebrington Gloucs ... 47 G3
Ebsworthy Town Devon ... 8 B4
Ecchinswell Hants ... 26 C5
Ecclaw Border ... 133 F2
Ecclefechan D & G ... 111 F2
Eccles Border ... 123 E4
Eccles Gt Man ... 82 C4
Eccles Kent ... 29 H2
Eccles Green Herefs ... 45 G4
Eccles on Sea Norfk ... 77 G3
Eccles Road Norfk ... 64 C4
Ecclesall S York ... 83 H3
Ecclesfield S York ... 84 A4
Eccleshall Staffs ... 70 C3
Eccleshill W York ... 90 C3
Ecclesmachan W Loth ... 131 G2
Eccleston Ches ... 81 F1
Eccleston Lancs ... 88 D1
Eccleston Mersyd ... 81 G4
Eccleston Green Lancs ... 88 D1
Echt Abers ... 149 E5
Eckford Border ... 122 D2
Eckington Derbys ... 84 B3
Eckington Worcs ... 47 E3
Ecton Nhants ... 60 D2
Ecton Staffs ... 71 F6
Edale Derbys ... 83 F3
Eday Airport Ork ... 169 c3
Edburton W Susx ... 16 C2
Edderside Cumb ... 103 E5
Edderton Highld ... 162 D2
Eddington Kent ... 31 E3
Eddleston Border ... 121 G4
Eddlewood S Lans ... 120 B5
Eden Mount Cumb ... 95 E3
Eden Park Gt Lon ... 28 D3
Edenbridge Kent ... 17 E6
Edenfield Lancs ... 89 F1
Edenhall Cumb ... 104 B3
Edenham Lincs ... 74 A2
Edensor Derbys ... 83 G2
Edentaggart Ag & B ... 129 E4
Edenthorpe S York ... 84 D5
Edern Gwynd ... 66 B4
Edgarley Somset ... 23 H3
Edgbaston W Mids ... 58 D4
Edgcombe Cnwll ... 3 E3
Edgcott Bucks ... 49 E1
Edgcott Somset ... 22 A3
Edge Gloucs ... 38 C5
Edge Shrops ... 69 F1
Edge End Gloucs ... 37 G6
Edge Green Ches ... 69 G5
Edgebolton Shrops ... 69 H2
Edgefield Norfk ... 76 D3
Edgefield Green Norfk ... 76 D3
Edgefold Gt Man ... 82 B5
Edgehill Warwks ... 48 B4
Edgerley Shrops ... 69 F2
Edgerton W York ... 90 B1
Edgeside Lancs ... 89 G2
Edgeworth Gloucs ... 38 D5
Edgeworthy Devon ... 9 E6
Edgiock Worcs ... 47 F5
Edgmond Shrops ... 70 B2
Edgmond Marsh Shrops ... 70 B2
Edgton Shrops ... 56 D4
Edgware Gt Lon ... 28 C5
Edgworth Lancs ... 89 F1
Edial Staffs ... 58 D6
Edinbane Highld ... 150 D1
Edinburgh C Edin ... 132 B2
Edinburgh Airport C Edin ... 131 H2
Edinburgh Castle C Edin ... 132 B2
Edinburgh Zoo C Edin ... 132 A2
Edingale Staffs ... 71 G1
Edingham D & G ... 110 C1
Edingley Notts ... 72 D6
Edingthorpe Norfk ... 77 F3
Edingthorpe Green Norfk ... 77 F3
Edington Border ... 123 F5
Edington Nthumb ... 114 C4
Edington Somset ... 23 G3
Edington Wilts ... 25 E5
Edington Burtle Somset ... 23 G4
Edingworth Somset ... 23 F5
Edith Weston Rutlnd ... 61 E6
Edithmead Somset ... 23 F4
Edlesborough Bucks ... 49 H1
Edlingham Nthumb ... 124 D2
Edlington Lincs ... 86 C2
Edmond Castle Cumb ... 104 B6
Edmondsham Dorset ... 12 D6
Edmondsley Dur ... 106 B6
Edmondthorpe Leics ... 73 F2
Edmonton Cnwll ... 4 C3
Edmonton Gt Lon ... 28 D5
Edmundbyers Dur ... 105 G5
Ednam Border ... 123 E3
Ednaston Derbys ... 71 G4
Edradynate P & K ... 139 F5
Edrom Border ... 123 E5
Edstaston Shrops ... 69 G3
Edstone Warwks ... 47 G5

Edvin Loach Herefs ... 46 B5
Edwalton Notts ... 72 D4
Edwardstone Suffk ... 52 C5
Edwardsville Myr Td ... 36 B4
Edwinsford Carmth ... 43 F3
Edwinstowe Notts ... 84 D1
Edworth Beds ... 50 C5
Edwyn Ralph Herefs ... 46 B5
Edzell Angus ... 148 D1
Efail Isaf Rhondd ... 36 B3
Efail-fach Neath ... 35 E4
Efail-Rhyd Powys ... 68 D3
Efailnewydd Gwynd ... 66 C4
Efailwen Carmth ... 33 F4
Efenechtyd Denbgs ... 68 C6
Effgill D & G ... 111 G4
Effingham Surrey ... 28 B1
Efflinch Staffs ... 71 G2
Efford Devon ... 9 F5
Egbury Hants ... 26 C4
Egdean W Susx ... 15 H6
Egerton Gt Man ... 89 E1
Egerton Kent ... 18 C6
Eggbuckland Devon ... 6 B3
Eggesford Devon ... 21 G2
Egginton Beds ... 49 H2
Egginton Derbys ... 71 G3
Egglescliffe Dur ... 106 D2
Eggleston Dur ... 105 G2
Egham Surrey ... 28 A3
Egham Wick Surrey ... 41 H1
Eginswell Devon ... 7 F4
Egleton Rutlnd ... 61 E6
Eglingham Nthumb ... 124 D3
Egloshayle Cnwll ... 4 D3
Egloskerry Cnwll ... 5 F5
Eglwys Cross Wrexhm ... 69 G4
Eglwys Fach Cerdgn ... 54 D5
Eglwys-Brewis V Glam ... 35 G1
Eglwysbach Conwy ... 79 G2
Eglwyswrw Pembks ... 42 B3
Egmanton Notts ... 85 E1
Egremont Cumb ... 102 D1
Egremont Mersyd ... 81 E4
Egton N York ... 98 D5
Egton Bridge N York ... 98 D5
Eight and Forty E R Yk ... 92 B3
Eight Ash Green Essex ... 52 C3
Eilanreach Highld ... 143 G6
Eilan Village Powys ... 55 G2
Elberton Gloucs ... 37 G3
Elbridge W Susx ... 15 G4
Elburton Devon ... 6 C3
Elcombe Wilts ... 39 F2
Elcot Berks ... 40 B1
Elder Street Essex ... 51 F4
Eldernell Cambs ... 62 B5
Eldersfield Worcs ... 46 C2
Elderslie Rens ... 129 F1
Eldmire N York ... 97 G2
Eldon Dur ... 106 B4
Eldwick W York ... 90 B4
Elfhill Abers ... 149 F3
Elford Nthumb ... 125 E4
Elford Staffs ... 71 G1
Elgin Moray ... 156 D5
Elgol Highld ... 143 E5
Elham Kent ... 19 E6
Elie Fife ... 132 D5
Elilaw Nthumb ... 124 C2
Elim IOA ... 78 C3
Eling Hants ... 14 B5
Elkesley Notts ... 85 E2
Elkstone Gloucs ... 38 D5
Ella Abers ... 158 B5
Ellacombe Devon ... 7 F4
Ellanbeich Ag & B ... 136 B1
Elland W York ... 90 B2
Elland Lower Edge W York ... 90 B2
Ellary Ag & B ... 127 F3
Ellastone Staffs ... 71 F4
Ellel Lancs ... 88 C5
Ellemford Border ... 122 D5
Ellen's Green Surrey ... 16 B5
Ellenborough Cumb ... 102 D4
Ellenbrook Gt Man ... 82 B5
Ellenhall Staffs ... 70 C3
Ellerbeck N York ... 97 G5
Ellerby N York ... 107 G2
Ellerdine Heath Shrops ... 70 A2
Ellerhayes Devon ... 9 G5
Elleric Ag & B ... 137 E5
Ellerker E R Yk ... 92 C2
Ellers N York ... 90 A4
Ellerton E R Yk ... 91 H4
Ellerton N York ... 97 F5
Ellerton Shrops ... 70 B3
Ellesborough Bucks ... 41 F5
Ellesmere Shrops ... 69 F3
Ellesmere Port Ches ... 81 F2
Ellicombe Somset ... 22 C4
Ellingham Hants ... 13 E5
Ellingham Norfk ... 65 F5
Ellingham Nthumb ... 125 E4
Ellingstring N York ... 97 E3
Ellington Cambs ... 61 G2
Ellington Nthumb ... 114 D5
Ellington Thorpe Cambs ... 61 G2
Elliots Green Somset ... 24 D4
Ellisfield Hants ... 27 E4
Ellishader Highld ... 151 E5
Ellistown Leics ... 72 B1
Ellon Abers ... 159 E2
Ellonby Cumb ... 104 A4
Ellough Suffk ... 65 G4
Elloughton E R Yk ... 92 C2
Ellwood Gloucs ... 37 G5
Elm Cambs ... 62 D6
Elm Green Essex ... 52 A1
Elm Grove Norfk ... 65 G6
Elm Park Gt Lon ... 29 F5
Elmbridge Worcs ... 58 B2
Elmdon Essex ... 51 E5
Elmdon W Mids ... 59 E4
Elmdon Heath W Mids ... 58 D3
Elmer W Susx ... 15 H4
Elmer's Green Lancs ... 81 G5
Elmers End Gt Lon ... 28 D3

Elmesthorpe Leics..... 59 G5
Elmhurst Staffs..... 71 F1
Elmley Castle Worcs..... 47 E3
Elmley Lovett Worcs..... 58 B2
Elmore Gloucs..... 38 C6
Elmore Back Gloucs..... 38 B6
Elms Green Worcs..... 57 G2
Elmscott Devon..... 20 C3
Elmsett Suffk..... 52 D5
Elmstead Green Essex..... 52 D3
Elmstead Heath Essex..... 52 D3
Elmstead Market Essex..... 52 D3
Elmstead Row Essex..... 52 D3
Elmsted Court Kent..... 19 E6
Elmstone Kent..... 31 F2
Elmstone Hardwicke Gloucs..... 47 E2
Elmswell E R Yk..... 92 D5
Elmswell Suffk..... 64 B2
Elmton Derbys..... 84 C2
Elphin Highld..... 161 F5
Elphinstone E Loth..... 132 C2
Elrick Abers..... 149 F5
Elrick D & G..... 101 E5
Elrington Nthumb..... 113 F1
Elsdon Nthumb..... 113 F4
Elsecar S York..... 84 B5
Elsenham Essex..... 51 F3
Elsfield Oxon..... 40 D5
Elsham Lincs..... 85 H6
Elsick House Abers..... 149 F4
Elsing Norfk..... 76 D2
Elslack N York..... 89 H4
Elson Hants..... 14 D4
Elson Shrops..... 69 F4
Elsrickle S Lans..... 121 E4
Elstead Surrey..... 27 G4
Elsted W Susx..... 15 F6
Elsthorpe Lincs..... 74 A2
Elstob Dur..... 106 C3
Elston Lancs..... 88 D3
Elston Notts..... 73 E5
Elston Wilts..... 25 F4
Elstone Devon..... 21 G2
Elstow Beds..... 50 A5
Elstree Herts..... 28 C6
Elstronwick E R Yk..... 93 F3
Elswick Lancs..... 88 C3
Elswick T & W..... 114 D2
Elsworth Cambs..... 62 B2
Elterwater Cumb..... 94 D5
Eltham Gt Lon..... 29 E3
Eltisley Cambs..... 62 B1
Elton Cambs..... 61 G5
Elton Ches..... 81 G2
Elton Derbys..... 71 G6
Elton Dur..... 106 C3
Elton Gloucs..... 38 B6
Elton Gt Man..... 82 C6
Elton Herefs..... 57 E2
Elton Notts..... 73 E4
Elton Green Ches..... 81 G2
Eltringham Nthumb..... 114 B2
Elvanfoot S Lans..... 120 D1
Elvaston Derbys..... 72 B3
Elveden Suffk..... 63 G3
Elvetham Heath Hants..... 27 F5
Elvingston E Loth..... 132 C2
Elvington Kent..... 31 F1
Elvington N York..... 91 H4
Elwell Devon..... 21 G4
Elwick Dur..... 106 D4
Elwick Nthumb..... 124 D5
Elworth Ches..... 70 B6
Elworthy Somset..... 22 D3
Ely Cambs..... 63 E3
Ely Cardif..... 36 C2
Emberton Bucks..... 49 G4
Embleton Cumb..... 103 F3
Embleton Dur..... 106 D4
Embleton Nthumb..... 125 E3
Embo Highld..... 163 E3
Embo Street Highld..... 163 E3
Emborough Somset..... 24 B4
Embsay N York..... 90 A5
Emery Down Hants..... 13 G5
Emley W York..... 83 G6
Emley Moor W York..... 83 G6
Emmbrook Berks..... 41 F1
Emmer Green Berks..... 41 E2
Emmett Carr Derbys..... 84 B2
Emmington Oxon..... 41 F4
Emneth Cambs..... 62 D6
Emneth Hungate Norfk..... 62 D6
Empingham Rutlnd..... 73 G1
Empshott Hants..... 27 F2
Empshott Green Hants..... 27 F2
Emsworth Hants..... 15 F4
Enborne Berks..... 26 C6
Enborne Row Hants..... 26 C6
Enchmarsh Shrops..... 57 E5
Enderby Leics..... 60 A5
Endmoor Cumb..... 95 F3
Endon Staffs..... 70 D5
Endon Bank Staffs..... 70 D5
Enfield Gt Lon..... 28 D6
Enfield Lock Gt Lon..... 28 D6
Enfield Wash Gt Lon..... 28 D6
Enford Wilts..... 25 F5
Engine Common Gloucs..... 38 B3
England's Gate Herefs..... 46 A4
Englefield Berks..... 40 D1
Englefield Green Surrey..... 41 H1
Englesea brook Ches..... 70 C5
English Bicknor Gloucs..... 37 G6
English Frankton Shrops..... 69 G3
Englishcombe Somset..... 24 C6
Engollan Cnwll..... 4 B3
Enham-Alamein Hants..... 26 B4
Enmore Somset..... 23 E3
Enmore Green Dorset..... 24 D1
Ennerdale Bridge Cumb..... 103 E2
Enniscaven Cnwll..... 4 C2
Enochdhu P & K..... 139 H6
Ensay Ag & B..... 135 E4
Ensbury Dorset..... 13 E4
Ensdon Shrops..... 69 F2
Ensis Devon..... 21 F3
Enson Staffs..... 70 D3
Enstone Oxon..... 48 B2

Enterkinfoot D & G..... 110 C5
Enterpen N York..... 97 H5
Enville Staffs..... 58 A4
Enys Cnwll..... 3 E3
Eolaigearraidh W Isls..... 168 b2
Epney Gloucs..... 38 B5
Epperstone Notts..... 72 D5
Epping Essex..... 51 E1
Epping Green Essex..... 51 E1
Epping Green Herts..... 50 D1
Epping Upland Essex..... 51 E1
Eppleby N York..... 106 A2
Eppleworth E R Yk..... 92 D3
Epsom Surrey..... 28 C2
Epwell Oxon..... 48 B3
Epworth Lincs..... 85 E5
Epworth Turbary Lincs..... 85 E5
Erbistock Wrexhm..... 69 F4
Erdington W Mids..... 58 D5
Eridge Green E Susx..... 17 F5
Eridge Station E Susx..... 17 F5
Erines Ag & B..... 127 G3
Erisey Cnwll..... 3 E1
Eriska Ag & B..... 136 D4
Eriswell Suffk..... 63 F3
Erith Gt Lon..... 29 F4
Erlestoke Wilts..... 25 E5
Ermington Devon..... 6 D3
Erpingham Norfk..... 77 E3
Erriottwood Kent..... 30 C2
Errogie Highld..... 154 D1
Errol P & K..... 140 B2
Erskine Rens..... 129 F2
Ervie D & G..... 108 B1
Erwarton Suffk..... 53 F4
Erwood Powys..... 44 D3
Eryholme N York..... 106 C2
Eryrys Denbgs..... 68 D6
Escalls Cnwll..... 2 A2
Escomb Dur..... 106 A4
Escott Somset..... 22 D3
Escrick N York..... 91 G4
Esgair Carmth..... 42 D2
Esgair Cerdgn..... 54 C2
Esgairgeiliog Powys..... 55 E6
Esgerdawe Carmth..... 43 F3
Esgyryn Conwy..... 79 G2
Esh Dur..... 106 A5
Esh Winning Dur..... 106 A5
Esher Surrey..... 28 B2
Esholt W York..... 90 C4
Eshott Nthumb..... 114 D5
Eshton N York..... 89 H5
Eskadale Highld..... 154 C3
Eskbank Mdloth..... 132 B2
Eskdale Green Cumb..... 94 B5
Eskdalemuir D & G..... 111 G4
Eskett Cumb..... 103 E2
Eskham Lincs..... 86 D4
Eskholme S York..... 91 G1
Esperley Lane Ends Dur..... 105 H2
Esprick Lancs..... 88 C3
Essendine Rutlnd..... 73 H1
Essendon Herts..... 50 D2
Essich Highld..... 155 E3
Essington Staffs..... 58 C6
Esslemont Abers..... 159 E2
Eston N York..... 107 E3
Etal Nthumb..... 123 F3
Etchilhampton Wilts..... 25 F5
Etchingham E Susx..... 17 H4
Etchinghill Kent..... 19 E5
Etchinghill Staffs..... 71 E2
Etchingwood E Susx..... 17 F4
Etherdwick E R Yk..... 93 F3
Etling Green Norfk..... 76 C1
Etloe Gloucs..... 38 B5
Eton Berks..... 41 H2
Eton Wick Berks..... 41 H2
Etruria Staffs..... 70 D5
Etteridge Highld..... 146 B4
Ettersgill Dur..... 105 E3
Ettiley Heath Ches..... 70 B6
Ettingshall W Mids..... 58 B5
Ettington Warwks..... 48 A4
Etton Cambs..... 61 G6
Etton E R Yk..... 92 D4
Ettrick Border..... 121 G1
Ettrickbridge Border..... 122 A2
Ettrickhill Border..... 111 G6
Etwall Derbys..... 71 G3
Eudon George Shrops..... 57 G4
Euston Suffk..... 64 B3
Euximoor Drove Cambs..... 62 D5
Euxton Lancs..... 88 D1
Evancoyd Powys..... 56 C2
Evanton Highld..... 154 D6
Evedon Lincs..... 74 A5
Evelith Shrops..... 57 H6
Evelix Highld..... 163 E3
Evenjobb Powys..... 45 E5
Evenley Oxon..... 48 D3
Evenlode Gloucs..... 47 H2
Evenwood Dur..... 106 A3
Evenwood Gate Dur..... 106 A3
Evercreech Somset..... 24 B3
Everingham E R Yk..... 92 B4
Everleigh Wilts..... 25 G5
Everley N York..... 99 E4
Eversholt Beds..... 49 H2
Evershot Dorset..... 11 F5
Eversley Hants..... 27 F5
Eversley Cross Hants..... 27 F5
Everthorpe E R Yk..... 92 C3
Everton Beds..... 50 C6
Everton Hants..... 13 G4
Everton Mersyd..... 81 F4
Everton Notts..... 85 E4
Evertown D & G..... 111 H2
Evesbatch Herefs..... 46 B4
Evesham Worcs..... 47 F4
Evington Leics..... 60 B6
Ewden Village S York..... 83 H4
Ewdness Shrops..... 57 G5
Ewell Surrey..... 28 C2
Ewell Minnis Kent..... 19 F6
Ewelme Oxon..... 41 E3

Ewen Gloucs..... 39 E4
Ewenny V Glam..... 35 F2
Ewerby Lincs..... 74 B5
Ewerby Thorpe Lincs..... 74 B5
Ewesley Nthumb..... 114 C6
Ewhurst Surrey..... 16 B5
Ewhurst Green E Susx..... 18 B4
Ewhurst Green Surrey..... 16 B5
Ewloe Flints..... 81 E1
Ewloe Green Flints..... 81 E1
Ewood Lancs..... 89 E2
Ewood Bridge Lancs..... 89 F2
Eworthy Devon..... 8 A4
Ewshot Hants..... 27 F4
Ewyas Harold Herefs..... 45 G2
Exbourne Devon..... 8 C5
Exbury Hants..... 14 C4
Exceat E Susx..... 17 F1
Exebridge Somset..... 22 B2
Exelby N York..... 97 F4
Exeter Devon..... 9 F4
Exeter Airport Devon..... 9 G4
Exford Somset..... 22 A3
Exfordsgreen Shrops..... 57 E6
Exhall Warwks..... 47 F5
Exhall Warwks..... 59 F4
Exlade Street Oxon..... 41 E2
Exley Head W York..... 90 B4
Exminster Devon..... 9 F3
Exmouth Devon..... 9 G4
Exning Suffk..... 63 E2
Exted Kent..... 19 E6
Exton Devon..... 9 G3
Exton Hants..... 14 D6
Exton Rutlnd..... 73 G1
Exton Somset..... 22 B3
Exwick Devon..... 9 F4
Eyam Derbys..... 83 G2
Eydon Nhants..... 48 D4
Eye Cambs..... 62 B6
Eye Herefs..... 57 E2
Eye Suffk..... 64 D3
Eye Green Cambs..... 62 B6
Eye Kettleby Leics..... 73 E2
Eyemouth Border..... 123 G6
Eyeworth Beds..... 50 C5
Eyhorne Street Kent..... 30 B1
Eyke Suffk..... 53 G6
Eynesbury Cambs..... 61 H1
Eynsford Kent..... 29 F3
Eynsham Oxon..... 40 C5
Eype Dorset..... 11 E4
Eyre Highld..... 150 D4
Eythorne Kent..... 31 F1
Eyton Herefs..... 45 G5
Eyton Shrops..... 69 F1
Eyton Shrops..... 69 G3
Eyton Shrops..... 56 D4
Eyton Wrexhm..... 69 F4
Eyton on Severn Shrops..... 57 F6
Eyton upon the Weald Moors
Shrops..... 70 B1

F

Faccombe Hants..... 26 B5
Faceby N York..... 97 H5
Fachwen Powys..... 68 C2
Facit Lancs..... 89 G1
Fackley Notts..... 72 B6
Faddiley Ches..... 69 H5
Fadmoor N York..... 98 B4
Faerdre Swans..... 34 D3
Fagwyr Swans..... 34 D4
Faifley W Duns..... 129 F2
Failand Somset..... 37 F1
Failford S Ayrs..... 119 F2
Failsworth Gt Man..... 82 D5
Fair Oak Hants..... 14 C5
Fair Oak Green Hants..... 27 E5
Fairbourne Gwynd..... 67 F1
Fairburn N York..... 91 F2
Fairfield Derbys..... 83 F2
Fairfield Kent..... 18 C4
Fairfield Worcs..... 58 B3
Fairford Gloucs..... 39 F4
Fairford Park Gloucs..... 39 F4
Fairgirth D & G..... 102 C6
Fairhaven Lancs..... 88 B2
Fairlie N Ayrs..... 118 D5
Fairlight E Susx..... 18 B3
Fairmile Devon..... 10 A4
Fairmile Surrey..... 28 B2
Fairnilee Border..... 122 B3
Fairoak Staffs..... 70 C3
Fairseat Kent..... 29 G3
Fairstead Essex..... 52 A2
Fairstead Norfk..... 77 F2
Fairwarp E Susx..... 17 E4
Fairwater Cardif..... 36 C2
Fairy Cross Devon..... 20 D3
Fakenham Norfk..... 76 B3
Fakenham Magna Suffk..... 64 B3
Fala Mdloth..... 122 B5
Fala Dam Mdloth..... 122 B6
Falcondale Cerdgn..... 43 F4
Falcut Nthumb..... 48 D3
Faldingworth Lincs..... 86 A3
Faldouet Jersey..... 174 d2
Falfield Gloucs..... 38 B4
Falkenham Suffk..... 53 F5
Falkirk Falk..... 131 E3
Falkland Fife..... 132 B6
Fallgate Derbys..... 72 A6
Fallin Stirlg..... 131 E4
Falloden Nthumb..... 125 E3
Fallowfield Gt Man..... 82 D4
Fallowfield Nthumb..... 113 F2
Falls of Blarghour Ag & B..... 137 E1
Falmer E Susx..... 16 D2
Falmouth Cnwll..... 3 F3
Falnash Border..... 112 A5
Falsgrave N York..... 99 F4

Falstone Nthumb..... 112 D3
Fanagmore Highld..... 164 C3
Fancott Beds..... 50 A3
Fanellan Highld..... 154 C3
Fangdale Beck N York..... 98 A4
Fangfoss E R Yk..... 92 B5
Fanmore Ag & B..... 135 F4
Fannich Lodge Highld..... 153 F6
Fans Border..... 122 C3
Far Bletchley Bucks..... 49 G3
Far Cotton Nhants..... 49 F5
Far End Cumb..... 94 D5
Far Forest Worcs..... 57 G3
Far Green Gloucs..... 38 C4
Far Moor Gt Man..... 81 G5
Far Oakridge Gloucs..... 38 D5
Far Sawrey Cumb..... 94 D4
Far Thorpe Lincs..... 86 C2
Farcet Cambs..... 62 A5
Farden Shrops..... 57 F3
Fareham Hants..... 14 D4
Farewell Staffs..... 71 F1
Farforth Lincs..... 86 D2
Faringdon Oxon..... 39 G4
Farington Lancs..... 88 D2
Farkhill P & K..... 139 H3
Farlam Cumb..... 104 B6
Farleigh Devon..... 7 E3
Farleigh Somset..... 37 F1
Farleigh Surrey..... 29 E2
Farleigh Hungerford Somset..... 24 D5
Farleigh Wallop Hants..... 26 D4
Farlesthorpe Lincs..... 87 E2
Farleton Cumb..... 95 F3
Farleton Lancs..... 95 F1
Farley Derbys..... 83 H1
Farley Staffs..... 71 F4
Farley Wilts..... 25 H2
Farley Green Suffk..... 52 A6
Farley Green Surrey..... 16 B6
Farley Hill Berks..... 27 F6
Farleys End Gloucs..... 38 B6
Farlington Hants..... 15 E4
Farlington N York..... 98 B2
Farlow Shrops..... 57 F3
Farmborough Somset..... 24 B5
Farmbridge End Essex..... 51 G2
Farmcote Gloucs..... 47 F2
Farmcote Shrops..... 57 H4
Farmers Carmth..... 43 G4
Farmington Gloucs..... 39 F6
Farmoor Oxon..... 40 C5
Farms Common Cnwll..... 2 D3
Farmtown Moray..... 157 G4
Farnachty Moray..... 157 F5
Farnah Green Derbys..... 72 A5
Farnborough Gt Lon..... 29 E2
Farnborough Berks..... 40 C2
Farnborough Hants..... 27 G5
Farnborough Warwks..... 48 C4
Farnborough Park Hants..... 27 G5
Farnborough Street Hants..... 27 G5
Farncombe Surrey..... 27 H4
Farndish Beds..... 61 E2
Farndon Ches..... 69 F5
Farndon Notts..... 73 E5
Farnell Angus..... 141 F5
Farnham Dorset..... 12 C6
Farnham Essex..... 51 F3
Farnham N York..... 91 E6
Farnham Suffk..... 65 F1
Farnham Surrey..... 27 F4
Farnham Common Bucks..... 41 H3
Farnham Green Essex..... 51 E3
Farnham Royal Bucks..... 41 H2
Farningham Kent..... 29 F3
Farnley N York..... 90 C4
Farnley W York..... 90 D3
Farnley Tyas W York..... 83 F6
Farnsfield Notts..... 72 D6
Farnworth Ches..... 81 G3
Farnworth Gt Man..... 82 B5
Farr Highld..... 166 A5
Farr Highld..... 155 E2
Farr Highld..... 146 C5
Farraline Highld..... 154 D1
Farringdon Devon..... 9 G4
Farrington Gurney Somset..... 24 B5
Farsley W York..... 90 C3
Farther Howegreen Essex..... 30 B6
Farthing Green Kent..... 18 B6
Farthing Street Gt Lon..... 29 E2
Farthinghoe Nhants..... 48 D3
Farthingloe Kent..... 19 F5
Farthingstone Nhants..... 48 D5
Fartown W York..... 90 C1
Fartown W York..... 90 C3
Farway Street Devon..... 10 B4
Fasnacloich Ag & B..... 137 E5
Fasnakyle Highld..... 153 G2
Fassfern Highld..... 144 C2
Fatfield T & W..... 115 E1
Faugh Cumb..... 104 B6
Fauld Staffs..... 71 G3
Fauldhouse W Loth..... 120 D5
Faulkbourne Essex..... 52 B2
Faulkland Somset..... 24 C5
Fauls Shrops..... 69 H3
Faversham Kent..... 30 D2
Fawdington N York..... 97 G2
Fawdon Nthumb..... 114 D2
Fawfieldhead Staffs..... 83 F1
Fawkham Green Kent..... 29 G3
Fawler Oxon..... 40 B6
Fawley Berks..... 40 B3
Fawley Bucks..... 41 F3
Fawley Hants..... 14 C4
Fawley Chapel Herefs..... 46 B2
Fawnog Flints..... 81 E1
Fawsley Nhants..... 48 D5
Faxfleet E R Yk..... 92 B2
Faygate W Susx..... 16 C5
Fazakerley Mersyd..... 81 F4
Fazeley Staffs..... 59 E6
Fearby N York..... 97 E3
Fearn Highld..... 163 G4

Fearnan P & K..... 138 D4
Fearnbeg Highld..... 151 E5
Fearnhead Ches..... 82 A4
Fearnmore Highld..... 151 G5
Fearnoch Ag & B..... 127 H3
Featherstone Staffs..... 58 B6
Featherstone W York..... 91 E2
Feckenham Worcs..... 47 F5
Feering Essex..... 52 B3
Feetham N York..... 96 C5
Feizor N York..... 96 A2
Felbridge Surrey..... 17 E5
Felbrigg Norfk..... 77 E4
Felcourt Surrey..... 17 E6
Felday Surrey..... 16 B6
Felden Herts..... 50 A1
Felin Fach Cerdgn..... 43 E5
Felin gwm Isaf Carmth..... 43 E1
Felin gwm Uchaf Carmth..... 43 E2
Felin-newydd Powys..... 44 D3
Felindre Carmth..... 43 F1
Felindre Carmth..... 43 G3
Felindre Carmth..... 42 D3
Felindre Cerdgn..... 43 F5
Felindre Powys..... 56 B3
Felindre Powys..... 45 E1
Felindre Swans..... 34 D4
Felindre Farchog Pembks..... 42 A3
Felinfach Powys..... 44 D2
Felinfoel Carmth..... 34 C4
Felixkirk N York..... 97 H3
Felixstowe Suffk..... 53 F4
Felixstowe Ferry Suffk..... 53 G4
Felkington Nthumb..... 123 G4
Felkirk W York..... 84 B6
Fell Foot Cumb..... 94 D5
Fell Lane W York..... 90 B4
Fell Side Cumb..... 103 G4
Felling T & W..... 114 D2
Felmersham Beds..... 49 H5
Felmingham Norfk..... 77 E3
Felpham W Susx..... 15 H3
Felsham Suffk..... 64 B1
Felsted Essex..... 51 G3
Feltham Gt Lon..... 28 B3
Felthamhill Gt Lon..... 28 B3
Felthorpe Norfk..... 77 E2
Felton Herefs..... 46 A4
Felton Nthumb..... 114 C6
Felton Somset..... 23 H6
Felton Butler Shrops..... 69 F2
Feltwell Norfk..... 63 F4
Fen Ditton Cambs..... 62 D1
Fen Drayton Cambs..... 62 C2
Fen End Lincs..... 74 C2
Fen End W Mids..... 59 E3
Fen Street Norfk..... 64 B5
Fen Street Norfk..... 64 D2
Fenay Bridge W York..... 90 C1
Fence Lancs..... 89 G3
Fence S York..... 84 B3
Fencehouses T & W..... 106 C1
Fencote N York..... 97 F4
Fencott Oxon..... 40 D6
Fendike Corner Lincs..... 75 E6
Fenham Nthumb..... 123 H3
Feniscliffe Lancs..... 89 E2
Feniscowles Lancs..... 89 E2
Feniton Devon..... 10 B4
Fenn Green Shrops..... 57 H4
Fenn Street Kent..... 30 B4
Fenny Bentley Derbys..... 71 G5
Fenny Bridges Devon..... 10 B4
Fenny Compton Warwks..... 48 B4
Fenny Drayton Leics..... 59 F5
Fenny Stratford Bucks..... 49 G3
Fenrother Nthumb..... 114 C5
Fenstanton Cambs..... 62 B2
Fenstead End Suffk..... 52 B6
Fenton Cambs..... 62 B3
Fenton Cumb..... 104 B6
Fenton Lincs..... 85 F2
Fenton Lincs..... 73 F5
Fenton Notts..... 85 E3
Fenton Nthumb..... 123 G3
Fenton Staffs..... 70 D4
Fenton Barns E Loth..... 132 D3
Fenwick E Ayrs..... 119 F4
Fenwick Nthumb..... 123 H3
Fenwick Nthumb..... 114 B3
Fenwick S York..... 91 G1
Feock Cnwll..... 3 F4
Feolin Ferry Ag & B..... 126 C2
Fergushill N Ayrs..... 119 E4
Feriniquarrie Highld..... 150 B4
Fermain Bay Guern..... 174 e2
Fern Angus..... 141 E6
Ferndale Rhondd..... 35 G4
Ferndown Dorset..... 13 E3
Ferness Moray..... 156 B4
Fernham Oxon..... 39 G3
Fernhill Heath Worcs..... 46 D5
Fernhurst W Susx..... 27 G2
Fernie Fife..... 140 C1
Ferniegair S Lans..... 120 B5
Fernilea Highld..... 150 D2
Fernilee Derbys..... 83 E2
Ferny Common Herefs..... 45 F4
Ferrensby N York..... 91 E6
Ferriby Sluice Lincs..... 92 D2
Ferrindonald Highld..... 143 F5
Ferring W Susx..... 16 B2
Ferrybridge W York..... 91 F2
Ferry Point Highld..... 162 D2
Ferryden Angus..... 141 G5
Ferryhill Dur..... 106 B4
Ferryside Carmth..... 33 H3
Ferrytown Highld..... 162 D2
Fersfield Norfk..... 64 C4
Fersit Highld..... 145 F2
Feshiebridge Highld..... 146 C5
Fetcham Surrey..... 28 B2
Fetterangus Abers..... 159 F4
Fettercairn Abers..... 148 D2
Fewcott Oxon..... 48 D2
Fewston N York..... 90 C5
Ffair Rhos Cerdgn..... 55 E2
Ffairfach Carmth..... 43 F1

Ffald-y-Brenin Carmth...... 43 F4
Ffawyddog Powys...... 36 C6
Ffestiniog Gwynd...... 67 G4
Ffestiniog Railway Gwynd...... 67 F4
Ffordd-las Denbgs...... 80 C1
Fforest Carmth...... 34 C5
Fforest Mons...... 45 F1
Fforest Fach Swans...... 34 D4
Fforest Goch Neath...... 35 E4
Ffostrasol Cerdgn...... 42 D4
Ffrith Flints...... 69 E6
Ffynnon-Oer Cerdgn...... 43 E5
Ffynnonddewi Cerdgn...... 42 D4
Ffynnongroyw Flints...... 80 D3
Fiag Lodge Highld...... 165 F1
Fickleshole Surrey...... 29 E2
Fiddington Gloucs...... 47 E2
Fiddington Somset...... 23 E3
Fiddleford Dorset...... 12 B6
Fiddlers Green Cnwll...... 3 F5
Fiddlers Hamlet Essex...... 29 F6
Field Staffs...... 71 E3
Field Broughton Cumb...... 95 E3
Field Dalling Norfk...... 76 C4
Field Head Leics...... 72 C1
Fieldhead Cumb...... 104 A4
Fife Keith Moray...... 157 F4
Fifehead Magdalen Dorset...... 24 C1
Fifehead Neville Dorset...... 12 B6
Fifehead St Quintin Dorset...... 12 B6
Fifield Berks...... 41 G2
Fifield Oxon...... 47 H1
Fifield Wilts...... 25 G4
Figheldean Wilts...... 25 G4
Filands Wilts...... 38 D3
Filby Norfk...... 77 H1
Filey N York...... 99 G3
Filgrave Bucks...... 49 G4
Filkins Oxon...... 39 G5
Filleigh Devon...... 21 G3
Filleigh Devon...... 21 G2
Fillingham Lincs...... 85 G3
Fillongley Warwks...... 59 F4
Filmore Hill Hants...... 27 E2
Filton Gloucs...... 37 G2
Fimber E R Yk...... 92 C6
Finavon Angus...... 141 E5
Fincham Norfk...... 63 F6
Finchampstead Berks...... 27 F6
Fincharn Ag & B...... 127 H5
Finchdean Hants...... 15 F5
Finchingfield Essex...... 51 H4
Finchley Gt Lon...... 28 D5
Findern Derbys...... 71 H3
Findhorn Moray...... 156 C5
Findhorn Bridge Highld...... 155 F2
Findo Gask P & K...... 139 G2
Findochty Moray...... 157 G6
Findon Abers...... 149 G4
Findon W Susx...... 16 B2
Findon Mains Highld...... 154 D5
Findrack House Abers...... 148 D5
Finedon Nhants...... 61 E3
Fineshade Nhants...... 61 F5
Fingal Street Suffk...... 65 E2
Fingask P & K...... 140 B2
Fingest Bucks...... 41 F3
Finghall N York...... 97 E4
Fingland Cumb...... 103 F6
Fingland D & G...... 120 B1
Finglesham Kent...... 31 G1
Fingringhoe Essex...... 52 D3
Finkle Green Essex...... 51 H5
Finkle Street S York...... 83 H5
Finlarig Stirlg...... 138 C3
Finmere Oxon...... 49 E2
Finnart P & K...... 138 B5
Finningham Suffk...... 64 C2
Finningley S York...... 84 D5
Finsbay W Isls...... 168 d6
Finstall Worcs...... 58 C2
Finsthwaite Cumb...... 94 D4
Finstock Oxon...... 40 B6
Finstown Ork...... 158 C4
Fintry Abers...... 158 C4
Fintry Stirlg...... 130 B4
Finzean Abers...... 148 D4
Fionnphort Ag & B...... 135 E2
Fionnsbhagh W Isls...... 168 d6
Fir Tree Dur...... 105 H3
Firbank Cumb...... 95 G4
Firbeck S York...... 84 C3
Firby N York...... 97 F3
Firby N York...... 98 C1
Firgrove Gt Man...... 82 D6
Firsby Lincs...... 87 E1
Firsdown Dorset...... 25 G3
Fishbourne IOW...... 14 D3
Fishbourne W Susx...... 15 F4
Fishbourne Roman Palace W Susx...... 15 F4
Fishburn Dur...... 106 C4
Fishcross Clacks...... 131 E5
Fisher W Susx...... 15 G4
Fisher's Pond Hants...... 14 C6
Fisher's Row Lancs...... 88 C4
Fisherford Abers...... 158 C3
Fisherrow E Loth...... 132 B2
Fisherstreet W Susx...... 27 H2
Fisherton Highld...... 155 H4
Fisherton S Ayrs...... 119 E1
Fisherton de la Mere Wilts...... 25 E3
Fisherwick Staffs...... 59 E6
Fishery Estate Berks...... 41 G2
Fishguard Pembks...... 32 D5
Fishlake S York...... 84 D6
Fishleigh Devon...... 8 B5
Fishmere End Lincs...... 74 C4
Fishnish Pier Ag & B...... 136 A4
Fishpond Bottom Dorset...... 10 D4
Fishponds Bristl...... 37 G2
Fishpool Gt Man...... 82 C6
Fishtoft Lincs...... 74 D4
Fishtoft Drove Lincs...... 74 D5
Fishwick Lancs...... 88 D2
Fiskavaig Highld...... 150 C2
Fiskerton Lincs...... 85 H2
Fiskerton Notts...... 73 E5
Fitling E R Yk...... 93 F3

Fittleton Wilts...... 25 G4
Fittleworth W Susx...... 16 A3
Fitton End Cambs...... 75 E1
Fitz Shrops...... 69 G2
Fitzhead Somset...... 22 D2
Fitzroy Somset...... 23 E2
Fitzwilliam W York...... 91 E1
Five Ash Down E Susx...... 17 F4
Five Ashes E Susx...... 17 F4
Five Bells Somset...... 22 D3
Five Bridges Herefs...... 46 B4
Five Lanes Mons...... 37 E3
Five Oak Green Kent...... 17 G6
Five Oaks Jersey...... 174 c2
Five Oaks W Susx...... 16 B4
Five Roads Carmth...... 34 B5
Five Wents Kent...... 30 B1
Fivecrosses Ches...... 81 G2
Fivehead Somset...... 23 F1
Fivelanes Cnwll...... 5 F4
Flack's Green Essex...... 52 A2
Flackwell Heath Bucks...... 41 G3
Fladbury Worcs...... 47 E4
Fladdabister Shet...... 169 j2
Flagg Derbys...... 83 F1
Flamborough E R Yk...... 99 H2
Flamingo Land Theme Park N York...... 98 C3
Flamstead Herts...... 50 B2
Flansham W Susx...... 15 H4
Flanshaw W York...... 90 D2
Flasby N York...... 89 H5
Flash Staffs...... 83 E1
Flashader Highld...... 150 D4
Flaunden Herts...... 28 A6
Flawborough Notts...... 73 E4
Flawith N York...... 97 H1
Flax Bourton Somset...... 37 F1
Flaxby N York...... 91 E5
Flaxley Gloucs...... 38 B6
Flaxmere Ches...... 81 H2
Flaxpool Somset...... 22 D3
Flaxton N York...... 91 H6
Fleckney Leics...... 60 C5
Flecknoe Warwks...... 60 A2
Fledborough Notts...... 85 F2
Fleet Dorset...... 11 G3
Fleet Hants...... 15 E4
Fleet Hants...... 27 F5
Fleet Lincs...... 74 D2
Fleet Hargate Lincs...... 74 D2
Fleetend Hants...... 14 C4
Fleetwood Lancs...... 88 B4
Flemingston V Glam...... 35 G1
Flemington S Lans...... 120 A5
Flempton Suffk...... 63 G2
Fletcher Green Kent...... 29 F1
Fletchersbridge Cnwll...... 5 E2
Fletchertown Cumb...... 103 F4
Fletching E Susx...... 17 E4
Fleur-de-lis Caerph...... 36 C4
Flexbury Cnwll...... 20 B1
Flexford Surrey...... 27 G4
Flimby Cumb...... 102 D3
Flimwell E Susx...... 17 H4
Flint Flints...... 81 E2
Flint Mountain Flints...... 81 E2
Flint's Green W Mids...... 59 E3
Flintham Notts...... 73 E5
Flinton E R Yk...... 93 F3
Flishinghurst Kent...... 18 A5
Flitcham Norfk...... 75 G3
Flitton Beds...... 50 B4
Flitwick Beds...... 50 A4
Flixborough Lincs...... 92 C1
Flixborough Stather Lincs...... 92 B1
Flixton Gt Man...... 82 B4
Flixton N York...... 99 F3
Flixton Suffk...... 65 F4
Flockton W York...... 90 D1
Flockton Green W York...... 90 D1
Flodden Nthumb...... 123 F3
Flodigarry Highld...... 151 E6
Flookburgh Cumb...... 94 D2
Flordon Norfk...... 64 D5
Flore Nhants...... 49 E5
Flotterton Nthumb...... 113 G5
Flowers Green E Susx...... 17 G2
Flowton Suffk...... 52 D5
Flushdyke W York...... 90 D2
Flushing Cnwll...... 3 F3
Fluxton Devon...... 10 A4
Flyford Flavell Worcs...... 47 E5
Fobbing Essex...... 29 H4
Fochabers Moray...... 157 G5
Fochriw Caerph...... 36 B5
Fockerby Lincs...... 92 B1
Foddington Somset...... 24 A2
Foel Powys...... 68 B1
Foel y Dyffryn Brdgnd...... 35 F4
Foelgastell Carmth...... 34 C6
Foggathorpe E R Yk...... 92 A3
Fogo Border...... 123 E4
Fogwatt Moray...... 156 D5
Folda Angus...... 140 B6
Fole Staffs...... 71 E4
Foleshill W Mids...... 59 F4
Foliejon Park Berks...... 41 G2
Folke Dorset...... 11 G6
Folkestone Kent...... 19 F5
Folkingham Lincs...... 74 A3
Folkington E Susx...... 17 F2
Folksworth Cambs...... 61 G4
Folkton N York...... 99 F3
Folla Rule Abers...... 158 C2
Follifoot N York...... 91 E5
Folly Gate Devon...... 8 C4
Folly Hill Surrey...... 27 F4
Fonmon V Glam...... 22 C6
Font-y-gary V Glam...... 22 C6
Fonthill Bishop Wilts...... 25 E2
Fonthill Gifford Wilts...... 25 E2
Fontmell Magna Dorset...... 24 D1
Fontmell Parva Dorset...... 12 B6
Fontwell W Susx...... 15 H4
Foolow Derbys...... 83 G2
Foots Cray Gt Lon...... 29 F5

Forbestown Abers...... 148 A6
Forcett N York...... 106 A2
Ford Ag & B...... 127 G5
Ford Bucks...... 41 F5
Ford Derbys...... 84 B3
Ford Devon...... 20 D3
Ford Devon...... 6 D3
Ford Devon...... 7 E2
Ford Gloucs...... 47 F2
Ford Nthumb...... 123 G3
Ford Shrops...... 69 F1
Ford Somset...... 22 D2
Ford Somset...... 24 B5
Ford Staffs...... 71 F5
Ford W Susx...... 15 H4
Ford Wilts...... 38 C2
Ford Wilts...... 25 G2
Ford End Essex...... 51 H2
Ford Green Lancs...... 88 C4
Ford Heath Shrops...... 69 F1
Ford Street Somset...... 22 D1
Ford's Green Suffk...... 64 C2
Forda Devon...... 8 B4
Fordcombe Kent...... 17 F5
Fordell Fife...... 131 H4
Forden Powys...... 56 C5
Forder Devon...... 8 D4
Forder Green Devon...... 7 E4
Fordham Cambs...... 63 E2
Fordham Essex...... 52 C3
Fordham Norfk...... 63 E5
Fordham Heath Essex...... 52 C3
Fordingbridge Hants...... 13 E6
Fordon E R Yk...... 99 F2
Fordoun Abers...... 149 E2
Fordstreet Essex...... 52 C3
Fordton Devon...... 9 E4
Fordwells Oxon...... 40 A6
Fordwich Kent...... 31 E2
Fordyce Abers...... 158 B5
Forebridge Staffs...... 70 D2
Foremark Derbys...... 72 A3
Forest Guern...... 174 g1
Forest N York...... 97 F5
Forest Becks Lancs...... 89 F5
Forest Chapel Ches...... 83 E2
Forest Gate Gt Lon...... 29 E5
Forest Green Surrey...... 16 B5
Forest Hall Cumb...... 95 F5
Forest Hall T & W...... 114 D2
Forest Head Cumb...... 104 C6
Forest Hill Gt Lon...... 28 D3
Forest Hill Oxon...... 40 D5
Forest Lane Head N York...... 90 D5
Forest Lodge Ag & B...... 137 G4
Forest Mill Clacks...... 131 F4
Forest Row E Susx...... 17 E5
Forest Side IOW...... 14 C2
Forest Town Notts...... 84 C1
Forest-in-Teesdale Dur...... 105 E3
Forestburn Gate Nthumb...... 114 B5
Forestside W Susx...... 15 F5
Forfar Angus...... 140 D5
Forgandenny P & K...... 139 H2
Forge Powys...... 55 E5
Forge Hammer Torfn...... 36 D4
Forge Side Torfn...... 36 D5
Forgie Moray...... 157 F4
Forgieside Moray...... 157 F4
Forgue Abers...... 158 B4
Forhill Worcs...... 58 C3
Formby Mersyd...... 81 E5
Forncett End Norfk...... 64 D5
Forncett St Mary Norfk...... 64 D5
Forncett St Peter Norfk...... 64 D5
Fornham All Saints Suffk...... 63 G2
Fornham St Martin Suffk...... 63 H2
Fornside Cumb...... 103 G2
Forres Moray...... 156 B5
Forsbrook Staffs...... 71 E4
Forse Highld...... 167 F2
Forse House Highld...... 167 F2
Forshaw Heath Warwks...... 58 D3
Forsinard Highld...... 166 C3
Forston Dorset...... 11 G4
Fort Augustus Highld...... 145 F5
Fort Hommet Guern...... 174 f2
Fort le Marchant Guern...... 174 h3
Fort William Highld...... 144 C2
Forteviot P & K...... 139 H1
Forth S Lans...... 120 D5
Forthampton Gloucs...... 46 D2
Fortingall P & K...... 139 E4
Fortnighty Highld...... 155 G4
Forton Hants...... 26 B4
Forton Lancs...... 88 C5
Forton Shrops...... 69 F2
Forton Somset...... 10 D5
Forton Staffs...... 70 C2
Fortrie Abers...... 158 C4
Fortrose Highld...... 155 E5
Fortuneswell Dorset...... 11 G2
Forty Green Bucks...... 41 G3
Forty Hill Gt Lon...... 28 D6
Forward Green Suffk...... 64 D1
Fosbury Wilts...... 26 A5
Foscote Nhants...... 49 E4
Foscot Oxon...... 47 H1
Fosdyke Lincs...... 74 C3
Fosdyke Bridge Lincs...... 74 D3
Foss P & K...... 139 E6
Foss-y-ffin Cerdgn...... 43 E5
Fossebridge Gloucs...... 39 E5
Foster Street Essex...... 51 F2
Fosterhouses S York...... 91 G1
Foston Derbys...... 71 G3
Foston Leics...... 60 B5
Foston Lincs...... 73 F4
Foston N York...... 98 C1
Foston on the Wolds E R Yk...... 93 E5
Fotherby Lincs...... 86 C4
Fothergill Cumb...... 102 D3
Fotheringhay Nhants...... 61 F5
Foul End Warwks...... 59 E5
Foul Mile E Susx...... 17 G3
Foulbridge Cumb...... 104 A5
Foulby W York...... 91 E1
Foulden Border...... 123 H4

Foulden Norfk...... 63 G5
Foulridge Lancs...... 89 G4
Foulsham Norfk...... 76 C2
Fountainhall Border...... 122 B4
Four Ashes Staffs...... 58 B6
Four Ashes Staffs...... 58 A4
Four Ashes Suffk...... 64 C2
Four Ashes W Mids...... 58 D3
Four Cabots Guern...... 174 g2
Four Crosses Powys...... 69 E2
Four Crosses Staffs...... 70 D1
Four Elms Kent...... 29 E1
Four Foot Somset...... 24 A3
Four Forks Somset...... 23 E3
Four Gates Gt Man...... 82 A5
Four Gotes Cambs...... 75 E2
Four Lane End S York...... 83 H5
Four Lane Ends Ches...... 69 H6
Four Lanes Cnwll...... 2 D4
Four Marks Hants...... 27 E3
Four Mile Bridge IOA...... 78 B2
Four Oaks E Susx...... 18 B4
Four Oaks Gloucs...... 46 C2
Four Oaks W Mids...... 58 D5
Four Oaks W Mids...... 59 E3
Four Points Berks...... 40 D2
Four Roads Carmth...... 34 B5
Four Shire Stone Warwks...... 47 H2
Four Throws Kent...... 18 A4
Four Wents Kent...... 29 G1
Fourlanes End Ches...... 70 C6
Fourpenny Highld...... 163 E3
Fourstones Nthumb...... 113 F1
Fovant Wilts...... 25 E2
Foveran Abers...... 159 F1
Fowey Cnwll...... 5 E1
Fowley Common Ches...... 82 B4
Fowlhall Kent...... 17 H6
Fowlis Angus...... 140 C3
Fowlis Wester P & K...... 139 F2
Fowlmere Cambs...... 51 E5
Fownhope Herefs...... 46 A3
Fox Corner Surrey...... 27 H5
Fox Hatch Essex...... 29 G6
Fox Street Essex...... 52 D3
Foxbar Rens...... 119 F6
Foxcombe Devon...... 8 B3
Foxcote Gloucs...... 39 E6
Foxcote Somset...... 24 C5
Foxdale IOM...... 174 k3
Foxearth Essex...... 52 B5
Foxendown Kent...... 29 G3
Foxfield Cumb...... 94 C3
Foxham Wilts...... 38 D2
Foxhills Hants...... 13 G6
Foxhole Cnwll...... 3 G5
Foxhole Swans...... 34 D4
Foxholes N York...... 99 F2
Foxhunt Green E Susx...... 17 F3
Foxley Nhants...... 49 E4
Foxley Norfk...... 76 C2
Foxley Wilts...... 38 D3
Foxley Green Wilts...... 38 D3
Foxlydiate Worcs...... 58 C2
Foxt Staffs...... 71 E5
Foxton Cambs...... 51 E6
Foxton Dur...... 106 C3
Foxton Leics...... 60 C4
Foxton N York...... 97 G4
Foxup N York...... 96 B2
Foxwist Green Ches...... 82 A1
Foxwood Shrops...... 57 F3
Foy Herefs...... 46 B2
Foyers Highld...... 154 C1
Foynesfield Highld...... 155 G4
Fraddam Cnwll...... 2 C3
Fraddon Cnwll...... 4 C2
Fradley Staffs...... 71 F1
Fradswell Staffs...... 71 E3
Fraisthorpe E R Yk...... 93 E6
Framfield E Susx...... 17 F3
Framingham Earl Norfk...... 65 E6
Framingham Pigot Norfk...... 65 E6
Framlingham Suffk...... 65 E2
Frampton Dorset...... 11 G4
Frampton Lincs...... 74 D4
Frampton Cotterell Gloucs...... 37 H2
Frampton Mansell Gloucs...... 38 D4
Frampton on Severn Gloucs...... 38 B5
Frampton West End Lincs...... 74 C4
Framsden Suffk...... 64 D1
Framwellgate Moor Dur...... 106 B5
Frances Green Lancs...... 89 E3
Franche Worcs...... 58 A3
Frandley Ches...... 82 A3
Frankaborough Devon...... 5 G5
Frankby Mersyd...... 81 E3
Frankfort Norfk...... 77 F2
Franklands Gate Herefs...... 45 H4
Frankley Worcs...... 58 C3
Franksbridge Powys...... 44 D5
Frankton Warwks...... 59 G2
Frant E Susx...... 17 G5
Fraserburgh Abers...... 159 F6
Frating Essex...... 52 D3
Frating Green Essex...... 52 D3
Fratton C Port...... 15 E4
Freathy Cnwll...... 5 G1
Freckenham Suffk...... 63 F3
Freckleton Lancs...... 88 C2
Freebirch Derbys...... 83 H2
Freeby Leics...... 73 F2
Freefolk Hants...... 26 C4
Freehay Staffs...... 71 E4
Freeland Oxon...... 40 B5
Freethorpe Norfk...... 65 F6
Freethorpe Common Norfk...... 65 F6
Freiston Lincs...... 74 D4
Fremington Devon...... 21 E4
Fremington N York...... 96 D5
French Street Kent...... 29 E1
Frenchay Gloucs...... 37 G2
Frenchbeer Devon...... 8 D3
Frenich P & K...... 139 E6
Frensham Surrey...... 27 G3
Freshfield Mersyd...... 81 E5
Freshford Somset...... 24 C5
Freshwater IOW...... 13 G3

Freshwater Bay IOW...... 13 G3
Freshwater East Pembks...... 32 D1
Fressingfield Suffk...... 65 E3
Freston Suffk...... 53 E5
Freswick Highld...... 167 G5
Fretherne Gloucs...... 38 B5
Frettenham Norfk...... 77 E2
Freuchie Fife...... 132 B6
Freystrop Pembks...... 32 D3
Friar Waddon Dorset...... 11 G3
Friar's Gate E Susx...... 17 F5
Friars' Hill N York...... 98 C3
Friday Bridge Cambs...... 62 D6
Friday Street E Susx...... 17 G2
Friday Street Suffk...... 65 E1
Friday Street Suffk...... 53 G6
Friday Street Suffk...... 65 F1
Friday Street Surrey...... 16 B6
Fridaythorpe E R Yk...... 92 C5
Friden Derbys...... 71 G6
Friendly W York...... 90 B2
Friern Barnet Gt Lon...... 28 D5
Friesland Bay Ag & B...... 134 D5
Friesthorpe Lincs...... 86 A3
Frieston Lincs...... 73 G5
Frieth Bucks...... 41 F3
Friezeland Notts...... 72 B5
Frilford Oxon...... 40 C4
Frilsham Berks...... 40 D1
Frimley Surrey...... 27 G5
Frimley Green Surrey...... 27 G5
Frindsbury Kent...... 30 A3
Fring Norfk...... 75 H3
Fringford Oxon...... 48 D2
Frinsted Kent...... 30 C2
Frinton-on-Sea Essex...... 53 F3
Friockheim Angus...... 141 F5
Friog Gwynd...... 67 F1
Frisby on the Wreake Leics...... 73 E2
Friskney Lincs...... 75 E6
Friskney Eaudike Lincs...... 75 E6
Friston E Susx...... 17 F1
Friston Suffk...... 65 G1
Fritchley Derbys...... 72 A5
Frith Bank Lincs...... 74 C5
Frith Common Worcs...... 57 G2
Fritham Hants...... 13 F6
Frithelstock Devon...... 21 E2
Frithelstock Stone Devon...... 21 E2
Frithend Hants...... 27 F3
Frithsden Herts...... 50 A2
Frithville Lincs...... 74 C5
Frittenden Kent...... 18 B5
Frittiscombe Devon...... 7 E2
Fritton Norfk...... 65 G5
Fritton Norfk...... 65 E5
Fritwell Oxon...... 48 C2
Frizinghall W York...... 90 C3
Frizington Cumb...... 102 D2
Frocester Gloucs...... 38 C5
Frodesley Shrops...... 57 E5
Frodsham Ches...... 81 G2
Frog End Cambs...... 51 E5
Frog End Cambs...... 63 E1
Frog Pool Worcs...... 58 A2
Frogden Border...... 123 E2
Froggatt Derbys...... 83 G2
Froghall Staffs...... 71 E5
Frogham Hants...... 13 E6
Frogham Kent...... 31 F1
Frogmore Devon...... 7 E2
Frognall Lincs...... 74 B1
Frogpool Cnwll...... 3 E4
Frogwell Cnwll...... 5 G3
Frolesworth Leics...... 59 H4
Frome Somset...... 24 C4
Frome St Quintin Dorset...... 11 F5
Frome Whitfield Dorset...... 11 G4
Fromes Hill Herefs...... 46 B4
Fron Denbgs...... 80 C1
Fron Gwynd...... 66 C4
Fron Gwynd...... 67 E5
Fron Powys...... 56 C6
Fron Powys...... 56 B5
Fron Isaf Wrexhm...... 69 E4
Fron-goch Gwynd...... 68 A4
Froncysyllte Denbgs...... 69 E4
Frostenden Suffk...... 65 G3
Frosterley Dur...... 105 G4
Froxfield Beds...... 49 H2
Froxfield Wilts...... 39 G1
Froxfield Green Hants...... 27 E2
Fryern Hill Hants...... 14 C6
Fryerning Essex...... 29 G6
Fryton N York...... 98 C2
Fuinary Highld...... 135 H4
Fulbeck Lincs...... 73 G5
Fulbourn Cambs...... 62 D1
Fulbrook Oxon...... 39 G6
Fulflood Hants...... 26 C2
Fulford N York...... 91 G4
Fulford Somset...... 23 E2
Fulford Staffs...... 70 D4
Fulham Gt Lon...... 28 C4
Fulking W Susx...... 16 C2
Full Sutton E R Yk...... 92 A5
Fullaford Devon...... 21 G4
Fullarton N Ayrs...... 119 E3
Fuller Street Essex...... 52 A2
Fuller Street Kent...... 29 F2
Fuller's End Essex...... 51 F3
Fuller's Moor Ches...... 69 G5
Fullerton Hants...... 26 B3
Fulletby Lincs...... 86 C2
Fullready Warwks...... 48 A4
Fullwood E Ayrs...... 119 F4
Fulmer Bucks...... 41 H3
Fulmodeston Norfk...... 76 C3
Fulnetby Lincs...... 86 A3
Fulney Lincs...... 74 C2
Fulstone W York...... 83 G6
Fulstow Lincs...... 86 D4
Fulwell Oxon...... 48 D1
Fulwood Lancs...... 88 D3
Fulwood Notts...... 72 B6
Fulwood S York...... 83 H3
Fulwood Somset...... 23 E1
Fundenhall Norfk...... 64 D5

Funtington W Susx 15 F4
Funtley Hants 14 D4
Funtullich P & K 139 E2
Furley Devon 10 C5
Furnace Ag & B 128 B5
Furnace Carmth 34 C4
Furnace Cerdgn 54 D5
Furnace End Warwks 59 E4
Furner's Green E Susx 17 E4
Furness Vale Derbys 83 E3
Furneux Pelham Herts 51 E3
Further Quarter Kent 18 C5
Furtho Nhants 49 F3
Furze Platt Berks 41 G2
Furzehill Devon 21 G5
Furzehill Dorset 12 D5
Furzehills Lincs 86 C2
Furzeley Corner Hants 15 E5
Furzley Hants 26 A1
Fyfett Somset 10 C6
Fyfield Essex 51 F1
Fyfield Hants 26 A4
Fyfield Oxon 40 B4
Fyfield Wilts 39 F1
Fyfield Wilts 25 G5
Fyfield Bavant Wilts 25 F2
Fyfield Wick Oxon 40 B4
Fylingthorpe N York 99 E5
Fyning W Susx 27 F2
Fyvie Abers 158 D3

G

Gabroc Hill E Ayrs 119 F4
Gaddesby Leics 72 D1
Gaddesden Row Herts 50 B2
Gadfa IOA 78 D4
Gadgirth S Ayrs 119 F2
Gadlas Shrops 69 F4
Gaer Powys 45 E1
Gaer-llwyd Mons 37 E4
Gaerwen IOA 78 D2
Gagingwell Oxon 48 B2
Gailes N Ayrs 119 E3
Gailey Staffs 70 D1
Gainford Dur 106 A2
Gainsborough Lincs 85 F4
Gainsford End Essex 51 H4
Gairloch Highld 160 B1
Gairlochy Highld 144 D3
Gairneybridge P & K 131 G5
Gaisby W York 90 C3
Gaisgill Cumb 95 G5
Gaitsgill Cumb 103 H5
Galashiels Border 122 B3
Galgate Lancs 88 C5
Galhampton Somset 24 B2
Gallanach Ag & B 136 C2
Gallantry Bank Ches 69 G5
Gallatown Fife 132 B4
Galley Common Warwks 59 F4
Galleywood Essex 51 H1
Gallovie Highld 145 H3
Gallowfauld Angus 140 D4
Gallowhill P & K 140 B3
Gallows Green Essex 52 C3
Gallows Green Worcs 58 B2
Gallowstree Common Oxon 41 E2
Gallt-y-foel Gwynd 79 E1
Galltair Highld 143 H6
Gally Hill Hants 27 H4
Gallypot Street E Susx 17 F5
Galmpton Devon 6 D2
Galmpton Devon 7 F3
Galphay N York 97 F2
Galston E Ayrs 119 G3
Galton Dorset 12 B3
Gamballs Green Staffs 83 E1
Gambles Green Essex 52 A2
Gamblesby Cumb 104 C4
Gamelsby Cumb 103 F5
Gamesley Gt Man 83 E4
Gamlingay Cambs 50 C6
Gamlingay Cinques Cambs 50 C6
Gamlingay Great Heath Beds 50 C6
Gammersgill N York 96 D3
Gamrie Abers 158 D5
Gamston Notts 85 E2
Gamston Notts 72 D4
Ganarew Herefs 37 F6
Ganavan Bay Ag & B 136 C3
Gang Cnwll 5 G3
Ganllwyd Gwynd 67 G2
Gannachy Angus 148 D1
Ganstead E R Yk 93 E3
Ganthorpe N York 98 C3
Ganton N York 99 F3
Ganwick Corner Herts 28 C6
Gappah Devon 9 E2
Garbity Moray 157 E4
Garboldisham Norfk 64 C3
Garchory Abers 147 H5
Garden City Flints 81 E2
Garden Village Derbys 83 G4
Gardeners Green Berks 27 F6
Gardenstown Abers 158 D5
Garderhouse Shet 169 h3
Gardham E R Yk 92 C4
Gare Hill Somset 24 C3
Garelochhead Ag & B 128 D4
Garford Oxon 40 C4
Garforth W York 91 E3
Garforth Bridge W York 91 E3
Gargrave N York 89 H5
Gargunnock Stirlg 130 C3
Garizim Conwy 79 F2
Garlic Street Norfk 65 E4
Garlieston D & G 101 F5
Garlinge Kent 31 G5
Garlinge Green Kent 31 E1
Garlogie Abers 149 E5
Garmond Abers 158 D4
Garmondsway Dur 106 C4

Garmouth Moray 157 E5
Garmston Shrops 57 F6
Garn Gwynd 66 B3
Garn-Dolbenmaen Gwynd 67 E4
Garnant Carmth 34 D6
Garnett Bridge Cumb 95 F5
Garnkirk N Lans 130 C2
Garnswllt Swans 34 D5
Garrabost W Isls 168 f8
Garras Cnwll 3 E2
Garreg Gwynd 67 F4
Garrigill Cumb 104 D4
Garriston N York 97 E4
Garroch D & G 109 H3
Garrochtrie D & G 100 B4
Garrochty Ag & B 118 C5
Garros Highld 151 E5
Garsdale Cumb 95 H4
Garsdale Head Cumb 96 A4
Garsdon Wilts 38 D3
Garshall Green Staffs 71 E3
Garsington Oxon 40 D4
Garstang Lancs 88 C4
Garston Herts 28 B6
Garston Mersyd 81 F3
Gartachossan Ag & B 126 B1
Gartcosh N Lans 130 C2
Garth Brdgnd 35 F3
Garth Denbgs 69 E4
Garth Mons 37 E3
Garth Powys 44 B4
Garth Powys 56 C3
Garth Penrhyncoch Cerdgn 54 D4
Garth Row Cumb 95 F5
Garthamlock C Glas 130 C2
Garthbrengy Powys 44 C2
Gartheli Cerdgn 43 F5
Garthmyl Powys 56 B5
Garths Cumb 95 F4
Gartly Abers 157 G2
Gartmore Stirlg 129 G5
Gartness N Lans 130 D1
Gartness Stirlg 129 F4
Gartocharn W Duns 129 F4
Garton E R Yk 93 F3
Garton-on-the-Wolds E R Yk 92 D5
Gartymore Highld 163 G5
Garvald E Loth 133 E2
Garvan Highld 144 B2
Garvard Ag & B 126 C4
Garve Highld 154 B5
Garvestone Norfk 64 C6
Garvock Inver 128 D2
Garway Herefs 45 G1
Garway Common Herefs 45 G1
Garway Hill Herefs 45 G2
Garyvard W Isls 168 e7
Gasper Wilts 24 C2
Gastard Wilts 38 D1
Gasthorpe Norfk 64 B3
Gaston Green Essex 51 F2
Gatcombe IOW 14 C2
Gate Burton Lincs 85 F3
Gate Helmsley N York 91 H5
Gatebeck Cumb 95 F3
Gateford Notts 84 C3
Gateforth N York 91 G2
Gatehead E Ayrs 119 F3
Gatehouse Nthumb 113 E4
Gatehouse of Fleet D & G 101 G6
Gateley Norfk 76 C2
Gatenby N York 97 F4
Gates Heath Ches 69 G6
Gatesgarth Cumb 103 F2
Gateshaw Border 123 E2
Gateshead T & W 114 D2
Gateside Angus 140 D4
Gateside E Rens 119 G5
Gateside Fife 131 H6
Gateside N Ayrs 119 E5
Gateslack D & G 110 C5
Gathurst Gt Man 81 H5
Gatley Gt Man 82 C3
Gatton Surrey 28 D1
Gattonside Border 122 C3
Gatwick Airport W Susx 16 D5
Gaufron Powys 55 G2
Gaulby Leics 60 C5
Gauldry Fife 140 D2
Gauldswell P & K 140 B5
Gaulkthorn Lancs 89 F2
Gaultree Norfk 62 D6
Gaunt's Common Dorset 12 D5
Gaunt's End Essex 51 F3
Gaunton's Bank Ches 69 H5
Gautby Lincs 86 B2
Gavinton Border 123 E5
Gawber S York 84 A5
Gawcott Bucks 49 E2
Gawsworth Ches 82 D2
Gawthorpe W York 90 D2
Gawthrop Cumb 95 H4
Gawthwaite Cumb 94 C3
Gay Bowers Essex 52 B1
Gay Street W Susx 16 B3
Gaydon Warwks 48 B5
Gayhurst Bucks 49 G4
Gayle N York 96 B4
Gayles N York 96 D6
Gayton Mersyd 81 E3
Gayton Nhants 49 E5
Gayton Norfk 75 G2
Gayton Staffs 71 E3
Gayton le Marsh Lincs 87 E3
Gayton Thorpe Norfk 75 H2
Gaywood Norfk 75 G2
Gazeley Suffk 63 F2
Gear Cnwll 3 E2
Gearraidh Bhaird W Isls 168 e7
Geary Highld 150 C5
Gedding Suffk 64 B1
Geddinge Kent 19 F6
Geddington Nhants 61 E4
Gedling Notts 72 D4

Gedney Lincs 74 D2
Gedney Broadgate Lincs 74 D2
Gedney Drove End Lincs 75 E3
Gedney Dyke Lincs 74 D3
Gedney Hill Lincs 74 D1
Gee Cross Gt Man 82 D4
Geeston Rutlnd 61 F6
Geldeston Norfk 65 F4
Gelli Rhondd 36 B3
Gelli Torfn 36 D3
Gellifor Denbgs 80 D1
Gelligaer Caerph 36 B4
Gelligroes Caerph 36 C4
Gellilydan Gwynd 67 F4
Gellinudd Neath 35 E5
Gelly Carmth 33 E4
Gellyburn P & K 140 A4
Gellywen Carmth 33 G4
Gelston D & G 102 B6
Gelston Lincs 73 G5
Gembling E R Yk 93 E5
Gentleshaw Staffs 71 E1
George Green Bucks 28 A4
George Nympton Devon 21 G3
Georgeham Devon 21 E5
Georgefield D & G 111 G4
Georgetown Blae G 36 C5
Georgia Cnwll 2 B3
Georth Ork 169 b3
Gerlan Gwynd 79 F1
Germansweek Devon 8 A4
Germoe Cnwll 2 C3
Gerrans Cnwll 3 F3
Gerrards Cross Bucks 28 A5
Gerrick N York 107 F2
Gestingthorpe Essex 52 B4
Geuffordd Powys 68 D1
Gib Hill Ches 82 A2
Gibraltar Lincs 75 F6
Gibsmere Notts 73 E5
Giddeahall Wilts 38 C2
Giddy Green Dorset 12 B3
Gidea Park Gt Lon 29 F5
Gidleigh Devon 8 D3
Giffnock E Rens 119 G5
Gifford E Loth 132 D2
Giffordtown Fife 132 B6
Giggleswick N York 96 A1
Gilberdyke E R Yk 92 B2
Gilbert Street Hants 27 E2
Gilbert's Cross Staffs 58 A4
Gilbert's End Worcs 46 D3
Gilchriston E Loth 132 D2
Gilcrux Cumb 103 E4
Gildersome W York 90 D2
Gildingwells S York 84 C3
Gilesgate Moor Dur 106 B5
Gileston V Glam 22 C6
Gilfach Caerph 36 C4
Gilfach Goch Brdgnd 35 G3
Gilfachrheda Cerdgn 42 D5
Gilgarran Cumb 102 D2
Gill Cumb 104 A3
Gill's Green Kent 18 A5
Gillamoor N York 98 C4
Gillan Cnwll 3 E2
Gillen Highld 150 C5
Gillesbie D & G 111 F4
Gilling East N York 98 B2
Gilling West N York 97 E5
Gillingham Dorset 24 D2
Gillingham Kent 30 A3
Gillingham Norfk 65 F4
Gillock Highld 167 F4
Gillow Heath Staffs 70 D6
Gills Highld 167 G6
Gilmanscleuch Border 121 H2
Gilmerton C Edin 132 B2
Gilmerton P & K 139 F2
Gilmonby Dur 105 G1
Gilmorton Leics 60 B4
Gilsland Nthumb 112 D1
Gilson Warwks 59 E4
Gilstead W York 90 B3
Gilston Herts 51 E2
Gilston Mdloth 122 B5
Giltbrook Notts 72 C5
Gilwern Mons 36 D6
Gimingham Norfk 77 F4
Ginclough Ches 83 E2
Gingers Green E Susx 17 G3
Gipping Suffk 64 C2
Gipsey Bridge Lincs 74 C5
Girdle Toll N Ayrs 119 E3
Girlington W York 90 C3
Girlsta Shet 169 h3
Girsby N York 106 C2
Girtford Beds 50 C6
Girthon D & G 101 G5
Girton Cambs 62 C2
Girton Notts 85 F1
Girvan S Ayrs 108 D4
Gisburn Lancs 89 G4
Gisleham Suffk 65 G4
Gislingham Suffk 64 C2
Gissing Norfk 64 D4
Gittisham Devon 10 B4
Gladestry Powys 45 E5
Gladsmuir E Loth 132 D2
Glais Swans 34 D4
Glaisdale N York 98 C5
Glamis Angus 140 D4
Glan-Duar Carmth 43 E4
Glan-Dwyfach Gwynd 66 D4
Glan-rhyd Powys 35 E5
Glan-y-don Flints 80 D3
Glan-y-llyn Rhondd 36 B3
Glan-y-nant Powys 55 G4
Glan-yr-afon Gwynd 68 A4
Glan-yr-afon Gwynd 68 B4
Glan-yr-afon IOA 79 F3
Glan-yr-afon Swans 34 D5
Glanaber Gwynd 67 F5
Glanafon Pembks 32 D3
Glanaman Carmth 34 D6
Glandford Norfk 76 C4
Glandwr Pembks 33 F5

Glandyfi Cerdgn 55 E5
Glangrwyney Powys 36 D6
Glanllynfi Brdgnd 35 F3
Glanmule Powys 56 B4
Glanrhyd Pembks 42 B3
Glanton Nthumb 124 D2
Glanton Pike Nthumb 124 D2
Glanvilles Wootton Dorset 11 G5
Glapthorn Nhants 61 F4
Glapwell Derbys 84 B1
Glasbury Powys 45 E3
Glascoed Denbgs 80 B2
Glascoed Mons 36 D4
Glascote Staffs 59 E6
Glascwm Powys 44 D4
Glasfryn Conwy 68 B5
Glasgow C Glas 130 B2
Glasgow Airport C Glas 129 F2
Glasgow Science Centre C Glas 129 G2
Glasinfryn Gwynd 79 E1
Glasnacardoch Bay Highld 143 F4
Glasnakille Highld 143 E5
Glaspwll Powys 55 E5
Glass Houghton W York 91 E2
Glassenbury Kent 18 A5
Glasserton D & G 101 F5
Glassford S Lans 120 B4
Glasshouse Gloucs 46 C1
Glasshouse Hill Gloucs 46 C1
Glasshouses N York 97 E1
Glasson Cumb 103 F6
Glasson Lancs 88 C5
Glassonby Cumb 104 C4
Glasterlaw Angus 141 F5
Glaston Rutlnd 61 E5
Glastonbury Somset 23 H3
Glatton Cambs 61 G4
Glazebrook Ches 82 B4
Glazebury Ches 82 B4
Glazeley Shrops 57 G4
Gleadsmoss Ches 82 C1
Gleaston Cumb 94 C2
Glebe Highld 154 C1
Gledhow W York 90 D3
Gledpark D & G 101 G5
Gledrid Shrops 69 E4
Glemsford Suffk 52 B6
Glen Auldyn IOM 174 m4
Glen Clunie Lodge Abers 147 E3
Glen Maye IOM 174 k3
Glen Mona IOM 174 m4
Glen Nevis House Highld 144 D2
Glen Parva Leics 60 B5
Glen Trool Lodge D & G 109 F3
Glen Vine IOM 174 l3
Glenallachie Highld 157 E3
Glenancross Highld 143 F3
Glenaros House Ag & B 135 G4
Glenbarr Ag & B 117 F4
Glenbarry Abers 158 B4
Glenbeg Highld 135 H6
Glenbeg Highld 156 B2
Glenbervie Abers 149 E2
Glenboig N Lans 130 C2
Glenborrodale Highld 135 H5
Glenbranter Ag & B 128 C5
Glenbreck Border 121 E2
Glenbrittle House Highld 142 D4
Glenbuck E Ayrs 120 B2
Glencally Angus 140 D6
Glencaple D & G 110 D2
Glencarron Lodge Highld 153 E4
Glencarse P & K 140 B2
Glenceitlein Highld 137 F5
Glencoe Highld 137 F6
Glencothe Border 121 E2
Glencraig Fife 131 H5
Glencrosh D & G 110 B4
Glendale Highld 150 B4
Glendaruel Ag & B 128 B3
Glendevon P & K 131 F6
Glendoe Lodge Highld 145 F5
Glendoick P & K 140 B2
Glenduckie Fife 140 C2
Gleneagles P & K 131 E6
Gleneagles Hotel P & K 139 F1
Glenegedale Ag & B 116 B5
Glenelg Highld 143 H6
Glenerney Moray 156 B4
Glenfarg P & K 131 G6
Glenfeshie Lodge Highld 146 C4
Glenfield Leics 60 B6
Glenfinnan Highld 144 A2
Glenfintaig Lodge Highld 144 D3
Glenfoot P & K 140 B1
Glenfyne Lodge Ag & B 137 G1
Glengarnock N Ayrs 119 E5
Glengolly Highld 167 E5
Glengorm Castle Ag & B 135 F3
Glengrasco Highld 150 D3
Glenholm Border 121 E3
Glenhoul D & G 109 H3
Glenisla Angus 140 B6
Glenkin Ag & B 128 C3
Glenkindie Abers 148 B6
Glenlivet Moray 156 D2
Glenlochar D & G 110 B1
Glenlomond P & K 131 H6
Glenluce D & G 100 C6
Glenmassen Ag & B 128 C4
Glenmavis N Lans 130 D2
Glenmore Highld 150 D3
Glenmore Lodge Highld 147 E5
Glenmuick Highld 140 D6
Glenralloch Ag & B 127 G2
Glenridding Cumb 103 H2
Glenrothes Fife 132 B5
Glenshee P & K 139 G3
Glenshera Lodge Highld 145 H4
Glenstriven Ag & B 128 B3
Glentham Lincs 85 H4
Glentromie Lodge Highld 146 C4
Glentrool Village D & G 109 E3
Glentruim House Highld 146 B4
Glentworth Lincs 85 G3
Glenuig Highld 143 F2
Glenure Ag & B 137 E5
Glenvarragill Highld 151 E3

Glenwhilly D & G 108 D2
Glespin S Lans 120 C2
Glewstone Herefs 46 A1
Glinton Cambs 61 G6
Glooston Leics 60 D5
Glororum Nthumb 125 E4
Glossop Derbys 83 E4
Gloster Hill Nthumb 125 F1
Gloucester Gloucs 46 D1
Gloucestershire Airport Gloucs 46 D1
Glusburn N York 90 A4
Glutt Lodge Highld 166 D2
Gluvian Cnwll 4 C2
Glympton Oxon 48 C1
Glyn Ceiriog Wrexhm 68 D4
Glyn-Neath Neath 35 F5
Glynarthen Cerdgn 42 C4
Glyncorrwg Neath 35 F4
Glynde E Susx 17 E2
Glyndebourne E Susx 17 E2
Glyndyfrdwy Denbgs 68 D4
Glyntaff Rhondd 36 B3
Glyntawe Powys 35 F6
Glynteg Carmth 42 D3
Gnosall Staffs 70 C2
Gnosall Heath Staffs 70 C2
Goadby Leics 60 D5
Goadby Marwood Leics 73 E3
Goat Lees Kent 18 D6
Goatacre Wilts 39 E2
Goatfield Ag & B 128 B5
Goatham Green E Susx 18 B3
Goathill Dorset 24 B1
Goathland N York 98 D5
Goathurst Somset 23 E3
Goathurst Common Kent 29 F1
Gobowen Shrops 69 E3
Godalming Surrey 27 H4
Goddard's Corner Suffk 65 E2
Goddard's Green Kent 18 B5
Godford Cross Devon 10 B5
Godington Bucks 49 E2
Godley Gt Man 82 D4
Godmanchester Cambs 62 B2
Godmanstone Dorset 11 G4
Godmersham Kent 30 D1
Godney Somset 23 H3
Godolphin Cross Cnwll 2 D3
Godre'r-graig Neath 35 E5
Godshill Hants 13 F6
Godshill IOW 14 C2
Godstone Staffs 71 E3
Godstone Surrey 28 D1
Godsworthy Devon 8 B2
Godwinscroft Hants 13 F4
Goetre Mons 36 D5
Goff's Oak Herts 50 D1
Gofilon Mons 36 D6
Gogar C Edin 131 H2
Goginan Cerdgn 54 D3
Golan Gwynd 67 E4
Golant Cnwll 5 E1
Golberdon Cnwll 5 G3
Golborne Gt Man 82 A4
Golcar W York 90 B1
Gold Hill Cambs 63 E5
Gold Hill Dorset 12 B6
Goldcliff Newpt 37 E3
Golden Cross E Susx 17 F3
Golden Green Kent 17 G6
Golden Grove Carmth 43 F1
Golden Hill Pembks 32 D2
Golden Pot Hants 27 E4
Golden Valley Derbys 72 B5
Goldenhill Staffs 70 D5
Golders Green Gt Lon 28 C5
Goldfinch Bottom Berks 26 C6
Goldhanger Essex 52 C2
Golding Shrops 57 F6
Goldington Beds 50 B6
Golds Green W Mids 58 C5
Goldsborough N York 107 H2
Goldsborough N York 91 E5
Goldsithney Cnwll 2 C3
Goldstone Kent 31 F2
Goldstone Shrops 70 B3
Goldsworth Park Surrey 27 H5
Goldthorpe S York 84 B5
Goldworthy Devon 20 D3
Golford Kent 18 B5
Golford Green Kent 18 B5
Gollanfield Highld 155 F4
Gollinglith Foot N York 97 E3
Golly Wrexhm 69 F6
Golsoncott Somset 22 C3
Golspie Highld 163 E4
Gomeldon Wilts 25 G3
Gomersal W York 90 C2
Gomshall Surrey 16 B6
Gonalston Notts 72 D5
Gonerby Hill Foot Lincs 73 G4
Gonfirth Shet 169 h3
Good Easter Essex 51 G2
Goodameavy Devon 6 C4
Gooderstone Norfk 63 G6
Goodleigh Devon 21 F4
Goodmanham E R Yk 92 C4
Goodmayes Gt Lon 29 E5
Goodnestone Kent 30 D2
Goodnestone Kent 31 F1
Goodrich Herefs 46 A1
Goodrich Castle Herefs 46 A1
Goodrington Devon 7 F3
Goodshaw Lancs 89 F2
Goodshaw Fold Lancs 89 F2
Goodstone Devon 7 E5
Goodwick Pembks 32 C5
Goodworth Clatford Hants 26 B3
Goodyers End Warwks 59 F4
Goole E R Yk 92 A2
Goole Fields E R Yk 92 A2
Goom's Hill Worcs 47 F5
Goonbell Cnwll 3 E5
Goonhavern Cnwll 3 E5
Goonvrea Cnwll 3 E5
Goose Green Essex 53 E3
Goose Green Essex 53 E3
Goose Green Gloucs 38 B2

288

Goose Green *Gt Man* ... 81 H5
Goose Green *Kent* ... 29 G1
Goose Green *Kent* ... 18 B5
Goose Green *W Susx* ... 16 B3
Goose Pool *Herefs* ... 45 G3
Goosecruives *Abers* ... 149 G5
Gooseford *Devon* ... 8 D4
Gooseham *Cnwll* ... 20 C2
Goosehill Green *Worcs* ... 47 E5
Goosemoor *Somset* ... 22 B3
Goosey *Oxon* ... 40 B3
Goosnargh *Lancs* ... 88 D3
Goostrey *Ches* ... 82 C2
Gorddinog *Conwy* ... 79 F2
Gordon *Border* ... 122 D4
Gordon Arms Hotel *Border* ... 121 G2
Gordonstown *Abers* ... 158 B5
Gordonstown *Abers* ... 158 D3
Gore *Powys* ... 45 E5
Gore Pit *Essex* ... 52 B3
Gore Street *Kent* ... 31 F2
Gorebridge *Mdloth* ... 121 H6
Gorefield *Cambs* ... 74 D1
Gores *Wilts* ... 25 G5
Gorey *Jersey* ... 174 d2
Goring *Oxon* ... 40 D2
Goring Heath *Oxon* ... 41 E2
Goring-by-Sea *W Susx* ... 16 B2
Gorleston on Sea *Norfk* ... 65 H6
Gorrachie *Abers* ... 158 C5
Gorran *Cnwll* ... 3 G4
Gorran Haven *Cnwll* ... 3 G4
Gorran High Lanes *Cnwll* ... 3 G4
Gorrig *Cerdgn* ... 42 D3
Gors *Cerdgn* ... 54 D3
Gorse Hill *Wilts* ... 39 F3
Gorsedd *Flints* ... 80 D2
Gorseinon *Swans* ... 34 C4
Gorseybank *Derbys* ... 71 H5
Gorsgoch *Cerdgn* ... 43 E4
Gorslas *Carmth* ... 34 C6
Gorsley *Gloucs* ... 46 B2
Gorsley Common *Gloucs* ... 46 B2
Gorst Hill *Worcs* ... 57 G3
Gorstage *Ches* ... 82 A2
Gorstan *Highld* ... 154 B5
Gorstello *Ches* ... 81 F1
Gorsty Hill *Staffs* ... 71 F3
Gorten *Ag & B* ... 136 B3
Gorthleck *Highld* ... 154 D1
Gorton *Gt Man* ... 82 D4
Gosbeck *Suffk* ... 64 D1
Gosberton *Lincs* ... 74 C3
Gosberton Clough *Lincs* ... 74 B3
Gosfield *Essex* ... 52 A4
Gosford *Devon* ... 10 A4
Gosforth *Cumb* ... 94 A5
Gosforth *T & W* ... 114 D2
Gosland Green *Ches* ... 69 H6
Gosling Street *Somset* ... 24 A2
Gosmore *Herts* ... 50 C3
Gospel End *Staffs* ... 58 B5
Gospel Green *W Susx* ... 27 G2
Gosport *Hants* ... 14 D4
Gossard's Green *Beds* ... 49 H4
Gossington *Gloucs* ... 38 B4
Goswick *Nthumb* ... 123 H4
Gotham *Notts* ... 72 C3
Gotherington *Gloucs* ... 47 E2
Gotton *Somset* ... 23 E2
Goudhurst *Kent* ... 17 H5
Goulceby *Lincs* ... 86 C3
Gourdas *Abers* ... 158 D3
Gourdie *Angus* ... 140 C3
Gourdon *Abers* ... 149 F1
Gourock *Inver* ... 128 D3
Govan *C Glas* ... 129 G2
Goveton *Devon* ... 7 E2
Gowdall *E R Yk* ... 91 G2
Gower *Highld* ... 154 C5
Gowerton *Swans* ... 34 C4
Gowkhall *Fife* ... 131 G4
Gowthorpe *E R Yk* ... 92 B5
Goxhill *E R Yk* ... 93 F4
Goxhill *Lincs* ... 93 E2
Grabhair *W Isls* ... 168 e7
Graby *Lincs* ... 74 A3
Grade *Cnwll* ... 3 E1
Gradeley Green *Ches* ... 69 H5
Graffham *W Susx* ... 15 G5
Grafham *Cambs* ... 61 G2
Grafham *Surrey* ... 16 A6
Grafton *Herefs* ... 45 H3
Grafton *N York* ... 97 G1
Grafton *Oxon* ... 39 G4
Grafton *Shrops* ... 69 F2
Grafton *Worcs* ... 46 A5
Grafton *Worcs* ... 47 E3
Grafton Flyford *Worcs* ... 47 E5
Grafton Regis *Nhants* ... 49 F4
Grafton Underwood *Nhants* ... 61 E3
Grafty Green *Kent* ... 30 B1
Graianrhyd *Denbgs* ... 68 D6
Graig *Conwy* ... 79 G2
Graig *Denbgs* ... 80 C2
Graig-fechan *Denbgs* ... 68 D5
Grain *Kent* ... 30 B4
Grains Bar *Gt Man* ... 83 E5
Grainsby *Lincs* ... 86 C5
Grainthorpe *Lincs* ... 86 D4
Grampound *Cnwll* ... 3 G5
Grampound Road *Cnwll* ... 3 G5
Gramsdal *W Isls* ... 168 b4
Gramsdale *W Isls* ... 168 b4
Granborough *Bucks* ... 49 F2
Granby *Notts* ... 73 E4
Grand Chemins *Jersey* ... 174 c2
Grand Prix Collection
  Donington *Leics* ... 72 B3
Grandborough *Warwks* ... 59 H2
Grandes Rocques *Guern* ... 174 a3
Grandtully *P & K* ... 139 F5
Grange *Cumb* ... 103 F2
Grange *Kent* ... 30 B4
Grange *Mersyd* ... 80 D3
Grange *P & K* ... 140 C2
Grange Crossroads *Moray* ... 157 G4
Grange Gate *Dorset* ... 12 C3

Grange Hall *Moray* ... 156 C5
Grange Hill *Gt Lon* ... 29 E5
Grange Moor *W York* ... 90 C1
Grange of Lindores *Fife* ... 140 C1
Grange Villa *Dur* ... 106 B6
Grange-over-Sands *Cumb* ... 95 E3
Grangehall *S Lans* ... 120 D4
Grangemill *Derbys* ... 71 G6
Grangemouth *Falk* ... 131 E3
Grangepans *Falk* ... 131 F3
Grangetown *Cardif* ... 37 E5
Grangetown *R & Cl* ... 107 E3
Grangetown *T & W* ... 115 F1
Gransmoor *E R Yk* ... 93 E5
Gransmore Green *Essex* ... 51 H3
Granston *Pembks* ... 32 C5
Grantchester *Cambs* ... 62 D1
Grantham *Lincs* ... 73 G4
Granton *C Edin* ... 132 A3
Grantown-on-Spey *Highld* ... 156 B2
Grantsfield *Herefs* ... 45 H5
Grantshouse *Border* ... 133 G2
Grappenhall *Ches* ... 82 A3
Grasby *Lincs* ... 86 A5
Grasmere *Cumb* ... 94 D6
Grass Green *Essex* ... 52 A4
Grasscroft *Gt Man* ... 83 E5
Grassendale *Mersyd* ... 81 F3
Grassgarth *Cumb* ... 103 G4
Grassington *N York* ... 96 C1
Grassmoor *Derbys* ... 84 B1
Grassthorpe *Notts* ... 85 F1
Grateley *Hants* ... 26 A3
Gratwich *Staffs* ... 71 E3
Graveley *Cambs* ... 62 B2
Graveley *Herts* ... 50 C3
Gravelly Hill *W Mids* ... 58 D4
Gravelsbank *Shrops* ... 56 D5
Graveney *Kent* ... 30 D2
Gravesend *Kent* ... 29 G3
Gravir *W Isls* ... 168 e7
Grayingham *Lincs* ... 85 G4
Grayrigg *Cumb* ... 95 F5
Grays *Essex* ... 29 G4
Grayshott *Hants* ... 27 G3
Grayson Green *Cumb* ... 102 D3
Grayswood *Surrey* ... 27 G3
Graythorpe *Dur* ... 107 E4
Grazeley *Berks* ... 27 E6
Greasbrough *S York* ... 84 B4
Greasby *Mersyd* ... 81 E4
Greasley *Notts* ... 72 C5
Great Abington *Cambs* ... 51 F6
Great Addington *Nhants* ... 61 F3
Great Alne *Warwks* ... 47 G5
Great Altcar *Lancs* ... 81 F5
Great Amwell *Herts* ... 51 E2
Great Asby *Cumb* ... 104 C1
Great Ashfield *Suffk* ... 64 C2
Great Ayton *N York* ... 107 E2
Great Baddow *Essex* ... 51 H1
Great Badminton *Gloucs* ... 38 C2
Great Bardfield *Essex* ... 51 G4
Great Barford *Beds* ... 50 B6
Great Barr *W Mids* ... 58 C5
Great Barrington *Gloucs* ... 39 G6
Great Barrow *Ches* ... 81 G1
Great Barton *Suffk* ... 64 A2
Great Barugh *N York* ... 98 C3
Great Bavington *Nthumb* ... 113 G3
Great Bealings *Suffk* ... 53 F6
Great Bedwyn *Wilts* ... 26 A6
Great Bentley *Essex* ... 53 E3
Great Billing *Nhants* ... 60 D2
Great Bircham *Norfk* ... 75 H3
Great Blakenham *Suffk* ... 53 E6
Great Blencow *Cumb* ... 104 A3
Great Bolas *Shrops* ... 70 B2
Great Bookham *Surrey* ... 28 B1
Great Bosullow *Cnwll* ... 2 B3
Great Bourton *Oxon* ... 48 C4
Great Bowden *Leics* ... 60 C4
Great Bradley *Suffk* ... 51 G6
Great Braxted *Essex* ... 52 B2
Great Bricett *Suffk* ... 52 D6
Great Brickhill *Bucks* ... 49 G2
Great Bridge *W Mids* ... 58 C5
Great Bridgeford *Staffs* ... 70 D3
Great Brington *Nhants* ... 60 C2
Great Bromley *Essex* ... 52 D3
Great Broughton *Cumb* ... 103 E3
Great Broughton *N York* ... 98 A5
Great Budworth *Ches* ... 82 B2
Great Burdon *Dur* ... 106 C2
Great Burstead *Essex* ... 29 H5
Great Busby *N York* ... 98 A5
Great Canfield *Essex* ... 51 G2
Great Carlton *Lincs* ... 86 D3
Great Casterton *Rutlnd* ... 73 G1
Great Chalfield *Wilts* ... 24 D6
Great Chart *Kent* ... 18 C6
Great Chatwell *Staffs* ... 70 C1
Great Chell *Staffs* ... 70 D5
Great Chesterford *Essex* ... 51 F5
Great Cheverell *Wilts* ... 25 E5
Great Chishill *Cambs* ... 51 E5
Great Clacton *Essex* ... 53 E2
Great Cliff *W York* ... 90 D1
Great Clifton *Cumb* ... 102 D3
Great Coates *Lincs* ... 86 C6
Great Comberton *Worcs* ... 47 E3
Great Comp *Kent* ... 29 G2
Great Corby *Cumb* ... 104 B6
Great Cornard *Suffk* ... 52 B5
Great Cowden *E R Yk* ... 93 F4
Great Coxwell *Oxon* ... 39 G4
Great Cransley *Nhants* ... 60 D3
Great Cressingham *Norfk* ... 63 H6
Great Crosthwaite *Cumb* ... 103 G2
Great Cubley *Derbys* ... 71 F4
Great Dalby *Leics* ... 73 E1
Great Doward *Herefs* ... 37 F6
Great Dunham *Norfk* ... 76 B1
Great Dunmow *Essex* ... 51 G3
Great Durnford *Wilts* ... 25 G3
Great Easton *Essex* ... 51 G3
Great Easton *Leics* ... 60 D5
Great Eccleston *Lancs* ... 88 C4

Great Edstone *N York* ... 98 C3
Great Ellingham *Norfk* ... 64 C5
Great Elm *Somset* ... 24 C4
Great Englebourne *Devon* ... 7 E3
Great Everdon *Nhants* ... 48 D5
Great Eversden *Cambs* ... 51 E6
Great Finborough *Suffk* ... 64 C1
Great Fransham *Norfk* ... 76 B1
Great Gaddesden *Herts* ... 50 A2
Great Gidding *Cambs* ... 61 G4
Great Givendale *E R Yk* ... 92 B5
Great Glemham *Suffk* ... 65 F1
Great Glen *Leics* ... 60 C5
Great Gonerby *Lincs* ... 73 G4
Great Gransden *Cambs* ... 62 B1
Great Green *Cambs* ... 50 D5
Great Green *Norfk* ... 65 E4
Great Green *Suffk* ... 64 B1
Great Green *Suffk* ... 64 B2
Great Habton *N York* ... 98 C2
Great Hale *Lincs* ... 74 B4
Great Hallingbury *Essex* ... 51 F3
Great Harrowden *Nhants* ... 61 E2
Great Harwood *Lancs* ... 89 F3
Great Haseley *Oxon* ... 41 E4
Great Hatfield *E R Yk* ... 93 F4
Great Haywood *Staffs* ... 71 E2
Great Heck *N York* ... 91 G2
Great Henny *Essex* ... 52 B4
Great Hinton *Wilts* ... 25 E5
Great Hockham *Norfk* ... 64 B5
Great Holland *Essex* ... 53 F3
Great Horkesley *Essex* ... 52 C4
Great Hormead *Herts* ... 51 E4
Great Horton *W York* ... 90 C3
Great Horwood *Bucks* ... 49 F2
Great Houghton *Nhants* ... 49 F5
Great Houghton *S York* ... 84 B5
Great Hucklow *Derbys* ... 83 G2
Great Kelk *E R Yk* ... 93 E5
Great Kimble *Bucks* ... 41 F5
Great Kingshill *Bucks* ... 41 G4
Great Langdale *Cumb* ... 94 D5
Great Langton *N York* ... 97 F4
Great Leighs *Essex* ... 51 H2
Great Limber *Lincs* ... 86 B6
Great Linford *Bucks* ... 49 G3
Great Livermere *Suffk* ... 64 A2
Great Longstone *Derbys* ... 83 G2
Great Lumley *Dur* ... 106 B6
Great Lyth *Shrops* ... 57 E6
Great Malvern *Worcs* ... 46 C4
Great Maplestead *Essex* ... 52 B4
Great Marton *Lancs* ... 88 B3
Great Massingham *Norfk* ... 76 A2
Great Meols *Mersyd* ... 81 E4
Great Milton *Oxon* ... 40 D4
Great Missenden *Bucks* ... 41 G4
Great Mitton *Lancs* ... 89 F3
Great Mongeham *Kent* ... 31 G1
Great Moulton *Norfk* ... 64 D4
Great Munden *Herts* ... 50 D3
Great Musgrave *Cumb* ... 104 D1
Great Ness *Shrops* ... 69 F2
Great Notley *Essex* ... 52 A3
Great Nurcott *Somset* ... 22 B3
Great Oak *Mons* ... 37 E5
Great Oakley *Essex* ... 53 E3
Great Oakley *Nhants* ... 61 E4
Great Offley *Herts* ... 50 B3
Great Ormside *Cumb* ... 104 D2
Great Orton *Cumb* ... 103 G6
Great Ouseburn *N York* ... 91 F6
Great Oxendon *Nhants* ... 60 C4
Great Oxney Green *Essex* ... 51 G1
Great Pattenden *Kent* ... 18 A6
Great Paxton *Cambs* ... 62 A2
Great Plumpton *Lancs* ... 88 B3
Great Plumstead *Norfk* ... 77 F1
Great Ponton *Lincs* ... 73 G3
Great Potheridge *Devon* ... 21 E2
Great Preston *W York* ... 91 E4
Great Purston *Nhants* ... 48 C3
Great Raveley *Cambs* ... 62 B3
Great Rissington *Gloucs* ... 39 G6
Great Rollright *Oxon* ... 48 B2
Great Rudbaxton *Pembks* ... 32 C4
Great Ryburgh *Norfk* ... 76 C3
Great Ryle *Nthumb* ... 124 C2
Great Ryton *Shrops* ... 57 E6
Great Saling *Essex* ... 51 H3
Great Salkeld *Cumb* ... 104 B4
Great Sampford *Essex* ... 51 G4
Great Sankey *Ches* ... 81 H3
Great Saredon *Staffs* ... 58 B6
Great Saughall *Ches* ... 81 F2
Great Saxham *Suffk* ... 63 G2
Great Shefford *Berks* ... 40 B2
Great Shelford *Cambs* ... 51 E6
Great Smeaton *N York* ... 97 G5
Great Snoring *Norfk* ... 76 C3
Great Somerford *Wilts* ... 38 D2
Great Soudley *Shrops* ... 70 B3
Great Stainton *Dur* ... 106 C3
Great Stambridge *Essex* ... 30 C5
Great Staughton *Cambs* ... 61 G2
Great Steeping *Lincs* ... 87 E1
Great Stoke *Bristl* ... 37 G2
Great Stonar *Kent* ... 31 G2
Great Strickland *Cumb* ... 104 B2
Great Stukeley *Cambs* ... 62 B3
Great Sturton *Lincs* ... 86 C2
Great Sutton *Ches* ... 81 F2
Great Sutton *Shrops* ... 57 E4
Great Swinburne *Nthumb* ... 113 F4
Great Tew *Oxon* ... 48 B2
Great Tey *Essex* ... 52 C3
Great Torrington *Devon* ... 21 E2
Great Tosson *Nthumb* ... 114 B6
Great Totham *Essex* ... 52 B2
Great Totham *Essex* ... 52 B2
Great Urswick *Cumb* ... 94 C3
Great Wakering *Essex* ... 30 C5
Great Waldingfield *Suffk* ... 52 C5
Great Walsingham *Norfk* ... 76 B4
Great Waltham *Essex* ... 51 H2

Great Warford *Ches* ... 82 C2
Great Warley *Essex* ... 29 G5
Great Washbourne *Gloucs* ... 47 E3
Great Weeke *Devon* ... 8 D3
Great Weldon *Nhants* ... 61 E4
Great Welnetham *Suffk* ... 64 A1
Great Wenham *Suffk* ... 52 D5
Great Whittington *Nthumb* ... 113 G2
Great Wigborough *Essex* ... 52 C2
Great Wilbraham *Cambs* ... 63 E1
Great Wishford *Wilts* ... 25 F3
Great Witchingham *Norfk* ... 76 D2
Great Witcombe *Gloucs* ... 38 D6
Great Witley *Worcs* ... 57 H2
Great Wolford *Warwks* ... 47 H3
Great Wratting *Suffk* ... 51 H5
Great Wymondley *Herts* ... 50 C4
Great Wyrley *Staffs* ... 58 C6
Great Wytheford *Shrops* ... 69 H2
Great Yarmouth *Norfk* ... 65 H6
Great Yeldham *Essex* ... 52 A5
Greatfield *Wilts* ... 39 E3
Greatford *Lincs* ... 74 A1
Greatgate *Staffs* ... 71 E4
Greatham *Dur* ... 106 D4
Greatham *Hants* ... 27 F2
Greatham *W Susx* ... 16 A3
Greatstone-on-Sea *Kent* ... 18 D4
Greatworth *Nhants* ... 48 D3
Grebby *Lincs* ... 87 E1
Greeba *IOM* ... 174 I3
Green *Denbgs* ... 80 C1
Green Bank *Cumb* ... 94 D3
Green Cross *Surrey* ... 27 G3
Green Down *Somset* ... 24 A5
Green End *Beds* ... 50 A5
Green End *Beds* ... 61 G2
Green End *Beds* ... 61 G2
Green End *Beds* ... 50 B6
Green End *Cambs* ... 62 B3
Green End *Cambs* ... 62 C1
Green End *Cambs* ... 62 D2
Green End *Cambs* ... 62 D1
Green End *Herts* ... 50 D4
Green End *Herts* ... 50 D3
Green End *Herts* ... 50 D4
Green End *Warwks* ... 59 E4
Green Hammerton *N York* ... 91 F5
Green Head *Cumb* ... 103 H5
Green Heath *Staffs* ... 71 E1
Green Hill *Wilts* ... 39 E3
Green Lane *Devon* ... 9 E2
Green Lane *Warwks* ... 58 D2
Green Moor *S York* ... 83 H5
Green Oak *E R Yk* ... 92 B2
Green Ore *Somset* ... 24 A4
Green Quarter *Cumb* ... 95 E5
Green Street *E Susx* ... 18 A3
Green Street *Gloucs* ... 38 D6
Green Street *Herts* ... 51 E3
Green Street *Herts* ... 28 C6
Green Street *Worcs* ... 46 D4
Green Street Green *Gt Lon* ... 29 E2
Green Street Green *Kent* ... 29 G3
Green Tye *Herts* ... 51 E3
Greencroft Hall *Dur* ... 106 A6
Greenend *Oxon* ... 48 B1
Greenfield *Ag & B* ... 128 C4
Greenfield *Beds* ... 50 B4
Greenfield *Flints* ... 80 D2
Greenfield *Gt Man* ... 83 E5
Greenfield *Highld* ... 144 D4
Greenfield *Oxon* ... 41 E3
Greenford *Gt Lon* ... 28 B4
Greengairs *N Lans* ... 130 D2
Greengates *W York* ... 90 C3
Greenhalgh *Lancs* ... 88 C3
Greenham *Berks* ... 26 C6
Greenham *Somset* ... 22 D1
Greenhaugh *Nthumb* ... 113 E3
Greenhead *Nthumb* ... 112 D1
Greenheys *Gt Man* ... 82 B5
Greenhill *D & G* ... 111 E3
Greenhill *Falk* ... 130 D3
Greenhill *Herefs* ... 46 C4
Greenhill *Kent* ... 31 E3
Greenhill *S Lans* ... 120 D3
Greenhillocks *Derbys* ... 72 B5
Greenhithe *Kent* ... 29 G3
Greenholm *E Ayrs* ... 119 G3
Greenholme *Cumb* ... 95 G5
Greenhouse *Border* ... 122 C2
Greenhow Hill *N York* ... 96 D1
Greenland *Highld* ... 167 F5
Greenland *S York* ... 84 B4
Greenlands *Bucks* ... 41 F3
Greenlaw *Border* ... 122 D4
Greenlea *D & G* ... 111 E3
Greenloaning *P & K* ... 131 G6
Greenmoor Hill *Oxon* ... 41 E2
Greenmount *Gt Man* ... 82 C6
Greenock *Inver* ... 128 D3
Greenodd *Cumb* ... 94 D3
Greens Norton *Nhants* ... 49 E4
Greensgate *Norfk* ... 76 D2
Greenshields *S Lans* ... 121 E4
Greenside *T & W* ... 114 C2
Greenside *W York* ... 90 C1
Greenstead *Essex* ... 52 D3
Greenstead Green *Essex* ... 52 B3
Greensted *Essex* ... 51 F1
Greenstreet Green *Suffk* ... 52 D6
Greenway *Gloucs* ... 46 C2
Greenway *Somset* ... 23 F2
Greenway *V Glam* ... 36 B2
Greenwich *Gt Lon* ... 29 E4
Greet *Gloucs* ... 47 F2
Greete *Shrops* ... 57 F2
Greetham *Lincs* ... 86 C2
Greetham *Rutlnd* ... 73 G1
Greetland *W York* ... 90 B2
Gregson Lane *Lancs* ... 88 D2
Greinton *Somset* ... 23 G3
Grenaby *IOM* ... 174 k2

Grendon *Nhants* ... 49 G5
Grendon *Warwks* ... 59 F5
Grendon Green *Herefs* ... 46 B5
Grendon Underwood *Bucks* ... 49 E1
Grenofen *Devon* ... 6 B5
Grenoside *S York* ... 84 A4
Greosabhagh *W Isls* ... 168 d6
Gresford *Wrexhm* ... 69 F5
Gresham *Norfk* ... 77 E4
Greshornish House Hotel *Highld* ... 150 D4
Gressenhall *Norfk* ... 76 C1
Gressenhall Green *Norfk* ... 76 C2
Gressingham *Lancs* ... 95 F2
Greta Bridge *Dur* ... 105 G1
Gretna *D & G* ... 111 H1
Gretna Green *D & G* ... 111 H1
Gretton *Gloucs* ... 47 F2
Gretton *Nhants* ... 61 E5
Gretton *Shrops* ... 57 E5
Grewelthorpe *N York* ... 97 E2
Grey Friars *Suffk* ... 65 G2
Grey Green *Lincs* ... 85 E5
Greygarth *N York* ... 97 E2
Greylake *Somset* ... 23 G3
Greyrigg *D & G* ... 111 E4
Greys Green *Oxon* ... 41 E2
Greysouthen *Cumb* ... 103 E3
Greystoke *Cumb* ... 104 A3
Greystone *Angus* ... 141 E4
Greywell *Hants* ... 27 E4
Gribb *Dorset* ... 10 D5
Gribthorpe *E R Yk* ... 92 B3
Griff *Warwks* ... 59 F4
Griffithstown *Torfn* ... 36 D4
Griffydam *Leics* ... 72 B2
Griggs Green *Hants* ... 27 F2
Grimeford Village *Lancs* ... 82 A6
Grimesthorpe *S York* ... 84 A4
Grimethorpe *S York* ... 84 B6
Grimley *Worcs* ... 46 D5
Grimmet *S Ayrs* ... 109 E6
Grimoldby *Lincs* ... 86 D3
Grimpo *Shrops* ... 69 F3
Grimsargh *Lancs* ... 88 D3
Grimsby *Lincs* ... 86 C6
Grimscote *Nhants* ... 49 E5
Grimscott *Cnwll* ... 20 C1
Grimshader *W Isls* ... 168 e8
Grimshaw *Lancs* ... 89 E2
Grimshaw Green *Lancs* ... 81 G6
Grimsthorpe *Lincs* ... 73 H2
Grimston *E R Yk* ... 93 F3
Grimston *Leics* ... 72 D2
Grimston *Norfk* ... 75 G2
Grimston Hill *Notts* ... 84 D1
Grimstone *Dorset* ... 11 G4
Grimstone End *Suffk* ... 64 B2
Grinacombe Moor *Devon* ... 5 H5
Grindale *E R Yk* ... 99 G2
Grindle *Shrops* ... 57 H6
Grindleford *Derbys* ... 83 G2
Grindleton *Lancs* ... 89 F4
Grindley Brook *Shrops* ... 69 G4
Grindlow *Derbys* ... 83 G2
Grindon *Dur* ... 106 C3
Grindon *Nthumb* ... 123 F4
Grindon *Staffs* ... 71 F5
Grindon *T & W* ... 115 E1
Grindon Hill *Nthumb* ... 113 E2
Grindonrigg *Nthumb* ... 123 F4
Gringley on the Hill *Notts* ... 85 E4
Grinsdale *Cumb* ... 103 H6
Grinshill *Shrops* ... 69 G2
Grinton *N York* ... 96 D5
Griomaisiader *W Isls* ... 168 e8
Griomsaigh *W Isls* ... 168 b4
Grishipoll *Ag & B* ... 134 D5
Grisling Common *E Susx* ... 17 E4
Gristhorpe *N York* ... 99 F3
Griston *Norfk* ... 64 B5
Gritley *Ork* ... 169 c2
Grittenham *Wilts* ... 39 E2
Grittleton *Wilts* ... 38 C2
Grizebeck *Cumb* ... 94 C3
Grizedale *Cumb* ... 94 D4
Groby *Leics* ... 60 A6
Groes *Denbgs* ... 80 B1
Groes-faen *Rhondd* ... 36 B2
Groes-Wen *Caerph* ... 36 B3
Groesffordd *Gwynd* ... 66 B4
Groesffordd Marli *Denbgs* ... 80 B2
Groesllwyd *Powys* ... 68 D1
Groeslon *Gwynd* ... 66 D6
Groeslon *Gwynd* ... 67 E6
Grogarry *W Isls* ... 168 b3
Grogport *Ag & B* ... 117 G5
Groigearraidh *W Isls* ... 168 b3
Gromford *Suffk* ... 65 F1
Gronant *Flints* ... 80 C3
Groombridge *E Susx* ... 17 F5
Grosebay *W Isls* ... 168 d6
Grosmont *Mons* ... 45 G2
Grosmont *N York* ... 98 D5
Groton *Suffk* ... 52 C5
Grotton *Gt Man* ... 83 E5
Grouville *Jersey* ... 174 d1
Grove *Bucks* ... 49 G1
Grove *Dorset* ... 11 G2
Grove *Kent* ... 31 F2
Grove *Notts* ... 85 E3
Grove *Oxon* ... 40 B3
Grove *Pembks* ... 32 D2
Grove Green *Kent* ... 30 A2
Grove Park *Gt Lon* ... 29 E3
Grove Vale *W Mids* ... 58 C5
Grovenhurst *Kent* ... 17 H5
Grovesend *Gloucs* ... 37 H3
Grovesend *Swans* ... 34 C4
Grubb Street *Kent* ... 29 G3
Gruinard *Highld* ... 160 D3
Gruinart *Ag & B* ... 126 B2
Grula *Highld* ... 150 D1
Gruline *Ag & B* ... 135 G3
Grumbla *Cnwll* ... 2 B3
Grundisburgh *Suffk* ... 53 F6
Gruting *Shet* ... 169 h3
Gualachulain *Highld* ... 137 F4

Guanockgate Lincs 74 D1
Guardbridge Fife 140 D2
Guarlford Worcs 46 D4
Guay P & K 139 G5
Guernsey Airport Guern 174 f1
Guestling Green E Susx 18 B3
Guestling Thorn E Susx 18 B3
Guestwick Norfk 76 D3
Guide Lancs 89 E2
Guide Bridge Gt Man 82 D4
Guide Post Nthumb 114 D4
Guilden Down Shrops 56 C4
Guilden Morden Cambs 50 D5
Guilden Sutton Ches 81 G1
Guildford Surrey 27 H4
Guildstead Kent 30 B2
Guildtown P & K 140 A3
Guilsborough Nhants 60 C3
Guilsfield Powys 68 D1
Guilton Kent 31 F2
Guiltreehill S Ayrs 109 E6
Guineaford Devon 21 F4
Guisborough N York 107 E2
Guiseley W York 90 C4
Guist Norfk 76 C3
Guiting Power Gloucs 47 F2
Gullane E Loth 132 D3
Gulling Green Suffk 63 G1
Gulval Cnwll 2 B3
Gulworthy Devon 6 B5
Gumfreston Pembks 33 E2
Gumley Leics 60 C4
Gummow's Shop Cnwll 4 B2
Gun Green Kent 18 A4
Gun Hill E Susx 17 F3
Gun Hill Warwks 59 F4
Gunby E R Yk 92 A3
Gunby Lincs 73 G2
Gunby Lincs 87 E1
Gundleton Hants 26 D3
Gunn Devon 21 F4
Gunnerside N York 96 C3
Gunnerton Nthumb 113 F2
Gunness Lincs 85 F6
Gunnislake Cnwll 6 B5
Gunnista Shet 169 j2
Gunthorpe Cambs 61 H6
Gunthorpe Lincs 85 F4
Gunthorpe Norfk 76 C3
Gunthorpe Notts 72 D4
Gunton Suffk 65 H5
Gunwalloe Cnwll 2 D2
Gupworthy Somset 22 C3
Gurnard IOW 14 C3
Gurnett Ches 82 D2
Gurney Slade Somset 24 B4
Gurnos Powys 35 E5
Gushmere Kent 30 D2
Gussage All Saints Dorset 12 D6
Gussage St Andrew Dorset 12 D6
Gussage St Michael Dorset 12 D6
Guston Kent 19 G6
Gutcher Shet 169 j5
Guthrie Angus 141 F3
Guy's Marsh Dorset 24 D1
Guyhirn Cambs 62 C6
Guyhirn Gull Cambs 62 C6
Guyzance Nthumb 125 E1
Gwaenysgor Flints 80 C3
Gwalchmai IOA 78 D2
Gwastadnant Gwynd 67 F6
Gwaun-Cae-Gurwen Carmth 34 D5
Gwbert on Sea Cerdgn 42 B4
Gwealavellan Cnwll 2 D4
Gwealeath Cnwll 2 D2
Gweek Cnwll 3 E2
Gwehelog Mons 37 E5
Gwenddwr Powys 44 D3
Gwendreath Cnwll 3 E1
Gwennap Cnwll 3 E4
Gwenter Cnwll 3 E1
Gwernaffield Flints 80 D1
Gwernesney Mons 37 E4
Gwernogle Carmth 43 E3
Gwernymynydd Flints 80 D1
Gwersyllt Wrexhm 69 E5
Gwespyr Flints 80 C3
Gwindra Cnwll 3 G5
Gwinear Cnwll 2 D3
Gwithian Cnwll 2 C4
Gwredog IOA 78 D3
Gwrhay Caerph 36 C4
Gwyddelwern Denbgs 68 C5
Gwyddgrug Carmth 43 E3
Gwynfryn Wrexhm 69 E5
Gwystre Powys 56 A2
Gwytherin Conwy 68 A6
Gyfelia Wrexhm 69 E5
Gyrn-goch Gwynd 66 D5

Habberley Shrops 56 D6
Habberley Worcs 58 A3
Habergham Lancs 89 F3
Habertoft Lincs 87 E2
Habin W Susx 27 F1
Habrough Lincs 86 B6
Hacconby Lincs 74 A2
Haceby Lincs 73 H4
Hacheston Suffk 65 E1
Hack Green Ches 70 D5
Hackbridge Gt Lon 28 D3
Hackenthorpe S York 84 B3
Hackford Norfk 64 C6
Hackforth N York 97 F4
Hackland Ork 169 b4
Hackleton Nhants 49 F5
Hacklinge Kent 31 G1
Hackman's Gate Worcs 58 B3
Hackness N York 99 E4
Hackness Somset 23 F4
Hackney Gt Lon 28 D4

Hackthorn Lincs 85 G3
Hackthorpe Cumb 104 B2
Hacton Gt Lon 29 F5
Hadden Border 123 E3
Haddenham Bucks 41 F3
Haddenham Cambs 62 D3
Haddington E Loth 132 D3
Haddington Lincs 85 G1
Haddiscoe Norfk 65 G5
Haddo Abers 158 D3
Haddon Cambs 61 G5
Hade Edge W York 83 F5
Hadfield Derbys 83 E4
Hadham Cross Herts 51 E3
Hadham Ford Herts 51 E3
Hadleigh Essex 30 B5
Hadleigh Suffk 52 D5
Hadleigh Heath Suffk 52 D5
Hadley Shrops 70 B1
Hadley Worcs 58 B2
Hadley End Staffs 71 F2
Hadley Wood Gt Lon 28 D6
Hadlow Kent 29 G1
Hadlow Down E Susx 17 F4
Hadnall Shrops 69 G2
Hadstock Essex 51 F5
Hadzor Worcs 47 E5
Haffenden Quarter Kent 18 B5
Hafod-y-bwch Wrexhm 69 E5
Hafod-y-coed Blae G 36 C4
Hafodunos Conwy 80 A1
Hafodyrynys Caerph 36 C4
Haggate Lancs 89 G3
Haggbeck Cumb 112 B2
Haggerston Nthumb 123 G4
Haggington Hill Devon 21 F5
Haggs Falk 130 D3
Hagley Herefs 46 A3
Hagley Worcs 58 B3
Hagmore Green Suffk 52 C5
Hagnaby Lincs 86 D1
Hagnaby Lincs 87 E3
Hagworthingham Lincs 86 D2
Haigh Gt Man 82 A6
Haighton Green Lancs 88 D3
Hail Weston Cambs 61 H2
Haile Cumb 94 A6
Hailes Gloucs 47 F2
Hailey Herts 51 E2
Hailey Oxon 41 E3
Hailey Oxon 40 B5
Hailsham E Susx 17 G2
Hainault Gt Lon 29 E5
Haine Kent 31 G3
Hainford Norfk 77 E2
Hainton Lincs 86 B3
Hainworth W York 90 B3
Haisthorpe E R Yk 99 G1
Hakin Pembks 32 C2
Halam Notts 72 D5
Halbeath Fife 131 G4
Halberton Devon 9 G6
Halcro Highld 167 F4
Hale Ches 81 G3
Hale Cumb 95 F3
Hale Gt Man 82 C3
Hale Hants 25 G1
Hale Somset 24 C2
Hale Surrey 27 G4
Hale Bank Ches 81 G3
Hale Green E Susx 17 F3
Hale Nook Lancs 88 B4
Hale Street Kent 29 G1
Halebarns Gt Man 82 C3
Hales Norfk 65 F5
Hales Staffs 70 B3
Hales Green Derbys 71 G4
Hales Place Kent 31 E2
Halesgate Lincs 74 D3
Halesowen W Mids 58 C4
Halesville Essex 30 C5
Halesworth Suffk 65 F3
Halewood Mersyd 81 G3
Halford Devon 7 E5
Halford Shrops 57 E4
Halford Warwks 47 H4
Halfpenny Cumb 95 F4
Halfpenny Green Staffs 58 A5
Halfpenny Houses N York 97 E3
Halfway Berks 40 B1
Halfway Carmth 43 G2
Halfway Carmth 44 A2
Halfway S York 84 B3
Halfway Bridge W Susx 27 G1
Halfway House Shrops 69 F1
Halfway Houses Kent 30 C3
Halifax W York 90 B2
Halkirk Highld 167 E4
Halkyn Flints 80 D2
Hall E Rens 119 F5
Hall Cliffe W York 90 D1
Hall Cross Lancs 88 C3
Hall Dunnerdale Cumb 94 C4
Hall End Beds 50 A5
Hall End Beds 50 B4
Hall End W Mids 58 C5
Hall Glen Falk 131 E3
Hall Green W Mids 58 D3
Hall's Green Essex 51 E1
Hall's Green Herts 50 D4
Hallam Fields Derbys 72 B4
Halland E Susx 17 F3
Hallaton Leics 60 D5
Hallatrow Somset 24 B5
Hallbankgate Cumb 104 C6
Hallbeck Cumb 95 G4
Hallen Gloucs 37 F2
Hallfield Gate Derbys 72 B6
Hallgarth Dur 106 C3
Hallglen Falk 131 E3
Hallin Highld 150 C5
Halling Kent 29 H2
Hallington Lincs 86 D3
Hallington Nthumb 113 G2
Halliwell Gt Man 82 B6
Halloughton Notts 73 E5
Hallow Worcs 46 B3
Hallow Heath Worcs 46 D5
Hallsands Devon 7 E1

Hallthwaites Cumb 94 C3
Halltoft End Lincs 74 D4
Hallworthy Cnwll 5 E5
Hallyne Border 121 F3
Halmer End Staffs 70 C4
Halmond's Frome Herefs 46 B4
Halmore Gloucs 38 B4
Halnaker W Susx 15 G4
Halsall Lancs 81 F6
Halse Nhants 48 D3
Halse Somset 22 D2
Halsetown Cnwll 2 C4
Halsham E R Yk 93 F2
Halsinger Devon 21 E4
Halstead Essex 52 B4
Halstead Kent 29 F2
Halstead Leics 60 D6
Halstock Dorset 11 F5
Halsway Somset 22 D3
Haltcliff Bridge Cumb 103 H4
Haltham Lincs 86 C1
Halton Bucks 41 G5
Halton Ches 81 H3
Halton Lancs 95 F1
Halton Nthumb 113 G1
Halton N York 91 E3
Halton Wrexhm 69 E4
Halton East N York 90 B5
Halton Fenside Lincs 87 E1
Halton Gill N York 96 B2
Halton Green Lancs 95 F1
Halton Holegate Lincs 86 D1
Halton Lea Gate Nthumb 104 C6
Halton Quay Cnwll 5 H2
Halton Shields Nthumb 113 G2
Halton West N York 89 G5
Haltwhistle Nthumb 112 D1
Halvergate Norfk 65 G6
Halwell Devon 7 E3
Halwill Devon 5 H6
Halwill Junction Devon 8 A5
Ham Devon 10 C5
Ham Gloucs 47 E1
Ham Gloucs 38 B4
Ham Gt Lon 28 C3
Ham Kent 31 G1
Ham Somset 23 F2
Ham Somset 24 B4
Ham Somset 24 B4
Ham Wilts 26 B5
Ham Common Dorset 24 D2
Ham Green Herefs 46 C4
Ham Green Kent 30 B3
Ham Green Kent 18 C4
Ham Green Somset 37 F2
Ham Green Worcs 58 C2
Ham Hill Kent 29 H2
Ham Street Somset 24 A3
Hamble-le-Rice Hants 14 C4
Hambleden Bucks 41 F3
Hambledon Hants 15 E5
Hambledon Surrey 27 H3
Hambleton Lancs 88 B4
Hambleton N York 91 G3
Hambleton Moss Side Lancs 88 B4
Hambridge Somset 23 G1
Hambridge Somset 24 B3
Hambrook Gloucs 37 G2
Hambrook W Susx 15 F4
Hameringham Lincs 86 C1
Hamerton Cambs 61 G3
Hamilton S Lans 120 B5
Hamlet Dorset 11 F5
Hamlins E Susx 17 G2
Hammerpot W Susx 16 B2
Hammersmith Gt Lon 28 C4
Hammerwich Staffs 58 D6
Hammerwood E Susx 17 E5
Hammond Street Herts 50 D1
Hammoor Dorset 12 B6
Hamnavoe Shet 169 h2
Hamnavoe Shet 169 j4
Hampden Park E Susx 17 G2
Hampden Row Bucks 41 G4
Hamperden End Essex 51 G4
Hampnett Gloucs 39 F6
Hampole S York 84 C6
Hampreston Dorset 12 D4
Hampsfield Cumb 95 E3
Hampson Green Lancs 88 C5
Hampstead Gt Lon 28 D5
Hampstead Norrey's Berks 40 D2
Hampsthwaite N York 90 D5
Hampt Cnwll 5 G3
Hampton Devon 10 C4
Hampton Gt Lon 28 B3
Hampton Kent 31 E3
Hampton Shrops 57 G4
Hampton Wilts 39 F3
Hampton Worcs 47 F3
Hampton Bishop Herefs 46 A3
Hampton Court Palace & Gardens Gt Lon 28 B3
Hampton Fields Gloucs 38 D4
Hampton Green Ches 69 G5
Hampton Heath Ches 69 G5
Hampton in Arden W Mids 59 E3
Hampton Loade Shrops 57 H4
Hampton Lovett Worcs 58 B2
Hampton Lucy Warwks 47 H5
Hampton Magna Warwks 59 E2
Hampton on the Hill Warwks 59 E2
Hampton Poyle Oxon 40 C6
Hampton Wick Gt Lon 28 C3
Hamptworth Wilts 25 H1
Hamrow Norfk 76 B2
Hamsey E Susx 17 E3
Hamsey Green Gt Lon 28 D2
Hamstall Ridware Staffs 71 F2
Hamstead IOW 14 B3
Hamstead W Mids 58 C5
Hamstead Marshall Berks 26 B6
Hamsterley Dur 105 H6
Hamsterley Dur 105 H3
Hamstreet Kent 18 D5
Hamwood Somset 23 F5
Hamworthy Dorset 12 D4
Hanbury Staffs 71 G3
Hanbury Worcs 58 C2

Hanby Lincs 73 H3
Hanchet End Suffk 51 G5
Hanchurch Staffs 70 C4
Hand and Pen Devon 9 G4
Hand Green Ches 69 H6
Handale N York 107 G2
Handbridge Ches 81 F1
Handcross W Susx 16 D4
Handforth Ches 82 D3
Handley Ches 69 G6
Handley Derbys 72 A6
Handley Green Essex 51 G1
Handsacre Staffs 71 F2
Handsworth S York 84 B3
Handsworth W Mids 58 C4
Handy Cross Bucks 41 G3
Hanford Dorset 12 B6
Hanford Staffs 70 D4
Hanging Houghton Nhants 60 D3
Hanging Langford Wilts 25 F3
Hangleton E Susx 16 D2
Hangleton W Susx 16 B2
Hanham Gloucs 37 G1
Hankelow Ches 70 B5
Hankerton Wilts 38 D3
Hankham E Susx 17 G2
Hanley Staffs 70 D5
Hanley Castle Worcs 46 D3
Hanley Child Worcs 57 G2
Hanley Swan Worcs 46 D3
Hanley William Worcs 57 G2
Hanlith N York 89 G6
Hanmer Wrexhm 69 G4
Hannaford Devon 21 F4
Hannah Lincs 87 E3
Hannington Hants 26 D5
Hannington Nhants 60 D2
Hannington Wilts 39 F4
Hannington Wick Wilts 39 F4
Hanscombe End Beds 50 B4
Hanslope Bucks 49 F4
Hanthorpe Lincs 74 A2
Hanwell Gt Lon 28 B4
Hanwell Oxon 48 C4
Hanwood Shrops 69 G1
Hanworth Gt Lon 28 B3
Hanworth Norfk 77 E4
Happendon S Lans 120 C3
Happisburgh Norfk 77 G3
Happisburgh Common Norfk 77 G3
Hapsford Ches 81 G2
Hapton Lancs 89 F3
Hapton Norfk 64 D5
Harberton Devon 7 E3
Harbertonford Devon 7 E3
Harbledown Kent 31 E2
Harborne W Mids 58 C4
Harborough Magna Warwks 59 H3
Harbottle Nthumb 113 F5
Harbourneford Devon 6 D4
Harbours Hill Worcs 58 C2
Harbridge Hants 13 E6
Harbridge Green Hants 13 E6
Harbury Warwks 48 B5
Harby Leics 73 E3
Harby Notts 85 F2
Harcombe Devon 9 F3
Harcombe Devon 10 B4
Harcombe Bottom Devon 10 D4
Harden W Mids 58 C5
Harden W York 90 B3
Hardenhuish Wilts 39 E5
Hardgate Abers 149 E5
Hardgate D & G 110 C1
Hardgate N York 90 D6
Hardgate W Duns 129 F2
Hardham W Susx 16 A3
Hardhorn Lancs 88 B3
Hardingham Norfk 64 C6
Hardingstone Nhants 49 F5
Hardington Somset 24 C4
Hardington Mandeville Somset 11 E6
Hardington Marsh Somset 11 E6
Hardington Moor Somset 11 E6
Hardisworthy Devon 20 C3
Hardley Hants 14 C4
Hardley Street Norfk 65 F5
Hardmead Bucks 49 G4
Hardraw N York 96 B4
Hardsough Lancs 89 F2
Hardstoft Derbys 84 B1
Hardway Hants 14 D4
Hardway Somset 24 C3
Hardwick Bucks 49 F1
Hardwick Cambs 62 C1
Hardwick Lincs 85 F2
Hardwick Nhants 60 D2
Hardwick Norfk 65 E4
Hardwick Oxon 40 B5
Hardwick Oxon 48 D2
Hardwick S York 84 C3
Hardwick W Mids 58 D5
Hardwick Green Worcs 46 D2
Hardwicke Gloucs 38 C5
Hardwicke Gloucs 47 E2
Hardy's Green Essex 52 C3
Hare Croft W York 90 B3
Hare Green Essex 53 E3
Hare Hatch Berks 41 F2
Hare Street Essex 51 E2
Hare Street Essex 29 F6
Hare Street Herts 51 E4
Harebeating E Susx 17 G2
Hareby Lincs 86 D1
Harefield Gt Lon 28 A5
Harehill Derbys 71 G4
Harehills W York 90 D3
Harehope Nthumb 124 D3
Harelaw Border 122 C2
Harelaw D & G 112 B3
Harelaw Dur 106 A6
Hareplain Kent 18 B5
Haresceugh Cumb 104 C4
Harescombe Gloucs 38 C5
Haresfield Gloucs 38 C5
Harestock Hants 26 C2
Harewood W York 90 D4
Harewood End Herefs 45 H2

Harford Devon 6 D3
Hargate Norfk 64 D4
Hargatewall Derbys 83 F2
Hargrave Ches 81 G1
Hargrave Nhants 61 F2
Hargrave Suffk 63 G1
Hargrave Green Suffk 63 G1
Harker Cumb 103 H6
Harkstead Suffk 53 E4
Harlaston Staffs 71 G1
Harlaxton Lincs 73 F3
Harle Syke Lancs 89 G3
Harlech Gwynd 67 E3
Harlescott Shrops 69 G2
Harlesden Gt Lon 28 C4
Harlestone Derbys 84 C2
Harleston Devon 7 E2
Harleston Norfk 65 E4
Harleston Suffk 64 C1
Harlestone Nhants 60 C2
Harley S York 84 A4
Harley Shrops 57 F5
Harlington Beds 50 A4
Harlington Gt Lon 28 B4
Harlington S York 84 C6
Harlosh Highld 150 C3
Harlow Essex 51 E2
Harlow Hill Nthumb 114 B2
Harlthorpe E R Yk 92 A3
Harlton Cambs 51 E6
Harlyn Bay Cnwll 4 B3
Harman's Cross Dorset 12 D3
Harmby N York 96 D4
Harmer Green Herts 50 C2
Harmer Hill Shrops 69 G2
Harmondsworth Gt Lon 28 B4
Harmston Lincs 85 G1
Harnage Shrops 57 F6
Harnham Nthumb 114 B4
Harnhill Gloucs 39 E4
Harold Hill Gt Lon 29 F5
Harold Wood Gt Lon 29 F5
Haroldston West Pembks 32 C3
Haroldswick Shet 169 k5
Harome N York 98 B3
Harpenden Herts 50 B2
Harpford Devon 10 A4
Harpham E R Yk 93 E6
Harpley Norfk 76 A3
Harpley Worcs 46 B5
Harpole Nhants 49 E5
Harpsdale Highld 167 E4
Harpsden Oxon 41 F2
Harpswell Lincs 85 G4
Harpur Hill Derbys 83 F2
Harpurhey Gt Man 82 D5
Harraby Cumb 104 A6
Harracott Devon 21 F3
Harrapool Highld 151 F3
Harrietfield P & K 139 G3
Harrietsham Kent 30 B1
Harringay Gt Lon 28 D5
Harrington Cumb 102 D3
Harrington Lincs 86 D2
Harrington Nhants 60 D3
Harringworth Nhants 61 E5
Harriseahead Staffs 70 D6
Harriston Cumb 103 F4
Harrogate N York 90 D5
Harrold Beds 49 H5
Harrop Dale Gt Man 83 E5
Harrow Gt Lon 28 B5
Harrow Green Suffk 52 B6
Harrow on the Hill Gt Lon 28 B5
Harrowbarrow Cnwll 5 G3
Harrowden Beds 50 B5
Harrowgate Village Dur 106 B3
Harston Cambs 51 E6
Harston Leics 73 F3
Harswell E R Yk 92 B4
Hart Dur 106 D4
Hart Station Dur 106 D4
Hartburn Nthumb 114 C4
Hartest Suffk 52 B6
Hartfield E Susx 17 F5
Hartford Cambs 62 B3
Hartford Ches 82 A2
Hartford Somset 22 B2
Hartford End Essex 51 H2
Hartfordbridge Hants 27 F5
Hartforth N York 97 E5
Hartgrove Dorset 24 D1
Harthill Ches 69 G6
Harthill N Lans 131 E1
Harthill S York 84 C3
Hartington Derbys 71 F6
Hartington Nthumb 114 B4
Hartland Devon 20 C3
Hartland Quay Devon 20 B3
Hartlebury Worcs 58 A2
Hartlepool Dur 106 D4
Hartley Cumb 96 A6
Hartley Kent 29 G3
Hartley Kent 18 A5
Hartley Nthumb 115 E3
Hartley Green Kent 29 G3
Hartley Green Staffs 71 E3
Hartley Wespall Hants 27 E5
Hartley Wintney Hants 27 F5
Hartlip Kent 30 B2
Hartlip Hill Kent 30 B2
Hartoft End N York 98 C4
Harton N York 91 H6
Harton Shrops 57 E4
Harton S T & W 115 E2
Hartpury Gloucs 46 D2
Hartshead W York 90 C2
Hartshead Moor Side W York 90 C2
Hartshill Staffs 70 D5
Hartshill Warwks 59 F5
Hartshorne Derbys 72 A2
Hartside Nthumb 124 C3
Hartswell Somset 22 D2
Hartwell Nhants 49 F4
Hartwith N York 90 C6
Hartwood N Lans 120 C5

290

H

Hartwoodmyres *Border* 122 B2
Harvel *Kent* 29 G2
Harvington *Worcs* 58 B3
Harvington *Worcs* 47 F4
Harwell *Notts* 84 D4
Harwell *Oxon* 40 C3
Harwich *Essex* 53 F4
Harwood *Dur* 105 E3
Harwood *Gt Man* 82 B6
Harwood *Nthumb* 113 G4
Harwood Dale *N York* 99 E4
Harwood Lee *Gt Man* 82 B6
Harworth *Notts* 84 D4
Hasbury *W Mids* 58 C4
Hascombe *Surrey* 16 A5
Haselbech *Nhants* 60 C3
Haselbury Plucknett *Somset* 11 E6
Haseley *Warwks* 59 E2
Haseley Green *Warwks* 59 E2
Haseley Knob *Warwks* 59 E2
Haselor *Warwks* 47 G5
Hasfield *Gloucs* 46 D2
Hasguard *Pembks* 32 C3
Haskayne *Lancs* 81 F5
Hasketon *Suffk* 53 F6
Hasland *Derbys* 84 B2
Hasland Green *Derbys* 84 B1
Haslemere *Surrey* 27 G2
Haslingden *Lancs* 89 F2
Haslingden Grane *Lancs* 89 F2
Haslingfield *Cambs* 51 E6
Haslington *Ches* 70 B6
Hassall *Ches* 70 C6
Hassall Green *Ches* 70 C6
Hassell Street *Kent* 18 D6
Hassingham *Norfk* 65 F6
Hassness *Cumb* 103 F2
Hassocks *W Susx* 16 D3
Hassop *Derbys* 83 G2
Haste Hill *Surrey* 27 G2
Haster *Highld* 167 G3
Hasthorpe *Lincs* 87 E2
Hastingleigh *Kent* 18 D6
Hastings *E Susx* 18 B2
Hastings *Somset* 10 D6
Hastingwood *Essex* 51 F1
Hastoe *Herts* 41 G5
Haswell *Dur* 106 C5
Haswell Plough *Dur* 106 C5
Hatch *Beds* 50 B5
Hatch Beauchamp *Somset* 23 F1
Hatch End *Beds* 61 G1
Hatch End *Gt Lon* 28 B5
Hatchet Gate *Hants* 14 B4
Hatching Green *Herts* 50 B2
Hatchmere *Ches* 81 H2
Hatcliffe *Lincs* 86 B5
Hatfield *Herefs* 46 B5
Hatfield *Herts* 50 C2
Hatfield *S York* 84 D6
Hatfield *Worcs* 46 D4
Hatfield Broad Oak *Essex* 51 F2
Hatfield Heath *Essex* 51 F2
Hatfield Peverel *Essex* 52 B2
Hatfield Woodhouse *S York* 84 D5
Hatford *Oxon* 40 B4
Hatherden *Hants* 26 B4
Hatherleigh *Devon* 8 B5
Hathern *Leics* 72 C2
Hatherop *Gloucs* 39 F5
Hathersage *Derbys* 83 G3
Hathersage Booths *Derbys* 83 G3
Hatherton *Ches* 70 B5
Hatherton *Staffs* 71 E1
Hatley St George *Cambs* 50 D6
Hatt *Cnwll* 5 G2
Hattersley *Gt Man* 83 E4
Hattingley *Hants* 27 E3
Hatton *Abers* 159 F3
Hatton *Angus* 141 E4
Hatton *Ches* 82 A3
Hatton *Derbys* 71 G3
Hatton *Gt Lon* 28 B3
Hatton *Lincs* 86 B2
Hatton *Shrops* 57 E4
Hatton *Warwks* 59 E2
Hatton Heath *Ches* 69 G6
Hatton of Fintray *Abers* 149 F6
Haugh *E Ayrs* 119 G2
Haugh *Lincs* 86 D2
Haugh *W York* 82 D6
Haugh Head *Nthumb* 124 C4
Haugh of Glass *Moray* 157 F3
Haugh of Urr *D & G* 110 C1
Haugham *Lincs* 86 D3
Haughhead Inn *E Duns* 130 B3
Haughley *Suffk* 64 C2
Haughley Green *Suffk* 64 C2
Haughton *Notts* 84 D2
Haughton *Powys* 69 E2
Haughton *Shrops* 69 F3
Haughton *Shrops* 69 H2
Haughton *Shrops* 70 B1
Haughton *Shrops* 57 G5
Haughton *Staffs* 70 D2
Haughton Green *Gt Man* 82 D4
Haughton le Skerne *Dur* 106 C2
Haughton Moss *Ches* 69 H6
Haultwick *Herts* 50 D3
Haunton *Staffs* 71 G1
Hautes Croix *Jersey* 174 c3
Hauxley *Nthumb* 125 F1
Hauxton *Cambs* 51 E6
Havannah *Ches* 82 D1
Havant *Hants* 15 E4
Haven *Herefs* 45 G5
Haven Bank *Lincs* 74 C5
Haven Side *E R Yk* 93 F2
Havenstreet *IOW* 14 D3
Havercroft *W York* 84 B6
Haverfordwest *Pembks* 32 D3
Haverhill *Suffk* 51 G3
Haverigg *Cumb* 94 B3
Havering-atte-Bower *Essex* 29 F5
Haversham *Bucks* 49 F3
Haverthwaite *Cumb* 94 D3
Haverton Hill *Dur* 106 D3
Havyat *Somset* 23 G5

Havyatt *Somset* 23 H3
Hawarden *Flints* 81 E1
Hawbridge *Worcs* 47 E4
Hawbush Green *Essex* 52 B3
Hawcoat *Cumb* 94 C2
Hawe's Green *Norfk* 65 E5
Hawen *Cerdgn* 42 D4
Hawford *Worcs* 46 D5
Hawick *Border* 112 B6
Hawkchurch *Devon* 10 D5
Hawkedon *Suffk* 52 B6
Hawkenbury *Kent* 18 B6
Hawkeridge *Wilts* 24 D5
Hawkerland *Devon* 9 G3
Hawkes End *W Mids* 59 F4
Hawkesbury *Gloucs* 38 B3
Hawkesbury *Warwks* 59 G4
Hawkesbury Upton *Gloucs* 38 C3
Hawkhill *Nthumb* 125 E2
Hawkhurst *Kent* 18 A4
Hawkhurst Common *E Susx* 17 F3
Hawkinge *Kent* 19 F5
Hawkley *Hants* 27 F2
Hawkridge *Somset* 22 B2
Hawksdale *Cumb* 103 H5
Hawkshaw *Gt Man* 89 F1
Hawkshead *Cumb* 94 D5
Hawkshead Hill *Cumb* 94 D5
Hawksland *S Lans* 120 C3
Hawkspur Green *Essex* 51 G4
Hawkstone *Shrops* 69 H3
Hawkswick *N York* 96 C2
Hawksworth *Notts* 73 E4
Hawksworth *W York* 90 C4
Hawkwell *Essex* 30 B5
Hawkwell *Nthumb* 114 B3
Hawley *Hants* 27 G5
Hawley *Kent* 29 F3
Hawling *Gloucs* 47 F1
Hawnby *N York* 98 A4
Haworth *W York* 90 B3
Hawstead *Suffk* 63 H1
Hawstead Green *Suffk* 63 H1
Hawthorn *Dur* 106 D5
Hawthorn *Hants* 27 E3
Hawthorn *Rhondd* 36 B3
Hawthorn Hill *Berks* 41 G2
Hawthorn Hill *Lincs* 74 C6
Hawthorpe *Lincs* 73 H3
Hawton *Notts* 73 E5
Haxby *N York* 91 G5
Haxby Gates *N York* 91 G5
Haxey *Lincs* 85 E5
Haxey Turbary *Lincs* 85 E5
Haxted *Surrey* 17 E6
Haxton *Wilts* 25 G4
Hay *Cnwll* 3 F5
Hay *Cnwll* 3 G4
Hay *Cnwll* 3 G5
Hay *Cnwll* 4 C3
Hay Green *Norfk* 75 F2
Hay Street *Herts* 51 E3
Hay-on-Wye *Powys* 45 E3
Haydock *Mersyd* 81 H4
Haydon *Dorset* 11 G6
Haydon *Somset* 23 E2
Haydon *Somset* 24 B5
Haydon Bridge *Nthumb* 113 F1
Haydon Wick *Wilts* 39 F3
Haye *Cnwll* 5 G3
Hayes *Gt Lon* 28 B4
Hayes *Gt Lon* 29 E3
Hayes End *Gt Lon* 28 B4
Hayfield *Ag & B* 137 E2
Hayfield *Derbys* 83 E3
Haygate *Shrops* 70 A1
Hayhillock *Angus* 141 E4
Hayle *Cnwll* 2 C3
Hayley Green *W Mids* 58 B4
Haymoor Green *Ches* 70 B5
Hayne *Devon* 9 F6
Hayne *Devon* 8 D3
Haynes (Church End) *Beds* 50 B5
Haynes (Northwood End) *Beds* 50 B5
Haynes (Silver End) *Beds* 50 B5
Haynes (West End) *Beds* 50 B5
Hayscastle *Pembks* 32 C4
Hayscastle Cross *Pembks* 32 C4
Haysden *Kent* 17 F6
Hayton *Cumb* 103 H4
Hayton *Cumb* 104 B6
Hayton *E R Yk* 92 B4
Hayton *Notts* 85 E3
Hayton's Bent *Shrops* 57 E3
Haytor Vale *Devon* 9 E2
Haytown *Devon* 20 D2
Haywards Heath *W Susx* 16 D4
Haywood *Herefs* 45 H3
Haywood *Herefs* 84 D6
Haywood Oaks *Notts* 72 D5
Hazards Green *E Susx* 17 H3
Hazel Grove *Gt Man* 82 D3
Hazel Street *Kent* 17 H5
Hazel Stub *Suffk* 51 G5
Hazelbank *S Lans* 120 C4
Hazelbury Bryan *Dorset* 12 A5
Hazeleigh *Essex* 52 B1
Hazeley *Hants* 27 F5
Hazelford *Notts* 73 E5
Hazelhurst *Gt Man* 83 E5
Hazelslade *Staffs* 71 E1
Hazelton Walls *Fife* 140 C2
Hazelwood *Derbys* 72 A5
Hazlemere *Bucks* 41 G4
Hazlerigg *T & W* 114 D3
Hazles *Staffs* 71 E5
Hazleton *Gloucs* 39 E6
Heacham *Norfk* 75 G4
Headbourne Worthy *Hants* 26 C2
Headcorn *Kent* 18 B6
Headingley *W York* 90 D3
Headington *Oxon* 40 D5
Headlam *Dur* 106 A3
Headland *Dur* 107 E4

Headless Cross *Worcs* 58 C2
Headlesscross *N Lans* 120 D5
Headley *Hants* 26 C5
Headley *Hants* 27 F3
Headley *Surrey* 28 C1
Headley Down *Hants* 27 F3
Headley Heath *Worcs* 58 D3
Headon *Notts* 85 E2
Heads *S Lans* 120 B4
Heads Nook *Cumb* 104 B6
Heage *Derbys* 72 A5
Healaugh *N York* 96 C5
Healaugh *N York* 91 F4
Heald Green *Gt Man* 82 C3
Heale *Devon* 21 G5
Heale *Somset* 23 E1
Heale *Somset* 23 G2
Healey *Lancs* 89 G1
Healey *N York* 97 E3
Healey *Nthumb* 114 B1
Healey *W York* 90 D1
Healeyfield *Dur* 105 G5
Healing *Lincs* 86 C6
Heamoor *Cnwll* 2 B3
Heanor *Derbys* 72 B5
Heanton Punchardon *Devon* 21 E4
Heapey *Lancs* 88 D2
Heapham *Lincs* 85 F3
Hearn *Hants* 27 F3
Hearts Delight *Kent* 30 B2
Heasley Mill *Devon* 21 G4
Heast *Highld* 143 F6
Heath *Derbys* 84 B1
Heath *W York* 91 E2
Heath and Reach *Beds* 49 G2
Heath Common *W Susx* 16 B3
Heath End *Bucks* 41 G4
Heath End *Hants* 26 B5
Heath End *Leics* 72 A2
Heath End *Surrey* 27 G4
Heath End *Warwks* 47 H5
Heath Green *Worcs* 58 D2
Heath Hall *D & G* 110 D3
Heath Hayes & Wimblebury
Staffs 71 E1
Heath Hill *Shrops* 70 C1
Heath House *Somset* 23 G4
Heath Town *W Mids* 58 B5
Heathbrook *Shrops* 70 A3
Heathcote *Derbys* 71 F6
Heathcote *Shrops* 70 B3
Heathencote *Nhants* 49 E4
Heather *Leics* 72 B1
Heathfield *Devon* 9 E2
Heathfield *E Susx* 17 G3
Heathfield *N York* 97 E2
Heathfield *Somset* 22 D2
Heathfield Village *Oxon* 40 C6
Heathrow Airport *Gt Lon* 28 B4
Heathstock *Devon* 10 C5
Heathton *Shrops* 58 A5
Heatley *Gt Man* 82 B3
Heatley *Staffs* 71 F3
Heaton *Gt Man* 82 B6
Heaton *Lancs* 88 C6
Heaton *Staffs* 82 D1
Heaton *T & W* 114 D2
Heaton *W York* 90 C3
Heaton Chapel *Gt Man* 82 D4
Heaton Mersey *Gt Man* 82 D4
Heaton Norris *Gt Man* 82 D4
Heaton's Bridge *Lancs* 81 F6
Heaverham *Kent* 29 F2
Heavitree *Devon* 9 F4
Hebburn *T & W* 115 E2
Hebden *N York* 90 A6
Hebden Bridge *W York* 90 A2
Hebden Green *Ches* 82 A1
Hebing End *Herts* 50 D3
Hebron *Carmth* 33 F4
Hebron *IOA* 78 D3
Hebron *Nthumb* 114 D4
Heckfield *Hants* 27 E5
Heckfield Green *Suffk* 64 D3
Heckfordbridge *Essex* 52 C3
Heckington *Lincs* 74 B4
Heckmondwike *W York* 90 C2
Heddington *Wilts* 25 E6
Heddon-on-the-Wall *Nthumb* 114 C2
Hedenham *Norfk* 65 F5
Hedge End *Hants* 14 C5
Hedgerley *Bucks* 41 H3
Hedgerley Green *Bucks* 41 H3
Hedging *Somset* 23 F2
Hedley on the Hill *Nthumb* 114 B1
Hednesford *Staffs* 71 E1
Hedon *E R Yk* 93 F2
Hedsor *Bucks* 41 G3
Hegdon Hill *Herefs* 46 A5
Heglibister *Shet* 169 h3
Heighington *Dur* 106 B3
Heighington *Lincs* 85 H2
Heightington *Worcs* 57 H2
Heiton *Border* 122 D2
Hele *Cnwll* 5 F6
Hele *Devon* 21 E5
Hele *Devon* 9 G5
Hele *Devon* 7 E5
Hele *Somset* 23 E2
Hele Lane *Devon* 21 H2
Helebridge *Cnwll* 20 B1
Helensburgh *Ag & B* 128 D3
Helenton *S Ayrs* 119 F2
Helford *Cnwll* 3 E2
Helford Passage *Cnwll* 3 E2
Helhoughton *Norfk* 76 B3
Helions Bumpstead *Essex* 51 G5
Hell Corner *Berks* 26 B6
Hellaby *S York* 84 C4
Helland *Cnwll* 4 D3
Hellandbridge *Cnwll* 4 D3
Hellescott *Cnwll* 5 F6
Hellesdon *Norfk* 77 E1
Hellesveor *Cnwll* 2 C4
Hellidon *Nhants* 48 C5
Hellifield *N York* 89 G5
Hellingly *E Susx* 17 G3

Hellington *Norfk* 65 F6
Helm *Nthumb* 114 D5
Helmdon *Nhants* 48 D4
Helme *W York* 83 F6
Helmingham *Suffk* 64 D1
Helmington Row *Dur* 106 A4
Helmsdale *Highld* 163 G5
Helmshore *Lancs* 89 F2
Helmsley *N York* 98 B3
Helperby *N York* 97 G2
Helperthorpe *N York* 99 E2
Helpringham *Lincs* 74 B4
Helpston *Cambs* 61 G6
Helsby *Ches* 81 G2
Helsey *Lincs* 87 E2
Helston *Cnwll* 2 D2
Helstone *Cnwll* 4 D4
Helton *Cumb* 104 B2
Helwith *N York* 96 D5
Helwith Bridge *N York* 96 A2
Hemblington *Norfk* 77 F1
Hemel Hempstead *Herts* 50 B1
Hemerdon *Devon* 6 C3
Hemingbrough *N York* 91 H3
Hemingby *Lincs* 86 C2
Hemingfield *S York* 84 B5
Hemingford Abbots *Cambs* 62 B2
Hemingford Grey *Cambs* 62 B2
Hemingstone *Suffk* 53 E6
Hemington *Nhants* 61 G4
Hemington *Somset* 24 C5
Hemley *Suffk* 53 F5
Hemlington *N York* 106 D2
Hempholme *E R Yk* 93 E5
Hempnall *Norfk* 65 E5
Hempnall Green *Norfk* 65 E5
Hempriggs *Moray* 156 C5
Hempstead *Essex* 51 G4
Hempstead *Kent* 30 B2
Hempstead *Norfk* 76 D4
Hempstead *Norfk* 77 G3
Hempsted *Gloucs* 38 C6
Hempton *Norfk* 76 B3
Hempton *Oxon* 48 C2
Hemsby *Norfk* 77 H2
Hemswell *Lincs* 85 G4
Hemswell Cliff *Lincs* 85 G4
Hemsworth *W York* 84 B6
Hemyock *Devon* 10 B6
Henbury *Bristl* 37 G2
Henbury *Ches* 82 D2
Hendersyde Park *Border* 123 E3
Hendham *Devon* 7 E3
Hendomen *Powys* 56 B5
Hendon *Gt Lon* 28 C5
Hendon *T & W* 115 F1
Hendra *Cnwll* 3 E3
Hendra *Cnwll* 4 D3
Hendre *Brdgnd* 35 G2
Hendre *Flints* 80 D1
Hendre Mons* 37 F6
Hendy *Carmth* 34 C5
Heneglwys *IOA* 78 D2
Henfield *W Susx* 16 C3
Henford *Devon* 5 G5
Henghurst *Kent* 18 C5
Hengoed *Caerph* 36 C4
Hengoed *Powys* 45 E4
Hengoed *Shrops* 69 E3
Hengrave *Suffk* 63 G2
Henham *Essex* 51 F3
Henhurst *Kent* 29 G3
Heniarth *Powys* 56 B6
Henlade *Somset* 23 E2
Henley *Dorset* 11 G5
Henley *Gloucs* 38 D6
Henley *Shrops* 57 E4
Henley *Shrops* 57 F3
Henley *Somset* 23 G2
Henley *Suffk* 53 E6
Henley *W Susx* 27 G2
Henley Green *W Mids* 59 F3
Henley Park *Surrey* 27 G4
Henley Street *Kent* 29 G3
Henley's Down *E Susx* 17 H3
Henley-in-Arden *Warwks* 58 D2
Henley-on-Thames *Oxon* 41 F2
Henllan *Cerdgn* 42 D3
Henllan *Denbgs* 80 C1
Henllan Amgoed *Carmth* 33 F4
Henllys *Torfn* 36 D3
Henlow *Beds* 50 C4
Hennock *Devon* 9 E3
Henny Street *Essex* 52 B4
Henry's Moat (Castell Hendre)
Pembks 33 E4
Henryd *Conwy* 79 G2
Hensall *N York* 91 G2
Henshaw *Nthumb* 113 E1
Hensingham *Cumb* 102 D2
Henstead *Suffk* 65 G4
Hensting *Hants* 26 C1
Henstridge *Somset* 24 C1
Henstridge Ash *Somset* 24 C1
Henstridge Marsh *Somset* 24 C1
Henton *Oxon* 41 F4
Henton *Somset* 23 H4
Henwick *Worcs* 46 D5
Henwood *Cnwll* 5 F3
Henwood *Oxon* 40 C4
Heol Senni *Powys* 44 B1
Heol-las *Swans* 34 D4
Heol-y-Cyw *Brdgnd* 35 G3
Hepburn *Nthumb* 124 D3
Hepple *Nthumb* 113 G5
Hepscott *Nthumb* 114 D4
Heptonstall *W York* 90 A2
Hepworth *Suffk* 64 B3
Hepworth *W York* 83 F5
Herbrandston *Pembks* 32 C2
Hereford *Herefs* 45 H3
Hereson *Kent* 31 G5
Hcribusta *Highld* 150 D0
Heriot *Border* 122 A3
Hermiston *C Edin* 131 H2
Hermit Hill *S York* 83 H5
Hermitage *Berks* 40 C1
Hermitage *Border* 112 B4

Hermitage *Dorset* 11 G5
Hermitage *Hants* 15 F4
Hermon *IOA* 78 D2
Hermon *Pembks* 42 B2
Herne *Kent* 31 E3
Herne Bay *Kent* 31 E3
Herne Common *Kent* 31 E2
Herne Hill *Gt Lon* 28 D3
Herne Pound *Kent* 29 G1
Herner *Devon* 21 F3
Hernhill *Kent* 30 D2
Herodsfoot *Cnwll* 5 F2
Heronden *Kent* 31 F1
Herongate *Essex* 29 G5
Heronsford *S Ayrs* 108 C3
Heronsgate *Herts* 28 A5
Herriard *Hants* 27 E4
Herring's Green *Beds* 50 B5
Herringfleet *Suffk* 65 G5
Herringswell *Suffk* 63 F2
Herringthorpe *S York* 84 B4
Herrington *T & W* 106 C6
Hersden *Kent* 31 F2
Hersham *Cnwll* 20 C1
Hersham *Surrey* 28 B2
Herstmonceux *E Susx* 17 G3
Herston *Dorset* 12 D2
Herston *Ork* 169 b1
Hertford *Herts* 50 D2
Hertford Heath *Herts* 50 D2
Hertingfordbury *Herts* 50 D2
Hesket Newmarket *Cumb* 103 G4
Hesketh Bank *Lancs* 88 C2
Hesketh Lane *Lancs* 89 E4
Heskin Green *Lancs* 88 D1
Hesleden *Dur* 106 D5
Hesleden *N York* 96 B2
Hesley *S York* 84 D4
Hesleyside *Nthumb* 113 E3
Heslington *N York* 91 G5
Hessay *N York* 91 F5
Hessenford *Cnwll* 5 G2
Hessett *Suffk* 64 B1
Hessle *E R Yk* 92 D2
Hessle *W York* 91 E1
Hest Bank *Lancs* 95 E1
Hestley Green *Suffk* 64 D2
Heston *Gt Lon* 28 B4
Hestwall *Ork* 169 a3
Heswall *Mersyd* 81 E3
Hethe *Oxon* 48 D2
Hethersett *Norfk* 64 D6
Hethersgill *Cumb* 112 B1
Hetherside *Cumb* 112 B1
Hetherson Green *Ches* 69 G5
Hethpool *Nthumb* 123 F2
Hett *Dur* 106 B4
Hetton *N York* 89 H5
Hetton Steads *Nthumb* 123 G3
Hetton-le-Hole *T & W* 106 C6
Heugh *Nthumb* 114 C3
Heugh Head *Border* 123 F6
Heughhead *Abers* 148 B6
Heveningham *Suffk* 65 F3
Hever *Kent* 17 F6
Heversham *Cumb* 95 F3
Hevingham *Norfk* 77 E2
Hewas Water *Cnwll* 3 G5
Hewelsfield *Gloucs* 37 G4
Hewenden *W York* 90 B3
Hewish *Somset* 23 G6
Hewish *Somset* 11 E5
Hewood *Dorset* 10 D5
Hexham *Nthumb* 113 F1
Hextable *Kent* 29 F3
Hexthorpe *S York* 84 C5
Hexton *Herts* 50 B4
Hexworthy *Cnwll* 5 G4
Hexworthy *Devon* 6 D5
Hey *Lancs* 89 G4
Hey Houses *Lancs* 88 B2
Heybridge *Essex* 52 B1
Heybridge *Essex* 29 G6
Heybridge Basin *Essex* 52 B1
Heybrook Bay *Devon* 6 B2
Heydon *Cambs* 51 E5
Heydon *Norfk* 76 D3
Heydour *Lincs* 73 H4
Heyhead *Gt Man* 82 C3
Heylipoll *Ag & B* 134 B4
Heylor *Shet* 169 h4
Heyrod *Gt Man* 83 E5
Heysham *Lancs* 88 C6
Heyshaw *N York* 90 C6
Heyshott *W Susx* 15 G5
Heyside *Gt Man* 82 D5
Heytesbury *Wilts* 25 E3
Heythrop *Oxon* 48 B2
Heywood *Gt Man* 82 D6
Heywood *Wilts* 24 D5
Hibaldstow *Lincs* 85 G5
Hickleton *S York* 84 B5
Hickling *Norfk* 77 G2
Hickling *Notts* 73 E3
Hickling Green *Norfk* 77 G2
Hickling Heath *Norfk* 77 G2
Hickmans Green *Kent* 30 D2
Hicks Forstal *Kent* 31 E2
Hickstead *W Susx* 16 D3
Hidcote Bartrim *Gloucs* 47 G3
Hidcote Boyce *Gloucs* 47 G3
High Ackworth *W York* 91 E1
High Angerton *Nthumb* 114 C4
High Ardwell *D & G* 100 B5
High Bankhill *Cumb* 104 B4
High Beach *Essex* 29 E6
High Bentham *N York* 95 G2
High Bewaldeth *Cumb* 103 F3
High Bickington *Devon* 21 F3
High Biggins *Cumb* 95 G3
High Blantyre *S Lans* .... 120 Ab
High Bonnybridge *Falk* 131 E3
High Borrans *Cumb* 95 E5
High Bradley *N York* 90 A4
High Bray *Devon* 21 G4
High Brooms *Kent* 17 G6

High Bullen Devon ... 21 E3
High Buston Nthumb ... 125 E2
High Callerton Nthumb ... 114 C3
High Casterton Cumb ... 95 G3
High Catton E R Yk ... 92 A5
High Close N York ... 106 A2
High Cogges Oxon ... 40 B5
High Common Norfk ... 64 B6
High Coniscliffe Dur ... 106 B2
High Crosby Cumb ... 104 A6
High Cross Cnwll ... 3 E3
High Cross E Ayrs ... 119 F4
High Cross Essex ... 27 E2
High Cross Herts ... 50 D3
High Cross W Susx ... 16 C3
High Cross Warwks ... 59 E2
High Cross Bank Derbys ... 71 H2
High Dubmire T & W ... 106 C6
High Drummore D & G ... 100 C4
High Easter Essex ... 51 G2
High Eggborough N York ... 91 G2
High Ellington N York ... 97 E3
High Ercall Shrops ... 70 A2
High Etherley Dur ... 106 A4
High Ferry Lincs ... 74 D5
High Flats W York ... 83 G5
High Garrett Essex ... 52 A3
High Grange Dur ... 106 A4
High Grantley N York ... 97 E2
High Green Cumb ... 95 E5
High Green Norfk ... 64 D6
High Green Norfk ... 64 D4
High Green Norfk ... 65 E5
High Green S York ... 84 A4
High Green Shrops ... 57 G4
High Green Suffk ... 63 H1
High Green W York ... 90 C1
High Green Worcs ... 46 D4
High Halden Kent ... 18 C5
High Halstow Kent ... 30 A4
High Ham Somset ... 23 G2
High Harrington Cumb ... 102 D3
High Harrogate N York ... 90 D5
High Haswell Dur ... 106 C5
High Hatton Shrops ... 70 A2
High Hawsker N York ... 99 E6
High Hesket Cumb ... 104 B5
High Hoyland S York ... 83 H6
High Hunsley E R Yk ... 92 C3
High Hutton N York ... 98 C2
High Ireby Cumb ... 103 F4
High Kelling Norfk ... 76 D4
High Kilburn N York ... 98 A3
High Killerby N York ... 99 F3
High Knipe Cumb ... 104 D3
High Lands Dur ... 105 H3
High Lane Gt Man ... 82 D3
High Lanes Cnwll ... 2 C3
High Laver Essex ... 51 F2
High Legh Ches ... 82 B3
High Leven N York ... 106 D2
High Littleton Somset ... 24 B5
High Lorton Cumb ... 103 F3
High Marnham Notts ... 85 F2
High Melton S York ... 84 C5
High Mickley Nthumb ... 114 B2
High Moorsley T & W ... 106 C5
High Newport T & W ... 115 E1
High Newton Cumb ... 95 E3
High Nibthwaite Cumb ... 94 D4
High Offley Staffs ... 70 C3
High Ongar Essex ... 51 F1
High Onn Staffs ... 70 C2
High Park Corner Essex ... 52 D3
High Pennyvenie E Ayrs ... 109 G5
High Post Wilts ... 25 G3
High Roding Essex ... 51 G2
High Row Cumb ... 103 G4
High Row Cumb ... 103 H2
High Salter Lancs ... 88 D6
High Salvington W Susx ... 16 B2
High Scales Cumb ... 103 F5
High Seaton Cumb ... 102 C3
High Shaw N York ... 96 B4
High Side Cumb ... 103 F3
High Spen T & W ... 114 C1
High Stoop Dur ... 105 H4
High Street Cnwll ... 3 G5
High Street Kent ... 18 A4
High Street Suffk ... 65 G2
High Street Suffk ... 65 G1
High Throston Dur ... 106 D4
High Town Staffs ... 71 E1
High Toynton Lincs ... 86 C2
High Trewhitt Nthumb ... 113 G5
High Urpeth Dur ... 114 D1
High Valleyfield Fife ... 131 G4
High Warden Nthumb ... 113 F1
High Westwood Dur ... 105 H6
High Woolaston Gloucs ... 37 G4
High Worsall N York ... 106 C2
High Wray Cumb ... 94 D5
High Wych Herts ... 51 E2
High Wycombe Bucks ... 41 G4
Higham Derbys ... 72 B6
Higham Kent ... 17 G6
Higham Kent ... 29 H3
Higham Lancs ... 89 F3
Higham S York ... 83 H5
Higham Suffk ... 63 G2
Higham Suffk ... 52 D4
Higham Dykes Nthumb ... 114 C3
Higham Ferrers Nhants ... 61 F2
Higham Gobion Beds ... 50 B4
Higham Hill Gt Lon ... 28 D5
Higham on the Hill Leics ... 59 G5
Highampton Devon ... 8 B5
Highams Park Gt Lon ... 29 E5
Highbridge Hants ... 26 C1
Highbridge Somset ... 23 F4
Highbrook W Susx ... 16 D4
Highburton W York ... 83 G6
Highbury Gt Lon ... 28 D5
Highbury Somset ... 24 B4
Highclere Hants ... 26 C5
Highcliffe Dorset ... 13 F4
Highcross Lancs ... 88 B3

Higher Alham Somset ... 24 B3
Higher Ansty Dorset ... 12 B5
Higher Ballam Lancs ... 88 B3
Higher Bartle Lancs ... 88 C3
Higher Berry End Beds ... 49 H3
Higher Bockhampton Dorset ... 11 G4
Higher Brixham Devon ... 7 F3
Higher Burrowton Devon ... 9 G4
Higher Burwardsley Ches ... 69 G6
Higher Chillington Somset ... 10 D6
Higher Clovelly Devon ... 20 C3
Higher Combe Somset ... 22 B2
Higher Coombe Dorset ... 11 F4
Higher Disley Ches ... 83 E3
Higher Gabwell Devon ... 7 F4
Higher Halstock Leigh Dorset ... 11 E5
Higher Harpers Lancs ... 89 G3
Higher Heysham Lancs ... 88 C6
Higher Hurdsfield Ches ... 82 D2
Higher Irlam Gt Man ... 82 B4
Higher Kingcombe Dorset ... 11 F5
Higher Kinnerton Flints ... 69 F6
Higher Melcombe Dorset ... 12 A5
Higher Muddiford Devon ... 21 F4
Higher Nyland Dorset ... 24 C1
Higher Ogden Gt Man ... 82 D6
Higher Pentire Cnwll ... 2 D2
Higher Penwortham Lancs ... 88 D2
Higher Studfold N York ... 96 A2
Higher Town Cnwll ... 3 F4
Higher Town Cnwll ... 4 D2
Higher Town IOS ... 2 b2
Higher Tregantle Cnwll ... 5 G1
Higher Walton Ches ... 82 A3
Higher Walton Lancs ... 88 D2
Higher Wambrook Somset ... 10 C5
Higher Waterston Dorset ... 11 G4
Higher Whatcombe Dorset ... 12 B5
Higher Wheelton Lancs ... 88 D2
Higher Whiteleigh Cnwll ... 5 F5
Higher Whitley Ches ... 82 A3
Higher Wraxhall Dorset ... 11 F5
Higher Wych Ches ... 69 G4
Higherford Lancs ... 89 G4
Highfield Devon ... 8 D4
Highfield E R Yk ... 92 A3
Highfield N Ayrs ... 119 E4
Highfield T & W ... 114 C1
Highfields S York ... 84 C5
Highgate E Susx ... 17 E5
Highgate Gt Lon ... 28 D5
Highgate Head Derbys ... 83 E3
Highgreen Manor Nthumb ... 113 E4
Highlane Ches ... 82 D1
Highlane S York ... 84 B3
Highlaws Cumb ... 103 E5
Highleadon Gloucs ... 46 C1
Highleigh W Susx ... 15 G3
Highley Shrops ... 57 G4
Highmoor Cumb ... 103 G5
Highmoor Oxon ... 41 E3
Highmoor Cross Oxon ... 41 E3
Highmoor Hill Mons ... 37 F3
Higham Gloucs ... 46 C1
Higham Green Gloucs ... 46 C1
Highridge Somset ... 24 A6
Highstead Kent ... 31 F3
Highstead Kent ... 30 C2
Highstreet Kent ... 30 D2
Highstreet Green Essex ... 52 A4
Highstreet Green Surrey ... 27 H3
Hightae D & G ... 111 E3
Highter's Heath W Mids ... 58 D3
Hightown Ches ... 82 D1
Hightown Hants ... 13 E5
Hightown Mersyd ... 81 E5
Hightown Green Suffk ... 64 B1
Highway Herefs ... 45 G4
Highway Wilts ... 39 E2
Highweek Devon ... 7 F5
Highwood Staffs ... 71 F3
Highwood Hill Gt Lon ... 28 C5
Highworth Wilts ... 39 G3
Hilborough Norfk ... 63 G5
Hilcote Derbys ... 72 B6
Hilden Park Kent ... 17 G6
Hildenborough Kent ... 29 F1
Hildersham Cambs ... 51 F6
Hilderstone Staffs ... 70 D3
Hilderthorpe E R Yk ... 99 G1
Hilfield Dorset ... 11 G5
Hilgay Norfk ... 63 G5
Hill Gloucs ... 37 G4
Hill Warwks ... 59 G2
Hill Brow Hants ... 27 F2
Hill Chorlton Staffs ... 70 C4
Hill Common Norfk ... 77 G2
Hill Common Somset ... 22 D2
Hill Deverill Wilts ... 24 D3
Hill Dyke Lincs ... 74 D5
Hill End Dur ... 105 G4
Hill End Fife ... 131 G5
Hill End Gloucs ... 47 E3
Hill Green Kent ... 30 B2
Hill Head Hants ... 14 D4
Hill of Beath Fife ... 131 H4
Hill of Fearn Highld ... 163 E1
Hill of Tarvit Mansion House Fife ... 140 D1
Hill Ridware Staffs ... 71 F2
Hill Side W York ... 90 C1
Hill Side Worcs ... 46 C5
Hill Top Dur ... 105 G2
Hill Top Hants ... 14 B4
Hill Top S York ... 84 B4
Hill Top W Mids ... 58 C5
Hill Top W York ... 83 F6
Hill Top W York ... 90 D1
Hillam N York ... 91 F2
Hillbeck Dur ... 105 E2
Hillborough Kent ... 31 F3
Hillbutts Dorset ... 12 D5
Hillclifflane Derbys ... 71 H5
Hillcott Wilts ... 25 G3
Hillend Fife ... 131 H3
Hillend Mdloth ... 132 B2
Hillend N Lans ... 131 E2
Hillend Swans ... 34 B3

Hillersland Gloucs ... 37 G6
Hillerton Devon ... 8 D4
Hillesden Bucks ... 49 E2
Hillesley Gloucs ... 38 B3
Hillfarrance Somset ... 22 D2
Hillgrove W Susx ... 27 G2
Hillhampton Herefs ... 46 B4
Hillhead Devon ... 7 F3
Hillhead S Lans ... 120 D3
Hillhead of Cocklaw Abers ... 159 G3
Hillhead of Durno Abers ... 158 C2
Hilliard's Cross Staffs ... 71 F1
Hilliclay Highld ... 167 E5
Hillingdon Gt Lon ... 28 B4
Hillington C Glas ... 129 G1
Hillington Norfk ... 75 G2
Hillis Corner IOW ... 14 C3
Hillmorton Warwks ... 60 A3
Hillock Vale Lancs ... 89 F3
Hillowton D & G ... 110 B1
Hillpool Worcs ... 58 B3
Hillpound Hants ... 14 D5
Hills Town Derbys ... 84 B2
Hillside Abers ... 149 G4
Hillside Angus ... 141 G6
Hillside Devon ... 6 D4
Hillstreet Hants ... 13 G6
Hillswick Shet ... 169 h4
Hilltown Devon ... 8 B3
Hilltown E Loth ... 132 B2
Hillwell Shet ... 169 h1
Hilmarton Wilts ... 39 E2
Hilperton Wilts ... 24 D5
Hilperton Marsh Wilts ... 24 D5
Hilsea Hants ... 15 E4
Hilston E R Yk ... 93 G3
Hilston Park Mons ... 45 G1
Hiltingbury Hants ... 26 C1
Hilton Border ... 123 F4
Hilton Cambs ... 62 B3
Hilton Cumb ... 104 D2
Hilton Derbys ... 71 G3
Hilton Dorset ... 12 B5
Hilton Dur ... 106 A3
Hilton Highld ... 163 E1
Hilton N York ... 106 D2
Hilton Shrops ... 57 H5
Himbleton Worcs ... 47 E5
Himley Staffs ... 58 B4
Hincaster Cumb ... 95 F3
Hinchley Wood Surrey ... 28 B3
Hinckley Leics ... 59 G5
Hinderclay Suffk ... 64 C3
Hinderwell N York ... 107 G2
Hindford Shrops ... 69 G3
Hindhead Surrey ... 27 G3
Hindle Fold Lancs ... 89 F3
Hindley Gt Man ... 82 A5
Hindley Nthumb ... 114 B1
Hindley Green Gt Man ... 82 A5
Hindlip Worcs ... 46 D5
Hindolveston Norfk ... 76 C3
Hindon Wilts ... 25 E2
Hindringham Norfk ... 76 C4
Hingham Norfk ... 64 C6
Hinksford Staffs ... 58 B4
Hinnington Shrops ... 57 H6
Hinstock Shrops ... 70 B3
Hintlesham Suffk ... 52 D5
Hinton Gloucs ... 38 B5
Hinton Gloucs ... 38 B2
Hinton Hants ... 13 F4
Hinton Herefs ... 45 F3
Hinton Shrops ... 57 G4
Hinton Admiral Hants ... 13 F4
Hinton Ampner Hants ... 26 D2
Hinton Blewett Somset ... 24 B5
Hinton Charterhouse Somset ... 24 C5
Hinton Green Worcs ... 47 F3
Hinton Marsh Hants ... 26 D2
Hinton Martell Dorset ... 12 D5
Hinton on the Green Worcs ... 47 F3
Hinton Parva Wilts ... 39 G3
Hinton St George Somset ... 11 E6
Hinton St Mary Dorset ... 12 B6
Hinton Waldrist Oxon ... 40 B4
Hinton-in-the-Hedges Nhants ... 48 D3
Hints Shrops ... 57 F3
Hints Staffs ... 58 D6
Hinwick Beds ... 49 G5
Hinxhill Kent ... 18 D6
Hinxton Cambs ... 51 F5
Hinxworth Herts ... 50 D5
Hipperholme W York ... 90 B2
Hipsburn Nthumb ... 125 E3
Hipswell N York ... 97 E5
Hirn Abers ... 149 E4
Hirnant Powys ... 68 C2
Hirst Nthumb ... 114 D4
Hirst Courtney N York ... 91 G2
Hirwaen Denbgs ... 68 D6
Hirwaun Rhondd ... 36 B3
Hiscott Devon ... 21 F3
Histon Cambs ... 62 D2
Hitcham Suffk ... 52 C6
Hitcham Causeway Suffk ... 52 C6
Hitcham Street Suffk ... 52 C6
Hitchin Herts ... 50 C5
Hither Green Gt Lon ... 29 E3
Hittisleigh Devon ... 8 D4
Hittisleigh Cross Devon ... 8 D4
Hive E R Yk ... 92 B3
Hixon Staffs ... 71 E3
Hoaden Kent ... 31 F2
Hoar Cross Staffs ... 71 F2
Hoarwithy Herefs ... 46 A2
Hoath Kent ... 31 F2
Hoathly Kent ... 17 G5
Hobarris Shrops ... 56 C3
Hobbles Green Suffk ... 51 H6
Hobbs Cross Essex ... 29 F6
Hobbs Cross Essex ... 51 F2
Hobkirk Border ... 112 C6
Hobland Hall Norfk ... 65 G5
Hobsic Notts ... 72 B5
Hobson Dur ... 114 C1
Hoby Leics ... 72 D2

Hoccombe Somset ... 22 D2
Hockering Norfk ... 76 D1
Hockerton Notts ... 73 E6
Hockley Ches ... 82 D3
Hockley Essex ... 30 B5
Hockley Staffs ... 59 E5
Hockley W Mids ... 59 F3
Hockley Heath W Mids ... 58 D3
Hockliffe Beds ... 49 H2
Hockwold cum Wilton Norfk ... 63 F4
Hockworthy Devon ... 22 C1
Hoddesdon Herts ... 51 E1
Hoddlesden Lancs ... 89 F2
Hoddom Cross D & G ... 111 F2
Hoddom Mains D & G ... 111 F2
Hodgehill Ches ... 82 C2
Hodgeston Pembks ... 32 D2
Hodnet Shrops ... 70 A3
Hodsall Street Kent ... 29 G2
Hodsock Notts ... 84 D3
Hodson Wilts ... 39 F2
Hodthorpe Derbys ... 84 C2
Hoe Hants ... 14 D5
Hoe Norfk ... 76 C2
Hoe Gate Hants ... 14 D5
Hoff Cumb ... 104 C2
Hog Hill E Susx ... 18 B3
Hogben's Hill Kent ... 30 D2
Hoggards Green Suffk ... 64 A1
Hoggeston Bucks ... 49 F2
Hoggrill's End Warwks ... 59 E5
Hoghton Lancs ... 89 E2
Hoghton Bottoms Lancs ... 89 E2
Hognaston Derbys ... 71 G5
Hogsthorpe Lincs ... 87 F2
Holbeach Lincs ... 74 D2
Holbeach Bank Lincs ... 74 D3
Holbeach Clough Lincs ... 74 D3
Holbeach Drove Lincs ... 74 D1
Holbeach Hurn Lincs ... 74 D2
Holbeach St Johns Lincs ... 74 D2
Holbeach St Mark's Lincs ... 74 D3
Holbeach St Matthew Lincs ... 74 D3
Holbeck Notts ... 84 C2
Holbeck Woodhouse Notts ... 84 C2
Holberrow Green Worcs ... 47 F5
Holbeton Devon ... 6 D3
Holborn Gt Lon ... 28 D4
Holborough Kent ... 29 H2
Holbrook Derbys ... 72 A4
Holbrook Suffk ... 53 E4
Holbrook Moor Derbys ... 72 A5
Holburn Nthumb ... 123 G3
Holbury Hants ... 14 C4
Holcombe Devon ... 9 F2
Holcombe Gt Man ... 89 F1
Holcombe Somset ... 24 B4
Holcombe Brook Gt Man ... 89 F1
Holcombe Rogus Devon ... 22 C1
Holcot Nhants ... 60 D2
Holden Lancs ... 89 F4
Holden Gate W York ... 89 G2
Holdenby Nhants ... 60 C2
Holder's Green Essex ... 51 G4
Holdgate Shrops ... 57 F4
Holdingham Lincs ... 74 A5
Holditch Dorset ... 10 D5
Holdsworth W York ... 90 B2
Hole Devon ... 20 D1
Hole Park Kent ... 18 B5
Hole Street W Susx ... 16 B3
Hole-in-the-Wall Herefs ... 46 B2
Holehouse Derbys ... 83 E4
Holemoor Devon ... 20 D1
Holford Somset ... 22 D3
Holgate N York ... 91 G5
Holker Cumb ... 94 D2
Holkham Norfk ... 76 B4
Holkham Hall Norfk ... 76 B4
Hollacombe Devon ... 5 G6
Holland Fen Lincs ... 74 C5
Holland Lees Lancs ... 81 G5
Holland-on-Sea Essex ... 53 E2
Hollandstoun Ork ... 169 d4
Hollee D & G ... 111 G2
Hollesley Suffk ... 53 G5
Hollicombe Devon ... 7 F4
Hollies Hill Worcs ... 58 B3
Hollin Green Ches ... 70 A5
Hollingbourne Kent ... 30 B1
Hollingbury E Susx ... 16 D2
Hollingdon Bucks ... 49 G2
Hollington Derbys ... 71 G4
Hollington Derbys ... 71 G4
Hollingworth Gt Man ... 83 E4
Hollinlane Ches ... 82 C3
Hollins Derbys ... 83 H2
Hollins Gt Man ... 82 C5
Hollins S York ... 84 B3
Hollins End S York ... 84 B3
Hollins Green Ches ... 82 B4
Hollins Lane Lancs ... 88 C5
Hollinsclough Staffs ... 83 F1
Hollinswood Shrops ... 70 B1
Hollinwood Gt Man ... 82 D5
Hollinwood Shrops ... 69 G4
Hollocombe Devon ... 21 F2
Holloway Derbys ... 72 A6
Holloway Gt Lon ... 28 D5
Holloway Wilts ... 24 D2
Hollowell Nhants ... 60 C1
Hollowmoor Heath Ches ... 81 G1
Hollows D & G ... 112 A3
Holly End Norfk ... 62 D6
Holly Green Worcs ... 46 D3
Hollybush Caerph ... 36 C5
Hollybush E Ayrs ... 119 F1
Hollybush Herefs ... 46 C3
Hollyhurst Ches ... 69 H4
Hollym E R Yk ... 93 G2
Hollywood Worcs ... 58 D3
Holmbridge W York ... 83 F5
Holmbury St Mary Surrey ... 16 B6
Holmbush Cnwll ... 3 H5
Holmcroft Staffs ... 70 D4

Holme Cambs ... 61 H4
Holme Cumb ... 95 F3
Holme Lincs ... 85 G5
Holme N York ... 97 G3
Holme Notts ... 73 F6
Holme W York ... 83 F5
Holme Chapel Lancs ... 89 G2
Holme Green N York ... 91 G4
Holme Hale Norfk ... 64 A6
Holme Lacy Herefs ... 46 A4
Holme Marsh Herefs ... 45 F5
Holme next the Sea Norfk ... 75 G4
Holme on the Wolds E R Yk ... 92 C4
Holme Pierrepont Notts ... 72 D4
Holme St Cuthbert Cumb ... 103 E5
Holme upon Spalding Moor E R Yk ... 92 B3
Holmer Herefs ... 45 H3
Holmer Green Bucks ... 41 G4
Holmes Chapel Ches ... 82 C1
Holmes Hill E Susx ... 17 F3
Holmesfield Derbys ... 83 H2
Holmeswood Lancs ... 88 C1
Holmewood Derbys ... 84 B1
Holmfield W York ... 90 B2
Holmfirth W York ... 83 F5
Holmgate Derbys ... 84 A1
Holmhead E Ayrs ... 119 G1
Holmpton E R Yk ... 93 G2
Holmrook Cumb ... 94 B5
Holmsey Green Suffk ... 63 F3
Holmshurst E Susx ... 17 G3
Holmside Dur ... 106 B6
Holmwrangle Cumb ... 104 B5
Holne Devon ... 6 D4
Holnest Dorset ... 11 G6
Holnicote Somset ... 22 B4
Holsworthy Devon ... 20 D1
Holsworthy Beacon Devon ... 20 D1
Holt Dorset ... 12 D5
Holt Norfk ... 76 D4
Holt Wilts ... 24 D5
Holt Worcs ... 58 A2
Holt Wrexhm ... 69 F5
Holt End Worcs ... 58 D2
Holt Fleet Worcs ... 58 A2
Holt Green Lancs ... 81 F5
Holt Heath Dorset ... 12 D5
Holt Heath Worcs ... 58 A2
Holt Street Kent ... 31 F1
Holtby N York ... 91 H5
Holton Oxon ... 40 D5
Holton Somset ... 24 B2
Holton Suffk ... 65 F3
Holton cum Beckering Lincs ... 86 B3
Holton Heath Dorset ... 12 C4
Holton Hill E Susx ... 17 G4
Holton le Clay Lincs ... 86 C5
Holton le Moor Lincs ... 86 A4
Holton St Mary Suffk ... 52 D4
Holtye E Susx ... 17 E5
Holway Flints ... 80 D2
Holwell Dorset ... 11 G6
Holwell Herts ... 50 C4
Holwell Leics ... 73 E2
Holwell Oxon ... 39 G5
Holwick Dur ... 105 F3
Holworth Dorset ... 12 B3
Holy Cross Worcs ... 58 B3
Holy Island Nthumb ... 124 D5
Holybourne Hants ... 27 E3
Holyfield Essex ... 51 E1
Holyhead IOA ... 78 B3
Holymoorside Derbys ... 84 A2
Holyport Berks ... 41 G2
Holystone Nthumb ... 113 G5
Holytown N Lans ... 120 B5
Holywell Cambs ... 62 C2
Holywell Cnwll ... 4 A4
Holywell Dorset ... 11 F5
Holywell Flints ... 80 D2
Holywell Nthumb ... 115 E3
Holywell Warwks ... 59 E2
Holywell Green W York ... 90 B1
Holywell Lake Somset ... 22 D1
Holywell Row Suffk ... 63 F3
Holywood D & G ... 110 D3
Holywood Village D & G ... 110 D3
Hom Green Herefs ... 46 A1
Homer Shrops ... 57 F5
Homer Green Mersyd ... 81 F5
Homersfield Suffk ... 65 E4
Homescales Cumb ... 95 F4
Homington Wilts ... 25 G2
Honey Hill Kent ... 31 E2
Honey Tye Suffk ... 52 C4
Honeyborough Pembks ... 32 D2
Honeybourne Worcs ... 47 G4
Honeychurch Devon ... 8 C5
Honeystreet Wilts ... 25 F5
Honiley Warwks ... 59 E3
Honing Norfk ... 77 F3
Honingham Norfk ... 76 D1
Honington Lincs ... 73 G4
Honington Suffk ... 64 B3
Honington Warwks ... 47 H3
Honiton Devon ... 10 B5
Honley W York ... 83 F5
Honnington Shrops ... 70 B1
Hoo Kent ... 31 F2
Hoo End Herts ... 50 C3
Hoo Green Ches ... 82 B3
Hoo Meavy Devon ... 6 C4
Hoo St Werburgh Kent ... 30 A3
Hoobrook Worcs ... 58 A3
Hood Green S York ... 83 H5
Hood Hill S York ... 84 A4
Hooe Devon ... 6 B3
Hooe E Susx ... 17 H2
Hoohill Lancs ... 88 B3
Hook Cambs ... 62 D5
Hook Devon ... 10 C5
Hook E R Yk ... 92 B2
Hook Hants ... 14 C4
Hook Hants ... 27 E5
Hook Kent ... 29 G2
Hook Pembks ... 32 D3

Hook Surrey 28 C2
Hook Wilts 39 E3
Hook Bank Worcs 46 D3
Hook End Essex 29 G6
Hook Green Kent 17 G5
Hook Norton Oxon 48 B2
Hook Street Gloucs 38 B4
Hook Street Wilts 39 E3
Hookagate Shrops 69 G1
Hooke Dorset 11 F5
Hookgate Staffs 70 B3
Hookway Devon 9 E4
Hookwood Surrey 16 D6
Hooley Surrey 28 D2
Hooley Bridge Gt Man 82 D6
Hooton Ches 81 F2
Hooton Levitt S York 84 C4
Hooton Pagnell S York 84 C5
Hooton Roberts S York 84 C4
Hop Pole Lincs 74 B1
Hopcrofts Holt Oxon 48 C2
Hope Derbys 83 G3
Hope Devon 6 D2
Hope Flints 69 E6
Hope Powys 56 C6
Hope Shrops 56 D5
Hope Shrops 57 F3
Hope Staffs 71 F5
Hope Bowdler Shrops 57 E5
Hope End Green Essex 51 G3
Hope Mansell Herefs 46 B1
Hope under Dinmore Herefs 45 H4
Hopehouse Border 121 G1
Hopeman Moray 156 D6
Hopesay Shrops 56 D4
Hopetown W York 91 E2
Hopgrove N York 91 G5
Hopperton N York 91 E5
Hopsford Warwks 59 G4
Hopstone Shrops 57 H5
Hopton Derbys 71 G5
Hopton Shrops 69 F2
Hopton Staffs 70 D3
Hopton Suffk 64 B3
Hopton Cangeford Shrops 57 F3
Hopton Castle Shrops 56 D3
Hopton on Sea Norfk 65 H5
Hopton Wafers Shrops 57 F3
Hoptonheath Shrops 56 D3
Hopwas Staffs 59 E6
Hopwood Gt Man 82 D6
Hopwood Worcs 58 C3
Horam E Susx 17 G3
Horbling Lincs 74 B3
Horbury W York 90 D1
Horcott Gloucs 39 F4
Horden Dur 106 D5
Horderley Shrops 56 D4
Hordle Hants 13 F4
Hordley Shrops 69 F3
Horeb Carmth 34 C5
Horeb Cerdgn 42 D3
Horfield Bristl 37 G2
Horham Suffk 65 E3
Horkesley Green Essex 52 C4
Horkesley Heath Essex 52 C4
Horkstow Lincs 92 D1
Horley Oxon 48 B4
Horley Surrey 16 D6
Horn Hill Bucks 28 A5
Horn Street Kent 19 E5
Hornblotton Green Somset 24 A3
Hornby Lancs 95 F2
Hornby N York 97 G5
Hornby N York 97 E4
Horncastle Lincs 86 C2
Hornchurch Gt Lon 29 F5
Horncliffe Nthumb 123 F4
Horndean Border 123 F4
Horndean Hants 15 E5
Horndon Devon 8 B3
Horndon on the Hill Essex 29 G4
Horne Surrey 16 D6
Horne Row Essex 52 A1
Horner Somset 22 B4
Horners Green Suffk 52 C5
Horney Common E Susx 17 E4
Horning Norfk 77 F2
Horninghold Leics 60 D5
Horninglow Staffs 71 G2
Horningsea Cambs 62 D2
Horningsham Wilts 24 D3
Horningtoft Norfk 76 B2
Horningtops Cnwll 5 F2
Horns Cross Devon 20 D3
Horns Cross E Susx 18 B4
Hornsbury Somset 10 D6
Hornsby Cumb 104 B5
Hornsbygate Cumb 104 B5
Hornsea E R Yk 93 F4
Hornsey Gt Lon 28 D5
Hornton Oxon 48 B4
Horpit Wilts 39 G3
Horra Shet 169 j5
Horrabridge Devon 6 C5
Horridge Devon 7 E5
Horringer Suffk 63 G1
Horringford IOW 14 D2
Horrocks Fold Gt Man 82 B6
Horrocksford Lancs 89 F4
Horsacott Devon 21 E4
Horsebridge Devon 5 G3
Horsebridge E Susx 17 G2
Horsebridge Hants 26 B2
Horsebridge Shrops 56 D6
Horsebridge Staffs 71 E5
Horsebrook Staffs 70 D1
Horsecastle Somset 23 G6
Horsedown Cnwll 2 D3
Horsegate Lincs 74 B1
Horsehay Shrops 57 G6
Horseheath Cambs 51 G5
Horsehouse N York 96 D3
Horsell Surrey 27 H5
Horseman's Green Wrexhm 69 G4
Horsenden Bucks 41 F4
Horsey Norfk 77 G2
Horsey Somset 23 E5

Horsey Corner Norfk 77 G2
Horsford Norfk 77 E2
Horsforth W York 90 D3
Horsham W Susx 16 C4
Horsham Worcs 46 C5
Horsham St Faith Norfk 77 E1
Horsington Lincs 86 B1
Horsington Somset 24 C2
Horsley Derbys 72 B4
Horsley Gloucs 38 C4
Horsley Nthumb 113 F4
Horsley Nthumb 114 C2
Horsley Cross Essex 53 E3
Horsley Woodhouse Derbys 72 B4
Horsley's Green Bucks 41 F4
Horsley-Gate Derbys 83 H2
Horsleycross Street Essex 53 E4
Horsleyhill Border 122 C1
Horsmonden Kent 17 H5
Horspath Oxon 40 D5
Horstead Norfk 77 F2
Horsted Keynes W Susx 17 E4
Horton Berks 28 A4
Horton Bucks 49 G1
Horton Dorset 12 D5
Horton Gloucs 38 B3
Horton Lancs 89 G5
Horton Nhants 49 F5
Horton Shrops 69 G3
Horton Shrops 70 B1
Horton Somset 10 D6
Horton Staffs 70 D6
Horton Surrey 28 C2
Horton Swans 34 B3
Horton Wilts 25 F6
Horton Cross Somset 10 D6
Horton Green Ches 69 G5
Horton Heath Hants 14 C5
Horton in Ribblesdale N York ... 96 A2
Horton Kirby Kent 29 F3
Horton-cum-Studley Oxon 40 D5
Horwich Gt Man 82 A6
Horwich End Derbys 83 E3
Horwood Devon 21 E3
Hoscar Lancs 81 G6
Hoscote Border 112 A6
Hose Leics 73 E3
Hosey Hill Kent 29 E1
Hosh P & K 139 F2
Hoswick Shet 169 h2
Hotham E R Yk 92 C3
Hothfield Kent 18 C6
Hoton Leics 72 C2
Hott Nthumb 113 E3
Hough Ches 70 B5
Hough Ches 82 D2
Hough End W York 90 D3
Hough Green Ches 81 G3
Hough-on-the-Hill Lincs 73 G5
Hougham Lincs 73 F4
Houghton Cambs 62 B3
Houghton Cumb 103 H6
Houghton Hants 26 B2
Houghton Nthumb 114 C2
Houghton Pembks 32 D2
Houghton W Susx 16 A2
Houghton Conquest Beds 50 A5
Houghton Gate T & W 106 B6
Houghton Green Ches 82 A4
Houghton Green E Susx 18 C4
Houghton le Side Dur 106 B3
Houghton le Spring T & W 106 C6
Houghton on the Hill Leics 60 C6
Houghton Regis Beds 50 A3
Houghton St Giles Norfk 76 B4
Hound Green Hants 27 E5
Houndslow Border 122 C4
Houndsmoor Somset 22 D2
Houndwood Border 133 G1
Hounslow Gt Lon 28 B4
Hounslow Green Essex 51 G2
Househill Highld 155 G5
Houses Hill W York 90 C1
Housesteads Roman Fort
  Nthumb 113 E2
Housieside Abers 159 E2
Houston Rens 129 E2
Houstry Highld 167 E2
Houton Ork 169 b2
Hove E Susx 16 D2
Hove Edge W York 90 C2
Hoveringham Notts 73 E5
Hoveton Norfk 77 F2
Hovingham N York 98 B2
How Caple Herefs 46 B2
How End Beds 50 A5
How Mill Cumb 104 B6
Howbrook S York 84 A4
Howden E R Yk 92 A2
Howden-le-Wear Dur 106 A4
Howe Highld 167 G5
Howe IOM 174 k2
Howe N York 97 G3
Howe Norfk 65 E5
Howe Bridge Gt Man 82 B5
Howe Green Essex 52 A1
Howe of Teuchar Abers 158 D4
Howe Street Essex 51 H2
Howe Street Essex 51 H4
Howegreen Essex 30 B6
Howell Lincs 74 B5
Howes D & G 111 F1
Howey Powys 44 C5
Howgill N York 89 G4
Howick Nthumb 125 F3
Howle Dur 105 G3
Howle Shrops 70 B2
Howle Hill Herefs 46 B1
Howlett End Essex 51 G4
Howley Somset 10 C6
Howmore W Isls 168 b3
Hownam Border 123 E1
Howrigg Cumb 103 G5
Howsham Lincs 85 H5
Howsham N York 92 A6
Howt Green Kent 30 C3
Howtel Nthumb 123 E3

Howton Devon 8 D3
Howton Herefs 45 G2
Howtown Cumb 104 A2
Howwood Rens 119 F5
Hoxne Suffk 64 D3
Hoylake Mersyd 80 D4
Hoyland Common S York 84 A5
Hoyland Nether S York 84 A5
Hoyland Swaine S York 83 G5
Hoyle W Susx 15 G5
Hoyle Mill S York 84 A5
Hubberholme N York 96 C3
Hubberston Pembks 32 C2
Hubbert's Bridge Lincs 74 C1
Huby N York 90 D4
Huby N York 98 A1
Huccaby Devon 6 D5
Hucclecote Gloucs 38 C6
Hucking Kent 30 B2
Hucknall Notts 72 C5
Huddersfield W York 90 C1
Huddington Worcs 47 E5
Hudswell N York 97 E5
Huggate E R Yk 92 C5
Hugglescote Leics 72 B1
Hugh Town IOS 2 a1
Hughenden Valley Bucks 41 G4
Hughley Shrops 57 F5
Huish Devon 21 E2
Huish Wilts 25 G6
Huish Champflower Somset 22 C2
Huish Episcopi Somset 23 G2
Hulberry Kent 29 F3
Hulcote Beds 49 G3
Hulcott Bucks 41 G6
Hulham Devon 9 G3
Hull E R Yk 93 E2
Hulland Derbys 71 G5
Hulland Ward Derbys 71 G5
Hullavington Wilts 38 D2
Hullbridge Essex 30 B6
Hulme Ches 82 A4
Hulme Gt Man 82 C4
Hulme Staffs 70 D5
Hulme End Staffs 71 F6
Hulme Walfield Ches 82 C1
Hulse Heath Ches 82 B3
Hulton Lane Ends Gt Man 82 B5
Hulver Street Norfk 76 B1
Hulver Street Suffk 65 G4
Hulverstone IOW 14 B2
Humber Devon 9 F2
Humber Herefs 46 A5
Humberside Airport Lincs 86 A6
Humberston Lincs 86 C5
Humberstone Leics 60 B6
Humberton N York 97 G2
Humbie E Loth 122 B6
Humbleton E R Yk 93 F3
Humbleton Nthumb 124 C4
Humby Lincs 73 H3
Hume Border 122 D4
Humshaugh Nthumb 113 F2
Huna Highld 167 G6
Huncoat Lancs 89 F3
Huncote Leics 60 A5
Hundalee Border 122 D1
Hundall Derbys 84 B2
Hunderthwaite Dur 105 F2
Hundle Houses Lincs 74 C5
Hundleby Lincs 86 D1
Hundleton Pembks 32 D2
Hundon Suffk 52 A6
Hundred Acres Hants 14 D5
Hundred End Lancs 88 C2
Hundred House Powys 44 D5
Hungarton Leics 60 C6
Hungate End Bucks 49 F4
Hunger Hill Lancs 81 H6
Hungerford Berks 40 B1
Hungerford Hants 13 E6
Hungerford Somset 22 C3
Hungerford Newtown Berks 40 B1
Hungerstone Herefs 45 G3
Hungerton Lincs 73 F3
Hungryhatton Shrops 70 B3
Hunmanby N York 99 G3
Hunningham Warwks 59 G2
Hunnington Worcs 58 C3
Hunsdon Herts 51 E2
Hunsingore N York 91 E5
Hunslet W York 90 D3
Hunsonby Cumb 104 C4
Hunstanton Norfk 75 G4
Hunstanworth Dur 105 F5
Hunster Ches 70 B5
Hunston W Susx 15 G4
Hunston Green Suffk 64 B2
Hunstrete Somset 24 B5
Hunsworth W York 90 C2
Hunt End Worcs 58 C2
Hunt's Corner Norfk 64 C4
Hunt's Cross Mersyd 81 F3
Hunter's Inn Devon 21 G5
Hunter's Quay Ag & B 128 C3
Huntham Somset 23 F2
Hunthill Lodge Angus 148 B2
Huntingdon Cambs 62 B2
Huntingfield Suffk 65 F3
Huntingford Dorset 24 D2
Huntington Ches 81 F1
Huntington E Loth 132 D3
Huntington Herefs 45 E5
Huntington Herefs 45 H3
Huntington N York 91 G5
Huntington Staffs 71 E1
Huntley Gloucs 46 C1
Huntly Abers 157 G3
Hunton Hants 26 C3
Hunton Kent 29 H1
Hunton N York 97 E4
Hunton Bridge Herts 28 B6
Hunts Green Bucks 41 G5
Hunts Green Warwks 59 E5
Huntscott Somset 22 B4
Huntsham Devon 22 C1
Huntshaw Devon 21 E3

Huntshaw Cross Devon 21 E3
Huntspill Somset 23 F4
Huntstile Somset 23 E3
Huntworth Somset 23 F3
Hunwick Dur 106 A4
Hunworth Norfk 76 D4
Hurcott Somset 10 D6
Hurdcott Wilts 25 G3
Hurdsfield Ches 82 D2
Hurley Berks 41 F3
Hurley Warwks 59 E5
Hurley Bottom Berks 41 F3
Hurley Common Warwks 59 E5
Hurlford E Ayrs 119 F3
Hurlston Green Lancs 81 F6
Hurn Dorset 13 E4
Hurn's End Lincs 75 E5
Hursley Hants 26 C2
Hurst Berks 41 F1
Hurst Dorset 12 B4
Hurst N York 96 D5
Hurst Somset 23 G1
Hurst Green E Susx 18 A4
Hurst Green Essex 52 D2
Hurst Green Lancs 89 E3
Hurst Green Surrey 29 E1
Hurst Hill W Mids 58 B5
Hurst Wickham W Susx 16 D3
Hurstbourne Priors Hants 26 C4
Hurstbourne Tarrant Hants 26 B5
Hurstley Herefs 45 F4
Hurstpierpoint W Susx 16 D3
Hurstway Common Herefs 45 F4
Hurstwood Lancs 89 G3
Hurtiso Ork 169 c2
Hurtmore Surrey 27 H4
Hurworth Burn Dur 106 C4
Hurworth Place Dur 106 B2
Hurworth-on-Tees Dur 106 B2
Hury Dur 105 F2
Husbands Bosworth Leics 60 C4
Husborne Crawley Beds 49 H3
Husthwaite N York 98 A2
Hut Green N York 91 G2
Hutcherleigh Devon 7 E3
Huthwaite N York 97 H5
Huthwaite Notts 72 B6
Huttoft Lincs 87 E2
Hutton Border 123 F5
Hutton Cumb 104 A3
Hutton E R Yk 92 D5
Hutton Essex 29 G6
Hutton Lancs 88 C2
Hutton Somset 23 F5
Hutton Bonville N York 97 F5
Hutton Buscel N York 99 E3
Hutton Conyers N York 97 F2
Hutton Cranswick E R Yk 92 D5
Hutton End Cumb 104 A4
Hutton Hall N York 107 E2
Hutton Hang N York 97 E4
Hutton Henry Dur 106 D4
Hutton Lowcross N York 107 E2
Hutton Magna Dur 105 H1
Hutton Mulgrave N York 107 H2
Hutton Roof Cumb 103 H3
Hutton Roof Cumb 95 F3
Hutton Rudby N York 97 H5
Hutton Sessay N York 97 H2
Hutton Wandesley N York 91 F5
Hutton-le-Hole N York 98 C4
Huxham Devon 9 F4
Huxham Green Somset 24 B3
Huxley Ches 69 G6
Huyton Mersyd 81 G4
Hycemoor Cumb 94 B4
Hyde Gloucs 38 D4
Hyde Gt Man 82 D4
Hyde Hants 13 E6
Hyde End Berks 27 E6
Hyde Heath Bucks 41 G4
Hyde Lea Staffs 70 D2
Hyde Park Corner Somset 23 F2
Hydestile Surrey 27 H3
Hykeham Moor Lincs 85 G1
Hyndford Bridge S Lans 120 D1
Hynish Ag & B 134 B3
Hyssington Powys 56 C5
Hystfield Gloucs 37 H4
Hythe Hants 14 B4
Hythe Kent 19 E5
Hythe Somset 23 G4
Hythe End Berks 28 A3
Hyton Cumb 94 B4

293

Ibberton Dorset 12 B5
Ible Derbys 71 G6
Ibsley Hants 13 E5
Ibstock Leics 72 B1
Ibstone Bucks 41 F4
Ibthorpe Hants 26 B5
Iburndale N York 107 H1
Ibworth Hants 26 D5
Icelton Somset 23 F6
Ickburgh Norfk 63 G5
Ickenham Gt Lon 28 B5
Ickford Bucks 41 E5
Ickham Kent 31 F2
Ickleford Herts 50 C4
Icklesham E Susx 18 B3
Ickleton Cambs 51 F5
Icklingham Suffk 63 G3
Ickornshaw N York 89 H4
Ickwell Green Beds 50 B5
Ickworth Suffk 63 G1
Icomb Gloucs 47 G1
Idbury Oxon 47 H1
Iddesleigh Devon 8 C5
Ide Devon 9 F4
Ide Hill Kent 29 F1
Ideford Devon 9 F2

Iden E Susx 18 C4
Iden Green Kent 18 A5
Iden Green Kent 18 B5
Idle W York 90 C3
Idless Cnwll 3 F4
Idlicote Warwks 48 A4
Idmiston Wilts 25 G3
Idridgehay Derbys 71 H5
Idrigill Highld 150 D5
Idstone Oxon 39 G3
Iffley Oxon 40 C5
Ifield W Susx 16 C5
Ifield Green W Susx 16 A4
Iford Dorset 13 E4
Iford E Susx 17 E2
Ifton Mons 37 F3
Ifton Heath Shrops 69 E4
Ightfield Shrops 70 A4
Ightham Kent 29 G2
Iken Suffk 65 G1
Ilam Staffs 71 F5
Ilchester Somset 23 H1
Ilderton Nthumb 124 C3
Ilford Gt Lon 29 E5
Ilford Somset 23 F1
Ilfracombe Devon 21 E5
Ilkeston Derbys 72 B4
Ilketshall St Andrew Suffk 65 F4
Ilketshall St Margaret Suffk 65 F4
Ilkley W York 90 B4
Illand Cnwll 5 F4
Illey W Mids 58 C3
Illidge Green Ches 82 C1
Illingworth W York 90 B2
Illogan Cnwll 2 D4
Illston on the Hill Leics 60 C5
Ilmer Bucks 41 F5
Ilmington Warwks 47 G3
Ilminster Somset 10 D6
Ilsington Devon 9 E2
Ilsington Dorset 12 A4
Ilston Swans 34 C3
Ilton N York 97 E3
Ilton Somset 23 F1
Imachar N Ayrs 117 H4
Immingham Lincs 93 F1
Immingham Dock Lincs 93 F1
Impington Cambs 62 D2
Ince Ches 81 G2
Ince Blundell Mersyd 81 E5
Ince-in-Makerfield Gt Man 82 A5
Inchbae Lodge Hotel Highld 154 B6
Inchbare Angus 148 D1
Inchberry Moray 157 E5
Inchinnan Rens 129 F2
Inchlaggan Highld 144 D5
Inchmichael P & K 140 B2
Inchnacardoch Hotel Highld 145 F5
Inchnadamph Highld 161 G6
Inchture P & K 140 C3
Inchvuilt Highld 153 F3
Inchyra P & K 140 B2
Indian Queens Cnwll 4 C2
Ingate Place Suffk 65 G4
Ingatestone Essex 29 G6
Ingbirchworth S York 83 G5
Ingerthorpe N York 97 F1
Ingestre Staffs 71 E2
Ingham Lincs 85 G3
Ingham Norfk 77 G3
Ingham Suffk 63 H2
Ingham Corner Norfk 77 G3
Ingleborough Norfk 75 E1
Ingleby Derbys 72 A3
Ingleby Arncliffe N York 97 H5
Ingleby Barwick N York 106 D2
Ingleby Cross N York 97 H5
Ingleby Greenhow N York 98 B5
Ingleigh Green Devon 8 C5
Inglesbatch Somset 24 C5
Inglesham Wilts 39 G4
Ingleton D & G 110 D1
Ingleton Dur 106 A3
Ingleton N York 95 H2
Inglewhite Lancs 88 D4
Ingmire Hall Cumb 95 G4
Ingoe Nthumb 114 B3
Ingoldisthorpe Norfk 75 G3
Ingoldmells Lincs 87 F1
Ingoldsby Lincs 73 H3
Ingram Nthumb 124 C3
Ingrave Essex 29 G5
Ingrow W York 90 B3
Ings Cumb 95 E5
Ingst Gloucs 37 G3
Ingthorpe Lincs 61 F6
Ingworth Norfk 77 E3
Inkberrow Worcs 47 F5
Inkerman Dur 105 H4
Inkhorn Abers 159 E3
Inkpen Berks 26 B6
Inkstack Highld 167 F5
Inmarsh Wilts 25 E5
Innellan Ag & B 128 C2
Innerleithen Border 121 H3
Innerleven Fife 132 C5
Innermessan D & G 108 C1
Innerwick E Loth 133 F2
Innesmill Moray 157 E5
Insch Abers 158 B2
Insh Highld 146 C5
Inskip Lancs 88 C3
Inskip Moss Side Lancs 88 C3
Instow Devon 21 E4
Insworke Cnwll 5 H1
Intake S York 84 B3
Inver Abers 147 G4
Inver Highld 163 E2
Inver P & K 139 G4
Inver-boyndie Abers 158 C5
Inverailort Highld 143 G2
Inveralligin Highld 152 C5
Inverallochy Abers 159 F6
Inveran Highld 162 C3
Inveraray Ag & B 128 B6
Inverarish Highld 151 F2
Inverarity Angus 140 D4
Inverarnan Stirlg 137 H2

Inverasdale *Highld* **160** B2
Inveravon *Falk* **131** F3
Inverawe *Ag & B* **137** E3
Inverbeg *Ag & B* **129** E5
Inverbervie *Abers* **149** F2
Inverbroom *Highld* **161** F2
Invercreran House Hotel *Ag & B* .. **137** E4
Inverdruie *Highld* **146** D5
Inveresk *E Loth* **132** B2
Inveresragan *Ag & B* **136** D3
Inverewe Garden *Highld* **160** C2
Inverey *Abers* **147** F3
Inverfarigaig *Highld* **154** C1
Inverfolla *Ag & B* **136** D4
Invergarry *Highld* **145** E4
Invergeldie *P & K* **139** E2
Invergloy *Highld* **144** D3
Invergordon *Highld* **155** E6
Invergowrie *P & K* **140** C3
Inverguseran *Highld* **143** G5
Inverhadden *P & K* **138** D5
Inverherive Hotel *Stirlg* **138** A2
Inverie *Highld* **143** G4
Inverinan *Ag & B* **136** D1
Inverinate *Highld* **152** C1
Inverkeilor *Angus* **141** G5
Inverkeithing *Fife* **131** G3
Inverkeithny *Abers* **158** B4
Inverkip *Inver* **128** D2
Inverkirkaig *Highld* **161** E6
Inverlael *Highld* **161** F2
Inverlair *Highld* **145** F2
Inverliever Lodge *Ag & B* **127** H6
Inverlochy *Ag & B* **137** F2
Invermark *Angus* **148** B2
Invermarkie *Abers* **157** F3
Invermoriston *Highld* **145** F6
Inverness *Highld* **155** E4
Inverness Dalcross Airport *Highld* .. **155** F4
Invernoaden *Ag & B* **128** C5
Inveroran Hotel *Ag & B* **137** G4
Inverquharity *Angus* **140** D5
Inverquhomery *Abers* **159** F4
Inverroy *Highld* **145** E3
Inversanda *Highld* **136** D6
Invershiel *Highld* **152** D1
Invershin *Highld* **162** C3
Invershore *Highld* **167** F2
Inversnaid Hotel *Stirlg* **129** E6
Inverugie *Abers* **159** G4
Inveruglas *Ag & B* **129** E6
Inveruglass *Highld* **146** C4
Inverurie *Abers* **158** D1
Inwardleigh *Devon* **8** C5
Inworth *Essex* **52** B2
Iochdar *W Isls* **168** b4
Iping *W Susx* **27** G1
Ipplepen *Devon* **7** F4
Ipsden *Oxon* **40** D3
Ipstones *Staffs* **71** E5
Ipswich *Suffk* **53** E5
Irby *Mersyd* **81** E3
Irby in the Marsh *Lincs* **87** E1
Irby upon Humber *Lincs* **86** B5
Irchester *Nhants* **61** E2
Ireby *Cumb* **103** F4
Ireby *Lancs* **95** G2
Ireland *Beds* **50** B5
Ireleth *Cumb* **94** C3
Ireshopeburn *Dur* **105** E4
Ireton Wood *Derbys* **71** H5
Irlam *Gt Man* **82** B4
Irnham *Lincs* **73** H3
Iron Acton *Gloucs* **38** B3
Iron Bridge *Cambs* **62** D5
Iron Bridge Museum *Shrops* .. **57** G6
Iron Cross *Warwks* **47** F4
Ironbridge *Shrops* **57** G6
Ironmacannie *D & G* **110** A2
Irons Bottom *Surrey* **16** C6
Ironville *Derbys* **72** B5
Irstead *Norfk* **77** G2
Irthington *Cumb* **112** B1
Irthlingborough *Nhants* **61** E2
Irton *N York* **99** F3
Irvine *N Ayrs* **119** E3
Isauld *Highld* **166** D5
Isbister *Shet* **169** h4
Isfield *E Susx* **17** E3
Isham *Nhants* **61** E3
Isington *Hants* **27** F3
Islandpool *Worcs* **58** B3
Islay Airport *Ag & B* **116** B5
Isle Abbotts *Somset* **23** F1
Isle Brewers *Somset* **23** F1
Isle of Dogs *Gt Lon* **29** E4
Isle of Man Ronaldsway Airport *IOM* .. **174** i2
Isle of Whithorn *D & G* **101** F4
Isleham *Cambs* **63** F3
Isleornsay *Highld* **143** F5
Isles of Scilly St Mary's Airport *IOS* .. **2** b1
Islesteps *D & G* **110** D2
Islet Village *Guern* **174** g3
Isleworth *Gt Lon* **28** C4
Isley Walton *Leics* **72** B2
Islibhig *W Isls* **168** c8
Islington *Gt Lon* **28** D4
Islip *Nhants* **61** F3
Islip *Oxon* **40** C6
Islivig *W Isls* **168** c8
Isombridge *Shrops* **70** A1
Istead Rise *Kent* **29** G3
Itchen Abbas *Hants* **26** D2
Itchen Stoke *Hants* **26** D2
Itchingfield *W Susx* **16** B4
Itchington *Gloucs* **37** H3
Itteringham *Norfk* **76** D3
Itton *Devon* **8** D4
Itton *Mons* **37** F4
Ivegill *Cumb* **103** H4
Ivelet *N York* **96** C5
Iver *Bucks* **28** A4
Iver Heath *Bucks* **28** A4
Iveston *Dur* **105** H5
Ivinghoe *Bucks* **41** G6
Ivinghoe Aston *Bucks* **41** H6

Ivington *Herefs* **45** G5
Ivington Green *Herefs* **45** G5
Ivy Cross *Dorset* **24** D2
Ivy Hatch *Kent* **29** G1
Ivy Todd *Norfk* **76** B1
Ivybridge *Devon* **6** D3
Ivychurch *Kent* **18** D4
Iwade *Kent* **30** C3
Iwerne Courtney or Shroton *Dorset* .. **12** B6
Iwerne Minster *Dorset* **12** C6
Ixworth *Suffk* **64** B2
Ixworth Thorpe *Suffk* **64** B3

J

Jack Green *Lancs* **88** D2
Jack Hill *N York* **90** C5
Jack's Bush *Hants* **26** A3
Jack-in-the-Green *Devon* **9** G4
Jacksdale *Notts* **72** B5
Jackson Bridge *W York* **83** G5
Jackton *S Lans* **119** H5
Jacobs Well *Surrey* **28** A1
Jacobstow *Cnwll* **5** E5
Jacobstowe *Devon* **8** C5
Jameston *Pembks* **33** E1
Jamestown *Highld* **154** C5
Jamestown *W Duns* **129** E3
Janets-town *Highld* **167** G3
Janetstown *Highld* **167** F2
Jardine Hall *D & G* **111** E4
Jarrow *T & W* **115** E2
Jarvis Brook *E Susx* **17** F4
Jasper's Green *Essex* **51** H3
Jawcraig *Falk* **131** E3
Jaywick *Essex* **53** E2
Jealott's Hill *Berks* **41** G2
Jeater Houses *N York* **97** G4
Jedburgh *Border* **122** D1
Jeffreyston *Pembks* **33** E2
Jemimaville *Highld* **155** E6
Jerbourg *Guern* **174** g1
Jersey Airport *Jersey* **174** b2
Jerusalem *Lincs* **85** G2
Jesmond *T & W* **114** D2
Jevington *E Susx* **17** F1
Jingle Street *Mons* **37** F5
Jockey End *Herts* **50** A2
Jodrell Bank *Ches* **82** C2
John o' Groats *Highld* **167** G6
John's Cross *E Susx* **18** A3
Johnby *Cumb* **104** A3
Johnshaven *Abers* **149** E1
Johnson's Street *Norfk* **77** G2
Johnston *Pembks* **32** D3
Johnstone *D & G* **111** G5
Johnstone *Rens* **129** F1
Johnstonebridge *D & G* **111** E4
Johnstown *Carmth* **42** D1
Johnstown *Wrexhm* **69** E5
Joppa *C Edin* **132** B2
Joppa *Cerdgn* **54** C2
Joppa *S Ayrs* **119** F1
Jordans *Bucks* **41** H3
Jordanston *Pembks* **32** C5
Jordanthorpe *S York* **84** A3
Joyden's Wood *Kent* **29** F3
Jump *S York* **84** B5
Jumper's Town *E Susx* **17** E5
Juniper *Nthumb* **105** F6
Juniper Green *C Edin* **132** A2
Jurby *IOM* **174** I5
Jurston *Devon* **8** D3

K

Kaber *Cumb* **105** E1
Kaimend *S Lans* **120** D4
Kames *Ag & B* **128** A2
Kames *E Ayrs* **120** B2
Kea *Cnwll* **3** F4
Keadby *Lincs* **85** F6
Keal Cotes *Lincs* **74** D6
Kearby Town End *N York* **91** E4
Kearsley *Gt Man* **82** C5
Kearsley *Nthumb* **114** B3
Kearsney *Kent* **19** F6
Kearstwick *Cumb* **95** G3
Kearton *N York* **96** C5
Keasden *N York* **95** H1
Keason *Cnwll* **5** G3
Keaton *Devon* **6** D3
Keckwick *Ches* **81** H3
Keddington *Lincs* **86** D4
Keddington Corner *Lincs* **86** D4
Kedington *Suffk* **51** H5
Kedleston *Derbys* **71** H4
Keelby *Lincs* **86** B6
Keele *Staffs* **70** C5
Keele University *Staffs* **70** C4
Keeley Green *Beds* **50** A5
Keelham *W York* **90** B3
Keeston *Pembks* **32** C4
Keevil *Wilts* **25** E5
Kegworth *Leics* **72** C3
Kehelland *Cnwll* **2** D4
Keig *Abers* **158** B1
Keighley *W York* **90** B4
Keilarsbrae *Clacks* **131** E4
Keillour *P & K* **139** G2
Keiloch *Abers* **147** G4
Keils *Ag & B* **126** D2
Keinton Mandeville *Somset* **24** A2
Keir Mill *D & G* **110** C4
Keirsleywell Row *Nthumb* **104** D5
Keisby *Lincs* **73** H3

Keisley *Cumb* **104** D2
Keiss *Highld* **167** G4
Keith *Moray* **157** F4
Keithick *P & K* **140** B4
Keithock *Angus* **141** F6
Keithtown *Highld* **154** C5
Kelbrook *Lancs* **89** G4
Kelburn *N Ayrs* **118** D5
Kelby *Lincs* **73** H4
Keld *Cumb* **104** B1
Keld *N York* **96** B5
Keld Head *N York* **98** D3
Keldholme *N York* **98** C3
Kelfield *Lincs* **85** F5
Kelfield *N York* **91** G3
Kelham *Notts* **73** E6
Kelhead *D & G* **111** F2
Kellacott *Devon* **5** G5
Kellamergh *Lancs* **88** C2
Kellas *Angus* **140** D3
Kellas *Moray* **156** D4
Kellaton *Devon* **7** E1
Kelleth *Cumb* **95** G5
Kelling *Norfk* **76** D4
Kellington *N York* **91** G2
Kelloe *Dur* **106** C4
Kelloholm *D & G* **110** B6
Kells *Cumb* **102** D2
Kelly *Devon* **5** G4
Kelly Bray *Cnwll* **5** G3
Kelmarsh *Nhants* **60** C3
Kelmscott *Oxon* **39** G4
Kelsale *Suffk* **65** F2
Kelsall *Ches* **81** G1
Kelshall *Herts* **50** D4
Kelsick *Cumb* **103** F5
Kelso *Border* **122** D3
Kelstedge *Derbys* **84** A1
Kelstern *Lincs* **86** C4
Kelsterton *Flints* **81** E2
Kelston *Somset* **24** C6
Keltneyburn *P & K* **139** E5
Kelton *D & G* **110** D2
Kelty *Fife* **131** H4
Kelvedon *Essex* **52** B3
Kelvedon Hatch *Essex* **29** F6
Kelynack *Cnwll* **2** A3
Kemacott *Devon* **21** G5
Kemback *Fife* **140** D1
Kemberton *Shrops* **57** G6
Kemble *Gloucs* **39** E4
Kemble Wick *Gloucs* **38** D4
Kemerton *Worcs* **47** E3
Kemeys Commander *Mons* **37** E5
Kemnay *Abers* **149** E6
Kemp Town *E Susx* **16** D2
Kempe's Corner *Kent* **18** D6
Kempley *Gloucs* **46** B2
Kempley Green *Gloucs* **46** B2
Kemps Green *Warwks* **58** D2
Kempsey *Worcs* **46** D4
Kempsford *Gloucs* **39** F4
Kempshott *Hants* **26** D4
Kempston *Beds* **50** A5
Kempston Hardwick *Beds* **50** A5
Kempton *Shrops* **56** D4
Kemsing *Kent* **29** F2
Kemsley *Kent* **30** C3
Kemsley Street *Kent* **30** B2
Kenardington *Kent* **18** C5
Kenchester *Herefs* **45** G3
Kencot *Oxon* **39** G5
Kendal *Cumb* **95** F4
Kenderchurch *Herefs* **45** G2
Kendleshire *Gloucs* **38** A2
Kenfig *Brdgnd* **35** E2
Kenfig Hill *Brdgnd* **35** F2
Kenidjack *Cnwll* **2** A3
Kenilworth *Warwks* **59** F2
Kenley *Gt Lon* **28** D2
Kenley *Shrops* **57** F5
Kenmore *Highld* **152** B5
Kenmore *P & K* **139** E4
Kenn *Devon* **9** F3
Kenn *Somset* **37** E1
Kennacraig *Ag & B* **127** G1
Kennards House *Cnwll* **5** F4
Kenneggy *Cnwll* **2** C3
Kennerleigh *Devon* **9** E5
Kennessee Green *Mersyd* **81** F5
Kennet *Clacks* **131** E4
Kennethmont *Abers* **157** G2
Kennett *Cambs* **63** F2
Kennford *Devon* **9** F3
Kenninghall *Norfk* **64** C4
Kennington *Kent* **18** D6
Kennington *Oxon* **40** C4
Kennoway *Fife* **132** C5
Kenny *Somset* **23** F1
Kennyhill *Suffk* **63** F3
Kennythorpe *N York* **98** D1
Kenovay *Ag & B* **134** B4
Kensaleyre *Highld* **150** D4
Kensham Green *Kent* **18** B4
Kensington *Gt Lon* **28** C4
Kensworth *Beds* **50** A3
Kensworth Common *Beds* **50** A2
Kent End *Wilts* **39** E4
Kent Green *Ches* **70** C6
Kent Street *E Susx* **18** A3
Kent Street *Kent* **29** G1
Kent's Green *Gloucs* **46** C2
Kent's Oak *Hants* **26** A2
Kentallen *Highld* **137** E5
Kentchurch *Herefs* **45** G2
Kentford *Suffk* **63** F2
Kentisbeare *Devon* **10** A5
Kentisbury *Devon* **21** F5
Kentisbury Ford *Devon* **21** F5
Kentish Town *Gt Lon* **28** D4
Kentmere *Cumb* **95** E5
Kenton *Devon* **9** F3
Kenton *Gt Lon* **28** C5
Kenton *Suffk* **64** D2
Kenton *T & W* **114** D2
Kenton Bankfoot *Nthumb* **114** D2
Kentra *Highld* **143** F1
Kents Bank *Cumb* **95** E2

Kenwick *Shrops* **69** F3
Kenwyn *Cnwll* **3** F4
Kenyon *Ches* **82** A4
Keoldale *Highld* **165** E5
Keppoch *Highld* **152** C1
Kepwick *N York* **97** H4
Keresley *W Mids* **59** F4
Keresley Green *Warwks* **59** F4
Kergilliak *Cnwll* **3** E3
Kernborough *Devon* **7** E2
Kerne Bridge *Herefs* **46** A1
Kerridge *Ches* **82** D2
Kerridge-end *Ches* **82** D2
Kerris *Cnwll* **2** B2
Kerry *Powys* **56** B4
Kerrycroy *Ag & B* **118** C6
Kersall *Notts* **85** E1
Kersbrook *Devon* **10** A3
Kerscott *Devon* **21** F3
Kersey *Suffk* **52** D5
Kersey Tye *Suffk* **52** C5
Kersey Upland *Suffk* **52** C5
Kershader *W Isls* **168** e7
Kershopefoot *Cumb* **112** B3
Kersoe *Worcs* **47** E3
Kerswell *Devon* **10** A5
Kerswell Green *Worcs* **46** D4
Kerthen Wood *Cnwll* **2** C3
Kesgrave *Suffk* **53** F5
Kessingland *Suffk* **65** H4
Kessingland Beach *Suffk* **65** H4
Kestle *Cnwll* **3** G4
Kestle Mill *Cnwll* **4** B2
Keston *Gt Lon* **29** E2
Keswick *Cumb* **103** G2
Keswick *Norfk* **65** E6
Ketsby *Lincs* **86** D2
Kettering *Nhants* **61** E3
Ketteringham *Norfk* **64** D6
Kettins *Angus* **140** B4
Kettle Green *Herts* **51** E2
Kettlebaston *Suffk* **52** C6
Kettlebridge *Fife* **132** B6
Kettlebrook *Staffs* **59** E6
Kettleburgh *Suffk* **65** E1
Kettleholm *D & G* **111** F2
Kettleness *N York* **107** H2
Kettleshulme *Ches* **83** E3
Kettlesing *N York* **90** C5
Kettlesing Bottom *N York* **90** C5
Kettlestone *Norfk* **76** C3
Kettlethorpe *Lincs* **85** F2
Kettletoft *Ork* **169** d4
Kettlewell *N York* **96** C2
Ketton *Rutlnd* **61** F6
Kew *Gt Lon* **28** C4
Kew Gardens *Gt Lon* **28** C4
Kewstoke *Somset* **23** F6
Kexbrough *S York* **83** H6
Kexby *Lincs* **85** F3
Kexby *N York* **91** H5
Key Green *Ches* **82** D1
Key Green *N York* **98** D5
Key Street *Kent* **30** B2
Key's Toft *Lincs* **75** E6
Keyham *Leics* **60** C6
Keyhaven *Hants* **13** G4
Keyingham *E R Yk* **93** F2
Keymer *W Susx* **16** D3
Keynsham *Somset* **37** G1
Keysoe *Beds* **61** G2
Keysoe Row *Beds* **61** G1
Keyston *Cambs* **61** F3
Keyworth *Notts* **72** D3
Kibbear *Somset* **23** E1
Kibblesworth *T & W* **114** D1
Kibworth Beauchamp *Leics* **60** C5
Kibworth Harcourt *Leics* **60** C5
Kidbrooke *Gt Lon* **29** E4
Kidburngill *Cumb* **103** E2
Kidd's Moor *Norfk* **64** D6
Kiddemore Green *Staffs* **70** C1
Kidderminster *Worcs* **58** A3
Kiddington *Oxon* **40** B6
Kidlington *Oxon* **40** C6
Kidmore End *Oxon* **41** E2
Kidsdale *D & G* **101** F4
Kidsgrove *Staffs* **70** C5
Kidstones *N York* **96** C3
Kidwelly *Carmth* **34** B5
Kiel Crofts *Ag & B* **136** D4
Kielder *Nthumb* **112** C4
Kiells *Ag & B* **126** C2
Kilbarchan *Rens* **129** E1
Kilbeg *Highld* **143** F5
Kilberry *Ag & B* **127** F1
Kilbirnie *N Ayrs* **119** E5
Kilbride *Ag & B* **136** C2
Kilbride *Ag & B* **127** F3
Kilbride *Ag & B* **128** B2
Kilbuiack *Moray* **156** C5
Kilburn *Derbys* **72** B5
Kilburn *Gt Lon* **28** C4
Kilburn *N York* **98** A3
Kilby *Leics* **60** B5
Kilchamaig *Ag & B* **127** G1
Kilchattan *Ag & B* **126** C5
Kilchattan *Ag & B* **118** C5
Kilcheran *Ag & B* **136** C4
Kilchoan *Highld* **135** G6
Kilchoman *Ag & B* **126** A1
Kilchrenan *Ag & B* **137** E2
Kilconquhar *Fife* **132** D5
Kilcot *Gloucs* **46** B2
Kilcoy *Highld* **154** D4
Kilcreggan *Ag & B* **128** D3
Kildale *N York* **107** E2
Kildalloig *Ag & B* **117** G2
Kildary *Highld* **162** D1
Kildavaig *Ag & B* **128** A3
Kildavanan *Ag & B* **128** B2
Kildonan *Highld* **163** F6
Kildonan *N Ayrs* **118** B1
Kildonan Lodge *Highld* **163** F6
Kildonnan *Highld* **142** D2
Kildrochet House *D & G* **100** B6
Kildrummy *Abers* **148** B6
Kildwick *N York* **90** A4

Kilfinan *Ag & B* **127** H3
Kilfinnan *Highld* **145** E4
Kilford *Denbgs* **80** C1
Kilgetty *Pembks* **33** E2
Kilgrammie *S Ayrs* **108** D5
Kilgwrrwg Common *Mons* **37** F4
Kilham *E R Yk* **99** F1
Kilham *Nthumb* **123** F4
Kilkenneth *Ag & B* **134** A4
Kilkenzie *Ag & B* **117** F3
Kilkhampton *Cnwll* **20** C2
Killamarsh *Derbys* **84** B3
Killay *Swans* **34** C3
Killearn *Stirlg* **129** G4
Killen *Highld* **155** E5
Killerby *Dur* **106** A3
Killerton *Devon* **9** G5
Killichonan *P & K* **138** C6
Killiechronan *Ag & B* **135** G3
Killiecrankie *P & K* **139** F6
Killilan *Highld* **152** D2
Killin *Stirlg* **138** C3
Killinghall *N York* **90** D5
Killington *Cumb* **95** G4
Killington *Devon* **21** G5
Killingworth *T & W* **114** D3
Killiow *Cnwll* **3** E4
Killivose *Cnwll* **3** E5
Killochyett *Border* **122** B4
Kilmacolm *Inver* **129** E2
Kilmahog *Stirlg* **130** B6
Kilmahumaig *Ag & B* **127** G4
Kilmaluag *Highld* **150** D6
Kilmany *Fife* **140** D2
Kilmarnock *E Ayrs* **119** F3
Kilmartin *Ag & B* **127** G5
Kilmaurs *E Ayrs* **119** F4
Kilmelford *Ag & B* **136** C1
Kilmersdon *Somset* **24** C4
Kilmeston *Hants* **26** D2
Kilmichael *Ag & B* **117** F3
Kilmichael Glassary *Ag & B* **127** G4
Kilmichael of Inverlussa *Ag & B* .. **127** F4
Kilmington *Devon* **10** C4
Kilmington *Wilts* **24** C3
Kilmington Common *Wilts* **24** C3
Kilmington Street *Wilts* **24** C3
Kilmorack *Highld* **154** C3
Kilmore *Ag & B* **136** C2
Kilmore *Highld* **143** F5
Kilmory *Ag & B* **127** F3
Kilmory *Ag & B* **143** E1
Kilmory *N Ayrs* **118** B2
Kilmuir *Highld* **150** C3
Kilmuir *Highld* **150** D6
Kilmuir *Highld* **162** D1
Kilmuir *Highld* **155** E4
Kiln Green *Berks* **41** F2
Kiln Pit Hill *Nthumb* **105** G6
Kilnave *Ag & B* **126** B2
Kilncadzow *S Lans* **120** C4
Kilndown *Kent* **17** H5
Kilnhill *Cumb* **103** F3
Kilnhouses *Ches* **82** A1
Kilnhurst *S York* **84** B4
Kilninver *Ag & B* **136** C2
Kilnsea *E R Yk* **93** H1
Kilnsey *N York* **96** C2
Kilnwick *E R Yk* **92** D4
Kilnwick Percy *E R Yk* **92** B5
Kiloran *Ag & B* **126** C5
Kilpatrick *N Ayrs* **117** H3
Kilpeck *Herefs* **45** G2
Kilpin *E R Yk* **92** B2
Kilpin Pike *E R Yk* **92** B2
Kilrenny *Fife* **133** E6
Kilsby *Nhants* **60** B2
Kilspindie *P & K* **140** B2
Kilstay *D & G* **100** C4
Kilsyth *N Lans* **130** C3
Kiltarlity *Highld* **154** C3
Kilton *N York* **107** F3
Kilton Thorpe *N York* **107** F3
Kilvaxter *Highld* **150** D6
Kilve *Somset* **22** D3
Kilvington *Notts* **73** F4
Kilwinning *N Ayrs* **119** E4
Kimberley *Norfk* **64** C6
Kimberley *Notts* **72** C4
Kimberworth *S York* **84** B4
Kimble Wick *Bucks* **41** F5
Kimblesworth *Dur* **106** B6
Kimbolton *Cambs* **61** G2
Kimbolton *Herefs* **45** H5
Kimcote *Leics* **60** B4
Kimmeridge *Dorset* **12** C2
Kimmerston *Nthumb* **123** G3
Kimpton *Hants* **26** A4
Kimpton *Herts* **50** C2
Kimworthy *Devon* **20** C2
Kinbrace *Highld* **166** B1
Kinbuck *Stirlg* **130** D6
Kincaple *Fife* **141** E2
Kincardine *Fife* **131** F4
Kincardine *Highld* **162** C3
Kincardine O'Neil *Abers* **148** D4
Kinclaven *P & K* **140** B4
Kincorth *Aber C* **149** G5
Kincorth House *Moray* **156** B5
Kincraig *Highld* **146** C5
Kincraigie *P & K* **139** G5
Kindallachan *P & K* **139** G5
Kineton *Gloucs* **47** E2
Kineton *Warwks* **48** B4
Kinfauns *P & K* **140** B2
Kinford *S Ayrs* **119** E3
King Arthur's Labyrinth *Gwynd* .. **55** E6
King Sterndale *Derbys* **83** F2
King's Acre *Herefs* **45** G3
King's Bromley *Staffs* **71** F2
King's Cliffe *Nhants* **61** F5
King's Coughton *Warwks* **47** F5
King's Heath *W Mids* **58** D3
King's Hill *Warwks* **59** F3
King's Lynn *Norfk* **75** F2
King's Mills *Guern* **174** f2

294

King's Moss Lancs — 81 G5
King's Newton Derbys — 72 B3
King's Norton Leics — 60 C5
King's Norton W Mids — 58 C5
King's Nympton Devon — 21 G2
King's Pyon Herefs — 45 G4
King's Somborne Hants — 26 B2
King's Stag Dorset — 11 G6
King's Stanley Gloucs — 38 C5
King's Sutton Oxon — 48 C3
King's Walden Herts — 50 C3
Kingarth Ag & B. — 118 C5
Kingcausie Abers — 149 F4
Kingcoed Mons — 37 E5
Kingerby Lincs — 85 H4
Kingford Devon — 20 C1
Kingham Oxon — 47 H2
Kingholm Quay D & G — 110 D2
Kinghorn Fife — 132 B4
Kinglassie Fife — 132 A5
Kingoldrum Angus — 140 C5
Kingoodie P & K — 140 C3
Kings Bridge Swans — 34 C4
Kings Caple Herefs — 46 A2
Kings Green Gloucs — 46 C3
Kings Hill Kent — 29 G2
Kings Hill W Mids — 58 C5
Kings House Hotel Highld — 137 G5
Kings Langley Herts — 50 B1
Kings Meaburn Cumb — 104 C2
Kings Muir Border — 121 G3
Kings Newnham Warwks — 59 G3
Kings Ripton Cambs — 62 B3
Kings Weston Bristl — 37 F2
Kings Worthy Hants — 26 C2
Kingsand Cnwll — 6 B3
Kingsash Bucks — 41 G5
Kingsbarns Fife — 141 F1
Kingsbridge Devon — 7 E2
Kingsbridge Somset — 22 C3
Kingsburgh Highld — 150 D4
Kingsbury Gt Lon — 28 C5
Kingsbury Warwks — 59 E5
Kingsbury Episcopi Somset — 23 G1
Kingsclere Hants — 26 C5
Kingscote Gloucs — 38 C4
Kingscott Devon — 21 E2
Kingscross N Ayrs — 118 B2
Kingsdon Somset — 23 H2
Kingsdown Kent — 31 G1
Kingsdown Wilts — 24 D6
Kingsdown Wilts — 39 F3
Kingseat Fife — 131 G4
Kingsey Bucks — 41 F5
Kingsfold W Susx — 16 C5
Kingsford Aber C — 149 F5
Kingsford E Ayrs — 119 F4
Kingsford Worcs — 58 A3
Kingsgate Kent — 31 G3
Kingshall Street Suffk — 64 B1
Kingsheanton Devon — 21 F4
Kingshouse Hotel Stirlg — 138 C2
Kingshurst W Mids — 59 E4
Kingside Hill Cumb — 103 F5
Kingskerswell Devon — 7 F4
Kingskettle Fife — 132 B6
Kingsland Dorset — 11 E4
Kingsland Herefs — 45 G5
Kingsland IOA — 78 B3
Kingsley Ches — 81 H2
Kingsley Hants — 27 F3
Kingsley Staffs — 71 E5
Kingsley Green W Susx — 27 G2
Kingsley Park Nhants — 60 D2
Kingslow Shrops — 57 H5
Kingsmead Hants — 14 D5
Kingsmuir Angus — 141 E5
Kingsmuir Fife — 132 D6
Kingsnorth Kent — 18 D5
Kingstanding W Mids — 58 D5
Kingsteignton Devon — 7 F5
Kingsthorne Herefs — 45 H2
Kingsthorpe Nhants — 60 D2
Kingston Cambs — 50 D6
Kingston Cnwll — 5 G3
Kingston Devon — 6 D2
Kingston Devon — 9 G3
Kingston Dorset — 12 A6
Kingston Dorset — 12 C2
Kingston E Loth — 132 D3
Kingston E Susx — 16 B2
Kingston Hants — 13 E5
Kingston IOW — 14 C2
Kingston Kent — 31 E1
Kingston Bagpuize Oxon — 40 R4
Kingston Blount Oxon — 41 F4
Kingston Deverill Wilts — 24 D3
Kingston Lisle Oxon — 40 B3
Kingston near Lewes E Susx — 17 E2
Kingston on Soar Notts — 72 C3
Kingston on Spey Moray — 157 E6
Kingston Russell Dorset — 11 F4
Kingston Seymour Somset — 23 G6
Kingston St Mary Somset — 23 E2
Kingston St Oxon — 41 E4
Kingston upon Thames Gt Lon — 28 C3
Kingstone Herefs — 45 G3
Kingstone Somset — 10 D6
Kingstone Staffs — 71 E3
Kingstone Winslow Oxon — 39 G3
Kingstown Cumb — 103 H6
Kingswear Devon — 7 F3
Kingswells Aber C — 149 F5
Kingswinford W Mids — 58 B4
Kingswood Bucks — 49 E1
Kingswood Gloucs — 37 G2
Kingswood Gloucs — 38 B3
Kingswood Kent — 30 B1
Kingswood Powys — 56 C6
Kingswood Somset — 22 D3
Kingswood Surrey — 28 C2
Kingswood Warwks — 59 E2
Kingswood Brook Warwks — 59 E2
Kingswood Common Herefs — 45 F5
Kingswood Common Staffs — 58 A6
Kingthorpe Lincs — 86 B2
Kington Gloucs — 37 G3
Kington Herefs — 45 F5

Kington Worcs — 47 E5
Kington Langley Wilts — 38 D2
Kington Magna Dorset — 24 C1
Kington St Michael Wilts — 38 D2
Kingussie Highld — 146 C4
Kingweston Somset — 23 H2
Kinharrachie Abers — 159 E2
Kinharvie D & G — 110 D1
Kinkell Bridge P & K — 139 F1
Kinknockie Abers — 159 F3
Kinleith C Edin — 131 H2
Kinlet Shrops — 57 G3
Kinloch Highld — 164 D2
Kinloch Highld — 165 F4
Kinloch Highld — 142 D4
Kinloch P & K — 140 B4
Kinloch P & K — 140 C4
Kinloch Hourn Highld — 144 B5
Kinloch Rannoch P & K — 138 D6
Kinlochard Stirlg — 129 F5
Kinlochbervie Highld — 164 C4
Kinlocheil Highld — 144 B2
Kinlochewe Highld — 152 D5
Kinlochlaggan Highld — 145 G3
Kinlochleven Highld — 137 F6
Kinlochmoidart Highld — 143 G1
Kinlochnanuagh Highld — 143 G2
Kinloss Moray — 156 C5
Kinmel Bay Conwy — 80 B3
Kinmuck Abers — 158 D1
Kinmundy Abers — 149 F6
Kinnabus Ag & B. — 116 B5
Kinnadie Abers — 159 F3
Kinnaird P & K — 139 G6
Kinnaird Castle Angus — 141 F5
Kinneddar Moray — 156 D6
Kinneff Abers — 149 F2
Kinnelhead D & G — 111 E5
Kinnell Angus — 141 F5
Kinnerley Shrops — 69 F2
Kinnersley Herefs — 45 F4
Kinnersley Worcs — 46 D4
Kinnerton Powys — 56 C2
Kinnerton Shrops — 56 D5
Kinnerton Green Flints — 69 F6
Kinnesswood P & K — 131 H5
Kinninvie Dur — 105 G2
Kinnordy Angus — 140 D5
Kinoulton Notts — 72 D3
Kinross P & K — 131 G5
Kinrossie P & K — 140 B3
Kinsbourne Green Herts — 50 B2
Kinsey Heath Ches — 70 B4
Kinsham Herefs — 56 D2
Kinsham Worcs — 47 E3
Kinsley W York — 91 E1
Kinson Dorset — 13 E4
Kintbury Berks — 26 B6
Kintessack Moray — 156 B5
Kintillo P & K — 140 A1
Kinton Herefs — 56 D3
Kinton Shrops — 69 F2
Kintore Abers — 149 E6
Kintour Ag & B. — 116 D5
Kintra Ag & B. — 135 E2
Kintraw Ag & B. — 127 G6
Kinveachy Highld — 155 G1
Kinver Staffs — 58 A4
Kiplin N York — 97 F5
Kippax W York — 91 E3
Kippen Stirlg — 130 C5
Kippford or Scaur D & G — 102 B6
Kipping's Cross Kent — 17 G5
Kirbister Ork — 169 b2
Kirburd Border — 121 F4
Kirby Bedon Norfk — 65 E6
Kirby Bellars Leics — 73 E2
Kirby Cane Norfk — 65 F5
Kirby Corner W Mids — 59 F3
Kirby Cross Essex — 53 F3
Kirby Fields Leics — 60 A6
Kirby Grindalythe N York — 99 E2
Kirby Hill N York — 97 E5
Kirby Hill N York — 97 G2
Kirby Knowle N York — 97 H4
Kirby le Soken Essex — 53 F3
Kirby Misperton N York — 98 C3
Kirby Muxloe Leics — 60 A6
Kirby Row Norfk — 65 F5
Kirby Sigston N York — 97 G4
Kirby Underdale E R Yk — 92 B5
Kirby Wiske N York — 97 G3
Kirconnel D & G — 110 D2
Kirdford W Susx — 16 A4
Kirk Highld — 167 F4
Kirk Bramwith S York — 84 D6
Kirk Deighton N York — 91 E5
Kirk Ella E R Yk — 92 D2
Kirk Hallam Derbys — 72 B4
Kirk Hammerton N York — 91 F5
Kirk Ireton Derbys — 71 G5
Kirk Langley Derbys — 71 H4
Kirk Merrington Dur — 106 B4
Kirk Michael IOM — 174 I4
Kirk of Shotts N Lans — 120 C6
Kirk Sandall S York — 84 D5
Kirk Smeaton N York — 91 F1
Kirk Yetholm Border — 123 E2
Kirkabister Shet — 169 j2
Kirkandrews D & G — 101 G3
Kirkandrews upon Eden Cumb — 103 G6
Kirkbampton Cumb — 103 G6
Kirkbean D & G — 102 D6
Kirkbride Cumb — 103 F6
Kirkbride N York — 97 F4
Kirkbuddo Angus — 141 E4
Kirkburn Border — 121 G3
Kirkburn E R Yk — 92 D5
Kirkburton W York — 83 G6
Kirkby Lincs — 86 A4
Kirkby Mersyd — 81 F5
Kirkby N York — 98 A5
Kirkby Fleetham N York — 97 F4
Kirkby Green Lincs — 74 A6
Kirkby Hall N York — 97 F4
Kirkby in Ashfield Notts — 72 C6
Kirkby la Thorpe Lincs — 74 A5
Kirkby Lonsdale Cumb — 95 G3

Kirkby Malham N York — 89 G6
Kirkby Mallory Leics — 59 G5
Kirkby Malzeard N York — 97 E2
Kirkby Mills N York — 98 C3
Kirkby on Bain Lincs — 86 C1
Kirkby Overblow N York — 90 D4
Kirkby Stephen Cumb — 96 A6
Kirkby Thore Cumb — 104 C3
Kirkby Underwood Lincs — 74 A3
Kirkby Wharf N York — 91 F4
Kirkby Woodhouse Notts — 72 C5
Kirkby-in-Furness Cumb — 94 C3
Kirkbymoorside N York — 98 C3
Kirkcaldy Fife — 132 B4
Kirkcambeck Cumb — 112 C2
Kirkchrist D & G — 101 H5
Kirkcolm D & G — 108 B2
Kirkconnel D & G — 110 B6
Kirkconnell D & G — 101 H6
Kirkcowan D & G — 101 E6
Kirkcudbright D & G — 101 H5
Kirkdale Mersyd — 81 F4
Kirkfieldbank S Lans — 120 C4
Kirkgunzeon D & G — 110 C1
Kirkham Lancs — 88 C3
Kirkham N York — 98 C1
Kirkhamgate W York — 90 D2
Kirkharle Nthumb — 113 G3
Kirkhaugh Nthumb — 104 D5
Kirkheaton Nthumb — 114 B3
Kirkheaton W York — 90 C1
Kirkhill Highld — 154 D4
Kirkhope S Lans — 110 D5
Kirkhouse Cumb — 104 B6
Kirkhouse Green S York — 84 D6
Kirkibost Highld — 143 E6
Kirkinch P & K — 140 C4
Kirkinner D & G — 101 E5
Kirkintilloch E Duns — 130 C2
Kirkland Cumb — 103 E2
Kirkland Cumb — 104 C3
Kirkland D & G — 110 B6
Kirkland D & G — 110 C4
Kirkland D & G — 111 E4
Kirkland Guards Cumb — 103 F4
Kirkleatham N York — 107 E3
Kirklevington N York — 106 D2
Kirkley Suffk — 65 H4
Kirklington N York — 97 F3
Kirklington Notts — 72 D6
Kirklinton Cumb — 112 B1
Kirkliston C Edin — 131 G2
Kirkmabreck D & G — 101 F6
Kirkmaiden D & G — 100 C4
Kirkmichael P & K — 139 H6
Kirkmichael S Ayrs — 109 G6
Kirkmuirhill S Lans — 120 B4
Kirknewton Nthumb — 123 F2
Kirknewton W Loth — 131 G2
Kirkney Abers — 157 G2
Kirkoswald Cumb — 104 B4
Kirkoswald S Ayrs — 108 D5
Kirkpatrick D & G — 110 D4
Kirkpatrick Durham D & G — 110 B2
Kirkpatrick-Fleming D & G — 111 G2
Kirksanton Cumb — 94 B3
Kirkstall W York — 90 D3
Kirkstead Lincs — 86 B1
Kirkstile Abers — 157 G3
Kirkstile D & G — 111 H4
Kirkstone Pass Inn Cumb — 95 E6
Kirkstyle Highld — 167 G6
Kirkthorpe W York — 91 E2
Kirkton Abers — 158 B2
Kirkton Abers — 158 D3
Kirkton D & G — 110 D3
Kirkton Fife — 140 D2
Kirkton Highld — 152 B2
Kirkton Highld — 152 C3
Kirkton P & K — 139 G2
Kirkton Manor Border — 121 G3
Kirkton of Airlie Angus — 140 C5
Kirkton of Auchterhouse Angus — 140 C4
Kirkton of Barevan Highld — 155 F4
Kirkton of Collace P & K — 140 B3
Kirkton of Glenbuchat Abers — 148 A6
Kirkton of Logie Buchan Abers — 159 F2
Kirkton of Menmuir Angus — 141 E6
Kirkton of Monikie Angus — 141 E4
Kirkton of Rayne Abers — 158 C2
Kirkton of Skene Abers — 149 F5
Kirkton of Strathmartine Angus — 140 D3
Kirkton of Tealing Angus — 140 D3
Kirktown Abers — 159 F6
Kirktown Abers — 159 G4
Kirktown of Bourtie Abers — 158 D2
Kirktown of Fetteresso Abers — 149 F3
Kirktown of Mortlach Moray — 157 E3
Kirktown of Slains Abers — 159 F2
Kirkwall Ork — 169 b2
Kirkwall Airport Ork — 169 c2
Kirkwhelpington Nthumb — 113 G3
Kirmincham Ches — 82 C1
Kirmington Lincs — 86 A6
Kirmond le Mire Lincs — 86 B4
Kirn Ag & B. — 128 C3
Kirriemuir Angus — 140 D5
Kirstead Green Norfk — 65 E5
Kirtlebridge D & G — 111 G2
Kirtling Cambs — 63 F1
Kirtling Green Suffk — 63 F1
Kirtlington Oxon — 48 C1
Kirtomy Highld — 166 A5
Kirton Abers — 148 D6
Kirton Lincs — 74 C4
Kirton Notts — 85 E2
Kirton Suffk — 53 F5
Kirton End Lincs — 74 C4
Kirton Holme Lincs — 74 C4
Kirton in Lindsey Lincs — 85 G4
Kirtonhill W Duns — 129 E3
Kirwaugh D & G — 101 E5
Kishorn Highld — 152 C3
Kislingbury Nhants — 49 E5
Kite Green Warwks — 59 G2
Kitebrook Warwks — 47 H2
Kites Hardwick Warwks — 59 G2

Kitleigh Cnwll — 5 F6
Kitt Green Gt Man — 81 H5
Kittisford Somset — 22 D1
Kittle Swans — 34 C3
Kitts Green W Mids — 58 D4
Kittybrewster Aber C — 149 G5
Kitwood Hants — 27 E2
Kivernoll Herefs — 45 G2
Kiveton Park S York — 84 C3
Knaith Lincs — 85 F3
Knaith Park Lincs — 85 F3
Knap Corner Dorset — 24 D2
Knaphill Surrey — 27 H5
Knaplock Somset — 22 B3
Knapp Somset — 23 F2
Knapp Hill Hants — 26 B2
Knapthorpe Notts — 73 E6
Knapton N York — 91 G5
Knapton N York — 98 D2
Knapton Norfk — 77 F3
Knapton Green Herefs — 45 G4
Knapwell Cambs — 62 C2
Knaresborough N York — 91 E5
Knarsdale Nthumb — 104 C5
Knaven Abers — 159 E3
Knayton N York — 97 G4
Knebworth Herts — 50 C3
Knedlington E R Yk — 92 A2
Kneesall Notts — 85 E1
Kneesworth Cambs — 50 D5
Kneeton Notts — 73 E5
Knelston Swans — 34 B3
Knenhall Staffs — 70 D4
Knettishall Suffk — 64 B3
Knightacott Devon — 21 G4
Knightcote Warwks — 48 B5
Knightley Staffs — 70 C2
Knightley Dale Staffs — 70 C2
Knighton Devon — 6 C2
Knighton Dorset — 11 F6
Knighton Dorset — 12 D4
Knighton Leics — 60 B5
Knighton Powys — 56 C3
Knighton Somset — 23 E4
Knighton Staffs — 70 B4
Knighton Staffs — 70 C3
Knighton Wilts — 39 G1
Knighton on Teme Worcs — 57 F2
Knightsbridge Gloucs — 46 D2
Knightsmill Cnwll — 4 D4
Knightwick Worcs — 46 C5
Knill Herefs — 45 F5
Knipton Leics — 73 F3
Knitsley Dur — 105 H5
Kniveton Derbys — 71 G5
Knock Cumb — 104 D3
Knock Highld — 143 F6
Knock Moray — 157 G4
Knock W Isls — 168 f8
Knock Castle N Ayrs — 128 C1
Knockally Highld — 167 E1
Knockan Highld — 161 F5
Knockando Moray — 156 D3
Knockbain Highld — 154 D3
Knockbain Highld — 154 D5
Knockdee Highld — 167 E4
Knockdown Wilts — 38 C3
Knockeen S Ayrs — 109 E4
Knockenkelly N Ayrs — 118 B2
Knockentiber E Ayrs — 119 F3
Knockhall Kent — 29 G3
Knockholt Kent — 29 E2
Knockholt Pound Kent — 29 F2
Knockin Shrops — 69 F2
Knockinlaw E Ayrs — 119 F3
Knockmill Kent — 29 G2
Knocknain D & G — 108 B1
Knocksheen D & G — 109 G3
Knockvennie Smithy D & G — 110 B2
Knodishall Suffk — 65 G2
Knole Somset — 23 H2
Knole Park Gloucs — 37 G3
Knolls Green Ches — 82 C3
Knolton Wrexhm — 69 F4
Knook Wilts — 25 E3
Knossington Leics — 73 F1
Knott End-on-Sea Lancs — 88 B4
Knotting Beds — 61 F2
Knotting Green Beds — 61 F2
Knottingley W York — 91 F2
Knotty Ash Mersyd — 81 F4
Knotty Green Bucks — 41 G3
Knowbury Shrops — 57 F3
Knowe D & G — 109 E2
Knowehead D & G — 109 H4
Knoweside S Ayrs — 108 D6
Knowl Green Essex — 52 A5
Knowl Hill Berks — 41 F2
Knowle Bristl — 37 G1
Knowle Devon — 21 E4
Knowle Devon — 9 E5
Knowle Devon — 9 G3
Knowle Shrops — 57 F3
Knowle Somset — 22 C4
Knowle W Mids — 59 E3
Knowle Cross Devon — 9 G4
Knowle Green Lancs — 89 E3
Knowle Hill Surrey — 27 H6
Knowle St Giles Somset — 10 D6
Knowlefield Cumb — 103 H6
Knowlton Dorset — 12 D6
Knowlton Kent — 31 F1
Knowsley Mersyd — 81 G4
Knowsley Safari Park Mersyd — 81 G4
Knowstone Devon — 22 A1
Knox N York — 90 D5
Knox Bridge Kent — 18 B5
Knucklas Powys — 56 C3
Knuston Nhants — 61 E2
Knutsford Ches — 82 C2
Knutton Staffs — 70 C5
Knypersley Staffs — 70 D6
Krumlin W York — 90 B1
Kuggar Cnwll — 3 E1
Kyle of Lochalsh Highld — 152 B2
Kyleakin Highld — 152 B2
Kylerhea Highld — 143 G6

Kyles Scalpay W Isls — 168 d6
Kylesku Highld — 164 C2
Kylesmorar Highld — 143 G3
Kylestrome Highld — 164 C2
Kyloe Nthumb — 123 H3
Kynaston Herefs — 46 B3
Kynaston Shrops — 69 F2
Kynnersley Shrops — 70 B2
Kyre Green Worcs — 46 B5
Kyre Park Worcs — 57 F2
Kyrewood Worcs — 57 F2
Kyrle Somset — 22 C1

L

L'Ancresse Guern — 174 g3
L'Eree Guern — 174 f2
L'Etacq Jersey — 174 a3
La Bellieuse Guern — 174 g1
La Fontenelle Guern — 174 h3
La Fosse Guern — 174 g1
La Greve Guern — 174 g3
La Greve de Lecq Jersey — 174 a3
La Hougue Bie Jersey — 174 d2
La Houguette Guern — 174 f2
La Passee Guern — 174 g3
La Pulente Jersey — 174 a2
La Rocque Jersey — 174 d1
La Rousaillerie Guern — 174 g2
La Villette Guern — 174 g1
Lacadal W Isls — 168 f8
Lacasaigh W Isls — 168 e7
Laceby Lincs — 86 B5
Lacey Green Bucks — 41 F4
Lach Dennis Ches — 82 B2
Lackenby N York — 107 E3
Lackford Suffk — 63 G2
Lackford Green Suffk — 63 G2
Lacock Wilts — 38 D1
Ladbroke Warwks — 48 B5
Ladderedge Staffs — 71 E5
Laddingford Kent — 17 H6
Lade Bank Lincs — 74 D5
Ladock Cnwll — 3 F5
Lady Hall Cumb — 94 C3
Lady Village Ork — 169 d4
Lady's Green Suffk — 63 G1
Ladybank Fife — 132 B6
Ladycross Cnwll — 5 G5
Ladygill S Lans — 120 D2
Ladykirk Border — 123 F4
Ladyridge Herefs — 46 B2
Ladywood W Mids — 58 C4
Ladywood Worcs — 46 D5
Lag D & G — 110 C3
Laga Highld — 136 A6
Lagavulin Ag & B. — 116 C5
Lagg N Ayrs — 118 A2
Laggan Highld — 145 E4
Laggan Highld — 146 A4
Laid Highld — 165 E4
Laide Highld — 160 C3
Laig Highld — 142 D3
Laigh Clunch E Ayrs — 119 F4
Laigh Fenwick E Ayrs — 119 F4
Laigh Glenmuir E Ayrs — 119 H1
Laighstonehall S Lans — 120 B5
Laindon Essex — 29 H5
Lairg Highld — 162 C4
Laisterdyke W York — 90 C3
Laithes Cumb — 104 A3
Lake Devon — 21 F4
Lake Devon — 8 B3
Lake Dorset — 12 D4
Lake IOW — 14 D2
Lake Wilts — 25 G3
Lakenheath Suffk — 63 F4
Laker's Green Surrey — 16 A5
Lakesend Norfk — 62 D5
Lakeside Cumb — 94 D4
Laleham Surrey — 28 A3
Laleston Brdgnd — 35 F2
Lamancha Border — 121 F5
Lamanva Cnwll — 3 E3
Lamarsh Essex — 52 B4
Lamas Norfk — 77 E2
Lamb Roe Lancs — 89 F3
Lambden Border — 123 E4
Lamberhurst Kent — 17 G5
Lamberhurst Down Kent — 17 G5
Lamberton Border — 123 G5
Lambeth Gt Lon — 28 D4
Lambfair Green Suffk — 51 H6
Lambley Notts — 72 D5
Lambley Nthumb — 104 C6
Lambourn Berks — 40 B2
Lambourne End Essex — 29 F5
Lambs Green W Susx — 16 C5
Lambston Pembks — 32 C3
Lamellion Cnwll — 5 F2
Lamerton Devon — 8 A2
Lamesley T & W — 114 D1
Lamington S Lans — 120 D2
Lamlash N Ayrs — 118 B2
Lamonby Cumb — 103 H4
Lamorick Cnwll — 4 D2
Lamorna Cnwll — 2 B2
Lamorran Cnwll — 3 F4
Lampen Cnwll — 5 E3
Lampeter Cerdgn — 43 F4
Lampeter Velfrey Pembks — 33 F3
Lamphey Pembks — 32 D2
Lamplugh Cumb — 103 E2
Lamport Nhants — 60 C2
Lamyatt Somset — 24 B3
Lana Devon — 20 C1
Lana Devon — 5 G6
Lanark S Lans — 120 C4
Lanarth Cnwll — 3 E2
Lancaster Lancs — 88 C6
Lancaut Gloucs — 37 F4
Lanchester Dur — 106 A6
Lancing W Susx — 16 C2

Land's End *Cnwll* ... 2 A2
Land's End Airport *Cnwll* ... 2 A3
Land-hallow *Highld* ... 167 F2
Landbeach *Cambs* ... 62 D2
Landcross *Devon* ... 21 F4
Landerberry *Abers* ... 149 E5
Landford *Wilts* ... 25 H1
Landimore *Swans* ... 34 B3
Landkey *Devon* ... 21 F4
Landkey Town *Devon* ... 21 F4
Landore *Swans* ... 34 D4
Landrake *Cnwll* ... 5 G2
Landscove *Devon* ... 7 E4
Landshipping *Pembks* ... 32 D3
Landue *Cnwll* ... 5 G4
Landulph *Cnwll* ... 6 B4
Landwade *Suffk* ... 63 E2
Landywood *Staffs* ... 58 C6
Lane *Cnwll* ... 4 B2
Lane Bottom *Lancs* ... 89 G3
Lane End *Bucks* ... 41 F3
Lane End *Ches* ... 82 B4
Lane End *Cnwll* ... 4 D3
Lane End *Hants* ... 26 D2
Lane End *Kent* ... 29 F3
Lane End *Lancs* ... 89 G4
Lane End *Wilts* ... 24 D4
Lane End Waberthwaite *Cumb* ... 94 B4
Lane Ends *Derbys* ... 71 G3
Lane Ends *Dur* ... 106 A4
Lane Ends *Lancs* ... 89 F3
Lane Ends *N York* ... 90 A4
Lane Green *Staffs* ... 58 B6
Lane Head *Dur* ... 105 H1
Lane Head *Gt Man* ... 82 A4
Lane Head *W Mids* ... 58 C5
Lane Heads *Lancs* ... 88 C3
Lane Side *Lancs* ... 89 F2
Laneast *Cnwll* ... 5 F4
Laneham *Notts* ... 85 E2
Lanehead *Dur* ... 105 E4
Lanehead *Nthumb* ... 113 E3
Laneshaw Bridge *Lancs* ... 89 H4
Langaford *Devon* ... 5 H6
Langaller *Somset* ... 23 E2
Langar *Notts* ... 73 E3
Langbank *Rens* ... 129 E2
Langbar *N York* ... 90 B5
Langbaurgh *N York* ... 107 E2
Langcliffe *N York* ... 96 B1
Langdale End *N York* ... 99 E4
Langdon *Cnwll* ... 5 G5
Langdon Beck *Dur* ... 105 E3
Langdown *Hants* ... 14 B4
Langdyke *Fife* ... 132 B6
Langenhoe *Essex* ... 52 D3
Langford *Beds* ... 50 C5
Langford *Devon* ... 9 G5
Langford *Essex* ... 52 B2
Langford *Notts* ... 73 F6
Langford *Oxon* ... 39 G4
Langford *Somset* ... 23 G5
Langford Budville *Somset* ... 22 D1
Langford End *Beds* ... 50 C6
Langham *Dorset* ... 24 C2
Langham *Essex* ... 52 D4
Langham *Norfk* ... 76 C4
Langham *Rutlnd* ... 73 F1
Langham *Suffk* ... 64 B2
Langham Moor *Essex* ... 52 D4
Langham Wick *Essex* ... 52 D4
Langho *Lancs* ... 89 E3
Langholm *D & G* ... 111 H3
Langland *Swans* ... 34 D3
Langlee *Border* ... 122 B3
Langley *Berks* ... 28 A4
Langley *Ches* ... 82 D2
Langley *Derbys* ... 72 B5
Langley *Gloucs* ... 47 E2
Langley *Gt Man* ... 82 D5
Langley *Hants* ... 14 C4
Langley *Herts* ... 50 C3
Langley *Kent* ... 30 B1
Langley *Nthumb* ... 105 E6
Langley *Oxon* ... 39 H6
Langley *Somset* ... 22 D2
Langley *W Susx* ... 27 F2
Langley *Warwks* ... 59 E2
Langley Burrell *Wilts* ... 38 D2
Langley Castle *Nthumb* ... 113 E1
Langley Common *Derbys* ... 71 H4
Langley Green *Derbys* ... 71 H4
Langley Green *Essex* ... 52 B3
Langley Green *Warwks* ... 47 G5
Langley Lower Green *Essex* ... 51 E4
Langley Marsh *Somset* ... 22 D2
Langley Mill *Derbys* ... 72 B5
Langley Moor *Dur* ... 106 B5
Langley Park *Dur* ... 106 B5
Langley Street *Norfk* ... 65 F6
Langley Upper Green *Essex* ... 51 E4
Langleybury *Herts* ... 28 B6
Langney *E Susx* ... 17 G2
Langold *Notts* ... 84 D3
Langore *Cnwll* ... 5 F5
Langport *Somset* ... 23 G2
Langrick *Lincs* ... 74 C5
Langridge *Somset* ... 38 B1
Langridge Ford *Devon* ... 21 F3
Langrigg *Cumb* ... 103 F5
Langrish *Hants* ... 27 E2
Langsett *S York* ... 83 G5
Langside *P & K* ... 139 E1
Langstone *Hants* ... 15 E4
Langstone *Newpt* ... 37 E3
Langthorne *N York* ... 97 F4
Langthorpe *N York* ... 97 G2
Langthwaite *N York* ... 96 C5
Langtoft *E R Yk* ... 99 F1
Langtoft *Lincs* ... 74 B1
Langton *Dur* ... 106 A3
Langton *Lincs* ... 86 C1
Langton *Lincs* ... 86 D2
Langton *N York* ... 98 D1
Langton by Wragby *Lincs* ... 86 B2
Langton Green *Kent* ... 17 F5
Langton Green *Suffk* ... 64 D3
Langton Herring *Dorset* ... 11 F3

Langton Matravers *Dorset* ... 12 D2
Langtree *Devon* ... 21 E2
Langtree Week *Devon* ... 21 E2
Langwathby *Cumb* ... 104 B3
Langwell House *Highld* ... 163 H6
Langworth *Lincs* ... 86 A2
Lanhydrock House & Gardens
  Cnwll ... 4 D2
Lanivet *Cnwll* ... 4 D2
Lanjeth *Cnwll* ... 3 G5
Lank *Cnwll* ... 4 D3
Lanlivery *Cnwll* ... 4 D2
Lanner *Cnwll* ... 3 E4
Lanoy *Cnwll* ... 5 F4
Lanreath *Cnwll* ... 5 E2
Lansallos *Cnwll* ... 5 E1
Lanteglos *Cnwll* ... 4 D4
Lanteglos Highway *Cnwll* ... 5 E1
Lanton *Border* ... 122 C2
Lanton *Nthumb* ... 123 F2
Lapford *Devon* ... 8 D5
Laphroaig *Ag & B* ... 116 C5
Lapley *Staffs* ... 70 D1
Lapworth *Warwks* ... 59 E2
Larachbeg *Highld* ... 136 B5
Larbert *Falk* ... 131 E3
Larbreck *Lancs* ... 88 C4
Largie *Abers* ... 158 D3
Largiemore *Ag & B* ... 128 A4
Largoward *Fife* ... 132 D6
Largs *N Ayrs* ... 118 D5
Largybeg *N Ayrs* ... 118 B2
Largymore *N Ayrs* ... 118 B2
Larkbeare *Devon* ... 10 A4
Larkfield *Inver* ... 128 D3
Larkfield *Kent* ... 29 H2
Larkhall *S Lans* ... 120 B4
Larkhill *Wilts* ... 25 G4
Larling *Norfk* ... 64 B4
Lartington *Dur* ... 105 G2
Lasborough *Gloucs* ... 38 C4
Lasham *Hants* ... 27 E3
Lashbrook *Devon* ... 8 A5
Lashenden *Kent* ... 18 B5
Lask Edge *Staffs* ... 70 D6
Lassodie *Fife* ... 131 G5
Lastingham *N York* ... 98 C4
Latcham *Somset* ... 23 G4
Latchford *Herts* ... 51 E3
Latchford *Oxon* ... 41 E4
Latchingdon *Essex* ... 30 B6
Latchley *Cnwll* ... 5 H3
Latebrook *Staffs* ... 70 C5
Lately Common *Gt Man* ... 82 B4
Lathbury *Bucks* ... 49 G4
Latheron *Highld* ... 167 F2
Latheronwheel *Highld* ... 167 G2
Lathones *Fife* ... 132 D6
Latimer *Bucks* ... 28 A6
Latteridge *Gloucs* ... 37 H3
Lattiford *Somset* ... 24 C2
Latton *Wilts* ... 39 F4
Lauder *Border* ... 122 C4
Laugharne *Carmth* ... 33 G3
Laughterton *Lincs* ... 85 F2
Laughton *E Susx* ... 17 F3
Laughton *Leics* ... 60 C4
Laughton *Lincs* ... 85 F4
Laughton *Lincs* ... 74 A3
Laughton-en-le-Morthen *S York* ... 84 C3
Launcells *Cnwll* ... 20 C1
Launcells Cross *Cnwll* ... 20 C1
Launceston *Cnwll* ... 5 G4
Launton *Oxon* ... 48 D1
Laurencekirk *Abers* ... 149 E2
Laurieston *D & G* ... 110 A1
Laurieston *Falk* ... 131 E3
Lavendon *Bucks* ... 49 G5
Lavenham *Suffk* ... 52 C6
Lavernock *V Glam* ... 36 C1
Laversdale *Cumb* ... 112 B1
Laverstock *Wilts* ... 25 G2
Laverstoke *Hants* ... 26 C4
Laverton *Gloucs* ... 47 F3
Laverton *N York* ... 97 E2
Laverton *Somset* ... 24 C5
Lavister *Wrexhm* ... 69 F6
Law *S Lans* ... 120 C5
Law Hill *S Lans* ... 120 C5
Lawers *P & K* ... 138 D2
Lawford *Essex* ... 52 D4
Lawford *Somset* ... 22 D3
Lawgrove *P & K* ... 140 A2
Lawhitton *Cnwll* ... 5 G4
Lawkland *N York* ... 96 A1
Lawkland Green *N York* ... 96 A1
Lawley *Shrops* ... 70 B1
Lawnhead *Staffs* ... 70 C2
Lawrence End *Herts* ... 50 B3
Lawrenny *Pembks* ... 32 D2
Lawshall *Suffk* ... 52 B6
Lawshall Green *Suffk* ... 52 B6
Lawton *Herefs* ... 45 G5
Laxay *W Isls* ... 168 e7
Laxdale *W Isls* ... 168 f8
Laxey *IOM* ... 174 m3
Laxfield *Suffk* ... 65 E3
Laxford Bridge *Highld* ... 164 C3
Laxo *Shet* ... 169 j3
Laxton *E R Yk* ... 92 B2
Laxton *Nhants* ... 61 E5
Laxton *Notts* ... 85 E1
Laycock *W York* ... 90 B4
Layer Breton *Essex* ... 52 C2
Layer Marney *Essex* ... 52 C2
Layer-de-la-Haye *Essex* ... 52 C3
Layham *Suffk* ... 52 D6
Layland's Green *Berks* ... 26 B6
Laymore *Dorset* ... 10 D5
Layter's Green *Bucks* ... 41 H3
Laytham *E R Yk* ... 92 A3
Laythes *Cumb* ... 103 F6
Lazenby *N York* ... 107 E3
Lazonby *Cumb* ... 104 B4
Le Bigard *Guern* ... 174 f1
Le Bourg *Guern* ... 174 g1

Le Bourg *Jersey* ... 174 d1
Le Gron *Guern* ... 174 f1
Le Haguais *Jersey* ... 174 c1
Le Hocq *Jersey* ... 174 d1
Le Villocq *Guern* ... 174 g2
Lea *Derbys* ... 72 A6
Lea *Herefs* ... 46 B1
Lea *Lincs* ... 85 F3
Lea *Shrops* ... 69 F1
Lea *Shrops* ... 56 D4
Lea *Wilts* ... 38 D3
Lea Bridge *Derbys* ... 71 H6
Lea Heath *Staffs* ... 71 E3
Lea Marston *Warwks* ... 59 E5
Lea Town *Lancs* ... 88 C3
Lea Yeat *Cumb* ... 96 A3
Leachkin *Highld* ... 155 E4
Leadburn *Mdloth* ... 121 G5
Leaden Roding *Essex* ... 51 G2
Leadenham *Lincs* ... 73 G5
Leadgate *Dur* ... 105 H5
Leadgate *Nthumb* ... 114 C1
Leadhills *S Lans* ... 120 C1
Leadingcross Green *Kent* ... 30 C1
Leadmill *Derbys* ... 83 G3
Leafield *Oxon* ... 40 A6
Leagrave *Beds* ... 50 B3
Leagreen *E R Yk* ... 93 F3
Leahead *Ches* ... 82 B1
Leake *N York* ... 97 G4
Leake Common Side *Lincs* ... 74 D5
Lealholm *N York* ... 107 G2
Lealholm Side *N York* ... 107 G2
Lealt *Highld* ... 151 E5
Leam *Derbys* ... 83 G3
Leamington Hastings *Warwks* ... 59 G2
Leamington Spa *Warwks* ... 59 F2
Leamonsley *Staffs* ... 71 F1
Leamside *Dur* ... 106 C5
Leap Cross *E Susx* ... 17 G2
Leasgill *Cumb* ... 95 F3
Leasingham *Lincs* ... 74 A5
Leasingthorne *Dur* ... 106 B4
Leatherhead *Surrey* ... 28 C2
Leathley *N York* ... 90 C4
Leaton *Shrops* ... 69 G2
Leaton *Shrops* ... 70 A1
Leaveland *Kent* ... 30 D1
Leavenheath *Suffk* ... 52 C4
Leavening *N York* ... 92 B6
Leaves Green *Gt Lon* ... 29 E2
Lebberston *N York* ... 99 F3
Lechlade *Gloucs* ... 39 G4
Leck Gruinart *Ag & B* ... 126 B2
Leck *Lancs* ... 95 G2
Leckbuie *P & K* ... 138 D4
Leckford *Hants* ... 26 B3
Leckhampstead *Berks* ... 40 C2
Leckhampstead *Bucks* ... 49 E3
Leckhampstead Thicket *Berks* ... 40 C2
Leckhampton *Gloucs* ... 47 E1
Leckmelm *Highld* ... 161 F3
Leckwith *V Glam* ... 36 C2
Leconfield *E R Yk* ... 92 D4
Ledaig *Ag & B* ... 136 D3
Ledburn *Bucks* ... 49 G1
Ledbury *Herefs* ... 46 C3
Leddington *Gloucs* ... 46 B3
Ledgemoor *Herefs* ... 45 G4
Ledicot *Herefs* ... 45 G5
Ledmore Junction *Highld* ... 161 G5
Ledsham *Ches* ... 81 F2
Ledsham *W York* ... 91 F2
Ledston *W York* ... 91 F2
Ledston Luck *W York* ... 91 E3
Ledstone *Devon* ... 7 E2
Ledwell *Oxon* ... 48 B2
Lee *Devon* ... 21 E5
Lee *Gt Lon* ... 29 E4
Lee *Hants* ... 14 B5
Lee *Shrops* ... 69 H3
Lee Brockhurst *Shrops* ... 69 H3
Lee Chapel *Essex* ... 29 H5
Lee Clump *Bucks* ... 41 G5
Lee Common *Bucks* ... 41 G5
Lee Green *Ches* ... 70 B6
Lee Mill *Devon* ... 6 C3
Lee Moor *Devon* ... 6 C4
Lee Street *Surrey* ... 16 D6
Lee-on-the-Solent *Hants* ... 14 D4
Leebotwood *Shrops* ... 57 E5
Leece *Cumb* ... 94 C2
Leedon *Beds* ... 49 G2
Leeds *Kent* ... 30 B1
Leeds *W York* ... 90 D3
Leeds Bradford Airport *W York* ... 90 C4
Leeds Castle *Kent* ... 30 B1
Leedstown *Cnwll* ... 2 D3
Leek *Staffs* ... 71 E6
Leek Wootton *Warwks* ... 59 F2
Leeming *N York* ... 97 F4
Leeming *W York* ... 90 B3
Leeming Bar *N York* ... 97 F4
Lees *Derbys* ... 71 G4
Lees *Gt Man* ... 82 D5
Lees Green *Derbys* ... 71 G4
Lees Hill *Cumb* ... 112 C2
Leesthorpe *Leics* ... 73 E1
Leeswood *Flints* ... 69 E6
Leetown *P & K* ... 140 B2
Leftwich *Ches* ... 82 B2
Legar *Powys* ... 36 C6
Legbourne *Lincs* ... 86 D3
Legburthwaite *Cumb* ... 103 G2
Legerwood *Border* ... 122 C4
Legoland *Berks* ... 41 G4
Legsby *Lincs* ... 86 B3
Leicester *Leics* ... 60 B6
Leicester Forest East *Leics* ... 60 A6
Leigh *Devon* ... 21 G2
Leigh *Dorset* ... 11 F5
Leigh *Gloucs* ... 46 D2
Leigh *Gt Man* ... 82 B5
Leigh *Kent* ... 17 F6
Leigh *Shrops* ... 56 D6
Leigh *Surrey* ... 16 C6
Leigh *Wilts* ... 39 E3
Leigh *Worcs* ... 46 C5

Leigh Beck *Essex* ... 30 B4
Leigh Delamere *Wilts* ... 38 D2
Leigh Green *Kent* ... 18 C5
Leigh Knoweglass *S Lans* ... 119 H4
Leigh Park *Dorset* ... 12 D5
Leigh Sinton *Worcs* ... 46 C4
Leigh upon Mendip *Somset* ... 24 B3
Leigh Woods *Somset* ... 37 G1
Leigh-on-Sea *Essex* ... 30 B5
Leighland Chapel *Somset* ... 22 C3
Leighterton *Gloucs* ... 38 C3
Leighton *N York* ... 97 E3
Leighton *Powys* ... 56 C6
Leighton *Shrops* ... 57 F6
Leighton *Somset* ... 24 C4
Leighton Bromswold *Cambs* ... 61 G3
Leighton Buzzard *Beds* ... 49 G2
Leinthall Earls *Herefs* ... 57 E2
Leinthall Starkes *Herefs* ... 57 E2
Leintwardine *Herefs* ... 56 D3
Leire *Leics* ... 60 A4
Leiston *Suffk* ... 65 G2
Leitfie *P & K* ... 140 C4
Leith *C Edin* ... 132 B3
Leitholm *Border* ... 123 E4
Lelant *Cnwll* ... 2 C3
Lelley *E R Yk* ... 93 F3
Lem Hill *Worcs* ... 57 G3
Lemmington Hall *Nthumb* ... 124 D2
Lempitlaw *Border* ... 123 E3
Lemreway *W Isls* ... 168 e7
Lemsford *Herts* ... 50 C2
Lenchwick *Worcs* ... 47 F4
Lendalfoot *S Ayrs* ... 108 C4
Lendrick *Stirlg* ... 129 G6
Lendrum Terrace *Abers* ... 159 G3
Lenham *Kent* ... 30 C1
Lenham Heath *Kent* ... 30 C1
Lenie *Highld* ... 154 C2
Lennel *Border* ... 123 F3
Lennox Plunton *D & G* ... 101 G5
Lennoxtown *E Duns* ... 130 C3
Lent *Bucks* ... 41 G2
Lenton *Lincs* ... 73 H3
Lenton *Notts* ... 72 C4
Lenwade *Norfk* ... 76 D2
Lenzie *E Duns* ... 130 C2
Leochel-Cushnie *Abers* ... 148 C5
Leominster *Herefs* ... 45 H5
Leonard Stanley *Gloucs* ... 38 C5
Leoville *Jersey* ... 174 a3
Lepe *Hants* ... 14 C3
Lephin *Highld* ... 150 B4
Leppington *N York* ... 92 B6
Lepton *W York* ... 90 C1
Lerryn *Cnwll* ... 5 E2
Lerwick *Shet* ... 169 j2
Les Arquets *Guern* ... 174 f1
Les Hubits *Guern* ... 174 g1
Les Lohiers *Guern* ... 174 f2
Les Murchez *Guern* ... 174 f1
Les Nicolles *Guern* ... 174 g1
Les Quartiers *Guern* ... 174 g2
Les Quennevais *Jersey* ... 174 a2
Les Sages *Guern* ... 174 f1
Les Villets *Guern* ... 174 f1
Lesbury *Nthumb* ... 125 E2
Leslie *Abers* ... 158 B1
Leslie *Fife* ... 132 B5
Lesmahagow *S Lans* ... 120 C3
Lesnewth *Cnwll* ... 5 E5
Lessingham *Norfk* ... 77 G3
Lessonhall *Cumb* ... 103 F5
Lestowder *Cnwll* ... 3 E2
Leswalt *D & G* ... 108 B1
Letchmore Heath *Herts* ... 28 B6
Letchworth *Herts* ... 50 C4
Letcombe Bassett *Oxon* ... 40 B3
Letcombe Regis *Oxon* ... 40 B3
Letham *Angus* ... 141 E5
Letham *Border* ... 112 D6
Letham *Falk* ... 131 E4
Letham *Fife* ... 140 C1
Letham Grange *Angus* ... 141 F4
Lethendy *P & K* ... 140 A4
Lethenty *Abers* ... 158 B1
Lethenty *Abers* ... 158 D3
Letheringham *Suffk* ... 65 E1
Letheringsett *Norfk* ... 76 D4
Lett's Green *Kent* ... 29 E2
Lettaford *Devon* ... 8 D3
Letterewe *Highld* ... 152 D6
Letterfearn *Highld* ... 152 C1
Letterfinlay Lodge Hotel *Highld* ... 145 E3
Lettermorar *Highld* ... 143 G3
Letters *Highld* ... 161 F2
Lettershaw *S Lans* ... 120 C1
Letterston *Pembks* ... 32 D5
Lettoch *Highld* ... 156 B1
Lettoch *Highld* ... 156 C2
Letton *Herefs* ... 45 F4
Letton *Herefs* ... 56 D2
Letty Green *Herts* ... 50 D2
Letwell *S York* ... 84 C3
Leuchars *Fife* ... 140 D2
Leumrabhagh *W Isls* ... 168 e7
Leurbost *W Isls* ... 168 e8
Levalsa Meor *Cnwll* ... 3 G5
Levedale *Staffs* ... 70 D2
Level's Green *Essex* ... 51 F3
Leven *E R Yk* ... 93 E4
Leven *Fife* ... 132 C5
Levencorroch *N Ayrs* ... 118 h1
Levens *Cumb* ... 95 F3
Levens Green *Herts* ... 50 D3
Levenshulme *Gt Man* ... 82 D4
Levenwick *Shet* ... 169 h1
Leverburgh *W Isls* ... 168 c6
Leverington *Cambs* ... 75 E1
Leverstock Green *Herts* ... 50 B1
Leverton *Lincs* ... 74 D5
Levington *Suffk* ... 53 F5
Levisham *N York* ... 98 D4
Lew *Oxon* ... 40 B5
Lewannick *Cnwll* ... 5 F4
Lewdown *Devon* ... 8 A3
Lewes *E Susx* ... 17 E2
Leweston *Pembks* ... 32 D4

Lewis Wych *Herefs* ... 45 F5
Lewisham *Gt Lon* ... 29 E3
Lewiston *Highld* ... 154 C2
Lewknor *Oxon* ... 41 E4
Leworthy *Devon* ... 5 G6
Leworthy *Devon* ... 21 G4
Lewson Street *Kent* ... 30 C2
Lewth *Lancs* ... 88 C3
Lewtrenchard *Devon* ... 8 B3
Lexden *Essex* ... 52 C3
Lexworthy *Somset* ... 23 E3
Ley *Cnwll* ... 5 E2
Ley Hill *Bucks* ... 41 H4
Leybourne *Kent* ... 29 H2
Leyburn *N York* ... 96 D5
Leycett *Staffs* ... 70 C5
Leygreen *Herts* ... 50 C3
Leyland *Lancs* ... 88 D2
Leyland Green *Mersyd* ... 81 H5
Leylodge *Abers* ... 149 E6
Leys *Abers* ... 159 F4
Leys *Angus* ... 140 C4
Leys of Cossans *Angus* ... 140 D5
Leysdown-on-Sea *Kent* ... 30 D3
Leysmill *Angus* ... 141 F4
Leysters *Herefs* ... 57 F2
Leyton *Gt Lon* ... 29 E5
Leytonstone *Gt Lon* ... 29 E5
Lezant *Cnwll* ... 5 G4
Lezayre *IOM* ... 174 m4
Lezerea *Cnwll* ... 2 D3
Lhanbryde *Moray* ... 157 E5
Libanus *Powys* ... 44 C2
Libberton *S Lans* ... 120 D4
Liberton *C Edin* ... 132 B2
Lichfield *Staffs* ... 71 F1
Lickey *Worcs* ... 58 C3
Lickey End *Worcs* ... 58 C3
Lickey Rock *Worcs* ... 58 C3
Lickfold *W Susx* ... 27 G2
Liddaton Green *Devon* ... 8 B3
Liddesdale *Highld* ... 136 B6
Liddington *Wilts* ... 39 G2
Lidgate *Derbys* ... 83 H2
Lidgate *Suffk* ... 63 F1
Lidget *S York* ... 84 D5
Lidgett *Notts* ... 84 D1
Lidham Hill *E Susx* ... 18 B3
Lidlington *Beds* ... 49 H3
Lidsing *Kent* ... 30 B2
Liff *Angus* ... 140 C3
Lifford *W Mids* ... 58 C3
Lifton *Devon* ... 5 G4
Liftondown *Devon* ... 5 G4
Lighthazles *W York* ... 90 A2
Lighthorne *Warwks* ... 48 B5
Lighthorne Heath *Warwks* ... 48 B5
Lightwater *Surrey* ... 27 G5
Lightwood *Staffs* ... 70 D4
Lightwood Green *Ches* ... 70 A4
Lightwood Green *Wrexhm* ... 69 F4
Lilbourne *Nhants* ... 60 B3
Lilburn Street *Nthumb* ... 124 C3
Lilleshall *Shrops* ... 70 B2
Lilley *Berks* ... 40 C2
Lilley *Herts* ... 50 B3
Lilliesleaf *Border* ... 122 C2
Lillingstone Dayrell *Bucks* ... 49 E3
Lillingstone Lovell *Bucks* ... 49 E3
Lillington *Dorset* ... 11 G6
Lilliput *Dorset* ... 12 D4
Lilstock *Somset* ... 22 D4
Lilyhurst *Shrops* ... 70 B1
Limbrick *Lancs* ... 88 D1
Limbury *Beds* ... 50 B3
Lime Street *Worcs* ... 46 D2
Limebrook *Herefs* ... 56 D2
Limefield *Gt Man* ... 82 C6
Limekilnburn *S Lans* ... 120 B4
Limekilns *Fife* ... 131 G3
Limerigg *Falk* ... 131 E2
Limerstone *IOW* ... 14 C2
Limestone Brae *Nthumb* ... 105 E5
Limington *Somset* ... 24 A1
Limmerhaugh *E Ayrs* ... 119 H2
Limpenhoe *Norfk* ... 65 F6
Limpley Stoke *Wilts* ... 24 C5
Limpsfield *Surrey* ... 29 E1
Limpsfield Chart *Surrey* ... 29 E1
Linby *Notts* ... 72 C5
Linchmere *W Susx* ... 27 G2
Lincluden *D & G* ... 110 D2
Lincoln *Lincs* ... 85 G2
Lincomb *Worcs* ... 58 A2
Lincombe *Devon* ... 7 E2
Lindal in Furness *Cumb* ... 94 C2
Lindale *Cumb* ... 95 E3
Lindfield *W Susx* ... 16 C4
Lindford *Hants* ... 27 F3
Lindley *W York* ... 90 B1
Lindley Green *N York* ... 90 C4
Lindow End *Ches* ... 82 C2
Lindridge *Worcs* ... 57 G2
Lindsell *Essex* ... 51 G3
Lindsey *Suffk* ... 52 C5
Lindsey Tye *Suffk* ... 52 C5
Liney *Somset* ... 23 F3
Linford *Essex* ... 29 G4
Linford *Hants* ... 13 F5
Lingbob *W York* ... 90 B3
Lingdale *N York* ... 107 F2
Lingen *Herefs* ... 56 D2
Lingfield *Surrey* ... 17 E6
Lingley Green *Ches* ... 81 H4
Lingwood *Norfk* ... 65 F6
Linicro *Highld* ... 150 D5
Linkend *Worcs* ... 46 D2
Linkenholt *Hants* ... 26 B5
Linkhill *Kent* ... 18 B4
Linkinhorne *Cnwll* ... 5 G3
Linktown *Fife* ... 132 B4
Linkwood *Moray* ... 156 D5
Linley *Shrops* ... 56 D5
Linley Green *Herefs* ... 46 C4
Linleygreen *Shrops* ... 57 G5
Linlithgow *W Loth* ... 131 F3
Linshiels *Nthumb* ... 113 F5
Linsidemore *Highld* ... 162 B4

Linslade

Llangelynin

297

Linslade Beds 49 G2
Linstead Parva Suffk 65 F3
Linstock Cumb 104 A6
Linthurst Worcs 58 C3
Linthwaite W York 90 B1
Lintlaw Border 123 E5
Lintmill Moray 157 G6
Linton Border 123 E2
Linton Cambs 51 F5
Linton Derbys 71 H2
Linton Herefs 46 B2
Linton Kent 30 A1
Linton N York 90 A6
Linton Nthumb 114 D5
Linton W York 91 E4
Linton Heath Derbys 71 H2
Linton Hill Gloucs 46 B2
Linton-on-Ouse N York 91 F6
Linwood Hants 13 F5
Linwood Lincs 86 B3
Linwood Rens 129 F2
Lionacleit W Isls 168 b4
Lional W Isls 168 f9
Lions Green E Susx 17 F3
Liphook Hants 27 F2
Lipley Shrops 70 B3
Liscard Mersyd 81 E4
Liscombe Somset 22 B2
Liskeard Cnwll 5 F2
Liss Hants 27 F2
Liss Forest Hants 27 F2
Lissett E R Yk 93 E5
Lissington Lincs 86 B3
Liston Essex 52 B5
Lisvane Cardif 36 C2
Liswerry Newpt 36 D3
Litcham Norfk 76 B2
Litchard Brdgnd 35 F2
Litchborough Nhants 48 D5
Litchfield Hants 26 C5
Litherland Mersyd 81 F4
Litlington Cambs 50 D5
Litlington E Susx 17 F1
Little Abington Cambs 51 F6
Little Addington Nhants 61 F3
Little Airies D & G 101 E5
Little Almshoe Herts 50 C3
Little Alne Warwks 47 G5
Little Altcar Mersyd 81 E5
Little Amwell Herts 50 D2
Little Asby Cumb 95 H6
Little Aston Staffs 58 D5
Little Atherfield IOW 14 C2
Little Ayton N York 107 E2
Little Baddow Essex 52 A1
Little Badminton Gloucs 38 C3
Little Bampton Cumb 103 G6
Little Bardfield Essex 51 G4
Little Barford Beds 61 H1
Little Barningham Norfk 76 D3
Little Barrington Gloucs 39 G5
Little Barrow Ches 81 G2
Little Barugh N York 98 C3
Little Bavington Nthumb 113 G3
Little Bayton Warwks 59 F4
Little Bealings Suffk 53 F5
Little Bedwyn Wilts 26 A6
Little Bentley Essex 53 E3
Little Berkhamsted Herts 50 D1
Little Billing Nhants 49 F5
Little Billington Beds 49 G1
Little Birch Herefs 45 H2
Little Bispham Lancs 88 B4
Little Blakenham Suffk 53 E6
Little Blencow Cumb 104 A3
Little Bloxwich W Mids 58 C6
Little Bognor W Susx 16 A3
Little Bolehill Derbys 71 H5
Little Bollington Ches 82 B3
Little Bookham Surrey 28 B1
Little Bourton Oxon 48 C4
Little Bowden Leics 60 C4
Little Bradley Suffk 51 H6
Little Brampton Herefs 45 F5
Little Brampton Shrops 56 D3
Little Braxted Essex 52 B2
Little Brechin Angus 141 F6
Little Brickhill Bucks 49 G2
Little Bridgeford Staffs 70 D3
Little Brington Nhants 60 C2
Little Bromley Essex 52 D4
Little Broughton Cumb 103 E3
Little Budworth Ches 82 A1
Little Burstead Essex 29 G5
Little Bytham Lincs 73 H2
Little Canfield Essex 51 G3
Little Carlton Lincs 86 D3
Little Carlton Notts 73 E6
Little Casterton Rutlnd 73 H1
Little Catwick E R Yk 93 E4
Little Catworth Cambs 61 G3
Little Cawthorpe Lincs 86 D3
Little Chalfield Wilts 24 D6
Little Chalfont Bucks 41 H4
Little Charlinch Somset 23 E3
Little Chart Kent 18 C6
Little Chesterford Essex 51 F5
Little Cheveney Kent 17 H6
Little Cheverell Wilts 25 E5
Little Chishill Cambs 51 E4
Little Clacton Essex 53 E3
Little Clanfield Oxon 39 G4
Little Clifton Cumb 103 E3
Little Coates Lincs 86 C6
Little Comberton Worcs 47 E3
Little Common E Susx 17 H2
Little Comp Kent 29 G2
Little Compton Warwks 47 H2
Little Corby Cumb 104 B6
Little Cornard Suffk 52 C5
Little Cowarne Herefs 46 B4
Little Coxwell Oxon 39 G4
Little Crakehall N York 97 F4
Little Cransley Nhants 60 D3
Little Cressingham Norfk 64 A5
Little Crosby Mersyd 81 E5
Little Crosthwaite Cumb 103 F3
Little Cubley Derbys 71 F4
Little Dalby Leics 73 E1
Little Dens Abers 159 F3
Little Dewchurch Herefs 45 H2
Little Ditton Cambs 63 F1
Little Doward Herefs 37 F6
Little Downham Cambs 62 D4
Little Driffield E R Yk 92 D5
Little Dunham Norfk 76 B1
Little Dunkeld P & K 139 G4
Little Dunmow Essex 51 G3
Little Durnford Wilts 25 G3
Little Easton Essex 51 G3
Little Eaton Derbys 72 A4
Little Ellingham Norfk 64 C5
Little Elm Somset 24 C4
Little Everdon Nhants 48 D5
Little Eversden Cambs 51 E6
Little Faringdon Oxon 39 G4
Little Fencote N York 97 F4
Little Fenton N York 91 F3
Little Fransham Norfk 76 B1
Little Gaddesden Herts 41 H6
Little Garway Herefs 45 G2
Little Gidding Cambs 61 G4
Little Glemham Suffk 65 F1
Little Gorsley Herefs 46 B2
Little Gransden Cambs 62 B1
Little Green Notts 73 E4
Little Green Somset 24 C4
Little Grimsby Lincs 86 D4
Little Gringley Notts 85 E3
Little Habton N York 98 C3
Little Hadham Herts 51 E3
Little Hale Lincs 74 B4
Little Hallam Derbys 72 B4
Little Hallingbury Essex 51 F2
Little Hanford Dorset 12 B6
Little Harrowden Nhants 61 E2
Little Haseley Oxon 41 E4
Little Hatfield E R Yk 93 E4
Little Hautbois Norfk 77 E2
Little Haven Pembks 32 C3
Little Hay Staffs 58 D6
Little Hayfield Derbys 83 E3
Little Haywood Staffs 71 E2
Little Heath Berks 41 E2
Little Heath Staffs 70 D2
Little Heath W Mids 59 F4
Little Hereford Herefs 57 F2
Little Hermitage Kent 29 H3
Little Horkesley Essex 52 C4
Little Hormead Herts 51 E4
Little Horsted E Susx 17 F3
Little Horton W York 90 C3
Little Horton Wilts 25 F5
Little Horwood Bucks 49 F2
Little Houghton Nhants 49 F5
Little Houghton S York 84 B5
Little Hucklow Derbys 83 F2
Little Hulton Gt Man 82 B5
Little Hungerford Berks 40 C2
Little Hutton N York 97 H2
Little Ingestre Staffs 71 E2
Little Irchester Nhants 61 E2
Little Kelk E R Yk 93 E5
Little Keyford Somset 24 C4
Little Kimble Bucks 41 F5
Little Kineton Warwks 48 B4
Little Kingshill Bucks 41 G4
Little Knox D & G 102 B6
Little Langdale Cumb 94 D5
Little Langford Wilts 25 F3
Little Lashbrook Devon 20 D1
Little Laver Essex 51 F2
Little Leigh Ches 82 A2
Little Leighs Essex 51 H2
Little Lever Gt Man 82 C5
Little Linford Bucks 49 G4
Little Linton Cambs 51 F5
Little Load Somset 23 G2
Little London Bucks 41 E5
Little London Cambs 62 C5
Little London E Susx 17 F3
Little London Essex 51 F4
Little London Essex 51 H4
Little London Gloucs 46 C1
Little London Hants 26 B4
Little London Hants 26 D5
Little London Lincs 74 C2
Little London Lincs 86 D2
Little London Lincs 75 E2
Little London Norfk 75 F2
Little London Powys 55 H4
Little London W York 90 C3
Little Longstone Derbys 83 G2
Little Madeley Staffs 70 C5
Little Malvern Worcs 46 C3
Little Mancot Flints 81 E1
Little Maplestead Essex 52 B4
Little Marcle Herefs 46 B3
Little Marland Devon 21 E2
Little Marlow Bucks 41 G3
Little Massingham Norfk 76 A2
Little Melton Norfk 64 D6
Little Mill Mons 36 D5
Little Milton Oxon 40 D4
Little Missenden Bucks 41 G4
Little Mongeham Kent 31 G1
Little Moor Somset 23 F2
Little Musgrave Cumb 104 D1
Little Ness Shrops 69 F2
Little Neston Ches 81 E2
Little Newcastle Pembks 32 D5
Little Newsham Dur 105 H2
Little Norton Somset 11 E6
Little Norton Staffs 58 C6
Little Oakley Essex 53 F4
Little Oakley Nhants 61 E4
Little Odell Beds 49 H5
Little Offley Herts 50 B3
Little Onn Staffs 70 C2
Little Ormside Cumb 104 D2
Little Orton Cumb 103 G6
Little Ouse Cambs 63 E4
Little Ouseburn N York 91 F6
Little Oxendon Nhants 60 C4
Little Packington Warwks 59 E4
Little Pattenden Kent 18 A6
Little Paxton Cambs 61 H2
Little Petherick Cnwll 4 C3
Little Plumpton Lancs 88 B3
Little Plumstead Norfk 77 F1
Little Ponton Lincs 73 G3
Little Posbrook Hants 14 D4
Little Potheridge Devon 21 E2
Little Preston Nhants 48 D5
Little Preston W York 91 E3
Little Raveley Cambs 62 B3
Little Reedness E R Yk 92 B2
Little Ribston N York 91 E5
Little Rissington Gloucs 47 G1
Little Rollright Oxon 48 A2
Little Rowsley Derbys 83 G1
Little Ryburgh Norfk 76 C3
Little Ryle Nthumb 124 C2
Little Ryton Shrops 57 E6
Little Salkeld Cumb 104 B4
Little Sampford Essex 51 G4
Little Sandhurst Berks 27 F5
Little Saredon Staffs 58 B6
Little Saughall Ches 81 F1
Little Saxham Suffk 63 G2
Little Scatwell Highld 154 B5
Little Sessay N York 97 H2
Little Shelford Cambs 51 E6
Little Silver Devon 9 E5
Little Silver Devon 9 F6
Little Singleton Lancs 88 B3
Little Skipwith N York 91 H3
Little Smeaton N York 91 F1
Little Snoring Norfk 76 C3
Little Sodbury Gloucs 38 B2
Little Sodbury End Gloucs 38 B3
Little Somborne Hants 26 B2
Little Somerford Wilts 38 D3
Little Soudley Shrops 70 B3
Little Stainforth N York 96 A1
Little Stainton Dur 106 C3
Little Stanney Ches 81 F2
Little Staughton Beds 61 G2
Little Steeping Lincs 87 E1
Little Stonham Suffk 64 D1
Little Stretton Leics 60 C5
Little Stretton Shrops 57 E5
Little Strickland Cumb 104 B2
Little Stukeley Cambs 62 A3
Little Sugnall Staffs 70 C3
Little Sutton Ches 81 F2
Little Sutton Shrops 57 E4
Little Swinburne Nthumb 113 G2
Little Sypland D & G 102 A5
Little Tew Oxon 48 B2
Little Tey Essex 52 C3
Little Thetford Cambs 63 E3
Little Thirkleby N York 97 H3
Little Thornage Norfk 76 D4
Little Thornton Lancs 88 B4
Little Thorpe Dur 106 D5
Little Thurlow Suffk 51 H6
Little Thurlow Green Suffk 51 H6
Little Thurrock Essex 29 G4
Little Torrington Devon 21 E2
Little Totham Essex 52 B2
Little Town Ches 82 A4
Little Town Cumb 103 F2
Little Town Lancs 89 E3
Little Twycross Leics 59 F6
Little Urswick Cumb 94 C2
Little Wakering Essex 30 C5
Little Walden Essex 51 F5
Little Waldingfield Suffk 52 C5
Little Walsingham Norfk 76 B4
Little Waltham Essex 51 H2
Little Warley Essex 29 G5
Little Washbourne Gloucs 47 E2
Little Weighton E R Yk 92 D3
Little Weldon Nhants 61 E4
Little Welnetham Suffk 64 A1
Little Welton Lincs 86 C3
Little Wenham Suffk 52 D5
Little Wenlock Shrops 57 G6
Little Weston Somset 24 B2
Little Whitefield IOW 14 D2
Little Whittington Nthumb 113 G2
Little Wilbraham Cambs 63 E1
Little Witcombe Gloucs 38 D6
Little Witley Worcs 57 H2
Little Wittenham Oxon 40 D4
Little Wolford Warwks 47 H3
Little Woodcote Surrey 28 D2
Little Wratting Suffk 51 H5
Little Wymington Beds 61 E2
Little Wymondley Herts 50 C3
Little Wyrley Staffs 58 C6
Little Wytheford Shrops 69 H2
Little Yeldham Essex 52 A5
Littlebeck N York 98 D5
Littleborough Devon 9 E6
Littleborough Gt Man 89 H1
Littleborough Notts 85 F3
Littlebourne Kent 31 F2
Littlebredy Dorset 11 F3
Littleburn Highld 155 E4
Littlebury Essex 51 F5
Littlebury Green Essex 51 F5
Littlecott Wilts 25 G4
Littledean Gloucs 38 B6
Littledown Hants 26 B5
Littleham Devon 21 E3
Littleham Devon 9 G3
Littlehampton W Susx 16 A2
Littleharle Tower Nthumb 113 G3
Littlehaven W Susx 16 C5
Littlehempston Devon 7 E4
Littlehoughton Nthumb 125 E3
Littlemill Abers 147 H4
Littlemill Highld 155 G4
Littlemoor Derbys 84 A1
Littlemore Oxon 40 D5
Littleover Derbys 72 A3
Littleport Cambs 63 E4
Littleport Bridge Cambs 63 E4
Littler Ches 82 A1
Littlestone-on-Sea Kent 18 D4
Littlethorpe Leics 60 B5
Littlethorpe N York 97 F2
Littleton Angus 140 C5
Littleton Ches 81 G1
Littleton D & G 101 G6
Littleton Dorset 12 C5
Littleton Hants 26 C2
Littleton Somset 23 H2
Littleton Somset 24 A6
Littleton Surrey 27 H4
Littleton Surrey 28 B3
Littleton Drew Wilts 38 C2
Littleton Pannell Wilts 25 E5
Littleton-on-Severn Gloucs 37 G3
Littletown Dur 106 C5
Littletown IOW 14 D3
Littlewick Green Berks 41 F2
Littlewindsor Dorset 11 E5
Littlewood Staffs 58 C6
Littleworth Bucks 49 G1
Littleworth Oxon 40 A4
Littleworth Staffs 70 D2
Littleworth Staffs 71 E1
Littleworth W Susx 16 C3
Littleworth Worcs 46 D4
Littleworth Worcs 58 C2
Littleworth Common Bucks 41 G3
Littleworth End Cambs 62 B2
Littley Green Essex 51 H2
Litton Derbys 83 G2
Litton N York 96 B2
Litton Somset 24 B5
Litton Cheney Dorset 11 F4
Liurbost W Isls 168 e8
Liverpool Mersyd 81 F4
Liverpool Airport Mersyd 81 F3
Liversedge W York 90 C2
Liverton Devon 9 E2
Liverton N York 107 F2
Liverton Mines N York 107 F3
Liverton Street Kent 30 B1
Livingston W Loth 131 G2
Livingston Village W Loth 131 G2
Lixton Devon 6 D3
Lixwm Flints 80 D2
Lizard Cnwll 3 E1
Llaingoch IOA 78 B3
Llaithddu Powys 56 A3
Llan Powys 55 F5
Llan-y-pwll Wrexhm 69 F5
Llanaber Gwynd 67 F2
Llanaelhaearn Gwynd 66 C4
Llanafan Cerdgn 54 D3
Llanafan-fechan Powys 44 C4
Llanallgo IOA 79 E3
Llanarmon Gwynd 66 D4
Llanarmon Dyffryn Ceiriog Wrexhm 68 D3
Llanarmon-yn-Ial Denbgs 68 D6
Llanarth Cerdgn 42 D5
Llanarth Mons 37 E5
Llanarthne Carmth 43 E1
Llanasa Flints 80 C3
Llanbabo IOA 78 C3
Llanbadarn Fawr Cerdgn 54 D3
Llanbadarn Fynydd Powys 56 A3
Llanbadarn-y-garreg Powys 44 D4
Llanbadoc Mons 37 E4
Llanbadrig IOA 78 C4
Llanbeder Newpt 37 E3
Llanbedr Gwynd 67 E3
Llanbedr Powys 44 D4
Llanbedr Powys 45 E1
Llanbedr-Dyffryn-Clwyd Denbgs 68 D6
Llanbedr-y-Cennin Conwy 79 G2
Llanbedrgoch IOA 79 E3
Llanbedrog Gwynd 66 C3
Llanberis Gwynd 67 E6
Llanbethery V Glam 36 B1
Llanbister Powys 56 A3
Llanblethian V Glam 35 G2
Llanboidy Carmth 33 F4
Llanbradach Caerph 36 C3
Llanbrynmair Powys 55 F6
Llancadle V Glam 36 B1
Llancarfan V Glam 36 B1
Llancayo Mons 37 E5
Llancillo Herefs 45 F2
Llancloudy Herefs 45 H1
Llancynfelyn Cerdgn 54 D5
Llandaff Cardif 36 C2
Llandanwg Gwynd 67 E3
Llandawke Carmth 33 G3
Llanddaniel Fab IOA 79 E2
Llanddarog Carmth 34 C6
Llanddeiniol Cerdgn 54 C2
Llanddeiniolen Gwynd 79 E1
Llandderfel Gwynd 68 B4
Llanddeusant Carmth 43 H2
Llanddeusant IOA 78 C3
Llanddew Powys 44 C2
Llanddewi Swans 34 B3
Llanddewi Brefi Cerdgn 43 G5
Llanddewi Rhydderch Mons 37 E6
Llanddewi Velfrey Pembks 33 F3
Llanddewi Ystradenni Powys 56 A2
Llanddewi'r Cwm Powys 44 C4
Llanddoget Conwy 79 G1
Llanddona IOA 79 E3
Llanddowror Carmth 33 G3
Llanddulas Conwy 80 A2
Llanddwywe Gwynd 67 E2
Llanddyfnan IOA 79 E2
Llandecwyn Gwynd 67 F4
Llandefaelog Powys 44 C2
Llandefaelog-Trer-Graig Powys 44 D2
Llandefalle Powys 44 D3
Llandegfan IOA 79 E2
Llandegla Denbgs 68 D5
Llandegley Powys 56 B2
Llandegveth Mons 36 D4
Llandegwning Gwynd 66 B3
Llandeilo Carmth 43 F1
Llandeilo Graban Powys 44 D4
Llandeilo'r Fan Powys 44 B3
Llandeloy Pembks 32 C4
Llandenny Mons 37 E5
Llandevaud Newpt 37 E3
Llandevenny Mons 37 E3
Llandinabo Herefs 45 H2
Llandinam Powys 55 H4
Llandissilio Pembks 33 E4
Llandogo Mons 37 F5
Llandough V Glam 35 G1
Llandough V Glam 36 C1
Llandovery Carmth 43 H3
Llandow V Glam 35 G2
Llandre Carmth 43 G3
Llandre Cerdgn 54 D4
Llandre Isaf Pembks 33 E4
Llandrillo Denbgs 68 C4
Llandrillo-yn-Rhos Conwy 79 H3
Llandrindod Wells Powys 44 C5
Llandrinio Powys 69 E2
Llandudno Conwy 79 G3
Llandudno Junction Conwy 79 G2
Llandudwen Gwynd 66 B4
Llandulas Powys 44 B3
Llandwrog Gwynd 66 D6
Llandybie Carmth 34 D6
Llandyfaelog Carmth 34 B5
Llandyfan Carmth 34 D6
Llandyfriog Cerdgn 42 C3
Llandyfrydog IOA 78 D3
Llandygai Gwynd 79 F2
Llandygwydd Cerdgn 42 C4
Llandynan Denbgs 68 D5
Llandyrnog Denbgs 80 C1
Llandyssil Powys 56 B5
Llandysul Cerdgn 42 D3
Llanedeyrn Cardif 36 C2
Llanedi Carmth 34 C5
Llaneglwys Powys 44 C3
Llanegryn Gwynd 54 D6
Llanegwad Carmth 43 E1
Llaneilian IOA 78 D4
Llanelian-yn-Rhos Conwy 80 A2
Llanelidan Denbgs 68 C5
Llanelieu Powys 45 E3
Llanellen Mons 36 D5
Llanelli Carmth 34 C4
Llanelltyd Gwynd 67 G2
Llanelly Mons 36 C6
Llanelwedd Powys 44 C4
Llanenddwyn Gwynd 67 E2
Llanengan Gwynd 66 C3
Llanerch Gwynd 68 A2
Llanerch Powys 56 C5
Llanerchymedd IOA 78 D3
Llanerfyl Powys 68 C1
Llanfachraeth IOA 78 C3
Llanfachreth Gwynd 67 G2
Llanfaelog IOA 78 C2
Llanfaelrhys Gwynd 66 B3
Llanfaenor Mons 37 E6
Llanfaes IOA 79 F2
Llanfaes Powys 44 C2
Llanfaethlu IOA 78 C3
Llanfair Gwynd 67 E3
Llanfair Caereinion Powys 56 A6
Llanfair Clydogau Cerdgn 43 F4
Llanfair Dyffryn Clwyd Denbgs 68 D6
Llanfair Kilgeddin Mons 37 E5
Llanfair P G IOA 79 E2
Llanfair Talhaiarn Conwy 80 B2
Llanfair Waterdine Shrops 56 C3
Llanfair-is-gaer Gwynd 79 E1
Llanfair-Nant-Gwyn Pembks 42 B3
Llanfair-y-Cwmwd IOA 78 D1
Llanfair-yn-Neubwll IOA 78 C2
Llanfairfechan Conwy 79 F2
Llanfairynghornwy IOA 78 C4
Llanfallteg Carmth 33 F4
Llanfallteg West Carmth 33 F4
Llanfarian Cerdgn 54 C3
Llanfechain Powys 68 D2
Llanfechell IOA 78 C4
Llanferres Denbgs 68 D6
Llanfflewyn IOA 78 C4
Llanfigael IOA 78 C3
Llanfihangel Glyn Myfyr Conwy 68 B5
Llanfihangel Nant Bran Powys 44 B3
Llanfihangel Rhydithon Powys 56 B2
Llanfihangel Rogiet Mons 37 F3
Llanfihangel Tal-y-llyn Powys 44 D2
Llanfihangel yn Nhowyn IOA 78 C2
Llanfihangel-ar-Arth Carmth 43 E3
Llanfihangel-nant-Melan Powys 45 E5
Llanfihangel-uwch-Gwili Carmth 43 E1
Llanfihangel-y-Creuddyn Cerdgn 54 D3
Llanfihangel-y-pennant Gwynd 67 E4
Llanfihangel-y-pennant Gwynd 67 F1
Llanfihangel-y-traethau Gwynd 67 E3
Llanfihangel-yng-Ngwynfa Powys 68 C2
Llanfilo Powys 44 D2
Llanfoist Mons 36 D6
Llanfor Gwynd 68 B4
Llanfrechfa Torfn 36 D4
Llanfrothen Gwynd 67 F4
Llanfrynach Powys 44 D2
Llanfwrog Denbgs 68 C6
Llanfwrog IOA 78 C3
Llanfyllin Powys 68 D2
Llanfynydd Carmth 43 F2
Llanfynydd Flints 69 E6
Llanfyrnach Pembks 42 B2
Llangadfan Powys 68 B1
Llangadog Carmth 34 B5
Llangadog Carmth 43 G2
Llangadwaladr IOA 78 C2
Llangadwaladr Powys 68 D3
Llangaffo IOA 78 D1
Llangain Carmth 34 A6
Llangammarch Wells Powys 44 B4
Llangan V Glam 35 G2
Llangarron Herefs 45 H1
Llangasty-Talyllyn Powys 44 D2
Llangathen Carmth 43 F1
Llangattock Powys 36 C6
Llangattock Lingoed Mons 45 F1
Llangattock-Vibon-Avel Mons 37 F6
Llangedwyn Powys 68 D2
Llangefni IOA 78 D2
Llangeinor Brdgnd 35 G3
Llangeinwen IOA 78 D1
Llangeitho Cerdgn 43 F5
Llangeler Carmth 42 D3
Llangelynin Gwynd 54 C6

298

Llangendeirne Carmth	34	B6
Llangennech Carmth	34	C4
Llangennith Swans	34	B3
Llangenny Powys	36	D6
Llangernyw Conwy	80	A1
Llangian Gwynd	66	C3
Llangiwg Neath	35	E5
Llangloffan Pembks	32	C5
Llanglydwen Carmth	33	F4
Llangoed IOA	79	F3
Llangoedmor Cerdgn	42	B4
Llangollen Denbgs	68	D4
Llangolman Pembks	33	E4
Llangors Powys	44	D2
Llangovan Mons	37	F5
Llangower Gwynd	68	A3
Llangranog Cerdgn	42	C5
Llangristiolus IOA	78	D2
Llangrove Herefs	45	H1
Llangua Mons	45	G2
Llangunllo Powys	56	B2
Llangunnor Carmth	42	D1
Llangurig Powys	55	G3
Llangwm Conwy	68	B4
Llangwm Mons	37	E4
Llangwm Pembks	32	D3
Llangwm-isaf Mons	37	E4
Llangwnnadl Gwynd	66	B3
Llangwyfan Denbgs	80	C1
Llangwyllog IOA	78	D3
Llangwyryfon Cerdgn	54	D2
Llangybi Cerdgn	43	F4
Llangybi Gwynd	66	D4
Llangybi Mons	37	E4
Llangyfelach Swans	34	D4
Llangynhafal Denbgs	80	D1
Llangynidr Powys	44	D1
Llangynin Carmth	33	G4
Llangynllo Cerdgn	42	D4
Llangynog Carmth	33	G3
Llangynog Powys	68	C3
Llangynog Powys	44	C4
Llangynwyd Brdgnd	35	F3
Llanhamlach Powys	44	D2
Llanharan Rhondd	35	G3
Llanharry Rhondd	35	G2
Llanhennock Mons	37	E3
Llanhilleth Blae G	36	C4
Llanidan IOA	78	D1
Llanidloes Powys	55	G4
Llaniestyn Gwynd	66	B3
Llanigon Powys	45	E3
Llanilar Cerdgn	54	D3
Llanilid Rhondd	35	G2
Llanina Cerdgn	42	D5
Llanio Cerdgn	43	F5
Llanishen Cardif	36	C2
Llanishen Mons	37	F5
Llanllechid Gwynd	79	F1
Llanlleonfel Powys	44	B4
Llanllowell Mons	37	E4
Llanllugan Powys	55	H6
Llanllwch Carmth	42	D1
Llanllwchaiarn Powys	56	B5
Llanllwni Carmth	43	E3
Llanllyfni Gwynd	66	D5
Llanmadoc Swans	34	B4
Llanmaes V Glam	35	G1
Llanmartin Newpt	37	E3
Llanmerewig Powys	56	B5
Llanmihangel V Glam	35	G1
Llanmiloe Carmth	33	G2
Llanmorlais Swans	34	C4
Llannefydd Conwy	80	B2
Llannon Carmth	34	C5
Llannor Gwynd	66	C4
Llanon Cerdgn	54	C2
Llanover Mons	36	D5
Llanpumsaint Carmth	42	D2
Llanrhaeadr-ym-Mochnant Powys	68	D3
Llanrhian Pembks	32	B5
Llanrhidian Swans	34	B3
Llanrhos Conwy	79	G3
Llanrhychwyn Conwy	67	G6
Llanrhyddlad IOA	78	C4
Llanrhystud Cerdgn	54	C2
Llanrothal Herefs	45	G1
Llanrug Gwynd	79	E1
Llanrumney Cardif	36	C2
Llanrwst Conwy	67	G6
Llansadurnen Carmth	33	G3
Llansadwrn Carmth	43	G2
Llansadwrn IOA	79	E2
Llansaint Carmth	34	A5
Llansamlet Swans	34	D4
Llansanffraid Glan Conwy Conwy	79	G2
Llansannan Conwy	80	B1
Llansannor V Glam	35	G2
Llansantffraed Powys	44	D1
Llansantffraed-Cwmdeuddwr Powys	55	G2
Llansantffraid-in-Elvel Powys	44	D5
Llansantffraid Cerdgn	54	C2
Llansantffraid-ym-Mechain Powys	68	D2
Llansawel Carmth	43	F3
Llansilin Powys	68	D3
Llansoy Mons	37	E4
Llanspyddid Powys	44	C2
Llanstadwell Pembks	32	D2
Llansteffan Carmth	33	H3
Llanstephan Powys	44	D3
Llantarnam Torfn	36	D4
Llanteg Pembks	33	F3
Llanthewy Skirrid Mons	37	E6
Llanthony Mons	45	F2
Llantilio Pertholey Mons	36	D6
Llantilio-Crossenny Mons	37	E6
Llantrisant IOA	78	C3
Llantrisant Mons	37	E4
Llantrisant Rhondd	36	B3
Llantrithyd V Glam	36	B1
Llantwit Fardre Rhondd	36	B3
Llantwit Major V Glam	35	G1
Llantysilio Denbgs	68	D4
Llanuwchllyn Gwynd	68	A3
Llanvaches Newpt	37	E3
Llanvair Discoed Mons	37	E3
Llanvapley Mons	37	E6
Llanvetherine Mons	37	E6
Llanveynoe Herefs	45	F2
Llanvihangel Crucorney Mons	45	F1
Llanvihangel Gobion Mons	37	E5
Llanvihangel-Ystern-Llewern Mons	37	E6
Llanwarne Herefs	45	H2
Llanwddyn Powys	68	C2
Llanwenarth Mons	36	D6
Llanwenog Cerdgn	43	E4
Llanwern Newpt	37	E3
Llanwinio Carmth	33	G4
Llanwnda Gwynd	66	D6
Llanwnda Pembks	32	D6
Llanwnnen Cerdgn	43	E4
Llanwnog Powys	55	H5
Llanwonno Rhondd	36	A4
Llanwrda Carmth	43	G2
Llanwrin Powys	55	E6
Llanwrthwl Powys	55	G2
Llanwrtyd Powys	44	B4
Llanwrtyd Wells Powys	44	B4
Llanwyddelan Powys	56	A5
Llanyblodwel Shrops	69	E2
Llanybri Carmth	33	G3
Llanybydder Carmth	43	E4
Llanycefn Pembks	33	E4
Llanychaer Bridge Pembks	32	D5
Llanycrwys Carmth	43	F4
Llanymawddwy Gwynd	68	A2
Llanymynech Powys	69	E2
Llanynghenedl IOA	78	C3
Llanynys Denbgs	80	C1
Llanyre Powys	44	C5
Llanystumdwy Gwynd	66	D4
Llanywern Powys	44	D2
Llawhaden Pembks	33	E3
Llawnt Shrops	69	E3
Llawryglyn Powys	55	G4
Llay Wrexhm	69	F6
Llechcynfarwy IOA	78	C3
Llechfaen Powys	44	D2
Llechrhyd Caerph	36	B5
Llechryd Cerdgn	42	B4
Llechylched IOA	78	C2
Lledrod Cerdgn	54	D2
Llidiardau Gwynd	68	A4
Llidiart-y-parc Denbgs	68	C4
Llidiartnenog Carmth	43	F3
Llithfaen Gwynd	66	C4
Lloc Flints	80	D2
Llong Flints	81	E1
Llowes Powys	45	E3
Llwydcoed Rhondd	35	G5
Llwydiarth Powys	68	C2
Llwyn Denbgs	80	C1
Llwyn-drain Pembks	42	C3
Llwyn-du Mons	36	D6
Llwyn-on Myr Td	35	G5
Llwyn-y-brain Carmth	33	F3
Llwyn-y-groes Cerdgn	43	F5
Llwyncelyn Cerdgn	43	E5
Llwydafydd Cerdgn	42	D5
Llwynderw Powys	56	B6
Llwyndyrys Gwynd	66	C4
Llwyngwril Gwynd	67	E1
Llwynhendy Carmth	34	C4
Llwynmawr Wrexhm	69	E4
Llwynypia Rhondd	35	G4
Llyn-y-pandy Flints	80	D1
Llynclys Shrops	69	E2
Llynfaes IOA	78	D2
Llys-y-fran Pembks	33	E4
Llysfaen Conwy	80	A2
Llyswen Cerdgn	43	E5
Llyswen Powys	44	D3
Llysworney V Glam	35	G2
Llywel Powys	44	B2
Load Brook S York	83	H3
Loan Falk	131	F3
Loanend Nthumb	123	G4
Loanhead Mdloth	132	B2
Loaningfoot D & G	102	D6
Loans S Ayrs	119	E3
Lobb Devon	21	E4
Lobhillcross Devon	8	B3
Loch Baghasdail W Isls	168	b2
Loch Euphoirt W Isls	168	b5
Loch Katrine Pier Stirlg	129	F6
Loch Maree Hotel Highld	152	C6
Loch nam Madadh W Isls	168	c5
Lochailort Highld	143	G2
Lochaline Highld	136	A4
Lochans D & G	100	B6
Locharbriggs D & G	110	D3
Lochavich Ag & B	136	D1
Lochawe Ag & B	137	F2
Lochboisdale W Isls	168	b2
Lochbuie Ag & B	135	H2
Lochcarron Highld	152	C3
Lochdon Ag & B	136	B3
Lochdonhead Ag & B	136	B3
Lochead Ag & B	127	F3
Lochearnhead Stirlg	138	C2
Lochee Dund C	140	D3
Locheilside Station Highld	144	B2
Lochend Highld	154	D3
Lochfoot D & G	110	C2
Lochgair Ag & B	127	H4
Lochgelly Fife	131	H4
Lochgilphead Ag & B	127	G4
Lochgoilhead Ag & B	128	C5
Lochieheads Fife	140	C1
Lochill Moray	157	E5
Lochindorb Lodge Highld	156	B3
Lochinver Highld	161	E6
Lochluichart Highld	153	G5
Lochmaben D & G	111	E3
Lochmaddy W Isls	168	c5
Lochore Fife	131	H5
Lochranza N Ayrs	118	A4
Lochside Abers	141	G6
Lochside D & G	110	D2
Lochside Highld	155	F4
Lochton S Ayrs	108	D3
Lochty Angus	141	E6
Lochty Fife	132	D6
Lochuisge Highld	136	C5
Lochwinnoch Rens	119	E5
Lochwood D & G	111	E4
Lockengate Cnwll	4	D2
Lockerbie D & G	111	E3
Lockeridge Wilts	25	G6
Lockerley Hants	26	A4
Locking Somset	23	F5
Locking Stumps Ches	82	A4
Lockington E R Yk	92	D4
Lockington Leics	72	B3
Lockleywood Shrops	70	B3
Locks Heath Hants	14	C4
Locksbottom Gt Lon	29	E2
Locksgreen IOW	14	C3
Lockton N York	98	D4
Loddington Leics	60	D6
Loddington Nhants	61	E2
Loddiswell Devon	7	E2
Loddon Norfk	65	F5
Lode Cambs	63	E2
Lode Heath W Mids	58	D3
Loders Dorset	11	E4
Lodge Green W Mids	59	E4
Lodsworth W Susx	27	G1
Lofthouse N York	96	C2
Lofthouse W York	90	D2
Lofthouse Gate W York	90	D2
Loftus N York	107	G3
Logan E Ayrs	119	H1
Loganbeck Cumb	94	C4
Loganlea W Loth	120	D6
Loggerheads Staffs	70	B4
Logie Angus	141	G6
Logie Fife	140	D2
Logie Moray	156	B4
Logie Coldstone Abers	148	B5
Logie Pert Angus	141	F6
Logierait P & K	139	G5
Logierieve Abers	159	F4
Login Carmth	33	F4
Lolworth Cambs	62	C2
Lon-las Swans	35	E4
Lonbain Highld	151	G4
Londesborough E R Yk	92	C4
London Gt Lon	28	D4
London Apprentice Cnwll	3	G5
London Beach Kent	18	B5
London Colney Herts	50	C1
London End Nhants	61	E2
Londonderry N York	97	F4
Londonthorpe Lincs	73	G4
Londubh Highld	160	C2
Lonemore Highld	160	B1
Long Ashton Somset	37	F1
Long Bank Worcs	57	H3
Long Bennington Lincs	73	F4
Long Bredy Dorset	11	F4
Long Buckby Nhants	60	B2
Long Cause Devon	7	E4
Long Clawson Leics	73	E3
Long Common Hants	14	C5
Long Compton Staffs	70	D2
Long Compton Warwks	48	A2
Long Crendon Bucks	41	E5
Long Crichel Dorset	12	D6
Long Ditton Surrey	28	C3
Long Drax N York	91	H2
Long Duckmanton Derbys	84	B2
Long Eaton Derbys	72	C3
Long Green Ches	81	G2
Long Green Worcs	46	D2
Long Hanborough Oxon	40	B6
Long Hedges Lincs	74	D5
Long Itchington Warwks	59	G2
Long Lane Shrops	70	A1
Long Lawford Warwks	59	G3
Long Load Somset	23	G1
Long Marston Herts	41	G6
Long Marston N York	91	F5
Long Marston Warwks	47	G4
Long Marton Cumb	104	C3
Long Meadow End Shrops	56	D4
Long Melford Suffk	52	B5
Long Newnton Gloucs	38	D3
Long Newton E Loth	132	D2
Long Preston N York	89	G5
Long Riston E R Yk	93	E4
Long Sight Gt Man	82	D5
Long Stratton Norfk	64	D5
Long Street Bucks	49	F4
Long Sutton Hants	27	F4
Long Sutton Lincs	75	E2
Long Sutton Somset	23	G2
Long Thurlow Suffk	64	C2
Long Waste Shrops	70	A1
Long Whatton Leics	72	B2
Long Wittenham Oxon	40	D4
Longbenton T & W	114	D2
Longborough Gloucs	47	G2
Longbridge W Mids	58	C3
Longbridge Warwks	59	F2
Longbridge Deverill Wilts	24	D3
Longburgh Cumb	103	G6
Longburton Dorset	11	G6
Longcliffe Derbys	71	G6
Longcombe Devon	7	F4
Longcot Oxon	39	G3
Longcroft Cumb	103	F6
Longcross Surrey	27	H6
Longden Shrops	57	E6
Longden Common Shrops	57	E6
Longdon Staffs	71	F1
Longdon Worcs	46	D3
Longdon Green Staffs	71	F1
Longdon Heath Worcs	46	D3
Longdon upon Tern Shrops	70	A2
Longdown Devon	9	E4
Longdowns Cnwll	3	E3
Longfield Kent	29	G3
Longford Derbys	71	G4
Longford Gloucs	46	D1
Longford Gt Lon	28	A4
Longford Kent	29	F2
Longford Shrops	70	A3
Longford Shrops	70	B2
Longford W Mids	59	F4
Longforgan P & K	140	C3
Longformacus Border	122	D5
Longframlington Nthumb	114	C6
Longham Dorset	12	D4
Longham Norfk	76	B2
Longhaven Abers	159	G3
Longhirst Nthumb	114	D4
Longhope Gloucs	46	B1
Longhope Ork	169	b1
Longhorsley Nthumb	114	C5
Longhoughton Nthumb	125	E2
Longlands Cumb	103	G4
Longlane Derbys	71	G4
Longleat Safari Park Wilts	24	D4
Longlevens Gloucs	46	D1
Longley W York	90	B2
Longley Green Worcs	46	C2
Longleys P & K	140	C4
Longmanhill Abers	158	C5
Longmoor Camp Hants	27	F2
Longmorn Moray	156	D5
Longmoss Ches	82	D2
Longnewton Border	122	C2
Longnewton Dur	106	C2
Longney Gloucs	38	B5
Longniddry E Loth	132	C3
Longnor Shrops	57	E5
Longnor Staffs	83	F1
Longparish Hants	26	C4
Longpark Cumb	112	B1
Longridge Lancs	88	D3
Longridge Staffs	70	D1
Longridge W Loth	120	D6
Longriggend N Lans	130	D2
Longrock Cnwll	2	C1
Longsdon Staffs	71	E5
Longshaw Common Gt Man	81	G5
Longside Abers	159	F4
Longslow Shrops	70	B4
Longstanton Cambs	62	C2
Longstock Hants	26	B3
Longstone Pembks	33	F3
Longstowe Cambs	50	D6
Longstreet Wilts	25	G4
Longthorpe Cambs	61	H5
Longthwaite Cumb	104	A2
Longton Lancs	88	C2
Longton Staffs	70	D4
Longtown Cumb	112	A2
Longtown Herefs	45	F2
Longueville Jersey	174	c1
Longville in the Dale Shrops	57	F5
Longwick Bucks	41	F5
Longwitton Nthumb	114	B4
Longwood D & G	102	A6
Longwood House Hants	26	D2
Longworth Oxon	40	B3
Longyester E Loth	132	D2
Lonmay Abers	159	F5
Lonmore Highld	150	C3
Looe Cnwll	5	F1
Loose Kent	30	A1
Loosebeare Devon	8	D5
Loosegate Lincs	74	C3
Loosley Row Bucks	41	F4
Lootcherbrae Abers	158	B4
Lopcombe Corner Wilts	25	H3
Lopen Somset	11	E6
Loppington Shrops	69	G3
Lorbottle Nthumb	124	C5
Lordington W Susx	15	F5
Lords Wood Kent	30	A2
Lordsbridge Norfk	75	F1
Lornty P & K	140	B4
Loscoe Derbys	72	B5
Loscombe Dorset	11	E4
Lossiemouth Moray	156	D6
Lost Gardens of Heligan Cnwll	3	G4
Lostford Shrops	70	A3
Lostock Gralam Ches	82	B2
Lostock Green Ches	82	B2
Lostock Hall Lancs	88	D2
Lostock Hall Fold Gt Man	82	B6
Lostock Junction Gt Man	82	B5
Lostwithiel Cnwll	5	E2
Lothbeg Highld	163	F5
Lothersdale N York	89	H4
Lothmore Highld	163	F5
Loudwater Bucks	41	G3
Loughborough Leics	72	C2
Loughor Swans	34	C4
Loughton Bucks	49	F3
Loughton Essex	29	E6
Loughton Shrops	57	F4
Lound Lincs	74	A2
Lound Notts	85	E3
Lound Suffk	65	H3
Lounston Devon	9	E2
Lount Leics	72	B2
Louth Lincs	86	D3
Love Clough Lancs	89	F2
Lovedean Hants	15	E5
Lover Wilts	25	G1
Loversall S York	84	C4
Loves Green Essex	51	G1
Lovesome Hill N York	97	G5
Loveston Pembks	33	E2
Lovington Somset	24	B2
Low Ackworth W York	91	F1
Low Angerton Nthumb	114	C4
Low Barbeth D & G	108	B1
Low Barlings Lincs	86	A2
Low Bell End N York	98	C5
Low Bentham N York	95	H4
Low Biggins Cumb	95	G3
Low Borrowbridge Cumb	95	G5
Low Bradfield S York	83	G4
Low Bradley N York	90	A4
Low Braithwaite Cumb	104	A4
Low Burnham N York	85	E5
Low Buston Nthumb	125	E3
Low Catton E R Yk	91	H5
Low Coniscliffe Dur	106	B2
Low Crosby Cumb	104	A6
Low Dinsdale Dur	106	C2
Low Eggborough N York	91	G2
Low Ellington N York	97	E3
Low Fell T & W	114	D1
Low Gartachorrans Stirlg	129	F4
Low Gate Nthumb	113	F1
Low Gettbridge Cumb	104	B6
Low Grantley N York	97	F2
Low Green N York	90	C5
Low Habberley Worcs	58	A3
Low Harrogate N York	90	D5
Low Hawsker N York	99	E6
Low Hesket Cumb	104	A5
Low Hill Worcs	58	A3
Low Hutton N York	98	C2
Low Knipe Cumb	104	B2
Low Laithe N York	97	E1
Low Langton Lincs	86	B2
Low Leighton Derbys	83	E3
Low Lorton Cumb	103	E3
Low Marnham Notts	85	F2
Low Middleton Nthumb	124	D5
Low Mill N York	98	B4
Low Moor Lancs	89	F4
Low Moor W York	90	C2
Low Moorsley T & W	106	C5
Low Mowthorpe N York	99	E1
Low Newton Cumb	95	E3
Low Rogerscales Cumb	103	E3
Low Row Cumb	103	F5
Low Row Cumb	103	G4
Low Row Cumb	112	C1
Low Row N York	96	C5
Low Salchrie D & G	108	B1
Low Santon Lincs	85	G6
Low Street Essex	29	G4
Low Street Norfk	77	F2
Low Tharston Norfk	64	D5
Low Torry Fife	131	H4
Low Toynton Lincs	86	C2
Low Valley S York	84	B5
Low Walworth Dur	106	B3
Low Wood Cumb	94	D3
Low Worsall N York	106	C2
Low Wray Cumb	94	D5
Lowbands Gloucs	46	C2
Lowca Cumb	102	D3
Lowdham Notts	72	D5
Lowe Shrops	69	G3
Lowe Hill Staffs	71	E6
Lower Aisholt Somset	23	E3
Lower Ansty Dorset	12	B5
Lower Apperley Gloucs	46	D2
Lower Arncott Oxon	40	D6
Lower Ashton Devon	9	E3
Lower Assendon Oxon	41	F3
Lower Ballam Lancs	88	B3
Lower Barewood Herefs	45	G5
Lower Bartle Lancs	88	C3
Lower Basildon Berks	40	D2
Lower Beeding W Susx	16	C4
Lower Benefield Nhants	61	F4
Lower Bentley Worcs	58	C2
Lower Beobridge Shrops	57	H4
Lower Birchwood Derbys	72	B5
Lower Boddington Nhants	48	C4
Lower Boscawell Cnwll	2	A3
Lower Bourne Surrey	27	G4
Lower Brailes Warwks	48	A3
Lower Breakish Highld	151	G1
Lower Bredbury Gt Man	82	D4
Lower Broadheath Worcs	46	D5
Lower Brockhampton Manor Herefs	46	B5
Lower Buckenhill Herefs	46	B2
Lower Bullingham Herefs	45	H3
Lower Burgate Hants	13	G6
Lower Burrowton Devon	9	G4
Lower Burton Herefs	45	G5
Lower Caldecote Beds	50	C5
Lower Cam Gloucs	38	B4
Lower Canada Somset	23	F5
Lower Catesby Nhants	48	C5
Lower Chapel Powys	44	C3
Lower Chicksgrove Wilts	25	E2
Lower Chute Wilts	26	A5
Lower Clapton Gt Lon	28	D4
Lower Clent Worcs	58	B3
Lower Clopton Warwks	47	G4
Lower Creedy Devon	9	E5
Lower Crossings Derbys	83	E3
Lower Cumberworth W York	83	G6
Lower Cwmtwrch Powys	35	F5
Lower Darwen Lancs	89	E2
Lower Dean Beds	61	F2
Lower Denby W York	83	G5
Lower Diabaig Highld	152	B5
Lower Dicker E Susx	17	F3
Lower Dinchope Shrops	57	E4
Lower Down Shrops	56	D4
Lower Dunsforth N York	97	G1
Lower Egleton Herefs	46	B4
Lower Elkstone Staffs	71	E6
Lower Ellastone Staffs	71	F4
Lower End Bucks	41	F5
Lower End Nhants	49	G3
Lower End Bucks	49	G5
Lower Everleigh Wilts	25	G5
Lower Exbury Hants	14	B3
Lower Eythorne Kent	31	F1
Lower Failand Somset	37	F2
Lower Farringdon Hants	27	E3
Lower Feltham Gt Lon	28	B3
Lower Fittleworth W Susx	16	A3
Lower Foxdale IOM	174	k3
Lower Frankton Shrops	69	F3
Lower Freystrop Pembks	32	D3
Lower Froyle Hants	27	F4
Lower Gabwell Devon	7	F5
Lower Gledfield Highld	162	C3
Lower Godney Somset	23	G3
Lower Gornal W Mids	58	B4
Lower Gravenhurst Beds	50	B4
Lower Green Gt Man	82	B5
Lower Green Herts	50	C4
Lower Green Herts	51	E4
Lower Green Kent	17	F5
Lower Green Kent	17	G6
Lower Green Nhants	49	F5
Lower Green Norfk	76	C4

Lower Green Staffs ... 58 B6
Lower Green Suffk ... 63 G2
Lower Hacheston Suffk ... 65 F1
Lower Halliford Surrey ... 28 B3
Lower Halstock Leigh Dorset ... 11 F5
Lower Halstow Kent ... 30 B3
Lower Hamworthy Dorset ... 12 D4
Lower Hardres Kent ... 31 E1
Lower Harpton Herefs ... 45 F5
Lower Hartlip Kent ... 30 B2
Lower Hartshay Derbys ... 72 B5
Lower Hartwell Bucks ... 41 F5
Lower Hatton Staffs ... 70 C4
Lower Hawthwaite Cumb ... 94 C4
Lower Hergest Herefs ... 45 F5
Lower Heyford Oxon ... 48 C2
Lower Heysham Lancs ... 88 C6
Lower Higham Kent ... 29 H3
Lower Holbrook Suffk ... 53 E4
Lower Hordley Shrops ... 69 F3
Lower Horncroft W Susx ... 16 A3
Lower Howsell Worcs ... 46 C4
Lower Irlam Gt Man ... 82 B4
Lower Kilburn Derbys ... 72 A4
Lower Kilcott Gloucs ... 38 C3
Lower Killeyan Ag & B ... 116 B5
Lower Kingcombe Dorset ... 11 F4
Lower Kingswood Surrey ... 28 C1
Lower Kinnerton Ches ... 81 F1
Lower Langford Somset ... 23 G5
Lower Largo Fife ... 132 C5
Lower Leigh Staffs ... 71 E4
Lower Lemington Gloucs ... 47 H3
Lower Llanfadog Powys ... 55 G2
Lower Lovacott Devon ... 21 E3
Lower Loxhore Devon ... 21 F4
Lower Lydbrook Gloucs ... 37 G6
Lower Lye Herefs ... 56 D2
Lower Machen Newpt ... 36 C3
Lower Maes-coed Herefs ... 45 F2
Lower Mannington Dorset ... 12 D5
Lower Marston Somset ... 24 C4
Lower Meend Gloucs ... 37 G5
Lower Merridge Somset ... 23 E3
Lower Middleton Cheney Nhants ... 48 C3
Lower Milton Somset ... 24 A4
Lower Moor W Mids ... 47 E4
Lower Morton Gloucs ... 37 G3
Lower Nazeing Essex ... 51 E1
Lower Norton Warwks ... 59 E2
Lower Nyland Dorset ... 24 C1
Lower Penarth V Glam ... 36 C1
Lower Penn Staffs ... 58 B5
Lower Pennington Hants ... 13 G4
Lower Penwortham Lancs ... 88 D2
Lower Peover Ches ... 82 B2
Lower Place Gt Man ... 82 D6
Lower Pollicott Bucks ... 41 E6
Lower Quinton Warwks ... 47 G4
Lower Rainham Kent ... 30 B3
Lower Raydon Suffk ... 52 D4
Lower Roadwater Somset ... 22 C3
Lower Salter Lancs ... 95 G1
Lower Seagry Wilts ... 38 D2
Lower Sheering Essex ... 51 F2
Lower Shelton Beds ... 49 H3
Lower Shiplake Oxon ... 41 F2
Lower Shuckburgh Warwks ... 48 C5
Lower Slaughter Gloucs ... 47 G1
Lower Soothill W York ... 90 D2
Lower Soudley Gloucs ... 38 A5
Lower Standen Kent ... 19 F5
Lower Stanton St Quintin Wilts ... 38 D2
Lower Stoke Kent ... 30 B4
Lower Stone Gloucs ... 38 B4
Lower Stonnall Staffs ... 58 D6
Lower Stow Bedon Norfk ... 64 B5
Lower Street Dorset ... 12 B4
Lower Street E Susx ... 17 H3
Lower Street Norfk ... 77 H4
Lower Street Suffk ... 52 A6
Lower Street Suffk ... 53 E6
Lower Stretton Ches ... 82 A3
Lower Stroud Dorset ... 11 E4
Lower Sundon Beds ... 50 A3
Lower Swanwick Hants ... 14 C5
Lower Swell Gloucs ... 47 G2
Lower Tadmarton Oxon ... 48 B3
Lower Tale Devon ... 10 A5
Lower Tean Staffs ... 71 E4
Lower Thurlton Norfk ... 65 G5
Lower Town Cnwll ... 2 D3
Lower Town Devon ... 6 D5
Lower Town Herefs ... 46 B3
Lower Town Pembks ... 32 D5
Lower Trebullett Cnwll ... 5 G4
Lower Tregantle Cnwll ... 5 G1
Lower Treluswell Cnwll ... 3 E3
Lower Tysoe Warwks ... 48 B4
Lower Ufford Suffk ... 53 F6
Lower Upcott Devon ... 9 F3
Lower Upham Hants ... 14 C5
Lower Upnor Kent ... 30 A3
Lower Vexford Somset ... 22 D3
Lower Walton Ches ... 82 A3
Lower Waterston Dorset ... 11 H4
Lower Weare Somset ... 23 G5
Lower Weedon Nhants ... 48 D5
Lower Welson Herefs ... 45 F4
Lower Westmancote Worcs ... 47 E3
Lower Whatcombe Dorset ... 12 B5
Lower Whatley Somset ... 24 C4
Lower Whitley Ches ... 82 A3
Lower Wick Gloucs ... 38 B4
Lower Wick Worcs ... 46 D4
Lower Wield Hants ... 27 E3
Lower Wigginton Herts ... 41 G5
Lower Willingdon E Susx ... 17 G2
Lower Withington Ches ... 82 C2
Lower Woodend Bucks ... 41 F3
Lower Woodford Wilts ... 25 G3
Lower Wraxhall Dorset ... 11 F5
Lower Wyche Worcs ... 46 C4
Lower Wyke W York ... 90 C2
Lowerhouse Lancs ... 89 F3
Lowesby Leics ... 60 C6
Lowestoft Suffk ... 65 H5
Loweswater Cumb ... 103 E3

Lowfield Heath W Susx ... 16 D5
Lowgill Cumb ... 95 G5
Lowgill Lancs ... 95 G1
Lowick Cumb ... 94 D3
Lowick Nhants ... 61 F3
Lowick Nthumb ... 123 G3
Lowick Bridge Cumb ... 94 D3
Lowick Green Cumb ... 94 D3
Lowlands Dur ... 105 H3
Lowlands Torfn ... 36 D4
Lowsonford Warwks ... 59 E2
Lowther Cumb ... 104 B2
Lowther Castle Cumb ... 104 B2
Lowthorpe E R Yk ... 93 E6
Lowton Devon ... 8 D5
Lowton Gt Man ... 82 A4
Lowton Somset ... 23 E1
Lowton Common Gt Man ... 82 A4
Lowton St Mary's Gt Man ... 82 A4
Loxbeare Devon ... 9 F6
Loxhill Surrey ... 16 A5
Loxhore Devon ... 21 F4
Loxhore Cott Devon ... 21 F4
Loxley Warwks ... 47 H4
Loxley Green Staffs ... 71 F3
Loxter Herefs ... 46 C3
Loxton Somset ... 23 F5
Loxwood W Susx ... 16 A4
Loyal Lodge Highld ... 165 G3
Lubenham Leics ... 60 C4
Lucasgate Lincs ... 74 D5
Luccombe Somset ... 22 B4
Luccombe Village IOW ... 14 D1
Lucker Nthumb ... 125 E4
Luckett Cnwll ... 5 G3
Lucking Street Essex ... 52 B4
Luckington Wilts ... 38 C3
Lucknam Wilts ... 38 C1
Luckwell Bridge Somset ... 22 B3
Lucott Somset ... 22 B4
Lucton Herefs ... 57 E2
Lucy Cross N York ... 106 B2
Ludag W Isls ... 168 b2
Ludborough Lincs ... 86 C4
Ludbrook Devon ... 6 D3
Ludchurch Pembks ... 33 F3
Luddenden W York ... 90 B2
Luddenden Foot W York ... 90 B2
Luddenham Court Kent ... 30 D2
Luddesdown Kent ... 29 G3
Luddington Lincs ... 92 B1
Luddington Warwks ... 47 G4
Luddington in the Brook Nhants ... 61 G4
Ludford Lincs ... 86 B4
Ludford Shrops ... 57 E3
Ludgershall Bucks ... 41 E6
Ludgershall Wilts ... 25 H4
Ludgvan Cnwll ... 2 C3
Ludham Norfk ... 77 G2
Ludlow Shrops ... 57 E3
Ludney Somset ... 10 D6
Ludwell Wilts ... 25 E1
Ludworth Dur ... 106 C5
Luffenhall Herts ... 50 D4
Luffincott Devon ... 5 G5
Luffness E Loth ... 132 D3
Lugar E Ayrs ... 119 H2
Lugg Green Herefs ... 45 G5
Luggate Burn E Loth ... 133 E2
Luggiebank N Lans ... 130 D2
Lugsdale Ches ... 81 G3
Lugton E Ayrs ... 119 F5
Lugwardine Herefs ... 46 A3
Luib Highld ... 151 F1
Lulham Herefs ... 45 G3
Lullington Derbys ... 71 G1
Lullington E Susx ... 17 F2
Lullington Somset ... 24 C4
Lulsgate Bottom Somset ... 23 H6
Lulsley Worcs ... 46 C5
Lulworth Camp Dorset ... 12 B3
Lumb Lancs ... 89 G2
Lumb W York ... 90 B2
Lumbutts W York ... 89 H2
Lumby N York ... 91 F3
Lumloch E Duns ... 130 C2
Lumphanan Abers ... 148 C5
Lumphinnans Fife ... 131 H4
Lumsden Abers ... 157 G1
Lunan Angus ... 141 G5
Lunanhead Angus ... 141 E5
Luncarty P & K ... 140 A3
Lund E R Yk ... 92 D4
Lund N York ... 91 H3
Lundie Angus ... 140 C3
Lundie Stirlg ... 130 D6
Lundin Links Fife ... 132 C5
Lundin Mill Fife ... 132 C5
Lundy Green Norfk ... 65 E5
Lunna Shet ... 169 j4
Lunsford Kent ... 29 H2
Lunsford's Cross E Susx ... 17 H2
Lunt Mersyd ... 81 F5
Luntley Herefs ... 45 G5
Luppitt Devon ... 10 B5
Lupridge Devon ... 7 E3
Lupset W York ... 90 D1
Lupton Cumb ... 95 F3
Lurgashall W Susx ... 27 G2
Lurley Devon ... 9 F6
Lusby Lincs ... 86 D1
Luscombe Devon ... 7 E3
Luson Devon ... 6 C3
Luss Ag & B ... 129 E4
Lusta Highld ... 150 C4
Lustleigh Devon ... 9 E3
Luston Herefs ... 57 E2
Luthermuir Abers ... 148 D1
Luthrie Fife ... 140 C2
Lutley Worcs ... 58 B4
Luton Beds ... 50 B3
Luton Devon ... 10 A5
Luton Devon ... 9 F2
Luton Kent ... 30 A3
Luton Airport Beds ... 50 B3
Lutterworth Leics ... 60 B4
Lutton Devon ... 6 C4

Lutton Devon ... 6 D4
Lutton Lincs ... 75 E3
Lutton Nhants ... 61 G4
Luxborough Somset ... 22 C3
Luxulyan Cnwll ... 4 D2
Luzley Gt Man ... 83 E5
Lybster Highld ... 167 F2
Lydbury North Shrops ... 56 D4
Lydcott Devon ... 21 G4
Lydd Kent ... 18 D3
Lydd Airport Kent ... 18 D3
Lydden Kent ... 19 F6
Lydden Kent ... 31 G3
Lyddington Rutlnd ... 61 E5
Lyde Green Hants ... 27 E5
Lydeard St Lawrence Somset ... 22 D2
Lydeway Wilts ... 25 F5
Lydford Devon ... 8 B3
Lydford on Fosse Somset ... 24 A2
Lydgate Gt Man ... 89 H1
Lydgate W York ... 89 H2
Lydham Shrops ... 56 D4
Lydiard Green Wilts ... 39 E3
Lydiard Millicent Wilts ... 39 F3
Lydiard Tregoze Wilts ... 39 F3
Lydiate Mersyd ... 81 F5
Lydiate Ash Worcs ... 58 C3
Lydlinch Dorset ... 12 A6
Lydney Gloucs ... 37 G5
Lydstep Pembks ... 33 E1
Lye W Mids ... 58 B4
Lye Cross Somset ... 23 H5
Lye Green Bucks ... 41 H5
Lye Green E Susx ... 17 F5
Lye Green Warwks ... 59 E2
Lye Head Worcs ... 57 H3
Lye's Green Wilts ... 24 D4
Lyford Oxon ... 40 B4
Lymbridge Green Kent ... 19 E6
Lyme Regis Dorset ... 10 D4
Lyminge Kent ... 19 E5
Lymington Hants ... 13 G4
Lyminster W Susx ... 16 A2
Lymm Ches ... 82 B3
Lympne Kent ... 19 E5
Lympsham Somset ... 23 F5
Lympstone Devon ... 9 G3
Lynbridge Devon ... 21 G5
Lynch Somset ... 22 B4
Lynch Green Norfk ... 64 D6
Lynchat Highld ... 146 C5
Lyndhurst Hants ... 13 G5
Lyndon Rutlnd ... 61 E6
Lyndon Green W Mids ... 58 D4
Lyne Border ... 121 F3
Lyne Surrey ... 28 A3
Lyne Down Herefs ... 46 B2
Lyne of Skene Abers ... 149 E5
Lyneal Shrops ... 69 G3
Lyneham Devon ... 9 E2
Lyneham Oxon ... 48 A1
Lyneham Wilts ... 39 E2
Lyneham Airport Wilts ... 39 E2
Lyneholmford Cumb ... 112 B2
Lynemouth Nthumb ... 115 E5
Lyness Ork ... 169 b2
Lyng Norfk ... 76 D2
Lyng Somset ... 23 F2
Lynhales Herefs ... 45 F5
Lynmouth Devon ... 21 G5
Lynn Shrops ... 70 C2
Lynn Staffs ... 58 D6
Lynn of Shenval Moray ... 156 D1
Lynsted Kent ... 30 C2
Lynstone Cnwll ... 20 B1
Lynton Devon ... 21 G5
Lyon's Gate Dorset ... 11 G5
Lyonshall Herefs ... 45 F5
Lytchett Matravers Dorset ... 12 C4
Lytchett Minster Dorset ... 12 C4
Lyth Highld ... 167 F5
Lytham Lancs ... 88 B2
Lytham St Anne's Lancs ... 88 B2
Lythbank Shrops ... 57 E6
Lythe N York ... 107 H2
Lythmore Highld ... 166 D5

M

Mabe Burnthouse Cnwll ... 3 E3
Mabie D & G ... 110 D2
Mablethorpe Lincs ... 87 E3
Macclesfield Ches ... 82 D2
Macduff Abers ... 158 C6
Machariock Ag & B ... 117 F1
Machen Caerph ... 36 C3
Machrie N Ayrs ... 117 H4
Machrihanish Ag & B ... 117 E2
Machrins Ag & B ... 126 C4
Machynlleth Powys ... 55 E5
Machynys Carmth ... 34 C4
Mackworth Derbys ... 71 H4
Macmerry E Loth ... 132 C2
Maddaford Devon ... 8 B4
Madderty P & K ... 139 G2
Maddington Wilts ... 25 F4
Maddiston Falk ... 131 F3
Madehurst W Susx ... 15 H5
Madeley Shrops ... 57 G6
Madeley Staffs ... 70 C4
Madeley Heath Staffs ... 70 C5
Madford Devon ... 10 B6
Madingley Cambs ... 62 C1
Madley Herefs ... 45 G3
Madresfield Worcs ... 46 D4
Madron Cnwll ... 2 B3
Maen-y-groes Cerdgn ... 42 D5
Maenaddwyn IOA ... 78 D3
Maenan Conwy ... 79 G1
Maenclochog Pembks ... 33 E4
Maendy V Glam ... 35 G2
Maenporth Cnwll ... 3 E3
Maentwrog Gwynd ... 67 F4

Maer Cnwll ... 20 B1
Maer Staffs ... 70 C4
Maerdy Carmth ... 43 G2
Maerdy Rhondd ... 35 G4
Maes-glas Newpt ... 36 D3
Maesbrook Shrops ... 69 E2
Maesbury Shrops ... 69 E3
Maesbury Marsh Shrops ... 69 E2
Maesgwynne Carmth ... 33 F4
Maeshafn Denbgs ... 68 D6
Maesllyn Cerdgn ... 42 D4
Maesmynis Powys ... 44 C4
Maesmynis Powys ... 44 C4
Maesteg Brdgnd ... 35 F3
Maesybont Carmth ... 34 C6
Maesycwmmer Caerph ... 36 C4
Magdalen Laver Essex ... 51 F1
Maggieknockater Moray ... 157 E4
Maggots End Essex ... 51 F3
Magham Down E Susx ... 17 G2
Maghull Mersyd ... 81 F5
Magor Mons ... 37 E3
Maiden Bradley Wilts ... 24 D3
Maiden Head Somset ... 24 A6
Maiden Law Dur ... 106 A6
Maiden Newton Dorset ... 11 F4
Maiden Wells Pembks ... 32 D2
Maidenbower W Susx ... 16 D5
Maidencombe Devon ... 7 F4
Maidenhayne Devon ... 10 C4
Maidenhead Berks ... 41 G2
Maidens S Ayrs ... 108 D6
Maidens Green Berks ... 41 G1
Maidenwell Lincs ... 86 D3
Maidford Nhants ... 48 D4
Maids Moreton Bucks ... 49 E3
Maidstone Kent ... 30 A2
Maidwell Nhants ... 60 D3
Mains of Balhall Angus ... 141 E6
Mains of Balnakettle Abers ... 148 D2
Mains of Dalvey Highld ... 156 C2
Mains of Haulkerton Abers ... 149 E2
Mainsforth Dur ... 106 C4
Mainsriddle D & G ... 102 C6
Mainstone Shrops ... 56 C4
Maisemore Gloucs ... 46 D1
Major's Green Worcs ... 58 D3
Makeney Derbys ... 72 A4
Malborough Devon ... 6 D1
Malcoff Derbys ... 83 F3
Malden Surrey ... 28 C3
Malden Rushett Gt Lon ... 28 C2
Maldon Essex ... 52 B1
Malham N York ... 89 G6
Mallaig Highld ... 143 F4
Mallaigvaig Highld ... 143 F4
Malleny Mills C Edin ... 131 H2
Mallows Green Essex ... 51 F3
Malltraeth IOA ... 78 D1
Mallwyd Gwynd ... 68 A1
Malmesbury Wilts ... 38 D3
Malmsmead Somset ... 21 H5
Malpas Ches ... 69 G5
Malpas Cnwll ... 3 F4
Malpas Newpt ... 36 D3
Malswick Gloucs ... 46 C2
Maltby Lincs ... 86 C3
Maltby N York ... 106 D2
Maltby S York ... 84 C4
Maltby le Marsh Lincs ... 87 E3
Malting Green Essex ... 52 C3
Maltman's Hill Kent ... 18 C6
Malton N York ... 98 D2
Malvern Link Worcs ... 46 C4
Malvern Wells Worcs ... 46 C3
Malzie D & G ... 101 E5
Mamble Worcs ... 57 G2
Mamhilad Mons ... 36 D5
Manaccan Cnwll ... 3 E2
Manafon Powys ... 56 A6
Manais W Isls ... 168 d6
Manaton Devon ... 8 D3
Manby Lincs ... 86 D3
Mancetter Warwks ... 59 F5
Manchester Gt Man ... 82 C4
Manchester Airport Gt Man ... 82 C3
Mancot Flints ... 81 E1
Mandally Highld ... 145 G4
Manderston House Border ... 123 E5
Manea Cambs ... 62 D4
Maney W Mids ... 58 D5
Manfield N York ... 106 B2
Mangerton Dorset ... 11 E4
Mangotsfield Gloucs ... 37 H2
Mangrove Green Herts ... 50 B3
Manhay Cnwll ... 2 D3
Manish W Isls ... 168 d6
Mankinholes W York ... 89 H2
Manley Ches ... 81 G2
Manmoel Caerph ... 36 C5
Mannel Ag & B ... 134 B3
Manning's Heath W Susx ... 16 C4
Manningford Bohune Wilts ... 25 G5
Manningford Bruce Wilts ... 25 G5
Manningham Brad ... 90 C3
Mannington Dorset ... 12 D5
Manningtree Essex ... 53 E4
Mannofield Aber C ... 149 G5
Manor Park Gt Lon ... 29 E5
Manorbier Pembks ... 33 E1
Manorbier Newton Pembks ... 33 E2
Manordeilo Carmth ... 43 G2
Manorhill Border ... 122 D3
Manorowen Pembks ... 32 D5
Mansell Gamage Herefs ... 45 G4
Mansell Lacy Herefs ... 45 G4
Mansergh Cumb ... 95 G3
Mansfield E Ayrs ... 109 H6
Mansfield Notts ... 72 C6
Mansfield Woodhouse Notts ... 84 C1
Mansriggs Cumb ... 94 D3
Manston Dorset ... 12 B6
Manston Kent ... 31 G3
Manston W York ... 91 E3
Manswood Dorset ... 12 D5
Manthorpe Lincs ... 73 G4

Manthorpe Lincs ... 74 A2
Manton Lincs ... 85 G5
Manton Notts ... 84 D2
Manton Rutlnd ... 61 E6
Manton Wilts ... 39 F1
Manuden Essex ... 51 F3
Manwood Green Essex ... 51 F2
Maperton Somset ... 24 B2
Maple Cross Herts ... 28 A5
Maplebeck Notts ... 73 E6
Mapledurham Oxon ... 41 E2
Mapledurwell Hants ... 27 E4
Maplehurst W Susx ... 16 C4
Maplescombe Kent ... 29 F2
Mapleton Derbys ... 71 F5
Mapleton Kent ... 29 E1
Mapperley Derbys ... 72 B4
Mapperley Park Notts ... 72 C4
Mapperton Dorset ... 11 E5
Mappleborough Green Warwks ... 58 D2
Mappleton E R Yk ... 93 F4
Mapplewell S York ... 84 A6
Mappowder Dorset ... 11 H5
Marazanvose Cnwll ... 3 E5
Marazion Cnwll ... 2 C3
Marbury Ches ... 69 H5
March Cambs ... 62 C5
March S Lans ... 110 D6
Marcham Oxon ... 40 C4
Marchamley Shrops ... 70 A3
Marchamley Wood Shrops ... 69 H3
Marchington Staffs ... 71 F3
Marchington Woodlands Staffs ... 71 F3
Marchros Gwynd ... 66 C3
Marchwiel Wrexhm ... 69 F5
Marchwood Hants ... 14 B5
Marcross V Glam ... 35 G1
Marden Herefs ... 45 H4
Marden Kent ... 18 A6
Marden Wilts ... 25 F5
Marden Ash Essex ... 51 F1
Marden Beech Kent ... 18 A6
Marden Thorn Kent ... 18 A6
Mardens Hill E Susx ... 17 F5
Mardlebury Herts ... 50 D2
Mardy Mons ... 36 D6
Marefield Leics ... 60 C6
Mareham le Fen Lincs ... 74 C6
Mareham on the Hill Lincs ... 86 C1
Marehay Derbys ... 72 B5
Marehill W Susx ... 16 B3
Maresfield E Susx ... 17 E4
Marfleet E R Yk ... 93 E2
Marford Wrexhm ... 69 F6
Margam Neath ... 35 E3
Margaret Marsh Dorset ... 24 D1
Margaret Roding Essex ... 51 G2
Margaretting Essex ... 29 G6
Margaretting Tye Essex ... 29 H6
Margate Kent ... 31 G3
Margnaheglish N Ayrs ... 118 D3
Margrie D & G ... 101 G5
Margrove Park N York ... 107 F2
Marham Norfk ... 75 G1
Marhamchurch Cnwll ... 20 B1
Marholm Cambs ... 61 G6
Marian-glas IOA ... 79 E3
Mariansleigh Devon ... 21 G3
Marine Town Kent ... 30 C3
Marionburgh Abers ... 149 E5
Marishader Highld ... 151 E5
Maristow Devon ... 6 B4
Maritime Centre Moray ... 119 E3
Marjoriebanks D & G ... 111 E3
Mark Somset ... 23 G4
Mark Causeway Somset ... 23 F4
Mark Cross E Susx ... 17 F2
Mark Cross E Susx ... 17 G4
Mark's Corner IOW ... 14 C3
Markbeech Kent ... 17 F6
Markby Lincs ... 87 E2
Markeaton Derbys ... 72 A4
Market Bosworth Leics ... 59 G6
Market Deeping Lincs ... 74 B1
Market Drayton Shrops ... 70 B3
Market Harborough Leics ... 60 C4
Market Lavington Wilts ... 25 F5
Market Overton Rutlnd ... 73 F2
Market Rasen Lincs ... 86 A4
Market Stainton Lincs ... 86 C3
Market Weighton E R Yk ... 92 C4
Market Weston Suffk ... 64 B3
Markfield Leics ... 72 C1
Markham Caerph ... 36 C4
Markham Moor Notts ... 85 E2
Markinch Fife ... 132 B5
Markington N York ... 97 F1
Markle E Loth ... 133 E3
Marks Tey Essex ... 52 C3
Marksbury Somset ... 24 B5
Markwell Cnwll ... 5 G2
Markyate Herts ... 50 B2
Marl Bank Worcs ... 46 C3
Marlborough Wilts ... 39 F1
Marlbrook Herefs ... 45 H5
Marlbrook Worcs ... 58 C3
Marlcliff Warwks ... 47 F4
Marldon Devon ... 7 F4
Marle Green E Susx ... 17 G3
Marlesford Suffk ... 65 F1
Marley Kent ... 31 E1
Marley Kent ... 31 G1
Marley Green Ches ... 69 H5
Marley Hill T & W ... 114 C2
Marlingford Norfk ... 76 D1
Marloes Pembks ... 32 B2
Marlow Bucks ... 41 G3
Marlow Herefs ... 56 D3
Marlow Bottom Bucks ... 41 G3
Marlpit Hill Kent ... 17 E6
Marlpits E Susx ... 17 E4
Marlpits E Susx ... 17 H3
Marlpool Derbys ... 72 B5
Marnhull Dorset ... 24 C1
Marple Gt Man ... 82 D3
Marple Bridge Gt Man ... 83 E4
Marr S York ... 84 C5
Marrick N York ... 96 D5

300

Marros Carmth 33 F2
Marsden T & W 115 F2
Marsden W York 83 E6
Marsden Height Lancs 89 G3
Marsett N York 96 B3
Marsh Bucks 41 F5
Marsh Devon 10 C6
Marsh W York 90 A3
Marsh Baldon Oxon 40 D4
Marsh Benham Berks 26 C6
Marsh Chapel Lincs 86 D5
Marsh Gibbon Bucks 49 E1
Marsh Green Devon 9 G4
Marsh Green Kent 17 E6
Marsh Green Shrops 70 A1
Marsh Green Staffs 70 D6
Marsh Lane Derbys 84 B3
Marsh Lane Gloucs 37 G5
Marsh Street Somset 22 C4
Marshall's Heath Herts 50 C2
Marshalswick Herts 50 C2
Marsham Norfk 77 E2
Marshborough Kent 31 G2
Marshbrook Shrops 57 E4
Marshfield Gloucs 38 C2
Marshfield Newpt 36 D2
Marshgate Cnwll 5 E5
Marshland Green Gt Man 82 B5
Marshland St James Norfk 75 E1
Marshside Mersyd 88 B1
Marshwood Dorset 10 D4
Marske N York 96 D5
Marske-by-the-Sea N York 107 F3
Marston Ches 82 B2
Marston Herefs 45 F5
Marston Lincs 73 F4
Marston Oxon 40 C5
Marston Staffs 70 C1
Marston Staffs 70 D3
Marston Warwks 59 E5
Marston Wilts 25 E5
Marston Green W Mids 59 E4
Marston Jabbet Warwks 59 G4
Marston Magna Somset 24 B1
Marston Meysey Wilts 39 F4
Marston Montgomery Derbys 71 F4
Marston Moretaine Beds 49 H3
Marston on Dove Derbys 71 G3
Marston St Lawrence Nhants 48 D3
Marston Stannett Herefs 46 A5
Marston Trussell Nhants 60 C4
Marstow Herefs 46 A1
Marsworth Bucks 41 G6
Marten Wilts 26 A5
Marthall Ches 82 C2
Martham Norfk 77 G2
Martin Hants 25 F1
Martin Kent 19 G6
Martin Lincs 74 B6
Martin Lincs 86 C1
Martin Dales Lincs 86 B1
Martin Drove End Hants 25 F1
Martin Hussingtree Worcs 46 D5
Martindale Cumb 104 A2
Martinhoe Devon 21 G5
Martinscroft Ches 82 B4
Martinstown Dorset 11 G3
Martlesham Suffk 53 F5
Martlesham Heath Suffk 53 F5
Martletwy Pembks 33 E3
Martley Worcs 46 C5
Martock Somset 23 G1
Marton Ches 82 A1
Marton Ches 82 C1
Marton Cumb 94 C3
Marton E R Yk 93 F3
Marton E R Yk 99 H2
Marton Lincs 85 F3
Marton N York 107 E2
Marton N York 91 E6
Marton N York 98 C3
Marton Shrops 56 C6
Marton Warwks 59 G2
Marton-le-Moor N York 97 G2
Martyr Worthy Hants 26 C2
Martyr's Green Surrey 28 B2
Marwick Ork 169 a3
Marwood Devon 21 F4
Mary Tavy Devon 8 B2
Marybank Highld 154 C4
Maryburgh Highld 154 D5
Maryculter Abers 149 F4
Marygold Border 123 E5
Maryhill Abers 158 D4
Maryhill C Glas 129 G2
Marykirk Abers 148 D1
Maryland Mons 37 F5
Marylebone Gt Lon 28 D4
Marylebone Gt Man 81 H5
Marypark Moray 156 D3
Maryport Cumb 102 D4
Maryport D & G 100 C4
Marystow Devon 8 A3
Maryton Angus 141 G5
Marywell Abers 148 C4
Marywell Abers 149 G4
Marywell Angus 141 F4
Masham N York 97 E3
Mashbury Essex 51 G2
Mason T & W 114 D3
Masongill N York 95 G2
Mastin Moor Derbys 84 B2
Matching Essex 51 F2
Matching Green Essex 51 F2
Matching Tye Essex 51 F2
Matfen Nthumb 114 B3
Matfield Kent 17 G6
Mathern Mons 37 F3
Mathon Herefs 46 C4
Mathry Pembks 32 C5
Matlask Norfk 76 D3
Matlock Derbys 71 H6
Matlock Bank Derbys 71 H6
Matlock Bath Derbys 71 H6
Matlock Dale Derbys 71 H6
Matson Gloucs 38 C6
Matterdale End Cumb 103 H2
Mattersey Notts 84 D4

Mattersey Thorpe Notts 84 D4
Mattingley Hants 27 L5
Mattishall Norfk 76 D1
Mattishall Burgh Norfk 76 D1
Mauchline E Ayrs 119 G2
Maud Abers 159 E4
Maufant Jersey 174 d2
Maugersbury Gloucs 47 G2
Maughold IOM 174 n4
Mauld Highld 154 B3
Maulden Beds 50 A4
Maulds Meaburn Cumb 104 C2
Maunby N York 97 G3
Maund Bryan Herefs 46 A4
Maundown Somset 22 C2
Mautby Norfk 77 H1
Mavesyn Ridware Staffs 71 F2
Mavis Enderby Lincs 86 D1
Maw Green Ches 70 B6
Maw Green W Mids 58 C5
Mawbray Cumb 103 E5
Mawdesley Lancs 88 C1
Mawdlam Brdgnd 35 E2
Mawgan Cnwll 3 E2
Mawgan Cross Cnwll 2 D2
Mawgan Porth Cnwll 4 B3
Mawla Cnwll 3 E4
Mawnan Cnwll 3 E2
Mawnan Smith Cnwll 3 E3
Maxey Cambs 61 G6
Maxstoke Warwks 59 E4
Maxted Street Kent 19 E6
Maxton Border 122 C2
Maxton Kent 19 F5
Maxwell Town D & G 110 D2
Maxworthy Cnwll 5 F5
May Bank Staffs 70 D5
May's Green Oxon 41 F2
May's Green Surrey 28 B2
Mayals Swans 34 D3
Maybole S Ayrs 109 E6
Maybury Surrey 28 A2
Mayes Green Surrey 16 B5
Mayfield E Susx 17 G4
Mayfield Mdloth 132 C2
Mayfield Staffs 71 F5
Mayford Surrey 27 H5
Mayland Essex 30 C6
Maynard's Green E Susx 17 G3
Maypole Kent 31 F2
Maypole Mons 37 F6
Maypole W Mids 58 D3
Maypole Green Norfk 65 G5
Maypole Green Suffk 64 B1
Maypole Green Suffk 65 E2
Mead Devon 20 B2
Meadgate Somset 24 B5
Meadle Bucks 41 F5
Meadowfield Dur 106 B5
Meadowtown Shrops 56 C5
Meadwell Devon 5 G4
Meal Bank Cumb 95 F4
Mealrigg Cumb 103 F3
Mealsgate Cumb 103 F4
Meanwood W York 90 D3
Mearbeck N York 89 G6
Meare Somset 23 G3
Meare Green Somset 23 F2
Meare Green Somset 23 F1
Mearns E Rens 119 G5
Mears Ashby Nhants 60 D2
Measham Leics 72 A1
Meathop Cumb 95 E3
Meaux E R Yk 93 E3
Meavy Devon 6 C4
Medbourne Leics 60 D5
Meddon Devon 20 C2
Meden Vale Notts 84 D2
Medlam Lincs 74 C6
Medlar Lancs 88 C3
Medmenham Berks 41 F3
Medomsley Dur 105 H6
Medstead Hants 27 E3
Meer Common Herefs 45 F4
Meerbrook Staffs 71 E6
Meesden Herts 51 E4
Meeson Shrops 70 B2
Meeth Devon 8 B5
Meeting Green Suffk 63 G1
Meeting House Hill Norfk 77 F3
Meidrim Carmth 33 G4
Meifod Powys 68 D1
Meigle P & K 140 D2
Meikle Carco D & G 110 B1
Meikle Earnock S Lans 120 B5
Meikle Kilmory Ag & B 118 B5
Meikle Obney P & K 139 H3
Meikle Wartle Abers 158 C2
Meikleour P & K 140 B4
Meinciau Carmth 34 B5
Meir Staffs 70 D4
Meir Heath Staffs 70 D4
Melbourn Cambs 51 E5
Melbourne Derbys 72 B2
Melbourne E R Yk 92 A4
Melbury Devon 20 D2
Melbury Abbas Dorset 24 D1
Melbury Bubb Dorset 11 F5
Melbury Osmond Dorset 11 F5
Melbury Sampford Dorset 11 F5
Melchbourne Beds 61 F2
Melcombe Bingham Dorset 12 B5
Meldon Devon 8 C4
Meldon Nthumb 114 C4
Meldon Park Nthumb 114 C4
Meldreth Cambs 51 E5
Meldrum Stirlg 130 C5
Meledor Cnwll 3 G3
Melfort Ag & B 136 C1
Melgund Castle Angus 141 E5
Meliden Denbgs 80 C3
Melin Court Neath 35 F4
Melin-byrhedyn Powys 55 F5
Melin-y-coed Conwy 67 H6
Melin-y-ddol Powys 56 A6
Melin-y-wig Denbgs 68 C5
Melinau Pembks 33 F3

Melkinthorpe Cumb 104 B3
Melkridge Nthumb 113 E1
Melksham Wilts 25 E6
Mell Green Berks 40 C2
Mellangoose Cnwll 2 D2
Mellguards Cumb 104 A5
Melling Lancs 95 G2
Melling Mersyd 81 F5
Melling Mount Mersyd 81 F5
Mellington Powys 56 C5
Mellis Suffk 64 C3
Mellon Charles Highld 160 C3
Mellon Udrigle Highld 160 C3
Mellor Gt Man 83 E3
Mellor Lancs 89 E3
Mellor Brook Lancs 89 E3
Mells Somset 24 C4
Mells Suffk 65 F3
Melmerby Cumb 104 C4
Melmerby N York 96 D3
Melmerby N York 97 F2
Melness Highld 165 G5
Melon Green Suffk 63 H1
Melplash Dorset 11 E4
Melrose Border 122 C3
Melsetter Ork 169 a1
Melsonby N York 106 A2
Meltham W York 83 F6
Meltham Mills W York 83 F6
Melton E R Yk 92 D2
Melton Suffk 53 F6
Melton Constable Norfk 76 D3
Melton Mowbray Leics 73 E2
Melton Ross Lincs 86 A6
Meltonby E R Yk 92 B5
Melvaig Highld 160 B2
Melverley Shrops 69 F2
Melverley Green Shrops 69 F2
Melvich Highld 166 C5
Membury Devon 10 C5
Memsie Abers 159 F5
Memus Angus 140 D6
Menabilly Cnwll 5 E1
Menagissey Cnwll 3 E4
Menai Bridge IOA 79 E2
Mendham Suffk 65 E4
Mendlesham Suffk 64 D2
Mendlesham Green Suffk 64 C2
Menheniot Cnwll 5 F2
Menithwood Worcs 57 G2
Mennock D & G 110 C6
Menston W York 90 C4
Menstrie Clacks 131 E5
Menthorpe N York 91 H3
Mentmore Bucks 49 G1
Meoble Highld 143 G3
Meole Brace Shrops 69 G1
Meonstoke Hants 14 D6
Meopham Kent 29 G3
Meopham Green Kent 29 G3
Meopham Station Kent 29 G3
Mepal Cambs 62 D3
Meppershall Beds 50 B4
Mere Ches 82 B3
Mere Wilts 24 D2
Mere Brow Lancs 88 C1
Mere Green W Mids 58 D5
Mere Green Worcs 58 B2
Mere Heath Ches 82 B2
Mereclough Lancs 89 G3
Meresborough Kent 30 B2
Mereworth Kent 29 G1
Meriden W Mids 59 E4
Merkadale Highld 150 D2
Merley Dorset 12 D4
Merlin's Bridge Pembks 32 D3
Merrifield Devon 7 E2
Merrington Shrops 69 G2
Merrion Pembks 32 C5
Merriott Somset 11 E6
Merrivale Devon 8 B2
Merrow Surrey 28 A1
Merry Field Hill Dorset 12 D5
Merry Hill Herts 28 B5
Merry Lees Leics 59 G6
Merryhill W Mids 58 B5
Merrymeet Cnwll 5 F2
Mersham Kent 18 D5
Merstham Surrey 28 D1
Merston W Susx 15 G4
Merstone IOW 14 C2
Merther Cnwll 3 F4
Merthyr Carmth 33 H4
Merthyr Cynog Powys 44 C3
Merthyr Dyfan V Glam 36 B1
Merthyr Mawr Brdgnd 35 F2
Merthyr Tydfil Myr Td 36 B5
Merthyr Vale Myr Td 36 B5
Merton Devon 21 E2
Merton Gt Lon 28 C3
Merton Norfk 64 B5
Merton Oxon 40 D6
Meshaw Devon 21 H2
Messing Essex 52 C3
Messingham Lincs 85 F5
Metfield Suffk 65 E3
Metherell Cnwll 5 H3
Metherin Cnwll 5 E3
Metheringham Lincs 74 A6
Methil Fife 132 C5
Methilhill Fife 132 C5
Methleigh Cnwll 2 D2
Methley W York 91 E2
Methley Junction W York 91 E2
Methlick Abers 158 D3
Methven P & K 139 G2
Methwold Norfk 63 F5
Methwold Hythe Norfk 63 F5
Mettingham Suffk 65 F4
Metton Norfk 77 E4
Mevagissey Cnwll 3 G4
Mexborough S York 84 B5
Mey Highld 167 F6
Meyllteyrn Gwynd 66 B3
Meysey Hampton Gloucs 39 F4
Miabhig W Isls 168 d3
Miavaig W Isls 168 d8
Michaelchurch Herefs 45 H2

Michaelchurch Escley Herefs 45 F3
Michaelchurch-on-Arrow Powys 45 E4
Michaelston-le-Pit V Glam 36 C1
Michaelstone-y-Fedw Newpt. 36 C3
Michaelstow Cnwll 4 D4
Michelcombe Devon 6 D4
Micheldever Hants 26 C3
Micheldever Station Hants 26 C3
Michelmersh Hants 26 B2
Mickfield Suffk 64 D1
Mickle Trafford Ches 81 G2
Micklebring S York 84 C4
Mickleby N York 107 G3
Micklefield W York 91 E3
Micklefield Green Herts 28 A6
Mickleham Surrey 28 C1
Mickleover Derbys 71 H3
Micklethwaite Cumb 103 G5
Micklethwaite W York 90 B4
Mickleton Dur 105 F2
Mickleton Gloucs 47 G3
Mickletown W York 91 E2
Mickley Derbys 84 A3
Mickley N York 97 F2
Mickley Green Suffk 63 G1
Mickley Square Nthumb 114 B2
Mid Ardlaw Abers 159 E5
Mid Beltie Abers 148 D4
Mid Bockhampton Hants 13 F4
Mid Calder W Loth 131 G2
Mid Clyth Highld 167 G6
Mid Holmwood Surrey 16 C6
Mid Lavant W Susx 15 G4
Mid Mains Highld 154 C3
Mid Thorpe Lincs 86 C2
Mid Yell Shet 169 j4
Midbea Ork 169 b4
Middle Assendon Oxon 41 F3
Middle Aston Oxon 48 C2
Middle Barton Oxon 48 C2
Middle Chinnock Somset 11 E6
Middle Claydon Bucks 49 E2
Middle Duntisbourne Gloucs 38 D5
Middle Handley Derbys 84 B2
Middle Harling Norfk 64 B4
Middle Kames Ag & B 127 H4
Middle Littleton Worcs 47 F4
Middle Madeley Staffs 70 C4
Middle Maes-coed Herefs 45 F3
Middle Mayfield Staffs 71 F4
Middle Mill Pembks 32 B4
Middle Quarter Kent 18 C5
Middle Rasen Lincs 86 A4
Middle Rocombe Devon 7 F5
Middle Salter Lancs 88 D6
Middle Stoford Somset 23 E1
Middle Stoke Kent 30 B4
Middle Stoughton Somset 23 G4
Middle Street Gloucs 38 C5
Middle Taphouse Cnwll 5 E2
Middle Town IOS 2 a1
Middle Tysoe Warwks 48 B4
Middle Wallop Hants 26 A3
Middle Winterslow Wilts 25 H2
Middle Woodford Wilts 25 G3
Middle Yard Gloucs 38 C5
Middlebie D & G 111 G2
Middlebridge P & K 146 D1
Middlecliffe S York 84 B5
Middlecott Devon 8 D3
Middleham N York 96 D4
Middlehill Cnwll 5 F3
Middlehill Wilts 38 C1
Middlehope Shrops 57 E4
Middlemarsh Dorset 11 G5
Middlemore Devon 6 B5
Middlesbrough N York 106 D3
Middleshaw Cumb 95 F4
Middlesmoor N York 96 D2
Middlestone Dur 106 B4
Middlestone Moor Dur 106 B4
Middlestown W York 90 D1
Middlethird Border 122 D4
Middleton Ag & B 134 A4
Middleton Cumb 95 G3
Middleton Derbys 83 G1
Middleton Derbys 71 H6
Middleton Essex 52 B5
Middleton Gt Man 82 D5
Middleton Hants 26 C4
Middleton Herefs 57 F2
Middleton Lancs 88 C5
Middleton N Ayrs 119 F5
Middleton N York 90 B4
Middleton N York 98 D3
Middleton Nhants 60 D4
Middleton Nthumb 75 G2
Middleton Nthumb 124 D5
Middleton Nthumb 114 B4
Middleton P & K 131 G6
Middleton Shrops 69 E3
Middleton Shrops 57 F3
Middleton Suffk 65 G2
Middleton Swans 34 B3
Middleton W York 90 D2
Middleton Warwks 59 E5
Middleton Cheney Nhants 48 C3
Middleton Green Staffs 71 E3
Middleton Hall Nthumb 124 C4
Middleton Moor Suffk 65 G2
Middleton on the Hill Herefs 57 F2
Middleton on the Wolds E R Yk 92 C4
Middleton One Row Dur 106 C2
Middleton Priors Shrops 57 F4
Middleton Quernhow N York 97 F2
Middleton Scriven Shrops 57 G4
Middleton St George Dur 106 C2
Middleton Stoney Oxon 48 D1
Middleton Tyas N York 97 E5
Middleton-in-Teesdale Dur 105 F3
Middleton-on-Leven N York 106 D2
Middleton-on-Sea W Susx 15 H4
Middletown Cumb 102 D1
Middletown Powys 69 E1
Middletown Somset 37 F1
Middlewich Ches 82 B1
Middlewood Cnwll 5 F3

Middlewood Herefs 45 F4
Middlewood Green Suffk 64 C1
Middleyard E Ayrs 119 G3
Middlezoy Somset 23 G2
Middridge Dur 106 B3
Midford Somset 24 C5
Midge Hall Lancs 88 D2
Midgeholme Cumb 104 C6
Midgham Berks 26 C6
Midgley W York 90 B2
Midgley W York 90 D1
Midhopestones S York 83 G5
Midhurst W Susx 15 G6
Midlem Border 122 B2
Midney Somset 23 F2
Midpark Ag & B 118 B5
Midsomer Norton Somset 24 B5
Midtown Highld 165 G5
Midville Lincs 74 D6
Midway Ches 82 D3
Migvie Abers 148 B5
Milborne Port Somset 24 B1
Milborne St Andrew Dorset 12 B4
Milborne Wick Somset 24 B1
Milbourne Nthumb 114 C3
Milbourne Wilts 38 D3
Milburn Cumb 104 C3
Milbury Heath Gloucs 38 B3
Milby N York 97 G2
Milcombe Oxon 48 B3
Milden Suffk 52 C5
Mildenhall Suffk 63 F3
Mildenhall Wilts 39 G1
Mile Elm Wilts 39 E1
Mile End Essex 52 C3
Mile End Gloucs 37 G5
Mile End Suffk 65 F4
Mile Oak E Susx 16 C2
Mile Oak Kent 17 H6
Mile Oak Staffs 59 E6
Mile Town Kent 30 C3
Milebrook Powys 56 C3
Milebush Kent 18 A6
Mileham Norfk 76 B2
Miles Hope Herefs 57 F2
Miles Platting Gt Man 82 D5
Milesmark Fife 131 G4
Milfield Nthumb 123 F3
Milford Derbys 72 A4
Milford Devon 20 C3
Milford Powys 56 A4
Milford Staffs 71 E2
Milford Surrey 27 H3
Milford Haven Pembks 32 C2
Milford on Sea Hants 13 G4
Milkwall Gloucs 37 G5
Mill Bank W York 90 B2
Mill Brow Gt Man 83 E4
Mill Common Norfk 65 F5
Mill Common Suffk 65 F3
Mill Cross Devon 7 E4
Mill End Bucks 41 F3
Mill End Cambs 62 B3
Mill End Herts 50 D4
Mill Green Cambs 51 G5
Mill Green Essex 29 G6
Mill Green Herts 50 C2
Mill Green Lincs 74 C2
Mill Green Norfk 64 D4
Mill Green Staffs 71 F2
Mill Green Suffk 52 C5
Mill Green Suffk 64 C1
Mill Green Suffk 64 D1
Mill Green Suffk 65 F1
Mill Green W Mids 58 D5
Mill Hill E Susx 17 G2
Mill Hill Gt Lon 28 C5
Mill Meece Staffs 70 C3
Mill of Drummond P & K 139 F1
Mill of Haldane W Duns 129 E3
Mill Side Cumb 95 E3
Mill Street Kent 29 H2
Mill Street Norfk 76 C2
Mill Street Norfk 76 D2
Mill Street Suffk 64 C2
Millais Jersey 174 a3
Milland W Susx 27 F2
Milland Marsh W Susx 27 F2
Millbeck Cumb 103 F3
Millbreck Abers 159 F3
Millbrex Abers 158 D3
Millbridge Surrey 27 G3
Millbrook Beds 50 A5
Millbrook Cnwll 5 H1
Millbrook Gt Man 83 E5
Millbrook Hants 14 B5
Millbrook Jersey 174 b2
Millbuie Abers 149 F5
Millbuie Highld 154 D4
Millburn S Ayrs 119 F2
Millcombe Devon 7 E3
Millcorner E Susx 18 B4
Millcraig Highld 155 H6
Milldale Staffs 71 F5
Millend Gloucs 37 G5
Millend Gloucs 38 B4
Miller's Dale Derbys 83 F2
Miller's Green Essex 51 G1
Millerhill Mdloth 132 B2
Millers Green Derbys 71 H5
Millerston N Lans 130 C2
Millgate Lancs 89 G1
Millgreen Shrops 70 B3
Millhalf Herefs 45 F4
Millhayes Devon 10 C5
Millhead Lancs 95 F2
Millheugh S Lans 120 B4
Millhouse Ag & B 128 A2
Millhouse Cumb 103 G4
Millhouse Green S York 83 G5
Millhousebridge D & G 111 E3
Millhouses S York 84 B5
Millhouses S York 84 A3
Milliken Park Rens 119 F6
Millin Cross Pembks 32 D3
Millington E R Yk 92 B5
Millness Cumb 95 F3
Millom Cumb 94 B3

Millook Cnwll............... 5 E6
Millpool Cnwll............... 2 C3
Millpool Cnwll............... 5 E3
Millport N Ayrs............... 118 C5
Millthorpe Derbys............... 83 H2
Millthrop Cumb............... 95 G4
Milltimber Aber C............... 149 F5
Milltown Abers............... 147 G5
Milltown Abers............... 148 B6
Milltown Cnwll............... 5 E2
Milltown D & G............... 111 H4
Milltown Derbys............... 72 A6
Milltown Devon............... 21 F4
Milltown of Campfield Abers............... 148 D4
Milltown of Edinville Moray............... 157 E3
Milltown of Learney Abers............... 148 D5
Milnathort P & K............... 131 G6
Milngavie W Duns............... 129 G3
Milnrow Gt Man............... 82 D6
Milnthorpe W York............... 90 D1
Milo15 Highld............... 150 B4
Milson Shrops............... 57 G3
Milstead Kent............... 30 C2
Milston Wilts............... 25 G4
Milthorpe Lincs............... 74 B3
Milthorpe Nhants............... 48 D4
Milton Cambs............... 62 D2
Milton Cumb............... 104 B6
Milton D & G............... 100 C6
Milton D & G............... 110 C2
Milton Derbys............... 71 H3
Milton Highld............... 167 G3
Milton Highld............... 151 G3
Milton Highld............... 154 C2
Milton Highld............... 154 D4
Milton Highld............... 162 D1
Milton Inver............... 129 E2
Milton Kent............... 29 G3
Milton Moray............... 157 G5
Milton Newpt............... 37 E3
Milton Notts............... 85 E2
Milton Oxon............... 48 C3
Milton Oxon............... 40 C3
Milton P & K............... 140 A5
Milton Pembks............... 33 E2
Milton Somset............... 23 F5
Milton Somset............... 23 G1
Milton Staffs............... 70 D5
Milton Stirlg............... 129 F5
Milton W Duns............... 129 F2
Milton Abbas Dorset............... 12 B5
Milton Abbot Devon............... 5 H4
Milton Bridge Mdloth............... 121 G6
Milton Bryan Beds............... 49 H2
Milton Clevedon Somset............... 24 B3
Milton Combe Devon............... 6 B4
Milton Common Oxon............... 41 E5
Milton Damerel Devon............... 20 D2
Milton End Gloucs............... 38 B5
Milton End Gloucs............... 39 F4
Milton Ernest Beds............... 61 F1
Milton Green Ches............... 69 G6
Milton Hill Oxon............... 40 C3
Milton Keynes Bucks............... 49 G3
Milton Lilbourne Wilts............... 25 G5
Milton Malsor Nhants............... 49 E5
Milton Morenish P & K............... 138 C3
Milton of Auchinhove Abers............... 148 C5
Milton of Balgonie Fife............... 132 B5
Milton of Buchanan Stirlg............... 129 F4
Milton of Campsie E Duns............... 130 C3
Milton of Leys Highld............... 155 E3
Milton of Tullich Abers............... 148 B4
Milton on Stour Dorset............... 24 D2
Milton Regis Kent............... 30 C2
Milton Street E Susx............... 17 F2
Milton-under-Wychwood Oxon............... 47 H1
Milverton Somset............... 22 D2
Milverton Warwks............... 59 F2
Milwich Staffs............... 71 E3
Milwr Flints............... 80 D2
Minard Ag & B............... 128 A5
Minchington Dorset............... 12 D6
Minchinhampton Gloucs............... 38 C4
Mindrum Nthumb............... 123 E3
Mindrum Mill Nthumb............... 123 F3
Minehead Somset............... 22 C4
Minera Wrexhm............... 69 E5
Minety Wilts............... 39 E3
Minffordd Gwynd............... 67 E4
Mingarrypark Highld............... 143 F1
Miningsby Lincs............... 86 D1
Minions Cnwll............... 5 F3
Minishant S Ayrs............... 109 E6
Minllyn Gwynd............... 67 H1
Minnigaff D & G............... 109 F1
Minnis Bay Kent............... 31 F3
Minnonie Abers............... 158 D5
Minskip N York............... 97 G1
Minstead Hants............... 13 G6
Minsted W Susx............... 15 G6
Minster Kent............... 30 C3
Minster Kent............... 31 G2
Minster Lovell Oxon............... 40 A5
Minsteracres Nthumb............... 105 G6
Minsterley Shrops............... 56 D6
Minsterworth Gloucs............... 38 C6
Minterne Magna Dorset............... 11 G5
Minterne Parva Dorset............... 11 G5
Minting Lincs............... 86 B2
Mintlaw Abers............... 159 F4
Minto Border............... 122 C1
Minton Shrops............... 57 E4
Minwear Pembks............... 33 E3
Minworth W Mids............... 58 D5
Mirehouse Cumb............... 102 D2
Mirfield W York............... 90 C2
Miserden Gloucs............... 38 D5
Miskin Rhondd............... 36 B2
Miskin Rhondd............... 36 B4
Misson Notts............... 84 D4
Misterton Leics............... 60 B4
Misterton Notts............... 85 E4
Misterton Somset............... 11 E5
Mistley Essex............... 53 E4
Mistley Heath Essex............... 53 E4
Mitcham Gt Lon............... 28 D3

Mitchel Troy Mons............... 37 F5
Mitcheldean Gloucs............... 46 B1
Mitchell Cnwll............... 3 F5
Mitchellslacks D & G............... 110 D4
Mitford Nthumb............... 114 C4
Mithian Cnwll............... 3 E5
Mitton Staffs............... 70 D1
Mixbury Oxon............... 48 D3
Mixenden W York............... 90 B2
Mixon Staffs............... 71 E6
Moats Tye Suffk............... 52 D6
Mobberley Ches............... 82 C3
Mobberley Staffs............... 71 E4
Moccas Herefs............... 45 F3
Mochdre Conwy............... 79 H2
Mochdre Powys............... 56 A4
Mochrum D & G............... 101 E5
Mockbeggar Hants............... 13 E5
Mockbeggar Kent............... 17 H6
Mockerkin Cumb............... 103 E2
Modbury Devon............... 6 D3
Moddershall Staffs............... 70 D4
Moel Tryfan Gwynd............... 67 E6
Moelfre IOA............... 79 E3
Moelfre Powys............... 68 D3
Moffat D & G............... 111 E5
Mogerhanger Beds............... 50 B6
Moira Leics............... 71 H1
Mol-chlach Highld............... 142 D5
Molash Kent............... 30 D1
Mold Flints............... 81 E1
Moldgreen W York............... 90 C1
Molehill Green Essex............... 51 F3
Molehill Green Essex............... 51 H3
Molescroft E R Yk............... 92 D4
Molesden Nthumb............... 114 C4
Molesworth Cambs............... 61 G3
Molland Devon............... 22 A2
Mollington Ches............... 81 F2
Mollington Oxon............... 48 C4
Mollinsburn N Lans............... 130 C2
Monachty Cerdgn............... 43 E5
Mondynes Abers............... 149 E2
Monewden Suffk............... 65 E1
Moneydie P & K............... 139 H3
Moneyrow Green Berks............... 41 G2
Moniaive D & G............... 110 B4
Monifieth Angus............... 141 E3
Monikie Angus............... 141 E4
Monimail Fife............... 140 C1
Monington Pembks............... 42 B4
Monk Bretton S York............... 84 A5
Monk Fryston N York............... 91 F2
Monk Sherborne Hants............... 26 D5
Monk Soham Suffk............... 65 E2
Monk Soham Green Suffk............... 65 E2
Monk Street Essex............... 51 G4
Monk's Gate W Susx............... 16 C4
Monken Hadley Gt Lon............... 28 C6
Monkhide Herefs............... 46 B4
Monkhill Cumb............... 103 G6
Monkhopton Shrops............... 57 F5
Monkland Herefs............... 45 G5
Monkleigh Devon............... 21 E3
Monknash V Glam............... 35 G1
Monkokehampton Devon............... 8 C5
Monks Eleigh Suffk............... 52 C5
Monks Heath Ches............... 82 C2
Monks Horton Kent............... 19 E5
Monks Kirby Warwks............... 59 G4
Monks Risborough Bucks............... 41 F5
Monkseaton T & W............... 115 E3
Monksilver Somset............... 22 D3
Monkspath W Mids............... 58 D3
Monksthorpe Lincs............... 87 E1
Monkswood Mons............... 37 E4
Monkton Devon............... 10 B5
Monkton Kent............... 31 F2
Monkton S Ayrs............... 119 E2
Monkton T & W............... 115 E2
Monkton V Glam............... 35 G1
Monkton Combe Somset............... 24 C5
Monkton Deverill Wilts............... 24 D3
Monkton Farleigh Wilts............... 24 D6
Monkton Heathfield Somset............... 23 E2
Monkton up Wimborne Dorset............... 12 D6
Monkton Wyld Dorset............... 10 D4
Monkwearmouth T & W............... 115 F1
Monkwood Hants............... 27 E2
Monmore Green W Mids............... 58 B5
Monmouth Mons............... 37 F6
Monnington on Wye Herefs............... 45 F3
Monreith D & G............... 101 E4
Mont Saint Guern............... 174 f2
Montacute Somset............... 23 H1
Montcliffe Gt Man............... 82 B6
Montford Shrops............... 69 F1
Montford Bridge Shrops............... 69 F1
Montgarrie Abers............... 148 C6
Montgarswood E Ayrs............... 119 G2
Montgomery Powys............... 56 C5
Montgreenan N Ayrs............... 119 E4
Monton Gt Man............... 82 C5
Montrose Angus............... 141 G6
Monxton Hants............... 26 A4
Monyash Derbys............... 83 F1
Monymusk Abers............... 148 D6
Monzie P & K............... 139 F2
Moodiesburn N Lans............... 130 C2
Moonzie Fife............... 140 C1
Moor Allerton W York............... 90 D3
Moor Crichel Dorset............... 12 D5
Moor End Beds............... 49 H1
Moor End Devon............... 8 D5
Moor End E R Yk............... 92 B3
Moor End Lancs............... 88 B4
Moor End N York............... 91 G3
Moor End W York............... 90 B2
Moor Green Herts............... 50 D3
Moor Head W York............... 90 D2
Moor Monkton N York............... 91 F5
Moor Row Cumb............... 102 D1
Moor Row Cumb............... 103 F6
Moor Row Dur............... 106 A2
Moor Side Lancs............... 88 C3
Moor Side Lancs............... 88 C3
Moor Side Lincs............... 74 C6
Moor Street Kent............... 30 B3

Moor Street W Mids............... 58 C4
Moorbath Dorset............... 11 E4
Moorby Lincs............... 86 C1
Moorcot Herefs............... 45 F5
Moordown Dorset............... 13 E4
Moore Ches............... 81 H3
Moorend Gloucs............... 38 B5
Moorends S York............... 91 H1
Moorgreen Hants............... 14 C5
Moorgreen Notts............... 72 C5
Moorhall Derbys............... 83 H2
Moorhampton Herefs............... 45 G4
Moorhead W York............... 90 C3
Moorhouse Cumb............... 103 F5
Moorhouse Cumb............... 103 G6
Moorhouse Notts............... 85 E1
Moorhouse Bank Surrey............... 29 E1
Moorland Somset............... 23 F2
Moorlinch Somset............... 23 G3
Moorsholm N York............... 107 F2
Moorside Cumb............... 94 B5
Moorside Dorset............... 24 D1
Moorside Gt Man............... 82 D5
Moorside W York............... 90 D3
Moorstock Kent............... 19 E5
Moorswater Cnwll............... 5 F2
Moorthorpe W York............... 84 B6
Moortown Devon............... 6 C5
Moortown Hants............... 13 E5
Moortown IOW............... 14 B2
Moortown Lincs............... 86 A5
Moortown Shrops............... 70 A2
Moortown W York............... 90 D3
Morangie Highld............... 162 D2
Morar Highld............... 143 F3
Morborne Cambs............... 61 G4
Morchard Bishop Devon............... 9 E5
Morcombelake Dorset............... 10 D4
Morcott Rutlnd............... 61 E2
Morda Shrops............... 69 E3
Morden Dorset............... 12 C4
Morden Gt Lon............... 28 C3
Mordiford Herefs............... 46 A3
Mordon Dur............... 106 C3
More Shrops............... 56 D4
Morebath Devon............... 22 B2
Morebattle Border............... 123 E2
Morecambe Lancs............... 95 E1
Moredon Wilts............... 39 F3
Morefield Highld............... 161 E3
Morehall Kent............... 19 F5
Moreleigh Devon............... 7 E3
Morenish P & K............... 138 C3
Moresby Cumb............... 102 D2
Moresby Parks Cumb............... 102 D2
Morestead Hants............... 26 C2
Moreton Ches............... 12 B3
Moreton Essex............... 51 F1
Moreton Herefs............... 57 E2
Moreton Mersyd............... 81 E4
Moreton Oxon............... 41 E5
Moreton Staffs............... 70 C2
Moreton Staffs............... 71 F3
Moreton Corbet Shrops............... 69 H2
Moreton Jeffries Herefs............... 46 B4
Moreton Morrell Warwks............... 48 A5
Moreton on Lugg Herefs............... 45 H4
Moreton Paddox Warwks............... 48 A5
Moreton Pinkney Nhants............... 48 D4
Moreton Say Shrops............... 70 A3
Moreton Valence Gloucs............... 38 C5
Moreton-in-Marsh Gloucs............... 47 G2
Moretonhampstead Devon............... 8 D3
Moretonmill Shrops............... 69 H2
Morfa Cerdgn............... 42 C4
Morfa Bychan Gwynd............... 67 E4
Morfa Dinlle Gwynd............... 66 D6
Morfa Glas Neath............... 35 F5
Morfa Nefyn Gwynd............... 66 C4
Morgan's Vale Wilts............... 25 G1
Morganstown Cardif............... 36 B2
Morham E Loth............... 132 D2
Moriah Cerdgn............... 54 D3
Morland Cumb............... 104 C2
Morley Ches............... 82 C3
Morley Derbys............... 72 B4
Morley Dur............... 105 H3
Morley W York............... 90 D2
Morley Green Ches............... 82 C3
Morley St Botolph Norfk............... 64 C5
Mornick Cnwll............... 5 G3
Morningside C Edin............... 132 A2
Morningside N Lans............... 120 C5
Morningthorpe Norfk............... 65 E5
Morpeth Nthumb............... 114 D4
Morphie Abers............... 141 G6
Morrey Staffs............... 71 F2
Morridge Side Staffs............... 71 E5
Morridge Top Staffs............... 83 E1
Morriston Swans............... 34 D4
Morston Norfk............... 76 C4
Mortehoe Devon............... 21 E5
Morthen S York............... 84 B4
Mortimer Berks............... 27 E6
Mortimer Common Berks............... 27 E6
Mortimer West End Hants............... 27 E6
Mortimer's Cross Herefs............... 56 D2
Mortlake Gt Lon............... 28 C4
Morton Cumb............... 103 H6
Morton Cumb............... 104 A4
Morton Derbys............... 72 B6
Morton IOW............... 14 D2
Morton Lincs............... 85 F4
Morton Lincs............... 74 A2
Morton Notts............... 73 E5
Morton Shrops............... 69 E2
Morton Hall Lincs............... 85 F1
Morton on the Hill Norfk............... 76 D2
Morton Tinmouth Dur............... 106 A3
Morton-on-Swale N York............... 97 F4
Morvah Cnwll............... 2 B3
Morval Cnwll............... 5 F2
Morvich Highld............... 152 D1
Morville Shrops............... 57 G5
Morville Heath Shrops............... 57 G5
Morwellham Quay Devon............... 6 B5
Morwenstow Cnwll............... 20 D2

Mosborough S York............... 84 B3
Moscow E Ayrs............... 119 G3
Mose Shrops............... 57 H4
Mosedale Cumb............... 103 G3
Moseley W Mids............... 58 B5
Moseley W Mids............... 58 D4
Moseley Worcs............... 46 D5
Moses Gate Gt Man............... 82 B5
Moss Ag & B............... 134 B4
Moss S York............... 84 D6
Moss Wrexhm............... 69 E5
Moss Bank Mersyd............... 81 G4
Moss Edge Lancs............... 88 C4
Moss End Bucks............... 82 B2
Moss Side Cumb............... 103 F5
Moss Side Lancs............... 88 B3
Moss Side Mersyd............... 81 F5
Moss Side Mersyd............... 81 F5
Moss-side Highld............... 155 G5
Mossat Abers............... 157 G1
Mossbank Shet............... 169 j4
Mossbay Cumb............... 102 D3
Mossblown S Ayrs............... 119 F2
Mossbrow Gt Man............... 82 B4
Mossburnford Border............... 122 D1
Mossdale D & G............... 110 A2
Mossdale E Ayrs............... 109 G5
Mossend N Lans............... 120 B5
Mosser Mains Cumb............... 103 E3
Mossley Ches............... 70 D6
Mossley Gt Man............... 83 E5
Mosspaul Hotel Border............... 112 A5
Mosstodloch Moray............... 157 G5
Mossy Lea Lancs............... 81 G6
Mossyard D & G............... 101 G5
Mosterton Dorset............... 11 E5
Moston Gt Man............... 82 D5
Moston Shrops............... 69 H3
Moston Green Ches............... 70 B6
Mostyn Flints............... 80 D3
Motcombe Dorset............... 24 D2
Mothecombe Devon............... 6 C2
Motherby Cumb............... 104 A3
Motherwell N Lans............... 120 B5
Motspur Park Gt Lon............... 28 C3
Mottingham Gt Lon............... 29 E3
Mottisfont Hants............... 26 B2
Mottistone IOW............... 14 B2
Mottram in Longdendale Gt Man............... 83 E4
Mottram St Andrew Ches............... 82 D2
Mouilpied Guern............... 174 g1
Mouldsworth Ches............... 81 G2
Moulin P & K............... 139 G6
Moulsecoomb E Susx............... 16 D2
Moulsford Oxon............... 40 D3
Moulsoe Bucks............... 49 G3
Moultavie Highld............... 155 E6
Moulton Ches............... 82 B2
Moulton Lincs............... 74 C2
Moulton N York............... 97 E5
Moulton Nhants............... 60 D2
Moulton Suffk............... 63 F2
Moulton V Glam............... 36 B1
Moulton Chapel Lincs............... 74 C2
Moulton Seas End Lincs............... 74 D3
Moulton St Mary Norfk............... 65 F6
Mount Cnwll............... 3 E5
Mount Cnwll............... 5 E3
Mount W York............... 90 B1
Mount Ambrose Cnwll............... 3 E4
Mount Bures Essex............... 52 C4
Mount Hawke Cnwll............... 3 E4
Mount Hermon Cnwll............... 2 D1
Mount Lothian Mdloth............... 121 G5
Mount Pleasant Ches............... 70 C6
Mount Pleasant Derbys............... 72 A5
Mount Pleasant Dur............... 106 B4
Mount Pleasant E Susx............... 17 E3
Mount Pleasant Norfk............... 64 B5
Mount Pleasant Suffk............... 52 A5
Mount Pleasant Worcs............... 58 C2
Mount Sorrel Wilts............... 25 F2
Mount Tabor W York............... 90 B2
Mountain W York............... 90 B3
Mountain Ash Rhondd............... 36 B4
Mountain Cross Border............... 121 F4
Mountain Street Kent............... 30 D1
Mountfield E Susx............... 18 A3
Mountgerald House Highld............... 154 D5
Mountjoy Cnwll............... 4 B2
Mountnessing Essex............... 29 G6
Mounton Mons............... 37 F4
Mountsorrel Leics............... 72 C1
Mousehill Surrey............... 27 G3
Mousehole Cnwll............... 2 B2
Mouswald D & G............... 111 E2
Mow Cop Ches............... 70 D6
Mowhaugh Border............... 123 E1
Mowmacre Hill Leics............... 60 B6
Mowsley Leics............... 60 C4
Mowtie Abers............... 149 F3
Moy Highld............... 155 F2
Moy Highld............... 145 H3
Moye Highld............... 152 C1
Moyles Court Hants............... 13 E5
Moylgrove Pembks............... 42 A4
Muasdale Ag & B............... 117 F4
Much Birch Herefs............... 45 H2
Much Cowarne Herefs............... 46 B4
Much Dewchurch Herefs............... 45 H2
Much Hadham Herts............... 51 E3
Much Hoole Lancs............... 88 C2
Much Hoole Town Lancs............... 88 C2
Much Marcle Herefs............... 46 B2
Much Wenlock Shrops............... 57 F5
Muchalls Abers............... 149 G4
Muchelney Somset............... 23 G4
Muchelney Ham Somset............... 23 G2
Muchlarnick Cnwll............... 5 F2
Mucking Essex............... 29 H4
Muckingford Essex............... 29 G4
Muckleburgh Collection Norfk............... 76 D4
Muckleford Dorset............... 11 G4
Mucklestone Staffs............... 70 B4
Muckley Shrops............... 57 G5
Muckton Lincs............... 86 D3
Mud Row Kent............... 30 D3
Muddiford Devon............... 21 F4

Muddles Green E Susx............... 17 F3
Mudeford Dorset............... 13 F4
Mudford Somset............... 24 A1
Mudford Sock Somset............... 24 A1
Mudgley Somset............... 23 G4
Mugdock Stirlg............... 129 G3
Mugeary Highld............... 150 D3
Mugginton Derbys............... 71 H4
Mugginton End Derbys............... 71 H4
Muggleswick Dur............... 105 G5
Muir of Fowlis Abers............... 148 C6
Muir of Miltonduff Moray............... 156 D5
Muir of Ord Highld............... 154 C4
Muir of Thorn P & K............... 139 H3
Muirden Abers............... 158 C4
Muirdrum Angus............... 141 F3
Muiresk Abers............... 158 C4
Muirhead Angus............... 140 C3
Muirhead Fife............... 132 B6
Muirhead N Lans............... 130 C2
Muirkirk E Ayrs............... 120 B2
Muirmill Stirlg............... 130 D3
Muirshearlich Highld............... 144 D2
Muirtack Abers............... 159 F3
Muirton P & K............... 139 F1
Muirton Mains Highld............... 154 C4
Muirton of Ardblair P & K............... 140 B4
Muker N York............... 96 B5
Mulbarton Norfk............... 64 D5
Mulben Moray............... 157 F4
Mulfra Cnwll............... 2 B3
Mullacott Cross Devon............... 21 E5
Mullion Cnwll............... 2 D2
Mullion Cove Cnwll............... 2 D1
Mumby Lincs............... 87 E2
Munderfield Row Herefs............... 46 B4
Munderfield Stocks Herefs............... 46 B4
Mundesley Norfk............... 77 F4
Mundford Norfk............... 63 G5
Mundham Norfk............... 65 F5
Mundon Hill Essex............... 52 B1
Mundy Bois Kent............... 18 C6
Mungrisdale Cumb............... 103 H3
Munlochy Highld............... 155 E4
Munnoch N Ayrs............... 118 D4
Munsley Herefs............... 46 B3
Munslow Shrops............... 57 E4
Murchington Devon............... 8 D3
Murcot Worcs............... 47 F3
Murcott Oxon............... 40 D6
Murcott Wilts............... 38 D3
Murkle Highld............... 167 E5
Murlaggan Highld............... 144 B4
Murrell Green Hants............... 27 F5
Murroes Angus............... 141 E3
Murrow Cambs............... 62 C6
Mursley Bucks............... 49 F2
Murston Kent............... 30 C2
Murthill Angus............... 141 E5
Murthly P & K............... 140 A4
Murton Cumb............... 104 C2
Murton Dur............... 106 C6
Murton N York............... 91 G5
Murton Nthumb............... 123 G4
Murton T & W............... 115 E3
Musbury Devon............... 10 C4
Muscoates N York............... 98 C3
Musselburgh E Loth............... 132 B2
Muston Leics............... 73 F4
Muston N York............... 99 G3
Mustow Green Worcs............... 58 B3
Muswell Hill Gt Lon............... 28 D5
Mutehill D & G............... 102 A5
Mutford Suffk............... 65 G4
Muthill P & K............... 139 F1
Mutterton Devon............... 9 G5
Muxton Shrops............... 70 B1
Mybster Highld............... 167 E4
Myddfai Carmth............... 43 H2
Myddle Shrops............... 69 G2
Mydroilyn Cerdgn............... 43 E5
Mylor Cnwll............... 3 F3
Mylor Bridge Cnwll............... 3 E3
Mynachlog ddu Pembks............... 33 F5
Mynd-llan Flints............... 80 D2
Myndtown Shrops............... 56 D4
Mynydd Buch Cerdgn............... 55 E3
Mynydd Isa Flints............... 81 E1
Mynydd Llandygai Gwynd............... 79 F1
Mynydd-bach Mons............... 37 F4
Mynydd-Bach Swans............... 34 D4
Mynyddgarreg Carmth............... 34 B5
Mynytho Gwynd............... 66 C3
Myrebird Abers............... 149 E4
Myredykes Border............... 112 C5
Mytchett Surrey............... 27 G5
Mytholm W York............... 90 A2
Mytholmroyd W York............... 90 A2
Mythop Lancs............... 88 B3
Myton-on-Swale N York............... 97 G1

Na Buirgh W Isls............... 168 c6
Naast Highld............... 160 B2
Nab's Head Lancs............... 89 E2
Naburn N York............... 91 G4
Naccolt Kent............... 18 D6
Nackington Kent............... 31 E1
Nacton Suffk............... 53 F5
Nafferton E R Yk............... 92 D3
Nag's Head Gloucs............... 38 D4
Nailbridge Gloucs............... 37 G6
Nailsbourne Somset............... 23 E2
Nailsea Somset............... 37 F1
Nailstone Leics............... 59 G6
Nailsworth Gloucs............... 38 C4
Nairn Highld............... 155 G5
Nalderswood Surrey............... 16 C6
Nancegollan Cnwll............... 2 D3
Nancledra Cnwll............... 2 C2
Nanhoron Gwynd............... 66 B3
Nannerch Flints............... 80 D2

Nanpantan Leics 72 C2
Nanpean Cnwll 3 G5
Nanquidno Cnwll 2 A3
Nanstallon Cnwll 4 D3
Nant Gwynant Gwynd 67 F5
Nant Peris Gwynd 67 F6
Nant-ddu Powys 35 G6
Nant-glas Powys 55 G2
Nant-y-Bwch Blae G 36 B5
Nant-y-caws Carmth 34 B6
Nant-y-derry Mons 36 D5
Nant-y-gollen Shrops 69 E3
Nant-y-moel Brdgnd 35 G3
Nant-y-pandy Conwy 79 F2
Nanternis Cerdgn 42 D5
Nantgaredig Carmth 43 E1
Nantgarw Rhondd 36 B3
Nantglyn Denbgs 68 B6
Nantgwyn Powys 55 G3
Nantile Gwynd 67 E5
Nantmawr Shrops 69 E2
Nantmel Powys 55 H2
Nantmor Gwynd 67 F5
Nantwich Ches 70 B5
Nantyffyllon Brdgnd 35 F3
Nantyglo Blae G 36 C5
Naphill Bucks 41 G4
Napleton Worcs 46 D4
Nappa N York 89 G5
Napton on the Hill Warwks 48 C5
Narberth Pembks 33 E3
Narborough Leics 60 B5
Narborough Norfk 75 H1
Narkurs Cnwll 5 G1
Nasareth Gwynd 66 D5
Naseby Nhants 60 C3
Nash Bucks 49 F3
Nash Gt Lon 29 E2
Nash Herefs 45 F5
Nash Newpt 36 D3
Nash Shrops 57 F2
Nash End Worcs 57 H4
Nash Lee Bucks 41 G5
Nash Street Kent 29 G3
Nash's Green Hants 27 E4
Nassington Nhants 61 G5
Nastend Gloucs 38 C5
Nasty Herts 50 D3
Nateby Cumb 96 A5
Nateby Lancs 88 C4
National Shire Horse Centre
        Devon 6 C3
National Space Science Centre
        Leics 60 B6
Natland Cumb 95 F4
Naughton Suffk 52 D6
Naunton Gloucs 47 G1
Naunton Worcs 46 D3
Naunton Beauchamp Worcs 47 E4
Navenby Lincs 73 G6
Navestock Essex 29 F6
Navestock Side Essex 29 F6
Navidale House Hotel Highld 163 G5
Navity Highld 155 F6
Nawton N York 98 B3
Nayland Suffk 52 C4
Nazeing Essex 51 E1
Nazeing Gate Essex 51 E1
Neacroft Hants 13 F4
Neal's Green Warwks 59 F4
Neap Shet 169 j3
Near Cotton Staffs 71 F5
Near Sawrey Cumb 94 D4
Neasden Gt Lon 28 C5
Neasham Dur 106 C2
Neath Neath 35 E4
Neatham Hants 27 F3
Neatishead Norfk 77 F2
Nebo Highld 164 B2
Nebo Conwy 67 H6
Nebo Gwynd 66 D5
Nebo IOA 78 D4
Necton Norfk 76 B1
Nedd Highld 164 B2
Nedderton Nthumb 114 D4
Nedging Suffk 52 D5
Nedging Tye Suffk 52 D6
Needham Norfk 65 E3
Needham Market Suffk 52 D6
Needham Street Suffk 63 F2
Needingworth Cambs 62 C3
Neen Savage Shrops 57 F3
Neen Sollars Shrops 57 G3
Neenton Shrops 57 G4
Nefyn Gwynd 66 C4
Neilston E Rens 119 G5
Nelson Caerph 36 B4
Nelson Lancs 89 G3
Nemphlar S Lans 120 C4
Nempnett Thrubwell Somset 23 H5
Nenthall Cumb 104 D5
Nenthead Cumb 104 D4
Nenthorn Border 122 D3
Neopardy Devon 9 E4
Nep Town W Susx 16 C3
Nercwys Flints 69 E6
Nereabolls Ag & B 116 A6
Nerston S Lans 120 A5
Nesbit Nthumb 123 G3
Nesfield N York 90 B5
Ness Ches 81 E2
Ness Botanic Gardens Ches 81 E2
Nesscliffe Shrops 69 F3
Neston Ches 81 E2
Neston Wilts 38 C1
Netchwood Shrops 57 F4
Nether Alderley Ches 82 C2
Nether Blainslie Border 122 C4
Nether Broughton Notts 73 E3
Nether Cerne Dorset 11 G4
Nether Compton Dorset 24 B1
Nether Crimond Abers 158 D1
Nether Dallachy Moray 157 F5
Nether Exe Devon 9 F5
Nether Fingland S Lans 110 D6
Nether Handley Derbys 84 B2
Nether Handwick Angus 140 C4
Nether Haugh S York 84 B4

Nether Headon Notts 85 E2
Nether Heage Derbys 72 A5
Nether Heyford Nhants 49 E3
Nether Howcleugh S Lans 111 E6
Nether Kellet Lancs 95 F2
Nether Kinmundy Abers 159 F3
Nether Langwith Notts 84 C2
Nether Moor Derbys 84 B1
Nether Padley Derbys 83 G2
Nether Poppleton N York 91 G5
Nether Row Cumb 103 G4
Nether Silton N York 97 H4
Nether Skyborry Shrops 56 C3
Nether Stowey Somset 23 E3
Nether Street Essex 51 G2
Nether Wallop Hants 26 A3
Nether Wasdale Cumb 94 B5
Nether Welton Cumb 103 G5
Nether Westcote Gloucs 47 H1
Nether Whitacre Warwks 59 E5
Nether Whitecleuch S Lans 120 C1
Nether Winchendon Bucks 41 E3
Netheravon Wilts 25 G4
Netherbrae Abers 158 D5
Netherburn S Lans 120 C4
Netherbury Dorset 11 E4
Netherby Cumb 112 A2
Netherby N York 90 D4
Nethercleuch D & G 111 F3
Nethercote Warwks 60 A2
Nethercott Devon 21 E4
Netherend Gloucs 5 G6
Netherend Gloucs 37 G4
Netherfield E Susx 17 H3
Netherfield Leics 72 D2
Netherfield Notts 72 D4
Netherfield Road E Susx 18 A3
Nethergate Norfk 76 D3
Netherhampton Wilts 25 F2
Netherhay Dorset 10 D5
Netherland Green Staffs 71 F3
Netherlaw D & G 102 B5
Netherley Abers 149 F4
Nethermill D & G 111 E3
Nethermuir Abers 159 E3
Netheroyd Hill W York 90 C1
Netherplace E Rens 119 G5
Netherseal Derbys 71 H1
Netherstreet Wilts 25 E6
Netherthong W York 83 F6
Netherthorpe Derbys 84 B2
Netherton Angus 141 E5
Netherton Devon 7 F5
Netherton Hants 26 B5
Netherton Herefs 45 H2
Netherton N Lans 120 B5
Netherton Nthumb 124 C2
Netherton Oxon 40 B4
Netherton P & K 140 A5
Netherton Shrops 57 G4
Netherton Stirlg 129 G3
Netherton W Mids 58 B4
Netherton W York 83 F6
Netherton W York 90 D1
Netherton Worcs 47 E3
Nethertown Cumb 102 D1
Nethertown Highld 167 G6
Nethertown Lancs 89 F3
Nethertown Staffs 71 F2
Netherurd Border 121 F4
Netherwitton Nthumb 114 C4
Nethy Bridge Highld 156 B1
Netley Hants 14 C4
Netley Marsh Hants 13 G6
Nettacott Devon 9 F5
Nettlebed Oxon 41 E3
Nettlebridge Somset 24 B4
Nettlecombe Dorset 11 E4
Nettlecombe IOW 14 C1
Nettleden Herts 50 A2
Nettleham Lincs 85 H2
Nettlestead Kent 29 H1
Nettlestead Green Kent 29 H1
Nettlestone IOW 14 D3
Nettlesworth Dur 106 B6
Nettleton Lincs 86 B5
Nettleton Wilts 38 C2
Nettleton Shrub Wilts 38 C2
Netton Devon 6 C2
Netton Wilts 25 G3
Neuadd Carmth 43 G1
Neuadd Fawr Carmth 43 H3
Neuadd-ddu Powys 55 G3
Nevendon Essex 30 A5
Nevern Pembks 42 A3
Nevill Holt Leics 60 D5
New Abbey D & G 110 D1
New Aberdour Abers 159 E5
New Addington Gt Lon 29 E2
New Alresford Hants 26 D2
New Alyth P & K 140 B4
New Arram E R Yk 92 D4
New Ash Green Kent 29 G3
New Balderton Notts 73 F5
New Barn Kent 29 G3
New Barnet Gt Lon 28 D6
New Barton Nhants 61 E2
New Bewick Nthumb 124 D3
New Bilton Warwks 59 H3
New Bolingbroke Lincs 74 C6
New Boultham Lincs 85 G2
New Bradwell Bucks 49 F3
New Brampton Derbys 84 A2
New Brancepeth Dur 106 B5
New Bridge N York 98 D1
New Brighton Flints 81 E1
New Brighton Mersyd 81 E4
New Brinsley Notts 72 B5
New Brotton N York 107 F3
New Broughton Wrexhm 69 E5
New Buckenham Norfk 64 C4
New Bury Gt Man 82 B5
New Byth Abers 158 D4
New Costessey Norfk 77 E1
New Cowper Cumb 103 G6
New Crofton W York 91 E1
New Cross Cerdgn 54 D3

New Cross Gt Lon 28 D4
New Cross Somset 23 G1
New Cumnock E Ayrs 109 H6
New Cut E Susx 18 B3
New Deer Abers 159 E4
New Delaval Nthumb 115 E3
New Delph Gt Man 83 E5
New Denham Bucks 28 A4
New Duston Nhants 60 C2
New Earswick N York 91 G5
New Eastwood Notts 72 B5
New Edlington S York 84 C5
New Elgin Moray 156 D5
New Ellerby E R Yk 93 E3
New Eltham Gt Lon 29 E3
New End Worcs 47 F5
New England Cambs 61 H5
New Farnley W York 90 D3
New Ferry Mersyd 81 F5
New Fletton Cambs 61 H5
New Fryston W York 91 F2
New Galloway D & G 109 H2
New Gilston Fife 132 C6
New Grimsby IOS 2 a2
New Hartley Nthumb 115 E3
New Haw Surrey 28 B2
New Hedges Pembks 33 E2
New Herrington T & W 106 C6
New Holkham Norfk 76 B4
New Holland Lincs 93 E2
New Houghton Derbys 84 C1
New Houghton Norfk 76 A3
New Houses Gt Man 81 H5
New Houses N York 96 A2
New Hutton Cumb 95 F4
New Hythe Kent 29 H2
New Inn Carmth 43 E3
New Inn Torfn 36 D4
New Invention Shrops 57 E6
New Lakenham Norfk 65 E6
New Lanark S Lans 120 C4
New Lane Lancs 81 F6
New Lane End Ches 82 A4
New Langholm D & G 111 H3
New Leake Lincs 74 D6
New Leeds Abers 159 F4
New Lodge S York 84 A6
New Longton Lancs 88 D2
New Luce D & G 108 D1
New Malden Gt Lon 28 C3
New Marske N York 107 E3
New Marston Oxon 40 C5
New Marton Shrops 69 F3
New Mill Abers 149 E3
New Mill Cnwll 2 B3
New Mill Herts 41 G5
New Mill W York 83 F6
New Mills Cnwll 3 F5
New Mills Derbys 83 E3
New Mills Powys 55 H3
New Milton Hants 13 F4
New Mistley Essex 53 E4
New Moat Pembks 33 E4
New Ollerton Notts 84 D1
New Oscott W Mids 58 D5
New Pitsligo Abers 159 E5
New Polzeath Cnwll 4 C4
New Prestwick S Ayrs 119 E2
New Quay Cerdgn 42 D5
New Quay Essex 52 D3
New Rackheath Norfk 77 F1
New Radnor Powys 45 E5
New Rent Cumb 104 A4
New Ridley Nthumb 114 B1
New Road Side N York 89 H4
New Romney Kent 18 D4
New Rossington S York 84 D4
New Row Cerdgn 55 E3
New Row Lancs 89 E3
New Sauchie Clacks 131 E6
New Sharlston W York 91 E2
New Shoreston Nthumb 125 E4
New Silksworth T & W 106 C6
New Skelton N York 107 F3
New Somerby Lincs 73 G4
New Spilsby Lincs 86 D1
New Springs Gt Man 82 A5
New Stevenston N Lans 120 B5
New Street Herefs 45 F5
New Swannington Leics 72 B2
New Thundersley Essex 30 A5
New Town Beds 50 C5
New Town Dorset 12 C6
New Town Dorset 12 D5
New Town E Loth 132 C2
New Town E Susx 17 F3
New Town Nhants 61 F3
New Town Wilts 39 G1
New Tredegar Caerph 36 C5
New Trows S Lans 120 C3
New Tupton Derbys 84 B1
New Village E R Yk 92 B3
New Walsoken Cambs 75 E1
New Waltham Lincs 86 C5
New Whittington Derbys 84 B2
New Winton E Loth 132 C2
New Yatt Oxon 40 B6
New York Lincs 74 C6
New York N York 90 C6
New York T & W 115 E2
Newall W York 90 C4
Newark Cambs 62 A5
Newark Ork 169 d4
Newark-on-Trent Notts 73 F5
Newarthill N Lans 120 B5
Newbarn Kent 19 E5
Newbattle Mdloth 132 B2
Newbie D & G 111 F1
Newbiggin Cumb 104 A3
Newbiggin Cumb 104 A4
Newbiggin Cumb 104 B5
Newbiggin Cumb 104 C3
Newbiggin Dur 105 F3
Newbiggin Dur 106 A6
Newbiggin N York 96 C4
Newbiggin N York 96 C3

Newbiggin-by-the-Sea Nthumb 115 E4
Newbiggin-on-Lune Cumb 95 H5
Newbigging Angus 140 C4
Newbigging Angus 140 D3
Newbigging Angus 141 E3
Newbigging S Lans 121 E4
Newbold Derbys 84 A2
Newbold Leics 72 B2
Newbold on Avon Warwks 59 H3
Newbold on Stour Warwks 47 H4
Newbold Pacey Warwks 48 A5
Newbold Revel Warwks 59 G3
Newbold Verdon Leics 59 G6
Newborough Cambs 62 A6
Newborough IOA 78 D1
Newborough Staffs 71 F2
Newbourne Suffk 53 F5
Newbridge C Edin 131 G2
Newbridge Caerph 36 C4
Newbridge Cerdgn 43 E5
Newbridge Cnwll 2 B3
Newbridge Cnwll 3 E4
Newbridge D & G 110 D3
Newbridge Hants 13 G6
Newbridge IOW 14 B2
Newbridge Oxon 40 B4
Newbridge Pembks 32 D5
Newbridge Wrexhm 69 E4
Newbridge Green Worcs 46 D3
Newbridge on Wye Powys 44 C5
Newbridge-on-Usk Mons 37 E4
Newbrough Nthumb 113 F1
Newbuildings Devon 9 E5
Newburgh Abers 159 E5
Newburgh Abers 159 F2
Newburgh Fife 140 B2
Newburgh Lancs 81 G6
Newburgh Priory N York 98 A2
Newburn T & W 114 C2
Newbury Berks 26 C6
Newbury Somset 24 C4
Newbury Wilts 24 D3
Newbury Park Gt Lon 29 E5
Newby Cumb 104 C2
Newby Lancs 89 G4
Newby N York 106 D2
Newby N York 95 H4
Newby N York 99 F4
Newby Bridge Cumb 94 D3
Newby Cross Cumb 103 H5
Newby East Cumb 104 B6
Newby Head Cumb 104 C2
Newby West Cumb 103 H5
Newby Wiske N York 97 G4
Newcastle Mons 37 E6
Newcastle Shrops 56 C4
Newcastle Airport Nthumb 114 C3
Newcastle Emlyn Carmth 42 C3
Newcastle upon Tyne T & W 114 D2
Newcastle-under-Lyme Staffs 70 C5
Newcastleton Border 112 B3
Newchapel Pembks 42 B3
Newchapel Staffs 70 D5
Newchapel Surrey 16 D6
Newchurch Blae G 36 C5
Newchurch Herefs 45 F4
Newchurch IOW 14 D2
Newchurch Kent 18 D4
Newchurch Mons 37 F4
Newchurch Powys 45 E5
Newchurch Staffs 71 F2
Newchurch in Pendle Lancs 89 G3
Newcraighall C Edin 132 B2
Newdigate Surrey 16 C6
Newell Green Berks 41 G1
Newenden Kent 18 B4
Newent Gloucs 46 C2
Newfield Dur 106 B4
Newfield Dur 106 B6
Newfield Highld 163 E1
Newfound Hants 26 D4
Newgale Pembks 32 C4
Newgate Norfk 76 D4
Newgate Street Herts 50 D1
Newhall Ches 70 A5
Newhall Derbys 71 H2
Newham Nthumb 125 E4
Newhaven Derbys 71 G6
Newhaven E Susx 17 E1
Newhey Gt Man 82 D6
Newholm N York 107 H2
Newhouse N Lans 120 B6
Newick E Susx 17 E3
Newingreen Kent 19 E5
Newington Kent 30 B2
Newington Kent 19 E5
Newington Oxon 40 D4
Newington Shrops 56 D4
Newington Bagpath Gloucs 38 C4
Newland Cumb 94 D3
Newland E R Yk 92 B2
Newland E R Yk 92 D3
Newland Gloucs 37 F5
Newland N York 91 H2
Newland Oxon 40 B5
Newland Somset 22 A3
Newland Worcs 46 C4
Newlandrig Mdloth 121 H6
Newlands Border 112 B4
Newlands Nthumb 114 A2
Newlands of Dundurcas Moray 157 E4
Newlyn Cnwll 2 B3
Newlyn East Cnwll 3 F5
Newmachar Abers 159 E1
Newmains N Lans 120 C5
Newman's End Essex 51 F2
Newman's Green Suffk 52 B5
Newmarket Suffk 63 F2
Newmarket W Isls 168 e8
Newmill Border 112 B6
Newmill Moray 157 F4
Newmill of Inshewan Angus 140 D6
Newmillerdam W York 90 D1
Newmills C Edin 131 H2
Newmills Fife 131 F4

Newmills Mons 37 F5
Newmiln P & K 140 A3
Newmilns E Ayrs 119 G3
Newnes Shrops 69 F3
Newney Green Essex 51 G1
Newnham Gloucs 38 B5
Newnham Hants 27 E5
Newnham Herts 50 C4
Newnham Kent 30 C2
Newnham Nhants 48 D5
Newnham Worcs 57 G2
Newnham Paddox Warwks 59 H4
Newport Cnwll 5 G4
Newport Devon 21 F4
Newport Dorset 12 C4
Newport E R Yk 92 B3
Newport Essex 51 F4
Newport Gloucs 38 B4
Newport Highld 163 H6
Newport IOW 14 C2
Newport Newpt 36 D3
Newport Norfk 77 H2
Newport Pembks 33 E6
Newport Shrops 70 B2
Newport Pagnell Bucks 49 G3
Newport-on-Tay Fife 140 D2
Newpound Common W Susx 16 B4
Newquay Cnwll 4 B2
Newquay Airport Cnwll 4 B2
Newsam Green W York 91 E3
Newsbank Ches 82 C1
Newseat Abers 158 C2
Newsham Lancs 88 D3
Newsham N York 96 D6
Newsham N York 97 G3
Newsham Nthumb 115 E3
Newsholme E R Yk 92 A2
Newsholme Lancs 89 G5
Newstead Border 122 C3
Newstead Notts 72 C5
Newstead Nthumb 125 E4
Newthorpe N York 91 F3
Newthorpe Notts 72 B5
Newtimber W Susx 16 D3
Newtoft Lincs 85 H3
Newton Ag & B 128 B5
Newton Beds 50 C5
Newton Border 122 C1
Newton Brdgnd 35 F2
Newton Cambs 75 E1
Newton Cambs 51 E6
Newton Cardif 36 C2
Newton Ches 81 F1
Newton Ches 69 G6
Newton Ches 81 G2
Newton Cumb 94 C2
Newton Derbys 72 B6
Newton Herefs 45 F2
Newton Herefs 56 D2
Newton Herefs 45 F4
Newton Highld 154 D4
Newton Highld 155 F4
Newton Highld 155 F6
Newton Lancs 88 B3
Newton Lancs 95 G2
Newton Lancs 89 E5
Newton Lincs 73 H4
Newton Mdloth 132 B2
Newton Moray 156 D5
Newton Moray 157 E5
Newton N York 99 E2
Newton Nhants 61 E4
Newton Norfk 76 A2
Newton Notts 72 D4
Newton Nthumb 124 C2
Newton Nthumb 114 B2
Newton S Lans 120 A5
Newton S Lans 120 D3
Newton Shrops 69 F3
Newton Somset 22 D3
Newton Staffs 71 E2
Newton Suffk 52 C5
Newton W Loth 131 G3
Newton W Mids 58 C5
Newton W York 91 F2
Newton Warwks 60 A3
Newton Wilts 25 H1
Newton Abbot Devon 7 F5
Newton Arlosh Cumb 103 F6
Newton Aycliffe Dur 106 B3
Newton Bewley Dur 106 D3
Newton Blossomville Bucks 49 G4
Newton Bromswold Beds 61 F2
Newton Burgoland Leics 72 A1
Newton by Toft Lincs 85 H3
Newton Ferrers Cnwll 5 G2
Newton Ferrers Devon 6 C2
Newton Ferry W Isls 168 c5
Newton Flotman Norfk 65 E5
Newton Green Mons 37 F3
Newton Harcourt Leics 60 B5
Newton Heath Gt Man 82 D5
Newton Hill W York 90 D2
Newton Kyme N York 91 F4
Newton Longville Bucks 49 G3
Newton Mearns E Rens 119 G5
Newton Morrell N York 106 B2
Newton Mountain Pembks 32 D2
Newton Mulgrave N York 107 G2
Newton of Balcanquhal P & K 131 H6
Newton of Balcormo Fife 132 D6
Newton on Ouse N York 91 F6
Newton on the Hill Shrops 69 G2
Newton on Trent Lincs 85 F2
Newton Poppleford Devon 10 A4
Newton Purcell Oxon 48 D2
Newton Regis Warwks 59 F6
Newton Reigny Cumb 104 B3
Newton Solney Derbys 71 H3
Newton St Cyres Devon 9 F4
Newton St Faith Norfk 77 E2
Newton St Loe Somset 24 C6
Newton St Petrock Devon 20 D2
Newton Stacey Hants 26 B4
Newton Stewart D & G 109 F1
Newton Toney Wilts 25 H3

Newton Tracey Devon 21 E3
Newton under Roseberry N York 107 E2
Newton Underwood Nthumb 114 C4
Newton upon Derwent E R Yk 92 A4
Newton Valence Hants 27 E2
Newton Wamphray D & G 111 F4
Newton with Scales Lancs 88 C3
Newton-by-the-Sea Nthumb 125 E4
Newton-le-Willows Mersyd 81 H4
Newton-le-Willows N York 97 E4
Newton-on-Rawcliffe N York 98 D4
Newton-on-the-Moor Nthumb 125 E1
Newtongarry Croft Abers 158 B3
Newtongrange Mdloth 132 B1
Newtonhill Abers 149 G4
Newtonloan Mdloth 121 H6
Newtonmill Angus 141 F6
Newtonmore Highld 146 B4
Newtown Blae G 36 C5
Newtown Ches 70 A5
Newtown Ches 70 D6
Newtown Ches 81 G2
Newtown Cnwll 2 C3
Newtown Cnwll 3 E2
Newtown Cnwll 5 E1
Newtown Cnwll 5 F4
Newtown Cumb 103 E5
Newtown Cumb 112 B1
Newtown Cumb 104 B2
Newtown Cumb 112 A1
Newtown D & G 110 B6
Newtown Derbys 83 E3
Newtown Devon 9 G4
Newtown Devon 21 H3
Newtown Dorset 11 E5
Newtown Dorset 12 D4
Newtown Gloucs 38 B4
Newtown Gt Man 81 H5
Newtown Hants 13 F6
Newtown Hants 26 C6
Newtown Hants 14 D5
Newtown Herefs 45 G5
Newtown Herefs 45 H2
Newtown Herefs 46 B4
Newtown Herefs 46 C3
Newtown Highld 145 F5
Newtown IOW 14 B3
Newtown Lancs 88 D1
Newtown Nthumb 123 G4
Newtown Nthumb 114 B6
Newtown Nthumb 124 D3
Newtown Powys 56 A4
Newtown Rhondd 36 B4
Newtown Shrops 69 F2
Newtown Shrops 69 G3
Newtown Somset 10 C6
Newtown Staffs 58 C6
Newtown Wilts 25 E2
Newtown Wilts 26 A6
Newtown Worcs 46 D5
Newtown Worcs 58 B3
Newtown Linford Leics 72 C1
Newtown of Beltrees Rens 119 F5
Newtown St Boswells Border 122 C3
Newtown Unthank Leics 59 H6
Newtyle Angus 140 C4
Newyears Green Gt Lon 28 B5
Newyork Ag & B 128 A6
Nextend Herefs 45 F5
Neyland Pembks 32 D2
Niarbyl IOM 174 k3
Nibley Gloucs 38 A5
Nibley Gloucs 38 B2
Nibley Green Gloucs 38 B4
Nicholashayne Devon 10 B6
Nicholaston Swans 34 C3
Nickies Hill Cumb 112 C1
Nidd N York 90 D6
Nigg Aber C 149 G5
Nigg Highld 163 E1
Nightcott Somset 22 B2
Nimlet Somset 38 B1
Nine Elms Wilts 39 F3
Nine Wells Pembks 32 B4
Ninebanks Nthumb 104 D5
Nineveh Worcs 57 F2
Ninfield E Susx 17 H3
Ningwood IOW 14 B2
Nisbet Border 122 D2
Nisbet Hill Border 123 E4
Niton IOW 14 C1
Nitshill C Glas 119 G5
No Man's Heath Ches 69 G5
No Man's Heath Warwks 71 H1
No Man's Land Cnwll 4 C3
No Man's Land Cnwll 5 F2
Noah's Ark Kent 29 F2
Noak Bridge Essex 29 H5
Noak Hill Essex 29 F5
Noblethorpe W York 83 H5
Nobold Shrops 69 G1
Nobottle Nhants 60 C2
Nocton Lincs 85 H1
Nogdam End Norfk 65 F5
Noke Oxon 40 D6
Nolton Pembks 32 C3
Nolton Haven Pembks 32 C4
Nomansland Devon 9 E6
Nomansland Wilts 25 H1
Noneley Shrops 69 G3
Nonington Kent 31 F1
Nook Cumb 112 B3
Nook Cumb 95 F3
Norbiton Gt Lon 28 C3
Norbreck Lancs 88 B4
Norbridge Herefs 46 C4
Norbury Ches 69 H5
Norbury Derbys 71 F4
Norbury Gt Lon 28 D3
Norbury Shrops 56 D5
Norbury Staffs 70 C2
Norbury Common Ches 69 H5
Norbury Junction Staffs 70 C2
Norchard Worcs 58 B2
Norcott Brook Ches 82 A3
Norcross Lancs 88 B4
Nordelph Norfk 63 E5
Norden Gt Man 89 G1
Nordley Shrops 57 G5
Norham Nthumb 123 F4
Norland Town W York 90 B2
Norley Ches 81 H2
Norleywood Hants 14 B3
Norlington E Susx 17 E3
Norman Cross Cambs 61 G4
Norman's Bay E Susx 17 H2
Norman's Green Devon 9 G5
Normanby Lincs 92 C1
Normanby Lincs 85 G3
Normanby N York 107 E3
Normanby N York 98 C3
Normanby le Wold Lincs 86 B4
Normandy Surrey 27 G4
Normanton Derbys 72 A3
Normanton Leics 73 F4
Normanton Lincs 73 G5
Normanton Notts 73 E5
Normanton Rutlnd 61 E6
Normanton W York 91 E2
Normanton Wilts 25 G3
Normanton le Heath Leics 72 A1
Normanton on Soar Notts 72 C2
Normanton on the Wolds Notts 72 D3
Normanton on Trent Notts 85 E1
Normoss Lancs 88 B3
Norney Surrey 27 G4
Norrington Common Wilts 24 D6
Norris Green Cnwll 5 H3
Norristhorpe W York 90 C2
North Anston S York 84 C3
North Aston Oxon 48 C2
North Baddesley Hants 14 B6
North Ballachulish Highld 137 E6
North Barrow Somset 24 B2
North Barsham Norfk 76 B3
North Benfleet Essex 30 A5
North Bersted W Susx 15 G4
North Berwick E Loth 132 D4
North Bitchburn Dur 106 A4
North Blyth Nthumb 115 E4
North Boarhunt Hants 14 D5
North Bockhampton Hants 13 F4
North Bovey Devon 8 D3
North Bradley Wilts 24 D5
North Brentor Devon 8 B3
North Brewham Somset 24 C3
North Bridge Surrey 27 H3
North Brook End Cambs 50 D5
North Buckland Devon 21 E5
North Burlingham Norfk 77 G1
North Cadbury Somset 24 B2
North Carlton Lincs 85 G2
North Carlton Notts 84 D3
North Cave E R Yk 92 C3
North Cerney Gloucs 39 E5
North Chailey E Susx 17 E3
North Charford Hants 25 G1
North Charlton Nthumb 125 E3
North Cheam Gt Lon 28 C3
North Cheriton Somset 24 B2
North Chideock Dorset 11 E4
North Cliffe E R Yk 92 C3
North Clifton Notts 85 F2
North Close Dur 106 B4
North Cockerington Lincs 86 D4
North Connel Ag & B 136 D3
North Cornelly Brdgnd 35 F2
North Corner Cnwll 3 E2
North Corry Highld 136 C5
North Cotes Lincs 86 D5
North Country Cnwll 2 D4
North Cove Suffk 65 G4
North Cowton N York 97 F5
North Crawley Bucks 49 G4
North Cray Gt Lon 29 F3
North Creake Norfk 76 B4
North Curry Somset 23 F2
North Dalton E R Yk 92 C5
North Deighton N York 91 E5
North Duffield N York 91 H3
North Duntulm Highld 150 D6
North Elham Kent 19 E6
North Elkington Lincs 86 C4
North Elmham Norfk 76 C2
North Elmsall W York 84 B6
North End Cumb 103 G6
North End Dorset 24 D2
North End E R Yk 93 F4
North End E R Yk 93 G3
North End Essex 51 G3
North End Hants 25 F1
North End Hants 26 D2
North End Hants 15 E4
North End Leics 72 C1
North End Lincs 93 E2
North End Lincs 86 C5
North End Lincs 85 H5
North End Lincs 74 C4
North End Lincs 87 E4
North End Mersyd 81 E5
North End Nhants 61 F2
North End Norfk 64 C5
North End Nthumb 114 C6
North End Somset 23 G6
North End W Susx 15 H4
North End W Susx 16 B2
North Erradale Highld 160 B2
North Evington Leics 60 B6
North Fambridge Essex 30 B6
North Ferriby E R Yk 92 D2
North Frodingham E R Yk 93 E5
North Gorley Hants 13 E6
North Green Norfk 65 E4
North Green Suffk 65 F2
North Green Suffk 65 F2
North Grimston N York 98 D2
North Halling Kent 29 H3
North Hayling Hants 15 E4
North Hazelrigg Nthumb 123 H3
North Heasley Devon 21 G4
North Heath W Susx 16 B3
North Hele Somset 22 C1
North Hill Cnwll 5 F4
North Hillingdon Gt Lon 28 B4
North Hinksey Oxon 40 C5
North Holmwood Surrey 16 C6
North Huish Devon 6 D3
North Hykeham Lincs 85 G1
North Kelsey Lincs 85 H5
North Kessock Highld 155 E4
North Killingholme Lincs 93 E1
North Kilvington N York 97 G3
North Kilworth Leics 60 B4
North Kingston Hants 13 E5
North Kyme Lincs 74 B5
North Landing E R Yk 99 H2
North Lee Bucks 41 F5
North Lees N York 97 F2
North Leigh Kent 19 E6
North Leigh Oxon 40 B6
North Leverton with Habblesthorpe Notts 85 E3
North Littleton Worcs 47 F4
North Lopham Norfk 64 C4
North Luffenham Rutlnd 61 E6
North Marden W Susx 15 F5
North Marston Bucks 49 F1
North Middleton Mdloth 121 H5
North Middleton Nthumb 124 C3
North Milmain D & G 100 B5
North Molton Devon 21 G4
North Moreton Oxon 40 D3
North Mundham W Susx 15 G4
North Muskham Notts 73 F6
North Newbald E R Yk 92 C3
North Newington Oxon 48 B3
North Newnton Wilts 25 G5
North Newton Somset 23 F2
North Nibley Gloucs 38 B4
North Oakley Hants 26 D5
North Ockendon Gt Lon 29 G5
North Ormesby N York 106 D3
North Ormsby Lincs 86 C4
North Otterington N York 97 G4
North Owersby Lincs 86 A4
North Perrott Somset 11 E5
North Petherton Somset 23 F2
North Petherwin Cnwll 5 F5
North Pickenham Norfk 63 H6
North Piddle Worcs 47 E5
North Pool Devon 7 E2
North Poorton Dorset 11 F4
North Poulner Hants 13 F5
North Quarme Somset 22 B3
North Queensferry C Edin 131 G3
North Radworthy Devon 21 H4
North Rauceby Lincs 73 H5
North Reston Lincs 86 D3
North Rigton N York 90 D4
North Ripley Hants 13 F5
North Rode Ches 82 D1
North Ronaldsay Airport Ork 169 d4
North Row Cumb 103 F3
North Runcton Norfk 75 G2
North Scale Cumb 94 C2
North Scarle Lincs 85 F1
North Seaton Nthumb 115 E4
North Seaton Colliery Nthumb 114 D4
North Shian Ag & B 136 D4
North Shields T & W 115 E2
North Shoebury Essex 30 C5
North Shore Lancs 88 B3
North Side Cambs 62 B5
North Side Cumb 102 D3
North Skelton N York 107 F3
North Somercotes Lincs 87 E4
North Stainley N York 97 F2
North Stainmore Cumb 105 E2
North Stifford Essex 29 G4
North Stoke Oxon 40 D3
North Stoke Somset 38 B1
North Stoke W Susx 16 A2
North Street Berks 41 E1
North Street Cambs 63 E2
North Street Hants 25 G1
North Street Hants 27 E3
North Street Kent 30 B3
North Street Kent 30 D2
North Sunderland Nthumb 125 E4
North Tamerton Cnwll 5 G6
North Tawton Devon 8 D5
North Third Stirlg 130 D4
North Thoresby Lincs 86 C4
North Tidworth Wilts 25 H4
North Town Berks 41 G2
North Town Devon 21 E1
North Town Somset 24 A3
North Tuddenham Norfk 76 C1
North Walbottle T & W 114 C2
North Walsham Norfk 77 F3
North Waltham Hants 26 D4
North Warnborough Hants 27 E4
North Weald Bassett Essex 51 F1
North Wheatley Notts 85 E3
North Whilborough Devon 7 F4
North Wick Somset 24 A6
North Widcombe Somset 24 A5
North Willingham Lincs 86 B3
North Wingfield Derbys 84 B1
North Witham Lincs 73 G2
North Wootton Dorset 11 G6
North Wootton Norfk 75 G2
North Wootton Somset 24 A3
North Wraxall Wilts 38 C2
North Wroughton Wilts 39 F2
Northacre Norfk 64 B5
Northall Bucks 49 H1
Northall Green Norfk 76 C1
Northallerton N York 97 G4
Northam Devon 21 E3
Northam Hants 14 C5
Northampton Nhants 49 F5
Northampton Worcs 58 A2
Northaw Herts 50 D1
Northay Somset 10 C6
Northborough Cambs 61 G6
Northbourne Kent 31 G1
Northbridge Street E Susx 18 A4
Northbrook Hants 26 C3
Northbrook Oxon 48 C1
Northchapel W Susx 27 H2
Northchurch Herts 41 H5
Northcott Devon 10 A6
Northcott Devon 10 B5
Northcott Devon 5 G5
Northcourt Oxon 40 C4
Northdown Kent 31 G3
Northedge Derbys 84 A1
Northend Bucks 41 E3
Northend Warwks 48 B4
Northend Woods Bucks 41 G3
Northenden Gt Man 82 C4
Northfield Aber C 149 G5
Northfield E R Yk 92 D2
Northfield W Mids 58 C3
Northfields Lincs 61 F6
Northfleet Kent 29 G3
Northiam E Susx 18 B4
Northill Beds 50 B5
Northington Gloucs 38 B5
Northington Hants 26 D3
Northlands Lincs 74 D5
Northleach Gloucs 39 F6
Northleigh Devon 21 F4
Northleigh Devon 10 B4
Northlew Devon 8 B4
Northload Bridge Somset 23 H3
Northmoor Oxon 40 B4
Northmoor Somset 22 B2
Northmuir Angus 140 D5
Northney Hants 15 E4
Northolt Gt Lon 28 B4
Northop Flints 81 E1
Northop Hall Flints 81 E1
Northorpe Lincs 85 F4
Northorpe Lincs 74 A2
Northorpe Lincs 74 B4
Northorpe W York 90 C2
Northover Somset 23 H3
Northover Somset 23 H2
Northowram W York 90 B2
Northport Dorset 12 C3
Northrepps Norfk 77 E4
Northton W Isls 168 c6
Northway Somset 22 D2
Northway Swans 34 C3
Northwich Ches 82 B2
Northwick Gloucs 37 G3
Northwick Somset 23 F4
Northwick Worcs 46 D5
Northwold Norfk 63 G5
Northwood Derbys 83 G1
Northwood Gt Lon 28 B5
Northwood IOW 14 C3
Northwood Shrops 69 G3
Northwood Staffs 70 D5
Northwood Green Gloucs 38 B6
Norton Ches 81 H3
Norton Cnwll 4 D3
Norton Dur 106 D3
Norton E Susx 17 F1
Norton Gloucs 46 D2
Norton Herts 50 C4
Norton IOW 13 G3
Norton Mons 45 G1
Norton N York 98 D2
Norton Nhants 60 B2
Norton Notts 84 C2
Norton Powys 56 C2
Norton S York 91 G1
Norton S York 84 A3
Norton Shrops 69 H1
Norton Shrops 57 G5
Norton Shrops 57 E3
Norton Shrops 57 G4
Norton Somset 23 F6
Norton Suffk 64 B2
Norton Swans 34 D3
Norton W Susx 15 G4
Norton Wilts 38 D3
Norton Worcs 46 D4
Norton Worcs 47 F4
Norton Bavant Wilts 25 E4
Norton Bridge Staffs 70 D3
Norton Canes Staffs 58 C6
Norton Canon Herefs 45 G4
Norton Corner Norfk 76 D3
Norton Disney Lincs 73 F6
Norton Ferris Wilts 24 C3
Norton Fitzwarren Somset 23 E2
Norton Green IOW 13 G3
Norton Green Staffs 58 C6
Norton Hawkfield Somset 24 B6
Norton Heath Essex 51 G1
Norton in Hales Shrops 70 B4
Norton in the Moors Staffs 70 D5
Norton Lindsey Warwks 59 E2
Norton Little Green Suffk 64 B2
Norton Malreward Somset 24 B6
Norton Mandeville Essex 51 G1
Norton St Philip Somset 24 C5
Norton sub Hamdon Somset 11 E6
Norton Subcourse Norfk 65 G5
Norton Wood Herefs 45 F4
Norton-Juxta-Twycross Leics 59 F6
Norton-le-Clay N York 97 G2
Norwell Notts 73 E6
Norwell Woodhouse Notts 85 E1
Norwich Norfk 77 E1
Norwich Airport Norfk 77 E1
Norwich Cathedral Norfk 77 E1
Norwick Shet 169 k6
Norwood Clacks 131 E4
Norwood Kent 18 D4
Norwood S York 84 B3
Norwood End Essex 51 F2
Norwood Green Gt Lon 28 B4
Norwood Green W York 90 C2
Norwood Hill Surrey 16 C6
Norwoodside Cambs 62 C5
Noseley Leics 60 C5
Noss Mayo Devon 6 C2
Nosterfield N York 97 F3
Nosterfield End Cambs 51 G5
Nostie Highld 152 C2
Notgrove Gloucs 47 F1
Nottage Brdgnd 35 F2
Notter Cnwll 5 G2
Nottingham Notts 72 C4
Nottington Dorset 11 G3
Notton W York 84 A6
Notton Wilts 38 D1
Nottswood Hill Gloucs 46 C1
Nounsley Essex 52 B2
Noutard's Green Worcs 58 A2
Nowton Suffk 63 H1
Nox Shrops 69 F1
Nuffield Oxon 41 E3
Nun Monkton N York 91 F5
Nunburnholme E R Yk 92 B4
Nuncargate Notts 72 C5
Nunclose Cumb 104 B5
Nuneaton Warwks 59 F5
Nuneham Courtenay Oxon 40 D4
Nunhead Gt Lon 28 D4
Nunkeeling E R Yk 93 E5
Nunney Somset 24 C4
Nunney Catch Somset 24 C4
Nunnington Herefs 46 A3
Nunnington N York 98 B3
Nunnykirk Nthumb 114 B5
Nunsthorpe Lincs 86 C5
Nunthorpe N York 91 G5
Nunthorpe N York 107 E2
Nunthorpe Village N York 107 E2
Nunton Wilts 25 G2
Nunwick N York 97 F2
Nunwick Nthumb 113 F2
Nup End Bucks 49 G1
Nupdown Gloucs 37 G4
Nupend Gloucs 38 C5
Nuptow Berks 41 G2
Nursling Hants 14 B5
Nursted Hants 15 F6
Nursteed Wilts 25 F5
Nurton Staffs 58 A5
Nutbourne W Susx 15 F4
Nutbourne W Susx 16 B3
Nutfield Surrey 28 D1
Nuthall Notts 72 C4
Nuthampstead Herts 51 E4
Nuthurst W Susx 16 C4
Nutley E Susx 17 E4
Nutley Hants 26 D4
Nuttal Lane Gt Man 89 F1
Nutwell S York 84 D5
Nybster Highld 167 G5
Nyetimber W Susx 15 G3
Nyewood W Susx 27 F1
Nymet Rowland Devon 8 D5
Nymet Tracey Devon 8 D5
Nympsfield Gloucs 38 C4
Nynehead Somset 22 D1
Nythe Somset 23 G3
Nyton W Susx 15 G4

O

Oad Street Kent 30 B2
Oadby Leics 60 B5
Oak Cross Devon 8 B4
Oak Tree Dur 106 C2
Oakall Green Worcs 46 D5
Oakamoor Staffs 71 E4
Oakbank W Loth 131 G2
Oakdale Caerph 36 C4
Oake Somset 22 D2
Oaken Staffs 58 B6
Oakenclough Lancs 88 D4
Oakengates Shrops 70 B1
Oakenholt Flints 81 E2
Oakenshaw Dur 106 A5
Oakenshaw W York 90 C2
Oaker Side Derbys 71 H6
Oakerthorpe Derbys 72 B5
Oakford Cerdgn 43 E5
Oakford Devon 22 B1
Oakfordbridge Devon 22 B1
Oakgrove Ches 82 D2
Oakham Rutlnd 61 E6
Oakhanger Ches 70 C5
Oakhanger Hants 27 F3
Oakhill Somset 24 B4
Oakhurst Kent 29 F1
Oakington Cambs 62 C2
Oaklands Powys 44 C4
Oakle Street Gloucs 38 B6
Oakley Beds 50 A6
Oakley Bucks 41 E5
Oakley Dorset 12 D4
Oakley Fife 131 F4
Oakley Hants 26 D4
Oakley Oxon 41 F4
Oakley Suffk 64 D3
Oakley Green Berks 41 G2
Oakley Park Powys 55 G4
Oakridge Gloucs 38 D5
Oaks Dur 106 A3
Oaks Lancs 89 E3
Oaks Shrops 56 D6
Oaks Green Derbys 71 F3
Oaksey Wilts 39 E4
Oakshaw Cumb 112 B2
Oakshott Hants 27 F2
Oakthorpe Leics 71 H1
Oakwood Derbys 72 B4
Oakwood Nthumb 113 F1
Oakwoodhill Surrey 16 B5
Oakworth W York 90 B3
Oare Kent 30 D2
Oare Somset 21 H5
Oare Wilts 25 G6
Oasby Lincs 73 H4
Oath Somset 23 G2
Oathlaw Angus 141 E5
Oatlands Park Surrey 28 B2
Oban Ag & B 136 C3
Obley Shrops 56 D3
Obney P & K 139 G3
Oborne Dorset 24 B1
Obthorpe Lincs 74 A1
Occold Suffk 64 D2
Occumster Highld 167 F2
Ochiltree E Ayrs 119 G1
Ockbrook Derbys 72 B4

Ocker Hill W Mids 58 C5
Ockeridge Worcs 46 C5
Ockham Surrey 28 B2
Ockle Highld 143 E1
Ockley Surrey 16 B5
Ocle Pychard Herefs 46 B4
Octon E R Yk 99 F2
Odcombe Somset 11 E6
Odd Down Somset 24 C5
Oddingley Worcs 47 E5
Oddington Gloucs 47 H2
Oddington Oxon 40 D6
Odell Beds 49 H5
Odham Devon 8 B5
Odiham Hants 27 F4
Odsal W York 90 C2
Odsey Herts 50 D5
Odstock Wilts 25 G2
Odstone Leics 59 G6
Offchurch Warwks 59 F2
Offenham Worcs 47 F4
Offerton T & W 115 E1
Offham E Susx 17 E3
Offham Kent 29 G2
Offham W Susx 16 A2
Offleymarsh Shrops 70 C3
Offord Cluny Cambs 62 B2
Offord Darcy Cambs 62 B2
Offton Suffk 52 D6
Offwell Devon 10 B4
Ogbourne Maizey Wilts 39 F1
Ogbourne St Andrew Wilts 39 F1
Ogbourne St George Wilts 39 G2
Ogden W York 90 B3
Ogle Nthumb 114 C3
Oglet Mersyd 81 G3
Ogmore V Glam 35 F2
Ogmore Vale Brdgnd 35 G3
Ogmore-by-Sea V Glam 35 F2
Ogwen Bank Gwynd 79 F1
Okeford Fitzpaine Dorset 12 B6
Okehampton Devon 8 C4
Olchard Devon 9 F2
Old Nhants 60 D3
Old Aberdeen Aber C 149 G5
Old Alresford Hants 26 D3
Old Auchenbrack D & G 110 A3
Old Basford Notts 72 C4
Old Basing Hants 27 E4
Old Bewick Nthumb 124 D3
Old Bolingbroke Lincs 86 D1
Old Bracknell Berks 41 E1
Old Bramhope W York 90 C4
Old Brampton Derbys 84 A2
Old Bridge of Urr D & G 110 B1
Old Buckenham Norfk 64 C4
Old Burghclere Hants 26 C5
Old Byland N York 98 A3
Old Cantley S York 84 D5
Old Cassop Dur 106 C5
Old Castle Brdgnd 35 F2
Old Churchstoke Powys 56 C5
Old Clee Lincs 86 C5
Old Cleeve Somset 22 C3
Old Clipstone Notts 84 D1
Old Colwyn Conwy 80 A2
Old Dailly S Ayrs 108 D5
Old Dalby Leics 72 D2
Old Dam Derbys 83 F3
Old Deer Abers 159 F4
Old Ditch Somset 23 H4
Old Edlington S York 84 C4
Old Eldon Dur 106 B4
Old Ellerby E R Yk 93 E3
Old Felixstowe Suffk 53 G4
Old Fletton Cambs 62 A5
Old Forge Herefs 46 A1
Old Furnace Herefs 45 H1
Old Glossop Derbys 83 E4
Old Goole E R Yk 92 A2
Old Grimsby IOS 2 a2
Old Hall Green Herts 51 E3
Old Hall Street Norfk 77 F3
Old Harlow Essex 51 F2
Old Heath Essex 52 D3
Old Hunstanton Norfk 75 G4
Old Hurst Cambs 62 B3
Old Hutton Cumb 95 F4
Old Kea Cnwll 3 F4
Old Kilpatrick W Duns 129 F2
Old Knebworth Herts 50 C3
Old Lakenham Norfk 65 E6
Old Langho Lancs 89 E3
Old Laxey IOM 174 m3
Old Leake Lincs 74 D5
Old Malton N York 98 D3
Old Micklefield W York 91 E3
Old Milverton Warwks 59 F2
Old Newton Suffk 64 C2
Old Quarrington Dur 106 C5
Old Radford Notts 72 C4
Old Radnor Powys 45 E5
Old Rayne Abers 158 C2
Old Romney Kent 18 D4
Old Shoreham W Susx 16 C2
Old Soar Kent 29 G1
Old Sodbury Gloucs 38 B2
Old Somerby Lincs 73 G3
Old Stratford Nhants 49 F3
Old Swinford W Mids 58 B4
Old Tebay Cumb 95 G5
Old Thirsk N York 97 G3
Old Town Cumb 104 B4
Old Town Cumb 95 G3
Old Town E Susx 17 G1
Old Town IOS 2 b1
Old Town Nthumb 113 F4
Old Town W York 90 A2
Old Trafford Gt Man 82 C4
Old Tupton Derbys 84 B1
Old Warden Beds 50 B5
Old Weston Cambs 61 G3
Old Wick Highld 167 G3
Old Windsor Berks 41 H2
Old Wives Lees Kent 30 D1
Old Woking Surrey 28 A2
Old Wolverton Bucks 49 F3
Old Woods Shrops 69 G2

Oldany Highld 164 B2
Oldberrow Warwks 58 D2
Oldbury Kent 29 G2
Oldbury Shrops 57 G5
Oldbury W Mids 58 C4
Oldbury Warwks 59 F5
Oldbury Naite Gloucs 37 G4
Oldbury on the Hill Gloucs 38 C3
Oldbury-on-Severn Gloucs 37 G3
Oldcastle Mons 45 F2
Oldcastle Heath Ches 69 G5
Oldcotes Notts 84 D3
Oldfield W York 90 A3
Oldfield Worcs 58 A2
Oldford Somset 24 C4
Oldhall Green Suffk 64 B1
Oldham Gt Man 82 D5
Oldhamstocks E Loth 133 F2
Oldland Gloucs 38 B1
Oldmill Cnwll 5 G3
Oldmixon Somset 23 F5
Oldridge Devon 9 E4
Oldshoremore Highld 164 C4
Oldstead N York 98 A3
Oldwall Cumb 112 B1
Oldwalls Swans 34 B3
Oldways End Somset 22 B2
Olive Green Staffs 71 F2
Oliver Border 121 E2
Oliver's Battery Hants 26 C2
Ollaberry Shet 169 h4
Ollach Highld 151 E2
Ollerton Ches 82 C2
Ollerton Notts 84 D1
Ollerton Shrops 70 B2
Olmarch Cerdgn 43 F5
Olmstead Green Cambs 51 G5
Olney Bucks 49 G4
Olrig House Highld 167 F5
Olton W Mids 58 D4
Olveston Gloucs 37 G3
Ombersley Worcs 58 A2
Ompton Notts 84 D1
Once Brewed Nthumb 113 E1
Onchan IOM 174 m3
Onecote Staffs 71 E6
Onehouse Suffk 64 C1
Onen Mons 37 E6
Ongar Street Herefs 56 D2
Onibury Shrops 57 E3
Onich Highld 137 E6
Onllwyn Neath 35 F5
Onneley Staffs 70 C4
Onslow Village Surrey 27 H4
Onston Ches 81 H2
Openwoodgate Derbys 72 A5
Opinan Highld 160 B1
Orbliston Moray 157 E5
Orbost Highld 150 C3
Orby Lincs 87 E1
Orchard Portman Somset 23 E1
Orcheston Wilts 25 F4
Orcop Herefs 45 G2
Orcop Hill Herefs 45 G2
Ord Abers 158 B5
Ordhead Abers 148 D5
Ordie Abers 148 B5
Ordiequish Moray 157 E5
Ordley Nthumb 105 F6
Ordsall Notts 85 E3
Ore E Susx 18 B2
Oreleton Common Herefs 57 E2
Oreton Shrops 57 G3
Orford Ches 82 A4
Orford Suffk 53 H6
Organford Dorset 12 C4
Orgreave Staffs 71 F2
Orlingbury Nhants 61 E3
Ormathwaite Cumb 103 G3
Ormesby N York 107 E2
Ormesby St Margaret Norfk 77 H1
Ormesby St Michael Norfk 77 H1
Ormiscaig Highld 160 D1
Ormiston E Loth 132 C2
Ormsaigmore Highld 135 G6
Ormsary Ag & B 127 F2
Ormskirk Lancs 81 F5
Ornsby Hill Dur 106 A6
Orphir Ork 169 b2
Orpington Gt Lon 29 E3
Orrell Gt Man 81 G4
Orrell Mersyd 81 F4
Orrell Post Gt Man 81 G5
Orrisdale IOM 174 I4
Orroland D & G 102 B5
Orsett Essex 29 G4
Orslow Staffs 70 C2
Orston Notts 73 E4
Orthwaite Cumb 103 F3
Orton Cumb 95 G6
Orton Nhants 60 D3
Orton Staffs 58 B5
Orton Longueville Cambs 61 H5
Orton Rigg Cumb 103 G5
Orton Waterville Cambs 61 G5
Orton-on-the-Hill Leics 59 F6
Orwell Cambs 50 D6
Osbaldeston Lancs 89 E3
Osbaldeston Green Lancs 89 E3
Osbaldwick N York 91 G5
Osbaston Leics 59 G6
Osbaston Shrops 69 E2
Osborne IOW 14 C3
Osborne House IOW 14 C3
Osbournby Lincs 74 A4
Oscroft Ches 81 G1
Ose Highld 150 C3
Osgathorpe Leics 72 B2
Osgodby Lincs 86 A4
Osgodby N York 91 G3
Osgodby N York 99 F3
Oskaig Highld 151 E2

Oskamull Ag & B 135 F3
Osmaston Derbys 71 G4
Osmington Dorset 11 G3
Osmington Mills Dorset 11 H3
Osmondthorpe W York 90 D3
Osmotherley N York 97 H5
Osney Oxon 40 C5
Ospringe Kent 30 D2
Ossett W York 90 D2
Ossington Notts 85 E1
Osterley Gt Lon 28 C4
Oswaldkirk N York 98 B3
Oswaldtwistle Lancs 89 F2
Oswestry Shrops 69 E3
Otford Kent 29 F2
Otham Kent 30 B1
Otham Hole Kent 30 B1
Othery Somset 23 G2
Otley Suffk 65 E1
Otley W York 90 C4
Otley Green Suffk 65 E1
Otter Ferry Ag & B 127 H3
Otterbourne Hants 26 C1
Otterburn N York 89 G5
Otterburn Nthumb 113 F4
Otterham Cnwll 5 E5
Otterham Quay Kent 30 B3
Otterhampton Somset 23 E4
Otternish W Isls 168 c5
Ottershaw Surrey 28 A2
Otterswick Shet 169 j4
Otterton Devon 10 A3
Otterwood Hants 14 B4
Ottery Devon 8 A2
Ottery St Mary Devon 10 A4
Ottinge Kent 19 E6
Ottringham E R Yk 93 F2
Oughterby Cumb 103 G6
Oughtershaw N York 96 B3
Oughterside Cumb 103 E4
Oughtibridge S York 83 H4
Oughtrington Ches 82 B3
Oulston N York 98 A2
Oulton Cumb 103 F5
Oulton Norfk 76 D3
Oulton Staffs 70 C2
Oulton Staffs 70 D4
Oulton Suffk 65 H5
Oulton W York 91 E2
Oulton Broad Suffk 65 H5
Oulton Street Norfk 76 D3
Oundle Nhants 61 F4
Ounsdale Staffs 58 B5
Ousby Cumb 104 C4
Ousden Suffk 63 G1
Ousefleet E R Yk 92 B2
Ouston Dur 114 D1
Out Elmstead Kent 31 F1
Out Newton E R Yk 93 G2
Out Rawcliffe Lancs 88 C3
Outchester Nthumb 124 D4
Outgate Cumb 94 D5
Outhgill Cumb 96 A5
Outhill Warwks 58 D2
Outlands Staffs 70 C2
Outlane W York 90 B1
Outwell Norfk 62 D6
Outwick Hants 25 G1
Outwood Surrey 16 D6
Outwood W York 90 D2
Outwood Gate Gt Man 82 C5
Outwoods Leics 72 B2
Outwoods Staffs 70 C2
Outwoods Warwks 59 E4
Ouzlewell Green W York 90 D2
Ovenden W York 90 B2
Over Cambs 62 C2
Over Ches 82 A1
Over Gloucs 46 D1
Over Gloucs 37 G2
Over Burrows Derbys 71 G4
Over Compton Dorset 24 A1
Over End Cambs 61 G5
Over Green Warwks 59 E5
Over Haddon Derbys 83 G1
Over Kellet Lancs 95 F2
Over Kiddington Oxon 48 B1
Over Monnow Mons 37 F5
Over Norton Oxon 48 A2
Over Peover Ches 82 C2
Over Silton N York 97 H4
Over Stowey Somset 23 E3
Over Stratton Somset 11 E6
Over Tabley Ches 82 B3
Over Wallop Hants 26 A3
Over Whitacre Warwks 59 E4
Over Woodhouse Derbys 84 B2
Over Worton Oxon 48 C2
Overbury Worcs 47 E3
Overcombe Dorset 11 G3
Evergreen Derbys 83 H2
Overleigh Somset 23 H3
Overley Staffs 71 F2
Overpool Ches 81 F2
Overscaig Hotel Highld 162 A6
Overseal Derbys 71 H1
Oversland Kent 30 D2
Oversley Green Warwks 47 F5
Overstone Nhants 60 D2
Overstrand Norfk 77 E4
Overstreet Wilts 25 F3
Overton Aber C 149 F6
Overton Ches 81 G2
Overton Hants 26 C4
Overton Lancs 88 C5
Overton N York 91 G5
Overton Shrops 57 E3
Overton Swans 34 B3
Overton Wrexhm 69 F4
Overton Bridge Wrexhm 69 F4
Overton Green Ches 70 C6
Overtown Lancs 95 G2
Overtown N Lans 120 C5
Overtown W York 91 E1
Overtown Wilts 39 F2

Overy Oxon 40 D4
Oving Bucks 49 F1
Oving W Susx 15 G4
Ovingdean E Susx 16 D2
Ovingham Nthumb 114 C2
Ovington Dur 105 H2
Ovington Essex 52 A5
Ovington Hants 26 D2
Ovington Norfk 64 B6
Ovington Nthumb 114 B2
Ower Hants 26 B1
Ower Hants 14 C4
Owermoigne Dorset 12 B3
Owl's Green Suffk 65 E2
Owlbury Shrops 56 C4
Owlerton S York 84 A4
Owlpen Gloucs 38 C4
Owlsmoor Berks 42 C5
Owlswick Bucks 41 F5
Owmby Lincs 86 A5
Owmby Lincs 85 H3
Owslebury Hants 26 C2
Owston Leics 60 D6
Owston S York 84 C6
Owston Ferry Lincs 85 F5
Owstwick E R Yk 93 F3
Owthorne E R Yk 93 G2
Owthorpe Notts 72 D3
Oxborough Norfk 63 G5
Oxbridge Dorset 11 E4
Oxcombe Lincs 86 C2
Oxcroft Derbys 84 B2
Oxen End Essex 51 G4
Oxen Park Cumb 94 D4
Oxenholme Cumb 95 F4
Oxenhope W York 90 B3
Oxenpill Somset 23 G3
Oxenton Gloucs 47 E2
Oxenwood Wilts 26 A5
Oxford Oxon 40 C5
Oxhey Herts 28 B6
Oxhill Dur 106 A6
Oxhill Warwks 48 A4
Oxley W Mids 58 B6
Oxley Green Essex 52 C2
Oxley's Green E Susx 17 H3
Oxlode Cambs 62 D4
Oxnam Border 122 D1
Oxnead Norfk 77 E2
Oxshott Surrey 28 B2
Oxshott Heath Surrey 28 B2
Oxspring S York 83 G5
Oxted Surrey 29 E1
Oxton Border 122 B5
Oxton N York 91 F4
Oxton Notts 72 D5
Oxwich Swans 34 C3
Oxwich Green Swans 34 B3
Oxwick Norfk 76 B2
Oykel Bridge Hotel Highld 161 H4
Oyne Abers 158 C2
Oystermouth Swans 34 D3
Ozleworth Gloucs 38 C4

P

Pabail W Isls 168 f8
Packers Hill Dorset 11 G6
Packington Leics 72 A1
Packmoor Staffs 70 D5
Packmores Warwks 59 F2
Padanaram Angus 140 D5
Padbury Bucks 49 E2
Paddington Gt Lon 28 D4
Paddlesworth Kent 29 H2
Paddlesworth Kent 19 E5
Paddock Wood Kent 17 G6
Paddolgreen Shrops 69 G3
Padeswood Flints 81 E1
Padfield Derbys 83 E4
Padgate Ches 82 A4
Padhams Green Essex 29 G6
Padiham Lancs 89 F3
Padside N York 90 C5
Padstow Cnwll 4 C3
Padworth Berks 26 D6
Page Bank Dur 106 B4
Pagham W Susx 15 G3
Paglesham Essex 30 C5
Paignton Devon 7 F4
Pailton Warwks 59 G3
Paine's Cross E Susx 17 G4
Painleyhill Staffs 71 E3
Painscastle Powys 44 D4
Painshawfield Nthumb 114 B1
Painsthorpe E R Yk 92 B5
Painswick Gloucs 38 C5
Painter's Forstal Kent 30 D2
Paisley Rens 129 F1
Pakefield Suffk 65 H4
Pakenham Suffk 64 B2
Pale Gwynd 68 B4
Pale Green Essex 51 G5
Palestine Hants 25 H3
Paley Street Berks 41 G2
Palfrey W Mids 58 C5
Palgrave Suffk 64 D3
Pallington Dorset 12 B4
Palmers Green Gt Lon 28 D5
Palmersbridge Cnwll 5 E4
Palmerston E Ayrs 119 G1
Palmerstown V Glam 36 B1
Palnackie D & G 102 B6
Palnure D & G 109 F1
Palterton Derbys 84 B1
Pamber End Hants 26 D5
Pamber Green Hants 26 D5
Pamber Heath Hants 26 D5
Pamington Gloucs 47 E2
Pamphill Dorset 12 D5
Pampisford Cambs 51 F5
Panborough Somset 23 G4

Panbride Angus 141 F3
Pancrasweek Devon 20 C1
Pancross V Glam 36 B1
Pandy Caerph 36 C3
Pandy Gwynd 54 D6
Pandy Gwynd 68 A3
Pandy Mons 45 F1
Pandy Powys 55 F6
Pandy Wrexhm 68 D4
Pandy Tudur Conwy 79 H1
Pandy'r Capel Denbgs 68 C5
Panfield Essex 52 A3
Pangbourne Berks 41 E2
Pangdean W Susx 16 D3
Panks Bridge Herefs 46 B4
Pannal N York 90 D5
Pannal Ash N York 90 D5
Pannanich Wells Hotel Abers 148 B4
Pant Shrops 69 E2
Pant Glas Gwynd 66 D5
Pant Mawr Powys 55 F4
Pant-ffrwyth Brdgnd 35 G3
Pant-Gwyn Carmth 43 F2
Pant-lasau Swans 34 D4
Pant-pastynog Denbgs 68 C6
Pant-y-dwr Powys 55 G3
Pant-y-ffridd Powys 56 B6
Pant-y-gog Brdgnd 35 F3
Pant-y-mwyn Flints 80 D1
Pantasaph Flints 80 D2
Panteg Pembks 32 C5
Pantersbridge Cnwll 5 E3
Pantglas Powys 55 E5
Panton Lincs 86 B3
Pantperthog Gwynd 55 E6
Pantyffynnon Carmth 34 D5
Pantygaseg Torfn 36 D4
Pantymenyn Carmth 33 F4
Panxworth Norfk 77 F1
Papa Westray Airport Ork 169 c4
Papcastle Cumb 103 E3
Papigoe Highld 167 G4
Papple E Loth 133 E2
Papplewick Notts 72 C5
Papworth Everard Cambs 62 B2
Papworth St Agnes Cambs 62 B2
Par Cnwll 4 D1
Paramour Street Kent 31 F2
Parbold Lancs 81 G6
Parbrook Somset 24 A3
Parbrook W Susx 16 B4
Parc Gwynd 68 A3
Parc Seymour Newpt 37 E3
Parcllyn Cerdgn 42 C4
Pardshaw Cumb 103 E3
Parham Suffk 65 E1
Park Abers 149 G5
Park D & G 110 D4
Park Nthumb 112 D1
Park Bottom Cnwll 2 D4
Park Bridge Gt Man 82 D5
Park Corner Berks 41 G2
Park Corner E Susx 17 F5
Park Corner Oxon 41 E3
Park End Beds 49 H4
Park End Nthumb 113 F2
Park End Staffs 70 C5
Park Gate Hants 14 C4
Park Gate W York 90 C4
Park Gate Worcs 58 B2
Park Green Essex 51 E4
Park Green Suffk 64 D2
Park Head Cumb 104 C4
Park Head Derbys 72 A5
Park Hill Gloucs 37 G4
Park Royal Gt Lon 28 C4
Park Street Herts 50 B1
Park Street W Susx 16 B4
Parkend Gloucs 37 G5
Parkers Green Kent 29 G1
Parkeston Essex 53 F4
Parkeston Quay Essex 53 F4
Parkfield Cnwll 5 G3
Parkgate Ches 81 E2
Parkgate Cumb 103 F5
Parkgate D & G 111 E4
Parkgate E Susx 17 H3
Parkgate Essex 51 H4
Parkgate Kent 29 F2
Parkgate Kent 18 B5
Parkgate Surrey 16 C6
Parkhall W Duns 129 F2
Parkham Devon 20 D3
Parkham Ash Devon 20 D3
Parkhill Nhants 73 E5
Parkhill House Abers 149 F6
Parkhouse Mons 37 F5
Parkmill Swans 34 C3
Parkside Dur 106 D6
Parkside N Lans 120 C5
Parkside Wrexhm 69 F6
Parkstone Dorset 12 D4
Parley Green Dorset 13 E4
Parlington W York 91 E3
Parmoor Bucks 41 F3
Parndon Essex 51 E1
Parracombe Devon 21 G5
Parrog Pembks 33 E6
Parson Drove Cambs 62 C6
Parson's Cross S York 84 A4
Parson's Heath Essex 52 D3
Parsonby Cumb 103 E4
Partick C Glas 129 G2
Partington Gt Man 82 B4
Partney Lincs 86 D1
Parton Cumb 102 D2
Partridge Green W Susx 16 C3
Partrishow Powys 45 F1
Parwich Derbys 71 G5
Paslow Wood Common Essex 51 G1
Passenham Nhants 49 F3
Passfield Hants 27 F3
Passingford Bridge Essex 29 F3
Paston Cambs 61 H6
Paston Norfk 77 F3
Pasturefields Staffs 71 E2
Patchacott Devon 8 B4

Name	Page	Grid
Patcham E Susx	16	D2
Patchetts Green Herts	28	B6
Patching W Susx	16	B2
Patchole Devon	21	F5
Patchway Gloucs	37	G2
Pateley Bridge N York	97	E1
Paternoster Heath Essex	52	C2
Pateshall Herefs	45	H5
Path of Condie P & K	139	H1
Pathe Somset	23	G2
Pathhead Fife	132	B4
Pathhead Mdloth	132	C1
Pathlow Warwks	47	G5
Patmore Heath Herts	51	E3
Patna E Ayrs	109	F6
Patney Wilts	25	F5
Patrick Brompton N York	97	E4
Patricroft Gt Man	82	C4
Patrington E R Yk	93	G2
Patrixbourne Kent	31	E1
Patterdale Cumb	103	H2
Pattingham Staffs	58	A5
Pattishall Nhants	49	E5
Pattiswick Green Essex	52	B3
Patton Shrops	57	F5
Paul Cnwll	2	B2
Paul's Dene Wilts	25	G2
Paulerspury Bucks	49	E4
Paull E R Yk	93	E2
Paulton Somset	24	B5
Paunton Herefs	46	B4
Pauperhaugh Nthumb	114	C5
Pave Lane Shrops	70	C2
Pavenham Beds	49	H5
Pawlett Somset	23	F3
Pawston Nthumb	123	F3
Paxford Gloucs	47	G3
Paxton Border	123	F5
Payden Street Kent	30	C1
Payhembury Devon	10	A5
Paythorne Lancs	89	G5
Paytoe Herefs	56	D2
Peacehaven E Susx	17	E1
Peak Dale Derbys	83	F2
Peak Forest Derbys	83	F3
Peak Hill Lincs	74	C2
Peakirk Cambs	61	H6
Peanmeanach Highld	143	G2
Pearson's Green Kent	17	H6
Peartree Green Herefs	46	B2
Pease Pottage W Susx	16	D5
Peasedown St John Somset	24	C5
Peasehill Derbys	72	B5
Peaseland Green Norfk	76	D2
Peasemore Berks	40	C2
Peasenhall Suffk	65	F2
Peaslake Surrey	16	B6
Peasley Cross Mersyd	81	G4
Peasmarsh E Susx	18	B4
Peasmarsh Somset	10	D6
Peasmarsh Surrey	27	H4
Peat Inn Fife	132	C6
Peathill Abers	159	E6
Peatling Magna Leics	60	B5
Peatling Parva Leics	60	B4
Peaton Shrops	57	E4
Pebmarsh Essex	52	B4
Pebworth Worcs	47	G4
Pecket Well W York	90	A2
Peckforton Ches	69	H6
Peckham Gt Lon	28	D4
Peckleton Leics	59	G5
Pedairffordd Powys	68	C2
Pedlinge Kent	19	E5
Pedmore W Mids	58	B4
Pedwell Somset	23	G3
Peebles Border	121	G3
Peel IOM	174	k3
Peel Lancs	88	B3
Peel Common Hants	14	D4
Peene Kent	19	E5
Peening Quarter Kent	18	B4
Peggs Green Leics	72	B2
Pegsdon Beds	50	B4
Pegswood Nthumb	114	D4
Pegwell Kent	31	G2
Peinchorran Highld	151	E2
Peinlich Highld	150	D5
Pelcomb Pembks	32	C3
Pelcomb Bridge Pembks	32	D3
Pelcomb Cross Pembks	32	C3
Peldon Essex	52	C2
Pell Green E Susx	17	G5
Pelsall W Mids	58	C6
Pelsall Wood W Mids	58	C6
Pelton Dur	106	B6
Pelton Fell Dur	106	B6
Pelutho Cumb	103	E5
Pelynt Cnwll	5	F1
Pemberton Carmth	34	C4
Pemberton Gt Man	81	H5
Pembles Cross Kent	18	C6
Pembrey Carmth	34	B4
Pembridge Herefs	45	G5
Pembroke Pembks	32	D2
Pembroke Dock Pembks	32	D2
Pembury Kent	17	G5
Pen Rhiwfawr Neath	35	E5
Pen-bont Rhydybeddau Cerdgn	54	D4
Pen-ffordd Pembks	33	E4
Pen-groes-oped Mons	36	D5
Pen-llyn IOA	78	C3
Pen-lon IOA	78	D1
Pen-rhiw Pembks	42	C3
Pen-twyn Caerph	36	C4
Pen-twyn Mons	37	F5
Pen-twyn Torfn	36	D5
Pen-y-bont Powys	68	D2
Pen-y-bont-fawr Powys	68	C2
Pen-y-bryn Neath	35	F3
Pen-y-bryn Pembks	42	B3
Pen-y-cae Powys	35	F6
Pen-y-cae-mawr Mons	37	E4
Pen-y-cefn Flints	80	C3
Pen-y-clawdd Mons	37	F5
Pen-y-cwn Pembks	32	C4
Pen-y-darren Myr Td	36	B5

Name	Page	Grid
Pen-y-fai Brdgnd	35	F2
Pen-y-felin Flints	80	D2
Pen-y-garn Cerdgn	54	D4
Pen-y-Garnedd Powys	68	C2
Pen-y-genffordd Powys	45	E2
Pen-y-graig Gwynd	66	B3
Pen-y-Gwryd Gwynd	67	F6
Pen-y-lan V Glam	35	G2
Pen-y-pass Gwynd	67	F6
Pen-y-stryt Denbgs	68	D5
Pen-yr-Heol Mons	37	E5
Pen-yr-Heolgerrig Myr Td	36	B5
Penair Cnwll	3	F4
Penallt Mons	37	F5
Penally Pembks	33	E1
Penare Cnwll	3	G4
Penarth V Glam	36	C1
Penblewin Pembks	33	E3
Penbryn Cerdgn	42	C4
Pencader Carmth	43	E3
Pencaenewydd Gwynd	66	D4
Pencaitland E Loth	132	C2
Pencalenick Cnwll	3	F4
Pencarnisiog IOA	78	C2
Pencarreg Carmth	43	E4
Pencarrow Cnwll	5	E4
Pencelli Powys	44	D2
Penclawdd Swans	34	C4
Pencoed Brdgnd	35	G2
Pencombe Herefs	46	B4
Pencoyd Herefs	45	H2
Pencraig Herefs	46	A1
Pencraig Powys	68	C3
Pendeen Cnwll	2	A3
Penderyn Rhondd	35	G5
Pendine Carmth	33	F2
Pendlebury Gt Man	82	C5
Pendleton Lancs	89	F3
Pendock Worcs	46	C2
Pendoggett Cnwll	4	D4
Pendomer Somset	11	F6
Pendoylan V Glam	36	B2
Penegoes Powys	55	E5
Penelewey Cnwll	3	F4
Pengam Caerph	36	C4
Pengam Cardif	36	C2
Penge Gt Lon	28	D3
Pengelly Cnwll	4	D4
Pengorffwysfa IOA	78	D4
Pengover Green Cnwll	5	F2
Pengrugla Cnwll	3	G4
Pengwern Denbgs	80	C2
Penhale Cnwll	2	D2
Penhale Cnwll	4	C2
Penhale Cnwll	4	D2
Penhale Cnwll	5	H1
Penhallow Cnwll	3	E5
Penhalurick Cnwll	3	E4
Penhalvean Cnwll	3	E4
Penhill Wilts	39	F3
Penhow Newpt	37	E3
Penhurst E Susx	17	H3
Peniarth Gwynd	54	D6
Penicuik Mdloth	121	G5
Peniel Carmth	42	D2
Peniel Denbgs	80	C1
Penifiler Highld	151	E3
Peninver Ag & B	117	G3
Penisar Waun Gwynd	79	E1
Penistone S York	83	G5
Penjerrick Cnwll	3	E3
Penkelly Cnwll	5	E1
Penketh Ches	81	H3
Penkill S Ayrs	108	D5
Penkridge Staffs	70	D1
Penlean Cnwll	5	F6
Penley Wrexhm	69	F4
Penllergaer Swans	34	C4
Penllyn V Glam	35	G2
Penmachno Conwy	67	G5
Penmaen Caerph	36	C4
Penmaen Swans	34	C3
Penmaenmawr Conwy	79	G2
Penmaenpool Gwynd	67	F2
Penmark V Glam	36	B1
Penmon IOA	79	F3
Penmorfa Gwynd	67	E4
Penmynydd IOA	79	E2
Penn Bucks	41	G4
Penn W Mids	58	B5
Penn Street Bucks	41	G4
Pennal Gwynd	55	E5
Pennan Abers	158	D6
Pennant Cerdgn	54	C2
Pennant Denbgs	68	C3
Pennant-Melangell Powys	68	C2
Pennard Swans	34	C3
Pennerley Shrops	56	D5
Pennicott Devon	9	F5
Pennington Cumb	94	C3
Pennington Hants	13	G4
Pennington Green Gt Man	82	A5
Pennorth Powys	44	D2
Pennsylvania Gloucs	38	B2
Penny Bridge Cumb	94	D3
Penny Bridge Pembks	32	D2
Penny Green Notts	84	C2
Penny Hill Lincs	74	D3
Pennycross Ag & B	135	C2
Pennygate Norfk	77	F2
Pennyghael Ag & B	135	G2
Pennyglen S Ayrs	108	D6
Pennymoor Devon	9	E6
Penparc Cerdgn	42	B4
Penparcau Cerdgn	54	C3
Penpedairheol Caerph	36	C4
Penpedairheol Mons	36	D5
Penperlleni Mons	36	D5
Penpillick Cnwll	4	D1
Penpol Cnwll	3	F4
Penpoll Cnwll	5	E1
Penponds Cnwll	2	D4

Name	Page	Grid
Penpont Cnwll	4	D3
Penpont D & G	110	C3
Penpont Powys	44	C2
Penquit Devon	6	D3
Penrest Cnwll	5	G4
Penrherber Carmth	42	C3
Penrhiw-pal Cerdgn	42	D4
Penrhiwceiber Rhondd	36	B4
Penrhiwllan Cerdgn	42	D3
Penrhos Gwynd	66	C3
Penrhos IOA	78	B3
Penrhos Mons	37	E5
Penrhos Powys	35	E5
Penrhos garnedd Gwynd	79	E2
Penrhyn Bay Conwy	79	H3
Penrhyn Castle Gwynd	79	F2
Penrhyn-side Conwy	79	H3
Penrhyncoch Cerdgn	54	D4
Penrhyndeudraeth Gwynd	67	F4
Penrice Swans	34	B3
Penrioch N Ayrs	117	H5
Penrith Cumb	104	B3
Penrose Cnwll	4	B3
Penrose Cnwll	5	F5
Penruddock Cumb	104	A3
Penryn Cnwll	3	E3
Pensarn Carmth	42	D1
Pensarn Conwy	80	B2
Pensax Worcs	57	G2
Pensby Mersyd	81	E3
Penselwood Somset	24	C2
Pensford Somset	24	B6
Pensham Worcs	47	E4
Penshaw T & W	106	C6
Penshurst Kent	17	F6
Penshurst Station Kent	17	F6
Pensilva Cnwll	5	F3
Pensnett W Mids	58	B4
Penstone Devon	9	E5
Penstrowed Powys	56	A4
Pentewan Cnwll	3	H4
Pentir Gwynd	79	E1
Pentire Cnwll	4	B2
Pentlepoir Pembks	33	E2
Pentlow Essex	52	B5
Pentlow Street Essex	52	B5
Pentney Norfk	75	G1
Penton Grafton Hants	26	B4
Penton Mewsey Hants	26	B4
Pentonbridge Cumb	112	B2
Pentraeth IOA	79	E2
Pentre Denbgs	80	C1
Pentre Flints	81	E1
Pentre Mons	36	D5
Pentre Powys	56	A4
Pentre Powys	56	B4
Pentre Powys	56	C5
Pentre Rhondd	35	G4
Pentre Shrops	69	F2
Pentre Wrexhm	69	E4
Pentre Bach Cerdgn	43	F4
Pentre Bach Flints	80	D2
Pentre Berw IOA	78	D2
Pentre Ffwrndan Flints	81	E2
Pentre Gwynfryn Gwynd	67	E3
Pentre Halkyn Flints	80	D2
Pentre Hodrey Shrops	56	D3
Pentre Isaf Conwy	80	B2
Pentre Llanrhaeadr Denbgs	80	C1
Pentre Llifior Powys	56	B5
Pentre Meyrick V Glam	35	G2
Pentre Saron Denbgs	68	C6
Pentre ty gwyn Carmth	44	A3
Pentre'r Felin Conwy	79	H2
Pentre'r-felin Cerdgn	43	F4
Pentre'r-felin Powys	44	B2
Pentre'rbryn Cerdgn	42	D5
Pentre-bach Powys	44	B2
Pentre-bont Conwy	67	G5
Pentre-cagel Cerdgn	42	D3
Pentre-celyn Denbgs	68	D5
Pentre-celyn Powys	55	F6
Pentre-chwyth Swans	34	C4
Pentre-clawdd Shrops	69	E3
Pentre-cwrt Carmth	42	D3
Pentre-dwr Swans	34	D4
Pentre-Gwenlais Carmth	34	D6
Pentre-llwyn-llwyd Powys	44	B5
Pentre-llyn Cerdgn	54	D3
Pentre-llyn-cymmer Conwy	68	B5
Pentre-Maw Powys	55	F6
Pentre-piod Torfn	36	D4
Pentre-poeth Newpt	36	D3
Pentre-tafarn-y-fedw Conwy	79	H1
Pentrebach Myr Td	36	B5
Pentrebeirdd Powys	68	D1
Pentredwr Denbgs	68	D5
Pentrefelin Gwynd	67	E4
Pentrefelin IOA	78	D4
Pentrefoelas Conwy	68	A5
Pentregalar Pembks	42	B2
Pentregat Cerdgn	42	D4
Pentrich Derbys	72	B5
Pentridge Hill Dorset	25	F1
Pentwynmaur Caerph	36	C4
Pentyrch Cardif	36	B2
Penwithick Cnwll	3	H5
Penwood Hants	26	C5
Penwyllt Powys	35	F6
Penybanc Carmth	43	F2
Penybont Powys	56	A2
Penycae Wrexhm	69	E4
Penycaerau Gwynd	66	B3
Penyffordd Flints	69	E6
Penygraig Rhondd	35	G3
Penygroes Carmth	34	C6
Penygroes Gwynd	66	D5
Penysarn IOA	78	D4
Penywaun Rhondd	35	G5
Penywern Neath	35	E5
Penzance Cnwll	2	B3
Penzance Heliport Cnwll	2	B3
Peopleton Worcs	47	E4
Peover Heath Ches	82	C2
Peper Harow Surrey	27	G4
Peplow Shrops	70	A2
Pepper's Green Essex	51	G2
Peppershill Oxon	41	E5

Name	Page	Grid
Pepperstock Beds	50	B2
Perceton N Ayrs	119	E3
Percie Abers	148	D4
Percyhorner Abers	159	E6
Perelle Guern	174	f2
Periton Somset	22	B4
Perivale Gt Lon	28	C4
Perkins Village Devon	9	G4
Perkinsville Dur	114	D1
Perlethorpe Notts	84	D2
Perran Wharf Cnwll	3	E4
Perranarworthal Cnwll	3	E4
Perranporth Cnwll	3	E5
Perranuthnoe Cnwll	2	C3
Perranwell Cnwll	3	E4
Perranwell Cnwll	3	E5
Perranzabuloe Cnwll	3	E5
Perrott's Brook Gloucs	39	E5
Perry W Mids	58	D5
Perry Barr W Mids	58	D4
Perry Green Essex	52	B3
Perry Green Herts	51	E2
Perry Green Wilts	38	D3
Perry Street Somset	10	D5
Pershall Staffs	70	C3
Pershore Worcs	47	E4
Pertenhall Beds	61	G2
Perth P & K	140	A2
Perthy Shrops	69	F3
Perton Herefs	46	B3
Perton Staffs	58	B5
Pertwood Wilts	24	D3
Pet Street Kent	18	D6
Peter Tavy Devon	8	B2
Peter's Green Herts	50	B3
Peterborough Cambs	62	A5
Peterchurch Herefs	45	F3
Peterculter Aber C	149	F4
Peterhead Abers	159	G4
Peterlee Dur	106	D5
Peters Marland Devon	21	E2
Petersfield Hants	27	F2
Petersham Gt Lon	28	C3
Peterston-super-Ely V Glam	36	B2
Peterstone Wentlooge Newpt	36	D2
Peterstow Herefs	46	A2
Petham Kent	31	E1
Petherwin Gate Cnwll	5	F5
Petrockstow Devon	8	B5
Petsoe End Bucks	49	G4
Pett E Susx	18	B3
Pett Bottom Kent	31	E1
Pettaugh Suffk	64	D1
Petterden Angus	140	D4
Pettinain S Lans	120	D1
Pettistree Suffk	53	F6
Petton Devon	22	C2
Petton Shrops	69	F3
Petts Wood Gt Lon	29	E3
Petty France Gloucs	38	C3
Pettycur Fife	132	B4
Pettymuk Abers	159	E1
Petworth W Susx	27	H1
Pevensey E Susx	17	G2
Pevensey Bay E Susx	17	G2
Pewsey Wilts	25	G5
Pheasant's Hill Bucks	41	F3
Phepson Worcs	47	E5
Philadelphia T & W	106	C6
Philham Devon	20	C3
Philiphaugh Border	122	B2
Phillack Cnwll	2	C4
Philleigh Cnwll	3	F4
Philpot End Essex	51	G2
Philpstoun W Loth	131	G3
Phocle Green Herefs	46	B2
Phoenix Green Hants	27	F5
Phoines Highld	146	B4
Pibsbury Somset	23	G2
Pica Cumb	102	D2
Piccadilly Warwks	59	E5
Piccotts End Herts	50	A2
Pickburn S York	84	C5
Pickering N York	98	D3
Picket Piece Hants	26	B4
Picket Post Hants	13	F5
Pickford W Mids	59	F3
Pickford Green W Mids	59	F3
Pickhill N York	97	G3
Picklescott Shrops	57	E5
Pickmere Ches	82	B2
Pickney Somset	23	E2
Pickstock Shrops	70	B2
Pickup Bank Lancs	89	F2
Pickwell Devon	21	E5
Pickwell Leics	73	E1
Pickwick Wilts	38	C1
Pickworth Lincs	73	G1
Pickworth Lincs	73	H3
Pict's Cross Herefs	46	A2
Pictillum Abers	149	E6
Picton Ches	81	G2
Picton Flints	80	C3
Picton N York	106	D1
Picton Ferry Carmth	33	G2
Piddinghoe E Susx	17	E2
Piddington Bucks	41	F4
Piddington Nhants	49	F5
Piddington Oxon	41	E6
Piddlehinton Dorset	11	G4
Piddletrenthide Dorset	11	G5
Pidley Cambs	62	C3
Pie Corner Herefs	46	B5
Piercebridge Dur	106	B2
Pierowall Ork	169	b4
Piff's Elm Gloucs	46	D2
Pig Oak Dorset	12	D5
Pig Street Herefs	45	F4
Pigdon Nthumb	114	C4
Pigeon Green Warwks	47	H5
Pikehall Derbys	71	G6
Pilford Dorset	12	D5
Pilgrims Hatch Essex	29	G6
Pilham Lincs	85	F4
Pill Somset	37	F2
Pillaton Cnwll	5	G2
Pillatonmill Cnwll	5	G2
Pillerton Hersey Warwks	48	A4

Name	Page	Grid
Pillerton Priors Warwks	48	A4
Pilleth Powys	56	C2
Pilley Hants	13	G4
Pilley S York	84	A5
Pilley Bailey Hants	13	G4
Pillgwenlly Newpt	36	D3
Pillhead Devon	21	E3
Pilling Lancs	88	C4
Pilling Lane Lancs	88	B4
Pilning Gloucs	37	G3
Pilot Inn Kent	18	D3
Pilsbury Derbys	83	F1
Pilsdon Dorset	10	D4
Pilsgate Cambs	61	G6
Pilsley Derbys	83	G2
Pilsley Derbys	84	B1
Pilson Green Norfk	77	G1
Piltdown E Susx	17	E4
Pilton Devon	21	F4
Pilton Nhants	61	F4
Pilton Rutlnd	61	E6
Pilton Somset	24	B3
Pilton Green Swans	34	B3
Pimlico Lancs	89	F4
Pimlico Nhants	48	D3
Pimperne Dorset	12	C5
Pin Green Herts	50	C3
Pinchbeck Lincs	74	C3
Pinchbeck Bars Lincs	74	B2
Pinchbeck West Lincs	74	B2
Pincheon Green S York	91	H1
Pinchinthorpe N York	107	E2
Pincock Lancs	88	D1
Pindon End Bucks	49	F4
Pinfold Lancs	81	F6
Pinford End Suffk	63	H1
Pinged Carmth	34	B5
Pingewood Berks	41	E1
Pinhoe Devon	9	F4
Pinkett's Booth W Mids	59	F3
Pinkney Wilts	38	C3
Pinley W Mids	59	F3
Pinley Green Warwks	59	E2
Pinmill Suffk	53	F4
Pinminnoch S Ayrs	108	D4
Pinmore S Ayrs	108	D4
Pinn Devon	10	A3
Pinner Gt Lon	28	B5
Pinner Green Gt Lon	28	B5
Pinsley Green Ches	69	H5
Pinvin Worcs	47	E4
Pinwherry S Ayrs	108	D3
Pinxton Derbys	72	B5
Pipe and Lyde Herefs	45	H4
Pipe Gate Shrops	70	B4
Piperhill Highld	155	G4
Pipers Pool Cnwll	5	F4
Pipewell Nhants	60	D4
Pippacott Devon	21	E4
Pippin Street Lancs	88	D2
Pipton Powys	44	D3
Pirbright Surrey	27	H5
Pirbright Camp Surrey	27	G5
Pirnie Border	122	D2
Pirnmill N Ayrs	117	H5
Pirton Herts	50	B4
Pirton Worcs	46	D4
Pishill Oxon	41	E3
Pistyll Gwynd	66	C4
Pitagowan P & K	146	C1
Pitblae Abers	159	F6
Pitcairngreen P & K	139	H2
Pitcalnie Highld	163	E1
Pitcaple Abers	158	C2
Pitcarity Angus	148	A1
Pitch Green Bucks	41	F5
Pitch Place Surrey	27	G3
Pitch Place Surrey	27	H4
Pitchcombe Gloucs	38	C5
Pitchcott Bucks	49	F1
Pitcher Row Lincs	74	C3
Pitchford Shrops	57	E6
Pitchroy Moray	156	D3
Pitcombe Somset	24	B2
Pitcot V Glam	35	F2
Pitcox E Loth	133	E3
Pitfichie Abers	148	D6
Pitglassie Abers	158	C3
Pitgrudy Highld	163	E3
Pitkennedy Angus	141	E5
Pitlessie Fife	132	B6
Pitlochry P & K	139	G6
Pitmachie Abers	158	C2
Pitmain Highld	146	B4
Pitmedden Abers	159	E2
Pitmedden Garden Abers	159	E2
Pitmuies Angus	141	E5
Pitmunie Abers	148	D6
Pitney Somset	23	G2
Pitroddie P & K	140	B2
Pitscottie Fife	140	D1
Pitsea Essex	30	A5
Pitses Gt Man	82	D5
Pitsford Nhants	60	D2
Pitstone Bucks	41	G6
Pitt Devon	9	G6
Pitt Hants	26	C2
Pitt Court Gloucs	38	B4
Pitt's Wood Kent	29	G1
Pittarrow Abers	149	E2
Pittentrail Highld	163	E5
Pittenweem Fife	132	D5
Pitteuchar Fife	132	B5
Pittington Dur	106	C5
Pittodrie House Hotel Abers	158	C1
Pitton Wilts	25	G2
Pittulie Abers	159	E6
Pity Me Dur	106	B5
Pityme Cnwll	4	C4
Pivington Kent	18	C6
Pixey Green Suffk	65	E3
Pixham Surrey	28	C1
Plain Street Cnwll	4	C4
Plains N Lans	130	D2
Plaish Shrops	57	E5
Plaistow Cnwll	72	A6
Plaistow Gt Lon	29	E4
Plaistow Herefs	46	C3

Plaistow W Susx 16 A4
Plaitford Hants 26 A1
Plank Lane Gt Man 82 A5
Plas Cymyran IOA 78 C2
Plastow Green Hants 26 D5
Platt Kent 29 G2
Platt Bridge Gt Man 82 A5
Platt Lane Shrops 69 G4
Platts Heath Kent 30 B1
Plawsworth Dur 106 B6
Plaxtol Kent 29 G1
Play Hatch Oxon 41 F2
Playden E Susx 18 C4
Playford Suffk 53 F5
Playing Place Cnwll 3 F4
Playley Green Gloucs 46 C2
Plealey Shrops 56 D6
Plean Stirlg 131 E4
Pleasance Fife 140 B1
Pleasington Lancs 89 E2
Pleasley Derbys 84 C1
Pleasleyhill Notts 84 C1
Pleck Dorset 11 G6
Pledgdon Green Essex 51 F3
Pledwick W York 90 D1
Pleinheaume Guern 174 g3
Plemont Jersey 174 a3
Plemstall Ches 81 G2
Plenmeller Nthumb 112 D1
Pleshey Essex 51 G2
Plockton Highld 152 B2
Plowden Shrops 56 D4
Plox Green Shrops 56 D6
Pluckley Kent 18 C6
Pluckley Station Kent 18 C6
Pluckley Thorne Kent 18 C6
Plucks Gutter Kent 31 F2
Plumbland Cumb 103 E4
Plumgarths Cumb 95 F4
Plumley Ches 82 B2
Plumpton Cumb 104 B4
Plumpton Cumb 94 D3
Plumpton E Susx 16 D3
Plumpton Nhants 48 D4
Plumpton End Nhants 49 E4
Plumpton Green E Susx 16 D3
Plumpton Head Cumb 104 B4
Plumstead Gt Lon 29 E4
Plumstead Norfk 76 D3
Plumstead Green Norfk 76 D3
Plumtree Notts 72 D3
Plumtree Green Kent 18 B6
Plungar Leics 73 E3
Plurenden Kent 18 C5
Plush Dorset 11 G5
Plusha Cnwll 5 F4
Plushabridge Cnwll 5 F3
Plwmp Cerdgn 42 D4
Plymouth Devon 6 B3
Plymouth Airport Devon 6 C4
Plympton Devon 6 C3
Plymstock Devon 6 C3
Plymtree Devon 9 G5
Pockley N York 98 B3
Pocklington E R Yk 92 B4
Pode Hole Lincs 74 C2
Podimore Somset 24 A2
Podington Beds 49 G5
Podmore Staffs 70 C4
Point Clear Essex 53 E2
Pointon Lincs 74 B3
Pokesdown Dorset 13 E4
Polapit Tamar Cnwll 5 G5
Polbain Highld 160 D5
Polbathic Cnwll 5 G2
Polbeth W Loth 131 F1
Polbrock Cnwll 4 D3
Poldark Mine Cnwll 2 D3
Pole Elm Worcs 46 D4
Pole Moor W York 90 B1
Polebrook Nhants 61 G4
Polegate E Susx 17 G2
Polelane Ends Ches 82 A3
Polesworth Warwks 59 E6
Polgigga Cnwll 2 A2
Polglass Highld 160 D4
Polgooth Cnwll 3 G5
Polgown D & G 110 B5
Poling W Susx 16 A2
Poling Corner W Susx 16 A2
Polkerris Cnwll 4 D1
Pollard Street Norfk 77 F3
Pollington E R Yk 91 G1
Polloch Highld 143 G1
Pollokshaws C Glas 119 G6
Pollokshields C Glas 130 B1
Polmassick Cnwll 3 G4
Polmear Cnwll 4 D1
Polmont Falk 131 F3
Polnish Highld 143 G2
Polperro Cnwll 5 F1
Polruan Cnwll 5 E1
Polsham Somset 23 H3
Polstead Suffk 52 C5
Polstead Heath Suffk 52 D5
Poltalloch Ag & B 127 G5
Poltescoe Cnwll 3 E1
Poltimore Devon 9 F4
Polton Mdloth 132 B1
Polwarth Border 123 E4
Polyphant Cnwll 5 F4
Polzeath Cnwll 4 C4
Pomathorn Mdloth 121 G5
Pomeroy Derbys 83 F1
Ponde Powys 44 D3
Ponders End Gt Lon 28 D6
Pondersbridge Cambs 62 B5
Ponsanooth Cnwll 3 E3
Ponsonby Cumb 94 A3
Ponsongath Cnwll 3 E1
Ponsworthy Devon 6 D5
Pont Cyfyng Conwy 67 G6
Pont Dolgarrog Conwy 79 G1
Pont Morlais Carmth 34 C5
Pont Pen-y-benglog Gwynd 67 F6
Pont Rhyd-sarn Gwynd 67 H3
Pont Rhyd-y-cyff Brdgnd 35 F3
Pont Robert Powys 68 C1

Pont Walby Neath 35 F5
Pont-ar-gothi Carmth 43 E1
Pont-ar-Hydfer Powys 44 B2
Pont-ar-llechau Carmth 43 G2
Pont-Ebbw Newpt 36 D3
Pont-faen Powys 44 C3
Pont-Nedd-Fechan Neath 35 F5
Pont-rhyd-y-fen Neath 35 E4
Pont-rug Gwynd 79 E1
Pont-y-blew Wrexhm 69 E4
Pont-y-pant Conwy 67 G5
Pont-yr-hafod Pembks 32 C4
Pont-yr-Rhyl Brdgnd 35 F3
Pontac Jersey 174 d1
Pontamman Carmth 34 D5
Pontantwn Carmth 34 B6
Pontardawe Neath 35 E5
Pontarddulais Swans 34 C5
Pontarsais Carmth 43 E2
Pontblyddyn Flints 69 E6
Pontdolgoch Powys 55 H5
Pontefract W York 91 F2
Ponteland Nthumb 114 C3
Ponterwyd Cerdgn 55 E3
Pontesbury Shrops 56 D6
Pontesbury Hill Shrops 56 D6
Pontesford Shrops 56 D6
Pontfadog Wrexhm 69 E4
Pontfaen Pembks 32 D5
Pontgarreg Cerdgn 42 D5
Pontgarreg Pembks 42 B3
Ponthenry Carmth 34 B5
Ponthir Torfn 36 D3
Ponthirwaun Cerdgn 42 C4
Pontlanfraith Caerph 36 C4
Pontlliw Swans 34 D4
Pontlottyn Caerph 36 B5
Pontlyfni Gwynd 66 D5
Pontnewydd Torfn 36 D4
Pontnewynydd Torfn 36 D4
Pontop Dur 105 H5
Pontrhydfendigaid Cerdgn 55 E2
Pontrhydygroes Cerdgn 55 E3
Pontrhydyrun Torfn 36 D4
Pontrilas Herefs 45 G2
Ponts Green E Susx 17 G3
Pontshaen Cerdgn 43 E4
Pontshill Herefs 46 B1
Pontsticill Powys 36 B5
Pontwelly Carmth 42 D3
Pontyates Carmth 34 B5
Pontyberem Carmth 34 C5
Pontybodkin Flints 69 E6
Pontyclun Rhondd 36 B3
Pontycymer Brdgnd 35 F3
Pontyglasier Pembks 42 B3
Pontygwaith Rhondd 35 G4
Pontygynon Pembks 42 B3
Pontymoel Torfn 36 D4
Pontypool Torfn 36 D4
Pontypool Road Torfn 36 D4
Pontypridd Rhondd 36 B3
Pontywaun Caerph 36 C3
Pool Cnwll 2 D4
Pool IOS 2 a2
Pool W York 90 D3
Pool Head Herefs 46 A4
Pool of Muckhart Clacks 131 F5
Pool Quay Powys 69 E1
Pool Street Essex 52 A4
Poole Dorset 12 C4
Poole Keynes Gloucs 39 E4
Poolewe Highld 160 C2
Pooley Bridge Cumb 104 B2
Pooley Street Norfk 64 C3
Poolfold Staffs 70 D6
Poolhill Gloucs 46 C2
Pooting's Kent 29 E1
Popham Hants 26 D4
Poplar Gt Lon 29 E4
Poplar Street Suffk 65 G2
Porchbrook Worcs 57 G2
Porchfield IOW 14 C3
Poringland Norfk 65 E5
Porkellis Cnwll 2 D3
Porlock Somset 22 B4
Porlock Weir Somset 22 B4
Port Appin Ag & B 136 D4
Port Askaig Ag & B 126 C2
Port Bannatyne Ag & B 128 B2
Port Carlisle Cumb 111 G1
Port Charlotte Ag & B 126 A1
Port Clarence Dur 106 D3
Port Driseach Ag & B 128 A2
Port e Vallen IOM 174 n4
Port Einon Swans 34 B3
Port Ellen Ag & B 116 C5
Port Elphinstone Abers 158 D1
Port Erin IOM 174 k2
Port Gaverne Cnwll 4 D4
Port Glasgow Inver 129 E2
Port Henderson Highld 160 B1
Port Isaac Cnwll 4 D4
Port Logan D & G 100 B4
Port Mor Highld 142 D2
Port Mulgrave N York 107 G3
Port nan Giuran W Isls 168 f8
Port nan Long W Isls 168 c5
Port Nis W Isls 168 f9
Port of Menteith Stirlg 130 B5
Port of Ness W Isls 168 f9
Port Quin Cnwll 4 D4
Port Ramsay Ag & B 136 C4
Port Soderick IOM 174 l2
Port Solent Hants 14 D4
Port St Mary IOM 174 k2
Port Sunlight Mersyd 81 F3
Port Talbot Neath 35 E3
Port Tennant Swans 34 D4
Port Wemyss Ag & B 116 A5
Port William D & G 101 E4
Port-an-Eorna Highld 152 B2
Portachoillan Ag & B 127 G6
Portavadie Ag & B 127 H2
Portbury Somset 37 F3
Portchester Hants 14 D4
Porteath Cnwll 4 C4
Portencalzie D & G 108 B2

Portencross N Ayrs 118 D4
Portesham Dorset 11 F3
Portessie Moray 157 F6
Portfield Gate Pembks 32 C3
Portgate Devon 5 H4
Portgordon Moray 157 F5
Portgower Highld 163 G5
Porth Cnwll 4 B2
Porth Rhondd 36 A3
Porth Dinllaen Gwynd 66 B4
Porth Navas Cnwll 3 E2
Porth-y-Waen Shrops 69 E2
Porthallow Cnwll 3 E2
Porthallow Cnwll 5 F1
Porthcawl Brdgnd 35 F2
Porthcothan Cnwll 4 B3
Porthcurno Cnwll 2 A2
Porthgain Pembks 32 B5
Porthgwarra Cnwll 2 A2
Porthill Staffs 70 C5
Porthkea Cnwll 3 F4
Porthkerry V Glam 22 D6
Porthleven Cnwll 2 D2
Porthmadog Gwynd 67 E4
Porthmeor Cnwll 2 B2
Portholland Cnwll 3 G4
Porthoustock Cnwll 3 F2
Porthpean Cnwll 3 G5
Porthtowan Cnwll 2 D4
Porthwgan Wrexhm 69 F5
Porthyrhyd Carmth 34 C6
Portincaple Ag & B 128 D4
Portinfer Jersey 174 a3
Portington E R Yk 92 B3
Portinnisherrich Ag & B 136 D1
Portinscale Cumb 103 F2
Portishead Somset 37 F2
Portknockie Moray 157 G6
Portlethen Abers 149 G4
Portling D & G 102 C5
Portloe Cnwll 3 G4
Portlooe Cnwll 5 F1
Portmahomack Highld 163 G4
Portmeirion Gwynd 67 E4
Portmellon Cnwll 3 H4
Portmore Hants 13 G4
Portnacroish Ag & B 136 D4
Portnaguran W Isls 168 f8
Portnahaven Ag & B 116 A6
Portnalong Highld 150 D2
Portobello C Edin 132 B2
Portobello T & W 114 D1
Portobello W Mids 58 C5
Porton Wilts 25 G3
Portontown Devon 5 H4
Portpatrick D & G 100 A5
Portreath Cnwll 2 D4
Portree Highld 151 E3
Portscatho Cnwll 3 F3
Portsea Hants 15 E4
Portskerra Highld 166 C5
Portskewett Mons 37 F3
Portslade E Susx 16 C2
Portslade-by-Sea E Susx 16 D2
Portslogan D & G 100 A6
Portsmouth Hants 15 E4
Portsmouth W York 89 G2
Portsonachan Hotel Ag & B 137 E2
Portsoy Abers 158 B6
Portswood Hants 14 C5
Portuairk Highld 135 F6
Portway Herefs 45 H4
Portway Herefs 45 H3
Portway W Mids 58 C4
Portway Worcs 58 D3
Portwrinkle Cnwll 5 G1
Portyerrock D & G 101 F4
Posbury Devon 9 E4
Posenhall Shrops 57 G6
Poslingford Suffk 52 A5
Posso Border 121 F3
Post Green Dorset 12 C4
Postbridge Devon 8 C2
Postcombe Oxon 41 E4
Postling Kent 19 E5
Postwick Norfk 65 E6
Potarch Abers 148 D4
Pothole Cnwll 3 G5
Potsgrove Beds 49 H2
Pott Row Norfk 75 G2
Pott Shrigley Ches 82 D3
Pott's Green Essex 52 C3
Potten End Herts 50 B5
Potter Brompton N York 99 E3
Potter Heigham Norfk 77 G2
Potter Row Bucks 41 G4
Potter Somersal Derbys 71 F4
Potter's Cross Staffs 58 A4
Potter's Forstal Kent 18 C6
Potter's Green E Susx 17 F4
Potters Green Herts 50 D3
Pottergate Street Norfk 64 D4
Potterhanworth Lincs 85 H1
Potterhanworth Booths Lincs 86 A1
Potterne Wilts 25 E5
Potterne Wick Wilts 25 E5
Potters Bar Herts 28 C6
Potters Brook Lancs 88 C5
Potters Crouch Herts 50 B5
Potters Green W Mids 59 G4
Potters Marston Leics 59 H5
Pottersheath Herts 50 C2
Potterspury Nhants 49 F3
Potterton Abers 149 G6
Potthorpe Norfk 76 B2
Pottle Street Wilts 24 D3
Potto N York 97 H5
Potton Beds 50 C6
Poughill Cnwll 20 B1
Poughill Devon 9 E5
Poulner Hants 13 E5
Poulshot Wilts 25 E5
Poulston Devon 7 E3
Poulton Gloucs 39 F4
Poulton Mersyd 81 E4
Poulton Priory Gloucs 39 F4

Poulton-le-Fylde Lancs 88 B3
Pound Bank Worcs 57 G3
Pound Green E Susx 17 F4
Pound Green Suffk 51 H6
Pound Green Worcs 57 H3
Pound Hill W Susx 16 B5
Pound Street Hants 26 C5
Poundffald Swans 34 C4
Poundgate E Susx 17 F4
Poundon Bucks 49 E2
Poundsbridge Kent 17 F6
Poundsgate Devon 6 D5
Poundstock Cnwll 5 F6
Pounsley E Susx 17 F4
Pouton D & G 101 F5
Pouy Street Suffk 65 F2
Povey Cross Surrey 16 D6
Pow Green Herefs 46 C4
Powburn Nthumb 124 D3
Powderham Devon 9 F3
Powerstock Dorset 11 E4
Powfoot D & G 111 F1
Powhill Cumb 103 F6
Powick Worcs 46 D4
Powmill P & K 131 F5
Poxwell Dorset 11 H3
Poyle Surrey 28 A4
Poynings W Susx 16 D3
Poynter's Lane End Cnwll 2 D4
Poyntington Dorset 24 B1
Poynton Ches 82 D3
Poynton Shrops 69 H2
Poynton Green Shrops 69 H2
Poyston Cross Pembks 32 D4
Poystreet Green Suffk 64 B1
Praa Sands Cnwll 2 C3
Pratt's Bottom Gt Lon 29 F2
Praze-an-Beeble Cnwll 2 D3
Predannack Wollas Cnwll 2 D1
Prees Shrops 69 H3
Prees Green Shrops 69 H3
Prees Heath Shrops 69 H4
Prees Higher Heath Shrops 69 H4
Prees Lower Heath Shrops 69 H3
Preesall Lancs 88 B4
Preesgweene Shrops 69 E4
Pren-gwyn Cerdgn 42 D4
Prendwick Nthumb 124 C2
Prenteg Gwynd 67 E4
Prenton Mersyd 81 E3
Prescot Mersyd 81 G4
Prescott Devon 10 A6
Prescott Shrops 69 F2
Prescott Shrops 57 G3
Presnerb Angus 147 G1
Prestatyn Denbgs 80 C3
Prestbury Ches 82 D2
Prestbury Gloucs 47 E2
Presteigne Powys 56 C2
Prestleigh Somset 24 B4
Prestolee Gt Man 82 C5
Preston Border 123 E5
Preston Devon 7 E3
Preston Devon 7 F5
Preston Devon 7 F4
Preston E Loth 133 E3
Preston E R Yk 93 F3
Preston E Susx 16 D2
Preston Gloucs 46 B3
Preston Gloucs 39 E4
Preston Herts 50 C3
Preston Kent 30 D2
Preston Kent 31 F2
Preston Lancs 88 D3
Preston Nthumb 125 E4
Preston Rutlnd 61 E6
Preston Shrops 69 G1
Preston Somset 22 D3
Preston Suffk 52 C6
Preston Wilts 39 G2
Preston Bagot Warwks 59 E2
Preston Bissett Bucks 49 E2
Preston Bowyer Somset 22 D2
Preston Brockhurst Shrops 69 H2
Preston Brook Ches 81 H3
Preston Candover Hants 26 D3
Preston Capes Nhants 48 D5
Preston Crowmarsh Oxon 40 D3
Preston Deanery Nhants 49 F5
Preston Green Warwks 59 E2
Preston Gubbals Shrops 69 G2
Preston Montford Shrops 69 F1
Preston on Stour Warwks 47 G4
Preston on Tees Dur 106 D2
Preston on the Hill Ches 81 H3
Preston on Wye Herefs 45 G3
Preston Patrick Cumb 95 F3
Preston Plucknett Somset 11 F6
Preston Street Kent 31 F2
Preston upon the Weald Moors
    Shrops 70 B1
Preston Wynne Herefs 46 A4
Preston-under-Scar N York 96 D4
Prestonpans E Loth 132 C2
Prestwich Gt Man 82 C5
Prestwick Nthumb 114 C3
Prestwick S Ayrs 119 E2
Prestwick Airport S Ayrs 119 E2
Prestwood Bucks 41 G4
Prestwood Staffs 58 B4
Price Town Brdgnd 35 G3
Prickwillow Cambs 63 E4
Priddy Somset 23 H4
Priest Hutton Lancs 95 F2
Priestacott Devon 20 D1
Priestcliffe Derbys 83 F2
Priestcliffe Ditch Derbys 83 F2
Priestend Bucks 41 E5
Priestland E Ayrs 119 G3
Priestley Green W York 90 C2
Priestweston Shrops 56 C5
Priestwood Green Kent 29 G2
Primethorpe Leics 60 A5
Primrose Green Norfk 76 D2
Primrose Hill Cambs 62 C4
Primrose Hill Derbys 72 B6

Primrose Hill Lancs 81 F6
Primrose Hill W Mids 58 B4
Primrosehill Border 123 E5
Primsidemill Border 123 E2
Princes Gate Pembks 33 F3
Princes Risborough Bucks 41 F5
Princethorpe Warwks 59 G2
Princetown Devon 6 C5
Prinsted W Susx 15 F4
Prion Denbgs 80 C1
Prior Rigg Cumb 112 B2
Priors Halton Shrops 57 E3
Priors Hardwick Warwks 48 C5
Priors Marston Warwks 48 C5
Priors Norton Gloucs 46 D2
Priory Wood Herefs 45 E4
Prisk V Glam 35 G2
Priston Somset 24 C5
Pristow Green Norfk 64 D4
Prittlewell Essex 30 B5
Privett Hants 27 E2
Prixford Devon 21 F4
Probus Cnwll 3 F4
Prora E Loth 132 C3
Prospect Cumb 103 E4
Prospidnick Cnwll 2 D3
Protstonhill Abers 158 D5
Providence Somset 37 F1
Prudhoe Nthumb 114 C2
Prussia Cove Cnwll 2 C3
Publow Somset 24 B6
Puckeridge Herts 51 E3
Puckington Somset 23 F1
Pucklechurch Gloucs 38 B2
Puckrup Gloucs 46 D3
Puddinglake Ches 82 B2
Puddington Ches 81 E2
Puddington Devon 9 E6
Puddledock Norfk 64 C5
Puddletown Dorset 12 A4
Pudleston Herefs 46 A5
Pudsey W York 90 C3
Pulborough W Susx 16 A3
Puleston Shrops 70 B2
Pulford Ches 69 F6
Pulham Dorset 11 G5
Pulham Market Norfk 64 D4
Pulham St Mary Norfk 65 E4
Pullens Green Gloucs 37 G3
Pulley Shrops 69 G1
Pulloxhill Beds 50 B4
Pumpherston W Loth 131 G2
Pumsaint Carmth 43 G3
Puncheston Pembks 32 D5
Punchknowle Dorset 11 F3
Punnett's Town E Susx 17 G3
Purbrook Hants 15 E4
Purfleet Essex 29 F4
Puriton Somset 23 F3
Purleigh Essex 52 B1
Purley Berks 41 E2
Purley Gt Lon 28 D2
Purlogue Shrops 56 C3
Purlpit Wilts 24 D6
Purls Bridge Cambs 62 D4
Purse Caundle Dorset 24 C1
Purshull Green Worcs 58 B2
Purslow Shrops 56 D3
Purston Jaglin W York 91 E1
Purtington Somset 10 D5
Purton Gloucs 38 B5
Purton Gloucs 38 B5
Purton Wilts 39 F3
Purton Stoke Wilts 39 F3
Pury End Nhants 49 E4
Pusey Oxon 40 B4
Putley Herefs 46 B3
Putley Green Herefs 46 B3
Putloe Gloucs 38 C5
Putney Gt Lon 28 C3
Putron Village Guern 174 g1
Putsborough Devon 21 E5
Puttenham Herts 41 G6
Puttenham Surrey 27 G4
Puttock End Essex 52 B5
Puttock's End Essex 51 F3
Putton Dorset 11 G3
Puxey Nhants 49 F3
Puxton Somset 23 G6
Pwll Carmth 34 B4
Pwll Trap Carmth 33 G3
Pwllcrochan Pembks 32 C2
Pwll-du Mons 36 D5
Pwll-glas Denbgs 68 C5
Pwll-y-glaw Neath 35 E4
Pwllgloyw Powys 44 C3
Pwllheli Gwynd 66 C3
Pwllmeyric Mons 37 F3
Pydew Conwy 79 H3
Pye Bridge Derbys 72 B5
Pye Corner Herts 51 E2
Pye Corner Newpt 37 E3
Pye Green Staffs 71 E1
Pyecombe W Susx 16 D3
Pyle Brdgnd 35 F2
Pyleigh Somset 22 D2
Pylle Somset 24 B4
Pymoor Cambs 62 D4
Pymore Dorset 11 E4
Pyrford Surrey 28 A2
Pyrton Oxon 41 E4
Pytchley Nhants 61 E3
Pyworthy Devon 5 G6

Q

Quabbs *Shrops* 56 B3
Quadring *Lincs* 74 C3
Quadring Eaudike *Lincs* 74 C3
Quainton *Bucks* 49 F1
Quaker's Yard *Myr Td* 36 B4
Quaking Houses *Dur* 106 A6
Quarley *Hants* 26 A4
Quarndon *Derbys* 72 A4
Quarr Hill *IOW* 14 D3
Quarrier's Village *Inver* 129 E2
Quarrington *Lincs* 74 A4
Quarrington Hill *Dur* 106 C5
Quarry Bank *W Mids* 58 B4
Quarrybank *Ches* 81 H1
Quarrywood *Moray* 156 D5
Quarter *N Ayrs* 118 D6
Quarter *S Lans* 120 B5
Quatford *Shrops* 57 G4
Quatt *Shrops* 57 H4
Quebec *Dur* 106 A5
Quedgeley *Gloucs* 38 C6
Queen Adelaide *Cambs* 63 E3
Queen Camel *Somset* 24 B2
Queen Charlton *Somset* 24 B6
Queen Dart *Devon* 22 A1
Queen Oak *Dorset* 24 C2
Queen Street *Kent* 17 H6
Queen Street *Wilts* 39 E3
Queen's Bower *IOW* 14 D2
Queen's Head *Shrops* 69 F3
Queen's Park *Beds* 50 A6
Queen's Park *Nhants* 49 F5
Queenborough *Kent* 30 C3
Queenhill *Worcs* 46 D3
Queensbury *W York* 90 B3
Queensferry *Flints* 81 E1
Queenslie *C Glas* 130 C2
Queenzieburn *N Lans* 130 C3
Quendon *Essex* 51 F4
Queniborough *Leics* 72 D1
Quenington *Gloucs* 39 F5
Quernmore *Lancs* 88 D6
Quernmore Park Hall *Lancs* .. 88 D6
Queslett *W Mids* 58 D5
Quethiock *Cnwll* 5 G2
Quick's Green *Berks* 40 D2
Quidenham *Norfk* 64 C4
Quidhampton *Hants* 26 C4
Quidhampton *Wilts* 25 F2
Quina Brook *Shrops* 69 G3
Quinbury End *Nhants* 48 D4
Quinton *Nhants* 49 F5
Quinton *W Mids* 58 C4
Quinton Green *Nhants* 49 F4
Quintrell Downs *Cnwll* 4 B2
Quither *Devon* 8 A3
Quixhall *Staffs* 71 F4
Quixwood *Border* 133 G1
Quoditch *Devon* 5 H6
Quorn *Leics* 72 C2
Quothquan *S Lans* 120 D3
Quoyburray *Ork* 169 c2
Quoyloo *Ork* 169 a3

R

Rabbit's Cross *Kent* 18 A6
Rableyheath *Herts* 50 C3
Raby *Cumb* 103 F5
Raby *Mersyd* 81 E3
Rachan Mill *Border* 121 F3
Rachub *Gwynd* 79 F1
Rackenford *Devon* 22 A1
Rackham *W Susx* 16 A3
Rackheath *Norfk* 77 F1
Racks *D & G* 111 E2
Rackwick *Ork* 169 a2
Radbourne *Derbys* 71 H4
Radcliffe *Gt Man* 82 C5
Radcliffe *Nthumb* 114 D6
Radcliffe on Trent *Notts* 72 D4
Radclive *Bucks* 49 E3
Radcot *Oxon* 39 G4
Raddery *Highld* 155 E5
Raddington *Somset* 22 C2
Radernie *Fife* 132 D6
Radford Semele *Warwks* 59 F2
Radlet *Somset* 23 E3
Radlett *Herts* 28 C6
Radley *Devon* 21 G3
Radley *Oxon* 40 D4
Radley Green *Essex* 51 G1
Radmore Green *Ches* 70 A6
Radnage *Bucks* 41 F4
Radstock *Somset* 24 B5
Radstone *Nhants* 48 D3
Radway *Warwks* 48 B4
Radway Green *Ches* 70 C5
Radwell *Beds* 61 F1
Radwell *Herts* 50 C4
Radwinter *Essex* 51 G4
Radwinter End *Essex* 51 G5
Radyr *Cardif* 36 B2
RAF College (Cranwell) *Lincs* .. 73 H5
Rafford *Moray* 156 C5
Ragdale *Leics* 72 D2
Ragdon *Shrops* 57 E4
Raginnis *Cnwll* 2 B2
Raglan *Mons* 37 E5
Ragnall *Notts* 85 F2
Raigbeg *Highld* 155 F2
Rainbow Hill *Worcs* 46 D5
Rainford *Mersyd* 81 G5
Rainham *Gt Lon* 29 F4
Rainham *Kent* 30 B3
Rainhill *Mersyd* 81 G4
Rainhill Stoops *Mersyd* 81 G4
Rainow *Ches* 82 D2

Rainsough *Gt Man* 82 C5
Rainton *N York* 97 G2
Rainworth *Notts* 72 D6
Raisbeck *Cumb* 95 G6
Raise *Cumb* 104 D5
Raisthorpe *N York* 92 B6
Rait *P & K* 140 B2
Raithby *Lincs* 86 C3
Raithby *Lincs* 86 D1
Raithwaite *N York* 107 H2
Rake *W Susx* 27 F2
Rakewood *Gt Man* 89 H1
Ralia *Highld* 146 B4
Ram *Carmth* 43 F4
Ram Hill *Gloucs* 38 B2
Ram Lane *Kent* 18 C6
Ramasaig *Highld* 150 B3
Rame *Cnwll* 3 B4
Rame *Cnwll* 5 H1
Rampisham *Dorset* 11 F5
Rampside *Cumb* 94 C1
Rampton *Cambs* 62 D2
Rampton *Notts* 85 F2
Ramsbottom *Gt Man* 89 F1
Ramsbury *Wilts* 39 G1
Ramscraigs *Highld* 167 E1
Ramsdean *Hants* 27 E1
Ramsdell *Hants* 26 D5
Ramsden *Oxon* 40 B6
Ramsden *Worcs* 47 E4
Ramsden Bellhouse *Essex* ... 29 H5
Ramsden Heath *Essex* 29 H6
Ramsey *Cambs* 62 B4
Ramsey *Essex* 53 F4
Ramsey *IOM* 174 m4
Ramsey Forty Foot *Cambs* .. 62 B4
Ramsey Heights *Cambs* ... 62 B4
Ramsey Island *Essex* 52 C1
Ramsey Mereside *Cambs* ... 62 B4
Ramsey St Mary's *Cambs* .. 62 B4
Ramsgate *Kent* 31 G2
Ramsgill *N York* 96 D2
Ramshaw *Dur* 105 F5
Ramsholt *Suffk* 53 G5
Ramshope *Nthumb* 112 D5
Ramshorn *Staffs* 71 F4
Ramsley *Devon* 8 C4
Ramsnest Common *Surrey* .. 27 H2
Ranby *Lincs* 86 C3
Ranby *Notts* 84 D3
Rand *Lincs* 86 A2
Randwick *Gloucs* 38 C5
Ranfurly *Rens* 129 E2
Rangemore *Staffs* 71 G2
Rangeworthy *Gloucs* 38 B3
Rank's Green *Essex* 52 A2
Rankinston *E Ayrs* 109 F6
Ranksborough *Rutlnd* 73 F1
Rann *Lancs* 89 F2
Rannoch Station *P & K* ... 138 B5
Ranscombe *Somset* 22 B4
Ranskill *Notts* 84 D3
Ranton *Staffs* 70 D2
Ranton Green *Staffs* 70 C2
Ranworth *Norfk* 77 F1
Raploch *Stirlg* 130 D5
Rapness *Ork* 169 c4
Rapps *Somset* 23 F1
Rascarrel *D & G* 102 B5
Rashfield *Ag & B* 128 C3
Rashwood *Worcs* 58 B2
Raskelf *N York* 97 H2
Rassau *Blae G* 36 C5
Rastrick *N York* 90 C2
Ratagan *Highld* 152 C1
Ratby *Leics* 60 A6
Ratcliffe Culey *Leics* 59 F5
Ratcliffe on Soar *Notts* 72 C3
Ratcliffe on the Wreake *Leics* . 72 D1
Ratfyn *Wilts* 25 G3
Rathen *Abers* 159 F5
Rathillet *Fife* 140 D2
Rathmell *N York* 89 F6
Ratho *C Edin* 131 H2
Ratho of Edin* 131 H2
Rathven *Moray* 157 F6
Ratlake *Hants* 26 B2
Ratley *Warwks* 48 B4
Ratling *Kent* 31 F1
Ratlinghope *Shrops* 56 D5
Rattan Row *Norfk* 75 E1
Rattar *Highld* 167 F6
Ratten Row *Cumb* 103 G4
Ratten Row *Cumb* 103 H5
Ratten Row *Lancs* 88 C4
Rattery *Devon* 7 E4
Rattlesden *Suffk* 64 B1
Ratton Village *E Susx* 17 G1
Rattray *P & K* 140 B4
Raughton *Cumb* 103 H5
Raughton Head *Cumb* 103 H5
Raunds *Nhants* 61 F3
Raven Meols *Mersyd* 81 E5
Ravenfield *S York* 84 C4
Ravenglass *Cumb* 94 B4
Raveningham *Norfk* 65 F3
Ravenscar *N York* 99 E5
Ravenscliffe *Staffs* 70 C5
Ravensdale *IOM* 174 l4
Ravensden *Beds* 50 B6
Ravenshead *Notts* 72 C5
Ravensmoor *Ches* 70 A5
Ravensthorpe *Nhants* 60 C2
Ravensthorpe *W York* 90 C2
Ravenstone *Bucks* 49 G4
Ravenstone *Leics* 72 B1
Ravenstonedale *Cumb* 95 H5
Ravenstruther *S Lans* 120 D4
Ravensworth *N York* 97 G6
Raw *N York* 99 E5
Rawcliffe *E R Yk* 91 H2
Rawcliffe *N York* 91 G5
Rawcliffe Bridge *E R Yk* .. 91 H2
Rawdon *W York* 90 B4
Rawling Street *Kent* 30 C2
Rawmarsh *S York* 84 B4
Rawnsley *Staffs* 71 E1
Rawreth *Essex* 30 A5

Rawridge *Devon* 10 B5
Rawtenstall *Lancs* 89 F2
Raydon *Suffk* 52 D5
Raylees *Nthumb* 113 F4
Rayleigh *Essex* 30 B5
Raymond's Hill *Devon* 10 D4
Rayne *Essex* 51 H3
Raynes Park *Gt Lon* 28 C3
Rea *Gloucs* 38 C6
Reach *Cambs* 63 E2
Read *Lancs* 89 F3
Reading *Berks* 41 E2
Reading Street *Kent* 18 C4
Reading Street *Kent* 31 G3
Reagill *Cumb* 104 C2
Rearquhar *Highld* 162 D3
Rearsby *Leics* 72 D1
Rease Heath *Shrops* 70 A5
Reay *Highld* 166 C5
Reculver *Kent* 31 F3
Red Ball *Somset* 22 D1
Red Bull *Ches* 70 C5
Red Cross *Cambs* 51 F6
Red Cross *Cnwll* 20 C1
Red Dial *Cumb* 103 F5
Red Hill *Dorset* 13 E4
Red Hill *Warwks* 47 G5
Red Lodge *Suffk* 63 F2
Red Lumb *Gt Man* 89 G1
Red Rock *Gt Man* 81 H6
Red Roses *Carmth* 33 F3
Red Row *T & W* 114 D5
Red Street *Staffs* 70 C5
Red Wharf Bay *IOA* 79 E3
Redberth *Pembks* 33 E2
Redbourn *Herts* 50 B2
Redbourne *Lincs* 85 G5
Redbrook *Gloucs* 37 F5
Redbrook *Wrexhm* 69 G4
Redbrook Street *Kent* 18 C5
Redburn *Highld* 156 B4
Redburn *Nthumb* 113 E1
Redcar *N York* 107 E3
Redcastle *D & G* 110 C1
Redcastle *Highld* 154 D4
Redding *Falk* 131 E3
Reddingmuirhead *Falk* ... 131 E3
Reddish *Gt Man* 82 D4
Redditch *Worcs* 58 C2
Rede *Suffk* 63 G1
Redenhall *Norfk* 65 E4
Redenham *Hants* 26 A4
Redesmouth *Nthumb* 113 F3
Redford *Abers* 149 E1
Redford *Angus* 141 F4
Redford *W Susx* 27 G2
Redfordgreen *Border* 121 H1
Redgate *Rhondd* 35 G3
Redgorton *P & K* 139 H3
Redgrave *Suffk* 64 C3
Redhill *Abers* 149 E5
Redhill *Herts* 50 D4
Redhill *Somset* 23 H6
Redhill *Surrey* 28 D1
Redisham *Suffk* 65 F4
Redland *Bristl* 37 G2
Redland *Ork* 169 b3
Redlingfield *Suffk* 64 D2
Redlingfield Green *Suffk* .. 64 D2
Redlynch *Somset* 24 C3
Redlynch *Wilts* 25 G1
Redmain *Cumb* 103 E3
Redmarley *Worcs* 57 H2
Redmarley D'Abitot *Gloucs* . 46 C2
Redmarshall *Dur* 106 C3
Redmile *Leics* 73 F4
Redmire *N York* 97 E4
Redmyre *Abers* 149 E2
Rednal *W Mids* 58 C3
Rednal *Shrops* 69 F3
Redpath *Border* 122 C3
Redpoint *Highld* 151 G6
Redruth *Cnwll* 2 D4
Redstocks *Wilts* 25 E5
Redstone *P & K* 140 B3
Redstone Cross *Pembks* .. 33 E3
Redvales *Gt Man* 82 C6
Redwick *Gloucs* 37 F3
Redwick *Newpt* 37 F3
Redworth *Dur* 106 B3
Reed *Herts* 51 E4
Reedham *Norfk* 65 G6
Reedness *E R Yk* 92 B2
Reeds Beck *Lincs* 86 B1
Reeds Holme *Lancs* 89 F2
Reepham *Lincs* 85 H2
Reepham *Norfk* 76 D2
Reeves Green *W Mids* 59 E3
Reiff *Highld* 160 D5
Reigate *Surrey* 28 C1
Reighton *N York* 99 G2
Reisque *Abers* 159 E1
Reiss *Highld* 167 G4
Rejerrah *Cnwll* 3 E5
Releath *Cnwll* 2 D3
Relubbus *Cnwll* 2 C3
Relugas *Moray* 156 M4
Remenham *Berks* 41 F3
Remenham Hill *Berks* 41 F2
Rempstone *Notts* 72 C2
Rendcomb *Gloucs* 39 E5
Rendham *Suffk* 65 F2
Rendlesham *Suffk* 53 G6
Renfrew *Rens* 129 F2
Renhold *Beds* 50 B6
Renishaw *Derbys* 84 B2
Rennington *Nthumb* 125 E3
Renton *W Duns* 129 E3
Renwick *Cumb* 104 C4
Repps *Norfk* 77 G2
Repton *Derbys* 71 H3
Resaurie *Highld* 155 E4
Rescassa *Cnwll* 3 G4
Rescorla *Cnwll* 3 H4
Resipole *Highld* 136 B6
Reskadinnick *Cnwll* 2 D4

Resolis *Highld* 155 E6
Resolven *Neath* 35 H4
Rest and be thankful *Ag & B* . 128 D6
Reston *Border* 123 F6
Restronguet *Cnwll* 3 F3
Reswallie *Angus* 141 E5
Reterth *Cnwll* 4 C2
Retew *Cnwll* 3 G5
Retford *Notts* 85 E3
Retire *Cnwll* 4 D2
Rettendon *Essex* 30 A6
Retyn *Cnwll* 4 B2
Revesby *Lincs* 74 C6
Rew *Devon* 7 E5
Rew *Devon* 6 D1
Rew Street *IOW* 14 C3
Rewe *Devon* 9 F4
Rexon *Devon* 5 H5
Reydon *Suffk* 65 G3
Reymerston *Norfk* 64 C6
Reynalton *Pembks* 33 E2
Reynoldston *Swans* 34 B3
Rezare *Cnwll* 5 G4
Rhadyr *Mons* 37 E4
Rhandirmwyn *Carmth* 43 H4
Rhayader *Powys* 55 G2
Rheindown *Highld* 154 C4
Rhes-y-cae *Flints* 80 D2
Rhewl *Denbgs* 68 C6
Rhewl *Denbgs* 68 D4
Rhewl Mostyn *Flints* 80 D3
Rhewl-fawr *Flints* 80 D3
Rhicarn *Highld* 164 B1
Rhiconich *Highld* 164 D4
Rhicullen *Highld* 162 D1
Rhigos *Rhondd* 35 G5
Rhireavach *Highld* 160 D3
Rhives *Highld* 163 E4
Rhiwbina *Cardif* 36 C2
Rhiwbryfdir *Gwynd* 67 F5
Rhiwderyn *Newpt* 36 D3
Rhiwen *Gwynd* 79 E1
Rhiwinder *Rhondd* 35 H3
Rhiwlas *Gwynd* 79 E1
Rhiwlas *Gwynd* 68 B4
Rhiwlas *Powys* 68 D3
Rhiwsaeson *Cardif* 36 B2
Rhode *Somset* 23 F3
Rhoden Green *Kent* 17 H6
Rhodes *Gt Man* 82 C5
Rhodes Minnis *Kent* 19 E6
Rhodesia *Notts* 84 C3
Rhodiad-y-brenin *Pembks* .. 32 B4
Rhonehouse *D & G* 102 B6
Rhoose *V Glam* 22 C6
Rhos *Carmth* 42 D3
Rhos *Denbgs* 68 D6
Rhos *Neath* 35 E5
Rhos *Powys* 45 E2
Rhos Haminiog *Cerdgn* ... 54 C2
Rhos Lligwy *IOA* 78 D3
Rhos-y-brithdir *Powys* 68 D2
Rhos-fawr *Gwynd* 66 C4
Rhos-on-Sea *Conwy* 79 H3
Rhos-y-garth *Cerdgn* 54 D3
Rhos-y-gwaliau *Gwynd* ... 68 B3
Rhos-y-llan *Gwynd* 66 B4
Rhos-y-meirch *Powys* 56 C2
Rhosbeirio *IOA* 78 C4
Rhoscefnhir *IOA* 79 E2
Rhoscolyn *IOA* 78 B2
Rhoscrowther *Pembks* 32 C2
Rhosesmor *Flints* 80 D1
Rhosgadfan *Gwynd* 67 E6
Rhosgoch *IOA* 78 D4
Rhosgoch *Powys* 45 E4
Rhoshill *Pembks* 42 B3
Rhoshirwaun *Gwynd* 66 B3
Rhoslan *Gwynd* 66 D4
Rhoslefain *Gwynd* 54 C6
Rhosllanerchrugog *Wrexhm* . 69 E5
Rhosmaen *Carmth* 43 F2
Rhosmeirch *IOA* 78 D2
Rhosneigr *IOA* 78 C2
Rhosnesni *Wrexhm* 69 F5
Rhosrobin *Wrexhm* 69 E5
Rhossili *Swans* 34 B3
Rhostryfan *Gwynd* 67 E6
Rhostyllen *Wrexhm* 69 E5
Rhosybol *IOA* 78 D4
Rhosygadfa *Shrops* 69 E3
Rhosymedre *Wrexhm* 69 E4
Rhu *Ag & B* 128 D3
Rhuallt *Denbgs* 80 C2
Rhubodach *Ag & B* 128 B2
Rhuddall Heath *Ches* 81 H1
Rhuddlan *Cerdgn* 43 E3
Rhuddlan *Denbgs* 80 C2
Rhulen *Powys* 44 D4
Rhunahaorine *Ag & B* ... 117 F5
Rhyd *Gwynd* 67 F5
Rhyd-Ddu *Gwynd* 67 E5
Rhyd-lydan *Conwy* 68 A5
Rhyd-uchaf *Gwynd* 68 A4
Rhyd-y pennau *Cerdgn* .. 54 D4
Rhyd-y-clafdy *Gwynd* 66 C3
Rhyd-y-foel *Conwy* 80 A2
Rhyd-y-groes *Gwynd* 79 E1
Rhyd-y-meirch *Mons* 36 D5
Rhyd-y-sarn *Gwynd* 67 F4
Rhyd-yr-onnen *Gwynd* ... 54 D6
Rhydargaeau *Carmth* 43 E3
Rhydcymerau *Carmth* 43 F3
Rhydd *Worcs* 46 D4
Rhydding *Neath* 35 E4
Rhydgaled *Conwy* 80 B1
Rhydlanfair *Conwy* 67 H5
Rhydlewis *Cerdgn* 42 D4
Rhydlios *Gwynd* 66 B3
Rhydowen *Cerdgn* 43 E4
Rhydroser *Cerdgn* 54 C2
Rhydspence *Herefs* 45 E4
Rhydtalog *Flints* 69 E6
Rhydycroesau *Shrops* 69 E3
Rhydyfelin *Cerdgn* 54 C3
Rhydyfelin *Rhondd* 36 B3
Rhydyfro *Neath* 35 E5
Rhydymain *Gwynd* 67 G2

Rhydymwyn *Flints* 80 D1
Rhyl *Denbgs* 80 B3
Rhymney *Caerph* 36 B5
Rhynd *P & K* 140 B2
Rhynie *Abers* 157 G2
Rhynie *Highld* 163 E2
Ribbesford *Worcs* 57 H3
Ribbleton *Lancs* 88 D3
Ribby *Lancs* 88 C3
Ribchester *Lancs* 89 E3
Riber *Derbys* 71 H6
Riby *Lincs* 86 B5
Riccall *N York* 91 G3
Riccarton *Border* 112 C4
Riccarton *E Ayrs* 119 F3
Rich's Holford *Somset* ... 22 D3
Richards Castle *Herefs* ... 57 E2
Richings Park *Bucks* 28 A4
Richmond *Gt Lon* 28 C3
Richmond *N York* 97 E5
Richmond *S York* 84 B3
Richmond Fort *Guern* ... 174 f2
Rickerscote *Staffs* 70 D2
Rickford *Somset* 23 H5
Rickham *Devon* 7 E1
Rickinghall *Suffk* 64 C3
Rickling *Essex* 51 F4
Rickling Green *Essex* 51 F4
Rickmansworth *Herts* 28 B5
Riddell *Border* 122 B2
Riddings *Cumb* 112 A2
Riddings *Derbys* 72 B5
Riddlecombe *Devon* 21 F2
Riddlesden *W York* 90 B4
Ridge *Dorset* 12 C3
Ridge *Herts* 28 C6
Ridge *Somset* 24 A5
Ridge *Wilts* 25 E2
Ridge Green *Surrey* 28 D1
Ridge Lane *Warwks* 59 F5
Ridge Row *Kent* 19 F6
Ridgebourne *Powys* 44 C5
Ridgehill *Somset* 24 A5
Ridgeway *Derbys* 72 A5
Ridgeway *Derbys* 84 B3
Ridgeway *Worcs* 47 F5
Ridgeway Cross *Herefs* .. 46 C4
Ridgewell *Essex* 52 A5
Ridgewood *E Susx* 17 F3
Ridgmont *Beds* 49 H3
Riding Mill *Nthumb* ... 114 B2
Ridley *Kent* 29 G2
Ridley *Nthumb* 113 E1
Ridley Green *Ches* 69 H5
Ridlington *Norfk* 77 F3
Ridlington *Rutlnd* 60 D6
Ridlington Street *Norfk* .. 77 F3
Ridsdale *Nthumb* 113 F3
Rievaulx *N York* 98 B3
Rievaulx Abbey *N York* .. 98 B3
Rigg *D & G* 111 G1
Riggend *N Lans* 130 D2
Righoul *Highld* 155 G4
Rigmadon Park *Cumb* ... 95 G3
Rigsby *Lincs* 87 E2
Rigside *S Lans* 120 C3
Riley Green *Lancs* 89 E2
Rileyhill *Staffs* 71 F1
Rilla Mill *Cnwll* 5 F3
Rillaton *Cnwll* 5 F3
Rillington *N York* 98 D2
Rimington *Lancs* 89 F4
Rimpton *Somset* 24 B1
Rimswell *E R Yk* 93 G2
Rinaston *Pembks* 32 D4
Rindleford *Shrops* 57 G5
Ring o'Bells *Lancs* 81 G6
Ring's End *Cambs* 62 C6
Ringford *D & G* 102 A6
Ringinglow *Derbys* 83 H3
Ringland *Norfk* 76 D1
Ringles Cross *E Susx* 17 F4
Ringlestone *Kent* 30 B2
Ringley *Gt Man* 82 C5
Ringmer *E Susx* 17 E3
Ringmore *Devon* 6 D2
Ringmore *Devon* 7 G5
Ringorm *Moray* 157 E2
Ringsfield *Suffk* 65 F4
Ringsfield Corner *Suffk* ... 65 F4
Ringshall *Bucks* 41 H6
Ringshall *Suffk* 52 D6
Ringshall Stocks *Suffk* ... 52 D6
Ringstead *Nhants* 61 F3
Ringstead *Norfk* 75 G4
Ringwood *Hants* 13 E5
Ringwould *Kent* 19 G6
Rinsey *Cnwll* 2 C2
Rinsey Croft *Cnwll* 2 D3
Ripe *E Susx* 17 F2
Ripley *Derbys* 72 B5
Ripley *Hants* 13 E4
Ripley *N York* 90 D6
Ripley *Surrey* 28 A2
Riplington *E R Yk* 92 C3
Riplington *Hants* 27 E2
Ripon *N York* 97 F2
Rippingale *Lincs* 74 A3
Ripple *Kent* 31 G1
Ripple *Worcs* 46 D3
Ripponden *W York* 90 B1
Risabus *Ag & B* 116 B5
Risbury *Herefs* 46 A5
Risby *Lincs* 92 C1
Risby *Suffk* 63 G2
Risca *Caerph* 36 C3
Rise *E R Yk* 93 E4
Riseden *E Susx* 17 G4
Riseden *Kent* 17 H5
Risegate *Lincs* 74 C3
Riseholme *Lincs* 85 G2
Risehow *Cumb* 102 D4
Riseley *Beds* 61 F2
Riseley *Berks* 27 E6
Rishangles *Suffk* 64 D2
Rishton *Lancs* 89 F3
Rishworth *W York* 90 B1
Rising Bridge *Lancs* 89 F2

307

Risley *Ches* 82 B4
Risley *Derbys* 72 B4
Risplith *N York* 97 F2
Rivar *Wilts* 26 A5
Rivenhall End *Essex* 52 B2
River *Kent* 19 F6
River *W Susx* 27 G1
River Bank *Cambs* 63 E2
Riverford *Highld* 154 D5
Riverhead *Kent* 29 F2
Rivers Corner *Dorset* 12 B6
Rivington *Lancs* 89 E1
Roachill *Devon* 22 A1
Road Ashton *Wilts* 24 D5
Road Green *Norfk* 65 E5
Roade *Nhants* 49 F4
Roadhead *Cumb* 112 B2
Roadmeetings *S Lans* 120 C4
Roadside *S Ayrs* 119 G1
Roadside *Highld* 167 E4
Roadwater *Somset* 22 C3
Roag *Highld* 150 C3
Roan of Craigoch *S Ayrs* 109 F5
Roast Green *Essex* 51 E4
Roath *Cardif* 36 C2
Roberton *Border* 112 B6
Roberton *S Lans* 120 D2
Robertsbridge *E Susx* 18 A4
Roberttown *W York* 90 C2
Robeston Wathen *Pembks* 33 E3
Robgill Tower *D & G* 111 G2
Robin Hill *Staffs* 70 D6
Robin Hood *Lancs* 81 G6
Robin Hood *W York* 90 D2
Robin Hood's Bay *N York* 99 E5
Robinhood End *Essex* 51 H4
Roborough *Devon* 21 F2
Roborough *Devon* 6 B4
Roby *Mersyd* 81 G4
Roby Mill *Lancs* 81 G5
Rocester *Staffs* 71 F4
Roch *Pembks* 32 C4
Roch Gate *Pembks* 32 C4
Rochdale *Gt Man* 82 D6
Roche *Cnwll* 4 C2
Rochester *Kent* 30 A3
Rochester *Nthumb* 113 E5
Rochford *Essex* 30 B5
Rochford *Worcs* 57 F2
Rock *Cnwll* 4 C3
Rock *Neath* 35 E4
Rock *Nthumb* 125 E3
Rock *W Susx* 16 B3
Rock *Worcs* 57 G2
Rock Ferry *Mersyd* 81 F3
Rock Hill *Worcs* 58 B2
Rockbeare *Devon* 9 G4
Rockbourne *Hants* 25 G1
Rockcliffe *Cumb* 111 H1
Rockcliffe *D & G* 102 C5
Rockcliffe Cross *Cumb* 111 H1
Rockend *Devon* 7 F4
Rockestal *Cnwll* 2 A2
Rockfield *Highld* 163 F2
Rockfield *Mons* 37 F6
Rockford *Devon* 21 H5
Rockford *Hants* 13 E5
Rockgreen *Shrops* 57 E3
Rockhampton *Gloucs* 37 G4
Rockhead *Cnwll* 4 D4
Rockhill *Shrops* 56 C3
Rockingham *Nhants* 61 E4
Rockland All Saints *Norfk* 64 B5
Rockland St Mary *Norfk* 65 F6
Rockland St Peter *Norfk* 64 B5
Rockley *Notts* 85 E2
Rockley *Wilts* 39 F1
Rockliffe *Lancs* 89 G2
Rockville *Ag & B* 128 D4
Rockwell End *Bucks* 41 F3
Rockwell Green *Somset* 22 D1
Rodborough *Gloucs* 38 C5
Rodbourne *Wilts* 39 F3
Rodbourne *Wilts* 38 D3
Rodd *Herefs* 45 F5
Roddam *Nthumb* 124 C3
Rodden *Dorset* 11 F3
Roddymoor *Dur* 106 A4
Rode *Somset* 24 D5
Rode Heath *Ches* 70 C6
Rode Heath *Ches* 82 D1
Rodel *W Isls* 168 c6
Roden *Shrops* 69 H2
Rodhuish *Somset* 22 C3
Rodington *Shrops* 69 H1
Rodington Heath *Shrops* 69 H1
Rodley *Gloucs* 38 B5
Rodley *W York* 90 C3
Rodmarton *Gloucs* 38 D4
Rodmell *E Susx* 17 E2
Rodmersham *Kent* 30 C2
Rodmersham Green *Kent* 30 C2
Rodney Stoke *Somset* 23 H4
Rodsley *Derbys* 71 G4
Rodway *Somset* 23 E3
Roe Cross *Gt Man* 83 E4
Roe Green *Gt Man* 82 C5
Roe Green *Herts* 50 C1
Roe Green *Herts* 50 D4
Roecliffe *N York* 97 G1
Roehampton *Gt Lon* 28 C3
Roffey *W Susx* 16 C5
Rogart *Highld* 162 D4
Rogate *W Susx* 27 F2
Roger Ground *Cumb* 94 D5
Rogerstone *Newpt* 36 D3
Roghadal *W Isls* 168 c6
Rogiet *Mons* 37 F3
Roke *Oxon* 40 D4
Roker *T & W* 115 H1
Rollesby *Norfk* 77 G2
Rolleston *Leics* 60 C5
Rolleston *Notts* 73 E5
Rolleston *Staffs* 71 G3
Rolston *E R Yk* 93 F4
Rolstone *Somset* 23 G5
Rolvenden *Kent* 18 B4
Rolvenden Layne *Kent* 18 B4

Romaldkirk *Dur* 105 G2
Roman Amphitheatre Caerleon *Newpt* 36 D3
Roman Baths & Pump Room *Somset* 24 C6
Romanby *N York* 97 G4
Romanno Bridge *Border* 121 F4
Romansleigh *Devon* 21 G3
Romden Castle *Kent* 18 C6
Romesdal *Highld* 150 D4
Romford *Dorset* 13 E6
Romford *Gt Lon* 29 F5
Romiley *Gt Man* 82 D4
Romney Street *Kent* 29 F2
Romsey *Hants* 14 B6
Romsley *Shrops* 57 H4
Romsley *Worcs* 58 C3
Ronachan *Ag & B* 117 F6
Rookhope *Dur* 105 F4
Rookley *IOW* 14 C2
Rookley Green *IOW* 14 C2
Rooks Bridge *Somset* 23 F4
Rooks Nest *Somset* 22 D3
Rookwith *N York* 97 E3
Roos *E R Yk* 93 G3
Roose *Cumb* 94 C2
Roosebeck *Cumb* 94 C2
Roothams Green *Beds* 61 G1
Ropley *Hants* 27 E2
Ropley Dean *Hants* 26 D2
Ropley Soke *Hants* 27 E3
Ropsley *Lincs* 73 G3
Rora *Abers* 159 F4
Rorrington *Shrops* 56 C5
Rosarie *Moray* 157 F4
Roscroggan *Cnwll* 2 D4
Rose *Cnwll* 3 E5
Rose Ash *Devon* 21 H3
Rose Green *Essex* 52 C3
Rose Green *Suffk* 52 C4
Rose Green *Suffk* 52 C5
Rose Green *W Susx* 15 G3
Rose Hill *E Susx* 17 E3
Rose Hill *Lancs* 89 G3
Roseacre *Lancs* 88 C3
Rosebank *S Lans* 120 C4
Rosebush *Pembks* 33 E5
Rosecare *Cnwll* 5 E5
Rosecliston *Cnwll* 4 B2
Rosedale Abbey *N York* 98 C4
Rosehall *Highld* 162 B4
Rosehearty *Abers* 159 E6
Rosehill *Shrops* 69 G2
Roseisle *Moray* 156 C6
Roselands *E Susx* 17 G1
Rosemarket *Pembks* 32 D2
Rosemarkie *Highld* 155 F5
Rosemary Lane *Devon* 10 B6
Rosemount *P & K* 140 B4
Rosenannon *Cnwll* 4 C2
Rosenithon *Cnwll* 3 E2
Roser's Cross *E Susx* 17 F3
Rosevean *Cnwll* 4 D2
Rosevine *Cnwll* 3 F3
Rosewarne *Cnwll* 2 D3
Rosewell *Mdloth* 121 G6
Roseworth *Dur* 106 D3
Roseworthy *Cnwll* 2 D4
Rosgill *Cumb* 104 B2
Roskhill *Highld* 150 C3
Roskorwell *Cnwll* 3 E2
Roskrow *Cnwll* 3 E3
Rosley *Cumb* 103 G5
Roslin *Mdloth* 132 B1
Rosliston *Derbys* 71 G2
Rosneath *Ag & B* 128 D3
Ross *D & G* 101 H5
Ross *Nthumb* 124 D5
Ross-on-Wye *Herefs* 46 B2
Rossett *Wrexhm* 69 F6
Rossett Green *N York* 90 D5
Rossington *S York* 84 D4
Rossland *Rens* 129 F2
Roster *Highld* 167 F2
Rostherne *Ches* 82 B3
Rosthwaite *Cumb* 103 F2
Roston *Derbys* 71 F4
Rosudgeon *Cnwll* 2 C3
Rosyth *Fife* 131 G3
Rothbury *Nthumb* 114 B6
Rotherby *Leics* 72 D2
Rotherfield *E Susx* 17 F4
Rotherfield Greys *Oxon* 41 E2
Rotherfield Peppard *Oxon* 41 E2
Rotherham *S York* 84 B4
Rothersthorpe *Nhants* 49 E5
Rotherwick *Hants* 27 E5
Rothes *Moray* 157 E4
Rothesay *Ag & B* 128 B1
Rothiebrisbane *Abers* 158 C3
Rothiemay *Moray* 157 H3
Rothiemurchus Lodge *Highld* 146 D5
Rothienorman *Abers* 158 C3
Rothley *Leics* 72 C1
Rothmaise *Abers* 158 C3
Rothwell *Lincs* 86 B5
Rothwell *Nhants* 60 D3
Rothwell *W York* 91 E2
Rothwell Haigh *W York* 90 D2
Rotsea *E R Yk* 92 D5
Rottal Lodge *Angus* 148 A1
Rottingdean *E Susx* 17 E2
Rottington *Cumb* 102 D1
Rou Island *Cumb* 94 C1
Roucan *D & G* 111 E3
Roud *IOW* 14 C2
Rough Close *Staffs* 70 D4
Rough Common *Kent* 31 E2
Rougham *Norfk* 76 A2
Rougham Green *Suffk* 64 B1
Roughlee *Lancs* 89 G4
Roughley *W Mids* 58 D5
Roughpark *Abers* 148 A6
Roughton *Lincs* 86 C1
Roughton *Norfk* 77 E4
Roughton *Shrops* 57 H5
Roughway *Kent* 29 G1

Round Bush *Herts* 28 B6
Round Green *Beds* 50 B3
Round Street *Kent* 29 G3
Roundbush *Essex* 30 B6
Roundbush Green *Essex* 51 G2
Roundham *Somset* 11 E6
Roundhay *W York* 90 D3
Rounds Green *W Mids* 58 C4
Roundstreet Common *W Susx* 16 A4
Roundway *Wilts* 25 F6
Roundyhill *Angus* 140 D5
Rous Lench *Worcs* 47 F5
Rousdon *Devon* 10 C4
Rousham *Oxon* 48 C2
Rout's Green *Bucks* 41 F4
Routenbeck *Cumb* 103 F3
Routenburn *N Ayrs* 118 D6
Routh *E R Yk* 93 E4
Row *Cnwll* 5 E4
Row *Cumb* 104 C4
Row *Cumb* 95 E4
Row Ash *Hants* 14 D5
Row Green *Essex* 52 A3
Row Town *Surrey* 28 A2
Rowanburn *D & G* 112 A2
Rowardennan Hotel *Stirlg* 129 E5
Rowardennan Lodge *Stirlg* 129 E5
Rowarth *Derbys* 83 E4
Rowberrow *Somset* 23 G5
Rowborough *IOW* 14 C2
Rowde *Wilts* 25 E5
Rowden *Devon* 8 C4
Rowen *Conwy* 79 G4
Rowfield *Derbys* 71 G5
Rowfoot *Nthumb* 104 D6
Rowford *Somset* 23 E2
Rowhedge *Essex* 52 D3
Rowhook *W Susx* 16 B5
Rowington *Warwks* 59 G1
Rowland *Derbys* 83 G2
Rowland's Castle *Hants* 15 E5
Rowland's Gill *T & W* 114 C1
Rowledge *Surrey* 27 F4
Rowley *Dur* 105 G5
Rowley *E R Yk* 92 D3
Rowley *Shrops* 56 C6
Rowley Green *W Mids* 59 F4
Rowley Hill *W York* 90 C1
Rowley Regis *W Mids* 58 C4
Rowlstone *Herefs* 45 F2
Rowly *Surrey* 16 A5
Rowner *Hants* 14 D4
Rowney Green *Worcs* 58 C2
Rownhams *Hants* 14 B5
Rowrah *Cumb* 103 E2
Rowsham *Bucks* 41 G6
Rowsley *Derbys* 83 G1
Rowstock *Oxon* 40 C3
Rowston *Lincs* 74 A6
Rowthorne *Derbys* 84 B1
Rowton *Ches* 81 G1
Rowton *Shrops* 69 F1
Rowton *Shrops* 70 A2
Rowton *Shrops* 56 D3
Roxburgh *Border* 122 D2
Roxby *Lincs* 92 C1
Roxby *N York* 107 G2
Roxton *Beds* 50 B6
Roxwell *Essex* 51 G1
Roy Bridge *Highld* 145 E2
Royal Botanic Gardens *C Edin* 141 E1
Royal Oak *Dur* 106 B3
Royal Oak *Lancs* 81 F5
Royal's Green *Ches* 70 A4
Roydhouse *W York* 83 G6
Roydon *Essex* 51 E2
Roydon *Norfk* 75 G2
Roydon *Norfk* 64 D3
Roydon Hamlet *Essex* 51 E1
Royston *Herts* 50 D5
Royston *S York* 84 A6
Royton *Gt Man* 82 D5
Ruabon *Wrexhm* 69 E4
Ruaig *Ag & B* 134 C4
Ruan High Lanes *Cnwll* 3 F4
Ruan Lanihorne *Cnwll* 3 F4
Ruan Major *Cnwll* 3 E1
Ruan Minor *Cnwll* 3 E1
Ruardean *Gloucs* 37 G6
Ruardean Hill *Gloucs* 37 G6
Ruardean Woodside *Gloucs* 37 G6
Rubery *Worcs* 58 C3
Rubha Ban *W Isls* 168 b2
Ruckcroft *Cumb* 104 B4
Ruckhall *Herefs* 45 G3
Ruckhall Common *Herefs* 45 G3
Ruckinge *Kent* 18 D5
Ruckland *Lincs* 86 D2
Ruckley *Shrops* 57 E5
Rudby *N York* 97 H5
Rudchester *Nthumb* 114 C2
Ruddington *Notts* 72 C3
Ruddle *Gloucs* 38 B5
Ruddlemoor *Cnwll* 3 G5
Rudford *Gloucs* 46 C1
Rudge *Somset* 24 D4
Rudgeway *Gloucs* 37 G3
Rudgwick *W Susx* 16 B5
Rudhall *Herefs* 46 B2
Rudheath *Ches* 82 B2
Rudley Green *Essex* 52 B1
Rudloe *Wilts* 38 C1
Rudry *Caerph* 36 C3
Rudston *E R Yk* 99 G2
Rudyard *Staffs* 70 D6
Ruecastle *Border* 122 C1
Rufford *Lancs* 88 C1
Rufforth *N York* 91 F3
Rug *Denbgs* 68 C4
Rugby *Warwks* 60 A3
Rugeley *Staffs* 71 E2
Ruggaton *Devon* 21 F5
Ruishton *Somset* 23 E2
Ruislip *Gt Lon* 28 B5
Rumbach *Moray* 157 F4
Rumbling Bridge *P & K* 131 F5

Rumburgh *Suffk* 65 F3
Rumby Hill *Dur* 106 A4
Rumford *Cnwll* 4 C3
Rumford *Falk* 131 F3
Rumney *Cardif* 36 C2
Rumwell *Somset* 23 E2
Runcorn *Ches* 81 G3
Runcton *W Susx* 15 G4
Runcton Holme *Norfk* 75 F1
Runfold *Surrey* 27 G4
Runhall *Norfk* 64 C6
Runham *Norfk* 77 G1
Runham *Norfk* 65 H6
Runnington *Somset* 22 D1
Runsell Green *Essex* 52 B1
Runshaw Moor *Lancs* 88 D1
Runswick *N York* 107 G2
Runtaleave *Angus* 147 H1
Runwell *Essex* 30 A5
Ruscombe *Berks* 41 F2
Rush Green *Ches* 82 B3
Rush Green *Essex* 53 E2
Rush Green *Gt Lon* 29 F5
Rush Green *Herts* 50 C3
Rush Green *Herts* 50 D3
Rushall *Herefs* 46 B3
Rushall *Norfk* 64 D4
Rushall *W Mids* 58 C5
Rushall *Wilts* 25 G5
Rushbrooke *Suffk* 64 B1
Rushbury *Shrops* 57 E5
Rushden *Herts* 50 D4
Rushden *Nhants* 61 F2
Rushenden *Kent* 30 C3
Rusher's Cross *E Susx* 17 G4
Rushett Common *Surrey* 16 A6
Rushford *Devon* 8 A2
Rushford *Norfk* 64 B3
Rushlake Green *E Susx* 17 G3
Rushmere *Suffk* 65 G4
Rushmere St Andrew *Suffk* 53 E5
Rushmoor *Surrey* 27 G3
Rushock *Herefs* 45 F5
Rushock *Worcs* 58 B2
Rusholme *Gt Man* 82 D4
Rushton *Ches* 81 H1
Rushton *Nhants* 60 D4
Rushton *Shrops* 57 F6
Rushton Spencer *Staffs* 82 D1
Rushwick *Worcs* 46 D5
Rushyford *Dur* 106 B4
Ruskie *Stirlg* 130 C5
Ruskington *Lincs* 74 A5
Rusland *Cumb* 94 D4
Rusper *W Susx* 16 C5
Ruspidge *Gloucs* 37 H5
Russ Hill *Surrey* 16 C5
Russel's Green *Suffk* 65 E3
Russell Green *Essex* 52 A2
Russell's Water *Oxon* 41 E3
Rusthall *Kent* 17 F5
Rustington *W Susx* 16 A2
Ruston *N York* 99 E3
Ruston Parva *E R Yk* 92 D6
Ruswarp *N York* 99 E6
Ruthall *Shrops* 57 F4
Rutherford *Border* 122 D2
Rutherglen *S Lans* 119 H6
Ruthernbridge *Cnwll* 4 D3
Ruthin *Denbgs* 68 D6
Ruthrieston *Aber C* 149 G5
Ruthven *Abers* 157 G4
Ruthven *Angus* 140 C5
Ruthven *Highld* 146 C4
Ruthven House *Angus* 140 C4
Ruthvoes *Cnwll* 4 C2
Ruthwaite *Cumb* 103 F4
Ruthwell *D & G* 111 E1
Ruxley Corner *Gt Lon* 29 F3
Ruxton Green *Herefs* 46 A1
Ruyton-XI-Towns *Shrops* 69 F2
Ryal *Nthumb* 114 B3
Ryall *Dorset* 10 D4
Ryall *Worcs* 46 D3
Ryarsh *Kent* 29 G2
Rycote *Oxon* 41 E5
Rydal *Cumb* 94 D5
Ryde *IOW* 14 D3
Rye *E Susx* 18 C3
Rye Cross *Worcs* 46 C3
Rye Foreign *E Susx* 18 C4
Rye Harbour *E Susx* 18 C3
Rye Street *Worcs* 46 C3
Ryebank *Shrops* 69 G3
Ryeford *Herefs* 46 B1
Ryehill *E R Yk* 93 F2
Ryeish Green *Nhants* 27 E6
Ryhall *Rutlnd* 73 H1
Ryhill *W York* 91 E1
Ryhope *T & W* 106 C6
Rylah *Derbys* 84 B1
Ryland *Lincs* 85 H3
Rylands *Notts* 72 C4
Rylstone *N York* 89 H5
Ryme Intrinseca *Dorset* 11 F6
Ryther *N York* 91 G3
Ryton *N York* 98 D2
Ryton *Shrops* 57 H6
Ryton *T & W* 114 C2
Ryton *Warwks* 59 G4
Ryton Woodside *T & W* 114 C2
Ryton-on-Dunsmore *Warwks* 59 G3

Sabden *Lancs* 89 F3
Sabine's Green *Essex* 29 F6
Sacombe *Herts* 50 D3
Sacombe Green *Herts* 50 D3
Sacriston *Dur* 106 B6
Sadberge *Dur* 106 C2
Saddell *Ag & B* 117 G4
Saddington *Leics* 60 C4

Saddle Bow *Norfk* 75 F2
Saddlescombe *W Susx* 16 D2
Sadgill *Cumb* 95 F5
Saffron Walden *Essex* 51 F4
Sageston *Pembks* 33 E2
Saham Hills *Norfk* 64 B6
Saham Toney *Norfk* 64 B6
Saighton *Ches* 81 G1
St Abbs *Border* 133 H2
St Agnes *Border* 133 F1
St Agnes *Cnwll* 3 E5
St Albans *Herts* 50 B1
St Allen *Cnwll* 3 F5
St Andrew *Guern* 174 g2
St Andrew's Major *V Glam* 36 C1
St Andrews *Fife* 141 E1
St Andrews Well *Dorset* 11 E4
St Ann's *D & G* 111 E4
St Ann's Chapel *Cnwll* 5 H3
St Ann's Chapel *Devon* 6 D2
St Anne's *Lancs* 88 B2
St Anthony *Cnwll* 3 E1
St Anthony's Hill *E Susx* 17 G1
St Arvans *Mons* 37 F4
St Asaph *Denbgs* 80 C2
St Athan *V Glam* 22 C6
St Aubin *Jersey* 174 b2
St Austell *Cnwll* 3 H5
St Bees *Cumb* 102 D1
St Blazey *Cnwll* 3 H5
St Blazey Gate *Cnwll* 3 H5
St Boswells *Border* 122 C2
St Brelade *Jersey* 174 a2
St Brelade's Bay *Jersey* 174 a1
St Breock *Cnwll* 4 C3
St Breward *Cnwll* 5 E4
St Briavels *Gloucs* 37 G5
St Bride's Major *V Glam* 35 F2
St Brides *Pembks* 32 B3
St Brides Netherwent *Mons* 37 E3
St Brides super-Ely *V Glam* 36 B2
St Brides Wentlooge *Newpt* 36 D2
St Budeaux *Devon* 6 B3
St Buryan *Cnwll* 2 B2
St Catherine *Somset* 38 C1
St Catherines *Ag & B* 128 C6
St Chloe *Gloucs* 38 C4
St Clears *Carmth* 33 G3
St Cleer *Cnwll* 5 F3
St Clement *Cnwll* 3 F4
St Clement *Jersey* 174 d1
St Clether *Cnwll* 5 F4
St Colmac *Ag & B* 128 B2
St Columb Major *Cnwll* 4 C2
St Columb Minor *Cnwll* 4 B2
St Columb Road *Cnwll* 4 C2
St Combs *Abers* 159 F5
St Cross South Elmham *Suffk* 65 E4
St Cyrus *Abers* 141 G6
St David's *P & K* 139 G2
St David's *Pembks* 32 B4
St Day *Cnwll* 3 E4
St Decumans *Somset* 22 D3
St Dennis *Cnwll* 4 C2
St Devereux *Herefs* 45 G2
St Dogmaels *Cerdgn* 42 B4
St Dogwells *Pembks* 32 D4
St Dominick *Cnwll* 5 G3
St Donats *V Glam* 35 G1
St Edith's Marsh *Wilts* 25 E6
St Endellion *Cnwll* 4 D4
St Enoder *Cnwll* 3 F5
St Erme *Cnwll* 3 F5
St Erney *Cnwll* 5 G2
St Erth *Cnwll* 2 C3
St Erth Praze *Cnwll* 2 C3
St Ervan *Cnwll* 4 C3
St Ewe *Cnwll* 3 G4
St Fagans *Cardif* 36 B2
St Fagans Welsh Life Museum *Cardif* 36 B2
St Fergus *Abers* 159 G4
St Fillans *P & K* 138 D2
St Florence *Pembks* 33 E2
St Gennys *Cnwll* 5 E6
St George *Conwy* 80 B2
St George's *V Glam* 36 B2
St George's Hill *Surrey* 28 B2
St Georges *Somset* 23 F5
St Germans *Cnwll* 5 G2
St Giles in the Wood *Devon* 21 E2
St Giles-on-the-Heath *Cnwll* 5 G5
St Gluvia's *Cnwll* 3 E3
St Harmon *Powys* 55 G3
St Helen Auckland *Dur* 106 A3
St Helena *Norfk* 77 E2
St Helens *Cumb* 102 D3
St Helens *E Susx* 18 B3
St Helens *IOW* 14 D2
St Helens *Mersyd* 81 G4
St Helier *Gt Lon* 28 C3
St Helier *Jersey* 174 c2
St Hilary *Cnwll* 2 C3
St Hilary *V Glam* 35 G1
St Hill *Devon* 10 A5
St Hill *W Susx* 17 E3
St Illtyd *Blae G* 36 C4
St Ippollitts *Herts* 50 C3
St Ishmael's *Pembks* 32 C2
St Issey *Cnwll* 4 C3
St Ive *Cnwll* 5 G3
St Ives *Cambs* 62 B2
St Ives *Cnwll* 2 C4
St Ives *Dorset* 13 E5
St James *Norfk* 77 F2
St James South Elmham *Suffk* 65 F3
St James's End *Nhants* 49 F5
St John *Cnwll* 5 H1
St John *Jersey* 174 b3
St John's *IOM* 174 k3
St John's Chapel *Devon* 21 E3
St John's Chapel *Dur* 105 E4
St John's Fen End *Norfk* 75 F1
St John's Highway *Norfk* 75 F1
St John's Kirk *S Lans* 120 D3
St John's Town of Dalry *D & G* 109 H3
St John's Wood *Gt Lon* 28 D4
St Johns *Dur* 105 G3

Place	Page	Grid
St Johns Kent	29	F2
St Johns Surrey	27	H5
St Johns Worcs	46	D5
St Jude's IOM	174	m5
St Just Cnwll	2	A3
St Just Lane Cnwll	3	F3
St Just-in-Roseland Cnwll	3	F3
St Katherines Abers	158	D2
St Keverne Cnwll	3	E2
St Kew Cnwll	4	D4
St Kew Highway Cnwll	4	D3
St Keyne Cnwll	5	F2
St Lawrence Cnwll	4	D3
St Lawrence Essex	52	C1
St Lawrence IOW	14	D1
St Lawrence Jersey	174	b2
St Lawrence Kent	31	G3
St Leonard's Street Kent	29	G2
St Leonards Bucks	41	G5
St Leonards Dorset	13	E5
St Leonards E Susx	18	B2
St Levan Cnwll	2	A2
St Lythans V Glam	36	B1
St Mabyn Cnwll	4	D3
St Madoes P & K	140	B2
St Margaret South Elmham Suffk	65	F4
St Margaret's at Cliffe Kent	19	G6
St Margaret's Hope Ork	169	b2
St Margarets Herefs	45	F3
St Margarets Herts	51	E2
St Marks IOM	174	I2
St Martin Cnwll	5	F1
St Martin Cnwll	3	E2
St Martin Guern	174	g1
St Martin Jersey	174	d2
St Martin's P & K	140	B3
St Martin's Moor Shrops	69	E4
St Martins Shrops	69	E4
St Mary Jersey	174	b3
St Mary Bourne Hants	26	B4
St Mary Church V Glam	35	G1
St Mary Cray Gt Lon	29	F3
St Mary Hill V Glam	35	G2
St Mary in the Marsh Kent	18	D4
St Mary's Ork	169	c2
St Mary's Bay Kent	18	D4
St Mary's Grove Somset	37	F1
St Mary's Hoo Kent	30	B4
St Marychurch Devon	7	F4
St Maughans Mons	37	F6
St Maughans Green Mons	37	F6
St Mawes Cnwll	3	F3
St Mawgan Cnwll	4	B2
St Mellion Cnwll	5	G2
St Mellons Cardif	36	C2
St Merryn Cnwll	4	C3
St Mewan Cnwll	3	G5
St Michael Caerhays Cnwll	3	G4
St Michael Church Somset	23	F2
St Michael Penkevil Cnwll	3	F4
St Michael South Elmham Suffk	65	F4
St Michael's on Wyre Lancs	88	C4
St Michaels Kent	18	B5
St Michaels Worcs	57	F2
St Minver Cnwll	4	C4
St Monans Fife	132	D5
St Neot Cnwll	5	E3
St Neots Cambs	61	H1
St Nicholas Pembks	32	C5
St Nicholas V Glam	36	B2
St Nicholas at Wade Kent	31	F3
St Ninians Stirlg	130	D4
St Olaves Norfk	65	G5
St Osyth Essex	53	E2
St Ouen Jersey	174	a2
St Owens Cross Herefs	46	A2
St Paul's Walden Herts	50	C3
St Pauls Cray Gt Lon	29	F3
St Peter Jersey	174	b2
St Peter Port Guern	174	g2
St Peter's Guern	174	f1
St Peter's Kent	31	G3
St Peter's Hill Cambs	62	B3
St Petrox Cnwll	32	D1
St Pinnock Cnwll	5	F2
St Quivox S Ayrs	119	E2
St Ruan Cnwll	3	E1
St Sampson Guern	174	h3
St Saviour Guern	174	f2
St Saviour Jersey	174	c2
St Stephen Cnwll	3	G5
St Stephen's Coombe Cnwll	3	G5
St Stephens Cnwll	5	G4
St Stephens Cnwll	5	H2
St Teath Cnwll	4	D4
St Tudy Cnwll	4	D4
St Twynnells Pembks	32	D1
St Veep Cnwll	5	E1
St Vigeans Angus	141	F4
St Wenn Cnwll	4	C2
St Weonards Herefs	45	H2
St y-Nyll V Glam	36	B2
Saintbury Gloucs	47	G3
Salachail Ag & B	137	E5
Salcombe Devon	7	E1
Salcombe Regis Devon	10	B3
Salcott Essex	52	C2
Sale Gt Man	82	C4
Sale Green Worcs	47	E5
Saleby Lincs	87	E2
Salehurst E Susx	18	A4
Salem Carmth	43	F2
Salem Cerdgn	54	D4
Salem Gwynd	67	E6
Salen Ag & B	135	H4
Salen Highld	136	B3
Salesbury Lancs	89	E3
Salford Beds	49	G3
Salford Gt Man	82	C4
Salford Oxon	48	A2
Salford Priors Warwks	47	F4
Salfords Surrey	16	D6
Salhouse Norfk	77	F1
Saline Fife	131	F4
Salisbury Wilts	25	G2
Salisbury Cathedral Wilts	25	G2
Salkeld Dykes Cumb	104	B4
Salle Norfk	76	D2
Salmonby Lincs	86	D2
Salperton Gloucs	47	F1
Salph End Beds	50	B6
Salsburgh N Lans	120	C6
Salt Staffs	70	D3
Salt Cotes Cumb	103	F5
Salta Cumb	103	E5
Saltaire W York	90	C3
Saltash Cnwll	5	H2
Saltburn Highld	155	E6
Saltburn-by-the-Sea N York	107	F3
Saltby Leics	73	F3
Saltcoats Cumb	94	B5
Saltcoats N Ayrs	118	D4
Saltcotes Lancs	88	B2
Saltdean E Susx	17	E2
Salterbeck Cumb	102	D3
Salterforth Lancs	89	G4
Salterswall Ches	82	A1
Salterton Wilts	25	G3
Saltfleet Lincs	87	E4
Saltfleetby All Saints Lincs	87	E4
Saltfleetby St Clement Lincs	87	E4
Saltfleetby St Peter Lincs	87	E4
Salford Somset	24	B6
Salthouse Norfk	76	D4
Saltley W Mids	58	D4
Saltmarsh Newpt	37	E2
Saltmarshe E R Yk	92	B2
Saltney Flints	81	F1
Salton N York	98	C3
Saltrens Devon	21	E3
Saltwick Nthumb	114	C3
Saltwood Kent	19	E5
Salvington W Susx	16	B2
Salwarpe Worcs	46	D5
Salwayash Worcs	11	E4
Sambourne Warwks	47	F5
Sambrook Shrops	70	B2
Samlesbury Lancs	88	D3
Samlesbury Bottoms Lancs	89	E2
Sampford Arundel Somset	22	D1
Sampford Brett Somset	22	D3
Sampford Courtenay Devon	8	C5
Sampford Moor Somset	22	D1
Sampford Peverell Devon	9	G6
Sampford Spiney Devon	6	C5
Samson's Corner Essex	52	D2
Samsonlane Ork	169	c3
Samuelston E Loth	132	D2
Sanaigmore Ag & B	126	A2
Sancreed Cnwll	2	B3
Sancton E R Yk	92	C3
Sand Somset	23	G4
Sand Hills W York	91	E3
Sand Hole E R Yk	92	B3
Sand Hutton N York	91	H5
Sand Side Cumb	94	C3
Sandaig Highld	143	G4
Sandal Magna W York	91	E1
Sandale Cumb	103	F4
Sandavore Highld	142	D2
Sanday Airport Ork	169	d4
Sandbach Ches	70	C6
Sandbank Ag & B	128	C3
Sandbanks Dorset	12	D3
Sandend Abers	157	G6
Sanderstead Gt Lon	28	D2
Sandford Cumb	104	D2
Sandford Devon	9	E5
Sandford Dorset	12	C3
Sandford Hants	13	E5
Sandford IOW	14	D2
Sandford S Lans	120	B4
Sandford Shrops	69	F2
Sandford Shrops	69	H3
Sandford Somset	23	G5
Sandford Orcas Dorset	24	B1
Sandford St Martin Oxon	48	B2
Sandford-on-Thames Oxon	40	D4
Sandgate Kent	19	F5
Sandhaven Abers	159	E6
Sandhead D & G	100	B5
Sandhills Dorset	11	F5
Sandhills Dorset	11	G6
Sandhills Oxon	40	D5
Sandhills Surrey	27	G3
Sandhills W Mids	58	D6
Sandhoe Nthumb	113	G1
Sandhole Ag & B	128	B5
Sandholme E R Yk	92	B3
Sandholme Lincs	74	D4
Sandhurst Berks	27	F5
Sandhurst Gloucs	46	D1
Sandhurst Kent	18	B4
Sandhurst Cross Kent	18	B4
Sandhutton N York	97	G3
Sandiacre Derbys	72	B4
Sandilands Lincs	87	F3
Sandiway Ches	82	A2
Sandleheath Hants	13	E6
Sandleigh Oxon	40	C4
Sandley Dorset	24	C2
Sandling Kent	30	A2
Sandlow Green Ches	82	C1
Sandness Shet	169	g3
Sandon Essex	52	A1
Sandon Herts	50	D4
Sandon Staffs	70	D3
Sandon Bank Staffs	70	D3
Sandown IOW	14	D2
Sandplace Cnwll	5	F2
Sandridge Herts	50	C2
Sandridge Wilts	25	E6
Sandringham Norfk	75	G3
Sands Bucks	41	G4
Sandsend N York	107	H2
Sandside Cumb	95	E3
Sandtoft Lincs	85	E5
Sandway Kent	30	C1
Sandwich Kent	31	G2
Sandwick Cumb	104	A2
Sandwick Shet	169	j2
Sandwick W Isls	168	f8
Sandwith Cumb	102	D2
Sandwith Newtown Cumb	102	D1
Sandy Beds	50	C6
Sandy Bank Lincs	74	C5
Sandy Cross E Susx	17	G3
Sandy Cross Herefs	46	B5
Sandy Haven Pembks	32	C2
Sandy Lane W York	90	B3
Sandy Lane Wilts	38	D1
Sandy Lane Wrexhm	69	F4
Sandy Park Devon	8	D4
Sandycroft Flints	81	F1
Sandyford D & G	111	F4
Sandygate Devon	9	E2
Sandygate IOM	174	m5
Sandyhills D & G	102	C6
Sandylands Lancs	88	C6
Sandylane Staffs	70	B4
Sandylane Swans	34	C3
Sandysike Cumb	112	A1
Sandyway Herefs	45	H2
Sangobeg Highld	165	E5
Sangomore Highld	165	E5
Sankey Bridges Ches	81	H3
Sankyn's Green Worcs	57	H2
Sanna Bay Highld	142	D1
Sanndabhaig W Isls	168	f8
Sannox N Ayrs	118	B4
Sanquhar D & G	110	B6
Santon Cumb	94	B5
Santon IOM	174	l2
Santon Bridge Cumb	94	B5
Santon Downham Suffk	63	G4
Sapcote Leics	59	H5
Sapey Common Herefs	57	G2
Sapiston Suffk	64	B3
Sapley Cambs	62	B3
Sapperton Derbys	71	G3
Sapperton Gloucs	38	D5
Sapperton Lincs	73	H3
Saracen's Head Lincs	74	D2
Sarclet Highld	167	G3
Sarisbury Hants	14	C4
Sarn Brdgnd	35	F3
Sarn Gwynd	66	B3
Sarn Powys	55	G5
Sarn Powys	56	B4
Sarn-bach Gwynd	66	C3
Sarn-wen Powys	69	E2
Sarnau Carmth	33	G3
Sarnau Cerdgn	42	C4
Sarnau Gwynd	68	B4
Sarnau Powys	69	E2
Sarnau Powys	44	C2
Sarnesfield Herefs	45	F4
Saron Carmth	42	D3
Saron Carmth	34	D5
Saron Gwynd	79	E1
Saron Gwynd	66	D6
Sarratt Herts	28	A6
Sarre Kent	31	F2
Sarsden Oxon	48	A1
Sarson Hants	26	A4
Satley Dur	105	H4
Satmar Kent	19	F5
Satron N York	96	C5
Satterleigh Devon	21	G3
Satterthwaite Cumb	94	D4
Satwell Oxon	41	E3
Sauchen Abers	149	E5
Saucher P & K	140	B3
Sauchieburn Abers	148	D1
Saul Gloucs	38	B5
Saundby Notts	85	E3
Saundersfoot Pembks	33	F2
Saunderton Bucks	41	F4
Saunton Devon	21	E4
Sausthorpe Lincs	86	D2
Saveock Water Cnwll	3	E4
Saverley Green Staffs	71	E4
Savile Town W York	90	D2
Sawbridge Warwks	59	H2
Sawbridgeworth Herts	51	F2
Sawdon N York	99	E3
Sawley Derbys	72	B3
Sawley Lancs	89	F4
Sawley N York	97	F2
Sawston Cambs	51	F6
Sawtry Cambs	61	H4
Saxby Leics	73	F2
Saxby Lincs	85	H3
Saxby All Saints Lincs	92	D1
Saxelbye Leics	73	E2
Saxham Street Suffk	64	C1
Saxilby Lincs	85	F2
Saxlingham Norfk	76	C4
Saxlingham Green Norfk	65	E5
Saxlingham Nethergate Norfk	65	E5
Saxlingham Thorpe Norfk	65	E5
Saxmundham Suffk	65	F2
Saxon Street Cambs	63	F1
Saxondale Notts	72	D4
Saxtead Suffk	65	E2
Saxtead Green Suffk	65	E2
Saxtead Little Green Suffk	65	E2
Saxthorpe Norfk	76	D3
Saxton N York	91	F3
Sayers Common W Susx	16	D3
Scackleton N York	98	B2
Scaftworth Notts	84	D4
Scagglethorpe N York	98	D2
Scalasaig Ag & B	126	C4
Scalby E R Yk	92	B2
Scalby N York	99	F4
Scald End Beds	61	F1
Scaldwell Nhants	60	D3
Scale Houses Cumb	104	C5
Scaleby Cumb	112	B1
Scalebyhill Cumb	112	B1
Scales Cumb	103	G3
Scales Cumb	94	C2
Scalesceugh Cumb	104	A5
Scalford Leics	73	E2
Scaling N York	107	G2
Scaling Dam N York	107	G2
Scalloway Shet	169	h2
Scamblesby Lincs	86	C2
Scammonden W York	90	B1
Scamodale Highld	143	H1
Scampston N York	98	D2
Scampton Lincs	85	G3
Scaniport Highld	154	D3
Scapegoat Hill W York	90	B1
Scarborough N York	99	F4
Scarcewater Cnwll	3	G5
Scarcliffe Derbys	84	C1
Scarcroft W York	91	E4
Scarcroft Hill W York	91	E4
Scarfskerry Highld	167	F6
Scargill Dur	105	G1
Scarinish Ag & B	134	B4
Scarisbrick Lancs	81	F6
Scarness Cumb	103	F3
Scarning Norfk	76	C1
Scarrington Notts	73	E4
Scarth Hill Lancs	81	F5
Scarthingwell N York	91	F3
Scartho Lincs	86	C5
Scatsta Airport Shet	169	h4
Scawby Lincs	85	G5
Scawsby S York	84	C5
Scawthorpe S York	84	C5
Scawton N York	98	A3
Scayne's Hill W Susx	17	E4
Scethrog Powys	44	D2
Scholar Green Ches	70	C6
Scholes Gt Man	82	A5
Scholes S York	84	B4
Scholes W York	83	F5
Scholes W York	90	C2
Scholes W York	91	E3
Scholes W York	91	E2
Scholey Hill W York	91	E2
School Aycliffe Dur	106	B3
School Green Ches	82	A1
School Green W York	90	B3
School House Dorset	10	D5
Schoolgreen Berks	27	E6
Scissett W York	83	G6
Scleddau Pembks	32	D5
Sco Ruston Norfk	77	F2
Scofton Notts	84	D3
Scole Norfk	64	D3
Scone P & K	140	A2
Sconser Highld	151	E2
Scoonie Fife	132	C5
Scopwick Lincs	74	A6
Scoraig Highld	160	D3
Scorborough E R Yk	92	D4
Scorrier Cnwll	3	E4
Scorriton Devon	6	D4
Scorton Lancs	88	C4
Scorton N York	97	F5
Scot Hay Staffs	70	C5
Scot Lane End Gt Man	82	A6
Scot's Gap Nthumb	114	B4
Scotby Cumb	104	A6
Scotch Corner N York	97	E5
Scotforth Lancs	88	C5
Scothern Lincs	85	H2
Scotland Lincs	73	G3
Scotland W York	90	C4
Scotland Gate T & W	114	D4
Scotlandwell P & K	131	H5
Scotscalder Station Highld	167	E4
Scotsdike Cumb	112	A2
Scotsmill Abers	158	B1
Scotstoun C Glas	129	G2
Scotswood T & W	114	D2
Scott Willoughby Lincs	73	H4
Scotter Lincs	85	F5
Scotterthorpe Lincs	85	F5
Scottlethorpe Lincs	73	H2
Scotton Lincs	85	F5
Scotton N York	97	E4
Scotton N York	90	D6
Scottow Norfk	77	F2
Scoulton Norfk	64	B5
Scounslow Green Staffs	71	F3
Scourie Highld	164	C3
Scourie More Highld	164	C3
Scousburgh Shet	169	h1
Scouthead Gt Man	83	E5
Scrabster Highld	167	E5
Scraesburgh Border	122	D1
Scrafield Lincs	86	C2
Scrainwood Nthumb	124	C2
Scrane End Lincs	74	D4
Scraptoft Leics	60	C6
Scratby Norfk	77	H1
Scrayingham N York	92	A6
Scrays E Susx	18	A3
Scredington Lincs	74	A4
Scremby Lincs	87	E1
Scremerston Nthumb	123	G4
Screveton Notts	73	E4
Scrivelsby Lincs	86	C1
Scriven N York	91	E5
Scrooby Notts	84	D4
Scropton Derbys	71	G3
Scrub Hill Lincs	74	C6
Scruschloch Angus	140	B5
Scruton N York	97	F4
Scuggate Cumb	112	B2
Scullomie Highld	165	G4
Sculthorpe Norfk	76	B3
Scunthorpe Lincs	85	F6
Scurlage Swans	34	B3
Sea Somset	10	D6
Sea Palling Norfk	77	G3
Seaborough Dorset	11	E5
Seabridge Staffs	70	C4
Seabrook Kent	19	E5
Seaburn T & W	115	F1
Seacombe Mersyd	81	E4
Seacroft Lincs	75	F6
Seacroft W York	91	E3
Seadyke Lincs	74	D4
Seafield Highld	151	E3
Seafield W Loth	131	F2
Seaford E Susx	17	F1
Seaforth Mersyd	81	E4
Seagrave Leics	72	D2
Seagry Heath Wilts	38	D2
Seaham Dur	106	D6
Seahouses Nthumb	125	E4
Seal Kent	29	F2
Seal Sands Dur	107	E3
Seale Surrey	27	G4
Seamer N York	106	D3
Seamer N York	99	F3
Seamill N Ayrs	118	D4
Searby Lincs	86	A5
Seasalter Kent	30	D2
Seascale Cumb	94	A5
Seathwaite Cumb	103	F1
Seathwaite Cumb	94	C4
Seatle Cumb	94	D3
Seatoller Cumb	103	F1
Seaton Cnwll	5	G1
Seaton Cumb	102	D3
Seaton Devon	10	C4
Seaton Dur	106	C6
Seaton E R Yk	93	E4
Seaton Kent	31	F3
Seaton Nthumb	115	E3
Seaton Rutlnd	61	E5
Seaton Burn T & W	114	D3
Seaton Carew Dur	107	E4
Seaton Delaval Nthumb	115	E3
Seaton Ross E R Yk	92	B4
Seaton Sluice Nthumb	115	E3
Seatown Dorset	11	E4
Seave Green N York	98	A5
Seaview IOW	14	D3
Seaville Cumb	103	F5
Seavington St Mary Somset	10	D6
Seavington St Michael Somset	10	D6
Sebastopol Torfn	36	D4
Sebergham Cumb	103	G4
Seckington Warwks	59	E6
Sedbergh Cumb	95	G4
Sedbury Gloucs	37	F4
Sedbusk N York	96	B4
Sedge Fen Suffk	63	F4
Sedgeberrow Worcs	47	F3
Sedgebrook Lincs	73	F4
Sedgefield Dur	106	C4
Sedgeford Norfk	75	G4
Sedgehill Wilts	24	D2
Sedgley W Mids	58	B5
Sedgley Park Gt Man	82	C5
Sedgwick Cumb	95	F3
Sedlescombe E Susx	18	A3
Sedrup Bucks	41	F5
Seed Kent	30	C2
Seend Wilts	25	E5
Seend Cleeve Wilts	25	E5
Seer Green Bucks	41	H3
Seething Norfk	65	F5
Sefton Mersyd	81	F5
Sefton Town Mersyd	81	F5
Seghill Nthumb	114	D3
Seighford Staffs	70	D2
Seion Gwynd	79	E1
Seisdon Staffs	58	A5
Selattyn Shrops	69	E3
Selborne Hants	27	F3
Selby N York	91	G3
Selham W Susx	15	G6
Selhurst Gt Lon	28	D3
Selkirk Border	122	B2
Sellack Herefs	46	A2
Sellafirth Shet	169	j5
Sellan Cnwll	2	B3
Sellick's Green Somset	23	E1
Sellindge Kent	19	E5
Selling Kent	30	D2
Sells Green Wilts	25	E5
Selly Oak W Mids	58	C4
Selmeston E Susx	17	F2
Selsdon Gt Lon	28	D2
Selsey W Susx	15	G3
Selsfield Common W Susx	16	D5
Selside Cumb	95	F5
Selside N York	96	A2
Selsley Gloucs	38	C5
Selsted Kent	19	F6
Selston Notts	72	B5
Selworthy Somset	22	B4
Semer Suffk	52	D5
Semington Wilts	24	D5
Semley Wilts	24	D2
Sempringham Lincs	74	B3
Send Surrey	28	A2
Send Marsh Surrey	28	A2
Senghenydd Caerph	36	B3
Sennen Cnwll	2	A2
Sennen Cove Cnwll	2	A2
Sennybridge Powys	44	B2
Serlby Notts	84	D4
Sessay N York	97	H2
Setchey Norfk	75	G1
Setley Hants	13	G5
Seton Mains E Loth	132	C3
Settle N York	96	A1
Settlingstones Nthumb	113	F2
Settrington N York	98	D2
Seven Ash Somset	22	D3
Seven Kings Gt Lon	29	E5
Seven Sisters Neath	35	F5
Seven Springs Gloucs	38	D6
Seven Star Green Essex	52	C3
Seven Wells Gloucs	47	G3
Sevenhampton Gloucs	47	F1
Sevenhampton Wilts	39	G3
Sevenoaks Kent	29	F1
Sevenoaks Weald Kent	29	F1
Severn Beach Gloucs	37	F3
Severn Stoke Worcs	46	D4
Sevick End Beds	50	B6
Sevington Kent	18	D5
Sewards End Essex	51	F4
Sewardstonebury Gt Lon	29	E6
Sewell Beds	49	H1
Sewerby E R Yk	99	H2
Seworgan Cnwll	3	E3
Sewstern Leics	73	F2
Sexhow N York	97	H5
Sezincote Gloucs	47	G2
Sgiogarstaigh W Isls	168	j9
Shabbington Bucks	41	E5
Shackerstone Leics	59	G6
Shacklecross Derbys	72	B3
Shackleford Surrey	27	G4
Shade W York	89	H2
Shader W Isls	168	e9
Shadforth Dur	106	C5

310

Shadingfield *Suffk* 65 G4
Shadoxhurst *Kent* 18 C5
Shadwell *Norfk* 64 B4
Shadwell *W York* 91 E4
Shaftenhoe End *Herts* 51 E4
Shaftesbury *Dorset* 24 D1
Shaftholme *S York* 84 C5
Shafton *S York* 84 B6
Shafton Two Gates *S York* 84 B6
Shalbourne *Wilts* 26 A6
Shalcombe *IOW* 14 B2
Shalden *Hants* 27 E3
Shalden Green *Hants* 27 E4
Shaldon *Devon* 7 G5
Shalfleet *IOW* 14 B2
Shalford *Essex* 51 H4
Shalford *Surrey* 16 A6
Shalford Green *Essex* 51 H3
Shallowford *Staffs* 70 D3
Shalmsford Street *Kent* 31 E1
Shalstone *Bucks* 49 E3
Shamley Green *Surrey* 16 A6
Shandford *Angus* 141 E6
Shandon *Ag & B* 128 D4
Shandwick *Highld* 163 E1
Shangton *Leics* 60 C5
Shankhouse *Nthumb* 114 D3
Shanklin *IOW* 14 D2
Shap *Cumb* 104 B2
Shapwick *Dorset* 12 C5
Shapwick *Somset* 23 G3
Shard End *W Mids* 58 D4
Shardlow *Derbys* 72 B3
Shareshill *Staffs* 58 B6
Sharlston *W York* 91 E1
Sharlston Common *W York* 91 E1
Sharman's Cross *W Mids* 58 D3
Sharnal Street *Kent* 30 B3
Sharnbrook *Beds* 49 H5
Sharneyford *Lancs* 89 G2
Sharnford *Leics* 59 H4
Sharnhill Green *Dorset* 11 G5
Sharoe Green *Lancs* 88 D3
Sharow *N York* 97 F2
Sharp Green *Norfk* 77 G2
Sharpenhoe *Beds* 50 B4
Sharperton *Nthumb* 113 G5
Sharpness *Gloucs* 38 A4
Sharpthorne *W Susx* 17 E5
Sharptor *Cnwll* 5 F3
Sharpway Gate *Worcs* 58 B2
Sharrington *Norfk* 76 C4
Shatterford *Worcs* 57 H3
Shatterling *Kent* 31 F2
Shaugh Prior *Devon* 6 C4
Shave Cross *Dorset* 10 D4
Shavington *Ches* 70 B5
Shaw *Berks* 40 C1
Shaw *Gt Man* 82 D6
Shaw *W York* 90 A3
Shaw *Wilts* 24 D3
Shaw *Wilts* 39 F3
Shaw Common *Gloucs* 46 B2
Shaw Green *Herts* 50 D4
Shaw Green *Lancs* 88 D1
Shaw Green *N York* 90 D5
Shaw Hill *Lancs* 88 D2
Shaw Mills *N York* 90 D6
Shawbost *W Isls* 168 e9
Shawbury *Shrops* 69 H2
Shawclough *Gt Man* 89 G1
Shawdon Hill *Nthumb* 124 D2
Shawell *Leics* 60 B3
Shawford *Hants* 26 C2
Shawforth *Lancs* 89 G2
Shawhead *D & G* 110 C2
Shawsburn *S Lans* 120 B4
Shear Cross *Wilts* 24 D3
Shearington *D & G* 111 E1
Shearsby *Leics* 60 B4
Shearston *Somset* 23 F2
Shebbear *Devon* 8 A5
Shebdon *Staffs* 70 C3
Shebster *Highld* 166 D5
Sheddens *E Rens* 119 G5
Shedfield *Hants* 14 D5
Sheen *Derbys* 71 F6
Sheep Hill *Dur* 114 C1
Sheep-ridge *W York* 90 C1
Sheepbridge *Derbys* 84 A2
Sheepscar *W York* 90 D3
Sheepscombe *Gloucs* 38 D5
Sheepstor *Devon* 6 C4
Sheepwash *Devon* 8 B5
Sheepwash *Nthumb* 114 D4
Sheepway *Somset* 37 F2
Sheepy Magna *Leics* 59 F5
Sheepy Parva *Leics* 59 F5
Sheering *Essex* 51 F2
Sheerness *Kent* 30 C3
Sheerwater *Surrey* 28 B3
Sheet *Hants* 27 F2
Sheffield *Cnwll* 2 B2
Sheffield *S York* 84 A3
Sheffield Bottom *Berks* 41 E1
Sheffield City Airport *S York* 84 B3
Sheffield Green *E Susx* 17 E4
Shefford *Beds* 50 B5
Sheigra *Highld* 164 C4
Sheinton *Shrops* 57 F6
Shelderton *Shrops* 56 D3
Sheldon *Derbys* 83 G1
Sheldon *Devon* 10 B5
Sheldon *W Mids* 58 D4
Sheldwich *Kent* 30 D2
Sheldwich Lees *Kent* 30 D2
Shelf *W York* 90 B2
Shelfanger *Norfk* 64 D4
Shelfield *W Mids* 58 C6
Shelfield *Warwks* 58 D2
Shelfield Green *Warwks* 47 G5
Shelford *Notts* 72 D4
Shelford *Warwks* 59 G5
Shellacres *Border* 123 F4
Shelley *Essex* 51 F1
Shelley *Suffk* 52 D5
Shelley *W York* 83 G6
Shelley Far Bank *W York* 83 G6

Shellingford *Oxon* 40 A4
Shellow Bowells *Essex* 51 G1
Shelsley Beauchamp *Worcs* 57 G2
Shelsley Walsh *Worcs* 57 G2
Shelton *Beds* 61 F2
Shelton *Norfk* 65 E4
Shelton *Notts* 73 E4
Shelton *Shrops* 69 G1
Shelton Green *Norfk* 65 E4
Shelton Lock *Derbys* 72 A3
Shelton Under Harley *Staffs* 70 C4
Shelve *Shrops* 56 D5
Shelwick *Herefs* 45 H3
Shenfield *Essex* 29 G6
Shenington *Oxon* 48 B3
Shenley *Herts* 28 C6
Shenley Brook End *Bucks* 49 F3
Shenley Church End *Bucks* 49 F3
Shenleybury *Herts* 50 C1
Shenmore *Herefs* 45 G3
Shennanton *D & G* 109 E1
Shenstone *Staffs* 58 D6
Shenstone *Worcs* 58 B3
Shenstone Woodend *Staffs* 58 D5
Shenton *Leics* 59 G5
Shepeau Stow *Lincs* 74 C1
Shephall *Herts* 50 D3
Shepherd's Bush *Gt Lon* 28 C4
Shepherd's Green *Oxon* 41 E3
Shepherds *Cnwll* 3 F5
Shepherds Patch *Gloucs* 38 B5
Shepherdswell *Kent* 19 F6
Shepley *W York* 83 G6
Shepperdine *Gloucs* 37 G4
Shepperton *Surrey* 28 B3
Shepperton Green *Surrey* 28 B3
Shepreth *Cambs* 51 E5
Shepshed *Leics* 72 B2
Shepton Beauchamp *Somset* 23 G1
Shepton Mallet *Somset* 24 B4
Shepton Montague *Somset* 24 B2
Shepway *Kent* 30 A1
Sheraton *Dur* 106 D4
Sherborne *Dorset* 24 B1
Sherborne *Gloucs* 39 F6
Sherborne *Somset* 24 A5
Sherborne Causeway *Dorset* 24 D1
Sherborne St John *Hants* 26 D5
Sherbourne *Warwks* 47 H5
Sherburn *Dur* 106 C5
Sherburn *N York* 99 E2
Sherburn Hill *Dur* 106 C5
Sherburn in Elmet *N York* 91 F3
Shere *Surrey* 16 B6
Shereford *Norfk* 76 B3
Sherfield English *Hants* 26 A1
Sherfield on Loddon *Hants* 27 E5
Sherfin *Lancs* 89 F2
Sherford *Devon* 7 E2
Sherford *Dorset* 12 C4
Sheriff Hutton *N York* 98 B1
Sheriffhales *Shrops* 70 C1
Sheringham *Norfk* 77 E4
Sherington *Bucks* 49 G4
Shermanbury *W Susx* 16 C3
Shernborne *Norfk* 75 G3
Sherrington *Wilts* 25 E3
Sherston *Wilts* 38 C3
Sherwood *Notts* 72 C4
Shettleston *C Glas* 130 C1
Shevington *Gt Man* 81 H6
Shevington Moor *Gt Man* 81 H6
Shevington Vale *Gt Man* 81 G6
Sheviock *Cnwll* 5 G1
Shibden Head *W York* 90 B2
Shide *IOW* 14 C2
Shidlaw *Nthumb* 123 E3
Shiel Bridge *Highld* 152 D1
Shieldaig *Highld* 152 B4
Shieldhill *D & G* 111 E3
Shieldhill *Falk* 131 E3
Shieldhill House Hotel *S Lans* 121 E3
Shields *N Lans* 120 B5
Shielfoot *Highld* 143 F1
Shielhill *Angus* 140 D5
Shielhill *Inver* 128 D2
Shifford *Oxon* 40 B4
Shifnal *Shrops* 57 H6
Shilbottle *Nthumb* 125 E3
Shildon *Dur* 106 B3
Shillford *E Rens* 119 F5
Shillingford *Devon* 22 C2
Shillingford *Oxon* 40 D3
Shillingford Abbot *Devon* 9 F3
Shillingford St George *Devon* 9 F3
Shillingstone *Dorset* 12 B6
Shillington *Beds* 50 B4
Shillmoor *Nthumb* 113 F6
Shilton *Oxon* 39 G5
Shilton *Warwks* 59 G4
Shilvinghampton *Dorset* 11 G3
Shimpling *Norfk* 64 D4
Shimpling *Suffk* 52 B6
Shimpling Street *Suffk* 52 B6
Shincliffe *Dur* 106 B5
Shiney Row *T & W* 106 C6
Shinfield *Berks* 41 E1
Shingay *Cambs* 50 D5
Shingle Street *Suffk* 53 G5
Shinnersbridge *Devon* 7 E4
Shinness *Highld* 162 B5
Shipbourne *Kent* 29 G1
Shipbrookhill *Ches* 82 B2
Shipdham *Norfk* 64 B6
Shipham *Somset* 23 G5
Shiphay *Devon* 7 F4
Shiplake *Oxon* 41 F2
Shiplake Row *Oxon* 41 F2
Shiplate *Somset* 23 F5
Shipley *Derbys* 72 B4
Shipley *Shrops* 58 A5
Shipley *W Susx* 16 B4
Shipley *W York* 90 C3
Shipley Bridge *Surrey* 16 D5
Shipley Hatch *Kent* 18 D5
Shipmeadow *Suffk* 65 F4
Shippea Hill Station *Cambs* 63 F4
Shippon *Oxon* 40 C4

Shipston on Stour *Warwks* 47 H3
Shipton *Bucks* 49 F2
Shipton *Gloucs* 47 F1
Shipton *N York* 91 H5
Shipton *Shrops* 57 F5
Shipton Bellinger *Hants* 25 H4
Shipton Gorge *Dorset* 11 E4
Shipton Green *W Susx* 15 F4
Shipton Moyne *Gloucs* 38 D3
Shipton-on-Cherwell *Oxon* 40 C6
Shipton-under-Wychwood *Oxon* 39 G6
Shiptonthorpe *E R Yk* 92 B4
Shirburn *Oxon* 41 E4
Shirdley Hill *Lancs* 81 F6
Shire *Cumb* 104 C4
Shire Oak *W Mids* 58 C6
Shirebrook *Derbys* 84 C1
Shiregreen *S York* 84 A4
Shirehampton *Bristl* 37 F2
Shiremoor *T & W* 115 E3
Shirenewton *Mons* 37 F4
Shireoaks *Notts* 84 C3
Shirkoak *Kent* 18 C5
Shirl Heath *Herefs* 45 G5
Shirland *Derbys* 72 B6
Shirlett *Shrops* 57 G5
Shirley *Derbys* 71 G4
Shirley *Gt Lon* 28 D3
Shirley *Hants* 14 B5
Shirley *W Mids* 58 D3
Shirrell Heath *Hants* 14 D5
Shirwell *Devon* 21 F4
Shirwell Cross *Devon* 21 F4
Shiskine *N Ayrs* 118 A2
Shittlehope *Dur* 105 G4
Shobdon *Herefs* 45 G5
Shobley *Hants* 13 F5
Shobrooke *Devon* 9 E5
Shoby *Leics* 72 D2
Shocklach *Ches* 69 G5
Shocklach Green *Ches* 69 F5
Shoeburyness *Essex* 30 C5
Sholden *Kent* 31 G1
Sholing *Hants* 14 C5
Shoose *Cumb* 102 D3
Shoot Hill *Shrops* 69 F1
Shop *Cnwll* 20 B2
Shop *Cnwll* 4 B3
Shop Street *Suffk* 65 E2
Shopwyke *W Susx* 15 G4
Shore *Gt Man* 89 H1
Shoreditch *Gt Lon* 28 D4
Shoreditch *Somset* 23 E1
Shoreham *Kent* 29 F2
Shoreham Airport *W Susx* 16 C2
Shoreham-by-Sea *W Susx* 16 C2
Shoreswood *Nthumb* 123 F4
Shorley *Hants* 26 D2
Shorncote *Gloucs* 39 E4
Shorne *Kent* 29 H3
Shorne Ridgeway *Kent* 29 H3
Short Heath *W Mids* 58 C5
Short Heath *W Mids* 58 D5
Shorta Cross *Cnwll* 5 F2
Shortbridge *E Susx* 17 E3
Shortfield Common *Surrey* 27 G3
Shortgate *E Susx* 17 F3
Shortheath *Hants* 27 F3
Shortlanesend *Cnwll* 3 F4
Shortstown *Beds* 50 B5
Shorwell *IOW* 14 C2
Shoscombe *Somset* 24 C5
Shotesham *Norfk* 65 E5
Shotgate *Essex* 30 A5
Shotley *Suffk* 53 F4
Shotley Bridge *Dur* 105 G5
Shotley Gate *Suffk* 53 F4
Shotley Street *Suffk* 53 F4
Shotleyfield *Nthumb* 105 G5
Shottenden *Kent* 30 D1
Shottermill *Surrey* 27 G2
Shottery *Warwks* 47 G5
Shotteswell *Warwks* 48 C4
Shottisham *Suffk* 53 G5
Shottle *Derbys* 71 H5
Shottlegate *Derbys* 71 H5
Shotton *Dur* 106 C3
Shotton *Dur* 106 D5
Shotton *Flints* 81 E1
Shotton *Nthumb* 123 F2
Shotton *Nthumb* 114 D3
Shotton Colliery *Dur* 106 C5
Shotts *N Lans* 120 C5
Shotwick *Ches* 81 F2
Shougle *Moray* 156 D5
Shouldham *Norfk* 75 G1
Shouldham Thorpe *Norfk* 63 F6
Shoulton *Worcs* 46 D5
Shover's Green *E Susx* 17 G4
Shraleybrook *Staffs* 70 C5
Shrawardine *Shrops* 69 F1
Shrawley *Worcs* 58 A2
Shreding Green *Bucks* 28 A4
Shrewley *Warwks* 59 E2
Shrewsbury *Shrops* 69 G1
Shrewton *Wilts* 25 F4
Shripney *W Susx* 15 G4
Shrivenham *Oxon* 39 G3
Shropham *Norfk* 64 B5
Shrub End *Essex* 52 C3
Shucknall *Herefs* 46 A3
Shudy Camps *Cambs* 51 G5
Shurdington *Gloucs* 47 E1
Shurlock Row *Berks* 41 F2
Shurnock *Worcs* 47 F5
Sixpenny Handley *Dorset* 25 E1
Shurrery *Highld* 166 D4
Shurrery Lodge *Highld* 166 D4
Shurton *Somset* 23 E4
Shustoke *Warwks* 59 E4
Shut Heath *Staffs* 70 D2
Shute *Devon* 9 F5
Shute *Devon* 9 E5
Shutford *Oxon* 48 B3
Shuthonger *Gloucs* 46 D3
Shutlanger *Nhants* 49 E4
Shutt Green *Staffs* 70 D1
Shutterton *Devon* 9 F2

Shuttington *Warwks* 59 E6
Shuttlewood *Derbys* 84 B2
Shuttlewood Common *Derbys* 84 B2
Shuttleworth *Lancs* 89 F1
Siabost *W Isls* 168 e9
Siadar *W Isls* 168 e9
Sibbertoft *Nhants* 60 C4
Sibdon Carwood *Shrops* 56 D4
Sibford Ferris *Oxon* 48 B3
Sibford Gower *Oxon* 48 B3
Sible Hedingham *Essex* 52 A4
Sibley's Green *Essex* 51 G3
Sibsey *Lincs* 74 D5
Sibsey Fenside *Lincs* 74 D5
Sibson *Cambs* 61 G5
Sibson *Leics* 59 F5
Sibster *Highld* 167 G4
Sibthorpe *Notts* 85 E2
Sibthorpe *Notts* 73 E5
Sibton *Suffk* 65 F2
Sicklesmere *Suffk* 64 A1
Sicklinghall *N York* 91 E4
Sid Cop *S York* 84 B6
Sidbrook *Somset* 23 E2
Sidbury *Devon* 10 B3
Sidbury *Shrops* 57 G4
Sidcot *Somset* 23 G5
Sidcup *Gt Lon* 29 E3
Siddick *Cumb* 102 D3
Siddington *Ches* 82 C2
Siddington *Gloucs* 39 E4
Sidemoor *Worcs* 58 B2
Sidestrand *Norfk* 77 F4
Sidford *Devon* 10 B3
Sidlesham *W Susx* 15 G3
Sidlesham Common *W Susx* 15 G4
Sidley *E Susx* 18 A2
Sidmouth *Devon* 10 B3
Siefton *Shrops* 57 E4
Sigford *Devon* 7 E5
Sigglesthorne *E R Yk* 93 E4
Sigingstone *V Glam* 35 G1
Signet *Oxon* 39 G5
Silchester *Hants* 26 D5
Sileby *Leics* 72 C1
Silecroft *Cumb* 94 B3
Silfield *Norfk* 64 D5
Silk Willoughby *Lincs* 74 A4
Silkstead *Hants* 26 C2
Silkstone *S York* 83 H5
Silkstone Common *S York* 83 H5
Silksworth *T & W* 106 C6
Silloth *Cumb* 103 E5
Silpho *N York* 99 E4
Silsden *W York* 90 B4
Silsoe *Beds* 50 B4
Silton *Dorset* 24 C2
Silver End *Essex* 52 B3
Silver Street *Kent* 30 B2
Silver Street *Somset* 24 A2
Silverdale *Lancs* 95 E4
Silverdale *Staffs* 70 C5
Silverdale Green *Lancs* 95 E2
Silverford *Abers* 158 D5
Silvergate *Norfk* 77 E3
Silverlace Green *Suffk* 65 F1
Silverley's Green *Suffk* 65 E3
Silverstone *Nhants* 49 E4
Silverton *Devon* 9 F5
Silverwell *Cnwll* 3 E5
Silvington *Shrops* 57 F3
Simmondley *Derbys* 83 E4
Simonburn *Nthumb* 113 F2
Simons Burrow *Devon* 22 D1
Simonsbath *Somset* 21 H4
Simonstone *Lancs* 89 F3
Simonstone *N York* 96 B4
Simprim *Border* 123 F4
Simpson *Bucks* 49 G3
Simpson Cross *Pembks* 32 C4
Sinclair's Hill *Border* 123 E4
Sinclairston *E Ayrs* 119 F1
Sinderby *N York* 97 G3
Sinderhope *Nthumb* 105 E5
Sinderland Green *Gt Man* 82 B4
Sindlesham *Berks* 41 F1
Sinfin *Derbys* 72 A3
Single Street *Gt Lon* 29 E2
Singleborough *Bucks* 49 F2
Singleton *Lancs* 88 B3
Singleton *W Susx* 15 G5
Singlewell *Kent* 29 G3
Sinkhurst Green *Kent* 18 B6
Sinnarhard *Abers* 148 B6
Sinnington *N York* 98 C3
Sinton *Worcs* 46 D5
Sinton Green *Worcs* 46 D5
Sipson *Gt Lon* 28 B4
Sirhowy *Blae G* 36 C5
Siron *Gloucs* 38 B2
Sissinghurst *Kent* 18 B5
Siston *Gloucs* 38 B2
Sitcott *Devon* 5 G5
Sithney *Cnwll* 2 D3
Sithney Common *Cnwll* 2 D3
Sithney Green *Cnwll* 2 D3
Sittingbourne *Kent* 30 C2
Six Ashes *Staffs* 57 H4
Six Bells *Blae G* 36 C5
Six Mile Bottom *Cambs* 51 F5
Six Rues *Jersey* 174 b3
Sixhills *Lincs* 86 B3
Sixmile Cottages *Kent* 19 E6
Sizergh Castle *Cumb* 95 F4
Sizewell *Suffk* 65 G2
Skaill *Ork* 169 c2
Skares *E Ayrs* 119 G1
Skateraw *Abers* 149 G6
Skateraw *E Loth* 133 F3
Skeabost *Highld* 150 D3
Skeeby *N York* 97 E5
Skeffington *Leics* 60 C6
Skeffling *E R Yk* 93 G1
Skegby *Notts* 72 C6
Skegby *Notts* 85 E2

Skegness *Lincs* 87 F1
Skelbo *Highld* 163 E3
Skelbo Street *Highld* 163 E3
Skelbrooke *S York* 84 C6
Skeldyke *Lincs* 74 D3
Skellingthorpe *Lincs* 85 G2
Skellorm Green *Ches* 82 D3
Skellow *S York* 84 C6
Skelmanthorpe *W York* 83 G6
Skelmersdale *Lancs* 81 G5
Skelmorlie *N Ayrs* 128 C2
Skelpick *Highld* 166 A4
Skelston *D & G* 110 C3
Skelton *Cumb* 104 A4
Skelton *E R Yk* 92 B3
Skelton *N York* 96 D5
Skelton *N York* 107 F3
Skelton *N York* 97 G2
Skelton *N York* 91 G5
Skelwith Bridge *Cumb* 94 D5
Skendleby *Lincs* 87 E2
Skene House *Abers* 149 E5
Skenfrith *Mons* 45 G1
Skerne *E R Yk* 92 D3
Skerray *Highld* 165 G5
Skerricha *Highld* 164 C3
Skerton *Lancs* 95 E1
Sketchley *Leics* 59 G5
Sketty *Swans* 34 D3
Skewen *Neath* 35 E4
Skewsby *N York* 98 B2
Skeyton *Norfk* 77 E3
Skeyton Corner *Norfk* 77 E3
Skiall *Highld* 166 D5
Skidbrooke *Lincs* 87 E4
Skidbrooke North End *Lincs* 87 E4
Skidby *E R Yk* 92 D3
Skigersta *W Isls* 168 f7
Skilgate *Somset* 22 C2
Skillington *Lincs* 73 F3
Skinburness *Cumb* 103 E6
Skinflats *Falk* 131 E3
Skinidin *Highld* 150 B3
Skinners Green *Berks* 26 C6
Skinningrove *N York* 107 F3
Skipness *Ag & B* 117 H6
Skipper's Bridge *Cumb* 112 A3
Skiprigg *Cumb* 103 H5
Skipsea *E R Yk* 93 E5
Skipsea Brough *E R Yk* 93 E5
Skipton *N York* 90 A5
Skipton-on-Swale *N York* 97 G3
Skipwith *N York* 91 H3
Skirlaugh *E R Yk* 93 E3
Skirling *Border* 121 E3
Skirmett *Bucks* 41 F3
Skirpenbeck *E R Yk* 92 A3
Skirwith *Cumb* 104 C3
Skirwith *N York* 95 H2
Skirza *Highld* 167 G5
Skitby *Cumb* 112 B1
Skittle Green *Bucks* 41 F5
Skulamus *Highld* 151 U1
Skyborry Green *Shrops* 56 C3
Skye Green *Essex* 52 B3
Skye of Curr *Highld* 156 B1
Skyreholme *N York* 90 B6
Slack *Derbys* 84 A1
Slack *W York* 90 A2
Slack Head *Cumb* 95 F3
Slackcote *Gt Man* 83 E6
Slackholme End *Lincs* 87 F2
Slacks of Cairnbanno *Abers* 158 D4
Slad *Gloucs* 38 C5
Slade *Devon* 21 F4
Slade *Devon* 10 B5
Slade *Somset* 22 A2
Slade End *Oxon* 40 D3
Slade Green *Kent* 29 F4
Slade Heath *Staffs* 58 B6
Slade Hooton *S York* 84 C4
Slades Green *Worcs* 46 D3
Sladesbridge *Cnwll* 4 D3
Slaggyford *Nthumb* 104 C5
Slaid Hill *W York* 90 D4
Slaidburn *Lancs* 89 E5
Slaithwaite *W York* 83 F6
Slaley *Derbys* 71 H6
Slaley *Nthumb* 105 F6
Slamannan *Falk* 131 E2
Slapton *Bucks* 49 G1
Slapton *Devon* 7 F2
Slapton *Nhants* 49 E4
Slattocks *Gt Man* 82 C6
Slaugham *W Susx* 16 C4
Slaughterford *Wilts* 38 C2
Slawston *Leics* 60 D5
Sleaford *Hants* 27 F3
Sleaford *Lincs* 74 A4
Sleagill *Cumb* 104 C2
Sleap *Shrops* 69 G3
Sleapford *Shrops* 70 A2
Sleasdairidh *Highld* 162 C3
Sledge Green *Worcs* 46 D3
Sledmere *E R Yk* 99 E1
Sleight *Dorset* 12 D4
Sleightholme *Dur* 96 C6
Sleights *N York* 107 F1
Slepe *Dorset* 12 D4
Slickly *Highld* 167 G5
Sliddery *N Ayrs* 118 A2
Sligachan *Ag & B* 128 C2
Slimbridge *Gloucs* 38 B5
Slindon *Staffs* 70 C3
Slindon *W Susx* 15 H4
Slinfold *W Susx* 16 B4
Sling *Gwynd* 79 F1
Slingsby *N York* 98 C2
Slip End *Beds* 50 B2
Slip End *Herts* 50 D4
Slipton *Nhants* 61 E3
Slitting Mill *Staffs* 71 E2
Slockavullin *Ag & B* 127 G5
Slogarie *D & G* 110 A2
Sloley *Norfk* 77 F2
Sloncombe *Devon* 8 D3
Sloothby *Lincs* 87 E2

Slough Berks ... 41 H2
Slough Green Somset ... 23 E1
Slough Green W Susx ... 16 D4
Slumbay Highld ... 152 C3
Slyfield Green Surrey ... 28 A1
Slyne Lancs ... 95 E1
Smailholm Border ... 122 D3
Small Dole W Susx ... 16 C3
Small Heath W Mids ... 58 D4
Small Hythe Kent ... 18 C4
Small Wood Hey Lancs ... 88 B4
Smallbridge Gt Man ... 89 G1
Smallbrook Devon ... 9 E4
Smallbrook Gloucs ... 37 G4
Smallburgh Norfk ... 77 F2
Smalldale Derbys ... 83 F2
Smalldale Derbys ... 83 G3
Smalley Derbys ... 72 B4
Smalley Common Derbys ... 72 B4
Smalley Green Derbys ... 72 B4
Smallfield Surrey ... 16 D6
Smallridge Devon ... 10 C5
Smallthorne Staffs ... 70 D5
Smallways N York ... 105 H1
Smallwood Ches ... 70 C6
Smallworth Norfk ... 64 C3
Smannell Hants ... 26 B4
Smardale Cumb ... 95 H6
Smarden Kent ... 18 B6
Smarden Bell Kent ... 18 B6
Smart's Hill Kent ... 17 F6
Smeafield Nthumb ... 124 D5
Smearisary Highld ... 143 F2
Smeeth Kent ... 18 D5
Smeeton Westerby Leics ... 60 C5
Smelthouses N York ... 97 E1
Smerral Highld ... 167 E2
Smestow Staffs ... 58 B5
Smethwick W Mids ... 58 C4
Smethwick Green Ches ... 82 C1
Smisby Derbys ... 72 A2
Smith End Green Worcs ... 46 C4
Smith Green Lancs ... 88 C5
Smith's End Herts ... 51 E4
Smith's Green Essex ... 51 G3
Smith's Green Essex ... 51 G5
Smitheclose IOW ... 14 D3
Smithfield Cumb ... 112 B1
Smithies S York ... 84 A5
Smithincott Devon ... 9 G6
Smithstown Highld ... 160 B1
Smithton Highld ... 155 E4
Smithy Bridge Gt Man ... 89 H1
Smithy Green Ches ... 82 B2
Smithy Green Gt Man ... 82 D3
Smithy Houses Derbys ... 72 B5
Smockington Leics ... 59 G4
Smoo Highld ... 165 E5
Smythe's Green Essex ... 52 C3
Snade D & G ... 110 C3
Snailbeach Shrops ... 56 D6
Snailwell Cambs ... 63 F2
Snainton N York ... 99 E3
Snaith E R Yk ... 91 G2
Snake Pass Inn Derbys ... 83 F4
Snape N York ... 97 F3
Snape Suffk ... 65 F1
Snape Green Mersyd ... 81 F6
Snape Street Suffk ... 65 F1
Snaresbrook Gt Lon ... 29 E5
Snarestone Leics ... 72 A1
Snarford Lincs ... 85 H3
Snargate Kent ... 18 C4
Snave Kent ... 18 D4
Sneachill Worcs ... 47 E4
Snead Powys ... 56 C5
Sneath Common Norfk ... 64 D4
Sneaton N York ... 99 E6
Sneatonthorpe N York ... 99 E5
Snelland Lincs ... 86 A3
Snelson Ches ... 82 C2
Snelston Derbys ... 71 F4
Snetterton Norfk ... 64 B4
Snettisham Norfk ... 75 G3
Snibston Leics ... 72 B1
Snig's End Gloucs ... 46 C2
Snitter Nthumb ... 124 C1
Snitterby Lincs ... 85 G4
Snitterfield Warwks ... 47 H5
Snitterton Derbys ... 71 H6
Snittlegarth Cumb ... 103 F4
Snitton Shrops ... 57 F3
Snoadhill Kent ... 18 C6
Snodhill Herefs ... 45 F3
Snodland Kent ... 29 H2
Snoll Hatch Kent ... 17 G6
Snow End Herts ... 51 E4
Snow Street Norfk ... 64 C3
Snowden Hill S York ... 83 G5
Snowshill Gloucs ... 47 F3
Soake Hants ... 15 E5
Soar Cardif ... 36 B3
Soar Devon ... 6 D1
Soar Powys ... 44 C2
Soberton Hants ... 14 D5
Soberton Heath Hants ... 14 D5
Sockbridge Cumb ... 104 B3
Sockburn Dur ... 97 G6
Sodom Denbgs ... 80 C2
Sodylt Bank Shrops ... 69 F4
Soham Cambs ... 63 E3
Soham Cotes Cambs ... 63 E3
Solas W Isls ... 168 b5
Soldon Pembks ... 32 C3
Soldon Devon ... 20 C2
Soldon Cross Devon ... 20 C2
Soldridge Hants ... 27 E3
Sole Street Kent ... 29 G3
Sole Street Kent ... 31 E1
Solihull W Mids ... 58 D3
Sollers Dilwyn Herefs ... 45 G5
Sollers Hope Herefs ... 46 B2
Sollom Lancs ... 88 C1
Solva Pembks ... 32 B4
Solwaybank D & G ... 111 G2
Somerby Leics ... 73 E1
Somerby Lincs ... 86 A1

Somercotes Derbys ... 72 B5
Somerford Dorset ... 13 F4
Somerford Keynes Gloucs ... 39 E4
Somerley W Susx ... 15 F3
Somerleyton Suffk ... 65 G5
Somersal Herbert Derbys ... 71 F3
Somersby Lincs ... 86 D2
Somersham Cambs ... 62 C3
Somersham Suffk ... 52 D6
Somerton Oxon ... 48 C2
Somerton Somset ... 23 H2
Somerton Suffk ... 52 B6
Somerwood Shrops ... 69 H1
Sompting W Susx ... 16 C2
Sonning Berks ... 41 F2
Sonning Common Oxon ... 41 F2
Sonning Eye Oxon ... 41 F2
Sontley Wrexhm ... 69 F5
Sopley Hants ... 13 E4
Sopworth Wilts ... 38 C3
Sorbie D & G ... 101 F5
Sordale Highld ... 167 E5
Sorisdale Ag & B ... 135 E6
Sorn E Ayrs ... 119 G2
Sortat Highld ... 167 F5
Sosgill Cumb ... 103 E2
Sotby Lincs ... 86 B2
Sots Hole Lincs ... 86 B1
Sotterly Suffk ... 65 G4
Soughton Flints ... 81 E1
Soulbury Bucks ... 49 G2
Soulby Cumb ... 104 A3
Soulby Cumb ... 104 D1
Souldern Oxon ... 48 C2
Souldrop Beds ... 49 H5
Sound Muir Moray ... 157 F4
Soundwell Gloucs ... 37 G2
Sourton Devon ... 8 B4
Soutergate Cumb ... 94 C3
South Acre Norfk ... 76 A1
South Alkham Kent ... 19 F6
South Allington Devon ... 7 E1
South Alloa Falk ... 131 E4
South Ambersham W Susx ... 15 G6
South Anston S York ... 84 C3
South Ascot Berks ... 27 G6
South Ashford Kent ... 18 D6
South Baddesley Hants ... 14 B3
South Bank N York ... 107 E3
South Bank N York ... 91 G5
South Barrow Somset ... 24 B2
South Beddington Gt Lon ... 28 D2
South Beer Cnwll ... 5 G5
South Benfleet Essex ... 30 A5
South Bersted W Susx ... 15 G4
South Bockhampton Dorset ... 13 F4
South Bowood Dorset ... 11 E4
South Bramwith S York ... 84 D6
South Brent Devon ... 6 D4
South Brewham Somset ... 24 C3
South Broomhill Nthumb ... 114 D5
South Burlingham Norfk ... 65 F6
South Cadbury Somset ... 24 B2
South Carlton Lincs ... 85 G2
South Carlton Notts ... 84 D3
South Cave E R Yk ... 92 C3
South Cerney Gloucs ... 39 E4
South Chailey E Susx ... 17 E3
South Chard Somset ... 10 D5
South Charlton Nthumb ... 125 E3
South Cheriton Somset ... 24 C2
South Church Dur ... 106 B4
South Cleatlam Dur ... 105 H2
South Cliffe E R Yk ... 92 C3
South Clifton Notts ... 85 F2
South Cockerington Lincs ... 86 D4
South Cornelly Brdgnd ... 35 F2
South Cove Suffk ... 65 G3
South Creake Norfk ... 76 B4
South Crosland W York ... 83 F6
South Croxton Leics ... 72 D1
South Dalton E R Yk ... 92 C4
South Darenth Kent ... 29 F3
South Duffield N York ... 91 H3
South Elkington Lincs ... 86 C3
South Elmsall W York ... 84 B6
South End E R Yk ... 93 H1
South End Hants ... 13 E6
South End Herefs ... 46 C4
South End Lincs ... 93 E2
South End Norfk ... 64 B4
South Erradale Highld ... 152 B6
South Fambridge Essex ... 30 B5
South Fawley Berks ... 40 B2
South Ferriby Lincs ... 92 D2
South Field E R Yk ... 92 D3
South Godstone Surrey ... 28 D1
South Gorley Hants ... 13 E6
South Green Essex ... 52 D3
South Green Essex ... 29 H5
South Green Kent ... 30 B2
South Green Norfk ... 76 D1
South Green Suffk ... 64 D3
South Gyle C Edin ... 131 H2
South Hanningfield Essex ... 30 A6
South Harting W Susx ... 15 F5
South Hayling Hants ... 15 E4
South Hazelrigg Nthumb ... 123 H3
South Heath Bucks ... 41 G4
South Heighton E Susx ... 17 E2
South Hetton Dur ... 106 C5
South Hiendley W York ... 84 B6
South Hill Cnwll ... 5 G3
South Hill Somset ... 23 G2
South Hinksey Oxon ... 40 C5
South Hole Devon ... 20 B3
South Holmwood Surrey ... 16 C6
South Hornchurch Gt Lon ... 29 F4
South Huish Devon ... 6 D2
South Hykeham Lincs ... 85 G1
South Hylton T & W ... 115 E1
South Kelsey Lincs ... 85 H4
South Kessock Highld ... 155 E4
South Killingholme Lincs ... 93 E1
South Kilvington N York ... 97 G3
South Kilworth Nhants ... 60 B3
South Kirkby W York ... 84 B6

South Knighton Devon ... 7 E5
South Kyme Lincs ... 74 B5
South Lawn Oxon ... 39 G6
South Leigh Oxon ... 40 B5
South Leverton Notts ... 85 E3
South Littleton Worcs ... 47 F4
South Lopham Norfk ... 64 C3
South Luffenham Rutlnd ... 61 E6
South Malling E Susx ... 17 E2
South Marston Wilts ... 39 G3
South Merstham Surrey ... 28 D1
South Middleton Nthumb ... 124 C3
South Milford N York ... 91 F3
South Milton Devon ... 6 D2
South Mimms Herts ... 28 C6
South Molton Devon ... 21 G3
South Moor Dur ... 106 A6
South Moreton Oxon ... 40 D3
South Mundham W Susx ... 15 G4
South Muskham Notts ... 73 E6
South Newbald E R Yk ... 92 C3
South Newington Oxon ... 48 B2
South Newton Wilts ... 25 F3
South Normanton Derbys ... 72 B6
South Norwood Gt Lon ... 28 D3
South Nutfield Surrey ... 28 D1
South Ockendon Essex ... 29 G4
South Ormsby Lincs ... 86 D2
South Ossett W York ... 90 D1
South Otterington N York ... 97 G4
South Owersby Lincs ... 86 A4
South Park Surrey ... 28 C1
South Perrott Dorset ... 11 E5
South Petherton Somset ... 23 G1
South Petherwin Cnwll ... 5 G4
South Pickenham Norfk ... 63 H6
South Pill Cnwll ... 5 H2
South Pool Devon ... 7 E2
South Poorton Dorset ... 11 F4
South Quarme Somset ... 22 B3
South Queensferry C Edin ... 131 G3
South Radworthy Devon ... 21 G4
South Rauceby Lincs ... 73 H5
South Raynham Norfk ... 76 B2
South Reddish Gt Man ... 82 D4
South Reston Lincs ... 86 D3
South Runcton Norfk ... 75 G1
South Scarle Notts ... 85 F1
South Shian Ag & B ... 136 D4
South Shields T & W ... 115 E2
South Shore Lancs ... 88 B3
South Somercotes Lincs ... 86 D4
South Stainley N York ... 97 F1
South Stifford Essex ... 29 G4
South Stoke Lincs ... 73 G3
South Stoke Oxon ... 40 D3
South Stoke Somset ... 24 C5
South Stoke W Susx ... 16 A2
South Stour Kent ... 18 D5
South Street Kent ... 29 G2
South Street Kent ... 30 D2
South Street Kent ... 31 E3
South Tarbrax S Lans ... 121 E5
South Tawton Devon ... 8 C4
South Thoresby Lincs ... 86 D2
South Thorpe Dur ... 105 H1
South Town Hants ... 27 E3
South Walsham Norfk ... 77 G1
South Warnborough Hants ... 27 E4
South Weald Essex ... 29 F5
South Weston Oxon ... 41 E4
South Widcombe Somset ... 24 A5
South Wigston Leics ... 60 B5
South Willesborough Kent ... 18 D5
South Willingham Lincs ... 86 B3
South Wingate Dur ... 106 D4
South Wingfield Derbys ... 72 A6
South Witham Lincs ... 73 G2
South Wonston Hants ... 26 C3
South Woodham Ferrers Essex ... 30 B6
South Wootton Norfk ... 75 G2
South Wraxall Wilts ... 24 D6
South Zeal Devon ... 8 C4
Southall Gt Lon ... 28 B4
Southam Gloucs ... 47 E2
Southam Warwks ... 48 B5
Southampton Hants ... 14 B5
Southampton Airport Hants ... 14 C5
Southborough Gt Lon ... 29 E3
Southborough Kent ... 17 G6
Southbourne Dorset ... 13 E4
Southbourne W Susx ... 15 F4
Southbrook Dorset ... 12 B4
Southburgh Norfk ... 64 C6
Southburn E R Yk ... 92 D5
Southchurch Essex ... 30 C5
Southcott Cnwll ... 5 E5
Southcott Devon ... 21 E2
Southcott Devon ... 8 B4
Southcott Devon ... 8 D3
Southcott Wilts ... 25 G5
Southcourt Bucks ... 41 F5
Southease E Susx ... 17 E2
Southend Ag & B ... 117 F1
Southend Wilts ... 39 G2
Southend Airport Essex ... 30 B5
Southend-on-Sea Essex ... 30 B5
Southernby Cumb ... 103 H4
Southernden Kent ... 18 B6
Southerndown V Glam ... 35 F2
Southerness D & G ... 102 D6
Southerton Devon ... 10 A4
Southery Norfk ... 63 E5
Southfield Falk ... 131 E2
Southfleet Kent ... 29 G3
Southford IOW ... 14 C1
Southgate Gt Lon ... 28 D5
Southgate Norfk ... 75 G3
Southgate Norfk ... 76 B3
Southgate Norfk ... 76 D2
Southgate Swans ... 34 C3
Southill Beds ... 50 B5
Southington Hants ... 26 C4
Southleigh Devon ... 10 B4
Southminster Essex ... 30 C6
Southmoor Oxon ... 40 B4
Southmuir Angus ... 140 D5

Southoe Cambs ... 61 H2
Southolt Suffk ... 64 D2
Southorpe Cambs ... 61 G6
Southover Dorset ... 11 F4
Southover E Susx ... 17 G4
Southowram W York ... 90 B2
Southport Mersyd ... 88 B1
Southrepps Norfk ... 77 E4
Southrey Lincs ... 86 B1
Southrop Gloucs ... 39 G5
Southrope Hants ... 27 E4
Southsea Hants ... 15 E3
Southsea Wrexhm ... 69 E5
Southside Dur ... 105 H3
Southtown Norfk ... 65 H6
Southtown Somset ... 23 F1
Southwaite Cumb ... 104 A5
Southwark Gt Lon ... 28 D4
Southwater W Susx ... 16 B4
Southwater Street W Susx ... 16 B4
Southway Somset ... 23 H3
Southwell Dorset ... 11 G2
Southwell Notts ... 73 E5
Southwick Hants ... 14 D4
Southwick Nhants ... 61 F5
Southwick Somset ... 23 F4
Southwick T & W ... 115 E1
Southwick W Susx ... 16 C2
Southwick Wilts ... 24 D5
Southwold Suffk ... 65 G3
Southwood Norfk ... 65 F6
Southwood Somset ... 24 A3
Sowe Common W Mids ... 59 G4
Sower Carr Lancs ... 88 B4
Sowerby N York ... 97 G3
Sowerby W York ... 90 B2
Sowerby Bridge W York ... 90 B2
Sowerby Row Cumb ... 103 H4
Sowerhill Somset ... 22 B2
Sowhill Torfn ... 36 D4
Sowley Green Suffk ... 51 H6
Sowood W York ... 90 B1
Sowton Devon ... 6 B4
Sowton Devon ... 9 G4
Soyland Town W York ... 90 B2
Spa Common Norfk ... 77 F3
Spain's End Essex ... 51 G4
Spalding Lincs ... 74 C2
Spaldington E R Yk ... 92 B3
Spaldwick Cambs ... 61 G3
Spalford Notts ... 85 F2
Spanby Lincs ... 74 A4
Spanish Green Hants ... 27 E5
Sparham Norfk ... 76 D2
Sparhamill Norfk ... 76 D2
Spark Bridge Cumb ... 94 D3
Sparket Cumb ... 104 A3
Sparkford Somset ... 24 B2
Sparkhill W Mids ... 58 D4
Sparkwell Devon ... 6 C3
Sparrow Green Norfk ... 76 C1
Sparrowpit Derbys ... 83 F3
Sparrows Green E Susx ... 17 G5
Sparsholt Hants ... 26 C2
Sparsholt Oxon ... 40 B3
Spartylea Cumb ... 105 E5
Spath Staffs ... 71 F4
Spaunton N York ... 98 C4
Spaxton Somset ... 23 E3
Spean Bridge Highld ... 144 D3
Spear Hill W Susx ... 16 B3
Spearywell Hants ... 26 A2
Speen Berks ... 26 C6
Speen Bucks ... 41 G4
Speeton N York ... 99 G2
Speke Mersyd ... 81 G3
Speldhurst Kent ... 17 F6
Spellbrook Herts ... 51 F2
Spelmonden Kent ... 17 H5
Spelsbury Oxon ... 48 B1
Spen W York ... 90 C2
Spen Green Ches ... 70 C6
Spencers Wood Berks ... 27 E6
Spennithorne N York ... 97 E4
Spennymoor Dur ... 106 B4
Spernall Warwks ... 47 F5
Spestos Devon ... 8 D4
Spetchley Worcs ... 46 D5
Spetisbury Dorset ... 12 C5
Spexhall Suffk ... 65 F3
Spey Bay Moray ... 157 F6
Speybridge Highld ... 156 B2
Speyview Moray ... 157 E3
Spilsby Lincs ... 86 D1
Spindlestone Nthumb ... 125 E4
Spinkhill Derbys ... 84 B2
Spinningdale Highld ... 162 D3
Spion Kop Notts ... 84 C1
Spirthill Wilts ... 39 E2
Spital Mersyd ... 81 F3
Spital Hill S York ... 84 D4
Spital in the Street Lincs ... 85 G4
Spithurst E Susx ... 17 E3
Spittal E Loth ... 132 D3
Spittal E R Yk ... 92 B5
Spittal Highld ... 167 E4
Spittal Nthumb ... 123 G5
Spittal Pembks ... 32 D4
Spittal of Glenmuick Abers ... 147 H3
Spittal of Glenshee P & K ... 147 F1
Spittal-on-Rule Border ... 122 C1
Spittalfield P & K ... 140 A1
Spixworth Norfk ... 77 E1
Splatt Cnwll ... 4 C4
Splatt Cnwll ... 5 F5
Splatt Cnwll ... 8 C5
Splayne's Green E Susx ... 17 E4
Splottlands Cardif ... 36 C2
Spodegreen Ches ... 82 B3
Spofforth N York ... 91 E5
Spon Green Flints ... 81 E1
Spondon Derbys ... 72 B4
Spooner Row Norfk ... 64 C5
Sporle Norfk ... 76 B1
Spott E Loth ... 133 F3
Spottiswoode Border ... 122 C4
Spratton Nhants ... 60 C2
Spreakley Surrey ... 27 F3

Spreyton Devon ... 8 D4
Spriddlestone Devon ... 6 C3
Spridlington Lincs ... 85 H3
Spring Gardens Dur ... 106 A3
Spring Vale S York ... 83 G5
Springburn C Glas ... 130 B2
Springfield D & G ... 111 H2
Springfield Essex ... 51 H1
Springfield Fife ... 140 C1
Springhill Staffs ... 58 C6
Springhill Staffs ... 58 D6
Springholm D & G ... 110 C2
Springside N Ayrs ... 119 E3
Springthorpe Lincs ... 85 F4
Sproatley E R Yk ... 93 F3
Sproston Green Ches ... 82 B1
Sprotbrough S York ... 84 C5
Sproughton Suffk ... 53 E5
Sprouston Border ... 123 E3
Sprowston Norfk ... 77 E1
Sproxton Leics ... 73 F2
Sproxton N York ... 98 B3
Sprytown Devon ... 5 H4
Spunhill Shrops ... 69 F3
Spurstow Ches ... 69 H6
Spyway Dorset ... 11 F4
Square & Compass Pembks ... 32 C5
Stableford Shrops ... 57 H5
Stableford Staffs ... 70 C4
Stacey Bank Derbys ... 83 H4
Stackhouse N York ... 96 A1
Stackpole Pembks ... 32 D1
Stacksford Norfk ... 64 C4
Stacksteads Lancs ... 89 G2
Staddiscombe Devon ... 6 C3
Staddlethorpe E R Yk ... 92 B2
Staden Derbys ... 83 F2
Stadhampton Oxon ... 40 D4
Stadhlaigearraidh W Isls ... 168 b3
Staffield Cumb ... 104 B4
Staffin Highld ... 151 E5
Stafford Staffs ... 70 D2
Stagsden Beds ... 49 H4
Stainborough S York ... 84 A5
Stainburn Cumb ... 102 D3
Stainburn N York ... 90 D4
Stainby Lincs ... 73 G2
Staincross S York ... 84 A6
Staindrop Dur ... 105 H2
Staines Surrey ... 28 A3
Stainfield Lincs ... 74 A2
Stainfield Lincs ... 86 B2
Stainforth N York ... 96 B2
Stainforth S York ... 84 D6
Staining Lancs ... 88 B3
Stainland W York ... 90 B1
Stainsacre N York ... 99 E6
Stainsby Derbys ... 84 B1
Stainton Cumb ... 103 H6
Stainton Cumb ... 104 B3
Stainton Cumb ... 95 F3
Stainton Dur ... 105 G2
Stainton N York ... 106 D2
Stainton N York ... 96 D4
Stainton S York ... 84 C4
Stainton by Langworth Lincs ... 86 A2
Stainton le Vale Lincs ... 86 B4
Stainton with Adgarley Cumb ... 94 C2
Staintondale N York ... 99 F5
Stair Cumb ... 103 F2
Stair E Ayrs ... 119 F2
Stair Haven D & G ... 100 C5
Stairfoot S York ... 84 A5
Staithes N York ... 107 G3
Stake Pool Lancs ... 88 C4
Stakeford Nthumb ... 114 D4
Stakes Hants ... 15 E4
Stalbridge Dorset ... 24 C1
Stalbridge Weston Dorset ... 24 C1
Stalham Norfk ... 77 G2
Stalham Green Norfk ... 77 G2
Stalisfield Green Kent ... 30 C1
Stallen Dorset ... 24 B1
Stalling Busk N York ... 96 B3
Stallingborough Lincs ... 86 B6
Stallington Staffs ... 70 D4
Stalmine Lancs ... 88 B4
Stalmine Moss Side Lancs ... 88 B4
Stalybridge Gt Man ... 83 E4
Stambourne Essex ... 51 H5
Stambourne Green Essex ... 51 H4
Stamford Lincs ... 61 F6
Stamford Nthumb ... 125 E3
Stamford Bridge Ches ... 81 G1
Stamford Bridge E R Yk ... 92 A5
Stamford Hill Gt Lon ... 28 D5
Stamfordham Nthumb ... 114 B3
Stanah Lancs ... 88 B4
Stanborough Herts ... 50 C2
Stanbridge Beds ... 49 H2
Stanbridge Dorset ... 12 D5
Stanbury W York ... 90 A3
Stand Gt Man ... 82 C5
Stand N Lans ... 130 D2
Standburn Falk ... 131 E3
Standeford Staffs ... 58 B6
Standen Kent ... 18 B5
Standen Street Kent ... 18 B4
Standerwick Somset ... 24 D4
Standford Hants ... 27 F3
Standingstone Cumb ... 102 D3
Standish Gloucs ... 38 C5
Standish Gt Man ... 81 H6
Standish Lower Ground Gt Man ... 81 H5
Standlake Oxon ... 40 B5
Standon Hants ... 26 C2
Standon Herts ... 51 E3
Standon Staffs ... 70 C3
Standon Green End Herts ... 50 D3
Standwell Green Suffk ... 64 D2
Stane N Lans ... 120 C5
Stanfield Norfk ... 76 B2
Stanford Beds ... 50 C5
Stanford Kent ... 19 E5
Stanford Shrops ... 69 F1
Stanford Bishop Herefs ... 46 B4
Stanford Bridge Shrops ... 70 B2

Stanford Bridge *Worcs* 57 G2
Stanford Dingley *Berks* 40 D1
Stanford in the Vale *Oxon* 40 B4
Stanford le Hope *Essex* 29 H4
Stanford on Avon *Nhants* 60 B3
Stanford on Soar *Notts* 72 C2
Stanford on Teme *Worcs* 57 G2
Stanfree *Derbys* 84 B2
Stanghow *N York* 107 F2
Stanground *Cambs* 62 A5
Stanhill *Lancs* 89 F2
Stanhoe *Norfk* 76 A4
Stanhope *Border* 121 F2
Stanhope *Dur* 105 G4
Stanhope Bretby *Derbys* 71 H2
Stanion *Nhants* 61 E4
Stanklin *Worcs* 58 B3
Stanley *Derbys* 72 B4
Stanley *Dur* 106 A6
Stanley *Notts* 84 B1
Stanley *P & K* 140 A3
Stanley *Staffs* 70 D5
Stanley *W York* 91 E2
Stanley Common *Derbys* 72 B4
Stanley Crook *Dur* 106 A5
Stanley Ferry *W York* 91 E2
Stanley Gate *Lancs* 81 G5
Stanley Moor *Staffs* 70 D5
Stanley Pontlarge *Gloucs* 47 E2
Stanmer *E Susx* 16 D2
Stanmore *Berks* 40 C2
Stanmore *Gt Lon* 28 C5
Stanmore *Hants* 26 C2
Stannersburn *Nthumb* 112 D3
Stanningfield *Suffk* 64 A1
Stanningley *W York* 90 C3
Stannington *Nthumb* 114 D3
Stannington *S York* 83 H3
Stannington Station *Nthumb* 114 D4
Stansbatch *Herefs* 45 F5
Stansfield *Suffk* 52 A6
Stanshope *Staffs* 71 F5
Stanstead *Suffk* 52 B6
Stanstead Abbotts *Herts* 51 E2
Stanstead Street *Suffk* 52 B6
Stansted *Kent* 29 G2
Stansted Airport *Essex* 51 F3
Stansted Mountfitchet *Essex* 51 F3
Stanton *Derbys* 71 H2
Stanton *Devon* 6 D3
Stanton *Gloucs* 47 F3
Stanton *Mons* 45 F1
Stanton *Nthumb* 114 C4
Stanton *Staffs* 71 F5
Stanton *Suffk* 64 B3
Stanton Butts *Cambs* 62 B3
Stanton by Bridge *Derbys* 72 A3
Stanton by Dale *Derbys* 72 B4
Stanton Drew *Somset* 24 B6
Stanton Fitzwarren *Wilts* 39 F3
Stanton Harcourt *Oxon* 40 B5
Stanton Hill *Notts* 72 B6
Stanton in Peak *Derbys* 83 G1
Stanton Lacy *Shrops* 57 E5
Stanton Lees *Derbys* 83 G1
Stanton Long *Shrops* 57 F4
Stanton on the Wolds *Notts* 72 D3
Stanton Prior *Somset* 24 B5
Stanton St Bernard *Wilts* 25 F5
Stanton St John *Oxon* 40 D5
Stanton St Quintin *Wilts* 38 D2
Stanton Street *Suffk* 64 B2
Stanton under Bardon *Leics* 72 B1
Stanton upon Hine Heath *Shrops* 69 H2
Stanton Wick *Somset* 24 B5
Stantway *Gloucs* 38 B6
Stanwardine in the Field *Shrops* 69 F2
Stanwardine in the Wood *Shrops* 69 F3
Stanway *Essex* 52 C3
Stanway *Gloucs* 47 F2
Stanway Green *Essex* 52 C3
Stanway Green *Suffk* 65 E2
Stanwell *Surrey* 28 B3
Stanwell Moor *Surrey* 28 A3
Stanwick *Nhants* 61 F2
Stanwix *Cumb* 103 H6
Staoinebrig *W Isls* 168 b3
Stape *N York* 98 D4
Stapehill *Dorset* 12 D5
Stapeley *Ches* 70 B5
Stapenhill *Staffs* 71 G2
Staple *Kent* 31 F2
Staple *Somset* 22 D3
Staple Cross *Devon* 22 C1
Staple Cross *E Susx* 18 A4
Staple Fitzpaine *Somset* 23 E1
Staple Hill *Worcs* 58 C3
Staplefield *W Susx* 16 D4
Stapleford *Cambs* 51 F6
Stapleford *Herts* 50 D2
Stapleford *Leics* 73 F2
Stapleford *Lincs* 73 F6
Stapleford *Notts* 72 C4
Stapleford *Wilts* 25 F3
Stapleford Abbotts *Essex* 29 F5
Stapleford Tawney *Essex* 29 F6
Staplegrove *Somset* 23 E2
Staplehay *Somset* 23 E1
Staplehurst *Kent* 18 A6
Staplers *IOW* 14 C2
Staplestreet *Kent* 30 D2
Staplet *Cumb* 112 B2
Stapleton *Herefs* 56 B2
Stapleton *Leics* 59 G5
Stapleton *N York* 106 B2
Stapleton *Shrops* 57 E6
Stapleton *Somset* 23 G1
Stapley *Somset* 10 B6
Staploe *Beds* 61 G1
Staplow *Herefs* 46 C3
Star *Fife* 132 B5
Star *Pembks* 42 C3
Star *Somset* 23 G5
Starbeck *N York* 90 D5
Starbotton *N York* 96 C2
Starcross *Devon* 9 G3

Stareton *Warwks* 59 F2
Starkholmes *Derbys* 71 H6
Starling *Gt Man* 82 C6
Starlings Green *Essex* 51 E4
Starr's Green *E Susx* 18 A3
Starston *Norfk* 65 E4
Start *Devon* 7 E2
Startforth *Dur* 105 G2
Startley *Wilts* 38 D2
Statenborough *Kent* 31 G2
Statham *Ches* 82 B3
Stathe *Somset* 23 F2
Stathern *Leics* 73 E3
Station Town *Dur* 106 C4
Staughton Green *Cambs* 61 G2
Staughton Highway *Cambs* 61 G2
Staunton *Gloucs* 37 F5
Staunton *Gloucs* 46 C2
Staunton Green *Herefs* 45 F5
Staunton in the Vale *Notts* 73 F4
Staunton on Arrow *Herefs* 45 F5
Staunton on Wye *Herefs* 45 F4
Staveley *Cumb* 94 D3
Staveley *Cumb* 95 E5
Staveley *Derbys* 84 B2
Staveley *N York* 91 E6
Staverton *Devon* 7 E4
Staverton *Gloucs* 46 D1
Staverton *Nhants* 48 D5
Staverton *Wilts* 24 D5
Staverton Bridge *Gloucs* 46 D1
Stawell *Somset* 23 F3
Stawley *Somset* 22 C1
Staxigoe *Highld* 167 G4
Staxton *N York* 99 F3
Staylittle *Cerdgn* 54 D4
Staylittle *Powys* 55 F5
Staynall *Lancs* 88 B4
Staythorpe *Notts* 73 E5
Stead *W York* 90 C4
Stean *N York* 96 D2
Steane *Nhants* 48 D3
Stearsby *N York* 98 B2
Steart *Somset* 23 E4
Stebbing *Essex* 51 G3
Stebbing Green *Essex* 51 H3
Stebbing Park *Essex* 51 G3
Stechford *W Mids* 58 D4
Stede Quarter *Kent* 18 B5
Stedham *W Susx* 27 G1
Steel *Nthumb* 105 F6
Steel Cross *E Susx* 17 F4
Steel Green *Cumb* 94 B3
Steel Heath *Shrops* 69 H4
Steele Road *Border* 112 B4
Steelend *Fife* 131 G4
Steen's Bridge *Herefs* 46 A5
Steep *Hants* 27 F2
Steep Lane *W York* 90 B2
Steephill *IOW* 14 D1
Steeple *Dorset* 12 C3
Steeple *Essex* 52 C1
Steeple Ashton *Wilts* 25 E5
Steeple Aston *Oxon* 48 C2
Steeple Barton *Oxon* 48 C2
Steeple Bumpstead *Essex* 51 H5
Steeple Claydon *Bucks* 49 E2
Steeple Gidding *Cambs* 61 G3
Steeple Langford *Wilts* 25 F3
Steeple Morden *Cambs* 50 D5
Steeton *W York* 90 B4
Stein *Highld* 150 C4
Stella *T & W* 114 C2
Stelling Minnis *Kent* 19 E6
Stembridge *Somset* 23 G1
Stenalees *Cnwll* 3 G5
Stenhouse *D & G* 110 C4
Stenhousemuir *Falk* 131 E3
Stenigot *Lincs* 86 C3
Stenscholl *Highld* 151 E5
Stenton *E Loth* 133 E2
Steornabhagh *W Isls* 168 f8
Stepaside *Pembks* 33 F2
Stepney *Gt Lon* 28 D4
Stepping Hill *Gt Man* 82 D3
Steppingley *Beds* 50 A4
Stepps *N Lans* 130 C2
Sternfield *Suffk* 65 F1
Sterridge *Devon* 21 F5
Stert *Wilts* 25 F5
Stetchworth *Cambs* 63 F1
Stevenage *Herts* 50 C3
Stevenston *N Ayrs* 118 C4
Steventon *Hants* 26 D4
Steventon *Oxon* 40 C3
Steventon End *Essex* 51 G5
Stevington *Beds* 49 H4
Stewartby *Beds* 50 A5
Stewartfield *S Lans* 119 H5
Stewarton *E Ayrs* 119 F4
Stewkley *Bucks* 49 G2
Stewley *Somset* 23 F1
Stewton *Lincs* 86 D3
Steyne Cross *IOW* 15 E2
Steyning *W Susx* 16 C2
Steynton *Pembks* 32 C2
Stibb *Cnwll* 20 B2
Stibb Cross *Devon* 20 B3
Stibb Green *Wilts* 25 H5
Stibbard *Norfk* 76 C3
Stibbington *Cambs* 61 G5
Stichill *Border* 122 D3
Sticker *Cnwll* 3 G5
Stickford *Lincs* 74 D6
Sticklepath *Devon* 8 C4
Sticklepath *Somset* 22 C4
Stickling Green *Essex* 51 F4
Stickney *Lincs* 74 D6
Stiff Street *Kent* 30 B2
Stiffkey *Norfk* 76 C4
Stifford's Bridge *Herefs* 46 C4
Stile Bridge *Kent* 18 A6
Stileway *Somset* 23 G3
Stillingfleet *N York* 91 G4
Stillington *Dur* 106 C3
Stillington *N York* 98 B2

Stilton *Cambs* 61 G4
Stinchcombe *Gloucs* 38 B4
Stinsford *Dorset* 11 G4
Stiperstones *Shrops* 56 D5
Stirchley *Shrops* 57 G6
Stirchley *W Mids* 58 C3
Stirling *Abers* 159 G3
Stirling *Stirlg* 130 D4
Stirtloe *Cambs* 62 A2
Stirton *N York* 89 H5
Stisted *Essex* 52 B3
Stitchcombe *Wilts* 39 G1
Stithians *Cnwll* 3 E3
Stivichall *W Mids* 59 F3
Stixwould *Lincs* 86 B1
Stoak *Ches* 81 F2
Stobo *Border* 121 F3
Stoborough *Dorset* 12 C3
Stoborough Green *Dorset* 12 C3
Stobs Castle *Border* 112 B6
Stobswood *Nthumb* 114 D5
Stock *Essex* 29 H6
Stock *Somset* 23 G5
Stock Green *Worcs* 47 E5
Stock Wood *Worcs* 47 E5
Stockbridge *Hants* 26 B3
Stockbriggs *S Lans* 120 B3
Stockbury *Kent* 30 B2
Stockcross *Berks* 40 C1
Stockdale *Cnwll* 3 E3
Stockdalewath *Cumb* 103 H5
Stocker's Hill *Kent* 30 C1
Stockerston *Leics* 60 D5
Stocking *Herefs* 46 B2
Stocking Green *Bucks* 49 F4
Stocking Pelham *Herts* 51 E4
Stockingford *Warwks* 59 F4
Stockland *Devon* 10 C5
Stockland Bristol *Somset* 23 E4
Stockland Green *Kent* 17 F6
Stockleigh English *Devon* 9 E5
Stockleigh Pomeroy *Devon* 9 F5
Stockley *Wilts* 25 E6
Stockley Hill *Herefs* 45 F3
Stocklinch *Somset* 23 G1
Stockmoor *Herefs* 45 G5
Stockport *Gt Man* 82 D4
Stocksbridge *S York* 83 G4
Stocksfield *Nthumb* 114 B2
Stockstreet *Essex* 52 B3
Stockton *Herefs* 45 H5
Stockton *Norfk* 65 F5
Stockton *Shrops* 56 C5
Stockton *Shrops* 70 C2
Stockton *Shrops* 57 G5
Stockton *Warwks* 59 G2
Stockton *Wilts* 25 E3
Stockton Brook *Staffs* 70 D5
Stockton Heath *Ches* 82 A3
Stockton on Teme *Worcs* 57 G2
Stockton on the Forest *N York* 91 H5
Stockton-on-Tees *Dur* 106 D3
Stockwell *Gloucs* 38 D6
Stockwell End *W Mids* 58 B5
Stockwell Heath *Staffs* 71 E2
Stockwood *Bristl* 37 G1
Stockwood *Dorset* 11 F5
Stodday *Lancs* 88 D3
Stodmarsh *Kent* 31 F2
Stody *Norfk* 76 D3
Stoer *Highld* 164 B1
Stoford *Somset* 11 F6
Stoford *Wilts* 25 F3
Stogumber *Somset* 22 D3
Stogursey *Somset* 23 E3
Stoke *Devon* 20 C3
Stoke *Hants* 26 B4
Stoke *Hants* 15 E4
Stoke *Kent* 30 B3
Stoke *W Mids* 59 G3
Stoke Abbott *Dorset* 11 E5
Stoke Albany *Nhants* 60 D4
Stoke Ash *Suffk* 64 D2
Stoke Bardolph *Notts* 72 D4
Stoke Bliss *Worcs* 57 G2
Stoke Bruerne *Nhants* 49 F4
Stoke by Clare *Suffk* 52 A5
Stoke Canon *Devon* 9 F4
Stoke Charity *Hants* 26 C3
Stoke Climsland *Cnwll* 5 G3
Stoke D'Abernon *Surrey* 28 B2
Stoke Doyle *Nhants* 61 H4
Stoke Dry *Rutlnd* 61 E5
Stoke Edith *Herefs* 46 B3
Stoke End *Warwks* 59 E5
Stoke Farthing *Wilts* 25 F2
Stoke Ferry *Norfk* 63 F5
Stoke Fleming *Devon* 7 E6
Stoke Gabriel *Devon* 7 F3
Stoke Gifford *Gloucs* 37 G2
Stoke Golding *Leics* 59 G5
Stoke Goldington *Bucks* 49 F4
Stoke Green *Bucks* 41 H2
Stoke Hammond *Bucks* 49 G2
Stoke Heath *Shrops* 70 B5
Stoke Heath *W Mids* 59 F3
Stoke Heath *Worcs* 58 B2
Stoke Holy Cross *Norfk* 65 E6
Stoke Lacy *Herefs* 46 B4
Stoke Lyne *Oxon* 48 D2
Stoke Mandeville *Bucks* 41 H5
Stoke Newington *Gt Lon* 28 D5
Stoke Orchard *Gloucs* 47 E2
Stoke Poges *Bucks* 41 H2
Stoke Pound *Worcs* 58 C2
Stoke Prior *Herefs* 45 H5
Stoke Prior *Worcs* 58 B2
Stoke Rivers *Devon* 21 F4
Stoke Row *Oxon* 41 E3
Stoke St Gregory *Somset* 23 F2
Stoke St Mary *Somset* 23 E1
Stoke St Michael *Somset* 24 B4
Stoke St Milborough *Shrops* 57 F4
Stoke sub Hamdon *Somset* 23 G1
Stoke Talmage *Oxon* 41 E4
Stoke Trister *Somset* 24 C2
Stoke upon Tern *Shrops* 70 A3

Stoke Wake *Dorset* 12 B5
Stoke Wharf *Worcs* 58 B2
Stoke-by-Nayland *Suffk* 52 C4
Stoke-on-Trent *Staffs* 70 D5
Stoke-upon-Trent *Staffs* 70 D5
Stokeford *Dorset* 12 C3
Stokeham *Notts* 85 E2
Stokeinteignhead *Devon* 7 F5
Stokenchurch *Bucks* 41 F4
Stokenham *Devon* 7 E6
Stokesay *Shrops* 57 E3
Stokesay Castle *Shrops* 57 E3
Stokesby *Norfk* 77 G1
Stokesley *N York* 107 E2
Stolford *Somset* 23 E4
Ston Easton *Somset* 24 B5
Stondon Massey *Essex* 29 G6
Stone *Bucks* 41 F5
Stone *Gloucs* 38 B4
Stone *Kent* 29 G3
Stone *Kent* 18 C4
Stone *S York* 84 C4
Stone *Somset* 24 A3
Stone *Staffs* 70 D3
Stone *Worcs* 58 B3
Stone Allerton *Somset* 23 G4
Stone Bridge Corner *Cambs* 62 B5
Stone Chair *W York* 90 B2
Stone Cross *E Susx* 17 F4
Stone Cross *E Susx* 17 G2
Stone Cross *E Susx* 17 G4
Stone Cross *Kent* 17 F5
Stone Cross *Kent* 18 D5
Stone Cross *Kent* 31 G2
Stone Hill *S York* 84 D6
Stone House *Cumb* 96 A3
Stone Street *Kent* 29 G1
Stone Street *Suffk* 52 C5
Stone Street *Suffk* 52 D5
Stone Street *Suffk* 65 F4
Stone-edge-Batch *Somset* 37 F1
Stonea *Cambs* 62 D5
Stonebridge *Norfk* 64 B4
Stonebridge *Somset* 23 G5
Stonebridge *W Mids* 59 E4
Stonebroom *Derbys* 72 B6
Stonecross Green *Suffk* 63 G1
Stonecrouch *Kent* 17 H5
Stoneferry *E R Yk* 93 E3
Stonefield Castle Hotel *Ag & B* 127 G2
Stonegate *E Susx* 17 G4
Stonegate *N York* 107 G2
Stonegrave *N York* 98 B3
Stonehall *Worcs* 46 D4
Stonehaugh *Nthumb* 113 E2
Stonehaven *Abers* 149 F3
Stonehenge *Wilts* 25 G3
Stonehill Green *Gt Lon* 29 F3
Stonehouse *Ches* 81 G2
Stonehouse *D & G* 110 C2
Stonehouse *Devon* 6 B3
Stonehouse *Gloucs* 38 C5
Stonehouse *Nthumb* 104 D6
Stonehouse *S Lans* 120 B4
Stoneleigh *Warwks* 59 F3
Stoneley Green *Ches* 70 A5
Stonely *Cambs* 61 G2
Stoner Hill *Hants* 27 E2
Stones Green *Essex* 53 E3
Stonesby *Leics* 73 F2
Stonesfield *Oxon* 40 B6
Stonestreet Green *Kent* 18 D5
Stonethwaite *Cumb* 103 G1
Stonewells *Moray* 157 E6
Stonewood *Kent* 29 G3
Stoney Cross *Hants* 13 F6
Stoney Middleton *Derbys* 83 G2
Stoney Stanton *Leics* 59 H5
Stoney Stoke *Somset* 24 C2
Stoney Stratton *Somset* 24 B3
Stoney Stretton *Shrops* 69 F1
Stoneybridge *W Isls* 168 b3
Stoneybridge *Worcs* 58 B3
Stoneyburn *W Loth* 120 D6
Stoneygate *Leics* 60 B6
Stoneyhills *Essex* 30 C6
Stoneykirk *D & G* 100 B5
Stoneywood *Aber C* 149 F5
Stoneywood *Falk* 130 D2
Stonham Aspal *Suffk* 64 D1
Stonnall *Staffs* 58 D6
Stonor *Oxon* 41 E3
Stonton Wyville *Leics* 60 C5
Stony Cross *Herefs* 57 F2
Stony Cross *Herefs* 46 C4
Stony Houghton *Derbys* 84 C1
Stony Stratford *Bucks* 49 F3
Stonyford *Hants* 13 G6
Stonywell *Staffs* 71 F1
Stoodleigh *Devon* 21 G4
Stoodleigh *Devon* 22 B1
Stopham *W Susx* 16 A3
Stopsley *Beds* 50 B3
Stoptide *Cnwll* 4 C3
Storeton *Mersyd* 81 E3
Storeyard Green *Herefs* 46 C4
Stormy Corner *Lancs* 81 G5
Stornoway *W Isls* 168 f8
Stornoway Airport *W Isls* 168 f8
Storridge *Herefs* 46 C4
Storrington *W Susx* 16 B3
Storth *Cumb* 95 E3
Storwood *E R Yk* 92 A4
Stotfield *Moray* 156 D6
Stotfold *Beds* 50 C4
Stottesdon *Shrops* 57 F3
Stoughton *Leics* 60 B6
Stoughton *Surrey* 27 H4
Stoughton *W Susx* 15 F5
Stoul *Highld* 143 G3
Stoulton *Worcs* 47 E4
Stour Provost *Dorset* 24 C1
Stour Row *Dorset* 24 D1
Stourbridge *W Mids* 58 B4
Stourpaine *Dorset* 12 C6
Stourport-on-Severn *Worcs* 58 A2
Stourton *Staffs* 58 B4
Stourton *W York* 90 D3

Stourton *Warwks* 48 A3
Stourton *Wilts* 24 C3
Stourton Caundle *Dorset* 11 G6
Stout *Somset* 23 G2
Stove *Shet* 169 h2
Stoven *Suffk* 65 G3
Stow *Border* 122 B4
Stow *Lincs* 85 F3
Stow Bardolph *Norfk* 63 E6
Stow Bedon *Norfk* 64 B5
Stow Longa *Cambs* 61 G2
Stow Maries *Essex* 30 B6
Stow-cum-Quy *Cambs* 62 D1
Stow-on-the-Wold *Gloucs* 47 G2
Stowbridge *Norfk* 63 E6
Stowe *Gloucs* 37 G5
Stowe *Shrops* 56 C3
Stowe by Chartley *Staffs* 71 E3
Stowehill *Nhants* 49 E5
Stowell *Somset* 24 B1
Stowey *Somset* 24 B5
Stowford *Devon* 8 A4
Stowford *Devon* 21 G5
Stowford *Devon* 8 A3
Stowford *Devon* 10 B4
Stowlangtoft *Suffk* 64 B2
Stowmarket *Suffk* 64 C1
Stowting *Kent* 19 E6
Stowting Common *Kent* 19 E6
Stowupland *Suffk* 64 C1
Straanruie *Moray* 147 E6
Strachan *Abers* 148 D4
Strachur *Ag & B* 128 B5
Stracthro Hospital *Angus* 148 D1
Stradbroke *Suffk* 65 E3
Stradishall *Wilts* 25 E3
Stradishall *Suffk* 52 A6
Stradsett *Norfk* 63 F6
Stragglethorpe *Lincs* 73 G5
Stragglethorpe *Notts* 72 D4
Straight Soley *Wilts* 40 A1
Straiton *Mdloth* 132 B2
Straiton *S Ayrs* 109 F5
Straloch *Abers* 158 D1
Straloch *P & K* 139 H6
Stramshall *Staffs* 71 F4
Strang *IOM* 174 I3
Strangford *Herefs* 46 A2
Stranraer *D & G* 100 B6
Strata Florida *Cerdgn* 55 E2
Stratfield Mortimer *Berks* 27 E6
Stratfield Saye *Hants* 27 E5
Stratfield Turgis *Hants* 27 E5
Stratford *Beds* 50 C5
Stratford *Gt Lon* 29 E4
Stratford St Andrew *Suffk* 65 F1
Stratford St Mary *Suffk* 52 D4
Stratford sub Castle *Wilts* 25 G2
Stratford Tony *Wilts* 25 F2
Stratford-upon-Avon *Warwks* 47 G5
Strath *Highld* 160 B3
Strathan *Highld* 161 E6
Strathan *Highld* 165 G5
Strathaven *S Lans* 120 B4
Strathblane *Stirlg* 129 G3
Strathcanaird *Highld* 161 F4
Strathcarron Station *Highld* 152 D3
Strathcoil *Ag & B* 136 B3
Strathdon *Abers* 148 A6
Strathkinness *Fife* 141 E1
Strathloanhead *W Loth* 131 E2
Strathmashie House *Highld* 145 H4
Strathmiglo *Fife* 132 A6
Strathpeffer *Highld* 154 C5
Strathtay *P & K* 139 F5
Strathwhillan *N Ayrs* 118 B3
Strathy *Highld* 166 B5
Strathy Inn *Highld* 166 B5
Strathyre *Stirlg* 138 C1
Stratton *Cnwll* 20 C1
Stratton *Dorset* 11 G4
Stratton *Gloucs* 39 E5
Stratton Audley *Oxon* 48 D2
Stratton St Margaret *Wilts* 39 F3
Stratton St Michael *Norfk* 64 D5
Stratton Strawless *Norfk* 77 E2
Stratton-on-the-Fosse *Somset* 24 B4
Stravithie *Fife* 141 E1
Stream *Somset* 22 D3
Streat *E Susx* 16 D3
Streatham *Gt Lon* 28 D3
Streatley *Beds* 50 B3
Streatley *Berks* 40 D2
Street *Devon* 10 B3
Street *Lancs* 88 D5
Street *N York* 98 C5
Street *Somset* 23 H3
Street Ashton *Warwks* 59 G4
Street Dinas *Shrops* 69 F4
Street End *E Susx* 17 G4
Street End *Kent* 31 E1
Street Gate *T & W* 114 C1
Street Houses *N York* 107 G3
Street Houses *N York* 91 F4
Street Lane *Derbys* 72 B5
Street on the Fosse *Somset* 24 B3
Streethay *Staffs* 71 F1
Streetlam *N York* 97 F5
Streetly *W Mids* 58 D5
Streetly End *Cambs* 51 G5
Strefford *Shrops* 57 E4
Strelitz *P & K* 140 C3
Strelley *Notts* 72 C4
Strensall *N York* 91 G6
Strensham *Worcs* 47 E3
Stretcholt *Somset* 23 F4
Strete *Devon* 7 F2
Stretford *Gt Man* 82 C4
Stretford *Herefs* 45 G5
Stretford *Herefs* 45 H5
Strethall *Essex* 51 F5
Stretham *Cambs* 62 D3
Strettington *W Susx* 15 G4
Stretton *Ches* 69 G5
Stretton *Ches* 82 A3
Stretton *Derbys* 72 B6
Stretton *Rutlnd* 73 G2

Stretton *Staffs* 70 D1
Stretton *Staffs* 71 G3
Stretton en le Field *Leics* 71 H1
Stretton Grandison *Herefs* 46 B4
Stretton Heath *Shrops* 69 F1
Stretton on Fosse *Warwks* 47 H3
Stretton Sugwas *Herefs* 45 G3
Stretton under Fosse *Warwks* 59 G3
Stretton Westwood *Shrops* 57 F5
Stretton-on-Dunsmore *Warwks* 59 G3
Strichen *Abers* 159 E5
Strines *Gt Man* 83 E3
Stringston *Somset* 23 E3
Strixton *Nhants* 49 G5
Stroat *Gloucs* 37 G4
Stromeferry *Highld* 152 C2
Stromness *Ork* 169 a2
Stronachlachar *Stirlg* 129 E6
Stronafian *Ag & B* 128 B3
Stronchrubie *Highld* 161 G6
Strone *Ag & B* 128 C3
Strone *Highld* 144 D2
Stronenaba *Highld* 144 D3
Stronmilchan *Ag & B* 137 F3
Stronsay Airport *Ork* 169 c3
Strontian *Highld* 136 C6
Strood *Kent* 29 H3
Strood *Kent* 18 B5
Strood Green *Surrey* 16 C6
Strood Green *W Susx* 16 A4
Stroud *Gloucs* 38 C5
Stroud *Hants* 27 E2
Stroud Green *Essex* 30 B5
Stroud Green *Gloucs* 38 C5
Stroude *Surrey* 28 A3
Stroxton *Lincs* 73 G3
Struan *Highld* 150 D2
Struan *P & K* 146 C1
Strubby *Lincs* 87 E3
Strumpshaw *Norfk* 65 F6
Strutherhill *S Lans* 120 B4
Struthers *Fife* 132 C6
Struy *Highld* 154 B3
Stryd-y-Facsen *IOA* 78 C3
Stryt-issa *Wrexhm* 69 E5
Stuartfield *Abers* 159 F4
Stubbers Green *W Mids* 58 C5
Stubbington *Hants* 14 D4
Stubbins *N York* 89 F1
Stubbs Green *Norfk* 65 E5
Stubhampton *Dorset* 12 C6
Stubley *Derbys* 84 A3
Stubshaw Cross *Gt Man* 81 H5
Stubton *Lincs* 73 F5
Stuchbury *Nhants* 48 D4
Stuckeridge *Devon* 22 B1
Stuckton *Hants* 13 E6
Stud Green *Berks* 41 G2
Studfold *N York* 96 A2
Studham *Beds* 50 A2
Studholme *Cumb* 103 F6
Studland *Dorset* 12 D3
Studley *Warwks* 58 D2
Studley *Wilts* 38 D1
Studley Common *Warwks* 58 D2
Studley Roger *N York* 97 F2
Studley Royal *N York* 97 F2
Stump Cross *Cambs* 51 F5
Stuntney *Cambs* 63 E3
Stunts Green *E Susx* 17 G3
Sturbridge *Staffs* 70 C3
Sturgate *Lincs* 85 F4
Sturmer *Essex* 51 H5
Sturminster Common *Dorset* 12 B6
Sturminster Marshall *Dorset* 12 C5
Sturminster Newton *Dorset* 12 B6
Sturry *Kent* 31 E2
Sturton *Lincs* 85 G5
Sturton by Stow *Lincs* 85 F3
Sturton le Steeple *Notts* 85 E3
Stuston *Suffk* 64 D3
Stutton *N York* 91 F4
Stutton *Suffk* 53 E4
Styal *Ches* 82 C3
Stydd *Lancs* 89 E3
Stynie *Moray* 157 E5
Styrrup *Notts* 84 D4
Succoth *Ag & B* 128 D6
Suckley *Worcs* 46 C4
Suckley Green *Worcs* 46 C5
Sudborough *Nhants* 61 F4
Sudbourne *Suffk* 53 H6
Sudbrook *Lincs* 73 G4
Sudbrook *Mons* 37 F3
Sudbrooke *Lincs* 85 H2
Sudbury *Derbys* 71 F3
Sudbury *Gt Lon* 28 C5
Sudbury *Suffk* 52 B5
Sudden *Gt Man* 82 D6
Suddington *Worcs* 58 A2
Sudgrove *Gloucs* 38 D5
Suffield *N York* 99 E4
Suffield *Norfk* 77 E3
Sugdon *Shrops* 70 A1
Sugnall *Staffs* 70 C3
Sugwas Pool *Herefs* 45 G3
Suisnish *Highld* 143 E6
Sulby *IOM* 174 m4
Sulgrave *Nhants* 48 D4
Sulgrave Manor *Nhants* 48 D4
Sulham *Berks* 41 E2
Sulhamstead *Berks* 40 D1
Sulhamstead Abbots *Berks* 27 E6
Sulhamstead Bannister *Berks* 41 E1
Sullington *W Susx* 16 B3
Sullom *Shet* 169 h4
Sullom Voe *Shet* 169 h4
Sully *V Glam* 36 C1
Sumburgh Airport *Shet* 169 h1
Summer Heath *Bucks* 41 F3
Summer Hill *Wrexhm* 69 E5
Summerbridge *N York* 90 C6
Summercourt *Cnwll* 3 F5
Summerfield *Norfk* 75 H4
Summerfield *Worcs* 58 A3
Summerhouse *Dur* 106 A3
Summerlands *Cumb* 95 F3
Summerley *Derbys* 84 A2

Summersdale *W Susx* 15 G4
Summerseat *Gt Man* 89 F1
Summertown *Oxon* 40 C5
Summit *Gt Man* 82 D6
Summit *N York* 89 H1
Sunbiggin *N York* 95 G6
Sunbury *Surrey* 28 B3
Sundaywell *D & G* 110 C3
Sunderland *Ag & B* 126 A1
Sunderland *Cumb* 103 F4
Sunderland *Lancs* 88 C5
Sunderland *T & W* 115 F1
Sunderland Bridge *Dur* 106 B5
Sundhope *Border* 121 H2
Sundon Park *Beds* 50 B3
Sundridge *Kent* 29 F1
Sunk Island *E R Yk* 93 F1
Sunningdale *Berks* 27 H6
Sunninghill *Surrey* 27 G6
Sunningwell *Oxon* 40 C4
Sunniside *Dur* 105 H4
Sunniside *T & W* 114 D1
Sunny Bank *Lancs* 89 F2
Sunny Brow *Dur* 106 A4
Sunnyhill *Derbys* 72 A3
Sunnyhurst *Lancs* 89 E2
Sunnylaw *Stirlg* 130 D5
Sunnymead *Oxon* 40 C5
Sunton *Wilts* 25 H5
Surbiton *Gt Lon* 28 C3
Surfleet *Lincs* 74 C3
Surfleet Seas End *Lincs* 74 C3
Surlingham *Norfk* 65 F6
Surrex *Essex* 52 B3
Sustead *Norfk* 77 E4
Susworth *Lincs* 85 F5
Sutcombe *Devon* 20 D2
Sutcombemill *Devon* 20 D2
Suton *Norfk* 64 C5
Sutterby *Lincs* 86 D2
Sutterton *Lincs* 74 C4
Sutton *Beds* 50 C5
Sutton *Cambs* 61 G5
Sutton *Cambs* 62 D3
Sutton *Devon* 8 D5
Sutton *Devon* 6 D2
Sutton *E Susx* 17 F1
Sutton *Gt Lon* 28 C2
Sutton *Kent* 31 G1
Sutton *Mersyd* 81 G4
Sutton *N York* 91 F2
Sutton *Norfk* 77 G2
Sutton *Notts* 73 E4
Sutton *Oxon* 40 B5
Sutton *Pembks* 32 C3
Sutton *S York* 84 C6
Sutton *Shrops* 69 F3
Sutton *Shrops* 69 G1
Sutton *Shrops* 70 B3
Sutton *Shrops* 57 G4
Sutton *Staffs* 70 C2
Sutton *Suffk* 53 G5
Sutton *W Susx* 15 H5
Sutton at Hone *Kent* 29 F3
Sutton Bassett *Nhants* 60 D4
Sutton Benger *Wilts* 38 D2
Sutton Bingham *Somset* 11 F6
Sutton Bonington *Notts* 72 C2
Sutton Bridge *Lincs* 75 E2
Sutton Cheney *Leics* 59 G5
Sutton Coldfield *W Mids* 58 D5
Sutton Courtenay *Oxon* 40 C4
Sutton Crosses *Lincs* 75 E2
Sutton cum Lound *Notts* 84 D3
Sutton Fields *Notts* 72 C3
Sutton Grange *N York* 97 F2
Sutton Green *Oxon* 40 B5
Sutton Green *Surrey* 28 A1
Sutton Green *Wrexhm* 69 F5
Sutton Howgrave *N York* 97 F3
Sutton in Ashfield *Notts* 72 C6
Sutton in the Elms *Leics* 60 A5
Sutton Lane Ends *Ches* 82 D2
Sutton Maddock *Shrops* 57 G5
Sutton Mallet *Somset* 23 F3
Sutton Mandeville *Wilts* 25 E2
Sutton Manor *Mersyd* 81 G4
Sutton Marsh *Herefs* 46 A4
Sutton Montis *Somset* 24 B2
Sutton on Sea *Lincs* 87 E3
Sutton on the Hill *Derbys* 71 G3
Sutton on Trent *Notts* 85 F1
Sutton Poyntz *Dorset* 11 G3
Sutton Scotney *Hants* 26 C3
Sutton St Edmund *Lincs* 74 D1
Sutton St James *Lincs* 74 D2
Sutton St Nicholas *Herefs* 45 H4
Sutton Street *Kent* 30 B2
Sutton upon Derwent *E R Yk* 92 A4
Sutton Valence *Kent* 30 B1
Sutton Veny *Wilts* 24 D3
Sutton Waldron *Dorset* 12 C6
Sutton Weaver *Ches* 81 H3
Sutton Wick *Oxon* 40 C4
Sutton Wick *Somset* 24 A5
Sutton-in-Craven *N York* 90 A4
Sutton-on-Hull *E R Yk* 93 E3
Sutton-on-the-Forest *N York* 98 B1
Sutton-under-Brailes *Warwks* 48 A3
Sutton-under-Whitestonecliffe
  N York 97 H3
Swaby *Lincs* 86 D2
Swadlincote *Derbys* 71 H2
Swaffham *Norfk* 76 A1
Swaffham Bulbeck *Cambs* 63 E2
Swaffham Prior *Cambs* 63 E2
Swafield *Norfk* 77 F3
Swainby *N York* 97 H5
Swainshill *Herefs* 45 G3
Swainsthorpe *Norfk* 65 E5
Swainswick *Somset* 38 B1
Swalcliffe *Oxon* 48 B3
Swalecliffe *Kent* 31 E3
Swallow *Lincs* 86 B5
Swallow Beck *Lincs* 85 G1
Swallow Nest *York* 84 B3
Swallowcliffe *Wilts* 25 E2
Swallowfield *Berks* 27 E6

Swallows Cross *Essex* 29 G6
Swampton *Hants* 26 B4
Swan Green *Ches* 82 B2
Swan Street *Essex* 52 C3
Swan Village *W Mids* 58 C5
Swanage *Dorset* 12 D2
Swanbourne *Bucks* 49 F2
Swanbridge *V Glam* 22 D6
Swancote *Shrops* 57 H5
Swanland *E R Yk* 92 D3
Swanley *Kent* 29 F3
Swanley Village *Kent* 29 F3
Swanmore *Hants* 14 D5
Swannington *Leics* 72 B2
Swannington *Norfk* 76 D2
Swanpool Garden Suburb *Lincs* 85 G2
Swanscombe *Kent* 29 G3
Swansea *Swans* 34 D3
Swansea Airport *Swans* 34 C3
Swanton Abbot *Norfk* 77 F3
Swanton Morley *Norfk* 76 C2
Swanton Novers *Norfk* 76 C3
Swanton Street *Kent* 30 B2
Swanwick *Derbys* 72 B5
Swanwick *Hants* 14 C4
Swarby *Lincs* 73 H4
Swardeston *Norfk* 64 D6
Swarkestone *Derbys* 72 A3
Swarland *Nthumb* 114 C6
Swarland Estate *Nthumb* 125 E1
Swarraton *Hants* 26 D3
Swartha *W York* 90 B4
Swarthmoor *Cumb* 94 C3
Swaton *Lincs* 74 B4
Swavesey *Cambs* 62 C2
Sway *Hants* 13 G4
Swayfield *Lincs* 73 G2
Swaythling *Hants* 14 C5
Sweet Green *Worcs* 46 B5
Sweetham *Devon* 9 F4
Sweethaws *E Susx* 17 F4
Sweetlands Corner *Kent* 18 B6
Sweets *Cnwll* 5 E5
Sweetshouse *Cnwll* 4 D2
Swefling *Suffk* 65 F2
Swepstone *Leics* 72 A1
Swerford *Oxon* 48 B2
Swettenham *Ches* 82 C1
Swffryd *Blae G* 36 C4
Swift's Green *Kent* 18 B6
Swilland *Suffk* 53 E6
Swillbrook *Lancs* 88 C3
Swillington *W York* 91 E3
Swimbridge *Devon* 21 F4
Swimbridge Newland *Devon* 21 F4
Swinbrook *Oxon* 39 G5
Swincliffe *N York* 90 D5
Swincliffe *W York* 90 C2
Swincombe *Devon* 21 G5
Swinden *N York* 89 G5
Swinderby *Lincs* 85 F1
Swindon *Gloucs* 47 E2
Swindon *Nthumb* 113 G5
Swindon *Staffs* 58 B4
Swindon *Wilts* 39 F3
Swine *E R Yk* 93 E3
Swinefleet *E R Yk* 92 B2
Swineford *Gloucs* 38 B1
Swineshead *Beds* 61 F2
Swineshead *Lincs* 74 C4
Swineshead Bridge *Lincs* 74 C4
Swiney *Highld* 167 F2
Swinford *Leics* 60 B3
Swinford *Oxon* 40 C5
Swingfield Minnis *Kent* 19 F6
Swingfield Street *Kent* 19 F6
Swingleton Green *Suffk* 52 C5
Swinhoe *Nthumb* 125 E4
Swinhope *Lincs* 86 C4
Swinithwaite *N York* 96 D4
Swinmore Common *Herefs* 46 B3
Swinscoe *Staffs* 71 F5
Swinside *Cumb* 103 F2
Swinstead *Lincs* 73 H2
Swinthorpe *Lincs* 86 A3
Swinton *Border* 123 E4
Swinton *Gt Man* 82 C5
Swinton *N York* 97 E3
Swinton *N York* 98 C2
Swinton *S York* 84 B5
Swithland *Leics* 72 C1
Swordale *Highld* 154 D6
Swordland *Highld* 143 G3
Swordly *Highld* 166 A5
Sworton Heath *Ches* 82 B3
Swydd-ffynnon *Cerdgn* 54 D2
Swyncombe *Oxon* 41 F6
Swynnerton *Staffs* 70 C4
Swyre *Dorset* 11 F5
Sycharth *Powys* 68 D2
Sychnant *Powys* 55 G3
Sychtyn *Powys* 55 G6
Sydallt *Flints* 69 E6
Syde *Gloucs* 38 D5
Sydenham *Gt Lon* 28 D3
Sydenham *Oxon* 41 E4
Sydenham Damerel *Devon* 5 H3
Sydenhurst *Surrey* 27 H3
Syderstone *Norfk* 76 A3
Sydling St Nicholas *Dorset* 11 G4
Sydmonton *Hants* 26 C5
Sydnal Lane *Shrops* 58 A6
Syerston *Notts* 73 E5
Sygun Copper Mine *Gwynd* 67 F5
Syke *Gt Man* 89 G1
Sykehouse *S York* 91 G1
Syleham *Suffk* 65 E3
Sylen *Carmth* 34 C5
Symbister *Shet* 169 j3
Symington *S Ayrs* 119 F2
Symington *S Lans* 120 D3
Symonds Yat *Herefs* 37 G6
Symondsbury *Dorset* 11 E4
Sympson Green *W York* 90 C3
Synderford *Dorset* 10 D5
Synod Inn *Cerdgn* 42 D5
Syre *Highld* 165 H3
Syreford *Gloucs* 47 F1
Syresham *Nhants* 48 D3

Syston *Leics* 72 D1
Syston *Lincs* 73 G4
Sytchampton *Worcs* 58 A2
Sywell *Nhants* 60 D2

Tabley Hill *Ches* 82 B3
Tackley *Oxon* 48 C1
Tacolneston *Norfk* 64 D5
Tadcaster *N York* 91 F4
Taddington *Derbys* 83 F2
Taddington *Gloucs* 47 F2
Taddiport *Devon* 21 E2
Tadley *Hants* 26 D5
Tadlow *Cambs* 50 D5
Tadmarton *Oxon* 48 B3
Tadwick *Somset* 38 B1
Tadworth *Surrey* 28 C2
Tafarn-y-bwlch *Pembks* 42 A3
Tafarn-y-Gelyn *Denbgs* 68 D6
Tafarnaubach *Blae G* 36 B5
Taff's Well *Cardif* 36 B3
Tafolwern *Powys* 55 F6
Tai'r Bull *Powys* 44 C2
Taibach *Neath* 35 E3
Tain *Highld* 167 F5
Tain *Highld* 163 F4
Tairbeart *W Isls* 168 d6
Takeley *Essex* 51 F3
Takeley Street *Essex* 51 F3
Tal-y-bont *Cerdgn* 54 D4
Tal-y-bont *Conwy* 79 G1
Tal-y-bont *Gwynd* 67 E2
Tal-y-bont *Gwynd* 79 F2
Tal-y-Cafn *Conwy* 79 G2
Tal-y-coed *Mons* 37 E6
Tal-y-garn *Rhondd* 36 A2
Tal-y-llyn *Gwynd* 67 G1
Tal-y-Waun *Torfn* 36 D5
Talachddu *Powys* 44 D2
Talacre *Flints* 80 C3
Talaton *Devon* 9 G5
Talbenny *Pembks* 32 C3
Talbot Green *Rhondd* 36 B2
Talbot Village *Dorset* 13 E4
Taleford *Devon* 10 A4
Talerddig *Powys* 55 G5
Talgarreg *Cerdgn* 42 D4
Talgarth *Powys* 44 D3
Talisker *Highld* 150 C2
Talke *Staffs* 70 C5
Talke Pits *Staffs* 70 C5
Talkin *Cumb* 104 B6
Talla Linnfoots *Border* 121 F1
Talladale *Highld* 152 C6
Tallaminnock *S Ayrs* 109 F5
Tallarn Green *Wrexhm* 69 G4
Tallentire *Cumb* 103 E4
Talley *Carmth* 43 F2
Tallington *Lincs* 61 G6
Tallwrn *Wrexhm* 69 E5
Talmine *Highld* 165 G3
Talog *Carmth* 33 G4
Talsarn *Cerdgn* 43 F5
Talsarnau *Gwynd* 67 F4
Talskiddy *Cnwll* 4 C2
Talwrn *IOA* 78 D2
Talwrn *Wrexhm* 69 F5
Talybont-on-Usk *Powys* 44 D1
Talysarn *Gwynd* 66 D5
Talywern *Gwynd* 55 F5
Tamer Lane End *Gt Man* 82 A5
Tamerton Foliot *Devon* 6 B4
Tamworth *Staffs* 59 E6
Tamworth Green *Lincs* 74 D4
Tan Hill *N York* 96 B5
Tan-y-Bwlch *Gwynd* 67 F4
Tan-y-fron *Conwy* 80 B1
Tan-y-fron *Wrexhm* 69 E5
Tan-y-Grisiau *Gwynd* 67 F5
Tan-y-groes *Cerdgn* 42 C4
Tancred *N York* 91 F5
Tancredston *Pembks* 32 C4
Tandridge *Surrey* 29 E1
Tanfield *Dur* 114 C1
Tanfield Lea *Dur* 114 D1
Tangiers *Pembks* 32 D3
Tangley *Hants* 26 B4
Tangmere *W Susx* 15 G4
Tangusdale *W Isls* 168 a2
Tankerness *Ork* 169 c2
Tankersley *S York* 84 A5
Tankerton *Kent* 31 E3
Tannach *Highld* 167 G3
Tannachie *Abers* 149 E3
Tannadice *Abers* 141 E6
Tanner's Green *Worcs* 58 D3
Tannington *Suffk* 65 E2
Tannochside *N Lans* 120 B6
Tansley *Derbys* 71 H6
Tansor *Nhants* 61 F4
Tantobie *Dur* 114 C1
Tanton *N York* 107 E2
Tanwood *Worcs* 58 B3
Tanworth in Arden *Warwks* 58 D2
Taobh Tuath *W Isls* 168 c6
Taplow *Bucks* 41 G4
Tarbert *Ag & B* 117 F6
Tarbert *Ag & B* 127 G2
Tarbert *W Isls* 168 d6
Tarbet *Ag & B* 129 E6
Tarbet *Highld* 164 C3
Tarbet *Highld* 143 G3
Tarbock Green *Mersyd* 81 G3
Tarbolton *S Ayrs* 119 F2
Tarbrax *S Lans* 121 F5
Tardebigge *Worcs* 58 C3
Tarfside *Angus* 148 C2
Tarland *Abers* 148 C5
Tarleton *Lancs* 88 C2
Tarlscough *Lancs* 81 G6
Tarlton *Gloucs* 38 D4

Tarnock *Somset* 23 G4
Tarns *Cumb* 103 E5
Tarnside *Cumb* 95 E4
Tarporley *Ches* 81 H1
Tarr *Somset* 22 B2
Tarr *Somset* 22 D2
Tarrant Crawford *Dorset* 12 C5
Tarrant Gunville *Dorset* 12 C6
Tarrant Hinton *Dorset* 12 C6
Tarrant Keyneston *Dorset* 12 C5
Tarrant Launceston *Dorset* 12 C5
Tarrant Monkton *Dorset* 12 C5
Tarrant Rawston *Dorset* 12 C5
Tarrant Rushton *Dorset* 12 C5
Tarring Neville *E Susx* 17 E2
Tarrington *Herefs* 46 B3
Tarskavaig *Highld* 143 F5
Tarves *Abers* 159 E2
Tarvie *P & K* 139 G6
Tarvin *Ches* 81 G1
Tarvin Sands *Ches* 81 G1
Tasburgh *Norfk* 64 D5
Tasley *Shrops* 57 G5
Taston *Oxon* 48 B1
Tatenhill *Staffs* 71 G2
Tathall End *Bucks* 49 F4
Tatham *Lancs* 95 G2
Tathwell *Lincs* 86 D3
Tatsfield *Surrey* 29 E2
Tattenhall *Ches* 69 G6
Tatterford *Norfk* 76 B3
Tattersett *Norfk* 76 B3
Tattershall *Lincs* 74 C6
Tattershall Bridge *Lincs* 74 B6
Tattershall Thorpe *Lincs* 74 C6
Tattingstone *Suffk* 53 E4
Tattingstone White Horse *Suffk* 53 E4
Tatworth *Somset* 10 D5
Tauchers *Moray* 157 F4
Taunton *Somset* 23 E2
Taverham *Norfk* 77 E1
Taverners Green *Essex* 51 F2
Tavernspite *Pembks* 33 F3
Tavistock *Devon* 6 B5
Taw Green *Devon* 8 C4
Tawstock *Devon* 21 F4
Taxal *Derbys* 83 E3
Taychreggan Hotel *Ag & B* 137 E2
Tayinloan *Ag & B* 117 F5
Taynton *Gloucs* 46 C1
Taynton *Oxon* 39 G6
Taynuilt *Ag & B* 137 E3
Tayport *Fife* 141 E3
Tayvallich *Ag & B* 127 E4
Tealby *Lincs* 86 B4
Team Valley *T & W* 114 D1
Teangue *Highld* 143 F5
Teanord *Highld* 154 D6
Tebay *Cumb* 95 G5
Tebworth *Beds* 49 H2
Tedburn St Mary *Devon* 9 E5
Teddington *Gloucs* 47 E2
Teddington *Gt Lon* 28 C3
Tedstone Delamere *Herefs* 46 C5
Tedstone Wafer *Herefs* 46 B5
Teesport *Cleve* 107 E3
Teesside Airport *Dur* 106 C2
Teesside Park *N York* 106 D4
Teeton *Nhants* 60 C2
Teffont Evias *Wilts* 25 E2
Teffont Magna *Wilts* 25 E2
Tegryn *Pembks* 42 B2
Teigh *Rutlnd* 73 F2
Teigncombe *Devon* 8 D3
Teigngrace *Devon* 7 F5
Teignmouth *Devon* 7 G5
Teindside *Border* 112 B6
Telford *Shrops* 70 B1
Tellisford *Somset* 24 D5
Telscombe *E Susx* 17 E2
Telscombe Cliffs *E Susx* 17 E1
Tempar *P & K* 138 D5
Templand *D & G* 111 E3
Temple *Cnwll* 5 E3
Temple *Mdloth* 121 G5
Temple Balsall *W Mids* 59 E3
Temple Bar *Cerdgn* 43 E5
Temple Cloud *Somset* 24 B5
Temple End *Suffk* 51 G6
Temple Ewell *Kent* 19 F6
Temple Grafton *Warwks* 47 G5
Temple Guiting *Gloucs* 47 F2
Temple Hirst *N York* 91 G2
Temple Normanton *Derbys* 84 B1
Temple of Fiddes *Abers* 149 F2
Temple Pier *Highld* 154 D2
Temple Sowerby *Cumb* 104 C3
Templecombe *Somset* 24 C1
Templeton *Devon* 9 F6
Templeton *Pembks* 33 E3
Templetown *Dur* 105 H5
Tempsford *Beds* 50 C6
Ten Mile Bank *Norfk* 63 E5
Tenbury Wells *Worcs* 57 F2
Tenby *Pembks* 33 E2
Tendring *Essex* 53 E3
Tendring Green *Essex* 53 E3
Tendring Heath *Essex* 53 E3
Tenpenny Heath *Essex* 52 D3
Tenterden *Kent* 18 B5
Terling *Essex* 52 A2
Tern *Shrops* 70 A2
Ternhill *Shrops* 70 A3
Terregles D & G 110 D2
Terrington *N York* 98 B2
Terrington St Clement *Norfk* 75 F2
Terrington St John *Norfk* 75 F1
Terry's Green *Warwks* 58 D3
Teston *Kent* 29 H1
Testwood *Hants* 14 B5
Tetbury *Gloucs* 38 D4
Tetbury Upton *Gloucs* 38 D4
Tetchill *Shrops* 69 F3
Tetcott *Devon* 5 G6
Tetford *Lincs* 86 D2
Tetney *Lincs* 86 C5
Tetney Lock *Lincs* 86 D5
Tetsworth *Oxon* 41 E4

Tettenhall W Mids 58 B5
Tettenhall Wood W Mids 58 B5
Tetworth Cambs 50 C6
Teversal Notts 72 C6
Teversham Cambs 62 D1
Teviothead Border 112 A5
Tewin Herts 50 D2
Tewkesbury Gloucs 46 D2
Teynham Kent 30 C2
Thackley W York 90 C3
Thackthwaite Cumb 103 E2
Thackthwaite Cumb 104 A3
Thakeham W Susx 16 B3
Thame Oxon 41 E5
Thames Ditton Surrey 28 C3
Thamesmead Gt Lon 29 F4
Thanington Kent 31 E2
Thankerton S Lans 120 D4
Tharston Norfk 64 D5
Thatcham Berks 26 C6
Thatto Heath Mersyd 81 G4
Thaxted Essex 51 G4
The Bank Ches 70 C6
The Bank Shrops 57 F5
The Beeches Gloucs 39 E4
The Blythe Staffs 71 E3
The Bog Shrops 56 D5
The Bourne Worcs 47 E5
The Braes Highld 151 E2
The Bratch Staffs 58 B5
The Broad Herefs 45 H5
The Brunt E Loth 133 F2
The Bungalow IOM 174 m4
The Butts Gloucs 38 D6
The Camp Gloucs 38 D5
The Chequer Wrexhm 69 G4
The City Beds 61 G1
The City Bucks 41 F4
The Common Oxon 48 A2
The Common Wilts 25 H2
The Common Wilts 39 E3
The Corner Kent 17 H6
The Corner Shrops 57 E4
The Cronk IOM 174 I5
The Den N Ayrs 119 E5
The Eden Project Cnwll 3 H5
The Flatt Cumb 112 C3
The Forge Herefs 45 F5
The Forstal E Susx 17 F5
The Forstal Kent 18 C6
The Forstal Kent 18 D5
The Fouralls Shrops 70 B3
The Green Cumb 94 C3
The Green Essex 52 A3
The Green N York 98 C5
The Grove Worcs 46 D3
The Haven W Susx 16 B4
The Haw Gloucs 46 D2
The Hill Cumb 94 C3
The Holt Berks 41 F2
The Hundred Herefs 57 E2
The Leacon Kent 18 C5
The Lee Bucks 41 G5
The Lhen IOM 174 m5
The Lochs Moray 157 G5
The Marsh Powys 56 C5
The Middles Dur 106 B6
The Moor Kent 18 A4
The Mumbles Swans 34 D3
The Murray S Lans 119 H5
The Mythe Gloucs 46 D3
The Narth Mons 37 F5
The Neuk Abers 149 E4
The Quarry Gloucs 38 B4
The Quarter Kent 18 B6
The Reddings Gloucs 47 E1
The Rookery Staffs 70 C6
The Ross P & K 139 E2
The Sands Surrey 27 G4
The Shoe Wilts 38 C2
The Smithies Shrops 57 G5
The Spike Cambs 51 F5
The Spring Warwks 59 F3
The Square Torfn 36 D4
The Stair Kent 17 G6
The Stocks Kent 18 C4
The Straits Hants 27 F3
The Strand Wilts 25 E5
The Towans Cnwll 2 C4
The Vauld Herefs 45 H4
The Wyke Shrops 57 G5
Theakston N York 97 F3
Thealby N Linc 92 C1
Theale Berks 41 E1
Theale Somset 23 G4
Thearne E R Yk 93 E3
Theberton Suffk 65 G2
Thedden Grange Hants 27 E5
Theddingworth Leics 60 C4
Theddlethorpe All Saints Lincs 87 E3
Theddlethorpe St Helen Lincs 87 E4
Thelbridge Cross Devon 21 H2
Thelnetham Suffk 64 C3
Thelveton Norfk 64 D3
Thelwall Ches 82 B3
Themelthorpe Norfk 76 D2
Thenford Nhants 48 C3
Theobald's Green Wilts 39 E1
Therfield Herts 50 D4
Thetford Norfk 64 A4
Thethwaite Cumb 103 H4
Theydon Bois Essex 29 E6
Thicket Priory E R Yk 91 H4
Thickwood Wilts 38 C1
Thimbleby Lincs 86 C2
Thimbleby N York 97 H4
Thingwall Mersyd 81 E4
Thirkleby N York 97 H3
Thirlby N York 97 H3
Thirlestane Border 122 C4
Thirlspot Cumb 103 G2
Thirn N York 97 E3
Thirsk N York 97 G3
Thirtleby E R Yk 93 E3
Thistleton Lancs 88 C3
Thistleton Rutlnd 73 G2
Thistley Green Suffk 63 F3
Thixendale N York 92 B6

Thockrington Nthumb 113 G3
Tholomas Drove Cambs 62 C6
Tholthorpe N York 97 H1
Thomas Chapel Pembks 33 E2
Thomas Close Cumb 104 A4
Thomas Town Warwks 58 D2
Thomastown Abers 158 B3
Thompson Norfk 64 B5
Thong Kent 29 G3
Thoralby N York 96 C3
Thoresby Notts 84 D2
Thoresthorpe Lincs 87 E2
Thoresway Lincs 86 B4
Thorganby Lincs 86 B4
Thorganby N York 91 H4
Thorgill N York 98 C4
Thorington Suffk 65 G3
Thorington Street Suffk 52 D4
Thorlby N York 89 H5
Thorley Herts 51 F3
Thorley IOW 14 B2
Thorley Houses Herts 51 E3
Thorley Street IOW 14 B2
Thormanby N York 97 H2
Thornaby-on-Tees N York 106 D3
Thornage Norfk 76 D4
Thornborough Bucks 49 F2
Thornborough N York 97 F3
Thornbury Devon 20 D1
Thornbury Gloucs 37 G3
Thornbury Herefs 46 B5
Thornbury W York 90 C3
Thornby Cumb 103 G5
Thornby Nhants 60 C3
Thorncliff Staffs 71 E6
Thorncombe Dorset 10 D5
Thorncombe Street Surrey 27 H3
Thorncott Green Beds 50 B5
Thorncross IOW 14 C2
Thorndon Suffk 64 D2
Thorndon Cross Devon 8 B4
Thorne S York 84 D6
Thorne Somset 23 H1
Thorne St Margaret Somset 22 D1
Thornecroft Devon 7 E4
Thornehillhead Devon 20 D2
Thorner W York 91 E4
Thornes Staffs 58 D6
Thornes W York 90 D1
Thorney Bucks 28 A4
Thorney Cambs 62 B6
Thorney Notts 85 F2
Thorney Somset 23 G1
Thorney Hill Hants 13 F5
Thorney Toll Cambs 62 C6
Thornfalcon Somset 23 F2
Thornford Dorset 11 F6
Thorngumbald E R Yk 93 F2
Thornham Norfk 75 H4
Thornham Magna Suffk 64 D2
Thornham Parva Suffk 64 D3
Thornhaugh Cambs 61 G5
Thornhill Caerph 36 C3
Thornhill D & G 110 C4
Thornhill Derbys 83 G3
Thornhill Hants 14 C5
Thornhill Stirlg 130 C5
Thornhill W York 90 D1
Thornhill Lees W York 90 D1
Thornhills W York 90 C2
Thornholme E R Yk 99 G1
Thornicombe Dorset 12 C5
Thornington Nthumb 123 F3
Thornley Dur 105 H4
Thornley Dur 106 C5
Thornley Gate Cumb 105 E6
Thornliebank E Rens 119 G5
Thorns Suffk 63 G1
Thorns Green Gt Man 82 C3
Thornsett Derbys 83 E3
Thornthwaite Cumb 103 F3
Thornthwaite N York 90 C5
Thornton Angus 140 D4
Thornton Bucks 49 F3
Thornton E R Yk 92 B4
Thornton Fife 132 B5
Thornton Lancs 88 B4
Thornton Leics 59 G6
Thornton Lincs 86 C1
Thornton Mersyd 81 F5
Thornton N York 106 D2
Thornton Nthumb 123 G4
Thornton Pembks 32 C2
Thornton W York 90 B3
Thornton Curtis Lincs 93 E1
Thornton Green Ches 81 G2
Thornton Hough Mersyd 81 E3
Thornton in Lonsdale N York 95 G2
Thornton le Dale N York 98 D3
Thornton le Moor Lincs 85 H4
Thornton Rust N York 96 C4
Thornton Steward N York 97 E4
Thornton Watlass N York 97 E3
Thornton-in-Craven N York 89 G4
Thornton-le-Beans N York 97 G4
Thornton-le-Clay N York 98 C1
Thornton-le-Moor N York 97 G4
Thornton-le-Moors Ches 81 G2
Thornton-le-Street N York 97 G3
Thorntonhall S Lans 119 H5
Thorntonloch E Loth 133 F2
Thornwood Common Essex 51 E1
Thornydykes Border 122 C4
Thornythwaite Cumb 103 H2
Thoroton Notts 73 E4
Thorp Arch W York 91 E4
Thorpe Derbys 71 F5
Thorpe E R Yk 92 D4
Thorpe Lincs 87 E3
Thorpe N York 90 A6
Thorpe Norfk 65 G5
Thorpe Notts 73 E5
Thorpe Surrey 28 A3
Thorpe Abbotts Norfk 64 D3
Thorpe Acre Leics 72 C2

Thorpe Arnold Leics 73 E2
Thorpe Audlin W York 91 F1
Thorpe Bassett N York 98 D2
Thorpe Bay Essex 30 C5
Thorpe Common S York 84 B4
Thorpe Constantine Staffs 59 E6
Thorpe End Norfk 77 F1
Thorpe Green Essex 53 E3
Thorpe Green Lancs 88 D2
Thorpe Green Suffk 52 C6
Thorpe Hesley S York 84 B4
Thorpe in Balne S York 84 D6
Thorpe in the Fallows Lincs 85 G3
Thorpe Langton Leics 60 C5
Thorpe Larches Dur 106 C3
Thorpe le Street E R Yk 92 B4
Thorpe Lea Surrey 28 A3
Thorpe Malsor Nhants 60 D3
Thorpe Mandeville Nhants 48 C4
Thorpe Market Norfk 77 E4
Thorpe Morieux Suffk 52 C6
Thorpe on the Hill Lincs 85 G1
Thorpe on the Hill W York 90 D2
Thorpe Park Surrey 28 A3
Thorpe Salvin S York 84 C3
Thorpe Satchville Leics 73 E1
Thorpe St Andrew Norfk 65 E6
Thorpe St Peter Lincs 75 E6
Thorpe Thewles Dur 106 C3
Thorpe Tilney Lincs 74 B6
Thorpe Underwood N York 91 F5
Thorpe Underwood Nhants 60 D3
Thorpe Waterville Nhants 61 F3
Thorpe Willoughby N York 91 G3
Thorpe-le-Soken Essex 53 E3
Thorpeness Suffk 65 G1
Thorpland Norfk 75 F1
Thorrington Essex 52 D3
Thorverton Devon 9 F5
Thrales End Beds 50 B2
Thrandeston Suffk 64 D3
Thrapston Nhants 61 F3
Threapland Cumb 103 F4
Threapland N York 90 A6
Threapwood Ches 69 G4
Threapwood Staffs 71 E4
Threapwood Head Staffs 71 E4
Threave S Ayrs 109 E5
Threave Castle D & G 110 B1
Three Ashes Herefs 45 H1
Three Bridges W Susx 16 D5
Three Burrows Cnwll 3 E4
Three Chimneys Kent 18 B5
Three Cocks Powys 45 E3
Three Crosses Swans 34 C4
Three Cups Corner E Susx 17 G3
Three Gates Worcs 46 B5
Three Hammers Cnwll 5 F5
Three Holes Norfk 62 D5
Three Lane Ends Gt Man 82 C6
Three Leg Cross E Susx 17 H4
Three Legged Cross Dorset 13 E5
Three Mile Cross Berks 27 E6
Three Mile Stone Cnwll 3 E4
Three Miletown W Loth 131 G3
Three Oaks E Susx 18 B3
Threehammer Common Norfk 77 F2
Threekingham Lincs 74 A4
Threepwood Border 122 B4
Threlkeld Cumb 103 G3
Threshfield N York 96 C1
Thrigby Norfk 77 G1
Thringarth Dur 105 F2
Thringstone Leics 72 B2
Thrintoft N York 97 F4
Thriplow Cambs 51 E5
Throapham S York 84 C3
Throckenhalt Lincs 74 D1
Throcking Herts 50 D4
Throckley T & W 114 C2
Throckmorton Worcs 47 E4
Throop Dorset 12 B4
Throop Dorset 13 E4
Throphill Nthumb 114 C4
Thropton Nthumb 114 B6
Throsk Stirlg 131 E4
Througham Gloucs 38 D5
Throughgate D & G 110 C3
Throwleigh Devon 8 D4
Throwley Kent 30 C2
Throwley Forstal Kent 30 C1
Thrumpton Notts 72 C3
Thrumpton Notts 85 E3
Thrumster Highld 167 G3
Thrunscoe Lincs 86 C5
Thrunton Nthumb 124 D2
Thrup Oxon 39 G4
Thrupp Gloucs 38 C5
Thrupp Oxon 40 C6
Thrushelton Devon 8 A3
Thrushesbush Essex 51 F2
Thrussington Leics 72 D2
Thruxton Hants 26 A4
Thruxton Herefs 45 G3
Thrybergh S York 84 B4
Thulston Derbys 72 B3
Thundersley Essex 30 B5
Thurcaston Leics 72 C1
Thurcroft S York 84 C4
Thurdon Cnwll 20 C2
Thurgarton Norfk 77 E3
Thurgarton Notts 73 E5
Thurgoland S York 83 H5
Thurlaston Leics 59 H5
Thurlaston Warwks 59 G2
Thurlbear Somset 23 E1
Thurlby Lincs 73 G6
Thurlby Lincs 74 A2
Thurlby Lincs 87 E2
Thurleigh Beds 61 F1
Thurlestone Devon 6 D2
Thurlow Suffk 51 H6
Thurloxton Somset 23 F2
Thurlstone S York 83 G5
Thurlton Norfk 65 G5
Thurlwood Ches 70 C6
Thurmaston Leics 72 D1

Thurnby Leics 60 C6
Thurne Norfk 77 G2
Thurnham Kent 30 B2
Thurning Nhants 61 G4
Thurning Norfk 76 D3
Thurnscoe S York 84 B5
Thursby Cumb 103 G6
Thursden Lancs 89 G3
Thursford Norfk 76 C3
Thursley Surrey 27 G3
Thurso Highld 167 E5
Thurstaston Mersyd 81 E3
Thurston Suffk 64 B2
Thurston Clough Gt Man 83 E5
Thurston Planch Suffk 64 B2
Thurstonfield Cumb 103 G6
Thurstonland W York 83 F6
Thurton Norfk 65 F5
Thurvaston Derbys 71 G4
Thuxton Norfk 64 C6
Thwaite N York 96 B5
Thwaite Suffk 64 D2
Thwaite Head Cumb 94 D4
Thwaite St Mary Norfk 65 F5
Thwaites W York 90 B4
Thwaites Brow W York 90 B4
Thwing E R Yk 99 F2
Tibbermore P & K 139 H2
Tibbers D & G 110 C4
Tibberton Gloucs 46 C1
Tibberton Shrops 70 B2
Tibberton Worcs 47 E5
Tibbie Shiels Inn Border 121 G1
Tibenham Norfk 64 D4
Tibshelf Derbys 72 B6
Tibthorpe E R Yk 92 C5
Ticehurst E Susx 17 H4
Tichborne Hants 26 D2
Tickencote Rutlnd 73 G1
Tickenham Somset 37 F1
Tickford End Bucks 49 G3
Tickhill S York 84 C4
Ticklerton Shrops 57 E4
Ticknall Derbys 72 A2
Tickton E R Yk 92 D4
Tidbury Green W Mids 58 D3
Tidcombe Wilts 26 A5
Tiddington Oxon 41 E5
Tiddington Warwks 47 H5
Tidebrook E Susx 17 G4
Tideford Cnwll 5 G2
Tideford Cross Cnwll 5 G2
Tidenham Gloucs 37 G4
Tideswell Derbys 83 F2
Tidmarsh Berks 41 E2
Tidmington Warwks 47 H3
Tidpit Hants 25 F1
Tiers Cross Pembks 32 C3
Tiffield Nhants 49 E4
Tigerton Angus 141 E6
Tigh a Ghearraidh W Isls 168 b5
Tigharry W Isls 168 b5
Tighnabruaich Ag & B 128 A2
Tigley Devon 7 E4
Tilbrook Cambs 61 G2
Tilbury Essex 29 G4
Tilbury Green Essex 52 A5
Tile Cross W Mids 59 E4
Tile Hill W Mids 59 F3
Tilehouse Green W Mids 59 E3
Tilehurst Berks 41 E2
Tilford Surrey 27 G4
Tilgate W Susx 16 D5
Tilgate Forest Row W Susx 16 D5
Tilham Street Somset 24 A3
Tillers Green Gloucs 46 C2
Tillicoultry Clacks 131 E5
Tillietudlem S Lans 120 C4
Tillingham Essex 52 C1
Tillington Herefs 45 G4
Tillington W Susx 27 H1
Tillington Common Herefs 45 G4
Tillybirloch Abers 148 D5
Tillycairn Abers 148 B4
Tillyfourie Abers 148 D6
Tillygreig Abers 159 E1
Tillyrie P & K 131 G6
Tilmanstone Kent 31 F1
Tiln Notts 85 E3
Tilney All Saints Norfk 75 F2
Tilney High End Norfk 75 F2
Tilney St Lawrence Norfk 75 F1
Tilshead Wilts 25 F4
Tilstock Shrops 69 H4
Tilston Ches 69 G5
Tilstone Bank Ches 69 H6
Tilstone Fearnall Ches 69 H6
Tilsworth Beds 49 H2
Tilton on the Hill Leics 60 C6
Tiltups End Gloucs 38 C4
Tilty Essex 51 G3
Timberland Lincs 74 B6
Timbersbrook Ches 82 D1
Timberscombe Somset 22 B3
Timble N York 90 C5
Timewell Devon 22 C2
Timpanheck D & G 111 H2
Timperley Gt Man 82 C4
Timsbury Hants 26 B2
Timsbury Somset 24 B5
Timsgarry W Isls 168 d8
Timsgearraidh W Isls 168 d8
Timworth Suffk 63 H2
Timworth Green Suffk 63 H2
Tincleton Dorset 12 B4
Tindale Cumb 104 C6
Tindale Crescent Dur 106 A4
Tingewick Bucks 49 E2
Tingrith Beds 50 A4
Tingwall Airport Shet 169 h3
Tinhay Devon 5 G4
Tinker's Hill Hants 26 B4
Tinkersley Derbys 83 G1
Tinsley S York 84 B4
Tinsley Green W Susx 16 D5
Tintagel Cnwll 4 D5
Tintagel Castle Cnwll 4 D5

Tintern Abbey Mons 37 F4
Tintern Parva Mons 37 F4
Tintinhull Somset 23 H1
Tintwistle Derbys 83 E4
Tinwald D & G 110 D3
Tinwell Rutlnd 61 F6
Tipp's End Norfk 62 D5
Tippacott Devon 21 H5
Tiptoe Hants 13 F4
Tipton W Mids 58 B5
Tipton Green W Mids 58 B5
Tipton St John Devon 10 A4
Tiptree Essex 52 C2
Tiptree Heath Essex 52 B2
Tir-y-fron Flints 69 E6
Tirabad Powys 44 B3
Tiree Airport Ag & B 134 B4
Tiretigan Ag & B 127 F1
Tirley Gloucs 46 D2
Tirphil Caerph 36 C5
Tirril Cumb 104 B3
Tisbury Wilts 25 E2
Tisman's Common W Susx 16 B5
Tissington Derbys 71 G5
Titchberry Devon 20 C3
Titchfield Hants 14 C4
Titchfield Common Hants 14 C4
Titchmarsh Nhants 61 F3
Titchwell Norfk 75 H4
Tithby Notts 73 E4
Titley Herefs 45 F5
Titmore Green Herts 50 C3
Titsey Surrey 29 E3
Tittensor Staffs 70 D4
Tittleshall Norfk 76 B2
Titton Worcs 58 A2
Tiverton Ches 69 H6
Tiverton Devon 9 F6
Tivetshall St Margaret Norfk 64 D4
Tivetshall St Mary Norfk 64 D4
Tivington Somset 22 B4
Tivy Dale S York 83 H5
Tixall Staffs 71 E2
Tixover Rutlnd 61 F5
Toadhole Derbys 72 B6
Toadmoor Derbys 72 A5
Tobermory Ag & B 135 G5
Toberonochy Ag & B 127 F6
Tobha Mor W Isls 168 b3
Tocher Abers 158 C2
Tochieneal Moray 157 G6
Tockenham Wilts 39 E3
Tockenham Wick Wilts 39 E2
Tocketts N York 107 F3
Tockholes Lancs 89 E2
Tockington S Gloucs 37 G3
Tockwith N York 91 F5
Todber Dorset 24 D1
Todburn Nthumb 114 C6
Toddington Beds 50 A4
Toddington Gloucs 47 F2
Todds Green Herts 50 C3
Todenham Gloucs 47 H3
Todhills Angus 140 D4
Todhills Cumb 112 A1
Todhills Dur 106 B4
Todmorden W York 89 H2
Todwick S York 84 C3
Toft Cambs 62 C1
Toft Ches 82 C2
Toft Lincs 74 A2
Toft Shet 169 j4
Toft Warwks 59 H2
Toft Hill Dur 106 A4
Toft Hill Lincs 86 C1
Toft Monks Norfk 65 G5
Toft next Newton Lincs 85 H3
Toftrees Norfk 76 B3
Toftwood Norfk 76 C1
Togston Nthumb 114 D6
Tokavaig Highld 143 F5
Tokers Green Oxon 41 E2
Tolastadh W Isls 168 f9
Toldish Cnwll 4 C2
Toll Bar S York 84 C5
Tolland Somset 22 D2
Tollard Farnham Dorset 12 C6
Tollard Royal Wilts 25 E1
Tollbar End W Mids 59 F3
Toller Fratrum Dorset 11 F4
Toller Porcorum Dorset 11 F4
Toller Whelme Dorset 11 E5
Tollerton N York 98 A1
Tollerton Notts 72 D3
Tollesbury Essex 52 C2
Tolleshunt D'Arcy Essex 52 C2
Tolleshunt Knights Essex 52 C2
Tolleshunt Major Essex 52 C2
Tolob Shet 169 h1
Tolpuddle Dorset 12 B4
Tolsta W Isls 168 f9
Tolvan Cnwll 3 E3
Tolver Cnwll 2 B3
Tolworth Gt Lon 28 C3
Tomatin Highld 155 F2
Tomchrasky Highld 145 E6
Tomdoun Highld 144 D4
Tomich Highld 162 C4
Tomich Highld 153 G2
Tomich Highld 154 D4
Tomich Highld 154 D4
Tomich Highld 162 D4
Tomintoul Moray 156 D1
Tomlow Warwks 59 G2
Tomnacross Highld 154 C3
Tomnavoulin Moray 156 D2
Tompkin Staffs 70 D5
Ton Mons 36 D4
Ton Mons 37 E4
Ton-teg Rhondd 36 B3
Tonbridge Kent 17 G6
Tondu Brdgnd 35 F3
Tonedale Somset 22 D2
Tong Kent 30 C2
Tong Shrops 57 H4
Tong W York 90 C3
Tong Green Kent 30 C1
Tong Norton Shrops 57 H4
Tong Street W York 90 C3

Tonge Leics ... 72 B2
Tongham Surrey ... 27 G4
Tongland D & G ... 102 A6
Tongue Highld ... 165 G4
Tongue End Lincs ... 74 B2
Tongwynlais Cardif ... 36 B2
Tonna Neath ... 35 E4
Tonwell Herts ... 50 D2
Tonypandy Rhondd ... 35 G3
Tonyrefail Rhondd ... 35 G3
Toot Baldon Oxon ... 40 D4
Toot Hill Essex ... 51 F1
Toot Hill Hants ... 14 B5
Toothill Wilts ... 39 F3
Tooting Gt Lon ... 28 D3
Tooting Bec Gt Lon ... 28 D3
Top End Beds ... 61 F2
Top of Hebers Gt Man ... 82 D5
Top-y-rhos Flints ... 69 E6
Topcliffe N York ... 97 G2
Topcroft Norfk ... 65 E5
Topcroft Street Norfk ... 65 E5
Topham S York ... 91 G1
Toppesfield Essex ... 52 A4
Toppings Gt Man ... 82 B6
Toprow Norfk ... 64 D5
Topsham Devon ... 9 F3
Torbeg N Ayrs ... 117 H3
Torboll Highld ... 162 D4
Torbreck Highld ... 155 E3
Torbryan Devon ... 7 F4
Torcastle Highld ... 144 D2
Torcross Devon ... 7 F2
Tore Highld ... 154 D4
Torfrey Cnwll ... 5 E1
Torinturk Ag & B ... 127 G1
Torksey Lincs ... 85 F2
Tormarton Gloucs ... 38 B2
Tormore N Ayrs ... 117 H4
Tornagrain Highld ... 155 F4
Tornaveen Abers ... 148 D5
Torness Highld ... 154 D2
Tornewton Devon ... 7 E4
Toronto Dur ... 106 A4
Torosay Castle Ag & B ... 136 B3
Torpenhow Cumb ... 103 F4
Torphichen W Loth ... 131 F2
Torphins Abers ... 148 D5
Torpoint Cnwll ... 6 B3
Torquay Devon ... 7 F4
Torquhan Border ... 122 B4
Torr Devon ... 6 C3
Torran Highld ... 151 F4
Torrance E Duns ... 130 C2
Torranyard N Ayrs ... 119 E4
Torre Somset ... 22 C3
Torridon Highld ... 152 C5
Torridon House Highld ... 152 C5
Torrin Highld ... 143 E6
Torrisdale Ag & B ... 117 G4
Torrisdale Highld ... 165 H5
Torrish Highld ... 163 F6
Torrisholme Lancs ... 95 E1
Torrobull Highld ... 162 C4
Torry Aber C ... 149 G5
Torryburn Fife ... 131 F4
Tortan Worcs ... 58 A3
Torteval Guern ... 174 f1
Torthorwald D & G ... 111 E3
Tortington W Susx ... 16 A2
Tortworth Gloucs ... 38 B4
Torvaig Highld ... 151 E3
Torver Cumb ... 94 D4
Torwood Falk ... 131 E4
Torwoodlee Border ... 122 B3
Torworth Notts ... 84 D3
Toscaig Highld ... 151 G2
Toseland Cambs ... 62 B2
Tosside N York ... 89 F5
Tostock Suffk ... 64 B2
Totaig Highld ... 150 B4
Tote Highld ... 150 D4
Tote Highld ... 151 E5
Tote Hill W Susx ... 27 G2
Tothill Lincs ... 86 D3
Totland IOW ... 13 G3
Totley S York ... 83 H3
Totley Brook S York ... 83 H3
Totnes Devon ... 7 E4
Toton Notts ... 72 C3
Totronald Ag & B ... 134 D5
Totscore Highld ... 150 D5
Tottenham Gt Lon ... 28 D5
Tottenhill Norfk ... 75 G1
Totteridge Gt Lon ... 28 C5
Totternhoe Beds ... 49 H1
Tottington Gt Man ... 82 C6
Tottleworth Lancs ... 89 F3
Totton Hants ... 14 B5
Touchen End Berks ... 41 G2
Toulston N York ... 91 F4
Toulton Somset ... 23 E2
Toulvaddie Highld ... 163 F2
Tovil Kent ... 30 A1
Tow Law Dur ... 105 H4
Towan Cnwll ... 4 B3
Towan Cnwll ... 3 H5
Toward Ag & B ... 128 C2
Toward Quay Ag & B ... 128 C2
Towcester Nhants ... 49 E4
Towednack Cnwll ... 2 B4
Towersey Oxon ... 41 E5
Towie Abers ... 148 B6
Town End Cambs ... 62 C5
Town End Cumb ... 94 C4
Town End Cumb ... 94 D6
Town End Cumb ... 104 C3
Town End Cumb ... 94 D4
Town End Cumb ... 95 E3
Town Green Lancs ... 81 F5
Town Green Norfk ... 77 G1
Town Head Cumb ... 95 E5
Town Head N York ... 89 G5
Town Head N York ... 90 C4
Town Kelloe Dur ... 106 C4
Town Lane Gt Man ... 82 B5
Town Littleworth E Susx ... 17 E3
Town of Lowdon Mersyd ... 82 A4

Town Row E Susx ... 17 F4
Town Street Suffk ... 63 G4
Town Yetholm Border ... 123 E2
Townend W Duns ... 129 E3
Towngate Cumb ... 104 B5
Towngate Lincs ... 74 B1
Townhead Cumb ... 103 E4
Townhead Cumb ... 104 C3
Townhead D & G ... 110 D4
Townhead S York ... 83 G5
Townhead of Greenlaw D & G ... 110 B1
Townhill Fife ... 131 G4
Townlake Devon ... 5 H3
Towns End Hants ... 26 D5
Townsend Somset ... 10 D6
Townshend Cnwll ... 2 C3
Townwell Gloucs ... 38 B3
Towthorpe E R Yk ... 92 C6
Towthorpe N York ... 91 G5
Towton N York ... 91 F3
Towyn Conwy ... 80 B3
Toxteth Mersyd ... 81 F3
Toy's Hill Kent ... 29 F1
Toynton All Saints Lincs ... 86 D1
Toynton Fen Side Lincs ... 74 D6
Toynton St Peter Lincs ... 86 D1
Trabboch E Ayrs ... 119 F2
Trabbochburn E Ayrs ... 119 F2
Traboe Cnwll ... 3 E2
Tracebridge Somset ... 22 D1
Tradespark Highld ... 155 G5
Traethsaith Cerdgn ... 42 C4
Trallong Powys ... 44 C2
Tramway Museum Derbys ... 72 A6
Tranent E Loth ... 132 C2
Tranmere Mersyd ... 81 E3
Trannack Cnwll ... 2 C3
Trantelbeg Highld ... 166 C4
Trantlemore Highld ... 166 C4
Tranwell Nthumb ... 114 C4
Trap's Green Warwks ... 58 D2
Trapp Carmth ... 43 G1
Traprain E Loth ... 133 E3
Traquair Border ... 121 H3
Trash Green Berks ... 41 E1
Traveller's Rest Devon ... 21 F3
Trawden Lancs ... 89 G3
Trawscoed Cerdgn ... 54 D3
Trawsfynydd Gwynd ... 67 G4
Tre Aubrey V Glam ... 36 B1
Tre Taliesin Cerdgn ... 54 D4
Tre'r-ddol Cerdgn ... 54 D5
Tre-gagle Mons ... 37 F5
Tre-Gibbon Rhondd ... 35 G5
Tre-groes Cerdgn ... 42 D4
Tre-Mostyn Flints ... 80 D3
Tre-Vaughan Carmth ... 42 D1
Tre-wyn Mons ... 45 F1
Trealaw Rhondd ... 35 G3
Treales Lancs ... 88 C3
Treamble Cnwll ... 3 E5
Trearddur Bay IOA ... 78 B3
Treaslane Highld ... 150 D4
Treator Cnwll ... 4 C3
Trebanog Rhondd ... 35 G3
Trebanos Neath ... 35 E5
Trebartha Cnwll ... 5 F4
Trebarvah Cnwll ... 3 E3
Trebarwith Cnwll ... 4 D4
Trebeath Cnwll ... 5 F5
Trebehor Cnwll ... 2 A2
Trebelzue Cnwll ... 4 B2
Trebetherick Cnwll ... 4 C4
Treborough Somset ... 22 C3
Trebudannon Cnwll ... 4 C2
Trebullett Cnwll ... 5 G4
Treburgett Cnwll ... 4 D4
Treburick Cnwll ... 4 C3
Treburley Cnwll ... 5 G4
Treburrick Cnwll ... 4 B3
Trebyan Cnwll ... 4 D2
Trecastle Powys ... 44 B2
Trecogo Cnwll ... 5 G4
Trecott Devon ... 8 C5
Trecwn Pembks ... 32 D5
Trecynon Rhondd ... 35 G5
Tredaule Cnwll ... 5 F4
Tredavoe Cnwll ... 2 B3
Tredegar Blae G ... 36 C5
Tredethy Cnwll ... 4 D3
Tredington Gloucs ... 47 E2
Tredington Warwks ... 47 H4
Tredinnick Cnwll ... 4 C3
Tredinnick Cnwll ... 4 D2
Tredinnick Cnwll ... 5 E2
Tredinnick Cnwll ... 5 F2
Tredinnick Cnwll ... 5 F2
Tredomen Powys ... 44 D2
Tredrissi Pembks ... 42 A3
Tredrizzick Cnwll ... 4 C4
Tredunhock Mons ... 37 E4
Tredustan Powys ... 44 D2
Treen Cnwll ... 2 B3
Treen Cnwll ... 2 B2
Treesmill Cnwll ... 4 D1
Treeton S York ... 84 B3
Trefasser Pembks ... 32 C5
Trefdraeth IOA ... 78 D2
Trefecca Powys ... 44 D2
Trefeglwys Powys ... 55 G4
Trefenter Cerdgn ... 54 D2
Treffgarne Pembks ... 32 D4
Treffgarne Owen Pembks ... 32 C4
Trefforest Rhondd ... 36 B3
Treffynnon Pembks ... 32 C5
Trefil Blae G ... 36 B5
Trefilan Cerdgn ... 43 F5
Trefin Pembks ... 32 C5
Treflach Wood Shrops ... 69 E3
Trefnannau Powys ... 69 E2
Trefnant Denbgs ... 80 C2
Trefonen Shrops ... 69 E3
Trefor Gwynd ... 66 C5
Trefor IOA ... 78 C3
Treforda Cnwll ... 4 D5
Trefrew Cnwll ... 5 E4
Trefriw Conwy ... 79 G4

Tregadillett Cnwll ... 5 F4
Tregaian IOA ... 78 D3
Tregare Mons ... 37 E5
Tregarne Cnwll ... 3 E2
Tregaron Cerdgn ... 43 G5
Tregarth Gwynd ... 79 F1
Tregaswith Cnwll ... 4 C2
Tregatta Cnwll ... 4 D5
Tregawne Cnwll ... 4 D2
Tregear Cnwll ... 3 F5
Tregeare Cnwll ... 5 F5
Tregeiriog Wrexhm ... 68 D3
Tregele IOA ... 78 C4
Tregellist Cnwll ... 4 D5
Tregenna Cnwll ... 3 F4
Tregenna Cnwll ... 4 D3
Tregeseal Cnwll ... 2 A3
Tregew Cnwll ... 3 E3
Tregidden Cnwll ... 3 E2
Tregiddle Cnwll ... 2 D2
Tregidgeo Cnwll ... 3 G4
Tregiskey Cnwll ... 3 G4
Treglemais Pembks ... 32 B5
Tregole Cnwll ... 5 E6
Tregolls Cnwll ... 5 F5
Tregonce Cnwll ... 4 C3
Tregonetha Cnwll ... 4 C2
Tregony Cnwll ... 3 G4
Tregoodwell Cnwll ... 5 E4
Tregoose Cnwll ... 2 D2
Tregoss Cnwll ... 4 C2
Tregowris Cnwll ... 3 E2
Tregoyd Powys ... 45 E3
Tregrehan Mills Cnwll ... 3 H5
Tregullon Cnwll ... 4 D2
Tregunna Cnwll ... 4 C3
Tregunnon Cnwll ... 5 F4
Tregurrian Cnwll ... 4 B2
Tregustick Cnwll ... 4 D2
Tregynon Powys ... 56 A5
Trehafod Rhondd ... 36 B3
Trehan Cnwll ... 5 G2
Treharris Myr Td ... 36 B4
Treharrock Cnwll ... 4 D4
Trehemborne Cnwll ... 4 B3
Ireherbert Carmth ... 43 F4
Treherbert Rhondd ... 35 G4
Treheveras Cnwll ... 3 F4
Trehunist Cnwll ... 5 G2
Trekelland Cnwll ... 5 G4
Trekenner Cnwll ... 5 G4
Treknow Cnwll ... 4 D5
Trelan Cnwll ... 3 E2
Trelash Cnwll ... 5 E5
Trelassick Cnwll ... 3 F5
Trelawne Cnwll ... 5 F1
Trelawnyd Flints ... 80 C3
Treleague Cnwll ... 3 E2
Treleaver Cnwll ... 3 E1
Trelech Carmth ... 33 G5
Trelech a'r Betws Carmth ... 33 G4
Treleddyd-fawr Pembks ... 32 B4
Trelew Cnwll ... 3 F3
Trelewis Myr Td ... 36 B4
Treligga Cnwll ... 4 C4
Trelights Cnwll ... 4 C4
Trelill Cnwll ... 4 D4
Trelinnoe Cnwll ... 5 G4
Trelion Cnwll ... 3 G5
Trelissick Cnwll ... 3 F4
Trelissick Garden Cnwll ... 3 F4
Trelleck Mons ... 37 F5
Trelleck Grange Mons ... 37 F4
Trelogan Flints ... 80 C3
Trelonk Cnwll ... 3 F4
Trelow Cnwll ... 4 C3
Trelowarren Cnwll ... 3 E1
Trelowia Cnwll ... 5 F2
Treluggan Cnwll ... 3 F4
Trelystan Powys ... 56 C6
Tremadog Gwynd ... 67 E4
Tremail Cnwll ... 5 E5
Tremaine Cnwll ... 5 F4
Tremar Cnwll ... 5 F3
Trematon Cnwll ... 5 G2
Trembraze Cnwll ... 5 F2
Tremeirchion Denbgs ... 80 C2
Tremethick Cross Cnwll ... 2 B3
Tremollett Cnwll ... 5 F3
Tremore Cnwll ... 4 D2
Trenance Cnwll ... 3 E2
Trenance Cnwll ... 4 B3
Trenance Cnwll ... 4 C3
Trenance Cnwll ... 2 D2
Trenarren Cnwll ... 3 H5
Trenault Cnwll ... 5 F4
Trench Shrops ... 70 B1
Trench Green Oxon ... 41 E2
Trencreek Cnwll ... 4 C2
Trencreek Cnwll ... 5 E6
Trendeal Cnwll ... 3 F5
Trendrine Cnwll ... 2 B4
Treneague Cnwll ... 4 C3
Trenear Cnwll ... 2 D3
Treneglos Cnwll ... 5 F5
Trenerth Cnwll ... 2 D3
Trenewan Cnwll ... 5 E1
Trenewth Cnwll ... 4 D5
Trengune Cnwll ... 5 E5
Treninnick Cnwll ... 4 B2
Trenoweth Cnwll ... 3 E3
Trent Dorset ... 24 B1
Trent Port Lincs ... 85 F3
Trent Vale Staffs ... 70 D4
Trentham Staffs ... 70 D4
Trentishoe Devon ... 21 G5
Trentlock Derbys ... 72 C3
Treoes V Glam ... 35 G2
Treorchy Rhondd ... 35 G4
Irequite Cnwll ... 4 D4
Trerhyngyll V Glam ... 35 G2
Trerulefoot Cnwll ... 5 G2
Tresahor Cnwll ... 3 E3
Tresawle Cnwll ... 3 F4
Tresco Heliport IOS ... 2 a2
Trescott Staffs ... 58 A5

Trescowe Cnwll ... 2 C3
Tresean Cnwll ... 4 B2
Tresham Gloucs ... 38 C3
Tresillian Cnwll ... 3 F4
Tresinney Cnwll ... 5 E4
Treskinnick Cross Cnwll ... 5 F6
Treslea Cnwll ... 5 E3
Tresmeer Cnwll ... 5 F5
Tresparrett Cnwll ... 5 E5
Tressait P & K ... 139 E6
Tresta Shet ... 169 h3
Tresta Shet ... 169 j4
Treswell Notts ... 85 E3
Treswithian Cnwll ... 2 D4
Trethawle Cnwll ... 5 F2
Trethevey Cnwll ... 4 D5
Trethewey Cnwll ... 2 A2
Trethomas Caerph ... 36 C3
Trethosa Cnwll ... 3 G5
Trethurgy Cnwll ... 3 H5
Tretio Pembks ... 32 B5
Tretire Herefs ... 45 H2
Tretower Powys ... 45 E1
Treuddyn Flints ... 69 E6
Trevadlock Cnwll ... 5 F4
Trevague Cnwll ... 5 F4
Trevalga Cnwll ... 4 D5
Trevalyn Wrexhm ... 69 F6
Trevanger Cnwll ... 4 C4
Trevanson Cnwll ... 4 C3
Trevarrack Cnwll ... 2 B3
Trevarren Cnwll ... 4 C2
Trevarrian Cnwll ... 4 B2
Trevarrick Cnwll ... 3 G4
Trevaughan Carmth ... 33 F3
Treveal Cnwll ... 2 B4
Treveal Cnwll ... 4 B2
Treveale Cnwll ... 3 F5
Treveighan Cnwll ... 4 D4
Trevellas Downs Cnwll ... 3 E5
Trevelmond Cnwll ... 5 F2
Trevemper Cnwll ... 4 B2
Treveneague Cnwll ... 2 C3
Treveor Cnwll ... 3 G4
Treverbyn Cnwll ... 3 H5
Treverbyn Cnwll ... 3 H5
Treverva Cnwll ... 3 E3
Trevescan Cnwll ... 2 A2
Trevethin Torfn ... 36 D4
Trevia Cnwll ... 5 E4
Trevigro Cnwll ... 5 G3
Trevilla Cnwll ... 3 E4
Trevilledor Cnwll ... 4 C3
Trevilson Cnwll ... 3 F5
Treviscoe Cnwll ... 3 G5
Treviskey Cnwll ... 3 G4
Trevissick Cnwll ... 3 H5
Trevithal Cnwll ... 2 B2
Trevithick Cnwll ... 4 B2
Trevithick Cnwll ... 3 G4
Trevivian Cnwll ... 5 E4
Trevoll Cnwll ... 4 B2
Trevone Cnwll ... 4 C3
Trevor Denbgs ... 69 E4
Trevorgans Cnwll ... 2 B2
Trevorrick Cnwll ... 4 C3
Trevorrick Cnwll ... 4 C3
Trevose Cnwll ... 4 B3
Trew Cnwll ... 2 D2
Trewalder Cnwll ... 4 D4
Trewalkin Powys ... 44 D2
Trewarlett Cnwll ... 5 G4
Trewarmett Cnwll ... 4 D5
Trewarthenick Cnwll ... 3 F4
Trewassa Cnwll ... 5 E5
Trewavas Cnwll ... 2 D2
Treween Cnwll ... 5 F4
Trewellard Cnwll ... 2 A3
Trewen Cnwll ... 5 F4
Trewen Cnwll ... 4 D4
Trewennack Cnwll ... 2 D3
Trewent Pembks ... 32 D1
Trewern Powys ... 69 E1
Trewetha Cnwll ... 4 D4
Trewethern Cnwll ... 4 D4
Trewidland Cnwll ... 5 F2
Trewillis Cnwll ... 3 E1
Trewince Cnwll ... 3 F3
Trewint Cnwll ... 5 E3
Trewint Cnwll ... 5 F4
Trewint Cnwll ... 5 F2
Trewirgie Cnwll ... 3 F4
Trewithian Cnwll ... 3 F3
Trewoodloe Cnwll ... 5 G3
Trewoofe Cnwll ... 2 B2
Trewoon Cnwll ... 2 D2
Trewoon Cnwll ... 3 G5
Treworga Cnwll ... 3 F5
Treworlas Cnwll ... 3 F4
Treworld Cnwll ... 5 E5
Treworthal Cnwll ... 3 F4
Treyarnon Cnwll ... 4 B3
Treyford W Susx ... 15 F5
Triangle W York ... 90 B2
Trickett's Cross Dorset ... 13 E5
Triermain Cumb ... 112 C1
Triffleton Pembks ... 32 D4
Trillacott Cnwll ... 5 F5
Trimdon Dur ... 106 C4
Trimdon Colliery Dur ... 106 C4
Trimdon Grange Dur ... 106 C4
Trimingham Norfk ... 77 F4
Trimley Lower Street Suffk ... 53 F4
Trimley Worcs ... 57 H3
Trimsaran Carmth ... 34 B5
Trimstone Devon ... 21 E5
Trinafour P & K ... 138 D6
Trinant Caerph ... 36 C4
Tring Herts ... 41 G5
Tring Wharf Herts ... 41 G6
Tringford Herts ... 41 G6
Trinity Angus ... 141 F6
Trinity Jersey ... 174 c3
Trinity Gask P & K ... 139 G2
Triscombe Somset ... 22 B3

Triscombe Somset ... 22 D3
Trislaig Highld ... 144 C2
Trispen Cnwll ... 3 F5
Tritlington Nthumb ... 114 D5
Troan Cnwll ... 4 C2
Trochry P & K ... 139 G4
Troedrhiwfuwch Caerph ... 36 B5
Troedyraur Cerdgn ... 42 C4
Troedyrhiw Myr Td ... 36 B4
Trofarth Conwy ... 80 A2
Trois Bois Jersey ... 174 b2
Troon Cnwll ... 2 D4
Troon S Ayrs ... 119 E2
Tropical World Roundhay Park W York ... 90 D3
Troston Suffk ... 64 B3
Troswell Cnwll ... 5 F5
Trotshill Worcs ... 46 D5
Trottiscliffe Kent ... 29 G2
Trotton W Susx ... 27 F1
Troughend Nthumb ... 113 F4
Troutbeck Cumb ... 103 H3
Troutbeck Cumb ... 95 E5
Troutbeck Bridge Cumb ... 95 E5
Troway Derbys ... 84 B3
Trowbridge Wilts ... 24 D5
Trowell Notts ... 72 C4
Trowle Common Wilts ... 24 D5
Trowse Newton Norfk ... 65 E6
Troy W York ... 90 D3
Trudoxhill Somset ... 24 C4
Trull Somset ... 23 E1
Trumfleet S York ... 84 D6
Trumpan Highld ... 150 B5
Trumpet Herefs ... 46 B3
Trumpington Cambs ... 51 E6
Trumpsgreen Surrey ... 27 H6
Trunch Norfk ... 77 F3
Trunnah Lancs ... 88 B4
Truro Cnwll ... 3 F4
Truro Cathedral Cnwll ... 3 F4
Truscott Cnwll ... 5 F4
Trusham Devon ... 9 E3
Trusley Derbys ... 71 G4
Trusthorpe Lincs ... 87 E3
Trysull Staffs ... 58 B5
Tubney Oxon ... 40 C4
Tuckenhay Devon ... 7 E3
Tuckhill Shrops ... 57 H4
Tuckingmill Cnwll ... 2 D4
Tuckingmill Wilts ... 25 E2
Tuckton Dorset ... 13 E4
Tucoyse Cnwll ... 3 G4
Tuddenham Suffk ... 63 F2
Tuddenham Suffk ... 53 E6
Tudeley Kent ... 17 G6
Tudhoe Dur ... 106 B4
Tudorville Herefs ... 46 B1
Tudweiloig Gwynd ... 66 B4
Tuesley Surrey ... 27 H3
Tuffley Gloucs ... 38 C6
Tufton Hants ... 26 C4
Tufton Pembks ... 33 E4
Tugby Leics ... 60 D5
Tugford Shrops ... 57 F4
Tughall Nthumb ... 125 E4
Tullibody Clacks ... 131 E5
Tullich Highld ... 155 E2
Tullich Highld ... 163 E1
Tulliemet P & K ... 139 G5
Tulloch Abers ... 158 D2
Tulloch Stirlg ... 138 B2
Tulloch Station Highld ... 145 F2
Tullochgorm Ag & B ... 128 A5
Tullybeagles Lodge P & K ... 139 G3
Tullynessle Abers ... 158 B1
Tulse Hill Gt Lon ... 28 D3
Tumble Carmth ... 34 C5
Tumbler's Green Essex ... 52 B3
Tumby Lincs ... 74 C6
Tumby Woodside Lincs ... 74 C6
Tummel Bridge P & K ... 139 E6
Tunbridge Wells Kent ... 17 G5
Tundergarth D & G ... 111 F3
Tungate Norfk ... 77 F3
Tunley Somset ... 24 C5
Tunstall E R Yk ... 93 G3
Tunstall Kent ... 30 C2
Tunstall Lancs ... 95 G2
Tunstall N York ... 97 E4
Tunstall Norfk ... 65 G6
Tunstall Staffs ... 70 C3
Tunstall Staffs ... 70 D5
Tunstall Suffk ... 65 F1
Tunstall T & W ... 106 C6
Tunstead Derbys ... 83 F2
Tunstead Norfk ... 77 F2
Tunstead Milton Derbys ... 83 E3
Tunworth Hants ... 27 E4
Tupsley Herefs ... 45 H3
Tur Langton Leics ... 60 C5
Turgis Green Hants ... 27 E5
Turkdean Gloucs ... 39 F6
Turleigh Wilts ... 24 D5
Turleygreen Shrops ... 57 H4
Turn Lancs ... 89 F1
Turnastone Herefs ... 45 F3
Turnberry S Ayrs ... 108 C5
Turnchapel Devon ... 6 B3
Turnditch Derbys ... 71 H5
Turners Green Lancs ... 88 D3
Turner's Green E Susx ... 17 G3
Turner's Green Warwks ... 59 E2
Turner's Hill W Susx ... 16 D5
Turners Puddle Dorset ... 12 B4
Turnford Herts ... 50 D1
Turnhouse C Edin ... 131 H2
Turnworth Dorset ... 12 B5
Turriff Abers ... 158 C4
Turton Bottoms Gt Man ... 89 F1
Turves Cambs ... 62 C5
Turvey Beds ... 49 G4
Turville Bucks ... 41 F3
Turville Heath Bucks ... 41 F3
Turweston Bucks ... 48 D3
Tushielaw Inn Border ... 121 G1
Tushingham cum Grindley Ches ... 69 G5

Tutbury Staffs 71 G3
Tutnall Worcs 58 C2
Tutshill Gloucs 37 F4
Tuttington Norfk 77 E3
Tutwell Cnwll 5 G3
Tuxford Notts 85 E2
Twatt Ork 169 a3
Twatt Shet 169 h3
Twechar E Duns 130 C3
Tweedmouth Nthumb 123 G5
Tweedsmuir Border 121 E2
Twelve Oaks E Susx 17 H3
Twelveheads Cnwll 3 E4
Twemlow Green Ches 82 C1
Twenty Lincs 74 B2
Twerton Somset 24 C6
Twickenham Gt Lon 28 C3
Twigworth Gloucs 46 D1
Twineham W Susx 16 C3
Twineham Green W Susx 16 C3
Twinhoe Somset 24 C5
Twinstead Essex 52 B4
Twitchen Devon 21 H4
Twitchen Shrops 56 D3
Twitham Kent 31 F2
Two Bridges Devon 8 C2
Two Dales Derbys 83 H1
Two Gates Staffs 59 E5
Two Mile Oak Cross Devon 7 F4
Two Pots Devon 21 E5
Two Waters Herts 50 B1
Twycross Leics 59 F6
Twycross Zoo Leics 59 F6
Twyford Berks 41 F2
Twyford Bucks 49 E2
Twyford Hants 26 C2
Twyford Leics 73 E1
Twyford Lincs 73 G3
Twyford Norfk 76 C2
Twyford Common Herefs 45 H3
Twyn-carno Caerph 36 B5
Twyn-y-Sheriff Mons 37 E5
Twyn-yr-Odyn V Glam 36 B2
Twynholm D & G 101 H5
Twyning Gloucs 46 D3
Twyning Green Gloucs 47 E3
Twynllanan Carmth 43 H2
Twywell Nhants 61 E3
Ty'n-dwr Denbgs 69 E4
Ty'n-y-bryn Rhondd 35 G3
Ty'n-y-coedcae Caerph 36 C3
Ty'n-y-Groes Conwy 79 G2
Ty-nant Conwy 68 B4
Ty-nant Gwynd 68 A3
Tyberton Herefs 45 G3
Tyburn W Mids 58 D4
Tycroes Carmth 34 D5
Tycrwyn Powys 68 C2
Tydd Gote Lincs 75 E2
Tydd St Giles Cambs 75 E2
Tydd St Mary Lincs 75 E2
Tye Hants 15 E4
Tye Green Essex 51 F3
Tye Green Essex 51 G4
Tye Green Essex 52 A3
Tyersal W York 90 C3
Tyldesley Gt Man 82 B5
Tyler Hill Kent 31 E2
Tyler's Green Essex 51 F1
Tylers Green Bucks 41 G4
Tylers Green Surrey 28 D1
Tylorstown Rhondd 35 G4
Tylwch Powys 55 G3
Tyn-y-nant Rhondd 36 B3
Tyndrum Stirlg 137 H3
Tynemouth T & W 115 E2
Tynewydd Rhondd 35 G4
Tyninghame E Loth 133 E3
Tynron D & G 110 C4
Tynygongl IOA 79 E3
Tynygraig Cerdgn 54 D2
Tyringham Bucks 49 G4
Tyseley W Mids 58 D4
Tythegston Brdgnd 35 F2
Tytherington Ches 82 D2
Tytherington Gloucs 38 A3
Tytherington Somset 24 C4
Tytherington Wilts 25 E3
Tytherleigh Devon 10 D5
Tytherton Lucas Wilts 38 D2
Tywardreath Cnwll 4 D1
Tywardreath Highway Cnwll 4 D1
Tywyn Conwy 79 G2
Tywyn Gwynd 54 C5

U

Ubbeston Green Suffk 65 F2
Ubley Somset 23 H5
Uckerby N York 97 F5
Uckfield E Susx 17 F3
Uckinghall Worcs 46 D3
Uckington Gloucs 47 E2
Uckington Shrops 69 H1
Uddingston S Lans 120 B5
Uddington S Lans 120 C3
Udimore E Susx 18 B3
Udny Green Abers 159 E2
Udny Station Abers 159 E1
Uffcott Wilts 39 F2
Uffculme Devon 10 A6
Uffington Lincs 61 F6
Uffington Oxon 39 H3
Uffington Shrops 69 G1
Ufford Cambs 61 G6
Ufford Suffk 53 F6
Ufton Warwks 48 B5
Ufton Nervet Berks 27 E6
Ugadale Ag & B 117 G3
Ugborough Devon 6 D3
Uggeshall Suffk 65 G3
Ugglebarnby N York 107 H1
Ughill Derbys 83 G4

Ugley Essex 51 F4
Ugley Green Essex 51 F3
Ugthorpe N York 107 G2
Uig Ag & B 134 D5
Uig Highld 150 B4
Uig Highld 150 D5
Uig W Isls 168 d8
Uigshader Highld 150 D3
Uisken Ag & B 135 F1
Ulbster Highld 167 G2
Ulcat Row Cumb 103 H2
Ulceby Lincs 93 E1
Ulceby Lincs 87 E2
Ulceby Cross Lincs 86 D2
Ulceby Skitter Lincs 93 E1
Ulcombe Kent 30 B1
Uldale Cumb 103 F4
Uley Gloucs 38 C4
Ulgham Nthumb 114 D5
Ullapool Highld 161 E3
Ullenhall Warwks 58 D2
Ullenwood Gloucs 38 D6
Ulleskelf N York 91 F4
Ullesthorpe Leics 59 H4
Ulley S York 84 B3
Ullingswick Herefs 46 B4
Ullinish Lodge Hotel Highld 150 C2
Ullock Cumb 103 E2
Ulpha Cumb 94 C4
Ulpha Cumb 95 E3
Ulrome E R Yk 93 E5
Ulting Wick Essex 52 B2
Ulverley Green W Mids 58 D4
Ulverston Cumb 94 D3
Ulwell Dorset 12 D3
Umachan Highld 151 F4
Umberleigh Devon 21 F3
Unapool Highld 164 C2
Under Burnmouth Border 112 B3
Under River Kent 29 F1
Underbarrow Cumb 95 E4
Undercliffe W York 90 C3
Underdale Shrops 69 G1
Underley Hall Cumb 95 G3
Underling Green Kent 18 A6
Underwood Notts 72 B5
Undley Suffk 63 F3
Undy Mons 37 E3
Union Mills IOM 174 I3
Union Street E Susx 17 H4
Unstone Derbys 84 A2
Unstone Green Derbys 84 A2
Unsworth Gt Man 82 C5
Unthank Cumb 103 H5
Unthank Cumb 104 A4
Unthank Cumb 104 C4
Unthank Derbys 83 H2
Unthank Nthumb 123 G4
Unthank End Cumb 104 A4
Up Cerne Dorset 11 G5
Up Exe Devon 9 F5
Up Holland Lancs 81 G5
Up Marden W Susx 15 F5
Up Mudford Somset 24 A1
Up Nately Hants 27 E4
Up Somborne Hants 26 B2
Up Sydling Dorset 11 G5
Upavon Wilts 25 G5
Upchurch Kent 30 B3
Upcott Devon 21 F4
Upcott Devon 21 H3
Upcott Herefs 45 F4
Upcott Somset 22 B2
Updown Hill Surrey 27 G6
Upend Cambs 63 F1
Upgate Norfk 76 D2
Upgate Street Norfk 64 C5
Upgate Street Norfk 65 E4
Uphall Dorset 11 F5
Uphall W Loth 131 G2
Upham Devon 9 F5
Upham Hants 14 D6
Uphampton Herefs 56 D2
Uphampton Worcs 58 A2
Uphill Somset 23 F5
Uplawmoor E Rens 119 F5
Upleadon Gloucs 46 C2
Upleatham N York 107 F3
Uplees Kent 30 D2
Uploders Dorset 11 E4
Uplowman Devon 9 G6
Uplyme Devon 10 D4
Upminster Gt Lon 29 F5
Upottery Devon 10 B5
Uppaton Devon 8 A3
Upper & Lower Stondon Beds 50 B4
Upper Affcot Shrops 57 E4
Upper Ardchronie Highld 162 C3
Upper Arley Worcs 57 H3
Upper Arncott Oxon 40 D6
Upper Astrop Nhants 48 C3
Upper Basildon Berks 40 D2
Upper Batley W York 90 D2
Upper Beeding W Susx 16 C2
Upper Benefield Nhants 61 F4
Upper Bentley Worcs 58 C2
Upper Bighouse Highld 166 C4
Upper Birchwood Derbys 72 B5
Upper Boat Rhondd 36 B3
Upper Boddington Nhants 48 C4
Upper Borth Cerdgn 54 D4
Upper Brailes Warwks 48 A3
Upper Breakish Highld 151 G1
Upper Breinton Herefs 45 G3
Upper Broadheath Worcs 46 D5
Upper Broughton Notts 72 D3
Upper Bucklebury Berks 40 D1
Upper Burgate Hants 13 E6
Upper Bush Kent 29 H3
Upper Caldecote Beds 50 C5
Upper Canada Somset 23 F5
Upper Canterton Hants 13 F6
Upper Catesby Nhants 48 C5
Upper Catshill Worcs 58 C3
Upper Chapel Powys 44 C3
Upper Cheddon Somset 23 E2
Upper Chicksgrove Wilts 25 E2

Upper Chute Wilts 26 A5
Upper Clapton Gt Lon 28 D5
Upper Clatford Hants 26 B4
Upper Clynnog Gwynd 66 D5
Upper Coberley Gloucs 38 D6
Upper Cokeham W Susx 16 C2
Upper Cotton Staffs 71 E5
Upper Cound Shrops 57 F6
Upper Cudworth S York 84 B6
Upper Cumberworth W York 83 G6
Upper Cwmtwrch Powys 35 E5
Upper Dallachy Moray 157 F5
Upper Deal Kent 31 G1
Upper Dean Beds 61 F2
Upper Denby W York 83 G5
Upper Denton Cumb 112 C1
Upper Dicker E Susx 17 F2
Upper Dinchope Shrops 57 E4
Upper Dounreay Highld 166 D5
Upper Dovercourt Essex 53 F4
Upper Drumbane Stirlg 130 C6
Upper Dunsforth N York 91 E6
Upper Eashing Surrey 27 H4
Upper Eathie Highld 155 F5
Upper Egleton Herefs 46 B4
Upper Elkstone Staffs 71 E6
Upper Ellastone Staffs 71 F4
Upper End Derbys 83 F2
Upper Enham Hants 26 B4
Upper Farmcote Shrops 57 H5
Upper Farringdon Hants 27 E3
Upper Framilode Gloucs 38 B5
Upper Froyle Hants 27 F3
Upper Godney Somset 23 H3
Upper Gravenhurst Beds 50 B4
Upper Green Berks 26 B6
Upper Green Essex 51 G4
Upper Green Mons 45 G1
Upper Green Suffk 63 G2
Upper Grove Common Herefs 46 A2
Upper Hackney Derbys 71 H6
Upper Hale Surrey 27 F4
Upper Halliford Surrey 28 B3
Upper Halling Kent 29 H2
Upper Hambleton Rutlnd 61 E6
Upper Harbledown Kent 31 E2
Upper Hardres Court Kent 31 E1
Upper Hardwick Herefs 45 G5
Upper Hartfield E Susx 17 E5
Upper Hartshay Derbys 72 B5
Upper Hatherley Gloucs 47 E1
Upper Hatton Staffs 70 C4
Upper Haugh S York 84 B4
Upper Hayton Shrops 57 E3
Upper Heaton W York 90 C1
Upper Helmsley N York 91 H5
Upper Hergest Herefs 45 E5
Upper Heyford Nhants 49 E5
Upper Heyford Oxon 48 C2
Upper Hill Herefs 45 G4
Upper Hockenden Kent 29 F3
Upper Hopton W York 90 C1
Upper Howsell Worcs 46 C4
Upper Hulme Staffs 71 E6
Upper Ifold Surrey 16 A5
Upper Inglesham Wilts 39 G4
Upper Kilcott Gloucs 38 C3
Upper Killay Swans 34 C3
Upper Kinchrackine Ag & B 137 F2
Upper Lambourn Berks 40 A2
Upper Landywood Staffs 58 C6
Upper Langford Somset 23 G5
Upper Langwith Derbys 84 C2
Upper Largo Fife 132 C5
Upper Leigh Staffs 71 E4
Upper Ley Gloucs 38 B6
Upper Littleton Somset 24 A6
Upper Longdon Staffs 71 F1
Upper Ludstone Shrops 58 A5
Upper Lybster Highld 167 F2
Upper Lydbrook Gloucs 37 G6
Upper Lyde Herefs 45 H4
Upper Lye Herefs 56 D2
Upper Maes-coed Herefs 45 F3
Upper Midhope Derbys 83 G5
Upper Milton Worcs 58 A3
Upper Minety Wilts 39 E3
Upper Moor Worcs 47 E4
Upper Moor Side W York 90 D3
Upper Mulben Moray 157 F4
Upper Netchwood Shrops 57 F5
Upper Nobut Staffs 71 E3
Upper Norwood W Susx 15 G5
Upper Padley Derbys 83 G3
Upper Pennington Hants 13 G4
Upper Pickwick Wilts 38 C1
Upper Pollicott Bucks 41 E6
Upper Poppleton N York 91 G5
Upper Quinton Warwks 47 G4
Upper Ratley Hants 26 B2
Upper Rochford Worcs 57 F2
Upper Ruscoe D & G 109 G1
Upper Sapey Herefs 57 G2
Upper Seagry Wilts 38 D2
Upper Shelton Beds 49 H3
Upper Sheringham Norfk 76 D4
Upper Shuckburgh Warwks 48 C5
Upper Skelmorlie N Ayrs 128 C2
Upper Slaughter Gloucs 47 G1
Upper Soudley Gloucs 37 H5
Upper Spond Herefs 45 F4
Upper Standen Kent 19 F5
Upper Staploe Beds 61 G1
Upper Stepford D & G 110 C3
Upper Stoke Norfk 65 E6
Upper Stowe Nhants 49 E5
Upper Street Hants 25 G1
Upper Street Norfk 77 F2
Upper Street Norfk 77 F2
Upper Street Norfk 64 D3
Upper Street Suffk 52 A6
Upper Street Suffk 53 E6
Upper Street Suffk 53 E4
Upper Strensham Worcs 46 D3
Upper Sundon Beds 50 A3
Upper Swell Gloucs 47 G2
Upper Tankersley S York 84 A5
Upper Tasburgh Norfk 65 E5

Upper Tean Staffs 71 E4
Upper Threapwood Ches 69 G4
Upper Town Ches 71 G5
Upper Town Derbys 71 G6
Upper Town Dur 105 G4
Upper Town Herefs 46 A4
Upper Town Somset 23 H6
Upper Town Suffk 64 B2
Upper Tumble Carmth 34 C5
Upper Tysoe Warwks 48 B4
Upper Ufford Suffk 53 F6
Upper Upham Wilts 39 G2
Upper Upnor Kent 30 A3
Upper Victoria Angus 141 E3
Upper Vobster Somset 24 C4
Upper Wardington Oxon 48 C4
Upper Weald Bucks 49 F3
Upper Weedon Nhants 48 D5
Upper Wellingham E Susx 17 E3
Upper Weston Somset 24 C6
Upper Weybread Suffk 65 E3
Upper Wick Worcs 46 D4
Upper Wield Hants 26 D3
Upper Winchendon Bucks 41 F6
Upper Woodford Wilts 25 G3
Upper Wootton Hants 26 D6
Upper Wraxall Wilts 38 C2
Upper Wyche Worcs 46 C4
Upperby Cumb 103 H5
Upperglen Highld 150 C4
Uppermill Gt Man 83 E5
Upperthong W York 83 F5
Upperthorpe Derbys 83 H1
Upperthorpe Lincs 85 E5
Upperton W Susx 27 H1
Uppertown Derbys 83 H1
Uppertown Highld 167 G6
Upperup Gloucs 39 E4
Upperwood Derbys 71 H6
Uppincott Devon 9 F5
Uppingham Rutlnd 61 E5
Uppington Shrops 70 A1
Upsall N York 97 H3
Upsettlington Border 123 G4
Upshire Essex 29 E6
Upstreet Kent 31 F2
Upthorpe Suffk 64 B3
Upton Berks 41 H2
Upton Bucks 41 F5
Upton Cambs 61 H3
Upton Ches 81 F2
Upton Ches 81 G3
Upton Cnwll 20 B1
Upton Cnwll 5 F3
Upton Cumb 103 G3
Upton Devon 10 A5
Upton Devon 6 D2
Upton Dorset 11 H3
Upton Dorset 12 D4
Upton E R Yk 93 E3
Upton Hants 26 B5
Upton Hants 14 B5
Upton Leics 59 F5
Upton Lincs 85 F3
Upton Mersyd 81 E3
Upton Nhants 49 E5
Upton Norfk 77 G1
Upton Notts 73 E5
Upton Notts 85 E2
Upton Oxon 39 G6
Upton Oxon 40 C3
Upton Pembks 32 D2
Upton Somset 22 C2
Upton Somset 23 G2
Upton Wilts 24 D2
Upton Warwks 47 G5
Upton Wilts 24 D2
Upton Bishop Herefs 46 B2
Upton Cheyney Gloucs 38 B1
Upton Cressett Shrops 57 G5
Upton Crews Herefs 46 B2
Upton Cross Cnwll 5 F3
Upton End Beds 50 B4
Upton Grey Hants 27 E4
Upton Heath Ches 81 F2
Upton Hellions Devon 9 E5
Upton Lovell Wilts 25 E3
Upton Magna Shrops 69 H1
Upton Noble Somset 24 C3
Upton Pyne Devon 9 F4
Upton Scudamore Wilts 24 D4
Upton Snodsbury Worcs 47 E5
Upton St Leonards Gloucs 38 C6
Upton Towans Cnwll 2 C4
Upton upon Severn Worcs 46 D3
Upton Warren Worcs 58 B2
Upwaltham W Susx 15 G5
Upware Cambs 63 E2
Upwell Norfk 62 D6
Upwey Dorset 11 G3
Upwick Green Herts 51 E3
Upwood Cambs 62 B4
Urchfont Wilts 25 F5
Urdimarsh Herefs 45 H4
Ure Bank N York 97 F2
Urlay Nook Dur 106 C2
Urmston Gt Man 82 C4
Urquhart Moray 157 F5
Urra N York 98 A5
Urray Highld 154 C4
Usan Angus 141 G4
Ushaw Moor Dur 106 B5
Usk Mons 37 E4
Usselby Lincs 86 A4
Usworth T & W 115 E1
Utkinton Ches 81 H1
Utley W York 90 B4
Uton Devon 9 E4
Utterby Lincs 86 C4
Uttoxeter Staffs 71 F3
Uwchmynydd Gwynd 66 A3
Uxbridge Gt Lon 28 B4
Uyeasound Shet 169 j5
Uzmaston Pembks 32 D3

V

Vale Guern 174 g3
Vale of Rheidol Railway Cerdgn 55 E3
Valley IOA 78 C3
Valley End Surrey 27 H6
Valley Truckle Cnwll 5 E4
Valtos Highld 151 E5
Valtos W Isls 168 d8
Van Caerph 36 C3
Vange Essex 29 H5
Varteg Torfn 36 D5
Vatsetter Shet 169 j4
Vatten Highld 150 C3
Vaynor Myr Td 36 B5
Vazon Bay Guern 174 f2
Velindre Powys 45 E3
Vellow Somset 22 D3
Velly Devon 20 C3
Venn Cnwll 20 C1
Venn Devon 7 F3
Venn Ottery Devon 10 A4
Venngreen Devon 20 D2
Vennington Shrops 69 F1
Venny Tedburn Devon 9 E4
Venterdon Cnwll 5 G3
Ventnor IOW 14 D1
Venton Devon 6 C3
Vernham Dean Hants 26 B5
Vernham Street Hants 26 B5
Vernolds Common Shrops 57 E3
Verwood Dorset 13 E5
Veryan Cnwll 3 G4
Veryan Green Cnwll 3 G4
Vickerstown Cumb 94 C2
Victoria Blae G 36 C5
Victoria Cnwll 4 C2
Victoria S York 83 G5
Vidlin Shet 169 j3
Viewfield Moray 157 F5
Viewpark N Lans 120 B6
Vigo Kent 29 G2
Ville la Bas Jersey 174 a3
Villiaze Guern 174 f1
Vinehall Street E Susx 18 A3
Vines Cross E Susx 17 G3
Virginia Water Surrey 28 A3
Virginstow Devon 5 G5
Virley Essex 52 C2
Vobster Somset 24 C4
Voe Shet 169 h3
Vowchurch Herefs 45 F3
Vulcan Village Lancs 81 H4

W

Wackerfield Dur 106 A3
Wacton Norfk 64 D5
Wadborough Worcs 47 E4
Waddesdon Bucks 41 F6
Waddeton Devon 7 F3
Waddicar Mersyd 81 F5
Waddingham Lincs 85 G4
Waddington Lancs 89 F4
Waddington Lincs 85 G1
Waddon Devon 9 F2
Waddon Dorset 11 F3
Wadebridge Cnwll 4 D3
Wadeford Somset 10 C6
Wadenhoe Nhants 61 F4
Wadesmill Herts 50 D2
Wadhurst E Susx 17 G5
Wadshelf Derbys 83 H2
Wadswick Wilts 24 D6
Wadworth S York 84 C4
Waen Denbgs 80 B1
Waen Denbgs 80 C1
Waen Powys 69 E2
Waen Fach Powys 68 D2
Waen-pentir Gwynd 79 E1
Waen-wen Gwynd 79 E1
Wagbeach Shrops 56 D6
Wainfelin Torfn 36 D4
Wainfleet All Saints Lincs 75 E6
Wainfleet Bank Lincs 75 E6
Wainford Norfk 65 F4
Wainhouse Corner Cnwll 5 E5
Wains Hill Somset 37 E1
Wainscott Kent 30 A3
Wainstalls W York 90 B2
Waitby Cumb 95 H6
Waithe Lincs 86 C5
Wake Green W Mids 58 D4
Wakefield W York 90 D2
Wakerley Nhants 61 E5
Wakes Colne Essex 52 C4
Wal-wen Flints 80 D2
Wal-wen Flints 80 D2
Walberswick Suffk 65 G3
Walberton W Susx 15 H4
Walbottle T & W 114 C2
Walbutt D & G 110 B3
Walby Cumb 104 A6
Walcombe Somset 24 A4
Walcot Lincs 92 C2
Walcot Lincs 74 A3
Walcot Shrops 69 H1
Walcot Shrops 56 D4
Walcot Warwks 47 G5
Walcot Wilts 39 F3
Walcot Green Norfk 64 D3
Walcote Leics 60 B4
Walcott Lincs 74 B6
Walcott Norfk 77 F3
Walden N York 96 C3
Walden Head N York 96 B3
Walden Stubbs N York 91 G1
Waldersdale Kent 30 A2
Walderton W Susx 15 F5
Walditch Dorset 11 E4

Waldley Derbys 71 F4
Waldridge Dur 106 B6
Waldringfield Suffk 53 F5
Waldron E Susx 17 F3
Wales S York 84 C3
Wales Somset 24 A2
Walesby Lincs 86 B4
Walesby Notts 84 D2
Walford Herefs 56 D3
Walford Herefs 46 A1
Walford Shrops 69 G2
Walford Staffs 70 C3
Walford Heath Shrops 69 G2
Walgherton Ches 70 B5
Walgrave Nhants 60 D2
Walhampton Hants 13 G4
Walk Mill Lancs 89 G2
Walkden Gt Man 82 B5
Walker T & W 114 D2
Walker Fold Lancs 89 E4
Walker's Green Herefs 45 H4
Walker's Heath W Mids 58 C3
Walkerburn Border 121 H3
Walkeringham Notts 85 E4
Walkerith Lincs 85 E4
Walkern Herts 50 D3
Walkerton Fife 132 A5
Walkford Dorset 13 F4
Walkhampton Devon 6 C5
Walkington E R Yk 92 D3
Walkley S York 84 A3
Walkwood Worcs 58 C2
Wall Cnwll 2 D3
Wall Nthumb 113 F2
Wall Staffs 58 D6
Wall End Cumb 94 C3
Wall End Herefs 45 G5
Wall Heath W Mids 58 B4
Wall Houses Nthumb 114 B2
Wall under Haywood Shrops 57 E5
Wallacetown S Ayrs 109 E5
Wallacetown S Ayrs 119 E4
Wallands Park E Susx 17 E2
Wallasey Mersyd 81 E4
Wallend Kent 30 B4
Waller's Green Herefs 46 B3
Wallhead Cumb 104 A6
Wallingford Oxon 40 D3
Wallington Gt Lon 28 D2
Wallington Hants 14 D4
Wallington Herts 50 D4
Wallington Heath W Mids 58 C6
Wallis Pembks 32 D4
Wallisdown Dorset 12 D4
Walliswood W Susx 16 B5
Walls Shet 169 g3
Wallsend T & W 115 E2
Wallthwaite Cumb 103 G3
Wallyford E Loth 132 C2
Walmer Kent 31 G1
Walmer Bridge Lancs 88 C2
Walmersley Gt Man 82 C6
Walmestone Kent 31 F2
Walmley W Mids 58 D5
Walmley Ash W Mids 58 D5
Walmsgate Lincs 86 D2
Walpole Somset 23 F3
Walpole Suffk 65 F3
Walpole Cross Keys Norfk 75 E2
Walpole Highway Norfk 75 E1
Walpole St Andrew Norfk 75 E2
Walpole St Peter Norfk 75 E2
Walrow Somset 23 F4
Walsall W Mids 58 C5
Walsall Wood W Mids 58 C6
Walsden W York 89 H2
Walsgrave on Sowe W Mids 59 G3
Walsham le Willows Suffk 64 C2
Walshaw Gt Man 82 C6
Walshaw W York 89 H3
Walshford N York 91 E5
Walsoken Norfk 75 E1
Walston S Lans 121 E4
Walsworth Herts 50 C4
Walter's Ash Bucks 41 F4
Walters Green Kent 17 F5
Walterston V Glam 36 B1
Walterstone Herefs 45 F2
Waltham Kent 31 E1
Waltham Lincs 86 C5
Waltham Abbey Essex 29 E6
Waltham Chase Hants 14 D5
Waltham Cross Herts 28 D6
Waltham on the Wolds Leics 73 F2
Waltham St Lawrence Berks 41 F2
Waltham's Cross Essex 51 H4
Walton Bucks 49 G3
Walton Cambs 61 H6
Walton Cumb 112 B1
Walton Derbys 84 A2
Walton Leics 60 B4
Walton Powys 45 E5
Walton Shrops 69 H2
Walton Shrops 57 E3
Walton Somset 23 G3
Walton Staffs 70 D3
Walton Staffs 70 D3
Walton Suffk 53 F4
Walton W Susx 15 F4
Walton W York 91 E1
Walton W York 91 E4
Walton Warwks 48 A4
Walton Cardiff Gloucs 47 E2
Walton East Pembks 32 D4
Walton Elm Dorset 24 C1
Walton Grounds Nhants 48 C3
Walton on the Hill Surrey 28 C1
Walton on the Naze Essex 53 F3
Walton on the Wolds Leics 72 D2
Walton Park Somset 37 E1
Walton West Pembks 32 C3
Walton-in-Gordano Somset 37 E2
Walton-le-Dale Lancs 88 D2
Walton-on-Thames Surrey 28 B3
Walton-on-the-Hill Staffs 70 D2
Walton-on-Trent Derbys 71 G2
Walwen Flints 80 D2
Walwick Nthumb 113 F2

Walworth Dur 106 B3
Walworth Gt Lon 28 D4
Walworth Gate Dur 106 B3
Walwyn's Castle Pembks 32 C3
Wambrook Somset 10 C5
Wampool Cumb 103 F6
Wanborough Surrey 27 G4
Wanborough Wilts 39 G2
Wandon End Herts 50 B3
Wandsworth Gt Lon 28 C3
Wangford Suffk 65 G3
Wanlip Leics 72 D1
Wanlockhead D & G 110 C6
Wannock E Susx 17 G2
Wansford Cambs 61 G5
Wansford E R Yk 92 D5
Wanshurst Green Kent 18 A6
Wanstead Gt Lon 29 E5
Wanstrow Somset 24 C3
Wanswell Gloucs 38 B4
Wantage Oxon 40 B3
Wants Green Worcs 46 C5
Wapley Gloucs 38 B2
Wappenbury Warwks 59 G2
Wappenham Nhants 48 D4
Warbleton E Susx 17 G3
Warborough Oxon 40 D4
Warboys Cambs 62 B3
Warbreck Lancs 88 B3
Warbstow Cnwll 5 F5
Warburton Gt Man 82 B4
Warcop Cumb 104 D2
Ward End W Mids 58 D4
Ward Green Suffk 64 C2
Warden Kent 30 D3
Warden Nthumb 113 F1
Warden Law T & W 106 C6
Warden Street Beds 50 B5
Wardhedges Beds 50 B4
Wardington Oxon 48 C4
Wardle Ches 70 A6
Wardle Gt Man 89 G1
Wardley Gt Man 82 C5
Wardley Rutlnd 60 D5
Wardley T & W 115 E2
Wardlow Derbys 83 G2
Wardsend Ches 82 D3
Wardy Hill Cambs 62 D4
Ware Herts 50 D2
Ware Street Kent 30 B2
Wareham Dorset 12 C3
Warehorne Kent 18 C5
Waren Mill Nthumb 125 E4
Warenford Nthumb 124 D4
Warenton Nthumb 124 D4
Wareside Herts 51 E2
Waresley Cambs 50 C6
Waresley Worcs 58 A2
Warfield Berks 41 G1
Warfleet Devon 7 F3
Wargate Lincs 74 C3
Wargrave Berks 41 F2
Warham Herefs 45 H3
Warham All Saints Norfk 76 C4
Warham St Mary Norfk 76 B4
Wark Nthumb 123 E3
Wark Nthumb 113 F2
Warkleigh Devon 21 F3
Warkton Nhants 61 E3
Warkworth Nhants 48 C3
Warkworth Nthumb 125 F2
Warlaby N York 97 G4
Warland W York 89 H2
Warleggan Cnwll 5 E3
Warleigh Somset 24 C6
Warley W York 90 B2
Warlingham Surrey 29 E2
Warmanbie D & G 111 F2
Warmbrook Derbys 71 H5
Warmfield W York 91 E2
Warmingham Ches 70 B6
Warmington Nhants 61 G4
Warmington Warwks 48 B4
Warminster Wilts 24 D4
Warmley Gloucs 38 A2
Warmsworth S York 84 C5
Warmwell Dorset 12 A3
Warndon Worcs 46 D5
Warnford Hants 26 D1
Warnham W Susx 16 B5
Warnham Court W Susx 16 C5
Warningcamp W Susx 16 A2
Warninglid W Susx 16 C4
Warren Ches 82 D2
Warren Pembks 32 D1
Warren Row Berks 41 F2
Warren Street Kent 30 C1
Warren's Green Herts 50 D4
Warrenby N York 107 E3
Warrenhill S Lans 120 D3
Warrington Bucks 49 G5
Warrington Ches 82 A3
Warriston C Edin 132 B3
Warsash Hants 14 C4
Warslow Staffs 71 F6
Warsop Notts 84 C1
Warsop Vale Notts 84 C1
Warter E R Yk 92 C5
Warter Priory E R Yk 92 B4
Warthermaske N York 97 E3
Warthill N York 91 H5
Wartling E Susx 17 G2
Wartnaby Leics 73 E2
Warton Lancs 88 C2
Warton Lancs 95 F2
Warton Nthumb 113 G6
Warton Warwks 59 F6
Warwick Cumb 104 A6
Warwick Warwks 59 F2
Warwick Bridge Cumb 104 B6
Warwick Castle Warwks 59 F2
Warwicksland Cumb 112 B2
Wasbister Ork 169 b3
Wasdale Head Cumb 94 C6
Wash Derbys 83 F3
Wash Devon 7 E4
Washall Green Herts 51 E4
Washaway Cnwll 4 D3

Washbourne Devon 7 E3
Washbrook Somset 23 G4
Washbrook Suffk 53 E5
Washfield Devon 9 F6
Washfold N York 96 D5
Washford Somset 22 C3
Washford Pyne Devon 9 E6
Washingborough Lincs 85 H2
Washington T & W 115 E1
Washington W Susx 16 B3
Washwood Heath W Mids 58 D4
Wasing Berks 26 D6
Waskerley Dur 105 G5
Wasperton Warwks 48 A5
Wasps Nest Lincs 86 A1
Wass N York 98 A3
Watchet Somset 22 D4
Watchfield Oxon 39 G3
Watchfield Somset 23 F4
Watchgate Cumb 95 F5
Watchill Cumb 103 F4
Watcombe Devon 7 F4
Watendlath Cumb 103 G2
Water Devon 8 D3
Water Lancs 89 G2
Water Eaton Oxon 40 C5
Water Eaton Staffs 70 D1
Water End Beds 50 B4
Water End Beds 50 B5
Water End Beds 50 B6
Water End E R Yk 92 B3
Water End Essex 51 G5
Water End Herts 50 A2
Water End Herts 50 C1
Water Fryston W York 91 F2
Water Newton Cambs 61 G5
Water Orton Warwks 59 E4
Water Stratford Bucks 49 E3
Water Street Neath 35 E3
Water Yeat Cumb 94 D4
Water's Nook Gt Man 82 B5
Waterbeach Cambs 62 D2
Waterbeach W Susx 15 G4
Waterbeck D & G 111 G2
Watercombe Dorset 12 A3
Waterden Norfk 76 B4
Waterend Cumb 103 E2
Waterfall Staffs 71 F5
Waterfoot E Ayrs 89 G2
Waterfoot S Lans 119 G5
Waterford Herts 50 D2
Watergate Cnwll 5 E4
Waterhead Cumb 94 D5
Waterhead E Ayrs 109 G6
Waterheads Border 121 G4
Waterhouses Dur 106 A5
Waterhouses Staffs 71 F5
Wateringbury Kent 29 H1
Waterlane Gloucs 38 D5
Waterloo Cnwll 5 G4
Waterloo Derbys 84 B1
Waterloo Dorset 12 D4
Waterloo Herefs 45 F4
Waterloo Highld 151 G1
Waterloo Mersyd 81 E4
Waterloo N Lans 120 C5
Waterloo N York 77 E2
Waterloo P & K 139 H3
Waterloo Pembks 32 D2
Waterloo Cross Devon 9 G6
Waterloo Port Gwynd 78 D1
Waterlooville Hants 15 E5
Watermillock Cumb 104 A2
Waterperry Oxon 40 D5
Waterrow Somset 22 C2
Waters Upton Shrops 70 A2
Watersfield W Susx 16 A3
Waterside Bucks 41 H4
Waterside Cumb 103 F5
Waterside E Ayrs 109 F6
Waterside E Ayrs 119 G4
Waterside E Duns 130 C2
Waterside E Duns 89 G2
Waterside S York 84 D6
Waterstein Highld 150 B3
Waterstock Oxon 41 E5
Waterston Pembks 32 D2
Watford Herts 28 B6
Watford Nhants 60 B2
Wath N York 97 E2
Wath N York 97 F2
Wath upon Dearne S York 84 B5
Watlington Norfk 75 F1
Watlington Oxon 41 E4
Watnall Notts 72 C5
Watten Highld 167 F4
Wattisfield Suffk 64 C3
Wattisham Suffk 52 D6
Watton Dorset 11 E4
Watton E R Yk 92 D5
Watton Norfk 64 B5
Watton Green Norfk 64 B5
Watton-at-Stone Herts 50 D3
Wattons Green Essex 29 F6
Wattston N Lans 130 D2
Wattstown Rhondd 35 H4
Wattsville Caerph 36 C3
Wauldby E R Yk 92 C2
Waulkmill Abers 148 D4
Waunarlwydd Swans 34 D4
Waunfawr Cerdgn 54 D4
Waunfawr Gwynd 67 E6
Waungron Swans 34 C4
Waunlwyd Blae G 36 C5
Wavendon Bucks 49 G3
Waverbridge Cumb 103 F5
Waverton Ches 81 G1
Waverton Cumb 103 F5
Wawne E R Yk 93 E3
Waxham Norfk 77 G3
Waxholme E R Yk 93 G3
Way Kent 31 G2
Way Village Devon 9 F6
Way Wick Somset 23 G5
Waye Devon 7 E5
Wayford Somset 10 D5
Waytown Dorset 11 E4
Weacombe Somset 22 D4

Weald Oxon 39 H4
Wealdstone Gt Lon 28 B5
Weardley W York 90 D4
Weare Somset 23 G4
Weare Giffard Devon 21 E3
Wearhead Dur 105 E4
Wearne Somset 23 G2
Weasdale Cumb 95 H5
Weasenham All Saints Norfk 76 B2
Weasenham St Peter Norfk 76 B2
Weaste Gt Man 82 C4
Weatheroak Hill Worcs 58 D3
Weaverham Ches 82 A2
Weaverslake Staffs 71 F2
Weaverthorpe N York 99 E2
Webb's Heath Gloucs 38 B2
Webbington Somset 23 G5
Webheath Worcs 58 C2
Webton Herefs 45 G3
Wedderlairs Abers 158 D2
Wedding Hall Fold N York 89 H4
Weddington Kent 31 F2
Weddington Warwks 59 F5
Wedhampton Wilts 25 F5
Wedmore Somset 23 G4
Wednesbury W Mids 58 C5
Wednesfield W Mids 58 B5
Weecar Notts 85 F1
Weedon Bucks 49 F1
Weedon Nhants 48 D5
Weedon Lois Nhants 48 D4
Weeford Staffs 58 D6
Week Devon 21 F3
Week Devon 21 G2
Week Devon 7 E4
Week Somset 22 B3
Week St Mary Cnwll 5 F6
Weeke Devon 8 D5
Weeke Hants 26 C2
Weekley Nhants 61 E3
Weel E R Yk 92 D3
Weeley Essex 53 E3
Weeley Heath Essex 53 E3
Weem P & K 139 F5
Weeping Cross Staffs 70 D2
Weethley Warwks 47 F5
Weeting Norfk 63 G4
Weeton E R Yk 93 G2
Weeton Lancs 88 B3
Weeton N York 90 D4
Weetwood W York 90 D3
Weir Lancs 89 G2
Weir Quay Devon 6 B4
Weirbrook Shrops 69 F2
Welbeck Abbey Notts 84 C2
Welborne Norfk 76 D1
Welbourn Lincs 73 G5
Welburn N York 98 C2
Welbury N York 97 G5
Welby Lincs 73 G4
Welches Dam Cambs 62 D4
Welcombe Devon 20 C2
Weldon Bridge Nthumb 114 C5
Welford Berks 40 B1
Welford Nhants 60 B3
Welford-on-Avon Warwks 47 G4
Welham Leics 60 D5
Welham Notts 85 E3
Welham Green Herts 50 C1
Well Hants 27 F4
Well Lincs 87 E2
Well N York 97 F3
Well End Bucks 41 G3
Well End Herts 28 C6
Well Fold W York 90 C2
Well Head Herts 50 C3
Well Hill Kent 29 F2
Well Town Devon 9 F6
Welland Worcs 46 C3
Welland Stone Worcs 46 D3
Wellbank Angus 141 E3
Wellbury Herts 50 B4
Wellesbourne Warwks 48 A5
Wellesbourne Mountford Warwks 48 A5
Wellhouse Berks 40 C1
Welling Gt Lon 29 E4
Wellingborough Nhants 61 E2
Wellingham Norfk 76 B2
Wellingore Lincs 73 G6
Wellington Cumb 94 B5
Wellington Herefs 45 H4
Wellington Shrops 70 B1
Wellington Somset 22 D1
Wellington Heath Herefs 46 C3
Wellington Marsh Herefs 45 H4
Wellow IOW 14 B2
Wellow Notts 84 D1
Wellow Somset 24 C5
Wellpond Green Herts 51 E3
Wells Somset 24 A4
Wells Green Ches 70 B5
Wells Head W York 90 B3
Wells-next-the-sea Norfk 76 B4
Wellsborough Leics 59 F6
Wellstye Green Essex 51 G3
Welltree P & K 139 G2
Wellwood Fife 131 G4
Welney Norfk 62 D5
Welsh Bicknor Herefs 37 G6
Welsh End Shrops 69 G4
Welsh Frankton Shrops 69 F3
Welsh Hook Pembks 32 D4
Welsh Newton Herefs 37 F6
Welsh St Donats V Glam 36 A2
Welshampton Shrops 69 G3
Welshpool Powys 56 C6
Welton Cumb 103 G5
Welton E R Yk 92 C2
Welton Lincs 85 H3
Welton Nhants 60 B2
Welton le Marsh Lincs 87 E1
Welton le Wold Lincs 86 C3
Welwick E R Yk 93 G2
Welwyn Herts 50 C2
Welwyn Garden City Herts 50 C2
Wem Shrops 69 G3
Wembdon Somset 23 F3
Wembley Gt Lon 28 C5

Wembury Devon 6 C2
Wembworthy Devon 21 G1
Wemyss Bay Inver 128 C2
Wenallt Cerdgn 54 D2
Wendens Ambo Essex 51 F4
Wendlebury Oxon 48 D1
Wendling Norfk 76 B1
Wendover Bucks 41 G5
Wendron Cnwll 2 D3
Wendy Cambs 50 D5
Wenfordbridge Cnwll 4 D3
Wenhaston Suffk 65 G3
Wennington Cambs 62 B3
Wennington Gt Lon 29 F4
Wennington Lancs 95 G2
Wensley Derbys 71 G6
Wensley N York 96 D4
Wentbridge W York 91 F1
Wentnor Shrops 56 D5
Wentworth Cambs 62 D3
Wentworth S York 84 B4
Wentworth Castle S York 83 H5
Wenvoe V Glam 36 B1
Weobley Herefs 45 G4
Weobley Marsh Herefs 45 G4
Wepham W Susx 16 A2
Wereham Norfk 63 F5
Wergs Staffs 58 B5
Wern Gwynd 67 E4
Wern Powys 68 B1
Wern Powys 69 E1
Wern Powys 36 B6
Wern Shrops 69 E3
Wern-y-gaer Flints 80 D1
Werneth Low Gt Man 83 E4
Wernffrwd Swans 34 C4
Werrington Cambs 61 H6
Werrington Cnwll 5 G5
Werrington Staffs 70 D5
Wervin Ches 81 F2
Wesham Lancs 88 C3
Wessington Derbys 72 A6
West Aberthaw V Glam 22 C6
West Acre Norfk 75 H1
West Allerdean Nthumb 123 G4
West Alvington Devon 7 E2
West Amesbury Wilts 25 G3
West Anstey Devon 22 A2
West Appleton N York 97 E4
West Ashby Lincs 86 C2
West Ashling W Susx 15 F4
West Ashton Wilts 24 D5
West Auckland Dur 106 A3
West Ayton N York 99 F3
West Bagborough Somset 23 E3
West Balsdon Cnwll 5 F6
West Bank Blae G 36 C5
West Bank Ches 81 G3
West Barkwith Lincs 86 B3
West Barnby N York 107 G2
West Barns E Loth 133 E3
West Barsham Norfk 76 B3
West Bay Dorset 11 E4
West Beckham Norfk 76 D4
West Bedfont Surrey 28 B3
West Bergholt Essex 52 C3
West Bexington Dorset 11 F3
West Bilney Norfk 75 G1
West Blatchington E Susx 16 D2
West Boldon T & W 115 E2
West Bourton Dorset 24 C2
West Bowling W York 90 C3
West Brabourne Kent 18 D6
West Bradenham Norfk 64 B6
West Bradford Lancs 89 F4
West Bradley Somset 24 A3
West Bretton W York 83 H6
West Bridgford Notts 72 C4
West Briscoe Dur 105 F2
West Bromwich W Mids 58 C4
West Buccleuch Hotel Border 111 H6
West Buckland Devon 21 G4
West Buckland Somset 23 E1
West Burton N York 96 C3
West Burton W Susx 16 A3
West Butsfield Dur 105 H5
West Butterwick Lincs 85 F5
West Byfleet Surrey 28 A2
West Cairngaan D & G 100 C3
West Caister Norfk 77 H1
West Calder W Loth 131 F1
West Camel Somset 24 A2
West Chaldon Dorset 12 B3
West Challow Oxon 40 B3
West Charleton Devon 7 E2
West Chelborough Dorset 11 F5
West Chevington Nthumb 114 D5
West Chiltington W Susx 16 B3
West Chinnock Somset 11 E6
West Chisenbury Wilts 25 G4
West Clandon Surrey 28 A1
West Cliffe Kent 19 G6
West Coker Somset 11 E6
West Combe Devon 7 E4
West Compton Somset 24 B3
West Compton Abbas Dorset 11 F4
West Cottingwith N York 91 H4
West Cowick E R Yk 91 G2
West Cross Swans 34 D3
West Curry Cnwll 5 F5
West Curthwaite Cumb 103 G5
West Dean W Susx 15 G3
West Dean Wilts 25 H2
West Deeping Lincs 74 A1
West Derby Mersyd 81 F4
West Dereham Norfk 63 F5
West Down Devon 21 E5
West Drayton Gt Lon 28 B4
West Drayton Notts 85 E2
West Dunnet Highld 167 F6
West Ella E R Yk 92 D2
West End Beds 49 H5
West End Berks 41 F2
West End Berks 41 G1
West End Caerph 36 C4
West End Cambs 62 B2
West End Cumb 103 G6
West End E R Yk 92 C3

West End E R Yk.............. 93 F3
West End E R Yk.............. 93 F2
West End Gloucs.............. 38 B3
West End Hants.............. 14 C5
West End Hants.............. 27 E3
West End Herts.............. 50 D1
West End Herts.............. 50 D1
West End Lancs.............. 89 F2
West End Lincs.............. 86 D4
West End N York.............. 90 C5
West End N York.............. 91 F4
West End Norfk.............. 76 B1
West End Norfk.............. 77 H1
West End Oxon.............. 40 D3
West End Somset.............. 37 F1
West End Somset.............. 24 B3
West End Surrey.............. 27 H5
West End Surrey.............. 28 B2
West End W Susx.............. 16 C3
West End W York.............. 90 C3
West End Wilts.............. 25 E2
West End Wilts.............. 38 D2
West End Wilts.............. 25 E2
West End Green Hants.............. 27 E5
West Ewell Surrey.............. 28 C2
West Farleigh Kent.............. 29 H1
West Farndon Nhants.............. 48 C4
West Felton Shrops.............. 69 F2
West Firle E Susx.............. 17 F2
West Firsby Lincs.............. 85 G3
West Flotmanby N York.............. 99 F3
West Garforth W York.............. 91 E3
West Ginge Oxon.............. 40 C3
West Grafton Wilts.............. 25 H5
West Green Hants.............. 27 F5
West Grimstead Wilts.............. 25 G2
West Grinstead W Susx.............. 16 C4
West Haddlesey N York.............. 91 G2
West Haddon Nhants.............. 60 B2
West Hagbourne Oxon.............. 40 C3
West Hagley Worcs.............. 58 B3
West Hallam Derbys.............. 72 B4
West Hallam Common Derbys.............. 72 B4
West Halton Lincs.............. 92 C2
West Ham Gt Lon.............. 29 E4
West Handley Derbys.............. 84 B2
West Hanney Oxon.............. 40 B3
West Hanningfield Essex.............. 30 A6
West Harnham Wilts.............. 25 G2
West Harptree Somset.............. 24 A5
West Harting W Susx.............. 15 F6
West Hatch Somset.............. 23 F1
West Hatch Wilts.............. 25 E2
West Haven Angus.............. 141 F3
West Head Norfk.............. 63 E6
West Heath Hants.............. 26 D5
West Heath W Mids.............. 58 C3
West Helmsdale Highld.............. 163 G5
West Hendred Oxon.............. 40 C3
West Heslerton N York.............. 99 E2
West Hewish Somset.............. 23 G6
West Hill Devon.............. 10 A4
West Hoathly W Susx.............. 16 D5
West Holme Dorset.............. 12 C3
West Horndon Essex.............. 29 G5
West Horrington Somset.............. 24 A4
West Horsley Surrey.............. 28 B1
West Horton Nthumb.............. 123 G2
West Hougham Kent.............. 19 F5
West Howe Dorset.............. 12 D4
West Howetown Somset.............. 22 B3
West Huntingtower P & K.............. 139 H2
West Huntspill Somset.............. 23 F4
West Hyde Beds.............. 50 B2
West Hyde Herts.............. 28 A5
West Hythe Kent.............. 19 E5
West Ilkerton Devon.............. 21 G5
West Ilsley Berks.............. 40 C2
West Itchenor W Susx.............. 15 F4
West Keal Lincs.............. 86 D1
West Kennett Wilts.............. 39 F1
West Kilbride N Ayrs.............. 118 D4
West Kingsdown Kent.............. 29 F2
West Kington Wilts.............. 38 C2
West Kirby Mersyd.............. 80 D3
West Knapton N York.............. 98 D2
West Knighton Dorset.............. 11 H3
West Knoyle Wilts.............. 24 D2
West Lambrook Somset.............. 23 G1
West Langdon Kent.............. 19 G6
West Laroch Highld.............. 137 G6
West Lavington W Susx.............. 15 G6
West Lavington Wilts.............. 25 F4
West Layton N York.............. 97 E6
West Leake Notts.............. 72 C3
West Learmouth Nthumb.............. 123 F3
West Lees N York.............. 97 H5
West Leigh Devon.............. 8 D5
West Leigh Devon.............. 7 E3
West Leigh Somset.............. 22 D2
West Lexham Norfk.............. 76 B2
West Lilling N York.............. 98 B1
West Linton Border.............. 121 F5
West Littleton Gloucs.............. 38 B2
West Lockinge Oxon.............. 40 B3
West Lulworth Dorset.............. 12 B3
West Lutton N York.............. 99 E2
West Lydford Somset.............. 24 A2
West Lyn Devon.............. 21 G5
West Lyng Somset.............. 23 F2
West Lynn Norfk.............. 75 F2
West Malling Kent.............. 29 H2
West Malvern Worcs.............. 46 C4
West Marden W Susx.............. 15 F5
West Markham Notts.............. 85 E2
West Marsh Lincs.............. 86 C4
West Marton N York.............. 89 G5
West Melbury Dorset.............. 24 D1
West Melton S York.............. 84 B5
West Meon Hants.............. 27 E2
West Meon Hut Hants.............. 27 E2
West Meon Woodlands Hants.............. 27 E2
West Mersea Essex.............. 52 D2
West Mickley Nthumb.............. 114 B2
West Midlands Safari Park Worcs.............. 58 A3
West Milton Dorset.............. 11 E4
West Minster Kent.............. 30 C1
West Molesey Surrey.............. 28 B3

West Monkton Somset.............. 23 E2
West Moors Dorset.............. 13 E5
West Morden Dorset.............. 12 C4
West Morriston Border.............. 122 C3
West Morton W York.............. 90 B4
West Mudford Somset.............. 24 A1
West Ness N York.............. 98 C3
West Newbiggin Dur.............. 106 C3
West Newton E R Yk.............. 93 F3
West Newton Norfk.............. 75 G3
West Newton Somset.............. 23 F2
West Norwood Gt Lon.............. 28 D3
West Ogwell Devon.............. 7 F5
West Orchard Dorset.............. 24 D1
West Overton Wilts.............. 25 G6
West Panson W Susx.............. 5 G5
West Parley Dorset.............. 13 E4
West Peckham Kent.............. 29 G1
West Pelton Dur.............. 106 B6
West Pennard Somset.............. 24 A3
West Pentire Cnwll.............. 4 A2
West Perry Cambs.............. 61 G2
West Porlock Somset.............. 22 B4
West Prawle Devon.............. 7 E1
West Pulham Dorset.............. 11 G5
West Putford Devon.............. 20 D2
West Quantoxhead Somset.............. 22 D3
West Raddon Devon.............. 9 F5
West Rainton Dur.............. 106 C6
West Rasen Lincs.............. 86 A4
West Ravendale Lincs.............. 86 C5
West Raynham Norfk.............. 76 B2
West Retford Notts.............. 85 E3
West Rounton N York.............. 97 G5
West Row Suffk.............. 63 F3
West Rudham Norfk.............. 76 A3
West Runton Norfk.............. 77 E4
West Saltoun E Loth.............. 132 D2
West Sandford Devon.............. 9 E5
West Sandwick Shet.............. 169 j4
West Scrafton N York.............. 96 D3
West Sleekburn Nthumb.............. 114 D4
West Somerton Norfk.............. 77 H2
West Stafford Dorset.............. 11 G4
West Stockwith Notts.............. 85 E4
West Stoke W Susx.............. 15 F4
West Stonesdale N York.............. 96 B5
West Stoughton Somset.............. 23 G4
West Stour Dorset.............. 24 C1
West Stourmouth Kent.............. 31 F2
West Stow Suffk.............. 63 G2
West Stowell Wilts.............. 25 G5
West Stratton Hants.............. 26 D3
West Street Kent.............. 29 H4
West Street Kent.............. 30 C1
West Street Kent.............. 31 G1
West Street Suffk.............. 64 B2
West Tanfield N York.............. 97 F3
West Taphouse Cnwll.............. 5 E2
West Tarbert Ag & B.............. 127 G2
West Tarring W Susx.............. 16 B2
West Thirston Nthumb.............. 114 C5
West Thorney W Susx.............. 15 F4
West Thorpe Notts.............. 72 D2
West Thurrock Essex.............. 29 G4
West Tilbury Essex.............. 29 G4
West Tisted Hants.............. 27 E2
West Torrington Lincs.............. 86 B3
West Town Hants.............. 15 E3
West Town Herefs.............. 45 G5
West Town Somset.............. 37 F1
West Town Somset.............. 23 H5
West Town Somset.............. 24 A3
West Town Somset.............. 24 C3
West Tytherley Hants.............. 26 A2
West Walton Norfk.............. 75 E1
West Walton Highway Norfk.............. 75 E1
West Wellow Hants.............. 26 A1
West Wembury Devon.............. 6 C2
West Wemyss Fife.............. 132 B5
West Wick Somset.............. 23 F5
West Wickham Cambs.............. 51 G6
West Wickham Gt Lon.............. 29 E3
West Williamston Pembks.............. 33 E2
West Winch Norfk.............. 75 G2
West Winterslow Wilts.............. 25 H2
West Wittering W Susx.............. 15 F3
West Witton N York.............. 96 D4
West Woodburn Nthumb.............. 113 F3
West Woodhay Berks.............. 26 B6
West Woodlands Somset.............. 24 C4
West Woodside Cumb.............. 103 G5
West Worldham Hants.............. 27 F4
West Worthing W Susx.............. 16 B2
West Wratting Essex.............. 51 G6
West Wycombe Bucks.............. 41 F4
West Wylam Nthumb.............. 114 C2
West Wyton N York.............. 96 D4
West Yatton Wilts.............. 38 C2
West Yoke Kent.............. 29 G3
West Youlstone Cnwll.............. 20 C2
Westbere Kent.............. 31 E2
Westborough Lincs.............. 73 F4
Westbourne Dorset.............. 13 E4
Westbourne W Susx.............. 15 F4
Westbrook Berks.............. 40 C1
Westbrook Kent.............. 31 G3
Westbrook Wilts.............. 25 E6
Westbury Bucks.............. 48 D3
Westbury Shrops.............. 69 F1
Westbury Wilts.............. 24 D4
Westbury Leigh Wilts.............. 24 D4
Westbury-on-Severn Gloucs.............. 38 B6
Westbury-on-Trym Bristl.............. 37 G2
Westbury-sub-Mendip Somset.............. 23 H4
Westby Lancs.............. 88 B3
Westcliff-on-Sea Essex.............. 30 B5
Westcombe Somset.............. 24 B3
Westcote Gloucs.............. 47 H1
Westcote Barton Oxon.............. 48 C6
Westcott Bucks.............. 41 E6
Westcott Devon.............. 9 G5
Westcott Surrey.............. 28 B1
Westcourt Wilts.............. 25 H5
Westdean E Susx.............. 17 F1
Westdown Camp Wilts.............. 25 F4
Westdowns Cnwll.............. 4 D4
Wested Kent.............. 29 F3

Westend Gloucs.............. 38 C5
Westend Town Nthumb.............. 113 E1
Westenhanger Kent.............. 19 E5
Wester Drumashie Highld.............. 154 D2
Wester Ochiltree W Loth.............. 131 F3
Wester Pitkierie Fife.............. 132 D6
Westerdale Highld.............. 167 E5
Westerdale N York.............. 98 B5
Westerfield Suffk.............. 53 E5
Westergate W Susx.............. 15 G4
Westerham Kent.............. 29 E1
Westerhope T & W.............. 114 D2
Westerland Devon.............. 7 F4
Westerleigh Gloucs.............. 38 B2
Westerton Angus.............. 141 G5
Westerton W Susx.............. 15 G4
Westfield Cumb.............. 102 D3
Westfield E Susx.............. 18 B3
Westfield Highld.............. 166 D5
Westfield N Lans.............. 130 D2
Westfield Norfk.............. 76 C1
Westfield Somset.............. 24 B5
Westfield W Loth.............. 131 F2
Westfield Sole Kent.............. 30 A2
Westfields Dorset.............. 11 G5
Westfields Herefs.............. 45 H3
Westfields of Rattray P & K.............. 140 B4
Westford Somset.............. 22 D1
Westgate Dur.............. 105 F4
Westgate Lincs.............. 85 E5
Westgate Norfk.............. 76 C4
Westgate Hill W York.............. 90 C2
Westgate on Sea Kent.............. 31 G3
Westgate Street Norfk.............. 77 E2
Westhall Suffk.............. 65 G3
Westham Dorset.............. 11 G2
Westham E Susx.............. 17 G2
Westham Somset.............. 23 G4
Westhampnett W Susx.............. 15 G4
Westhay Somset.............. 23 G3
Westhead Lancs.............. 81 G5
Westhide Herefs.............. 46 A4
Westhill Abers.............. 149 F5
Westholme Somset.............. 24 A3
Westhope Herefs.............. 45 G4
Westhope Shrops.............. 57 E4
Westhorp Nhants.............. 48 C4
Westhorpe Lincs.............. 74 C3
Westhorpe Suffk.............. 64 C2
Westhoughton Gt Man.............. 82 B5
Westhouse N York.............. 95 G2
Westhouses Derbys.............. 72 B6
Westhumble Surrey.............. 28 C1
Westlake Devon.............. 6 D3
Westland Green Herts.............. 51 E3
Westleigh Devon.............. 21 E3
Westleigh Devon.............. 22 C1
Westleton Suffk.............. 65 G2
Westley Shrops.............. 56 D6
Westley Suffk.............. 63 G2
Westley Waterless Cambs.............. 63 E1
Westlington Bucks.............. 41 F5
Westlinton Cumb.............. 112 A1
Westmarsh Kent.............. 31 F2
Westmeston E Susx.............. 16 D3
Westmill Herts.............. 51 E3
Westminster Gt Lon.............. 28 D4
Westmuir Angus.............. 140 D5
Westnewton Cumb.............. 103 E4
Westoe T & W.............. 115 E2
Weston Berks.............. 40 B2
Weston Ches.............. 81 G3
Weston Ches.............. 70 B5
Weston Devon.............. 10 B5
Weston Devon.............. 10 B3
Weston Dorset.............. 11 G2
Weston Hants.............. 27 E1
Weston Herefs.............. 45 F5
Weston Herts.............. 50 C4
Weston Lincs.............. 74 C2
Weston N York.............. 90 C4
Weston Nhants.............. 48 D4
Weston Notts.............. 85 E1
Weston Shrops.............. 57 F5
Weston Shrops.............. 69 E3
Weston Shrops.............. 56 D3
Weston Somset.............. 24 C6
Weston Staffs.............. 71 E3
Weston Beggard Herefs.............. 46 A3
Weston by Welland Nhants.............. 60 D4
Weston Colley Hants.............. 26 C3
Weston Colville Cambs.............. 51 G6
Weston Corbett Hants.............. 27 E4
Weston Coyney Staffs.............. 70 D4
Weston Favell Nhants.............. 49 F5
Weston Green Cambs.............. 51 G6
Weston Heath Shrops.............. 70 C1
Weston Hills Lincs.............. 74 C2
Weston in Arden Warwks.............. 59 G4
Weston Jones Staffs.............. 70 C2
Weston Longville Norfk.............. 76 D2
Weston Lullingfields Shrops.............. 69 F2
Weston Patrick Hants.............. 27 E4
Weston Rhyn Shrops.............. 69 E4
Weston Subedge Gloucs.............. 47 G3
Weston Turville Bucks.............. 41 G5
Weston under Penyard Herefs.............. 46 B1
Weston under Wetherley Warwks.............. 59 F2
Weston Underwood Bucks.............. 49 G4
Weston Underwood Derbys.............. 71 H4
Weston-in-Gordano Somset.............. 37 F2
Weston-on-the-Green Oxon.............. 48 D1
Weston-Super-Mare Somset.............. 23 F5
Westonbirt Gloucs.............. 38 C3
Westoning Beds.............. 50 A4
Westoning Woodend Beds.............. 50 A4
Westonzoyland Somset.............. 23 F3
Westow N York.............. 98 C1
Westport Somset.............. 23 G1
Westquarter Falk.............. 131 E3
Westra V Glam.............. 36 C1
Westray Airport Ork.............. 169 b4
Westridge Green Berks.............. 40 D2
Westrigg W Loth.............. 131 E2

Westrop Wilts.............. 39 G4
Westruther Border.............. 122 D4
Westry Cambs.............. 62 C5
Westthorpe Derbys.............. 84 B3
Westward Cumb.............. 103 G5
Westward Ho! Devon.............. 20 D3
Westwell Kent.............. 18 C6
Westwell Oxon.............. 39 G5
Westwell Leacon Kent.............. 18 C6
Westwick Cambs.............. 62 C2
Westwick Dur.............. 105 G2
Westwick Norfk.............. 77 F3
Westwood Devon.............. 9 G4
Westwood Kent.............. 31 G3
Westwood Notts.............. 72 B5
Westwood Wilts.............. 24 D5
Westwood Heath W Mids.............. 59 F3
Westwoodside Lincs.............. 85 E5
Wetham Green Kent.............. 30 B3
Wetheral Cumb.............. 104 A6
Wetherby W York.............. 91 E4
Wetherden Suffk.............. 64 C2
Wetheringsett Suffk.............. 64 D2
Wethersfield Essex.............. 51 H4
Wetherup Street Suffk.............. 64 D2
Wetley Rocks Staffs.............. 71 E5
Wettenhall Ches.............. 70 A6
Wetton Staffs.............. 71 F6
Wetwang E R Yk.............. 92 C5
Wetwood Staffs.............. 70 C3
Wexcombe Wilts.............. 26 A5
Wexham Bucks.............. 41 H2
Wexham Street Bucks.............. 41 H3
Weybourne Norfk.............. 76 D4
Weybread Suffk.............. 65 E3
Weybread Street Suffk.............. 65 E3
Weybridge Surrey.............. 28 B2
Weycroft Devon.............. 10 C5
Weydale Highld.............. 167 E5
Weyhill Hants.............. 26 A4
Weymouth Dorset.............. 11 G2
Whaddon Bucks.............. 49 F3
Whaddon Cambs.............. 50 D5
Whaddon Gloucs.............. 38 C6
Whaddon Wilts.............. 24 D5
Whaddon Wilts.............. 25 G2
Whale Cumb.............. 104 B2
Whaley Derbys.............. 84 C2
Whaley Bridge Derbys.............. 83 E3
Whaley Thorns Derbys.............. 84 C2
Whaligoe Highld.............. 167 G2
Whalley Lancs.............. 89 F3
Whalley Banks Lancs.............. 89 F3
Whalton Nthumb.............. 114 C4
Whaplode Lincs.............. 74 D2
Whaplode Drove Lincs.............. 74 D1
Wharf Warwks.............. 48 C4
Wharfe N York.............. 96 A2
Wharles Lancs.............. 88 C3
Wharley End Beds.............. 49 G3
Wharncliffe Side S York.............. 83 H4
Wharram-le-Street N York.............. 98 D1
Wharton Ches.............. 82 B1
Wharton Herefs.............. 45 H5
Whashton N York.............. 97 E5
Whashton Green N York.............. 97 E5
Whasset Cumb.............. 95 F3
Whatcote Warwks.............. 48 A4
Whateley Warwks.............. 59 E5
Whatfield Suffk.............. 52 D5
Whatley Somset.............. 10 D5
Whatley Somset.............. 24 C4
Whatley's End Gloucs.............. 37 H2
Whatlington E Susx.............. 18 A3
Whatsole Street Kent.............. 19 E6
Whatstandwell Derbys.............. 72 A5
Whatton Notts.............. 73 E4
Whauphill D & G.............. 101 E5
Whaw N York.............. 96 C5
Wheal Rose Cnwll.............. 3 E4
Wheatacre Norfk.............. 65 G5
Wheatfield Oxon.............. 41 E4
Wheathampstead Herts.............. 50 C2
Wheathill Shrops.............. 57 F4
Wheathill Somset.............. 24 A2
Wheatley Hants.............. 27 F3
Wheatley Oxon.............. 40 D5
Wheatley W York.............. 90 B2
Wheatley Hill Dur.............. 106 C5
Wheatley Hills S York.............. 84 D5
Wheatley Lane Lancs.............. 89 G3
Wheaton Aston Staffs.............. 70 C1
Wheatsheaf Wrexhm.............. 69 E5
Wheddon Cross Somset.............. 22 B3
Wheel Inn Cnwll.............. 2 D2
Wheelbarrow Town Kent.............. 19 E6
Wheeler's Green Oxon.............. 41 F1
Wheeler's Street Kent.............. 18 B6
Wheelerend Common Bucks.............. 41 F4
Wheelerstreet Surrey.............. 27 H3
Wheelock Ches.............. 70 C6
Wheelock Heath Ches.............. 70 C6
Wheelton Lancs.............. 88 D2
Wheldale N York.............. 91 F2
Wheldrake N York.............. 91 H4
Whelford Gloucs.............. 39 F4
Whelpley Hill Bucks.............. 50 A1
Whelpo Cumb.............. 103 G4
Whelston Flints.............. 80 D2
Whempstead Herts.............. 50 D3
Whenby N York.............. 98 B2
Whepstead Suffk.............. 63 G1
Wherstead Suffk.............. 53 E5
Wherwell Hants.............. 26 B3
Wheston Derbys.............. 83 F2
Whetsted Kent.............. 17 G6
Whetstone Gt Lon.............. 28 D5
Whetstone Leics.............. 60 B5
Wheyrigg Cumb.............. 103 F5
Whicham Cumb.............. 94 B3
Whichford Warwks.............. 48 A3
Whickham T & W.............. 114 D2
Whiddon Devon.............. 8 B5
Whiddon Down Devon.............. 8 D4
Whight's Corner Suffk.............. 53 E5

Whigstreet Angus.............. 141 E4
Whilton Nhants.............. 60 B2
Whimble Devon.............. 20 D1
Whimple Devon.............. 9 G4
Whimpwell Green Norfk.............. 77 G3
Whin Lane End Lancs.............. 88 B4
Whinburgh Norfk.............. 76 C1
Whinnie Liggate D & G.............. 102 A5
Whinnow Cumb.............. 103 G5
Whinny Hill Dur.............. 106 C3
Whinnyfold Abers.............. 159 G2
Whippingham IOW.............. 14 C3
Whipsnade Beds.............. 50 A2
Whipsnade Wild Animal Park Bucks.............. 50 A2
Whipton Devon.............. 9 F4
Whirlow S York.............. 83 H3
Whisby Lincs.............. 85 G1
Whissendine Rutlnd.............. 73 F1
Whissonsett Norfk.............. 76 B2
Whistlefield Ag & B.............. 128 D4
Whistlefield Inn Ag & B.............. 128 C4
Whistley Green Berks.............. 41 F2
Whiston Mersyd.............. 81 G4
Whiston Nhants.............. 49 G5
Whiston S York.............. 84 B3
Whiston Staffs.............. 70 D1
Whiston Staffs.............. 71 E5
Whiston Cross Shrops.............. 57 H6
Whiston Eaves Staffs.............. 71 E5
Whiston Lane End Mersyd.............. 81 G4
Whitacre Fields Warwks.............. 59 E5
Whitbeck Cumb.............. 94 B3
Whitbourne Herefs.............. 46 C5
Whitburn T & W.............. 115 F2
Whitburn W Loth.............. 131 F2
Whitby Ches.............. 81 F2
Whitby N York.............. 99 E6
Whitbyheath Ches.............. 81 F2
Whitchester Border.............. 122 D5
Whitchurch Bucks.............. 49 F1
Whitchurch Cardif.............. 36 C2
Whitchurch Devon.............. 6 B5
Whitchurch Hants.............. 26 C4
Whitchurch Herefs.............. 37 F6
Whitchurch Oxon.............. 41 E2
Whitchurch Pembks.............. 32 B4
Whitchurch Shrops.............. 69 H4
Whitchurch Somset.............. 24 B6
Whitchurch Canonicorum Dorset.............. 10 D4
Whitchurch Hill Oxon.............. 41 E2
Whitcombe Dorset.............. 11 G3
Whitcot Shrops.............. 56 D4
Whitcott Keysett Shrops.............. 56 C4
White Ball Somset.............. 22 D1
White Chapel Lancs.............. 88 D4
White Chapel Worcs.............. 47 F3
White Colne Essex.............. 52 B4
White Coppice Lancs.............. 89 E1
White Cross Cnwll.............. 2 D2
White End Worcs.............. 46 C3
White Kirkley Dur.............. 105 G4
White Lackington Dorset.............. 11 G4
White Ladies Aston Worcs.............. 47 E4
White Mill Carmth.............. 43 E1
White Notley Essex.............. 52 A2
White Ox Mead Somset.............. 24 C5
White Pit Lincs.............. 86 D2
White Roding Essex.............. 51 F2
White Stake Lancs.............. 88 D2
White Stone Herefs.............. 46 A3
White Waltham Berks.............. 41 F2
White-le-Head Dur.............. 114 C1
Whiteacre Kent.............. 19 E6
Whiteacre Heath Warwks.............. 59 E5
Whiteash Green Essex.............. 52 B4
Whitebirk Lancs.............. 89 E2
Whitebridge Highld.............. 145 G6
Whitebrook Mons.............. 37 F5
Whitecairns Abers.............. 149 G6
Whitechapel Gt Lon.............. 28 D4
Whitechurch Pembks.............. 42 B3
Whitecliffe Gloucs.............. 37 G5
Whitecraig E Loth.............. 132 B2
Whitecroft Gloucs.............. 37 G5
Whitecrook D & G.............. 100 C6
Whitecross Cnwll.............. 2 C3
Whitecross Cnwll.............. 4 C3
Whitecross Falk.............. 131 F3
Whiteface Highld.............. 162 D3
Whitefarland N Ayrs.............. 117 H5
Whitefaulds S Ayrs.............. 109 E6
Whitefield Devon.............. 21 G4
Whitefield Gt Man.............. 82 C5
Whitefield Somset.............. 22 D2
Whitefield Lane End Mersyd.............. 81 G4
Whiteford Abers.............. 158 C2
Whitegate Ches.............. 82 A2
Whitehall Hants.............. 27 F4
Whitehall Ork.............. 169 c3
Whitehall W Susx.............. 16 B3
Whitehaven Cumb.............. 102 D2
Whitehill Hants.............. 27 F3
Whitehill Kent.............. 30 D2
Whitehill Leics.............. 72 B1
Whitehills Abers.............. 158 B6
Whitehouse Abers.............. 148 D6
Whitehouse Ag & B.............. 127 G1
Whitehouse Common W Mids.............. 58 D5
Whitekirk E Loth.............. 133 E3
Whitelackington Somset.............. 10 D6
Whiteley Hants.............. 14 D4
Whiteley Bank IOW.............. 14 D2
Whiteley Green Ches.............. 82 D2
Whiteley Village Surrey.............. 28 B2
Whitemans Green W Susx.............. 16 D4
Whitemire Moray.............. 156 B4
Whitemoor Cnwll.............. 4 C2
Whitemoor Derbys.............. 72 A5
Whitemoor Notts.............. 72 C4
Whitemoor Staffs.............. 70 D6
Whiteness Shet.............. 169 h2
Whiteoak Green Oxon.............. 40 B6
Whiteparish Wilts.............. 25 H2
Whiterashes Abers.............. 158 D1
Whiterow Highld.............. 167 G3
Whiterow Moray.............. 156 B5
Whiteshill Gloucs.............. 38 C5

Whitesmith E Susx — 17 F3
Whitestaunton Somset — 10 C6
Whitestone Devon — 9 E4
Whitestone Cross Devon — 9 F4
Whitestreet Green Suffk — 52 C5
Whitewall Corner N York — 98 D2
Whiteway Gloucs — 38 D5
Whiteway Somset — 24 C6
Whitewell Lancs — 89 E4
Whiteworks Devon — 6 C5
Whitfield Gloucs — 38 B3
Whitfield Kent — 19 F6
Whitfield Nthumb — 104 D6
Whitfield Nhants — 48 D3
Whitfield Hall Nthumb — 104 D6
Whitford Devon — 10 C4
Whitford Flints — 80 D2
Whitgift E R Yk — 92 B2
Whitgreave Staffs — 70 D3
Whithorn D & G — 101 F4
Whiting Bay N Ayrs — 118 B2
Whitkirk W York — 91 E3
Whitland Carmth — 33 F3
Whitlaw Border — 112 B6
Whitletts S Ayrs — 119 E2
Whitley Berks — 41 E1
Whitley N York — 91 G2
Whitley S York — 84 A4
Whitley Wilts — 24 D6
Whitley Bay T & W — 115 E3
Whitley Chapel Nthumb — 105 F6
Whitley Heath Staffs — 70 C3
Whitley Lower W York — 90 C1
Whitley Row Kent — 29 F1
Whitlock's End W Mids — 58 D3
Whitminster Gloucs — 38 C5
Whitmore Dorset — 12 D5
Whitmore Staffs — 70 C4
Whitnage Devon — 9 G6
Whitnash Warwks — 59 F2
Whitney-on-Wye Herefs — 45 E4
Whitrigg Cumb — 103 F4
Whitrigg Cumb — 103 F6
Whitrigglees Cumb — 103 F6
Whitsbury Hants — 25 G1
Whitsford Devon — 21 G4
Whitsome Border — 123 F4
Whitson Newpt — 37 E3
Whitstable Kent — 31 E3
Whitstone Cnwll — 5 F6
Whittingham Nthumb — 124 D2
Whittingslow Shrops — 57 E4
Whittington Derbys — 84 B2
Whittington Gloucs — 47 F1
Whittington Lancs — 95 G2
Whittington Norfk — 63 F5
Whittington Shrops — 69 E3
Whittington Staffs — 58 D6
Whittington Staffs — 58 B4
Whittington Warwks — 59 F5
Whittington Worcs — 46 D4
Whittington Moor Derbys — 84 A2
Whittle-le-Woods Lancs — 88 D2
Whittlebury Nhants — 49 E4
Whittlesey Cambs — 62 B5
Whittlesford Cambs — 51 F5
Whittlestone Head Lancs — 89 F1
Whitton Dur — 106 C3
Whitton Lincs — 92 C2
Whitton Nthumb — 114 B6
Whitton Powys — 56 C2
Whitton Shrops — 57 F3
Whitton Suffk — 53 E5
Whittonditch Wilts — 39 G1
Whittonstall Nthumb — 105 G6
Whitway Hants — 26 C5
Whitwell Derbys — 84 C2
Whitwell Herts — 50 C3
Whitwell IOW — 14 C1
Whitwell N York — 97 F5
Whitwell Rutlnd — 73 G1
Whitwell Street Norfk — 76 D2
Whitwell-on-the-Hill N York — 98 C1
Whitwick Leics — 72 B2
Whitwood W York — 91 E2
Whitworth Lancs — 89 G1
Whixall Shrops — 69 G3
Whixley N York — 91 E5
Whorlton Dur — 105 H2
Whorlton N York — 97 H5
Whyle Herefs — 46 A5
Whyteleafe Surrey — 28 D2
Wibdon Gloucs — 37 G4
Wibsey W York — 90 C3
Wibtoft Warwks — 59 H4
Wichenford Worcs — 46 C5
Wichling Kent — 30 C2
Wick Devon — 10 B5
Wick Dorset — 13 E4
Wick Gloucs — 38 B1
Wick Highld — 167 G3
Wick Somset — 23 E4
Wick Somset — 23 G2
Wick V Glam — 35 G1
Wick W Susx — 16 A2
Wick Wilts — 25 G1
Wick Worcs — 47 E4
Wick Airport Highld — 167 G4
Wick End Beds — 49 H4
Wick St Lawrence Somset — 23 F6
Wicken Cambs — 63 E2
Wicken Nhants — 49 F3
Wicken Bonhunt Essex — 51 F4
Wickenby Lincs — 86 A3
Wicker Street Green Suffk — 52 C5
Wickersley S York — 84 B4
Wickford Essex — 30 A5
Wickham Berks — 40 B1
Wickham Hants — 14 D5
Wickham Bishops Essex — 52 B2
Wickham Green Berks — 40 B1
Wickham Green Suffk — 64 C2
Wickham Heath Berks — 40 B1
Wickham Market Suffk — 65 E1
Wickham Skeith Suffk — 64 C2
Wickham St Paul Essex — 52 B4
Wickham Street Suffk — 52 A6
Wickham Street Suffk — 64 C2

Wickhambreaux Kent — 31 F2
Wickhambrook Suffk — 52 A6
Wickhamford Worcs — 47 F3
Wickhampton Norfk — 65 G6
Wicklewood Norfk — 64 C6
Wickmere Norfk — 77 E3
Wickstreet E Susx — 17 F2
Widdington Essex — 51 F4
Widdop Lancs — 89 H3
Widdrington Nthumb — 114 D5
Widdrington Station T & W — 114 D5
Wide Open T & W — 114 D3
Widecombe in the Moor Devon — 8 D2
Widegates Cnwll — 5 F2
Widemouth Bay Cnwll — 5 F6
Widford Essex — 51 H1
Widford Herts — 51 E2
Widford Oxon — 39 G5
Widham Wilts — 39 F3
Widley Hants — 15 E4
Widmer End Bucks — 41 G4
Widmerpool Notts — 72 D3
Widmore Gt Lon — 29 E3
Widnes Ches — 81 G3
Widworthy Devon — 10 C4
Wigan Gt Man — 81 H5
Wigborough Somset — 11 E6
Wiggaton Devon — 10 A4
Wiggenhall St Germans Norfk — 75 F1
Wiggenhall St Mary Magdalen Norfk — 75 F1
Wiggenhall St Mary the Virgin Norfk — 75 F1
Wiggens Green Essex — 51 G5
Wiggenstall Staffs — 71 F6
Wiggington Shrops — 69 F4
Wigginton Herts — 41 G5
Wigginton N York — 91 G5
Wigginton Oxon — 48 B2
Wigginton Staffs — 59 E6
Wigglesworth N York — 89 F3
Wiggold Gloucs — 39 E5
Wiggonby Cumb — 103 G5
Wiggonholt W Susx — 16 B3
Wighill N York — 91 F4
Wighton Norfk — 76 B4
Wightwick Staffs — 58 B5
Wigley Derbys — 83 H2
Wigley Hants — 26 B1
Wigmore Herefs — 56 D2
Wigmore Kent — 30 B2
Wigsley Notts — 85 F2
Wigsthorpe Nhants — 61 F4
Wigston Leics — 60 B5
Wigston Fields Leics — 60 B5
Wigston Parva Leics — 59 G4
Wigthorpe Notts — 84 D3
Wigtoft Lincs — 74 C4
Wigton Cumb — 103 F5
Wigtown D & G — 101 F6
Wigtwizzle S York — 83 G4
Wike W York — 90 D4
Wilbarston Nhants — 60 D4
Wilberfoss E R Yk — 92 A5
Wilburton Cambs — 62 D3
Wilby Nhants — 61 E2
Wilby Norfk — 64 C4
Wilby Suffk — 65 E3
Wilcot Wilts — 25 G5
Wilcott Shrops — 69 F2
Wilcrick Newpt — 37 E3
Wilday Green Derbys — 84 A2
Wildboarclough Ches — 83 E1
Wilden Beds — 50 B6
Wilden Worcs — 58 A3
Wildhern Hants — 26 B4
Wildhill Herts — 50 D1
Wildmanbridge S Lans — 120 C5
Wildmoor Worcs — 58 C3
Wildsworth Lincs — 85 F4
Wilford Notts — 72 C4
Wilkesley Ches — 70 A4
Wilkhaven Highld — 163 F2
Wilkieston W Loth — 131 G2
Wilkin's Green Herts — 50 C1
Wilksby Lincs — 86 C1
Willand Devon — 9 G6
Willaston Ches — 81 F2
Willaston Ches — 70 B5
Willen Bucks — 49 G3
Willenhall W Mids — 58 C5
Willenhall W Mids — 59 F3
Willerby E R Yk — 92 D3
Willerby N York — 99 F3
Willersey Gloucs — 47 F3
Willersley Herefs — 45 F4
Willesborough Kent — 18 D6
Willesborough Lees Kent — 18 D6
Willesden Gt Lon — 28 C4
Willesleigh Devon — 21 F4
Willesley Wilts — 38 C3
Willett Somset — 22 D3
Willey Shrops — 57 G5
Willey Warwks — 59 H4
Willey Green Surrey — 27 G4
Williamscot Oxon — 48 C4
Williamstown Rhondd — 35 G3
Willian Herts — 50 C4
Willicote Warwks — 47 G4
Willingale Essex — 51 G1
Willingdon E Susx — 17 G2
Willingham Cambs — 62 C2
Willingham by Stow Lincs — 85 F3
Willingham Green Cambs — 51 G6
Willington Beds — 50 B6
Willington Derbys — 71 H3
Willington Dur — 106 A4
Willington Kent — 30 A1
Willington Warwks — 48 A3
Willington Corner Ches — 81 G1
Willington Quay T & W — 115 E2
Williton Somset — 22 D3
Willoughby Lincs — 87 E2
Willoughby Warwks — 60 A2
Willoughby Hills Lincs — 74 D5

Willoughby Waterleys Leics — 60 B5
Willoughby-on-the-Wolds Notts — 72 D2
Willoughton Lincs — 85 G4
Willow Green Ches — 82 A2
Willows Green Essex — 51 H3
Willsbridge Gloucs — 38 A1
Willsworthy Devon — 8 B3
Willtown Somset — 23 G2
Wilmcote Warwks — 47 G5
Wilmington Devon — 10 C5
Wilmington E Susx — 17 F2
Wilmington Kent — 29 F3
Wilmington Somset — 24 C5
Wilmslow Ches — 82 C3
Wilnecote Staffs — 59 E5
Wilpshire Lancs — 89 E3
Wilsden W York — 90 B3
Wilsford Lincs — 73 H4
Wilsford Wilts — 25 F5
Wilsford Wilts — 25 G5
Wilsham Devon — 21 H5
Wilshaw W York — 83 F6
Wilsill N York — 97 E1
Wilsley Green Kent — 18 A5
Wilsley Pound Kent — 18 A5
Wilson Herefs — 46 A1
Wilson Leics — 72 B2
Wilsontown S Lans — 120 D5
Wilstead Beds — 50 B5
Wilsthorpe Lincs — 74 A1
Wilstone Herts — 41 G6
Wilstone Green Herts — 41 G6
Wilton Cumb — 102 D1
Wilton Herefs — 46 A2
Wilton N York — 107 E3
Wilton N York — 98 D3
Wilton Wilts — 25 F2
Wilton Wilts — 25 H5
Wilton Dean Border — 122 B1
Wimbish Essex — 51 G4
Wimbish Green Essex — 51 G4
Wimbledon Gt Lon — 28 C3
Wimblington Cambs — 62 C5
Wimboldsley Ches — 82 B1
Wimborne Minster Dorset — 12 D5
Wimborne St Giles Dorset — 12 D6
Wimbotsham Norfk — 63 E6
Wimpole Cambs — 50 D6
Wimpstone Warwks — 47 H4
Wincanton Somset — 24 C2
Winceby Lincs — 86 D1
Wincham Ches — 82 B2
Winchburgh W Loth — 131 G3
Winchcombe Gloucs — 47 F2
Winchelsea E Susx — 18 C3
Winchelsea Beach E Susx — 18 C3
Winchester Hants — 26 C2
Winchet Hill Kent — 18 A5
Winchfield Hants — 27 F5
Winchmore Hill Bucks — 41 G4
Winchmore Hill Gt Lon — 28 D5
Wincle Ches — 83 E1
Wincobank S York — 84 B4
Winder Cumb — 102 D2
Windermere Cumb — 95 E5
Winderton Warwks — 48 B3
Windhill Highld — 154 D4
Windlehurst Gt Man — 82 D3
Windlesham Surrey — 27 G6
Windmill Cnwll — 4 C3
Windmill Derbys — 83 G2
Windmill Hill E Susx — 17 G3
Windmill Hill Somset — 23 F1
Windrush Gloucs — 39 G6
Windsole Abers — 158 B5
Windsor Berks — 41 H2
Windsor Castle Berks — 41 H2
Windsor Green Suffk — 52 C6
Windsoredge Gloucs — 38 C4
Windy Arbour Warwks — 59 F2
Windy Hill Wrexhm — 69 E5
Windygates Fife — 132 B5
Windyharbour Ches — 82 C2
Wineham W Susx — 16 C3
Winestead E R Yk — 93 G2
Winewall Lancs — 89 G4
Winfarthing Norfk — 64 D4
Winford IOW — 14 D2
Winford Somset — 24 A6
Winforton Herefs — 45 F4
Winfrith Newburgh Dorset — 12 B3
Wing Bucks — 49 G1
Wing Rutlnd — 61 E6
Wingate Dur — 106 C4
Wingates Gt Man — 82 B5
Wingates Nthumb — 114 C5
Wingerworth Derbys — 84 B1
Wingfield Beds — 50 A3
Wingfield Suffk — 65 E3
Wingfield Wilts — 24 D5
Wingfield Green Suffk — 65 E3
Wingham Kent — 31 F2
Wingmore Kent — 19 E6
Wingrave Bucks — 49 G1
Winkburn Notts — 73 E6
Winkfield Berks — 41 G1
Winkfield Row Berks — 41 G1
Winkfield Street Berks — 41 G1
Winkhill Staffs — 71 E5
Winkhurst Green Kent — 29 F1
Winkleigh Devon — 8 C5
Winksley N York — 97 F2
Winkton Dorset — 13 E4
Winlaton T & W — 114 C2
Winlaton Mill T & W — 114 C2
Winless Highld — 167 G4
Winllan Powys — 68 D2
Winmarleigh Lancs — 88 C2
Winnall Hants — 26 C2
Winnall Worcs — 58 A2
Winnersh Berks — 41 F1
Winnington Ches — 82 A2
Winscales Cumb — 102 D3
Winscombe Somset — 23 G5
Winsford Ches — 82 B1
Winsford Somset — 22 B3
Winsham Devon — 21 E4
Winsham Somset — 10 D5

Winshill Staffs — 71 G2
Winshwen Swans — 34 D4
Winskill Cumb — 104 C4
Winslade Hants — 27 E4
Winsley Wilts — 24 D5
Wisley Gardens Surrey — 28 B2
Winslow Bucks — 49 F2
Winson Gloucs — 39 F5
Winsor Hants — 13 G6
Winster Cumb — 95 E4
Winster Derbys — 71 G6
Winston Dur — 105 H2
Winston Suffk — 64 D1
Winston Green Suffk — 64 D1
Winstone Gloucs — 38 D5
Winswell Devon — 21 E2
Winterborne Came Dorset — 11 G3
Winterborne Clenston Dorset — 12 B5
Winterborne Herringston Dorset — 11 G3
Winterborne Houghton Dorset — 12 B5
Winterborne Kingston Dorset — 12 C4
Winterborne Monkton Dorset — 11 G3
Winterborne Stickland Dorset — 12 B5
Winterborne Tomson Dorset — 12 C4
Winterborne Whitechurch Dorset — 12 C4
Winterborne Zelston Dorset — 12 C4
Winterbourne Berks — 40 C1
Winterbourne Gloucs — 37 G2
Winterbourne Abbas Dorset — 11 F4
Winterbourne Bassett Wilts — 39 F2
Winterbourne Dauntsey Wilts — 25 G3
Winterbourne Earls Wilts — 25 G3
Winterbourne Gunner Wilts — 25 G3
Winterbourne Monkton Wilts — 39 F1
Winterbourne Steepleton Dorset — 11 G4
Winterbourne Stoke Wilts — 25 F3
Winterbrook Oxon — 40 D3
Winterburn N York — 89 H5
Wintering ham Lincs — 92 C2
Winterley Ches — 70 B6
Wintersett W York — 91 E1
Winterslow Wilts — 25 H2
Winterton Lincs — 92 C1
Winterton-on-Sea Norfk — 77 H2
Winthorpe Lincs — 87 F1
Winthorpe Notts — 73 F6
Winton Cumb — 96 A6
Winton Dorset — 13 E4
Winton E Susx — 17 F2
Winton N York — 97 G4
Wintringham N York — 99 E2
Winwick Cambs — 61 G3
Winwick Ches — 82 A4
Winwick Nhants — 60 B3
Wirksworth Derbys — 71 H5
Wirswall Ches — 69 H4
Wisbech Cambs — 75 E1
Wisbech St Mary Cambs — 62 C6
Wisborough Green W Susx — 16 A4
Wiseman's Bridge Pembks — 33 F2
Wiseton Notts — 85 E4
Wishanger Gloucs — 38 D5
Wishaw N Lans — 120 B5
Wishaw Warwks — 59 E5
Wisley Surrey — 28 B2
Wispington Lincs — 86 B2
Wissenden Kent — 18 C5
Wissett Suffk — 65 F3
Wissington Suffk — 52 C4
Wistanstow Shrops — 57 E4
Wistanswick Shrops — 70 B3
Wistaston Ches — 70 B5
Wistaston Green Ches — 70 B5
Wisterfield Ches — 82 C2
Wiston Pembks — 32 D3
Wiston S Lans — 120 D3
Wiston W Susx — 16 B3
Wistow Cambs — 62 B3
Wistow Leics — 60 C5
Wistow N York — 91 G3
Wiswell Lancs — 89 F3
Witcham Cambs — 62 C3
Witchampton Dorset — 12 D5
Witchford Cambs — 62 D3
Witcombe Somset — 23 G1
Witham Essex — 52 B2
Witham Friary Somset — 24 C3
Witham on the Hill Lincs — 73 H2
Withcall Lincs — 86 C3
Withdean E Susx — 16 D2
Witherenden Hill E Susx — 17 G4
Witheridge Devon — 9 E6
Witherley Leics — 59 F5
Withern Lincs — 87 E3
Withernsea E R Yk — 93 G2
Withernwick E R Yk — 93 F4
Withersdale Street Suffk — 65 E3
Withersfield Essex — 51 G5
Witherslack Cumb — 95 E3
Witherslack Hall Cumb — 95 E3
Withiel Cnwll — 4 D2
Withiel Florey Somset — 22 C3
Withielgoose Cnwll — 4 D2
Withington Gloucs — 39 E6
Withington Gt Man — 82 C4
Withington Herefs — 46 A3
Withington Shrops — 69 H1
Withington Staffs — 71 E3
Withington Green Ches — 82 C2
Withington Marsh Herefs — 46 A4
Withleigh Devon — 9 F6
Withnell Lancs — 89 E2
Withy Mills Somset — 24 B5
Withybed Green Worcs — 58 C3
Withybrook Warwks — 59 G4
Withycombe Somset — 22 C3
Withyham E Susx — 17 F5
Withypool Somset — 22 A3
Withywood Bristl — 24 A6
Witley Surrey — 27 H3
Witnesham Suffk — 53 E6
Witney Oxon — 40 B5
Wittering Cambs — 61 F6
Wittersham Kent — 18 C4
Witton Norfk — 77 F1
Witton Norfk — 77 F3
Witton W Mids — 58 D4

Witton Gilbert Dur — 106 B5
Witton Green Norfk — 65 G6
Witton le Wear Dur — 105 H3
Witton Park Dur — 106 A4
Wiveliscombe Somset — 22 D2
Wivelrod Hants — 27 E3
Wivelsfield E Susx — 16 D3
Wivelsfield Green E Susx — 16 D3
Wivelsfield Station W Susx — 16 D3
Wivenhoe Essex — 52 D3
Wivenhoe Cross Essex — 52 D3
Wiveton Norfk — 76 C4
Wix Essex — 53 E4
Wix Green Essex — 53 E3
Wixford Warwks — 47 F5
Wixhill Shrops — 69 H3
Wixoe Essex — 51 H5
Woburn Beds — 49 H2
Woburn Abbey Beds — 49 H2
Woburn Sands Bucks — 49 G3
Wokefield Park Berks — 27 E6
Woking Surrey — 28 A2
Wokingham Berks — 41 F1
Wolborough Devon — 7 F5
Wold Newton E R Yk — 99 F2
Wold Newton Lincs — 86 C4
Woldingham Surrey — 29 E2
Wolf Hills Nthumb — 104 D6
Wolf's Castle Pembks — 32 D4
Wolfclyde S Lans — 121 E3
Wolferlow Herefs — 46 B5
Wolferton Norfk — 75 G3
Wolfhampcote Warwks — 60 A2
Wolfhill P & K — 140 B3
Wolfsdale Pembks — 32 D4
Wollaston Nhants — 61 E2
Wollaston Shrops — 69 E1
Wollaston W Mids — 58 B4
Wollaton Notts — 72 C4
Wolleigh Devon — 9 E3
Wollerton Shrops — 70 A3
Wollescote W Mids — 58 B4
Wolseley Bridge Staffs — 71 E2
Wolsingham Dur — 105 G4
Wolstanton Staffs — 70 D5
Wolstenholme Gt Man — 89 G1
Wolston Warwks — 59 G3
Wolsty Cumb — 103 E5
Wolvercote Oxon — 40 C5
Wolverhampton W Mids — 58 B5
Wolverley Shrops — 69 G3
Wolverley Worcs — 58 A3
Wolverton Bucks — 49 F3
Wolverton Hants — 26 D5
Wolverton Kent — 19 F6
Wolverton Warwks — 47 G5
Wolverton Wilts — 24 C2
Wolverton Common Hants — 26 D5
Wolvesnewton Mons — 37 F4
Wolvey Warwks — 59 G4
Wolvey Heath Warwks — 59 G4
Wolviston Dur — 106 D3
Wombleton N York — 98 B3
Wombourne Staffs — 58 B5
Wombwell S York — 84 B5
Womenswold Kent — 31 F1
Womersley N York — 91 F1
Wonastow Mons — 37 F5
Wonersh Surrey — 16 A6
Wonford Devon — 9 F4
Wonson Devon — 8 D4
Wonston Hants — 26 C3
Wooburn Bucks — 41 G3
Wooburn Green Bucks — 41 G3
Wooburn Moor Bucks — 41 G3
Wood Bevington Warwks — 47 F5
Wood Burcot Nhants — 49 E4
Wood Dalling Norfk — 76 D3
Wood Eaton Staffs — 70 C2
Wood End Beds — 50 A5
Wood End Beds — 61 G2
Wood End Cambs — 62 C3
Wood End Gt Lon — 28 B4
Wood End Herts — 50 D3
Wood End W Mids — 58 B5
Wood End Warwks — 58 D2
Wood End Warwks — 59 E5
Wood End Warwks — 59 F4
Wood Enderby Lincs — 86 C1
Wood Green Gt Lon — 28 D5
Wood Hayes W Mids — 58 B6
Wood Lane Shrops — 69 F3
Wood Lane Staffs — 70 C5
Wood Norton Norfk — 76 C3
Wood Row W York — 91 E2
Wood Street Norfk — 77 G2
Wood Street Surrey — 27 H4
Wood Top Lancs — 88 D4
Wood Walton Cambs — 62 A3
Wood's Corner E Susx — 17 G3
Wood's Green E Susx — 17 G5
Woodale N York — 96 C3
Woodall S York — 84 B3
Woodbastwick Norfk — 77 F1
Woodbeck Notts — 85 E2
Woodborough Notts — 72 D5
Woodborough Wilts — 25 G5
Woodbridge Devon — 10 B4
Woodbridge Dorset — 24 D1
Woodbridge Suffk — 53 F6
Woodbury Devon — 9 G3
Woodbury Salterton Devon — 9 G3
Woodchester Gloucs — 38 C5
Woodchurch Kent — 18 C5
Woodchurch Mersyd — 81 E3
Woodcombe Somset — 22 B4
Woodcote Gt Lon — 28 D2
Woodcote Oxon — 41 E2
Woodcote Shrops — 70 C1
Woodcote Green Worcs — 58 B3
Woodcott Hants — 26 C5
Woodcroft Gloucs — 37 F4
Woodcutts Dorset — 25 E1
Woodditton Cambs — 63 F1
Woodeaton Oxon — 40 D5
Wooden Pembks — 33 E2
Woodend Highld — 136 B6
Woodend Nhants — 48 D4

Woodend Staffs 71 G3
Woodend W Loth 131 E2
Woodend W Susx 15 F4
Woodend Green Essex 51 F4
Woodfalls Wilts 25 G1
Woodford Devon 7 E3
Woodford Gloucs 38 B4
Woodford Gt Lon 29 E5
Woodford Gt Man 82 D3
Woodford Nhants 61 F3
Woodford Bridge Gt Lon 29 E5
Woodford Halse Nhants 48 D4
Woodford Wells Gt Lon 29 E5
Woodgate Devon 10 B6
Woodgate Norfk 76 B1
Woodgate Norfk 76 C2
Woodgate W Mids 58 C4
Woodgate W Susx 15 G4
Woodgate Worcs 58 C2
Woodgreen Hants 25 G1
Woodgreen Oxon 40 B5
Woodhall Lincs 86 C1
Woodhall N York 96 C4
Woodhall Hill W York 90 C3
Woodhall Spa Lincs 86 B1
Woodham Bucks 49 E1
Woodham Dur 106 B3
Woodham Surrey 28 A2
Woodham Ferrers Essex 30 B6
Woodham Mortimer Essex 52 B1
Woodham Walter Essex 52 B1
Woodhead Abers 158 D3
Woodhill Somset 23 F2
Woodhorn Nthumb 115 E4
Woodhorn Demesne Nthumb 115 E4
Woodhouse Leics 72 C1
Woodhouse S York 84 B3
Woodhouse W York 90 D3
Woodhouse W York 91 E2
Woodhouse Eaves Leics 72 C1
Woodhouse Green Staffs 82 D1
Woodhouse Mill S York 84 B3
Woodhouselee Mdloth 132 A1
Woodhouselees D & G 112 A2
Woodhouses Cumb 103 G5
Woodhouses Gt Man 82 D5
Woodhouses Staffs 71 F1
Woodhouses Staffs 71 F2
Woodhuish Devon 7 F3
Woodhurst Cambs 62 B3
Woodingdean E Susx 16 D2
Woodkirk W York 90 D2
Woodland Abers 159 E1
Woodland Devon 7 E4
Woodland Devon 6 D3
Woodland Dur 105 G3
Woodland Kent 19 E5
Woodland S Ayrs 108 D4
Woodland Head Devon 9 E4
Woodland Street Somset 24 A3
Woodland View S York 83 H3
Woodlands Abers 149 E4
Woodlands Dorset 12 D5
Woodlands Hants 13 G6
Woodlands Kent 29 F2
Woodlands N York 90 D5
Woodlands S York 84 C5
Woodlands Somset 22 D3
Woodlands Park Berks 41 G2
Woodlands St Mary Berks 40 B2
Woodleigh Devon 7 E2
Woodlesford W York 91 E2
Woodley Berks 41 F2
Woodley Gt Man 82 D4
Woodmancote Gloucs 47 E2
Woodmancote Gloucs 39 E5
Woodmancote Gloucs 38 B4
Woodmancote W Susx 15 F4
Woodmancote W Susx 16 C3
Woodmancote Worcs 47 E3
Woodmancott Hants 26 D3
Woodmansey E R Yk 92 D3
Woodmansgreen W Susx 27 G2
Woodmansterne Surrey 28 D2
Woodmanton Devon 9 G3
Woodmarsh Wilts 24 D5
Woodmill Staffs 71 F2
Woodminton Wilts 25 F1
Woodnesborough Kent 31 G2
Woodnewton Nhants 61 F5
Woodnook Notts 72 B5
Woodplumpton Lancs 88 C3
Woodrising Norfk 64 B6
Woodrow Worcs 58 B3
Woodseaves Shrops 70 B3
Woodseaves Staffs 70 C3
Woodsend Wilts 39 G2
Woodsetts S York 84 C3
Woodsford Dorset 12 B4
Woodside Berks 41 G1
Woodside Cumb 102 D3
Woodside Essex 51 F1
Woodside Fife 132 C6
Woodside Gt Lon 28 D3
Woodside Hants 13 G4
Woodside Herts 50 C1
Woodside P & K 140 B3
Woodside Green Kent 30 C1
Woodstock Oxon 40 C6
Woodstock Pembks 33 E4
Woodston Cambs 61 H5
Woodthorpe Derbys 84 B2
Woodthorpe Leics 72 C2
Woodthorpe Lincs 87 E3
Woodton Norfk 65 E5
Woodtown Devon 20 C4
Woodvale Mersyd 81 E6
Woodville Derbys 71 H2
Woodwall Green Staffs 70 C3
Woody Bay Devon 21 G5
Woodyates Dorset 25 F1
Woofferton Shrops 57 E2
Wookey Somset 23 H4
Wookey Hole Somset 23 H4
Wool Dorset 12 B3
Woolacombe Devon 21 E5
Woolage Green Kent 31 F1
Woolage Village Kent 31 F1

Woolaston Gloucs 37 G4
Woolaston Common Gloucs 37 G4
Woolavington Somset 23 F3
Woolbeding W Susx 27 G1
Woolbrook Devon 10 B3
Woolcotts Somset 22 C2
Wooldale W York 83 H6
Wooler Nthumb 124 C4
Woolfardisworthy Devon 20 C3
Woolfardisworthy Devon 9 E5
Woolfold Gt Man 82 C6
Woolfords S Lans 121 E5
Woolhampton Berks 26 D6
Woolhanger Devon 21 G5
Woolhope Herefs 46 B3
Woolland Dorset 12 B5
Woollard Somset 24 B6
Woollensbrook Herts 50 D2
Woolley Cambs 61 G3
Woolley Cnwll 20 C2
Woolley Derbys 72 A6
Woolley Somset 38 B1
Woolley W York 83 H6
Woolley Bridge Derbys 83 E4
Woolley Green Berks 41 G2
Woolmer Green Herts 50 C3
Woolmere Green Worcs 58 C2
Woolmerston Somset 23 F3
Woolminstone Somset 10 D5
Woolpack Kent 18 B5
Woolpit Suffk 64 B2
Woolpit Green Suffk 64 B1
Woolscott Warwks 59 H2
Woolsgrove Devon 9 E5
Woolsington T & W 114 D2
Woolstaston Shrops 57 E5
Woolsthorpe Lincs 73 F3
Woolsthorpe-by-Colsterworth
Lincs 73 G2
Woolston Ches 82 B4
Woolston Devon 7 E2
Woolston Devon 7 E3
Woolston Hants 14 C5
Woolston Shrops 69 E2
Woolston Shrops 56 D4
Woolston Somset 22 D3
Woolston Somset 24 B2
Woolston Green Devon 7 E4
Woolstone Bucks 49 G3
Woolstone Gloucs 47 E2
Woolstone Oxon 39 G3
Woolton Mersyd 81 F3
Woolton Hill Hants 26 C5
Woolverstone Suffk 53 E5
Woolverton Somset 24 C5
Woolwich Gt Lon 29 E4
Woonton Herefs 45 F4
Woonton Herefs 46 A5
Wooperton Nthumb 124 D3
Woore Shrops 70 B4
Wootten Green Suffk 65 E3
Wootton Beds 50 A5
Wootton Hants 13 F4
Wootton Herefs 45 F4
Wootton IOW 14 D3
Wootton Kent 19 F6
Wootton Lincs 93 E1
Wootton Nhants 49 F5
Wootton Oxon 48 C1
Wootton Oxon 40 C4
Wootton Shrops 69 F3
Wootton Staffs 70 C3
Wootton Staffs 71 F4
Wootton Bassett Wilts 39 E2
Wootton Bridge IOW 14 D3
Wootton Broadmead Beds 50 A5
Wootton Common IOW 14 D3
Wootton Courtenay Somset 22 B4
Wootton Fitzpaine Dorset 10 D4
Wootton Rivers Wilts 25 G6
Wootton St Lawrence Hants 26 D5
Wootton Wawen Warwks 58 D2
Worcester Worcs 46 D5
Worcester Park Gt Lon 28 C3
Wordsley W Mids 58 B4
Worfield Shrops 57 H5
Worgret Dorset 12 C3
Workhouse End Beds 50 B6
Workington Cumb 102 D3
Worksop Notts 84 C3
Worlaby Lincs 85 H6
Worlaby Lincs 86 D2
World's End Berks 40 C2
Worlds End Bucks 41 G5
Worlds End Hants 14 D5
Worlds End W Susx 16 D3
Worle Somset 23 F6
Worleston Ches 70 B6
Worlingham Suffk 65 G4
Worlington Devon 21 H2
Worlington Suffk 63 F3
Worlingworth Suffk 65 E2
Wormald Green N York 97 F1
Wormbridge Herefs 45 G2
Wormegay Norfk 75 G1
Wormelow Tump Herefs 45 H2
Wormhill Derbys 83 F2
Wormhill Herefs 45 G3
Worminghall Bucks 41 E5
Wormingford Essex 52 C4
Wormington Gloucs 47 F3
Worminster Somset 24 A3
Wormit Fife 140 D2
Wormleighton Warwks 48 C5
Wormley Herts 50 D1
Wormley Surrey 27 H3
Wormley Hill S York 91 H1
Wormleybury Herts 50 D1
Wormshill Kent 30 B2
Wormsley Herefs 45 G4
Worplesdon Surrey 27 H5
Worrall S York 83 H4
Worrall Hill Gloucs 37 G6
Worsbrough S York 84 A5
Worsbrough Bridge S York 84 A5
Worsbrough Dale S York 84 A5
Worsley Gt Man 82 C5
Worsley Mesnes Gt Man 81 H5

Worstead Norfk 77 F3
Worsthorne Lancs 89 G3
Worston Devon 6 C3
Worston Lancs 89 F4
Worth Kent 31 G2
Worth Somset 23 H4
Worth W Susx 16 D5
Worth Abbey Surrey 16 D5
Worth Matravers Dorset 12 D2
Wortham Suffk 64 C3
Worthen Shrops 56 D6
Worthenbury Wrexhm 69 F5
Worthing Norfk 76 C2
Worthing W Susx 16 B2
Worthington Leics 72 B2
Worthybrook Mons 37 F5
Worting Hants 26 D4
Wortley S York 83 H5
Wortley W York 90 D3
Worton N York 96 C4
Worton Wilts 25 E5
Wortwell Norfk 65 E4
Wotherton Shrops 56 C5
Wothorpe Cambs 61 F6
Wotter Devon 6 C4
Wotton Surrey 16 B6
Wotton Underwood Bucks 41 E6
Wotton-under-Edge Gloucs 38 B4
Woughton on the Green Bucks 49 G3
Wouldham Kent 29 H2
Woundale Shrops 57 H5
Wrabness Essex 53 E4
Wrafton Devon 21 E4
Wragby Lincs 86 B2
Wragby W York 91 E1
Wramplingham Norfk 64 D6
Wrangaton Devon 6 D3
Wrangbrook W York 84 C6
Wrangle Lincs 75 E5
Wrangle Common Lincs 75 E5
Wrangle Lowgate Lincs 75 E5
Wrangway Somset 22 D1
Wrantage Somset 23 F1
Wrawby Lincs 85 H6
Wraxall Somset 37 F1
Wraxall Somset 24 B3
Wray Lancs 95 G2
Wray Castle Cumb 94 D5
Wraysbury Berks 43 G4
Wrayton Lancs 95 G2
Wrea Green Lancs 88 B3
Wreaks End Cumb 94 C3
Wreay Cumb 104 A5
Wreay Cumb 104 A2
Wrecclesham Surrey 27 F4
Wrekenton T & W 114 D1
Wrelton N York 98 C3
Wrenbury Ches 70 A5
Wrench Green N York 99 E4
Wreningham Norfk 64 D5
Wrentham Suffk 65 G4
Wrenthorpe W York 90 D2
Wrentnall Shrops 56 D6
Wressle E R Yk 92 A3
Wressle Lincs 85 G6
Wrestlingworth Beds 50 C5
Wretton Norfk 63 F5
Wrexham Wrexhm 69 F5
Wribbenhall Worcs 57 H3
Wrickton Shrops 57 G4
Wright's Green Essex 51 F2
Wrightington Bar Lancs 81 G6
Wrinehill Staffs 70 C5
Wrington Somset 23 G5
Wrington Somset 23 G5
Writhlington Somset 24 C5
Writtle Essex 51 H1
Wrockwardine Shrops 70 A1
Wroot Lincs 85 E5
Wrose W York 90 C3
Wrotham Kent 29 G2
Wrotham Heath Kent 29 G2
Wrottesley Staffs 58 A5
Wroughton Wilts 39 F2
Wroxall IOW 14 D1
Wroxall Warwks 59 E2
Wroxeter Shrops 57 F6
Wroxham Norfk 77 F2
Wroxton Oxon 48 B3
Wyaston Derbys 71 G4
Wyatt's Green Essex 29 G6
Wyberton East Lincs 74 D4
Wyberton West Lincs 74 C4
Wyboston Beds 61 H1
Wybunbury Ches 70 B5
Wych Dorset 11 E4
Wych Cross E Susx 17 E5
Wychbold Worcs 58 B2
Wychnor Staffs 71 G2
Wyck Hants 27 F3
Wyck Rissington Gloucs 47 G1
Wycliffe Dur 105 H1
Wycoller Lancs 89 H3
Wycomb Leics 73 E2
Wycombe Marsh Bucks 41 G3
Wyddial Herts 51 E4
Wye Kent 18 D6
Wyesham Mons 37 F5
Wyfordby Leics 73 E2
Wyke Devon 9 F5
Wyke Devon 10 C4
Wyke Dorset 24 D2
Wyke Shrops 57 G6
Wyke Surrey 27 G4
Wyke W York 90 C2
Wyke Champflower Somset 24 B3
Wyke Regis Dorset 11 G2
Wykeham N York 98 D2
Wykeham N York 99 E3
Wyken Shrops 57 H5
Wyken W Mids 59 G3
Wykey Shrops 69 F2
Wykin Leics 59 G5
Wylam Nthumb 114 C4
Wylde Green W Mids 58 D5
Wylye Wilts 25 F3
Wymeswold Leics 72 D2
Wymington Beds 61 F2

Wymondham Leics 73 F2
Wymondham Norfk 64 D5
Wyndham Brdgnd 35 G3
Wynford Eagle Dorset 11 E4
Wynyard Park Dur 106 D3
Wyre Piddle Worcs 47 E4
Wysall Notts 72 D3
Wyson Herefs 57 E2
Wythall Worcs 58 D3
Wytham Oxon 40 C5
Wythburn Cumb 103 G1
Wythenshawe Gt Man 82 C3
Wythop Mill Cumb 103 F3
Wyton Cambs 62 B3
Wyton E R Yk 93 F3
Wyverstone Suffk 64 C2
Wyverstone Street Suffk 64 C2
Wyville Lincs 73 F3

Y

Y Felinheli Gwynd 79 E1
Y Ferwig Cerdgn 42 B4
Y Ffor Gwynd 66 D4
Y Gyffylliog Denbgs 68 C6
Y Maerdy Conwy 68 B4
Y Nant Wrexhm 69 E5
Y Rhiw Gwynd 66 B3
Yaddlethorpe Lincs 85 F5
Yafford IOW 14 C2
Yafforth N York 97 G4
Yalberton Devon 7 F3
Yalding Kent 29 H1
Yanwath Cumb 104 B3
Yanworth Gloucs 39 E6
Yapham E R Yk 92 B5
Yapton W Susx 15 H4
Yarborough Somset 23 G5
Yarbridge IOW 14 D2
Yarburgh Lincs 86 D4
Yarcombe Devon 10 C5
Yard Devon 21 H3
Yardley W Mids 58 D4
Yardley Gobion Nhants 49 F4
Yardley Hastings Nhants 49 G5
Yardley Wood W Mids 58 D3
Yardro Powys 45 E3
Yarford Somset 23 E2
Yarkhill Herefs 46 B3
Yarley Somset 23 H4
Yarlington Somset 24 B2
Yarlsber N York 95 H2
Yarm N York 106 D2
Yarmouth IOW 14 B2
Yarnacott Devon 21 F4
Yarnbrook Wilts 24 D5
Yarner Devon 9 E2
Yarnfield Staffs 70 D3
Yarnscombe Devon 21 F3
Yarnton Oxon 40 C5
Yarpole Herefs 57 E2
Yarrow Border 121 H2
Yarrow Somset 23 G4
Yarrow Feus Border 121 H2
Yarrowford Border 122 A2
Yarsop Herefs 45 G4
Yarwell Nhants 61 G5
Yate Gloucs 38 B2
Yateley Hants 27 F5
Yatesbury Wilts 39 E1
Yattendon Berks 40 D2
Yatton Herefs 57 E2
Yatton Herefs 46 B2
Yatton Somset 23 G6
Yatton Keynell Wilts 38 C2
Yaverland IOW 14 D2
Yawl Devon 10 D4
Yawthorpe Lincs 85 F4
Yaxham Norfk 76 C1
Yaxley Cambs 61 H5
Yaxley Suffk 64 D3
Yazor Herefs 45 G4
Yeading Gt Lon 28 B4
Yeadon W York 90 C4
Yealand Conyers Lancs 95 F2
Yealand Redmayne Lancs 95 F2
Yealand Storrs Lancs 95 F2
Yealmbridge Devon 6 C3
Yealmpton Devon 6 C3
Yearby N York 107 E3
Yearngill Cumb 103 E4
Yearsley N York 98 B2
Yeaton Shrops 69 G2
Yeaveley Derbys 71 G4
Yeavering Nthumb 123 F2
Yedingham N York 99 E3
Yelford Oxon 40 B5
Yelland Devon 21 E4
Yelling Cambs 62 B2
Yelvertoft Nhants 60 B3
Yelverton Devon 6 C4
Yelverton Norfk 65 E6
Yenston Somset 24 C1
Yeo Mill Somset 22 A2
Yeo Vale Devon 20 D3
Yeoford Devon 9 E4
Yeolmbridge Cnwll 5 G5
Yeovil Somset 24 A1
Yeovil Marsh Somset 24 A1
Yeovilton Somset 24 A1
Yeovilton Fleet Air Arm Museum
Somset 24 A2
Yerbeston Pembks 33 E3
Yesnaby Ork 169 a3
Yetlington Nthumb 124 C2
Yetminster Dorset 11 F6
Yetson Devon 7 E3
Yettington Devon 9 G3
Yetts o' Muckhart Clacks 131 F5
Yew Green Warwks 59 E2
Yews Green W York 90 B3
Yielden Beds 61 F2
Yieldingtree Worcs 58 B3

Yieldshields S Lans 120 C4
Yiewsley Gt Lon 28 B4
Ynysboeth Rhondd 36 B4
Ynysddu Caerph 36 C3
Ynysforgan Swans 34 D4
Ynyshir Rhondd 35 H3
Ynyslas Cerdgn 54 D5
Ynysmaerdy Rhondd 36 B3
Ynysmeudwy Neath 35 E5
Ynystawe Swans 34 D4
Ynyswen Powys 35 F6
Ynyswen Rhondd 35 G4
Ynysybwl Rhondd 36 B4
Ynysymaengwyn Gwynd 54 D6
Yockenthwaite N York 96 B3
Yockleton Shrops 69 F1
Yokefleet E R Yk 92 B2
Yoker C Glas 129 F2
York Lancs 89 E3
York N York 91 G5
York Minster N York 91 G5
York Town Surrey 27 G5
Yorkletts Kent 30 D2
Yorkley Gloucs 37 G5
Yorton Heath Shrops 69 G2
Youlgreave Derbys 83 G1
Youlthorpe E R Yk 92 B5
Youlton N York 97 H1
Young's End Essex 52 A3
Youngsbury Herts 51 F2
Yoxall Staffs 71 F2
Yoxford Suffk 65 F2
Yoxford Little Street Suffk 65 F2
Ysbyty Cynfyn Cerdgn 55 E3
Ysbyty Ifan Conwy 67 H3
Ysbyty Ystwyth Cerdgn 55 E2
Ysceifiog Flints 80 D2
Ysgubor-y-Coed Cerdgn 54 D5
Ystalyfera Powys 35 E5
Ystrad Rhondd 35 G4
Ystrad Aeron Cerdgn 43 E5
Ystrad Ffin Carmth 43 H4
Ystrad Meurig Cerdgn 55 E2
Ystrad Mynach Caerph 36 C4
Ystradfellte Powys 35 F5
Ystradgynlais Powys 35 E5
Ystradowen V Glam 35 G3
Ystumtuen Cerdgn 55 E3
Ythanbank Abers 159 E1
Ythanwells Abers 158 B3
Ythsie Abers 159 E2

Z

Zeal Monachorum Devon 8 D3
Zeals Wilts 24 C2
Zelah Cnwll 3 F5
Zennor Cnwll 2 B4
Zoar Cnwll 3 E2
Zouch Notts 72 C2

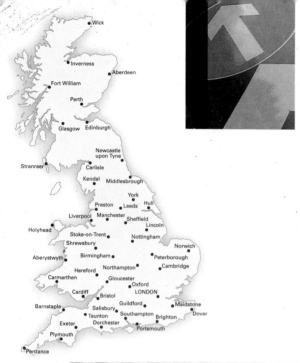

distances and journey times

The distances between towns on the mileage chart are given to the nearest mile, and are measured along the normal AA-recommended routes. It should be noted that AA-recommended routes do not necessarily follow the shortest distance between places but are based on the quickest travelling time, making maximum use of motorways and dual carriageways.

These times are average off-peak journey times based on normal AA-recommended routes. The times given do not take into account rest breaks, fuel stops or any unforeseen traffic delays, and therefore should be used as a guide only.

Example: Glasgow to Norwich, a journey of 379 miles taking approximately 7 hours 29 minutes.

journey times

The chart is a triangular matrix of place names running diagonally, with journey times in the upper-right section and distances in the lower-left section. The place names along the diagonal are:

Aberdeen, Aberystwyth, Barnstaple, Birmingham, Brighton, Bristol, Cambridge, Cardiff, Carlisle, Carmarthen, Dorchester, Dover, Edinburgh, Exeter, Fort William, Glasgow, Gloucester, Guildford, Hereford, Holyhead, Hull, Inverness, Kendal, Leeds, Lincoln, Liverpool, Maidstone, Manchester, Middlesbrough, Newcastle, Northampton, Norwich, Nottingham, Oxford, Penzance, Perth, Peterborough, Plymouth, Portsmouth, Preston, Salisbury, Sheffield, Shrewsbury, Southampton, Stoke-on-Trent, Stranraer, Taunton, Wick, York, LONDON

distances